Florida

Kim Grant

Paige R Penland

Elaine Merrill

LONELY PLANET PUBLICATIONS
Melbourne · Oakland · London · Paris

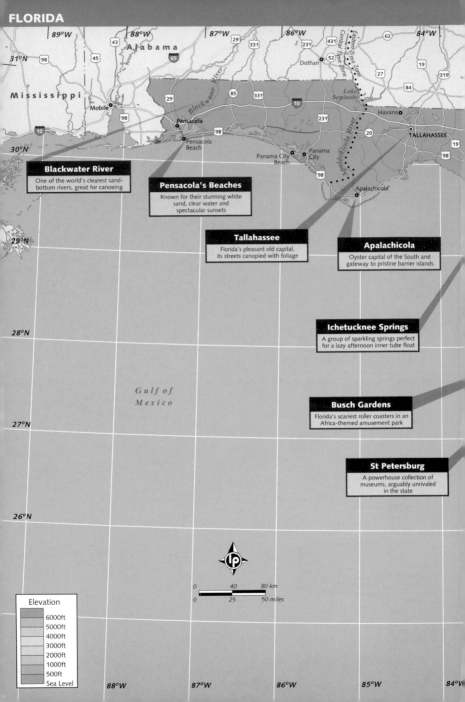

FLORIDA

Blackwater River
One of the world's clearest sand-bottom rivers, great for canoeing

Pensacola's Beaches
Known for their stunning white sand, clear water and spectacular sunsets

Tallahassee
Florida's pleasant old capital, its streets canopied with foliage

Apalachicola
Oyster capital of the South and gateway to pristine barrier islands

Ichetucknee Springs
A group of sparkling springs perfect for a lazy afternoon inner tube float

Busch Gardens
Florida's scariest roller coasters in an Africa-themed amusement park

St Petersburg
A powerhouse collection of museums, arguably unrivaled in the state

Gulf of Mexico

Elevation
6000ft
5000ft
4000ft
3000ft
2000ft
1000ft
500ft
Sea Level

0   40   80 km
0   25   50 miles

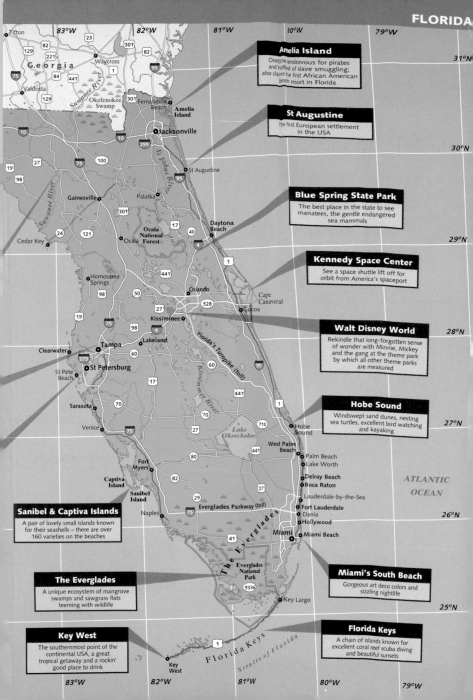

FLORIDA

Amelia Island
One-time rendezvous for pirates and hotbed of slave smuggling; also claims the first African American beach resort in Florida

St Augustine
The first European settlement in the USA

Blue Spring State Park
The best place in the state to see manatees, the gentle endangered sea mammals

Kennedy Space Center
See a space shuttle lift off for orbit from America's spaceport

Walt Disney World
Rekindle that long-forgotten sense of wonder with Minnie, Mickey and the gang at the theme park by which all other theme parks are measured

Hobe Sound
Windswept sand dunes, nesting sea turtles, excellent bird watching and kayaking

Sanibel & Captiva Islands
A pair of lovely small islands known for their seashells – there are over 160 varieties on the beaches

Miami's South Beach
Gorgeous art deco colors and sizzling nightlife

The Everglades
A unique ecosystem of mangrove swamps and sawgrass flats teeming with wildlife

Key West
The southernmost point of the continental USA, a great tropical getaway and a rockin' good place to drink

Florida Keys
A chain of islands known for excellent coral reef scuba diving and beautiful sunsets

Florida
3rd edition – January 2003
First published – January 1997

Published by
Lonely Planet Publications Pty Ltd ABN 36 005 607 983
90 Maribyrnong St, Footscray, Victoria 3011, Australia

Lonely Planet Offices
Australia Locked Bag 1, Footscray, Victoria 3011
USA 150 Linden St, Oakland, CA 94607
UK 10a Spring Place, London NW5 3BH
France 1 rue du Dahomey, 75011 Paris

Photographs
Many of the images in this guide are available for licensing from
Lonely Planet Images.
[W] www.lonelyplanetimages.com

Front cover photograph
White ibis, Everglades National Park (Joseph Van Os/Image Bank)

ISBN 1 74059 136 4

text & maps © Lonely Planet Publications Pty Ltd 2003
photos © photographers as indicated 2003

Printed by The Bookmaker International Ltd
Printed in China

Contents

MIAMI & MIAMI BEACH · 123

THE EVERGLADES · 205

FLORIDA KEYS · 221

SOUTHEAST FLORIDA · 258

CENTRAL FLORIDA · 312

SPACE COAST 374

NORTHEAST FLORIDA 393

SOUTHWEST FLORIDA 438

NORTHWEST FLORIDA & THE PANHANDLE 506

INDEX 553

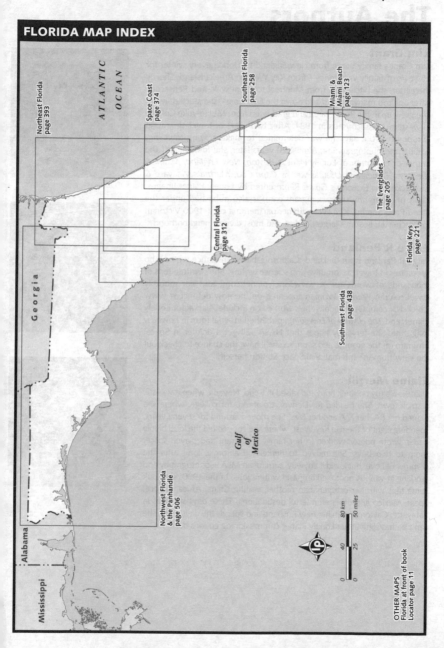

FLORIDA MAP INDEX

ATLANTIC OCEAN

Northeast Florida
page 393

Space Coast
page 374

Southeast Florida
page 258

Miami & Miami Beach
page 123

The Everglades
page 205

Central Florida
page 312

Florida Keys
page 221

Georgia

Southwest Florida
page 438

Gulf of Mexico

Northwest Florida & the Panhandle
page 506

Alabama

Mississippi

0   40   80 km
0   25   50 miles

OTHER MAPS
Florida at front of book
Locator page 11

The Authors

Kim Grant

Kim Grant's family drove from New England to Florida every winter for 15 years of family vacations — from Key West to Amelia Island. Shortly thereafter, she hitchhiked from Montreal to Gainesville and Pensacola. After one too many trips up and down the East Coast, she started flying. She grew up in the Boston area and graduated from Mt Holyoke College in western Massachusetts in 1984. After two years of traveling around Europe on $10 a day, she was determined to make a living traveling, writing and photographing. Almost 20 years later, she finds herself the author or co-author of Lonely Planet's *Boston, New England, Miami & the Keys, Florida* and *USA*, as well as *Cape Cod, Martha's Vineyard & Nantucket: An Explorer's Guide*. Represented by Lonely Planet Images, Kim's photography (www.kimgrant.com) is also published under the Bindu Press imprint. Kim lives with her partner in a circa-1900 Victorian in Dorchester, Boston's largest, oldest and most diverse neighborhood.

Paige R Penland

Paige R Penland is an Oakland, California-based freelance writer who specializes in travel, automotive and science writing. She's written tens of thousands of words for **w** www.lonelyplanet.com, and her monthly travel column *Wander Woman* appeared on the now defunct **w** www .chickclick.com. Other books she's worked on include *Alaska*, for Lonely Planet, and *The History of Lowriding*, published in serial form in *Lowrider* magazine. She fervently hopes that NASA will get a 'Writer in Space' program off the ground, and soon, so she'll have the chance to check out the view from the International Space Station herself.

Elaine Merrill

Elaine is a baby boomer, born and raised in Reno, Nevada, when it was still a small town. She headed for Denver, Colorado, for college, where she earned her BA, her MA and her Mrs. She moved around for several years, spending eight of them in Key West, where she copyedited the local hippie paper, wrote poetry, worked in her family restaurant and played soccer mom to two boys. She moved to Berkeley, California, long after the Summer of Love, but loved it anyway, earning an MFA in photography and working at various photo, editing and writing jobs. In the 1990s she took some trips with her octogenarian mother, visiting China, Africa, Greece, Spain, Mexico and other wonderful destinations. These days she lives in Lafayette, California with her new husband and spends the days when she can't be traveling at her Lonely Planet commissioning editor's desk.

FROM THE AUTHORS

Kim Grant First and foremost, thanks to co-authors Paige Penland (one of the sharpest wits and keenest observers I've encountered) and Elaine Merrill (now a fine Senior Editor in her own right). Three chicks on the road is a tough trio to beat! Lonely Planet should try this combo more often. Paige and Elaine made my coordinating job a breeze. As for Senior Editor David Zingarelli, he's so good that I might consider changing my beat to Central America and the Caribbean in order to work with him again. Project editors Ben Greensfelder (whose knowledge of minutiae is astonishing) and Kanani Kauka (whose manner embodies the Aloha spirit) made the editing process practically painless. Thanks also go to editors and proofers Wade Fox, Wendy Taylor and Kathryn Ettinger. Thanks to new papa Sean Brandt and his entire carto team; LP maps rule! Thanks, Mom, for all your tips since moving to the Sunshine State. And finally, thanks — as always — to the infinitely supportive Lisa Otero, for walking the walk with me.

Paige R Penland I couldn't have done this book without many, many Floridians who dropped what they were doing just to offer recommendations and guidance so you all would have a great trip. Feel free to return the favor by tipping much more than our books suggest.

Thanks especially to Linda and Ben Shuler for their hospitality and insight into the Space Coast and Central Florida; Beth Penland for her help covering Gay Day at Disney; Barbara Brannan and Jason Callahan for the guided tours of Gainesville and the Kennedy Space Center (many of the jokes and insights from the KSC coverage should be attributed to Jason); and Patrick Huerta for his help covering Daytona and making sure all the maps for my portions of the book were as useful as possible. Thanks, too, to Kim and Elaine, as well as the entire LP editorial and cartographic staff that helped hammer my work into place. You all rock. Let's go surfing.

Elaine Merrill On the road, thanks to the friendly folks at HoJo's in Tallahassee (my first home away from home) and to the two gallant gentlemen at the US Air Force Armament Museum who saved the day when I locked my keys in the car. Thanks also to Nick and Corinna Selby for providing a great text base in the 2nd edition of *Florida* and to co-authors Kim Grant and Paige Penland for their ongoing support. In the office, thanks to David Zingarelli for getting me the gig and being there all the way through it, to Maria Donohoe and Ruth Askevold for their phone presence in times of crisis and to Kanani Kauka, editor extraordinaire. At home, thanks to Mike Zinser and to Chris and David Merrill, the people who give meaning to everything I do.

This Book

This is the 3rd edition of Lonely Planet's *Florida*. The 1st and 2nd editions were researched and written by Nick and Corinna Selby.

Kim Grant, Paige Penland and Elaine Merrill updated this edition of the book. Kim acted as coordinating author and updated the introductory chapters as well as the Miami & Miami Beach, Everglades, Florida Keys, and Southwest Florida chapters. She also covered Fort Lauderdale for the Southeast Florida chapter. Paige tackled the rest of Southeast Florida as well as the Central Florida, Northeast Florida and Space Coast chapters. Elaine researched and authored the Northwest Florida & the Panhandle chapter.

Some material in this book was drawn from Lonely Planet's *Miami & the Keys*, which was also authored by Kim Grant.

FROM THE PUBLISHER

David Zingarelli was the in-house mastermind behind *Florida* 3's development and oversaw its US production. Text was edited with keen eyes and deft hands by Ben Greensfelder, Kanani Kauka and Wade Fox. Wendy Taylor and Kathryn Ettinger proofed the pages, Tammy Fortin proofed a mountain of maps and Wendy coordinated the editorial effort. Production assistance was generously provided by Elaine Merrill, Erin Corrigan, Graham Neale, Maria Donohoe, Michele Posner, Susan Rimerman, Vivek Waglé and Wendy Smith.

Cartography was a global effort thanks to Laurie Mikkelsen, Karen Fry, Natasha Valleley, Alison Lyall, Graham Neale, Sean Brandt, Annette Olson and Bart Wright. Thanks also go to Chris LeeAck and Lachlan Ross for their invaluable technical support.

The book pages were impeccably designed by Emily Douglas, who also crafted the colorwraps. Andreas Schueller provided production support. Justin Marler designed the cover and Ruth Askevold handled its production. Susan Rimerman graciously provided guidance during the layout process. Illustrations were created by Justin, Hugh D'Andrade, Hannah Reineck, Hayden Foell and Jennifer Steffey.

Foreword

ABOUT LONELY PLANET GUIDEBOOKS

The story begins with a classic travel adventure: Tony and Maureen Wheeler's 1972 journey across Europe and Asia to Australia. There was no useful information about the overland trail then, so Tony and Maureen published the first Lonely Planet guidebook to meet a growing need.

From a kitchen table, Lonely Planet has grown to become the largest independent travel publisher in the world, with offices in Melbourne (Australia), Oakland (USA), London (UK) and Paris (France).

Today Lonely Planet guidebooks cover the globe. There is an ever-growing list of books and information in a variety of media. Some things haven't changed. The main aim is still to make it possible for adventurous travelers to get out there – to explore and better understand the world.

At Lonely Planet we believe travelers can make a positive contribution to the countries they visit – if they respect their host communities and spend their money wisely. Since 1986 a percentage of the income from each book has been donated to aid projects and human rights campaigns, and, more recently, to wildlife conservation.

UPDATES & READER FEEDBACK

Things change – prices go up, schedules change, good places go bad and bad places go bankrupt. Nothing stays the same. So, if you find things better or worse, recently opened or long-since closed, please tell us and help make the next edition even more accurate and useful.

Lonely Planet thoroughly updates each guidebook as often as possible – usually every two years, although for some destinations the gap can be longer. Between editions, up-to-date information is available in our free, quarterly *Planet Talk* newsletter and monthly email bulletin *Comet*. The *Upgrades* section of our website (W www.lonelyplanet.com) is also regularly updated by Lonely Planet authors, and the site's *Scoop* section covers news and current affairs relevant to travelers. Lastly, the *Thorn Tree* bulletin board and *Postcards* section carry unverified, but fascinating, reports from travelers.

Tell us about it! We genuinely value your feedback. A well-traveled team at Lonely Planet reads and acknowledges every email and letter we receive and ensures that every morsel of information finds its way to the relevant authors, editors and cartographers.

Everyone who writes to us will find their name listed in the next edition of the appropriate guidebook and will receive the latest issue of *Comet* or *Planet Talk*. The very best contributions will be rewarded with a free guidebook.

We may edit, reproduce and incorporate your comments in Lonely Planet products such as guidebooks, websites and digital products, so let us know if you don't want your comments reproduced or your name acknowledged.

How to contact Lonely Planet:
Online: e talk2us@lonelyplanet.com.au, W www.lonelyplanet.com
Australia: Locked Bag 1, Footscray, Victoria 3011
UK: 10a Spring Place, London NW5 3BH
USA: 150 Linden St, Oakland, CA 94607

Introduction

There are only four things you really need to know about Florida. The sun, sea and sand are just as incredible as they are in your mind's eye; fun lurks around most corners. Number two: Everyone is from somewhere else. Number three: Quirky, bizarre and surreal things happen in Florida first (and often nowhere else). And, number four: as the *New York Times* says, 'As Florida goes, so goes a nation.'

Let's start with the most superficial one, the main reason you're drawn to this state in the first place: Florida is an absolutely great vacation destination. It doesn't matter if you're a nuclear family from the Midwest, backpackers from Europe, a straight guy from DC, lesbians from the Bay Area, merrymakers from Oz, college students from

the Northeast or retirees from Canada. It may sound trite, but it's true: Florida offers something for everyone.

You can build entire vacations around a diversity of wilderness areas or beaches, attractive cities or over-the-top theme parks. It's your call. This is a state where a designated historic district can be as young as 60 years old (think Miami Beach's Art Deco District) or older than 400 (think charming St Augustine, the first settlement founded in the New World by the Europeans in 1565).

Hundreds of miles of exceptional beaches have turned the Panhandle into a top destination for sun worshipers. Eastern shore Atlantic beaches are as long as the day is sunny; western shore Gulf beaches are as powdery as confectioner's sugar. And at least a half

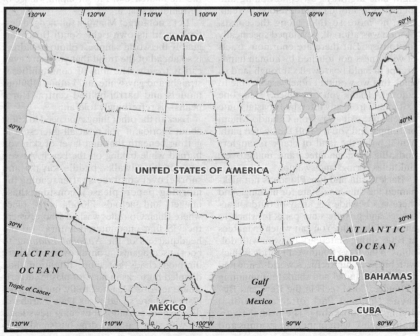

dozen beaches around the state make Dr. Beach's annual top US beaches list.

As a family destination, nothing else in the world can quite compete with the powerhouse confluence of Walt Disney World (and its Magic-Mouse-Kingdom, Epcot, MGM Studios and Animal Kingdom), Universal Studios, Islands of Adventure and SeaWorld in Orlando; Busch Gardens in Tampa; Daytona Beach; and Cape Canaveral's Kennedy Space Center.

Perhaps surprisingly, for a destination known throughout the world for beaches and theme parks, the 'real' Florida – beautiful, challenging and bizarre natural attractions – astounds those who set out to find it. So when your last nerve is trounced by a bright-faced French teenager in a fur suit urging you to 'have a Disney day,' it's nice to know that even in the heart of Walt Disney World, the real Florida is as close as a 40-minute drive. It's accessible.

It's easier than you might think to escape eight-lane highways, air conditioning and high-rises. Is Florida overdeveloped? Yeah, sure, no more so than along the coasts. Florida was, after all, developed specifically for tourists. But there are enormous tracts of wilderness not touched by human hands except to build boardwalks through land so thick that we wouldn't otherwise be able to enjoy it. (Thank you very much.) Head one exit inland from any interstate coastal route or head one exit away from Orlando, Miami or Tampa, and you'll be off the beaten path. You'll be in the land of crackers; anglers and alligators; manatees and mangroves; sinkholes, springs and swamps.

Back to sun and fun: Florida is not nicknamed the Sunshine State for nothing. And there is a bewildering array of outdoor activities and pristine state parks in which to enjoy all that sun. You can watch manatees at Blue Spring State Park or swim with dolphins in the Keys. Southwest Florida is thick with bird-watching refuges, world-renowned shelling in Sanibel and shark-tooth hunting in Venice. Coral reefs in the Keys and Biscayne National Park offer exceptional diving and snorkeling. The primal Everglades, dense with mangrove swamps and

saw-grass flats, offer rare ecotourism opportunities. Then there's rafting, tubing, boating and every other conceivable water sport. In addition to hundreds of miles of shoreline, including a (dare we say) picturesque Intracoastal Waterway, Florida also has 30,000 lakes and rivers, including spring-fed rivers that are so clear, you can easily make out details 60 feet under water.

The 'real' Florida, where the action is, also has wonderfully weird tourist attractions that are as goofy as anything Disney could dream up. Head for psychic fulfillment at Cassadaga, the nation's only township made up entirely of spiritualists. Or check out the nation's only bordello museum in Yeehaw Junction, or an underwater performance of dancing mermaids at Weeki Wachee. Watch residents of a state that saw very little Civil War action as they stage fantastically complex Civil War reenactments. It's the little stuff that'll lodge in your memory: oysters from tiny Apalachicola, fishing on the Steinhatchee or the shrimping village of Fernandina Beach.

Let's not forget Miami, a full-fledged destination in its own right. South Beach, arguably the world's hippest photo backdrop, is so ahead of the trend that you can't even call it trendy. The mix of communities – straight and gay, white and Latino, fabulous models and barrel-bellied central Europeans – is refreshingly tolerant.

Back to the other things you need to know about Florida, if you're at all interested in getting beneath that first layer of skin you burned while baking on the beach. As you wander boardwalks, paddle kayaks and snorkel over coral reefs (after reading the morning paper, please), consider these nuggets and factoids. Florida is the place where Elian Gonzales washed ashore; where the US first encountered anthrax (at the headquarters of the *National Enquirer* to boot) used against it on its own soil; where dimpled chads got more attention than dimpled buttocks in need of plastic surgery; where terrorists learned to fly, but not land, planes; where speed racer Dale Earnhardt died; where sensational evening news leads off with shark attacks, drug busts and abortion doctors getting killed. This is a place that needs your tourist sales-tax dollars because there is no state income tax. As the money flows (or doesn't), so flows a state/nation. This is a place, remember, where everyone is from somewhere else, so all are welcome – even OJ Simpson … but then again, not stable gay couples who want to adopt orphans. This is the place where people ignore their past and re-create themselves, or where they come to die. (To be fair, only 20% of the population consists of retirees.)

Florida's population statistics mirror those of the US as a whole; it has the exact same percentages of whites, Hispanics and African Americans. And as Florida figures out how to create opportunities (or not) for all groups, the nation might sit up and take notice. If Florida can figure out how to deal with ecology *and* development, and not just pay political lip service to the issues during election years, the nation might sit up and take notice. If Florida can assuage its conservative northern brethren (which resemble those in the Deep South) *and* its liberal southern populace (which feels for all the world like the 'Sixth Borough' of Manhattan), perhaps there's hope after all. If not, consider changing your last name to Bush, unfolding a beach chair, peeling an orange and humming along after me: 'It's a small world after all…it's a small, small world.'

Facts about Florida

HISTORY
Early Inhabitants
Discounting beguiling theories of direct transpacific crossings from Southeast Asia, historians now believe that, except for a few Vikings in the north, the pre-Hispanic inhabitants of the Americas arrived from Siberia in waves of migrations between about 60,000 and 8000 BC, crossing land now submerged beneath the Bering Strait. (The earliest known human traces in the US date from about 50,000 BC.) These tribes were highly mobile and, once they crossed into Alaska, moved south to warmer climates.

While there was settlement throughout Florida, the highest concentration of groups was in the coastal areas, as it remains today. In the late Archaic period, about 3000 BC, populations were heaviest in the Panhandle, in the northeast and southwest portions of the state and around present-day Tampa. Shell middens (mounds), created from a riotous abundance of snails, mussels and oysters, are evidence of settlements. One wonders how it was possible to eat that much shellfish. The only way to get a grasp on the quantities is to see it for yourself: See the Southwest Florida chapter for information on Mound Key, where shell mounds reach heights of 30 feet and were dense enough to provide the foundation for an entire village.

By 600 to 500 BC, more defined cultures began to develop ceramic, shell and copper items. In northeast Florida, the St Johns River villages had sand burial mounds and highly developed village life that for the first time showed signs of dependence on agriculture (corn) as opposed to hunting.

Indian Peoples
Little written history exists on the various groups of Florida natives, but it seems clear that by the time the first Europeans arrived, in the 16th century, distinct groups of Indians had settled in the region.

The largest northern group was the Timucuan, described as being very tall (it is said that height was inbred, by mating the tallest males and females) and very beautiful.

The 20,000 or so Calusa were the largest group on the southwest part of the peninsula. There's tantalizing speculation concerning the origin of the Calusa's hatred of the Spaniards, which suggests contact earlier than is recorded, but one thing is clear: the Calusa didn't much care for the Spanish and were highly demonstrative of their animosity.

Other groups included the Tequesta, who lived at the southern tip of the peninsula between the 10,000 Islands and present-day Miami; the Ais and Jeaga, on the southeast coast; the Tocobaga, on the Gulf Coast north of the Calusa; and the 25,000 Apalachee who occupied the eastern end of the Panhandle.

Spanish Exploration
Juan Ponce de León, an explorer on Christopher Columbus' second voyage (1493) and fighter in the Spanish siege of Puerto Rico (1506–7), sailed northwest from Spanish settlements in the Caribbean and wound up running smack into central Florida's Atlantic coastline in 1513, probably near present-day Cape Canaveral. In honor of Pascua Florida, the Easter Feast of Flowers, Ponce de León named this new land Florida.

Ponce de León didn't see anyone on the shores of what he thought was an island, but he claimed the land for Spain just in case and then tried to sail around it. After making his way around the Florida Keys, he ended up at San Carlos, near present-day Tampa, where he was welcomed by the Calusa with arms – not open ones, just arms.

The Calusa attacked until he sailed away, but Ponce de León had discovered a good source of freshwater and, he presumed, a line on all the riches the area undoubtedly held. He returned to Spain, and on the way he discovered the arid keys west of Key West and named them *Las Tortugas* for the huge numbers of turtles there (see Dry Tortugas National Park in the Florida Keys chapter).

Who Are the Seminole?

The native group with the most name recognition in Florida, the Seminole, is neither a single tribe nor one that existed when the first Europeans landed in Florida. Instead, the Seminole began as breakaways from other Indian tribes, as well as all kinds of runaways, including black slaves. The origin of the name Seminole is a tricky one: the Florida Department of State says it derives from the Spanish *cimarrone*, while most historical texts claim it was a Creek Indian word, sim-in-ole or sem-in-ole. In any case, in both languages it means 'wild one' or 'runaway' or even 'one who camps at a distance' and reflects the origins of the Seminole nation.

The Muskhogean Indians once existed all around the Gulf Coast of the present-day USA. A subgroup, the Creek Confederacy, settled in Georgia and Alabama and gained in number and strength by the turn of the 19th century, when skirmishes with the ever-encroaching Americans escalated into mass killings on both sides. Andrew Jackson enlisted the help of the American-friendly Lower Creeks against the Upper Creeks in the Battle of Horseshoe Bend, on March 27, 1814. It all but wiped them out. The surviving Red Sticks, a faction of the Upper Creeks, escaped south into still-Spanish Florida, where they were joined by other groups of Indians escaping similar treatment. The Seminole welcomed them, as well as runaway slaves, with open arms.

All these groups eventually became the Seminole and Miccosukee nations, and though technically in Spanish territory, they were far from safe from Andrew Jackson's purges. Partly in the interest of reclaiming escaped black slaves living among the Seminole, the Americans continued to pursue the Indians across the border. See Seminole Wars, later in this section.

King Ferdinand V named Ponce de León governor of Florida in 1514. Ponce de León was unable to return to the land until 1521, when he brought settlers, animals and missionaries back to San Carlos. You can guess what the Calusa did. Ponce de León died shortly thereafter in Cuba from a poison-arrow wound. But this did not discourage the Spanish, who were convinced – based on their experiences in South America and the recent discoveries in Mexico – that Florida was a land of untold mineral wealth.

After Ponce de León's death, several other attempts were made by the Spanish to suss out just what Florida (the area now encompassing much of the present-day southeastern USA) had to offer. Attempts were made by the feckless Pánfilo de Narváez, who blew it in 1528 and lost everything – four ships, 400 men (including himself) and 80 horses. Despite the disaster, a greater understanding about the land was gained from the diaries of Narváez's treasurer, Álvar Núñez Cabeza de Vaca, who survived among the Indians for eight years before rejoining his own people in Mexico City. Considerably more successful was the approximately 4000-mile expedition by Hernando de Soto in 1539. De Soto explored a huge area of the southeastern USA, and when he died in 1542, he was buried in the Mississippi River.

The French & British Sniff Around

Over the next 20 years, the Spanish were still unable to make a permanent settlement in Florida. Meanwhile, the British and French were sniffing around the region, looking for minerals and possible colonial lands.

Despite the Spanish claim on the region, the French arrived in 1562 under the command of Jean Ribault and established a colony on Parris Island, at the southern end of present-day South Carolina. It failed, and Ribault's deputy, René de Laudonnière, pushed on to establish Fort Caroline in 1564 on the St Johns River near present-day Jacksonville.

Never one to let the French pull a fast one, Spain's King Philip II sent Pedro Menéndez de Avilés to stomp the French and establish a fort of his own. In 1565 Menéndez arrived at Cape Canaveral with about 1500 soldiers and settlers. They made their way north and established St Augustine, named for the day on which they arrived on the Florida coast: August 28, the Feast Day of Saint Augustine, Bishop of Hippo. St Augustine was established on September 4; it was the USA's first permanent European settlement.

Menéndez and his troops headed north, where they were whupped by the French; they then retreated south to St Augustine. Soon after, the French, in an effort to fight *fuego* with *feu*, launched a fleet to take on the pesky Spaniards. But the French fell victim to one of Florida's famous coastal storms, and their fleet was destroyed. Menéndez, always optimistic, immediately forged north to the relatively unpopulated French fort and destroyed it. He executed all prisoners, as well as survivors from the French fleet washed ashore south of St Augustine. In all, almost 600 people were butchered, giving the inlet its name: *Matanzas* (massacres).

And so a full 50 years before the Pilgrims lurched upon Plymouth Rock, and 40 before even the establishment at Jamestown, Florida was finally settled for the Spanish by Menéndez.

Florida would become to North America what Poland is to Europe: the flattest piece of land between battling superpowers. Before it was ceded to the USA by Spain in 1821, the area was occupied by several armies – a total of eight flags have flown over Amelia Island.

A Good Christian Colony

In addition to chasing away Frenchmen and seeking to get rich, Menéndez also sought to convert the Indians to Christianity and to generally show them what swell folks the Spanish were. His goal was to establish a territory-wide series of missions, forts and trade posts.

All did not go as planned. Missionaries were murdered, and Indian uprisings became as common as one would expect when a new force comes in and tells you everything you believe in is wrong, and in any case it belongs

to them. To make matters worse, in 1568 a new bunch of Frenchmen showed up to avenge the deaths at Fort Caroline; they were assisted by turncoat Timucuans, who led them right into the fort.

Menéndez regained control of the situation in a method still common today: he threw money and people at it. He tidied up problems that were delaying his supply lines from Cuba and offered highly attractive conditions to settlers, who came in droves. St Augustine became a bustling and wealthy trading town.

The French & British in North America

In the late 16th century, the French and British were both making overtures to settle the New World, or at least to keep their hands in it. In 1584, Elizabeth I granted Sir Walter Raleigh a charter to settle lands in North America. His colony, on Roanoke Island in North Carolina's Outer Banks, is remembered today as the 'Lost Colony' for the mysterious disappearance of its settlers.

Meanwhile, Spanish St Augustine was under constant pressure from the Brits: the city was attacked and burned by troops led by Sir Francis Drake in 1586. Later, in 1702, the British returned and attacked the city for 52 days, burning it down – but the Castillo de San Marcos fort held. (See St Augustine, in the Northeast Florida chapter.)

The 1607 settlement of Jamestown, Virginia (which generally gets Anglocentric textbook honors for being the first European settlement in the New World, despite the presence of St Augustine) was a problem-plagued English colony. Half the party died during its first winter.

Meanwhile, the French were wondering how to get their hands on the Louisiana Territory, which they would claim in the late 17th century.

From Settlement to Colony

St Augustine grew, and life gained a degree of normalcy. Even the original missionary activities were gaining a foothold, and Spain was forging relations with Indians throughout the territory. With a few notable exceptions near the turn of the 17th century, including rebellions by Guale and Ais Indians, Florida was humming right along. But it was still a very dangerous place, fraught with the peril of Indian or European attacks, fires set either by invading armies or drunken card players and a sense that it could all end at a moment's notice.

The population of St Augustine was mainly soldiers and traders, and the city limits at the time were far smaller than they are today. As the Indians and settlers began to pair off (and as prostitution became more common), the Indians found themselves looking at a slew of new diseases. These diseases would, over the next 100 years, finish what the early explorers had started and exterminate all but a smattering of Florida's once-thriving Indian population.

Superpower Shift

During the 17th century, the shape of the world superpowers was altered, with Spain losing control of many colonies and possessions, and Britain and France gaining more power. While the British and French sent troops and explorers scurrying all over the new territories, the Spanish seemed perfectly content to maintain their itsy-bitsy settlements at St Augustine and Pensacola, at the western end of the state.

By the end of the 17th century, the Brits, who were in possession of well-established colonies in the northeast, were continually pressing the Spanish on the southern boundaries of the British territory. In 1670 a demarcation line was established on what are roughly the present-day borders of Georgia and South Carolina, but the line was taken more as a suggestion than a rule, and the Brits repeatedly ran raids into the Spanish territory – either overtly or covertly.

To the west, the French were quickly establishing colonies along the Mississippi River, trying to link up the South with their new Canadian territories. Alliances between the powers were formed as quickly as they were scrapped – and they were scrapped as soon as they were formed.

Throughout the 18th century, the very proximity of the British in Georgia, the French in Louisiana and the Spanish in Florida heightened tensions. By 1700 there were 12 British colonies, and the British were definitely setting their sights on Florida. In 1732 James Oglethorpe settled Savannah, Georgia, and after a trip to England for supplies and armaments, he attacked St Augustine in 1740. That attack, which laid siege to the city for 27 days before Oglethorpe's troops ran out of supplies and were forced to retreat, led the Spanish to build tiny Fort Matanzas, at the southern end of St Augustine. While the Spanish repelled the attack again, their position continued to be under constant pressure from the British.

French & Indian War

As pressure on Spain mounted, so too did the friction between the other two big boys in the fray, England and France. As they began feeling the urge to stretch their legs to the west and east, respectively, hostilities

That's Dedication

When the first Europeans arrived in Florida, they could not have imagined a less welcoming place. Aside from hostile natives and the unforgiving heat, the land itself was swampy, overgrown and fraught with dangers. Early settlers had to contend with alligators, poisonous snakes, thick undergrowth and vegetation, and perhaps worst of all, biting insects in such prodigious quantities that the explorers wondered if they had arrived in hell.

As settlers pushed southward in Florida, workers related stories about black clouds of mosquitoes swarming from sunrise to sunset. And the swamplike conditions throughout the state, especially in the south, made reclaiming land a nightmare.

As we look at Florida today, with its winding ribbons of asphalt and its urban sprawl, it's easy to forget just how recently much of the state was uninhabitable by any but the most dedicated backwoods travelers.

broke out between them in 1754. Known as the French & Indian War for the French alliance with Indian groups against the British, it was the first war between European powers fought outside of Europe.

Choosing the marginally lesser of two evils, the Spanish chose to side with France in 1761, to which England replied, 'Fine, and by the way, we hope you liked Havana 'cause we just took it.' In the First Treaty of Paris (1763), ending the seven-year-long war, Spain was offered a swap of Cuba for Florida, and they jumped at the chance.

American Revolution

England tried to force the 13 original colonies to float the cost of its war with France in the form of new taxes. But tax hikes aren't the best way to win votes in America; higher taxes – including tariffs on just about anything Americans held dear, a hated Stamp Act and taxes on iron goods – precipitated a break from England. America's rallying cry was 'No taxation without representation' (taxation imposed on the colonists while they had no ability to plead their own case to the Court of St James). Today, of course, content in their ample congressional representation, Americans happily chip in and pay all new taxes. Ha!

Officially declared in 1776, the American Revolution barely affected Florida, which remained avidly loyalist. Florida's governor at the time invited other loyalists to move down to the region.

But after just 20 years of British rule – during which Florida developed a social structure the Spanish had never succeeded in creating – the Second Treaty of Paris (1783) ended the Revolution and returned Florida to the hands of Spain.

US Expansion

The northernmost portion of Florida was becoming quite alluring indeed to expansionist Americans toward the end of the 18th century; in 1795 some Georgian hotheads attacked the San Nicolás mission in present-day Jacksonville. They held it for several months before being beaten back to Georgia. And in 1800 Spain finally gave up

the Louisiana Territory to Napoleon, who promptly gave it up to the Americans!

A little later, Amelia Island, northeast of Jacksonville, became a key strategic locale. In 1807–08 President Thomas Jefferson imposed his wildly unpopular Embargo Act, which banned the importation of French and British products and prohibited slave importation. Amelia Island morphed into black-market central.

As the superpowers – and the USA was fast on its way to becoming one, at least in this region – squared off for what was to become the War of 1812 (1812–15), the Spanish ended up allied with the British against the US and France. The War of 1812, aside from being a power struggle between the Americans and British, was an aggressive campaign of US expansion – north into Canada, westward across the plains and south into Florida.

The 1814 Battle of Horseshoe Bend, in Alabama, proved pivotal for Florida. There, notorious (and heroic to his compatriots) Indian-hunter Andrew Jackson (1767–1845) defeated the Creeks in an overwhelming massacre, and then took half of their huge territory for the US. The battle also gave him an excuse to chase fleeing Creeks into Spanish Florida under the guise of defense. In late 1817 Jackson instigated the First Seminole War; see below.

As the US sent more and more troops into the region on Indian-hunting and Spanish-harassing missions, the pressure became too much for Spain. It gradually lost its grip on East Florida settlements – Amelia Island was a Sodom-like den of smuggling, piracy, prostitution and debauchery – and the Spanish government's inability to adequately supply and police the area led to its decision to cede the territory to the US in 1819.

But an itchy Spanish King Ferdinand VII began to waiver. After the US told the Spanish to give up and get out or face US troops, a renegotiated treaty was signed, specifying among other things that the US would assume Spanish debt in the region. The Spanish finally gave up control of Florida in 1821. The debts, by the way, were never repaid. And who do you think was made governor of the new American territory? Yep, Jackson himself.

Seminole Wars

The treaty signed in 1814, at the end of the Battle of Horseshoe Bend, opened to white settlers some 20 million acres of land in the region owned by the Creeks. Tensions ran very high, and skirmishes periodically broke out. There would be a total of three Seminole Wars.

Instigated by Andrew Jackson, the first began in 1817, when Indians in the Miccosukee settlement of Fowltown had the audacity to respond to an attack by whites, killing about 50, including some women and children. Enter Jackson, who late that year stormed through Florida with a force of 5000, destroying Seminole villages and, while he was at it, engaging in a totally unsanctioned attack on Pensacola. (He actually took it, but the US gave it back – see Pensacola, in the Northwest Florida chapter.)

Jackson was elected president of the USA in 1828, and the extermination of the American Indian was accelerated by his Indian Removal Act of 1830. The Treaty of Moultrie Creek of 1823 and the Treaty of Payne's Landing of 1832 were both signed by *some* Seminole, who agreed to give up their Florida lands and move west to reservations, but the provisions of the treaties were flouted by both sides. When the US began moving troops in 1835 to enforce the Treaty of Payne's Landing, Osceola, a Seminole leader, planned an attack on an army detachment. Major Francis Dade and 108 of his men were ambushed by the Seminole as they marched between Tampa and Fort King – only three survived. The attack triggered the beginning of the Second Seminole War, which lasted seven years.

The war dragged on so long because it was fought guerrilla-style by the Seminole in swamps and hammocks. (This was highly atypical of the traditional European tactics employed by US soldiers.) Creek Indian warriors from Alabama were engaged to fight for the US, in exchange for promises of federal protection of their families while they were away fighting. Not surprisingly, they returned to pillaged homes and were interned in camps and gradually forced west.

Osceola was captured on October 27, 1837, as he approached US Major General Thomas Jesup, commander of the Florida troops, both traveling under white flags. Jesup snatched Osceola, who later died at Fort Moultrie in South Carolina.

By 1842, thousands of Seminole had been displaced, marched to reservations in the west by army troops. As the war wound down, the surviving Florida Seminole took refuge in the Everglades. Despite their relegation to the swamps, the Seminole weren't really left alone, and in 1853 they were actually outlawed – a law proclaiming Indians illegal in Florida called for their removal to any place west of the Mississippi River.

In 1855, a party of surveyors were killed after they encroached on Seminole territory. The resulting backlash turned into the Third Seminole War, which ended after Chief Billy Bowlegs agreed to go west (he was paid) in 1858. He and about 100 Seminole did migrate, but about 200 or 300 refused to acknowledge the agreement and retreated into the Everglades. There was never a full treaty ending the war, and some Seminole today say they are technically still at war with the USA.

Statehood & the Civil War

With the Indians out of the way, Florida became the 27th state admitted to the Union on March 3, 1845, only to secede 16 years later with the onset of the Civil War. Admitted to the Union as a slave-owning, agricultural state, Florida seceded from the USA along with the Confederacy on January 10, 1861.

The US Civil War (1861–65) stemmed from a number of issues, but a few rise to the fore. There was a profound debate over the moral and economic issues surrounding slavery. In the 19th century, public opinion against it – and in favor of 'free labor' – in the northern states and in England was quickly rising. Compounding this issue were the distinct economic differences between the northern and southern states.

Northern states, while maintaining an agrarian base, were moving quickly over to manufacturing and industry. The South depended on selling raw materials, principally cotton, to manufacturing nations such as Britain, but the North was in favor of instituting trade tariffs to protect its fledgling industry.

Additionally, the introduction of new territories to the USA through westward expansion potentially introduced a tilt in the balance of power between free and slave states within the US Congress. That issue was underscored by the admittance of California in 1850 as a free state.

Florida's Role Aside from providing troops, Florida's role in the Civil War was mainly one of supplying the ever-growing food needs of the Confederate war machine. As Yossarian explained to Milo in *Catch-22,* troops just can't eat cotton (even when chocolate covered), and since cotton was the South's main crop, the Confederate army pressed Florida's citrus and cattle farmers into heavy overtime.

All did not go well. Cattle ranchers and packing plants were heavily overburdened. Florida cattle were so valuable to the Confederates that the Union's attentions focused on Florida in an effort to cripple the South – the largest battle of the war held on Florida soil, at Olustee, began as a Union effort to cut off beef supplies.

Civil War battles in Florida included the following:

Santa Rosa Island – October 9, 1861
    1200 Union soldiers captured Fort Pickens at Pensacola.

St Johns Bluff – October 1 to 3, 1862
    A Union flotilla carrying about 1500 troops on ships steamed into the mouth of the St Johns River. They were joined by infantry forces at Mt Pleasant Creek and then landed forces at Mayport. The Confederates got out of Dodge.

Fort Brooke – October 16 to 18, 1863
    Under covering fire from two Union ships, the Union marched to the Hillsborough River and captured the *Scottish Chief* and *Kate Dale.*

Olustee – February 20, 1864
    After a fine start sacking several Confederate encampments, Union General Truman Seymour's troops ran into the decidedly unimpressed Brigadier General Joseph Finegan and 5000 of his closest friends. Finegan broke the Union line but allowed the troops to retreat to Jacksonville in this, the largest battle in Florida.

Natural Bridge – March 6, 1865
    Major General John Newton went after Confederate troops who had attacked at Cedar Keys and Fort Myers. The Union army advanced and tried to cross the river at Natural Bridge, near St Marks, but the Confederates (Home Guard as well as a 'Baby Corps' of adolescent boy cadets) held their position.

At the end of the war, Tallahassee was the only Confederate state capital that hadn't fallen to Federal troops.

Reconstruction

The Civil War was one of the bloodiest conflicts in the history of modern warfare, and wounds ran incredibly deep. From the early stages of the conflict until his assassination, President Abraham Lincoln (1809–65) had been putting together a framework for reconstruction of the Union – the 10% Plan. Under it, the Union would federally recognize states in which as few as 10% of the populace had taken oaths of loyalty to the USA – a plan designed to grant political viability to dependable groups (in the Union's opinion) as quickly as possible.

But with Lincoln's assassination, all bets were off, and a political void opened; Florida was ruled by martial law under Union troops. Any semblance of a state government disappeared after the war. Florida's governor, John Milton, killed himself, preferring death to Reconstruction. The state was then run by troops carrying out orders from Washington. In the confusion that followed, dozens of factions struggled for power – from labor organizers to the Ku Klux Klan, an organized gang of white supremacists who began a campaign of violence against blacks that continues to this day.

But as the federal government established and maintained order, the return to normalcy progressed. Farmers scrambled to reestablish farms, and Florida blacks, though technically free, found themselves working as hired hands for the same plantations as before. As businessmen and former politicians struggled to re-create a state government, heated arguments arose on what role, freedoms and recognition blacks in Florida would receive.

President Andrew Johnson, a Southerner and former slave owner who succeeded Lincoln, devised a compromise between Lincoln's and the more radical southern proposals. While his presidential reconstruction granted many concessions, it remained firm that state constitutions must ratify the 13th Amendment, abolishing slavery, before being readmitted to the Union.

The contentious issue was black suffrage, something the southern states were loath to

Florida Black Heritage Trail

Florida's pointed political geography has afforded it an exotic and intricate history, nowhere more apparent than along the Black Heritage Trail. This collection of 141 sites scattered throughout the state commemorates the trials and triumphs of blacks in Florida, from the free founders of St Augustine through the artists and scientists of the last century. The Department of State publishes the 32-page *Florida Black Heritage Trail*, with maps and commentaries, as well as recommended driving tours. Order a free copy by calling ☎ 888-735-2872, or download maps and a four-day driving tour at ⓦ www.flausa.com/interests/tours/aa.php.

During the 18th and early 19th centuries the British, Spanish, French and finally the Confederacy imported enslaved Africans to clear the swamps and cull from the earth the agricultural bounty that has kept Florida in doubloons and dollars since the colonial era. But Florida's patchwork of political spheres, pirate empires and uncharted outback offered unusual opportunities for blacks willing to risk everything for freedom. Slaves who escaped Georgia to Spanish-held Florida were often granted their freedom upon arrival in St Augustine, where they founded Fort Mose, a military stronghold for black freedom fighters.

During the War of 1812, the British used Fort Gadsden, near Apalachicola, to recruit escaped slaves and disgruntled Seminole and Choctaw Indians to their side. After being defeated, Britain abandoned its new troops, who held the fort until US forces invaded, slaughtering almost half of them.

During the Civil War, blacks also played a major role in the brutal Battle of Olustee, east of Jacksonville. Union forces, 30% of which were African American, lost almost 2000 men in five hours; the Confederacy lost about half that. The battlefield is now the site of one of the country's largest reenactments; it takes place every February 20.

Following the Civil War, Henry Flagler, Addison Mizner and Abrams L Lewis began building resort communities up and down the coastline. Lewis, who had made his fortune in Jacksonville as owner of the Afro American Insurance Company, had an edge attracting a crowd to American Beach, on Amelia Island, in the 1930s. Segregation kept African Americans off the nicest bits of the northern coastline, so they rolled south, where they could enjoy this sweet stretch of sand all day, then listen to Duke Ellington, Count Basie and, in later years, Florida native Ray Charles do their thing all night in black-owned clubs, restaurants and resorts.

These are just a few of the sites along Florida's Black Heritage Trail, along which baseball legend Jackie Robinson played his first major-league game (Daytona) and writer Zora Neale Hurston found inspiration on the porch of Joe Clark's store (Eatonville).

Freedom was hard won in this country, and not wasted in Florida. Add a little inspiration to your sun-soaked vacation and check out some of the sites preserved along this fascinating tribute to some of Florida's finest folk.

– Paige Penland

grant, but under the congressional Reconstruction plan, martial law was eventually imposed to install it. When Florida was readmitted in 1868, it had technically granted the vote to blacks, but the state's new constitution was carefully worded to ensure Florida did not get a 'negro government.' After Federal troops left, discriminatory laws were enacted – including one forbidding a black man to testify at a white man's trial – and a poll tax was imposed, which kept droves of black and poor white voters away from the voting booth.

The new Florida government began what in many ways continues to this day: an agenda of pro-business, pro-development activities to open up Florida's natural resources to exploitation at the expense of social programs. While schools went underfunded and overcrowded, developers and tourists were enticed to the area – the former by criminally cheap land prices (25¢ an acre was not unheard of) and the latter by hotels and resorts built by the former.

Development

At the end of the 18th century, real-estate developers were creating holiday resorts throughout Florida. As the state's agricultural trade – especially citrus and cattle – expanded, the need for railroads increased. As communications advanced, the ability to shuttle tourists to hitherto remote areas of Florida became feasible.

The first trans-state railroad was constructed just prior to the Civil War by David Yulee (the first Jewish member of the US Senate), but sadly, it remained open for only about a month, running from Fernandina Beach to Cedar Key before being rerouted north during the war. After the war, railroads popped up throughout the state, and much of Florida was finally connected to the Atlantic coast railroads and thus with the northern states for the first time.

Henry Flagler (1830–1913), who was partners with John D Rockefeller in Standard Oil, was arguably the most important developer, turning Florida into a holiday destination juggernaut. Flagler, whose real-estate career began in Westchester County,

New York, became convinced that Florida's Atlantic coast was the perfect playground for the rich and famous, and by golly, he was the man to bring them there.

Flagler first purchased the existing railroad between Jacksonville and St Augustine, and from that, he created what would become the Florida East Coast (FEC) Railway. It eventually traversed the entire east coast from Jacksonville to Key West.

Flagler built resorts in each of the railway's main terminals, beginning in St Augustine, where he constructed the Ponce de León Hotel (now Flagler College) and helped spur a boom of area resorts. The railroad extended southward; Flagler also planned a southern terminus in Palm Beach, where he built an even more lavish resort, the Royal Poinciana Hotel, and the Palm Beach Inn (now known as The Breakers).

After a record freeze in 1895 that shocked tourists and stunned the fledgling Florida citrus industry, Flagler took Julia Tuttle (a major landowner in Miami) up on her offer to extend the FEC to Miami, and eventually to Key West, across Flagler's crown jewel, the Overseas Highway. Although the highway connected Key West to the mainland over a series of causeways, it wasn't profitable. It was also destroyed by a hurricane in 1935. The foundations of the FEC's bridges were incorporated in the second incarnation of the Overseas Highway (the road that exists today) over the next several years.

Addison Mizner (1872–1933) also made a major contribution to South Florida's development. Just after WWI, the favored architect developed Mediterranean-style, pastel-colored mansions for rich vacationers and homeowners in Palm Beach and especially Boca Raton. Mizner was wiped out in the land bust of 1926.

Spanish-American War

The USA showed it was a power to be reckoned with during the 10-week Spanish-American War in 1898. As Cuba struggled for independence from Spanish rule, and as

Railroads in Florida

Railroads were the single most important factor in the development of Florida. Most people associate railroads in Florida with Henry Flagler, who owned the Florida East Coast (FEC) Railway, but Flagler was a latecomer.

Henry B Plant (1819–99) was probably the biggest player in the railroad scene; his Plant Railroad System ran up the southwest coast and across Florida, connecting with steamships between Tampa, Key West and Havana. By the time he sold his railroad empire in 1902, his system included or connected with a network including the East Florida Railway from Jacksonville to the St Mary's River, the Savannah, Florida & Western Line and the Louisville & Nashville line running across the Panhandle.

After the land bust in 1926, several lines folded. WWII breathed life into John Williams' Seaboard Air Line Railway for a while, but business stayed slow even after a merger of competing rail lines in the late 1960s. The beginning of the end was the arrival in 1971 of Amtrak, which gobbled up remaining companies, cut service and raised prices. The merger of the remaining lines, Seaboard Coast Line and the Chessie System, created the CSX Corporation in 1980.

Today Florida railroad museums pop up here and there, and if you do find a functional line – like the Seminole Gulf Railway in Fort Myers – it's probably only a tourist attraction, for dinner excursions rather than for transportation.

reports drifted back of Cuban farmers being gathered into prison camps, newspapers like William Randolph Hearst's *New York Journal* began a propaganda campaign of 'yellow journalism,' which successfully riled the American public.

The news stories ostensibly supported the 'humanitarian annexation' of Cuba, which perhaps not coincidentally would have been the culmination of the USA's Manifest Destiny – a doctrine that held that it was destined to control all of North America – and a happy windfall to US businessmen.

President William McKinley resisted intervention, but when the battleship *Maine* was destroyed in Havana harbor, McKinley declared war on Spain; Congress ratified the declaration on April 25. (Debate rages today about the *Maine*'s destruction. On one hand, suspiciously, all the ship's officers were ashore at the time of the detonation. On the other, there's new evidence that the explosion was accidental.)

The main fighting took place in two theaters: the South Pacific and Cuba. After handy victories in Manila and Guam, US army and volunteer regiments landed in Cuba in late June, including the Rough Riders (who had to leave their horses in Florida), led by Leonard Wood and Theodore Roosevelt.

With the military buildup, many Florida towns – especially Tampa, Key West, Miami and Jacksonville – had people pouring in to receive plots of homesteading land. And as reports filtered north, Florida gained a reputation as a paradisiacal location affordable to all: tourists came in droves. Because it became the most important staging area for the fight in Cuba, South Florida experienced something of a mini-boom.

The Spanish-American War itself was something of a letdown to war buffs; the Spanish surrendered on July 17.

Social Conditions

As developers moved into Florida, conditions for the poor grew worse as railroad and land barons practically bought the state outright. Government was rife with corruption, land deals were questionable, and social services were at an appallingly low level. But as farmers and workers organized, a distinct antideveloper mood infiltrated Florida's political system. The organization and collective protests of farmers, blacks and women resulted in the election of Napoleon Bonaparte Broward as governor in 1905.

A populist, antideveloper/pro-little-guy candidate, Broward actually followed through with many social programs, including child labor laws, an inspired education system, labor law reforms and new jobs. Unfortunately, his theories on how to create new jobs were the very cause of the destruction of the Everglades: it was he who initiated drainage and canals throughout the Everglades in an effort to expose mucklands necessary for growing sugar.

WWI & the Roaring '20s

Once again war helped Florida. By the time the USA entered WWI in 1917, there was a large naval presence at Key West, Pensacola, Tampa and Jacksonville. By the time the war was over, Florida's new permanent residents led the state into the '20s with great momentum.

During Prohibition (the ban on the sale or manufacturing of alcohol in the USA), Florida became a smuggler's haven. Consider all the unguarded coastline, the convenient proximity to Cuba and Puerto Rico, and the endless supply of vacationing imbibers. Miami especially never took much to Prohibition; Al Capone moved in to grab a piece of the action, and Miami Beach became one constant party, packing in gamblers and drinkers.

The entire state was booming on a huge scale, one never before seen in the USA. Hundreds of thousands of people were migrating to Florida; land prices soared. Railroads and roads were popping up everywhere, and cities were expanding at staggering rates.

Land Bust

In a manner similar to the stock markets of the '20s, buying Florida land on margin was the ticket; shysters bought land with incredibly small down payments and shucked it onto settlers at huge profits. With such buying and construction, transportation became ever more important. But several disasters were straining the limits of existing communications – among them, a debilitating rail strike and a sunken supply ship in Miami harbor that blocked the entrance to the Miami River and kept other boats from dropping off their loads.

But the end came in a flash: a major hurricane hit South Florida in late 1926, wiping out construction, killing 400 and injuring thousands. In the aftermath, hordes of people who thought they were getting the deal of a lifetime found the catch – deadly storms. They pulled out quickly, taking their money with them. Land prices plummeted, and banks folded like books. And as if to hammer the nails in the coffin, the area was hit by another devastating hurricane and several smaller storms a little more than a year later.

Great Depression

Florida businesses pretty much followed the national trend during the Great Depression, after the stock market crash of 1929. As banks failed, businesses failed, and many of Florida's rich developers ran home with their tails between their legs. Since Florida's economy was already suffering because of the land bust, the Depression hit it harder than other states, and as such, it needed more federal bail-outs.

Florida was a major supporter of Franklin Delano Roosevelt. In the President's first '100 Days,' he called an emergency session of Congress to create dozens of new government agencies that would have a profound effect on Florida and the nation. As part of Roosevelt's New Deal, the Works Progress Administration (WPA) and the Civilian Conservation Corps (CCC) were created. The WPA sent armies of workers to construct buildings, roads, dams, trails and housing, while the CCC worked to restore state and national parks. Other federal programs included Social Security, which gives money to the elderly and infirm (memo to Republicans: if you don't like it, give yours back). It was the largest campaign of government-created jobs in the USA, and while critics at the time called it busywork, projects by the WPA and CCC stand today, many as national landmarks.

1940s & 1950s

After the Japanese attack on Pearl Harbor, Hawaii, on December 7, 1941, the USA began work on its war machine. Though it sounds cruel, WWII was just what Florida needed. In early 1942, U-boats off the coast of Florida were sinking US freighters at an alarming rate. Almost overnight, Florida turned into one of the biggest war factories and training grounds in the Union: almost every US pilot who flew in WWII trained in Florida; the Army's anti-U-boat school was in Miami; Key West's naval base overflowed with sailors.

As the war ended, soldiers and sailors returned to settle in the region. Once again, Florida experienced a boom initiated by war. Miami Beach experienced yet another boom, as it became known as the 'Cuba of America' and was driven by gangsters and gamblers.

The area was also the beneficiary of increased demand for agricultural products, and Florida farmers raked in big bucks. During the war, Florida's citrus production was the highest in the nation.

In 1954, Leroy Collins became the first Southern governor to declare racial segregation 'morally wrong.'

When the aerospace industry moved into Florida near the end of the '50s, an entire 'Space Coast' was created to support the highfalutin goals of the National Aeronautics & Space Administration (NASA) in its race to beat the Russkies into space – see the Space Coast chapter for a full history of the US space program.

Bay of Pigs

After the 1959 Cuban revolution, Miami and South Florida became flooded with many anti-Castro immigrants, who, in gathering to arrange a counterrevolutionary (CR) force, managed to establish a permanent Cuban community in Miami.

A group of exiles formed the 2506th Brigade, sanctioned by the US government, which provided weapons and CIA training for the purpose of launching an attack on Cuba. In April 1961, the CRs landed on the beaches at Playa Giróin, a town on the Bay of Pigs. But a warning had somehow leaked

to the Cubans – a *New York Times* correspondent says he heard about the impending attack weeks before it happened – and the pathetic, half-baked, poorly planned and badly executed attack found itself up against forces who were waiting in a virtual ambush.

To add insult to injury, when the magnitude of the botch-up became clear, President Kennedy, in the name of 'plausible deniability,' refused to send air cover or naval support. The first wave of CRs was left on the beach with no reinforcements or supplies. The CRs were all captured or killed (though all prisoners were released by Cuba about three months later).

Kennedy vs Krushchev

Kennedy and the CIA both looked rather silly after the fiasco, and that is probably why Kennedy stood his ground so firmly when the world was brought to the brink of nuclear war during the Cuban Missile Crisis.

Smelling blood after the Bay of Pigs, the USSR's General Secretary Nikita Krushchev began secretly installing missile bases in Cuba. By some stroke of luck or accident, the CIA managed to take photographs of the activities, which were shown to Kennedy on October 16, 1962. The Kennedy administration debated what to do, and for almost a week after Kennedy saw the photos, the Soviet embassy denied the existence of the bases.

On October 22, Kennedy went on national television and announced that the USSR was installing missiles on Cuba, 90 miles south of Key West, and that this was a direct threat to the safety and security of the country. He announced a naval 'quarantine' of Cuba (a euphemism for a naval blockade, which would have been an act of war) and further, that any attack on the USA from Cuba would be regarded as an attack by the USSR.

Tensions mounted, and a flurry of letters passed between Washington and Moscow, beginning with 'Well, okay, we *do* have missiles, but they're there as a deterrent and not as an offensive threat' and culminating in two offers from the Soviets to end the stalemate.

The first, dated October 26, agreed to remove the missiles in exchange for a

Cuban Revolutions

While most people peg the influx of Cubans to the rise of Fidel Castro in 1959, Cubans have been flocking to Miami – and Florida in general – for more than a century. The first large wave of immigration was in 1868, when socialist-minded cigar workers fleeing the Ten Years' War made Key West sort of an 'enlightened-masses tobacco combine.'

Those enlightened masses, educated about Cuban struggles, began demanding more money and benefits at a time when the economy was in a downturn. Cigar-maker Vicente Martínez Ybor almost single-handedly squashed Key West's cigar industry by moving his factory to Tampa and bringing Cuban laborers from Havana.

The move by Cubans to Miami began during the Spanish-American War but took off after Cuban independence. It really soared after regular aviation between Miami and Havana was established in the late 1920s.

From then until Castro's Revolution – despite intrigue and the murderous Batista regime – the Cuban-American relationship thrived. Gamblers and hot shots poured into Cuba on hourly flights from Miami, and wealthy Cubans flocked to Miami for clothes and American products.

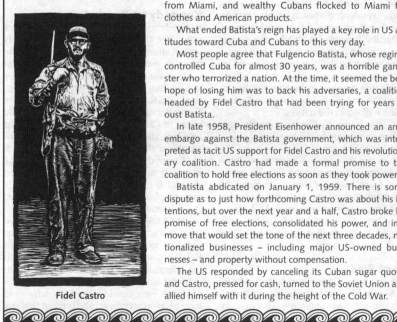

Fidel Castro

What ended Batista's reign has played a key role in US attitudes toward Cuba and Cubans to this very day.

Most people agree that Fulgencio Batista, whose regime controlled Cuba for almost 30 years, was a horrible gangster who terrorized a nation. At the time, it seemed the best hope of losing him was to back his adversaries, a coalition headed by Fidel Castro that had been trying for years to oust Batista.

In late 1958, President Eisenhower announced an arms embargo against the Batista government, which was interpreted as tacit US support for Fidel Castro and his revolutionary coalition. Castro had made a formal promise to the coalition to hold free elections as soon as they took power.

Batista abdicated on January 1, 1959. There is some dispute as to just how forthcoming Castro was about his intentions, but over the next year and a half, Castro broke his promise of free elections, consolidated his power, and in a move that would set the tone of the next three decades, nationalized businesses – including major US-owned businesses – and property without compensation.

The US responded by canceling its Cuban sugar quota, and Castro, pressed for cash, turned to the Soviet Union and allied himself with it during the height of the Cold War.

promise by the USA not to attack Cuba. The second, on October 27, tied that removal to the USA's removal of similar sites it had in Turkey.

Kennedy responded to the first offer publicly; it was ·announced that the USA would not invade Cuba, and the Soviets began removing their missiles. Several months later, and with markedly less fanfare, the US removed its missiles from Turkey.

Miami's Cuban population swelled as Cubans emigrated to the USA. A special immigration center was established to handle the overflow in Miami's Freedom Tower – the Ellis Island of the South.

During the mid-'60s, the 'freedom flights' running between Miami and Havana brought in large numbers of Cuban refugees, creating high tensions between blacks and Cubans.

1970s & the Mariel Boatlift

Something happened to Florida in the 1970s that would change the face of its tourism market forever: Walt Disney World. Hundreds of thousands of tourist-related, service-sector jobs spurted up around this massive entertainment and resort center. Hangers-on and imitators also moved in.

In the late 1970s, as Florida's economy began to recover from the oil crisis and recession, Fidel pulled a fast one: He opened the floodgates and allowed anyone who wanted to leave Cuba access to the docks at Mariel. Before the ink was dry on the proclamation, the largest flotilla ever launched for nonmilitary purposes set sail (or paddle) in practically anything that would float to cover the 90 miles between Cuba and Florida. The Mariel Boatlift, as the largest of these would be called, brought 150,000 Cubans to Florida, including an estimated 25,000 prisoners and mental patients that Fidel cleverly decided to foist off on the US. The resulting economic and logistical strain on South Florida only added to still-simmering racial tensions, which would explode on May 17, 1980, in Liberty City, a Miami neighborhood – see the Miami chapter for information on the Liberty City Riots.

Also in the late 1970s, Florida distinguished itself by becoming the first state to reinstate the death penalty, and Tampa became the first place where a Led Zeppelin concert turned into a major riot. Music must have really irritated Florida judges, and one of them rang in the 1980s by declaring a 2 Live Crew album 'obscene' and banning its sale within the state.

1980s & Drugs

In the 1980s, Florida was gaining recognition as an economic powerhouse both in banking and drug dealing – which, despite an unsavory reputation, happened to be a major force in the rejuvenation of South Florida. Jacksonville was becoming an insurance capital, and tourism was playing an ever more important role statewide. Key West, rescued from bankruptcy after the Great Depression, was becoming as romantic to tourists as Paris, and terrorist activity targeting Americans abroad in the mid-'80s put Florida in an enviable position: it was 'nearby, easy to get to, no passports required and they talk good English like us.'

While technology began booming throughout the country, the Space Coast and its support industries between the Kennedy Space Center and Orlando began gaining importance as simulation-technology businesses set up shop. (See the Orlando section in the Central Florida chapter and the Space Coast chapter for more information.)

'Cocaine,' Robin Williams once said, 'is God's way of telling us we're making too damn much money.' If ever a nation was making too much money, it was America in the '80s. All that blow had to come from somewhere, and Miami's excellent Caribbean location made it a major source of America's incoming drugs. As pink-clad detectives made the whole thing look sexy on *Miami Vice* (see the Miami chapter), South Florida began looking more and more like an armed camp. I-95 and US Hwy 1 were patrolled by officers from an alphabet soup of agencies, empowered to stop pretty much anyone who fit 'drug-runner profiles.' The Conch Republic was one form of public protest against this (see the Florida Keys chapter), but more serious problems were developing in Miami and Ybor City, where drug use and displacement of the poor were becoming very serious problems.

By the late 1980s, Miami Beach had risen to international Fabulousness on a comet of big-name models and movie stars coming to the area to be 'seen,' and the rest of South Florida was riding its coattails.

1990s

Haitian Coup In late September 1991, the Haitian military, led by Lieutenant General Raoul Cedras, overthrew the government of the constitutionally elected President

Jean-Bertrand Aristide. The US response was economic sanctions, to be removed only after the return of Aristide to power.

Under Cedras' leadership, Haitian armed forces, which at that time were given extreme legal and institutional autonomy, were responsible for law enforcement and 'public safety.' As human-rights abuses – beatings, torture, executions and 'disappearances' – escalated, refugees began to flee to the relative (they thought) safety of the USA in anything that would float. Many refugees ended up in Little Haiti, and as many as possible were rounded up by the Immigration and Naturalization Service (INS) for deportation. Signs posted throughout Miami urged people 'Don't Be a Snitch,' meaning don't report Haitians to the police, but rather point them in the direction of Little Haiti.

For the next three years, media images of Haitians being rounded up by the US Coast Guard permeated local media: in the first seven months of 1992 alone, the UN High Commissioner for Refugees (UNHCR) said the US Coast Guard had intercepted and detained a total of 38,315 Haitian refugees at Guantanamo Bay, Cuba. Of those, only 11,617 were given the INS stamp of approval as 'potentially qualified for political asylum.'

As pressure mounted from Miami's Haitian groups, who pointed out the historical carte blanche given any Cuban who manages to wash up on US soil, the US Supreme Court upheld a detestable Bush-administration policy that allows the Coast Guard to return refugees it has intercepted on the high seas directly to their home country without the benefit of an asylum hearing. And that's what the Coast Guard did.

Through a series of maneuvers (including, some say, covert payment of a cool $1 million by the USA to Cedras), Aristide was returned to power. Cedras resigned and was granted political amnesty. For the second time in a century, the US sent troops to Haiti to restore democracy.

This event allowed the Clinton administration to say to the rest of the Haitians who were being held at Guantanamo Bay, in essence, 'Please go home now; you no longer have a claim of asylum as your country is again a model democracy.' As if to accentuate the divergent treatment of Haitians and Cubans, Clinton made that move the day after agreeing to allow some 20,000 Cubans at Guantanamo entry to the USA.

Cuban Run-Ins & Embargos Also in the early 1990s, the US stopped instantly accepting Cuban refugees in an effort to keep the hotheads with Fidel rather than on Miami streets. The US started its Communism death watch as anti-Castro demonstrators stepped up pressure and as Cuba sank deeper into debt and became more desperate for hard currency. Pundits predicting Castro's imminent fall were generally disappointed; the dictator kept fighting back.

In early 1995, Castro may have made things far more difficult, though, by shooting down two American planes flown by Brothers to the Rescue (BTTR). A Miami-based group that patrols the Caribbean looking

Radio & TV Martí

When the Soviet Union fell in 1991, a shriveled-up import market crippled Cuba's economy. And the USA cranked up pressure to isolate and bring down Castro through a number of measures. The looniest of these was Radio and TV Martí, a Reagan-era project lasting through to the Clinton administration. In 1985 Martí began wasting about $50,000 a day on broadcasts of American 'cultural offerings' – *Days of Our Lives, Kate & Allie, Cheers* and *Lifestyles of the Rich & Famous* – between 3am and 6am from a blimp hovering off the Keys. Yes, a blimp.

In some of the finest of Cold War justifications, Martí was considered to be a high priority to show US determination – despite the fact that Cubans didn't know about it, didn't watch it, didn't have the equipment to watch it, and even if they had, the Cuban government jammed the broadcasts anyway. *The Nation* magazine said that less than 1% of Cubans had seen Martí.

Rosie Heeds the Battle Cry

By her own admission, part-time Miami resident Rosie O'Donnell is a sucker for helping kids and for causes she believes in. Look out, state of Florida, because Rosie – former talk-show celeb and gay-activist-by-default – is taking on the issue of gays being unable to adopt children in Florida's foster-care system. It's been that way since a 1977 ban was enacted by the state legislature, during the same era in which orange-juice spokesperson Anita Bryant brought her anti-gay attacks to breakfast tables around the country.

To this day, Florida is one of only three states that prohibit gays from adopting (the other two are Utah and Mississippi). A dozen others have recently considered ways to restrict gays from adopting. Rosie, a gay parent who adopted her children *outside* of Florida, decided to use her star status to bring attention to the prejudiced practice. Miami-Dade County, where she lives, has one of the worst foster-care systems in the US; thousands of children languish (and worse: are lost) without families. To paraphrase Rosie, Florida gays are 'good enough' to become temporary foster parents (especially of sick children who no one else wants) but apparently 'unworthy' for full-fledged adoptions.

Rosie, appearing on the ABC television program *20/20* in March 2002 to talk publicly about her sexuality for the first time, said that to be an adoptive parent, 'you have to really want to save a child who others have deemed unsaveable. And for the state of Florida to tell anyone who's willing, capable, and able to do that, that they're unworthy, is wrong.' She continued, ' All I'm saying is don't let these children suffer without a family because of your bias.'

Rosie chose to speak out because of a specific case making its way through the courts, that of longtime partners Steve Lofton and Roger Croteau, who are raising five HIV-positive children. Two of their children were adopted in Oregon, but three are Florida foster children. Of these three, Ernie (who they've raised for more than 10 years) no longer tests positive for HIV, and he's still under the magic age of 14. In other words, Florida deems him 'adoptable' and is searching for a new family for him. In other words, gays no longer need apply. Lofton and Croteau mounted a legal challenge to adopt Ernie, but a lower-court judge dismissed the case before it could be tried. Enter Rosie. Enter the American Civil Liberties Union (ʷ www.lethimstay.com), which is mounting an appeal. It's an important crossroads for gay rights, and a personal one for Ernie, his dads and his brothers and sisters.

– Kim Grant

for refugee rafters, these rabid anti-Castro, Miami-based Cubans characterize their work as 'humanitarian aid.' BTTR claims to have rescued thousands of rafters and boat people, who, it also claims, are shot at by Cuban patrol boats and helicopters. After BTTR planes skirted Cuban airspace as part of a flotilla and airborne demonstration, they were downed by the Cuban Air Force. The US government's outrage over the attack raised one of the biggest flaps between the countries since the Bay of Pigs.

Though most foreign governments permit their citizens to travel and do business with Cuba, the USA does not. Americans, though, can still surreptitiously visit Cuba via Cancún, Jamaica and the Bahamas. Journalists, academics and families with close kin can officially visit (although families can only visit once yearly). In 1998 sweeping trade embargos were lightly loosened for the first time since commercial transactions ceased in 1963. Medical supplies were first allowed, then came agricultural products, as long as Cuba paid in cash. Although Cuba was struck hard by a hurricane, Fidel's pronouncement in 2000 that he'd not take 'one grain of rice' from the US was tempered by his cash acquisition in 2002 of $17 million worth of grain from the US.

While the US House of Representatives has voted twice to allow the resumption of travel to Cuba, the US Senate has squashed it twice. President Bush, mindful of his brother's bid for reelection as governor in 2002 and his own close call in Florida in 2000 (and bid in 2004), has ordered a top-to-bottom review of the government's policies toward Cuba. The expatriate population always watches with great interest.

Hurricanes & More Trouble Florida entered the 1990s with a few other 'bumps.' On August 24, 1992, Hurricane Andrew, with sustained 145 mph winds and gusts of up to 170 mph, slammed Homestead. By the time it passed, the costliest disaster to ever hit the USA had damages pegged at $30 billion. It could have been worse, but people had had time to prepare and evacuate, and the Category 4 storm was obliging enough to keep moving and not sit on the area. Had the storm been 20 miles farther north when it hit land (as was expected), the surge would have destroyed Miami Beach. See the Dangers & Annoyances section in the Facts for the Visitor chapter for complete hurricane information.

Coup and chaos in Haiti led to waves of refugees washing up on South Florida's shores, and further upheaval in Cuba led to several new waves of Cuban raft refugees as well. Florida also leapt to the national spotlight in the abortion fight when, in 1993, Dr David Gunn was shot dead by Paul Hill outside a Pensacola abortion clinic.

There was also a heavily publicized spree of foreign-tourist-related crimes in 1993. With several shootings and many robberies, Florida was in a deserved panic over the potential loss of its tourism market, which was fast becoming the state's most important industry. Heightened security and the creation of a Tourist Police Force helped to substantially reduce attacks against tourists.

South Florida's image as some sort of wild, wild west was brought to light again, though, on July 15, 1997. Fashion designer Gianni Versace was gunned down in front of his Miami Beach mansion. The publicity was instant and worldwide. (See the Miami Beach section in the Miami chapter for more information.)

Elian Gonzales Is there a soul in the world who doesn't know the story of the little boy whose mother died at sea while trying to flee Cuba for a better life in America? Of a little boy who was rescued from an inner tube 2 miles off the coast of Fort Lauderdale on Thanksgiving Day 1999, then protectively mothered by his cousin Marisleysis while he rode around with an impish grin on bicycles in the front yard of his great-uncle Lazaro Gonzalez, whom he'd not met before his arrival? And who was later seized at gunpoint from his closet in an early-morning raid by US Border Patrol agents and then reunited with his Cuban father and his second family, who remained in the US for another two months while all the political wrangling played itself out? Is there anyone?

It quickly became a struggle between the exiles and Fidel. Is it better for a boy to grow up under communism or capitalism? Is capitalism stronger than blood? Underlying this was an uglier polarization of the local Miami community. Other immigrant groups had long resented the inordinate influence Cubans had and preference they were shown. On a national level, the debate raged between taking a hard-line approach or appeasing Castro. Democratic attorney general Janet Reno, a former federal prosecutor and current Miami-Dade resident, took a lot of flak for the decision, and it may have haunted her in her unsuccessful run for the governorship in 2002.

21st Century

At the outset of the new century, Florida is poised to be a state with both clout and complex problems. From oil drilling in the Gulf of Mexico to reclaiming the Everglades; from gay adoptions (see the boxed text 'Rosie Heeds the Battle Cry') to terrorists training at flight schools; from failed educational policies and the nation's first anthrax attack to the high cost of prescription-drug prices for the bursting

For Want of a Chad

December 9, 2000: The US presidential elections held on November 7th had come down to the wire, a question of some 600 votes in a nation of 280 million. Citizens who had long suspected that their voice didn't count were suddenly proven wrong. Vice President Al Gore, candidate for the barely center-left Democratic Party, had already secured a slim (539,898) majority of the popular vote. But to win in the Electoral College, which actually decides presidential elections, he needed Florida.

But Florida was enemy territory, presided over by Governor Jeb Bush (the brother of George W Bush, presidential candidate for the conservative Republican Party) and Secretary of State Katherine Harris (Bush's campaign co-chair). Gore voters would be presented with an unusual set of roadblocks.

In 1999, Harris had used $4 million of taxpayer money to wipe 181,000 'suspected felons' from Florida's voting rolls. Most were black; 'coincidentally,' nine out of 10 Florida blacks just happen to be Democrats. As a result, many African Americans were barred from voting, including Madison County elections supervisor Linda Howell, who was not a felon. Somehow, other felons, including Jeb Bush's wife, Columba (she had unsuccessfully attempted to smuggle $19,000 worth of French jewelry into the USA), remained on the rolls.

More famously, the West Palm Beach 'butterfly ballot' had placed Gore's name almost exactly opposite that of arch-conservative Pat Buchanan. Consequently, an estimated 3000 confused voters punched the wrong hole.

Anyone tempted to make Alzheimer's jokes (the area is known for its retirees) should note that a study in Alberta, Canada, offered potential voters a similar choice on mock ballots for prime minister. Replacing Gore was center-left candidate Jean Chrétien, while Pat Buchanan's slot was occupied by the not-quite-fascist Joe Clark. On the list ballot, no errors were reported. On the butterfly ballot, Canadian voters punched the wrong name 7.5% of the time – within one percentage point of the estimated error in West Palm Beach.

Buchanan – well known for his occasional anti-Semitic outbursts – stated publicly that there was no way he'd done so well among West Palm's largely Jewish constituency. Republican spin doctors pointed out that Theresa LePore, who had designed the ballot, was a Democrat. But it soon came to light that she'd been registered Republican until 1996; shortly after the election, she re-registered as Independent.

As the world watched, bemused but nervous, Florida began a recount. They were given 36 days by the US Supreme Court to manually examine West Palm Beach's ballots, searching for evidence that mistakes had been made. The word 'chad,' which refers to the bits of paper punched through by voters, entered public parlance: Hanging chads, partially separated from the ballot, would be counted; pregnant chads, with a dimple but no separation, would not. Volunteers worked around the clock.

The Bush lead slimmed daily, but time was running out. The law firm Gibson, Dunn and Crutcher (which employs US Supreme Court Justice Antonin Scalia's son) argued before the Supreme Court that it was important for the USA to have a clear leader as soon as possible, regardless of the actual number of votes received. At 2:45pm December 9, the Supreme Court voted, with a majority of exactly one, to halt the recount.

Bush won with 537 votes. The *Miami Herald* noted that if the most inclusive standards had been used to complete the recount, Gore would have won by some 300 votes.

On Inauguration Day in January 2001, Bush became the first president-elect in 25 years to forego the final four-block walk to the podium, where he would be sworn in as president and the self-proclaimed leader of the free world. The hissing crowd had pelted his limo with eggs, trapping him inside. And Americans who'd complained that their votes didn't really count were finally vindicated.

– Paige Penland

elderly population; from balancing the interests of agriculture and developers, and of Cubans and Hispanics and African Americans, Florida has its hands full. To say the least! But as we've seen, if a politician can address these problems with just the right election-year rhetoric (and a few well-placed friends on the Supreme Court), he or she can have the ear of the White House, if not the Lincoln Bedroom.

Miami and Orlando are still the powerhouse tourism draws, but other cities – notably Key West, Fort Lauderdale, Tampa, St Petersburg, St Augustine and Pensacola – have been seeing an uptick recently, thanks to downtown renewal and renovation. Theme parks account for a huge percentage of visitors: While Disney is still decidedly king of the hill, there's tough competition from Universal Studios, SeaWorld, Islands of Adventure, Busch Gardens and smaller entries, like Wet 'n' Wild and Splendid China. Furthermore, folks are discovering just how accessible and incredible the state and national parks can be.

GEOGRAPHY

Florida's terrain is mainly flat, with coastal lowlands. Although it's slightly hilly in the center, you won't find anything over 350 feet above sea level in Florida. The south-central portion is all wetlands and reclaimed wetlands. As nature intended it, the sheet-flow ecosystem of water from the Kissimmee River fed Lake Okeechobee at the southeast center of Florida, which then overflowed, feeding sheets of freshwater to the Everglades. But nature was overruled by man in South Florida, and the Kissimmee was dammed, diked, canaled and diverted – see the Everglades chapter for more information.

The coasts are buttressed by natural barrier islands. The waterways between the barrier islands and the mainland were deepened and widened by the Army Corps of Engineers to create a sheltered inland route from Miami to Virginia: the Atlantic Intracoastal Waterway, one of the country's most important commercial and recreational waterways. A similar waterway, the Gulf Intracoastal Waterway, stretches along the Gulf Coast.

The Panhandle refers to the handle-like strip of land jutting off to the northwest. Florida's northern borders are Alabama and Georgia; the Atlantic Ocean and the Gulf of Mexico on the east and west, respectively, surround the rest of it.

Florida is the 22nd-largest state in the USA: it's more than 600 miles from Miami to Pensacola. Key West is closer to Havana than to Miami, and Tallahassee (the state capital) is 239 miles from Tampa, which is almost 200 miles from St Augustine.

GEOLOGY

On the face of it, geologically speaking, Florida's not much to jump up and down about. It's essentially an enormous arched slab of porous limestone. However, when the seas receded and exposed the Florida peninsula – recently enough that dinosaurs never made it here – the limestone caused some interesting things to happen.

First, the saltwater that saturated the limestone was forced out by freshwater from rainfall. Decaying plant matter that was washed into the ground by rainfall created a carbonic acid, which ate away at the limestone, forming tunnels and caverns and eventually entire underground freshwater systems of rivers and streams. The entire system is called the Florida Aquifer, the source of the state's freshwater supply.

Weaknesses and cracks in the limestone, combined with the pressure of the circulating water, result in springs, of which Florida has hundreds, if not thousands. And those same weaknesses are responsible for sinkholes – amusing when they're not on your property – which occur when the carbonic acid eats away at a section of limestone that's not thin enough to become a spring. When enough stone is dissolved, entire sections of ground simply sink into, well, a hole. One of the best examples of a fascinating Florida sinkhole is the Devil's Millhopper, just north of Gainesville.

CLIMATE

Florida's warm weather may have been the only reason anyone dreamed of inhabiting the place at all.

Ideal conditions in South Florida exist between December and May, when temperatures average between 59° and 75°F (15° to 24°C), and average rainfall is a scant 2.01 inches. But in northern Florida, the winter months are cool and, in recent years, have been downright cold – not just Florida cold: northern Florida always has a few nights each winter in the teens.

Florida summers are summed like this: very hot and humid, with thunderstorms at 3pm. There's a cats-and-dogs quality to Florida rain, and it comes on quickly. Summer rainstorms are preceded by inhuman rises in humidity, closely followed by fantastically ominous clouds, which sweep in and reduce daylight to twilight in a matter of minutes. The rain – copious doses of fist-sized raindrops – has a ferocity that floods streets in minutes and causes drivers to pull over and cower. But the rains rarely last very long, and the raindrops are so warm that they can actually be refreshing.

June is the rainiest month, with an average of 9.33 inches, and temperatures average between 75° and 88°F (24° to 31°C). August is probably the hottest month, with average temperatures between 77° and 89°F (25° to 31°C), but with all these temperatures you have to take into account the heat index, a product of heat and humidity. It feels a *lot* hotter than 89°F when there's 90% humidity!

See the climate charts below for more detailed information.

ECOLOGY & ENVIRONMENT
While this will sound grim, keep in mind that things are improving and that government is

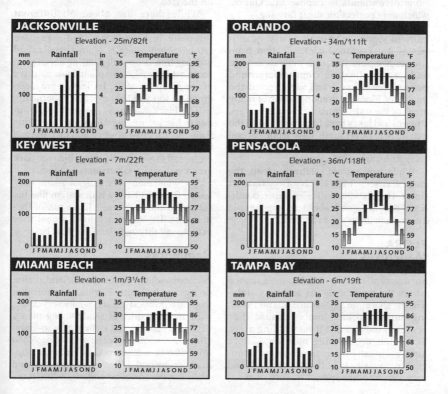

now taking an active role in limiting and re-pairing damage and managing land use.

The *Encyclopedia of Florida* says that Florida's state motto, 'In God We Trust,' was 'evidently taken from the inscription on American currency.' In that spirit lies the fundamental philosophy behind Florida's environmental and ecological policies. The destruction of vast tracts of Florida's natural balance was a direct result of the government's encouragement.

From the mid-1800s, when developers 'discovered' the paradise of South Florida, state government supported irresponsible large-scale agricultural projects and real-estate development. The destruction of the Everglades began in an effort to create jobs, by controlling the flow of water from Lake Okeechobee and draining significant portions of wetlands to expose mucklands, which were perfect for sugar farming.

While the Florida Aquifer has the capability to supply unbelievably large quantities of water, ground contamination from sources like pesticides, heavy metals, sewage and gasoline (leaking from underground storage tanks) has drastically affected the quality of Florida's drinking water in many areas of the state. Similarly, Florida's rivers, streams and lakes have been polluted to the extent that largemouth bass from several lakes are inedible. Mercury levels in the Everglades are startlingly high.

While beaches are relatively clean, the coast has seen high levels of bacteria at times. Health authorities monitor conditions and are good about letting people know when limits are exceeded.

FLORA
Mangroves

Mangrove trees are halophytes, plants that are tolerant of salty conditions. Located where the land meets the sea, they stabilize the shoreline and reduce inland flooding during storms, simply because they prevent sand and dirt from washing away. Silt builds up, forming more and more land; eventually the mangroves are strangled by the very land they've created, and they die. Another special quality of man-

There are three species of mangrove in Florida.

groves is that their seeds sprout while still on the tree.

While there are about 50 different species of mangrove around the world, three are in Florida. The red mangrove *(Rhizophora mangle)*, sometimes called walking tree, drops salt-filtering aerial prop roots, which make the plant look as if it's propped up on stilts. Its leaves are deep green on top and lighter green underneath.

The black mangrove *(Avicennia germinans)* has *pneumatophores*, or 'breathing roots,' which grow upward and take oxygen into the system. This kind of mangrove excretes salt through its leaves, which are dark green with white salt crystals on them.

The white mangrove *(Laguncularia racemosa)* does not have a root system like the other two and looks more like a run-of-the-mill tree. Its leaves are light green; they excrete salt through glands at their base.

Hammocks

Hammocks are tracts of forested land that rise above adjacent marshes, pineland, prairie or swamp. In South Florida, they're often tropical hardwood forests, usually very dense, with an understory of shade-loving plants. Common plant species include gumbo-limbo *(Bursera simaruba)*, pigeon plum *(Coccoloba diversifolia)*, soldierwood *(Colubrina elliptica)*, crabwood *(Psychotria undata)* and white stopper *(Eugenia axillaris)*, which is the bush that produces that skunk aroma you'll smell all over South Florida.

Sea Oats

Sea oats *(Uniola paniculata)* get their name from the large plumes they produce. They're protected vegetation in Florida because they trap wind-blown sand and thereby stabilize sand dunes. It's illegal to pick or disturb them in any way.

Sea Grapes

Sea grapes *(Coccoloba uvifera)* are coastal landscape plants native to Florida that stand up to wind and saltwater. They have large, round leaves and produce a small, purple, edible fruit that braver people eat or make into jelly.

Pine Flatwoods

Pine flatwoods usually don't have very rich soil and are home to mainly slash pine and saw palmetto, though sometimes cabbage palms (see below) grow in these as well.

Spanish Moss

The most surprising thing about Spanish moss *(Tillandsia usneoides)*, the ubiquitous, spooky stuff attached to trees in the northern areas of Florida, is that it's not a moss at all. It's an air plant and a member of the pineapple family. That's right, pineapple. Its seeds have tiny parachutes that carry them from tree to tree. In some areas, notably Tallahassee and on St George Island, Spanish moss can get so thick and tangled that it jumps from treetop to treetop across roads, creating a canopy.

Saw Grass

Named for its fine teethlike edges, saw grass is the principal Everglades vegetation but it grows wherever it's wet. It's rough, firm, stiff and green.

Strangler Figs

The rope-like roots you'll see growing on cypress trees or cabbage palms are the strangler fig *(Ficus aurea)*, whose seeds start growing as an air plant. As the strangler fig grows, it sends off roots, which wrap around the trunk of its host, eventually strangling and killing it.

Palms

Florida has many species of palm, which are tropical evergreen trees and shrubs with branchless trunks and fanned leaves in clumps at their top. The following are the most common palms you'll run into:

Cabbage palm *(Sabal palmetto)*
These are tall and sometimes bent at fantastic angles, as on Lincoln Road Mall in Miami Beach.

Coconut palm *(Cocos nucifera)*
This classic desert-island fantasy, tall and gracefully curved, does indeed produce coconuts. It's rare to find mature fruit in Florida, as landscapers hack them off as soon as they're large enough to hurt someone if the fruit should fall during a windstorm. If you do find one large enough (it's about the size and shape of an American football), hack off the top with a machete, and use a straw to drink the juice. You'll sometimes see this offered from carts on the street in Miami's Little Havana.

King palm *(Archontophoenix alexandrae)*
Native to Australia, this introduced ornamental is a knobby-trunked beast that can reach heights of up to 75 feet.

Royal palm *(Roystonea regia)*
Native to South Florida and Cuba, this enormous and very straight-growing palm has a white trunk and very long foliage. They line Palm Beach's Royal Palm Way.

Sago palm *(Cycas revoluta)*
Short-trunked with leaves spreading out like a Japanese fan, these introduced ornamentals look as if they're playing a game of cards.

Yellow butterfly/areca palm *(Chrysalidocarpus lutescens)*
Another introduced ornamental, native to Asia, these grow in clumps of several plants, which look as if they're racing their siblings to attain maximum height. Look for curved trunks and lush leaves.

Flowering Plants

The following are some of the (not necessarily native) flowering plants and trees you're most likely to encounter in Florida:

Allamanda – White or pink, trumpet-shaped flower; toxic

Bougainvillea – A vine with clusters of red, pink, white or orange flowers

Cassia – Also called golden or pink shower tree, depending on the color of the flowers, which appear before the leaves of the tree do

Cup of gold – An 8- to 10-inch-diameter flower that opens white and turns bright yellow; toxic

Frangipani – An evergreen shrub with delicious-smelling white, pink or red flowers; instantly recognizable to anyone who's ever seen a movie or TV show featuring somebody getting off a plane in Hawaii

Hibiscus – A big, delicate, trumpet-shaped flower in red, white, yellow or pink; each flower blooms only for one day

Ixora – Red, sometimes white, clusters of starlike flowers; an evergreen perennial

Jacaranda – Purplish-blue bell-shaped flowers on a tree with fernlike leaves; one of our absolute favorites

Oleander – Pink, white, red or yellow flowers; a very toxic shrub

Royal poinciana – Also called flame tree, with reddish-orange flowers; also a favorite of ours

Spider lily – You'll see many different kinds of lilies, but we particularly like the smell of this one; it's white and spider-like and toxic

Fruit Trees

Throughout Florida, you'll run into orange, grapefruit, lemon, lime and tangerine groves (see Economy, later in the chapter). Wonder why all the fruit you see in Publix and Winn-Dixie supermarkets stinks? The good stuff is sent up north! There are also wild banana, mango and papaya trees almost everywhere you go. Most people are a little touchy about strangers walking up to their trees and snatching fruit, so ask first.

FAUNA
Crocodilians

Crocodilians are the world's largest living reptiles, and two species are native to the USA: the American alligator *(Alligator mississippiensis)* and the American crocodile *(Crocodylus acutus)*. Crocodiles are very rare in Florida, so if you see a crocodilian here, it's probably an alligator. This can be considered a good thing by visitors: crocs are the more aggressive of the two.

Alligators The name derives from the Spanish *el lagarto*, the lizard. Alligators are carnivorous; hatchlings eat insects, frogs, small fish, snails and the like. As they grow, they move on to bigger game, but they're never above small snacks like crickets or grasshoppers. Alligators' jaws close on reflex: when open (the muscles to open their mouths are far weaker than those that close them), their closing mechanisms are triggered by anything touching the inside of their mouths.

When that something is edible, the alligator clamps down upon it, raises its head and gulps – swallowing prey small enough in one gulp, and crushing and tearing larger prey repeatedly until swallowable. Stories of alligators dragging prey underwater to drown it are hooey.

Appearance Alligators indeed look like long and scary lizards. Most males grow to between 9 and 12 feet, females 6 to 8 feet; the largest found in Florida was a terrifying 17½ feet. Alligators generally live to an age of 30 to 35 years in the wild, longer when raised in captivity.

Young alligators are black, with bright stripes and blotches of yellow on their backs and cream-colored bellies. As they grow older, they lose the stripes, but the stomach remains light-colored. It's said that Indians believed rubbing a gator's stomach would make it fall asleep – volunteers?

Alligators have a broad snout (the most obvious difference between alligators and crocodiles, which have narrow ones), and a socket in the upper jaw hides their fourth tooth (which is visible on crocs). There's nothing external to distinguish male and female alligators to the casual observer.

Alligators have large corneas that enhance their night vision. They can see underwater, too: transparent, protective membranes cover their eyes when submerged.

Habitat Alligators are usually (but not exclusively) found in freshwater such as shallow lakes, marshes, swamps, rivers, creeks, ponds and manmade canals. American alligators are found primarily in

Louisiana, Florida and southern Georgia. They're a common sight along Florida riverbanks, where they like to sun themselves, and occasionally you can catch a glimpse of the lazy reptiles swimming across rivers and streams.

Gators are warm-weather fans and will rarely feed when the temperature dips below 68°F; their metabolism slows considerably in cold weather. But gators are cold-blooded and can die when the temperature is more than 100°F. To cool themselves, alligators sit on riverbanks or in the shade with their mouths wide open, which dissipates heat.

In the Everglades, where deep, open water is limited, females live in ponds, venturing into open areas for breeding. Males prowl, and during mating season make house calls on many ponds, searching for female companionship. Nesting occurs in June and July; hatching in August.

In the winter dry season, alligators become a crucial factor in the survival of many species by digging 'gator holes' – artificial ponds. They dig with their mouths and legs, sweeping out mud and vegetation with lashes of their tails. As the hole fills with water, the gators keep it free of vegetation with further tail-lashing housekeeping. When the dry season comes, gator holes are often the only source of freshwater for many other animals, and many come to hang out. Rent, however, can be expensive: some of the visitors become gator dinner.

Threats to Alligators While alligator eggs and infants are eaten by raccoons, otters and sometimes even other alligators, generally speaking, humankind is the alligator's only natural enemy. Formerly abundant in the wild in Florida, an estimated 10 million alligators were killed from hunting and the draining of wetlands in the late 19th century until the Mason-Smith Act, which banned the sale of endangered species in 1969. Alligators had been considered endangered since the mid-1940s. Thanks to protection, the alligator population has recovered to

Alligator Attacks

Generally speaking, alligators don't pose a threat to humans; they attack from hunger, not maliciousness. But certain activities will cause alligators to become aggressive.

The most common mistake people make is feeding alligators, which is about as stupid as climbing a zoo fence to pet a cute tiger. When humans feed alligators, the gators naturally begin to associate humans with food – and if you're not holding out a cheeseburger, an alligator used to being fed by people might then consider making a snack of your arm. It is illegal in Florida to feed alligators.

Alligators – males and females – are also very protective of their young and will descend upon any threat to any young alligator, not just their own, with great vigor. Acts seen as threatening can be as inadvertent as coming between a parent and child, say, in a canoe. The chief warning that you've behaved offensively is a loud hissing sound – a call for assistance, answered by other gators with as much enthusiasm as cops to an 'officer down' radio call. Get away as fast as possible and do not look back until you are safe – in a bar.

such an extent it was reclassified as 'threatened' in 1985. It is still illegal to hunt or molest alligators in the wild, and strict penalties apply to violators.

Current threats to alligators include cars and loss of habitat.

Crocodiles The crocodile is classified as an endangered species. While there have never been as many crocs as alligators in Florida, there are only an estimated 400 to 500 left in the wild, and their numbers are not substantially increasing.

Crocodiles are more aggressive than alligators (though the American crocodile is not particularly aggressive) and will attack humans with relatively less provocation. They can be smaller than alligators but range in size from 3 to 15 feet; males are larger than females. Crocodiles nest on marl banks, porous sand or shell beaches.

American crocodiles prefer coastal, brackish and saltwater habitats (but they can live in freshwater). Their snouts are more tapered and triangular than those of alligators, and their fourth tooth is exposed. Their bodies are grayish-green, with a light-colored underside; young crocs have dark bands on their backs and tails.

Adult crocodiles feed at night in the water. They eat fish, crabs, birds, turtles, snakes and small mammals. In daytime they rest in creeks or in dens, which they build within vegetation.

Females build their nests – which you really don't want to approach, okay? – near deep water. They lay eggs April and May, and after the hatch in July and August, mothers carry their newborns to the water in their mouths.

As with alligators, humans are the full-grown croc's only natural enemies.

Turtles

Florida turtles, both sea and land, are either threatened or endangered species, protected by state and federal law. The sea turtle most commonly found in Florida is the threatened loggerhead turtle (*Caretta caretta*). Also seen, but far more rarely, is the green sea turtle (*Chelonia midas*) and,

rarer still, the leatherback (*Dermochelys coriacea*), the largest of the sea turtles. Both of the latter are endangered. Disturbing turtle nests or possession of live or dead turtles can result in fines or imprisonment.

Nesting Florida's beaches are a perfect nesting ground for sea turtles. Nesting occurs from May to September. Turtles swim ashore at night, preferably onto a wide beach, and pull themselves forward using their foreflippers to find a suitable (the drier the better) area for laying eggs. They hollow a pit with their front flippers, which helps them settle into the sand, and then dig a cylindrical cavity of about 20 inches with their rear flippers.

The turtle raises its hind flippers and releases two to three eggs at a time; she'll lay about 100 in all, each about the size of a ping-pong ball. The eggs have a leathery shell, which prevents them from breaking when they hit the sand. Using her front flippers, the turtle covers the eggs with sand and returns to the water. Sea turtles don't guard their nests, but loggerheads build four to five nests per season at intervals of 10 to 12 days.

The eggs fall victim to raccoons and other small animals that dig them up for food. Surviving to the hatching stage is really a matter of luck, and only one in 1000 turtles will reach maturity.

Hatching Hatching occurs after about 60 days. Baby turtles orient themselves by moonlight to find the water, and here is yet another instance of humankind's development leading to tragedy for nature: turtle hatchlings are frequently disoriented by the lights from the condominiums and hotels that line the beaches, and often crawl off in the wrong direction.

Volunteers in Turtle Watch programs throughout Florida (see especially the John D MacArthur State Park section in the Southeast Florida chapter as well as the Canaveral National Seashore section in the Space Coast chapter) stand by at hatching time and try to point the turtles in the right direction, employing any method they can – including flashlights and search lights – to get them into the sea.

Manatees

The endangered Florida manatee *(Trichechus manatus)*, also called the sea cow, is a subspecies of the West Indian manatee. Once abundant throughout the tropical and sub-tropical Caribbean waters, only an estimated 4000 to 5000 manatees are left in the wild today. Manatees have large, plump, grayish-brown bodies with two small forelimbs and a tail shaped like a beaver's. Their large, flexible upper lip is covered with small whiskers. Manatees range in size from about 9 to 12 feet and weigh between 1000 to 2500 pounds. These herbivores consume 10% to 15% of their body weight daily. After 13 months of pregnancy, females give birth to only one calf – every two to five years. They have no natural enemies except humans.

Dolphins

Florida's most common dolphin species is the bottle-nosed dolphin *(Tursiops truncatus)*, which isn't as shy as a common dolphin. It's very easy to see them throughout Florida, even in Biscayne Bay! If you're ca-noeing or kayaking in the Everglades and notice playful critters leaping out of the water alongside your boat, you may be looking at bottle-nosed dolphins or por-poises – look for the long snout (bottle-nosed) or no snout (porpoise).

To identify an individual bottle-nosed dolphin, look at its dorsal fin – when dolphins fight (and they do -- they're not all Flipper friendly), they take chunks out of their fins. Every dorsal fin is shaped differently.

Florida Panthers

These beautiful creatures *(Felis concolor coryi)* have been on the endangered species list since 1973. In the past decade, hunting, habitat loss and automobiles had decreased the wild population to some 30 to 50 animals. To make things worse, these sur-vivors were inbreeding, resulting in genetic defects. Land has now been set aside specif-ically to preserve panther habitat, however, and an innovative breeding program has re-

Mad about Manatees

A cute little nose barely breaks the surface of the water, with a 'pfft' and spray of water and air. Below that nose stretches a big gray mass with a walruslike body that tapers to a beaverlike tail. For all their size and weight, West Indian manatees, which are related to the elephant, are shy and elusive. So shy, in fact, that early explorers who glimpsed them thought they were mermaids. Later, after they'd been seen grazing on underwater vegetation, they were called 'sea cows.'

These slow, nearly blind mammals are protected by federal and state laws, but their numbers are threatened by loss of habitat, careless anglers and increasing boat traffic. When they come to the water's surface to breathe, manatees are vulnerable to being hit by boats. It's not uncommon to see pro-peller scars across their backs. Frequently they are also injured or killed by fishing lines, which strangle them or tangle their fins.

The best places to see manatees are Blue Springs State Park, Homosassa Springs State Wildlife Park and along the Crystal River. They winter (November to March) in the parks' 72°F springs. In warmer periods, they also swim in the St Johns River.

There are several organizations throughout Florida that rescue and rehabilitate injured manatees; they keep busy. The two largest are SeaWorld in Orlando and Seaquarium in Miami. See the Central Florida and Miami chapters for more information.

leased some Texas cougars into the Florida wild to improve the gene pool. A recent census yielded estimates of 75 to 100 animals. These brave few are found prima-rily in South Florida, in the Everglades and Big Cypress parks.

In 1982, the panther became the official mammal of Florida. They are large, light-brown, sleek and very elegant. The solitary cats grow to about 7 feet long and 4 feet high, and weigh up to 150 pounds. They feed on deer, hogs, raccoons and sometimes even alligators. Three kittens is an average litter; the gestation period is about three months.

Birds

Pelicans are large birds that live an average age of 30 years, weigh 5lb to 8lb and eat about half their body weight in fish daily. They're also prehistoric looking, resembling pterodactyls, and are hilarious – especially when one has grabbed a fish and is carrying it around in the sack beneath its chin.

Florida has several types of heron, long-necked wading birds who fold their necks over their backs in flight. Throughout the state, you'll see snowy egrets and great white herons, along with ibis and the pink and orange roseate spoonbill. You'll only find pink flamingos in zoos, on lawns, and in John Waters movies, and in the latter two instances, they're made out of plastic.

There are only about 600 pairs of endangered bald eagles, the US national symbol, left in Florida. Adults have a white head and tail a dark body and yellow eyes, legs and bill. They grow to about 3 feet high and have a wingspan of up to 8 feet. Although they're visible in several Atlantic coast state parks, you'll have to be patient.

Wood storks, large wading birds with a dark featherless head, a stout bill, and a 5-foot wingspan, have been classified as endangered since 1985, when they were recognized as victims of wetlands draining.

Coral Reef

Florida's coral reef is the largest in North America and the third-largest in the world. Corals belong to the phylum Cnidaria; they look like plants, but they're actually animals. Individual members of coral (polyps) attach themselves to reefs and form a coral colony by producing calcium carbonate. The sea fans and whips found here – the ones that make it all seem like plant life – are unique to coral reefs in this area.

Coral reefs are to the underwater world what sea oats (see earlier) are to sand dunes: their rigidity catches sand and protects the shoreline from erosion by violent seas or storms. Coral reefs have an ecological diversity equal to, if not greater than, an entire tropical rain forest and are home to thousands of varieties of plant and animal life, many of which have a symbiotic relationship with the coral.

To exist, coral reefs require very stable warm temperatures and pure water, conditions threatened on several fronts. Storms and radical upward temperature shifts have both affected the area. This heat is causing bleaching of the reefs in Indonesia and the Seychelles, and bleaching is expected to occur in Florida and the Caribbean as well.

The purity of the water may have been threatened by a decline in freshwater in Florida Bay, a result of diverting water from the Everglades. In an effort to rebalance the salinity in Florida Bay, 'fresh' – that is, non-saline – water was pumped into it. But that water was full of agricultural runoff, including phosphates and nitrates, which disturbed the area's ecological balance.

All this, combined with humankind's meddling, is killing Keys coral. It has long since died in areas to the north. Other reef's enemies include boaters carelessly dropping anchor or running aground on coral; swimmers, divers and snorkelers standing on it or taking pieces of it; fishing and overfishing; and 'nutrient' – that's sewage to you and me – being pumped into South Florida water from the Florida Keys (where the sewage is only partially treated before being pumped directly into the ocean).

GOVERNMENT & POLITICS

With the exception of its long and proud history of open and seemingly encouraged graft, corruption and conflict of interest (which dates to Spanish explorers and pirates of all nationalities), the Florida state government is a miniature replica of the US federal government. The US legislature is made up of the bicameral Congress – the Senate and the House of Representatives. The Senate has two senators from each of the 50 states, while the 435-member House has one or more members from each state, depending on the state's population. Florida, the USA's fourth most-populous state, has 23 representatives.

The Florida legislature mimics the national one. Bills are introduced by representatives and go through several subcommittees before being argued and amended on the floor of the House, which then passes them on to the Senate, which sends them through several subcommittees and argues and amends them further. They're then sent back to the House for even *further* amendment, and, finally, to the governor, who can sign the bills into law or veto them About half of all bills die in the process.

The capital city of Florida is Tallahassee, in the northwest central section of the state, a geographical compromise reached when Florida had two capitals, St Augustine and Pensacola.

At press time in 2002, with a statewide election looming on the horizon, Governor Jeb Bush, brother of the current President Bush (No 43, or the 43rd president of the USA, also know as 'W') and son of the former President George Bush (No 41), held the highest office in Florida and certainly had the ear of the nation's Commander-in-Chief. It's convenient to have family in such high places, especially when it comes to crucial electoral votes. (See the boxed text 'For Want of a Chad,' earlier.)

ECONOMY

Florida's economy relies heavily on tourism, its most lucrative and important business. Almost 72 million tourists visited Florida in 2001.

Miami's position as gateway to Latin America has given it powerhouse status as an international business city. More than 150 multinational companies have operations in Miami, and at least 100 have their Latin American headquarters here. Among the top 20 are Johnson & Johnson, The Gap, American Airlines, Sony, IBM, Cisco, Canon, Oracle, UPS, FedEx, ExxonMobil and Chevron-Texaco.

Miami customs processes 30% of all US exports to South America and 50% of all US exports to Central America and the Caribbean. The city is also establishing itself as an international banking center: almost 45 international banks call it home. To be sure, brokerage houses, banking, imports, exports and commodities drive the local economy. But then again, more than a few people

The Florida Lottery

Florida has no state income tax and relies heavily on tourists (who pay a hotel tax), consumers (who pay state sales tax) and lottery players to support itself. The Florida Lottery is unbelievably crafty, bringing in hundreds of millions of dollars annually by promising – and sometimes even delivering – huge payoffs. While we think lotteries unconscionably suck money from the poor, the Florida Lottery is too big to ignore.

All lottery games are variations of the centuries-old numbers racket, in which the player picks numbers and hopes to match them to those chosen at random (at least in official games) on live television by large-breasted women supervised by hulking thugs. You can buy tickets at supermarkets, liquor stores and even in video stores.

Games played include the following:

Lotto – Choose six from 48 numbers. The weekly Lotto drawing has a minimum payoff of $7 million – and if no one wins it, the pot increases weekly until someone does.

Fantasy 5 – Pick five from 26 numbers from Monday to Friday; payoffs start at $20,000.

Scratching games – Laminated cards you scratch to see if you've won. Prizes range from another ticket to a gazillion dollars. Win for Life is a scratch-off game that pays winners $1000 a week for the rest of their lives.

admit in hushed tones that 'Miami is the city that drugs built.' If there is a kilo of truth to that, it's worth noting that there is more high-rise construction here than in any major metropolitan center I've visited in the last few years. To paraphrase a James Carville adage: It's the drugs, stupid.

Other important economic activities in Florida include sugar production; the $8-billion-a-year citrus industry, which produces much of the country's frozen concentrated orange juice, bottled juice, grapefruit sections and citrus salad; electronics, programming and simulation technology; space exploration and space-related industry.

Minerals are important to Florida's economy as well. In fact, Florida mines about a quarter of the world's phosphate. Other products extracted from the earth include limestone, peat, zircon, dolomite and sulfur. Until quite recently, oil and gas exploration had also been big in three wildlife areas (including Big Cypress National Preserve) and the Gulf of Mexico, about 25 miles south of Pensacola. Under the terms of a federal agreement reached during Governor Jeb Bush's reelection year (2002), and perhaps as payback for Jeb handing the 2000 Presidential election to his brother 'W' on a sliver platter, W and Jeb are buying back those oil leases. Furthermore, they're paying the leaseholders twice what they paid in the first place. Great deal: Jeb looks good to environmentalists (and, more importantly, the majority of Florida voters, who oppose drilling) *and* to oil companies. That's what politicians call a 'win-win situation.'

POPULATION & PEOPLE

The official Census 2000 pegs Florida's population at about 16 million, a 26% increase from 1990. That's a lot of extra people in one decade. Most of Florida's populace is concentrated on the coasts, and of those, more than a quarter of them live south of Alligator Alley (Hwy 84/I-75).

In Miami there are slightly more Hispanics or Latinos than whites. An astounding 45% of Miamians are foreign born: Cubans are the largest group (at 60%), followed by Canadians, Haitians, Germans and Jamaicans.

Native Americans number 49,200, constituting 0.3% of Florida's population. Two federally recognized Indian tribes in Florida have reservations: the **Seminole Tribe** (☎ 800-617-7516, [W] www.seminoletribe.com), in Hollywood, Tampa, Dania, Big Cypress National Preserve and Brighton, near Lake Okeechobee; and the **Miccosukee Tribe** (☎ 305-223-8380), with a reservation and convention center on the Tamiami Trail.

The Seminole Tribe has expanded its efforts to preserve and interpret the culture, language and customs of the Florida Seminole. Their Web site (see above) is a great starting point, as is the Ah-Tah-Thi-Ki Museum on the Big Cypress National Preserve. See the Everglades chapter for more information.

EDUCATION

Florida's public grade schools and Florida's students fall short of the national average in many areas, notably in Scholastic Aptitude Tests (SATs), the criterion for college and university admissions in the USA. And the number of students who drop out before graduation is higher than the national average. It's not surprising: Florida spends less than almost any other state on its education system, though it spends more than any other state on prison construction. As one local said, 'You can't blame the state for that; they're executing prisoners as quickly as they can!'

Florida has several state and private universities: the University of Florida in Gainesville, the University of Miami, Florida International University in Miami and Florida State University in Tallahassee are the major players.

ARTS

Much of Florida's arts – with the exception of local crafts, which can be found all over – emanate from South Florida, the vast majority from Miami. Since the mid-1980s, Miami's redevelopment has resulted in an explosion of artistic and cultural activity. Many artists based in other areas of the country, notably the northeast, headed down to take advantage of lower real-estate prices and quirky and affluent visitors. The influx of foreigners has also resulted in a boom in Caribbean and South American art.

Literature

Fiction While inroads are being made in poetry and experimental fiction, the Miami literature scene remains primarily a hotbed of mystery, scandal and detective novels. But no list of Florida writers would be complete without mention of Florida's best known: Marjorie Kinnan Rawlings, Ernest Hemingway and Zora Neale Hurston.

Rawlings' books contain beautiful descriptions of rural Florida life. She's best known for *The Yearling*, the story of Jodie Baxter's love for a fawn, which alienates the boy from his family. But Rawlings is also author of books including *Cross Creek*, which describes her home in a town near Gainesville, and *Jacob's Ladder*.

Ernest Hemingway, known as much (in Florida, anyway) for his drinking in Key West bars as for his distinctive style and riveting tales of moral dilemmas, lived in that city during one of his most fertile periods. It was there that he completed many of his best-loved works, including *A Farewell to Arms*. Key West is rife with Hemingway-abilia. See the Florida Keys chapter for more information.

Author of seven books, Zora Neale Hurston (1903–60) is best known for *Their Eyes Were Watching God*, her 1937 novel about an independent black woman in rural Florida. Hurston, born in Eatonville, also compiled southern black folklore. Also see the Central Florida chapter.

South Florida has more than a dozen international superstar suspense/thriller writers, and more are appearing every day. Heavy Miami hitters include Carl Hiaasen, whose books *(Stormy Weather, Native Tongue* and *Striptease)* offer snarling satire of South Florida, especially its tourists and developers. Hiaasen's *Team Rodent: How Disney Devours the World* is an eminently readable rant against the Magic Kingdom.

Of course, Elmore Leonard, the author of dozens of books, including *Get Shorty,*

Gold Coast, Stick and *Maximum Bob*, is not to be forgotten. Charles Willeford, the quintessential grizzled Miami author, is best known for *Miami Blues*.

Other bright stars include Pulitzer Prize–winning *Miami Herald* columnist Edna Buchanan *(Miami, It's Murder)*; Pulitzer Prize–winning columnist Liz Balmaseda; Les Standiford, author of eco-thriller *Spill* and several other novels that star building contractor John Deal in *Deal to Die for, Done Deal* and *Book Deal*.

Tampa-based Randy Wayne White writes richly detailed thrillers set on Sanibel Island, an enclave of weirdness on the Florida gulf coast; his hero, Doc Ford, stars in books including *North of Havana, Captiva* and *Sanibel Flats*.

Also incredibly well known is the 1988 Pulitzer Prize winner Dave Barry, the humorist whose columns at the *Miami Herald* (since 1983) are syndicated throughout the world. He's the author of numerous books, including *Dave Barry Is Not Making This Up, Dave Barry Turns 40, Dave Barry's Only Travel Guide You'll Ever Need, Dave Barry's Guide to Cyberspace* and *Dave Barry's Greatest Hits*.

Nonfiction Those scant on time, or who can't read on the beach, might pick up *The Florida Reader*, edited by Maurice O'Sullivan & Jack Lane.

Reality is more colorful than fiction in Miami. Look for Edna Buchanan's *The Corpse Had a Familiar Face*; Buchanan's *Herald* beat was grisly crime, and this is her story of covering those stories. The irrepressible Joan Didion's *Miami* expresses her take on the Cuban community (fiction or nonfiction?). Arva Moore Parks' *Miami, the Magic City* chronicles local lore with a good dose of historic photos. David Leon Chandler's *Henry Flagler* chronicles the story of Miami's 'Robber Baron,' who laid out the city. Rolf Shields' *Bought and Sold* tells the history of Miami like it was.

In the same vein, John Rothchild's *Up for Grabs* exposes the state's wacky commercial transactions. *Dreamers, Schemers & Scallawags: The Florida Chronicles*, by

Stuart McIver, gives the lowdown on the state's colorful underground characters.

Marjorie Stoneman Douglas' *The Everglades: River of Grass* is a must-read for anyone remotely interested in the complex ecological issues. Michael Gannon's *The New History of Florida* tells the state's story by way of historical themes.

Music

While classical music has a local hero in the innovative New World Symphony (see the Miami chapter), and some local bands are gaining recognition, the biggest story in Florida is Latin- and Caribbean-influenced music, including salsa, reggae, merengue, mambo, rumba, cha-cha and calypso. And as if to prove it, most major recording companies have offices in Miami. The best times to see ensemble Cuban bands – often with up to 20 musicians and singers – is during special celebrations, like the Calle Ocho Festival (see the Facts for the Visitor chapter).

Throughout the state, regional orchestras, such as the Florida Symphony and the Jacksonville Symphony, perform classical concerts regularly; performances and venues are listed throughout the book.

Dance

Miami nourishes start-ups. There are dozens of nonprofit dance organizations, and hundreds of dance-related businesses like studios, schools and production companies. And the mix of American, African, Cuban, Haitian, European and Latin American cultures is obvious in the productions you'll see here. The biggest players in Florida are the Miami City Ballet, one of the top 10 funded companies in the country (see the Entertainment section of the Miami chapter for more information), and the Miami-based Florida Dance Association (W www.fldance.org), which holds and coordinates many performances throughout Florida.

Painting & Sculpture

Perhaps surprisingly, as recently as the early 1980s, Miami's art scene was virtually nonexistent. But in the mid-1980s, artists discovered that they could get more space and live more cheaply in South Beach than in other art centers like New York and Los Angeles. At about the same time, the South Beach boom began, which in turn supplied the cash to fuel an explosion in local art. Even today, though, the lack of many major galleries or a truly world-class museum is still an issue, and the Miami arts market is still only one notch above fledgling.

That said, head to Miami's ArtCenter/South Florida, showcasing affordable studios and an exhibition space. The Museum of Contemporary Art is a schlep to visit, but worth it. The Rubell Family houses their modern art collection downtown in what was once a warehouse for drugs confiscated by the DEA. As you can imagine, Cuban and Latin American artists have a major impact on Miami's growing art community. Watch for group shows, and check out the monthly exhibits at the Latin American Art Museum, in Little Havana. The Miami Art Museum also specializes in post-WWII art of the Western hemisphere. For more Euro-centric art, the Bass Museum and the Lowe Art Museum will satisfy your cravings.

In Southeast Florida, the big collections include Fort Lauderdale's Museum of Art, with outstanding works by Picasso, Matisse, Moore, and Warhol. The Boca Raton Museum of Art and West Palm Beach's Norton Museum of Art aren't to be sneezed at either.

The major player in Northeast Florida is the Cummer Museum of Art, in Jacksonville, while the Southwest has many options: chief among them is the John & Mable Ringling Museum of Art, in Sarasota. St Petersburg, though, boasts a trip of powerhouse collections: The Dalí Museum, St Petersburg Fine Arts Museum and the Florida International Museum, with rotating international blockbuster exhibitions.

Film

At the turn of the 20th century, before Hollywood, California became film-making central, places like Jacksonville and even Hollywood, Florida, were cranking out films. These days, filmmakers are flocking back to the area with a vengeance. In the last few years, Miami Beach has starred in staggeringly successful films, including *There's Something About Mary*, *The Bodyguard*, *Donnie Brasco*, *Ace Ventura: Pet Detective*, *True Lies*, *Get Shorty* and *The Birdcage*.

For a wonderful glimpse of Miami Beach during the worst of its recent troubles, rent *Black Sunday,* which features a car and foot chase through the South Beach of the early 1980s – as witnessed by thousands of octogenarians in beach chairs. The glitzy and glamorous world of cocaine dealing and organized crime was explored in *Scarface,* a classic Miami movie starring Al Pacino.

From the beginning of filmmaking, Miami has provided a backdrop for some of America's most beloved classics, such as *The Cocoanuts* (the Marx Brothers' first feature); *Where the Sidewalk Ends,* filmed entirely at Miami Studios; *Citizen Kane,* which used the South Florida coastline as the setting for Xanadu, the largest pleasure palace in the world; *Key Largo,* with Bogie and Bacall; Elvis Presley's *Clambake; The Bellboy,* with funnyman Jerry Lewis doing his schtick at the gaudy Fontainebleau Hotel; *The Barefoot Mailman*; and three Bond films, *Dr No, Live and Let Die* and *Goldfinger.*

Architecture

Florida's architecture can be referred to as 'prosaic,' but we'd rather call it 'spectacularly unspectacular.' With very few exceptions – notably Key West, Miami's Art Deco District, Ybor City in Tampa, and the historic districts in Pensacola and especially St Augustine – the architecture you'll run into is run-of-the-mill, post-1950s urban sprawl. Buildings that don't look like shopping centers are probably condos – high-rise monsters that line the coasts.

There are several exceptions. The Spanish colonial and revival styles, predominant in St Augustine and Pensacola, resemble more the grand buildings of Mediterranean Spain (with archways, adobe, wood and terra-cotta tile) than the relatively stark version of Spanish Mission architecture found in the USA's Southwest. A perfect example, we hate to say it,

is taste-bastion Donald Trump's Mar-a-Lago, in Palm Beach.

Pockets of Victorian and Queen Anne pop up here and there, recognizable by their riotous colors and baubles, gingerbread towers, doodads and hoo-has. If you feel as if you've just walked into an expensive soap shop – or a B&B – it's probably a Victorian.

Cracker architecture, also called Florida vernacular, is classic pioneer homesteading architecture with a twist: enormous sun porches. Early 'single pen' houses – simple boxes with porches – were later expanded by adding a wall that either straddled the existing chimney (saddlebag) or was adjacent to the wall opposite the fireplace (double pen). Cracker homes run from quaint to enormous and are wood inside and out.

Miami Art Deco While famous for three distinct architectural styles – Mediterranean, towering skyscrapers and art deco – Miami is made up mainly of boom-era construction, with vibrant pockets of style here and there.

Miami Beach is best known, of course, for its art deco buildings. The term was a

NEIL SETCHFIELD

Well-preserved art deco in South Beach

contraction of the 1925 Parisian *Exposition Internationale des Arts Décoratifs et Industriels Modernes,* in which a strong emphasis was placed upon *arts décoratifs,* or decorative arts. The exposition wasn't the starting point, but rather the dawn of a style that combined many existing forms. These mostly included turn-of-the-century and pre-WWI European movements like art nouveau, Arts and Crafts, the Vienna secession and Italian futurism, and the more geometric modernism.

From the mid-1930s to early 1940s, Miami Beach developed what came to be known as Tropical Deco architecture. It organically reflected the natural world around it. For example, glass architectural blocks let bright Florida light in, but kept sweltering heat out. They also served a geometric or Cubist aesthetic. Floral reliefs, popular during the art nouveau period, appeared here too. Friezes on façades or etched into glass reflected native flora and fauna such as palm trees, pelicans and flamingos. Friezes also took their cues from the uniquely American jazz movement – harmonious and lyrical. Surrounded by the water, Miami Beach deco also developed a rhythmic language with scalloped waves and fountains.

Whereas Northeast deco buildings had socialist overtones, the clean lines of Miami Beach architecture still made room for joyful, playful, hopeful characteristics. Dreaming about the future began to take hold. Space travel was explored through design; buildings began to loosely resemble rockets, and rooflines embodied fantasies about space travel. Curved walls enhanced aerodynamic principles. Racing stripes alluded to the new speed of cars and trains. Nautical elements from the dawning era of ocean liners found expression through porthole windows and metal railings. Geometric and abstract zigzag (or ziggurat) patterns not only reflected the ancient Aztec and Egyptian cultures, they also symbolized lightning bolts of electricity, which was being harnessed in bigger ways. Sun rays, more imagery borrowed from ancient cultures, are used as life-affirming

elements that countered the dark days of Depression.

It's important to note that the colors you now see are more garish than they originally were. Earlier, many of the buildings were white with only a color trim, and more pastels were used as opposed to the neon colors of today. Also interestingly, the value of these Miami Beach buildings is based more on the sheer number of protected historic structures: individually, the inexpensively constructed houses would be worth far less.

SOCIETY & CONDUCT

'People in New York and Los Angeles,' said former *Miami Herald* columnist Eugene J Patron, 'have a lifestyle. Floridians have a life.' Northerners are often pleasantly surprised when interacting with Floridians (at least outside Miami), who tend to be more laid-back and friendly. Southern hospitality is as good as its reputation, but remember, the farther *north* you go, the farther *south* you get. The Panhandle may as well be Alabama, and Miami may as well be Brooklyn.

Outside the major cities, especially in rural areas, Floridians tend to be more conservative; their politics and attitudes are old-fashioned and right wing. In rural areas, travelers should avoid behavior or dress that may be considered offensive. It's also not a good idea for women to wear revealing clothing or go braless. Gay and lesbian travelers in these areas should do their best to behave as 'straight' as possible.

Rednecks, who refer to themselves as just that, can be found in many areas of northern Florida, easily identified by their foul and racially derogatory language. Leave them in peace to wallow in ignorance. While travelers may hear remarks directed at Cubans, Jews, blacks, Asians and Native Americans, racially motivated crimes are rare.

RELIGION
Western
Floridians are mostly Christians, but there are significant numbers of Jews too. Many are transplants from the northeastern USA, but there are also a healthy number of

Russian-Jewish and Cuban-Jewish immigrants. Many area Jews are Reform (they don't adhere as strictly to religious and social teachings of the Torah) as opposed to Conservative (more religious and ceremonial) or extremely religious Orthodox.

Chabad Lubovitchers, a faction of Orthodox Judaism that proselytizes within the Jewish faith, are also represented. If a long-haired, bearded man dressed in a black suit and white shirt and wearing a black hat or *yarmulke* asks you a) if you're Jewish and b) to step inside a recreational vehicle, you've just met a Lubovitcher.

Afro-Caribbean

These religions include Santería, a synchronism of the West African Yoruba religion with Catholicism. It was brought to Cuba by slaves who settled there and is primarily practiced in Cuba. Voodoo is Yoruba, as practiced by Haitians. Both of these religions practice animal sacrifice as a token of fidelity to the gods and spirits, and it's not uncommon to come upon animal remains at various places around the city, like along the Miami River, in parks and, strangely, near the Bass Museum.

Afro-Brazilian

Afro-Brazilian religions, or cults, do not follow the ideas of major European or Asian religions. Neither do they use doctrines to define good and evil. One of the things that was most shocking to Europeans in their first contact with the African images and rituals was the cult of Exú. This entity was generally represented by combined human and animal images, complete with a horn and an erect penis. Seeking parallels between their own beliefs and African religions, European Catholics and Puritans identified Exú as Satan. For Africans, however, Exú represents the transition between the material and the spiritual worlds.

Floridisms

You'll hear generic southern vernacular, as well as slang peculiar to Florida:

Anymore – In the South, 'anymore' refers to the present as well as past tense, meaning both 'any longer' ('I don't love you anymore') and 'nowadays' ('We used to take US Hwy 1 but anymore we take I-95').

Bubba – Standard Key West catch-all greeting or reference ('Hey, Bubba, howzit goin?').

Chickee – Thatched open-air structures, derived from Indian word for house. Pseudo-chickees are usually found in picnic areas in parks, but real chickees, suitable for sleeping (as long as you have a free-standing tent or mosquito netting), are found in the 10,000 Islands, in the Everglades.

Conch - Native Key West resident; see the Key West chapter for information on the Conch Republic.

Cracker – Named for the sound of the cracking whips of cattle drivers, this is a term for white native Floridians whom you'd otherwise call rednecks. It can be pejorative if you need it to be.

CST - Cuban Standard Time; a Miami excuse implying that Cubans are always late ('Sorry, I'm on CST').

Gorby – Derogative Key West term for tourists.

Parrothead – Jimmy Buffet fan.

Snowbird – Vacationing Northerner.

Touron – Derogative Key West term for tourists.

Y'all – Contraction of 'you all'; a generic reference to one or more people ('Y'all ain't got no grits where you come from?').

YUCA – Young Urban Cuban American; a Cuban Yuppie.

Candomblé, an African word denoting a dance in honor of the gods, is the most orthodox of the cults brought to Brazil from Africa by the Nago, Yoruba and Jeje peoples. In the ritual of Candomblé, Exú acts as a messenger between the gods and human beings. For example, everything related to money, love and protection against thieves comes under the watchful eye of Exú. Ultimately, Exú's responsibility is the temporal world.

LANGUAGE

'One of the nicest things about Miami,' goes an old joke, 'is how close it is to the USA.' Indeed, while English is the predominant language in the USA, Miami has an above-average number of non–English-speaking, and some may say intentionally unassimilated, foreigners. It's a somewhat unique situation in the USA. While pockets of foreigners have gravitated to other large cities, there seems to be a lesser degree of linguistic assimilation here, where, as some put it, 'Them Cubans just won't talk English like everybody else.'

Visitors can get away with English only, but to do that is to essentially write off experiencing a huge chunk of Miami culture and life. Spanish is the main language in almost every shop, café, coin laundry and restaurant in Little Havana and in a surprising number of businesses elsewhere in the city.

Spanish

Pronunciation Spanish has five vowels: **a**, **e**, **i**, **o** and **u**. They are pronounced something like the highlighted letters of the following English words: f**a**ther, **e**nd, mar**i**ne, **o**r and tr**u**th. The stress is placed on the syllable with an accent over it (México=**meh**-hiko) In the absence of a written accent, if the word ends in a vowel, **n**, or **s**, stress is on the second to last syllable (hasta luego=**ah**-sta loo-**eh**-go). Words ending in any other letter take stress on the final syllable.

Useful Words & Phrases

yes	*sí*
no	*no*
good/OK	*bueno*
bad	*malo*
better	*mejor*
best	*lo mejor*
more	*más*
less	*menos*
very little	*poco* or *poquito*

Greetings & Civilities

hello/hi	*hola*
good morning/day	*buenos días*
good evening/night	*buenas noches*
see you later	*hasta luego*
goodbye	*adiós*
pleased to meet you	*mucho gusto*
please	*por favor*
thank you	*gracias*
you're welcome	*de nada*
excuse me	*perdóneme*

Shopping

How much does it cost?	*¿Cuánto cuesta?*
I want…	*Quiero…*
What do you want?	*¿Qué quiere?*
Do you have…?	*¿Tiene…?*
Is/Are there…?	*¿Hay…?*
I understand.	*Entiendo.*
I do not understand.	*No entiendo.*
Do you understand?	*¿Entiende usted?*
Please speak slowly.	*Por favor hable despacio.*

Getting Around

street	*calle*
avenue	*avenida*
corner (of)	*esquina (de)*
block	*cuadra*
to the left	*a la izquierda*
to the right	*a la derecha*
straight ahead	*adelante*
Where is…?	*¿Dónde está…?*
the bus station	*el terminal de gua gua**
the train station	*la estación del ferrocarril*
bus	*gua gua* or *autobús**
train	*tren*
taxi	*taxi*
toilet	*sanitario*

**Gua gua* is Latin American slang for *autobús.* The former is universally understood in Miami; the latter is not.

Numbers

0	*cero*	14	*catorce*
1	*un, uno* (m), *una* (f)	15	*quince*
2	*dos*	16	*dieciséis*
3	*tres*	17	*diecisiete*
4	*cuatro*	18	*dieciocho*
5	*cinco*	19	*diecinueve*
6	*seis*	20	*veinte*
7	*siete*	30	*treinta*
8	*ocho*	40	*cuarenta*
9	*nueve*	50	*cincuenta*
10	*diez*	100	*cien*
11	*once*	200	*doscientos*
12	*doce*	500	*quinientos*
13	*trece*	1000	*mil*
		1,000,000	*millón*

Facts for the Visitor

PLANNING

When to Go

See the Climate section in the Facts about Florida chapter for specifics on temperature and rainfall. While Florida used to be thought of as a winter destination, many areas in the northern reaches of the state, notably St Augustine, Gainesville, Tallahassee and the Panhandle, are booming summer destinations. Northern Florida gets quite cool in winter, during which time the waters really aren't warm enough for swimming. But, alas, certain events happen only during winter – manatees, for example, seek warm water springs throughout northern Florida in winter (in summer you'll only find them in South Florida).

The Orlando area is a year-round destination, though there is heavy rainfall in summer. It is always crowded, especially during holidays, so reserve early if you plan to go there.

Miami and South Florida are most visited in winter, when the weather is pleasantly warm and the humidity isn't too high, so be prepared for higher prices and larger crowds. In summer, humidity and mosquitoes can be a problem (especially in the Everglades). But then again, the crowds will be thinner and the prices cheaper. Again, though, there are seasonal events: summertime is the only time to see turtles lay eggs on the beaches, for example.

The hurricane season – from June through November – can also be a perfectly pleasant time to visit, but remember, one little hurricane can ruin a holiday. See Dangers & Annoyances, later, for more information.

What Kind of Trip?

This really depends on what you're after and how much time you have. If you're here for a short visit, your trip will probably center around the Miami area, Orlando or Key West. But if you have time to explore, Florida's surprising diversity and wonderful parks are really memorable. With some

The Best & the Worst
The Best
1 Visiting Miami's South Beach
2 Canoeing in the 10,000 Islands
3 Exploring (and picking strawberries) in old St Augustine
4 Broiling on Pensacola beaches
5 Manatee-watching at Blue Spring State Park
6 Lunching at the Florida House Inn on Amelia Island
7 Shelling in Sanibel
8 Viewing a space shuttle launch at Cape Canaveral
9 Seeing St Petersburg's powerhouse collection of museums
10 Visiting Walt Disney World and the Orlando theme parks
The Worst
10 Summertime humidity
9 Public transport (except in Orlando)
8 Rednecks
7 Seething golf courses enveloping the state
6 The horror of Hwy 192 in Kissimmee
5 Miami Immigration & Naturalization Service (INS)
4 Hurricanes, tornadoes and mosquitoes
3 Urban sprawl eating at the Everglades
2 Big white cars with Palm Beach County plates and retirees driving 5 mph
1 Dimpled chads and ballot fraud

time, you'll be able to explore the Panhandle area, go tubing on the Blackwater River or Itchetucknee Springs, see the majesty of southwest Florida and perhaps even take a jaunt to the Bahamas or Cuba.

It's easy to plan thematic trips through the state. From B&B holidays to biking treks to Everglades adventures, Florida's information and tourism infrastructure is highly developed and easy to navigate.

Travel, including solo travel, is generally easy and safe going. But it's always easier with a car or motorcycle, and Florida is a good place to buy a used car (see the Getting Around chapter).

What to Bring

What to bring depends very much on where and when you go. Generally, if you visit in summer, you'll only need light clothing (it rarely gets cool enough for a sweater), but you'll need to be prepared for sudden downpours. Keep in mind, this is a first-world destination, so anything you might forget is readily available. Here is a list of suggested things to pack.

In summer, bring a pair of lightweight long pants and a light shirt to protect yourself against mosquitoes and no-see-ums (see Dangers & Annoyances, later). If you plan on going north in winter, bring slightly heavier items.

A key item at any time is sunscreen. Bring lots of this stuff (again, see the Dangers & Annoyances section), as well as good sunglasses and mosquito repellent (and/or a mosquito net with no-see-um netting). Swimming and snorkeling gear, a raincoat or an umbrella (especially in summer), a daypack for hiking trips or other excursions, solid shoes (if you're a walking kind of person) and flip-flops or sandals (sometimes beach sand really heats up) will definitely make your trip more pleasant.

See the Outdoor Activities chapter for the equipment you'll need for hiking, canoeing, kayaking or backpacking in the wilderness.

Florida is very casual for the most part. The minimal requirement is a pair of shorts and a bathing suit, with an optional set of in-line skates, but people wear just about anything they want. That casualness, however, is a tricky bugger: Cubans in Miami dress very fashionably for a night out, and for South Beach, Palm Beach, Boca Raton, Sarasota or Tampa nightlife, you'll want to dress to the nines.

Toiletries, hygiene and first-aid products are readily available, and Florida is an inexpensive place to buy clothes, so plan on leaving with more than you arrived with.

MAPS

Free state maps are easy to come by. The free *Official State Transportation Map* is a road map that's probably better than most commercial maps covering the same area. It's available through Visit Florida (see State Tourist Offices, below) and through some larger convention & visitor's bureaus. Members of the American Automobile Association (AAA) can request free Florida maps from their local AAA office; members of foreign affiliates can pick up maps once they arrive in the States.

For city maps, many convention & visitor's bureaus and chambers of commerce have free or inexpensive maps, invariably created by the *Dolph Map Company,* which covers every major city in the state. Its maps usually sell for $3 in bookstores, gas stations and map shops.

Hikers and backpackers can purchase topographical maps from specialty map shops, such as **A World of Maps** (☎ 954-267-9000; w www.aworldofmaps.com; 6820 N Florida Ave, Tampa, FL 33604). You can also purchase topographical maps directly from the **US Geological Survey** (USGS; ☎ 703-648-4090; w www.usgs.gov; Map & Book Sales, Denver, CO 80225). The USGS is an agency of the federal Department of the Interior that publishes very detailed maps of the entire country at different scales, up to 1:250,000. Many camping stores and national park and national forest ranger stations sell USGS maps of their immediate area. Maps at 1:62,500, or approximately 1 inch=1 mile, are ideal for backcountry hiking and backpacking. Some private cartographers are producing updated versions of old USGS maps at 1:62,500.

Boaters, canoers and kayakers can figure out which charts they'll need from the Web site for FAA NACO (w www.naco.faa.gov) and then call them (☎ 301-436-6990, 800-638-8972) directly to order by credit card. Or write to the NACO Distribution Division, Public Sales and Service, 6501 Lafayette Ave, Riverdale, MD 20737.

For getting off the beaten path, De-Lorme's *Florida Atlas & Gazetteer* (**w** www .delorme.com; scale 1:150,000) is the best all-around source for really tiny roads, though it's useless for navigating in cities. It also has listings – some dated but others useful – of campgrounds, historic sites, parks, natural features and even scenic drives.

Two good map companies to contact for all kinds of maps are **MapLink** (☎ 805-692-6777, 800-962-1394; **w** www.maplink.com; 30 S La Patera Lane, No 5, Santa Barbara, CA 93117) and **Omni Resources** (☎ 336-227-8300; **w** www.omnimap.com; 1004 S Mebane St, PO Box 2096, Burlington, NC 27216).

TOURIST OFFICES
Local Tourist Offices
Many towns don't have tourist offices per se. Chambers of commerce, or, in larger cities, the convention & visitor's bureau (sometimes called a visitor's & convention bureau and abbreviated as CVB/VCB) can provide you with local information about what to see and do. One underutilized service often performed by CVB/VCBs is, if you're stuck in a place and don't know what to do with yourself, they can set up an itinerary for you, tailored to your interests (travel with kids, ecotourism, organized tours etc). Do note, though, that CVB/VCBs vary in usefulness from place to place. In this book, the address and telephone number of each chamber of commerce and/or other tourist offices are given in the Information heading under the town.

If you're in a town with useless or hateful chamber or CVB/VCB personnel, and you don't know where to turn for reliable information (which is doubtful if you have this book!), head to the research desk at the main branch of the public library. They can tell you about local organizations that specialize in whatever you're interested in. In this book, we list libraries where possible.

State Tourist Offices
Visit Florida (☎ 850-488-5607, 888-735-2872; **w** www.flausa.com; 661 E Jefferson St, Suite 300, Tallahassee, FL 32301) is the state's pri-vatized tourism agency, and it does a very good job. Its Web site is first rate, and Visit Florida will send you a shiny, colorful folder of information about the state. The brochures and vacation guide also include numbers of local convention & visitor's bureaus and tourist development councils. If you have a specific need or question, state tourist offices may be able to answer it or refer you to the appropriate office.

Visit Florida offices include the following:

Campbellton Welcome Center (☎ 850-263-3510)
Hwy 231, 3 miles north of Campbellton

Capitol Welcome Center (☎ 850-488-6167)
Florida Capitol Building, W Plaza Level, Tallahassee

Jennings Welcome Center (☎ 386-938-2981)
4 miles north of Jennings on I-75 South

Pensacola Welcome Center (☎ 850-944-0442)
16 miles west of Pensacola on I-10 East

Yulee Welcome Center (☎ 904-225-9182)
7 miles north of Yulee on I-95 South

Tourist Offices Abroad
International tourist offices for Florida include the following:

Brazil (☎ 11-3069-9559)
Alameda Lorena, 800 (11th floor, Suite 1111) 01424-001, São Paulo

Canada (☎ 416-485-2573)
512 Duplex Ave, Toronto, Ontario, M4R2E3

Germany (☎ 69-131-0091)
Schillerstrasse 10, D60313 Frankfurt am Main

Japan (☎ 03-5276-0260)
Ichibancho KK Building, SF, 13-8, Ichibancho, Chiyoda-ku, Tokyo 102-0082

UK (☎ 20-7932-2406)
28 Eccleston Square, London SW1V 1NZ

France (☎ 01 53 69 00 64)
8-10, Boulevard du Montparnasse, 75015 Paris

VISAS & DOCUMENTS
Passport
All foreign visitors (other than Canadians) must bring a passport. Most visitors also require a US visa. Canadians must have proper proof of Canadian citizenship, such as a citizenship card with photo ID or a passport. All visitors should bring their

driver's license and any health-insurance or travel-insurance cards.

If you could, on the best of days, be mistaken as being under 30, carry a photo ID card with your age on it, or a national ID card. Anyone who appears to be under 30 is asked for identification at bars and nightclubs.

It's a good idea to make a photocopy of your passport and international ID to carry around instead of the original (though you can't use the photocopy to get into a bar). There's nothing worse than losing your identity on a trip.

Visas

Apart from Canadians, and those entering under the Visa Waiver Pilot Program (see below), all foreign visitors need to obtain a visa from a US consulate or embassy. In most countries, the process can be done by mail or through a travel agent.

Your passport should be valid for at least six months longer than your intended stay in the USA, and you'll need to submit a recent photo (37mm x 37mm) with the application. Documents of financial stability and/or guarantees from a US resident are sometimes required, particularly for those from developing, Eastern European and former Soviet-bloc countries.

The most common visa is a Non-Immigrant Visitors Visa, B1 for business purposes, B2 for tourism or visiting friends and relatives. A visitor's visa is good for one or five years with multiple entries, and it specifically prohibits the visitor from taking paid employment in the USA. The validity period depends on what country you're from. The length of time you'll be allowed to stay in the USA is ultimately determined by US immigration authorities at the port of entry. If you're coming to the USA to work or study, you will probably need a different type of visa, and the company or institution you're going to be with should make the arrangements. Allow six months for processing the application.

Visa Waiver Pilot Program Citizens of certain countries may enter the USA without a US visa, for stays of 90 days or less, under the Visa Waiver Pilot Program (**W** www .travel.state.gov/vwp.html). Currently these countries are Andorra, Austria, Australia, Belgium, Brunei, Denmark, Finland, France, Germany, Iceland, Ireland, Italy, Japan, Liechtenstein, Luxembourg, Monaco, the Netherlands, New Zealand, Norway, Portugal, San Marino, Singapore, Slovenia, Spain, Sweden, Switzerland, the United Kingdom and Uruguay. Under this program, you must have a roundtrip ticket that is nonrefundable in the USA, and you will not be allowed to extend your stay beyond 90 days. Check with the US embassy in your home country for any other requirements.

Visa Extensions Tourists are usually granted a three-month stay on arrival. If you try to extend at that time, the first assumption will be that you are working illegally, so come prepared with concrete evidence that you've been traveling extensively and will continue to be a model tourist. Extensions are manhandled by the US Government Justice Department's Immigration & Naturalization Service (INS; ☎ 800-375-5283, **W** www.ins.usdoj.gov), at 7880 Biscayne Blvd in Miami. Get there early, bring along a good, long book and pack a lunch.

Travel Insurance

No matter how you're traveling, consider travel insurance. This not only covers you for medical expenses and luggage theft or loss but also for cancellation or delays in your travel arrangements (you might fall seriously ill two days before departure, for example). If you're planning to travel a long time, the insurance may seem very expensive – but if you can't afford it, you certainly won't be able to afford a medical emergency in the USA. Everyone should be covered for the worst possible scenario, such as an accident that requires hospital treatment and a flight home. Coverage depends on your insurance and type of ticket, so ask both your insurer and your ticket-issuing agency to explain the finer points.

STA Travel offers a variety of insurance options at reasonable prices. Ticket loss is also covered by travel insurance. Make sure you have a separate record of all your ticket details – or better still, a photocopy of your ticket. Also make a copy of your policy, in case the original is lost. Buy travel insurance as early as possible. If you buy it the week before you fly, you may find, for instance, that you're not covered for delays to your flight caused by strikes or other industrial actions that may have been in force before you took out the insurance.

International Driving Permit

Bring your driver's license if you intend to rent a car; visitors from some countries may find it wise to back up their national license with an International Driving Permit, available from their local auto club for a nominal fee. Note that your foreign driver's license *is* valid in the USA. An IDP is not a license but rather an official translation of yours (valid for one year, and you still need to carry your license), and while the major rental companies are used to seeing foreign licenses, local traffic police are more likely to accept an IDP as valid identification than an unfamiliar document from another country.

Automobile Association Card

If you plan on driving a lot in Florida, consider joining your national automobile association or the American Automobile Association (AAA; Ⓦ www.aaa.com), which costs $45 annually. Members of the AAA or an affiliated automobile club can get car-rental, maps and sightseeing-admission discounts with membership cards. More important, membership gives you access to AAA road service in case of an emergency, from locking your keys in the car to having major engine problems.

Hostel Card

About half the hostels in Florida are members of Hostelling International/American Youth Hostel (HI/AYH), which is affiliated with the International Youth Hostel Federation (IYHF). You can purchase membership on the spot when checking in, although it's advisable to purchase it before you leave home. The card will save you

about $2 to $3 off nonmember rates. Some non-HI hostels will also extend a discount to HI cardholders.

Student & Youth Card

Students should get an international student ID (ISIC), or bring along a school or university ID card (not as good). You can get an ISIC from STA Travel offices around the world with proof of enrollment. The ISIC secures substantial discounts at museums and tourist attractions and on some airfares.

Seniors' Card

British Railways and the American Association of Retired People (AARP; Ⓦ www .aarp.com) issue identification cards for seniors, usually people over 55. These are absolutely key in Florida, where almost all major attractions, most hotel chains and some smaller hotels offer seniors' discounts. Discounts can be substantial – up to 20% off on a room. You'll also save on some transport, including airfare.

Photocopies

All important documents (passport data page and visa page, credit cards, travel insurance policy, air/bus/train tickets, driving license etc) should be photocopied before you leave home. Leave one copy with someone at home and keep another with you, separate from the originals.

EMBASSIES & CONSULATES

As a tourist, it's important to realize what your own embassy – the embassy of the country of which you are a citizen – can and can't do to help you if you get into trouble. Generally speaking, it won't be much help in emergencies if the trouble you're in is remotely your own fault. Remember that you are bound by the laws of the country you are in. Your embassy will not be sympathetic if you end up in jail after committing a crime locally, even if such actions are legal in your own country.

In genuine emergencies you might get some assistance, but only if other channels have been exhausted. For example, if you need to get home urgently, a free ticket home is exceedingly unlikely – the embassy would expect you to have insurance. If your money and documents are stolen, it might assist you with getting a new passport, but a loan for onward travel is out of the question.

US Embassies & Consulates

To find US embassies in countries other than those listed below, visit Ⓦ www.usembassy.state.gov. US diplomatic offices abroad include the following:

Australia (☎ 2-6214-5600)
  21 Moonah Place, Yarralumla ACT 2600
  (☎ 2-9373-9200) Level 59 MLC Center,
  19-29 Martin Place, Sydney NSW 2000
  (☎ 3-9526-5900) 553 St Kilda Rd, Melbourne,
  Victoria 3004

Austria (☎ 1-313-39)
  Boltzmanngasse 16, A-1091, Vienna

Belgium (☎ 2-508-21-11)
  Blvd du Regent 27, B-1000, Brussels

Canada (☎ 613-238-5335)
  490 Sussex Dr, Ottawa, Ontario, K1N 1G8
  (☎ 604-685-4311) 1095 W Pender St,
  Vancouver, BC, V6E 2M6
  (☎ 514-398-9695) 1155 Rue St-Alexandre,
  Montréal, Québec, H2Z 1Z2

Denmark (☎ 45-3555-3144)
  Dag Hammarskjolds Allé 24, Copenhagen

Finland (☎ 9-171-931)
  Itainen Puistotie 14A, Helsinki

France (☎ 1 43 12 22 22)
  2 Av Gabriel, 75382 Paris

Germany (☎ 30-238-5174)
  Neustaedtische Kirchstrasse 4-5, 10017 Berlin

Greece (☎ 1-721-2951)
  91 Vasilissis Sophias Blvd, 10160 Athens

India (☎ 11-419-8000)
  Shanti Path, Chanakyapuri 110021,
  New Delhi

Ireland (☎ 1-668-8777)
  42 Elgin Rd, Ballsbridge, Dublin

Israel (☎ 3-519-7575)
  71 Hayarkon St, Tel Aviv

Italy (☎ 6-46-741)
  Via Vittorio Veneto 119A-121, 00187 Rome

Japan (☎ 3-224-5000)
  1-10-5 Akasaka, Minato-ku, Tokyo

Kenya (☎ 2-537-800)
  Mombasa Rd, Unit 64100, Nairobi (E)

Korea (☎ 2-397-4114)
  82 Sejong-Ro, Chongro-ku, Seoul

Malaysia (☎ 3-2168-5000)
  376 Jalan Tun Razak, 50400 Kuala Lumpur

Mexico (☎ 5-209-9100)
  Paseo de la Reforma 305, Cuauhtémoc,
  06500 Mexico City

Netherlands (☎ 70-310-9209)
  Lange Voorhout 102, 2514 EJ The Hague
  (☎ 20-5755-309) Museumplein 19,
  1071 DJ Amsterdam

New Zealand (☎ 4-472-2068)
  29 Fitzherbert Terrace, Thorndon, Wellington

Norway (☎ 22-44-85-50)
  Drammensvein 18, Oslo

Russia (☎ 95-728-5000)
  Bolshoy Devyatinskiy Pereulok No 8,
  121099 Moscow

Singapore (☎ 476-9100)
  27 Napier Rd, Singapore 258508

South Africa (☎ 12-342-1048)
  877 Pretorius St, Box 9536, Pretoria 0001

Spain (☎ 1-91587-2200)
  Calle Serrano 75, 28006 Madrid

Sweden (☎ 8-783-5300)
  Dag Hammarskjolds Vag 31, S-115 89
  Stockholm

Switzerland (☎ 31-357-7011)
  Jubilaumsstrasse 93, 3005 Berne

Thailand (☎ 2-255-4365)
  120 Wireless Rd, Bangkok

United Kingdom (☎ 020-7499-9000)
  24/31 Grosvenor Square, London W1A 1AE
  (☎ 131-556-8315) 3 Regent Terrace,
  Edinburgh EH7 5BW
  (☎ 2890-328-239) Queens House, 14 Queens St,
  Belfast BT1 6EQ

Consulates in Florida

Check under Consulates in the white pages of the telephone book for diplomatic representation in Miami. Be patient: Miami is considered a cushy post by the always hardworking diplomatic set, and some consular offices have ridiculously limited hours and act as if you're really interfering with their day if you ask for things. Most consulates are in Miami, but a few are in Coral Gables. Citizens of Australia and New Zealand may contact the British or Canadian consulates for emergency assistance, as neither country maintains consular offices in Miami.

Consulates include the following:

Antigua & Barbuda (☎ 305-381-6762)
25 SE 2nd Ave, Suite 300

Argentina (☎ 305-373-7794)
800 Brickell Ave

Austria (☎ 305-325-1561)
1454 NW 17th Ave, Suite 200

Bahamas (☎ 305-373-6295)
25 SE 2nd Ave, Suite 818

Belgium (☎ 305-932-4263)
4100 N Miami Ave

Bolivia (☎ 305-670-0709)
9100 S Dadeland Blvd, Suite 406

Brazil (☎ 305-285-6200)
2601 S Bayshore Dr, Suite 800,
Coconut Grove

Canada (☎ 305-579-1600)
200 S Biscayne Blvd, Suite 1600

Chile (☎ 305-373-8623)
800 Brickell Ave, Suite 1230

Colombia (☎ 305-448-5558)
280 Aragon Ave, Coral Gables

Costa Rica (☎ 305-871-7485)
1600 NW Le Jeune Rd, Suite 102

Denmark (☎ 305-446-4284)
2655 Le Jeune Rd, Coral Gables

Dominican Republic (☎ 305-358-3220)
1038 Brickell Ave

Ecuador (☎ 305-539-8214)
1101 Brickell Ave, Suite 102

El Salvador (☎ 305-371-8850)
300 Biscayne Blvd Way, Suite 1020

France (☎ 305-372-9798)
2S Biscayne Blvd, Suite 1710

Germany (☎ 305-358-0290)
100 Biscayne Blvd

Guatemala (☎ 305-443-4828)
300 Sevilla Ave, Suite 210, Coral Gables

Haiti (☎ 305-859-2003)
259 SW 13th St

Honduras (☎ 305-447-8927)
300 Sevilla Ave, Coral Gables

Israel (☎ 305-925-9400)
100 N Biscayne Blvd, Suite 1800

Italy (☎ 305-374-6322)
1200 Brickell Ave, 7th floor

Jamaica (☎ 305-374-8431)
25 SE 2nd Ave, Suite 842

Mexico (☎ 305-716-4977)
1200 NW 78th Ave, Suite 200

Netherlands (☎ 305-789-6646)
801 Brickell Ave, 9th floor

Nicaragua (☎ 305-220-6900)
8532 SW 8th St, Suite 201

Norway (☎ 305-358-4386)
1007 N American Way

Panama (☎ 305-371-7031)
2800 Ponce de León Blvd, Suite 1050

Paraguay (☎ 305-374-9090)
300 Biscayne Blvd Way, Suite 907

Peru (☎ 305-374-1305)
444 Brickell Ave, Suite 135

Portugal (☎ 305-444-6311)
1901 Ponce de León Blvd, Coral Gables

Spain (☎ 305-446-5511)
2655 Le Jeune Rd, Suite 203, Coral Gables

Switzerland (☎ 305-377-6700)
825 Brickell Bay Dr, Suite 1450

Trinidad & Tobago (☎ 305-374-2199)
1000 Brickell Ave, Suite 800

United Kingdom (☎ 305-374-1522)
1001 Brickell Bay Dr, Suite 2880

Uruguay (☎ 305-443-9764)
1077 Ponce de León Blvd, Suite B, Coral
Gables

Venezuela (☎ 305-577-3834)
1101 Brickell Ave, Suite 901

CUSTOMS

US customs allows each person over the age of 21 to bring one liter of liquor and 200 cigarettes duty-free into the country. US citizens are allowed to import, duty-free, $400 worth of gifts from abroad, while non–US citizens are allowed to bring in $100 worth. US law permits you to bring in, or take out, as much as $10,000 in American or foreign currency, traveler's checks or letters of credit without formality. Larger amounts of any or all of the above – there are no limits – must be declared to customs.

It's forbidden to bring in to the USA chocolate liqueurs, pornography, lottery tickets, items with fake brand names and goods made in Cuba or Iraq. Any fruit, vegetables or other food or plant material must be declared or left in the bins in the arrival area. Most food items are prohibited to prevent the introduction of pests or diseases.

The USA, like 140 other countries, is a signatory to CITES, the Convention on International Trade in Endangered Species. As such, it prohibits the import and export of products made from species that may be endangered in any part of the world, including ivory, tortoiseshell, coral, and many fur, skin and feather products. If you want to bring a snakeskin belt with you, you may have to show a certificate that it was not made from an endangered species. The easiest option is not to bring anything even remotely suspect. CITES restrictions apply to what you take home, too. Alligator-skin boots might be a great souvenir, but be ready to convince customs authorities that they're not made from endangered gators.

Due to Miami's infamous popularity as a drug-smuggling gateway, customs officers in Miami are known to be...let's call them *thorough* in their examination of backpackers and other travelers who may fit a profile officers have of a 'mule,' or someone ferrying narcotics. They may not be very polite – but you should be, and you should dress neatly and carry lots of traveler's checks and credit cards, or show other signs of prosperity lest they think you're here to work illegally.

Both customs and immigration officers have the right to drag you into a room for questioning, or worse. If you are taken back there, make certain that a representative of your airline (who can call your relatives and get you information) knows you're there and who you want told of your predicament.

MONEY
Currency
The US dollar (US$ or just $) is divided into 100 cents with coins of one cent (penny), five cents (nickel), 10 cents (dime), 25 cents (quarter) and relatively rare 50 cents (half dollar). There are even a few $1 coins in circulation; they're gold-colored and feature a design by American artist Glenda Goodacre.

Banknotes are called bills. Be sure to check the corners for amounts, as they're all the same size and color. Circulated bills come in denominations of $1, $2 (rare), $5, $10, $20, $50 and $100. The US has two designs of bills in circulation, but you'd have to study

them closely to notice. On the newer bills the central portrait is bigger and off-center.

There are three straightforward ways to handle payments: cash, US-dollar traveler's checks and credit cards. The ubiquitous ATMs (automated teller machines; see that section, later) facilitate the process of acquiring cash.

Exchange Rates
These are particularly volatile, but at press time exchange rates were as follows:

country	unit		US dollars
Australia	A$1	=	$0.55
Canada	C$1	=	$0.63
EU	E€1	=	$0.98
Hong Kong	HK$10	=	$1.28
Japan	Y100	=	$0.83
New Zealand	NZ$1	=	$0.47
UK	£1	=	$1.56

Daily exchange rates are listed in the *New York Times*, *Wall Street Journal* and *International Herald Tribune*. You can also get up-to-the-second exchange rates, if you're so inclined, on the Internet from sites such as W www.xe.com/ucc/convert.cgi.

Note that the exchange rates listed in newspapers and on the Web are those for chunks of currency; actual street exchange rates will always be lower (unless you bring in a suitcase full of cash).

Exchanging Money
Cash The best advice for people who need to exchange a foreign currency for US$ is to do so at home, before you arrive. Exchange rates are generally worse in the US than in other countries. If you must change money in the States, head to a real bank, rather than an exchange office. **Bank of America** (☎ 305-350-6350) offers foreign-exchange services in all its branches and has branches all through the state.

Private exchange offices generally offer the least competitive rates and charge the highest commissions. There are private exchange offices around town, in places such as drugstores and record shops.

Traveler's Checks Denominated in US dollars, traveler's checks are often as good as cash in the USA; many establishments (not just banks) will accept them just like cash. The major advantage of traveler's checks over cash is that they can be replaced if lost or stolen. But changing traveler's checks denominated in a foreign currency is rarely convenient, economical or practical. Get larger denomination US$100 checks, as you may be charged service fees per check when cashing them at banks.

For refunds on lost or stolen traveler's checks (not cards) call American Express at ☎ 800-221-7282; MasterCard at ☎ 800-223-9920; Thomas Cook at ☎ 800-223-7373; or Visa at ☎ 800-227-6811.

ATMs You can usually withdraw money straight from your bank account at home at these ubiquitous machines. Most ATMs (automated teller machines) in the Miami area accept bank cards from the Plus and Cirrus systems, the two largest ATM networks in the USA, as well as Visa and MasterCard credit cards.

Keep in mind that you will be charged a fee from the bank that is dispensing the money as well as your bank at home. These can add up if you are withdrawing money daily. As for credit-card cash advances, remember that you are charged interest on the withdrawal, often at a higher rate than for a standard purchase, beginning immediately and until you pay it back.

Credit & Debit Cards Major credit cards are accepted at hotels, most restaurants, gas stations, shops and car rental agencies throughout the USA. In fact, you'll find it hard to perform certain transactions, such as renting a car or purchasing tickets to performances, without one. Visa and Master-Card are the most widely accepted.

Even if you loathe credit cards and prefer to rely on traveler's checks and ATMs, carry one for emergencies. Banks in Australia, New Zealand and the UK are now selling Visa Travel Money, a pre-paid Visa card similar to a telephone card: Your credit limit is the amount you buy the card with, and

while it's not rechargeable, it's accepted like a regular Visa card. It charges a fee that is usually around 2% of the card's purchase price, so it's more expensive than traveler's checks, but is also more accessible.

Places that accept Visa and MasterCard are also likely to accept debit cards. Unlike a credit card, a debit card deducts payment directly from the user's checking account. Instead of an interest rate, users are charged a minimal fee for the transaction. Be sure to check with your bank to confirm that your debit card will be accepted in other states or countries. Debit cards from large commercial banks can often be used worldwide.

Carry copies of your credit card numbers separately from the cards. If they are lost or stolen, contact the company immediately. Following are toll-free numbers for the main credit card companies. Contact your bank if you lose your ATM card.

American Express	☎ 800-528-4800
Diners Club	☎ 800-234-6377
Discover	☎ 800-347-2683
MasterCard	☎ 800-826-2181
Visa	☎ 800-336-8472

Costs
Luxury or penury, both are accommodated in Florida. Cheap hotels and digs with all the fixins abound; there are good choices for everyone from backpackers to business travelers.

Getting here is often very cheap, especially from the UK, where package deals are readily available. It's also cheap from within the USA, especially if you take a bus or drive here. See the Getting There & Away chapter for more information.

Rental cars in Florida tend to be cheaper than elsewhere. Rates start at around $25 a day or $125 a week, but you really have to seek those out; an average rate can be figured at $35/175 a day/week.

Budget Ranges The most inexpensive way to see Florida is to camp at state parks with a tent, share a rental car among four people, food shop at grocery stores and have a lot of picnics. Traveling this way, your daily budget for food, lodging and transport can be as low as $25 to $35 per person; figure an additional $20 or so per person if you'll be spending lots of time in big cities.

Traveling frugally outside of a tent, a couple can expect to spend between $75 and $85 per person per day. Such travel entails staying in budget motels, eating breakfast and lunch in fast-food places (or lunchrooms), taking dinner in moderately priced restaurants and getting around by rental car. Two people touring in a rental car, staying at fancier hotels or B&Bs and dining pretty much as they please should expect to spend *at least* $130 to $180 per person per day.

Accommodation rates range widely and, as with so many things here, depend a lot on when and where you go. Generally, you'll find the cheapest beds in the Orlando/Kissimmee area, where competition is so fierce that motel rooms start at about $35 in summer; $60 in winter. Elsewhere, decent but very basic hotel rooms generally start at about $75 in winter and range to, well, anything really. Youth hostels are the cheapest option if you're traveling alone (rates are as low as $13 for a bed in a dorm).

The cheaper-end restaurants usually have breakfast for about $2 to $4; lunch can be $4 to $6 and dinner $5 to $8. A beer in a supermarket costs $1 (a six-pack is $4 to $6, depending on the brand); in a bar, it's $2.50 to $4.

Tipping
Tipping is a US institution that can, initially, be a little confusing for foreign visitors. Wait-staff at restaurants, bartenders, taxi drivers, bellhops, hotel cleaning staff and others are paid a mere stipend. Customers are expected to compensate these people directly: Tips are actually part of their salary.

So tipping is not really an option; the service has to be absolutely *appalling* before you should consider not tipping. In a bar or restaurant, a tip is customarily 15% (for a standard tip, double the tax and add a smidge) of the bill; a tip for outstanding service in a restaurant is 20%. You needn't

tip at fast-food restaurants or self-serve cafeterias. Hotel cleaning staff should be tipped about $2 a day, unless they don't deserve it. Tip daily, as they rotate shifts. Add about 10% to taxi fares even if you think your driver should be institutionalized. Hotel porters who carry bags a long way expect $3 to $5, or add it up at $1 per bag. Valet parking is worth about $2, to be given when your car is returned to you.

Special Deals
The USA is probably the most promotion-oriented society on earth. Though the bargaining common in many other countries is not generally accepted in the US, you can work angles to cut costs. For example, at hotels in the off-season, casually and respectfully mentioning a competitor's rate may prompt a manager to lower the quoted rate. Artisans may consider a negotiated price for large purchases. Discount coupons are widely available – check circulars in Sunday papers and at supermarkets, tourist offices or chambers of commerce.

Taxes
There is no national sales tax (such as VAT) in the USA. Most states levy sales taxes (Florida's is 6%), but some communities also tack on a bit more for their fair share (Miami, for instance, adds another 0.5%). States and cities/towns also usually levy taxes on hotel rooms and restaurant meals. Rooms and meal taxes are not normally included in prices quoted to you, even though (or perhaps because) they may increase your final bill by as much as 9.5% to 11.5%. You must add tax to rates listed in this book. If you eat and drink in a hotel the same percentage tax is also added. Rental cars are subjected to the 6% sales tax and a myriad of other surcharges, which add up quickly.

POST & COMMUNICATIONS
Postal Rates
For 24-hour postal information call ☎ 800-275-8777 or check **w** www.usps.gov. Private shippers such as United Parcel Service (UPS; ☎ 800742-5877) and Federal Express (FedEx; ☎ 800-463-3339) ship much of the

nation's load of parcels and important time-sensitive documents to both domestic and foreign destinations.

Currently, rates for 1st-class mail within the USA are 37¢ for letters up to 1oz (28g; 23¢ for each additional ounce) and 23¢ for postcards. Parcels airmailed anywhere within the USA are $3.85 for 1lb or less. For heavier items, rates differ according to the distance mailed. Books, periodicals and computer disks can be sent by a cheaper 4th-class rate.

With the exception of mail to Canada and Mexico, international airmail rates start at 80¢ for a 1oz letter; postcards cost 70¢. Aerograms to anywhere are 70¢. Letters to Canada and Mexico are 60¢ for a 1oz letter and 85¢ for a letter up to 2oz; postcards cost 40¢.

Sending Mail

Mail within the USA generally takes two to three days, and mail to destinations within Florida takes from one to two days – except in St Augustine, where delivery time ranges from three days to never. Not to sound like a postal pamphlet, but it *does* help speed delivery to put the correct 9-digit zip (postal) code on the envelope (though the first five will usually suffice). If you know the address but not the zip code, you can find a list at the post office or on the Internet (W www.usps.gov/ncsc).

Allow mail at least a week to reach Europe, and up to two weeks at peak times of the year like Christmas. If you have the correct postage, you can drop your mail into any official blue mailbox, found in such places as shopping centers and street corners. Mail pickup times are written on the inside of the mailbox lid.

Receiving Mail

You can have mail sent to you care of General Delivery at any post office that has its own zip (postal) code. It's best to have your intended date of arrival (if the sender knows it) clearly marked on the envelope. Mail is usually held for 30 days before it's returned to sender; you might request that your correspondents write 'hold for arrival' on letters. Have them address mail to you like so:

Your Name
c/o USPS Miami Beach General Delivery
1300 Washington Ave
Miami Beach, FL 33139

Your Name
c/o USPS Orlando General Delivery
46 E Robinson St
Orlando, FL 32802

Alternatively, have mail sent to the local representative of American Express or Thomas Cook, both of which provide mail service for their members. Call ☎ 800-275-8777 for postal zip codes and post offices nearest you.

Telephone

With the ongoing overlay of new area codes all around Florida, making a local phone call is more confusing than ever. For instance, if you are calling locally in Miami (or Fort Lauderdale, the Everglades or the Orlando area, among lots of other places), you must dial the area code + the seven-digit number. Leave off the preceding 1 before local calls – just start with ☎ 305 or ☎ 786. If you are calling locally in the Keys or Key West (or West Palm Beach or Naples, among lots of other places), you only have to dial the seven-digit number.

But how do you know which to do where? Make the call using the area code, and if it goes through, great. If it doesn't, a recorded voice will tell you to hang up and dial again without using the area code. Only in America.

If you are calling long distance, dial 1 + the three-digit area code + the seven-digit number. If you're calling from abroad, the international country code for the USA is 1.

The ☎ 800, 888, 877 and 866 area codes are toll-free numbers within the USA and sometimes from Canada as well.

The ☎ 900 and 976 area codes have a reputation for catering to sleazy operations – a smorgasbord of phone sex at $2.99 a minute, perhaps. Regardless of the nature of the business, you will be charged a fee when calling ☎ 900 or 976 numbers.

Directory assistance is reached locally by dialing ☎ 411. This is free from many pay phones, but costs as much as $1.25 from a private phone. For directory assistance outside your area code, dial ☎ 1 + the three-digit area code + 555-1212.

Pay Phones Local calls cost 50¢ at pay phones, which don't give change. Most hotels add a service charge of 50¢ to $1 for each local – and sometimes toll-free – call made from a room phone. Many also add hefty surcharges for long-distance calls, 50% or even 100% on top of their carrier's rates. Public pay phones, which can be found in many lobbies, are always cheaper. Many area pay phones accept incoming calls; the number will be posted on the phone.

Long-distance rates vary depending on the destination and which telephone company you use. There are literally hundreds of long-distance companies in the US, and rates vary by several hundred percent – call the operator (☎ 0, 3050 or 00) for rate information. Don't ask the operator to put your call through, however, because operator-assisted calls are much more expensive than calls dialed directly. Generally, nights (11pm to 8am) and all day Saturday and Sunday are the cheapest times to call. Smaller discounts apply in the evening from 5pm to 11pm daily.

Phone Debit Cards Phone debit cards in denominations of $5, $10, $20 and $50 allow purchasers to pay in advance, with access through a toll-free number. Look for these ubiquitous cards in small convenience stores and large drugstores. You shouldn't have to pay more than 25¢ per minute on domestic long-distance calls, but some are as high as 45¢ per minute. Wal-Mart and other discount retailers sell them for as little as 6¢ a minute. If a card merely says that you'll 'save up to 60%,' move on. When using phone debit or calling cards, be cautious of people watching you dial in the numbers – thieves will memorize numbers and use your card to make calls to all corners of the earth.

International Calls To place an international call direct, dial ☎ 011 + country code + area code (dropping the leading 0) + number. From a pay phone, dial all those numbers before inserting coins; a voice will come on telling you how much to put in the phone after you dial the number. For international operator assistance and rates, dial ☎ 00. Calls to Canada are treated like domestic calls.

In general, it's cheaper to make international calls at night, but this varies with the country you're calling and the long-distance company. Calls from a private phone to Australia or Europe, from a nondiscounted long-distance carrier, should be about $1 for the first minute and 50¢ for each subsequent minute. Calls to other continents usually cost about twice that. From private phones with a discount plan for long-distance service, the cost could be as low as 20¢ a minute to Europe, 50¢ a minute to Australia – check before you dial!

eKno Communication Service Lonely Planet's eKno global communication service provides low-cost international calls – for local calls, you're usually better off with a local phone card. eKno also offers free messaging services, email, travel information and an online travel vault, where you can securely store all your important documents. You can join online at ⓦ www.ekno.lonely planet.com, where you will find the local-access numbers for the 24-hour customer-service center. Once you have joined, check the eKno Web site for the latest access numbers for each country and for updates on new features.

Collect & Country Direct You can call collect (reverse charges) from any phone. There are increasing numbers of providers, but beware that there really is a difference in price, so check before you dial. The main players at the time of writing were AT&T (☎ 800-225-5288) and MCI (☎ 800-265-5328). You can also just dial ☎ 0 + the area code and number, eg, 0+212+555-4567, but this is generally the most expensive option of all.

Country-direct service connects you, toll-free, with an operator from another country and allows you to make collect calls via that country's phone system, which may be cheaper than doing it from the USA. With country direct, you may also use your telephone-company charge card from home. The following are some country-direct numbers:

Australia	☎ 800-682-2878
Austria	☎ 800-624-0043
Belgium	☎ 800-472-0032
Denmark	☎ 800-762-0045
France	☎ 800-537-2623
Germany	☎ 800-292-0049
Ireland	☎ 800-562-6262
Italy	☎ 800-543-7662
Japan	☎ 800-543-0051
Netherlands	☎ 800-432-0031
Norway	☎ 800-292-0047
New Zealand	☎ 800-248-0064
Portugal	☎ 800-822-2776
Spain	☎ 800-247-7246
Sweden	☎ 800-345-0046

Fax & Telegram

Fax machines are easy to find in the USA; they're at shipping outlets such as Mail Boxes Etc, as well as most hotel business service centers and photocopy shops like Kinko's. Be prepared to pay high prices (more than $1 a page to US numbers, $4 or more to Europe and elsewhere). Prices for incoming faxes are usually half the outgoing domestic rate. You can send telegrams from Western Union offices; call for information (☎ 800-325-6000).

Email & Internet Access

Email is probably the preferred method of communication for travelers. However, unless you have a laptop and modem that can be plugged into a telephone socket, it's sometimes difficult to get online. See the Digital Resources section, following, for a variety of helpful suggestions on how to stay connected.

Before heading off, consider signing up for a free email account with any of the larger providers. Companies such as Yahoo! (ᴡ www.yahoo.com), Microsoft (ᴡ www.hotmail.com), Pobox (ᴡ www.pobox.com) and Excite (ᴡ www.excite.com) will give you a free email address (for example, ⓔ janedoe@excite.com). You can then access your email account from any Web browser, such as those at Internet cafés or libraries. Don't forget your user name and password, and remember to log off before you leave to avoid misuse of your account.

DIGITAL RESOURCES

The World Wide Web is a rich resource for travelers. You can research your trip, hunt down bargain airfares, book hotels, check on weather conditions and chat with locals and other travelers about the best places to visit (or avoid!).

There's no better place to start your Web exploration than the Lonely Planet Web site (ᴡ www.lonelyplanet.com). Here you'll find succinct summaries on traveling to most places on earth, postcards from other travelers and the Thorn Tree bulletin board, where you can ask questions before you go or dispense advice when you get back. You can also find travel news, and the subWWWay section links you to the most useful travel resources elsewhere on the Web.

Lonely Planet produces a guide to Miami as part of its *CitySync* series of digital city guides for handheld computers. *CitySync* lets travelers and locals use their Palm OS handheld to search and sort hundreds of detailed listings. For more information, go to ᴡ www.citysync.com.

BOOKS

Many books are published in different editions by different publishers in different countries. As a result, a book might be a hardcover rarity in one country but readily available in paperback in another. Fortunately, bookstores and libraries can search by title or author, so your local bookstore or library is best placed to advise you on the availability of the following recommendations. Most of the books listed here are available locally, some nationally and internationally. One of the best publishers of books on Florida and its regions is **Pineapple Press** (☎ 800-746-3275; W www.pineapplepress .com; PO Box 3889, Sarasota, FL 34230). See the Facts about Florida chapter for works by local writers.

Lonely Planet

Lonely Planet publishes guides to *Miami & the Keys,* the *USA,* the neighboring states of *Louisiana & the Deep South,* and Pisces diving & snorkeling guides to the *Florida Keys* as well as guides to nearby destinations including *Eastern Caribbean, Cuba* and *Mexico.* LP also publishes a complete series of guides to Central and South America, including several French-language titles to those regions. Lonely Planet's *Travel with Children* is a parent must-read for preparation and strategy.

Guidebooks

One of our favorites is Frank Zoretich's *Cheap Thrills Florida* (Pineapple Press), written by an admittedly very stingy man and containing lots of cheap things to do around here. If you're coming with kids, don't miss the excellent *Places to Go with Children in Miami & South Florida* by Cheryl Lani Juárez & Deborah Ann Johnson (Chronicle Books), which is indispensable in keeping the little darlings calm and entertained. Chelle Koster Walton's excellent *Fun with the Family in Florida* is just what it sounds like.

Backcountry Travel

For getting out in nature, don't miss the late Marjory Stoneman Douglas' classic *The Everglades* (Pineapple Press), which should be required reading for those heading out into the Glades. Also check out Susan D Jewell's excellent *Exploring Wild South Florida* (Pineapple Press) and Allen de Hart's *Adventuring in Florida* (The Sierra Club).

History

The best book on Florida history is *The New History of Florida* (University Press of Florida), edited by Michael Gannon and written by Gannon and many experts in Florida history. The book is a concise and complete, beautifully written, flawlessly edited masterpiece of a good read – in many chapters, actually reading more like a novel than a history. Another great read, though it's a bit more stilted, is *Adventures into the Unknown Interior of America,* by Cabeza de Vaca and translated by Cyclone Cavey, describing the doomed expedition of Pánfilo de Narváez, the first European to explore Florida thoroughly (see the History section of Facts about Florida).

The standard work on the history of Florida is the ever-so-dry *A History of Florida* by Charlton W Tebeau (pronounced **tee**-bow); though it's patchy on pre-European history, Tebeau's book has been the classic reference for years. For a breezier read, Michael Gannon's *Florida: A Short History* (University Press) is a good bet.

Architecture

For a thorough exploration of Miami Beach deco in words and pictures, pick up *Tropical Deco: The Architecture and Design of Old Miami Beach* by Laura Cerwinske & David Kaminsky; and *Deco Delights: Preserving the Beauty and Joy of Miami Beach Architecture* by Barbara Baer Capitman & Steven Brooke.

Flora & Fauna

David W Nellis' *Seashore Plants of South Florida & the Caribbean* (Pineapple Press) is filled with color photos and good descriptions. A more scholarly and complete – yet accessible – guide is Ralph W Tiner's *Field Guide to Coastal Wetland Plants of the Southeastern United States* (University of Massachusetts Press).

NEWSPAPERS & MAGAZINES

There is usually at least one place in every city, town and village that carries, besides the local papers, national papers like the *New York Times,* the *Wall Street Journal* and *USA Today.* For excellent, unbiased and thoughtful coverage of international news, pick up a copy of the *Christian Science Monitor.* Most major Western European newspapers are available at good newsstands. Speaking of newsstands, they're almost nonexistent in Florida outside the big cities, having been replaced by steel boxes on street corners.

The *Miami Herald,* the flagship of the Knight Ridder newspaper group, has the largest circulation of any paper in the state, and it's available in many cities around the state. In cities around Florida, look for local tabloids like Miami's *New Times* or Fort Lauderdale's *City Link,* which have features and hard-hitting investigative journalism.

The *Miami Herald* publishes *El Nuevo Herald,* an excellent Spanish daily (in fact, if you speak Spanish, you should look here first for coverage of Latin America).

RADIO

All rental cars have radios, and travelers can choose from hundreds of radio stations. In South Florida, Spanish-language broadcasts are common, and in major cities there's usually a good mix of rock, disco, Top 40, dance, adult contemporary and easy-listening, and usually there's at least one AM all-news station (at least in South Florida).

National Public Radio (NPR) is an excellent source of balanced news coverage, with a more international approach than most US stations. Its *All Things Considered* and *Morning Edition* are three-hour news programs in the evening and morning that take the time to cover stories in a way that commercial radio simply can't. NPR broadcasts on the lower end of the FM dial.

In most Florida cities, you'll also have the opportunity to listen to hate and political radio, featuring fat blabbermouths, convicted felons and former high-school football coaches touting conservative political values. And Christian radio is big in the rural areas.

TELEVISION

American television is a hodgepodge of talk shows, cop shows, dramas, melodramas, sit-coms, soap operas, game shows and commercials. The five major broadcast television networks are ABC, CBS, Fox, NBC and PBS. Of them, Fox shows the most sensationalis-

tic – but also the most groundbreaking – TV shows. CBS, ABC and NBC all show a mix of quasi-current films, news and news-magazine shows, sit-coms and dramas. ABC, CBS and NBC broadcast national news at 6:30pm eastern standard time (EST). PBS, the Public Broadcasting System, shows mainly educational programs, foreign programs and films, and excellent current-affairs shows like *Newshour with Jim Lehrer.* And the best part of it all is, it's mostly viewer supported – there are no standard commercial interruptions but rather a list of corporate sponsors is read at the end of each program.

On local Florida TV stations, gore springs eternal: the local news motto is 'If it bleeds, it leads.' If you're accustomed to the sensationalism of a British daily newspaper, you'll feel right at home with local broadcasts. In the Tampa Bay area, tune into Bay News 9, the nation's first all Spanish cable station.

Cable TV is available at almost every hotel, which gives you access to, at the very least, ESPN (sports), CNN and CNN Headline News, the Weather Channel and Comedy Central. Some offer premium channels like HBO and Showtime (feature films).

PHOTOGRAPHY & VIDEO

Color print film, widely available at supermarkets and discount drugstores, has greater latitude than color slide film. This means that print film can handle a wider range of light and shadow than slide film, and that the printer can fix your mistakes. However, slide film, particularly the slower speeds (under 100 ASA), has better resolution than print film. B&W film is most likely to be found at camera shops. Both B&W film and slide film are rarely sold outside of major cities and, when available, are more expensive. With the abundance of reflective surfaces in Miami, consider using a polarizing filter.

Drugstores process film cheaply. If you drop it off by noon, you can usually pick it up the next day. Processing a roll of 100 ASA 35mm color film with 24 exposures costs about $6 to $8. One-hour processing services are listed in the Yellow Pages under 'Photo Processing.' Expect to pay double the drugstore price.

Hawksbill turtle

Face to face with a dolphin

Endangered West Indian manatee

Everglades alligator

Katydid

West Indian flamingoes

Purple gallinule

Cabbage butterfly

Great blue heron

WILLIAM HARRIGAN

Elkhorn coral

CHRISTOPHER P BAKER

Hibiscus flower

Palm leaf

RICHARD CUMMINS

MARK NEWMAN

Swamps of Big Cypress National Preserve

Film can be damaged by excessive heat, so don't leave your camera and film in the sun (next to you on the beach towel) or car on hot days (read: most of the year). It's worth carrying a spare battery for your camera in case it dies in the middle of nowhere. If you're buying a new camera for your trip, practice using it before taking it on the trip.

A note on video equipment for overseas visitors: Remember that the USA uses the National Television System Committee (NTSC) color TV and video standard, which, unless converted, is not compatible with the PAL and SECAM standards used in Africa, Europe, Asia and Australia.

Since the terrorist attacks of 9-11, security is *very* serious business at US airports. If you'd like to bypass the X-ray scanner for your film, prepare ahead of time: Unpack your film from boxes and plastic film canisters, and have all the film readily visible in a plastic bag. You really only need to do this for very high speed film (1600 ASA and above).

TIME

Except for the western section of the Panhandle, Florida is in the US eastern time zone, three hours ahead of San Francisco and Los Angeles, and five hours behind GMT/UTC. West of the Apalachicola River, the Panhandle is in the US central time zone, one hour behind the rest of the state, two hours ahead of San Francisco and Los Angeles, and six hours behind GMT/UTC. Daylight saving time takes place from the first Sunday in April through the last Sunday in October. The clocks 'spring forward' one hour in April and 'fall back' one hour in October. Clocks are reset at 1am.

ELECTRICITY

Electric current in the USA is 110V-115V, 60Hz. Outlets may be suited for flat two- or three-prong plugs. If your appliance is made for another electrical system, you will need a transformer or adapter; if you didn't bring one along, check Radio Shack or another consumer electronics store.

WEIGHTS & MEASURES

The US continues to resist the imposition of the metric system. Distances are in feet, yards and miles; weights are in ounces, pounds and tons. Gasoline is measured in US gallons, about 20% smaller than the Imperial gallon and equivalent to 3.79L. Temperatures are given in degrees Fahrenheit. See the conversion chart on the inside back cover for more information.

LAUNDRY

There are coin laundries in almost every city in the state. Generally, the cost is $1.50 to wash, and there is either a flat rate (like $1.25) to dry, or it costs 25¢ for each five or 10 minutes in dryers. Some laundries have attendants who will wash, dry and fold your clothes for an additional charge. To find a laundry, look under 'Laundries' or 'Laundries – Self-Service' in the Yellow Pages. Dry cleaners are also listed under 'Laundries' or 'Cleaners.'

RECYCLING

It is illegal to litter highways, streets, sidewalks or other public spaces. Fines can be stiff, through enforcement is usually lax. Virtually all commercial beverage containers sold in the USA are recyclable. Some campgrounds and a few roadside rest areas have recycling bins next to the trash bins. Materials accepted are usually plastic and glass bottles, aluminum and tin cans, and newspapers.

Perhaps better than recycling is reducing your use of these products. Many gas stations and convenience stores sell large plastic insulated cups with lids, which are inexpensive and ideal for hot and cold drinks. You can usually save a few cents by using your cup to buy drinks.

When hiking and camping in the wilderness, take out everything you bring in – this includes *any* kind of garbage you may create.

TOILETS

Americans have many names for public toilet facilities. The most common names are 'restroom' or 'bathroom.' Other popular names include 'ladies'/men's room,' 'comfort station,' 'facility' and 'sanitary facility.' Of course, you can just ask for 'the toilet.'

You will find public toilets in airports, bars, large stores, museums, state and national parks, restaurants, hotels, and tourist information offices, as well as at bus, train and highway gas stations. Public toilets in city parks and other public places have mostly been closed due to criminal and sexual misuse.

HEALTH

Florida is a typical first-world destination when it comes to health. For most foreign visitors, no immunizations are required for entry, though cholera and yellow fever vaccinations may be required of travelers from areas with a history of those diseases. There are no unexpected health dangers, excellent medical attention is readily available, and the only real health concern is that a collision with the medical system can cause severe injuries to your financial state.

Hospitals and medical centers, walk-in clinics and referral services are easily found throughout the state of Florida.

In a serious emergency, call ☎ 911 for an ambulance to take you to the nearest hospital's emergency room.

Predeparture Preparations

Make sure you're healthy before you start traveling. If you are embarking on a long trip, make sure your teeth are in good shape. If you wear glasses, take a spare pair and your prescription. You can get new spectacles made up quickly and competently for about $100, depending on the prescription and frame you choose. If you require a particular medication, take an adequate supply, and bring a prescription.

Health Insurance A travel insurance policy to cover theft, lost tickets and medical problems is a good idea, especially in the USA, where some privately run hospitals will refuse care without evidence of insurance. (Public hospitals must treat everyone, though standards are lower, and waits can carry on for hours before you're looked at, except in the most serious of cases.) There are a wide

variety of policies; your travel agent will have recommendations. International student travel policies handled by STA Travel and other student travel organizations are usually a good value. Some policies offer lower and higher medical-expenses options, and the higher one is chiefly for countries like the USA with extremely high medical costs. Check the fine print.

Some policies specifically exclude 'dangerous activities' like scuba diving, motorcycling and trekking. If these activities are on your agenda, avoid this sort of policy. You may prefer a policy that pays doctors or hospitals directly, rather than requiring you to pay on the spot and claim later. If you have to claim later, keep *all* documentation. Some policies ask you to call back (reverse charges) to a center in your home country for an immediate assessment of your problem. Check whether the policy covers ambulance fees or an emergency flight home. If you have to stretch out, you will need two seats, and somebody has to pay for them!

Food & Water

Here's the most important health rule: take care in what you eat and drink. Stomach upsets are the most common travel health problem (between 30% and 50% of travelers on a two-week stay experience this), but the majority of these upsets will be relatively minor. American standards of cleanliness in places serving food and drink are very high.

Bottled drinking water, both carbonated and noncarbonated, is widely available in the USA. You can get a gallon of filtered drinking water (bring your own jug) from dispensers at Publix and Winn-Dixie supermarkets for 25¢. Tap water in Florida is usually OK to drink (though it tastes lousy).

Everyday Health

Normal body temperature is 98.6°F or 37°C; more than 4°F or 2°C higher indicates a high fever. The normal adult pulse rate is 60 to 100 per minute (children 80 to 100, babies 100 to 140). You should know how to take a temperature and a pulse rate.

Respiration (breathing) rate is also an indicator of illness. Count the number of breaths per minute: between 12 and 20 is normal for adults and older children (up to 30 for younger children, 40 for babies). People with a high fever or serious respiratory illness (like pneumonia) breathe more quickly than normal. More than 40 shallow breaths a minute usually means pneumonia.

Travel & Climate-Related Problems

Motion Sickness Eat lightly before and during a trip to reduce the chances of motion sickness. If you are prone to motion sickness, try to find a place that minimizes disturbance, for example, near the wing on aircraft or near the center on buses. Fresh air helps. Commercial anti–motion-sickness preparations, which can cause drowsiness, must be taken before the trip commences; once you feel sick, it's too late. Ginger, a natural preventative, is available in capsule form from health-food stores.

Jet Lag People experience jet lag when traveling by air across more than three time zones (each time zone usually represents a one-hour time difference). It occurs because many of the functions of the human body are regulated by internal 24-hour cycles called circadian rhythms. When we travel long distances rapidly, our bodies take time to adjust to the 'new time' of our destination, and we may experience fatigue, disorientation, insomnia, anxiety, impaired concentration and loss of appetite. These effects will usually be gone within three days of arrival, but there are ways to minimize the impact of jet lag:

- Rest for a couple of days prior to departure; try to avoid late nights and last-minute dashes for traveler's checks or your passport.
- Try to select flight schedules that minimize sleep deprivation; arriving in the early evening means you can go to sleep soon after you arrive. For very long flights, try to organize a stopover.
- Avoid excessive eating (which bloats the stomach) and alcohol (which causes dehydration) during the flight. Instead, drink plenty of noncarbonated, nonalcoholic drinks such as fruit juice or water.

- Make yourself comfortable by wearing loose-fitting clothes and perhaps bringing an eye mask and earplugs to help you sleep.

Sunburn Use a good sunscreen and take your time. Don't try to become a bronzed demigod or goddess on the first day (or for that matter, the first week). Most doctors recommend sunscreen with a sun protection factor (SPF) of 40 for easily burned areas like your shoulders and nose. Nude sunbathers hanging out at Haulover Beach in Miami or other nude beaches throughout the state need to slather the stuff *everywhere.*

Heat Exhaustion Dehydration or salt deficiency can cause heat exhaustion. Take time to acclimatize to high temperatures, and make sure you get enough liquids. Salt deficiency is characterized by fatigue, lethargy, headaches, giddiness and muscle cramps. Salt tablets may help. Vomiting or diarrhea can also deplete your liquid and salt levels. Anhydrotic heat exhaustion, caused by the inability to sweat, is quite rare, but unlike the other forms of heat exhaustion, it is likely to strike people who have been in a hot climate for some time, rather than newcomers. Always carry – and use – a water bottle on long trips.

Heat Stroke Long, continuous periods of exposure to high temperatures can leave you vulnerable to this serious, sometimes fatal, condition, which occurs when the body's heat-regulating mechanism breaks down and body temperature rises to dangerous levels. Avoid excessive alcohol intake or strenuous activity when you first arrive in a hot climate.

Symptoms include feeling unwell, lack of perspiration and a high body temperature of 102° to 105°F (39° to 41°C). Hospitalization is essential for extreme cases, but meanwhile, get out of the sun, remove clothing, cover with a wet sheet or towel and fan continually.

Fungal Infections Fungal infections, which occur with greater frequency in hot weather, are most likely to occur on the scalp, between the fingers or toes (athlete's foot), in the groin (jock itch or crotch rot) and on the body (ringworm). You get ringworm (which is a fungal infection, not a worm) from infected animals or by walking on damp areas such as shower floors.

To prevent fungal infections, wear loose, comfortable clothes, avoid artificial fibers, wash frequently and dry carefully. If you do get an infection, wash the infected area daily with a disinfectant or medicated soap and water, and rinse and dry well. Apply an antifungal powder, and try to expose the infected area to air or sunlight as much as possible. Change underwear and towels frequently, and wash them often in hot water.

Infectious Diseases
Diarrhea A change of water, food or climate can cause 'the runs'; diarrhea caused by contaminated food or water is more serious. It's unlikely in the USA but common in Mexico. Despite all your precautions, you may still get a mild bout of traveler's diarrhea from exotic food or drink. Dehydration is the main danger with any diarrhea, particularly for children, who can get dehydrated quite quickly. Fluid replacement remains the mainstay of management. Weak black tea with a little sugar, soda water or soft drinks diluted 50% with water are all good. With severe diarrhea, a rehydrating solution is necessary to replace minerals and salts. Such solutions, like Pedialyte, are available at pharmacies.

Hepatitis Hepatitis is a general term for inflammation of the liver. There are many causes of this condition: poor sanitation, contact with infected blood products, drugs, alcohol and contact with an infected person are but a few. The symptoms are fever, chills, headache, fatigue, and aches and pains, followed by loss of appetite, nausea, vomiting, abdominal pain, dark urine, light-colored feces and jaundiced skin. The whites of the eyes may also turn yellow.

Hepatitis A is the most common strain. You should seek medical advice, but there is not much you can do apart from resting, drinking lots of fluids, eating lightly and avoiding fatty foods. People who have had hepatitis should avoid alcohol for some time after the illness, as the liver needs time to recover. Viral hepatitis is an infection of the liver, which can have several unpleasant symptoms, or no symptoms at all, with the infected person not knowing they have the disease.

HIV/AIDS HIV, the Human Immunodeficiency Virus, develops into AIDS, Acquired Immune Deficiency Syndrome, which is a fatal disease. Any exposure to blood, blood products or body fluids may put the individual at risk. The disease is often transmitted through sexual contact or dirty needles – vaccinations, acupuncture, tattooing and body piercing can be potentially as dangerous as intravenous drug use.

Fear of HIV infection should never preclude treatment for serious medical conditions. One good resource for help and information is the hotline for the **US Center for Disease Control AIDS** (☎ 800-342-2437, 800-344-7432 in Spanish). AIDS support groups are listed in the front of phone books.

Cuts, Bites & Stings
In hot climates, skin punctures heal slowly and can easily become infected. Treat any cut with an antiseptic such as Betadine. Where possible, avoid bandages and Band-Aids, which can keep wounds wet.

Bee and wasp stings and nonpoisonous spider bites are usually painful but not dangerous. Calamine lotion will give relief, and ice packs will reduce the pain and swelling. Avoid bites by not using bare hands to turn over rocks or large pieces of wood (see also Treating Bites in Dangers & Annoyances).

Ticks are a parasitic arachnid that may be present in brush, forest and grasslands, where hikers often get them on their legs or in their boots. The adults suck blood from hosts by burying their heads into skin, but they are often found unattached and can simply be brushed off. However, if one has attached itself to you, pulling it off and leaving the head in the skin increases the likelihood of infection or disease, such as Rocky Mountain spotted fever or Lyme disease.

Always check your body for ticks after walking through a high-grass or thickly forested area. If you do find a tick attached to you, grasp its head (not the body, as this will squeeze material from the tick into the wound) with a pair of tweezers and pull gently until the little bugger comes loose. If you get sick in the next couple of weeks, consult a doctor.

WOMEN TRAVELERS
Women often face different situations when traveling than do men. If you are a woman traveler, especially a woman traveling alone, get in the habit of traveling with a little extra awareness of your surroundings.

Women must recognize the extra threat of rape, which is a problem not only in urban but also in rural areas. The best way to deal with the threat of rape is to avoid putting yourself in vulnerable situations. Conducting yourself in a commonsense manner will help you avoid most problems. It's said that shouting 'Fire!' may draw assistance more effectively than yelling 'Help!'

If despite all precautions you are assaulted, call the police. In any emergency, phoning ☎ 911 will connect you with the emergency operator for police, fire and ambulance services.

Men may interpret a woman drinking alone in a bar as a bid for male company, whether you intend it that way or not. If you don't want the company, most men will respect a firm but polite 'no thank you.'

Don't hitchhike alone, and don't pick up hitchhikers if driving alone. If you get stuck on a road and need help, it's a good idea to have a premade sign to signal for help. At night, avoid getting out of your car to flag down help; turn on your hazard lights and wait for the police to arrive. Be extra careful at night on public transit, and remember to check the times of the last bus or train before you go out at night.

Never accept drinks offered by strangers in bars. In the mid-1990s (especially), Rohypnol, a tasteless sedative 10 times more powerful than Valium, was being added to women's drinks in Florida bars by the men who bought them – the women were sedated and raped.

To deal with potential dangers, many women protect themselves with a whistle, Mace, cayenne-pepper spray or some self-defense training. If you do decide to purchase a spray, contact a police station to find out about regulations and training classes. Laws regarding sprays vary from state to state, so be informed based on your destination. It's a federal felony to carry sprays on airplanes (because of their combustibility).

The headquarters for the **National Organization for Women** (NOW; ☎ 202-331-0066; w www.now.org; 1000 16th St NW, Suite 700, Washington, DC 20036) is a good resource for any woman-related information, and it can refer you to state and local chapters. **Planned Parenthood** (☎ 212-541-7800; w www.plannedparenthood.org; 810 7th Ave, New York, NY 10019) can refer you to clinics throughout the country and offer advice on medical issues. Check the Yellow Pages under 'Women's Organizations & Services' for local resources.

GAY & LESBIAN TRAVELERS
In the 1970s, Miami was one of the first municipalities in the USA to pass legislation barring discrimination against homosexuals in the workplace and housing. Before long came the backlash. Miami then became the highly publicized target of a campaign by conservative witch Anita Bryant in 1977, and the law was repealed. The biggest news in the Miami gay and lesbian scene was the 1998 reinstatement of the law after a close vote.

Gay and lesbian visitors account for nearly $100 million in annual revenues to the Miami area. And with financial clout comes respect. Ah, capitalism; it runs deep in Miami. Partying also runs deep. South Beach hosts two flamboyant circuit parties; see the boxed text 'Circuit Parties' in the Miami chapter.

Florida appears to be a very gay-friendly destination, but outside the major cities like Miami, Fort Lauderdale, Key West or even Orlando, it might be wise to keep the closet door slightly closed. In rural areas especially, gay travelers may occasionally find hostility or open rudeness. Gay-bashing is not common in Florida, but it's not unheard of anywhere in the USA. You should always use caution in strange situations.

Outside South Beach and Key West, there are cities with gay and lesbian bars, clubs and community centers, but there aren't any 'gay neighborhoods' like you'd find in New York or San Francisco.

In this book, we list gay and lesbian resources wherever possible. On the Internet, head to **QueerAmerica** (W www.queer america.com), which lists gay and lesbian resources and community groups within specified areas – enter a zip code or area code, and the Web site will spit out as much as it knows (which is usually a lot!). Other good sources are college and university campuses.

A few well-known national gay publications with sections on South Florida are worth checking out. Try Damron's *Women's Traveller,* with listings for lesbians; *Men's Travel Guide,* for men; and *Damron Accommodations,* listing gay-owned and gay-friendly hotels, B&Bs and guest houses nationwide. All three are published by Damron Company (☎ 415-255-0404, 800-462-6654, W www.damron.com). *Ferrari's Places for Women* is also useful. Out & About (☎ 212-645-6922, 800-929-2268, W www.outandabout.com) publishes books and a newsletter.

The **Gay & Lesbian Yellow Pages** (☎ 212-674-0120, W www.glyp.com), another good resource, has national and regional editions. You can also contact the **National AIDS/HIV Hotline** (☎ 800-342-2437), the **National Gay and Lesbian Task Force** (☎ 202-332-6483, W www.ngltf.org) or the **Lambda Legal Defense Fund** (☎ 212-995-8585 in New York City, ☎ 213-937-2728 in Los Angeles).

DISABLED TRAVELERS

Travel within the USA is becoming easier for people with disabilities. Public buildings (including hotels, restaurants, theaters and museums) are now required by law to be wheelchair accessible and have special toilet facilities. Public transportation services (buses, trains and taxis) must be made accessible to all, including those in wheelchairs, and telephone companies are required to provide relay operators

for the hearing impaired. Many banks now provide ATM instructions in braille, and you will find audible crossing signals, as well as dropped curbs, at busier roadway intersections.

Larger private and chain hotels (see Accommodations later in this chapter for listings) have rooms for disabled guests. Major car rental agencies offer hand-controlled models at no extra charge. All major airlines, Greyhound buses and Amtrak trains will allow service animals to accompany passengers and will frequently sell two-for-one packages to accommodate attendants of seriously disabled passengers. Airlines will also provide assistance for connecting, boarding and deplaning – just ask for assistance when making your reservation. (Note that airlines must accept wheelchairs as checked baggage and have an onboard chair available, though some advance notice may be required on smaller aircraft.) Of course, the more populous the area, the greater the likelihood of facilities for the disabled, so it's important to call ahead to see what is available.

A number of organizations and tour providers specialize in the needs of disabled travelers:

Access-Able Travel Source (☎ 303-232-2979, W www.access-able.com), PO Box 1796, Wheat Ridge, CO 80034 – an excellent Web site with many links

Mobility International USA (☎ 541-343-1284, W www.miusa.org), PO Box 10767, Eugene, OR 97440 – advises disabled travelers on mobility issues and runs an educational exchange program

MossRehab ResourceNet (☎ 215-456-9600, 215-456-9602 TTY, W www.mossresourcenet.org/travel.htm), 1200 W Tabor Rd, Philadelphia, PA 19141 – a concise list of useful contacts for disabled travelers

Society for Accessible Travel & Hospitality (SATH; ☎ 212-447-7284, W www.sath.org), 347 Fifth Ave, No 610, New York, NY 10016 – lobbies for better facilities and publishes *Open World* magazine

Travelin' Talk Network (☎ 615-552-6670, W www.travelintalk.net), PO Box 3534, Clarksville, TN 37047 – offers a global network of people providing services to disabled people

Twin Peaks Press (☎ 360-694-2462, W home .pacifier.com/~twinpeak), PO Box 129, Vancouver, WA 98666 – publishes a quarterly newsletter, plus directories and access guides

SENIOR TRAVELERS

Though the age at which senior benefits kick in changes from place to place, travelers aged 50 and up can expect to receive cut rates at such places as hotels, museums and restaurants. Be sure to inquire about these rates at hotels, museums and restaurants *before* you make your reservation.

Visitors to national parks and campgrounds can cut costs greatly by using the Golden Age Passport (see Golden Passports, under Useful Organizations, later).

Some national advocacy groups that can help seniors in planning their travels include the following:

AARP (formerly known as the American Association of Retired Persons; ☎ 800-424-3410, W www.aarp.org), 601 E St NW, Washington, DC 20049 – an advocacy group for Americans 50 years and older, and a good resource for travel bargains. A one-year membership costs $10.

Elderhostel (☎ 877-426-8056, W www.elder hostel.org), 11 Ave de Lafayette, Boston, MA 02111 – a nonprofit organization that offers people 55 years and older the opportunity to attend academic college courses and study tours throughout the USA and Canada.

FLORIDA FOR CHILDREN

Florida is very kid-friendly – especially with all those beaches. (Watch out for the topless spots if that sort of thing bothers you.) We list, as often as possible, attractions kids might like, as well as children's admission prices. There's almost never an extra charge for kids in hotels. There are museums specifically targeted to children's interests in many large cities and even in some smaller ones. There are also public playgrounds in every city, especially along the beaches, and there are public toilets and water fountains at most of them. Every sizable Florida city has a municipal swimming pool with organized programs and free-swim periods.

Cities with outstanding children's museums (many focusing on science and technology) are Orlando (of course), Miami, Tampa, Fort Lauderdale, Sarasota, Boca Raton, St Augustine, Key West and West Palm Beach. Some cities also have good circuses (Sarasota) and zoos (Palm Beach, Miami, Jacksonville, Tampa, Pensacola and Panama City Beach). Lion Country Safari in West Palm Beach is definitely a fun stop.

Pick up Lonely Planet's excellent *Travel with Children* for general information and encouragement. If you're stuck for ideas on what to do with the kids, contact the nearest convention & visitor's bureau. They'll be more than happy to help you work out an itinerary.

Ask at your hotel about babysitters. If you really need a day (or week) of peace, there are a variety of cool programs that'll take the kids off your hands. The US Space Camp is a fantastic weeklong educational program for kids interested in science and space exploration; see the Titusville section of the Space Coast chapter.

Walt Disney World, in the Central Florida chapter, might as well be labeled 'Fun for the Kids.'

USEFUL ORGANIZATIONS
American Automobile Association

AAA (☎ 800-564-6222; W www.aaa.com), with offices in all major cities and many smaller towns, provides useful information, free maps and routine road services – like tire repair and towing (free within a limited radius) – to its members for $49 annually. Members of its foreign affiliates, like the Automobile Association in Canada and the UK and ADAC in Germany, are entitled to the same services. The basic membership fee is an excellent investment, simply for the maps. Its nationwide toll-free roadside assistance number is ☎ 800-222-4357.

National Park Service (NPS) & US Forest Service (USFS)

The NPS and USFS administer the use of parks and forests. National forests are less protected than parks, allowing commercial exploitation in some areas (usually logging or privately owned recreational facilities).

National parks most often surround spectacular natural features and cover hundreds of square miles. A full range of accommodations can be found in and around national parks; contact individual parks for more specific information. National park campground and reservations information can be obtained by contacting **National Park Reservation Service** (☎ 800-365-2267; http://reservations.nps.gov).

Current information about national forests can be obtained from ranger stations, which are also listed in the text. National forest campground and reservation information can be obtained by calling ☎ 877-444-6777 (**W** www.reserveusa.com). General information about federal lands is also available from the **US Fish & Wildlife Service** (☎ 404-679-7289), whose Georgia office fields Florida-related questions.

Golden Passports For a one-time $10 processing fee, Golden Age Passports allow permanent US residents 62 years and older unlimited entry to all sites in the national park system, with discounts on camping (50%) and other fees. Golden Access Passports offer the same benefits to US residents who are legally blind or permanently disabled. Golden Eagle Passports, which cost $50 annually, are available to any permanent US residents under age 62. This pass allows you free and unlimited entry for 12 consecutive months to all national parks and national monuments in the country. Those accompanying Golden Eagle and Golden Age Passport holders also gain free entrance into national parks. All three passports can be obtained in person at any national park or regional office of the USFS or NPS.

DANGERS & ANNOYANCES
Crime
The cities of Florida generally have lower levels of violent crime than larger, better-known cities such as Washington, DC; New York; and Los Angeles. Nevertheless, violent crime is present, and you should take the usual precautions, especially in the cities.

Always lock cars and put valuables out of sight, whether leaving the car for a few minutes or longer, and whether you are in town or in the remote backcountry.

Be aware of your surroundings and of who may be watching you. Avoid walking on dimly lit streets at night, particularly if you are alone. Walk purposefully. Exercise particular caution in large parking lots or parking structures at night. Avoid unnecessary displays of money or jewelry. Split up your money and credit cards to avoid losing everything, and try to use ATM machines in well-trafficked areas.

In hotels, don't leave valuables lying around your room. Use safety deposit boxes, or at least place valuables in a locked bag. Don't open your door to strangers – check the peephole or call the front desk if unexpected people are trying to enter.

Highway Robbery & Carjacking
In the early 1990s, several highly publicized attacks on tourists in Miami made international headlines. As a result, tourism revenue dropped off considerably. Because money talks, action was taken, and since then, the number of attacks has been halved. You'd still do well to use caution. Official police cars have flashing blue *and* red lights; if any other vehicle attempts to pull you over, keep driving until you get to a well-lighted area, such as a gas station, and call the police. That's also what you should do if someone rams your car from behind. Forget about stopping to exchange insurance information; just get to someplace safe and call the police. Consider the situation carefully if you are inclined to stop for a stranded motorist.

When someone approaches you at a stoplight, points a gun at you, orders you out of the vehicle and drives off with your car, it's called a carjacking. It's a federal offense. Police say that resisting a gun-wielding person is not wise; just follow instructions and hope for the best.

Credit Card Scams
When using phone credit cards, be aware of people watching you, especially in public places. Thieves can memorize your numbers

and then make calls without having the actual card. Shield the telephone with your body when punching in your number. Use touch-tone key pads to avoid actually saying your credit card number aloud in a public place. Some walls do have ears.

Try to limit the situations in which you give your credit card number out over the phone. People can charge anything they want if they have your name, card number and expiration date. Destroy any carbons generated by a credit card sale.

Hotels customarily ask for a credit card imprint when you check in to cover incidental expenses. Make certain that this imprint is destroyed if not used.

Enter a '$' sign before, and make certain there's a decimal point in, numbers written in the 'total' box on a credit card slip. You don't want to be charged $1500 for a T-shirt instead of $15.

Panhandlers & the Homeless

Miami has a serious problem. Waves of refugees from poor countries and the northeastern US have resulted in a high number of homeless people and panhandlers. What you, as a tourist, should and can do is a very touchy issue. The official Lonely Planet line: Don't encourage them – it only helps to make visitors an easy mark. If you're really concerned, volunteer at a homeless shelter, or donate to homeless-relief programs at local churches and synagogues.

Hurricanes

Every year during hurricane season (June through November) storms form over the Atlantic Ocean and the Gulf of Mexico and gather strength – and some roll right over Florida. Some years – most notably 1992, when Hurricane Andrew flattened the land, decimating the city of Homestead just south of Miami – are worse than others.

A hurricane is a concentrated system of very strong thunderstorms with high circulation. The 74mph to 160mph winds created by a hurricane can extend for hundreds of miles around the eye (center) of a hurricane system. Floods and flash floods caused by the torrential rains it produces cause addi-tional property damage. Perhaps most dangerous of all, though, hurricanes can cause a storm surge, forcing the level of the ocean to rise between 4 and 18 feet above normal. If the 13- to 18-foot storm surge caused by Category-4 Andrew had hit Miami instead of Homestead in 1992, it would have easily destroyed the entire city of Miami Beach.

Hurricanes are generally sighted well in advance, and there's time to prepare. When a hurricane threatens, listen to radio and TV news reports. Give credence only to forecasts attributed to the National Weather Center (shortwave radio listeners can tune to 162.55MHz), and dismiss anything else as rumor. There's a hurricane hot line (☎ 305-229-4483), which will give you information about approaching storms, storm tracks, warnings, estimated time till touchdown...all the things you need to make a decision about if and when to leave.

There are two distinct stages of alert: A Hurricane Watch is given when a hurricane *may* strike the area within the next 36 to 48 hours; a Hurricane Warning is given when a hurricane is likely to strike the area. If a Hurricane Warning is issued during your stay, you may be placed under an evacuation order. Hotels generally follow these orders and ask guests to leave. The Red Cross operates hurricane shelters, but they're just that – shelter: They do not provide food. You must bring your own food, first-aid kit, blanket or sleeping bag – and hey, bring a book. Ask your hotel or hostel for more information about the logistics of evacuation.

If you're determined to sit out a hurricane warning, you will need the following:

- Flashlight
- As much fresh drinking water as possible (storms knock out water supply)
- Butane lighter and candles
- Canned food, peanut butter, powdered or UHT (ultra-pasteurized, long-life) milk
- Cash (ATMs might not function)
- Portable, battery-powered radio

Stay in a closet or other windowless room. Cover yourself with a mattress to prevent injury from flying glass. Taping windows

Hurricane Categories

Floridians are very hurricane conscious: schoolchildren participate in hurricane evacuation drills and take preparedness classes, and many Floridians have committed to memory facts and statistics on meteorological phenomena matched perhaps only by San Franciscans' knowledge of plate-tectonics theory.

The Saffir/Simpson scale breaks hurricanes into five levels of intensity, based on the speed of circular wind intensity. Storms circulate counterclockwise in the northern hemisphere.

The following is some hurricane and storm terminology:

Tropical depression – Formative stage of a storm. The winds of this organized cloud system are clocked at less than 39mph.

Tropical storm – Strengthened tropical depression. This organized system of powerful thunderstorms has high circulation and wind speeds between 39mph and 73mph.

Category-1 hurricane – Winds between 74mph and 95mph. This level of storm primarily affects plants, small piers and small boats, and can produce a storm surge of between 4 and 5 feet, flooding coastal roads. A category-1 hurricane is still a hurricane; do not treat it lightly.

Category-2 hurricane – Winds between 96mph and 110mph. In addition to causing major damage to plants and uprooting trees, it can damage and destroy mobile homes, roofs, doors and windows. It can also cause a 6- to 8-foot storm surge.

Category-3 hurricane – Winds between 111mph and 130mph. Large trees are uprooted and knocked over; signs, mobile homes and small buildings near the coast are destroyed; roofs, windows, doors and building structures are damaged. A 9- to 12-foot storm surge cuts off coastal escape routes three to five hours before the storm.

Category-4 hurricane – Winds between 131mph and 155mph. Mobile homes, plants, trees and signs are ripped up and destroyed; roofs, windows and doors are damaged; buildings suffer major structural damage. A 13- to 18-foot storm surge cuts off coastal escape routes three to five hours before the storm.

Category-5 hurricane – Winds above 155mph. Buildings and roofs are destroyed. An 18-foot storm surge cuts off coastal escape routes three to five hours before the storm.

does not stop them from breaking, but it does reduce shatter. For a full list of tips on preparedness, check the local white-pages telephone directory.

Tornadoes

For a brief period after a hurricane, as if to add insult to injury, conditions become just ducky for a tornado. A Tornado Watch is generally issued as standard operating procedure after a hurricane, but actual twisters do pop up in Florida even without hurricanes. There's not much you can do about a tornado except be aware of the situation and follow the instructions of local radio and television stations and police.

Ocean Dangers

Florida's Atlantic coastline isn't, for the most part, very rough. But there are a few areas of rough surf, rip tides (see below) and undertows. The entire coast is dangerous before and after storms, when it is inconceivably stupid to go in the water. The most important thing to keep in the water is your calm. And use your head: Human versus Ocean is no contest.

Rip Tides Rips, rip currents or rip tides are fast-flowing currents of water within the ocean, moving from shallow areas out to sea. They are most common in conditions of high surf, forming when water from incoming waves builds up near the shore – essentially, when the waves are coming in faster than they can flow back out.

The water then runs along the shoreline until it finds an escape route out to sea, usually through a channel or out along a point. Swimmers caught up in the current can be ripped out to deeper water. Though rips can be powerful, they usually dissipate 50 to 100 yards offshore. Here's where that Don't Panic thing comes in. Even if you're stuck in what seems like a bad rip tide, you're just a few minutes away from an easy swim back to shore. Anyone caught in one should either go with the flow until it loses power, or swim parallel to shore to slip out of it. Trying to swim against a rip current will exhaust the strongest of swimmers. Repeat after me: ride, don't fight, a rip tide.

Undertows Undertows are common along steeply sloped beaches when large waves backwash directly into incoming surf. The outflowing water picks up speed as it flows down the slopes. When it hits an incoming wave, the water pulls under it, creating an undertow. Swimmers caught in an undertow can be pulled beneath the surface. Once again, remain calm and go with the current until you get beyond the wave.

Jellyfish Take a peek into the water before you plunge in to make certain it's not jellyfish territory. These gelatinous creatures with saclike bodies and stinging tentacles are fairly common on Florida's Atlantic coast. They're most often found drifting near the shore or washed up on the beach. The sting of a jellyfish varies from mild to severe, depending on the type of jellyfish. But unless you have an allergic reaction to jellyfish venom, the stings are not generally dangerous.

The Portuguese man-of-war is the worst type to encounter. Not technically a jellyfish, the man-of-war is a colonial hydrozoan, or a colony of coelenterates, rather than a solitary coelenterate like a true jellyfish. Its body consists of a translucent, bluish bladderlike float, which generally grows to about 4 to 5 inches long. A man-of-war sting is very painful, similar to a bad bee sting, except you're likely to get stung more than once from clusters of their incredibly long tentacles, containing hundreds of stinging cells. Even touching a man-of-war a few hours after it's washed up on shore can result in burning stings.

If you do get stung, quickly remove the tentacles and apply vinegar or a meat tenderizer containing papain (derived from papaya), which neutralizes the toxins. For serious reactions, including chest pains or difficulty in breathing, seek medical attention.

Snakes

Five of Florida's native snakes are venomous. The first four are members of the *Crotalidae* family (pit vipers), which inject venom that destroys red blood cells and the walls of blood vessels. Coral snakes are in the family of *Elapidae,* producing venom that paralyzes the victim, whom they then begin to nibble. Before you freak out, you should know that encountering poisonous snakes in Florida is rare.

The diamondback rattlesnake *(Crotalus adamanteus)* is the largest, most dangerous of the pit vipers and can grow to 8 feet long. They have a big, heavy, brownish body, marked with dark (almost black) diamond shapes, set off by yellowish-white borders. Diamondbacks usually rattle before they attack.

The pygmy rattlesnake *(Sistrurus miliarius)* is much smaller (from 1½ to 2 feet), and has grayish-brown with round black and reddish-orange markings. It also rattles before an attack, but its rattle is so quiet, one can usually only hear it when it's very close. The pygmy rattlesnake's poison generally isn't fatal.

The copperhead snake *(Agkistrodon contortrix)* is only found in the northwestern section of Florida and is not very aggressive. It grows to about 4 feet and has an hourglass-shaped head. It too is grayish-brown with chestnut-colored bands; the head is more copper-toned.

The cottonmouth (sometimes also called water moccasin; *Agkistrodon piscivorus conanti)* is named for the white interior of its mouth. (Hopefully you'll never get close enough to properly identify one!) This olive-green to brown snake with a dark stripe from its eyes to jaws grows to about 5 feet and has a heavy body ending in a thin, pointy tail. They live near lakes and streams and are very venomous.

The coral snake *(Micrurus fulvius)*, a relative of the cobra, is small and deadly: its poison is the most potent of any North American snake. They are very pretty – their slim bodies have sections of black and red divided by thin orange-yellow stripes. They can easily be mistaken for the harmless scarlet king snake. To keep them apart, remember this little rhyme: Red on yellow, kill a fellow; red on black, venom lack. Fortunately, coral snakes are very shy and generally nocturnal.

Snake Bites In the unlikely event of a bite by a poisonous snake, the main thing is to stay calm – easy for us to say! If you can get to a telephone, call ☎ 800-222-1222 to be connected to the nearest Poison Control Center. If you can, find a ranger. If you're alone, stave off panic with knowledge: snake bites don't, no matter what you've seen in

the movies, cause instantaneous death. But they are dangerous, and you need to keep a good, clear head on your shoulders.

Wrap the bitten limb as you would a sprained ankle (not too tightly), and then attach a splint to immobilize the limb. Get medical help as soon as possible, and if you can, bring along the dead snake for identification – but *do not* attempt to catch the snake if there's *any* chance of being bitten again. Sucking out the poison and attaching tourniquets have been widely discredited as treatment for snakebites, so do not apply ice or a tourniquet and do not elevate the limb or attempt to suck out the poison yourself. Instead, keep the affected area below the level of the heart and move it as little as possible. Do not ingest alcohol or any drugs. Antivenins are available in hospitals.

Alligators

Alligators generally only eat when they're hungry – unless they think they're being attacked. They've been known to munch on small animals or things that look like them, such as small children or people crouching down real small to snap a photo. Fairly common in suburban and rural lakes, alligators move around but generally mind their own business. 'Nuisance alligators' – those that eat pets or livestock – become the bailiwick of the police (call ☎ 911 if you see an alligator in a city). Generally speaking, the best thing to do with an alligator is stay away from it completely.

Biting Insects

Florida has about 70 types of mosquitoes and other biting insects like deerflies and fleas. They're bloody annoying, but there are some steps you can take to minimize your chances of getting bitten. Most larger Florida cities have mosquito-control boards that supervise spraying to reduce the problem, but in low-lying cities like St Augustine, insects abound – especially in summer.

Prime biting hours are around sunrise and sunset. Cover up – wear long pants, socks and long-sleeved shirts. The better brands of insect repellent in the USA are

Sparks & Sharks

Not to alarm you further, but there are two more natural perils to consider: lightning and sharks. More people are struck by lightning in the Sunshine State than in any other. If you're caught in the open during a thunderstorm, stay as low as possible to avoid attracting Zeus' wrath.

More than half the world's reported shark attacks occur off the coast of Florida. Even though there are more sharks out there than you would like to think, other than staying out of the water, there's not much one can do about it. So, like, don't go see *Jaws* right before you come, okay? Seriously, though, when swimming, make sure that there are lifeguards present (or at least a swimming companion), and heed shark-attack warnings.

Off! and Cutter for city use, and industrial-strength products like REI Jungle Juice or any repellent that contains a high percentage of DEET for more severe situations, such as the Everglades or the backwoods.

Treating Bites In Florida, aloe vera grows wild. If you've been bitten, grab an aloe vera leaf, break off a piece, squeeze out the juice and rub it on bites – it's great stuff. Calamine lotion, available at all drugstores, works okay but you'll get pink globs all over your skin. Tiger Balm, available in better drugstores and health-food shops, reduces itch and swelling from bites. Rub it on the bite and try to control yourself from scratching for about five minutes, when the itch should be gone. If that doesn't work, try cortisone cream or antihistamine tablets, both available at drugstores.

EMERGENCIES

Dial ☎ 911 for police, fire and ambulance emergencies – it's a free call from any phone. Check the inside front cover of the Miami white pages for a slew of emergency numbers.

If you're robbed, report the theft to police on a nonemergency number. You'll need a police report in order to make an insurance claim back home.

If your credit cards, debit cards or traveler's checks have been stolen, notify your bank or the relevant company as soon as possible. See the Money section, earlier in this chapter, for telephone numbers.

Foreign visitors who have lost their passports should contact their consulate. Having a photocopy of the important pages of your passport will make replacement much easier.

LEGAL MATTERS

Florida law tends to be tougher than most northern states when it comes to drug possession or use. It's less strict in the far south of the state than in the north. In Miami, the police are more tolerant than in, say, St Augustine, where someone arrested for carrying a pot pipe makes the newspaper. But the late 1990s saw an increase in police raids on nightclubs, and dozens of people are arrested on minor drug charges each week. Possession of small quantities of marijuana or speed (amphetamines) is a misdemeanor and technically punishable by up to one year in prison *and* a $1000 fine.

It's illegal to walk with an open alcoholic drink – including beer – on the street, unless you're on Panama City Beach. If you're driving, all liquor has to be unopened (not just sealed, but new and untouched) and, technically, stored in the trunk of the car.

See below for more on the severe penalties for drinking and driving in Florida.

If you are stopped by the police for any reason, there is no system of paying fines on the spot. Attempting to pay the fine to the officer is frowned upon (at best) and may lead to a charge of attempted bribery to compound your troubles. Should the officer decide you need to pay up front, he or she can take you directly to the magistrate instead of allowing you the usual 30-day period to pay the fine.

Everyone arrested legally has (and should be given) the right to remain silent, to make one phone call and to representation by an attorney. If you don't have a lawyer or family member to help you, call your embassy. The police will give you the number upon request. You are presumed innocent until proven guilty.

Note that police officers in Florida are allowed to search you if they have 'probable cause' – an intentionally vague condition that can almost be defined as 'if they want to.' The police will likely be able to search your car, under many different circumstances. There is no legal reason for you to speak to a police officer if you don't want to (although the officer may try to offer compelling reasons – like hand-cuffs – if they wish to speak with you and you ignore them).

Florida law upholds the death penalty for capital crimes.

Driving Laws

The maximum permissible speed is 70mph on interstate highways and between 55mph and 65mph on state highways unless other-wise posted. You can usually drive about 5mph over the limit without much likeli-hood of being pulled over by the police, but if you're doing 10mph over the limit, you'll be caught sooner or later.

Speed limits on smaller highways are 55mph or less, and in cities they can vary from 25mph to 45mph. Watch for school zones, where speed limits can be as low as 15mph during school hours – these limits are strictly enforced. Passengers should wear a seat belt (mandatory) and motor-cyclists a helmet (not mandatory).

Drinking & Driving

The USA is one of the least tolerant coun-tries in the world when it comes to drunk driving. During festive holidays and special events, police roadblocks are sometimes set up to check for drunk drivers.

While alcohol levels vary from person to person, generally speaking, if you have *one* beer, you're pushing Florida's legal limit (.08%). If you're pulled over and an officer suspects you're drunk, you'll be given a 'field sobriety test.' If you fail, you'll be placed under arrest immediately. In the police station, you'll be offered a breath test. Refusal isn't admission of guilt, but if you refuse, they'll probably find some charge on which to hold you even longer. If you fail the breath test, your license will be immediately suspended pending a hearing, and you'll be fined hundreds of dollars. De-pending on alcohol level and whether you've had an accident, this fine could easily reach $5000. Don't bother drinking and driving; it's not worth it.

BUSINESS HOURS

Office hours are generally 9am to 5pm, though there can be a variance of half an hour or so. In large cities, a few supermar-kets and 'convenience stores' (selling food, beverages, newspapers and some household items) are open 24 hours a day. Shops are usually open from 9am or 10am to 5pm or 6pm but are often open until 9pm in shop-ping malls, except on Sundays, when hours are generally noon to 5pm.

Post offices are generally open Monday to Friday from 8am to 5pm, and some are also open Saturday from 8am to 3pm. Banks are usually open Monday to Friday from 9am or 10am to 4pm or 5pm. A few banks are open Saturday from 9am to 2pm (hours are decided by the individual bank branches).

Gas stations on major highways are open 24 hours a day, seven days a week. City gas stations usually open at 6am or 7am and stay open until 8pm or 9pm. In small towns and villages, hours will proba-bly be slightly shorter.

PUBLIC HOLIDAYS

National public holidays are celebrated throughout the USA. Banks, schools and government offices (including post offices) are closed, and transportation, museums and other services are on a Sunday sched-ule. If public holidays fall on a weekday or weekend, they are often celebrated on the nearest Friday or Monday, to create a three-day weekend.

The following are the current national holidays:

New Year's Day – January 1
Martin Luther King Jr Day – 3rd Monday in January
Presidents' Day – 3rd Monday in February
Easter – a Sunday in April or late March
Memorial Day – last Monday in May
Independence Day – July 4
Labor Day – 1st Monday in September
Columbus Day – 2nd Monday in October
Veterans Day – November 11
Thanksgiving – 4th Thursday in November
Christmas Day – December 25

CULTURAL EVENTS

The USA is always ready to call a day an event. Retailers remind the masses of coming events with huge advertising binges running for months before the actual day. Because of this tacky overexposure, some of these events are nicknamed 'Hallmark Holidays' (after the greeting-card manufacturer). Some of these are also public holidays (see above), and therefore, banks, schools and government buildings are closed. In larger cities with diverse cultures, traditional holidays of other countries are also celebrated with as much, if not more, fanfare.

January

Chinese New Year – Starting in late January or early February, this two-week event begins with parades, firecrackers, fireworks and lots of food.

February

Valentine's Day – February 14. No one knows why St Valentine is associated with romance in the USA, but this is the day of roses, sappy greeting cards and packed restaurants. Some people wear red and give out 'Be My Valentine' candies.

March

St Patrick's Day – March 17. The patron saint of Ireland is honored by those who feel the Irish in their blood – and by those who have Irish beer in their blood. Everyone wears green, stores sell green bread, bars serve green beer, and towns and cities put on frolicking parades of marching bands and community groups.

April

Easter – Observers go to church and often paint eggs, which are usually hidden (by the 'Easter Bunny') for children to find. Chocolate eggs and bunnies are also eaten. Travel during this weekend is usually expensive and crowded. Incidentally, Good Friday is not a public holiday and often goes unnoticed.

Passover – Celebrated in March or April, depending on the Jewish calendar. Jewish families get together during Passover to partake in the traditional Seder dinner, which commemorates the liberation of Jews from their slavery in Egypt.

May

Cinco de Mayo – On May 5, 1862, the Mexicans won a decisive battle against the French army. Now it's the day on which Americans eat lots of Mexican food and drink margaritas.

Mother's Day – Held on the second Sunday of the month, the day is celebrated with cards, flowers and restaurant reservations.

June

Father's Day – Held on the third Sunday of the month, it's the same idea but with a different parent.

July

Independence Day – On this day, often called the Fourth of July, flags are flown, barbecues abound, parades storm small-town streets, fireworks litter the air and ground – all intended to commemorate America's Declaration of Independence.

October

Halloween – October 31. Kids and adults dress in costumes. In safer neighborhoods, children go door to door 'trick-or-treating' for candy, and adults go to parties and act out their alter egos. Miami and Orlando are especially good places to be on Halloween, as the gay communities hold parades with wild and lavish costumes.

November

Day of the Dead – November 2. Observed in areas with Mexican communities, this is a day for families to honor dead relatives. People make breads and sweets resembling skeletons, skulls and such.

Election Day – Held on the first Tuesday of the month, this is the chance for US citizens to perform their patriotic duty by voting. Shamefully, only about 45% of them do. Even more flags are flown than on the Fourth of July, and signs with corny photos of candidates decorate the land. In retrospect, Election Day was never bigger in Florida than on November 7, 2000.

Thanksgiving – Held on the last Thursday of the month, this is a day for giving thanks, and ostensibly commemorating the short-lived harvesting cooperation between the original Pilgrims and Native Americans. The important family gathering, celebrated with a bounty of food and football games on TV, is followed by the biggest shopping day of the year, where everyone burns off pumpkin pie by running shopping relays through the malls. The day before Thanksgiving is often the heaviest travel day in the country.

December

Chanukah – This eight-day Jewish holiday commemorates the victory of the Maccabees over the armies of Syria. The date of Chanukah changes year to year, as it's tied to Kislev 25 to Tevet 2 in the Jewish calendar.

Christmas – December 25. The day before is as much of an event as Christmas itself, with church services, caroling in the streets, people cruising neighborhoods looking for the best light displays and stores full of procrastinators.

Kwanzaa – This seven-day celebration, held from December 26 to 31, is based on an African holiday that gives thanks to the harvest. Families join together for a feast and practice seven different principles corresponding to the seven days of celebration.

New Year's Eve – December 31. People celebrate with little tradition other than dressing up and drinking champagne, or staying home and watching the festivities on TV. The following day, people stay home to nurse their hangovers and watch college football.

SPECIAL EVENTS

There are special events all the time in Florida; the Florida Division of Tourism has a complete list, updated annually, and each city's CVB/VCB or chamber of commerce publishes a list of its own celebrations.

January

Outback Bowl (Tampa; ☎ 813-874-2695, 223-1111) This football match takes place at the Raymond James Stadium on January 1.

Florida Citrus Bowl (Orlando; ☎ 407-849-2020) This college football game is played at the Florida Citrus Bowl Stadium on or close to New Year's Day.

Circus Sarasota (Sarasota; ☎ 941-355-9805; W www.circussarasota.org) Performers, acrobats, magicians and artists get together in Ringling Country for the entire month of February at the Sarasota County Fairgrounds.

Art Deco Weekend Festival (Miami; ☎ 305-672-2014) This weekend fair in mid-January is thick with arts and crafts, food stalls and the usual block-party types clogging the roads between 1st and 23rd Sts.

Martin Luther King Jr Festival (actually festivals) MLK's birthday is celebrated throughout the state in mid-January.

Miami Film Festival (Miami; ☎ 305-377-3456; W www.miamifilmfestival.com) This two-week festival from late January to early February is sponsored by FIU.

February

Rodeo (Homestead; ☎ 305-247-3515; W www.homesteadrodeo.com) Since the late 1940s, this full-fledged rodeo (from late January to early February) has featured bull riding, bareback and saddle bronco riding, team roping, steer wrestling and women's barrel racing.

Edison Festival of Lights (Fort Myers; ☎ 941-334-2999; W www.edisonfestival.org) During the first two weeks of February, this festival celebrates the famous inventor. Arts & crafts are sold, and at the end, there is a parade of lights.

Speed Weeks (Daytona; ☎ 386-253-7223; W www.daytonabeach.com) This three-week auto-race celebration begins in early February and leads up to the Daytona 500 at Daytona International Speedway.

Florida State Fair (Tampa; ☎ 800-345-3247) During the second week of February, fruits, vegetables, and arts & crafts are displayed and sold at the Florida State Fairgrounds.

International Boat Show (Miami; ☎ 305-531-8410) With over 250,000 attendees, this eagerly anticipated late-February show is held at the Miami Beach Convention Center.

March

Bike Week (Daytona; ☎ 386-255-0981; W www.bikeweek.com) During the first week in March, lawyers, Hell's Angels, speed heads, accountants and others saddle up for a wild party, based around motorcycle races at the Daytona Speedway.

Sanibel Shell Fair (Sanibel Island; ☎ 239-472-2155) A tradition since 1937, this three-day celebration concerns all things shells and starts the first Thursday of March.

Winter Party (Miami; ☎ 305-572-1841; W www.winterparty.com) From early to mid-March, this big gay circuit party bonanza benefits the Dade Human Rights Foundation.

Calle Ocho Festival (Miami; ☎ 305-644-8888; W www.carnaval-miami.org) This mid-March festival is not for the claustrophobic, since over a million people attend the Little Havana party, with 23 blocks of concerts, giveaways, Cuban food and more.

Italian Renaissance Festival (Miami; ☎ 305-250-9133) With period plays and concerts, and people dressed in traditional Italian costume, this mid-March event is held at the Vizcaya Museum & Gardens.

Orchid Show (Miami; ☎ 305-255-3656) Since the mid-1940s, this mid-March show of flowers from statewide growers has been held at the Coconut Grove Exhibition Center.

South Beach Wine & Food Festival (Miami; ☎ 877-649-8325; W www.sobewineandfoodfest.com) This big and glittery two-day, mid-March event is sponsored by FIU at Lummus Park, and boasts over 200 wine producers and seminars and dinners.

Miami-Dade County Fair & Expo (Miami; ☎ 305-223-7060; W www.fairexpo.com) This 18-day extravaganza from mid- to late March showcases the area's agricultural roots at the Fair Expo Center, SW 112th Ave at 24th St.

Sarasota Jazz Festival (☎ 941-366-1552) This is a weeklong jazz, blues and big-band festival during the last week of March.

Nasdaq 100 Tennis Open (Miami; ☎ 305-442-3367) Top-ranked tennis pros play before millions of spectators in late March.

Springtime Tallahassee (☎ 850-224-5012; W www .seetallahassee.com) Lasting from late March to early April, this large festival features ubiquitous arts & crafts, a balloon rally, a parade and music.

April

Festival of the States (St Petersburg; ☎ 727-898-3654; W www.festivalofstates.com) Taking place in early April, this 50-year tradition offers competitions, music performances, an antique car show and the like.

Fun 'n' Sun Festival (Clearwater; ☎ 727-562-4804) Sport contests, musical events and lots of action on the beach and in town mark this mid-April to early May attraction.

Pompano Beach Seafood Festival (☎ 954-941-2940) One of Florida's countless seafood celebrations, this late April event offers a great opportunity to taste local fish, oysters, crabs and regional cooking.

Kissimmee Jazz Festival (☎ 407-908-3263) This free two-stage festival takes place on the last Sunday in April at Kissimmee Lakefront.

Gay & Lesbian Film Festival (Miami; ☎ 305-534-9924; W www.miamigaylesbianfilm.com) From late April to early May, this annual event screens at the Colony Theatre.

May

Conch Republic Days (Key West; ☎ 305-294-2587; W www.flakeys.com) The founders of this island

nation are toasted in true Key West style in late April. The 10-day event overlaps with April 23, the actual day of succession.

International Hispanic Theatre Festival (Miami; ☎ 305-445-8877; W www.teatroavante.com) From late May to mid-June, this is one of the largest Hispanic theater celebrations in the USA, featuring US, Latin American, Caribbean and European companies.

June

Fiesta of Five Flags (Pensacola; ☎ 850-433-6512; W www.fiestaoffiveflags.org) The arrival of the Spanish is celebrated in early June, complete with reenactments and Spanish food and music.

July

America's Birthday Bash (Miami; ☎ 305-358-7550) Held on the Fourth of July at Bayfront Park, this excellent fireworks and laser show with live music and celebrations draws crowds of more than 100,000.

Underwater Music Festival (Big Pine Key; ☎ 800-872-3722) Held in mid-July, this underwater symphony is staged for divers.

Hemingway Days Festival (Key West; ☎ 305-294-2587; W www.hemingwaydays.com) The best thing about this mid- to late-July event, celebrated to coincide with Papa's birthday on the 21st, is the Hemingway look-alike contest sponsored by Sloppy Joe's, but there are also short-story competitions judged by Hemingway's granddaughter. The event has been held since 1981.

August

Bon Festival (Delray Beach; ☎ 561-495-0233; W www.morikami.org) This evening Japanese cultural celebration with folk music, food and dancing is held at the excellent Morikami Gardens in mid-August.

September

Festival Miami (Miami; ☎ 305-284-4940; W www .music.miami.edu) This late-September to late-October annual concert series is held at the University of Miami Campus in Coral Gables.

October

Hispanic Heritage Festival (Miami; ☎ 305-541-5023; W www.hispanicfestival.com) In late October, this large festival commemorates the discovery of the Americas with concerts, food, games and folkloric groups; it takes place along Sunset Dr between SW 57th Ave and US Hwy 1.

Miami Reggae Festival (Miami; ☎ 305-891-2944) Since the early 1980s, this late-October event has been one of the country's largest reggae events; it's held at Bayfront Park.

Fantasy Fest (Key West; ☎ 305-296-1817; W www .fantasyfest.net) One of many Florida Halloween celebrations, this 10-day late-October event is perhaps Florida's most outrageous, with drag queens and other wacky entrants.

Biketoberfest (Daytona Beach; ☎ 800-854-1234; W www.daytonabeach.com) Mid-October sees another week of motorcycle celebration.

Fifth Avenue Oktoberfest (Naples; ☎ 941-435-3742; W www.fifthavenuesouth.com) This three-day German-style beer festival in Naples is held erroneously in mid-October (in Germany, it's held in September).

November

Book Fair International (Miami; ☎ 305-237-3258; W www.miamibookfair.com) From mid- to late November, this is among the most important and well-attended such fairs in the USA, with hundreds of nationally known writers joining hundreds of publishers and hundreds of thousands of visitors; don't miss it.

Lincolnville Festival (St Augustine; ☎ 904-829-8379, 825-1000) This early-November festival features ethnic foods, live entertainment, and arts & crafts shows.

South Miami Art Festival (Miami; ☎ 305-661-1621) Since the early 1980s, this early-November event has featured over 150 exhibitors along Sunset Dr between SW 57th Ave and US Hwy 1.

Winston Cup (Homestead; ☎ 305-230-7223; W www .homesteadmiamispeedway.com) This mid-November Nascar weekend is held at the Homestead Miami Speedway.

White Party (Miami; ☎ 305-667-9296; W www .whiteparty.net) This weeklong extravaganza from mid- to late November draws more than 15,000 gays for nonstop partying.

December

Winterfest Boat Parade (Fort Lauderdale; ☎ 954-767-0686; W www.winterfestparade.com) This parade features almost a hundred decorated boats cruising up the Intracoastal Waterway in early December.

Grand Illuminations/Night of Lights (St Augustine; ☎ 904-824-9550) The entire historic district is lit with tens of thousands of little lights from late November until early February – you'll feel as if you're in a fairy tale. There are also reenactments and other shows and events.

Art Basel Miami Beach (Miami; ☎ 305-674-1292; W www.artbasel.com/miami_beach) In early December, this important international art show features works at over 150 galleries.

Jewish Film Festival (Miami; ☎ 305-576-4030; W www.caje-miami.org/filmfestival) Sponsored by FIU in early to mid-December, almost 30 films and documentaries from all over the world are screened.

First Night New Year's celebrations for all ages are held in larger Florida cities.

WORK

Foreigners cannot work legally in the USA without the appropriate work visa, and recent legislative changes specifically target illegal immigrants, which is what you will be if you try to work while on a tourist visa.

Miami has been ground zero for large numbers of refugees from the Caribbean area, notably Haiti and Cuba, so INS checks are frequent. Local businesses are probably more concerned here than anywhere (except for Southern California and Texas) when it comes to verifying your legal status. See Visa Extensions under Documents, earlier in this chapter, for warnings about longer stays.

ACCOMMODATIONS
Reservations

The cheapest bottom-end motels may not accept reservations, but at least you can call to see if they have a room. Even if they don't take reservations, they'll often hold a room for an hour or two.

Chain hotels accept reservations days or months ahead. Normally, you have to give a credit card number to hold the room. If you don't show and don't call to cancel, you will be charged the first night's rental. Cancellation policies vary; ask for details when you book. Some places let you cancel at no charge 24 hours or 72 hours in advance; others are less forgiving. Also, tell the hotel if you plan to arrive late – many places will rent your room if you haven't arrived or called by 6pm. Chains often have a toll-free number (see Hotels, later), but their central reservation system might not know about local discounts.

Camping

While it's less convenient than in Europe, opportunities for camping abound in Florida. There are three types of campsites available in the state: undeveloped, public, and privately owned. Both privately owned and public campgrounds – usually located within or close to state parks – are clean and, generally speaking, very safe. Both usually have hot showers and sewage hookups for recreational vehicles (RVs). Your fellow campers will include an interesting mix of foreigners and rural Americans – American city dwellers tend to camp less than rural dwellers.

Undeveloped Campgrounds You can camp in some backwoods areas, along riverbanks and in fields within state or national parks or forests. Undeveloped campsites obviously have no running water, toilets or any other facilities, and generally accommodate only tents. Basic responsibility (ie, hauling out every speck of your trash, digging pit toilets, not defecating near streams, and generally not leaving behind a single trace of your presence) is required for camping in undeveloped areas along the Florida National Scenic Trail, in the Everglades, Big Cypress National Preserve, Ocala National Forest or along rivers like the Blackwater River. See the Outdoor Activities chapter for proper outdoor etiquette.

Public Campgrounds Although public campgrounds are more spartan than their private counterparts (there are usually no swimming pools, laundry facilities or other niceties), they are generally more fun. Not only are public campgrounds inexpensive, but park rangers usually operate educational programs at least once a week. Think along the lines of campfire talks or organized nature walks. Public campgrounds usually accommodate tents, RVs and vans.

Most public campgrounds have toilets, fire pits (or charcoal grills), picnic benches, and, usually, drinking water (it's always a good idea to have a few gallons of water with you out in the boonies, just in case). These basic campgrounds usually cost between $7 and $20 a night. Areas costing several dollars more have showers or RV hookups. Make reservations for Florida state parks by calling ☎ 800-326-3521 or visiting W www.florida parks.com.

Costs given in the text are per site and normally include two people and one vehicle. If there are more of you, you'll need to pay more; if there are more than

---

It's the Water

The Sunshine State's water attracts many tourists – so why not vacation on it? Houseboats and sailboats are two cost-effective ways to enjoy the water: It's far more fun to spend your days island-hopping, or anchored and looking toward the shore, rather than sitting on the shore looking toward the water.

No boating skills? Few are needed with houseboats, which chug along slowly. However, you'll be given some basic instruction before you're given the keys. Two options are Houseboat Vacations of the Florida Keys (☎ 305-664-4009; W www.thefloridakeys.com/houseboats) and Flamingo Lodge Marina & Outpost Resort (☎ 239-695-3101, 800-600-3813; W www.flamingo lodge.com) in the Everglades. Two days in the winter with a fully equipped boat will run about $475 per boat. For more information, see the boxed text 'Houseboating' in the Everglades chapter.

Lack of seafaring skills shouldn't stop you from chartering a sailboat, at least not at Southwest Florida Yachts, which offers live-aboard sailing classes. By day you sail and learn to work the lines; by night you relax, cook dinner, watch the stars and sleep on board. For details, contact Southwest Florida Yachts (☎ 941-656-1339, 800-262-7939; W www.swfyachts.com). Two days of lessons and accommodations run $395 per person.

six of you, you'll need two sites. Public campgrounds often have seven- or 14-night limits.

Private Campgrounds Privately owned campgrounds are the most expensive camping option and are usually located several miles from town. Most are designed for RVs but will also have a small section for tenters. Sites always cost more than public campgrounds, but private campgrounds have many more amenities: swimming pools, laundries, shuffleboard areas, restaurants, convenience stores and bars. The better ones have lakes with boating and fishing.

Kampgrounds of America (KOA; ☎ 406-248-7444; W www.koa.com), a national network of private campgrounds, sets the standard for quality and price, with sites in or near most Florida cities. Each KOA facility has a pool, laundry, restaurant, bar, games area (shuffleboard, volleyball and the like) as well as tent, RV and van sites and Kamping Kabins – small log cabins with air conditioning and sometimes full kitchens. Kamping Kabins come in one- and two-bedroom flavors and average about $35 a night. KOA sites average $25 to $35, with electricity, cable TV and sewage hookups costing more. Most KOA campsites have toll-free 800 numbers, and all accept reservations.

Other privately owned campsites are listed in the text when they aren't obnoxiously geared toward RVs. Coupon books and advertising-heavy magazines at welcome centers and tourist information booths have exhaustive listings.

Crew Houses

These private guest houses are designed for those who work aboard boats and are waiting for the next gig. Crew houses are found mainly in Fort Lauderdale, the yachting capital of the East Coast, and generally charge around $105 to $135 weekly. They're usually clean and comfortable, and are a great places to get information and to network for crewing opportunities. See the boxed text 'Joining a Crew' in the Southeast Florida chapter for more information.

Hostels

Hostels are not just for youth; rather, they're places where travelers of all ages can get a cheap bed and exchange travel tales and information on where to do what.

There are hostels in Key West, Florida City, Miami Beach, Clearwater Beach, St Petersburg, Fort Lauderdale, Orlando, Kissimmee and St Augustine. About half of them are affiliated with **Hostelling International/American Youth Hostels** (HI/AYH; ☎ 202-783-6161; W www.hiayh.org; 733 15th St NW, Suite 840, Washington, DC 20005). These affiliates offer discounts to members and usually allow nonmembers to stay for a few dollars more. To use HI's code-based reservation service (☎ 800-909-4776), you'll need the hostel's access code, available from the HI/AYH handbook or the actual hostel. Reservations are advised during the high season, during which time there may be a limit of a three-night stay.

It's important to note that while HI/AYH hostels maintain that organization's standards, some private hostels meet or exceed them. Don't pass on a place just because it is or is not an HI hostel: check out the rooms and speak to travelers staying there before paying.

HI/AYH hostels expect you to rent or carry a sheet or sleeping bag to keep the beds clean. In all hostels, there are information and advertising boards, TV rooms and lounge areas. Most hostels have a common kitchen, available to everyone staying there. There's a common room where travelers can hang out, and often there are inexpensive coin-operated laundry facilities. Books and games are also often available.

Independent hostels may offer a discount to HI/AYH members. They often have a few private single/double rooms available, although bathroom facilities are still usually shared.

Dormitory beds at both types of hostels cost about $12 to $17 nightly. Private rooms cost in the low to mid-$30s for one or two people. Dorms generally have between four and eight single beds, mostly bunk beds, and are often segregated by sex. You'll usually have to share a bathroom. Alcohol is banned in some hostels.

B&Bs

Bed & breakfast inns in Florida really try hard to provide personal attention, excellent rooms, great service and local advice, and on many occasions, the owners are absolutely lovely people. Indeed, the B&B concept – spending a night or so in someone's house as opposed to a hotel – is a very nice one. But reviewing B&Bs is tricky business, so we've resorted to this catchall, which we're sure you'll find accurate as you travel the state:

This charming (Victorian house/Key West mansion/art deco delight/Spanish colonial villa/renovated turn-of-the-century hunting lodge) is run by a lovely (American/English/German/Uruguayan) (husband-and-wife team/gay couple) who make certain all the rooms – which feature (four-poster beds/sleek modern beds), coffeemakers, (TV and telephone/no TV or telephone) and (fireplaces/wood-burning stoves) – are ship-shape.

The four (dogs/cats) that live here are named (Harris, Tudor, Rex and Fluffy/Calvin, Siamesey, Pirate and Tom), and breakfast is a (full, hot affair with pancakes, waffles, omelets and bacon/Continental affair with freshly made muffins, breads, cakes and fruit) and coffee and tea. In the afternoon, there's (a free cocktail hour/free wine and beer). Out (front/back), there's a lovely (veranda/screened-in porch/sundeck), and there (is/is not) a pool and Jacuzzi. In-season room rates range from $90 to $190 a night, and (all/no) major credit cards are accepted.

Motels

Motels, a creation of the 1950s, are relatively inexpensive hotels designed for short stays by motorists (the name is a contraction of 'motor hotel') and other travelers, and for trysts (often involving television evangelists). A typical mid-range Florida motel is a one- or two-story building with a large parking lot and is often located just off a highway exit, near an airport or along a major road. The entryway will smell like old coffee and have discount-coupon and pamphlet racks against a wall.

Motels are usually at least 15 years old, and some rooms show their age more than others. The more run-down ones might have cigarette burns in the sink or a scruffy carpet, but they're usually clean enough. The better – not necessarily the more expensive – ones can be spotless. Rooms have private bathrooms; towels, washcloths and soap are provided. There are either one or two double or queen-size beds, and there is almost always color cable TV. Some offer pay-per-view movies ($6 to $9 per movie), and many have free HBO or Showtime (see Television, earlier in this chapter). All rooms have air conditioning.

Breakfast is rarely included – though many motels offer free coffee and donuts in the morning – and there are almost always soda- and snack-vending machines and free ice (wash that ice bucket before you fill it up). Daily maid service is standard, and you should leave a tip if the service is good (see Tipping, earlier in this chapter).

Budget These rooms, advertised as '$29.99,' are the cheesiest offering, and only to be explored by hardcore budget travelers. Mattresses are saggy, 'decor' is preposterous, and the cleanliness is absolutely minimum – that means clean sheets and towels.

Motel 6 (☎ 800-466-8356; W www.motel6 .com) is one of the cheapest national chains and a noticeable step up in quality. Rooms are small and bland, but the beds are usually OK. Every room has a TV and phone (local calls are free), and most properties have a swimming pool. Rooms start in the $30s in smaller towns, in the $40s in larger towns. They usually charge a flat $6 for each extra person.

Mid-Range Rooms from $40 to about $60 are often perfectly pleasant: furniture and televisions are newer; there may be a clock radio, a fridge and a microwave; the decor is better (though where they buy their paintings is unfathomable); and carpets are newer. Several different motel chains compete with one another at this price level.

The main difference between these and Motel 6 rooms is the size – there's more space to spread out. Beds are always reliably firm, the front desk is often staffed 24 hours, and little extras like free coffee, a table, cable TV, rental movies, or a bathtub with your shower may be offered.

If these sorts of things are worth an extra $10 to $20 a night to you, try **Super 8 Motel** (☎ 800-800-8000; W www.super8.com), **Days Inn** (☎ 800-329-7466; W www.daysinn.com), **Best Western** (☎ 800-528-1234; W www.bestwestern.com), **Red Roof Inns** (☎ 800-733-7663; W www.redroof.com) or **Econo Lodge** (☎ 800-553-2666; W www.choicehotels.com). Not all of these have pools, however.

Top End The larger and more expensive chains, charging in the $70 to $100 range, make a motel almost as nice as a hotel. Their clean and fresh rooms have lots of amenities, like better soap, shampoo, conditioner, in-room safes, more towels and more space. Usually a buffet Continental breakfast is included, and cafés, restaurants or bars may be on the premises or adjacent to them. The swimming pool is often indoor, with a spa or exercise room also available. Very good choices include the **Quality Suites** (☎ 800-228-5151; W www.choice hotels.com), **Comfort Inns** (☎ 800-228-5150; W www.comfortinn.com), **Sleep Inns** (☎ 800-627-5337; W www.sleepinns.com) and **Rodeway Inns** (☎ 800-228-2000; W www.hotelchoice.com).

Hotels

Hotels are traditionally located within cities and offer more and better service than motels. This means there will be doormen, valet parking, room service, a copy of *USA Today* in the morning, laundry and dry cleaning, a pool and perhaps a health club, a business center and other niceties. The perks come at a price, to be sure: Want a shirt washed? It's gonna cost you six bucks.

The basic hotel room differs little from the basic motel room, except that the furnishings should be newer and cleaner. Surprisingly, rooms at expensive hotels – like Hyatt and Sheraton – usually aren't much nicer than high-quality motel rooms, and they usually cost at least twice as much.

The exceptions are privately owned, smaller hotels in unique settings, and larger hotels in larger cities, which have reduced their prices and increased their services to compete with better motels and resorts. Specialty hotels – like The Hotel or the Whitelaw Hotel in Miami Beach, The Breakers in Palm Beach and the Ritz-Carltons anywhere – offer decadence and a hotel experience that's worth it if you can afford it.

Chain-owned hotels in Florida include the following:

Hilton	☎ 800-445-8667
	(W www.hilton.com)
Holiday Inn	☎ 800-465-4329
	(W www.holiday-inn.com)
Marriott	☎ 800-228-9290
	(W www.marriott.com)
Radisson	☎ 800-333-3333
	(W www.radisson.com)
Ritz-Carlton	☎ 800-241-3333
	(W www.ritzcarlton.com)
Sheraton	☎ 800-325-3535
	(W www.starwood.com/sheraton)

There are, of course, nonchain establishments in all price ranges. Some are quirky historical hotels, full of turn-of-the-century furniture. Others are privately run establishments that just don't want to be part of a chain. In smaller towns, complexes of cabins are available – these often come complete with a fireplace, kitchen and an outdoor area with trees and maybe a stream a few steps away.

Prices The bottom end for hotels is about $90 a night (in-season) throughout the state, usually at Holiday Inns and Marriotts. These offer basic amenities, room service, restaurants and nightclubs.

Full-service hotels, with bellhops and doormen, restaurants and bars, exercise rooms and saunas, room service and concierges, are found in the main cities. Aimed at those with expense accounts, in-season prices range from about $150 to $200 per room per night.

Rack Rates

The 'rack rate' is the standard price a person walking in off the street will pay for hotel accommodations. It is not necessarily the final price, though. This is especially true in the larger, more expensive places. Sometimes a simple 'Do you have anything cheaper?' will result in an immediate price reduction. Sometimes, in chain hotels, it may help to walk to the telephone booth in the lobby and call that chain's toll-free reservation number and ask for specials. At other times, the toll-free line may quote you a price much higher than that particular hotel offers. Always try both tactics whenever possible. It's never bad form to negotiate in an American hotel, and the savings can be substantial if you do.

Resorts

Florida resorts aim to keep you entertained on the premises for your entire holiday. They offer good service and add-ons like golf, tennis, water sports, health clubs, several pools, game rooms, activities for kids and adults, restaurants, cafés, and sometimes even convenience stores. Resort prices are higher than hotel prices – count on at least $185 to $250 a night for these places – and all the activities, except those for kids, usually cost extra.

FOOD

Florida's smorgasbord of multicultural cuisine can leave some visitors scratching their heads. The first thing that at least Europeans will find surprising is the unbelievable quantity of food you get at American restaurants. A plate of food in Florida groans under its own weight. Two light eaters may do perfectly well by sharing one main dish – though some restaurants charge a 'sharing fee,' usually about $2 to $3.

Listen up: you'll see dolphin on restaurant menus throughout Florida. This is dolphin *fish* – not the friendly and protected sea mammal. The other name for dolphin fish is mahi mahi. The alligator tail that's also served is not from protected alligators but from those raised on federally licensed alligator farms. Although it's mainly found as deep-fried nuggets, marinated and grilled alligator is quite tasty.

Florida cuisine is a mixture of seafood, American Southern, Cuban, Spanish, Caribbean, African and European foods. Chinese food in Florida is generally poor, but Thai and Japanese are often very good, sometimes excellent. Korean, Malaysian, Indonesian and Indian restaurants are very rare, and when you do find them, they are often very expensive. The most common foreign cuisine is Italian, which has been considerably Americanized to include dishes that never even existed in Italy (like veal parmigiana: breaded fried veal covered with melted mozzarella cheese and tomato sauce).

Highlights include Jamaican jerk dishes – fierily spiced, marinated and grilled dishes with chicken (which is most common), beef or fish. Traditional Creole dishes, usually featuring shrimp but also made with chicken, have a tomato-based sauce with peppers, garlic, onion and celery served on rice. Jambalaya is a tomatoey rice dish with ham or sausage, onions, garlic and peppers.

Gumbo, a stewlike substance served over rice, is thickened first with browned flour and then with either okra (a slimy vegetable) or filé powder, made from sassafras leaves. The most popular variations are made with shrimp and crab.

Note that Haitian and Cuban dishes sometimes use goat, which can be stringy. Various types of food are described in the following paragraphs, but for a complete discussion of Cuban cooking, see the boxed text 'Cuban Cuisine' in the Miami chapter.

Main Meals

See Fast Food below for chain restaurants serving breakfast, lunch and dinner throughout Florida.

Breakfast This meal in America is heavier than in many other countries, though Brits and the Irish will feel right at home tucking into eggs, toast, bacon, ham or sausage and fried potatoes. (Home fries are fried chunks of potato with onions and sometimes bell peppers; hash browns are shredded potatoes fried with any combination of stuff.) Europeans looking for traditional breakfasts (cheeses, ham, salami and assorted breads) will have no luck outside Orlando and Miami. 'Continental breakfast' is a euphemism for anything from a donut and a cup of coffee to a European-like spread of cheese, bread, muffins and croissants.

Many upscale fast-food places and some steak houses in Orlando have all-you-can-eat breakfast buffets for around $10. Be suspicious of these, and calculate how much the same thing would cost at a diner, where your meal would probably be cheaper and definitely made to order.

Lunch Traditionally, lunch is the least important meal in the USA. Many office workers have lunch at their desks, and most people simply grab something on the run – which is precisely why America has the best sandwiches in the world: we know how to eat on the go. Sandwiches are usually packed with stuff, including fresh vegetables, meats (like roast beef, ham or turkey) and cheeses. Subway routinely offers sandwiches with any of the following at no extra charge: lettuce, tomato, onion, peppers, hot peppers, oil, vinegar, salt, pepper, mayonnaise, ketchup and mustard.

Lunch is almost always a better value than dinner. The same $7 lunch dish will often cost $15 at dinner. Early-bird dinners, offered from around 4pm to 6pm, try to lure customers in by offering similar discounts.

Dinner The main, largest and most social meal of the day in the USA is dinner. Americans tend to eat at about 7pm or 8pm. It's the time when restaurants are the most expensive and the most crowded.

Fast Food

McDonald's, Burger King and Wendy's are the big players. In cities like Miami, though, it may come as a surprise to learn that fast food at lunch and dinner can be more expensive than cheap local restaurants. But generally speaking, the fast-food places have the cheapest breakfasts.

Other fast-food chains operating in Florida include Taco Bell, with good and cheap Mexican-style food, Subway (good, huge sandwiches), KFC (Kentucky Fried Chicken) and more upscale entries like Denny's (open 24 hours), Shoney's, and Cracker Barrel for bland American food. Chili's has Southwesternish fare, Red Lobster has seafood, Pollo Tropical serves chicken with a Cuban twist, Boston Market and Kenny Rogers serve roasted chicken, and Waffle House has good breakfasts 24 hours a day.

Look in discount booklets for coupons to fast-food places – usually two-for-one deals or reduced-price combination meals. Most fast-food places honor their competitor's coupons: a coupon for two-for-one Burger King Whoppers will usually get you two Big Macs.

Vegetarian

Non–meat-eaters will have an easy time in cities. In rural areas, though, it can be more difficult, as meat plays a key role in most Southern cooking. You may need to ask twice whether something contains meat – some crackers don't consider things like sausage seasoning, bacon bits or chicken to

---

Bagels

A bagel is a disk-shaped bread product made from heavy dough that has been boiled and then baked. The result is a substantial and chewy roll with a uniquely textured coating – the closest comparison would be a real Bavarian Brez'n, but that's not really it. Just eat one. Originally ethnic Jewish, the bagel has insinuated itself into the American menu and can now be bought in most big cities from coast to coast. They are usually offered in plain, sesame, poppy, onion, garlic and various combinations of the previous. They're available in any diner and in most restaurants that serve breakfast.

be meat! Salad bars are a good way to stave off hunger, and many restaurants serve large salads as main courses.

American

'Standard' American food is so influenced by cuisines from other countries that it's difficult to nail down other than the obvious: hamburgers. But modern American cooking can be summed up as combining American portions and homegrown foods with foreign sensibilities and techniques. There are many styles of American cooking that borrow heavily from French, Italian (the most popular foreign food in the USA), Asian and, to a lesser extent, Turkish and Greek cuisines.

Southern

Southern cuisine is heavy on fat and meats; typical specialties include biscuits (faintly similar to scones), mashed potatoes, collard greens (served with hot-pepper-infused vinegar) and black-eyed peas, all of which are prepared with chunks of pork or ham. Main courses include fried chicken, roasted ham, pork in any variety of ways and gravies with cornbread (a dry cakelike bread made from yellow cornmeal). If you're here on New Year's Day, have a plate of black-eyed peas for good luck in the coming year (every restaurant will be serving them); it's a Southern tradition.

Perhaps the biggest shock comes in the form of grits, a corn-derived white glop that's peculiar to the South. Treat grits as a hot cereal and add cream and sugar, or treat them as a side dish and add salt and pepper. Grits are served in lieu of potatoes at breakfast, and they're best when totally smooth and very hot.

Barbecue Barbecuing is a Southern tradition that has been entirely deconstructed in the hands of Australians, who can't even get the fire going and who depend on the women to cook while the men drink beer and give (faulty) instructions. Barbecue (purists say the proper pronunciation is 'bubbuh-kyu') consists mainly of seasoned pork, chicken and baby back ribs cooked over an open flame – brutal, but, meat-eaters say, delicious. Barbecue is served with sweet-and-tangy sauce that has smoky overtones. The idea is that the meat is cooked and smoked simultaneously, so by the time it's done, it falls off the joints and bones.

There are many places in Florida to experiment with this cuisine, and the best of them are in small towns with cheesy signs. One sure-fire way to tell if a restaurant is good is the number of police cars, ambulances and other vehicles parked in front – if it's packed, it's good.

The best chain in Florida for ribs is Sonny's, with branches all over northern Florida. Even if you don't partake, buy a bottle of Sonny's Sweet BBQ Sauce to take with you, and put it on everything.

Seafood

Florida has more than 8000 miles of coastline, so it's no surprise that seafood is omnipresent. Most common are grouper, dolphin fish (mahi mahi), tuna, salmon and swordfish, all served grilled or deep-fried. Blackened seafood is thrown into a red-hot frying pan filled with black pepper so the outside is burned to a crisp while the inside is cooked to medium. Incidentally, one sure-fire indicator of a town's sophistication is the availability of non–deep-fried foods – in some towns, everything is fried.

Another Florida favorite is stone crab, indigenous to South Florida and available in the winter only. Florida lobster doesn't hold a candle to Maine lobster, so if you like the latter, avoid the former. Many towns along the southwest and the Panhandle, especially the Apalachicola area (renowned for the eponymous variety of oysters found there), have 'raw bars,' where raw clams and oysters are served on the half shell. Be careful and make certain everything's fresh before digging in. (It is usually *very* fresh, but food poisoning isn't any fun, so look before you gulp.)

Supermarkets

To the first-time visitor, American supermarkets are daunting and over-the-top. Often large enough to house a regulation football field, American supermarkets are one-stop shopping extravaganzas that stock everything from auto parts to garbage cans, electronics to pharmaceuticals, school supplies to contraceptives, wine to beer, and, oh yes, food (including fresh produce, seafood and meats).

The two biggest supermarket chains are Publix and Winn-Dixie. Most supermarkets have bakeries, but they also sell dozens of types of packaged breads. Some supermarkets also have full-service delicatessen counters; newer ones have full-service cafés.

DRINKS
Nonalcoholic Drinks
Familiar soft drinks are readily available, although they sometimes are called 'tonic' or 'pop' rather than soda or soft drinks. You can also select from a host of bottled fruit juices, iced tea and spring water. Most drinks come in cups or glasses filled with ice, so you're paying mostly for frozen water. You might want to order your drinks without ice or with 'just a little' ice. Tap water is safe to drink virtually everywhere and usually is palatable.

Smoothies are made from yogurt and fresh fruits blended into a type of shake. A shake, or milkshake, is fast-blended ice cream, milk and flavoring (usually chocolate, vanilla or strawberry). The biggest surprise for many non-Latino foreign visitors is *guarapo,* or sugarcane juice.

Traditionally, American coffee comes from a light-brown roasted bean and is weaker than that preferred in Europe. In some parts of Florida, 'regular' coffee means coffee with sugar and milk or cream, so specify 'black coffee' if that's what you want.

Espresso is readily available (Starbucks has made inroads in Florida), as are American versions of other European favorites such as café au lait, cappuccino and caffe latte. The American versions are often elaborate concoctions with endless variations – vanilla, raspberry or cinnamon flavoring, for instance. Cities and most larger towns have specialty coffee shops where beans are roasted frequently, ground shortly before brewing and brewed by bean variety or origin, to order.

Tea, likewise, comes in bewildering variety. It is often served with lemon, unless milk is specified. Herbal teas of many kinds are readily available; as is decaffeinated tea. Iced tea with lemon is a popular summer drink.

Alcoholic Drinks
The strictly enforced minimum drinking age in Florida is 21. Carry a driver's license or passport as proof of age to enter a bar, to buy alcohol or to order it at a restaurant. Servers have the right to ask to see your ID and may refuse service without it – they're instructed to proof anyone who appears to be under 30. Minors are not allowed in bars and pubs, even to order nonalcoholic beverages. Unfortunately, this means most dance clubs are also off-limits to minors, although a few clubs have solved the under-age problem with a segregated drinking area. Minors are, however, welcome in the dining areas of restaurants where alcohol is served.

Beer and wine are sold in supermarkets in Florida, while harder stuff is sold in liquor stores. One shocking sight in Florida is the drive-through liquor stand, where customers pull in, order a bottle and zip away. There are several chain liquor stores in Florida, among them Walgreens (a pharmacy/liquor store) and regional chains like ABC. Liquor stores also stock a bewildering variety of 'coolers' – flavored sparkling wines and beers, which might be best described as alcoholic pop.

Beer Commercially available American 'beer,' for lack of a better term, is weaker and sweeter than its equivalent around the world, perhaps to encourage drinking more of it. Indeed, the marketing of 'light' beer – with fewer calories than regular beer – stalled until savvy marketers were able to convince the public that 'less filling' meant one could suck down many more beers on the same stomach.

Bottles of beer range from ponies (8oz) to standard 12oz, to long-neck (12oz as well, but the bottle neck is longer), to 40oz bottles. American beer also comes in 12oz and 16oz (1 pint) cans. Bottles and cans are generally sold in bundles of six (six-packs) or 12, or in cases of 24.

Six-packs of major brands (Budweiser, Michelob and Miller) cost $4 to $5 in supermarkets. You can visit the Anheuser-Busch Brewery in Jacksonville (see the Northeast Florida chapter), the Anheuser-Busch Beer School at Sea World in Orlando (see the Central Florida chapter) or the Hospitality Center at Busch Gardens in Tampa (see the Southwest Florida chapter).

Ice brew implies a 'cold filtration process,' but it adds up to beer with about 5.5% alcohol. Microbrewed beers, made by smaller companies with limited production, are usually excellent and taste much like their European counterparts. Look for Samuel Adams (Boston) and Anchor Steam (San Francisco), both of which are so popular that their 'micro' status could probably come under challenge. There are about a dozen mi-crobrewers in Florida, mentioned in the text where possible. Microbrews and ice brews cost between $5 and $8 a six-pack but are worth the extra cost.

Wine Wine is also available in supermarkets, and foreign visitors will often find that wine from their home country is cheaper here – many Australian wines are about 20% less in Florida than at home. But while perfectly drinkable wine is available in supermarkets, connoisseurs will do far better in proper liquor stores, which sell a better range of higher-end wines.

ENTERTAINMENT
Clubs

Nightclubs in Florida are located in larger cities. In most, you'll want to dress for the occasion – especially in Miami Beach, where you'd better look as if you own the place or forget even getting in. In fact, competition is so fierce here that nightclubs open and go out of business constantly.

Smoking

The USA, which gave the world tobacco, is now mostly a huge no-smoking zone. Government regulations have banished smokers from virtually all public spaces except bars and the out-of-doors, and have also banished most tobacco advertising from the media. Several state governments banded together and sued tobacco companies in order to reclaim the millions of public-health dollars they have had to spend dealing with tobacco-related illnesses. The trial revealed that the tobacco companies had indeed designed their products to be particularly addictive and had suppressed evidence that tobacco use causes various diseases. In short, tobacco products, their manufacturers and their uses are now in high disrepute.

Many Americans find smoking unpleasant and know that heavy or habitual smoking is unhealthy and harmful not only to the smoker, but also those nearby (particularly children and people with asthma or other pulmonary impairments). If you are a smoker from a country that permits smoking in public places, you should be aware of American regulations and social customs.

Smoking is prohibited in most public buildings, such as airports, train and bus stations, offices, hospitals and stores, and on public conveyances (subways, trains, buses, planes etc). Except for the designated smoking areas in some restaurants, bars and a few other enclosed places, you must step outside to smoke.

Most cities and towns require restaurants to have nonsmoking sections, but there is no requirement that there be smoking sections. Hotels offer 'nonsmoking' rooms – that is, rooms used only by nonsmoking guest so that the rooms have no stale tobacco smell.

If you are in an enclosed space (a room or car, for example) with other people, it's polite to ask permission of all others before you smoke and to refrain from smoking if anyone protests.

In larger clubs, entry fees are between $10 and $15; in Orlando, admission to hootchaterias (with loud music and cheap alcohol) like Church St Station and Pleasure Island is about $15 to $20, while local clubs charge less than average to try and draw people away from their huge competitors. In most cities, bars turn into nightclubbish places in the evenings, with live music of some sort or contests.

Gay and lesbian nightclubs generally have live performances that range from drag shows to amateur nights to strippers.

Bars

Bars range from down-and-dirty to chic, and the prices range accordingly. Most American bartenders (except in tonier places that spend money on automatic pourers) free-hand pour in a manner that would make British publicans blanch. A 'shot,' ostensibly 1oz, is often larger than that. American custom says that you tip the bartender for each drink – generally $1 – and that (except in very crowded nightclubs) you place your cash on the bar and leave it there while you drink.

'Happy hours,' usually a lot longer than an hour and sometimes all day, are periods in which drink prices are reduced, sometimes substantially. Two drinks for the price of one is a common deal. 'Ladies' night' – a clever ploy that allows women to drink for free, thus luring horny, thirsty males – is usually held once a week.

Performing Arts

The biggest destination for music, dance and theater is Miami, though Fort Lauderdale, Tampa, Sarasota and the Palm Beaches are also noteworthy centers of activity. See the individual chapter sections for information on what performing arts are available.

Cinemas

Americans have been known to make a movie or two, and every Florida city has at least one chain theater. American movie houses have taken the as-many-as-possible approach, and the quaint one-movie cinema is practically extinct. The best place to look

for six-, nine- and up to 18-multiplex cinemas is in the nearest shopping mall. Prices are usually from about $4.50 before 4pm and from $6 and $8 in the evening. Miami has several independent film outlets offering smaller-budget, foreign or cult films, and we list others where they exist. Mostly, though, you should expect only mass-appeal Hollywood films.

SPECTATOR SPORTS

Sports in the USA developed separately from the rest of the world, and baseball (with its clone, softball), football and basketball dominate the scene, both for spectators and participants. Football and basketball, in particular, are huge. In professional basketball, key players are the Orlando Magic and Miami Heat.

Florida has three NFL football teams: the winning Miami Dolphins, the Tampa Bay Buccaneers and the Jacksonville Jaguars. If you've ever wondered whether it was true that the word fan derives from 'fanatic,' attend a Florida pro football game. And if you think that's bad, wait till you see the fanaticism associated with *college* football: the state has several good college teams, chief among them the University of Miami Hurricanes and the FSU Seminoles.

Baseball is so embedded in the country's psyche that – despite its complex rules, the difficulty and expense of maintaining playing fields with an irregular configuration, and labor-management problems at the highest professional levels – the sport continues to flourish. Many of the most meaningful metaphors in American English and even political discourse – such as 'getting to first base' or the debased 'three strikes and you're out' – come from baseball. Softball, which requires less space than baseball, draws more participants, both men and women, than any other organized sport in the country. Many professional baseball teams come to the warmth of South Florida for spring training in March, and minor-league teams play here throughout the baseball season, from April to October. There are major-league baseball teams in Miami (Marlins) and St Petersburg/ Tampa Bay (Devil Rays, whose future is uncertain following a bid to decrease the number of major-league teams).

Jai alai, a fascinating and dangerous Basque game in which teams hurl a *pelota* – a *very* hard ball – at more than 150 mph, can be seen (and wagered on) in South Florida stadiums.

Soccer has made limited inroads, and will probably remain a relatively minor diversion until the Americans can consistently make a name for themselves at the World Cup.

SHOPPING

Other than handicrafts and art in the major cities, there really isn't a big 'Florida product.' The main things to buy here, especially if you're coming from Europe or even Australia, are clothing and consumer goods, all of which are cheaper than at home (see the boxed text 'Cheaper in the States').

Tourist-crap stands abound in major cities and in gas stations along highways. The big offerings are 'funny' T-shirts, lacquered alligator heads (they're real, culled from alligator farms) and other standard schlocky stuff.

Large Specialty Chain Stores

There are several large specialty retailers that often have less-expensive prices than mom-and-pop establishments. Check advertisements in local newspapers for special deals and sales. Many of these stores have more than one location in any given town, so call and ask for the location nearest you. The larger clothing specialty stores are listed below under Shopping Malls.

Circuit City sells electronics, computers, appliances and other gizmotronics.

Some *Eckerd* pharmacies are open 24 hours.

Sports Authority sells sporting goods, backpacks, bicycles and running, hiking and climbing equipment.

Walgreens, a chain of combination pharmacy/liquor stores, sells both pints of whiskey *and* bandages. Makes sense.

Wal-Mart, K-Mart and *Sears* are one-stop shopping centers for just about anything you'd need, from padlocks to plates, diapers to garbage disposals (pronounced 'dispose-all' in the South) and everything in between.

Cheaper in the States

While you'll have trouble finding a jar of Vegemite, the USA has the world's best prices (with the possible exception of Hong Kong) on some other items. They include:

Jeans – New blue jeans (like unwashed Levi's and faded Gap jeans) start at $35.

Sunglasses – Ray-Bans and other premium brands can be found for as low as $35.

Zippo lighters – These flashy babies start at about $12.

Running shoes – Name-brand sneakers start at $40.

Camping equipment – From tents and sleeping bags to heavy-duty backpacks, everything costs less here.

Computers – Though you'll probably have to pay an import tariff when you get home, it will be certainly be offset by great American bargains. Between falling prices and equipment upgrades, it doesn't do any good to quote prices here.

Cameras – Ditto on cameras, especially digital.

CDs – If you're lucky, the new CDs you want will cost $12 to $14; harder-to-come-by titles reach up to $20, though.

If you're buying electric or electronic appliances here (such as kitchen gadgets, telephones, CD players, etc), you'll need a step-down transformer – not an adapter – to allow the item to work at home.

Shopping Malls

Massive shopping malls have so saturated the shopping scene it's difficult to find many items without entering one. And the insidious nature of the malls and the huge shops is that lower wages lead to higher employee turnover and less-informed staff. Major shops in malls usually sell clothing (eg, Neiman-Marcus, Saks Fifth Avenue, Gap, Burdines) and general merchandise (eg, Sears, K-Mart, Wal-Mart, JC Penney), while all malls will have a food court (a collection of fast-food joints), a Sunglass Hut, shoe shops, some specialty jean and women's clothing shops, and bookstores.

Factory outlet malls, usually located several miles from a major city, sell old or overstocked items that manufacturers are trying to unload. It could be last season's gear, ugly as sin, damaged or 'irregular.' Most of the time, prices in a true factory outlet can be up to 70% lower than retail.

Believe it or not, the number-two tourist destination in Florida is Sawgrass Mills Mall, in Sunrise, 10 miles west of Fort Lauderdale. See the Southeast Florida chapter for details on this shopper's paradise.

Thrift Shops

Thrift and secondhand shops, found in most Florida cities, are usually affiliated with churches or relief organizations, to which items are donated. The items range from used books (usually a buck apiece) to used clothing, which is always clean and sometimes fantastic vintage stuff. Look for Goodwill, Salvation Army and St Vincent de Paul outlets. The best selections are found in more affluent neighborhoods, where donations are of higher quality. For instance, you might find a pair of original Pucci pants in amazing condition for $10 in a Palm Beach thrift shop. Check in the local Yellow Pages under 'Thrift Shops' for listings.

Flea Markets

True flea markets are bazaars, usually held on weekends in huge parking lots, where merchants from all over the state get together to sell stuff. Prices are negotiable, and you should always bargain. In some cities, like Kissimmee, organized flea markets occur daily during the tourist season. Prices at these are higher.

Outdoor Activities

Ah, the great outdoors – from broiling on a beach to canoeing in the backcountry. With so much water, the opportunities for swimming, snorkeling, scuba diving, fishing and kayaking are almost unparalleled.

Florida road warriors are faced with some of the world's most monotonous highways: endless ribbons of shimmering, straight blacktop, lined on either side with a uniform dark-green canopy. Cruising at 60mph it would appear that there's absolutely nothing on either side of you until you get to the next major city. But nothing could be further from the truth. Just off the major roads lies an astonishing array of wilderness areas, thousands of rivers and lakes, and subtropical flora and fauna unseen elsewhere in the continental USA. You may be surprised to learn that Florida has more state parks per capita and per square mile than most other states.

HIKING

There is no better way to appreciate Florida's beauty – its beaches, parks and scenic trails, peaceful hammocks and marshes – than on foot and on the trail. Taking a few days' (or even just a few hours') break from the highway to explore the outdoors refreshes road-weary travelers and heightens their appreciation of the scenery that whizzes past day after day. Some travelers experience one good hike and then plan the rest of their trip around wilderness or hiking areas.

Safety

Major forces to be reckoned with are weather (which is uncontrollable) and your own frame of mind. Be prepared for unpredictable weather – you may go to bed under a clear sky and wake up in a thunderstorm the likes of which you haven't seen since watching *Moby Dick*. Afternoon summer thunderstorms are very common. Carry a rain jacket at all times. Backpackers should have a pack-liner (heavy-duty garbage bags

work well), a full set of rain gear and food that does not require cooking. A positive attitude is helpful in any situation. If a hot shower, comfortable mattress and clean clothes are essential to your well-being, don't head out into the wilderness for five days – stick to day hikes.

Highest safety measures suggest never hiking alone, but solo travelers should not be discouraged, especially if they value solitude. The important thing is to always let someone know where you are going and how long you plan to be gone. Use sign-in boards at trailheads or ranger stations. Travelers looking for hiking companions can inquire or post notices at ranger stations, outdoors stores, campgrounds and youth hostels.

Fording rivers and streams is potentially dangerous but often necessary. In national parks and along maintained trails in national forests, bridges usually cross large bodies of water (this is not the case in designated wilderness areas, where bridges are taboo). Upon reaching a river, unclip all of your pack straps – your pack is expendable, you are not. Avoid crossing barefoot – you don't know where that bottom's been. Bring a pair of lightweight canvas sneakers or Teva-style sandals for crossing, or you'll be stuck sloshing around in wet boots for the rest of your hike.

Using a staff for balance is helpful, but don't rely on it to support all your weight. Don't enter water higher than mid-thigh; any higher than that and your body gives the current a large mass to work against.

If you get wet in cool weather, wring your clothes out immediately, wipe off all the excess water on your body and hair and put on any dry clothes you (or your partner) might have.

People with little hiking or backpacking experience should not attempt to do too much, too soon, or they might end up being nonhikers. Know your limitations, know the route and pace yourself accordingly. Remember, there is absolutely nothing wrong with turning back or not going as far as you had originally planned.

Treading Lightly

Backcountry areas are fragile and cannot support an inundation of human activity, especially insensitive and careless activity. Treat the backcountry like you would your own backyard – minus the barbecue pit and kids trampling the shrubs.

A code of backcountry ethics has evolved to deal with the growing number of people in the wilderness. There are a few important principles: minimizing the impact on the land, leaving no trace and taking nothing but photographs and memories. Above all, stay on the main trail, stay on the main trail and, lastly, even if it means walking through mud, *stay on the main trail.*

Wilderness Camping Camping in undeveloped areas is rewarding for its peacefulness but presents special concerns. Take care to ensure that the area you choose can comfortably support your presence and to leave the surroundings in better condition than they were on your arrival. The following list of guidelines should help.

- Bury human waste in holes dug 6 to 8 inches deep. The salt and minerals in urine attract deer; use a tent-bottle (funnel attachments are available for women) if you are prone to middle-of-the-night calls by Mother Nature. Camouflage the hole when finished.

- Use soaps and detergents sparingly or not at all, and never allow these things to enter streams or lakes. When washing yourself (a backcountry luxury, not a necessity), lather up (with biodegradable soap) and rinse yourself off with cans of water as far away as possible from your water source. Scatter dishwater after removing all food particles.

- Carry a lightweight stove for cooking and use a lantern instead of a campfire.

- If a fire is allowed and appropriate, dig a hole and build a fire in it. On islands or beach areas, build fires below the high-tide line. Gather sticks no thicker than an adult's wrist from the ground. Use only dead and down wood; do not twist branches off live or dead and standing trees. Pour wastewater from meals around the perim-

eter of the campfire to prevent the fire from spreading, and thoroughly douse it before leaving or going to bed.

- Designate cooking clothes to leave in the food bag, away from your tent, so that wild animals, if they smell food on the clothes, won't trash the tent looking for it.

- Burn cans to get rid of their odor, and then remove them from the ashes and pack them out.

- Pack out what you pack in, including all trash – yours *and* that of others less considerate than you.

What to Bring

Equipment The following list is a general guideline for backpackers, not an 'if-I-have-everything-here-I'll-be-fine' guarantee. Know yourself and what special things you may need on the trail; consider the area and climatic conditions in which you will be traveling.

- Boots – light- to medium-weight are recommended for day hikes, while sturdy boots are necessary for extended trips with a heavy pack. Most importantly, they should be well broken in and have a good heel. Waterproof boots are preferable.

- Alternative footwear – thongs or sandals or running shoes for wearing around camp, and canvas sneakers for crossing streams.

- Socks – frequent changes during the day reduce the chance of blisters but are usually impractical and inconvenient.

- Subdued colors are usually recommended, but if hiking during hunting season, blaze orange is a necessity.

- Shorts, light shirt – for everyday wear; remember heavy cotton takes a long time to dry and is very cold when wet.

- Long-sleeve shirt – light cotton or polypropylene. A buttoned front makes layering easy and can be left open when the weather is hot and your arms need protection from the sun.

- Long pants – denim takes forever to dry, and hey, this is the subtropics. Sturdy cotton or canvas pants are good for trekking through brush, and cotton or nylon sweats are comfortable to wear around camp.

- Rain gear – light, breathable and waterproof is the ideal combination, but it doesn't exist no matter what those catalogs say. You need plastic, not Gore-Tex, for Florida rain. If nothing else is

Another beautiful day at Miami's South Beach

Activity-minded folk on South Beach Promenade

Miami's MacArthur Causeway

South Beach leisure takes many forms.

Dining al fresco at Miami's South Beach

Cuban iconography, Little Havana

Lifeguard and his art deco hut, South Beach

Deco signage on Ocean Drive, South Beach

Miami's signature art deco architecture

Classic wheels on Ocean Drive

available, use heavy-duty trash bags to cover you and your packs.

- Hat – a cotton hat with a brim is good for sun protection.

- Bandanna or handkerchief – good for a runny nose, dirty face, unmanageable hair, and to use as a tablecloth for picnic lunches or a signal flag (especially a red bandanna).

- Small towel – one that is indestructible and will dry quickly.

- First-aid kit – should include, at the least, self-adhesive bandages and adhesive tape, disinfectant, antibiotic salve or cream, gauze, small scissors and tweezers. An elastic bandage never hurts.

- Knife, fork, spoon and mug – a double-layer plastic mug with a lid is best. A mug acts as eating and drinking vehicle, mixing bowl and wash basin; the plastic handle protects you from getting burned.

- Pots and pans – aluminum cook sets are best, but any sturdy 1-quart pot is sufficient. True gourmands who want more than pasta, soup and freeze-dried food will need a skillet or frying pan. A metal pot-scrubber is helpful for removing stubborn oatmeal, especially when using cold water and no soap.

- Stove – lightweight and easy to operate is ideal. Most outfitters rent propane or butane stoves; test the stove before you head out, even cook a meal on it, to familiarize yourself with any quirks it may have.

- Water purifier – optional but really nice; water can also be purified by boiling for at least 10 minutes.

- Matches or lighter – waterproof matches are good; several lighters are smart.

- Candle or lantern – candles don't stay lit when they are dropped or wet and can be hazardous inside a tent. Outdoors stores will rent you lanterns; test them before hitting the trail.

- Flashlight – each person should have their own; be sure its batteries are fresh. Lightweight head-lamps that hold spare bulbs are a good choice.

- Sleeping bag – goose-down bags are warm and lightweight but worthless if they get wet; most outdoors stores rent synthetic bags.

- Sleeping pad – Lightweight foam pads that also fill up with air when unrolled work well. Use a sweater or sleeping-bag sack stuffed with clothes as a pillow.

- Tent – make sure it's waterproof, or has a water-proof cover, and has no-see-um – *not just mosquito* – netting. Learn how to put it up *before* you reach camp. Remember that your packs will be sharing the tent with you.

- Camera and binoculars – don't forget extra film and waterproof film canisters (sealable plastic bags work well).

- Compass, GPS device and maps – each person should have their own.

- Eyeglasses – contact-lens wearers should always bring a back-up set.

- Sundries – biodegradable toilet paper, small sealable plastic bags, insect repellent, sunscreen, lip balm, unscented moisturizing cream, mole-skin for foot blisters, dental floss (burnable and good when there is no water for brushing), sunglasses, deck of cards, pen or pencil and paper or notebook, books and nature guides.

Food Keeping your energy up is important, but so is keeping your pack light. If you pack loads of food, you'll probably use it all, but if you have just enough, you will probably not miss anything. Consider these basic staples: packaged instant oatmeal, bread (the denser the better), rice or pasta, instant soup or ramen noodles, dehydrated meat (jerky), dried fruit, energy bars, chocolate, trail mix and peanut butter and honey or jam (in plastic jars or squeeze bottles). See Sea Kayaking later in this chapter for information on freeze-dried meals. Don't forget the wet-wipes, but be sure to dispose of them properly or pack them out.

Books

There are quite a few good how-to and where-to books on the market, usually found in outdoors stores, or bookstores' Sports & Recreation or Outdoors sections. Chris Townsend's *Backpacker's Handbook* (Ragged Mountain Press/McGraw Hill, 1997) is a beefy collection of tips for the trail.

Maps

A good map is essential for any hiking trip. NPS and US Forest Service (USFS) ranger stations usually stock topographical maps that cost $2 to $6. In the absence of a ranger station, try a stationery or hardware store.

Longer hikes require two types of maps: US Geological Survey (USGS) quadrangles and US Department of Agriculture-Forest

Service maps. To order a map index and price list, contact the **US Geological Survey** (W www.usgs.gov; PO Box 25286, Denver, CO 80225). For general information on maps, see also the Facts for the Visitor chapter. For information regarding maps of specific forests, wilderness areas or national parks, see the appropriate geographic entry.

Florida National Scenic Trail (FNST)

At press time, the 1300-mile FNST was about 80% complete; the remaining 20% still ran along roadways. The trail runs north from the Big Cypress National Preserve in the Everglades National Park, around Lake Okeechobee, up through the central part of the state, through the Ocala National Forest, and then west to the Gulf Island National Seashore near Pensacola.

Though trail conditions can be unpredictable – due to flooding, mud or a shortage of volunteers for maintenance – many segments are excellent. Through-hikers need to note that 260 of the 1300 miles are on roads or connectors, and 400 miles are on private property, which is only open to members of the **Florida Trail Association** (FNST; ☎ 352-378-8823, 877-445-3352; W www.florida-trail.org; 5415 SW 13th St, Gainesville, FL 32608). The FNST is an all-volunteer organization that maintains the trail network, provides information on it and sells maps and companion guides. Memberships are $25 per person, $30 per family.

Before setting out, contact the FNST to purchase map packs ($25) for the nine regions. Each invaluable map has lots of trail data, including information on camping and parking. When hiking the trail, you should bring everything you'll need to be entirely self-sufficient.

State Parks

With 156 state parks (☎ 850-488-9872) encompassing more than 570,000 acres, Florida ranks number five among US states for the sheer number of acres set aside. Its parks are visited by over 18 million people annually. We detail the interesting parks throughout this guide, but you may wish to consult the

state's Web site (W www.dep.state.fl.us/parks) for super-thorough information.

National Parks

Unless you have a few days to get into the backcountry of a national park, or are visiting between late May and early September, outside of the tourist season, expect the parks to be crowded.

Travelers with little hiking experience will appreciate well-marked, well-maintained trails, often with toilets at either end and interpretive displays along the way. The trails give access to the parks' natural features and usually show up on **National Park Service** (NPS; ☎ 800-365-2267 for reservations; W www.nps.gov) maps as nature trails or self-guided interpretive trails. These hikes are generally no longer than 2 miles.

Most national parks require overnight hikers to carry backcountry permits, available from visitor's centers or ranger stations. These permits must be obtained 24 hours in advance, and using one requires that you follow a specific itinerary. While this system reduces the chance of people getting lost in the backcountry and limits the number of people using one area at any given time, it may detract from the sense of space and freedom hiking can give. In backcountry areas of the Everglades and Big Cypress, a ranger will determine if you're an experienced wilderness explorer or a misinformed yahoo. For more information, call the NPS.

BICYCLING

Florida is flat as a pancake, with plenty of bicycle trails in and around cities and in parks. Also, rail-trails – bicycle paths on the track beds of former railway lines – pop up here and there: in Tallahassee, Gainesville and along the southwest coast north of St Pete Beach. In cities like Miami Beach, Fernandina Beach on Amelia Island, St Augustine, Tallahassee, Pensacola and Pensacola Beach and Key West, a bike is a great way to get around, and rentals are readily available.

Information

Members of the **League of American Bicyclists** (LAB; ☎ 202-822-1333; W www

.bikeleague.org; 1612 K St NW, Suite 800, Washington, DC 20006) may transport their bikes free on selected airlines. (It's not as simple as it sounds, though; contact them for details.) The LAB also publishes, and posts on its Web site, an annual almanac that lists contacts in each state, along with information about bicycle routes, special events, local clubs, tons of helpful tips on safe biking, maintenance and things to do prior to a big trip.

Bicycle tourists will also want the *Cyclosource Catalog,* listing books and maps, and *The Cyclist's Yellow Pages,* a trip-planning resource, both published by the **Adventure Cycling Association** (☎ 406-721-1776; W www.adventurecycling.org; 150 E Pine St, Missoula, MT 59802).

For further information, see the Bicycle section of the Getting Around chapter.

Laws & Regulations

Trail etiquette requires that cyclists yield to other users. Helmets should always be worn to reduce the risk of head injury, but they are not mandated by law. National parks, however, require that all riders under 18 years old wear helmets.

HORSEBACK RIDING

Horseback riding is not as popular here as elsewhere in the country, and it tends to be expensive. Experienced riders may want to let the owners know, or else risk being saddled with an excessively docile stable nag. Horse country in Florida is just south of Gainesville (see Ocala in the Central Florida chapter).

CANOEING

Florida's covered with, and almost surrounded by, water – there are canoeing opportunities practically everywhere. The best opportunities for adventure are in the Everglades, where the 99-mile Wilderness Waterway and trips around the 10,000 Islands are fantastic. The biggest concentration of other waterways for paddling are sprinkled throughout southwestern Florida, and there are great places to paddle throughout the state. In this book we've included fine possibilities where we found them.

Most state and county parks with good, easygoing rivers offer canoe rentals; private concessionaires operate in or near parks that don't. Generally speaking, rentals cost about $7 an hour, or $15 for four hours, and

---

Sand & Sun Fun

It's official: Dr Beach's list of the USA's best beaches puts four of Florida's in the top 10. Since 1991, Dr Beach (Stephen Leatherman) has annually ranked the country's beaches, taking into consideration 50 criteria, from sand softness and water temperature to rip currents and vistas. The following are the Florida winners:

1   St Joseph Peninsula State Park
4   Fort DeSoto Park
5   Caladesi Island State Park
9   Cape Florida State Recreation Area

Excluded from the running were the past No 1–ranked beaches, including Bahia Honda State Park in the Florida Keys, Grayton Beach State Park in Santa Rosa and St Andrews State Park in Panama City.

Incidentally, South Beach (Miami) and Panama City Beach come in near the top in the 'best beaches with nightlife' category.

You can check out Dr Beach in cyberspace (W www.drbeach.org) or in print *(America's Best Beaches).*

from \$25 for a full day or 24 hours. Rangers are invariably forthcoming with information about how you can maximize your wildlife-viewing possibilities.

What to Bring

Consider the following for individual back-country canoe trips (obviously the overnight stuff is only if you plan to camp):

- good, sightable compass and GPS device
- good flashlight (Petzl headlamps and Mini Maglite brands are good)
- nautical charts and tide chart
- tent with no-see-um – not just mosquito – netting
- sleeping bag
- 1 gallon of water per person per day, preferably in heavy-duty or army-surplus water containers, not store-bought 1-gallon jugs
- as much food as you'll need plus an extra day's food per person
- a solid plastic sealable cooler, like a Coleman or Eskimo – *not* Styrofoam – for food storage
- portable cooking stove, pot and utensils
- industrial-strength insect repellent like REI Jungle Juice
- sunscreen, sunglasses and a hat
- strong plastic garbage bags – Hefty-brand lawn bags are nice
- biodegradable toilet paper and a small spade to dig a waste pit
- binoculars (to see route markers) and a camera
- dry change of clothes for *when* you fall in the water
- good shoes or boots

Packing

Canoeists have more flexibility than back-packers; take the important stuff, size and weight be damned (well, sorta). Consider these criteria: You'll want to a) be comfortable when you get where you're going; b) not cheat yourself on meals; and c) have the right equipment to avoid getting into trouble.

Pack as much food and gear as you can into sealable coolers and try this trick: fill cleaned-out half-gallon milk jugs with water, freeze them and put them in the coolers; block ice lasts longer than cubes,

and you'll have cold drinking water as it melts. Several of those can last for two to three days.

Consider skimping on clothes: assume you'll get wet, and pack as little as possible. But always pack lightweight long pants, lightweight long-sleeve shirts and clean, dry socks and underwear. Keep these in the plastic garbage bags. Heavy-duty Ziploc-brand freezer bags are good for wallets and small items. Wrap your sleeping bag, tent, clothes and cameras and other electronics in the heavy-duty garbage bags, remove the air from the bags, tie them off twice and place them in a backpack.

Tie everything – backpacks, coolers, water jugs – together in a daisy chain (that is, with lines between each piece of gear, rather than around one big clump), and then tie one end to the inside of the canoe. In the unlikely event that you flip, you'll still have your stuff.

SEA KAYAKING

This quiet, unobtrusive sport allows you to check out unexplored islands, coastline and marine life at close range. Sea kayaks, which hold one or two people, are larger and more stable than whitewater boats, making them safer and easier to navigate. They also have decent storage capacity, so you can take them on overnight, or even weeklong trips. Imagine paddling to a secluded beach on one of the Gulf Coast or Everglades islands and setting up camp for a week.

What to Bring

There's enough room in one Sea Lion sea kayak for seven days' worth of supplies – if you're a good packer. Bring the same type of stuff that you would on a canoe trip, but scale everything down. Take smaller bottles of water, or a collapsible water container, since you'll be able to seal the boat. Also, you can use the kayak's sealable hatch instead of a heavy and bulky plastic cooler, which saves on space. You'll need to economize on size on things like your tent, stove and sleeping bag. Take only exactly what you need, and in the smallest form possible.

Freeze-dried food is the order of the day for overnight trips. If you've yet to sample it, you may be in for a shock: freeze-dried food, available from several companies, actually tastes a lot better than you'd expect. Companies like Richmoor/Natural High make a huge array of dishes. Some you dump into a pot of boiling water; with others you add the water directly to the bag. For side dishes, such as green beans or corn, expect to pay about $2 a bag. Breakfast items like a cheese omelet are about $3, and full dinners (including a main course and a side dish that's said to feed two but probably feeds only 1½), expect to pay from $5.50 (for beef stew or chicken teriyaki) to $6.50 (for honey-lime chicken and whole-grain rice).

SURFING

Florida surfing isn't much to speak of compared to California or Hawaii, but you can surf along the entire Atlantic coast. The best places are between Miami Beach and Fort Lauderdale, and around the central Florida coast, where conditions are usually decent, or actually good if you're a longboarder. Count on 2- to 3-foot surf unless there's a storm, when it can get big. Playalinda Beach and around the Space Coast (see the Space Coast chapter) is great for surfing, as is Daytona Beach, around Amelia Island and Fort George Island and the area from Flagler Beach up to St Augustine (see the Northeast chapter for all these).

Surf shops may be loath to rent out boards because of insurance problems, but they might sell you a board and buy it back at the end of the day for a bit less than you paid…Get it? Wink wink.

WINDSURFING

Though you can put in at any beach or public boat launch, there are surprisingly few places that rent windsurfing equipment, making it necessary for serious boarders to bring their own. Beginners and casual boarders will find relatively calm conditions and rental facilities at Biscayne Bay, near Miami's Rickenbacker Causeway, and at resorts. Generally speaking, the best places for windsurfing are along the southeast and southwest coasts, though it's popular in the northeast as well; local weather forecasts give wind and surf conditions.

SCUBA DIVING & SNORKELING

Diving in Florida requires at least an Open Water I certificate, for which you'll need several open-water dives. You'll also need to work in the pool before even getting to the ocean. If you push yourself, and the weather and seas are right, you can certify in three days.

For information on dive courses and standards, contact the **Professional Diving Instructors Corporation** (PDIC; ☎ 570-342-1480; W www.pdis-intl.com; PO Box 3633, Scranton, PA 18505), or the **National Association for Underwater Instruction** (NAUI; ☎ 813-628-6284, 800-553-6284; W www.naui.org; PO Box 89789, Tampa, FL 89789). Note that medical-grade oxygen is now available in Florida without a prescription.

Quick one- to three-day certification courses can get you into shallow waters to see the underwater world for as little as $250, though you might want to buy your own snorkel, fins and various other gear and books, which can add up to a $400 to $500 total cost. Shallow diving is especially satisfying in the Florida Keys, where the protected coral reefs house a rich marine environment close to the surface. Lonely Planet's *Diving & Snorkeling Florida Keys* is packed with information. Local dive shops are the best resource for equipment, guides and instructors. *Scuba Diving* (W www.scubadiving.com) and *Sport Diver* (W www.sportdiver.com) are widely available magazines dedicated entirely to underwater pursuits.

If you don't have the time, money or desire to dive deep, you can often rent a snorkel, mask and fins for about $10 an hour. In touristy spots such as South Beach, people set up equipment-rental stands along the beach. If you'll do it more than three times, though, it pays to invest $30 or so in an inexpensive mask and snorkel from a decent source, such as one of the Sports Authority superstores scattered throughout the state.

FISHING

Florida saltwater fishing is an obsession, and every city along the coast has a marina packed with charter fishing boats. Freshwater fishing (or more specifically, bass fishing), inland on lakes throughout the state and especially near Orlando, is as much a Florida tradition as grits or speeding. There are complex limits on catches in Florida; licenses are issued and fees and validity set on a county-by-county basis. Fishing boats are available at practically every marina in the state, but especially on both coasts in South Florida. Charters run regularly from Miami Beach, Fort Lauderdale, The Keys, Key West, Naples and Marco Island. Since we rarely recommend specific charters, it's best to wander around the docks and see which captains float your boat.

Barracuda Danger

Do not eat barracuda in Florida no matter what size – they may carry ciguatera toxin (CTX), produced by microscopic algae. This is eaten by smaller fish, then travels up the food chain and accumulates in larger fish, who pass it on to humans. It can cause severe illness, with symptoms including diarrhea, nausea, cramps, numbness of the mouth, chills, headaches, dizziness and convulsions. Don't believe local legends about the weight of the fish or cooking tests using a dime in the boiling water – this toxin can be deadly.

SAILING

Charter sailboats, with or without crew, are available from marinas throughout Florida. Prices vary unbelievably, depending on the size of the boat, the season, the mood of the owner and your level of experience. The best place to start is probably Fort Lauderdale. See the boxed text 'Joining a Crew' in the Southeast Florida chapter for suggestions on how to hook up with crew positions.

TENNIS

Almost every Florida city has municipal courts; check in the blue-pages section of the telephone directory under Parks Department for local numbers. All resorts and many hotels have courts as well. You also may be able to get time on the courts at college or university campuses simply by asking.

GOLF

There are courses are all over Florida, and some rank among the best in the country. In many ways that's unfortunate: Golf courses waste colossal amounts of water for irrigation, and runoffs of fertilizer and pesticides poison the very source of the state's freshwater supply (the Florida Aquifer). Golf courses also eat up huge tracts of land, and environmentalists charge that the damage to local flora and fauna is irretrievable. The development associated with golf courses – condominiums and resorts – only adds to the damage.

We don't include golf courses in this book. But there are many other sources – practically every pamphlet handed out by CVBs (convention & visitor's bureaus) and chambers of commerce lists all area golf courses.

HOT-AIR BALLOONING

Floating above Florida in a wicker gondola has its attractions, given the scenery, but it's not cheap at the relatively few locations that offer it commercially. Most flights leave at dawn or at sunset and go 1000 to 2000 feet above the ground. They're available in southwest Florida but pop up almost everywhere; check in local airports, where people will know of balloonists in the area. A one-hour flight for two people typically costs at least $175.

JET SKIING & MOTORBOATING

Jet skis and motorboats kill manatees and fish, rip up sea plants and protected sea grass (destroying the manatees' food supply), scare swimmers, annoy locals and result in several deaths a year. Further-more, some of Florida's bays and canals are very shallow and tricky to navigate. Further*most*, many areas are protected Manatee Zones. You can rent these hateful machines around the beach, but we wish you wouldn't. If that's not strong enough for you, consider this: You wouldn't want to take a spill on your wave runner and have it run off without you, leaving you bobbing deep in shark-infested waters, would you?

Getting There & Away

AIR
Airports
The state's two major international airports are Miami International Airport (MIA) and Orlando International Airport (MCO). But if you're looking for a really cheap deal to Miami, consider Fort Lauderdale (FLL), about 30 miles north.

Other airports with increased international traffic include Tampa/St Petersburg (TPA), Daytona Beach (DAB) and Jacksonville (JAX), which are becoming important domestic hubs as well.

Most Florida cities have regional airports and offer connecting service to other US cities; these include Palm Beach (PBI, actually in West Palm Beach), Sarasota (SRQ), Tallahassee (TLH), Gainesville (GNV), Fort Myers (RSW) and Pensacola (PNS).

With the exception of major tourist destinations like Miami, Fort Lauderdale, Palm Beach and Orlando, there is rarely public transportation between airports and downtown; you're at the mercy of car rental agencies, taxis or, more rarely, shuttle services. In this book we include as many options as we've found.

Airlines
Airlines are listed in the Yellow Pages under 'Airlines.' Important offices in Miami include the following:

US-Based Airlines
Air Tran ☎ 800-247-8726,
W www.airtran.com

America West ☎ 800-235-9292,
W www.americawest.com

American Airlines ☎ 800-433-7300,
W www.aa.com

Cape Air ☎ 800-352-0714,
W www.flycapeair.com

Continental Airlines ☎ 800-525-0280,
W www.flycontinental.com

Delta Air Lines ☎ 800-221-1212,
W www.delta.com

Frontier ☎ 800-432-1359,
W www.frontierairlines.com

Jet Blue ☎ 800-538-2583,
W www.jetblue.com

Midway Airlines ☎ 800-446-4392,
W www.midwayair.com

Northwest Airlines ☎ 800-225-2525,
W www.nwa.com

Spirit Airlines ☎ 800-772-7117,
W www.spiritair.com

Southwest Airlines ☎ 800-435-9792,
W www.southwest.com

United Airlines ☎ 800-241-6522,
W www.ual.com

USAirways ☎ 800-428-4322,
W www.usairways.com

International Airlines
Aeromexico ☎ 800-237-6639,
W www.aeromexico.com

Aerolineas Argentinas ☎ 800-333-0276,
W www.aerolineas.com

Air Canada ☎ 888-247-2262,
W www.aircanada.ca

Air France ☎ 800-237-2747,
W www.airfrance.fr

Air New Zealand ☎ 800-262-1234,
W www.airnewzealand.com

Alitalia ☎ 800-223-5730,
W www.alitalia.it

Air Jamaica ☎ 800-523-5585,
W www.airjamaica.com

Bahamas Air ☎ 800-222-4262,
W www.bahamasair.com

British Airways ☎ 800-247-9297,
W www.britishairways.com

Cayman Airways ☎ 800 422-9626,
W www.caymanairlines.com

El Al ☎ 800-223-6700,
W www.elal.co.il

Iberia ☎ 800-772-4642,
W www.iberia.com

KLM ☎ 800-374-7747,
W www.klm.com

LAB Bolivia ☎ 800-337-0918,
W www.labairlines.com

LanChile   ☎ 305-670-9999,
W www.lanchile.com

Lan Peru   ☎ 800-735-5590,
W www.lanperu.com

Lufthansa   ☎ 800-645-3880,
W www.lufthansa.com

Mexicana   ☎ 800-531-7921,
W www.mexicana.com

Qantas Airways   ☎ 800-227-4500,
W www.qantas.com.au

Sun Country   ☎ 800-359-6786,
W www.suncountry.com

Swissair   ☎ 800-221-4750,
W www.swissair.com

Varig Brazilian Airlines ☎ 800-468-2744,
W www.varig.co.uk

Virgin Atlantic   ☎ 800-862-8621,
W www.virgin-atlantic.com

Buying Tickets

Numerous airlines fly to the USA, and a variety of fares are available. In addition to a straightforward roundtrip ticket, you can also get a Round-the-World ticket or a Visit USA pass (see those headings, later). So rather than walking into the nearest travel agent or airline office and buying a ticket, it pays to shop around first. Consult reference books and check the travel sections of magazines like *Time Out* and *TNT* in the UK, or the Saturday editions of newspapers like the *Sydney Morning Herald* and *The Age* in Australia. Ads in these publications offer cheap fares, usually low-season fares on obscure airlines with conditions attached. But don't be surprised if agents are sold out.

The plane ticket will probably be the single most expensive item in your budget, and buying it can be intimidating. Research the current state of the market and start shopping for a ticket early – some of the cheapest tickets must be bought months in advance, and some popular flights sell out quickly. Talk to acquaintances who traveled recently – they may be able to stop you from making some obvious mistakes.

Note that high season in the USA is mid-June to mid-September (summer) and the two weeks around Christmas. The best rates for travel to and within the USA are offered November through March, except for major

holidays – especially Thanksgiving (the third Thursday in November) – which account for the heaviest travel days of the year.

Call travel agents for bargains. Airlines can supply information on routes and timetables; however, except during fare wars, they do not supply the cheapest tickets. Airlines often have competitive low-season student and senior citizens' fares. Before you buy, confirm the fare, the route, the dates and any restrictions on the ticket.

Cheap tickets are available in two distinct categories: official and unofficial. Official ones have a variety of names, including budget, advance-purchase, advance-purchase excursion (Apex) and super-Apex fares. Unofficial tickets are simply discounted tickets that the airlines release through selected travel agents (not through airline offices). The cheapest tickets are often nonrefundable and require an extra fee for changing your flight. (Many insurance policies will cover this loss if you have to change your

Warning

The information in this chapter is particularly vulnerable to change, especially after the 9/11 tragedy in 2001. Prices for international travel are volatile, routes are introduced and canceled, schedules change, special deals come and go, and rules and visa requirements are amended. Airlines and governments seem to take a perverse pleasure in making price structures and regulations as complicated as possible. You should check directly with the airline or a travel agent to make sure you understand how a fare (and any ticket you may buy) works. In addition, the travel industry is highly competitive, and there are many lurks and perks.

The upshot of this is you should get opinions, quotes and advice from as many airlines and travel agents as possible before you part with your hard-earned cash. The details given in this chapter should be regarded only as pointers and cannot substitute for your own careful, up-to-date research.

flight in an emergency.) Roundtrip (return) tickets usually work out cheaper than two one-way fares – often *much* cheaper.

Use the fares quoted in this book as a guide only. They are approximate and based on the rates advertised by travel agents and airlines at press time. Quoted airfares do not necessarily constitute a recommendation for the carrier.

You may decide to pay more than the rock-bottom fare by opting for the safety of a better-known travel agent. Established firms such as STA Travel, which has offices worldwide, Council Travel in the USA and Travel CUTS in Canada are valid alternatives, and they offer good prices to most destinations.

Once you have your ticket, make copies of it and your itinerary, and keep them separately from the originals (it doesn't hurt to leave extra copies with someone at home). If the ticket is lost or stolen, the copies will help you get a replacement.

Remember to buy travel insurance as early as possible (see the Visas & Documents section of the Facts for the Visitor chapter).

Travel Web Sites

Commercial reservation networks offer airline ticketing as well as information and bookings for hotels, car rental and other services. To buy a ticket via the Web, you'll need a credit card; this should be straightforward and secure, as card details are encrypted. Search these Web sites that, in turn, search multiple airlines for good fares:

Atevo Travel	w www.atevo.com
Cheap Tickets	w www.cheaptickets.com
Excite Travel	w www.city.net
Internet Travel Network	w www.itn.net
Lowest Fare	w www.lowestairfare.com
Microsoft Expedia	w www.expedia.com
Orbitz	w www.orbitz.com
Priceline	w www.priceline.com
Travelocity	w www.travelocity.com
Travel Library	w www.travel-library.com

Getting Bumped

Airlines try to guarantee themselves consistently full planes by overbooking, assuming some passengers will not show up. When everyone who's booked actually does show up, some passengers can be 'bumped' off the full plane, but they are usually compensated for the inconvenience. Getting bumped can be a nuisance because you have to wait around for the next flight, but if your schedule is flexible, you might be able to make the system work for you.

When you check in at the airline counter, ask if they will need volunteers to be bumped, and ask what the compensation will be. Depending on the desirability of the flight, this can range from a $200 voucher toward your next flight to a fully paid roundtrip ticket. Try to confirm a later flight so you don't get stuck in the airport on standby. If you have to spend the night, airlines frequently foot the hotel bill for their bumpees. All in all, it can be a great deal, and many people plan their trips with a day to spare, hoping to get a free ticket that will cover their next trip.

Be aware that, due to this same system, being just a little late for boarding can get you bumped with none of these benefits.

Visit USA Passes

Many domestic carriers offer Visit USA passes to non-US citizens. The passes are actually coupons that you buy – each coupon equals a flight. You have to book each of these, including your return flight, outside of the US.

Contact the bigger carriers like Continental, American Airlines and Delta in your home country. Some will let you fly standby, while others require you to reserve flights in advance (and penalize you if you need to change the fare). When flying standby, call the airline a day or two before the flight and make a 'standby reservation.' This way you get priority over others who just appear at the airport and hope to get on the flight the same day.

Round-the-World Tickets

Round-the-World (RTW) tickets are very popular since they can work out to be no more expensive, or even cheaper, than an ordinary return ticket. Official airline RTW tickets are usually put together by combining passage from two airlines. You can fly anywhere on their route systems as long as you do not backtrack. Read the small print; other restrictions and time limits often apply. Your best bet is to find a travel agent that advertises or specializes in RTW tickets. Start your search with the best by contacting the experts at **Air Treks** (☎ 415-365-1665, W www.airtreks.com) in San Francisco.

Travelers with Special Needs

If you have special needs of any sort – dietary restrictions, dependence on a wheelchair, responsibility for a baby, fear of flying – you should let the airline know as soon as possible so they can make arrangements accordingly. You should remind them when you reconfirm your booking (at least 72 hours before departure) and again when you check in at the airport.

Guide dogs for the blind will often have to travel in a specially pressurized baggage compartment with other animals, away from their owner, though smaller guide dogs may be admitted to the cabin. Guide dogs are not subject to quarantine as long as they have proof of vaccination against rabies.

Deaf travelers can request airport and inflight announcements in written form.

Children under the age of two travel for 10% of the standard fare (or free on some airlines), as long as they don't occupy a seat. (They don't get a baggage allowance.) 'Skycots' should be provided by the airline if requested in advance; these will take a child weighing up to about 22lb. Children between two and 12 can usually occupy a seat for half to two-thirds of the full fare, and they do get a baggage allowance. Strollers usually must be checked at the aircraft door; they are returned at the door upon disembarking.

Departure Tax

A departure tax is charged to all passengers bound for a foreign destination from the USA. A North American Free Trade Agreement (NAFTA) tax is charged to passengers entering the USA from a foreign country.

Depending upon the airport, there may be other small airport usage and security fees (you can almost count on these, as the ramifications of 9/11 continue to impact the airlines' bottom line). Departure taxes are normally included in the cost of tickets bought in the USA. If you bought your ticket outside the USA, you may have to pay the tax when you check in for your departing flight.

Baggage & Other Restrictions

Baggage regulations are set by each airline but usually allow you to check two bags of average size and weight and to carry one smaller bag (in addition to a purse or computer) onto the plane. If you are carrying many pieces of luggage, or pieces that are particularly big, bulky, fragile or heavy (such as a bicycle or other sports equipment), check with the airline about special procedures and extra charges.

If your luggage is delayed upon arrival (which is rare), some airlines will give you a cash advance to purchase necessities. If sporting equipment is misplaced, the airline may pay for rentals. Should the luggage be lost, it is important to submit a claim. The airline doesn't have to pay the full amount of the claim; rather, they can estimate the value of your lost items. It may take them anywhere from six weeks to three months to process the claim and pay you.

A number of items are illegal to carry on airplanes, either in checked baggage or on your person. These include weapons, knives of *any* kind, scissors, aerosols, tear gas and pepper spray, camp-stove fuel canisters and full oxygen tanks. After 9/11 anything bizarre (like a stapler) or pointy (like a nail file) may be confiscated. Life will be much simpler if you're able to check all your baggage rather than carry on anything. All bags are subject to random searches.

Smoking is prohibited on all domestic flights within the USA and on most international flights to and from the USA. Most airports in the USA prohibit smoking except in designated areas.

Since 9/11, only ticketed passengers are allowed beyond the X-ray machines.

Within the USA

Check the weekly travel sections of major newspapers like the *New York Times*, *Los Angeles Times*, *Chicago Tribune*, *San Francisco Examiner*, and the *Boston Globe* for discount fares. From Miami, scan *New Times* and the *Miami Herald* advertisements for discounted flights that leave from Miami.

Reputable nationwide, budget travel agents include **STA Travel** (☎ 800-777-0112; w www.sta.com). While STA caters to students, they happily serve people of all ages.

The best deals to Miami are from the New York metropolitan area, but this route is also the most crowded: reserve early, as planes sell out well in advance of the date of departure. Currently, Southwest Airlines has the lowest *scheduled* airfares between Fort Lauderdale and their metro New York hub, which is actually in Islip on Long Island. With a bit of luck in the winter, you can get a roundtrip ticket for as little as $150. On other scheduled airlines departing from JFK and La Guardia, expect to pay at least $225 (roundtrip) advance purchase; $300 from Los Angeles; and $350 to $450 from San Francisco.

Canada

The Canadian Federation of Students' **Travel CUTS** (☎ 416-966-2887; w www.travelcuts.com; Toronto) has offices in major Canadian cities. Also check the Toronto *Globe & Mail* and *Vancouver Sun*, which carry travel agents' ads. With a little luck (midweek, with a 14-day advance purchase and seven-day stay), you might find a roundtrip ticket price of C$475 from Toronto and C$625 from Vancouver, regardless of season.

Bahamas

American and Bahamas Air run many flights between Miami and Nassau, and typical roundtrip fares are about US$200 (BSD$200).

Elsewhere in the Caribbean

Miami is the gateway to the Caribbean, and the vast majority of flights to and from Caribbean destinations are serviced by American Airlines, with daily flights between many destinations, including San Juan, Puerto Rico; Santo Domingo, Dominican Republic; Montego Bay, Jamaica; St Martin and Barbados. Prices change dramatically, but last-minute deals are always a possibility. Use the following roundtrip fares to Miami as a starting point only:

destination	winter/summer
Barbados	$945/900 (US$475/US$450)
Montego Bay	$15,700/23,000 (US$475/US$325)
San Juan	US$460/US$275
Santo Domingo	US$525/US$340

Central & South America

Miami is the main US/Latin American gateway, and MIA is served by everyone and his brother's airlines. You can sometimes get incredible deals through discount brokers in Latin America, but they come and go quickly. By scheduled air, the average roundtrip tickets available through Web sites like w www.expedia.com are US$400 to US$450 from major Central American cities.

From Rio de Janeiro, Brazil, economy fares often have to be purchased two weeks in advance, and minimum-stay restrictions

---

Travel Between Miami & Cuba

Because of deep historical ties and the strong influence of Cubans on Miami's culture, it only seems natural to pop over to Havana from Miami and check out the scene. Ah, if it were only that simple or easy. There are regular charter flights between the two cities, but despite the fact that the political winds might be changing, there is a very technical and oh-so-legal list of criteria of who can go to Cuba and for what purposes. Quite honestly, if you're considering it, the best thing to do is check out Lonely Planet's very thorough *Cuba* guide.

apply. You can probably find a flight from Rio for around US$750 in the winter.

From Caracas, Venezuela, count on prices of around US$400 to US$550 in the winter.

UK

Start by perusing the travel sections of *Time Out*, *Evening Standard* and *TNT*. UK travelers will probably find the cheapest flights are advertised by obscure bucket shops. Many are honest and solvent, but some are rogues who will take your money and disappear. If you feel suspicious about a firm, don't give them all the money at once – leave a deposit of 20% or so and pay the balance on receiving the ticket. If they insist on cash in advance, go elsewhere. Once you have the ticket, ring the airline to confirm that you are booked on the flight.

Good, reliable agents for cheap tickets in the UK include **Trailfinders** (☎ 020-7938-3939; W www.trailfinders.co.uk; 194 Kensington High St, London W8 7RG) and **STA Travel** (☎ 020-7581-4132; W www.statravel .co.uk; 86 Old Brompton Rd, London SW7 3LQ). The **Globetrotters Club** (W www .globetrotters.co.uk; BCM Roving, London WC1N 3XX) publishes the newsletter *Globe* that covers obscure destinations and can help you find traveling companions.

Don't forget that most British travel agents are registered with the **Association of British Travel Agents** (ABTA; W www.abta .com) and are bonded under agreements such as the Air Transport Operators License (ATOL). If you buy a ticket from such an agent and the airline then goes out of business, ATOL guarantees a refund or an alternative flight.

In January a roundtrip air ticket from London to Miami might run £125 to £285. In July, the same ticket would cost £550.

Continental Europe

Most major European airlines service Miami or Orlando, many with nonstop service. In January/June, expect to pay €450/650 from Amsterdam; €450/700 from Paris; €600/650 from Madrid; €470/650 from Munich or Frankfurt.

NBBS, the Dutch Student Travel Service, is probably your best bet in the Netherlands, but also check out W www.budgettravel.com/ amsterta.htm for a complete list of Dutch travel agents near you.

STA (☎ 49-69-703035; W www.statravel .de; Frankfurt) and **Travel Overland** (☎ 89-272-76300; W www.travel-overland.de; München) have many popular offices throughout Germany.

For great student fares from France, contact **USIT** (☎ 33 1 42 44 14 00; W www.usit connections.fr) in Paris, which has many outlets in the city and around the country. For USIT locations around the world, check out W www.usitnow.ie.

Australia & New Zealand

Neither Qantas nor Air New Zealand have direct service to Florida; you'll have to change planes and/or carriers in Los Angeles or San Francisco, on the West Coast. From Auckland to Los Angeles, it takes 12 to 13 hours; from Sydney to Los Angeles, 13½ to 14½ hours. From the West Coast to Miami or Orlando takes four to eight hours, depending on the connections (or lack thereof). From the Australian east coast, typical Apex roundtrip fares vary from A$2500 to A$2800 to Miami or Orlando. On Air New Zealand, expect to spend about NZ$2200 to NZ$2600 from December to April, but don't forget to add another NZ$600 for the last leg to Miami. The whole trip is only about NZ$200 less expensive during the US winter.

STA Travel, which sells tickets to everyone but has special deals for students and travelers under 30, has offices in major cities in Australia and New Zealand. Head offices are located at 224 Faraday St, Carlton South, Melbourne, VIC 3053, Australia (☎ 1300-360-960, 9347-6911), and 10 High St, Auckland, New Zealand (☎ 0800-100-677, 309-0458). In Australia, don't forget to peruse the Saturday editions of newspapers like the *Sydney Morning Herald* and the *Age*. Kiwis, pick up your *New Zealand Herald*.

South Africa

A reasonably easy-to-get discounted flight between Johannesburg and Miami would be about R5000/5800 in low/high season. **STA Travel** (☎ 27-21-418-6570; **W** www.sta travel.co.za; Cape Town) has offices all over the country, as does **Rennies Travel** (☎ 27-21-215-013; Johannesburg).

Asia

Hong Kong is the discount plane ticket capital of the region, but its bucket shops can be unreliable. Ask other travelers for advice before buying a ticket. The dependable **STA Travel** (**W** www.statravel.com) has branches in Hong Kong, Tokyo, Singapore, Bangkok and Kuala Lumpur.

United Airlines, Northwest and Japan Air Lines have daily flights to the West Coast, where you can get a connecting flight to Miami. Airfares as low as HKD$7400 may be available from Hong Kong to Miami, with a West Coast connection, but more normal fares might hover around HKD$9400.

Arriving in the USA

As you approach the USA, your flight's cabin crew will hand out a customs and immigration form for you to fill in.

Arriving from outside North America, you must complete customs and immigration formalities at the airport where you first land, whether or not it is your final destination. Choose the proper immigration line: US citizens or non-US citizens.

After you have cleared immigration procedures, pick up your luggage in the customs area and proceed to an officer, who will ask you questions concerning your destination and length of stay, and perhaps check your luggage. The dog sniffing around the luggage is looking for drugs, explosives and restricted agricultural and food products.

After passing through immigration, you collect your baggage and then pass through customs. If you have nothing to declare, there is a good chance you can clear customs quickly and without a luggage search, but you can't rely on it. After passing through customs, you are officially in the country. If your flight is continuing to another city or you have a connecting

flight, it is your responsibility to get your bags to the right place. Normally, there are airline counters just outside the customs area that will help you.

Also see Customs & Immigration in the Facts for the Visitor chapter.

Leaving the USA

You should check in three hours early for international flights. All passengers must present photo identification at check-in. During check-in procedures, you may be asked questions about whether you have packed your own bags, whether anyone else has had access to them since you packed them and whether you have received any parcels to carry. These questions are for security reasons.

LAND
Bus

Greyhound (☎ 800-231-2222; **W** www.grey hound.com) is the main bus (coach) operator in the USA, and it's the only scheduled statewide service. In other words, Greyhound is the carless traveler's best friend, serving all major cities and many second-tier ones. But bus travel can often be tiring, inconvenient and expensive, so look at all your options.

Getting to places off Greyhound's main routes is impossible without a car. Furthermore, buses tend to run infrequently; schedules are often inconveniently timed; buses are often late; and stations are sometimes in sleazy areas. Fares can be relatively high: bargain airfares can undercut buses on long-distance routes; on shorter routes, renting a car can be cheaper. Nonetheless, long-distance bus trips are often available at bargain prices by purchasing or reserving tickets three to seven days in advance. Then, once you've arrived at your far-flung destination, you can rent a car to get around.

In an effort to boost ticket sales, Greyhound offers a series of incentive fares to a variety of locations around the country. These change frequently, so it pays to ask. Seven-day advance purchase fares from Miami to some other major US destinations (one way/roundtrip) include the following:

destination	daily frequency	duration	price
Atlanta	11	17-19 hrs	$59/118
New Orleans	5	24 hrs	$55/109
New York City	8	23-28 hrs	$69/133
Washington, DC	8	24 hrs	$69/129

Greyhound's AmeriPass is an unlimited travel pass available to anyone (not just non-US residents). It's available in seven-day ($199), 10-day ($249), 15-day ($299), 30-day ($389), 45-day ($439) and 60-day ($549) increments, but unless you're going to be doing a whole lot of travel, it's probably not worth it.

Train

Amtrak (☎ 800-872-7245; 🖥 www.amtrak .com) has been, since 1971, the US national railway system. It connects Florida with cities all over the continental USA and Canada, and two main routes serve Florida. The pricing structure is based on the date you're traveling, not just the time of year. You should always ask Amtrak if you can get a better deal by leaving a couple of days later or earlier. Having said that, in the winter months it's generally cheaper to go northbound and pricier to go southbound, and vice versa in spring. The cheapest period is usually summer.

On all Amtrak trains, each adult paying full fare can bring two children ages two to 15 for half price. Seniors 62 and over get a 15% discount on tickets. There are two types of seating: reclining, airline-style seats, and cabins. Cabins come in four flavors: single, double, family (sleeping two adults and two children under 12) and 1st-class. Cabins always command a surcharge, which varies depending on the date you're traveling.

Routes If you're coming to Florida by train from anywhere except Los Angeles, you will at some point have to connect with Amtrak's *Palmetto* or Silver Service. The *Silver Meteor* and *Silver Star* trains

run between New York City and Miami, Orlando and Tampa.

The *Silver Meteor* runs directly to Miami via Orlando; the *Silver Star* splits after Orlando: half the train's cars head to Miami, and the other half go to Tampa. The average travel time from New York City to Miami is 28 hours, to Orlando 22 hours, to Tampa 23 hours, and the cost ranges (rather unhelpfully) from $86 to $235 one-way. You can pick up the Silver Service anywhere on the route, which has stops in major cities on the East Coast. The *Silver Star* leaves New York City's Penn Station at 11:30am daily, the *Silver Meteor* at 7:05pm and the *Palmetto* at 7:45am.

From Los Angeles, the *Southwest Chief* train runs three times a week (currently on Sunday, Wednesday and Friday), passing through Phoenix, Tucson and El Paso to New Orleans and across the Panhandle to Florida's east coast, where it turns south to Miami. The train departs LA at 10:30pm and arrives in Orlando three days later at 8:45pm. For onward service to Miami, you'll have to overnight (at your own cost) in Orlando and continue the trip the next day, departing at 8:45am and arriving in Miami at 11:44am. One-way coach tickets, with reclining seats, cost $170 to $301.

Another option is the *AutoTrain*, which runs between Lorton, Virginia (near Washington, DC) to Sanford, Florida (20 miles from Orlando). The trains leave both stations at 4pm daily, arriving the following morning at 9:30am. On the *AutoTrain,* you pay for your passage, your cabin and your car separately.

Explore USA Tickets These special tickets allow you to make Miami a stopover. The peak seasons are from mid-June to early September and mid-December to early January. At press time, a 45-day Explore USA ticket cost $430 off-peak and $500 in peak season, including unlimited (but scheduled) stopovers. This is not a rail pass, though; it's a glorified roundtrip ticket, and you have to know exact dates and stops before you buy it.

Car & Motorcycle

Florida is served by three main interstate highways that connect it with the north and the west: I-95 is the main East Coast interstate, extending from Miami to Maine; I-10 extends from Jacksonville (where it intersects with I-95) west to Pensacola and onward all the way to Los Angeles; I-75 runs west from metro Miami across Alligator Alley and northward to Michigan. For a particularly rewarding drive from points west of Florida, take I-10, which passes near luscious Pensacola beaches as you cross the Florida Panhandle. Here are a few sample distances and times from other points in the USA:

city	distance	driving time
Atlanta	658 miles	11½ hours
New Orleans	863 miles	14½ hours
Washington, DC	1064 miles	18 hours
New York City	1282 miles	21½ hours
Chicago	1394 miles	23½ hours
Los Angeles	2754 miles	46 hours
San Francisco	3108 miles	52½ hours

SEA

There are very few ways to hop aboard a tramp steamer these days. Fort Lauderdale, America's largest transatlantic yacht harbor, may offer your chance. For complete information on crews, agencies, when to go, special consideration for women crew members and what to bring, see the boxed text 'Joining a Crew,' under Fort Lauderdale in the Southeast Florida chapter.

ORGANIZED TOURS

Tours of the USA are so numerous that it's impossible to include a comprehensive listing here. For overseas visitors, perhaps the most reliable sources of information on the constantly changing offerings are major international travel agents such as Thomas Cook and American Express. For those who have limited time, package tours can be an efficient and relatively inexpensive way to travel.

Trek America (☎ 973-983-1144, 800-221-0596, ⓦ www.trekamerica.com; PO Box 189, Rockaway, NJ 07866, USA; ☎ 1295-256 777, 4 Water Perry Court, Middleton Rd, Banbury, Oxon OX16 8QG, England) offers roundtrip camping tours to different areas of the country.

Adventure World (☎ 02-8913-0755, ⓦ www.adventureworld.com.au; 73 Walker St, North Sydney, NSW 2060) is the place to contact in Australia.

Suntrek (☎ 707-523-1800, 800-786-8735, ⓦ www.suntrek.com; Sun Plaza, 77 W

A Free Loaner Car

Want some temporary wheels? Try Auto Driveaway (☎ 212-967-2344; New York City), which has locations in major cities around the country, including the Washington, DC area (☎ 703-360-8250; ⓦ www.autodriveawaydc.com; Alexandria, VA) and Pennsylvania (☎ 215-540-2466, 800-351-4723; ⓦ www.autodriveawaypa.com). People who want their car moved from city A to city B, but don't have the time or inclination to do it themselves, leave it to this organization. As long as you're willing to drive from city A to city B in four days and pay for the gas (the first tank's free), the car's yours. To qualify, drivers must be 21 years old and must have a valid driver's license and one other form of ID. Non-US citizens can use an international driver's license, but must show a valid entry visa and passport as well.

Auto Driveaway requires a $300 refundable deposit (which acts as your collision damage waiver in the event of an accident) and a $15 nonrefundable registration fee. They provide $1 million of insurance. The only downside: Auto Driveaway suggests calling them 10 to 14 days prior to your intended departure date, which will put a damper on trying to get a cheap plane ticket if no car is available.

Third St, Santa Rosa, CA 95401, USA; ☎ 08024-474 490, Marktplatz 17, 83607 Holzkirchen, Germany) tours are for the 'young at heart' and attract predominantly young international travelers, although there is no age limit. They have representatives all over the world.

AmeriCan Adventures (☎ 800-864-0335 in California, ⓦ www.americanadventures.com; ☎ 1295-756 200 in Oxon, England) offers seven- to 21-day trips to different parts of the USA, usually following a theme like Route 66 or the Wild West.

Specialized Tours

Elderhostel (☎ 877-426-8056; ⓦ www.elderhostel.org; 11 Avenue de Lafayette, Boston, MA 02111) is a nonprofit organization offering educational programs for those aged 60 and above and has programs throughout the USA.

Backroads (☎ 510-527-1555, 800-462-2848; ⓦ www.backroads.com; 801 Cedar St, Berkeley, CA 94710) and companies like it have bicycling, hiking and walking, cross-country skiing, running and multisport tours.

Getting Around

The best way to get around most US states – and Florida is no exception – is by car. But most modes of transportation are possible; it might even be desirable to combine a couple of modes.

AIR

Flying within Florida is convenient if you're trying to save time (it's 650 miles from Miami to Pensacola), but the cost is usually higher than that of driving. Most airlines operating within Florida fly small commuter planes, so expect propellers!

There is service between most major cities in Florida (Pensacola and Tallahassee in the Panhandle; Jacksonville and Daytona Beach in the northeast; Gainesville and Orlando in central Florida; Tampa, Sarasota, Fort Myers and Naples in the southwest; Miami and Key West in South Florida; Fort Lauderdale and West Palm Beach in the southeast). See individual city sections for specific information.

The following main airlines operate within Florida:

American Airlines ☎ 800-433-7300
W www.aa.com

American Trans Air ☎ 800-435-9282
W www.ata.com

Continental Airlines ☎ 800-525-0280
W www.continental.com

Delta Air Lines ☎ 800-221-1212
W www.delta.com

Northwest Airlines ☎ 800-225-2525
W www.nwa.com

Southwest Airlines ☎ 800-435-9792
W www.southwest.com

US Airways ☎ 800-428-4322
W www.usairways.com

BUS

Greyhound (☎ 800-231-2222, ☎ 01342-317-317 Greyhound International in the UK; W www.greyhound.com) offers bus service between all major Florida cities. Individual city sections within this book include the telephone number and address of the local Greyhound depot. Since the permutations for itinerary planning with regards to bus routes are almost infinite, call Greyhound for specific information. It's always a bit cheaper to take the bus during the week than on the weekend. Also, fares for children are usually about half the adult fare. To get you started, here are some one-way fares and travel times around Florida:

route	duration (hours)	price
Miami to Key West	4¾	$32
Miami to Naples	3	$23
Naples to Sarasota	3-4	$26
Sarasota to Tampa	2	$11
Tampa to Orlando	2-3	$16
Miami to Fort Lauderdale	1	$5.50
Fort Lauderdale to Cocoa	5-6	$40
Cocoa to Daytona Beach	2	$16
Daytona Beach to St Augustine	1	$14
St Augustine to Jacksonville	1	$10
Jacksonville to Tallahassee	4	$28
Tallahassee to Panama City	2	$18
Panama City to Pensacola	3-4	$21

TRAIN
Amtrak

You can use Amtrak (☎ 800-872-7245; W www.amtrak.com) for intra-Florida transport for some major cities (except between Miami and Palm Beach, which is covered by Tri-Rail – see below), but it's generally more expensive and less convenient. Always inquire about special discount fares (offered only on a space-available basis), for which one-way and roundtrip tickets are usually priced the same. For destinations that require connecting bus service, don't forget, you'll have to factor in the additional expense and inconvenience of getting from Amtrak into the center of town.

The *Silver Palm* runs daily from Miami to Tampa (with stops in Fort Lauderdale and West Palm Beach and smaller towns). The trip from Miami to Tampa takes five hours and costs $38 to $73 one way, depending on the fares available at the time of purchase. Roundtrip prices are doubled. Three daily Silver Service trains run from Miami up Florida's east coast to Jacksonville (and onward up through major East Coast cities, for that matter). The Florida segment takes eight to nine hours and costs $56 to $107 one way. On Sunday, Tuesday and Thursday, the *Sunset Limited* heads from Orlando up Florida's east coast to Jacksonville (3½ hours, $22 one way), before cutting west to Tallahassee and Pensacola and onward to Los Angeles. Orlando to Pensacola takes 12 hours and costs $52 to $112.

Tri-Rail

This commuter rail system (☎ 800-874-7245, W www.tri-rail.com) runs between three Florida counties: Dade, Broward and Palm Beach (see the appropriate Getting Around sections of the Miami and Southeast Florida chapters for particulars). Folks who answer the information lines are usually quite helpful in providing details pertinent to your proposed itinerary. The double-decker trains are a marvel of cleanliness and often are very cheap; fares are calculated on a six-zone basis. However, more lengthy trips (like from Palm Beach to Miami) take about four times longer than driving.

There are Tri-Rail stations at the following: Miami Airport, Tri-Rail/Metrorail Transfer Center (in Miami's neighborhood of Hialeah), Hollywood, Fort Lauderdale Airport, Fort Lauderdale, Pompano Beach, Boca Raton, Delray Beach, Lake Worth and Palm Beach International Airport (in West Palm Beach).

CAR & MOTORCYCLE

By far the most convenient and popular way to get around Florida is by car. In fact, in many cities it's nearly impossible to get by without one. Even if you're in a small town like St Augustine, getting to a supermarket will require a car or an expensive taxi. Motorcycles are very popular in Florida, and with the exception of the rain in the summer, conditions are perfect: good flat roads and warm weather.

Overseas visitors: Unless you're coming here from Saudi Arabia or Indonesia, American gasoline prices are a gift from heaven. But remember to always use self-service gas pumps, as full-service ones cost about 25¢ more per gallon.

Road Rules

Americans drive on the right (and yes, that also means *correct*) side of the road and are supposed to pass on the left. (In Florida, that means that they pass on both sides!) Right turns on a red light are permitted after a full stop. At four-way stop signs, the car that reaches the intersection first has the right of way. If it's a tie, the car on the right has the right-of-way. Flashing yellow lights mean caution; flashing red lights mean stop. Speed limits in the city are between 15mph and 45mph. Be especially careful in school zones, which are limited to 15mph when the lights are flashing, and on causeways, which – no matter how fast cars actually travel – are limited to no more than 45mph.

Tri-Rail Rent-A-Cops

Europeans on Tri-Rail might be pleasantly reminded of home. As you wait for the train, you buy your ticket from Swiss-made ticket machines (the same ones used in U-Bahn stations throughout Germany). And when you board, it looks much the same as in Europe – basically it's the honor system, but when an inspector comes around and asks for your ticket and you don't have one, you're hit with a fine.

The key difference between Tri-Rail and metros in Europe is that the ticket inspectors come around each and every time, and they're armed and provided with hearts of stone by the Wackenhut Company, which hires them. Don't mess with Tri-Rail.

The US Highway System

There are five main categories of roads in Florida: Interstate highways are usually high-speed, multilane roads that cross several states; odd-numbered roads generally go north-south; even-numbered ones generally go east-west (in this book, interstates are abbreviated as, for example, I-95 or I-4). US highways are smaller roads that nonetheless cross several states; they are lined with businesses and have stoplights (and are abbreviated in this book as, for example, US Hwy 1). State roads are about the same size as US highways, and county roads are smaller still (both are abbreviated simply as Hwy, such as Hwy 84). Finally, there are city streets.

Most roads in Florida are excellent for driving, motorcycling, bicycling or even in-line skating: they are flat, smooth, well maintained and well signed.

Note that bicyclists and travelers using wheelchairs may be frustrated by the distinct lack of shoulders on the roads.

Florida police officers are merciless when it comes to speed-limit enforcement; see Legal Matters in the Facts for the Visitor chapter for more information on speed limits. Speeding tickets are outrageous: for example, if you're clocked at 50mph in a 40mph zone, the fine is about $150. Radar detectors are legal in Florida (hint-nudge-wink).

All passengers in a car must wear seatbelts; the fine for not wearing a seatbelt can be as high as $150. All children under three must be in a child safety seat (the rental car companies will rent you one for about $5 a day).

Parking

Always park in the shade if possible. Furthermore, it may pay to invest in a windshield shade – even a cardboard one – to filter sunlight. Cars heat up to unbelievable temperatures very quickly.

Outside cities, park wherever you want, within reason. A red-painted curb means that no parking is allowed. Parking in designated handicapped parking spaces or in front of a fire station, fire hydrant, taxi stand or police station is always illegal and your car may be towed. Believe it or not, in many cases it's also illegal to park in front of a church.

In cities, parking is often a challenge, especially in places like Miami, Miami Beach, Coral Gables, St Augustine, Ybor City in Tampa and Key West. In those places, look for metered parking or, if none is available, city or private parking lots. In city lots, parking is generally about 75¢ an hour; private lots can charge a lot more, especially during special events.

Valet parking is available at many finer restaurants and in front of hotels in Miami Beach and in Miami. It's usually at least $10.

There's always free parking in supermarkets and shopping malls, and parking is usually available for a small (perhaps $5) fee at stadiums and theme parks.

Floridians are generally careful about not knocking over bikes parked on the street, but there aren't many motorcycle-only parking lots.

Towing

If your car is towed, call the nearest police station and ask them which towing company they use. Or look for a phone number plastered on a nearby sign (that you probably ignored) that says 'if your car has been towed, call XYZ.' The tow will cost at least $80 plus the cost of the ticket to unimpound your car. It's not a pleasant experience, and the location of the towing contractor is seldom convenient.

Theft

Car theft is a popular sport in Miami and throughout South Florida, where boats to the Caribbean are waiting to ship your car off to somewhere other than your garage. If you own a car, it may pay to invest in an antitheft device like the Club. But note that in Miami some car thieves have found a simple yet effective method of getting around the Club: they hacksaw through your steering wheel.

Obviously, don't tempt thieves by leaving your keys in the car or your doors unlocked, and remove valuables from plain sight before leaving your vehicle.

So if, despite all precautions, you come back and find your car gone, call the police on a nonemergency number to see if they had it towed. If they didn't, don't hang up; report it stolen immediately.

Breakdown

Most rental cars are covered for breakdown; your rental agreement will have a toll-free breakdown number. Depending on the company, someone will come rescue you soon or next to soon. If they can't get to you

until the next day, ask if your motel costs can be covered. Even if they say no, keep your receipts for food and lodging while you wait, and take the matter up with a manager when you return the car. You may get reimbursed, or perhaps get a coupon for a free rental next time.

If you break down in a privately owned vehicle, check the Yellow Pages under 'Towing.' If you're on the road, find a pay phone, call ☎ 411 or ☎ 555-1212 for directory assistance and ask them for a towing company. If they argue and say they can't, ask for a supervisor and explain your situation. They'll usually look up a company in the Yellow Pages for you. Members of the American Automobile Association and its foreign affiliates can call ☎ 800-222-4357 (W www.aaa.com), and a tow truck will be sent out quickly.

It may pay to rent or buy a cellular telephone, especially if you'll be traveling to remote areas. Many rental car agencies rent phones for about $1 a day plus a $10 one-time rental fee, plus expensive air time ($1 per minute).

Rental

All major US car rental companies have offices throughout Florida. Rates go up and down like the stock market, and it's always worth phoning around to see what's available. Booking ahead usually ensures the best rates – and booking ahead can mean calling the company's 800 number from the pay phone in the rental office. (Sometimes the head office can get you a better price than the branch office.) If you're a member of a frequent-flyer club, be sure to check whether the rental company has a promotion with your airline. Most car rental agencies require that you be at least 25 years of age and have a major credit card in your own name.

Major rental companies in Florida include the following:

Alamo   ☎ 800-327-9633;
  W www.alamo.com
Avis   ☎ 800-831-2847;
  W www.avis.com

Road Distances from Miami

Although Miami is at the southern tip of the state, many passengers begin their travels there. For drivers, it's convenient to know the distances from Miami to various points around the state (although it's obviously highly unlikely if you've just flown into Miami that you'll be driving to Pensacola, for instance). Distances from Miami are as follows:

  22 miles to Fort Lauderdale

  39 miles to Boca Raton

  64 miles to the Palm Beaches

  141 miles to Fort Myers

  155 miles to Key West

  228 miles to Orlando

  245 miles to Tampa

  251 miles to Daytona Beach

  302 miles to St Augustine

  331 miles to Gainesville

  649 miles to Pensacola

Budget   ☎ 800-527-0700;
  🅆 www.budget.com
Dollar   ☎ 800-800-4000;
  🅆 www.dollar.com
Enterprise   ☎ 800-325-8007;
  🅆 www.enterprise.com
Hertz   ☎ 800-654-3131;
  🅆 www.hertz.com
National   ☎ 800-227-7368;
  🅆 www.nationalcar.com
Thrifty   ☎ 800-367-2277;
  🅆 www.thrifty.com

Rates & Fuel In Florida, a typical small car costs $25 to $45 a day or $129 to $229 a week. On top of that there is a 6.5% state sales tax, 9.89% airport fee (in Miami), $2.05 per day Florida road surcharge, $0.43 per day 'license recoupment charge,' and $7 to $18 a day for each insurance option you take. If you can manage it, consider renting at a nonairport location, as you'll save the exorbitant airport fees.

Generally speaking, the best deals are for weekly or weekend rentals. It pays to shop around carefully; the same car can vary from company to company by as much as $20 a day or $75 a week. If you're planning on dropping off at a different location than the one you picked up from, make certain there won't be any penalty. Enough companies offer this option that you shouldn't have to pay additional charges.

Most car rental companies in Florida include unlimited mileage at no extra cost. Be sure to check whether you get unlimited mileage, as you can rack up hundreds of miles *within* a city. At 25¢ per mile, this could be an unhappy surprise.

You may be offered a choice of 'fuel plans': You can pick up and return the car with a full tank of fuel, or you can pay for the gas that's in the car and return it empty. The full tank is always the better choice. As it's virtually impossible to return a car empty of gas, you will end up turning over several gallons of fuel to the rental company, which will then try to sell it to the next renter.

Gas stations are ubiquitous and many are open 24 hours a day. Small-town stations may be open only from 7am to 8pm or 9pm. At some stations you must pay before you pump; at others, you may pump before you pay. The more modern pumps have credit/debit card terminals built into them, so you can pay with plastic right at the pump. At more expensive, 'full service' stations, an attendant will pump your gas for you; no tip is expected. Plan on spending $1.40 to $1.60 per US gallon, more for higher-octane fuels.

Insurance Note that in Florida, liability insurance is not included in rental costs. Some credit cards cover Loss/Damage-Waiver (LDW, sometimes called CDW, or Collision/Damage Waiver), which means you won't have to pay if you damage the car itself. But liability insurance means you won't have to pay if you hit someone and they sue you. If you own a car and have insurance at home, your liability insurance may extend to coverage of rental cars, but be *absolutely* certain before driving on the roads in the litigious USA.

Note that in case of damage, a rental company might require that you not only pay for repairs, but also that you pay normal rental fees for all the time that the rental car is off the road for repairs. Your policy should cover this loss as well.

If you aren't already covered, you should pay the extra money for liability and/or LDW insurance (at $7-18 daily).

Motorcycle Rental
American Road Collection (☎ 305-871-1040; 🅆 www.budgetharley.com; 1416 18th St, Miami Beach; ☎ 954-522-2723; 1880 S Federal Hwy (US 1), Fort Lauderdale) rents motorcycles. Its fleet includes many Harley-Davidsons, including Fat Boy, Heritage Softail, Road King and Road King Classic models. Prices run from $109 to $169 a day depending on the day of the week (weekends are more expensive) and model. It also does multiday, weekly and monthly rates – for example, a Heritage Softail runs approximately $700 a week. Liability is included, but CDW is not, and it costs $25 a day. You

beds and a dinette that converts to a single bed, a bathroom with shower and a full kitchen – cost $875 a week in low season and $1095 in high season (for three weeks around Christmas). A thousand miles are included; after that you're billed 29¢ a mile. You can prepurchase additional miles at 500 miles for $130, but there is no refund for unused miles. One-way drop-off charges within Florida add another $50. Inquire about their long-term rentals and buy-back programs.

Recreational Vehicle Rental Association (RVRA; ☎ 703-591-7130, 800-336-0355; Ⓦ www.rvra.org; 3930 University Dr, Fairfax, VA 22030) is a great resource for anyone considering renting an RV. Or, consult the Yellow Pages of the phone book under 'Recreational Vehicles-Renting & Leasing,' 'Trailers-Camping & Travel' and 'Motor Homes-Renting & Leasing.'

must wear a helmet, provided by American Road Collection, out of the driveway, but they are not mandated by Florida law. Please wear one.

CruiseAmerica (☎ 800-327-7799; Ⓦ www .cruiseamerica.com) has several Florida locations and rents Honda motorcycles from $149 to $179 per day, including unlimited mileage, CDW and liability insurance. Helmets are also mandatory with CruiseAmerica. Renters must be over 21, have a valid motorcycle license and a credit card.

RV Rental
A recreational vehicle (RV) can be a great way to get out into Florida. Renting an RV makes sense if you meet one of two conditions: a) you're as rich as Croesus or b) there are several of you. RVs are surprisingly roomy and flexible, and even the smaller ones can sleep four comfortably – as long as you're close friends. If you're not, don't despair: many RV sites are large enough to accommodate the RV and still leave room for a tent outside.

The downside is you'll probably need additional transportation when you get where you're going. At an average highway gas consumption of between 8 and 10 miles per gallon, RVs are not exactly a good method of city transport. You can, of course, get a bicycle rack or, if you also have a car, a tow-hitch to bring it along, but that makes your already dismal gas mileage even worse.

CruiseAmerica (☎ 800-327-7799; Ⓦ www .cruiseamerica.com) is the largest and best known of the nationwide RV-rental firms. It has a huge variety of rentals available. The standard – 21 to 25 feet with two double

Car & Motorcycle Purchase
One way to beat the high cost of renting a car is to buy a used vehicle on arrival and then sell it when you leave. If you go this route, it helps to either have a bit of the auto mechanic in you or to find a mechanic you can trust; you won't get much return value on a 'lemon' or a gas guzzler. Don't ask yourself, 'Do I feel lucky?' because even minor repairs could cost well over $250.

Any used-car owner who won't bring or let you take the car to a mechanic is hiding something. While you're there, tell the mechanic how much the seller wants for it, and if things look good, ask them to run an emissions test – it's no good finding out after you've bought it that the car won't pass state emissions levels. As a general idea of how much you'll spend on that, **Shorty & Fred's Garage** (☎ 305-672-1047; Miami Beach) will check out a car from top to bottom for $65.

Once you've bought the car, you must buy a rather costly auto insurance policy (generally $600 to $900 a year, depending on your age and driving record) and take the smog certificate and proof of insurance, along with the ownership title and bill of sale, to any office of the Department of Motor Vehicles (DMV). For full listings, check in the blue government section of the white pages under Florida State Department of Highways and Motor Vehicles. It normally takes a full morning or afternoon to get your auto registration, which costs anywhere from 7% to 12% of the cost of the car.

As your departure from the USA approaches, you must set aside time to sell the car, which could require laying out additional money to place a classified ad in a newspaper.

If you don't object to a little wind, you might consider buying a motorcycle, which is cheaper than a car and tends to be easier to sell. But note that motorcycle insurance costs more. Although helmets are not required by Florida law, you really should wear one.

BICYCLE

If you can stand the heat, Florida's not a bad place for cycling. Absolutely flat roads make it easy going, and biking is a convenient mode of transportation. Helmets are not required under Florida law, but they're a good idea, as are highly reflective everything-you-can-think-of. Since Florida drivers are not used to seeing bicyclists, the more you can do to make them see you, the better chance you have of getting where you're going.

If you do get tired of biking, you can pack your bike. Most international airlines, and flights within Florida, allow you to bring a bike at no extra charge as checked luggage. They charge a fee ($50 to $100) if it's in addition to your checked-luggage limit. Bike boxes cost about $10 if you buy them from an airline, Greyhound or Amtrak (but Amtrak doesn't always require them – it depends on the route). You'll have to remove the handlebars and pedals to box it, but you may also get away with bagging it. Greyhound charges an additional $15 extra for your boxed bike.

Many cities in Florida have outlets for bicycle rentals – at hostels, hotels, resorts or bike shops. Sports Authority, Sears, K-Mart and Wal-Mart all carry bicycle parts, so if you're in a town without a bike shop, there's still reason to hope.

Bicyclists are charged $1 each for admission to most state parks.

Especially in Miami Beach, where bicycle theft is common, make certain to lock your bike. If you can remove the front wheel and take it with you, do so. Also remove the seat if it has a quick-release height adjust. Use a sturdy U-type lock, not a chain and padlock.

Organizations & Resources

State organizations include the **Florida Bicycle Association** (w www.floridabicycle .org; PO Box 1547, Orlando, FL 32802) and the **Office of the State Bicycle/Pedestrian Coordinator** (☎ 850-410-4927; w www11.my florida.com/safety; Florida Department of Transportation, 605 S Suwannee St, MS 82, Tallahassee, FL 32399-0450).

Bike Florida (☎ 407-343-1992 ; w www .bikeflorida.org; PO Box 451514, Kissimmee, FL 34745) is the best all-around source for information about bicycling in the state. They'll assist with reservations for accommodations, help you plan itineraries, and counsel you on the realities of a bike trip through Florida.

For further information, see the Bicycling section in the Outdoor Activities chapter.

HITCHHIKING

It is never entirely safe to hitchhike anywhere in the world, and we don't recommend it. Travelers who decide to hitchhike should understand that they are taking a small but potentially serious risk – creeps and criminals might see a hitchhiker as easy prey.

Universities have ride-sharing programs, as well as bulletin boards, which can be a useful alternative, especially at the end of semesters and during school holidays. Once you arrive in Florida, check for rides to or near where you're headed.

In Fort Lauderdale and in several of Florida's larger counties, there are share-a-ride programs designed to assist commuters. They can act, in a pinch, as the American equivalent of the German *Mitfahrzentrale* – a central source that pairs up drivers and passengers. You'll have to chip in for gas and tolls, and it usually doesn't work for very long distances.

BOAT

There's water-taxi service in Fort Lauderdale, which you should take simply because its fun to see Fort Lauderdale from the Intracoastal Waterway. See that Getting There & Away section for more information.

Each coastal city, of course, has sightseeing boats that cruise harbors and coastlines. And it really pays (in memories) to get out on the water.

Florida is a world center for two major types of boat transport: crewing aboard privately owned yachts and the fast-growing cruise ship industry. See the boxed text 'Joining a Crew,' under Fort Lauderdale in the Southeast Florida chapter, for information on crewing.

Cruises

A number of Web sites specialize in cruising, a multibillion-dollar business. Check out the following, and look for last minute specials for multi-night and -day cruises:

W www.cruise.com

W www.vacationstogo.com

W www.bestpricescruises.com

W www.cheapncl.com

W www.cruisesonly.com

Here is a list of some of the lines cruising out of Florida:

Carnival Cruise Lines ☎ 800-327-9501;
 W www.carnival.com

Celebrity Cruises ☎ 800-437-3111;
 W www.celebritycruises.com

Cunard Line ☎ 800-528-6273;
 W www.cunard.com

Disney Cruise Line ☎ 800-951-3532;
 W www.disneycruise.disney.go.com

Holland America ☎ 800-426-0327;
 W www.hollandamerica.com

Norwegian Cruise Line ☎ 800-327-7030;
 W www.ncl.com

Princess Cruises ☎ 800-421-0522;
 W www.princesscruises.com

Royal Caribbean ☎ 800-327-6700;
 W www.royalcaribbean.com

Royal Olympic Cruises ☎ 800-368-3888;
 W www.royalolympiccruises.com

Sea Escape Cruises ☎ 800-327-2005;
 W www.seaescape.com

Port of Miami The Port of Miami (W www.co.miami-dade.fl.us/portofmiami/so_cruise.htm), on Dodge Island just south of the MacArthur Causeway, is the largest cruise-ship port in the world, serving more than three million passengers yearly. You can book everything from simple day trips to elaborate round-the-world voyages. The most common are three-day cruises to the Bahamas, and four- and seven-day trips to Caribbean ports of call like San Juan, Puerto Rico, and the islands of St Thomas, St John and St Martin.

Rates fluctuate daily and a number of discounts apply – they're yours for the asking…so ask. The definition of cruise high season (summertime and during school vacations) and cruise low season (winter, with the exception of holidays) varies with each carrier; low-season prices can be 15% to 30% less than high season. Port charges and taxes are included in the following high-season prices, which should simply be used as a basis for comparison and are based on double occupancy. Following are the major cruise operators.

The most popular line, **Carnival Cruise Lines** (☎ 305-599-2600) offers three-night tours (Friday to Monday) on the *Fascination* visiting Nassau, Bahamas. An inside cabin (category four) costs $370 per person, while large suites (category 12) run $790 per person. A four-night cruise (Monday to Friday) on the *Imagination* to Key West and Cozumel, Mexico, runs $510 per person for an inside cabin, $1040 per person for a large suite.

Norwegian Cruise Line (☎ 305-436-4000) is the leader in 'freestyle cruising,' which provides greater flexibility in meal times, dress codes and tipping options. Three-night tours aboard the *Majesty* to the Bahamas run from $290 (category L, the cheapest inside cabin) to $320 (category HH, the cheapest outer cabin with a picture window) per person. Four-night *Majesty* voyages to Key West and Cozumel run from $340 to $395 per person. Note that this ship only sails from mid-November to mid-April.

Royal Caribbean (☎ 305-539-6000) offers three-night Bahamas trips on the *Majesty of the Seas,* which run from $375 (category Q, inside) to $1200 (category C, with a verandah) per person. The seven-night Eastern Caribbean cruise aboard the very nice *Explorer of the Seas* is $1175 to $1625 per person.

Port Canaveral As the closest port to Orlando, **Port Canaveral** (☎ 321-783-7831, 888-767-8226; ⓦ www.portcanaveral.org) has been giving Miami a run for its money as the number-one port in the world since Scandinavian World Cruises established a home base here in 1982. Its mainstay is popular three- and four-night cruises with the Carnival, Norwegian, Disney, Holland America and Royal Caribbean lines.

Port Everglades The third-busiest port after Miami and Port Canaveral, **Port Everglades** (☎ 954-523-3404; ⓦ www.broward .org/port; 18050 Eller Drive, Fort Lauderdale) offers a very similar range of cruises. Day trips to the Bahamas are quite popular. For one-stop shopping out of Port Everglades, contact ⓦ www.fort-lauderdale-cruises.com. The following cruise companies operate out of Port Everglades: Celebrity,

Cunard, Holland America, Princess, Royal Caribbean, Royal Olympic and Sea Escape.

Tampa The **Port of Tampa** (☎ 813-905-7678, 800-741-2297; ⓦ www.tampaport.com; 1101 Channelside Dr) is still a small player by Florida standards, but it's rapidly gaining a foothold in the market with half a million passengers projected to pass through terminal turnstiles in 2002–03. Currently it has berths for Carnival Cruise Lines, Celebrity Cruises, Holland America and Royal Caribbean. For details on Carnival and Holland America cruises, see Activities under Tampa in the Southwest Florida chapter.

PUBLIC TRANSPORTATION
Local bus service is available only in larger cities; generally, bus fare is between 75¢ and $1.25. Fares in Florida are paid as you board (you always board through the front doors), and exact change is usually required, though some buses take $1 bills. Transfers – slips of paper that will allow you to change buses – range from free to 25¢. Operating hours differ from city to city, but generally buses run from about 6am to 10pm.

Wheelchair-bound passengers should contact the local bus company to inquire about special transport services. Most buses in Florida are wheelchair accessible, though some bus companies offer individual transit services in addition to regular service for those with physical or mental disabilities. See the Facts for the Visitor chapter for information on organizations that assist with travel for the disabled.

Miami & Miami Beach

There's more to Miami than sex in South Beach. Certainly, this city is sultry. It attracts a wildly diverse cauldron of pleasure-seekers – happy hedonists who'd rather gyrate the night away (not to mention the dawn!) at discos and doze on the beach during the day than go to a museum. And there are plenty of justifiably trendy and wonderfully shallow reasons why exotic models, celebrities and *you* are drawn to SoBe's circuit of chichi nightclubs, mod martini bars, sophisticated restaurants and renovated art deco hotels. When we say it's the hottest and steamiest city in America, we're not just talking weather.

And yet, if you limit yourself to sensuous pastimes and don't venture beyond the physical and psychological parameters of South Beach, you'll miss the outrageously opulent Coconut Grove villas and the industrial chic of the seedy Miami River area; diverse contemporary art collections and the haunting Holocaust Memorial; Little Havana's religious *botánicas*, funky monkeys and performing parrots.

HISTORY

Miami Beach and Miami are very new cities, even by American standards. They were developed mainly during the 20th century.

The City's Beginnings

In 1895, a record freeze enveloped most of the north of Florida, where Henry Flagler's railroads were bringing thousands of wealthy Northerners to stay at his hotels and resorts. The freeze wiped out citrus crops and sent vacationers scurrying, and legend has it that Julia Tuttle (who owned large tracts of property here and had approached Flagler with the offer of partnership in exchange for the extension of his railroad to Miami, which he'd refused) went into her garden, snipped off some orange blossoms and sent them to Flagler, who then hightailed it down to Miami.

What he found was a tropical paradise that was very warm indeed. Flagler and Tuttle came to terms, and Flagler announced the extension of the railroad. Not long after, thousands of people whose livelihoods had been wiped out by the big freeze – including citrus growers and workers, and service

Highlights

- Take a walking tour of South Beach's delightful and colorful Deco District

- Visit the Holocaust Memorial in South Beach for a sobering but stunning reminder of WWII atrocities

- Take a refreshing dip in Coral Gables' extraordinarily beautiful Venetian Pool

- Hop aboard the Metromover at dusk to fully appreciate downtown Miami's neon buildings at night

- Head to Little Havana to watch old men rolling cigars in small 'factories' or playing dominoes in Domino Park on SW 8th St (Calle Ocho)

- Drink in the splendor of Coconut Grove's opulent Italian Renaissance–style villa, the Vizcaya Museum & Gardens

- Enjoy a panoply of outdoor pursuits at Key Biscayne's Bill Baggs Cape Florida State Recreation Area

industry professionals such as doctors and merchants – headed down to Miami in anticipation of the boom that was to come.

Passenger train service to Miami began April 22, 1896, the year the city of Miami became incorporated. The wave peaked during WWI, when the US military established an aviation training facility here. Many of the thousands who came to work and train here also settled in the area.

After the war, the first full-fledged Miami boom (1923–25) was fueled not just by the area's idyllic beachfront location and perfect weather, but also by gambling and a lax implementation of Prohibition. Though it was illegal, liquor flowed freely throughout the entire Prohibition period.

But the boom was cut short by a devastating hurricane, which was immediately followed by a statewide recession and national depression. After the boom, though, Miami remained a favorite haunt of gangsters. Al Capone's Palm Island mansion was a pleasure palace, and he wasn't alone.

In the mid-1930s, a mini-boom resulted in the creation and development of Miami Beach's famous art deco buildings. This reasonably prosperous period continued until 1942, when a German U-boat sank a US tanker off Florida's coast. The ensuing reaction created a full-scale conversion of South Florida into a massive military base, training facility and staging area. Miami Beach's hotels were full of soldiers, who marched up and down the beach in full combat gear.

The 1950s Boom

In the 1950s, Miami Beach had another boom, as the area became known as the 'Cuba of America.' Gamblers and gangsters, enticed by Miami's gaming, as well as by its proximity to the fun, sun and fast times of Batista-run Cuba, moved in en masse. Even a hurricane didn't discourage people *that* much.

Racial Tensions

In 1954, Leroy Collins became the first Southern governor to declare racial segregation 'morally wrong.' But despite the declaration, Miami's record of harmonious race relations has not been altogether impressive. Blacks were segregated to an area north of downtown known as Colored Town, later called Overtown. And in the 1950s, as the city grew, many were displaced to the federal housing projects at Liberty City, a misnomer if ever there was one. (See Elsewhere in Miami later in this chapter for more information.)

During 1965, the two 'freedom flights' that ran daily between Miami and Havana disgorged more than 100,000 Cuban refugees. Sensing the tension that was building between blacks and Cubans, Dr Martin Luther King, Jr pleaded with the two sides not to let animosity lead to bloodshed.

Riots and skirmishes broke out nonetheless, and acts of gang-style violence occurred. But not all were caused by simmering Cuban/black tensions: Whites got into the fray as well. In 1968, a riot broke out after two white police officers arrested a 17-year-old black male, stripped him naked and hung him by his ankles from a bridge.

In 1970, the 'rotten meat' riot began when blacks picketed a white-owned shop they had accused of selling spoiled meat. After three days of picketing, white officers attempted to disperse the crowds and fired on them with tear gas. During the 1970s, there were 13 other race-related violent confrontations.

The Mariel Boatlift (see the History section in the Facts about Florida chapter) brought 150,000 Cubans to Florida. This included an estimated 25,000 prisoners and mental patients that Fidel had cleverly decided to foist off on the Cuban-American population. The resulting strain on the economy, logistics and infrastructure of South Florida only added to still-simmering racial tensions.

Miami's racial tensions would explode on May 17, 1980, when four white police officers, being tried on charges that they beat a black suspect to death while he was in custody, were acquitted by an all-white jury. When the verdict was announced, severe race riots broke out all over Miami and lasted for three days. The riots resulted in 18 deaths, $80 million in property damage and 1100 arrests.

The 1980s

In the indulgent 1980s, the area gained prominence as the major East Coast entry port for drug dealers, their products and the unbelievable sums of money that went along with them. As if to keep up, many savings and loans (S&Ls) opened here in newly built headquarters. While *Newsweek* magazine called Miami 'America's Casablanca,' locals dubbed it the 'City with the S&L Skyline.' Downtown was completely reborn while in the grip of drug smugglers. Shootouts were common, as were gangland slayings by cocaine cowboys. The police, Coast Guard, Drug Enforcement Agency (DEA), Border Patrol and FBI were in a tizzy trying to keep track of it all.

Then it happened: *Miami Vice.*

The show starred Don Johnson and Philip Michael Thomas as two narcotics detectives dressed in outrageously expensive (and yet pastel-colored) outfits driving around in a Ferrari Testarossa and million-dollar cigarette boats. It was single-handedly responsible for Miami Beach rising to international attention in the mid-1980s. The show's unique look, slick soundtrack and music video–style montages glamorized the rich South Florida lifestyle. Before long, people were coming down to check it out for themselves.

Photographer Bruce Weber began using South Beach as a grittily fashionable backdrop for modeling shoots in the early 1980s, leading to imitators and eventually to the situation that exists today: model-jam.

By the late 1980s, Miami Beach had risen to international Fabulousness. Celebrities were wintering in Miami, international photographers were shooting here, and the Art Deco District, having been granted federal protection, was going through a renovation and renaissance. A city filled with drug addicts was fast becoming a showpiece of fashion and trendiness.

The Roaring '90s & Beyond

Miami rode the peak of a boom during most of the 1990s. The city hosted the Summit of the Americas in 1994 (everyone attended but Castro), celebrated its centennial in 1996 and jumped for joy as the US military moved its Central and South American command center to Miami. Hurricane Andrew barely affected the tourist industry, which is the city's economic backbone. And despite highly publicized crimes against tourists in 1993, Miami is now the third most popular city for international tourists after Los Angeles and New York.

As the very fabulous South Beach scene sprouted, so did a drug-dependent club culture. Ecstasy, ketamine and GHB were as popular as topless models. It finally got so bad in the late 1990s that the police couldn't avoid it any longer and started cracking down. While politicians knew the value of clubs to the local economy, they didn't want to be seen as condoning drug use. Very popular clubs were closed. These days, if Miami Beach won't issue 24-hour liquor licenses, the city of Miami will. New clubs are springing up downtown, but there have been problems with policing. The saga continues. One-ton drug busts regularly feed nightly news reports.

The highly publicized murder of fashion designer Gianni Versace in 1997 stunned the celebrity world and once again brought negative media coverage to the area (see the Miami Beach section for more information). Yet still the boom continued. Creeping gentrification has made inroads, and South Beach has long since left the growing stages of a funky, hip destination and become a multinational hot spot. Small, family-run shops and restaurants are out, the Gap and Starbucks are in.

What Now? How long the boom will last is subject to conjecture but not really to heated debate. To be sure, South Beach simultaneously excels at reinventing itself and maintaining a central core. Gay travelers are very loyal; the sun still shines and the beach is still golden; hotels get groovier by the minute; kitchens churn out celebrity chefs faster than one-minute eggs; and the club scene stays hot to the Touch, distinct like Rain and Liquid, morphing faster than you can BED Lola (see Entertainment for more on these clubs).

On the one hand, more people than ever are coming. Miami remains the hottest American city, and Americans always relish a good night on the town. On the other hand, though, there are murmurs among Europeans and the supermodel crowd that South Beach is imploding and getting – gasp – passé.

Locals are not worried. After the film, TV and European fashion shoots are over; after the Stallones and Schwarzeneggers, Rosies and Madonnas, and the thousands who swarm the neon-emblazoned cafés and boutiques of SoBe depart, South Beach will still be here. And it will be better than ever.

ORIENTATION

The city of Miami covers an enormous, sprawling area that's subdivided into neighborhoods and sections and is adjacent to several cities. Miami is on the mainland, while the city of Miami Beach is on a thin barrier island about 3 miles east, across Biscayne Bay.

South Beach (Maps 3 & 4)

The southern part of the city of Miami Beach encompasses the widest section of the island. Streets run east-west, avenues run north-south. Unlike the city of Miami, major arteries (Washington, Collins, Alton and Ocean) are named rather than numbered. There are no directional sectors such as NW or SE.

Washington Ave is the bustling main drag, and Collins Ave is the famous deco hotel–lined thoroughfare. The chic outdoor cafés and restaurants along Ocean Drive overlook the wide Atlantic beach shorefront.

Alton Rd is the utilitarian main drag on the west side, gaining in popularity as the sexier eastern end becomes more and more crowded.

Lincoln Road is pedestrian-only between Washington Ave and Alton Rd.

South Pointe is below 5th St at the southern tip of Miami Beach, directly across Government Cut from Fisher Island.

Northern Miami Beach (Map 5)

Northern Miami Beach (which for our mapping purposes lies north of the Collins Canal) should not be confused with an entirely different city on the mainland called North Miami Beach. Indian Creek separates Collins Ave, almost exclusively lined with high-rise condominiums and luxury hotels, from the residential districts at the west. Alton Rd winds through this exclusive neighborhood and connects with Collins Ave at 63rd St.

The official northern border of Miami Beach is 96th St. But for our purposes we've mapped a large stretch of the beach – including the neighborhoods of Surfside, Bal Harbour, Sunny Isles and some of Golden Beach.

Downtown Miami (Map 6)

Downtown Miami is a fairly straightforward grid, with Flagler St as much the main drag as any. The downtown area is divided by the lazy Miami River, which is crossed by the Brickell Ave Bridge. Biscayne Blvd runs north from the river, and Brickell Ave runs south of it; both are on the eastern side of the district.

The north-south divider is Flagler St, and the east-west divider is Miami Ave; prefixes are given to streets – N, S, E, W, NW, NE, SW, SE – based on that street's position relative to the intersection of Flagler St and Miami Ave.

Most avenues and streets are numbered: Avenues begin at 1st and count upward the farther east and west they are from Miami Ave, so E 1st Ave would be one block east of Miami Ave, while W 42nd Ave would be 42 blocks west of Miami Ave. Streets are numbered similarly, increasing in number progressively the farther north or south of Flagler St they are, so N 1st St would be one block north of Flagler St etc.

Key Biscayne (Map 7)

The Rickenbacker Causeway ($1 toll), with exits off US Hwy 1 and I-95 and most directly accessible from Biscayne Blvd, leads over to Key Biscayne. It turns into Crandon Park Blvd, the key's only real main road, which runs all the way to the southernmost tip and the Cape Florida Lighthouse.

Little Havana (Map 8)

Calle Ocho, or SW 8th St, doesn't just cut *through* the heart of the neighborhood, it *is* the heart of the neighborhood. For the purposes of our exploration, the neighborhood extends roughly from W Flagler St to SW 13th St and from SW 3rd Ave to SW 37th Ave. The Miami River separates Little Havana from downtown on the northeast border.

Coconut Grove (Map 9)

The Grove unfolds along S Bayshore Dr (south of the Rickenbacker Causeway). S Bayshore hugs the shoreline and becomes McFarlane Rd as you approach the main part of town, where it then becomes Main Hwy and eventually leads to Douglas Rd (SW 37th Ave), Ingraham Hwy, Old Cutler Rd and attractions in South Dade. US Hwy 1 acts as the northern boundary for the Grove.

Coral Gables (Map 10)

The lovely Mediterranean-style city of Coral Gables is essentially bordered by Calle Ocho to the north, Sunset Dr (SW 72nd St/Hwy 986) to the south, Le Jeune Rd (SW 42nd Ave) to the east and Red Rd (SW 57th Ave/Hwy 959) to the west. US Hwy 1 slashes through at a 45-degree angle from northeast to southwest. The main campus of the University of Miami is located just south of the enormous Coral Gables Biltmore Golf Course, north of US Hwy 1. The address system in Coral Gables is bass-ackwards when compared to Miami; avenues here run east-west, while streets run north-south.

Maps

All rental car companies are required by law to hand out decent city and area maps when they rent a car. Rand McNally, AAA and Dolph Map Company all make maps of the Miami area. Lonely Planet produces a laminated foldout map of the Miami area that includes Key West and Fort Lauderdale. The best free map is from the Greater Miami & the Beaches Convention & Visitor's Bureau (see below).

INFORMATION
Tourist Offices

The Greater Miami & the Beaches Convention & Visitor's Bureau (☎ 305-539-3000, 800-933-8448, W www.miamiandbeaches .com; Map 6) has luxurious headquarters on the 27th floor of 701 Brickell Ave, a five-minute walk south of the Miami River. The office is open 8:30am to 5pm Monday to Friday.

Run by the Miami Design Preservation League (MDPL), the Art Deco Welcome Center (☎ 305-672-2014, W www.mdpl.org; Map 4), 1001 Ocean Dr, has tons of Deco District information. It's open 10am to 10pm daily. The MDPL also organizes walking tours of the District (see Organized Tours later in this chapter).

The informative Miami Beach Chamber of Commerce (☎ 305-672-1270, W www .miamibeachchamber.com; Map 3), 1920 Meridian Ave, is open 9am to 5pm Monday to Friday.

The Coconut Grove Chamber of Commerce (☎ 305-444-7270, W www.coconut grove.com; Map 9), 2820 McFarlane Rd, is open 9am to 5pm Monday to Friday.

Coral Gables Chamber of Commerce (☎ 305-446-1657, W www.gableschamber .org; Map 10), inside the Omni-Colonnade Hotel, at 2333 Ponce de León Blvd, Suite 650, is open 9am to 5pm Monday to Friday.

The Black Archives History & Research Center of South Florida (☎ 305-636-2390; Map 2), at 5400 NW 22nd Ave, Suite 101, in Liberty City, has information about black culture and can arrange tours of Liberty City and other areas of Miami.

Money

Bank of America has branch offices all over Miami and Miami Beach. Some private exchange offices include American Express (☎ 305-358-7350, 100 N Biscayne Blvd; Map 6); Thomas Cook (☎ 305-285-2348, 800-287-7362, 80 N Biscayne Blvd; Map 6); and SunTrust Bank (☎ 305-591-6000, 777 Brickell Ave) and (☎ 305-591-6743, 1111 Lincoln Road; Map 3).

Continued on page 146

1 Wings Over Miami
2 X-Treme Rock Climbing
3 Gold Coast Railroad
  Museum
4 Miami Metrozoo
5 Miami-Homestead-
  Everglades KOA
6 Monkey Jungle
7 Bur's Berry Farm
8 Cutler Ridge Mall;
  Greyhound Bus Station
9 Fruit & Spice Park
10 Knauss Berry Farm
11 Coral Castle

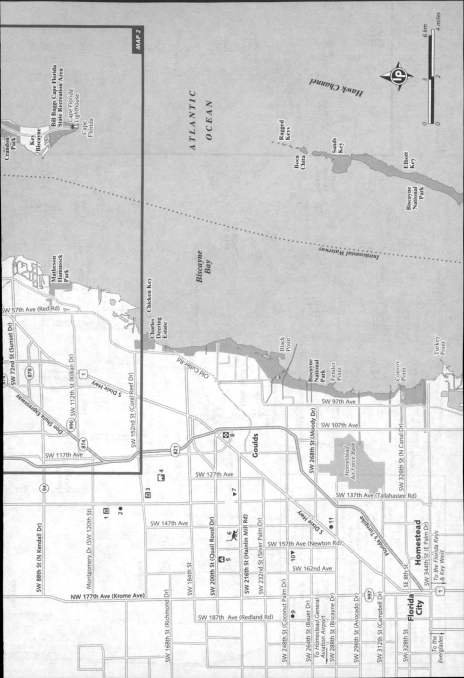

ATLANTIC OCEAN

Hawk Channel

Ragged Keys

Sands Key

Boca Chita

Elliott Key

Biscayne National Park

Bill Baggs Cape Florida State Recreation Area
Cape Florida Lighthouse
Cape Florida
Key Biscayne
Crandon Park

MAP 2

Matheson Hammock Park

Biscayne Bay

Charles Chicken Key

Charles / Chicken Key
Charles Deering Estate

Intracoastal Waterway

Black Point

Biscayne National Park
Fender Point

Convoy Point

Turkey Point

SW 57th Ave (Red Rd)

Old Cutler Rd

S Dixie Hwy

SW 112th St (Killian Dr)

SW 152nd St (Coral Reef Dr)

SW 72nd St (Sunset Dr)

Don Shula Expressway

878

990

874

SW 117th Ave

SW 97th Ave

SW 107th Ave

SW 268th St (Moody Dr)

821

8

Goulds

94

4

3

1

2

Montgomery Dr (SW 120th St)

SW 127th Ave

SW 137th Ave (Tallahassee Rd)

Homestead Air Force Base

SW 328th St (N Canal Rd)

SW 147th Ave

7

SW 88th St (N Kendall Dr)

SW 200th St (Quail Roost Dr)

6

5

S Dixie Hwy

11

Florida's Turnpike

SW 216th St (Hainlin Mill Rd)

SW 232nd St (Silver Palm Dr)

SW 157th Ave (Newton Rd)

10

SW 162nd Ave

Homestead

SE 8th St (E Palm Dr)

To the Florida Keys & Key West

1

NW 177th Ave (Krome Ave)

SW 184th St

SW 168th St (Richmond Dr)

SW 187th Ave (Redland Rd)

9

SW 248th St (Coconut Palm Dr)

SW 264th St (Bauer Dr)
To Homestead General Aviation Airport

SW 288th St (Biscayne Dr)

SW 296th St (Avocado Dr)

SW 312th St (Campbell Dr)

997

SW 328th St

SW 344th St (E Palm Dr)

Florida City

To the Everglades

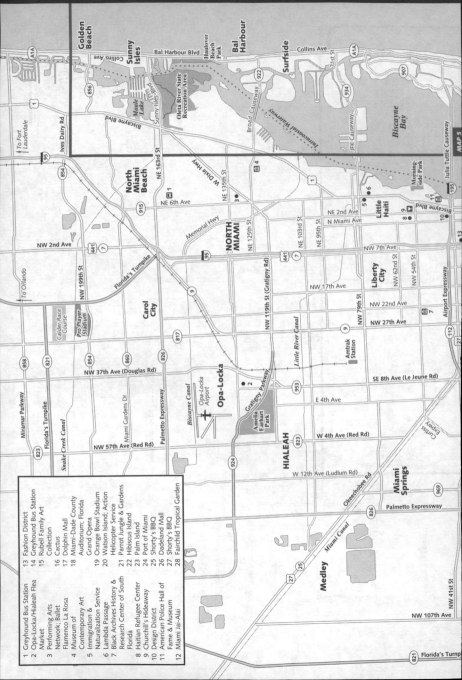

MAP 2 MIAMI

MAP 5

MAP 5

Golden
Beach

Sunny
Isles

Bal Harbour Blvd

Bal
Harbour

Surfside

Collins Ave

Haulover
Beach
Park

Collins Ave

71st St

A1A

907

934

922

Oleta River State
Recreation Area

Broad Causeway

Intracoastal Waterway

JFK Causeway

Biscayne
Bay

Julia Tuttle Causeway

195

13

A1A

1

To Fort
Lauderdale

Ives Dairy Rd

95

886

Maule
Lake

Sunny Isles Blvd

Biscayne Blvd

North
Miami
Beach

NE 163rd St

W Dixie Hwy

854

915

NE 6th Ave

4

1

Morning-
side Park

6
5

5

Little
Haiti

8

10

11

Biscayne Blvd

NW 2nd Ave

441

7

Memorial Hwy

NE 135th St

NORTH
MIAMI

NE 125th St

3

NE 103rd St

N Miami Ave

NE 95th St

NW 7th Ave

Liberty
City

NW 62nd St

NW 54th St

Airport Expressway

To Orlando

NW 199th St

Florida's Turnpike

95

441

7

NW 17th Ave

NW 119th St (Gratigny Rd)

NW 79th St

NW 22nd Ave

NW 27th Ave

112

27

858

821

Calder Race
Course

Pro Player
Stadium

Carol
City

9

817

Little River Canal

9

953

Amtrak
Station

7

SE 8th Ave (Le Jeune Rd)

Miramar Parkway

Florida's Turnpike

823

Snake Creek Canal

854

860

826

NW 37th Ave (Douglas Rd)

Miami Gardens Dr

Palmetto Expressway

Biscayne Canal

Opa-Locka
Airport

Opa-Locka

2

Gratigny Parkway

Amelia
Earhart
Park

E 4th Ave

Curtiss
Expwy

NW 57th Ave (Red Rd)

924

HIALEAH

823

W 4th Ave (Red Rd)

W 12th Ave (Ludlum Rd)

Miami
Springs

969

Okeechobee Rd

826

Palmetto Expressway

Medley

Miami Canal

25

27

NW 41st Ave

NW 107th Ave

821

Florida's Turnp

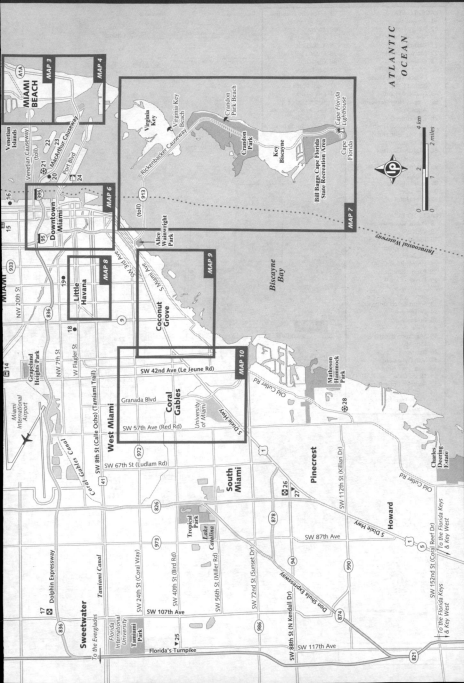

ATLANTIC OCEAN

MAP 3
MAP 4

Venetian Islands
Venetian Causeway (toll)
21
22 MacArthur Causeway
23
20 Port Blvd
24

A1A
MIAMI BEACH

Virginia Key
Virginia Key Beach
Crandon Park Beach

Rickenbacker Causeway

Crandon Park

Cape Florida Lighthouse

Key Biscayne

Bill Baggs Cape Florida State Recreation Area
Cape Florida

MAP 7

Intracoastal Waterway

4 km
2 miles
2
1
0
0

16
15
933
395
95
MAP 6
Downtown Miami
913 (toll)

Alice Wainwright Park

MIAMI
NW 20th St
836
9
MAP 8
Little Havana
SW 3rd Ave
S Miami Ave
19
18

MAP 9
Coconut Grove

Biscayne Bay

14
Miami International Airport
Grapeland Heights Park
NW 7th St
W Flagler St

MAP 10

SW 42nd Ave (Le Jeune Rd)

Granada Blvd
Coral Gables
University of Miami
SW 57th Ave (Red Rd)
S Dixie Hwy

Old Cutler Rd
Matheson Hammock Park
28
Charles Deering Estate

West Miami
SW 8th St (Calle Ocho) (Tamiami Trail)
41
972
SW 67th St (Ludlam Rd)
Coral Gables Canal

826
973
South Miami
Tropical Park
Lake Catalina
878
26
27
Pinecrest
SW 112th St (Killian Dr)

Howard
SW 87th Ave
S Dixie Hwy
1
5
To the Florida Keys & Key West

17
Dolphin Expressway
Sweetwater
Tamiami Canal
To the Everglades
836
Florida International University
Tamiami Park
25
Florida's Turnpike

SW 24th St (Coral Way)
SW 40th St (Bird Rd)
SW 56th St (Miller Rd)
SW 72nd St (Sunset Dr)
Don Shula Expressway
94
SW 107th Ave
SW 8th St (N Kendall Dr)
986
874
SW 117th Ave
990
SW 152nd St (Coral Reef Dr)
To the Florida Keys & Key West
821

MAP 3 SOUTH BEACH (11TH TO 23RD ST)

PLACES TO STAY
1 Banana Bungalow
12 Abbey Hotel
14 The Dorchester Hotel
21 Raleigh Hotel
22 Marseilles Hotel
39 Greenview
40 Crest Hotel Suites
42 Delano Hotel; David Barton Gym
43 National Hotel
62 Tropics Hotel & Hostel
63 Aqua Hotel
75 Clay Hotel & International Hostel
83 Nassau Suite Hotel
85 Villa Paradiso
86 Brigham Gardens Guesthouse
95 Cardozo Hotel; Café Cardozo
99 Hotel Impala; Spiga
104 The Tides
112 Kent Hotel

59 El Rancho Grande
65 Pollo Tropical
68 Tantra
71 Pizza Rustica
76 Kafka Kafé
78 Osteria del Teatro
80 Grillfish
81 San Loco
84 La Sandwicherie
87 Front Porch Cafe
94 Escopazzo
97 Toni's Sushi Bar
103 Les Deux Fontaines
110 Thai House
111 Mark's South Beach

PLACES TO EAT
8 Publix Supermarket
13 Wolfie's
16 Joe Allen Miami Beach
24 Epicure Market
25 Ice Box Cafe
26 Lincoln Road Café
28 Pacific Time
29 David's Cafe II
30 Paninoteca
32 Spris
33 South Beach Stone Crabs
34 La Terrasse
36 Rosinella
37 Yuca
45 Segafredo Zanetti Espresso
46 Balans
47 Van Dyke Cafe
48 Van Dyke News
51 Nexxt Cafe
52 Joffrey's Coffee Co
54 Sushi Samba
57 Texas Taco Factory; Pucci's Pizza

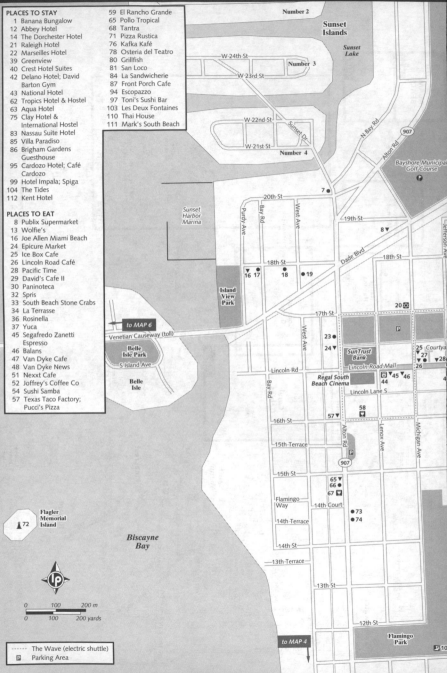

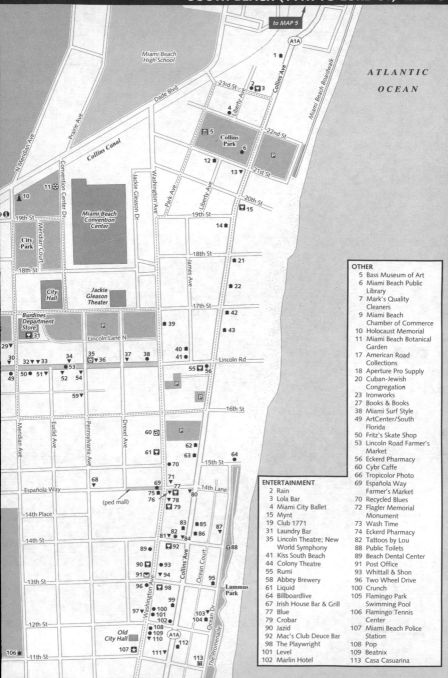

to MAP 5

A1A

ATLANTIC OCEAN

Miami Beach High School

Miami Beach Boardwalk

Dade Blvd

Collins Canal

Collins Park

Convention Center Dr

N Meridian Ave

Prairie Ave

Jackie Gleason Dr

Washington Ave

Park Ave

Liberty Ave

Collins Ave

23rd St

22nd St

21st St

20th St

19th St

18th St

17th St

Lincoln Rd

Lincoln Lane N

16th St

15th St

14th Lane

14th Place

14th St

13th St

12th St

11th St

Miami Beach Convention Center

Jackie Gleason Theater

Burdines Department Store

Española Way (ped mall)

Old City Hall

Lummus Park

The Promenade

Ocean Dr

Ocean Court

Collins Court

Washington Ave

Pennsylvania Ave

Drexel Ave

Euclid Ave

Meridian Ave

James Ave

Meridian Court

City Park

City Hall

OTHER
5 Bass Museum of Art
6 Miami Beach Public Library
7 Mark's Quality Cleaners
9 Miami Beach Chamber of Commerce
10 Holocaust Memorial
11 Miami Beach Botanical Garden
17 American Road Collections
18 Aperture Pro Supply
20 Cuban-Jewish Congregation
23 Ironworks
27 Books & Books
38 Miami Surf Style
49 ArtCenter/South Florida
50 Fritz's Skate Shop
53 Lincoln Road Farmer's Market
56 Eckerd Pharmacy
60 Cybr Caffe
66 Tropicolor Photo
69 Española Way Farmer's Market
70 Recycled Blues
72 Flagler Memorial Monument
73 Wash Time
74 Eckerd Pharmacy
82 Tattoos by Lou
88 Public Toilets
89 Beach Dental Center
91 Post Office
93 Whittall & Shon
96 Two Wheel Drive
100 Crunch
105 Flamingo Park Swimming Pool
106 Flamingo Tennis Center
107 Miami Beach Police Station
108 Pop
109 Beatnix
113 Casa Casuarina

ENTERTAINMENT
2 Rain
3 Lola Bar
4 Miami City Ballet
15 Mynt
19 Club 1771
31 Laundry Bar
35 Lincoln Theatre; New World Symphony
41 Kiss South Beach
44 Colony Theatre
55 Rumi
58 Abbey Brewery
61 Liquid
64 Billboardlive
67 Irish House Bar & Grill
77 Blue
79 Crobar
90 Jazid
92 Mac's Club Deuce Bar
98 The Playwright
101 Level
102 Marlin Hotel

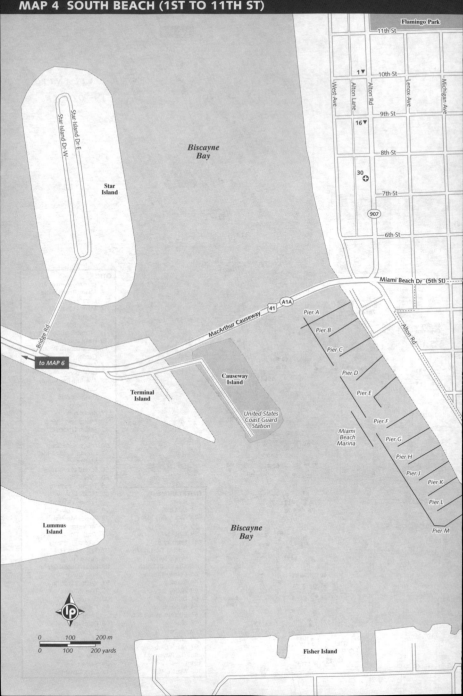

MAP 4 SOUTH BEACH (1ST TO 11TH ST)

Flamingo Park

11th St

10th St
1 ▼

9th St
16 ▼

8th St

30 ✛

7th St

907

6th St

West Ave
Alton Lane
Alton Rd
Lenox Ave
Michigan Ave

Miami Beach Dr (5th St)

Biscayne
Bay

Star Island Dr E
Star Island Dr W

Star
Island

Bridge Rd

to MAP 6

Terminal
Island

Causeway
Island

MacArthur Causeway

41 A1A

United States
Coast Guard
Station

Pier A
Pier B
Pier C
Pier D
Pier E
Pier F
Pier G
Pier H
Pier J
Pier K
Pier L
Pier M

Miami
Beach
Marina

Alton Rd

Lummus
Island

Biscayne
Bay

Fisher Island

0   100   200 m
0   100   200 yards

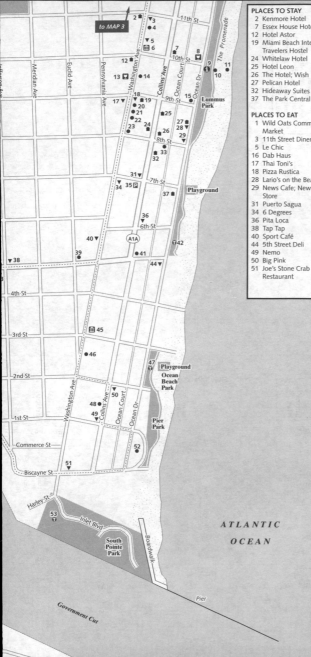

PLACES TO STAY
2 Kenmore Hotel
7 Essex House Hotel
12 Hotel Astor
19 Miami Beach International
   Travelers Hostel
24 Whitelaw Hotel
25 Hotel Leon
26 The Hotel; Wish
27 Pelican Hotel
32 Hideaway Suites
37 The Park Central

PLACES TO EAT
1 Wild Oats Community
   Market
3 11th Street Diner
5 Le Chic
16 Dab Haus
17 Thai Toni's
21 Pizza Rustica
28 Lario's on the Beach
29 News Cafe; News Cafe
   Store
31 Puerto Sagua
34 6 Degrees
36 Pita Loca
38 Tap Tap
40 Sport Café
44 5th Street Deli
50 Nemo
50 Big Pink
51 Joe's Stone Crab
   Restaurant

ENTERTAINMENT
4 Twist
8 The Clevelander Bar
13 Chelsea Hotel
14 BED
15 Mango's Tropical Cafe
22 Pump
48 Opium Garden
52 Penrod's Entertainment
   Complex; Pearl Restaurant
   & Champagne Lounge;
   Nikki Beach

OTHER
6 Wolfsonian Foundation
9 Art Deco Welcome Center;
   Miami Design Preservation
   League
10 Beach Patrol Headquarters
11 Lifeguard Tower
20 South Beach Tattoo
21 LIB Color Labs
23 Betsey Johnson
30 Miami Beach Community
   Health Center
33 Ritchie Swimwear
35 Parking
39 Eckerd Pharmacy
41 Spec's Music
42 Public Toilets
43 Estefan Enterprises
45 Sanford L Ziff Jewish
   Museum of Florida
46 Library
47 Public Toilets
53 Public Toilets

------ The Wave (electric shuttle)

MAP 5 NORTHERN MIAMI BEACH

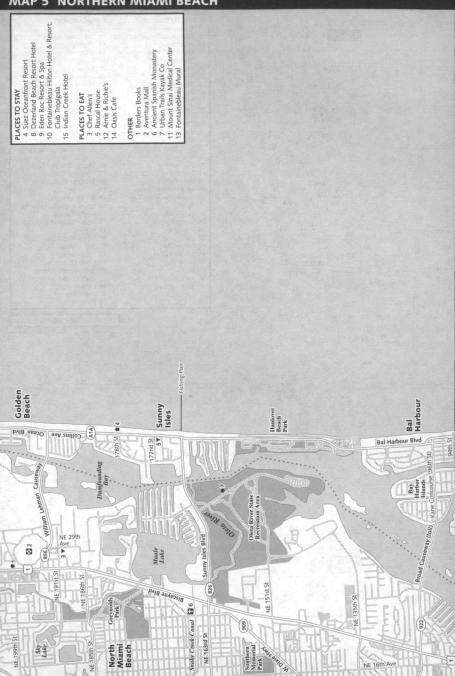

PLACES TO STAY
4 Suez Oceanfront Resort
8 Dezerland Beach Resort Hotel
9 Eden Roc Resort & Spa
10 Fontainebleau Hilton Hotel & Resort;
   Club Tropigala
15 Indian Creek Hotel

PLACES TO EAT
3 Chef Allen's
5 Rascal House
12 Arnie & Richie's
14 Oasis Cafe

OTHER
1 Borders Books
2 Aventura Mall
6 Ancient Spanish Monastery
7 Urban Trails Kayak Co
11 Mount Sinai Medical Center
13 Fontainebleau Mural

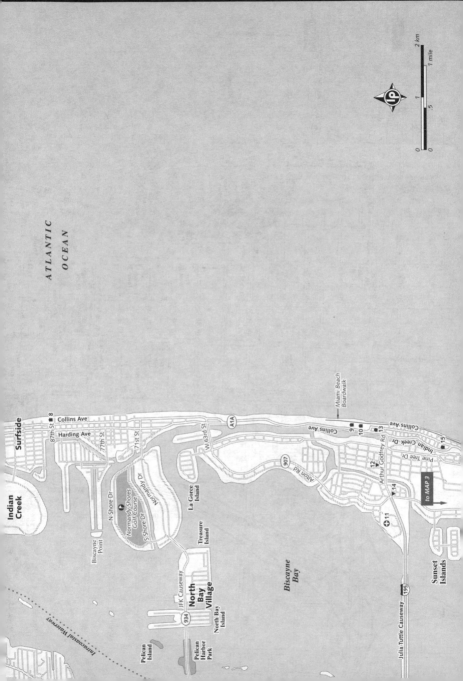

ATLANTIC
OCEAN

Surfside

Indian Creek

Collins Ave
Harding Ave

87th St

77th St

71st St

N Shore Dr

Normandy Shores
Golf Course

S Shore Dr

Normandy Dr

Biscayne Point

W 63rd St

A1A

La Gorce Island

Treasure Island

JFK Causeway

North Bay Village

Pelican Harbor Park

North Bay Island

Pelican Island

Intracoastal Waterway

Biscayne Bay

907

Alton Rd

Miami Beach Boardwalk

Collins Ave

Collins Ave

Indian Creek Dr

Arthur Godfrey Rd

Pine Tree Dr

to MAP 3

Sunset Islands

Julia Tuttle Causeway

195

0 .5 1 2 km
0   1 mile

MAP 6 DOWNTOWN MIAMI

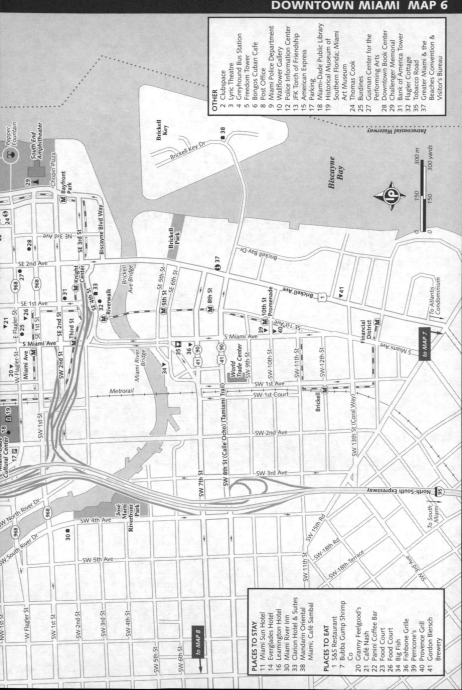

OTHER
2 Clubspace
3 Lyric Theatre
4 Greyhound Bus Station
5 Freedom Tower
6 Bongos Cuban Cafe
8 Post Office
9 Miami Police Department
10 Wallflower Gallery
12 Police Information Center
13 JFK Torch of Friendship
15 American Express
17 Parking
18 Miami-Dade Public Library
19 Historical Museum of
    Southern Florida; Miami
    Art Museum
24 Thomas Cook
25 Burdines
27 Gusman Center for the
    Performing Arts
28 Downtown Book Center
29 Challenger Memorial
31 Bank of America Tower
32 Flagler Cottage
35 Tobacco Road
37 Greater Miami & the
    Beaches Convention &
    Visitor's Bureau

PLACES TO STAY
11 Miami Sun Hotel
14 Everglades Hotel
16 Leamington Hotel
30 Miami River Inn
33 Clarion Hotel & Suites
38 Mandarin Oriental
    Miami; Café Sambal

PLACES TO EAT
1 S&S Restaurant
7 Bubba Gump Shrimp
    Co
20 Granny Feelgood's
21 Café Nash
22 Panini Coffee Bar
23 Food Court
26 Food Court
34 Big Fish
36 Fishbone Grille
39 Perricone's
40 Provence Grill
41 Gordon Biersch
    Brewery

to MAP 8

to MAP 7

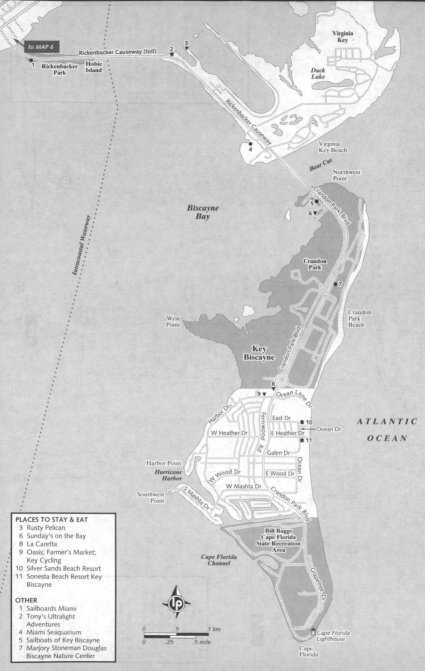

MAP 7 KEY BISCAYNE

Virginia
Key

Duck
Lake

to MAP 6

Rickenbacker Causeway (toll)

1 Rickenbacker
Park

Hobie
Island

Rickenbacker Causeway

Virginia
Key Beach

Bear Cut

Northwest
Point

Biscayne
Bay

Intracoastal Waterway

Crandon Park Blvd

Crandon
Park

Crandon
Park
Beach

West
Point

Key
Biscayne

Crandon Park Blvd

ATLANTIC
OCEAN

Ocean Lane Dr

Harbor Dr

Fernwood Rd

East Dr

E Heather Dr

Ocean Dr

W Heather Dr

Galen Dr

Ocean Dr

Harbor Point
Hurricane
Harbor

W Wood Dr

E Wood Dr

Southwest
Point

S Mashta Dr

W Mashta Dr

Crandon Park Blvd

Bill Baggs
Cape Florida
State Recreation
Area

Cape Florida
Channel

Grapetree Dr

Cape Florida
Lighthouse

Cape
Florida

PLACES TO STAY & EAT
3 Rusty Pelican
6 Sunday's on the Bay
8 La Caretta
9 Oasis; Farmer's Market;
   Key Cycling
10 Silver Sands Beach Resort
11 Sonesta Beach Resort Key
   Biscayne

OTHER
1 Sailboards Miami
2 Tony's Ultralight
   Adventures
4 Miami Seaquarium
5 Sailboats of Key Biscayne
7 Marjory Stoneman Douglas
   Biscayne Nature Center

0   .5   1 km
0   .25   .5 mile

MAP 8 LITTLE HAVANA

SW-10th Ave
SW-11th Ave
To Taquerías
el Mexicano
to MAP 6

SW-12th Ave
SW-12th Court
Cuban Memorial Blvd
to MAP 9

NW 12th Ave
SW-13th Ave
SW-13th Court
SW-14th Ave
SW-14th Ave
SW-15th Ave
SW-16th Ave
NW-16th Ave
SW 17th Ave
NW 17th Ave
SW-17th Court
SW-18th Ave
SW-18th Court
SW-11th Terrace
SW-19th Ave
SW-20th Ave
Calle Ocho (SW 8th St) (Tamiami Trail)
SW-21st Ave
SW-22nd Ave
NW 22nd Ave
SW-23rd Ave

W-Flagler St
SW-Flagler Terrace
NW-1st St
SW 1st St
SW-2nd St
SW-3rd St
SW-4th St
SW-5th St
SW-6th St

NW-2nd St
NW-1st-Terrace
NW-1st-St
W-Flagler-Terrace
SW-1st St
SW-2nd St
SW-3rd St
SW-4th-St
SW-5th St
SW-6th St
SW 7th St
SW-9th St
SW-10th St
SW-11th Terrace
SW-12th St
SW-13th St

SW-10th-St
SW-11th-St
SW-12th-St
SW-13th-St

968
968
933

90 41
90 41

To Versailles, La Carreta,
Hy Vong Vietnamese
Restaurant, Botánica Las
Mercedes, Versailles Bakery
& La Casa de las Guayaberas

(Beacon Blvd)
SW 22nd Ave Rd

400 m
400 yards
0   200
0   200

PLACES TO EAT
2 Guayacan
3 El Pescador
8 Casa Panza

OTHER
1 Unidos en Casa Elian
4 Hoy Como Ayer
5 Latin American Art Museum
6 Cervantes Book Store;
  Botánica El Camino; La
  Tradición Cubana
7 Bay of Pigs Museum
9 Máximo Gómez Park
  (Domino Park)
10 Little Havana To-Go
11 Eternal Torch in Honor of
   the 2506th Brigade
12 Nestor Izquierdo Statue
13 Cuba Brass Relief Map
14 José Martí Memorial
15 Casino
16 El Crédito Cigars

MAP 9 COCONUT GROVE

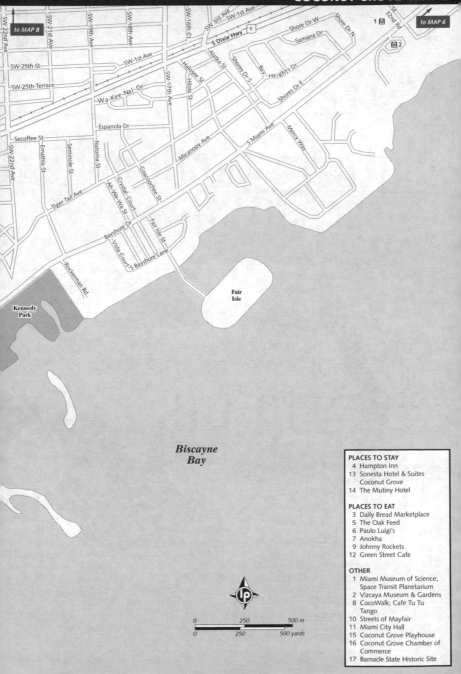

to MAP 8

to MAP 6

1

2

SW-22nd Ave

SW-21st Ave

SW-19th Ave

SW-8th Ave

SW-16th Ct.

SW-3rd Ave

SW-1st Ave

Shore Dr W

Shore Dr N

SE-32nd Rd

SE-32nd Rd

S Dixie Hwy

Samana Dr

SW-25th St

SW-1st Ave

Alatka St

Shores Dr S

Bay

Heights Dr

SW-25th Terrace

Wa-Kee-Nal-Dr

Halissee St

Hilola St

Shores Dr E

SW-17th Ave

Espanola Dr

S Miami Ave

Mercy Way

Secoffee St

Micanopy Ave

SW-22nd Ave

Emathla St

Seminole St

Natoma St

Coucoochee St

Crystal Court

Tiger Tail Ave

Ah-We-Wa St

Bayshore Dr

Vista Court

Fair Isle St

S Bayshore Lane

Rockerman Rd

Kennedy Park

Fair Isle

Biscayne Bay

0   250   500 m

0   250   500 yards

LP

PLACES TO STAY
4 Hampton Inn
13 Sonesta Hotel & Suites
   Coconut Grove
14 The Mutiny Hotel

PLACES TO EAT
3 Daily Bread Marketplace
5 The Oak Feed
6 Paulo Luigi's
7 Anokha
9 Johnny Rockets
12 Green Street Cafe

OTHER
1 Miami Museum of Science;
   Space Transit Planetarium
2 Vizcaya Museum & Gardens
8 CocoWalk; Cafe Tu Tu
   Tango
10 Streets of Mayfair
11 Miami City Hall
15 Coconut Grove Playhouse
16 Coconut Grove Chamber of
   Commerce
17 Barnacle State Historic Site

MAP 10 CORAL GABLES

see MAP 9

SW 22nd-Terrace
SW 23rd St
SW 24th St

SW 37th Ave (Douglas Rd)

15 ▽

SW 37th Court

SW-38th Ave

SW 38th Court

SW 39th Ave

Monego St

Ponce de León Blvd

Douglas Road

M

To Douglas Entrance

Alhambra Entrance Monuments

Alhambra Circle

Alhambra Plaza

Merrick Way

Galiano St

Almeria Ave

Ponce Circle Park

Ponce de León Blvd

7 ▼

10 ⊞ ▼ 11

14 ●

3

To Hotel Chateau Bleau

Navarre Ave

Minorca Ave

Alcazar Ave

2 ⊞

Alhambra Circle

5

6 ●

Giralda Ave

Aragon Ave

9

13 ⊞

Salzedo St

Andalusia Ave

Palermo Ave

Malaga Ave

San Sebastian Ave

Romano Ave

Sarto Ave

Camilo Ave

Aledo Ave

Cadima Ave

Alesio Ave

Viscaya Ave

Fluvia Ave

Candia Ave

Velarde Ave

Laguna St

SW 40th St (Bird Rd)

San Lorezo Ave

Altara Ave

953

976

Viscaya Court

4 ▼

SW 22nd St (Miracle Mile)

SW 42nd Ave (Le Jeune Rd)

12 ●

Hernando St

972

Valencia Ave

Almeria Ave

Sevilla Ave

Palermo Ave

Catalonia Ave

Malaga Ave

Santander Ave

Anastasia Ave

Biltmore Way

Segovia St

Cardena St

Segovia Circle

Greenway Dr

Riviera Dr

University Dr

San Antonio Ave

Altara Ave

San Lorenzo Ave

Anderson Rd

Monserrate St

Toledo St

Toledo St

8 ⊞

SW 24th St (Coral Way)

De Soto Blvd

16 ⊞

17 ●

Granada Blvd

Granada Entrance Monuments

Granada Golf Course

Andalusia Ave

Palermo Ave

Catalonia Ave

Malaga Ave

Anastasia Ave

Coral Gables Canal

Cordova St

Columbus Blvd

Asturia Ave

Castile Ave

Madrid St

San Domingo St

N Greenway Dr

18 ●

Biltmore Golf Course

Mariola Court

Algardi Ave

San Amaro Ave

San Amaro Ave

Alhambra Circle

N Greenway Dr

S Greenway Dr

Indian Mound Trail

Alhambra Circle

SW 40th St (Bird Rd)

Algardi Ave

Cantoria Ave

Greenway Court

1 ●

Ferdinand St

To Country Club Prado

Country Club Prado

Coral Way Entrance Monuments

SW 57th Ave (Red Rd)

Valencia Ave

Sevilla Ave

19 ▼

PLACES TO STAY
3 Hotel Place St Michel
18 The Biltmore Hotel
24 Terrace Inn
25 Holiday Inn

PLACES TO EAT
4 Café Demetrio
5 Meza Fine Art Gallery &
   Cafe
7 Miss Saigon Bistro
9 Caffe Abbracci
11 Miracle Mile Cafeteria
15 Norman's
19 Allen's Drug Store

OTHER
1 Alhambra Watertower
2 Absinthe House
6 Books & Books
8 Merrick House
10 Coral Gables Chamber
   of Commerce
12 City Hall
13 Miracle Theater; Actors'
   Playhouse
14 Barnes & Noble
   Bookstore
16 Venetian Pool
17 DeSoto Fountain
20 Bill Cosford Cinema
21 Jerry Herman Ring
   Theatre
22 Lowe Art Museum
23 Mark Light Stadium
26 The Shops at Sunset
   Place (Gameworks,
   Virgin Megastore)

MIAMI

Continued from page 127

Post & Communications

You can have mail sent to you care of General Delivery at any post office that has its own zip (postal) code. In South Beach, send it to: USPS, General Delivery, 1300 Washington Ave, Miami Beach, FL 33139 (Map 3). If you're staying elsewhere in Miami, send it to: USPS, General Delivery, Miami FL 33101. Pick this mail up at the Flagler Station, 500 NW 2nd Ave (Map 6).

Anyone who's anyone in Miami has a cell phone, and you can often rent one in larger hotels and at rental car agencies. Unicom (☎ 305-538-9494, W www.unicom .com), 742 Alton Rd, in South Beach, rents phones.

Email & Internet Access

Most hostels have computers with Internet connections for a minimal fee. Otherwise, the appropriately cluttered Kafka Kafé (☎ 305-673-9669; Map 3), 1464 Washington Ave, is the Beach's biggest Internet café; it charges $7 an hour for access.

The austere Cybr Caffe (☎ 305-534-0057; Map 3), 1574 Washington Ave, has a similar number of terminals and the same rates.

Bookstores

The best locally owned bookstores are the two branches of Books & Books (☎ 305-

Local Calls

To make up for the huge numbers of cell-phone and fax numbers crowding the ☎ 305 area code, the local telephone companies had to overlay another area code to the city. Now, even if you are calling the restaurant next door to your hotel in Miami, you must dial ☎ 305 + the seven-digit number, or in the case of the new numbers being doled out, ☎ 786 + the seven-digit number. Leave off the preceding '1' before local calls – just start with ☎ 305 or ☎ 786.

532-3222, W www.booksandbooks.com, 933 Lincoln Road, South Beach, Map 3; ☎ 305-442-4408, 265 Aragon Ave, Coral Gables, Map 10). Both branches have a café and excellent fiction and Florida-related sections.

When you're downtown, look for the Downtown Book Center (☎ 305-377-9941, 247 SE 1st St; Map 6).

Other than those bookstores, there is an excellent Borders (☎ 305-935-4712, 19925 Biscayne Blvd, Aventura; Map 5) and Barnes & Noble (☎ 305-446-4152, 152 Miracle Mile; Map 10).

One of the best places for Spanish-language books is Cervantes Book Store (Map 8; see the boxed text 'Calle Ocho: Cigars, Botánicas & More' later in this chapter).

Periodicals & Foreign Press

The News Cafe Store (☎ 305-538-6397, 800 Ocean Dr; Map 4) is open 24 hrs daily. Look for the separate 24-hour newsstand between News Cafe's restaurant and bar. It has a good selection of international and domestic papers.

Libraries

The Miami-Dade Public Library (☎ 305-375-2665/5184, W www.mdpls.org; Map 6), 101 W Flagler St, is an excellent resource. It has an enormous Florida room containing thousands of books on all aspects of Florida life, history and travel, as well as a large video- and audio-tape library. The library is open 9am to 6pm Monday to Wednesday, Friday and Saturday, 9am to 9pm Thursday, and 1pm to 5pm Sunday.

A good branch library is on Miami Beach (☎ 305-535-4219; Map 3), at 2100 Collins Ave. It's open 10am to 8pm Monday and Wednesday, 10am to 5:30pm Tuesday and Thursday to Saturday, closed Sunday.

Media

The *Miami Herald* is the city's only major daily. While local coverage tends to draw fire from all sides, it's a good source of international and national news. The Friday *Herald* features a pullout *Weekend* section with a whole lot of timely listings. Not to be outdone, they also publish a very good free weekly, the *Street*.

The weekly free alternative *New Times* has the best coverage of local issues, along with superb entertainment and restaurant listings.

Wire, a gay freebie, is more focused on partying at the beach.

The *Miami Herald* publishes *El Nuevo Herald*, an excellent Spanish daily (in fact, if you speak Spanish, you should look here first for coverage of Latin America).

National Public Radio (NPR) can be found at 91.3 FM.

Universities

The state-run liberal arts Florida International University (FIU; Map 2) has an enrollment of more than 26,000 students. Its University Park campus is located on US Hwy 41 (west of Calle Ocho) between SW 107th Ave and Florida's Turnpike. The North Campus is located off US Hwy 1 at NE 151st St.

The University of Miami's Coral Gables campus (made up of two colleges and 10 schools) occupies 260 acres within the city of Coral Gables. Founded in 1925, UM has a total enrollment of about 13,000 full- and part-time students.

Gay & Lesbian Travelers

The best source for unbiased information is the bookstore Lambda Passage (☎ 305-754-6900; Map 2), 7545 Biscayne Blvd, a fixture in Miami since the mid-1980s. Look for the rainbow flag at their store, park behind the building, and enter through the back door. It's open 11am to 9pm Monday to Saturday, noon to 6pm Sunday.

A local weekly newspaper focusing on gay and lesbian community issues is *twn* ('the weekly news'). The weekly *Hotspots*, packed with ads from discos to straight-forward classifieds, concentrates more on Fort Lauderdale than Miami. *She Times*, a lesbian-oriented monthly, has a hodge-podge of self-help, poetry, useful listings and personals (from a mix of men, women, drag queens and others).

Contact the gay and lesbian Dade Human Rights Foundation (☎ 305-572-1841, W www.dhrf.com) for a calendar of events they participate in and sponsor.

Photography

On South Beach, head to Tropicolor Photo (☎ 305-672-3720; Map 3), at 1442 Alton Rd, or LIB Color Labs (☎ 305-538-5600; Map 4), at 851 Washington Ave, for film and processing.

Pros patronize Aperture Pro Supply (☎ 305-673-4327; Map 3), at 1330 18th St. If you're a stickler for fresh film, picky about processing film quickly (film wilting in the humidity), or need another camera body or some studio space to rent, contact these folks.

Laundry

On the Beach, head to Wash Time (☎ 305-672-7110; Map 3), Alton Rd at 14th Court. Mark's Quality Cleaners (☎ 305-538-6275; Map 3), at 1201 20th St, has same-day service if you drop off your clothes by 10am. For a good time *and* clean clothes, head to the Laundry Bar, 721 Lincoln Lane (Map 3; see Bars, under Entertainment, later in this chapter).

Medical Attention

For physician referrals 24 hours daily, contact the Mount Sinai Medical Center Visitor's Medical Line (☎ 305-674-2222).

The Miami Beach Community Health Center (☎ 305-538-8835; Map 4), 710 Alton Rd, charges fees based on your income. Get there early (it's open 7am to 3:30pm Monday to Friday), since walk-in clinic lines are usually very long. Bring ID. If you're foreign born, bring your passport and I-94 card; US citizens should bring proof of residence and income.

If you need dental attention, head to the 2nd-floor Beach Dental Center (☎ 305-532-3300; Map 3), 1370 Washington Ave.

In a serious emergency, call ☎ 911 for an ambulance to take you to the nearest hospital's emergency room. Mount Sinai Medical Center (☎ 305-674-2121; Map 5), 4300 Alton Rd, is the area's best.

Some shops in the statewide Eckerd pharmacy (☎ 305-538-1571) chain are open 24 hours daily; call for the nearest location.

Dangers & Annoyances

If you encounter any problems with hotels, restaurants or businesses during your stay, you aren't powerless. For incidents in Miami Beach, contact Michael Aller (☎ 305-673-7010), also known as 'Mr Miami Beach.' He's the city of Miami Beach's lovable Tourism & Convention coordinator.

Unsafe Areas Many locals will warn you against visiting Liberty City and Little Haiti (see that section, later). While they may not be as dangerous as some people think, you should avoid walking around in them late at night. Deserted areas below 5th St in South Beach are more dangerous at night. In downtown Miami, use particular caution near the Greyhound station and around causeways, bridges and overpasses where homeless people and some refugees have set up shantytowns.

If you're considering sex on the beach or in Miami's public toilets, it's not a very original idea: Both the police and muggers patrol, albeit for different reasons.

Bad Service Miami has arguably the worst service in the USA. Service in some South Beach restaurants can be atrocious. Many waitstaff and others in the 'service' industry are really here to be discovered by a talent agent. When they decide that you're not one, you are of no value to them. Petulant and pouty wannabe models of both sexes can be seen at practically every Ocean Drive restaurant acting as 'hosts.' There's nothing much you can do about it except keep your dignity and remember: Real models don't hand out menus.

MIAMI BEACH

Most people come to Miami for beaches, clubs and bars, but there are other compelling attractions within the city of Miami Beach, and specifically the subset of South Beach. From tattoo parlors to tony salons, and from laid-back Larry to high-energy

Harry, the Beach has all extremes covered. Yes, America's Riviera is gay, but it also has a heavily Jewish culture and a decidedly Latin flair. In fact, there's even a **Cuban-Jewish Congregation** (☎ *305-534-7213, 1700 Michigan Ave*).

South Beach (Maps 3 & 4)

Art Deco Historic District South Beach's heart is its Art Deco Historic District, one of the largest areas in the USA on the National Register of Historic Places. In fact, the District's rejuvenation and rebirth as a major tourist destination results directly from its protection as a historic place in 1979. The National Register designation prevents developers from wholeheartedly razing significant portions of what was, in the 1980s, a crime-ridden collection of crumbling eyesores populated primarily by drug-crazed lunatics, Cuban refugees and elderly residents. It's a far cry from that now. Today, hotel and apartment façades are decidedly colorful, with pastel architectural details. Depending on your perspective, the bright buildings catapult you back to the Roaring Twenties or onto a wacky tour of American kitsch.

The Deco District is bounded by Dade Blvd to the north, 6th St to the south, the Atlantic Ocean to the east and Lenox Ave to the west. One of the best things about these 1000 or so buildings is their scale: Most are no taller than the palm trees. And, while the architecture is by no means uniform – you'll see streamline moderne, Mediterranean revival and tropical art deco designs – it's all quite harmonious. The 1-sq-mile district feels like a small village.

Ocean Beach Historic District & South Pointe The Historic District boundaries zigzag from 6th to 1st St and exclude a number of blocks. While construction rumbles, **South Pointe Park** is still a wonderful place to spend a sunny afternoon. It has a nice little playground, a fishing pier from which kids (illegally) dive into Government Cut, a short boardwalk and an excellent stretch of beach that's less crowded during the week than those to the near north. (On weekends it's overrun by families.)

You can't miss the dramatic architecture of **Estefan Enterprises** *(420 Jefferson Ave),* designed by the internationally renowned firm of Arquitectonica (which has its own offices on Brickell Ave). The dynamic musical duo of Gloria and Emilio Estefan, dubbed 'Miami's Royal Family,' operate their ever-increasing business ventures from here (see Bongos Cuban Cafe under Dance Clubs & Nightclubs in the Entertainment section).

Ocean Drive Strolling along Ocean Drive from north to south is a safari through the trendy. On the beach, low-flying planes trail advertisements for nightclubs, restaurants and performances. As the day progresses, the clicking, flashing and whirring of high-fashion photo shoots is replaced by in-line skaters and volleyball players. Across from the beach, hotels and sidewalk cafés threaten to spill into the street. Models and wannabes, actors and wannabes, and bedazzled tourists swarm the sidewalks. Vehicular traffic appears to be limited to vintage roadsters, '65 Mustangs and grandiose Harley-Davidsons.

The fashion-impaired needn't worry; despite Ocean Drive's undeniable chic, it's definitely a come-as-you-are affair. Dozens of cafés and bistros line the Drive. Grab a sidewalk table if one's available. As the masses strut, sashay, skate and groove their way past, order a *café con leche,* keep an eye peeled for famous models and try to look a tad pretentious and self-congratulatory to fit in. It's great fun.

For those who want one last glimpse of the ocean without getting salty prior to their departure, a **boardwalk** runs from 21st to 46th St.

The **Promenade**, though, is a wavy concrete ribbon between the beach and Ocean Drive, from 5th to 15th St. If you've ever flipped through a fashion magazine, you've seen it: It's *the* Beach location for photo shoots. If you show up here before 9am, you can watch the glamorous, motor-driven events unfold 1/250 of a second at a time. Other times throughout the day and late into the night, in-line skaters, bicyclists, roller skaters, skateboarders, dog walkers,

yahoos, locals and tourists mill about and occasionally bump into each other. Around 8th St, there's a nice shady stretch with a kids' play area.

The main 'sight' on Ocean Drive is **Casa Casuarina**, the former residence of slain fashion designer Gianni Versace. Built in 1930 with Florida keystone (coral from the Keys), it was originally known as the Amsterdam Palace *(1114 Ocean Dr; no entry).* The Mediterranean revival house, a three-story Spanish-style palace with exposed timbers, was modeled after the Governor's House in Santo Domingo. When Versace purchased the property in the early 1980s, poor artists had been living there, and the house was a mess. During Versace's tenure, he renovated the large mahogany front doors, an interior atrium that wraps around a courtyard, and a small copper rooftop observatory; plus, he hired artists to cover every inch of the place with elaborate tile.

The house has always attracted fashion plates, but it's now a morbid destination for ghoulish tourists, who pose for photographs on the very steps where the designer was gunned down in 1997. As Versace was unlocking the gate, his murderer shot two bullets through the back of his head.

Washington Avenue Washington Ave is the Beach's engine room, its main commercial artery. Make it a point to mail a postcard at the 1937 **post office** *(1300 Washington Ave).* This Depression moderne building was constructed under President Franklin Roosevelt's reign with WPA funds, which supported artists who were out of work during the Great Depression.

Collins Avenue This busy road runs parallel to Ocean Drive and is thick with designer shops between 6th and 9th Sts. Collins has lots of good hotels that aren't as noisy as those on Ocean Drive.

Lincoln Road Mall Ocean Drive may have a firm choke hold on the 'fabulous,' but locals own the Lincoln Road Mall. (OK, we'll be realistic; locals do have to share Lincoln Road with every single tourist, conventioneer and professional who comes to Miami.) 'The Road' was laid out by designer and architect Morris Lapides in the 1950s; look for his trademark wavy and futuristic sculptures all along Lincoln. The Beach's cultural epicenter, The Road is a wide, pedestrian-only sidewalk that's hallowed ground for in-line skaters. It's plastered with galleries and outdoor cafés filled with off-duty models trying to relax. It's also lined with lush planters and imposing palms, perfect for a picnic-style late-afternoon snack.

Don't miss the **ArtCenter/South Florida** *(☎ 305-538-7887, 800 Lincoln Road; open 1pm-10pm daily).* With over 70 artists, this nonprofit collective is fantastic. It's the most exciting place on Lincoln. Tour the more structured gallery, as well as the maze of working studios where dozens of diverse artists pursue their inner demons and outer expressions of spirituality. It's great fun to peer down into their minimal spaces, trying to understand their creative processes.

A **farmer's market** *(between Alton Rd & Pennsylvania Ave; held 9am-6pm Sun)* provides a good diversion, with fresh fruits, veggies, juices, breads and more.

Española Way Designed as a Spanish-style village in the early to mid-1920s, Española Way is lined with charming, pink Spanish-style buildings between Washington and Drexel Aves. Originally intended as an artists' colony, it sort of is something of one today, kind of. Little galleries and cafés line the narrow, shaded enclave. A flea market operates Friday through Sunday. Look for everything from garage-sale stuff to handmade crafts. For further details, see Shopping, later in this chapter.

The rambling 1920s Clay Hotel & International Hostel (see Places to Stay later in this chapter), complete with wrought-iron balconies, was formerly the home of Desi Arnaz. The Cuban bandleader, who started the rumba phenomenon, had a conga club here. In its heyday, the ritzy place doubled s a gambling casino. Mobster Al Capone's H Gambling Syndicate took over the 'le wing (now Rooms 128 to 138).

Bass Museum of Art This museum *(☎ 305-673-7530,* W *www.bassmuseum.org, 2121 Park Ave; admission $6/4 adult/senior & student; open 10am-5pm Tues, Wed, Fri & Sat, 10am-9pm Thur, 11am-5pm Sun)* has permanent collections ranging from 16th-century European religious works, to Northern European and Renaissance paintings, to impressive old masters like Peter Paul Rubens. Look for Albrecht Durer, Toulouse-Lautrec and perhaps the finest Flemish tapestries in an American museum.

Wolfsonian Foundation The forbidding Mediterranean-style building that houses the Wolfsonian collection *(☎ 305-531-1001,* W *www.wolfsonian.fiu.edu, 1001 Washington Ave; admission $5/3.50 adult/senior, student & youth 6-18 yrs, admission free 6pm-9pm Thur; open 11am-6pm Mon, Tues, Fri & Sat, 11am-9pm Thur, noon-5pm Sun)* used to be a storage facility for Miami native Mitchell Wolfson's fascinating collection of art nouveau, Arts and Crafts, and art moderne. Now the 14-room gallery, under the auspices of Florida International University, rotates through 70,000 pieces (dating from 1885 to 1945). They range from industrial design to decorative arts to advertising and propaganda. Be sure to check out the tremendous deco 'waterfall' in the lobby.

Holocaust Memorial It's impossible to overstate the impact of this memorial *(☎ 305-538-1663,* W *www.holocaustmmb.com, Cnr Meridian Ave & Dade Blvd; admission free; open 9am-9pm daily),* dedicated to the six million Jews who were killed during the Holocaust. Created through the efforts of Miami Beach Holocaust survivors and dramatically realized by sculptor Kenneth Treister, this elaborate and exquisitely detailed memorial is quite moving. Like the Kaddish, the Jewish prayer for the dead that speaks only of life, the memorial is a testament to humankind's perseverance and the hope for a better world.

Sanford L Ziff Jewish Museum of Florida Jews have been officially 'allowed' to live in Florida since 1763, but evidence suggests that Jews who had converted to Christianity to escape persecution and death were here as early as the 1500s. This museum (☎ 305-672-5044, ⓦ www.jewishmuseum .com, 301 Washington Ave; admission $5/4 adult/senior & student, free Sat; open 10am-5pm Tues-Sun except during Jewish holidays), housed in a 1936 Orthodox synagogue (Miami's first congregation), is dedicated to the history of Florida Jews.

Miami Beach Botanical Garden This secret garden (☎ 305-673-7256, 2000 Convention Center Dr; admission free; open 9am-5pm daily) contains 4 acres of lush plantings that most people don't even realize are here. It's a contemplative place after the Holocaust Memorial.

Northern Miami Beach (Map 5)
North of 21st St on Collins Ave, the world of 1950s and '60s Miami Beach comes alive. It's still the kind of place where people say 'love you, kid…and I mean that.' Back then, all the schmoozers, stars and tourists were heading to high-rise hotels lining Collins Ave. With a few notable exceptions, architecture from here to the northern city limits consists of a never-ending string of high-rise condos, hotels and apartments. The style is known as MiMo, or Miami Modern; it's characterized by fancy and glamour.

The iconic 1954 **Fontainebleau Hilton Hotel & Resort** (4441 Collins Ave) remains the other architectural highlight. Another brainchild of architect Morris Lapidus, this over-the-top leviathan is unmatched. Just before Collins Ave makes a little jog to the left, note the two magnificent pillars, through which the Fontainebleau's pool is visible. Fooled again. It's actually a spectacular trompe l'oeil **mural**, designed by Richard Hass and painted over an eight-week period by Edwin Abreu. It covers 13,016 sq ft of what was, before 1986, a big blank wall.

The enormous **Eden Roc Resort** (4525 Collins Ave), another notable '50s-era Lapidus resort (this with a decidedly Caribbean flair), has a fancy pool and indoor rock-climbing facilities (see Activities, later

in this chapter). Try to stop in to both; they are windows to another world.

Backtrack a bit and head west on **41st St**, also called Arthur Godfrey Rd, which is lined with kosher shops, delicatessens and even a kosher pizzeria. It's the 5th Avenue of the Orthodox Jewish South. Head north on **North Bay Rd**, which from 40th to 60th St is lined with mansions.

As you continue north, you'll pass the community of **Surfside**, a predominately French-Canadian one, and then the ultra-swanky **Bal Harbour Shops**, which epitomizes a segment of *Lifestyles of the Rich and Famous*. This stretch of northern Miami Beach has great expanses of sandy beachfront that is tailor-made for family outings

Haulover Beach Park (☎ 305-947-3525, 10800 Collins Ave; admission $4 per car; open sunrise-sunset daily) has scads of barbecues, picnic tables, and volleyball and tennis courts. You can rent canoes and kayaks nearby at Urban Trails Kayak Co (see Activities, later in this chapter). Thanks to dense plant growth, it's also relatively hidden from the condos. This is also a good beach for surfing and windsurfing, as well as nude sunbathing.

As early as 500 BC, the rich Oleta River estuary was home to Tequesta Indians. Today, the **Oleta River State Recreation Area** (☎ 305-919-1846, 3400 NE 163rd St; admission $2 for 1 person, $4 for 2-4 people, $1 per each additional person over 4; open 8am-sunset daily), coming in at almost 1000 acres and certainly the largest urban park in the state, provides a perfect refuge from posing. There are lots of canoe, kayak and bicycle trails (and kayak rentals), a sandy swimming beach and shady picnic areas.

DOWNTOWN MIAMI (MAP 6)
Downtown Miami is not the most exciting American city you'll ever encounter, but if you've never been outside the USA, it will feel more like São Paulo than Seattle. Most streets are lined with shops selling electronics, luggage and clothing to Latin American visitors. Throngs of Brazilians, Colombians and Venezuelans heave bags of electronic goods from shop to shop. But the place dies

down quickly after 5pm, when office towers disgorge their worker bees.

Parking can be nightmarish, but public transportation is good, so it definitely pays to park adjacent to the Bayside Marketplace and hop onto the Metromover (most sites are within one or two blocks of the elevated tram); see Getting Around, later in this chapter, for more information. Driving can also be nightmarish, since just one or two blocks often separate mildly seedy areas from really seedy areas. Find yourself on the outskirts of downtown, take the wrong turn off the expressway, and you'll be reliving the opening sequence of *Bonfire of the Vanities*. Highways on stilts and concrete-jungle overpasses provide protective cover for communities of homeless people and addicts.

The Waterfront

The barren waterfront **Bicentennial Park** *(Biscayne Blvd; Metromover: Bicentennial Park)* has an amphitheater with occasional free concerts and events. The adjacent **American Airlines Arena** hosts big concerts and Miami Heat and Miami Sol (WNBA) basketball games.

Just south of the American Airlines Arena, the **Bayside Marketplace** (☎ 305-577-3344, Ⓦ *www.baysidemarketplace.com*, *401 Biscayne Blvd; Metromover: Freedom Tower)*, a waterfront pantheon to consumerism, is adored by hordes of tourists and cruise-ship passengers who dock nearby. Don't be a mall snob: Order a frozen daiquiri or margarita here and take in the scene. It's vibrant, with small shops, free daily concerts, lots of restaurants and sightseeing boat trips.

Bayfront Park (☎ 305-358-7550; Metromover: Bayfront Park), a freight port during the first 1920s building boom, is a somewhat calm downtown oasis, with two performance venues. The amphitheater is a great perch for the Fourth of July and New Year's Eve festivities, while the smaller 200-seat South End Amphitheater hosts free springtime performances featuring local talent. Also look for the **JFK Torch of Friendship**, a fountain recognizing the accomplishments of longtime US congressman Claude Pepper, and the **Challenger Memorial**, a monument to the astronauts killed in the 1986 space shuttle explosion.

Historical Museum of Southern Florida

Within the Mediterranean-style Miami-Dade Cultural Center, this historical

---

Bright Lights, Big City

Downtown Miami, glowing with nighttime neon, easily ranks among the nation's most beautiful and colorful skylines. Although there are upward of 40 buildings lit up at night, the downtown skyline is dominated by the **Bank of America Tower** *(100 SE 2nd St; Metromover: Knight Center)*. Designed by IM Pei in 1987, this unmistakable symbol is illuminated nightly and for special events. Orange and aqua probably indicates a home game for the Miami Dolphins; snowflakes show up in December. The lights, in fact, are changed every few days. The building's seven faces can be custom lit with a combination of seven colors per face. Unfortunately, there's no observation deck.

You can't miss the humble **MacArthur Causeway** (also called the I-395 bridge), which runs parallel to the Port of Miami cruise ships, its pilings magnificently awash in fuchsia. When the full moon makes its monthly appearance over Miami, the bridge is positively enchanting.

Other funky downtown neon lighting comes courtesy of the Metromover's rainbow-illuminated 4.4-mile track, which makes a downtown circuit. It's trippy. It looks like a child took the fluorescent colors from her crayon box and sketched a long ribbon of light beams as far as the eye can see. The ride is spectacular, and spectacularly cheap (25¢), allowing a city tour sans traffic and blaring horns. Several stations have public artwork, such as Brickell's patchwork ceiling celebrating Miami's multicultural 'quilt.'

museum (☎ 305-375-1492, Ⓦ www.historical-museum.org, 101 W Flagler St; Metromover: Government Center; admission $5/4/2 adult/senior/child 6-12 yrs; open 10am-5pm Mon-Wed & Sat, 10am-9pm Thur, noon-5pm Sun) celebrates the multicultural roots that nourish South Florida. It's particularly interesting for kids. Covering a whopping 10,000 years of state history, the far-reaching exhibits start with natural habitats, wetlands, coasts and ridges. They then move through prehistoric Florida, the Spanish invaders and a Spanish galleon before continuing on to wreckers, the cigar industry, Indian tribes and the railroad's importance during the Flagler Boom.

Exhibits then proceed through the Great Depression, 1930s tourism, WWII and to the present day. The installations aren't huge, but they're very informative. Historical tours led by Dr Paul George are in conjunction with this museum (see Organized Tours under Getting Around later in this chapter).

Miami Art Museum

Adjacent within the Miami-Dade Cultural Center, the MAM (☎ 305-375-3000, Ⓦ www.miamiartmuseum.org, 101 W Flagler St; Metromover: Government Center; admission $5/2.50 adult/senior & student, child under 12 yrs free, admission free Sun; open 10am-5pm Tues-Fri, noon-5pm Sat & Sun) is ensconced in spectacular Philip Johnson–designed digs. Without a permanent collection, its fine rotating exhibits concentrate on post-WWII international art.

Gusman Center for the Performing Arts

Try to see a concert or almost anything being held here (174 E Flagler St), since the interior of the former movie palace is stunning. (See Performing Arts under Entertainment, later, for more information.)

Miami-Dade Community College

There are two art galleries with rotating exhibitions at the Wolfson Campus of the Miami-Dade Community College (☎ 305-237-3696, 300 NE 2nd Ave; Metromover: College/Bayside; admission free; both open 10am-6pm Mon-Fri). Both the 3rd-floor Centre Gallery and the 5th-floor Frances Wolfson Gallery often have photography shows.

Freedom Tower

Designed by the New York architectural firm of Shultz & Weaver in 1925, this tower (600 Biscayne Blvd; Metromover: Freedom Tower) is one of two surviving area towers modeled after the Giralda bell tower in Spain's Cathedral of Seville. (The second is at the Biltmore Hotel, discussed in the Coral Gables section, later.) The 'Ellis Island of the South,' it served as an immigration processing center for almost half a million Cuban refugees in the 1960s. Placed on the National Register of Historic Places in 1979, it was also home to the Miami Daily News for 32 years. Despite being restored, it remains empty, but the Cuban National Foundation does have plans for a museum here.

Lyric Theatre

A local mural depicts prominent black Miamians on the side of this theater (☎ 305-358-1146, 819 NW 2nd Ave). Built in 1913, the 400-seat Lyric used to be a prime venue for silent movies, talkies, vaudeville and live performances by jazz greats like Duke Ellington and his contemporaries. It's the only symbol left of the once-vibrant neighborhood of Overtown (for more information, see Liberty City, later).

Miami River

The colorful, seedy riverfront is one of Miami's most fascinating places – but drive: You won't want to walk around here by night or day. Much of the shore is lined with makeshift warehouses, where goods move between shore and small tugboats bound for and from the Caribbean and other foreign ports. What exactly is in those containers is best not to ask. But unsavory images of drug smugglers and other rogue elements certainly leap to the imagination. It's all quite alluring and compelling in a mysterious way. Fisherfolk float in with their daily catch, fancy yachts 'slumming it' dock at restaurants, and nonconformists hang out on their houseboats. In order to have an excuse to linger in the neighborhood, where you are bound to get lost, enjoy lunch or dinner at one of the atmospheric seafood restaurants along the shores (see Places to Eat).

The river, by the way, was fed by the Everglades until the early 20th century. But for the time being at least, it's fed by canals starting at about the 32nd Ave bridge in Little Havana.

The 1897 **Flagler cottage** (*66 SE 4th St; no entry*), next to Bijan's on the River restaurant, was moved to this location in 1980 from SW 2nd St. It's one of just 14 simple pine houses that were built by railroad magnate and developer Henry Flagler. He rented them to workers for $15 to $22 month.

KEY BISCAYNE (MAP 7)
Basically the city's playground, Key Biscayne is a prime center for windsurfing, swimming, biking, boating, fishing and other outdoor pursuits (see Activities, later). **Virginia Key Beach**, a lovely city park with picnic tables, barbecue grills and relative peace and quiet, is a perfect for families. **Hobie Beach**, on the eponymous island, is great for windsurfing. And after a long, hard day of playing, there are lots of waterfront restaurants boasting dramatic skyline views perfect for sunset drinks.

Crandon Park
Definitely worth a visit, this 1200-acre park boasts the **Marjory Stoneman Douglas Biscayne Nature Center** (☎ 305-361-6767, Ⓦ *www.biscaynenaturecenter.org, 4000 Crandon Park Blvd; admission free; open 10am-4pm daily*), and **Crandon Park Beach**, a glorious but crowded white-sand beach that stretches for 3 miles. Much of the park consists of a dense coastal hammock and mangrove swamps. The nature center, especially fun for children, can teach you all about it.

Bill Baggs Cape Florida State Recreation Area
is wildish 494-acre wetland park (☎ 305-5811, *entrance 1200 S Crandon Park admission $2 per person, $4 for 2-8*

people; open 8am-sundown daily) is planted with native species (ever since Hurricane Andrew wiped out every single exotic species, that is). The barrier-island ecosystem is extensive, and there are plenty of walkways, boardwalks, bike trails, relatively secluded beaches, covered picnic areas and a little café selling decent soups and sandwiches. You'll also encounter hungry raccoons who like sandwiches (we don't need to tell you to keep your food to yourself, though, right?). A concession shack rents kayaks, bikes, in-line skates, beach chairs and umbrellas.

At the park's southernmost tip, the 1845 brick **Cape Florida Lighthouse** (☎ 305-361-8779), the oldest surviving lighthouse in Florida, replaced one that was severely damaged in 1836 by attacking Seminole Indians. You can tour it at 10am and 1pm Thursday to Monday (free). Tours are limited to about 12 people, so put your name on a sign-up list at least 30 minutes prior to the tour.

Miami Seaquarium
This fine 38-acre marine-life park (☎ 305-361-5705, Ⓦ *www.miamiseaquarium.com, 4400 Rickenbacker Causeway; admission $23/18 adult/child 3-9 yrs; open 9:30am-6pm daily, ticket booth closes at 4:30pm*) excels in preserving and protecting aquatic creatures, as well as educating us about them. It was one of the country's first such parks dedicated to sea life. There are dozens of shows and exhibits – easily a morning's worth if you're thorough – including a tropical reef; the Shark Channel, with feeding presentations; Faces of the Rainforest, with exotic birds and reptiles; and Discovery Bay, a natural mangrove habitat that serves as a refuge for rehabilitating rescued sea turtles. Check out the Pacific white-sided dolphins or visit the injured West Indian manatees being nursed back to health; some are released.

You can also swim and interact with the dolphins through Seaquarium's WADE, the Water and Dolphin Exploration Program (☎ 305-365-2501; $125; twice daily Wed-Sun).

LITTLE HAVANA (MAP 8)

After the Mariel Boatlift (see the History section in the Facts about Florida chapter), Little Havana exploded with Cuban exiles into a distinctly traditional Cuban neighborhood. Spanish is the predominant language, and you will encounter folks who speak no English. The borders of Little Havana are arguable, but for the purposes of this book, they extend *roughly* from W Flagler St to SW 13th St and from SW 3rd Ave to SW 37th Ave (Douglas Rd). The Miami River also meanders through Little Havana; see the Miami River discussion under Downtown, earlier.

The last Friday night of each month is the most happening in Little Havana. From 6pm to 11pm all the shops and restaurants fling their doors open, and café tables and merchandise spill out onto the sidewalks. Artists and craftspeople show their wares. Folks young and old, well-dressed and not, salsa to live and recorded music in the streets, on sidewalks and in shops.

Calle Ocho

The heart of Little Havana is Calle Ocho, Spanish for SW 8th St, which runs one-way from west to east. It's teeming with action and lined with Cuban shops, cafés, record stores, pharmacies and clothing stores. Of particular note are the cigar shops and *botánicas* selling Santería-related items like perfumed waters named 'Money' or 'Love Me,' or the more esoteric 'Keep Dead Resting.' See the boxed text 'Calle Ocho: Cigars, Botánicas & More,' later in this chapter, for details about many of these storefronts.

Little Havana as a tourist attraction is an elusive bugger; in fact, it's not really a tourist attraction at all. It's just a very Cuban neighborhood, which is exactly its attraction. It's real; it's not putting on airs for anyone; and it couldn't care less whether you visit. So, except for the occasional street fair or celebration, don't expect Celia Cruz or a ghostly Tito Puente leading a parade of colorfully attired, tight-trousered men. More likely you'll see old men wearing boxy *guayaberas* (shirts) arguing politics and playing dominoes.

On your way to a few of the sights discussed below, stop for a *guarapo* (sugarcane juice), *café con leche* or thimbleful of Cuban espresso.

Máximo Gómez Park

Perhaps better known as **Domino Park** *(Cnr SW 15th Ave & SW 8th St; open 9am-6pm daily)* because of the scores of elderly Cuban men playing dominoes, this is a highly sensory place to soak in the local scene. The clack-clack-clack sounds of hundreds of black-and-white dominoes being slapped on cement tables is downright musical. The park's namesake, Máximo Gómez y Báez, was the Dominican-born general of the Cuban revolutionary forces in the late 19th century.

Cuban Memorial Blvd

The two blocks of SW 13th Ave south of SW 8th St contain a series of monuments to Cuban patriots and freedom fighters (read: anti-Castro Cubans), including the **Eternal Torch in Honor of the 2506th Brigade**. It's dedicated to the counterrevolutionaries who died during the botched Bay of Pigs invasion on April 17, 1961 (see the History section in the Facts about Florida chapter). Other monuments include a huge brass relief map of Cuba, which is dedicated to the 'ideals of people who will never forget the pledge of making their Fatherland free,' and a bust of José Martí.

Unidos en Casa Elian

The Elian Gonzales house *(no ☎, 2319 NW 2nd St; donations requested; open 10am-6pm daily)*, where his life unfolded before cable news channels on a daily basis, is now a museum. You've undoubtedly seen the little house, on an ordinary street, on television many times. Elian's great-uncle Delfin bought the house in late 2000 and opened it in late 2001 as a shrine honoring Elian's time in the States. The place is filled, floor-to-ceiling, with hundreds of photographs, magazine covers, Elian's toys, his four bicycles and the pedal car he rode around the front yard. His bedroom is a time capsule: Clothes hang in the closet, the inner tube that saved his life at sea hangs on the wall, Spiderman pajamas are laid out on the bed. And then there's the life-sized enlargement of the Pulitzer prize–winning photograph of Elian hiding in the closet and being seized by federal border-patrol agents at gunpoint. The photo hangs right next to the real closet. It's like folks are waiting for him to return one day – the same boy, the same size, with the same impish grin.

Bay of Pigs Museum

This memorial museum (☎ 305-649-4719, 1821 SW 9th St; open Mon-Fri), also called the Juan Peruyero Museum and Manuel Artime Library, is named after two leaders of the ill-fated Bay of Pigs invasion. The walls are lined with pictures of comrades who were killed during combat and those who participated but have died over the years, without seeing a free Havana. The invasion is documented with memorabilia, flight charts and newspaper clippings. It's all quite personal and moving.

Latin American Art Museum

With 11 rotating exhibits yearly, this museum (☎ 305-644-1127, W www.latinartmuseum.org, 2206 SW 8th St; admission free; open 11am-5pm Tues-Fri & 11am-4pm Sat Sept-July) is one of the few in the country dedicated solely to the art and culture of Latinos.

COCONUT GROVE (MAP 9)

The Grove has much to recommend it: lots of lush parkland along S Bayshore Dr, including the 28-acre Kennedy Park; two great museums and an excellent playhouse; mod, multimillion-dollar waterfront homes next to modest cottages; good people-watching in the village center; and a great bicycling route along Old Cutler Rd (see Activities, later). At least Sylvester Stallone and Madonna thought so; they are among the famous who chose to live here at one point or another.

Miami's first major settlement dates back to 1834, but it wasn't formally established until 1873, when the population included blacks from the Bahamas, whites from Key West and intellectuals from New England. While the Grove became a big-time bohemian hangout in the 1960s and '70s, its nucleus has morphed into a highly commercialized district. Visitors are lured to CocoWalk, a stylized mall with restaurants and a cinema, and the adjacent Streets of Mayfair, another upscale shopper's paradise. It's really packed on weekends.

Pan Am 'Clipper' Air Travel

Pan Am 'Clippers,' big, luxurious flying boats really, began taking to the skies off Dinner Key Marina, 3500 Pan American Dr, in 1939. It was a romantic time for air travel, when then-exotic locales like Honolulu and the shores of South America were filled with wonder and newness. It was a time when overnight flights to China carried only 18 passengers, all in 1st class (the only class). It was a time when, on flights to Cuba and Key West, pilots would bring along carrier pigeons (rather than radios) to notify the terminal if there was trouble during the flight and if the plane had to make an emergency landing.

Although originally headquartered in a houseboat, Pan Am built an art deco terminal graced with nautical exterior details on Dinner Key in 1930, when it began flying to South America. It was the talk of the town. Although it has been unceremoniously converted into Miami City Hall (open 9am-5pm Mon-Fri), you can still see a 1938 Pan Am dinner menu and models of the clippers and other seaplanes that flew from here. Head into the lobby and turn left, and left again. You'll get a palpable sense of history sitting near the hangars, which are now used for boatyards. The seaplanes stopped flying in 1945, after WWII had fast-forwarded the development of long-distance land-based planes. Suddenly the exotic locales weren't so remote, and dare we say, the planet not so lonely.

Barnacle State Historic Site
Surrounded by 5 acres of ground, a pioneer residence (☎ 305-448-9445, 3485 Main Hwy; admission $1; house open 9am-4pm Fri-Sun, park open 8am-sundown daily) sits here on its original foundations, which date back to 1891. Owned by homesteader Ralph Monroe, often called Miami's first snowbird (a nickname for Northerners who fly south for the winter), the house is open for guided tours at 10am, 11:30am, 1pm and 2:30pm. Inquire about the great monthly moonlight concerts.

Vizcaya Museum & Gardens
This opulent Italian Renaissance–style villa (☎ 305-250-9133, W www.vizcayamuseum .com, 3251 S Miami Ave; admission $10/5 adult/child 6-12 yrs; museum open 9:30am-5pm daily, last admission 4:30pm; gardens open 9:30am-5:30pm daily) was built for industrialist James Deering in 1916. The villa itself is brimming with 15th- to 19th-century furniture, tapestries, paintings and decorative arts. Although the seaside grounds, which once spread for 180 acres, have been reduced to a mere 30, they're a poetic 30 acres. They feature splendid gardens, beautiful fountains, sculptures, elegant pools, a charming gazebo, canals running everywhere and lots of trails.

Tours of the 1st floor can be inconsistent (since they are led by volunteer guides), but they're included with the price of admission, so definitely take one. You'll get to peek into 34 of the 70 rooms. Tours last 45 minutes and run every 15 minutes from 10am to 2pm.

Miami Museum of Science & Space Transit Planetarium
The highly recommended science and space museum (☎ 305-646-4200, 646-4420 cosmic hot line for planetarium, W www.miamisci .org, 3280 S Miami Ave; admission to both $10/8/6 adult/senior & student/child 3-12 yrs; both open 10am-6pm daily) has great hands-on, creative exhibits: from turbulent weather phenomena and the mysterious universe to creepy crawlers and coral-reef exhibits. Yes, the virtual reality games are fun, but this museum also shows that gravity can be, too.

Even special exhibits like 'microbes: hard to live with, impossible to live without,' which might sound deadly (no pun intended), are interesting. Kids also tend to love the outdoor Wildlife Center, which features dangerous animals of South Florida and exotic birds of prey.

From outer space to cyberspace, the planetarium shines. On Friday and Saturday nights there are laser shows (the first show, at 7:30pm, is free, but later shows cost $7/4 adult/senior & child) set to the Beatles, Led Zeppelin and Pink Floyd.

Admission is half-price at 4pm on weekdays, because the last laser show has already begun, and at that point, you can only get into the science museum.

CORAL GABLES (MAP 10)
This lovely, leafy 'City Beautiful' exudes opulence and comfort, thanks to the vision of developer George Merrick. He took 1600 acres of inherited family land (planted with citrus and avocado trees), purchased 1400 more in 1921 and then went on an architect-hiring spree. His goal was simple: Create a planned 'model suburb' with a decidedly Mediterranean theme, magnificent gateways, impressive plazas, fountains and wide tree-lined streets. The city was in full bloom a mere three years later, and by 1925 it was incorporated. Today, Coral Gables, while exciting to multinational corporations and resident diplomats, is a quiet place with spreading banyan trees, fine restaurants, some very notable sites and an upscale arts scene.

There are really two faces to Coral Gables: the southern neighborhood around the University of Miami, which educates about 14,000 students, and the northern neighborhood along the Miracle Mile and off Coral Way (the same street where it's Miracle Mile).

The winding side streets can be confusing in Coral Gables, but go ahead and get lost. You'll stumble onto some beautiful scenery. A farmer's market (☎ 305-460-5311, 8am-1pm mid-Jan–Mar), with lots of gourmet picnic-style prepared foods, is held in front of the Coral Gables City Hall, 405 Biltmore Way.

Lowe Art Museum

On the University of Miami campus, works at the Lowe (☎ 305-284-3535, Ⓦ www.lowe museum.org, 1301 Stanford Dr; admission $5/3 adult/student; open 10am-5pm Tues, Wed, Fri & Sat, noon-7pm Thur, noon-5pm Sun) cover the spectrum, including: Renaissance and Baroque art; Western sculpture from the 18th to the 20th centuries; European paintings by Gauguin, Picasso and Monet; Egyptian, Greek and Roman antiquities; African, pre-Columbian and Asian entries (textiles, paintings, ceramics); and a collection of Southwestern weavings and Guatemalan textiles. The Central and South American collection reaches from Chile to Mexico in all media.

Biltmore Hotel

The city's crown jewel is the 16-story (315-foot) tower of the Mediterranean revival Biltmore (☎ 305-445-1926, 800-727-1926, Ⓦ www.biltmorehotel.com, 1200 Anastasia Ave), modeled after the Giralda bell tower at the Cathedral of Seville in Spain. Al Capone had a speakeasy here, and the Capone Suite is still haunted by the spirit of Fats Walsh, who was murdered here. More recently, the hotel hosted the 1994 Summit of the Americas. It's that kind of place. A palpable sense of enormity pervades the hotel. The pool is the largest hotel pool in the continental USA.

Don't miss the guided tour (☎ 305-445-1926; admission free; tours 1:30pm, 2:30pm & 3:30pm Sun), run by the Dade Heritage Trust, of the hotel and grounds. Tours leave from the upper lobby concierge desk and include the Capone and Merrick Suites, if they're unoccupied. For in-depth, well-spun yarns about ghosts, visiting celebs and the hotel's construction, check out the fascinating storytelling (☎ 305-445-1926; admission free; 7pm Thur).

Venetian Pool

As tons of earth and rock were taken for Merrick's building boom, a very large limestone quarry formed. Then a creative thinker thought: Why not transform this eyesore by letting it fill with water and

become a beautiful swimming hole? On the National Register of Historic Places, this 1924 spring-fed pool (☎ 305-460-5356, 2701 DeSoto Blvd; admission $5.50/2.50 adult/child 3-12 yrs Nov-Mar, $8.50/4.50 Apr-Oct; open 10am-4:30pm Tues-Sun Nov-Mar; open 11am-5:30pm Tues-Fri, 10am-4:30pm Sat & Sun Apr-May & Sept-Oct; open 11am-7:30pm Mon-Fri, 10am-4:30pm Sat & Sun June-Aug) boasts coral rock caves, cascading waterfalls, a palm-fringed island, vine-covered loggias and Venetian-style moorings. During its 1920s heyday, it hosted synchronized swimmer Esther Williams and Johnny 'Tarzan' Weismuller, both seen in historic photos at the pool.

While you're in the neighborhood, check out the adjacent DeSoto Fountain, about four blocks south of Coral Way. Denman Fink designed this four-faced fountain in the early 1920s.

Merrick House

When George Merrick's father purchased the land sight unseen for $1100 in 1899, it was a rocky plot with a rustic wooden cabin and some guava trees. George and his father certainly developed it, but Merrick's boyhood homestead does not have the same grand style that would later mark his adult vision. Today the modest family residence (☎ 305-460-5361, 907 Coral Way; admission $5/3/1 adult/senior & student/child 6-12 yrs; open for tours 1pm-4pm Sun & Wed) looks as it did in 1925.

Entrances & Watertower

Merrick planned a series of elaborate entry gates to the city, but the real-estate bust meant that projects went unfinished. Among the completed gates worth noting are: Country Club Prado (1927; SW 8th St & the Prado Country Club); the Douglas Entrance (1927; SW 8th St & Douglas Rd); the Granada Entrance (Alhambra Circle & Granada Blvd); the Alhambra Entrance (Alhambra Circle & Douglas Rd) and the Coral Way Entrance (Red Rd & Coral Way).

The Alhambra Watertower (1931), where Greenway Court and Ferdinand St meet Alhambra Circle, looks for all the world like a

Moorish lighthouse. The copper dome and frescoes were restored in 1993.

ELSEWHERE IN MIAMI

Just because these sights don't fall within any distinct neighborhood district doesn't mean they aren't worth checking out. On the contrary, some of the following sites are Miami's most intriguing, thought-provoking, wacky, evocative, historic or fun. Keep in mind, however, that sights within this section are spread out for 20 miles from north to south. Plan your travel time around rush-hour traffic, and think carefully about combining sights with visits to adjacent neighborhoods.

Biscayne Bay

Between Miami and Miami Beach there are about a dozen islands, some more exclusive than others, but all visible from the Mac-Arthur, Julia Tuttle and JFK Causeways. Most are accessible by bridges.

Flagler Memorial Monument (Map 4) Accessible only by private boat, this little speck of an island serves as a monument to Henry Flagler, one of Florida's leading pioneers, who, it could be argued, was single-handedly responsible for the development of South Florida. Who ever said no man is an island?

Fisher Island (Map 4) One of the Beach's pioneering developers, Carl Fisher, purchased this glorious little island and planned on dying here. He even built a mausoleum. As is wont to happen, though, he got bored with it after a while. When William K Vanderbilt II fell in love with the place, Fisher traded the island for Vanderbilt's 250-foot yacht *and* its crew. Things were like that in those days. Vanderbilt proceeded to build a splendiferous Spanish-Mediterranean-style mansion, with guest houses, studios, tennis courts and a golf course.

Today, this exclusive resort is accessible only by air and private ferry. The condominiums that line the mile-long private beach range from $1 million hovels to a $7-plus-million pad President Clinton once borrowed. It's said that the sun shines over the island even when it's raining in Miami Beach. Perhaps when you play with Nature by importing boatloads of sugary white sand from the Bahamas as they did on Fisher Island, you have some sway over the weather, too. Monied readers can overnight on Fisher Island at the **Inn at the Fisher Island Club** (☎ 305-535-6080, 800-537-3708).

The island is usually open only to paying guests and residents, but you can arrange a tour if you're especially persistent. Ferries leave from the Fisher Island Ferry Terminal off the MacArthur Causeway. The air-conditioned ferries depart every 15 minutes around the clock (yup, that's 24/7), and the trip takes 10 minutes.

Hibiscus, Palm & Star Islands Hibiscus (Map 2), Palm (Map 2) and Star (Map 4) Islands, though far less exclusive than Fisher Island, are three little bastions of wealth. There aren't *as many* very famous people living there now – just very rich ones – although Star Island is home to Miami's favorite star, Gloria Estefan. For a short time (he died here), Al Capone lived on Palm Island. The islands' circular drives are guarded by security booths, but they're also public, so if you ask politely and don't look like a hoodlum, you should be able to get in. Star Island consists of little more than one elliptical road lined with royal palms, sculpted 8-foot ficus hedges and fancy gates guarding houses you can't see. It will occur to you: So this is how the other 0.0009% of the population lives. But as one gatekeeper told me: We're probably a lot happier than these folks are, and they probably don't even know their neighbors.

Watson Island (Map 2) The island nearest to downtown Miami is the grungiest of the lot and is divided in half by the MacArthur Causeway. **Parrot Jungle & Gardens** (see below) occupies the northern side of Watson Island, while the southern side is home to some fishing and air charters.

Parrot Jungle & Gardens (Map 2) More than just a squawking-parrot show, Parrot Jungle (☎ 305-666-7834, ☒ www.parrot

jungle.com, Watson Island; admission $16/14/12 adult/senior & student/child 3-10 yrs; open 9:30am-6pm daily, last admission 5pm) has been a figure in South Florida kitsch since 1936, but at press time, it was in the middle of a move to Watson Island. The 20-acre location will be set in a coral-rock facility with a petting zoo and show area. Check the Web site for updates on the move. With more than 1200 varieties of exotic and tropical plants, the gardens are home to crocodiles, a rare albino alligator, orangutans, chimps, tortoises and very pink flamingos. The bird show is held five times daily; 'highlights' include showy parrots, macaws and cockatoos riding bicycles, roller-skating and playing cards.

Port of Miami (Map 2) Miami is the world's cruise capital, and when these 14-story floating behemoths are docked at the Port, it's a pretty amazing sight. The traffic jams on Thursday, Friday and Sunday, when the ships are loading and unloading weekend merrymakers, are pretty amazing, too. You also can't help but notice lines of semis hauling containers of goods, stacked like cereal boxes in a supermarket, bound for distant ports.

Fairchild Tropical Garden (Map 2)
The country's largest tropical botanical garden, the Fairchild *(☎ 305-667-1651, W www.ftg.org, 10901 Old Cutler Rd; admission $8/4 adult/child 3-12 yrs; open 9:30am-4:30pm daily)* covers 83 acres of lush rain-forest greenery. It has 11 lakes, plus streams, grottoes, waterfalls and hundreds of varieties of rare and exotic flowers. In addition to three easy-to-follow self-guided walking tours, there's a good, free 40-minute tram tour of the entire park (on the hour 10am to 3pm).

Matheson Hammock Park (Map 2)
This 100-acre county park *(☎ 305-665-5475, 9610 Old Cutler Rd; admission $4 per car; open 6am-sunset daily)* is the city's oldest and one of the most scenic. It offers good swimming for children in a closed tidal pool,

lots of hungry raccoons, dense mangrove swamps, crocodile spotting areas and the notable waterfront restaurant **Redfish Grill** *(☎ 305-668-8788).* There's a nice picnic area at the front end of the park, before you to pay to enter.

Miami Metrozoo (Map 1)
This worthy zoo *(☎ 305-251-0400, W www.miamimetrozoo.com, 12400 SW 152nd St; admission $9/4.75 adult/child 3-12 yrs; open 9:30am-5:30pm daily; last admission 4pm)* boasts 900 animals of more than 200 species. Keep your eyes peeled for informative zookeeper talks in front of some exhibits. At the children's petting area, kids can play with potbellied pigs, sheep, ferrets, chickens, lizards and more. There are also good wildlife shows in the amphitheater.

For a quick overview (and because the zoo is so big and can be so tiring), hop on the Zoofari Monorail for a good orientation; it departs every 20 minutes. If you have time, take the Behind the Scenes Tram Tour ($2), a 45-minute ride that takes you past the veterinary hospital, quarantine pens and brooder and hatchery building. It's wildly interesting. In general, though, try to visit the zoo in the morning, when the animals are more active. This is especially true in summertime.

Monkey Jungle (Map 1)
Monkey Jungle *(☎ 305-235-1611, W www.monkeyjungle.com, 14805 SW 216th St; admission $15/10 adult/child 4-12 yrs; open 9:30am-5pm daily, last admission 4pm)* brochures have a tag line: 'where humans are caged and monkeys run free.' It might conjure up images from *Planet of the Apes.* Indeed, you will be walking through screened-in trails, with primates swinging freely, screeching and chattering all around you. But it's not scary, just a bit odiferous, especially on warm days (read: most days).

Fruit & Spice Park (Map 1)
This 35-acre tropical public park *(☎ 305-247-5727, 24801 SW 187th Ave; admission $3.50/1 adult/child; free tours; open 10am-5pm daily)* has more than 100 varieties of citrus, 80 varieties of bananas, 40 types of grapes and a lot

more exotic tropical fruits, plants and spices. In the heart of South Florida's agricultural district, some of the species that grow here can't survive anywhere else. Best of all, while walking along the aromatic paths, you can take anything that falls (naturally) to the ground. Barring that, you can buy the exotic offerings at the **Redland Fruit Store**.

Coral Castle (Map 1)

South Florida has its share of strange attractions, half-truths, embellishments and wacky stories, and this castle (☎ *305-248-6345*, W *www.coralcastle.com, 28655 S Dixie Hwy; admission $9.75/6.50/5 adult/senior & student/youth 7-18 yrs; open 7am-8pm daily)*, on the National Register of Historic Places, is one if not all of the above. Here's the rumor and legend: After a Latvian was snubbed at the altar by a younger woman, he was so distraught he fled the country and immigrated to the States. He then spent the next 28 years (from 1923 to 1951), using only handmade tools, to single-handedly carve these coral rocks into a monument to unrequited love.

The largest stone weighs 29 tons, and the swinging gate weighs 9 tons. Strangely, no one ever saw him actually building the prehistoric-looking structures. But scholars have come here hoping to unlock the mysteries of how the pyramids were built. It's a misnomer to refer to it as a castle, since there are no turrets, ramparts or other architectural elements typical of castles.

Gold Coast Railroad Museum (Map 1)

South Florida would still be a swamp today without the introduction of train service. Primarily of interest to serious train buffs, this museum (☎ *305-253-0063*, W *www.gold coast-railroad.org, 12450 SW 152nd St; admission $5/3 adult/child 3-11 yrs; open 11am-3pm Mon-Fri, 11am-4pm Sat & Sun)* was set up in the 1950s by the Miami Railroad Historical Society. It displays more than 30 antique railway cars, including the Ferdinand Magellan presidential car, which is featured prominently in the famous photograph of newly elected president Harry

Truman. He's standing at the rear holding a newspaper bearing the famous erroneous headline 'Dewey Defeats Truman.'

Wings over Miami (Map 1)

Air and history buffs will be delighted at this Tamiami Airport museum (☎ *305-233-5197*, W *www.wingsovermiami.com, 14710 SW 128th St; admission $10/6 adult/senior & child under 13 yrs; open 10am-5pm Thur-Sun)*, which chronicles the history of aviation. Highlights include a propeller collection, J47 jet engine, a Soviet bomber from Smolensk and the nose section of 'Fertile Myrtle.' An impressive exhibit on the Tuskeegee Airmen features videos of the black pilots telling their own stories. The staff is knowledgeable and dedicated.

Ancient Spanish Monastery (Map 5)

The Episcopal Church of St Bernard de Clairvaux (☎ *305-945-1461*, W *www.spanish monastery.com, 16711 W Dixie Hwy; admission $5/2.50/2 adult/senior/child under 12 yrs; open to visitors 9am-5pm Mon-Sat)* is a stunning early Gothic and Romanesque building. Constructed in 1141 in Segovia, Spain, it was converted to a granary 700 years later, and eventually bought by newspaper tycoon William Randolph Hearst. He dismantled it and shipped it to the USA in more than 10,000 crates, intending to reconstruct it at his sprawling estate near San Luis Obispo, California. But construction was never approved by the government, and the stones sat in boxes until 1954, when a group of Miami developers purchased the dismantled monastery from Hearst and reassembled it here. It's a lovely, albeit popular, oasis, claimed (incorrectly) to be the oldest building in the Western Hemisphere.

Museum of Contemporary Art (Map 2)

The MoCA (☎ *305-893-6211*, W *www.moca nomi.org, 770 NE 125th St; admission $5/3 adult/senior & student; open 11am-5pm Tues-Sat, noon-5pm Sun)* features excellent rotating exhibitions of contemporary art by local, national and international artists.

Think along the lines of a Keith Haring retrospective and the first US appearances of Mexican masterpieces by Frida Kahlo and Diego Rivera. The reincarnated MoCA also has a strong permanent collection; look for work by Jasper Johns, Duane Michaels and Roy Lichtenstein. Good films usually accompany and enhance the exhibits.

Rubell Family Art Collection (Map 2)

The Rubell family operates a number of top-end hotels on the Beach, but they have also amassed an impressive and pioneering contemporary art collection (☎ 305-573-6090, 95 NW 29th St; admission $5/2.50 adult/senior & student; open 10am-6pm Wed-Sun) that spans the last 30 years. Opened in 1996, the 40,000-sq-foot facility houses works by Cindy Sherman, Keith Haring, Damien Hirst and Jeff Koons. But don't expect just one or two pieces by each artist; the aim is to focus on an artist's entire career.

American Police Hall of Fame & Museum (Map 2)

A police officer is killed in the USA every 57 hours, and this museum (☎ 305-573-0070, W www.aphf.org, 3801 Biscayne Blvd; admission $12/9/6 adult/senior/child 12 yrs & under; open 10am-5:30pm daily) memorializes them. You can't miss the boxy building with a 1995 Chevy Caprice Classic police car glued to the museum wall fronting Biscayne Blvd. In this extraordinarily violent culture in which we live, kids seem to be attracted to the gore and execution devices. (Florida recently discontinued the use of the electric chair, as it constitutes cruel and unusual punishment, but the state still enforces the death penalty.) While it has some 'fun' collections, like the cop car from Blade Runner, gangster memorabilia, confiscated weapons and restraint devices, it's mainly a tribute to slain officers.

Liberty City (Map 2)

From the birth of Miami until the 1950s, blacks were permitted to live only in the northwest quarter of downtown, called Colored Town. Since it was 'over the tracks,' the name was later changed to Overtown

and was eventually decimated by the construction of freeways and bypasses.

In 1934, a Miami Herald series on Overtown's appalling living conditions led to the first federal public-housing project in the southeastern USA. Subsequently, Overtown's residents were shoved into the projects, as whites needed the space. The 1950s concrete apartment blocks in Liberty City were built by white contractors to meet the housing demands of the expanding black community.

Liberty City, north and west of downtown, is misnamed. Made infamous by the Liberty City Riots in 1980 (see Racial Tensions, under History, earlier in this chapter), the area is very poor, and crime is higher than in other parts of the city. And while plans exist to renovate the area by creating a village of cultural and tourist attractions, the prospects of that happening in the near future look doubtful.

Whites, fearing 'black encroachment' on their neighborhoods, actually went so far as to build a wall at the then-border of Liberty City – NW 12th Ave from NW 62nd to NW 67th Sts – to separate their neighborhoods. Part of the wall still stands, at NW 12th Ave between NW 63rd and 64th Sts.

For information on Liberty City, Overtown and other areas significant to black history, contact the very helpful **Black Archives History & Research Center of South Florida (Map 2)** (☎ 305-636-2390, 5400 NW 22nd Ave; open 9am-5pm Mon-Fri, from 1pm-5pm for specific research projects), in the Caleb Center.

Little Haiti (Map 2)

As with Little Havana, Little Haiti has absorbed waves of refugees during times of political strife in the homeland. Haitians are the third-largest group of foreign-born residents in Florida, after Cubans and (surprisingly) snowbird Canadians. Although Little Haiti has had limited success in marketing itself as a tourist attraction, check in at the **Haitian Refugee Center** (☎ 305-757-8538, 119 NE 54th St; open 9am-5pm Mon-Fri), a community center that disseminates information about Haitian life in Haiti and

Miami. It's also a good resource for information about community events.

This colorful neighborhood is very roughly bounded by Biscayne Blvd to the east, I-95 to the west, 90th St to the north and 54th St to south. While you're up here, keep an eye peeled for Haitian **botánicas** that sell Voodoo-related items. They're worth visiting for beautiful bottles, beads and sequined banners with Voodoo symbols. While they may seem pricey at $100 to $200, they're far cheaper here than at galleries around the country, where they sell as art.

ACTIVITIES
Health Clubs
Bronze bods praise the sun, while buff bods bow to free weights. For those who can't go a day or week without flexing some serious muscle, plenty of gyms open their doors for daily and weekly memberships. Some might allow the use of nearby hotel pools; it's always worth asking.

Try **Crunch (Map 3)** (☎ *305-674-8222, 674-0247 class hot line, 1253 Washington Ave; $21/99 day/week)*, a gay fave that's also particularly popular with supermodels and offers wacky classes like Rear Attitude and Kardio Kombat. Devotees worship Crunch with the same fervor that others attend Mass.

Ironworks (Map 3) (☎ *305-531-4743, 1676 Alton Rd; $15/25/56 day/three days/week)*, popular with locals who size one another up discreetly, offers lots of yoga and aerobics classes. Ten visits for $80 is a great deal.

The truly chic head to the ultra stylish **David Barton Gym (Map 3)** (☎ *305-672-2000, 1685 Collins Ave; $20/75 day/week, 10-visit pass $150)*, on the lower level of the fiercely fashionable Delano Hotel. The nightclub of health clubs, where celebrity-spotting is a frowned-upon sport, delights in dim lighting, designer furniture, loud house music and…oh yes, state-of-the-art exercise equipment. Pumping iron and crunching abs is a bona fide recreational activity. Ask for the pass that gains access to the sexy pool.

Bicycling
The weather's fine and the roads are flat (elevation: sea level). What more could you

want? Well, you could call the **Miami-Dade County Bicycle Coordinator** (☎ *305-375-1647)* for a map highlighting the best metro roads. A leafy canopy lures cyclists in Coral Gables and Coconut Grove, where there's a particularly nice route. Follow the dedicated bike path and lane along S Miami Ave through Coconut Grove and down Old Cutler Rd to Matheson Hammock Park. Key Biscayne and the Bill Baggs Cape Florida State Recreation Area are popular places, as is the Oleta River State Recreation Area. On Key Biscayne you can rent at **Key Cycling (Map 7)** (☎ *305-361-0061, 61 Harbor Dr)*.

Biking in South Beach, especially on the Promenade and the boardwalk along the beach, is an excellent way to get around. Several places rent bicycles, including **Two Wheel Drive (Map 3)** (☎ *305-534-2177, 1260 Washington Ave; $5/15/45 per hour/day/week; open 10am-7pm Mon-Fri, 10am-6pm Sat & 11am-4pm Sun)*. It's also a nice ride from South Beach over the Venetian Causeway to Bayside Marketplace and back.

In-Line Skating
In-line skating is the most popular form of South Beach transportation. Everyone seems to have a pair of skates, and most streets are excellent for it. Three caveats for babes on blades: You can't ride on the café and hotel side of Ocean Ave or on the boardwalk that starts on 21st St, and you should use extra caution on Washington Ave. Lincoln Road and The Promenade resemble the Daytona 500 racetrack in sheer volume (if not speed, since riders generally skate at a moderate pace – all the better to see and be seen). Since some shops balk at letting you in with skates on, carry some sandals with you.

For rentals, roll over to **Fritz's Skate Shop (Map 3)** (☎ *305-532-1954, 730 Lincoln Road; $7.50/14/22.50 hour/6pm-noon/10am-10pm)*. Fritz gives free lessons on Sunday morning at 10:30am, when the streets have no name and late-night clubbers have just barely gone to bed.

Swimming Pools
Water, water everywhere, not a drop to drink. True and not true: These fresh and

salty waters are made for swimming, and you can always get a beverage poolside. Plus, sitting poolside sipping a cool drink is a worthy and noble Miami tradition. The spring-fed **Venetian Pool (Map 10)** (see Coral Gables, earlier) wins hands down.

The excellent T-shaped **Flamingo Park Swimming Pool (Map 3)** (*☎ 305-673-7750, 11th St)* has six lanes in its 25-yard lap-swimming area and a deep-water area. At press time the pool was closed for recon-struction; call for hours and fees.

Tennis

The **Flamingo Tennis Center (Map 3)** (*☎ 305-673-7761, 1000 12th St; open 7:45am-9pm Mon-Fri, 7:45am-8pm Sat & Sun)* has 19 popular clay courts that are open to the public for $2.50 per person per hour. On weekends and evenings after 5pm, the place is like a zoo.

Kayaking & Canoeing

Kayaking through mangroves is magical, and you can do it at Haulover Beach Park (Map 5) or Key Biscayne. Equipment rental is cheap, and you won't even need lessons to make the boat go where you want it to. Make a bee line for **Urban Trails Kayak Co (Map 5)** (*☎ 305-947-1302, 3400 NE 163rd St; singles $8/20/25 hr/4hrs/ day, tandem $12/30/35 including paddles,*

Beaches

Miami Beach has perhaps the best city beaches in the country. The water is relatively clear and warm, and the imported sand is relatively white. It's wide, firm and long enough to accommodate the throngs. A whopping 12 miles from South Pointe to 192nd St (William Lehman Causeway), the city is said to have an astonishing 35 miles of shoreline when taking into consideration Key Biscayne and the like.

Like a large, accommodating restaurant, the Beach is wordlessly zoned to provide everyone with what they want without offending anyone else. So, if you find yourself somewhere where the people around you make you uncomfortable, just move a little and you'll be fine. Perhaps surpris-ingly, topless bathing is legal in most places, a happy result of Miami Beach's popularity with Eu-ropeans and South Americans. In general, skimpy seems to be the order of the day, and you'll see plenty of thongs and other minuscule coverings on the bronzed gods and goddesses. Fear not ye in traditional bathing suits, you won't feel out of place.

The most crowded sections of the Beach are from about 5th St to 21st St. You'll see lots of models preening for photo shoots between 6th and 14th Sts, also known as Glitter Beach. Week-ends are usually more crowded than weekdays, but (except during special events), it's usually not too difficult to find a quiet spot. From 21st St to 46th St, the 1½-mile boardwalk is a nice way to see the beach without getting sand between your toes – perhaps for a sunset stroll before heading out to an early dinner?

Don't forget to check out the funky, Ken Scharf–designed **lifeguard tower** at 10th St. Other good, locally designed lifeguard towers dot 5th St to 14th St.

Elsewhere, notwithstanding the weekend traffic snarls (read: crawls) across the Rickenbacker Causeway, Key Biscayne (Map 7) is a key place to go. The 5 miles of Key beaches are relatively un-developed, commercial-free zones. Joy, ecstasy, delight, rapture.

Surfing & Windsurfing Beaches

First things first: This isn't Hawaii. In Miami Beach, head north to Haulover Beach Park in Sunny Isles (Map 5) or as far south as you can. The breaks between 5th St and South Pointe can actually give pretty good rides (by Florida standards, like 2 to 4 feet). You'll do well with a longboard. Hobie Beach (also called Windsurfing Beach; Map 7) rules for windsurfing.

life jacket & instructions; open 9am-5pm daily, weather permitting). Add $5 per single and $10 per tandem if you want to keep the kayaks overnight. This friendly outfitter can help plan and map your trip to some 19 Intracoastal Waterway islands, many with barbecue facilities. You can even camp on some for nothing. Ask about guided two- to four-hour trips (☎ 305-491-0221) for four or more people ($45 per person).

Sailboards Miami (Map 7) *(☎ 305-361-7245, 1 Rickenbacker Causeway; singles/tandem $13/18 hr)* also rents kayaks. See Windsurfing, below, for directions. You can also purchase a 10-hour card for $90. To get

some exercise for your lower body, you could try renting water bikes, which sit in a kayak-type boat and rent for the same prices as the kayaks. In either case, if you're goal-oriented and need a destination, head for the little offshore sandbar.

Windsurfing

Head immediately to Hobie Beach, also known as Windsurfing Beach. For board rentals, try the friendly folks at **Sailboards Miami (Map 7)** *(☎ 305-361-7245, 1 Rickenbacker Causeway; rentals $20-26/hr, lots of multi-hour specials; open 10am-4:30pm daily).* They offer short- and long-board rentals and also feature two-hour

---

Beaches

Gay Beaches
The tides wash up gay sand around 12th St, especially after the clubs close on Friday and Saturday. It's not like there's sex going on (there isn't); it's just a spot where gay men happen to congregate. Though outnumbered, lesbians gather here, too. Sunday afternoon volleyball at 4pm, after everyone has had a decent night's (morning's) sleep, is packed with fun-loving locals.

Swimming Beaches
What? You actually want to swim? Head to 85th St in Surfside (Map 5), devoid of high-rise condos and safely watched by lifeguards.

Nude Beaches
Nude bathing is legal at Haulover Beach Park in Sunny Isles (Map 5). Head to the northern end of the park between the two northernmost parking lots. The area north of the lifeguard tower is predominantly gay, south is straight. Sex is not tolerated on these beaches and you'll get arrested if you're seen heading into the bushes.

Latino Beaches
Latino families, predominantly Cuban, congregate between 5th St and South Pointe (Map 4). Topless bathing is unwise and can be considered offensive here.

Party Scene Beaches
Key Biscayne's ever-popular Crandon Park Beach (Map 7) attracts tons of families, locals blaring dueling stereos and tried-and-true beach bums to its barbecue grills. Admission is $2 per carload.

Quiet Beaches
It's pretty low-key up around 53rd St (despite the presence of families; Map 5) and down at Matheson Hammock Park (Map 2).

Family-Fun Beaches
Families head to beaches north of 21st St – especially the one at 53rd St, with a playground and public toilets – and the dune-backed one around 73rd St. They also head south to Matheson Hammock Park (Map 2), which has calm artificial lagoons.

'guaranteed-to-learn' windsurfing lessons for $69 (more advanced lessons cost $30/50 half-hour/hour, including equipment). Take the first right turn after the tollbooths for the Rickenbacker Causeway to Key Biscayne, where the water is calm.

Sailing

If you're a bona fide seaworthy sailor, **Sailboats of Key Biscayne (Map 7)** *(☎ 305-361-0328, 4000 Crandon Park Blvd; $27/81/129 hour/half-day/day for a 22-foot Catalina)* will rent you a vessel.

Rock Climbing

X-Treme Rock Climbing (Map 1) *(☎ 305-233-6623, 13972 SW 139th Court; $12 per day; open 3pm-10pm Mon-Fri, 10am-10pm Sat, 10am-8pm Sun)* boasts over 11,000 feet of climbing surfaces, including beginning routes and expert roof overhangs. Classes ($35) are offered by appointment only.

The Eden Roc Resort's **Spa of Eden (Map 5)** (see Northern Miami, under Places to Stay) has a very good indoor climbing wall.

Ultralight Aircraft & Skydiving

Over the years, ultralights have become so popular in South Florida that Miami-Dade County built a field specifically for them at **Homestead General Aviation Airport** *(HGAA; ☎ 305-247-48833; W www.airnav .com; 28700 SW 217th Ave)*. Although the small aircraft are regulated, you don't need a pilot's license to fly them. Lessons cost about $100 an hour, and you'll need 10 to 12 hours of training before you can fly solo. Contact the **Light Aircraft Flyers Association** *(☎ 305-460-3356)* for information about lessons and upcoming events.

Also at the airport, check out **Skydive Miami** *(☎ 305-759-3483)* will train you and push you out of a plane for $169.

In Miami proper, check out **Tony's Ultralight Adventures (Map 7)** *(☎ 305-361-3909, Rickenbacker Causeway; open 10am-sundown Sat & Sun, by appointment weekdays)*, which offers sightseeing flights and lessons in its nice, two-seater ultralight seaplane. First come, first served.

ORGANIZED TOURS

The **Miami Design Preservation League** *(MDPL; ☎ 305-672-2014, W www.mdpl.org)* is still ferociously active in protecting and restoring South Beach. They offer first-rate tours that depart from the **Art Deco Welcome Center (Map 4)** *(☎ 305-531-3484, 1001 Ocean Dr; tours $15; building open 9am-6pm daily, tours 10:30am Sat & 6:30pm Thur)*. The 1950s building has a space for deco-related exhibits and a gift shop with memorabilia, books and gifts. Volunteer guides of varying strengths illuminate the importance of and reasoning behind certain architecture details on many distinct buildings. Reservations are not required for the 1½-hour walking tours, but you should show up 15 minutes prior to the tour. Tours get crowded during February and March, but otherwise groups usually coalesce with about 15 to 20 people. The morning tour is preferable, since it's difficult to make out building details at night.

For a really great perspective on many different aspects of the city, call Dr Paul George (☎ 305-237-3723, 375-1492), a history professor at Miami-Dade Community College and former head of the Florida Historical Society. He really makes history jump off the page (or in his case, the streets). In conjunction with the Historical Museum of South Florida, he leads about 70 different very popular tours of Dade County between September and late June. Tours are conducted by bus and boat (three hours, $37), by foot and bike (two hours, $15) and by public transportation. Tours usually depart at 10am on Saturday and 11am on Sunday; they're always from different locations.

PLACES TO STAY

There are a few visitors who don't sleep much in Miami, but even *they* will need a place to change their clothes. Fortunately, metro Miami is blessed with a range of places to stay.

The Beach has upwards of 100 hotels with about 8000 beds ranging in price from $13 to $2000 nightly. The hotels below are categorized based on the price of a room in

The perfect accommodation

the wintertime high season; expensive suites skew the practical range. So-called budget rooms are less than $100, mid-range $100 to $200, and top end over $200. But remember, these prices are just guidelines; you should be able to get a room for less, unless you visit during a circuit party or other special event. Once you've arrived, it never hurts to ask to see a room before hauling your bag upstairs.

You'll have to swallow hard to absorb the 12.5% room tax. A few places even tack on an obligatory 15% service charge; ask before making a reservation. Hotel parking costs extra, but at least it includes in-and-out privileges.

South Beach
(11th to 23rd St; Map 3)

From rock bottom to top dollar, South Beach booms with choices. There are still a few places where you can pay less than $75 a night, but you'll sacrifice quality. Shop the budget places carefully, and check the rooms before committing. Even at the height of high season, you'll have a choice. Don't let anyone convince you otherwise. Also note that true deco style is compact by modern standards, so the more 'landmark' deco a hotel is, the smaller its rooms are likely to be. Unless otherwise noted, assume all South Beach hotels are two- to four-story low-rise hotels.

Budget **Banana Bungalow** (☎ 305-538-1951, 800-746-7835, fax 305-531-3217,

W www.bananabungalow.com, 2360 Collins Ave) Dorm beds $15-19; singles/doubles $45-99/56-102 off-season, $84-116/91-130 Dec-Apr. That the fun Bungalow has a big canalside pool surrounded by a concrete slab doesn't deter a bevy of bathing beauties. Perhaps that's because of the loud music, as well as the adjacent happening bar with a seriously rowdy international crowd. There are 60 spartan private rooms and 30 dorm rooms (most with six beds), a borderline inadequate communal kitchen and two Internet terminals.

Clay Hotel & International Hostel (☎ 305-534-2988, 800-379-2529, fax 305-673-0346, W www.clayhotel.com, 1438 Washington Ave) Dorm beds $15/18 with/without card, singles/doubles $40-54/42-60 off-season, $42-64/46-76 mid-Dec–mid-Apr. Perhaps the country's most beautiful HI hostel, this 100-year-old Spanish-style villa is also the Beach's most established. The Clay has an array of clean and comfortable rooms, from single-sex dorms with four to eight beds, to spacious VIP rooms with balconies to family rooms and decent private rooms with TV, phone, bath and air-con. Many are located in a medina-like maze of adjacent buildings. The excellent kitchen is large but very warm in summer.

Tropics Hotel & Hostel (☎ 305-531-0361, fax 305-531-8676, W www.tropicshotel

Reservation Agencies

Agencies usually have access to cheaper rates than you. Try the *Greater Miami & the Beaches Hotel Association* (☎ 305-531-3553, 800-733-6426, W *www.gmbha.org*), which sends out information on their members; *Hotel Reservation Service* (☎ 888-429-4290, W *www.hotelresservice.com*) or the *Central Reservation Service* (☎ 407-740-6442, W *www.reservation-services.com*), which both book rooms; or the *Florida Hotel Network* (☎ 305-538-3616, 800-538-3616, W *www.hotels.com*), which also makes reservations.

.com, 1550 Collins Ave) Dorm beds $16, private rooms $50/63/75 double/triple/quad Apr–mid-Feb, $75/88/100 high season. The surprisingly nice Tropics sports an Olympic-sized swimming pool, spacious brick patio, barbecue area and a full kitchen. Its clean dorms have four beds and attached bath, while the nice private rooms have firm mattresses, TV and phone. Some have great views of the pool. Lockers and Internet access ($1 per five minutes) are available.

Mid-Range Brigham Gardens Guesthouse (☎ 305-531-1331, fax 305-538-9898, W www.brighamgardens.com, 1411 Collins Ave) Rooms $70-110 off-season, $100-145 mid-Nov–May. Weekly discounts. This charming guest house, built around a lush garden that attracts tropical birds, feels like a sanctuary. Perhaps it's the bamboo, hammocks, fountains and patio chairs. Or perhaps it's the attention paid by the hosts to ensure you a restful respite. Choose from among 23 large and airy guest rooms (most with kitchens and bathrooms), studios and apartments.

Aqua Hotel (☎ 305-538-4361, fax 305-673-9109, W www.aquamiami.com, 1530 Collins Ave) Rooms & suites $75-295 off-season, $95-395 Oct–May. Renovated in 2001, this hip place utilizes wood and concrete for flooring, and marble and stainless steel in the bathrooms. Mod kitchenettes and Web TV are also appealing. Giant palms and teak furnishings surround the pool and courtyard, off which all 50 rooms are located. A second-story patio, where you can bring your Continental breakfast buffet goodies, overlooks the street.

The Dorchester Hotel (☎ 305-531-5745, 800-327-4739, fax 305-673-1006, W www.suitesofdorchester.com, 1850 Collins Ave) Rooms/suites $89/219 off-season, $115/269 late Dec–mid-Apr. Even though these 94 rooms are clean, they could stand some renovating, and the squeaky beds could be a bit firmer. Still, for the price, they're a good value. As for the 35 nicely renovated one-bedroom suites, they boast bona fide full kitchens and separate living rooms; some have sofa beds. The staff is very nice.

Abbey Hotel (☎ 305-531-0031, fax 305-672-1663, W www.abbeyhotel.com, 300 21st St) Rooms $95-165 off-season; $120-185 Dec-Mar. Insulated from the partying throngs, these 50 rooms manage to make timeless deco feel contemporary and warm. For the price, they're a very good value. Rooms feature touches of burnished chrome, platform beds and an earth-tone color scheme. There's no pool, but there is a nice garden. (A rooftop solarium is in the works.)

Villa Paradiso (☎ 305-532-0616, fax 305-667-0074, W www.villaparadisohotel.com, 1415 Collins Ave) Studios $79-115 off-season, $125-135 late Dec–mid-Apr. Similar in its upscale style and friendly personality to its neighborly competitor (Brigham Gardens), Villa Paradiso is another very good choice for studios and one-bedrooms with kitchens.

Marseilles Hotel (☎ 305-538-5711, 800-327-4739, fax 305-673-1006, W www.marseilleshotel.com, 1741 Collins Ave) Rooms/suites $95-115/169-189 off-season, $139-189/199-229 Jan–mid-Apr. This oceanfront property has eight very nicely renovated suites and 104 comfortable regular rooms. For the money, they're a very good deal.

Kent Hotel (☎ 305-531-6771, 800-688-7678, fax 305-531-0720, W www.thekenthotel.com, 1131 Collins Ave) Rooms $130 off-season, $145 Oct–May. The hipster Kent was one of the Beach's best values at press time. Completely gutted in 2000, these 54 rooms have warm-wood floors, blonde-wood furnishings and stainless steel accents. You'd better like lilac if you stay here, though: The walls, bedspreads and robes are all lilac. Besides the funky lobby, other common space includes a side garden with Indonesian-style tables, bamboo and hammocks.

Crest Hotel Suites (☎ 305-531-0321, 800-531-3880, fax 305-531-8180, W www.crestgrouphotels.com, 1670 James Ave) Rooms/suites $115-140/145-195 off-season, $155/195-235 Dec-Apr. This family-owned place, with 61 rooms in two buildings, is an excellent choice. Studios and one-bedroom suites feature custom galley-kitchens, combo living/dining areas, modern bathrooms and small work spaces. Don't overlook the added value of a pool and rooftop solarium.

Greenview (☎ 305-531-6588, 877-782-3557, fax 305-535-8602, W www.rubell hotels.com, 1671 Washington Ave) Rooms/suites $95-150/175-230 off-season, $160/260 late Dec–Apr. With only 40 rooms, this delightful find is at once homey and elegant. Furnishings are spare, with black-and-white photos on the walls and piles of white bedding. A Continental breakfast is included, as are the pool facilities at its sister hotel, the Albion.

Top End **Nassau Suite Hotel** (☎ 305-532-0043, 866-859-4177, fax 305-534-3133, W www.nassausuite.com, 1414 Collins Ave) Suites $150-260 off-season, $190-300 Nov-May. All of these 22 homey, contemporary pads feature shellacked hardwood floors, comfy pull-out sofas, fully equipped kitchens and walk-in closets. The rooms also have DSL connections and entertainment centers. You could easily imagine living here a while.

Cardozo Hotel (☎ 305-535-6500, 800-782-6500, fax 305-532-3563, W www.cardozo hotel.com, 1300 Ocean Dr) Rooms/suites $150-285/300-400 off-season, $195-310/395-450 Nov-May. The leopard-patterned hallway carpet sets the tone for singer Gloria Estefan's hotel, which looks every bit as distinctive and pricey as it is. Many of its 43 large, elegant rooms have dark hardwood floors and handmade furniture. Triple sheeting is but one of the typically luxurious amenities. The small bathrooms are outfitted with cool porcelain sinks and lots of glass and marble. Yessiree, this place is nice indeed.

Hotel Impala (☎ 305-673-2021, 800-646-7252, fax 305-673-5984, W www.hotel impalamiamibeach.com, 1228 Collins Ave) Rooms/suites $185-220/250-340 off-season, $225-250/300-400 Oct-May. Accessed through its lush courtyard, this lovely European-style hotel features 17 rooms with oversize bathtubs, and the requisite VCR, stereo with CD player etc. The friendly staff has managed to create atmos-

pheric elegance without arrogance. Rates include Continental breakfast.

National Hotel (☎ 305-532-2311, 800-327-8370, fax 305-534-1426, W www.national hotel.com, 1677 Collins Ave) Rooms $255-355 off-season, $315-450 Oct-May. (Suites are about twice the room rate.) This deco landmark doubles as a super-chic South Beach hangout. While the rooms aren't as mod as the lobby, they're lovely, with wood furnishings and shiny bathrooms. About a quarter of the 152 guest rooms in this mid-rise have balconies overlooking the pool. One palm-lined pool, which is a spectacular 250 feet long, leads to another, which in turn leads to a beachside tiki bar.

Raleigh Hotel (☎ 305-534-6300, 800-848-1775, fax 305-538-8140, W www.raleigh hotel.com, 1775 Collins Ave) Rooms $209-359 off-season, $319-499 Oct-May. If not at the National, then drop some of your hard-earned cash here. A hands-down fave, the mid-rise Raleigh is high-style deco luxe all the way. The 107 rooms' low platform beds make rolling out of bed in the morning very easy. We won't bother saying the pool is 'arguably' the best in town because no one would argue. It's swanky; you'd better suit up with self-confidence to bare your skin here.

Delano Hotel (☎ 305-672-2000, 800-555-5001, fax 305-674-6499, W www.ianschrager hotels.com, 1685 Collins Ave) Rooms $205-475 off-season, $325-575 Jan-Apr. To enter this fiercely fashionable sanctum, you must confidently stride past two hyper-tanned doormen dressed in white. Once inside, the self-congratulatory staff will politely rent you one of their 208 slick, sparse and minimally appointed rooms. A theater-set designer clearly worked the lobby: A Euro dance beat pulses, and floor-to-outrageously-high-ceiling curtains billow around enormously round pillars. Get into the groove.

The Tides (☎ 305-604-5070, 800-688-7678, fax 305-605-5180, W www.thetideshotel.com, 1220 Ocean Dr) Rooms/suites $475/575 off-season, $525/625 mid-Dec–May, penthouses up to $3000. Everything's chic and chichi at The Tides, where service is ultra-cool but surprisingly gracious. The lobby is awash in Latin jazz, equally soft lighting and overstuffed couches. Guest rooms – all 45 of which face the ocean – are wonderfully soothing, decorated in a rich (yes, rich) palette of beige, cream and a paler shade of white. They all have telescopes for planetary or Hollywood stargazing. The excellent pool is open around the clock.

South Beach
(1st to 11th St; Map 4)
Budget Miami Beach International Travelers Hostel (☎ 305-534-0268, 800-978-6787, fax 305-534-5862, W www.sobehostel.com, 236 9th St) Dorm beds $13-15 year-round, private rooms $32-59 off-season, $49-89 Jan-Apr. This 9th St hostel, not an HI member, has a little less of everything than the competition, but that applies to the digits on the prices as well. Rooms are a tad worn, but security is good and the staff friendly. Half the 100 rooms are private; dorms have four beds. The kitchen is big, the video-rental library decent and the Internet access speedy. You'll need either an out-of-state university ID, HI card, US or foreign passport with a recent entry stamp, or an onward ticket to get a room, but these rules are only enforced when it's crowded.

Mid-Range Kenmore Hotel (☎ 305-674-1930, 800-937-8376, fax 888-972-4666, W www.bestwestern.com/southbeach, 1050 Washington Ave) Rooms $85 off-season, $125 Dec-Apr. Best Western manages the Kenmore and its adjacent three properties (Park Washington, Taft and Belaire), which collectively take up an entire block. The Kenmore has a distinctive deco look, with a wavy concrete wall and a figure 8–shaped pool. You'll appreciate the relative remoteness of these 1930s establishments, close enough to the scene but just beyond the demarcation line for partiers.

Hideaway Suites (☎ 305-538-5955, 888-881-5955, fax 305-531-2464, W www.hideawaysuites.com, 751 Collins Ave) Units $99 off-season, $128-158 Dec-May. These 10 spotless apartments, tucked away in a little courtyard insulated from street noise, feature a washer/dryer, full kitchens, free local calls, daily maid service and a very

friendly staff. One wish would be that the units had more than one window.

Hotel Leon (☎ 305-673-3767, fax 305-673-5866, W www.hotelleon.com, 841 Collins Ave) Rooms/suites $100/145-195 off-season, $145/185-245 Oct-May. This 18-room Mediterranean hideaway is another hands-down fave for its friendly service and impeccable attention to detail. The hotel boasts (actually, it's too understated to boast, but we will) refreshing features like in-room fireplaces, deep bathtubs, *saltillo* tiles, exposed rafters, rattan furnishings, high ceilings and textured walls. The warmth continues into a communal buffet-breakfast room (add $7 per person).

Essex House Hotel (☎ 305-534-2700, 800-553-7739, fax 305 532-3827, W www.essexhotel.com, 1001 Collins Ave) Rooms/suites $129/189 off-season, $175/239 Nov-Apr. The lovingly restored Essex, with its ever-so-authentic deco lobby, is a friendly place with a helpful staff, a small pool and large rooms furnished with soft, subdued colors. The side verandah, filled with rattan furnishings, is a particularly pleasant place to people-watch. A Continental breakfast is included with the 58 rooms and 18 suites.

Top End The Park Central (☎ 305-538-1611, 800-727-5236, fax 305-534-7520, W www.theparkcentral.com, 640 Ocean Dr) Rooms/suites $95-165/145-195 off-season, $185-250/295-350 Nov-Apr. This 1937 art deco classic is a consummate SoBe hot spot; its pool is fabulous (if small), and its rooftop deck is a must-see even if you're not staying here. The 127 guest rooms and bathrooms are small but first-rate. To reach the roof, walk past reception, take the elevator to the top floor and walk out to the right. Go around 4pm, when cruise ships chug down Government Cut, or on any weekend night, for a great view of the Drive's action.

Whitelaw Hotel (☎ 305-398-7000, fax 305-398-7010, W www.southbeachgroup.com, 808 Collins Ave) Rooms $95 off-season, $195 Nov-Apr. The brochure promises 'clean sheets, hot water, stiff drinks,' but the 49-room Whitelaw goes a tad beyond that. The crisp bedding is Belgian, the bathrooms marble, and the alcohol complimentary from 8pm to 10pm. After white sheets, white robes, billowy white curtains and white antiqued floors, the sea-blue bathrooms come as a welcome shock. Oh, and could the retro vinyl lobby furniture get any whiter?

Hotel Astor (☎ 305-531-8081, fax 305-531-3193, W www.hotelastor.com, 956 Washington Ave) Rooms/suites $110-230/220-600 off-season, $195-290/390-900 Jan-Mar. An easy favorite, these 40 oh-so-inviting rooms are done in soothing earth tones. Note that 'regular' rooms are indeed small. But the bathrooms, with plenty of marble and mirrors, are bigger than most. The Astor has a small pool with a very cool 'water wall' surrounded by lots of comfy chaise lounges and a low-key bar with funky music.

Pelican Hotel (☎ 305-673-3373, 800-773-5422, fax 305-673-3255, W www.pelican hotel.com, 826 Ocean Dr) Rooms/suites $135/230-310 off-season, $180-200/300-400 Nov-May. Theme rooms rule here like nowhere else on the Beach. When the owners of Diesel jeans purchased the hotel in 1999, they scoured garage sales looking for just the right stuff. They found it – in spades. From 'born in the stars and stripes' and Western motifs to 'some like it wet' and psychedelic themes, each of the 30 rooms is completely different and fun.

The Hotel (☎/fax 305-531-2222, W www .thehotelofsouthbeach.com, 801 Collins Ave) Rooms/suites $255-295/395 off-season, $275-325/425 Jan-May. Another fine boutique hotel, with only 48 rooms and four suites, this Todd Oldham–designed accommodation boasts the best rooftop pool in South Beach, with cabanas, a fitness facility and showers. The casually elegant guest rooms feature handmade and artisanal detailing, like mosaic doorknobs and shower stalls, stylishly lush fabrics, and wood furnishings, along with modern amenities like data ports.

Northern Miami Beach (Map 5)

The following places are also convenient to South Beach.

Budget Urban Trails Kayak Co (☎ 305-947-1302, W www.kayakmiami.com, 3400 NE

163rd St) This is a rare innercity treat: You can camp for free on a myriad of little uninhabited intracoastal islands. But how to reach them? The airline wouldn't check your kayak as legit luggage? Luckily, this facility (see Activities) rents kayaks overnight, and they'll show you the way.

Mid-Range Suez Oceanfront Resort (☎ 305-932-0661, 800-327-5278, fax 305-937-0058, W www.suezresort.com, 18215 Collins Ave) Rooms $65-125 off-season, $82-135 mid-Dec–mid-Apr. This family-friendly 200-room motel would have to be underwater to be closer to the ocean. A throwback to an earlier era, the hotel boasts two pools, tennis courts and a tropical patio with lots of tables, umbrellas and palm trees. Spring for a room overlooking the patio rather than one of the annex rooms on the parking lot.

Dezerland Beach Resort Hotel (☎ 305-865-6661, 800-331-9346, fax 305-866-2630, W www.dezerhotels.com, 8701 Collins Ave) Rooms $89-139. The common areas of this 10-story hotel are mired in the past, too. The fabulous '50s roar to life in the form of car seats, oversized antique gas station signs and fin-backed cars that have been converted into dining tables. But while the hotel lobby-as-theme-park is decidedly retro, the 225 largish guest rooms are newly renovated, with tile floors. Some have a balcony, and all are adjacent to a 50-acre park. The hotel provides a convenient shuttle to South Beach.

Indian Creek Hotel (☎ 305-531-2727, 800-491-2772, fax 305-531-5651, W www.indian creekhotel.com, 2727 Indian Creek Dr) Rooms/suites $90/150 off-season, $140/240 Oct-Apr. The rustically civilized lobby and tropical courtyard here are delightfully serene places to while away a few hours. Mix in a friendly staff, a cool pool and a location just far enough from the madness, and you've got a recipe for a restful retreat. The 61 deco-style rooms are a tad dark, but you won't be in them during the day anyway.

Top End Eden Roc Resort (☎ 305-531-0000, 800-228-9290, fax 305-674-5555, W www .edenrocresort.com, 4525 Collins Ave)

Rooms starting at $189 off-season, $259 late Dec–mid-Apr. The gloriously renovated Eden Roc Resort is giving the Fontainebleau Hilton (see next listing) a run for its money. With extras such as an indoor rock-climbing complex, an Olympic-sized pool and an oceanfront spa and health club, it's a great place to get away. There are 349 rooms from which to choose.

Fontainebleau Hilton Hotel & Resort (☎ 305-538-2000, 800-445-8667, fax 305-673-5351, W www.hiltons.com, 4441 Collins Ave) Rooms starting at $189 off-season, $239 late Dec–May. Probably the Beach's most recognizable landmark, the 1200-room Fontainebleau opened in 1954 and was purchased by Hilton in 1978. It could be a bit more stylish, even though it has every conceivable amenity, including restaurants and bars galore, beachside cabanas, seven tennis courts, a kids' activity program, grand ballroom, business center, marina, shopping mall and an ab-fab swimming pool.

Downtown Miami (Map 6)

Downtown isn't the most exciting or beautiful place to stay, but the neighborhood might be centrally located for those exploring the farther reaches of the city with a car.

Budget Miami Sun Hotel (☎ 305-375-0786, 226 NE 1st Ave) Singles $39, doubles $45. This centrally located hostelry, adjacent to the courthouses and an undeveloped city block, is clean. Yup; that's about it. Oh, there are 80 rooms.

Leamington Hotel (☎ 305-373-7783, fax 305-536-2208, 307 NE 1st St) Doubles $46. Not a bad option, this decent place has 90 rooms and features an old-fashioned elevator. Whoopee.

Everglades Hotel (☎ 305-379-5461, 800-327-5700, fax 305-577-8390, W www.miami gate.com/everglades, 244 Biscayne Blvd) Doubles $99, less in summer. This 300-room behemoth looks like a three-star tourist hotel in post-embargo Havana: The lobby is suitably dark, the staff suitably morose, the decor suitably clunky. As you might expect, the rooms are below average. Still,

it's a worthwhile budget option in the heart of downtown.

Mid-Range Miami River Inn (☎ 305-325-0045, 800-468-3589, fax 305-325-9227, W www.miamiriverinn.com, 118 SW South River Dr) Doubles $69-129 off-season, $109-199 Dec-Mar. This complex in the middle of a colorful, unsafe nowhere, is gated out of necessity (see Miami River, under Downtown Miami, earlier in this chapter). It has charming New England–style rooms with wicker, brass and antiques. In addition to friendly service and fluffy comforters, you'll enjoy the lushly landscaped pool and Continental breakfast. There are 40 rooms, including a couple of apartments, within four wooden buildings from the early 20th century. Check out the treasure trove of Miami books in the guest library.

Clarion Hotel & Suites (☎ 305-374-5100, 800-252-7466, fax 305-381-9826, W www .clarionmiaconctr.com, 100 SE 4th St) Doubles $79-119 off-season, $129-189 Jan-Mar. Alongside the river in a location that can be maddeningly difficult to find, this 150-room Clarion has large, well-appointed rooms and suites. Some have microwaves and fridges. The hotel is adjacent to the Knight Center Metromover station.

Top End Mandarin Oriental Miami (☎ 305-913-8288, 800-526-6566, fax 305-913-8317, W www.mandarinoriental.com, 500 Brickell Key Dr) Doubles starting at $395 off-season, $550 Dec-May. This premier Asian hotel chain always takes top honors in my books, and this exclusive, extravagant Miami location is no exception. Don't worry about the sticker shock; with 324 rooms, you'll rarely have to pay rack rates. You might be able to get an entry-level $550 room with a balcony and breakfast for about $269. The full-service spa is outstanding.

Key Biscayne (Map 7)

Seriously consider staying on the sandy shores of Key Biscayne.

Silver Sands Beach Resort (☎ 305-361-5441, fax 305-361-5477, W www.silver sandsmiami.com, 301 Ocean Dr) Rooms/

cottages $129-149/279 off-season, $169-189/329 mid-Dec–late Apr; weekly rates available; kids free under age 14 when sharing a room with their parents. Hidden in a quiet neighborhood just steps from the beach, this 60-room single-story motel is a quiet gem. The simple rooms, half of which spill out onto a garden courtyard (they're worth the extra $20), have clean bathrooms, tile rather than carpeting, firm mattresses and mini-kitchens. Of course there's a pool.

Sonesta Beach Resort Key Biscayne (☎ 305-361-2021, 800-766-3782, fax 305-361-3096, W www.sonesta.com, 350 Ocean Dr) Rooms $195-330 off-season, $295-425 late Dec–Apr. On a wide stretch of powdery sand, this 295-room mid-rise hotel works hard and successfully to make you never want to leave the property. It's a really fine place to relax and boasts an oceanfront pool, a kids' activity program, bicycle rentals, plenty of bars and restaurants, contemporary rooms, tennis courts and a fitness center.

Coconut Grove (Map 9)
A waterside neighborhood with lots of options, Coconut Grove offers a couple of distinct alternatives.

Hampton Inn (☎ 305-448-2800, 800-426-7866, fax 305-442-8655, W www.hampton inn.com, 2800 SW 28th Terrace) Rooms $89 off-season, $129 late Dec–late Apr. This modest 136-room hotel, easily accessible off US Hwy 1, but not within walking distance of the Grove, includes a Continental breakfast buffet in its rates. Many rooms have refrigerators and microwaves. Will wonders never cease: They also offer free local calls.

The Mutiny Hotel (☎ 305-441-2100, 888-868-8469, fax 305-441-2822, W www.mutiny hotel.com, 2951 S Bayshore Dr) Suites $149-325 mid-June–Sept, $199-399 mid-season, $219-429 Jan-Mar. This small luxury hotel, with 120 one- and two-bedroom suites featuring balconies, boasts an indulgent staff, luxe bedding, gracious appointments, fine amenities and a small heated pool. Although it's on a busy street, you won't hear the traffic noises once inside.

Sonesta Hotel & Suites Coconut Grove (☎ 305-529-2828, 800-766-3782, W www

.sonesta.com, 2889 McFarlane Rd) Rooms $165-185 off-season, $175-295 late Dec–mid-Apr; one-bedroom suites are more expensive. Opened in March 2002, this 300-room hotel is the excellent sister property to the one on Key Biscayne (see that entry, earlier).

Coral Gables (Map 10)
A tony and leafy neighborhood, Coral Gables offers a little of everything.

Terrace Inn (☎ 305-662-8845, fax 305-662-5562, 1430 S Dixie Hwy) Rooms $59 off-season, $69-89 Nov-Apr. This bi-level place, just far enough off US Hwy 1 to make it quieter than its competitors, used to be a Howard Johnson. You'll recognize the trademark hotel roofline. The 80 rooms are modest.

Holiday Inn (☎ 305-667-5611, 800-465-4329, fax 305-669-3151, 1350 S Dixie Hwy) Rooms $99-129 off-season, $119-169 mid-Dec–mid-Apr. A gargantuan chain hotel with 155 standard-issue rooms, Holiday Inn has newly renovated rooms near the university. You'll find the requisite kidney-shaped pool and a fitness center on the premises.

Hotel Chateau Bleau (☎ 305-448-2634, 888-642-6442, fax 305-448-2017, 1111 Ponce de León Blvd) Rooms $69 off-season, $89-109 Dec-Mar. Although the name has grander aspirations than the rooms deliver, this is still a commendable lodging choice. Operated by Best Western, this low-rise motel has a friendly staff and 120 newly renovated rooms, most of which overlook a parking lot. For what it's worth, though, there are balconies and a small pool. A few rooms have kitchenettes.

Hotel Place St Michel (☎ 305-444-1666, 800-848-4683, fax 305-529-0074, W www .hotelplacestmichel.com, 162 Alcazar Ave) Rooms/suites $125/160 off-season, $150-165/185-200 Nov-Apr. The first things you'll notice at this charming Old World, European-style hotel are the vaulted ceilings, fancy tile work and inlaid wood floors. With only 27 rooms, though, the hotel's hallmark is excellent service. You can also expect amenities like Continental breakfast, a morning newspaper and evening turndown service. The plush furnishings are a welcome relief from the omnipresent, stark deco look.

The Biltmore Hotel (☎ 305-445-1926, 800-727-1926, fax 305-913-3159, W www.biltmorehotel.com, 1200 Anastasia Ave) Doubles starting at $359 Jan-Mar (with four seasonal price changes throughout the year), suites a heck of a lot more. The brochure buzzwords here are apt and don't overstate the hotel's case: splendor, glamour, opulence, bygone era, exquisite style, pampered luxury. You get the idea. This 1926 National Historic Landmark, built in a Mediterranean style, also has the largest hotel pool in the country. Promise to stop by even if you haven't packed in high style. There are 280 rooms. The popular Capone Suite (see the Coral Gables section, earlier) is priced according to availability, but it hovers in the $1000 to $2000 range.

Greater Miami (Map 1)

Miami-Homestead-Everglades KOA (☎ 305-233-5300, 800-562-7732, W www.miamicamp.com, 20675 SW 162nd Ave) Tents/hookups $26/30, 'kamping kabins' $45 (2-4 people), 1-/2-room lodges $59/89. The area's only KOA has almost 300 sites (only 13 of which are specifically for tenters), a pool, game room, shuffleboard, bike rentals, laundry facilities etc. Cabins have bunk beds, a porch and barbecue grills. Lodges sleep four to eight people and have almost-full kitchens. If you intend to 'commute' to Miami from here, note that it's 25 miles south of downtown.

PLACES TO EAT

Miami restaurants enliven the palate and eyes. From authentic hole-in-the-wall Cuban joints to haute New World fusion that'll knock your sockless sandals off, there is something for every budget and trendy taste bud. Cuisine can be as sophisticated as you are, as lowbrow as Uncle Mike or as campy as Aunt Mildred. Certainly, the experience of dining out can be as much about being seen as it is about being nourished. You decide. Miami eateries benefit from a cultural connection to Latin America and the

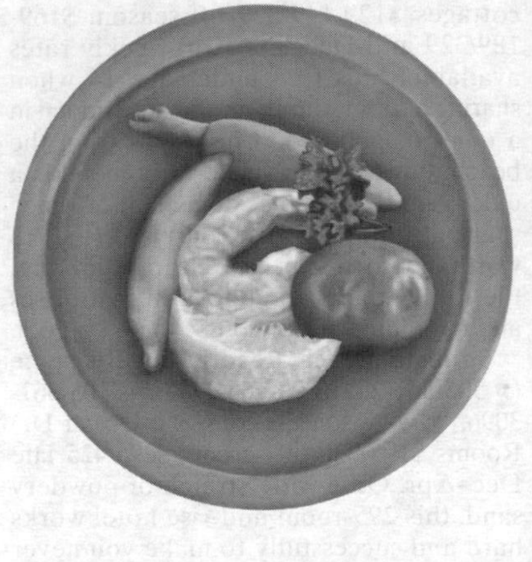

Caribbean that's simply not matched elsewhere in the country. Take advantage of it.

Establishments are categorized according to the restaurant's average main courses at dinner: budget (up to $10), mid-range ($10-19) and top end ($20 and up). A general rule of thumb for calculating the price of a full meal with a glass of wine, tax, tip and an appetizer *or* dessert is to double the entrée price. Don't rule out the top-end places just because you're budget conscious. Consider getting a couple of appetizers and sharing an entrée. You don't think rail-thin models *ever* eat full meals, do you? In an effort to draw folks in, many restaurants offer early specials. Don't be demure about asking.

South Beach (Maps 3 & 4)

The restaurant scene in South Beach is so varied that this section has been organized by the type of food served – Mexican, Italian, seafood etc, then price subcategories where necessary.

There are two caveats worth noting about South Beach dining: Service can be poor if you're not a VIP, or at least a VBP (very beautiful person). And many places – such as the News Cafe – include the tip automatically. Be vigilant and don't tip twice!

Markets Hit Alton Rd for moderately priced picnic fixings consisting of extraordinary delights.

Wild Oats Community Market (☎ 305-532-1707, 1020 Alton Rd) **Map 4** Open 7am-11pm daily. This has got to be the best natural-food market on earth, and grazing is the order of the day here. With aisles and aisles of wonderful stuff, it's South Beach's primo place to assemble a fantastic and healthy meal. There's also a magnificent salad bar and pre-made vegetarian, vegan, organic and even meat entrées. Get the food at the deli counter and sit at the tables in front, where there's even free spring water. Or belly up to the juice bar, where the tonics will cure whatever ails you.

Epicure Market (☎ 305-672-1861, 1656 Alton Rd) **Map 3** Dishes $5-8. Open 10am-8pm Mon-Fri, 10am-7pm Sat, 10am-6pm Sun. Head to the kosher deli counter for excellent prepared salads and pasta dishes, which can be heated if you want.

There are only a couple of real American-style supermarkets in the area. Look for **Publix** (☎ 305-538-7250, 1045 Dade Blvd; Map 3) on Miami Beach; **Publix** and **Winn-Dixie** markets are scattered all over the area.

Bakeries & Delicatessens 5th Street Deli (☎ 305-604-0555, 458 Ocean Dr) **Map 4** Dishes $5-7. Open 8am-8pm Mon-Thur, 8am-9pm Fri-Sun. Another purveyor of tasty deli-style sandwiches, 5th Street features Boar's Head meats, as well as some vegetarian options like roasted vegetables, avocado and brie.

Le Chic (☎ 305-673-5522, 1043 Washington Ave) **Map 4** Sandwiches $5-7. Open 6:30am-7:30pm Mon-Sat, 6:30am-2:30pm Sun. This authentic French bakery serves sandwiches on fresh baguettes or croissants. Treat yourself to a delectable pastry, unless you model in your spare time.

Seafood There are plenty of places for a variety of great seafood.

Mid-Range Les Deux Fontaines (☎ 305-672-7878, 1230 Ocean Dr) **Map 3** Breakfast mains $5-10, dinner dishes $10-20. Open 7:30am-midnight daily. Open for breakfast, light lunches and more substantial dinners, this restaurant has its terrace perfectly perched above Ocean Drive – just close enough to people-watch but far enough to keep the 'riffraff' from your food. Seafood is the specialty, but don't expect fancy preparations. Prices shoot upward at dinnertime, although it's not as expensive as it looks or feels.

South Beach Stone Crabs (☎ 305-538-5888, 723 Lincoln Road) **Map 3** Stone crabs $25 & up, mains $12-34. Open noon-midnight daily. A fine alternative to the

SoBe Coffee Bars

This is not Seattle, or even Atlanta, when it comes to the coffeehouse scene. But while most small coffee bars on the Beach have fallen victim to Starbucks, there are alternatives to the super sugary, high-octane joe served at Cuban places around town.

Segafredo Zanetti Espresso (☎ 305-673-0047, 1040 Lincoln Road; Map 3) is an honest-to-goodness, bona fide Italian café, serving Italian sweets and heavenly espresso drinks. It's open 11am to midnight Sunday to Thursday, until 1am on Friday and Saturday.

Kafka Kafé (☎ 305-673-9669, 1464 Washington Ave; Map 3) has Internet access and a bookish coffeehouse vibe. It's open 8:30am to midnight daily.

Joffrey's Coffee Co (☎ 305-445-5116, 660 Lincoln Road; Map 3), a newer chain than Starbucks, is trying to give them a run for your coffee dollars. The digs are still unpretentious, and the staff is friendly. It's open 11am to midnight Sunday to Wednesday, until 2am Thursday to Saturday.

If you blink you'll miss *Van Dyke News* (☎ 305-534-3600, 846 Lincoln Road; Map 3). Around the corner from the busy Van Dyke Cafe, this little convenience store–cum-newsstand-cum-sidewalk-espresso bar is frequented by locals reading the paper and sipping cappuccino in peace.

interminable line at Joe's, this sidewalk eatery offers the same crustaceans, with a prime view of the Lincoln Road *passagiato*. When crabs are out of season, you can feast on other seafood and pasta specials.

Grillfish (☎ 305-538-9908, 1444 Collins Ave) **Map 3** Mains $13-22. Open 6pm-11pm Sun-Thur, 6pm-midnight Fri & Sat. Grillfish has a wonderful atmosphere. Greek? Mediterranean? 'Gay,' said the cute waiter. It's elegant, but tuxedos are fortunately forbidden. The mainly Italian-inspired seafood dishes are very good, but they also do chicken. Try the salmon or rainbow trout served over pasta. If you have an appetite, the mussels and shrimp scampi 'apps' are tasty, too.

Top End **Joe's Stone Crab Restaurant** (☎ 305-673-0365, 227 Biscayne St) **Map 4** Open 11:30am-2:30pm Tues-Sat & 5pm-10pm daily mid-Oct–mid-May (stone crab season); closed mid-May–mid-Oct. As close as Miami Beach gets to a world-famous restaurant, Joe's has been around since 1913. No reservations are accepted and the line is a mile long – tip the mai\tre d' or be prepared to wait and wait, and wait some more. The quality and high profile come at a price: Medium-sized stone crab claws cost $20 (eight per order), 'selects' $27 (seven per order) and large ones $37 (five per order).

Tantra (☎ 305-672-4765, 1445 Pennsylvania Ave) **Map 3** Mains $32 & up (market price for seafood). Open 7pm-1am daily. One of South Beach's coolest celebrity hot spots also serves some of its most creative and exciting cuisine. Based on the premise that all senses are to be awakened, Tantra delivers in the visual, aural and taste departments. Large portions of eclectic cuisine like Thai spiced duck confit with an orange-scented cucumber salad share the stage with Moroccan spiced lamb with mint and mango. The lobby features freshly cut grass, while the bar pulses to tantric music as sweet somethings wander around offering aphrodisiac cocktails.

American Sandwiches rule this category, but you still have to choose whether to eat in chic or diner-like surroundings.

Budget There are lots of great places to get a quick sandwich.

La Sandwicherie (☎ 305-532-8934, 229 14th St) **Map 3** Dishes $5-9. Open 9am-5am daily, delivery available until 10pm. Despite its faux-French name, baguettes and pretentious translations *(cornichons*=French pickles), La Sandwicherie is as American as a sex scandal over nothing. This means that it has great – and great-big – sandwiches. The fruit juices, smoothies and shakes are also good. Located in an alley (which smells a bit ripe now and then), the shop has about four stools and a small sandwich bar.

Ice Box Cafe (☎ 305-538-8448, 1657 Michigan Ave) **Map 3** Open 11am-11pm Tues-Thur & Sun, 11am-midnight Fri & Sat. This catering operation-cum-ultra-chic-café serves beautifully prepared sandwiches and salads and luscious desserts in an intimate storefront setting. You can eat in or take out.

Van Dyke Cafe (☎ 305-534-3600, 846 Lincoln Road) **Map 3** Dishes $6-15. Open 8am-2am daily. One of Lincoln Road's most touristed spots, the Van Dyke serves adequate food in a cool setting. It's usually packed to the rafters and co-opts half the sidewalk. Service is very friendly, even efficient, and if you could just avoid the models preening and posing, it would be a far better place to enjoy the burgers, open roast beef sandwiches and eggplant parmigiana (a house specialty). There's nightly jazz upstairs.

Mid-Range **News Cafe** (☎ 305-538-6397, 800 Ocean Dr) **Map 4** Dishes $9-12. Open 24 hrs daily. It's worth spending part of an afternoon at this painfully trendy South Beach landmark. The food almost rivals the street-side perch. It has terrific salads, plain omelets and pasta dishes but is perhaps more well known for tomato bruschetta. Pair it with an iced tea to sip while watching the skaters wiggle and glide down Ocean Drive. A 15% tip is added to all checks, but if you're really unhappy with the service, they'll remove it upon request.

11th Street Diner (☎ 305-534-6373, 1065 Washington Ave) **Map 4** Dishes $5-15. Open 24 hrs daily. This original art deco diner, trucked down from Wilkes-Barre,

Pennsylvania, has been renovated and serves really good three-egg omelets, sandwiches and down-home favorites like fried chicken and meatloaf. The service is leisurely but cheery.

Front Porch Cafe (☎ 305-531-8300, 1418 Ocean Dr) **Map 3** Lunch mains $8-9, dinner mains $11-14. Open 8am-10:30pm daily. Since 1990 (eons by South Beach standards), the Front Porch has been noteworthy for its low-key, pleasant atmosphere and its good sampler salads and sandwiches. It's a quiet place to meet for a fashionable breakfast without the side order of attitude.

Big Pink (☎ 305-532-4700, 157 Collins Ave) **Map 4** Dishes $7-20. Open 9am-1am Sun-Thur, 9am-2am Fri & Sat. Big Pink is big fun '50s style. What can you say about a place whose signature dish is an authentic, American-style 'TV dinner' served on a six-compartment steel tray? Burgers, sandwiches, pizza, meal-sized salads, nacho platters, buckets of fries and chicken wings are served in a cavernous, convivial atmosphere. Breakfast is available all day. Dine inside or at sidewalk tables. Either way, save room for the Key lime pie.

Balans (☎ 305-534-9191, 1022 Lincoln Road) **Map 3** Mains $8-18. Open 8am-midnight Sun-Thur, 8am-1am Fri & Sat. This chic, British-owned, oh-so-Soho bistro has a modern-yet-comfortable atmosphere. The menu fuses Mediterranean and Asian cuisines; their signature lobster club sandwich is worth every penny. Sidewalk seating appeals to those who prefer open-air people-watching.

Café Cardozo (☎ 305-695-2822, 1300 Ocean Dr) **Map 3** Breakfast & lunch $3-12, dinner mains $10-18. Open 8am-midnight Sun-Thur, 8am-2am Fri & Sat. This offshoot of the popular News Cafe features tasty appetizers like conch fritters and black-bean cakes, as well as burgers, sandwiches, salads, pizza, grilled fish and pasta dishes. Breakfast is served until 4pm. On warm days, a cooling mist falls from the terrace above to gently spritz the diners at sidewalk tables. Sounds like a cooling idea, but on breezy days, the cars driving down Ocean Ave get most of the benefit.

Nexxt Cafe (☎ 305-532-6643, 700 Lincoln Road) **Map 3** Mains $12-20. Open 11am-11pm Mon-Thur, 11:30am-midnight Fri-Sun. You can't go wrong with the wide-ranging salads, pastas, grilled fish and meat dishes here. And the immense menu mirrors equally immense servings; entrées are big enough to share. It's a struggle, but leave room for a luscious dessert. Sidewalk seating provides a full view of the Lincoln Road parade.

***Top End* Joe Allen Miami Beach** (☎ 305-531-7007, 1787 Purdy Ave) **Map 3** Mains $15-25. Open 11:30am-11:30pm daily. South Beach's hidden gem is located in an under-developed bayside neighborhood. This hip and decidedly low-key restaurant serves outstanding food to an upbeat, unpretentious crowd. Great steaks, fresh fish, salads, pizza and smooth service keep everyone well fed and happy.

Pearl Restaurant & Champagne Lounge (☎ 305-538-1111, 1 Ocean Dr) **Map 4** Mains $17-37. Open 7pm-midnight Wed-Sun. Situated within Penrod's Entertainment Complex, this upscale, groovy eatery is orange. You can't avoid it, and you'll soon be basking in it. Just give in to it. Perhaps you'll head straight to the centerpiece of the lounge/club/restaurant, a champagne bar with high-backed, sculpturally molded chairs. As for the first-rate creative cuisine, it ranges from miso-marinated sea bass to garlic-and-herb–crusted rack of lamb. Save room for dessert.

Places to Eat 24/7

When hunger strikes in the middle of the night, after clubbing or a bad dream, you have options. These places are open 24 hours a day, seven days a week.

11th Street Diner	Map 4
News Cafe	Map 4
Rascal House	Map 5
La Carreta	just off Map 8,
(in Little Havana)	3632 SW 8th St

Wish (☎ 305-531-2222, 801 Collins Ave) **Map 4** Breakfast $8-15, dinner mains $23-34. Open 7am-11pm Sun-Thur, 7am-midnight Fri & Sat. Put Wish on the top of your wish list for a quiet, romantic dinner spot. Within the Todd Oldham–designed 'The Hotel,' highly acclaimed chef Michael Reidt takes contemporary French-Brazilian cuisine to the next level, emphasizing fresh fish, savory flesh and fancy fowl. The elegantly understated dining room is lovely, with Persian-inspired decor, but the adjoining candlelit courtyard may be the Beach's most romantic dining spot.

Mark's South Beach (☎ 305-604-9050, 1120 Collins Ave) **Map 3** Lunch mains $15-17, dinner mains $25-38, five-course tasting menu $65. Open noon-3pm & 7pm-11pm daily. The most innovative kitchen in South Beach lies within the chic Nash Hotel. Chef-owner Mark Militello, one of the original trio of chefs known as the Mango Gang, is forever pushing the proverbial envelope. Although the menu, which changes nightly, tilts toward seafood, meat eaters will be intrigued, too. Desserts are as beautiful as the clientele. The subterranean dining room is cozy and elegant, the service helpful and assured.

Cuban David's Cafe II (☎ 305-672-8707, 1654 Meridian Ave) **Map 3** Dishes $3-6, buffet lunch $7.50. Open 7am-11pm daily. Most folks come for a quick shot of Cuban coffee from the take-out window, but the place is also popular for cheap breakfasts, taken at bar stools, and a bountiful lunch buffet, served in the dining room.

Lincoln Road Café (☎ 305-538-8066, 941 Lincoln Road) **Map 3** Dishes $3-6, buffet lunch $7.50. Open 8am-1am daily. This longtime, famous Cuban spot is known for infuriatingly slow service and reliably decent food (the poultry dishes are very good).

Pollo Tropical (☎ 305-672-8888, 1454 Alton Rd) **Map 3** Dishes $7-13. Open 11am-midnight daily. The most nutritious fast food in the country is served here. Yes, it's fast food in fast-food surroundings, but it's great.

Puerto Sagua (☎ 305-673-1115, 700 Collins Ave) **Map 4** Dishes $6-25. Open 7:30am-2am daily. An anomaly on this stretch of Collins Ave – its neighbors are the Gap and Benetton – this authentic Cuban diner and restaurant serves humongous portions at reasonable prices. Try the black bean soup, *arroz con pollo* (rice with chicken) or *ropa vieja* (shredded beef), or specialties like *filete de pargo grillet* (grilled red snapper). Stick to the low-end and moderately priced dishes; this is not the place to drop $25 on an entrée. If you haven't had Cuban café con leche yet, this is the place to do it, because they serve the espresso and steamed milk in separate cups and let you add the sugar.

Lario's on the Beach (☎ 305-532-9577, 820 Ocean Dr) **Map 4** Dishes $10-30. Open 11am-3am daily. This Cuban-themed restaurant and salsa club, co-owned by singer Gloria Estefan, draws folks more for the atmosphere than the food (which is good but not outstanding). Still, if you are into the scene, it's definitely worth a visit. Try the paella (for two people; it takes 45 minutes) or the less expensive fish Creole. Otherwise, a couple can squeak out for $25 or so by sharing three or four appetizers (like a huge Cuban sandwich) and getting a drink apiece.

Yuca (☎ 305-532-9822, 501 Lincoln Road) **Map 3** Lunch mains $13-30, dinner mains $22-40. Open noon-11pm Mon-Sat, noon-10pm Sun. Reviews are mixed: When it opened, Yuca was the Beach's best Cuban Nouveau place (actually it was and remains the *only* one, but let's not get picky). But then its star chef decamped for Manhattan and he may have taken a good deal of the magic with him. The menu still features Cuban-inspired dishes and certainly, it still has its admirers, but many patrons simply head upstairs to the chic lounge for drinks and live music.

Other Caribbean Tap Tap (☎ 305-672-2898, 819 5th St) **Map 4** Dishes $9-13. Open 11am-11pm Mon-Fri, 4pm-midnight Sat & Sun. No doubt about it: Tap Tap's tropical fruit and vegetable salads and dishes like stewed goat and pumpkin soup should be experienced. It's also fun for a drink; try anything with Haitian Barbancourt rum.

The atmosphere is charming and vibrant, the decor colorful, with handmade Haitian furniture and murals throughout. Live music and other entertainment rotates through quite often.

6 Degrees (☎ 305-538-2212, 685 Washington Ave) **Map 4** Mains $13-20. Open 7pm-2am Sun-Thur, 7pm-5am Fri & Sat. Executive chef Jason Strom's inviting menu features tasty appetizers like crab cakes and coconut-crusted shrimp. His pork tenderloin signature dish cures for 18 hours in a mixture of salt, brown sugar, *mirepois,* and juniper berries and is then grilled to perfection. The bar, which runs the length of the deep red dining room, attracts an increasingly bustling crowd as the night progresses.

Asian There are surprisingly few good, cheap choices.

Thai House (☎ 305-531-4841, 1137 Washington Ave) **Map 3** Dishes $7-13. Open noon-3pm & 5pm-midnight Mon-Fri, 2pm-midnight Sat & Sun. This family-run place features friendly service and a number of veggie dishes, tasty pad thai and higher-priced specialties.

Mid-Range **Toni's Sushi Bar** (☎ 305-673-9368, 1208 Washington Ave) **Map 3** Mains $13-25. Open 6pm-midnight Sun-Thur, 6pm-1am Fri & Sat. Sushi starts simple and runs to an extravagant sushi boat here. On the scene for a long time, Toni's remains wildly popular, though some think the quality has slipped as Toni has extended his empire. Cooked seafood shares the stage with sushi.

Thai Toni's (☎ 305-538-8424, 890 Washington Ave) **Map 4** Mains $10-20. Open 6pm-11:30pm daily. Renowned for pricey seafood specialties, chic clientele and a dramatically lit and understated open dining room, Thai Toni's has indisputably very good food – especially the soups. Curry dishes also share the stage with a good selection of vegetarian meals. The more exotic palates can munch on frog's legs prepared with basil or garlic.

Sushi Samba (☎ 305-673-5337, 600 Lincoln Road) **Map 3** Starters $7-12, dinner mains $17-29. Open noon-2am daily. New in late 2001, this wildly different eatery successfully blends Japanese with Brazilian and Peruvian flavors in a mod setting that emphasizes the sensual rhythms of samba music. For sure, it's a very fun restaurant with a novel cuisine that's highly evolved and well executed. Definitely try the sashimi seviche; one-of-a-kind sushi rolls; *tiradito,* a Peruvian-inspired dish similar to seviche; blue-cornmeal–crusted calamari; and a *sake-tini* (martini with sake) or *sakegria,* made with plum sake.

Top End **Nemo** (☎ 305-532-4550, 100 Collins Ave) **Map 4** Lunch mains $10-19, dinner mains $21-32. Open noon-3pm & 7pm-midnight Mon-Fri, 7pm-midnight Sat, 11am-3pm & 6pm-11pm Sun. Foodies love Nemo, where culinary wizard Michael Schwartz conjures up a Mediterranean-inspired pan-Asian menu featuring dishes like wok-charred salmon and grilled Indian-spiced pork chops. The dining room is perhaps a bit too cozy; the most sought-after tables are in the lovely courtyard. Dress to kill.

Pacific Time (☎ 305-534-5979, 915 Lincoln Road) **Map 3** Mains $21-32. Open 6pm-11pm Sun-Thur, 6pm-midnight Fri & Sat. Chef/owner Jonathan Eismann's time-tested favorite dazzles with Pacific Rim–inspired food served in a chic and bustling (noisy) setting. Seafood dishes are consistently dynamite; try any preparation featuring locally caught dolphin fish. The wine list spans the world.

Italian (& Pizza) For a quick bite on the go, pizza is always a good bet. It's also hard to go wrong with Italian cuisine.

Budget **Spris** (☎ 305-673-2020, 731 Lincoln Road) **Map 3** Dishes $7-15. Open noon-1am daily. Spris' innovative early bird special, known as 'Beat the Clock,' begins at 5:30pm and ends at 7:30pm sharp. Here's how it works: The price you pay is determined by the time you place your order for one of three specials. Order at 6:15pm, pay $6.15. Specials consist of individual-sized, wood oven–baked pizzas and a beverage (wine, beer or soda). Adding a delicious salad won't add much to the bill, but it will sure round out your meal. Spris is a great addition to the al fresco Lincoln Road scene.

Rosinella (☎ 305-672-8777, 525 Lincoln Road) **Map 3** Dishes $8-11. Open 11:20am-midnight Sun-Thur, 11:30am-1am Fri & Sat. Under the same ownership as Sport Café, this small, cozy place has wonderful organic soups and vegetarian dishes. The fresh pastas and sauces taste like they were made by the Italian grandmother of your dreams. The antipasti and salads are assembled with beautiful produce and imported gourmet ingredients. As if that wasn't enough, you'll be greeted warmly, in Italian, by a friendly staff.

Paninoteca (☎ 305-538-0058, 809 Lincoln Road) **Map 3** Dishes $4-9. Open 11am-11:30pm daily. An Italian sandwich bar with salads and individual-sized focaccia pizzas (*pizzini*), Paninoteca also has hot and cold sandwiches (*panini*) with tasty toppings, fillings and spreads like black olive, onion confit and sun-dried tomatoes.

Pizza wars are in full swing. The only decisions are: by the slice, by the pie, take-out, delivery or eat-in.

Pizza Rustica (☎ 305-538-6009, 1447 Washington Ave, **Map 3**; ☎ 305-674-8244, 863 Washington Ave, Map 4) Slices $2.50-3.50. Open 11am-6am daily. South Beach's favorite pizza bar has two locations to satisfy the demand for Roman-style crusty/chewy slices topped with an array of exotic offerings. A slice is a meal unto itself. There's free delivery from the lower Washington Ave location only.

Pucci's Pizza (☎ 305-674-1110, 1608B Alton Rd) **Map 3** Slices $3, pies $10-25. Open 'until we close,' usually 11am-3am Sun-Thur, 11am-5am Fri & Sat. This popular pizza bar serves thin-crust New York–style pizzas with traditional toppings.

Mid-Range **Sport Café** (☎ 305-674-9700, 560 Washington Ave) **Map 4** Specials $7-16. Open 11:30am-1am daily. The name of this unpretentious and comfortable café disguises its true nature. The family-run place feels more like a Roman café – not a slicked-up American version of a Roman café, but a

real one! Try any of the excellent homemade pastas, and of the daily specials, don't miss the crab ravioli in pink cream sauce topped with freshly ground Romano cheese and black pepper. The first-rate Roman-style pizza boasts a perfectly thin crust.

Spiga (☎ 305-534-0079, 1228 Collins Ave) **Map 3** Mains $12-19. Open 6pm-11:30pm. The lovely, intimate dining room of the Hotel Impala is an oasis of elegant tranquility on bustling Collins Ave. The menu features homemade tagliolini pasta and endive with a light gorgonzola sauce, as well as veal scaloppini with prosciutto and sage in a white-wine sauce.

Osteria del Teatro (☎ 305-538-7850, 1443 Washington Ave) **Map 3** Mains $16-42. Open 6pm-11pm Mon-Thur, 6pm-midnight Fri & Sat. Considered Miami's best Italian restaurant by many, the Osteria offers pricey but very delicious northern Italian meals and gracious service. If you arrive between 6pm and 7pm or after 10pm, the three-course fixed-price dinner with a glass of wine is worth every penny (it's discounted then).

Top End **Escopazzo** (☎ 305-674-9450, 1311 Washington Ave) **Map 3** Mains $18-28. Open 6pm-midnight Sun-Thur, 6pm-1am Fri & Sat. Head here for the best value in this price range. The authentic Italian restaurant earns its reputation nightly with delectable dishes and friendly service. The homemade pasta dishes are exceptional. Reservations are a must – the dining room only seats 70 or so.

French **La Terrasse** (☎ 305-695-9191, 639 Lincoln Road) **Map 3** Dishes $10-23. Open noon-midnight daily. This authentic French bistro meshes seamlessly among Lincoln Road's sidewalk cafés. One bite of the *tarte Tatin* (upside-down caramelized apple tart) and you'll think you're on the Left Bank. At times la Terrasse offers a three-course dinner menu ($17.50).

Mexican The bout for best South Beach burrito has several worthy contenders.

Texas Taco Factory (☎ 305-535-5757, 1608 Alton Rd) **Map 3** Dishes $1.50-5.50. Open 7am-11pm daily. This Tex-Mex joint features fresh ingredients and rock-bottom prices. The 'fat boy' burrito has beans, cheese, lettuce, tomatoes, sour cream and guacamole; add meat for an extra 75¢. Fajita platters (half a pound of grilled meat and all the accompaniments) are big enough to share.

San Loco (☎ 305-538-3009, 235 14th St) **Map 3** Dishes $2-7. Open 11am-5am Sun-Thur, 11am-6am Fri & Sat. San Loco still has the Beach's best burrito, hands down. The restaurant also makes enchiladas, tacos, nachos (free of bushels of cilantro) and really excellent taco salads. The lovely staff will take good care of you.

El Rancho Grande (☎ 305-673-0480, 1626 Pennsylvania Ave) Lunch mains $5-7, dinner mains $9.50-18. Open 11:30am-11pm daily. This comfortable and cozy restaurant, where dishes are served in terracotta dishware, is more formal than its competition. While burritos come smothered with two types of melted cheese, sour cream, rice, beans and guacamole, salads are a bit skimpier. Lunch specials and margaritas are key. If you love cilantro, you'll love El Rancho; they put it in everything they serve (except the margaritas).

And the heavyweight medal goes to whom?

German Dab Haus (☎ 305-534-9557, 852 Alton Rd) **Map 4** Dishes $7-13. Open 4pm-'closing' daily. Beyond the drab exterior lies a quick trip to Munich, with excellent German dishes like bratwurst, *currywurst, knoblauchwurst, sauerbraten* and pork and chicken schnitzel. It also has cre\pes with mushrooms, potatoes, red cabbage and cheese. Don't miss the honey-garlic brie. Wash it all down with a hearty Bavarian ale, preferably when there's live music and a lively crowd.

Israeli Pita Loca (☎ 305-673-3388, 601 Collins Ave) **Map 4** Dishes $4-9. Open noon-11:45pm Sun-Thur, noon-4:30pm Fri, 8pm-1am Sat. This Israeli shawarma-and-falafel joint is perfect for a quick bite, but service can be a bit brusque. Note the hours (closed during Shabbat).

Northern Miami Beach (Map 5)

Not to be confused with North Miami Beach, which is a distinct entity, these places lie east of the Intracoastal Waterway, in the communities of Surfside, Bal Harbour and Sunny Isles.

Rascal House (☎ 305-947-4581, 17190 Collins Ave) Dishes $7-15. Open 24 hrs daily. Wolfie Cohen's nostalgic 1954 Miami eatery has sassy service, classic swivel stools at the counter and Naugahyde booths. It bustles with older patrons, Northeastern snowbirds and curious tourists who relish roast brisket, latkes, blintzes, borscht and Lake Erie whitefish salad.

Arnie & Richie's (☎ 305-531-7691, 525 Arthur Godfrey Rd) Dishes $4-24. Open 6:30am-8:45pm Mon-Fri, 7am-4pm Sat & Sun. Smoked whitefish, corned beef and other Jewish deli staples rule the roost at this authentic deli.

Oasis Cafe (☎ 305-674-7676, 976 41st St) Lunch $7-10, dinner mains $7-16. Open 11am-10pm Mon-Sat, 5pm-10pm Sun. Tired of all the South Beach hype? This Mediterranean vegetarian café will treat you right, right down to the healthful dolmas, eggplant salad and hummus. Try the grilled fish on focaccia for more substance.

Downtown Miami (Map 6)

Most downtown places cater to 9-to-5ers, but an increasing number attract a burgeoning pleasure-seeking crowd. You'll find some surprising choices worth searching out.

Budget Food courts (SE 1st Ave between E Flagler St & SE 1st St; Biscayne Blvd between NE 1st St & E Flagler St) Dishes $1-6. Open weekdays. Chinese, Mexican and Indian food, as well as pizza, sandwiches, and other fast foods, fit the bill at these two food courts.

Panini Coffee Bar (☎ 305-377-2888, 16 NE 3rd Ave) Dishes $4-7. Open 8:30am-6pm Mon-Fri, 9am-4:30pm Sat. This indoor/outdoor café, Frenchish and trendy by downtown standards, has requisite coffee and pastries. But they also have sandwiches on French bread, salads and soup by the cup and bowl.

S&S Restaurant (☎ 305-373-4291, 1757 NE 2nd Ave) Dishes $4-10. Open 5:30am-6pm Mon-Fri, 6am-2pm Sat & Sun. Step back into the past at this classic '40s-style diner with downright sassy service ('Keep yer shirt on, hon!') and great old-fashioned choices that define 'comfort food.' You'll be happy with humongous burgers, meatloaf and baked macaroni and cheese, or more adventurous entries like shrimp Creole. It's no wonder the small horseshoe-shaped linoleum lunch counter is always very crowded, especially with cops.

Granny Feelgood's (☎ 305-377-9600, 25 W Flagler St) Breakfast $3-7, lunch $4-12. Open 7am-4pm Mon-Fri. A neighborhood staple since the mid-1970s, this health-food emporium has great chicken, fish and veggie dishes. If you 'feel good' after your meal (and you will), consider purchasing some of Granny's vitamins and herbal goods next door.

Café Nash (☎ 305-371-8871, 37 E Flagler St) Dishes $7-10. Open 8am-4pm Mon-Fri, 9am-4pm Sat. Within the Seybold Building Arcade, Nash is a fairly small place that appeals to businessfolk. The fare ranges from omelets and salads to sandwiches and combo platters.

Tobacco Road (☎ 305-374-1198, 626 S Miami Ave) Dishes $7-11. Open 11:30am-5am daily (kitchen stops serving at 2am). Miami's oldest bar, on the scene since the 1920s (and a speakeasy during Prohibition), Tobacco Road is primarily a blues and jazz joint, but it also has excellent burgers, with toppings ranging from mundane (cheese) to

strange (eggs). During the Friday happy hour, it is indeed a happy place to be ($5 cover). But Tuesday nights are even better, when the Road has lobsters for $11 from 5:30pm until they run out (about 7:30pm).

Mid-Range Fishbone Grille (☎ 305-530-1915, 650 S Miami Ave) Lunch mains $9-16, dinner mains $9-25. Open noon-4pm & 5:30pm-10pm Mon-Fri, 5:30pm-10pm Sat. Arguably Miami's best cheap fish house, this casual place with an open kitchen features grilled, blackened, sautéed, baked or *française* seafood preparations. Prices fluctuate with the market; check the long chalkboard list for the prime catches-of-the-day.

Bubba Gump Shrimp Co (☎ 305-379-8866, Bayside Marketplace) Dishes $10-19. Open 11:30am-10:30pm daily. You'll dine at picnic tables under thousands of white lights and outstretched banyan tree limbs at this open-air eatery. Feast on large portions of shrimp cooked every which way, described with the wackiest names and served by the wackiest waiters you'll ever have to affectionately endure. True fans of the movie *Forrest Gump* (on which this themed chain restaurant is based) won't overlook the gift store, which rivals the size of the restaurant section.

Perricone's (☎ 305-374-9449, 15 SE 10th St) Lunch mains $8-9, dinner mains $12-20. Open 7am-10pm Sun-Wed, 7am-11pm Thur-Sat. Ensconced in a huge Vermont barn trucked down for a new lease on life, Perricone's has a winning formula in its combo deli-restaurant. Purchase some wine from the market and they'll uncork it (for a fee that's much less than the normal mark-up on wine) at the restaurant. Sandwiches, pastas and grilled dishes are popular. The outdoor terrace, offering much-appreciated relief from the downtown bustle, attracts more suits than travelers, but don't let that stop you. The all-you-can-eat Sunday buffet ($15), with pasta, omelets and fruit, is a bargain.

Provence Grill (☎ 305-373-1940, 1001 S Miami Ave) Lunch mains $5-12, dinner mains $13-20. Open 11:30am-3pm & 5:30pm-10:30pm daily. Ooh-la-la! If you didn't get to France this year, no worries, mate. One bite of the Grill's mussels in garlic, or one whiff of the lavender-laced crème bru\lée, and you'll be transported across the Atlantic before you can say *mais oui*. The setting, complete with a lush outdoor bar (where you'll wait, since service at this popular restaurant breezes by slower than an escargot), is surprisingly countrified for the locale. *C'est bon.*

Gordon Biersch Brewery (☎ 786-425-1130, 1201 Brickell Ave) Lunch mains $9-13, dinner mains $18-22. Open 11:30am-11pm Sun-Thur, 11:30am-midnight Fri & Sat (bar open until 2am Fri & Sat). This cavernous chain brewpub, with great German-style beer, has an eclectic menu. Stick to the brick-oven pizzas, burgers and garlic-laden french fries rather than trying the more elaborate offerings. Friday afternoon happy hour resembles Ivy League fraternity parties, which will bring back fond memories for some.

Top End Big Fish (☎ 305-373-1770, 55 SW Miami Ave) Lunch mains $8-20, dinner mains $11-35. Open noon-3pm & 6:30pm-11:30pm Mon-Fri, noon-11:30pm Sat & Sun. It's got riverfront competition, but the big fish on the block grills some tasty denizens of the deep. (Some dependable Italian dishes grace the menu, too.) Waiting at the congenial bar for dramatic skyline views and a funky atmosphere won't be difficult, but you will have to do it. It's a little tough to find, with all the one-way streets, but don't give up.

Café Sambal (☎ 305-913-8251, 500 Brickell Key Dr) Lunch mains $12-20, dinner mains $18-30. Open 6:30am-11pm daily. Within the luxe Mandarin Oriental Miami hotel on Brickell Key, this nouveau Asian bistro pairs exceptional food (including crab cakes) with 'relaxed' service. But who cares. You can savor the skyline while you sip a martini and drink in the view.

Key Biscayne (Map 7)
Peckish at the Seaquarium? Need a post-beach pick-me-up? Or a sunset drink? Or picnic fixings for a lighthouse excursion? Few of these places win 'best of' awards, but they're all respectable.

Farmer's Market (☎ 305-361-1300, 91 Harbor Dr) Open 9am-8pm Mon-Fri, 8am-8pm Sat & Sun. This upscale market carries smoked salmon, hot and cold prepared foods, Old World cheeses, olives and luscious pastries and breads.

La Carreta (☎ 305-365-1177, 12 Crandon Park Blvd) Dishes $4-5. Open 7am-11pm daily. For quick, no-frills Cuban-style snacks, this Miami chain offers dependably filling and cheap choices – from big breakfasts to sandwiches.

Oasis (☎ 305-361-5709, 19 Harbor Dr) Dishes $4-12. Open 6am-9pm daily. From blue-collar workers to blue-blood pols, socioeconomic barriers come tumbling down at this Cuban coffee oasis. More aptly described as a hole-in-the-wall with a take-out coffee window, Oasis serves sandwiches, paella and the like.

Sunday's on the Bay (☎ 305-361-6777, 5420 Crandon Park Blvd) Mains $15-24. Open 11am-11pm Mon-Thur, 11am-3am Fri, 11am-5am Sat & Sun. The bountiful Sunday buffet ($24 per person) draws crowds, but then again so do the tropical bar, marina views and large outdoor terrace. Drinks are fun anytime, but Sundays on the bay are better than any other day on the bay. The predictable seafood dishes are just that: predictable, but fine.

Rusty Pelican (☎ 305-361-3818, 3201 Rickenbacker Causeway) Lunch mains $8-19, dinner mains $18-25. Open 11:30am-4pm & 5pm-11pm Mon-Thur, 11:30am-4pm & 5pm-midnight Fri & Sat, 10:30am-3pm & 5pm-11pm Sun. Panoramic skyline views, perhaps the best in Miami, draw the faithful and romantic to this airy, tropical restaurant. Come for a sunset drink, then head into the sunset somewhere else for dinner. The average surf-and-turf menu is nothing to scream hysterically (positively or negatively) about.

Little Havana (Map 8)
Cuban, Cuban and more Cuban. Only Fidel's island nation has more authentic eateries, and none of Miami's will strain your budget. If you don't speak Spanish, bring a Spanish-English dictionary with you – many places have only Spanish menus and monolingual waitstaff.

Cuban Cuisine

There's nothing delicate about Cuban cooking; it's hearty and hefty. The most common ingredients are pork, beef, rice, beans, eggs, tomatoes, lettuce, lemons and oranges. Cuban food isn't generally spicy either. Garlic and onions, rather than chili peppers, are used for seasoning. Floridian Cuban cuisine utilizes *mojo*, a garlic-citrus sauce.

The most common dishes are *carne asada* (roasted beef), *puerco asado* (roast pork), *carne de cerdo* (pork), *bistec* (steak), *arroz con pollo* (chicken and rice), *filete de pescado* (fish filet) and *ropa vieja* (literally 'old clothes,' but actually shredded skirt-steak stew served with rice and plantains). Other meat and poultry dishes include *bistec de res* (beefsteak), *cabra* (goat), *cabrito* (kid goat), *chorizo* (spicy pork sausage), *cordero* (lamb) and *jamón* (ham). Seafood dishes include *ceviche* (raw seafood, marinated in citrus juice), *calamar* (squid), *camarones* (shrimp), *jaiba* (small crab), *langosta* (lobster), *mariscos* (shellfish) and *ostiones* (oysters).

Common side dishes include *arroz* (rice); *moros y christianos* (literally 'Moors and Christians,' gastronomically black beans and rice); *frijoles negros o rojos* (black or red beans); *yuca* (manioc or cassava), a starchy root vegetable that's boiled, baked or fried, like french fries; and *maduros* (fried plantains), a larger cousin of the banana. When done right, fried plantains are crispy outside and sweet and starchy inside.

Sandwiches

Cuban sandwiches from *loncherías* (snack bars) are in a class of their own. They're made by slicing Cuban loaves lengthwise, filling them with ingredients and toasting (also known as smashing) them in a *plancha* – a heated press. The most popular ones include the *cubano* (pork or ham and cheese, sometimes with mustard and pickles, depending on how much you look like a gringo), *pan con lechón* (extra crispity-crunchy pork and mojo), *palomilla* (steak with fried onions) and *medianoche* (literally 'midnight'; actually with ham, cheese and roast pork).

Desserts

Most desserts *(postres)* are small afterthoughts. They include *arroz con leche* (rice pudding), *crepa* (thin pancakes or crêpes), *flan* or *crème caramel* (custard), *galletas* (cookies or biscuits), *gelatina* (jello), *helado* (ice cream) and *pastel* (pastry or cake). Watch out for *tres leches* (literally 'three-milk' cake), which is actually a glucose-tolerance test disguised as pudding.

Tea & Coffee

The big players are *café con leche* (half coffee and half hot steamed milk); *café con crema* (coffee with cream served separately); *cafecito* (espresso served in thimble-sized shots); *té de manzanilla* (chamomile tea); and *té negro* (black tea). When ordering coffee don't expect a Seattle-style look-alike. The Cuban version is an industrial-strength, over-sweetened beverage (they pour, really pour, in the sugar for you unless you specifically request they don't). Non-Cuban palates may find it ghastly.

Fruit & Vegetable Drinks

Pure fresh juices *(jugos)*, where the nectar is squeezed right in front of you, are popular and readily available. Every fruit and many vegetables are used. Ever tried pure beet juice? Another local favorite is *guarapo* (sugarcane juice). *Licuados* blend fruit or juice with water and sugar. *Licuados con leche* use milk in lieu of water. Consider adding raw egg, ice, and flavorings like vanilla and nutmeg. *Aguas frescas* or *aguas de fruta* combine fruit juice or a syrup made from mashed grains or seeds with sugar and water.

Budget Versailles Bakery (☎ 305-441-2500, 3501 SW 8th St) Open 8am-10pm daily. This bakery, where rum cake is a favorite, adjoins the famed restaurant (see below).

Taquerías el Mexicano (☎ 305-858-1160, 521 SW 8th St) Dishes $5-10. Open 9am-11pm daily. This casual, friendly joint serves tasty Mexican food; a number of choices are vegetarian. For a Mexicano-style breakfast of champions, order *chilaquiles* – tortilla chips simmered in green sauce mixed with scrambled eggs and covered with cheese, sour cream, rice and beans.

El Pescador (☎ 305-541-9224, 1543 SW 8th St) Dishes $4.50-13. Open 10:30am-10pm Tues-Sun. This little storefront eatery is bright and cheerful and the service friendly. It's a real winner for seafood lovers. Daily specials might include grilled dolphin fish and shrimp Creole accompanied by rice and black beans, fried plantains or potatoes.

Versailles (☎ 305-444-0240, 3555 SW 8th St) Dishes $8-10. Open 8am-2am Mon-Thur, 8am-3:30am Fri, 8am-4:30am Sat, 9am-2am Sun. Don't be fooled by the name; there's nothing French here but the chandeliers (and those aren't really either). The cavernous and glitzy (in a 1980s *Scarface/Miami Vice* kind of way) restaurant is a landmark. And since it's a favorite among Cuban power brokers and families alike, you might want to go out of your way to eat here. It can be fun with a group and a pitcher of (weak) sangria. Service is fine but the food barely reaches average. Live with it.

Guayacan (☎ 305-649-2015, 1933 SW 8th St) Dishes $7-15. Open 11am-10pm Sun-Thur, 11am-11pm Fri & Sat. For Nicaraguan cooking, served by friendly folks in a pleasantly homey atmosphere, you'll like Guayacan. Along with the hearty specialty soups, you could make a meal of the *antojitos* (appetizers) like *chorizo de cerdo* (pork sausages) and Nicaraguan tamales. Or order the house special: *pescado a la Tipitapa* (whole red snapper, de-boned and deep fried, served with a zingy pepper-and-onion sauce). You certainly won't leave hungry.

Hy Vong Vietnamese Restaurant (☎ 305-446-3674, 3458 SW 8th St) Dishes $8-15. Open 6pm-10:30pm Tues-Sun; closed mid–late Aug. Little Havana's culinary anomaly rocks Miami's food world. Hy Vong really does serve some of the best Vietnamese food in the USA. Favorites include *bun* – thin sliced meat with vermicelli – and the squid salad marinated in lime juice and onions. Most dishes are quite spicy, and portions are generous. Get to the tiny storefront eatery early; it may look like a dive, but it's no secret.

Mid-Range Casa Panza (☎ 305-643-5343, 1620 SW 8th St) Tapas $3.50-6, mains $12-15. Open 11:30am-10pm Sun & Mon, 11:30am-2am Tues-Sat. Dark and cozy and more than a little kitschy, Casa Panza serves authentically prepared and presented dishes. Start with a bowl of *caldo gallego* (white-bean soup with pork sausage). Then order some tapas like *tortilla de patatas* (potato and onion omelet, served at room temperature), *gambas al ajillo* (shrimp in garlic sauce) and *boquerones en vinagre* (fresh anchovies in vinaigrette).

La Carreta (☎ 305-444-7501, 3632 SW 8th St) Dishes $5-20. Open 24 hrs daily. The original link in a Cuban chain, La Carreta features all the traditional Cuban dishes you'll find at Versailles. The decor is a little less glaring and in-your-face, though no less kitschy in its country farmhouse way. Open around the clock, the Carreta is popular for *medianoches* (Cuban-style grilled ham-and-cheese sandwiches) and *café cubano*. If you just need a caffeine and sugar fix, order from the take-out window in the back.

Coconut Grove (Map 9)

The Grove can satisfy every conceivable culinary desire, from cheap Middle Eastern to authentic French to what may be Miami's best Indian.

Budget The Oak Feed (☎ 305-448-7595, 2830 Oak Ave) Open 9am-10pm daily. Miami's first natural-foods store is still going strong. Instead of serving 1960s flower children, though, the Oak Feed's clientele is yuppies and boomers.

Daily Bread Marketplace (☎ 305-856-5893, 2400 SW 27th St) Dishes $3-6. Open

9am-8pm Mon-Sat, 11am-5pm Sun. Essentially a small grocery store with tables, this family-run Middle Eastern deli has superb lentil soup, lamb kebabs, spanakopita, falafel and gyro sandwiches. Otherwise, assemble a picnic with olives, baba ghanoush, baklava and homemade pita bread. There are a few outdoor tables.

Johnny Rockets (☎ 305-444-1000, 3036 Grand Ave) Dishes $4-6. Open 11am-midnight Mon-Thur, 11am-2am Fri & Sat, 11am-midnight Sun. This 1950s-style chain hamburger joint, with a soda fountain and old-fashioned Coca-Cola glasses, is cramped inside but has plenty of sidewalk tables. The No 12 cheeseburger (with red sauce, pickles, lettuce and tomato) is terrific, but get the red sauce on the side before committing. The chicken breast sandwiches are also good.

Mid-Range Cafe Tu Tu Tango (☎ 305-529-2222, CocoWalk) Dishes $4-10. Open 11am-midnight Sun-Wed, 11am-1am Thur, 11am-2am Fri & Sat. This wacky, 2nd-floor theme restaurant resembles an artist's studio or garret, deliberately cluttered with half-finished paintings. While munching on eclectic Spanish tapas, have a tarot-card reading and watch the artists painting at their easels.

Green Street Cafe (☎ 305-567-0662, 3110 Commodore Plaza) Breakfast $4-7, lunch & dinner $10-17. Open 7:30am-11pm Sun-Thur, 7:30am-midnight Fri & Sat. People-watching takes precedence over the food at this longtime corner café. But still, you can get good American-style breakfasts until 3pm. Pizza, salads, elaborate pasta dishes and salmon filets are offered at lunch and dinner.

Paulo Luigi's (☎ 305-445-9000, 3324 Virginia St) Lunch mains $7-9, dinner mains $10-30. Open 11:45am-2:35pm & 5pm-11pm Mon-Thur, 11:45am-2:35pm & 5pm-1am Fri, 5pm-1am Sat & Sun. Practically obliterated by CocoWalk, this now-hidden family-friendly (and all-around friendly) Italian restaurant has been a local favorite since the mid-1970s. Why? It offers decent pizza and creative pasta dishes for reasonable prices, in a homey environment. Jeez. It's a rarity.

Anokha (☎ 786-552-1030, 3195 Commodore Plaza) Veggie dishes average $11, other mains average $14. Open 6:30pm-10:30pm Tues, Wed & Sun, 6pm-11:30pm Thur-Sat. Perhaps Miami's best Indian cuisine, this family-run phenom goes beyond excellent vindaloos, curries and tandooris. It's small in size but huge in my estimation.

Coral Gables (Map 10)

Most Coral Gables restaurants are clustered near 'Restaurant Row,' on Giralda Ave between Ponce de León Blvd and Miller Ave, but that's not the only game in town. You'll want to cruise Miracle Mile, too. In all, there are dozens of places serving dozens of types of cuisine from Italian to bistro-style French. The upscale ones are worth every penny.

Budget Allen's Drug Store (☎ 305-665-6964, 4000 Red Rd) Dishes $3-6. Open 6am-8pm Mon-Fri, 6am-5pm Sat, 6am-3pm Sun. For drugstore chic and retro cheesiness, Allen's 'Picnics Cafe' boasts cheap and reliably good burgers, meatloaf, diner specials and a cool jukebox. Since the actual drugstore caters to elderly patrons, you'll be chowing down next to walkers and other paraphernalia that aids seniors. It's a trip, a fun one.

Miracle Mile Cafeteria (☎ 305-444-9005, 147 Miracle Mile) Dishes $4-6. Open 11am-8:30pm daily. It's astonishing that some national retailer hasn't invaded this space, full of kitsch, Formica and a friendly staff. They're deservedly proud of their old-fashioned Southern fare, like brisket of roast beef and barbecue ribs. Enjoy a slice of history with a slice of pie; one day they'll both be gobbled up for good.

Café Demetrio (☎ 305-448-4949, 300 Alhambra Circle) Dishes $4-7. Open 7:30am-9pm Mon-Thur, 7:30am-midnight Fri & Sat. Decidedly European, from Spanish omelets and Italian coffee to Greek salads and Linzer tortes, this unpretentious place is a breath of fresh air in Coral Gables. Sandwiches and salads are menu mainstays.

Mid-Range Miss Saigon Bistro (☎ 305-446-8006, 148 Giralda Ave) Lunch mains $7-10, dinner mains $10-16. Open 11:30am-10pm daily. For great soups, noodle dishes and other Vietnamese food, you can't beat this solid family-run place. Portions are hefty. Since it's small, there are always people waiting to feast here.

Top End Caffe Abbracci (☎ 305-441-0700, 318 Aragon Ave) Lunch mains $14-16, dinner mains $16-24. Open 11:30am-3:30pm Mon-Fri, 6:30pm-11:30pm daily. The most reasonably priced of these pricey restaurants, Abbracci embraces you warmly, from the time you make a reservation to the moment you're walking out the door a satisfied customer. The dark, elegant and upscale eatery is decidedly trendy, but it serves some of the best northern Italian food in the city. Pastas are fresh, antipasti plentiful, veal a specialty and the tiramisu a delight. The daily lunch special of pasta and fish is a bargain at $15.50.

Meza Fine Art Gallery & Cafe (☎ 305-461-2733, 275 Giralda Ave) Lunch mains $6-12, dinner mains $16-29. Open 11:30am-2:30pm & 6pm-'who knows' Mon-Sat. Tired of fussy food but still want the dining room to have an energetic buzz? This artful place puts as much creativity on the plates as it does in the sleek space, which doubles as a performance space and gallery. The cuisine blends Mediterranean, Cuban and Mexican flavors in dishes like guava-chili sirloin and salmon with a mango-ginger sauce. The bar scene picks up with a younger crowd later in the evening, when there is often live music.

Norman's (☎ 305-446-6767, 21 Almeria Ave) Mains $20-40. Open 6pm-10:30pm Mon-Sat. The hype about chef-owner Norman Van Aken's restaurant – that it's *the* best restaurant in Miami and perhaps the best in the southeastern US – is no hyperbole. If you're going to blow some bucks, this is the right place (as long as you have reservations). With gracious service, handsome surroundings, an open kitchen and creative New World cuisine that fuses Caribbean, Asian, Latin and North American, Norman's delights the senses. Look for something delectable, like pecan-crusted Louisiana catfish with fried green tomatoes

and mashed sweet potatoes. The wine pairing is exceptional.

Greater Miami

You might not go out of your way to eat at these places (except one!), but if you're in their neighborhoods at lunch or dinner, you'll appreciate knowing they're there.

Chef Allen's (☎ 305-935-2900, 19088 NE 29th Ave) **Map 5** Mains $26-40. Open 6pm-'until the last guest leaves' daily. Welcome to his world, and thus by extension yours: Chef Allen was dubbed James Beard's 'Best American Chef in the Southeast' in 1994.

Master of his universe (which clearly reaches far beyond this Aventura neighborhood), Allen Susser reigns with New World–Floribbean cuisine, which pairs fresh local ingredients with tantalizing global flavors. If you splurge just once, Susser will not disappoint. A special trek to Chef Allen's will reward you with a mountain of memories. Speaking of mountains, save room for Susser's trademark soufflé.

The following are *way* out but worth the trip, especially if you're visiting the Monkey Jungle, the Fruit & Spice Park, Fairchild Tropical Gardens, Matheson Hammock Park or the Miami Metrozoo.

Bur's Berry Farm (no ☎, 12741 SW 216th St, Goulds) **Map 1** Open 9am-5:30pm daily Dec-May. This berry farm surely has the country's best strawberries: fist-sized, sumptuously sweet, breathtakingly fresh, unbelievably satisfying strawberries. Bur's also makes a killer strawberry shake.

Knauss Berry Farm (☎ 305-247-0668, 15980 SW 248th St) **Map 1** Open late Nov–Apr. This farm has similarly heavenly cinnamon rolls that create similarly long lines, especially on Saturday. It also has lush strawberries and luscious breads, cakes and brownies. Sugar high, anyone?

Shorty's BBQ (☎ 305-670-7732, 9200 S Dixie Hwy) **Map 2** Dishes $6-16. Open 11am-10pm Sun-Thur, 11am-11pm Fri & Sat. This South Dade institution has enjoyed buckets of fame since the early 1950s. Long before deco became de rigueur, and probably long after the vibe settles over South Beach, this rustic place will still be dishing out sweet baby back ribs ($16), cobbed corn, barbecued spare ribs ($9) and tender chicken ($6) on picnic tables. Look for the branch at 11575 SW 40th St (☎ 305-227-3196; Map 2) when you're heading back into the city from the Everglades.

ENTERTAINMENT
Calling Miami a trendy nightspot is a little like calling New York a fairly large city. Miami Beach is one of the most fashionable places in the country for clubbing. But nightlife encompasses far more than just nightclubs, bars and lounges. The New World Symphony is a delightful treat, and legitimate theater is also very active. Sports fans go nuts in a city with professional football, baseball, basketball and hockey, plus jai alai, NASCAR and horse racing.

Bars
Pubs Mac's Club Deuce Bar (☎ 305-673-9537, 222 14th St) **Map 3** Open 8am-5am daily. The oldest bar in Miami Beach, established in 1926, 'the Deuce' is a real

neighborhood bar and hype-free zone. There's no posing going on here and the atmosphere, though seedy, feels *real*. The clientele defies categorization. Every conceivable affiliate of the South Beach community hangs here, from transvestites to construction workers, stars to star-gazers, hipsters to yupsters to bikers. The dark but friendly and welcoming room has a pool table, jukebox, reasonably priced beer and no-nonsense service.

Irish House Bar & Grill (☎ 305-534-5667, 1430 Alton Rd) **Map 3** Open 11am-5am daily. This comfy bar is another local fave, featuring half-price weekday happy hours (4pm to 7pm), pool tables, video games, dart boards and a jukebox. Pitchers (depending on the brew) cost $12 to $16.

The Playwright (☎ 305-534-0667, 1265 Washington Ave) **Map 3** Open 11am-5am daily. This authentic Irish pub features a large selection of imported beers, a big-screen TV for sporting events, live music and weekday happy hours from 4pm to 7pm. Down $6 pitchers from Sunday to Thursday.

See also **Churchill's Hideaway** under Live Music, later.

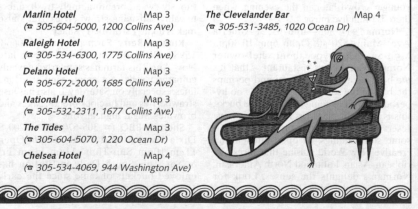

Hotel Lounges, Lobbies & Bars

Some hotels offer complimentary cocktails to their guests for a limited period each night. Inquire to find out if your hotel is among them. Otherwise, check out the following groovy places, some of which are on the map under Places to Stay, and others under Entertainment:

Marlin Hotel   Map 3
(☎ 305-604-5000, 1200 Collins Ave)

Raleigh Hotel   Map 3
(☎ 305-534-6300, 1775 Collins Ave)

Delano Hotel   Map 3
(☎ 305-672-2000, 1685 Collins Ave)

National Hotel   Map 3
(☎ 305-532-2311, 1677 Collins Ave)

The Tides   Map 3
(☎ 305-604-5070, 1220 Ocean Dr)

Chelsea Hotel   Map 4
(☎ 305-534-4069, 944 Washington Ave)

The Clevelander Bar   Map 4
(☎ 305-531-3485, 1020 Ocean Dr)

Restaurant & Theme Bars Laundry Bar (☎ 305-531-7700, ⓦ www.laundrybar.com, 721 Lincoln Lane N) **Map 3** Open noon-5am daily. This bar/billiards parlor/coin Laundromat is a hoot. As they say, 'get sloshed while you wash.' The place has a decidedly gay (and lesbian) vibe, but it's certainly relaxed and welcomes all. In addition to two-for-one drinks daily until 9pm, they offer different nightly specials and themes.

Blue (☎ 305-534-1009, 222 Española Way) **Map 3** Open 10pm-5am daily. Everything is blue but the patrons at this ultra-chic cocktail bar and lounge. Even the music is a bluesy mix of deep house and sultry soul.

Tantra (☎ 305-672-4765, ⓦ www.tantra restaurant.com, 1445 Pennsylvania Ave) **Map 3** Open until 1am nightly. This exotic restaurant (see the South Beach section of Places to Eat) is also a great place to hang out after dinner, when it becomes a late-night lounge. Guest DJs spin music to complement the sensual, candlelit ambience and aphrodisiac cocktails.

Tap Tap (☎ 305-672-2898, 819 5th St) **Map 4** Open 11am-11pm Sun-Thur, 11am-midnight Fri, 5pm-midnight Sat, 5pm-10pm Sun. This Haitian restaurant and bar (see the South Beach section of Places to Eat) is a cool and colorful place to hang out drinking Haitian Barbancourt rum or African Ngoma beer. There is often live Haitian and other Caribbean music. The restaurant also exhibits art and hosts community meetings.

Dab Haus (☎ 305-534-9557, 852 Alton Rd) **Map 4** Open 4pm-11pm Sun-Thur, 11am-midnight Fri & Sat. This honest-to-goodness German pub has the area's best German beer, wine and schnapps. Try the Dortmunder pils, Alt Tucher hefe weizen, dark hefe weizen, Kristall weizen, Königs pils and/or Hacker-Pschorr. They also have wine by the glass, but that's not why you came. It's a darned serviceable German restaurant, too – see the South Beach section of Places to Eat.

Pearl Restaurant & Champagne Lounge (☎ 305-538-1111, ⓦ www.pearlsouthbeach .com, 1 Ocean Dr) **Map 4** Open 7pm-5am daily. Champagne-sippers recline on fur-trimmed designer chairs, enjoying a variety of bubblies by the glass, complemented by caviar hors d'oeuvres. DJs spin lounge classics and R&B at this decadent, deep-orange haven within Penrod's Entertainment Complex; see also the South Beach section of Places to Eat.

The Ever-Changing Scene

The club and entertainment scene changes faster than a chameleon facing imminent danger. Although I have tried to primarily include venues that have withstood the test of time, it is ironically the very nature of time that can imperil these very same venues. Longevity can kill, can breed boredom. A buzz is created by newness, not oldness. Today's hot club is tomorrow's closed club. Replacing one kind of logic for another, clubs thrive on reinventing the wheel. Reinvention is paramount – just look at Madonna (the singer, not the club).

So, for up-to-date info on the ever-changing entertainment scene, pick up the *New Times*, a weekly fave published on Thursday, and *Wire*, the weekly gay bible that comes out on Thursday. Also look for the *Miami Herald's* Friday 'Weekend' section and the free weekly, *The Street*.

Also, consider cruising the Internet before cruising the clubs. Check these sites for daily listings of what's going on:

City Search
ⓦ www.miami.citysearch.com

Entertainment News & Views
ⓦ www.entnews.com

Miami Night Guide
ⓦ www.miami.nightguide.com

New Times
ⓦ www.miaminewtimes.com

Street
ⓦ www.streetmiami.com

SunPost
ⓦ www.miamisunpost.com

Microbreweries Abbey Brewery (☎ 305-538-8110, 1115 16th St) **Map 3** Open 1pm-5am daily. Abbey Brewery makes really good beer, including Abbey Brown, Oatmeal Stout, Porter Christmas and India Pale Ale (all are $4.25 a pint). But it also has some dozen more beers on tap and a little pub grub.

See also Tobacco Road under Live Music, later.

Live Music

Latin/Tropical Mango's Tropical Cafe (☎ 305-673-4422, 900 Ocean Dr) **Map 4** Cover $10-20. Open 11am-5am daily. From the street you can feel the spicy beat and catch a glimpse into the open-air courtyard. Or you can shed your inhibitions, make your way in and join the bumping, grinding and booty-shaking. Live bands play salsa, reggae and merengue into the early morning hours. The first band starts at 6:45pm nightly, and the last one goes on at 2am on weekends.

Club Tropigala (☎ 305-541-2631, 538-2000, 4441 Collins Ave) **Map 5** Cover $20. Open 7pm-'till the last person leaves' Wed-Sun. The Fountainbleau Hotel houses this '50s era, kitschy Cubano supper club featuring highly produced dance shows at 8pm or 8:30pm. Put yourself in a Desi Arnaz frame of mind and ba-ba-loo the night away.

Hoy Como Ayer (☎ 305-541-2631, 2212 SW 8th St) **Map 8** Cover $5-10. Open 8pm-5am Wed-Sun. This hot spot, with authentic Cuban music and a small dance floor, is enhanced by Cuban memorabilia and cigar smoke. A house band is often complemented by other musicians who stop in to jam. The café also plays vintage Cuban music videos and film clips.

Jazz & Blues Jazid (☎ 305-673-9372, 1342 Washington Ave) **Map 3** Cover $10 Fri & Sat, free Sun-Thur. Open 9pm-5am daily. Live jazz, soul and funk bands play in this sophisticated and intimate candlelit lounge. It's smooth.

Wallflower Gallery (☎ 305-579-0069, W www.wallflowergallery.com, 10 NE 3rd St) **Map 6** Open Thur-Sat (generally). This gallery hosts a variety of programs; it's always best to call ahead.

Tobacco Road (☎ 305-374-1198, W www .tobacco-road.com, 626 S Miami Ave) **Map 6** Cover about $5, after 9pm only. Open 11:30am-5am daily. This venerable bar and live music venue serves several of its own microbrews in addition to jazz, blues and classic-rock bands. The kitchen satisfies cravings with bar food until 2am (see the Downtown Miami section of Places to Eat). Friday night happy hours are popular.

Rock Churchill's Hideaway (☎ 305-757-1807, W www.churchillspub.com, 5501 NE 2nd Ave) **Map 2** Cover $10-15. Open 11am-3am Mon-Sat, noon-3am Sun. A rockin' English pub in Little Haiti, Churchill's Hideaway has been around since the 1950s. This place feels like an authentic English bar, not some gussied-up tourist trap. It features satellite TV broadcasts of UK football and rugby, dozens of beers and local rock and punk bands on weekend nights.

See also Tobacco Road, above.

Dance Clubs & Nightclubs

Clubs rise and fall like the Nasdaq composite after a tech bubble bursts. It's like on *The Jetsons* when the daughter tells her father, 'No, Daddy, that band was groovy *last* week!' If it isn't obvious already, the information in this section is the most volatile in the book.

Drugs are illegal, and the law is strictly enforced by undercover narcotics cops who pose as barflies. That said, never leave your drink unattended; you never know who might slip what into it.

The club scene gets going late and doesn't wind down until the wee hours of the morning. Arriving when the doors open at 11pm tags you a dreaded early bird, but it may help you get in. To increase your chances of going the distance, take a 'disco nap' in the evening, and as you hop from club to club, refuel with a *cafecito* or two or three.

South Beach nightclubs are generally a healthy mix of gay, lesbian and straight, though several are more exclusively gay. We list the mixed and straight ones together, as the lines are very blurry. If a place is predominantly gay, they'll politely let you know.

There is a club to suit every taste, and some clubs change their ambience and musical style on a nightly basis; for an idea of what's available, see the boxed text 'The Ever-Changing Scene' earlier.

Straight & Mixed Rain (☎ 786-295-9540, 305-674-7447 guest list, 323 23rd St) **Map 3** Cover $20. Open 10pm-5am Tues, Fri & Sat. Far from the maddening crowds, but not too far, the stage is set at Rain with white couches, multi-hued ceilings and energetic dance music. A beautiful crowd dances up a storm on indoor and outdoor dance floors. It's a very dancey place.

Billboardlive (☎ 305-538-2251, **W** www .billboardlive.com, 15th St & Ocean Dr at

---

Don't You Know Who I Am?!?

For reasons best left to psychologists, the more offensively and breathtakingly rude a doorman, and the more ruthlessly exclusive a club, the larger the clamoring hordes of short-skirted women and big-tipping men trying to gain entry.

When the average nightclub cover charge on the Beach is about $20 (except when it's free), why anyone would lay out cold hard cash or certain parts of their warm bodies to get into a place where drinks cost $10 a pop is beyond reason. But there it is.

To get into some of the more popular clubs, ask the concierge or bellperson at your hotel to get you on the guest list. Or try calling and putting yourself on the guest list. Or try one or more of the following strategies:

Be polite: Don't be meek, but don't act as if you're Sean Penn.

Have attitude: You're a lean, mean, partying machine, and no one's gonna mess with you. Oh yeah, you're gorgeous, too.

Be cool: When the competition is as fierce as it is here (think gigantic sale at a department store two days before Christmas), a nanosecond of hesitation will keep you milling about on a crowded sidewalk filled with wannabes.

Dress properly: Standard Miami nightclub garb mirrors New York, Paris or any other fashion center: look expensive, but understatedly so. Dress in black, unless it's a White Party. Or at least dress interestingly – drag queens and other outrageously dressed people get in as well.

Get there early: Yeah, we know; cool people are not the first ones in line. But do you want to be cool or do you want to get in?

Know someone

Be famous

None of the above worked last night? This is only a hint, but you could try 'Hi, this is – [your name here] – with South African Vogue; I'm in town doing a piece on...'Don't say you're from Lonely Planet.

Ocean Steps) **Map 3** Cover $20. Open Fri-Sun. As a general rule, this three-story space starts the evening slowly, with ambient lounge music that builds in tempo and volume as the night progresses. The club often reaches its 1500-person capacity for the Sunday afternoon tea dances (doors open at 5pm). Local and nationally known DJs and bands are booked.

Crobar (☎ 305-531-5027, **W** www.crobar miami.com, 1445 Washington Ave) **Map 3** Cover $25. Open 10:30pm-5am Thur-Sun. This Chicago import has breathed new nocturnal verve into the renovated art deco Cameo Theatre. You may need an actual crowbar to get past the doormen, but once in you'll be part of the hottest scene on South Beach. The sound and light show alone is worth the price of admission. 'Anthem' Sunday nights are gay and feature local superstar DJ Abel.

Level (☎ 305-532-1525, **W** www.levelnight club.com, 1235 Washington Ave) **Map 3** Cover $20. Open 10pm-5am Mon, Thur-Sat. This art deco palace is a clubland smorgasbord – too huge and sprawling to be truly exclusive. With 40,000-plus sq ft of space spread out over three floors, you can take your pick of dance floors, VIP lounges (if you can gain admittance) and bars. Themes vary from room to room, and the crowd is young and exuberant. Friday nights are gay.

Liquid (☎ 305-531-9411, **W** www.liquid nightclub.com, 1532 Washington Ave) **Map 3** Cover usually $10. Open 11pm-5am Tues-Sat. Liquid has stayed fluid, reincarnating itself through new ownership and retaining its much-vaunted exclusivity in new digs. Unless you are dressed very smartly, forget it. Once you're admitted, however, the vibe is pretty democratic: Everyone is assumed to be worthy. Thursday nights are gay, as is the after-hours party on Sunday morning (from 8am until 'whenever everyone's left or passes out'). Yes, you read that correctly; the party *starts* at 8am on Sunday morning.

Lola Bar (☎ 305-695-8697, **W** www.lolabar .com, 247 23rd St) **Map 3** No cover. Open 11pm-5am Tues, Thur-Sat. A little off the beaten path, Lola rewards those in the know with a cozy atmosphere, comfy lounge chairs,

pool tables and great music. The DJ spins music you can actually dance to, not just pose to. Tuesdays are quite popular. What you save with free admission, you'll no doubt spend on overpriced bar drinks. You can't win 'em all.

Mynt (☎ 786-276-6132, 1921 Collins Ave) **Map 3** Cover $20 for men Fri & Sat. Open 10pm-5am Wed-Sat. Whatever you do, don't wear something that will clash with the mint-green palette. Likewise, since the air-conditioning system doubles as an aromatherapy conduit (guess the scent), wear perfume that complements a minty-fresh ambience. Chocolate perfume might be in order. To carry the theme to its natural conclusion, order a *mojito,* and try not to go green with envy while drinking in all the beautiful people. Be forewarned: green is also the color of American greenbacks (money). You may need to 'mynt' your own to afford an evening here.

Kiss South Beach (☎ 305-695-4445, 301 Lincoln Road) **Map 3** No cover. Open 7pm-4am Mon-Sat. Within the Albion Hotel, this club aims to titillate with red decor and red accents. The pervasive atmosphere is sex, sex, sex. Actually, when it was still a design concept waiting to be fulfilled, the place was meant to be even racier, with topless dancers and female waitstaff trained to suggest service of a more personal variety. Even though the original plan was nixed, Kiss still closes the gap between Miami's dance and sex clubs with DJs and dancers.

Rumi (☎ 305-672-4353, 330 Lincoln Road) **Map 3** No cover. Open 7pm-5am Tues-Sun. Named for the 13th-century Sufi mystic whose poetry is currently in vogue, Rumi is like a scene out of the Arabian Nights. Its numerous dining rooms, decorated in dark, rich red and earth tones, are transformed into intimate lounges and dance areas as the night wears on (after 11:30pm or so).

Opium Garden (☎ 305-531-5535, 136 Collins Ave) **Map 4** Cover $20. Open 11pm-5am Fri-Sun (and sometimes Thur). This decadent den is not for the faint-of-ego. If you are either drop-dead gorgeous or up for a challenge, sashay to the velvet ropes and try to gain *entrée.* Once in, strike your most

Cypress trees

Pa-hay-okee boardwalk, Everglades National Park

Everglades waterbirds take flight.

Great blue heron stalking fish along the Anhinga Trail, Everglades

Key West's Duval Street

'So, this giant lobster walks into a bar…'

Islamorada from above

Sunset-watching at Key West's Mallory Square

disinterested pose and glide through the various levels until you find a perch that suits you. Dancing and drinking take second and third place to watching people who are watching people who are people-watching.

Nikki Beach (☎ 305-538-1111, **w** www .penrods.com, 1 Ocean Dr) **Map 4** Cover $20 after 10pm Fri & Sat and after 4pm Sun. Open 11am-5pm Mon-Thur, 11am-5am Fri-Sun. Part of Penrod's Entertainment Complex, this beach-blanket-bimbo–themed beach party is for adults reliving their college spring-break experiences – assuming, that is, that any memories survived the drunken haze of yore. If you can gain entrance to the semiprivate stretch of sand, you can party with the glamorous throngs in thongs. On Monday night an open-air movie screening is followed by the infamous Beehive Party. Friday night happy hour features discount cocktails, a buffet and free champagne for the ladies (5pm to 7pm). A bonfire takes place at 7:30pm.

BED (☎ 305-532-9070, 929 Washington Ave) **Map 4** No cover. Open 8pm-5am Wed-Sun; reservations open at 10am (call early!). What will they think of next? Anything to get a little press between the sheets, eh? Except for the dancing, you do everything here while comfortably ensconced on an actual bed. Take off your shoes and stay awhile. Drop by on Thursday for 'dream girls dinner theater,' a drag cabaret show.

Bongos Cuban Cafe (☎ 786-777-2100, **w** www.bongoscubancafe.com, 601 Biscayne Blvd) **Map 6** Cover $10 before midnight, $20 after. Nightclub open 11pm-5am Fri & Sat. Singer Gloria Estefan's family-style Cuban-themed restaurant transforms itself into a hot-hot-hot salsa club. For the price of the cover, you get the liveliest show in town. It's packed, and once the joint starts jumping, the rhythm is gonna get ya (if claustrophobia doesn't first).

Clubspace (☎ 305-375-0001, **w** www.club space.com, 142 NE 11th St) **Map 6** Cover $20. Open 10pm-10am Fri & Sat. This gargantuan warehouse, located in a former no-man's-land downtown, is the current late-night/early morning club of choice. With 30,000 sq ft to fan out, dancers really have

room to strut their stuff. An around-the-clock liquor license redefines the concept of after-hours.

Gay & Lesbian The gay South Beach nightclub scene is sizzling, but lesbians take note: gay means male in this case. There are no exclusively lesbian clubs in Miami. Although lesbians (and straight women, generally) are welcome in most gay clubs, the vibe in these places is decidedly driven by high-octane testosterone.

For up-to-date listings, check out *Wire,* or log on to the following sites: Express (**w** www.expressgaynews.com), Wire (**w** www.thewireonline.com) and Weekly News (**w** www.twnonline.org).

Cactus (☎ 305-438-0662, **w** www.cactus miami.com, 2041 Biscayne Blvd) **Map 2** Cover $3 on Sat. Open 4pm-2am Sun-Thur, 4pm-3am Fri & Sat. With different themes, happy hours and drag shows nightly, Cactus boasts seven gay clubs in one. One size fits all? Check out the popular Latin-themed 'Ay Papi!' show on Saturday night, complete with male go-go dancers.

Club 1771 (☎ 305-673-6508, 1771 West Ave) **Map 3** Cover varies depending on when you arrive. Open 10pm-4am Sat. These warehouse digs are mammoth, yet somehow this club manages to fill to the brim on Saturday night, when groovy professional dancers entertain the throngs upstairs and nationally known DJs spin downstairs. If you don't mind being unfashionably early, there are free drinks from 10pm to 11pm.

Twist (☎ 305-538-9478, 1057 Washington Ave) **Map 4** Never a cover, always a groove. Open 1pm-5am daily. Twist has more depth than the other flavor-of-the-month clubs; it has staying power. This two-story club has six different bars, including a rooftop bar and patio, a lively and fun place to hang out. Themes change nightly.

Pump (☎ 305-538-7867, 841 Washington Ave) **Map 4** Cover $15-20. Open 4am-'whenever' Sat & Sun morning. Yes, you read that right. Ready for bed? NOT. Only true nocturnal creatures need apply to this antidote for insomnia.

See also Laundry Bar (under Theme Bars, earlier), and Crobar, Level and Liquid (above).

Cinemas

Regal South Beach Cinema (☎ 305-674-6766, 1100 Lincoln Road) **Map 3** This mod, state-of-the-art, 21-screen theater anchors the western end of Lincoln Road. It shows foreign, independent and critically acclaimed mass-appeal movies.

Absinthe House (☎ 305-446-7144, 235 Alcazar Ave) **Map 10** Ah, the good old days...this art house has only one screen for independent and foreign films.

Bill Cosford Cinema (☎ 305-284-4861, w www.miami.edu/cosford, Memorial Classroom Building, 2nd Floor, off University Dr) **Map 10** On the UM campus, this newly renovated art house was launched in memory of the *Miami Herald* film critic. Catch some-

thing here if you can; they always deliver a good lineup of international films, in addition to hosting the Cuban Film Festival. Be sure to call to see what's playing; the chatty film descriptions are enthusiastic and informative.

Performing Arts

Venues You'll see a huge 'coming soon' billboard on the downtown side of the MacArthur Causeway promoting a gigantic, $250 million performing arts center. Someday it will house the city's homeless (but resident) performing arts companies. It's been in the works since the early 1990s.

Colony Theatre (☎ 305-674-1026, 1040 Lincoln Road) **Map 3** A stunning deco showpiece, this small 1934 performing arts center has 465 seats with great acoustics. It's a treasure. And it hosts everything from movies and an occasional musical to

Circuit Parties

Not since ancient Rome have so many men gathered together for a common purpose (or so it appears on the streets of South Beach). In case you didn't know, Miami boasts two huge parties – extravagant annual affairs that last a week (and longer) – that are must-attends on the national circuit. And hallelujah, it's raining men.

With buns far tighter than anything you'd see at the supermarket bread aisle, buff knights dressed in white descend for The White Party (w www.whiteparty.net), a lavish 10-day spectacle held mid- to late November. Why white? As Frank Wagner, the event's co-founder says 'White stands for purity. White is elegant, nonpolitical, noncombative and makes people look just plain beautiful.' Known as the 'Jewel of the Circuit Parties,' the main event is held on the Sunday after Thanksgiving at Vizcaya Museum & Gardens (see the Coconut Grove section). Tickets can be very hard to come by – the sophisticated event attracts upwards of 3000 people. They pour in to support a very vital cause: Care Resource, South Florida's oldest and largest HIV/AIDS service organization. Renowned around the world, the actual party sees folks arriving in yachts, and there's plenty of live music. Ancillary parties at hotels and clubs attract gays by the tens of thousands, and the atmosphere is wild. Let the rhythm move you.

Dancing queens, leave your tambourine at home during the Winter Party (w www.winterparty.com), a weeklong dance fest in early March benefiting the Dade Human Rights Foundation. Growing out of a 1993 response to statewide threats to gay and lesbian civil rights, the party's unofficial mantra: Dance till you can dance no more. Venues and events, from the well-known Ice Palace Party and Miami Light Project show to tea dances and film festivals, are held around South Beach and Miami. If the idea of pink palm trees and 5000 nearly naked men dancing on the beach gets you all sizzling and steamy, make your reservations right this minute. You'll return home bronzed and boozy after having a blast givin' it up for nationally known DJs and supporting a good cause. Enjoy.

theatrical dramas, ballet and off-Broadway productions.

Lincoln Theatre (☎ 305-531-3442, 555 Lincoln Road) **Map 3** The Beach's theatrical jewel hosts a wide variety of performances from local groups to visiting artists. It's somewhat intimate, with only 785 seats.

Jackie Gleason Theater of the Performing Arts (☎ 305-673-7300, W www.gleason theater.com, 1700 Washington Ave) **Map 3** Built in 1951, the Beach's premiere showcase for touring Broadway shows, orchestras and other big musical productions has 2700 seats and very good acoustics. They were so good, in fact, that Jackie Gleason chose to make the theater home to his long-running 1960s television show.

Gusman Center for the Performing Arts (☎ 305-374-2444, W www.gusmancenter.org, 174 E Flagler St) **Map 6** This ornate venue, within an elegantly renovated 1920s movie palace, services a huge variety of performing arts – film festivals, symphonies, ballet and touring shows. The acoustics are excellent, and the fresco ceiling is covered in twinkling stars and clouds. Even though the 1700-seat center isn't as fully booked as it should be, if you get a chance to attend something here, by all means, do.

Theater Actors' Playhouse (☎ 305-444-9293, W www.actorsplayhouse.org, 280 Miracle Mile) **Map 10** Tickets $30-32. Performances Wed-Sun. Within the 1948 deco Miracle Theater, this 600-seat venue stages well-known musicals and comedies. Their smaller venue is perfect for children's theater.

Jerry Herman Ring Theatre (☎ 305-284-3355, W www.miami.edu/ring, 1321 Miller Dr) **Map 10** Tickets $14/10 adult/senior. This University of Miami troupe stages musicals, dramas and comedies from September to May. Alumni actors include Sylvester Stallone, Steven Bauer, Saundra Santiago and Ray Liotta. One-act 'summer shorts' from June to August are fun.

Coconut Grove Playhouse (☎ 305-442-4000, W www.cgplayhouse.com, 3500 Main Hwy) **Map 9** Tickets $40-45/15 adult/youth under 24 yrs, day-of-performance $15 off when paying with cash (they rarely sell out).

This lovely state-owned theater, anchoring the Grove since 1956, gained fame from the moment it opened by premiering Samuel Beckett's *Waiting for Godot*. The main stage, with 1100 seats, features highly regarded earnest and experimental productions by local and international playwrights. The smaller Encore Room features theater-in-the-round cabaret.

Classical Music New World Symphony (☎ 305-673-3331, 800-597-3331, W www.nws .org, 555 Lincoln Road) **Map 3** Tickets $24-70, students half-price, $20 standby tickets for any age (one hour prior to performance; take any empty seat). Performances Oct-May. Sometimes described as 'America's training orchestra,' the deservedly heralded NWS serves as a three- to four-year preparatory program for very talented musicians who've already graduated from prestigious music schools. Founded in 1987, the NSW is led by artistic director Michael Tilson Thomas, who still conducts performances for 12 weeks a year despite his national fame and fortune.

Opera The Florida Grand Opera (☎ 305-854-1643, W www.fgo.org, 2901 W Flagler St) **Map 2** Tickets $19-135. Performances Dec-May. Founded in the 1940s, this highly respected opera performs five nights a week, alternating between its Miami-Dade County Auditorium venue (above) and the Broward Center in Fort Lauderdale (see the Southeast Florida chapter). Even though they stage the operas in their original languages, don't worry: English subtitles are projected.

Dance The Performing Arts Network and Ballet Flamenco La Rosa (☎ 305-672-0552, W www.panmiami.org, 13126 NW Dixie Hwy) **Map 2** This professional flamenco, salsa and merengue dance company performs on a very loose schedule. Call for performance dates and prices. PAN instructors will teach beginners (6:30pm Thursday) and intermediates (7:30pm Thursday) how to salsa for $8 per class, and flamenco (Tuesday, Thursday and Saturday; call for class time) for $12 per class. You can dance if you want to, but can you dance well? The red-hot dancers will make sure you can.

Miami City Ballet (☎ 305-929-7010, 877-929-7010, **W** www.miamicityballet.org, 2200 Liberty Ave) **Map 3** Tickets $19-59. Performances Sept-Mar. Formed in 1985, this resident troupe is guided by artistic director Edward Villella, who studied under the great George Balanchine at the New York City Ballet. You can buy tickets from their new headquarters (10am to 5pm Monday to Friday) and watch the dancers rehearsing through big picture windows.

SPECTATOR SPORTS
Professional Sports
Football Miami Dolphins (☎ 305-620-2578, **W** www.miamidolphins.com) Tickets $20-54. Season Aug-Dec, with home games about twice a month. Attending an American football game may be one of the most intense experiences in spectator sports, and 'Dol-fans' get more than a little crazy when it comes to their team. The Dolphins play at **Pro Player Stadium** (2269 NW 199th St) **Map 2**, a mile south of the Dade-Broward county line. On game days there is bus service between downtown Miami and the stadium (contact Metrobus at ☎ 305-770-3131 or check www.co.miami-dade.fl.us/transit/).

Basketball Miami Heat (☎ 786-777-4328, **W** www.nba.com/heat) Tickets $33-100. Season Nov-Apr. Since 1996, the Armani-clad celebrity coach Pat Riley has led the Miami Heat to five straight playoff berths. They play at the **American Airlines Arena** (601 Biscayne Blvd) **Map 6**, where Madonna and other elusive stars have been sighted courtside.

Miami Sol (☎ 786-777-4765, **W** www.wnba.com/sol) Tickets $6-52. Season June-Aug. This women's team also plays pro hoops at the American Airlines Arena in downtown.

Baseball Florida Marlins (☎ 305-626-7400, **W** www.marlins.mlb.com) Tickets $4-55/2-55 adult/child. Season May-Sept. Founded in 1993, the Florida Marlins were the fastest

franchise in the history of baseball to win a World Series (1997). The triumph disgusted baseball purists, who loudly shouted that their hallowed series had been bought – a reference to the team's then-outlandish payroll. As if to prove them right, the owner sold the star players immediately after winning the World Series. Tickets are easy to come by, since it's hot down here in the summer, and since the Marlins are once again doormats, losing quite often at **Pro Player Stadium** (**Map 2**).

Hockey Florida Panthers (**W** www.floridapanthers.com) Tickets $14-67. Season mid-Oct–mid-Apr. The Panthers, who picked up the Stanley Cup in 1996, play National Hockey League games at the **National Car Rental Center** (☎ 954-835-8000, 2555 Panther Pkwy), in Sunrise, Florida. From Miami, take the Palmetto Expressway (SR 826) or Florida's Turnpike to I-75 north, to the Sawgrass Expressway (toll road 869). After the toll plaza, stay in the far right lane and take exit 1B.

Jai Alai Miami Jai-Alai (☎ 305-633-6400, 3500 NW 37th Ave) **Map 2** Tickets $1-5. Matches noon-5pm Wed-Mon, 7pm-midnight Mon, Fri & Sat. Jai alai (pronounced **high**-aligh, which roughly translates as 'merry festival') is a fascinating and dangerous game. Something of a cross between racquetball and lacrosse, it originated in the Basque region of the Pyrenees in the 17th century, and was introduced to Miami in 1924. The fronton where the games are held is the oldest in the States, having been built just two years after the game was introduced. What *is* the game? Well, players hurl a *pelota* (very hard ball) at more than 170mph to their opponents, who try to catch it with a *cesta*, or woven basket, attached to their glove. Audiences wager on the lightning-fast games, said to be the fastest on earth. No kidding. Bus No 36 stops right in front of the arena.

College Sports
University of Miami Hurricanes (☎ 800-462-2637, **W** www.hurricanesports.com) The

UM Hurricanes dominate college area sports, especially the football squad (tickets $25 to $45). Watch the 'Canes at the famed **Orange Bowl Stadium** (1145 NW 11th St; Map 2).

Hurricane baseball (tickets $7 to $15) is played at **Mark Light Stadium** (**Map 10**). Hurricane basketball (tickets $15 to $20) is played downtown at the **Miami Arena** (**Map 6**).

SHOPPING

Conspicuous consumption, a favored American pastime, is alive and well in Greater Miami. It appears most readily in sprawling mega-malls, modern pantheons that inhabit every city neighborhood.

Art

Wallflower Gallery (☎ 305-579-0069, 10 NE 3rd St) **Map 6** Open 10am-8pm Tues-Fri. Put this funky, cool gallery on your short list of places to check out. Between performance pieces, live music and 'regular' art shows featuring local talent, this cultural oasis is worthy of your support. The staff is also particularly friendly. Wandering around the upstairs space with a drink is not at all intimidating. Special events are held on most Thursday, Friday and Saturday nights.

See also ArtCenter, under Lincoln Road Mall, in South Beach, earlier.

Collectibles

Kitsch in Miami is like mountains in Alaska, steak in Texas and jazz in New Orleans. It's everywhere you look. Cheezoid '50s and '60s Americana and martini-chic rule.

Beatnix (☎ 305-532-8733, 1149 Washington Ave) **Map 3**. Open noon-midnight daily. This shop has a monstrous collection of kitsch, including clothes, coasters, postcards, glasses and the like.

Pop (☎ 305-604-9604, 1151 Washington Ave) **Map 3** Open noon-10pm daily. Dare we say that kitsch doesn't get more collectible than at Pop? From George Jetson and his nuclear family to Ken and Barbie, the traditional household unit is covered.

Indies Company (☎ 305-375-1492, 101 W Flagler St) **Map 6** Open 10am-5pm Mon-

Wed, Fri & Sat, 10am-9pm Thur, noon-5pm Sun. The gift shop at the Historical Museum of Southern Florida thrives on Florida, Florida and more Florida: Think faux alligators and tacky postcards. Actually, the shop has fine souvenirs and a great collection of Miami and South Florida books, too.

Fashion

Fashion and South Beach stroll arm in arm. Upmarket chain stores and designer boutiques saturate Collins Ave between 6th and 9th Sts. It's a veritable ground zero for fashionistas.

Ritchie Swimwear (☎ 305-538-0201, 160 8th St) **Map 4** Open 9am-9pm Mon-Sat, 10am-7pm Sun. Ritchie comes through for every woman who needs a separate size top and bottom.

Whittall & Shon (☎ 305-538-2606, 1319 Washington Ave) **Map 3** Open 11am-8:30pm Mon-Thur, 11am-10:30pm Fri-Sun. When the disco beat here gets your gay blood pumping, shake your gay booty while flipping through gay tank tops. (What makes a tank top gay, you ask? Only what's inside it.) Don't get us wrong, heterosexuals are certainly welcome, but they'll be in the minority for once.

Recycled Blues (☎ 305-538-0656, 1507 Washington Ave) **Map 3** Open 1am-9pm daily. Got budgetary blues? South Beach is actually a great place to buy used clothing.

These folks have Levi's for $12, shorts for $8 and jackets for $20.

Betsey Johnson (☎ 305-673-0023, 805 Washington Ave) **Map 4** Open 11am-7pm Mon-Fri, 11am-8pm Sat, noon-6pm Sun. This hugely popular line of women's wear has a few pieces of clothing so revealing that they may as well be ribbons with pockets. But one former Lonely Planet editor swears by Betsey's clothes, ribbons and all.

Miami Surf Style (☎ 305-532-6928, 421 Lincoln Road) **Map 3** Open 9am-midnight daily. Dude, cheap jeans, hats and T-shirts rule this roost.

See also the boxed text 'Calle Ocho: Cigars, Botánicas & More,' below.

Music

With regards to the recording industry, Miami is right up there with LA, New York and Nashville these days. All the major labels have offices here. And it would be embarrassing for *any* music store to have anything less than a wide selection of imports, as well as listening stations.

Spec's Music (☎ 305-534-3667, 501 Collins Ave) **Map 4** Open 10am-midnight Sun-Thur, 10am-1am Fri & Sat. Spec's, the Tower Records of Miami, has almost 20 supershops around town (for a list, check **w** www .fye.com). This location has a café, lots of listening booths and Latin dance tunes for their clientele: dancing queens.

Calle Ocho: Cigars, Botánicas & More (Map 8)

Little Havana's main thoroughfare, filled with tiny shops you will not find anywhere else in the States, is certainly distinct. Check it out.

Cigars

Although it's illegal to import cigars (and anything else) from Cuba, shops still market Cuban cigars. How can they do that? Simple: They use tobacco that comes from Cuban seeds but is grown in the Dominican Republic. Despite the documented relationship between smoking and various cancers, cigar smoking is igniting passions across the USA. Miami is in its own world; cigar smoking borders on a sacred privilege here.

According to an article in *Cigar Aficionado*, Ernesto Curillo, the owner of **El Crédito Cigars** (☎ 305-858-4162, 1106 SW 8th St; open 8am-6pm Mon-Fri, 8am-4pm Sat), is one of the leaders of the Renaissance. The store, supplied by perhaps Miami's most successful cigar factory, offers several lines, one of the hottest of which is La Gloria Cubana. Peer into the store's picture windows, watching a dozen or so Cuban *tabaqueros* hand-rolling cigars on well-worn wooden benches, then cutting and pressing them. Or go inside to flex your olfactory senses (tobacco smells heady and sweet) and purchase some fat stogies either in bulk or singles. The folks are nice about letting people take photos; ask if you want one.

La Tradición Cubana (☎ 305-643-4005, 1894 SW 8th St) Open 9am-5pm Mon-Fri, 10am-2pm Sat. This little cigar factory is the real thing, not some gussied-up showroom for tourists. You can watch workers roll the cigars you are about to buy. The cigars made here are known for their robust aroma and taste.

What? Don't know how to smoke a cigar? Cut off the end closest to the band with a sharp knife and light that end so that it burns evenly. Draw, but don't inhale the smoke; let it roll around your mouth before exhaling. By all means don't gnaw or suck on the cigar. Don't take more than one or two puffs per minute; if it burns too quickly it'll taste sour. Practice a studied, conversational look.

Botánicas

The spiritual shops of Santería, *botánicas* sell a variety of lotions, potions, sprays, candles and soap to assist in worship and prayer. Bad news coming? Try 'Door Evil Stopper.' Tighten the lips of loose

Virgin Megastore (☎ 305-665-4445, 5701 Sunset Place) **Map 10** Open 10am-midnight Mon, 10am-11pm Tues-Thur, 10am-midnight Fri & Sat, 11am-11pm Sun. You'll find the standard wide selection and de rigueur listening stations at this Miami branch of the chain.

See also the boxed text 'Calle Ocho: Cigars, Botánicas & More,' later.

Piercings & Tattoos

Everyone in Miami Beach and their dog seems to have a tattoo. And while piercings aren't as popular here as they are in some other large cities, Beach piercers can put a pin through it with the best of

them – from eyebrows and tongues to nipples and navels.

Tattoos by Lou (☎ 305-532-7300, 231 14th St) **Map 3** Open noon-1am Mon-Thur, noon-2am Fri & Sat, noon-midnight Sun. Not surprisingly, the most famous Beach tattoo parlor has been here the longest. Since you must be 18 years old, bring an ID. Lou's has three other Miami locations (9820 S Dixie Hwy, 456 NE 167th St, and 1193 W 37th St).

South Beach Tattoo (☎ 305-538-0104, 861 Washington Ave) **Map 4** Open 11am-2am daily. From body piercing and tattoos for a minimum of $50 to a good selection of T-shirts for $15, this place covers your skin one way or another.

Calle Ocho: Cigars, Botánicas & More (Map 8)

mouthed relatives with a bath using 'Stop Gossip' soap. Friend on trial? Pick up some 'Court Case.' Keep Miami's finest at bay with 'Law: Stay Away' candles. Kids won't listen? You need 'Do As I Say' floor wash. Botánicas also sell books, incense, good-luck charms and other Santería and related items.

Everything in these religious supply shops is taken very seriously, so show the same respect you would in a Christian Science Reading Room or, say, a bible shop. The following are some of the better-known Calle Ocho botánicas.

Botánica El Camino (☎ 305-643-9135, 1896 SW 8th St) is the place to stock up on candles and aerosol sprays; it's delightfully welcoming to browsers from out of town. **Botánica Las Mercedes** (☎ 305-631-0606, 2742 SW 8th St), located in a little strip mall, is run by Mercedes, who speaks English and is warmly welcoming to anyone with a genuine interest in her craft.

More

La Casa de las Guayaberas (☎ 305-266-9683, 5840 SW 8th St) Open 10am-7pm Mon-Sat. You, too, can dress like the legendary musicians in the Buena Vista Social Club. Handmade *guayaberas*, traditional Cuban dress shirts for men, start at $15 for a cotton-poly blend and go up to $130 for linen.

Little Havana-To-Go (☎ 305-857-9720, ⓦ www.littlehavanatogo.com, 1440 SW 8th St) Open 10:30am-6pm Mon-Sat, noon-4pm Sun. Little Havana's official souvenir store is not as cheesy as you might think. They actually have some cool authentic stuff, and the folks who work here are very friendly and helpful.

Cervantes Book Store (☎ 305-642-5222, 1898 SW 8th St) Open 9:30am-5:30pm Mon-Sat, noon-4pm Sun. This is *the* place to purchase Spanish-language books.

Casino (☎ 305-856-6888, 1208 SW 8th St) Open 9am-9pm Mon-Sat, 10am-5pm Sun. Cuban musicians have a friend in Casino. You can find Cuban music here that can't even be purchased in Havana. Knowledgeable salespeople oversee a hefty Latin selection.

Flea Markets

Opa-Locka/Hialeah Flea Market (☎ 305-688-8080, 12705 NW 42nd Ave) **Map 2** Open 6am-7pm Mon-Fri, 8am-5pm Sat & Sun. With about 1200 vendors, this is a biggie.

Española Way (between Washington & Drexel Aves) **Map 3** Held 7pm-midnight Fri, 9am-midnight Sat, 11am-9pm Sun. This hippie-style market has handcrafted items, clothing, food vendors and Latin music. On Friday and Saturday evenings, it turns more artsy.

Malls

There are dozens, but these are some of the biggest and best.

Dadeland Mall (☎ 305-665-6226, W www .shopsimon.com, 7535 N Kendall Dr) **Map 2** Open 10am-9:30pm Mon-Sat, noon-7pm Sun. In addition to 175 or so other stores, this Kendall mall boasts Florida's first and largest Burdines department store, plus another Burdines devoted solely to home furnishings. The Spanish-challenged should note that many store employees here speak limited English.

Dolphin Mall (☎ 305-365-7446, W www .shopdolphinmall.com, Florida's Turnpike & Dolphin Expressway) **Map 2** Open 11am-10pm Mon-Sat, noon-8pm Sun. The largest discount outlet center within city limits, this bargain mall boasts an Off Saks Fifth Ave, Marshall's Megastore, a big sporting goods store, a 28-screen movie theater, a huge food court and a roller coaster to keep the kids occupied – it's fun for the whole family. Mall developers expect you to make a day of it.

Aventura Mall (☎ 305-935-1110, W www .shopaventuramall.com, 19501 Biscayne Blvd) **Map 5** Open 10am-9:30pm Mon-Sat, noon-8pm Sun. This upscale granddaddy of a mall, which attracts families with its enormous indoor playground, has a Macy's, Lord & Taylor, Burdines, Bloomingdale's and a 24-screen movie theater with newfangled stadium seating. Look for South Beach shuttles from many hotels (including Loews Miami Beach).

The Shops at Sunset Place (☎ 305-663-0482, W www.shopsimon.com, 5701 Sunset Place) **Map 10** Open 10am-10pm Mon-Fri, 11am-10pm Sat, 11am-9pm Sun. This mall-as-theme-park features faux trees and waterfalls and bird sounds, an IMAX theater, the virtual-reality Gameworks emporium, NikeTown, FAO Schwarz, a teen skating ramp and a 24-screen movie complex.

Design District (Map 2)

Just north of our downtown map borders, between N Miami and NE 2nd Aves and NE 37th and 42nd Sts, the Design District (W www.designdistrict.com) is Miami's epicenter for the interior decorating and design industry. It's an amalgam of international showrooms for antiques, tiles, furniture and art. If it has to do with outfitting or redesigning a home or office, you name it, it's here. Start your exploration at NE 2nd Ave and NE 40th St.

Fashion District (Map 2)

Also just north of our downtown borders, along NW 6th Ave between 23rd and 29th Sts, the less fashionable Fashion District has outlets for about 30 of the 500 or so garment manufactures in the Miami area. From holes-in-the-wall with handbags to a few chic boutiques, patient shoppers will enjoy the adrenaline rush that comes with finding a bargain.

Downtown Miami (Map 6)

The heart of downtown, especially along **Flagler St**, is crammed with dozens and dozens of shops selling…well, selling export-ready electronics mainly to Latin American visitors. Head downtown if you're up for haggling and you speak a modicum of Spanish. Cuban coffee windows will keep the buzz up as you wing it.

Bayside Marketplace (☎ 305-577-3344, W www.baysidemarketplace.com, 401 Biscayne Blvd) Open 10am-10pm Mon-Thur, 10am-11pm Fri & Sat, 11am-9pm Sun. This touristy bayfront mall has entertainment, restaurants, bars, tour-boat docks, pushcart vendors and name-brand shops. There are no surprises, except for the nice views.

There's a downtown branch of **Burdines** (☎ 305-577-2312, 22 E Flagler St), a grand Southern department store.

GETTING THERE & AWAY
Air
Miami is served by two main airports: Miami International Airport (MIA) and the Fort Lauderdale-Hollywood International Airport (FLL). See the following Getting Around section for information about getting to and from MIA; see the Getting Around section in the Fort Lauderdale chapter for information about getting to and from FLL.

Miami International Airport (MIA; ☎ 305-876-7000/7770, W www.miami-airport .com) is one of the country's busiest. There are plenty of ATMs and information booths throughout the airport. The central information booth is located on Concourse E, in the main lobby on the 2nd floor. Check here for lost and found, too. The 24-hour currency exchange office, at International Arrivals, yields typically awful rates. Smoking is prohibited anywhere inside the terminal except in the members-only airline lounges.

Bus
There are four Greyhound (☎ 800-231-2222, W www.greyhound.com) terminals in Miami, which seem to connect to every conceivable Florida town. The main downtown terminal (☎ 305-374-6160; Map 6), 100 NW 6th St, is open from 5am to 11pm daily. Greyhound's airport terminal (☎ 305-871-1810; Map 2), 4111 NW 27th St, is open 24 hours daily. The North Miami terminal (☎ 305-945-0801; Map 2), 16560 NE 6th Ave, is open 6am to 11:30pm daily. The southern Miami terminal (☎ 305-296-9072), 20505 S Dixie Hwy, at the Cutler Ridge Mall (Map 1), has more limited service. It's open from 9am to 6pm Monday through Saturday and from noon to 6pm Sunday.

See the Getting Around chapter for Greyhound fares between Miami and other Florida destinations.

Train
Amtrak's main Miami terminal (☎ 305-835-1223, 800-872-7245, W www.amtrak.com; Map 2), 8303 NW 37th Ave, connects the city with the rest of the continental USA and Canada. The trip from Miami to Tampa takes five hours and costs $36 to $71 one way. Orlando takes six hours and costs $35 to $68. Roundtrip fares are twice the one-way fares.

You can pick up a taxi to your hotel or the airport right outside the Amtrak station. The airport, where you can rent a car, is just 5 miles away; the fare will be about $12 plus tip. Or take the 'L' bus to Miami Beach and No 42 to the airport.

Car & Motorcycle
Miami is 28 miles and 30 minutes south of Ft Lauderdale via I-95; 124 miles and 2 hours east of Naples via US41 or I-75; almost 4 hours north of Key West via US1; and 4½ hours southeast of Orlando via Florida's Turnpike to West Palm Beach and I-95.

GETTING AROUND
To/From MIA
MIA is about 6 miles west of downtown, sandwiched between the Airport Expressway (Hwy 112) and the Dolphin Expressway (Hwy 836). Public transportation from MIA to downtown and Miami Beach is tricky at best, a pain in the rear at worst. SuperShuttle is the best option.

Bus Metrobus (☎ 305-770-3131, W www.co .miami-dade.fl.us/transit/) departs from the lower level of Concourse E ostensibly every 40 minutes between 5:30am and 9pm weekdays, 6:30am to 7:30pm weekends. Take the No 7 to Government Center (where you can catch a connecting bus to your final destination). The ride takes 35 minutes and costs $1.25. The J bus leaves from the same place, ostensibly every 30 minutes, and takes a circuitous route that ends up in Miami Beach more than an hour later. Ostensibly, there is service from 4:30am to 11:30pm daily, but after 7pm, there's only one bus per hour.

Greyhound from MIA is also a pain. I wouldn't bother under any circumstances.

Shuttle Blue SuperShuttle (☎ 305-871-2000, 800-874-8885, W www.supershuttle .com) vans constantly prowl the lower level outside the baggage claim area. The Super-Shuttle operates 24 hours daily and takes credit cards. The only drawback is that it makes a lot of stops, letting people off at various hotels along the way. Your hotel could be the closest to the airport or the farthest. Costs vary depending on destination. From MIA to South Beach, it'll be about $13 to $16 per person.

Car & Motorcycle From MIA to downtown, take Hwy 112 (Airport Expressway; small toll) east and I-95 south and follow signs. To South Beach, take 37th Ave south to Hwy 836 east (Dolphin Expressway) to I-395 east, which leads to the MacArthur Causeway. For Northern Miami Beach, take Hwy 112 east directly to I-195 east, the Julia Tuttle Causeway. For Coconut Grove, take Hwy 112 east to I-95 south to US1 south and follow signs. For Coral Gables, head south on NW 42nd Ave, which is also Le Jeune Rd.

Taxi There are flat rates between MIA and five zones around the city. It costs $31 to go from MIA to Key Biscayne; $24 to anywhere between Government Cut and 63rd St (zone 4, which includes all of South Beach and takes about 20 to 25 minutes). These rates are per carload, not per person.

The Wave

For a mere 25¢ per ride, this South Beach electric shuttle bus (☎ 305-843-9283) runs north-south along Washington Ave from 17th St to South Pointe Dr and east-west along 17th St. A second route runs from the Holocaust Memorial over to Collins Ave and up to the Bass Museum of Art. Pick up a copy of the exact route from the Chamber of Commerce (1920 Meridian Ave; Map 3). It's the best and easiest way to get around.

Metrobus

First things first, and you can't say we didn't warn you: You'll spend more time *waiting for* a bus than *riding on* a bus and you'll probably describe the experience as 'grueling.' Seriously consider if that's how you want to spend your holiday.

For specific route information or travel planning assistance, call ☎ 305-770-3131 (W www.co.miami-dade.fl.us/transit/) Monday to Friday from 6am to 10pm, weekends

9am to 5pm. To order an advance transit map by mail, call ☎ 305-654-6586 Monday to Friday, 8:30am to 4:30pm.

In Miami, get maps, scheduling information and tokens at transit booths located at Government Center, on NW 1st St, between NW 1st and 2nd Aves; at the corner of E Flagler and E 1st Aves; and at the Omni Metromover Terminal, near Biscayne Blvd just south of NE 15th St. The Omni and Government Center terminals are main junction points for buses downtown. Pay as you board. Bus fare is $1.25.

Some major routes include the following:

bus	between
C, K	Miami Beach and Government Center
S, M	Miami Beach and Omni Mall
S	Omni Mall to South Beach, north on Alton Rd then east on 17th St and north on Collins Ave past the Bass Museum & up to the Aventura Mall
8	downtown transit booth and Calle Ocho
17, 6, 22	Government Center and Vizcaya Museum & Gardens (and Museum of Science & Space Transit Planetarium)/ Coconut Grove
B	downtown transit booth and Seaquarium on Key Biscayne
24	downtown transit booth and Miracle Mile, Coral Gables

Metromover

Equal parts bus, monorail and train, the Metromover (W www.co.miami-dade.fl.us/transit/; fare 25¢) offers visitors a great perspective and a cheap orientation tour of downtown. For local taxpayers, it's a boondoggle, losing money every day it operates. Consider riding it at night, when the city is lit with neon. Besides, the city needs every quarter it can get.

You can change between Metrorail and Metromover at Government Center.

Metrorail

This 21-mile-long heavy rail system (W www.co.miami-dade.fl.us/transit/) has one elevated line running from Hialeah through downtown Miami and south to Kendall/

Dadeland. Trains run every 5 to 15 minutes from 6am to midnight. The Metrorail connects with Tri-Rail (at the Tri-Rail/Metrorail Transfer Center at NW 79th St and E 11th Ave, Hialeah) and Metromover and Metrobus (at Government Center). The fare is $1.25, or $1 with a Metromover transfer. Transfers to either Tri-Rail or Metromover are free; transfers from Metrorail to Metrobus are 25¢. It costs $2 to park at most stations.

Tri-Rail

Clean and cheap, Tri-Rail (☎ 800-874-7245, Ⓦ www.tri-rail.com) double-decker commuter trains run along 71 miles of track between Dade, Broward and Palm Beach Counties. For longer trips, to Palm Beach, for instance, Tri-Rail is painfully inefficient (it takes four times longer to take Tri-Rail to Palm Beach than to drive).

Car & Motorcycle

The urban sprawl of metro Miami means that most visitors will end up driving. Unless you'll be in South Beach, downtown or Coconut Grove exclusively, get a car. Expect serious rush hour traffic from 7am to 9am and 4pm to 6pm on weekdays.

Major Thoroughfares Miami Beach is connected to the mainland by four causeways built over Biscayne Bay. They are, from south to north: the MacArthur (also the extension of Hwys 41 and A1A), Venetian (50¢ toll), Julia Tuttle Causeway and John F Kennedy Causeway.

The most important highway is I-95, which runs north-south until it ends at US Hwy 1 south of downtown. US Hwy 1, which runs from Key West all the way north to Maine, hugs the coastline. It's called Dixie Hwy south of downtown and Biscayne Blvd north of downtown.

Hwy A1A goes by the name of Collins Ave in Miami Beach.

Besides the causeways to Miami Beach, the major eastern roads are Calle Ocho (also called SW 8th St); Hwy 112 (aka the Airport Expressway); and Hwy 836 (also called the Dolphin Expressway), which runs

east from the Turnpike Extension, crosses the Palmetto Expressway and skirts the southern edge of the airport before slicing through downtown and connecting with I-395 and the MacArthur Causeway.

Parking Except in Coral Gables, South Beach and downtown, parking is pretty straightforward. Regulations are well signed, and meters are plentiful.

Parking downtown can be a nightmare, or at least expensive. Park in the Cultural Center Garage at SW 2nd Ave, just west of the Miami-Dade Cultural Center. If you visit the Historical Museum of Southern Florida, Miami Art Museum or main public library in that complex, they'll validate your parking ticket so that parking costs $2.40.

On Miami Beach there are many municipal parking lots; look for giant blue 'P' signs. Big garages are located at Collins Ave and 7th St; Collins Ave and 14th St; Washington Ave and 12th St; Washington Ave and 16th St; and 17th St across from the Jackie Gleason Theater of the Performing Arts. If you park illegally or if a sidewalk meter runs out, parking fines are about $20, but a tow could cost $75. Call Beach Towing (☎ 305-534-2128) if you think your car has been towed.

Miami Beach is tough on enforcement, but Coral Gables is positively Orwellian: Metered parking is everywhere that valet parking is not. If you're even a second late, you'll be hit with varyingly outrageous fines.

Meter Cards These magnetic cards are a parker's best friend. Instead of collecting quarters everywhere you go and running back to feed the meters every two to 10 hours (meters cost $1 per hour), purchase a card from the Miami Beach City Hall (1700 Convention Center Dr, 1st floor, weekdays; Map 3), the Chamber of Commerce (1920 Meridian Ave; open 9am-5pm Mon-Fri, 10am-4pm Sat-Sun; Map 3) or any Publix grocery store (Dade Blvd at 19th St). Cards come in denominations of $10, $20 and $25.

Rentals All the big operators, and a host of smaller or local ones, have bases in the

MIAMI

Miami area. If you only want to rent a car for a day or two and are staying in South Beach, ask the agency if they have a location there. Check the Yellow Pages for listings besides Thrifty (☎ 800-367-2277, W www .thrifty.com).

CruiseAmerica (☎ 305-828-1198, 800-327-7799, W www.cruiseamerica.com), with several area locations, rents motorcycles and recreational vehicles.

Taxi

In an effort to provide better service and change the reputation of Miami cabbies, a consortium of drivers has banded together; call their 'Dispatch Service' (☎ 305-888-4444) for a ride. Taxis in Miami have flat and metered rates. The metered fare is $3.25 for the first mile, $2 each additional mile. Regular routes like the South Beach Convention Center to Coconut Grove cost $16. You will not have to pay extra for luggage or extra people in the cab.

Bicycle

Miami is as flat as a pancake and as smooth as a baby's behind, so biking around the Beach makes a lot of sense. In fact, it makes so much sense that people who don't have bikes will try to steal yours. Use a sturdy U-type bike lock. Mere chains and padlocks do not deter people in Miami Beach, where bike theft rates rival those of Amsterdam.

Bicycles are not allowed on buses, Metrorail or Tri-Rail, but you can bike across the causeways. There are several places in South Beach and on Key Biscayne to rent bicycles; see the Activities section, earlier in this chapter, for bike rentals.

The Everglades

Flying over South Florida makes it obvious: Vast tracts of the Everglades are completely inaccessible to the public. But the remainder, within Everglades National Park, contains some of the most accessible wilderness areas in the state. You'll find developed canoeing and kayaking routes, hiking and biking trails, and a very good information infrastructure.

Don't overlook Big Cypress National Preserve, a protected area at the northern end of the Everglades that is also open to hikers and drivers, or the colorful underwater Biscayne National Park, on the eastern shore.

The Tamiami Trail (US Hwy 41), the main artery linking Miami and the southwest Florida coast, is the easiest place to dip into the park. If you only have time to do one thing in the Everglades, stop at Shark Valley on the Tamiami Trail. At some point you will end up in Flamingo or Everglades City, which is near the 10,000 Islands; both make good bases for richer exploration.

Getting There & Around
The only sensible way to explore the area is by car. From Miami, take Florida's Turnpike Extension (toll) or US Hwy 1 to reach Florida City and Homestead; it's about 45 minutes with light traffic. From there to the entrance of Everglades National Park, it's another 15 minutes. And from there to Flamingo along Hwy 9336, add another hour without stopping.

From downtown Miami (assuming moderate traffic), it takes about 45 minutes to an hour to reach Shark Valley. There's no public transportation along the Tamiami Trail.

To reach Everglades City from the Tamiami Trail, head south on Hwy 29 until you're forced to turn right. At the traffic circle, turn left, and the road leads you to the Gulf Coast Visitor Center. The whole trip from Miami takes a little less than two hours.

To reach Marco Island (the unofficial capitol of the 10,000 Islands region) from I-75, take the last Naples exit, and then take Hwy 951 west to the island. Alternately, it's about 30 miles west of Everglades City, via Hwy 92 off the Tamiami Trail, across the Goodland Bridge over Goodland Bay and up to San Marco Drive.

Greyhound (☎ 800-231-2222) services Homestead, but not Florida City, Everglades City, Flamingo or Marco Island. There are four daily buses ($9.25/18.25 one-way/roundtrip) from Miami. The only other

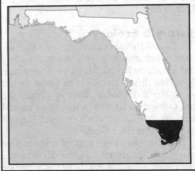

THE EVERGLADES

Highlights

- Cross paths with an alligator – look, but DON'T FEED!

- Take the excellent 17-mile narrated tram tour (or hike or bike) to the Shark Valley Observation Tower for a 50-foot-high overview of the prairie

- Explore the 10,000 Islands by kayak and camp on secluded island chickees (open-air thatched huts)

- Visit the Ah-Tah-Thi-Ki Museum to learn about Seminole life

- Take a glass-bottom boat tour in Biscayne National Park

- Send a postcard from the nation's smallest post office in Ochopee

- Visit the Big Cypress Gallery, a stunning black-and-white photography gallery

way to reach Florida City by public transportation is idiotic: You can take Metrorail to Dadeland North, then bus No 1 to the Cutler Ridge Mall and then No 35 or No 70 to Florida City.

EVERGLADES NATIONAL PARK

The second-largest US national park (after Yellowstone) and largest subtropical wilderness in the continental USA, the Everglades are a unique and delicate ecosystem made up of swamps and marshes at the southern tip of the Florida peninsula. It's also one of the most well-known and poorly understood areas of the USA. Visitors to South Florida hear about airboat tours and the Shark Valley Tram Tour, and of ecological threats to the area, but many don't have time to find out more. Or they're scared off by tales of renegade alligators and poisonous snakes lurking in the muck.

Whether you visit the Ernest Coe Visitor Center for an afternoon, take the Shark Valley Tram Tour, or embrace canoeing and camping in the 10,000 Islands and on the Wilderness Waterway, we can't urge you enough to visit.

Though the threat to the Everglades is very real, it is a spectacular place to get into the real nature of South Florida. From the brackish waters of the mangrove and cypress swamps; to hardwood hammocks, saw-grass flats, Dade County pinelands and marshes; to creatures like crocodiles, alligators, bottle-nosed dolphins, manatees, snowy egrets, bald eagles and ospreys, there is simply no other place like the Everglades.

History & Ecology

The Calusa Indians called the area Pa-hay-okee, which means 'grassy water.' The late and much-beloved Marjory Stoneman Douglas called it the River of Grass. In her book *The Everglades: River of Grass,* she says Gerard de Brahm (a surveyor) named them River Glades, which on later English maps became Ever Glades.

The Everglades are part of a sheet-flow ecosystem, beginning at the Kissimmee River, which empties into Lake Okeechobee

at the south center of the state. Before humankind's meddling, Okeechobee overflowed and sent sheets of water through the Everglades and finally into the Gulf of Mexico. The resulting ecosystem was home to thousands of species of flora and wildlife. Wading birds, amphibians, reptiles and mammals flourished.

Enter business, stage right. Sugar growers, attracted by mucky waters, swarmed in and pressured the government to make land available to them. In 1905, Florida governor Napoleon Bonaparte Broward personally dug the first shovelful of dirt for what was to become one of the largest and most destructive diversions of water in the world. The Caloosahatchee River was diverted and connected to Lake Okeechobee. Hundreds of canals were dug, slicing through the Everglades to the coastline to 'reclaim' the land. The flow of lake water was then restricted by a series of dikes. Farmland began to sprout up in areas previously uninhabited by humans.

Unfortunately, farming diverted the freshwater desperately needed by nature in the Everglades, and it produced fertilizer-rich wastewater, which promotes foliage growth, which in turn clogs waterways and further complicates matters. More recently, as chemicals spill into the Glades and local waters, the Florida Aquifer (the source of Florida's freshwater supply) is in great danger of being contaminated. Autopsies of local animals, including Florida panthers, have shown that mercury levels are extremely high. Pollution from industry and farming is killing foliage, and because of the freshwater diversion, saltwater from the Gulf of Mexico is flowing deeper into the park than ever before. There are 16 endangered and five threatened animal species within the park.

Restoration Efforts to save the Everglades began as early as the late 1920s, but they were sidelined by the Great Depression. In 1926 and 1928, two major hurricanes caused Okeechobee to burst its banks; the resulting floods killed hundreds. So the Army Corps of Engineers came in and did a *really* good job of damming the lake: They constructed the Hoover Dike. Through the efforts of conservationists and prominent citizens like Marjorie Stoneman Douglas, the Everglades was declared a national park in 1947. But the threat is far from over.

Everglades restoration is one of the hottest potatoes in the USA's environmental community. In the mid-1990s, Congress voted to cut subsidies to Florida sugar growers by a penny a pound and to use the savings to buy 126,000 acres of land to restore a natural flow of water through South Florida. About one-fifth of Florida's sugar-producing land was purchased and allowed to revert to marshland. Additionally, the federal and state governments would then spend $100 million to reroute and reconstruct South Florida's dikes, dams and levees, from northern Lake Okeechobee through the Glades.

The basic idea of restoration is to increase the quantity of freshwater within the Everglades, remove upstream phosphorus, employ mitigation projects to enhance the Everglades with restoration objectives, and maintain a diverse habitat to meet the needs of wildlife. It sounds great, but it's easier said than done. And the politics are highly divisive.

Thousands of scientists, environmentalists and business groups are still arguing about the best way to meet the goals of restoration. The Everglades Coalition, with 42 subgroups, is the primary environmental group. They want to restore the remaining Everglades lands to conditions prior to developmental impacts while maintaining flood protection and providing freshwater needs for the growing South Florida populous. The Coalition also wants to continue restoring the Kissimmee River Basin, return Lake Okeechobee to a more natural state, proceed with land acquisition to preserve as much of the system as possible and control urban sprawl.

The Coalition has been working closely with local, state and federal officials about the best way to proceed, and the federal government has earmarked funds for restoration.

Planning

The Everglades' seasons consist of the dry season (roughly November to May) and the mosquitoes and no-see-ums season (June to October). While the park is open year-round, it's best to visit in the dry season. The summer season is brutal.

Rangers can help you develop specific itineraries with the assistance of the *Wilderness Trip Planner,* a very good National Park Service (NPS) guide to the park. Molloy's *A Paddler's Guide to Everglades National Park* is an excellent guide to waterway trails. For nature information and identification, look for *Florida's Fabulous Birds,* by Winston Williams; *Florida's Fabulous Reptiles & Amphibians,* by Peter Carmichael and Winston Williams; the National Geographic's *Field Guide to Birds of North America;* and *Peterson Field Guide to the Birds,* by Roger Tory Peterson.

Visitor's Centers

The main park entry points have visitor's centers where you can get maps, camping permits and ranger information. The principal one, the Ernest Coe Visitor Center (☎ 305-242-7700, W www.nps.gov/ever), on Hwy 9336, is packed with excellent information. It's open 8am to 5pm daily; the gate is open 24 hours daily. Admission is $10 per carload, $5 for pedestrians and cyclists. A quick stop here is the fastest and easiest way to see some of the Everglades. The center is about 15 miles south of Florida City and 38 miles north of Flamingo. The adjacent Royal Palm Visitor Center (☎ 305-242-7700), on Hwy 9336, is open from 8am to 4:15pm daily.

The Shark Valley Visitor Center (☎ 305-221-8776), on the Tamiami Trail, is open from 8:30am to 5pm daily. The Flamingo Visitor Center (☎ 239-695-3094), at the park's southern coast, is open from 7:30am to 5pm daily. The Gulf Coast Visitor Center (☎ 239-695-3311), on Hwy 29 in Everglades City, is the northwesternmost ranger station. It's open from 8:30am to 5pm daily and provides the best access to the 10,000 Islands area (see the boxed text 'Canoe Camping on 10,000 Islands').

THE EVERGLADES

THE EVERGLADES

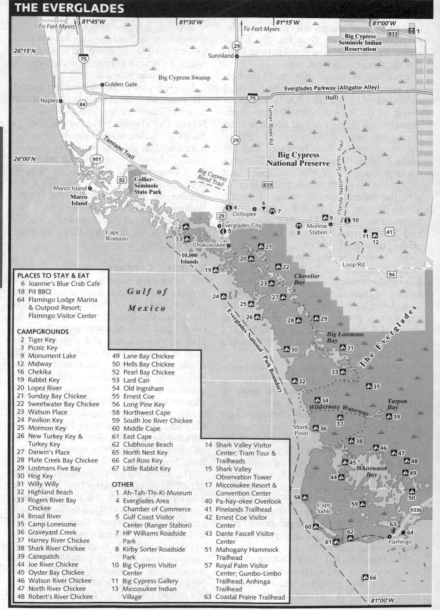

PLACES TO STAY & EAT
6 Joannie's Blue Crab Cafe
18 Pit BBQ
64 Flamingo Lodge Marina
   & Outpost Resort;
   Flamingo Visitor Center

CAMPGROUNDS
2 Tiger Key
3 Picnic Key
9 Monument Lake
16 Midway
16 Chekika
19 Rabbit Key
20 Lopez River
21 Sunday Bay Chickee
22 Sweetwater Bay Chickee
23 Watson Place
24 Pavilion Key
25 Mormon Key
26 New Turkey Key &
   Turkey Key
27 Darwin's Place
28 Plate Creek Bay Chickee
29 Lostmans Five Bay
30 Hog Key
31 Willy Willy
32 Highland Beach
33 Rogers River Bay
   Chickee
34 Broad River
35 Camp Lonesome
36 Graveyard Creek
37 Harney River Chickee
38 Shark River Chickee
39 Canepatch
44 Joe River Chickee
45 Oyster Bay Chickee
46 Watson River Chickee
47 North River Chickee
48 Robert's River Chickee

49 Lane Bay Chickee
50 Hells Bay Chickee
52 Pearl Bay Chickee
53 Lard Can
54 Old Ingraham
55 Ernest Coe
56 Long Pine Key
58 Northwest Cape
59 South Joe River Chickee
60 Middle Cape
61 East Cape
62 Clubhouse Beach
65 North Nest Key
66 Carl Ross Key
67 Little Rabbit Key

OTHER
1 Ah-Tah-Thi-Ki Museum
4 Everglades Area
   Chamber of Commerce
5 Gulf Coast Visitor
   Center (Ranger Station)
7 HP Williams Roadside
   Park
8 Kirby Sorter Roadside
   Park
10 Big Cypress Visitor
   Center
11 Big Cypress Gallery
13 Miccosukee Indian
   Village

14 Shark Valley Visitor
   Center; Tram Tour &
   Trailheads
15 Shark Valley
   Observation Tower
17 Miccosukee Resort &
   Convention Center
40 Pa-hay-oke Overlook
41 Pinelands Trailhead
42 Ernest Coe Visitor
   Center
43 Dante Fascell Visitor
   Center
51 Mahogany Hammock
   Trailhead
57 Royal Palm Visitor
   Center; Gumbo-Limbo
   Trailhead; Anhinga
   Trailhead
63 Coastal Prairie Trailhead

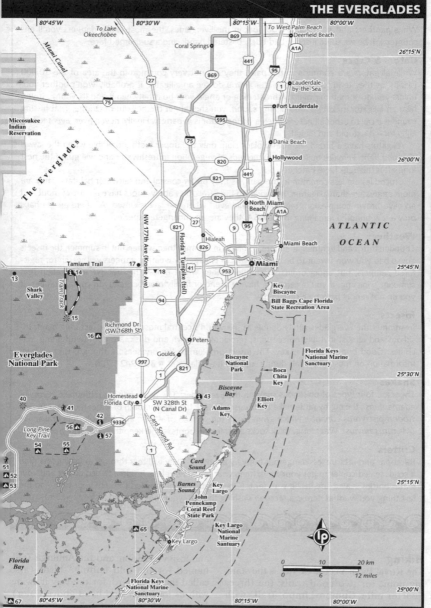

THE EVERGLADES

To Lake Okeechobee
Miami Canal
80°45'W 80°30'W 80°15'W 80°00'W
26°15'N
Coral Springs
To West Palm Beach
Deerfield Beach
869
441
95
1
Lauderdale-by-the-Sea
27
869
Fort Lauderdale
75
595
Miccosukee Indian Reservation
75
Dania Beach
The Everglades
820
Hollywood 26°00'N
821
441
826
27
North Miami Beach A1A
821
9 95 1
Hialeah
826
NW 177th Ave (Krone Ave)
Florida's Turnpike (toll)
ATLANTIC OCEAN
41
Miami Beach
Tamiami Trail 17 953 Miami 25°45'N
13
14
Shark Valley
Tram Track
18
94
Key Biscayne
Bill Baggs Cape Florida State Recreation Area
15
Richmond Dr (SW 168th St)
16
Peters
Florida Keys National Marine Sanctuary
Everglades National Park
Goulds
997
Biscayne National Park
Boca Chita Key
1 821 25°30'N
40
Homestead Biscayne Bay
41 Florida City SW 328th St (N Canal Dr) 43 Elliott Key
Long Pine Key Trail 56 42 9336
Adams Key
54 57
Card Sound Rd
51
55
52
Card Sound
53
1
Barnes Sound 25°15'N
Key Largo
John Pennekamp Coral Reef State Park
65
Key Largo National Marine Sanctuary
Key Largo
Florida Bay
0 10 20 km
0 6 12 miles
67
80°45'W 80°30'W 860°15'W 80°00'W 25°00'N

Panthers & Gators & Crocs, Oh My!

While panthers and gators and crocs lurk in the Everglades, the most exotic dangers you'll encounter will be weather, insects, bad tides, blistered hands and a sunburned face.

Gators & Crocs

While alligators are common in the park, they are not very common in the area of the 10,000 Islands, as they tend to avoid saltwater. If you do see an alligator, it probably won't bother you, unless you do something overtly threatening or angle your boat between it and its young. If you hear an alligator making a loud hissing sound, you should get the hell out of Dodge. That hissing sound is a call to other alligators when a young gator is in danger. Finally, never, ever, *ever* feed an alligator – it's stupid and illegal.

Alligators have a broad snout and black skin; only the upper teeth are visible when the jaw is clamped tight. Females build nests on mounds of vegetation in freshwater and will guard the nest long after the eggs have hatched.

Crocodiles are less common in the park, as they prefer coastal and saltwater habitats. They are more aggressive than alligators, however, so the same rules apply. Crocs have a narrow snout and an olive-brown complexion; teeth are visible even when the jaw is closed. As there are perhaps only a few hundred remaining in the USA, they are an endangered species.

Weather

Thunderstorms and lightning are more common in summer than winter. But in summer, the insects are so bad you won't want to be out anyway. In emergency weather, rangers will search for registered campers, but under ordinary conditions, they won't unless they receive information that someone's missing. If you're camping, have a friend or family member ready to contact rangers if you do not report back by a certain day.

Insects

In summer the Everglades surely double as the world's central mosquito-manufacturing plant. Insidious and almost invisible no-see-ums, ferocious at dawn and dusk, are god-awful biting machines. Good bug repellant is key. The insect problem in the dry season, though, isn't so bad. Information on mosquito levels during summer is available at ☎ 305-242-7700.

Snakes

There are four types of poisonous snake in the Everglades: The diamondback rattlesnake *(Crotalus adamanteus);* the pigmy rattlesnake *(Sistrurus miliarius);* the cottonmouth or water moccasin *(Agkistrodon piscivorus conanti)*, which swim along the surface of water; and the colorful coral snake *(Micrurus fulvius)*. Wear long, thick socks and lace-up boots – and keep the hell away from them.

Critters

Raccoons and rats are less dangerous but very annoying. They will tear through anything less than a solid, sealed cooler to get your food. Keep your food and refuse inside a sealed cooler and your water bottles sealed and inside your tent. (Open water can be smelled through your tent, and the last thing you want at 4am is a raccoon slashing through your tent for a sip of fresh water.)

Hiking

The Royal Palm Visitor Center is the starting point for two good trails: the three-quarter-mile **Gumbo-Limbo Trail**, with gumbo-limbo and royal palm trees, orchids and lush vegetation; and the **Anhinga Trail**, named for the odd anhinga birds (also called the snake bird, for the way it swims with its long neck and head above water). You'll probably run into alligators, turtles, waterfowl, lizards and snakes on this half-mile trail.

All along Hwy 9336 between the visitor's center and Flamingo, the 38-mile main road offers lots of opportunities for hiking, including: the **Pinelands**, a half-mile trail through Dade County pine forest – look for exposed limestone bedrock; **Pa-hay-okee Overlook**, a quarter-mile boardwalk trail with an observation tower; and **Mahogany Hammock**, a half-mile boardwalk leading into lush and overgrown vegetation. **Long Pine Key** is the starting point of a 15-mile series of walking trails where you may see many species indigenous to the Everglades, including, if you're very quiet and patient, Florida panthers.

Camping
In addition to camping in Flamingo and Big Cypress (see those sections, later), car campers shouldn't overlook *Long Pine Key* (☎ *800-365-2267, free off-season, sites $14 Nov-Apr)*, just west of the Royal Palm Visitor Center. Reservations are a good idea in the high season. Sites are suitable for both RV (no hookups, but there are dump stations) and tent campers; you'll find drinking water, fire rings, barbecue areas and picnic tables. For information about backcountry camping and permits, see National Parks in the Outdoor Activities chapter.

Attention canoe campers: See the boxed text 'Canoe Camping on 10,000 Islands.'

FLORIDA CITY & HOMESTEAD
Hurricane Andrew ripped through Homestead in 1992 at speeds of 200mph, leveling everything in its path. Even though the town has been rebuilt, Homestead's economy never completely recovered. But this is still the 'gateway to the Everglades,' and the countryside still supports lots of farms, nurseries and 'u-pick' farm stands.

Krome Ave (Hwy 997) cuts through both towns; you'll find a few motels and fast-food restaurants here. In Homestead, the Chamber of Commerce (☎ 305-247-2332), 43 N Krome Ave, is open 9am to noon and 1pm to 5pm weekdays.

Places to Stay & Eat
Everglades International Hostel (☎ *305-248-1122, 800-372-3874,* **w** *www.everglades hostel.com, 20 SW 2nd Ave, Florida City)* Dorm beds $13-16, doubles $33-39; add $1 per person for air-con in summer. This hostel, in a 1930s boarding house and operated by the super-friendly Owhnn, has six-bedded dorm rooms and private doubles with shared bath. You'll find lots of information about Glades canoeing, kayaking and bicycling. (They also rent canoes and kayaks and give tours.) The hostel has a full kitchen, a garden, Internet connections and laundry facilities.

Best Western Florida City/Homestead Gateway to the Keys (☎ *305-246-5100, 800-937-8376,* **w** *www.bestwestern.com, 411 S Krome Ave, Florida City)* Rooms $74-89 off-season, $94-109 Dec-May. This two-story motel has a pool and 114 standard-issue rooms with either two queens or one king bed. Some rooms have a microwave, refrigerator and desk.

Robert Is Here (☎ *305-246-1592, 19200 SW 344th St, Homestead)* Open 8am-7pm daily Nov-Aug. For a slice of Old Florida, not to mention some exotic fruits and slices of heady mango (in summer), stop at Robert's, surely one of the best-known farmer's markets in the country. The mango shakes are otherworldly, but if you're here in the winter, try a Key lime milkshake.

El Toro Taco (☎ *305-245-8182, 1 S Krome Ave, Homestead)* Dishes $2-9. Open 11am-9pm Tues-Thur & Sun, 11am-10pm Fri & Sat. The mythical aura surrounding El Toro Taco has a basis in reality, and it's reason enough for some to drive to Homestead from Miami. The fajitas, burritos, other Mexican specialties and fresh salsa are exceptional at this family-run restaurant. Bring your own beer.

Farmer's Market Restaurant (☎ *305-242-0008, 300 N Krome Ave, Florida City)* Lunch $8-10, dinner $12-14. Open 5:30am-9pm daily. This simple restaurant prepares homemade everything, from hotcakes and hearty breakfasts, to fried-fish baskets at lunch, to seafood combos and snapper at dinner.

FLAMINGO

From the Coe and Royal Palm visitor's centers, follow Hwy 9336 to the bitter end. Welcome to Flamingo, the most developed and least authentic Everglades experience you can get. With sightseeing and bay cruises, it's really geared toward holidaymakers. You'll find camping, houseboat rentals and a lodge, in addition to nature and bike paths, picnic tables and short canoe trails.

If you 're overnighting in Flamingo, pick up the NPS brochure, which details nearby canoe and hiking trails. The 7.5-mile (one way) **Coastal Prairie Trail** follows an old road once used by cotton pickers; it's only partially shaded by buttonwood trees, so bring plenty of sunscreen. Also see the boxed text 'Canoe Camping on 10,000 Islands' and Canoeing & Kayaking in the Everglades City section, later, for more opportunities to canoe and kayak in the Everglades.

Flamingo Lodge Marina & Outpost Resort (☎ 239-695-3101, 800-600-3813, W www.flamingolodge.com, Hwy 9336, open daily) does it all. They rent kayaks for $27 for four hours, $43 for a full day and $50 overnight. A tandem costs $38/54/60. They also rent bicycles for $8/14 for four/eight hours. The outfit also leads sightseeing tours for two hours ($16/8 adult/child, departs 10am, 1pm & 3:30pm) and four hours ($39 per person,

departs at 8:30am & 1:30pm). The longer trips aren't really worth the extra time and money. In fact, the scenery is better out of Everglades City, so if you have time, head west. The lodge also has laundry facilities, a post office, coolers, binoculars and fishing gear.

Places to Stay & Eat

National Park Service (☎ 800-365-2267, W reservations.nps.gov) Sites free off-season, $14 Nov-Apr. The campgrounds here are run by the NPS. None of these primitive, barely shaded sites have hookups. Depending on the time of year, cold-water showers are either bracing or a welcome relief.

Flamingo Lodge Marina & Outpost Resort (see above) Rooms $65/95 off-season/ mid-Dec–Mar, suites & cottages $89-110/135-145. All 102 perfunctory units have two double beds, TV and air-con. It's better than camping in a rainstorm or with the mosquitoes. Suite and cottage rates are for four people (so they're a bargain, really), and the cottages have full kitchens.

BISCAYNE NATIONAL PARK

Call it a living, breathing work of art, or a dazzling and garish spectacle of life. Either way, it's the world's third-largest reef (second to Australia's Great Barrier Reef

---

Houseboating

One of the laziest, easiest and most fun ways to explore parts of the Everglades is on a houseboat. They're surprisingly simple to navigate and only reach cruising speeds of 6mph, so you needn't worry if your skills don't match a Nascar driver's. Contact the **Flamingo Lodge Marina & Outpost Resort** (☎ 239-695-3101, 800-600-3813, W www.flamingolodge.com, Hwy 9336). These folks rent two types of houseboat, which, if you're with five other people, is cheaper than you might think. Even with the top luxury model (the Gibsons), it only ends up being $41 per person per night. And the longer you keep it out, the cheaper it gets. All boats have a refrigerator/freezer, stove and oven, bathrooms with showers, propane, linen, kitchen utensils, pots, life vests and charts. The luxury boats have air-con and generators, while the pontoon boats do not.

Boxier pontoon boats, which can sleep six comfortably, cost $275 nightly or $340 for two nights off-season. From November to April the two-night minimum is $475. The Gibsons have a two-night minimum year-round, and cost $525 off-season, $575 November to April. Expect to pay an extra $40 a day for fuel. You don't need a special license; if you've never driven a boat before, they'll give you an hour-long orientation course and set you free with a seafaring RV.

and offshore Belize), and it contains the continental USA's only living coral. Fortunately, this unique 300-sq-mile park, 95% of which is under water, is very easy to explore independently with a canoe or via a glass-bottom–boat tour. Its offshore keys, accessible only by boat, also offer pristine opportunities for camping.

First things first though: Head straight to Convoy Point and the **Dante Fascell Visitor Center** (☎ 305-230-7275, W www.nps.gov/ bisc, 9700 SW 328th St, open 8:30am-5pm daily) to watch a great introductory film for a good overview of the park. Generally, summer and fall are the best times to visit the park; you'll want to snorkel when the water is calm.

Long **Elliott Key** has picnicking, camping and hiking among mangrove forests; tiny **Adams Key** has only picnicking; and equally tiny **Boca Chita Key** has an ornamental lighthouse, picnicking and camping. No-see-ums (tiny biting flies) are invasive, and their bites are devastating. Make sure your tent is devoid of miniscule entry points. Primitive *camping* costs $10 per night; self-pay with exact change on the harbor (rangers cruise the Keys to check your receipt). Bring in all supplies, including water, and carry everything out. There is no water on Boca Chita (only saltwater toilets), and since it has a deeper port, it tends to attract bigger (and louder) boaters. There are cold-water showers and potable water on Elliott, but it's always good to bring your own, since the generator might go out.

Biscayne National Underwater Park (☎ 305-230-1100) offers glass-bottom–boat viewing of the exceptional reefs, canoe rentals, transportation to the keys, and snorkeling and scuba diving trips. Here's the lowdown on the myriad services offered: All tours require a minimum of six people, so call to make reservations. Three-hour glass-bottom–boat trips depart at 10am daily ($20/18/13 adult/senior/child under 12 yrs). Canoe rentals cost $8 hourly, and kayaks cost $16; they're rented from 9am to 3pm. Transportation to Elliott Key for hiking or camping costs $25 per person roundtrip (make reservations at least a day

in advance). A three-hour snorkeling trip ($30 per person) departs at 10am Monday to Thursday and at 1:30pm daily; you'll have about 1½ hours in the water. Scuba trips depart at 8:30am Friday to Sunday ($45). Two points of caution: Coral rock is very sharp (be careful wading in the water), and mosquitoes are fierce (bring lots of repellent).

ALONG THE TAMIAMI TRAIL

Although Shark Valley is the main attraction on the Tamiami Trail (allegedly a contraction of Tampa and Miami; the trail blazes between the two cities), a few other stops are worthy of your time. For the most part, it's straight as an arrow through monotonous swampland. Unless you're desperate, skip the Miccosukee Cultural Center – it's not the best introduction to Florida Native American life (think fried food, alligator wrestling and expensive gasoline). For a more friendly and accessible introduction to Native American traditions and customs, see the Ah-Tah-Thi-Ki Museum section, later.

Miccosukee Resort & Convention Center

About 15 minutes west of the Miami airport, this resort (☎ 305-925-2555, 877-242-6464, W www.miccosukee.com, 500 SW 177th Ave) has 302 contemporary guest rooms and suites ($99 Nov-Apr, inquire about off-season packages); wall-to-wall gaming tables that are open around the clock; second-tier nationally known entertainers; and five restaurants, including a deli and an all-you-can-eat buffet. Hotel guests have access to a nice fitness center. Inquire about special packages.

Shark Valley

This Everglades National Park entrance (☎ 305-221-8776, admission $8 per car, open 8:30am-5pm daily) offers a very popular and painless way to immerse yourself in the Everglades prairie. You can bike ($4.75 per hour), walk or take a tram tour along the 17-mile **trail** between the entrance and the 50-foot-high **Shark Valley Observation Tower**, which offers a dramatic vantage point overlooking the park. The place is teeming with flora and fauna, including plenty of gators sunning themselves on the asphalt roadway. Give them wide berth.

The naturalist-led **Shark Valley Tram Tour** (☎ *305-221-8455, tours $11/10/6.50 adult/senior/child under 12 yrs*) takes two hours and is extremely worthwhile. If you only have time for one Everglades activity, this should be it. Trams leave hourly between 9am and 4pm in winter; and at 9am, 11am, 1pm and 3pm in summer. Reservations are recommended in high season. Shark Valley is 25 miles west of Florida's Turnpike.

Big Cypress Gallery

Clyde Butcher's photography gallery (☎ *239-695-2428,* **w** *www.clydebutcher.com, Tamiami Trail, open 10am-5pm Wed-Mon*) is a sanctified highlight of any trip to the Everglades. By all means stop here. In the great tradition of Ansel Adams, Clyde's large-format black-and-white images elevate the swamps to a higher level. He has found a quiet spirituality in the brackish waters, and you just might too, with the help of his eyes.

Patient wildlife watchers may get a chance to spot the Florida panther in Big Cypress.

Big Cypress National Preserve

This 1139-sq-mile, federally protected preserve is the result of a compromise between environmentalists, cattle ranchers and oil-and-gas explorers. While allowing preexisting development to proceed to a certain extent, the preserve generally protects the land. The area is integral to the Everglades' ecosystem: Rains that flood the prairies and wetlands here slowly filter down through the Glades.

About 45% of the cypress swamp (which is not a swamp at all, but a group of mangrove islands, hardwood hammocks, islands of slash pine, prairie and marshes) is protected preserve. Great bald cypress trees are nearly gone from the area, as lumber and other industries took their toll before the preserve was established. These days, dwarf pond cypress trees fill the area.

Why is it called Big Cypress then? Because of the size of the preserve, not the cypress trees within it. Resident fauna include alligators, snakes, wading birds (white ibis, wood storks, tri-color herons and egrets), Florida panthers (rarely seen), wild turkeys and red cockaded woodpeckers.

Information The Big Cypress Visitor Center (☎ 239-695-4111), about 20 miles west

---

Air Boats & Swamp Buggies

Air boats are flat-bottomed skiffs that use powerful fans to propel themselves in the water. While capable of traveling in shallow water, they are very loud, and their environmental impact has not been determined. One thing is clear: Air boats in the hands of responsible operators have little impact, but irresponsible operators cause lots of direct and collateral damage to the ecosystem.

Swamp buggies are enormous balloon-tired vehicles that can go through swamps, causing ruts and damaging wildlife.

Air-boat and swamp-buggy rides are offered all along US Hwy 41 (Tamiami Trail). Please assess the motives behind the operator's existence before just getting on a 'nature' tour. You may be helping to disturb the Everglades' delicate balance.

of Shark Valley, sells off-road vehicle permits (4WDs are permitted; $50 annual permit required). It's open from 8:30am to 4:30pm daily. The National Preserve Headquarters (☎ 239-695-2000) is just east of Ochopee. It's open from 8am to 4:30pm weekdays.

Hiking You'll find 31 miles of the Florida National Scenic Trail (FNST), maintained by the Florida Trail Association, within Big Cypress National Preserve. From the southern terminus, which can be accessed by car via Loop Rd, the trail runs 8.3 miles north to the Tamiami Trail, passing the Big Cypress Visitor Center. There are two primitive campsites with water wells along the trail. Off-road vehicles are permitted to cross, but not operate on, the FNST. For the less adventurous, there's the short Tree Snail Hammock Nature Trail, off Loop Rd.

Driving On-road vehicles can drive on Loop Rd, a potholed dirt road, and Turner River Rd, which shoots straight as an arrow north off the Tamiami Trail. There are excellent wildlife-viewing opportunities along the entire stretch of Turner River Rd, especially in the Turner River Canal, which runs along the east side of it. The road leads to the northern area of the preserve, where off-road vehicles are permitted.

Camping In addition to the two sites on the FNST, there are six primitive campgrounds on the preserve. You can pick up a map at the visitor's center. Be sure to bring your own water and food. Most campsites – *Bear Island*, *Midway*, *Loop Rd*, *Mitchell Landing* and *Pinecrest* – are free, and you needn't register. Mitchell Landing, Loop Rd and Pinecrest do not accommodate RVs. *Monument Lake (free off-season, $14 Nov-Apr)* has water and toilets.

For information about backcountry camping and permits, see National Parks in the Outdoor Activities chapter.

Ochopee

Driving through the tiny hamlet of Ochopee (population about 4)…no…wait…turn around, you missed it. That's right, folks,

break out the cameras: Ochopee's claim to fame is that it has the USA's smallest official post office! In a former toolshed, a friendly postal worker patiently poses for snapshots. For the cost of a stamp, you can send a postcard or letter from here.

Places to Eat

Pit BBQ (☎ 305-226-2272, 16400 SW 8th St, between Miami & Shark Valley) Dishes $4-9. Open 11am-11:30pm daily. It doesn't get more real than this: authentic barbecue served on picnic tables in a dumpy joint with country & western music on the juke box. You gotta love it (otherwise, don't stop).

Joannie's Blue Crab Cafe (☎ 239-695-2682, Tamiami Trail, east of Ochopee) Dishes $10-13. Open 9am-5pm daily. This quintessential shack, with open rafters, shellacked picnic tables, wooden floors and alligator kitsch, couldn't be more atmospheric – in a *Deliverance* sort of way. Although the food served on paper plates is just so-so, the down-home charm of the place makes up for it. While stone crabs are a decided specialty, you can also get swamp dinners (with gator nuggets, gator fritters, frogs legs and Indian fry bread) and peel-and-eat shrimp.

Collier-Seminole State Park

This state park and wilderness preserve (☎ 239-394-3397, admission $3.25 per carload, $1 per pedestrian or cyclist, open 8am-sunset), perhaps the only memorial that celebrates man's conquering of the Everglades, is named after Barron Gift Collier, one of the main developers of the Tamiami Trail. The 4070-acre preserve, where freshwater and saltwater meet, is filled with red, black and white mangrove and buttonwood trees. You'll also see manatees (especially in winter), white ibis, snowy egrets, alligators, over 40 tree species and three species of lizard.

Also within the park, the Blackwater River sports a 13-mile **canoe trail**. Inquire about ranger-led canoe trips on Sunday mornings, or you can rent canoes *($3/15 hourly/daily)* at the entrance station. You can also canoe, with reservations, down to **Grocery Place** *(primitive campsite adult/*

THE EVERGLADES

child $3/2), but the site is basically just a clearing, and you'll have to dig a pit to do your business. Keep in mind that January through March are the most desirable months (mosquitoes make it unbearable in summer), and reservations are advisable. There is also more **developed camping** (☎ *800-326-3521, without/with electricity $11/14)*, with full bathrooms, within the state park (not within the preserve section).

On the reserve, look for a 6½-mile **hiking trail** that winds through pine flatwood and cypress swamp, a 3½-mile **biking trail** and an interpretive center near the main campsites.

The park entrance is about 15 miles northwest of the intersection of Hwy 29 and the Tamiami Trail.

EVERGLADES CITY

Everglades City survives rather than thrives on the trade of fisherfolk who pull into the marina and live in RVs, and tourists passing through to visit the Everglades. It's a perfectly pleasant community, in a fisherfolk's paradise kind of way, and it's a sensible place to spend the night in order to get an early start on canoe trips in the 10,000 Islands. Hwy 29 runs south through town.

Canoe Camping on 10,000 Islands

The finest way to experience the serenity and beauty of the Everglades – which are somehow desolate yet lush, tropical yet foreboding – is by canoeing or kayaking through the excellent network of waterways that skirt the northwest portion of the park. The **10,000 Islands** consist of many (but not really 10,000) tiny islands and a mangrove swamp that hugs the southwestern-most border of Florida.

The **Wilderness Waterway**, a 99-mile path between Everglades City and Flamingo, is the longest canoe trail in the area, but there are shorter canoe trails near Flamingo.

Most islands are fringed by narrow beaches with sugar-white sand, but note that the water is brackish, not clear, and very shallow most of the time. It's not Tahiti, but it's fascinating. The best part is that you can camp on your own island for up to a week. Some campsites come with 'chickees' – wooden platforms built above the waterline on which you can pitch a free-standing (no spikes) tent.

Getting around the 10,000 Islands is pretty straightforward if you religiously adhere to NOAA tide and nautical charts. Going against the tides is the fastest way to make it a miserable trip. The Gulf Coast Visitor Center in Everglades City (see that section, later, for more information) sells **nautical charts** and gives out free **tidal charts**. You can also purchase charts prior to your visit – call ☎ 305-247-1216 and ask for chart Nos 11430, 11432 and 11433.

Canoe & Kayak Itineraries

Near Everglades City, you can take a downstream trip on the Turner River alone or with a group. Take a drift-with-the-current trip to Chokoloskee Island, or add a bit of a challenge at the end and paddle upstream in the boating canal to the Gulf Coast Visitor Center.

For an easy day of paddling, just cross the bay from the Gulf Coast Visitor Center (ranger station) and paddle out and around the mangroves to Sandfly Island or on the Chokoloskee Bay Loop.

For an easy one- or two-night trip, head to islands closest to the ranger station: Tiger, Picnic, Rabbit, New Turkey, Turkey and Hog Keys – all with beach campsites.

For a nice few days of canoeing, head south from the Gulf Coast Visitor Center, past Chokoloskee and up the Lopez River, north near Sunday Bay, and then southeast to Sweetwater Bay, where there's a chickee at which you can spend the night. The next morning head toward Watson Place and southwest to Pavilion Key for an overnight at the beach campsite. Then head north to Rabbit Key for a final night on the beach. In the morning, head back north to the ranger station.

At the corner of US Hwy 41 and Hwy 29, the Everglades Area Chamber of Commerce (☎ 239-695-3239), open 9am to 5pm daily, dispenses basic information. The Gulf Coast Visitor Center (☎ 239-695-3311), at the southern end of town, has loads of information on the 10,000 Islands and the Everglades. It's open 8:30am to 5pm daily.

You can wash clothes at the coin laundry next to the Right Choice Market (it's the only choice, actually).

Bike rentals are available at the Ivey House Hotel (see Places to Stay & Eat, later) for $3/15 per hour/day.

Canoeing & Kayaking

Rangers with the **National Park Service** (☎ 239-695-3311, *Gulf Coast Visitor Center, tours free, open mid-Nov–mid-Apr*) lead two different canoe trips through overhanging mangrove tunnels along the Turner River. Tours designed for more experienced paddlers depart at 9am on Saturday and last for seven hours; the Sunday morning trips, at 9:30am, last four hours and are geared toward paddlers with average abilities.

The NPS also rents canoes by the day and for overnights ($24), and provides shuttle service ($150) if you'll be paddling from

---

Canoe Camping on 10,000 Islands

There are hundreds of other combinations; check with a ranger at the Gulf Coast Visitor Center for more recommendations.

If you're going to make the eight- to 10-day Wilderness Waterway trek between Everglades City and Flamingo, you'll probably need help portaging (shuttling your car from one point to the other). Contact the very nice folks at the Everglades International Hostel (☎ 305-248-1122, 800-372-3874, W www.evergladeshostel.com), 20 SW 2nd Ave, Florida City. They're the only ones in the area who provide this service ($200 if you rent with them, $300 if you don't). However you cut it, count on sacrificing one day for logistics: One person ferries the car around while another pulls permits for the backcountry trip.

Wilderness Camping

Three types of backcountry campsites are available from the Flamingo and Gulf Coast Visitor Centers: beach sites, on coastal shell beaches and in the 10,000 Islands; ground sites, which are basically mounds of dirt built up above the mangroves along the interior bays and rivers; and chickees.

Chickees, which have toilets, are the most civilized; they're certainly unique. There's a serenity in sleeping on what feels like a raft levitating above the water in the middle of nature. Beach sites are the most comfortable, though biting insects are rife, even in winter. Ground sites tend to be the most bug-infested.

Warning: If you're just paddling around and you see an island that looks perfectly pleasant for camping but it's not a designated campsite, beware – you may end up submerged when the tides change.

From November to April, camping permits cost $10; in the off-season, sites are free, but you must still self-register at the Flamingo and Gulf Coast Visitor Centers.

All the park's resources are protected, including the plants, shells, artifacts and buildings. You can fish, but *only* with a state fishing license; check at any ranger station for information. Free permits, available at ranger stations, are required for overnight stays. In areas without toilets, you'll need to dig a hole at least 6 inches deep for waste. Campfires are prohibited except at certain beach sites: Use dead and down wood only, and build your fire below the high-tide line. Remove all your garbage from the park when you leave.

Everglades City to Flamingo and need to get back to pick up your car.

Everglades National Park Boat Tours (☎ 239-695-2591, 800-445-7724, *Gulf Coast Visitor Center, tours $16/8 adult/child 6-12 yrs*) offer the simplest tours. Large pleasure boats depart every 30 minutes (9am to 4:30pm) from mid-December to mid-April and every hour or so in the off-season. Tours last 1¾ hours.

North American Canoe Tours (*NACT*; ☎ 239-695-3299, W *www.evergladesadventures .com, Ivey House Hotel, 107 Camellia St, open Nov–mid-Apr*) rents camping equipment, first-rate canoes ($25/35/25 half/full/each additional day), recreational kayaks ($35/55/45 half/full/each additional day) and touring kayaks ($45/65/55 half/full/each additional day), which have rudders and upgraded paddles that make going against the current a whole lot easier. You get 20% off most of these services and rentals if you're staying at the Ivey House Hotel, which NACT owns.

NACT is the best outfit for regular guided tours. For $75 to $95 per person (depending on whether you want to go out in a canoe or kayak), you get a guided six-hour canoe trip, with lunch, on the Turner River; daily tours depart at 9am. NACT also offers interesting day tours within the 10,000 Islands for approximately the same price. NACT will also customize multinight excursions.

For those making the eight- to 10-day trip between the Gulf Coast and Flamingo Visitor Centers with an NACT rental boat, they will pick up boats in Flamingo for $100, but you'll still have to get yourself back to Everglades City. Call the Everglades International Hostel (☎ 305-248-1122, 800-372-3874) to make arrangements for that.

See the boxed text 'Canoe Camping on 10,000 Islands' for more information on opportunities to canoe and kayak in the Everglades.

Places to Stay & Eat

Glades Haven (☎ 239-695-2746, *Hwy 29*) Tent/RV sites $20/30. Across from the Gulf Coast Visitor Center, this 30-site commercial campground is geared more toward RVs than tents, but tenters are welcome.

Ivey House Hotel (☎ 239-695-3299, W *www.iveyhouse.com, 107 Camellia St*) Rooms $50-90 Nov–mid-Dec, $70-125 mid-Dec–Apr; closed May-Oct. Deli open 7am-2pm. The town's premier lodging feels a tad institutional because of its newness, but this fine choice should be your first choice. In its former life, the low-slung hotel served as a recreation hall for Tamiami Trail laborers, but now the family-run hostelry has good meals (breakfast is included, and there's not a deep fryer in sight), comfortable rooms and free use of bicycles (on a first-come, first-served basis). The newer inn rooms are more expensive, but they're much nicer. The older B&B rooms are smaller, with shared bath. Guests staying in these rooms do not have access to the pool at the inn. These folks also run NACT, which operates some of the best nature trips around; see the Canoeing & Kayaking section, earlier.

Rod & Gun Club Lodge (☎ 239-695-2101, *200 Riverside Dr*) Rooms $75 off-season, $105 mid-Oct–June. Built in the 1920s as a hunting lodge by Barron Collier (who needed a place to chill after watching workers dig his Tamiami Trail), this lodge is handsome and masculine, but the 17 guesthouse rooms aren't as much so. It sure harkens back to Olde Florida.

Captain's Table (☎ 239-695-4211, 800-741-6430, *Hwy 29*) Rooms $45-75 off-season, $70-95 late Dec–Apr. At the jig in Hwy 29 east of the downtown traffic circle, Captain's Table has a nice staff and 48 barely tidy rooms and suites (with kitchen facilities).

Cheryl's Deli/Glades Haven (☎ 239-695-2746, *Hwy 29*) Dishes $4-5. Open 6am-9pm daily. Across from the Gulf Coast Visitor Center, Cheryl's/Glades has decent cold-cut sandwiches with lots o' toppings.

Susie's Station (*no* ☎, *Hwy 29*) Dishes $6-9. The atmosphere at Susie's is pleasant enough, but she only serves fried stuff: chicken strips, fried shrimp, french fries and the like. It's on the west side of the traffic circle.

Stock up on groceries before you come, since the *Right Choice Market*, just east of the traffic circle, is about 25% more expensive than any Publix.

AH-TAH-THI-KI MUSEUM

The best Everglades tourism news in years is the advent of this Seminole museum (☎ 863-902-1113, W www.seminoletribe.com/museum, Big Cypress Seminole Indian Reservation, admission $6/4 adult/senior & child, open 9am-5pm Tues-Sun), 17 miles north of I-75. With educational exhibits on Seminole life, history and the tribe today, the museum was founded with Seminole gaming proceeds. Gambling receipts – an economic powerhouse – provide most of the Seminole tribe's multimillion-dollar operating budget.

Never before have the Seminoles opened so much up to the public. Sure, it's good for business, but they really are dedicated to giving visitors a closer understanding of the Seminole and Miccosukee people, and enabling them to experience Seminole life. It's not the wild wild Glades, and there are aspects, like alligator wrestling, that leave something to be desired, but it's a breakthrough for the tribe. Until recently, they had kept to themselves where tourism was concerned.

Seminole Safari (☎ 239-949-6101, 800-617-7516, W www.seminoletours.com) offers day ($45) and overnight ($110) packages. Overnights include sleeping in a screened-in chickee hut, listening to campfire storytelling, taking an air-boat or swamp-buggy ride and having Indian meals (catfish, fry bread, gator nuggets). It's touristy, certainly, but the package is a rather unique opportunity.

MARCO ISLAND

The only inhabited island in the 10,000 Islands, Marco Island has a gorgeous Gulf Coast beach and highly developed resorts that are popular with overseas visitors – especially English and German. If you have cash and like resort life, this is a great place to kick back on a dazzling white-sand beach and have a nice rest.

The island is at the very southwestern edge of Florida. San Marco Dr cuts straight west to Collier Blvd, which shoots up the Gulf Coast and becomes Hwy 951, crossing

East Marco Bay and reconnecting with the Tamiami Trail. The main resorts are at the southwestern end of the island.

The **Marco Island Chamber of Commerce** (☎ 239-394-7549, 800-788-6272, www.marcoislandchamber.org, 1102 N Collier Blvd), with good information and maps, is open 9am to 5pm Monday through Saturday. Wash up at **Marco Island Laundry** (☎ 239-642-6635, 277 N Collier Blvd).

The Marco Island Trolley (☎ 239-394-1600) tootles around the island on several loops from about 10am to 5pm Monday through Saturday. For $16 adults, $7 children, you can get on and off as many times as you like. But you can also use it as a narrated orientation tour (1½ hours) by staying on for one complete loop.

Official public **beaches** include Marco South, at the southernmost end of S Collier Blvd before it cuts east, and Tigertail Beach, the more developed of the two. At Tigertail, about three-quarters of the way up the western side of the island, there are public toilets, showers and a snack bar.

Places to Stay
Mar-Good RV Park (☎ 239-394-6383, 321 Pear Tree Ave, Goodland) Tent sites $20, RV sites $30, cottages $50. With 50 friendly campsites (mostly geared toward RVs, since the sites are open), this waterfront, but not beachfront, park has a convenience store and a little bar. Take San Marco Dr to Goodland Dr, then take a right turn just before the Goodland Bridge back to the Tamiami Trail, down to Goodland Dr W, and make a left on Pear Tree Ave.

Resorts & Condos For condos, contact the Chamber of Commerce, which publishes the realtor-filled *Marco Island & the Everglades*.

The following resorts are enormous places with health clubs; swimming pools; great beach access with cabanas; wave runner, bicycle and other sports equipment rentals; and, of course, kids' activities, nightclubs and restaurants. As with any resort, note that these prices are the standard rack rates for those who question nothing, except 'Where do I sign?'

You can always get better deals through a travel agent.

Radisson Suites Beach Resort (☎ 239-394-4100, 800-333-3333, Ⓦ *www.radisson .com, 600 S Collier Blvd*) Rooms from $125 summer, $195 winter. The southernmost of the big three resorts has the best prices and very good services. Though it's not as swank as the Hilton or Marriott, it's awfully respectable, with friendly and attentive staff, an enormous pool and a beach that's every bit as good as those of their neighbors. Always ask about their 'super-saver' rates.

Marco Island Hilton Beach Resort (☎ 239-394-5000, 800-443-4550, Ⓦ *www .hilton.com, 560 S Collier Ave*) Suites from $149 summer, $309 winter. If you've got the bucks, you can't go wrong with these 300 junior suites, complete with mini-fridges and sleeper sofas.

Marco Island Marriott Resort & Golf Club (☎ 239-394-2511, 800-438-4373, Ⓦ *www .marriott.com/mrkfl, 400 S Collier Blvd*) Rooms from $129 summer, $259 winter. This mega-resort, with 770 rooms and suites, boasts 16 tennis courts, four swimming pools

and lots of spa treatments. Be sure to ask about their summer getaway rates.

Places to Eat

Empire Bagel Factory (☎ 239-642-4141, 277 N Collier Ave) Open 6:30am Tues-Sun. Next to the laundry, Empire has quick snacks, with good bagels and sandwiches.

Taste of Chicago (☎ 239-394-1368, 297 S Collier Ave) Dishes $5-12. Open 7am-10pm daily. This family-run place with good service also has great breakfasts, chili, pasta dishes and beer-batter fish fry; their grouper is very good.

Olde Marco Island Inn (☎ 239-394-3131, 100 Palm St) Lunch $8, dinner $19-22. Open 8am-10pm daily. Built as the family home for Captain William D Collier (not Barron Gift Collier), the island's first hotel is now a restaurant. And most island visitors come here at least once. Main courses revolve around seafood, from sautéed snapper to baked seafood combos with scallops, lobster, shrimp and fish. They also have a huge selection of boozy coffees, from Irish to Swiss to Mexican.

Florida Keys

The string of islands south of Miami have fascinated visitors since the Spanish explorers arrived in the early 16th century. But while divers and fisherfolk will have a great time here, the Florida Keys aren't exactly a romantic, untouched and steamy paradise (unless you have some cash to spare). If, however, you gear your expectations realistically, and take the time to unearth its treasures, there is an alluring, quirky and, yes, even sultry side to the Keys. Just bring the bug repellent and some cash.

Still, nowhere else in the world can you wake up in an underwater hotel, snorkel along spectacular reefs and see adorable but endangered Key deer. And even though it's under duress, the coral reef off the Keys is one of the world's most beautiful and ecologically diverse.

Outside Key West, you'll drive many miles between places of interest, and mostly you'll see innumerable islands and unbroken blue sky and ocean. And don't forget Key lime pie and conch chowder; when they're good, they *are* delightful.

About 90 miles north of Havana, Cuba, Key West is the legendary land of Hemingway, sunset celebrations, Jimmy Buffet's *Margaritaville* and Key lime pie.

After Juan Ponce de León first sailed around the Keys in 1513 ('key' is the Anglicized version of the Spanish *cayo,* or cay), he was attacked by fierce Calusa Indians at the southwest corner of the state. Today, tourists might feel attacked by hawkers of T-shirts, sponges, seashells and wind chimes.

Early Keys settlers farmed limes, tamarind, breadfruit and pineapple, while over on Big Pine Key, locals caught and skinned sharks, salted the hides and prepared them for processing into shagreen leather. In Islamorada and Key West, the nonfarming population became 'wreckers,' salvaging goods from sinking or sunken ships. But they weren't pirates; they were federally licensed workers who scavenged wrecks and brought the cargo into Key West for auction.

However, tourism – especially after Henry Flagler extended his FEC Railway all the way through the Keys to Key West in the late 19th century – became the Keys' main moneymaker and remains such today.

Highlights

- Swim with bottle-nosed dolphins
- Scuba dive or snorkel around coral reefs and sunken Spanish galleons
- Find the best conch chowder and Key lime pie
- Watch the sunset, then spend the night barhopping in Key West
- Stand at the southernmost point of the continental USA in Key West
- See rare sea turtles in the Dry Tortugas archipelago
- Help save the coral reef by volunteering with Reef Relief

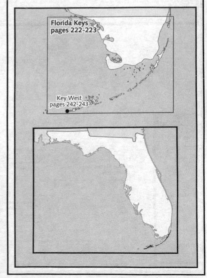

Florida Keys
pages 222-223

Key West
pages 242-243

FLORIDA KEYS

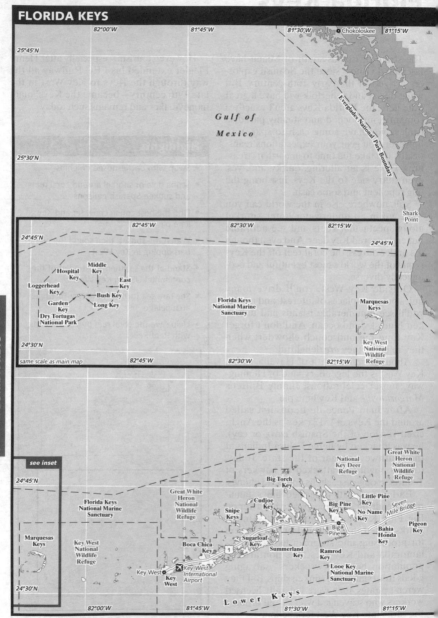

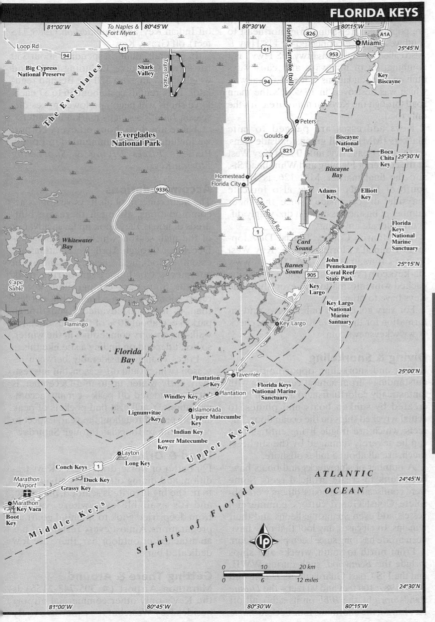

81°00'W
To Naples &
Fort Myers
80°45'W
80°30'W
80°15'W

826

Loop Rd
94

41

953

A1A

Miami
25°45'N

Big Cypress
National Preserve

Shark
Valley

Train Track

41

94

Key
Biscayne

The Everglades

Everglades
National Park

997

Goulds

Peters

821

Biscayne
National
Park

Boca
Chita
Key
25°30'N

Homestead
Florida City

9336

Card Sound Rd

Biscayne
Bay

Adams
Key

Elliott
Key

Florida
Keys
National
Marine
Sanctuary

Whitewater
Bay

Card
Sound

John
Pennekamp
Coral Reef
State Park

25°15'N

Cape
Sable

Barnes
Sound

905

Key
Largo

Key Largo
National
Marine
Sanctuary

Flamingo

Florida
Bay

Key Largo

25°00'N

Plantation
Key

Tavernier

Windley Key

Plantation

Florida Keys
National Marine
Sanctuary

Lignumvitae
Key

Islamorada

Upper Matecumbe
Key

Indian Key

Upper Keys

Lower Matecumbe
Key

Layton

Long Key

ATLANTIC
OCEAN

24°45'N

Conch Keys

Marathon
Airport

Duck Key

Grassy Key

Straits of Florida

Marathon

Key Vaca

Boot
Key

Middle Keys

0   10   20 km
0   6   12 miles

81°00'W

80°45'W

80°30'W

80°15'W

24°30'N

Orientation & Information

Hundreds of tiny islands, about 45 of which are populated, are strung from northeast to southwest and are connected by US Hwy 1. Also called the Overseas Hwy, US Hwy 1 is a combination of highways and causeways built on the foundations of the FEC Railway, which was destroyed in 1935. It's the main road through the Keys. In many areas it's the only road.

Keys addresses are pegged to mile markers (MM), small green roadside signs, on the Overseas Hwy: mile 0 is in Key West at the corner of Fleming and Whitehead Sts, and the final marker, MM 126, is 1 mile south of Florida City. We also indicate 'bayside' or 'oceanside,' since the sheer number of businesses make it dizzyingly difficult to locate anything.

The Monroe County Tourist Development Council's Florida Keys & Key West Visitor's Bureau (☎ 305-296-1552, Ⓦ www .fla-keys.com) runs this excellent Web site, packed with information on everything the Keys have to offer.

For very good daily online news and information for the whole Keys region, check Ⓦ www.keysnews.com

Diving & Snorkeling

Diving and snorkeling opportunities are outstanding – from natural coral reefs with fantastically colorful fish, to artificial reefs created by sunken boats and planes, to actual wrecked ships on the ocean floor. The reefs, which are fragile living entities that can be severely damaged by the slightest touch, are all about 5 miles offshore.

A number of shipwrecks and boats have been sunk to create artificial reefs. Some were confiscated drug boats, others were obsolete Coast Guard cutters, commercial vessels and even Spanish galleons and their remains. In all cases, any loot that may have been inside has long since been picked clean.

From north to south, wrecks and ships include the *Bentwood*, sunk during WWII, and the US Coast Guard cutters *Duane* and *Bibb* (1987; 100 feet and 90 feet – the *Duane* stands upright, the *Bibb* on its side), all off Key Largo; the enormous four-decked *Eagle*

(1985; 110 feet), on Alligator Reef off Islamorada; portions of a Spanish galleon (1733), off Indian Key; and *Thunderbolt* (1986; 115 feet), off Grassy Key.

In general, count on spending about $50 for a two-tank dive, including tanks and weights; add an extra $20 for BC and regulator. Tank rentals cost about $6 to $7 each. Dive shops will negotiate lower prices off-season, but it's a seller's market in winter.

There are dive shops on every corner; we include ones recommended in Lonely Planet's *Pisces Diving & Snorkeling Florida Keys*.

Accommodations

The main concern of all Keys visitors is accommodations; although there are hundreds of hotels, they book up far in advance of the high season, which runs from mid-December through April. Reservations are essential. Booking agencies at chambers of commerce can help, even during peak periods. State-park campgrounds accept reservations a year in advance, but not less than 48 hours in advance. Even though parks keep about 10% of the sites open for walk-ins, it's very competitive in the winter, so don't depend on finding a site like this.

Prices change considerably between in-season (winter) and off-season, but interestingly, early winter, up to mid-December, is often considered off-peak at many accommodations. You'll also find pockets of peak and off-peak throughout the year. Expect to pay a bit more Thursday through Saturday.

Food & Drink

For better or worse, drinking is a Keys tradition, and dining often takes a back seat to it. The big favorite is seafood, of course, and it's available everywhere, varying from deep-fried gook to splendid gourmet preparations. Almost every restaurant has an attached or outdoor bar; there are few dedicated bars.

Getting There & Around

Marathon Airport (☎ 305-743-2155) is the Key's only other commercial airport besides Key West, but it's expensive to fly

US Coast Guard cutter *Duane*, Upper Keys

WILLIAM HARRIGAN

Upper Keys sunset

WILLIAM HARRIGAN

Sailboats seeking sailors, Islamorada

LEE FOSTER

Snorkeling at Elbow Reef

WILLIAM HARRIGAN

The graces of Christ of the Deep, Key Largo

WILLIAM HARRIGAN

Kayaking in the Keys

LEE FOSTER

Fort Lauderdale's riverwalk and craft market

Beachside, Fort Lauderdale

Boat moored on the Intracoastal Waterway

here, so most people make the two-hour drive from Miami.

In essence, Greyhound (☎ 305-296-9072, W www.greyhound.com) serves all Keys destinations along US Hwy 1. Buses depart downtown Miami for the Keys and Key West at 6:30am, 12:30pm, 4pm and 7pm. There are official stops with signs, but just tell the driver where you want to get off and they'll stop. Once you're on the Keys, just stand anywhere on the Overseas Hwy (US Hwy 1) and when you see the bus in the distance, signal firmly and visibly, using all methods at your disposal – and the bus will stop to pick you up…if the driver sees you. To be really safe, ask Greyhound about the official stops.

By car, there are two options: From Miami take I-95 south to US Hwy 1 and follow that until you can't go any farther – that'd be Key West. A shorter route is Florida's Turnpike Extension (toll) south to US Hwy 1 south from Florida City. Most of the route is just two lanes, often with a center turning lane, so traffic can crawl and dart in and out. Be patient.

Unless you're staying in one place the entire time, you'll need wheels to get around. There's no public transportation, and distances are too far to make bicycling a real option for anyone except experienced riders. You can rent bicycles in most larger Keys. Most major car rental companies have offices in Marathon and Key Largo.

Swimming with Dolphins

Experts say 'structured' programs – in which staff accompany swimmers in controlled areas for swims with dolphins that are accustomed to human contact – are safer and more humane than 'unstructured' ones. There are three swim-with-dolphins programs on the Keys.

Theater of the Sea

This Islamorada attraction (☎ 305-664-2431; W www.theaterofthesea.com; MM 84.5 bayside; admission $18/11 adult/child 3-12 yrs; open 9:30am-4pm) might look cheesy, but it's been here since 1946. Structured dolphin swims and sea-lion programs include 30 minutes of instruction and 30 minutes of supervised swim. The swims ($135/95 for the dolphin/sea lion program) are by reservation only at 9:30am, noon and 2pm. They also run some other nice programs, including continuous dolphin and sea-lion shows; a marine exhibit with sharks, stingrays and tropical fish; a living shell exhibit; and a five-minute boat ride in the dolphin lagoon.

Dolphin Research Center

Near Marathon on Grassy Key, this open-lagoon, nonprofit educational center (☎ 305-289-1121; W www.dolphins.org; MM 59 bayside; admission $15/12.50/10 adult/senior/child 4-12 yrs; open 9am-4pm) is dedicated to spreading understanding about dolphins. You can join a Dolphin Encounter program, in which you'll learn about and then swim with their dolphins for $135. Dolphin Splash programs, during which you'll stand on a submerged platform while a dolphin comes up to meet you, include 10 minutes in the water and 20 minutes spent preparing for it. General admission gets you into the center, where narrated demos are given every 30 minutes.

Dolphins Plus

This Key Largo center (☎ 305-451-1993, 866-860-7946; W www.dolphinsplus.com; off MM 99.5 bayside; admission $10/7 adult/child 7-17 yrs) specializes in recreational and educational unstructured swims. They expect you to already know a good deal before embarking upon the swim, even though a classroom session is included. Daily 30 minute natural swims ($100) are held at 9am and 1:45pm. Structured swims ($150), with a classroom session and hands-on interaction, are offered at 8:30am, 10:45am, 1pm and 3:15pm. It's tricky to find; call for specific directions.

Upper Keys

The Upper Keys stretch from Key Largo south to Long Key. Most visitors head down US Hwy 1 from Florida City, but you could also take the less trafficked FL 997 to FL 905 (toll $1), which passes the very colorful Alabama Jack's (see Places to Eat & Drink in the Key Largo section).

KEY LARGO

Key Largo is the name of the island (at 33 miles, the longest in the Keys) and the town, which stretches from about MM 106 to MM 97.

After Bogart and Bacall starred in the 1948 film *Key Largo*, shot almost entirely on sound stages in Hollywood, California, the Key was suddenly known far and wide. The savvy town, formerly known as Rock Harbor, swiftly changed its name to capitalize on the increased fame. Despite the in-town presence of *The African Queen*, from the Bogart movie of *that* name, Bogie himself never came here to shoot anything; the boat was just brought in as a tourist attraction.

Key Largo is blessed with the largest concentration of dive sites in the Keys, and its biggest allure is justifiably the underwater John Pennekamp Coral Reef State Park, the most accessible place to see the Florida reef. Divers will also love Jules' Undersea Lodge, an underwater hotel (see Places to Stay, later in this section). But then again, don't forget about Dolphins Plus (see the boxed text 'Swimming with Dolphins').

Information

Greyhound stops at the Key Largo Shopper grocery store, MM 99.6 oceanside.

The helpful Key Largo Chamber of Commerce (☎ 305-451-1414, 800-822-1088, ⓦ www.keylargo.org), MM 106 bayside, has area-wide information. It's open 9am to 6pm.

The Key Largo post office is located at MM 100 bayside. In Tavernier there's a post office at MM 91.5 bayside.

The Book Nook (☎ 305-451-1468), MM 99.6 oceanside, in Waldorf Plaza, sells nature, travel and Florida books. Cover to Cover Books (☎ 305-852-1415), MM 91.5 bayside, in Tavernier, is another general bookstore with Florida and travel sections. Key Chain Books in Tavernier (☎ 305-852-1415) is also worthy.

The public library (☎ 305-451-2396), MM 101 bayside, is in Tradewinds Plaza, where there's also a Publix grocery store.

Head to Mariner Hospital (☎ 305-852-4418), MM 91.5 bayside, in Tavernier, for health problems.

There are dozens of dive shops in Key Largo, most of which are located within Pennekamp Park (see below). Two others come recommended: **Silent World Dive Center** *(☎ 305-451-3252, 800-966-3483, MM 103.2 bayside)* and **Amoray Dive Resort** *(☎ 305-451-3595, 800-426-6729, MM 104.2 bayside)*.

John Pennekamp Coral Reef State Park

The first underwater park in the USA, Pennekamp *(☎ 305-451-1202, ⓦ www.penne kamppark.com, MM 102.5 oceanside; admission $4 per vehicle plus 50¢ per person or $2.50 for one person, $1.50 per pedestrian or cyclist; open 8am-sunset)* covers 75 sq miles of ocean containing living coral reef. It also has 170 acres of land with walking trails, including the Wild Tamarind Nature Trail, home to air plants, gumbo-limbo, wild bamboo, Jamaica dogwood, crabwood and, of course, wild tamarind.

Most importantly, the park's ranger-led programs and concession offer very convenient ways to experience the Florida reef. You can rent snorkeling or diving gear; take a glass-bottom–boat, snorkeling or diving trip; or rent canoes and kayaks and explore a 3-mile network of canoe trails. And if you don't have the inclination to jump into the water, the **visitor's center** is billed as 'the reef you can walk out to.' You can't miss the 30,000-gallon aquarium showcasing living coral and tropical fish and plant life. Don't overlook the theater showing continuous nature videos. The park offers great ranger-led programs, including nature walks through mangrove and hardwood hammocks, a campfire program, and a lecture series discussing a range of environmental subjects, from crocodiles and raising bananas to native versus non-native vegetation.

Diving & Snorkeling Administratively speaking, the reef isn't within the state park at all; it's out past the 3-mile limit in the federally managed **Key Largo National Marine Sanctuary** (☎ 305-852-7717), which extends for about 20 miles southwest along a line 3 miles off the Keys' Atlantic shore to Broad Creek (see Looe Key National Marine Sanctuary, later).

Rangers and folks at the **scuba concession** (☎ 305-451-6322) are very helpful and will assist you in planning specific trips.

The main snorkeling and diving areas within the sanctuary are Carysfort Reef, where you'll also find the 100-foot Carysfort Lighthouse (1852); Carysfort South, the biggest shallow reef in the area, whose calm waters are perfect for snorkeling; the popular Elbow Reef, with three major wrecks; and the sunken USCG cutters *Duane* and *Bibb;* see Diving & Snorkeling, earlier. But the park's most famous snorkel and dive site is at Key Largo Dry Rocks: the Christ of the Deep Statue. It's a 9-foot-high, 4000lb, algae-covered bronze statue of Christ built in Italy by Guido Galletti, installed as an underwater shrine to sailors and those lost at sea.

You can rent a full scuba outfit – mask, two tanks, regulator, BC and weight belt – for $38 a day. Four-hour, two-dive trips leave at 9:30am and 1:30pm and cost $41. They also offer certification in resort ($160), advanced ($325) and open-water ($450) diving.

The **snorkel concession** (☎ 305-451-1621) rents equipment for $7 a day. They also operate 2½-hour snorkeling tours at 9am, noon and 3pm; adults/children cost $26/21, and it costs $3 extra for equipment. Four-hour sailboat snorkeling trips leave at 9am and 1:30pm for $32/27, plus $3 for equipment rental.

Canoeing & Kayaking Well-marked, easy **canoe trails** through mangroves begin at the marina. Canoes and kayaks (singles $10 hourly, doubles $15) are available from the park concession (☎ 305-451-1621).

Boat Tours This 2½-hour *glass-bottom boat tour* (☎ 305-451-1621; $18/10 adult/child under 12 yrs; departures at 9:15am, 12:15pm & 3pm) goes out to Molasses Reef (named for a wrecked Jamaican ship carrying sugarcane molasses), which extends from Fort Lauderdale through the Dry Tortugas. If this is your only chance to see the reef, you'll be amazed by brilliant colors, the abundance of soft and hard coral and the sheer variety of tropical fish, from stingrays and turtles to barracuda and angelfish.

Key Largo Princess (☎ 305-451-4655, MM 100 oceanside) Departures at 10am, 1pm and 4pm. Cost $18/8.50 adult/child. These two-hour cruises depart from the Holiday Inn docks.

Key Largo Undersea Park

This place is a trip. Within a sheltered natural mangrove lagoon, the park (☎ 305-451-2353, W www.jul.com, MM 103.2 oceanside; office open 8am-4pm) is home to Jules' Undersea Lodge, an underwater hotel (see Places to Stay, later), which can be reached only by diving. The 50-by-20-foot, steel-and-acrylic structure, permanently anchored 30 feet beneath the surface of the lagoon, originally served as an underwater research lab off the coast of Puerto Rico.

Keys to Happiness

Think marriage is overrated? Apparently, so do many folks in the Florida Keys, where the 2000 US census ranked the Keys first among Florida's 67 counties in percentage of households headed by unmarried partners – nearly 10% of the county's 35,086 households. Almost one-third of them live in Key West, which has a large gay and lesbian population. Nationwide, the Keys rank 23rd among 3,141 counties.

The numbers don't surprise Keys residents, who attribute the numbers to a laid-back population, a large gay community and a high cost of living that forces adults to share living space.

FLORIDA KEYS

The lab was home to aquanauts exploring the continental shelf.

You can stay at the hotel or visit it during the day (by reservation only). Divers can use their own tanks or rent equipment here (a one-tank dive is $34 to $45). If you want to enter the hotel, sign up for a three-hour mini-adventure ($60), which also gives access to its facilities and three breathing hookahs – 120-foot-long air hoses for tankless diving. The lodge also offers many specialty diving courses, like diver propulsion vehicles, underwater archaeology and photography.

Snorkelers can use the area for $15, including gear. It's not in a coral reef, but you will see some reef fish. You may get lucky and see some of their local snorkeling Elvises.

African Queen

This antique steam-engine vessel (☎ 305-451-4655, 800-843-5397, MM 100 oceanside; open when it's in port, call ahead), the one used in the movie with Hepburn and Bogart, carries up to 15 people for a nostalgic cruise up the Port Largo Canal.

Florida Keys Wild Bird Rehabilitation Center

In nearby Tavernier, this rehab center for our fine feathered friends (☎ 305-852-4486, MM 93.6 bayside; admission $5 suggested; open 8am-5pm) has a boardwalk, self-guided nature trails and a bird rescue program. Call them if you spot an injured bird. Expect to spend about 30 minutes on the well-signed habitats for herons, pelicans, hawks and ospreys. Try to time your visit with the excellent wild-bird feedings at 3:30pm.

Organized Tours

Florida Bay Outfitters (☎ 305-451-3018, W www.kayakfloridakeys.com, MM 104 bayside) Open 9am-6pm. These folks rent canoes ($35 a half-day, $45 for 24 hours), single kayaks ($35/45) and double kayaks ($50/60). They also rent so-so snorkeling and camping gear. From November to April (only in winter, simply because in summer there are too many bugs), they offer very good half-day and overnight backcountry tours.

Captain Sterling's (☎ 305-853-5161, W www.captainsterling.com, MM 102 bayside) If you don't have time to get up to the Everglades, these folks lead 1½ hour Florida Bay ecology tours ($39/29 adult/child, maximum six people), where you'll see a beautiful mangrove tunnel, petrified coral reef, dolphins and manatees. There are also adventurous crocodile-spotting tours at night ($249 for up to six people). There are only about 500 crocs in the park, and you'll spot between one and three of them.

Places to Stay

Camping The *John Pennekamp Coral Reef State Park* (☎ 305-451-1202, 800-326-3521 reservations, W www.reserveamerica.com, MM 102.5 bayside) Sites without/with electricity $19/21. These 47 nonwaterfront sites, most of which have water, are always in demand. If you come by boat, overnight moorings on buoys cost $17.50, which includes use of the dump station and showers (call ☎ 305-451-6322).

Calusa Camp Resort (☎ 305-451-0232, MM 101.5 bayside) Sites without/with hookups $25/45-65. These 350 sites aren't on the beach (some are canalside and bayside, though), and you can't make open fires. But they do have a pool, and you can bring your own grill. The office closes at 5pm, so get there early to check in.

America Outdoors Campground (☎ 305-852-8054, MM 97.5 bayside) Sites without/with hookups $45-60/60-85. Camping here is big business. These 155 sites, in a tropical hardwood hammock, don't have grills, but you can bring your own.

Hotels & Resorts The *Sunset Cove Resort* (☎ 305-451-0705, fax 305-451-5609, MM 99.5 bayside) Rooms & cottages $85-100, waterfront suites $130-140. You'll know you've arrived when you spot the kitschy oversized dino guarding this family-friendly place. This good value offers 20 tidy rooms (some with full kitchen), lots of barbecue grills, a beach area and the free use of canoes and paddleboats. Inquire about their more unusual accommodations, like the Airstream trailer and motor home.

Bay Harbor Lodge (☎ 305-852-5695, 800-385-0986, MM 97.7 bayside) Rooms $50-155 off-season, $75-165 mid-Dec–mid-Apr. This good complex has 16 clean cottages, efficiencies and rooms (many with kitchens, some waterside). They also offer a small pool, free use of various watercrafts and free lodging to children under age 18 (when they share their parents' room).

Largo Lodge (☎ 305-451-0424, 800-468-4378, MM 102 bayside) Apartments $95 off-season, $115 Dec-Apr. These six hidden cottages, tucked into a lush setting, feature efficiency kitchens, a living-dining room combination and a bedroom with two queen-size beds. A private swimming cove has enough tables and chairs for relaxing.

Westin Beach Resort (☎ 305-852-5553, 800-826-1006, fax 305-852-5198, W www .westin.com, MM 97 bayside) Rooms $109-309 off-season, $169-379 late Dec–Apr. This first-rate resort has 200 airy rooms with balconies, two main restaurants, nature trails, two pools, a bar with happy-hour specials, a myriad of water sports, a white-sand beach and a kids' program. The least expensive rooms face the parking lot, but at least they're mini-suites.

Marriott Beach Resort (☎ 305-453-0000, 800-932-9332, fax 305-453-0093, W www .marriottkeylargo.com, MM 103.8 bayside) Rooms $189-249 off-season, $249-319 Jan-May. This more developed, 153-room resort has upscale services including massage, spa therapies, an on-site dive shop, children's program, many restaurants, a fitness center, tennis, boat rentals and a pool. There's no beach though.

Kona Kai Resort & Gallery (☎ 305-852-7200, 800-365-7829, fax 305-852-4629, W www.konakairesort.com, MM 97.8 bayside) Rooms $109-168 off-season, $212-268 mid-Dec–mid-Apr, suites $146-319 off-season, $257-421 mid-Dec–mid-Apr. This intimate and magical hideaway features 11 airy rooms and suites (with full kitchens), all warmly contemporary and newly renovated. There's plenty to do – from nothing on your private patio to tennis, kayaking and paddleboating. A white-sand beach, dotted with palms and hammocks, is more tempting than

the curvaceous pool. The gallery, where you check in, is first rate, too.

Jules' Undersea Lodge (☎ 305-451-2353, fax 305-451-4789, W www.jul.com, MM 103.2 oceanside, 51 Shoreland Dr) Permanently anchored 30 feet beneath the water's surface, Jules' Undersea Lodge can accommodate six guests. The first question on everyone's mind is: Is it safe? Well, it was designed for scientists who lived onboard it for long periods of time. Even if all the backup generators and systems failed, there would still be about 12 hours of breathing time inside the hotel. Staff members are on duty 24 hours a day. In addition to two fairly luxurious private guest rooms, there are two common rooms, including a fully stocked kitchen/dining room and a wet room with hot showers and gear storage. Telephones and an intercom connect guests with the surface.

Noncertified divers can also stay here, but you'll have to get a quick limited certificate ($75). There are several accommodation packages, all of which require a reservation. The cheapest costs $250 per person; check-in at 5pm, out at 9am. The 'luxury aquanaut' package costs $350 per person and includes dinner and breakfast; check-in at 1pm, out at 11am. The 'ultimate romantic getaway' package costs $1050 for two people – for that, you get the place all to yourselves, with flowers and caviar and other little extras. Guests must be at least 10 years old; smoking and alcohol are not permitted.

Places to Eat & Drink

Ganim's (☎ 305-451-3337, MM102 bayside) Dishes $4-10. Open 6am-9pm Mon-Sat, 6am-2pm Sun. Nothing beats this place for reliable, quick, no-frills American diner food.

Mrs Mac's Kitchen (☎ 305-451-3722, MM 99.4 bayside) Breakfast & lunch $4-5, dinner $6-12. Open 7:30am-9:30pm Mon-Sat. Serving home-style cooking by and for locals, this packed diner (plastered with license plates and beer cans) leans toward meat and potatoes, stuffed pita pockets, steak sandwiches, Cajun shrimp baskets and burgers. Each night's menu is also supplemented by themed specials like Mexican or Italian.

Señor Frijoles *(☎ 305-451-1592, MM 104 bayside)* Dishes $8-12. Open 11am-10:15pm. Tequila is the main event at this waterfront eatery, but you can't drink on an empty stomach. Look for run-of-the-mill, south-of-the-border fare like all-you-can eat tacos (on Wednesday nights), burritos and camarones rancheros.

Crack'd Conch *(☎ 305-451-0732, MM 105 bayside)* Lunch $9-15, dinner mains $11-25. Open noon-10pm. This fun seafood restaurant, with over 100 types of beer, has lunchtime sandwiches like crab cakes with bacon and cheddar or steamed shrimp in a basket. The dinnertime mixed seafood platter is an appetite buster and a wallet killer, but well worth it.

Alabama Jack's *(no ☎, 58000 Card Sound Rd)* Dishes $10-16. This funky joint, on the banks of a mangrove swamp on the back road between Florida City and Key Largo, is a trip. More bar than eatery, it attracts everyone from Harley Davidson and pickup drivers to boaters and rich folks in stretch limos. Seafood and conch fritters take center stage under the open-air awnings.

The Fish House *(☎ 305-451-4665, MM 102.4 oceanside)* Lunch dishes $8-13, dinner mains $15-22. Open 11:30am-10pm. An easy favorite and a good value, this friendly and fun place has a nice tiled bar, fish nets hanging from the ceiling and hundreds of little holiday lights enlivening the scene. All the restaurants down here boast that they sell fresh fish, but this place *really* delivers. The smoked fish is a worthy specialty! Then again, oysters and clams from the raw bar are primo, too. Then again, so is the ceviche. Hmmmm.

Calypso's *(☎ 305-451-0600, Ocean Bay Dr, off MM 99.5 oceanside)* Lunch dishes $6-10, dinner mains $16-21. Open 11:30am-9:45pm Wed, Thur, Sun & Mon, 11:30am-10:45pm Fri & Sat. This waterside eatery serves creative dishes at decent prices in a casual atmosphere. What more could you want, really?

Sundowners *(☎ 305-451-4502, MM 104 bayside)* Lunch $10, dinner $20. Open 11am-10:15pm. Certainly pleasant enough, the restaurant's name suggests its real raison d'etre: To paraphrase an election mantra,

'it's the sunsets, stupid.' The wide ranging menu will satisfy everyone in your party, with conventional pasta, chicken, seafood and steak dishes. Yellowtail is a specialty.

ISLAMORADA

Islamorada (eye-luh-murr-**ah**-da) is located on Upper Matecumbe Key, but the whole area spans about 20 miles from Plantation Key south to Long Key. Home to some significant state historic sites and the fun Theater of the Sea (see the boxed text 'Swimming with Dolphins'), Islamorada is worth a stop simply for its good restaurants; Manny & Isa's Kitchen (see Places to Eat, later) is always on the shortlist of 'Best Key Lime Pie.' It's also the self-proclaimed sportfishing capital of the world. The promoters just might be right about that.

Greyhound stops at the Burger King at MM 82.5 oceanside.

Look for the Islamorada Chamber of Commerce (☎ 305-664-4503, 800-322-5397, W www.fla-keys.com), MM 82.5 bayside, in an old caboose. It's open 9am to 5pm Monday to Friday, 10am to 3pm Saturday and Sunday.

The post office is at MM 82.9 oceanside.

Area dive shops include **Holiday Isle Dive Shop** *(☎ 305-664-3483, 800-327-7070, MM 84.5 oceanside)* and **Lady Cyana Divers** *(☎ 305-664-8717, 800-221-8717, MM 85.9 bayside)*.

Lignumvitae Key State Botanical Site

Only accessible by boat, this site (lignum-vite-ee; ☎ 305-664-2540) encompasses a 280-acre island of virgin tropical forest. Bring mosquito repellent! The simple attractions are the Matheson House (1919), with its windmill and cistern. The forest features strangler fig, mastic, gumbo-limbo and poisonwood trees, as well as native lignumvitae trees, known for their extremely hard wood.

On the island, 1¼-hour guided walking tours are given at 10am and 2pm Thursday to Monday, but you can only visit by boat. From Robbie's Marina (later in this section), boats depart for the 15-minute trip ($15/10 adult/child under 12 yrs) about 30

FLORIDA KEYS

minutes prior to each tour; reservations are highly recommended.

Indian Key State Historic Site
Also accessible only by boat, this 23-acre historic island (☎ *305-664-2540*) has an interesting history. In 1831, renegade wrecker Jacob Housman bought the island and opened his own wrecker station after falling out with Key West wreckers. Housman developed it into a thriving little city, complete with a warehouse, docks, streets, a hotel and about 40 to 50 permanent residents. By 1836 Indian Key was the seat of Dade County. But Housman eventually lost his wrecker's license, and in 1840 he lost the entire island after an attack during the Second Seminole War.

There's not much here today – just foundation remains, some cisterns, Housman's grave and lots of plant life. But there are trails and an observation tower. Free 1½-hour ranger-led tours (Thursday to Monday at 9am and 1pm) detail the fascinating history – not just of the wrecking operation, but also of the island's geological and natural history. There's a catch, though: You need to have a boat or take a 10-minute shuttle ($15/10 adult/child under 12 yrs) from Robbie's Marina (see below). Shuttles depart about 30 minutes before the tours begin. Show up early, since the boat can hold only six people.

Robbie's Marina
Robbie's (☎ *305-664-9814*, W *www.robbies .com, MM 77.5 bayside; open 8am to 6pm*) rents all sorts of boats. Rates for a 15-foot boat start at $70 for half a day and, depending on the boat size and number of people, rise briskly from there. You can also feed tarpons right from the dock here ($1 to $2 per bucket of fish food); the best time is midmorning.

Organized Tours
The ever-opportunistic **Robbie's** also operates tours to Lignumvitae Key State Botanical Site (see earlier in this section), and two-hour scenic sunset cruises on Florida Bay ($25/15 adult/child under 12 yrs).

Schooner Freya (☎ *305-664-8582, MM 82 bayside*) offers great two-hour sunset cruises aboard a traditional vessel ($25/10 adult/child under 12 yrs) from February through April.

Fishing
A big sportfishing outfitter *World Wide Sportsman* (☎ *305-664-4615, MM 81.5 bayside*) also has fly tying and casting demos; a complete selection of rods, reels and bait; and a full-service marina.

Robbie's (☎ *305-664-8070, 877-664-8498, MM 84.5 oceanside*) operates 'party' fishing boats (as opposed to more expensive charters) that head out for a half day ($25; 9:30am and 1:45pm), all day ($40) and at night ($30; 7:30pm). These large boats usually hold about 40 to 50 people, whereas charters are limited to six people and generally cost $300 for a half day of backcountry fishing, $450 for deep-sea fishing. You need reservations for charters but not party boats; they're docked at the southern end of Holiday Isle Docks.

Places to Stay
Camping *Long Key State Recreation Area* (☎ *305-664-4815, 800-326-3521 reservations,* W *www.reserveamerica.com, MM 67.5 oceanside*) Sites without/with electricity $24/26. Make reservations right this minute: It's tough to get one of these 60 sites, but once you do, you'll never want to leave. Most of the waterfront sites offer decent wooded privacy between one another.

Fiesta Key Resort KOA (☎ *305-664-4922,* W *www.koa.com, MM 70 bayside*) Sites without/with hookups $40-50/58-78 off-season, $43-53/68-88 mid-Nov–mid-Apr; motel rooms & efficiencies $105-125 off-season, $143-163 mid-Nov–mid-Apr. For resort-style camping complete with organized social activities, nothing beats this highly developed campground, which has 350 sites, 20 motel rooms and seven efficiencies with kitchens. They also have an Olympic-sized pool, beach and full-service marina.

Motels & Hotels *Key Lantern* (☎ *305-664-4572,* W *www.keylantern.com, MM 82 bayside*) Rooms $50-75. These 24 simple and really cheap rooms aren't oceanfront, and the place doesn't have a pool, but the staff is friendly, and rooms have a TV and fridge.

Ragged Edge Resort (☎ *305-852-5389,* W *www.ragged-edge.com, 243 Treasure Harbor Rd*) Rooms $48-83 off-season, $69-119 mid-Dec–mid-Apr. This low-key and popular efficiency and apartment complex, far from the maddening traffic jams, has 10 quiet units and friendly hosts. The larger studios, with screened-in porches, are the most desirable. There's no beach, but you can swim off the dock and at the pool.

Drop Anchor Motel (☎ *305-664-4863, MM 85 oceanside*) Rooms $50-100 off-season, $85-105 mid-Dec–mid-Apr. The bi-level motel has a little pool, barbecue grills, friendly hosts and lots of hard-packed white sand and palms, but no beach. The 16 rooms, some of which have screened porches and kitchenettes, have refrigerators and coffee-makers but no phones. Inquire about weekly rates.

White Gate Court (☎ *305-664-4136, 800-645-4283, fax 305-664-9746,* W *www.white gatecourt.com, MM 76 bayside*) Units $110-195 off-season, $120-210 mid-Dec–Apr. With only seven studios and villas, these family-friendly places go fast – with good reason. Each well-equipped unit has a full kitchen, laundry, free local calls, barbecue grill and nice garden area with torch lights. Guests have free use of paddleboats, snorkeling gear and bicycles. You can swim off the dock.

Casa Morada (☎ *305-664-0044, 888-881-3030, fax 305-664-0674,* W *www.casamorada .com, 136 Madeira Rd, off MM 82.2*) Suites $155-190 off-season, $200-230 mid-Dec–mid-May. This hidden enclave of 16 contemporary suites – decorated in an upscale, urbane, beachy sort of way, with iron beds and lots of periwinkle accents – is a romantic fave. A pool with lots of beach chairs and palm trees occupies some prime real estate on a point. Weekend Continental breakfasts are included.

Cheeca Lodge & Spa (☎ *305-664-4651, 800-327-2888,* W *www.cheeca.com, MM 82 oceanside*) Rooms $149-450 off-season, $199-650 late Dec–mid-Apr. If you like angling, par-3 golf, tennis, spa amenities and kids' programs, this conference-style Rock-

resort will fully satisfy you. The 203 upscale rooms are located in the main hotel or outlying villas; some are oceanfront, and most have balconies. Their dive shop arranges all sorts of trips, or you can just wander the nature trails, rent a bike or kayak, laze by the seductive pool, kick around some white sand or retreat to the spa.

Holiday Isle Resort (☎ *305-664-2321, 800-327-7070,* W *www.holidayisle.com, MM 84 oceanside*) Rates are complex, but expect to pay from $110 off-season, $130 Feb–mid-Apr. This mini asphalt city of four hotels and a dozen eateries (including tiki bars, raw bars, barbecue joints and sandwich shops) also has playgrounds, volleyball, basketball and live music. Activities are based around partying, fishing, diving and parasailing. The rates above are for a simple room; if you want something nicer, search elsewhere for better values.

Places to Eat & Drink

Village Gourmet (☎ *305-664-4030, MM 82.7 oceanside*) Sandwiches $5-8. Open 5:30am-9pm Mon-Thur, 5:30am-10pm Fri & Sat, 6am-2pm Sun. With only about a dozen seats, this takeout place has tasty baked goods at breakfast, plus cold pastas, pizzas, sandwiches and perhaps a special, like chicken parmigiana. The espresso is watery, though.

Manny & Isa's Kitchen (☎ *305-664-5019, MM 81.6 oceanside*) Lunch $5-8, dinner mains $11-18. Open 11am-9pm Wed-Mon. This value-packed, no-frills Spanish/American joint has good daily specials, lobster enchiladas, *ropa vieja* (shredded beef) and chili con carne. Their Key lime pie rules.

Time Out Barbecue (☎ *305-664-8911, MM 81.5 oceanside*) Lunch $5-6, dinner $10-14. Open 11am-10pm. This low-brow eatery with linoleum floors dishes up killer barbecue. The smoky aroma wafts into your car the moment you pull up to the front door.

Papa Joe's (☎ *305-664-8109, MM 79.7 bayside*) Lunch dishes $8-13, dinner mains $13-23. Open 10am-10pm. Since the mid-1930s, this rustic, nautical landmark with sloping floors has offered value-conscious lunches ($6) and dinner specials ($11). But it's perhaps more popular for its rockin' outdoor tiki-style raw bar and sunset happy hours.

Mile Marker 88 (☎ 305-852-9315, MM 88 bayside) Mains $15-24. Open 5pm-9pm Tues-Sun. This longtime, chef-owned institution serves creative seafood preparations – it's hard to go wrong when ordering. Delectable stone crabs will set you back about $38.

Islamorada Fish Company (☎ 305-664-9271, MM 81.5 bayside) Dishes $9-15. Open 11am-9pm. This lively waterfront bar is a happening scene at sunset. You know the menu: fried fish baskets, fish sandwiches, seafood and a raw bar.

Green Turtle Inn (☎ 305-664-9031, MM 81.5 oceanside) Lunch $4-10, dinner mains $13-19. Open noon-10pm Tues-Sun. This kitschy, lantern-lit eatery has been dishing up homemade turtle consommé, conch chowder and steaks since 1947. The nightly pianist or 'master mentalist' certainly conjure up another era.

Ziggie's Crab Shack (☎ 305-664-3391, MM 83 bayside) Lunch $7-10, dinner mains $13-19, crabs $20-22. Open 11am-10pm. Tacky in a festive way, and intentionally downscale, with Naughahide chairs and picnic-table booths, Ziggie's specializes in crabs served every which way – from cakes to Alaskan Kings to stone crabs. If you're in a hurry, they do a 'lunch express.'

Bentley's (☎ 305-664-9094, MM 82.8 oceanside) Mains $15-20. Open 4pm-10pm Mon-Sat. Early specials, good seafood, friendly service and decent prices pack 'em in year after year. The menu isn't going to surprise you, but that's the draw.

Lorelei (☎ 305-664-4656, MM 82 bayside) Lunch $6-9, dinner mains $15-22. Open 7am-10pm. You'll want to dine (or drink like the throngs) at sunset at the cabana bar, which serves less expensive fare like conch fritters, popcorn shrimp, Philly cheese steaks and salads until early evening.

Atlantic's Edge (☎ 305-664-4651, MM 82 oceanside) Mains $18-36. Open 6pm-10pm. Cheeca Lodge's fine dining restaurant specializes in panoramic ocean views, seafood and steaks. They'll prepare the daily catch any way you want or cook your catch and serve it with side dishes (for $15.50).

Morada Bay (☎ 305-664-0604, MM 81.6 bayside) Lunch $9-16, dinner mains $21-27. Open 11:30am-10pm. If you can ignore the overwhelmed service, there's no more atmospheric and romantic beachfront place on the Keys. A whitewashed preppy boathouse ethos merges with a laid-back Caribbean setting, complete with powdery white sand, palm trees and nighttime torches. What, you want to know about the food? Patrons come for the drinks (served in jelly jars) and the sunsets, but the 'Floribbean' seafood (Caribbean and Floridian influenced) is A-OK, too.

Whale Harbor (☎ 305-664-4959, MM 83.5 oceanside) Buffet $25 adult, $10-19 child. Open 4pm-9pm Mon-Sat, noon-9pm Sun. When quantity reigns over other attributes, hit this all-you-can-eat seafood buffet. You can't miss their kitschy lighthouse.

Pierre's (☎ 305-664-3225, MM 81.6 bayside) Mains $25-30. Open 5:30pm-10pm. If you're only going to splurge once, let it be here. This two-story waterfront plantation house, owned by the wildly successful and adjacent Morada Bay, specializes in creative seafood preparations. At the very least, clean yourself up a bit and hang out in the handsome lounge with oversized rattan chairs or on the verandah.

LONG KEY STATE RECREATION AREA

Opened in 1969, this 965-acre recreation area (☎ 305-664-4815, MM 67.5 oceanside; admission $3.25 per car plus 50¢ per person), about 30 minutes south of Islamorada's midsection, is filled with gumbo-limbo trees, crabwood, poisonwood and lots of wading birds in the mangroves. Two short nature trails head through distinct plant communities. In addition to ranger-led programs a couple of times a week, Friday evening campfire programs and a two-hour guided nature walk on Wednesday mornings (10am), the park also has a 1½-mile canoe trail through a saltwater tidal lagoon, and canoes can be rented ($4 hourly, $10 daily). While the park has both gulf and oceanside sections, its beach is small at low tide and gone at high tide.

Beaches of the Keys

The Keys are not well known for their beaches. Some are plagued by sandflies, but all are lapped by calm waters. Most are really narrow ribbons of white sand that tend to be even narrower in winter because of tides. For better or worse, the water is usually very shallow close to shore. The following are good public beaches, most with picnic tables, some with grills and all with toilets.

destination	mile marker
Harry Harris County Park	MM 92.5
Lower Matecumbe Beach	MM 73.5
Anne's Beach	MM 73
Long Key	MM 67.5
Sombrero Beach	MM 50
Little Duck Key Beach	MM 38
Bahia Honda State Park	MM 37

Middle Keys

The Keys midsection runs from the tiny Conch Keys and Duck Key (MM 63 to MM 61), through Grassy Key (MM 60 to MM 57) and Key Vaca (MM 54 to MM 47), on which Marathon is located. The region ends with Pigeon Key (a National Historic District), which explores the building of the Overseas Hwy (the lifeline of the Florida Keys), and the famed Old Seven Mile Bridge (MM 46.5 to MM 40).

MARATHON

People come to Marathon to fish, which is not to say that nonfishers will be bored. It's just that the area is really geared toward fishing. The second-largest town in the Keys (after Key West) also boasts the Dolphin Research Center (actually on Grassy Key), where you can swim with dolphins in supervised programs (see the boxed text 'Swimming with Dolphins').

Greyhound stops at the Marathon Airport, MM 50.5 bayside.

The Marathon Visitors Center Chamber of Commerce (☎ 305-743-5417, 800-262-7284, W www.floridakeysmarathon.com), MM 53.5 bayside, has a mother lode of information and sells Greyhound tickets. It's open 9am to 5pm.

Fisherman's Hospital (☎ 305-743-5533), MM 48.7 oceanside, has a major emergency room.

The post office (MM 52.5 bayside) is in the Town Square Mall.

Food for Thought (☎ 305-743-3297), MM 51 bayside, in Gulfside Village Shopping Center, is a combination bookstore/health-food shop. Marathon Discount Book Center (☎ 305-289-2066, MM 48.5 oceanside) has inexpensive closeout books and books on tape.

Good dive shops include **Sombrero Reef Explorers** (☎ 305-743-0536, 19 Sombrero Rd, off MM 50 oceanside) and **Aquatic Adventures Dive Center** (☎ 305-743-2421, 800-978-3483, MM 54 oceanside).

Museums of Crane Point Hammock

This fun 63-acre complex (☎ 305-743-9100, W www.cranepoint.org, MM 50 bayside; admission $7.50/6/4 adult/senior/student or child over 6 yrs; open 9am-5pm Mon-Sat, noon-5pm Sun) encompasses both the Museum of Natural History of the Florida Keys and the Children's Museum of the Florida Keys. It provides a geological and geographical history of the Keys, a rare early-20th-century Bahamian-style house, exhibits on pirates and wrecking, a treasure chest filled with dress-up clothes and a walk-through coral reef tunnel featuring underwater sounds. There are short (1½ mile) but nice walking trails through the hammock, and the staff is very helpful and friendly.

Beaches & Wrecks

Sombrero Beach, at the end of Sombrero Beach Rd about 2 miles east of US Hwy 1 from MM 50, has public bathrooms, a picnic area, barbecue grills, a little playground and volleyball nets.

Divers will want to note Sombrero Reef's wreck of the slave ship *Ivory Coast* (1853); it's marked by a light tower. An artificial reef built by Flagler supports the Overseas Highway.

Activities

Kayaking Adventures (☎ 305-743-0561, 19 Sombrero Blvd, off MM 50 oceanside) provides three-hour guided mangrove ecotours ($40 per person), three-hour sunset tours ($40 per person), instruction (included) and rentals (single/double $30/40 half-day, $45/60 full day).

Places to Stay

Camping *Jolly Rogers Trailer Park* (☎ 305-289-0404, 800-995-1525, MM 59.5 bayside) Sites $25 off-season, $40-50 mid-Nov–mid-Apr. There are 225 sites, all with hookups, here. Many tent sites are waterfront.

Knights Key Campground (☎ 305-743-4343, 800-348-2267, MM 47 oceanside) Tent sites without/with hookups $23/28, oceanfront/marina sites with hookups $55/65-70; sites cost less mid-Apr–Nov. On the northern end of the Seven Mile Bridge, this 200-site campground has only 17 sites specifically for tenters. It provides friendly service and 10% off for weekly summertime stays.

Motels & Hotels *Siesta Motel* (☎ 305-743-5671, W www.siestamotel.net, MM 51 oceanside) Rooms average $65 year-round. For the best, cheapest, cleanest place in the Keys, head here. The seven-room motel also provides great service.

Blue Waters Motel (☎ 305-743-4832, 800-222-4832, MM 48.5 bayside) Rooms $60-89 off-season, $90-150 Jan-Mar. A friendly place with a pool and docks, the motel's 16 nice rooms have large bathrooms, free local calls and covered car ports.

Royal Hawaiian Motel Botel (☎ 305-743-7500, MM 53 bayside) Rooms $69-79 off-season, $105-115 mid-Jan–Mar. This family-run canalside place, with a boat dock and pool, has eight rooms that have waterfront balconies and sleep four. It's a very good inexpensive choice.

Lime Tree Bay Resort (☎ 305-664-0750, 800-723-4519, fax 305-664-0750, W www.lime treebayresort.com, MM 68.5 bayside) Rooms and 1-bedroom suites $72-180 off-season,

$102-205 in high season. This excellent, intimate, 29-unit motel complex has basic rooms, studios with kitchens and patios, suites and one- and two-bedroom cottages. There are plenty of palm trees with hammocks, barbecue grills, tiki covered sitting areas, a decent beach, pool, tennis court and on-site boating activities.

Coral Lagoon Resort (☎ 305-289-0121, W www.corallagoonresort.com, MM 53.5 oceanside) Efficiencies $75-100 off-season, $125 late Dec–late Apr. This lush, canalside complex, with 18 spacious units, boasts semiprivate outdoor decks with hammocks and grills for each unit. Tennis racquets, rods and reels, and plenty of personalized services are included. They also have slightly smaller units for $15 less and slightly bigger two-bedroom units for $25 more.

Conch Key Cottages (☎ 305-289-1377, 800-330-1577, W www.conchkeycottages .com, MM 62.3 oceanside) Units $74-147 off-season, $110-235 mid-Dec–early Sept, more for two-bedroom units; inquire about weekly rates. Nicely hidden from US Hwy 1 by a short pebbly causeway, this popular and nicely landscaped complex is comprised of 12 freestanding pastel cottages furnished with rattan, wicker and local pine. Each cottage has its own hammock and kayak; and all enjoy the small but lushly private pool.

Banana Bay Resort (☎ 305-743-3500, 800-226-2621, fax 305-743-2670, W www .bananabay.com, MM 49.5 bayside) Rooms $75-175 off-season, $125-225 late Dec–Apr; ask about the myriad of packages. Rates vary with the view, but regardless, this 60-room resort has a friendly staff, lush setting and a nice pool. A poolside breakfast buffet is included.

Seascape Ocean Resort (☎ 305-743-6455, fax 305-743-8469, 1075 75th St, off MM 50.5 oceanside) Rooms $150-225. These nine rooms, several of which have a kitchen, hearken back to the 1950s, but with updated amenities and a B&B ambience. Seascape, with a lovely waterfront pool and little sitting areas, was originally a private estate, and the current residential neighborhood lends it a rare quietness. Rates include Continental breakfast and afternoon wine and snacks.

FLORIDA KEYS

Hawk's Cay Resort (☎ 305-743-9000, 800-432-2242, w www.hawkscay.com, 61 Hawk's Cay Blvd, off MM 61 oceanside, Duck Key) Rooms $200-325 off-season, $240-295 Jan–mid-Apr, suites & villas much more. This five-story 400-room hotel, with tightly packed townhouse villas, is decorated in an upscale Caribbean style. The most developed, self-contained resort in the Keys offers a sailing school, snorkeling, tennis, boat and kayak rentals, fishing programs, dolphin encounters and scuba lessons.

Places to Eat & Drink

Herbie's (☎ 305-743-6373, MM 50.5 bayside) Dishes $5-10. Open 11am-10pm Tues-Sat. This popular locals' place has been serving burgers, fried-fish sandwiches, and seafood platters and baskets since the early 1970s. It's casual and small, with shellacked picnic tables inside a screened-in porch.

Leigh Ann's Coffee House (☎ 305-743-2001, MM 50.5 oceanside) Dishes $4-7. Open 7am-4pm. From breakfast frittatas to lunchtime bruschettas to smoothies and salads, the pleasant and friendly Leigh Ann's is a delightful oasis from the omnipresent conch fritters and seafood platters. The espresso is downright decent, unless you're a bean addict from Seattle.

7 Mile Grill (☎ 305-743-4481, MM 45 bayside) Breakfast $3-9, dinner $8-11. Open 7am-9pm Fri-Tues. This popular short-order place has bar service and some covered tables overlooking the parking lot. Go for a hearty morning serving of two eggs and a Delmonico steak, or lunchtime grilled-fish sandwiches or dinnertime shrimp steamed in beer.

Island City Fish Market (☎ 305-743-9196, MM 53 oceanside) Dishes $7-16. Open 11:30am-8:30pm Wed-Mon. This retail fish market and restaurant gets daily shipments from local charter boats. It's not much to look at (or smell), so you're better off at an outdoor picnic table (even though they're at the parking lot) or grilling the fish yourself (they have condiments). They'll cook your fish, too.

Water's Edge (☎ 305-743-7000, MM 61 oceanside) Mains $19-31. Open 5pm-9:45pm.

Within the upscale Hawk's Cay Resort, this dress-up restaurant with nice water views serves everything from stuffed filet and black Angus strip steak to vegetarian curry and yellowfin-tuna Caesar salads.

Barracuda Grill (☎ 305-743-3314, MM 49.5 bayside) Mains $15-20. Open 5:55pm-10pm-ish Mon-Sat. This stylishly casual and chef-owned New American grill is making waves with its creative dishes and friendly service. If the timing is right, make it a point to eat here.

Shucker's (☎ 305-743-8686, MM 50.5 bayside) Lunch dishes $7-14, dinner mains $17-20. Open 11:30am-10pm Mon-Fri, 5pm-10pm Sat-Sun. When you're in the mood for a 'normal' restaurant (that's meant in a complimentary way), Shucker's delivers with friendly service, an airy atmosphere and better than decent food. Lunch revolves around fish sandwiches and Cajun chicken salad, while dinner specialties highlight shrimp, yellowfin tuna and the catch-of-the-day prepared pan fried, almondine or française.

PIGEON KEY & OLD SEVEN MILE BRIDGE

This 5-acre island, about 2 miles west of Marathon and basically below the Old Seven Mile Bridge, is a National Historic District. As Henry Flagler's FEC Railway progressed southward, the construction of the Seven Mile Bridge between Marathon and Bahia Honda Key (actually Little Duck Key) became an immense project. From 1908 to 1912, Pigeon Key housed about 400 workers. Then it housed the railroad maintenance workers. And after the hurricane that wiped out Flagler's railroad in 1935, the Key housed workers who converted the railroad to automobile bridges.

After a brief stint in the 1970s as a research facility leased by the University of Miami, the Pigeon Key Foundation preserved the island's buildings and began telling the story of the railroad and its workers. Today the Key (☎ 305-289-0025, w www.pigeonkey.org; admission $8.50/5 adult/child; tours 10am-3pm) is open for touring, and you can visit the old town, including the 'honeymoon cottage,' the assistant bridge tender's and bridge tender's houses, the section gang's quarters and the 'negro quarters.'

Park at the southwestern end of Marathon (MM 47), and take the hourly shuttle out to the island; it runs from 10am to 3pm, with the last shuttle returning at 4:45pm. You can also ride or walk across the bridge.

The **Old Seven Mile Bridge** (*admission free*) serves as 'the World's Longest Fishing Bridge;' park at the northeastern foot of the bridge.

Lower Keys

The Lower Keys extend from Bahia Honda Key (MM 40) to Boca Chica Key (MM 7). Accommodation and dining choices in this stretch suffer in their proximity to Key West; most are located on Big Pine Key. As for things to do, the National Key Deer Refuge is the main attraction, but you'll also find skydiving and great diving and snorkeling, especially at Looe Key National Marine Sanctuary and Bahia Honda State Park. You can also arrange wonderful kayak trips among the mangroves within the Great White Heron National Wildlife Refuge.

Information

The helpful Lower Keys Chamber of Commerce (☎ 305-872-3580, 800-872-3722, W www.lowerkeyschamber.com), MM 31 oceanside, is on Big Pine Key. It's open 9am to 5pm Monday to Friday, 9am to 3pm Saturday.

The post office is at MM 30 bayside, on Big Pine Key.

Big Pine Shopping Center, at MM 30.5 bayside (turn northwest on Key Deer Blvd), has a Winn-Dixie, the biggest food market in the area, and the Big Pine Key public library (☎ 305-289-6303).

For emergencies, the closest facility is Lower Keys Medical Center (☎ 305-294-5531, 800-233-3119), 5900 College Rd, near MM 5, on Stock Island; it has a 24-hour emergency room.

Dive shops include **Looe Key Reef Resort & Dive Center** (☎ 305-872-2215, 800-942-5397, MM 27.5 oceanside), on Ramrod Key, and **Paradise Divers** (☎ 305-872-1114, MM 38.5 bayside), on Big Pine Key.

BAHIA HONDA STATE PARK

With one of the Keys' best sparkling-white-sand beaches, this 524-acre park (☎ 305-872-2353, W www.bahiahonda park.com, MM 36.8 oceanside; admission $4 per car plus 50¢ per person; open 8am-sunset) sits at the foot of the Seven Mile Bridge. (In summer sand flies are rife!) Even though it's very popular, the 2½-mile expanse and the shape of the beach allow for privacy. Don't get too private though: Topless and nude bathing are prohibited. Rangers will tell you once to put on clothes, after which you could be fined and ejected from the park. Bahia Honda is the southernmost Key with exposed limestone, and along its nature trails you'll find silver palms, yellow satinwood and endangered lily thorns.

Snorkeling & Kayaking

The **park concession** (☎ 305-872-3210) rents equipment ($10 for a mask, fins and snorkel) and offers daily excursions at 9:30am and 1:30pm ($26/21 adult/child under 18 yrs). Reservations are a good idea in high season. The concession also rents kayaks (singles/doubles cost $10/18 an hour and $30/54 per half day) and has a grocery store.

Organized Tours

Big Pine Kayak Adventures (☎ 305-872-7474, W www.keyskayaktours.com), run by nature photographer Bill Keogh, offers guided kayak journeys into both the Great White Heron and Key Deer Refuges. Regularly scheduled morning and afternoon trips usually last three to four hours ($50), though you may wish to take a slightly shorter sunset journey ($50). You'll paddle along the shallow red-mangrove coastlines, checking out what's what. Bill usually limits trips to six people to ensure that it's peaceful enough for all. He also rents kayaks and customizes backcountry trips.

FLORIDA KEYS

Bat Tower

On the National Register of Historic Places, this wooden tower *(off MM 17 bayside, Lower Sugarloaf Key)* was built in 1929 by Righter Clyde Perky. He thought the tower would attract bats, which would then eat the swarming masses of mosquitoes and make the Keys a wonderful place. The bats never came.

Reflections Nature Tours *(☎ 305-872-4668,* W *www.floridakeyskayaktours.com)* If you'd prefer a woman's take on the natural scene, Emily Graves also takes folks on guided tours for similar prices. She also rents kayaks and delivers them anywhere between Sunshine and Cudjoe Keys.

Sky Dive Key West *(☎ 305-745-4386)*, near Bat Tower off MM 17 at the Sugarloaf Key Airport, offers tandem skydives for $219. Add $1 per pound over 200lbs, and add $99 if you want a videotape for posterity. **Fantasy Dan's** *(☎ 305-745-2217)*, at the same location, offers airplane tours for $20 to $50, depending on how much time you spend in the air. It's amazing to see these little strips of land from above; it helps you to fully understand how fragile their existence is.

LOOE KEY NATIONAL MARINE SANCTUARY

Pronounced 'loo,' this isn't a Key but rather a grove reef off Ramrod Key, and you can only visit with an organized trip. The Key Largo (see the John Pennekamp Coral Reef State Park section, earlier) and Looe Key National Marine Sanctuaries were established in 1971 and 1981, respectively, to protect sensitive areas within the Keys. In reality, they are a compromise between commercial activities and environmental protection. Named for an English frigate that sank here in 1744, the Looe Key reef contains the 210-foot *Adolphus Busch* – used in the film *Fire Down Below* – which was sunk 60 to 120 feet in 1998. Permissible

activities include limited lobster-catching, crabbing and hook-and-line sport and commercial fishing. The sanctuary designation protects against damaging the natural features (which includes standing on, anchoring on or touching coral).

Diving & Snorkeling

Thousands of varieties of hugely colorful tropical fish, coral and sea life abound in the sanctuary. **Strike Zone Charters** *(☎ 305-872-9863, 800-654-9560, MM 29.5 bayside)* has four-hour snorkeling and diving trips aboard glass-bottom boats that depart at 9:30am and 1:30pm. Snorkeling trips cost $25 per person, plus $5 for equipment; diving trips are $40, plus $25 for equipment.

Looe Key Reef Resort *(☎ 305-872-2215, MM 27.5 oceanside)* (see Places to Stay below) runs snorkeling/diving trips aboard a catamaran for $22.50/35 without equipment. If you need rental gear, add $9 for snorkeling and $47 for diving. The four-hour trip hits two different reef locations.

NATIONAL KEY DEER REFUGE

Key deer, an endangered subspecies of white-tailed deer, live primarily on Big Pine and No Name Keys.

The National Key Deer Refuge *(headquarters: ☎ 305-872-2239/0774, MM 30.5 bayside, Big Pine Shopping Center; admission free; open 8am-5pm Mon-Fri)* sprawls over several Keys, but the sections that are open to the public – Blue Hole, Watson's Hammock and Watson's Nature Trail – are on Big Pine and No Name Keys. Besides these areas, all areas marked with signs that read 'US Fish & Wildlife Service – Unauthorized Entry Prohibited' are open to the public from a half-hour before sunrise to a half-hour after sunset. Key deer are best spotted in early morning and late afternoon.

From MM 30.5, take Key Deer Blvd north for 3½ miles. You'll first come to Blue Hole; Watson's Nature Trail and Watson's Hammock are a quarter mile farther on the same road. Less than a mile long, **Watson's Nature Trail** winds through the Key deer's natural habitat.

No Name Key gets fewer visitors than the Blue Hole or Watson's Nature Trail. Take Key Deer Blvd to Watson Blvd, turn right, go about 1½ miles to Wilder Blvd, turn left, follow it for 2 miles to Bogie Bridge, cross that, and you'll be on No Name.

Blue Hole, an old quarry that's now the largest freshwater body in the Keys, has lots of alligators, turtles, fish and wading birds. Please don't feed the wildlife; many visitors do, and it's illegal and irresponsible.

GREAT WHITE HERON NATIONAL WILDLIFE REFUGE

This refuge (☎ 305-872-2239) consists of two large but little-visited wading-bird nesting areas where you can see herons, ibis, egrets, ospreys, hawks and even eagles, as well as fish, crabs, sponges, coral and mangroves. Kayaks and canoes are permitted, but there are no services. For more information, contact the National Key Deer Refuge headquarters in the Big Pine Shopping Center (see above). Also see Organized Tours in the Bahia Honda State Park section, earlier, for organized refuge trips.

PLACES TO STAY
Camping

Bahia Honda State Park (☎ 305-872-2353, 800-326-3521 reservations, **W** www.reserve america.com, MM 37) Sites without/with electricity $24/26, cabins $97 mid-Sept–mid-Dec, $125 other times; waterfront sites (reserve far in advance or forget it) are an additional $2. One of the Key's best camping places, this excellent park has 200 almost bayside and oceanside sites and six cabins, each sleeping six.

Big Pine Key Fishing Lodge (☎ 305-872-2351, MM 33 oceanside) Sites without/with hookups $30/37, motel efficiencies $89-115. This well-maintained canalside place has 60 tent sites, 97 RV sites and 16 efficiencies. Even with an artificial beach, ocean swimming isn't great, but there is a pool. The lodge, geared toward fishing and diving, also has boat rentals.

Sugarloaf Key Resort KOA (☎ 305-745-3549, 800-562-7731, 251 County Rd, off MM 20 oceanside) Tent sites $40-43 off-season, $44-47 mid-Jan–mid-Mar, RV sites $60-80 off-season, $69-87 mid-Jan–mid-Mar. This

Key Deer

This endangered species, a subspecies of white-tail deer, live primarily on Big Pine and No Name Keys. Once mainland-dwelling animals, the formation of the Keys stranded them on the islands, and evolution has wrought changes on their stature. Since it's warmer here than on the mainland, the deer don't need as much body mass. And to compensate for reduced grazing lands and scarce freshwater, the deer now have single births rather than multiple litters.

Key deer are only really threatened by humans, who can't stop feeding them. This causes Key deer to fearlessly approach humans and, unfortunately, their vehicles. About 65% of the vehicular deaths occur along US Hwy 1. Contrary to their nature, they have also begun traveling in herds in pursuit of handouts.

Key deer are generally light to 'dead leaf' brown with black tails and a white rump. Fawns have white spots on their backs and ribs for the first month. Some full-grown deer have a black mask over the eyes and the forehead. Full-grown bucks normally weigh about 75lb; does about 65lb. Bucks are about 30 inches high at the shoulders, does are about 25 inches, and fawns weigh just 2lb to 3½lb at birth. Mating season is from September to December, and the Key deer's gestation period is 204 days (fawning occurs in April and May).

Please slow down when you're in their habitat. Speed limits are strictly enforced, and while there is no penalty for hitting a Key deer inadvertently, if you're speeding, you're in violation of state and federal laws. Fines run in the hundreds of dollars. And please don't feed them. It's illegal, and if you're caught, fines can reach $25,000.

highly developed KOA has about 200 tent sites and 200 RV sites.

Motels & Hotels

Parmer's Place Guesthouse (☎ 305-872-2157, W www.parmersresort.com, 565 Barry Ave, off MM 28.5 bayside) Units $55-130 off-season, $75-140 Jan-Aug. On 5 acres of Little Torch Key (call for directions), this lush and well-maintained 45-room waterfront resort has motel rooms, efficiencies, one- and two-bedroom units, and lots of aviaries with chattering birds. Rates include Continental breakfast, a large pool and gas grills. You can swim from the docks.

Looe Key Reef Resort (☎ 305-872-2215, 800-942-5397, W www.diveflakeys.com, MM 27.5 oceanside) Rooms $70-75 off-season, $95 Feb-Apr & July-Aug. Since the focus of this motel is diving, their 20 rooms are quite basic.

Sugarloaf Lodge (☎ 305-745-3211, 800-553-6097, fax 305-745-3389, W www.sugarloaflodge.com, MM 17 bayside) Rooms $90-100 off-season, $130-140 Dec-May. These 55 waterfront rooms, geared toward fisherpeople and divers, are basic but fine.

Little Palm Island Resort & Spa (☎ 305-872-2524, 800-343-8567, fax 305-872-4843, W www.littlepalmisland.com) Suites $795. Accessible only by plane or boat, this 30-bungalow luxe retreat rewards guests with pampering service, romantic surroundings, white-sand beaches, a lagoonlike pool and Zen-style gardens. And for that price, it should! Spa services and the dining room are phenomenal. There's no better 6-acre place to stay if you can pay....

B&Bs

Both these places are on the northern edge of Big Pine Key.

The Barnacle (☎ 305-872-3298, 800-465-9100, 1557 Long Beach Dr, off MM 33 oceanside) Rooms $95-150. This Caribbean-style hideaway has three rooms (one with a small kitchen) and one cottage, as well as a hot tub and hammocks.

Casa Grande (☎ 305-872-2878, Long Beach Dr, off MM 33 oceanside) Rooms $90-105 off-season, $119 mid-Dec–Apr. Within a hacienda-style house, these three rooms include breakfast, use of the Jacuzzi and lots of thoughtful extras.

PLACES TO EAT & DRINK

Baby's Coffee (☎ 800-523-2326, MM 15 oceanside) Open 7am-6pm Mon-Fri, 7am-5pm Sat & Sun. It's the only coffee place in the area; they roast their own, and luckily it's OK.

Good Food Conspiracy (☎ 305-872-3945, MM 30 oceanside) Open 9:30am-7pm Mon-Sat, 9:30am-5pm Sun. This health-food place has a limited amount of prepared foods, a juice bar, smoothies, vitamins and the like. If you're camping, they have healthful food supplies.

Big Pine Restaurant (☎ 305-872-2790, MM 30 bayside) Dishes $3-7, dinner mains $9-15. Open 6am-9pm Tues-Sun, 6am-2pm Mon. Next to the Big Pine Post Office, this place transports you into the past with cheap breakfast specials, cheeseburgers with all the fixings and sandwiches.

No Name Pub (☎ 305-872-9115, N Watson Blvd, off MM 30.5 bayside) Dishes $5-15. Open 11am-11pm. Perhaps the most colorful eatery around these parts, this smoky and hidden locals' roadhouse is wall-papered with dollar bills. The bar-cum-rustic restaurant serves great pizzas to families and drinkers.

Montes (☎ 305-745-3731, MM 25 bayside) Lunch dishes $8-10, dinner mains $8-18. Open 9am-10pm Mon-Sat, 10:30am-9pm Sun. On Summerland Key, this weather-beaten and screened-in hangout serves the requisite fried-fish dinners, sandwich platters and seafood baskets.

Montego Bay (☎ 305-872-3009, MM 30.2 bayside) Lunch $7, dinner $17. Open 11am-10pm. On Big Pine Key, this Caribbean-style waterfront restaurant is more a bar than eatery. Nonetheless, they dish up plenty of *yah-mon* attitude and jerk chicken.

Mangrove Mama's (☎ 305-745-3030, MM 20 oceanside) Lunch $10-15, dinner mains $19-25. Open 11:30am-3:30pm & 5:30pm-10pm. This hippish roadside eatery and rustic bar occasionally has live reggae. Check it out.

As for the food, think good, Caribbean-inspired seafood, coconut shrimp, spicy conch stew and surf-and-turf. Even the locals hang out here, especially at happy hour.

Key West

The capital of the Conch Republic, Key West has a well-earned reputation as a tropical paradise with gorgeous sunsets and raucous nightlife. Jimmy Buffet *does* serve up a mean margarita; Ernest Hemingway *did* live, work and drink here; Sloppy Joe's Bar pours up a mean Hemingway Hammer; and there is certainly plenty of juggling and acrobatic nonsense around the sunset celebration.

Yes, Key West is overrun by tourists, and its Conchs have become cynical, but they're also some of the most fun-loving, quirky, radical, reactionary, friendly and downright interesting people you'll come across. And if you look carefully, you'll find fleeting images of the former Key West. Walking through narrow side streets away from Truman Ave or Duval St, you'll see lovely Keys architecture and get a sense of how the locals live (at least, those who aren't there to sell you a T-shirt or a seat on a glass-bottom boat).

History

The area's first European settlers were the Spanish, who upon finding Indian burial sites, named the place *Cayo Hueso* (kah-ya **way**-so) – Bone Island, a name that was later Anglicized into Key West. Purchased from a Spaniard by John Simonton in 1821, Key West was developed as a naval base in 1822. It then served as the naval base for David Porter's Anti-Pirate Squadron, which by 1826 had substantially reduced pirate activity in the region. From then on, Key West's times of boom and bust were closely tied to a military presence.

The construction of forts at Key West and on the Dry Tortugas brought men and money. As well, the island's proximity to busy and treacherous shipping lanes (which attracted the pirates in the first place) created a wrecking industry – salvaging goods from downed ships.

In the late 1800s, the area became the focus of mass immigration and political activity for Cubans, who were fleeing oppressive conditions under Spanish rule and trying to form a revolutionary army. Along with them came cigar manufacturers, who turned Key West into the USA's cigar manufacturing center. That would end when workers' demands convinced several large manufacturers, notably Vicénte Martínez Ybor and Ignacio Haya, to relocate to Tampa, in southwest Florida.

During the Spanish-American War, Key West may have been the most important staging point for US troops, and the military buildup lasted through WWI. All of the Keys began to boom when Henry Flagler's Overseas Highway – running over a series of causeways from the mainland to Key West – was constructed.

The Conch Republic

Conchs (pronounced 'conk' as in 'bonk,' not 'contsh' as in 'paunch') are people who were born and raised in Key West. It's a rare and difficult title to achieve. Even after seven years of living here, residents only rise to the rank of 'Freshwater Conch.' You will hear reference to, and see the flag of, the Conch Republic, and therein lies an interesting tale.

In 1982, the US border patrol and US customs erected a roadblock at Key Largo to catch drug smugglers and illegal aliens. As traffic jams and anger mounted, many tourists disappeared: They decided they'd rather take the Shark Valley Tram in the Everglades, thank you very much.

To voice their outrage, a bunch of fiery Conchs decided to secede from the USA. After forming the Conch Republic, they made three declarations (in this order): secede from the USA, declare war on the USA and surrender, and request $1 million in foreign aid.

Every February, Conchs celebrate the anniversary of those heady days with non-stop parties.

KEY WEST

PLACES TO STAY
5 Jabour's Camp & Lodge
24 Curry House
30 Frances St Bottle Inn
39 Crowne Plaza La Concha
41 Marrero's
42 Big Rubys Guesthouse
44 Pegasus Hotel
48 The Gardens Hotel
52 Merlin Guesthouse
56 Andrews Inn
57 Wicker Guesthouse
58 Key Lodge Motel
59 Duval Gardens
66 Conch House Heritage Inn
68 Chelsea House
69 Red Rooster
70 The Mermaid & The
     Alligator
71 La Pensione
77 Pearl's Rainbow
78 Spindrift Motel
79 Best Western Hibiscus
80 Key West Youth Hostel &
     SeaShell Motel
82 Southernmost Point
     Guesthouse
83 Atlantic Shores Resort
84 Santa Maria Motel
86 Wyndham Casa Marina
     Resort & Beach House

PLACES TO EAT
2 Turtle Kraals Restaurant &
    Bar
4 Java Lounge; Key West
    Lime Shoppe
6 Waterfront Market;
    Schooner Wharf Bar; Reef
    Relief
7 BO's Fish Wagon
8 Pepe's Cafe
9 PT's Late Night
13 Bagatelle
27 Mangia Mangia
28 5 Brothers Grocery &
     Sandwich Shop
32 Kelly's
49 Mangoes
62 The Deli Restaurant
67 Cafe des Artistes
72 El Siboney
73 Mo's Restaurant
74 Alice's; La Te Da
75 Banana Café
76 Camille's
85 Louie's Backyard

OTHER
1 Yankee Freedom II
3 Key West Aloe
10 Parking
11 Key West Chamber of
     Commerce
12 Billie's Bar
14 Old Town Trolley Tours
15 Key West Aquarium
16 Key West Shipwreck
     Historeum
17 Key West Cigar Factory
18 Mel Fisher Maritime
     Museum

19 Audubon House & Tropical
     Gardens
20 Captain Tony's Saloon
21 Rick's/Durty Harry's;
     Upstairs at Rick's
22 Sloppy Joe's Bar
23 Curry Mansion
25 Helio Gallery
26 Flaming Maggie's
29 Haitian Art Co
31 Little White House
33 Jessie Porter's Heritage
     House Museum & Robert
     Frost Cottage
34 Mosquito Coast Island
     Outfitters & Kayak Guides
35 Wreckers' Museum/ Oldest
     House
36 Red Barn Theatre
37 Public Library
38 Post Office
43 Margaritaville Café
45 Bank of America
46 Green Parrot
47 Bourbon St Pub
50 Key West Business Guild
51 801 Bourbon Bar
53 Pandemonium
54 Key West Lighthouse
55 Hemingway House
60 Gay & Lesbian Community
     Center
61 Keys Mopeds & Scooters
63 Donnie's Club International
64 Truman Medical Center
65 Moped Hospital
81 Southernmost Point
87 West Martello Tower

FLORIDA KEYS

Gulf of

Mexico

Key West Bight

Front St.

Simonton St.

Greene St.

Duval St.

Ann St.

Dey St.

Caroline St.

Mallory
Square

Wall St.

Bahama St.

Pier B

Eaton St.

Truman
Annex

Fleming St.

Front St.

Southard St.

*Submarine
Basin*

Angela St.

Whitehead St.

Thomas St.

Covington Ave.

Emma St.

Fort St.

Dekalb Ave.

Angela St.

*Harry S Truman
US Naval Reservation*

**Fort Zachary
Taylor State
Historic Site**

Whitehead Spit

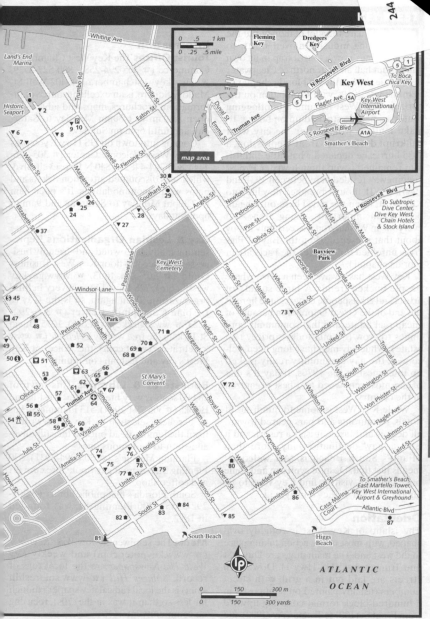

Key West was also a center for the sponge-diving industry. Today you can still buy them in Mallory Square for a lot of money, but the main sponging industry moved north to Tarpon Springs, now a tourist trap in its own right, about half an hour north of Clearwater Beach (see the Southwest Florida chapter).

In the late 1910s, with Prohibition on the horizon, Key West became a bootlegging center, as people stocked up on booze. To make matters worse, after the city went bankrupt during the Great Depression, a 1935 hurricane depleted what little enthusiasm remained (even though writer Ernest Hemingway resided here between 1931 and 1940). WWII, though, breathed new life into Key West, when the naval base once again became an important staging area. And everyone in Washington was certainly happy about that presence when the Bay of Pigs crisis unfolded in 1961 (see the Facts about Florida chapter).

Key West has always been a place where people bucked trends. A large society of artists and craftspeople congregated here at the end of the Great Depression because of cheap real estate, and that community continues to grow (despite today's pricey real estate). While gay men have long been welcomed, the gay community really picked up in earnest in the 1970s. Today it's one of the most renowned and best organized in the country.

While Key West is home to hundreds of hotels, restaurants and bars geared toward all desires and tastes, it isn't a resort, and it isn't a 'gay' destination any more than Miami's South Beach is. 'All welcome' means just that. Despite cynicism and some price gouging, visitors find Key West to be almost as good as they'd imagined.

Orientation

The island of Key West is roughly oval shaped, with most of the action taking place in the west end. The main drags are Duval St and Truman Ave (US Hwy 1). Downtown streets are laid out in a grid, with street numbers (usually painted on lampposts) in a hundred-block format counting upward from Front St (100) to Truman Ave (900) and

so on. Mallory Square, at the far northwestern tip, hosts nightly sunset celebrations.

Information

Tourist Offices The Key West Chamber of Commerce (☎ 305-294-2587, 800-527-8539, Ⓦ www.keywestchamber.org), 402 Wall St, Mallory Square, is an excellent source of information, brochures, maps and advice. It's open 8:30am to 6:30pm Monday to Saturday, and until 6pm on Sunday.

Coming into town on US Hwy 1, you pass the Key West Welcome Center (☎ 305-296-4444, 800-284-4482), 3840 N Roosevelt Blvd, which sells discounted attraction tickets and helps with accommodations. It's open 8am to 7:30pm Monday to Saturday and 9am to 6pm Sunday.

Gay & Lesbian Organizations Representing many gay-owned and -friendly businesses, the second-floor Key West Business Guild (☎ 305-294-4603, Ⓦ www.gaykeywestfl.com), 728 Duval St, is a very helpful organization. Then again, so is the Gay & Lesbian Community Center (☎ 305-292-3223, Ⓦ www.glcckeywest.org), 1075 Duval St. Pick up the free weekly *Celebrate* (Ⓦ www.celebratekeywest.com), the 'voice' of Key West's gay and lesbian community.

Bookstores & Libraries This town of 28,000 souls is very literary. Key West Island Books (☎ 305-294-2904), 513 Fleming St, has an excellent selection of Key West writers, from the famous dead ones to the still-alive-and-soon-to-be-famous ones.

Flaming Maggie's (☎ 305-294-3931), 830 Fleming St, is a great gay bookstore cum art and coffee shop.

South Florida's first public library (☎ 305-292-3535), 700 Fleming St, was founded in 1892.

Media The semiweekly *Key West Keynoter* (Ⓦ www.keynoter.com) and weekly *Key West: The Newspaper* are the local rags of record. *Solares Hill* (Ⓦ www.solareshill.com) is the local radical newspaper (though far less so than it was in the '70s), focusing on community interest.

National Public Radio (NPR) is broadcast at 91.3 FM.

Emergency The Key West Visitor Assistance Program (☎ 800-771-5397) is a 24-hour, multilingual switchboard that puts travelers in touch with authorities in any kind of emergency – from passport loss to rape to hotel complaints.

Medical Services Lower Keys Medical Center (☎ 305-294-5531), 5900 College Rd, Stock Island, near MM 5, has a 24-hour emergency room. For less-critical problems, Truman Medical Center (☎ 305-296-4399), 540 Truman Ave, is open 9am to 4:45pm Monday to Friday and 9:30am to noon Saturday.

THINGS TO SEE & DO
Mallory Square
This cobblestone square hosts Key West's famous nightly sunset celebrations, a uniquely Key West carnival featuring jugglers, acrobats, well-trained parrots and artisans. The atmosphere seems designed to get as many people as possible near the bars, restaurants, trinket shops and sidewalk stalls. But despite the cynicism, the event *is* interesting – once. Show up an hour beforehand to get the full effect.

Key West Aquarium
Though its age shows a bit, this 1932 aquarium (☎ *305-296-2051,* **w** *www.keywest aquarium.com, Mallory Square, 1 Whitehead St; admission $9/4.50 adult/child 4-12 yrs; open 10am-6pm)* has a friendly and helpful staff. Kids like the touch tanks, with starfish, conchs and sea cucumbers; and the fish tanks, with catfish, snappers and angelfish. The aquarium also has a 'Pet a Shark' program! Outdoor tanks hold barracudas, sharks and sawfish. Tours at 11am, 1pm, 3pm and 4:30pm last 40 minutes and are included with admission. Tickets are valid for two consecutive days.

Hemingway House
One of Key West's great attractions, this lovely Spanish-colonial house (☎ *305-294-*

Ernest Hemingway, aka Papa

FLORIDA KEYS

1575, **w** *www.hemingwayhome.com, 907 Whitehead St; admission $9/5 adult/child 6-12 yrs; open 9am-5pm)* was Hemingway's house from 1931 to 1940. It was here that he wrote *The Short Happy Life of Francis Macomber, A Farewell to Arms, Death in the Afternoon* and *To Have and Have Not,* and where he began *For Whom the Bell Tolls.* But he didn't just write here; he procrastinated by installing Key West's first saltwater swimming pool in a kind of romantic garden. The construction project set him back so much that he pressed 'my last penny' into the cement on the pool's deck. It's still there today. Hemingway retained ownership of the house until his death in 1961; the descendants of his famous six-toed cat still rule the house and grounds. Tours, departing every 15 minutes and lasting about 30 minutes, include fun stories about his wives, the chandeliers and the old overgrown gardens.

Key West Cemetery
One of the country's more fascinating cemeteries contains tombstone epitaphs like 'I told you I was sick' and 'At least I

know where he is sleeping tonight.' You'll have to hunt for them, but that's the fun of it. Guided tours are available on Tuesday and Thursday at 9:30am (☎ 305-292-6829; *tours $10 per person*) from the main gate at Margaret and Angela Sts.

Curry Mansion

This 100-year-old Victorian mansion (☎ 305-294-5349, W *www.currymansion.com, 511 Caroline St*), with extraordinary woodwork and Tiffany sliding glass doors, was built by Milton Curry, one of Florida's first millionaires; it's now a guest house. On most days you can take a self-guided tour of the antique-packed rooms from 8:30am to 5pm; it's $5 for adults, $1 for children. If you're impressed enough that you want to stay, rooms range from $150 to $250 nightly off-season, $240 to $325 from mid-January to mid-April. Be careful, though; only four rooms are in the main house (16 more are out back, and eight others are across the street). Note that Curry Mansion is not Curry House (see the Places to Stay section).

Wreckers' Museums

Two small museums are dedicated to study of the wreckers. The home of Confederate blockade-runner Francis B Watlington's house, the **Wreckers' Museum/Oldest House** (☎ 305-294-9502, 322 Duval St; admission $5/1 adult/child; open 10am-4pm), is filled with period antiques and has enjoyable, volunteer-led tours.

The **Key West Shipwreck Historeum** (☎ 305-292-8990, 1 Whitehead St; admission $8/4 adult/child 4-12 yrs; open 9:45am-4:45pm) is more interesting. A narrated film portrays the lives and times of the wreckers, and knowledgeable volunteers explain how Key West developed as a port. Allow about 30 to 45 minutes to see and do everything.

Southernmost Point

An official marker at the corner of South and Whitehead Sts indicates the southernmost point in the continental USA (technically there's land farther south, but it's within the naval base, which is private property and therefore doesn't count) and draws hundreds of photo-seeking tourists. You gotta be able to prove 'I was there,' after all.

Jessie Porter's Heritage House Museum & Robert Frost Cottage

This Caribbean-colonial house (☎ 305-296-3573, W *www.heritagehousemuseum.org, 410 Caroline St; admission $6/5 adult/senior, student & child over 12 yrs; open 10am-3pm Thur-Sat & Tues*), open for guided tours only, contains the original furnishings and antiques of a Key West family who lived here. Spoken-word recordings of Robert Frost's poetry play in the garden.

Key West Lighthouse

This functioning lighthouse (☎ 305-294-0012, W *www.kwahs.com, 938 Whitehead St; admission $8/6/4 adult/senior/student over 7 yrs; open 9:30am-4:30pm*) is farther inland than you might expect for two reasons. First, the navy filled in about 2000 yards between here and Fort Taylor. Second, lighthouse placement isn't all that important when you consider that it sits at the high point (10 feet above sea level) on a flat island in the middle of the ocean. Lighthouses are designed so boats know that if they're lined up with the lighthouse's red lens, they're in trouble. The adjacent keeper's house contains a little museum, but visitors can also climb the 88 steps to the top of the lighthouse.

Audubon House & Tropical Gardens

This lovely early-19th-century house (☎ 305-294-2116, W *www.audubonhouse.com, 205 Whitehead St; admission $8.50/7.50/3.50 adult/senior/child 6-12 yrs; open 9:30am-5pm*) was built by ship's carpenters for Captain John H Geiger, whose family lived here for about 120 years. In 1958 it became Key West's first restored building and was named after John James Audubon, who painted in the garden in 1832, before the house had been built.

Take a free, self-guided, half-hour tour with narration, which is supplied courtesy of a CD player. The rooms are furnished with authentic 19th-century Key West furniture and many Audubon lithographs.

The tropical gardens are especially nice – rife with birds of paradise, star-fruit trees, fishtail ferns and palms, hibiscus and jasmine.

Mel Fisher Maritime Museum

This fascinating museum (☎ 305-294-2633, W *www.melfisher.org, 200 Greene St; admission $7.50/3.75 adult/child 6-12 yrs; open 9:30am-5pm*) exhibits the rich 17th-century galleon treasures of Spain's *Santa Margarita* and the *Atocha,* discovered by the late Mel Fisher in 1980–85 (he started his galleon search in 1969). Various jewels, tools, coins and navigational pieces are displayed on the ground floor, along with a world map showing shipping routes that the boats took. The 2nd floor features a slave ship and interesting changing exhibits. Mel, whose motto was 'Today's the day,' took walks through the museum until just months before he died in 1998.

Little White House

President Harry S Truman's former vacation house (☎ 305-294-9911, 111 Front St; admission $10/5 adult/child 5-12 yrs; open 9am-5pm*), with restful, lush and lovely grounds, is open only for guided tours. You'll see Truman's piano, lots of original furnishings and a 15-minute video about Truman's life. The knowledgeable guides rattle out trivia and fun facts for everyone from children to serious history buffs. It's located in the Harry S Truman Annex (in which you can wander around by yourself).

East Martello Tower

This Civil War citadel (☎ 305-296-3913, 3501 S Roosevelt Blvd; admission $6/4/2 adult/senior/child; open 9:30am-4:30pm*), across from Key West Airport, houses a gallery with local artwork and an interesting Key West history museum. Diehards can climb the central tower to a watchtower with horrible airport views and unimpressive beach views. Metal sculptures, originally stored within the tower for lack of space elsewhere, have turned into an attraction in and of themselves.

West Martello Tower

The ruins of the western old brick fort (☎ 305-294-3210, cnr Atlantic Blvd & White St; admission free; open 9:30am-3:15pm Mon-Sat*) now flourish with local plant life from the Key West Garden Club headquartered here. Since it's staffed by volunteers, the opening hours are a little iffy.

Fort Zachary Taylor State Historic Site

Fort Zachary Taylor (☎ 305-292-6713; admission $2.50 for one person in a car, $5 for two, plus 50¢ for each additional person in a car, $1.50 per pedestrian; open 8am-sunset*), at the southwestern end of the island, operated from 1845 to 1866 and defended against blockade-running Union ships during the Civil War. Today the state historic site and park has showers, picnic tables, a very good beach and the deepest, clearest water on the island – it's great for swimming. Ranger-led tours depart at noon and 2pm.

ACTIVITIES
Beaches

All three city beaches on the southern side of the island are narrow, with calm and clear water. **South Beach** is at the end of Simonton St. **Higgs Beach**, at the end of Reynolds St and Casa Marina Court, has barbecue grills, picnic tables and a long wooden pier that draws gay sunbathers. **Smathers Beach**, farther east off S Roosevelt Blvd, is more popular with jet skiers, parasailers, teens and college students. Don't forget Key

West's best beach, at Fort Zachary Taylor (see above), favored by gay locals.

Diving & Snorkeling

Near-shore dive opportunities aren't as plentiful as elsewhere in the Keys, but they are definitely here. Because of pollution and activity, there's no snorkeling to speak of on Key West beaches. Most dive companies take you west, to sites including Cottrell, Barracuda, Boca Grande, Woman, Sand, Rock and Marquesas Keys. At some dive sites – especially around the Marquesas – nondivers can go along and snorkel. Don't touch the coral.

The best opportunities for diving (with the skill levels required to dive them) include the following:

Cayman Salvage Master (advanced) – 67 to 90 feet; a coral- and plant-covered fish farm

Eastern Dry Rocks (beginner) – 20 to 25 feet; there's snorkeling here, too

Joe's Tug (intermediate) – a submerged tugboat at a depth of about 65 feet

Western Dry Rocks (beginner) – massive coral and mounds of brain

Dive companies set up at kiosks around Mallory Square and other places in town, notably the corner of Truman and Duval Sts. Shop around carefully, as prices vary greatly. Check these well-established places: **Subtropic Dive Center** (☎ 305-296-9914, 800-853-3483, 1605 N Roosevelt Blvd) and **Dive Key West** (☎ 305-296-3823, 800-426-0707, 3128 N Roosevelt Blvd).

Reef Relief At the end of William St within the Waterfront Market (see Places to Eat, later in this section), the nonprofit Reef Relief (☎ 305-294-3100, W www.reefrelief.org) maintains a network of anchoring buoys along the Keys. The idea is that if boaters have alternate anchoring spots, they won't lower their anchors onto the coral, thus damaging it. Buoys are free for all. Experienced divers interested in volunteering to clean the buoys, which is frequently necessary, should contact Reef Relief. The headquarters has free exhibits on coral and the Florida reef system, as well as knowledgeable volunteers and staff who can give you detailed ecological information.

ORGANIZED TOURS

Old Town Trolley Tours (☎ 305-296-6688; tours $20/10 adult/child 4-12 yrs) runs 90-minute narrated tram tours starting at Mallory Square and making a large, lazy circle around the whole city (both the old and new town), with nine stops along the way. You can get on and off, going in the same direction, as often as you want for one rotation. Trolleys depart every 15 to 30 minutes from 9am to 4:30pm. Narration is hokey and touristy, but you'll get a good overview of Key West, its history and gossipy dirt about local issues and people in the news.

Conch Train Tour (☎ 305-294-5161; tours $20/10 adult/child 4-12 yrs) Also run by Old Town Trolley, these trams operate between 9am and 4:30pm and depart every 30 minutes. You'll stay on board the trolley, stay within old town and listen to narration about 100 so-called points of interest. Pick up the trolley at Duval and Front Sts.

Mosquito Coast Island Outfitters & Kayak Guides (☎ 305-294-7178, 310 Duval St; trips $55) These four-hour, near-shore, natural-history and geology tours head to Sugarloaf Keys. Show up at their Lazy Dog shop at 8:45am, and the friendly folks will drive you to Sugarloaf, where you lazily paddle in single or double kayaks. The cost includes snorkel equipment, energy bars, bottled water and the guide.

PLACES TO STAY

Key West is packed with rooms, but picking the right one takes some forethought. Key West also has one hostel and one in-town campground. But B&Bs offer the most authentic Key West experience. Although a number of guest houses are exclusively gay and lesbian, all of the city's guest houses welcome gay and lesbian couples – hey, it's Key West.

Except for the hostel, plan on spending at least $85 in summer and $130 in winter. Room rates in all nonhostel accommodations are often negotiable and change with the crowds. It's usually cheaper midweek than on weekends. Most hotel booking agencies push prices to the limit of what the market will bear – a hotel room that rents for $120 on Saturday may be $50 on Sunday. And as a rule, prices drop about 40% in summer.

Camping
There's a $20 difference between staying right in town as opposed to just outside of town.

Boyd's Key West Campground (☎ 305-294-1465, 6401 Maloney Ave) Sites $35/41 nonwaterfront/waterfront off-season, $41/48 mid-Nov–mid-Apr; water and electricity $10. Just outside town on Stock Island (turn south at MM 5), Boyd's has upward of 300 sites. There's a bus stop for downtown practically at their front door.

Jabour's Camp & Lodge (☎ 305-294-5723, 223 Elizabeth St) Sites $46 off-season, $60 mid-Dec–mid-Apr, 4- to 6-person motor homes $57 off-season, $75 winter. The only campground actually in Key West is near Key West Bight.

Hostels
Key West Youth Hostel & SeaShell Motel (☎ 305-296-5719, W www.keywesthostel.com, 718 South St) Dorms $19.50/22.50 members/nonmembers, motel rooms $75 off-season, $110-150 Dec–mid-Apr. At the cheapest place in town, rates include sheets and use of the communal kitchen, but the hostel also sells cheap breakfasts and dinners. Alcohol is prohibited. Since a taxi between here and the main Greyhound station costs $7 per person, you'd be better off getting off at the downtown Key West stop (at Caroline and Grinnell Sts) and then calling a taxi, for about $4 per carload.

Motels & Hotels
Chain hotels include *Courtyard By Marriott* (☎ 305-294-5541, 3420 N Roosevelt Blvd); *Best Western Hibiscus* (☎ 305-294-3763, 1313 Simonton St at United St); *Days Inn* (☎ 305-294-3742, 3852 N Roosevelt Blvd), one of the cheapest places in town; *Radisson*

(☎ 305-294-5511, 3820 N Roosevelt Blvd); and *Crowne Plaza La Concha* (☎ 305-296-2991, 430 Duval St).

Spindrift Motel (☎ 305-296-3432, 800-501-7824, W www.keywestspindrift.com, 1212 Simonton St) Rooms $79-119 off-season, $119-189 late Dec–Apr. This perfectly average motel has 18 rooms.

Pegasus Hotel (☎ 305-294-9323, fax 305-294-4741, W www.pegasuskeywest.com, 501 Southard St) Rooms $95-129 off-season, $139-199 late Dec–late Apr. Well-situated, clean and friendly, this hotel has 25 guest rooms and the added benefits of a nice rooftop pool, deck, Jacuzzi and limited free parking.

Santa Maria Motel (☎ 305-296-5678, fax 305-294-0010, 1435 Simonton St) Rooms and efficiencies vary month-to-month: $89-129 June, $109-149 Oct, $215-245 Mar. This 51-unit motel has a nice pool; apartments have small kitchens.

Key Lodge Motel (☎ 305-296-9915, 800-458-1296, fax 305-292-4886, W www.stayinkeywest.com, 1004 Duval St) Rooms $99-120 Apr–mid-Dec, $209-229 mid-Feb–Mar. This 21-room motel has large, clean rooms, most of which have fridges and microwaves. Pluses include a heated pool and free parking.

Wyndham Casa Marina Resort & Beach House (☎ 305-296-3535, fax 305-296-4633, W www.casamarinakeywest.com, 1500 Reynolds St) Rooms $169-359 off-season, $169-409 late Dec–Mar, suites more. Next to Higgs Beach, this first-rate 311-room resort was built in the 1920s by railroad magnate Henry Flager. Of course he chose *the* prime location; the present-day resort has the Key West's largest private beach. Look for three oceanside pools, every recreational pursuit imaginable, a kid's program, daily activities and plenty of dining and entertainment choices. Guest rooms and suites have private balconies or terraces.

B&Bs
Unless otherwise noted, a Continental breakfast is included in the rates; it's usually served pool- or gardenside.

Southernmost Point Guesthouse (☎ 305-294-0715, fax 305-296-0641, W www.southern

mostpoint.com, 1327 Duval St) Rooms and efficiencies $65-105 off-season, $115-165 late Dec–Apr. This foofy 10-room Victorian house has large rooms (many of which have beds draped with mosquito netting and a heavy dose of air freshener) and a nice garden and porch.

The Mermaid & the Alligator *(☎ 305-294-1894, 800-773-1894, fax 305-295-9925, W www.kwmermaid.com, 729 Truman Ave)* Rooms $88-168 off-season, $118-228 late Dec–Apr. Casually elegant, this early-20th-century Victorian house has nine individually decorated rooms, lots of character, off-street parking, full breakfast, complementary evening wine and a small pool surrounded by tropical plantings and a charming brick patio. It's a very good choice.

Red Rooster *(☎ 305-296-6558, 800-845-0825, fax 305-296-4822, W www.redrooster inn.com, 709 Truman Ave)* Rooms $69-155 off-season, $120-195 late Dec–Apr. This gay-staffed place, with classical music piped throughout, was more famous in its last incarnation: It served as a notorious brothel whose wanton activities forced the nuns at St Mary's Church, across the street, to shade the windows so students couldn't peer across. It's been renovated and cleaned up, though a little of the former atmosphere remains. The staff is friendly, and the side garden and pool is quite nice.

Chelsea House *(☎ 305-296-2211, 800-845-8859, fax 305-296-4822, W www.chelsea housekw.com, 707 Truman Ave)* Rooms $79-190 off-season, $160-255 late Dec–Apr. With an atmosphere more akin to a college dorm than a traditional Victorian mansion, this 1870 house defies a 'gay' or 'straight' categorization. The majority of guests on any given day may be gay or straight – the Chelsea House welcomes all at this 18-room complex. Rooms have TV, air conditioning, fridge and bath. There's a clothing-optional sun deck, paperback library, free parking and brick paths that lead to a small pool and tropical garden.

Wicker Guesthouse *(☎ 305-296-4275, 800-880-4275, fax 305-294-7240, W www.wicker housekw.com, 913 Duval St)* Rooms $85-98 off-season, $130-150 mid-Dec–May, studios

& suites $105-135 off-season, $185-235 winter. Despite a location in the middle of everything, this modern 18-unit guest-house complex has a secluded garden, a nice pool and off-street parking. Wicker and wood furnishings abound. While some rooms have a kitchenette, there's also a shared kitchen. Rates for two-bedroom suites include four people.

Merlin Guesthouse *(☎ 305-296-3336, 800-642-4753, fax 305-296-3524, W www.merlinn keywest.com, 811 Simonton St)* Rooms $89-109 off-season, $135-169 late Dec–mid-Apr, suites & cottages $119-225 off-season, $169-300 late Dec–mid-Apr. Set in a secluded garden with a pool and elevated wooden walkways, this 20-room B&B boasts airy, light and very tidy guest rooms. Everything is made from bamboo, rattan and wood; many rooms have high ceilings or exposed rafters.

Frances St Bottle Inn *(☎ 305-294-8530, 800-294-8530, fax 305-294-1628, W www .bottleinn.com, 535 Frances St)* Rooms $80-135 off-season, $139-169 mid-Dec–Apr. Gay-friendly and with a welcoming staff, this small inn has eight updated rooms, very tidy and clean bathrooms, a two-story verandah and a small patio with hot tub. Cheaper rooms have a shared bath across the hall. Rental bikes are available.

Duval Gardens *(☎ 305-292-3379, 800-867-1234, fax 305-294-7470, W www.duval gardens.com, 1012 Duval St)* Units $109-159 off-season, $150-200 Jan–mid-Apr. This modest 10-room B&B with efficiencies and suites has lots of wicker and rattan, a Jacuzzi, a sun deck and a small pool.

Conch House Heritage Inn *(☎ 305-293-0020, fax 305-293-8447, W www.conchhouse .com, 625 Truman Ave)* Rooms $98-168 off-season, $148-228 Jan-Apr. Built in 1875 and family-owned since 1889, this six-room place with a small pool is very clean and nice. It's gay- and lesbian-friendly.

La Pensione *(☎ 305-292-9923, fax 305-296-6509, W www.lapensione.com, 809 Truman Ave)* Rooms $108-138 off-season, $168 Jan–mid-May. A very good value for the price, this elegant 1891 revival mansion has nine well-kept rooms and a friendly staff. A very full breakfast buffet taken on the verandah or in the communal dining room will stand you in good stead, as will the pool and off-street parking.

Andrews Inn (☎ 305-294-7730, fax 305-294-0021, ⓦ www.andrewsinn.com, Zero Whalton Lane) Rooms $115-149 off-season, $169-189 late Dec–Apr. Draws include a tranquil backyard, small pool, friendly hosts, lots of cats and a tropical feel; some of the six wicker-filled rooms have decks. Evening cocktails are included for inn guests.

The Gardens Hotel (☎ 305-294-2661, 800-526-2664, fax 305-292-1007, ⓦ www.gardens hotel.com, 526 Angela St) Rooms $155-285 off-season, $265-355 mid-Dec–Apr, suites at least $100 more. Occupying almost an entire city block, this walled, private and chichi enclave was formerly Key West's largest private residence. It boasts botanical-garden–quality grounds, a kidney-shaped pool and plantation-style houses. The 17 guest rooms are romantic, elegantly furnished, understated with floral motifs and filled with indulgent amenities. A full breakfast is included.

PLACES TO EAT

Even though Key West cuisine often takes a backseat to drinking, you'll find more than a few culinary delights here. Most restaurants offer reliably good food, fresh seafood and decent portions. Interestingly, a good percentage of that 'local' seafood comes from somewhere other than the Keys.

Gay Accommodations in Key West

Again, unless otherwise noted, a Continental breakfast is included in the rates; it's usually served pool- or gardenside.

Pearl's Rainbow (☎ 305-292-1450, 800-749-6696, ⓦ www.pearlsrainbow.com, 525 United St) Rooms & suites $69-199 off-season, $109-249 mid-Dec–Apr. Key West's only women-only place (gay or straight) is welcoming and well-maintained. The 38 rooms range from small third-floor cubbies to deluxe poolside suites with balconies. In addition to a popular bar (see the Entertainment section, later), look for two sun/shade decks, two pools and two hot tubs. Double the fun, eh?

Atlantic Shores Resort (☎ 305-296-2491, 800-526-3559, fax 305-294-2753, ⓦ www.atlantic shoresresort.com, 510 South St) Rooms $80-145 off-season, $110-250 Jan–late Apr. Defying a sexual-orientation categorization, all are welcome at this clean, motelish, faux-art-decoish place. It boasts a clothing-optional pool, popular tea dances (see the Entertainment section, later) and an adjacent liquor store, which pretty much sums up the emphasis at this resort. No breakfast here, folks.

Marrero's (☎ 305-294-6977, 800-459-6212, fax 305-292-9030, ⓦ www.marreros.com, 410 Fleming St) Rooms $90-170 off-season, $120-210 mid-Dec–Apr. This late-19th-century mansion, once owned by a prominent cigar manufacturer, has 13 rooms and suites. All are decorated quite differently, but you can expect high ceilings, antiques, wood floors and modern amenities like refrigerators and phones. Two verandahs and a large pool (clothing-optional area) are nice.

Curry House (☎ 305-294-6777, 800-633-7439, fax 305-294-5322, 806 Fleming St) Rooms $85-140 off-season, $140-190 mid-Dec–Apr. Key West's oldest exclusively gay men's guest house is housed in a 100-year-old, Victorian-style, three-story mansion. Two of the nine rooms have shared bath. Rates include a full hot breakfast and daily happy hour; there's a clothing-optional pool and Jacuzzi.

Big Rubys Guesthouse (☎ 305-296-2323, 800-477-7829, fax 305-296-0281, ⓦ www.big rubys.com, 409 Appelrouth Lane) Rooms $85-187 off-season, $145-255 mid-Dec–Mar. Upscale and sleek, in an Architectural Digest sort of way, this impeccable 17-room complex has a lagoon pool area with elegant decking and tropical palms, luxuriously full breakfasts, fine linens and lots of privacy. 'Low-key luxe' sums it up.

Budget

Java Lounge (☎ 305-296-7877, 622 Greene St) Referring to it as a lounge is a stretch; it's only big enough for a few patrons to order at a time. Still, for strong espresso and sweet treats, make a beeline here.

Waterfront Market (☎ 305-296-0778, 201 William St) Open 7am-6pm Sat-Thur, 7am-8pm Fri. Not simply a breakfast place, this market has bagels, coffee, sandwiches, organic produce, health foods, wine, beer and a juice bar. The dockside entrance doors open before the front entrance.

5 Brothers Grocery & Sandwich Shop (☎ 305-296-5205, 913 Southard St) Dishes $4-7. Open 6am-6pm Mon-Fri & 6am-5pm Sat. This local Cuban market has conch chowder, burgers and Cuban and pork sandwiches.

BO's Fish Wagon (☎ 305-294-9272, 801 Caroline St) Dishes $8-10. Open 11am-8pm Mon-Sat, 11am-5pm Sun. For fried fish, catch-of-the-day, grilled sandwiches and a cool atmosphere, BO's is your place.

Mid-Range

The Deli Restaurant (☎ 305-294-1464, 531 Truman Ave) Lunch $5-10, dinner mains $7-20. Open 7:30am-10pm. For friendly service and well-prepared 'comfort food,' head to this biscuit-and-corn-bread sort of place. A local hangout, operated by the same family since 1950, it serves killer breakfasts, filling seafood dishes and meatloaf. Vegetarians can pile on side dishes like mashed potatoes, rice and beans, zucchini, carrots and other veggies.

Camille's (☎ 305-296-4811, 1202 Simonton St) Breakfast $3-7, lunch $6-12, dinner $14-25. Open 8am-3pm, 4pm-10:30pm. An island fave since forever, Camille's is packed all day because of good, friendly service and creative dishes. Breakfast is particularly renowned; lunchtime salads are refreshing; dinner specials are always fresh. During the afternoon happy hour (4pm to 6pm), you can only get light fare like burgers and sandwiches.

Mo's Restaurant (☎ 305-296-8955, 1116 White St) Lunch $5-7, dinner mains $10-14. Open 11:30am-3pm & 5pm-10pm Mon-Fri. Good service and inexpensive, well-prepared meals (from sandwiches to casseroles to leg of lamb) abound. It's a little small (let's call it intimate), and you may have to wait a while for a table on weekends, but if you'd rather dine with locals than tourists, who cares.

PT's Late Night (☎ 305-296-4245, 920 Caroline St) Lunch $7-9, dinner mains $9-16. Open 11am-3am. When they say late night, they mean it. When you're finished drinking and have worked up a good appetite, PT's serves hearty portions of diner fare, salads and nachos. As much sports bar as eatery, burger aficionados will nonetheless be quite pleased.

El Siboney (☎ 305-296-4184, 900 Catherine St) Dishes $5-13. Open 11am-9:30pm Mon-Sat. Sure, authentic Cuban cuisine can be found in Miami's Little Havana, but in Key West? Yup. Ignore the unstylish environs to dine on large portions, with locals, at this family-style place. Catch some Old Key West flavor while it's still here.

Turtle Kraals Restaurant & Bar (☎ 305-294-2640, 1 Land's End Village) Lunch dishes $6-11, dinner mains $10-18. Open 11am-10:30pm Mon-Fri, noon-11pm Sat & Sun. A rustic marina-front eatery housed in an open-air warehouse, Turtle Kraals specializes in fish prepared with a Cuban-Caribbean-Southwestern twist. It's popular with locals as well as tourists. Try the excellent mango crab cakes with fried plantains, mojo grilled shrimp or lobster chili rellenos. Lunch is more simple, with, perhaps, a char-grilled fish sandwich.

Kelly's (☎ 305-293-8484, 301 Whitehead St) Lunch dishes $6-11, dinner mains $12-23. Open noon-4pm & 5pm-10pm. Kelly's is a cool bar and grill owned by actress Kelly McGillis (who sometimes works here). The restaurant is housed in the former home of Pan American Airways. The first Pan Am flight (001) departed to Havana, Cuba, from here on October 27, 1927. It has prime outdoor tables, its own brewery, decent lunch specials, a raw bar and a tapas-style menu. Yeah, it's a bit touristy, but it'll admirably satisfy most everyone.

Banana Café (☎ 305-294-7227, 1211 Duval St) Breakfast and lunch $5-12, dinner mains $14-25. Open 8am-3pm daily, 7pm-

11pm Wed-Sun. From scrambled eggs with vegetables at breakfast (served all day), to lunchtime crêpes, to steamed salmon and beef tenderloin at dinner, Banana Café has something for everyone. There's also live jazz on Wednesday and Thursday nights.

Pepe's Cafe *(☎ 305-294-7192, 806 Caroline St)* Lunch dishes under $10, dinner mains $17-20. Open 6:30am-10:30pm. Key West's oldest restaurant dates back to 1909. It's a rustic institution with a great locals' bar and outdoor patio – perfect for margaritas made with fresh-squeezed lime juice. As for the food, the barbecue specials on Sunday night are primo, as are the oysters, burgers and steaks. Lunch revolves around soups, sandwiches, chili and conch chowder. The breakfasts are huge.

Mangia Mangia *(☎ 305-294-2469, 900 Southard St)* Mains $10-16. Open 5:30pm-10pm. Popular among locals, this small spot is one of the absolute best places for cheap, homemade pastas, but the seafood specials are also very fresh.

Top End
Consistency tops the attributes of these fine places.

Mangoes *(☎ 305-292-4606, 700 Duval St)* Lunch mains $8-15, dinner mains $15-30. Open 11am-3:30pm & 5:30pm-11pm. At first glance, you might expect the brick patio on Duval to be Mangoes' best feature; it could probably get away with it. But Mangoes is far better than that. It delivers upscale, creative Florida cooking with a sprinkling of Caribbean influence. The wood-fired pizzas served at dinner are very good, too.

Bagatelle *(☎ 305-296-6609, 115 Duval St)* Lunch dishes $7-14, dinner mains $17-24. Open 11:30am-3:30pm & 5pm-10:30pm. Within a late-19th-century sea captain's house, this romantic dining room features a blow-the-budget surf-and-turf ($47) and lots of Florida fish prepared with tropical overtones. Lunchtime salads are quite good. Even though it's a tad touristy, the second-floor balcony perch always affords good people-watching.

Alice's *(☎ 305-296-6706, 1125 Duval St)* Mains $20-27. Open 6pm-11pm. Chef-owned

Alice's restaurant wins rave reviews hand over fist for its creative, eclectic menu. Patrons have been singing her praises for years and follow her to the ends of the earth (ie, around Key West). You will too.

Louie's Backyard *(☎ 305-294-1061, 700 Waddell Ave)* Lunch $15, dinner $30. Open 11:30am-3:30pm & 6pm-10:30pm. Started by a Conch in his house, Louie's is one of Key West's most popular places, as much for its romantic location, location, location as its excellent and highly creative Caribbean-American cuisine. In fact, the setting is as much a feast for the eyes as the seafood is for the stomach. If your wallet can't take it, though, at least have a drink at the waterfront bar (it closes at 2am). You'll remember it for years.

Cafe des Artistes *(☎ 305-294-7100, 1007 Simonton St)* Mains $25-35. Open 6pm-9pm. Tired of seafood, however flawlessly prepared, in rustic surroundings? A treat for serious foodies, this longtime nouveau French restaurant is arguably the best in Key West. Daily specials are always creative and often tropically influenced; perhaps you'll find sautéed yellowtail snapper with shrimp and scallops or raspberry duckling. With a little luck, you'll snag a table on the rooftop deck.

ENTERTAINMENT
Theater
Stop in at the Chamber of Commerce to see what's going at the ***Tennessee Williams Fine Arts Center***, the ***Waterfront*** or the ***San Carlos*** theaters.

Red Barn Theatre *(☎ 305-296-9911, 319 Duval St)* Tickets $25. This tiny little playhouse has staged a variety of well-known and original plays and comedies since the mid-1980s.

Bars & Live Music
Drinking is a Key West institution with a long and illustrious history of lushes, from rumrunners (the people, not the drink) to Hemingway. And the tradition is immortalized in Jimmy Buffet's song 'Margaritaville.' Spring break (mid-March) is a big deal here. Pub crawls are another institution, but

FLORIDA KEYS

The Secret of Key Lime Pie

No person who considers him- or herself a true Conch (Key West native) would ever give out their secret recipe for Key lime pie, but Kim Dyer went to an awful lot of trouble to compile all the recipes she could find and publish them (believe it or not) in a FAQ on an Internet newsgroup for Jimmy Buffet fans. Thanks, Kim!

We've gone with the simple, basic 'Key Lime Pie: Variant No 1.'

9-inch pie crust:

1 cup flour (Wondra if possible)   ⅓ cup and 1 tbsp shortening
½ tsp salt   3 tbsp cold water

Combine flour, salt and shortening, then while still mixing, add water. Roll out dough onto a floured board and bake in a pie pan in a preheated 375°F oven for 10 minutes or until lightly brown.

Filling:

1½ cups sugar   2 tbsp cornstarch
Juice from 1½ Key limes*   2 tbsp flour
Grated peel of one lime   2 cups milk (yes, milk)
3 eggs   1 tbsp butter

Combine all this and then cook in a double boiler – not on direct heat, or it will burn – and stir until thickened, about 20 to 25 minutes.

Meringue:

5 tbsp sugar   3 egg whites
1 tbsp cornstarch   ½ tsp cream of tartar
½ cup water

Combine 2 tbsp sugar, cornstarch and water. Cook on direct heat until it thickens and becomes clear. Set aside. Combine the egg whites with the 3 tbsp sugar and the cream of tartar and mix with an electric beater on high until smooth. Add the cooked sugar, water and cornstarch, and beat the entire mixture until fluffy.

Add filling to the pie crust, then pile on the meringue. Bake at 300°F for 10 minutes, then at 350°F until the meringue browns. Cool and serve.

*If you can't get Key limes, the next best option is to buy some Key lime juice through a company such as Key West Aloe (☎ 305-294-5592, ⓦ www.keywestaloe.com) – a 16oz bottle costs $4.20 (add $6.95 shipping). Failing that, use a mixture that's half lemon juice and half lime juice.

bar owners freaked out when police enforced the open-container laws hindering customers from walking between bars carrying drinks. Enforcement isn't as gung-ho now, but it is illegal to walk with an open container holding an alcoholic drink – even if it's in a plastic cup.

Most bars have live music most nights; happy hours and drink specials happen all the time. Bars stay open until people leave, at least until 2am and sometimes later. These watering holes are the most legendary.

Sloppy Joe's Bar (☎ *305-294-5717, 201 Duval St*) The Hemingway hangout of record, since 1937, has live entertainment nightly. Their Hemingway Hammer is made from 151-proof rum, banana and strawberry liqueur, blackberry brandy and a dash of white rum.

Margaritaville Café (☎ 305-292-1435, 500 Duval St) Jimmy Buffet's very touristy place mixes its requisite namesake drink (there are better elsewhere), serves the requisite 'cheeseburgers in paradise' (there are better elsewhere) and puts on nightly bands. But, hey, Parrotheads will be Parrotheads.

Schooner Wharf Bar (☎ 305-292-9520, 202 William St) With a fairly authentic 'sailor's bar' feeling, this real Conch hangout is great for waterside-sunset or post-cruise drinks. Local musicians – playing everything from banjos to reggae – perform nightly.

Rick's/Durty Harry's (☎ 305-296-4890, 202/208 Duval St) This joint has nine bars and nightly live music that draws faithful tourists. People really like this meat market, and not just for their Wednesday and Thursday night specials: For $7 (low season) or $10 (high season) you get a wristband allowing you to drink all you can from 9pm to 11:30pm (bring your ID). If you can maneuver the stairs, *Upstairs at Rick's* has dancing.

Billie's Bar (☎ 305-294-9292, 407 Front St) Open until 4am when it's busy. Billie's sunset happy hour has wicked-cheap draft, domestic beers and well drinks.

Captain Tony's Saloon (☎ 305-294-1838, 428 Greene St) This old-fashioned saloon features live music almost daily and nightly.

Green Parrot (☎ 305-294-6133, 601 Whitehead St) Open to the street, this locals' bar has been pickling its patron's livers with booze since 1890. Yup, this is what Key West is all about.

Gay & Lesbian Venues

The 'straight,' serious-drinking and partying section of town runs from Mallory Square to the 500 block of Duval St. From then on, it's a healthy mix of straight and gay. Gay and lesbian bars change as quickly as they do in Miami's South Beach, so ask around when you arrive. Check the Key West Business Guild's map and *Key West*

Columbia Fun Map, available at local gay-friendly businesses.

Atlantic Shores Resort (☎ 305-296-2491, 510 South St) This popular local spot for men and women and au naturel sunning has a small snack bar, grill, pool, beach and Key West's largest tea dance on Sunday (7pm to 11pm). It's so popular that they added one on Wednesday, too (6pm to 10pm). And don't forget their Thursday night outdoor movies.

Donnie's Club International (☎ 305-294-2655, 900 Simonton St) This locals' bar has a long happy hour (noon to 7pm) and Tuesday night pool tourneys (7pm).

Bourbon St Pub (no ☎, 724 Duval St) With three bars, this place dishes hot dancing, nightly videos and good 2nd-floor people-watching down onto Duval St.

801 Bourbon Bar (no ☎, 801 Duval St) This great hangout has three bars, the island's longest happy hour (from noon to 8pm) and nightly drag and cabaret shows (11pm).

La Te Da (☎ 305-296-6706, 1125 Duval St) Locals head over for the happy hour, live entertainment Thursday to Sunday and a few different bars.

Pearl's Rainbow (☎ 305-292-1450, 525 United St) This outdoor patio bar, within a guest house, is Key West's only women-only bar.

SHOPPING

There is so much tourist stuff that you won't be able to avoid it. But hidden among the crud and T-shirt shops are some much cooler galleries and shops, including *Helio Gallery* (☎ 305-294-7901, 814 Fleming St), *Haitian Art Co* (☎ 305-296-8932, 600 Frances St), *Key West Lime Shoppe* (☎ 800-376-0806, cnr Greene & Elizabeth Sts), *Pandemonium* (☎ 305-294-0351, 825 Duval St), *Key West Cigar Factory* (☎ 305-294-3470, 306 Front St) and *Key West Aloe* (☎ 305-294-5592, 524 Front St). You might want to procure a pair of Kino sandals, the classic Key West footwear. These Naugahyde sandals are slippery when wet, but they're cheap. If they ever break, bring them in and they'll be repaired.

GETTING THERE & AWAY
Air
Key West International Airport (EYK) is off S Roosevelt Blvd on the west side of the island. Expect to spend $150 to $180 for a roundtrip flight between Miami and Key West. With a little luck and good timing, you can get a direct, roundtrip flight between New York City and Key West for as low as $300. Flights from LA ($350 in summer, $575 in winter) and San Francisco ($400 year-round) usually have to stop in Tampa, Orlando or Miami first.

American Airlines (☎ 800-433-7300) and US Airways (☎ 800-428-4322) all have several flights a day. Cape Air (☎ 305-352-0714, 800-352-0714, W www.flycapeair.com) flies between Key West and Naples ($109/160-200 one-way/roundtrip), Fort Myers ($118/180-230) and Fort Lauderdale ($129/170-230).

Bus
Based at the Key West Airport, Greyhound (☎ 305-296-9072, W www.greyhound.com), 3535 S Roosevelt Blvd, has four buses daily between Key West and downtown Miami. Buses leave Key West at 6am (arriving at 10:55am), 8:45am (arriving 1:40pm), 11:30am (arriving 4:25pm) and 5:45pm (arriving 10:40pm). Fares are $32.25 weekdays; a tad more on weekends.

Car & Motorcycle
The 160 miles (3½ hours) from Miami to Key West along US Hwy 1 is as much the journey as the destination. Seriously. Take Florida's Turnpike Extension (toll) south and then pick up US Hwy 1 south at Florida City. Don't be in a hurry; enjoy the views. Besides, there are keenly enforced speed limits, high speeding fines, and you might hit a Key deer while speeding (see National Key Deer Refuge, in the Lower Keys section).

GETTING AROUND
A city bus (75¢) runs between the airport and Duval and Caroline Sts every 40 minutes or so; take the blue route into Old Town. A taxi from the airport to the city will cost about $7.

The City Transit System (☎ 305-292-8160, W www.keywestcity.com) has six color-coded bus routes. Depending on the route, buses run every 15 minutes or so, from about 6:30am to 10pm. Printed schedules are available on the bus and from the Web site, under transportation. The fare is 75¢ for adults, 35¢ for seniors.

The best thing to do with a car in Key West is to sell it: Parking is tough, the city is quick to ticket and tow, and traffic is restricted. Look for the main public-parking garage, at Caroline and Grinnell Sts ($1.25 hourly/$8 daily).

You don't need a license to rent a moped or scooter; prices average $18 a day (9am to 5pm or 6pm) or $25 for 24 hours. Try Keys Mopeds & Scooters (☎ 305-294-0399), 523 Truman Ave, or Moped Hospital (☎ 305-296-3344), 601 Truman Ave.

Bicycle rentals are also available many places, where prices average $10 daily, but the Key West Youth Hostel rents them for a bit less ($6 daily, $8 for 24 hours).

Dry Tortugas National Park

The Dry Tortugas (tor-**too**-guzz), a tiny archipelago of seven islands about 69 miles southwest of Key West, was first 'developed' 300 years after its discovery by Juan Ponce de León. He named it Las Tortugas (the Turtles) for the hawksbill, green, leatherback and loggerhead sea turtles that roam the islands. Sailors later changed it to Dry Tortugas, since there was no freshwater here. Today it's a national park under the control of the Everglades National Park office (☎ 305-242-7700, W www.nps.gov/drto). You can only reach it by boat or plane.

Since the island was surrounded by rocky shoals, the first item of business was to build a lighthouse at **Garden Key**. When the US saw a need to protect and control the traffic flowing into the Gulf of Mexico, they began constructing **Fort Jefferson** in 1846. A federal garrison during the Civil War, Fort Jefferson was also a prison for Union deserters and for at least four people, among them Dr Samuel Mudd, arrested for complicity in the assassination of Abraham Lincoln. In 1867, a yellow-fever outbreak killed 38 people, and after a hurricane in 1873, the fort was abandoned. It reopened in 1886 as a quarantine station for smallpox and cholera victims. Although it was declared a national monument in 1935 by President Roosevelt, George Bush Sr upped its status to a National Park in 1992.

The park is open for day trips and overnight camping, which provides a rare perspective – it's so close to the hubbub of Key West and yet so blissfully removed and peaceful. The sparkling waters offer excellent **snorkeling and diving** opportunities. A visitor's center is located within the fascinating Fort Jefferson.

PLACES TO STAY & EAT

Garden Key has 13 *campsites* ($3 per person, per night) given out on a first-come, first-served basis. Reserve early by calling the Everglades National Park office (☎ 305-242-7700, ⓦ www.nps.gov/drto). There are toilets, but no freshwater showers or drinking water; bring everything you'll need.

Since there is no freshwater, mosquitoes will not mar your trip. Even no-see-ums, tiny biting flies, are kept at bay most of the time; they only come out for about 15 minutes prior to sunset.

As for *food*, most of the time you'll find Cuban-American fishing boats trolling the waters. They'll happily trade for lobster, crab and shrimp; you'll have the most leverage trading beverages. Paddle up to them and start bargaining for your supper. In March and April, there is stupendous bird watching, including aerial fighting. Stargazing is mind-blowing any time of the year.

GETTING THERE & AWAY

If you have your own boat, the Dry Tortugas are covered under National Ocean Survey chart No 11438.

Otherwise, the experienced and knowledgeable crew of the *Yankee Freedom II* (☎ 305-294-7009, 800-634-0939, ⓦ www.yankeefreedom.com) operates a fast ferry between Garden Key and the Key West Seaport (at the northern end of Margaret St). Roundtrip fare costs $109/99/69 adult/senior/child under 16 yrs. For an overnight drop-off (including gear), the cost is $130/99 adult/child. Board at the marina at 7:30am (the ferry leaves at 8am), and return at 5:30pm. Reservations are recommended. Continental breakfast, a picnic lunch, snorkeling gear and a 45-minute tour of the fort are all included.

If you don't have gear, the extraordinarily excellent folks at Dry Tortugas Kayak Outfitters (☎ 305-296-3009) rent first-rate kayaks and sometimes tents, coolers, grills etc. Prices depend on how much gear you need.

Seaplanes of Key West (☎ 305-294-0709, ⓦ www.seaplanesofkeywest.com) can take up to 10 passengers (flight time 40 minutes each way). A four-hour trip costs $179/129 adult/child under 12 yrs, and an eight-hour trip costs $305/225. They'll also fly you out to camp for $329/235 per person, including snorkeling equipment; reserve at least a week in advance.

Southeast Florida

Between the hubbub of Miami and the Right Stuff of the Space Coast lie some of Florida's most famous – and infamous – beaches. To be sure, you'll find a lot of opulence: from the USA's yachting capital in Fort Lauderdale to the staggering (even swaggering) mansions at Palm Beach, this is a moneyed area.

But it's also very accessible. Even the most exclusive places are usually polite to travelers, and you can find ways to experience the glamour vicariously without paying through the nose. For instance, you can window-shop on Palm Beach's Worth Ave (looking at $600 pants!) and still find a motel room for $70 in southern West Palm Beach or Lake Worth. You can get great Thai food for under $7 in West Palm Beach and loll on Fort Lauderdale's spiffy beaches while spending no more than $16 for a bed.

The natural coastal gems lie between Stuart and north Palm Beach, where pristine wilderness awaits in state parks and the Hobe Sound National Wildlife Refuge. The area is wide open for exploration and a wonderful way to get away from golf courses, developments and highways. You can also kayak around St Lucie Inlet State Park, canoe along the Loxahatchee River and camp in Jonathan Dickinson State Park.

And finally, Florida's southeast coast has a prize of such value, such eminence…well, you simply *must* snap a photograph of the world headquarters of the *National Enquirer* in Lantana.

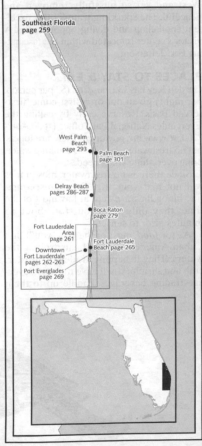

Southeast Florida
page 259

West Palm Beach
page 293

Palm Beach
page 301

Delray Beach
pages 286-287

Boca Raton
page 279

Fort Lauderdale Area
page 261

Fort Lauderdale Beach page 265

Downtown Fort Lauderdale
pages 262-263

Port Everglades
page 269

Fort Lauderdale & the Southeast Coast

FORT LAUDERDALE
pop 152,000
As recently as the mid-1980s, Fort Lauderdale was the unofficial spring break capital of the country. At the peak, more

American university students partook of this rite of passage in Fort Lauderdale than anywhere else in the country. The sand was sticky from beer, and the streets were full of students drinking cheap drafts until they passed out. But since the late '80s, the town has divested itself completely of this scene. In essence, it's been outlawed. And the powers that be have done an exceedingly good job at renovating and grooming the whole place.

That's not to say this is not a partying town. There are dozens of clubs, pubs and beach nightspots, where you should dress respectably and behave yourself. These days, though, Fort Lauderdale is known more as an international yachting center than a party spot. Ships owned around the world are built and repaired here; huge yachts winter here; and some of the wealthiest European, Asian and American sailors can be seen fussing over details with the city's countless support staff.

Fort Lauderdale has some worthy cultural and historical sites (especially the museum of art) and lovely areas for walking – notably the district along E Las Olas Blvd and Riverwalk. There's also the Hugh Taylor Birch State Recreation Area and a river cruise to provide natural distractions.

History

Small bands of Indians lived in this region for about 4000 years before the arrival of the Spanish in the 16th century. During the early period of Spanish control and the later occupation of Florida by the British, fighting between the Europeans and Indian groups on the west coast of Florida kept settlers at bay. But during the second era of Spanish rule, European settlers slowly began to gain a regional foothold. In 1821 the USA took control of Florida, and by 1825, families had settled on the north banks of the New River.

In 1836, in the midst of the Second Seminole War, Seminoles attacked the Cooley family residence, killing all but Mr Cooley, who was away. The Cooley Massacre, a milestone in the city's history, led Major William Lauderdale (for whom the city is named)

SOUTHEAST FLORIDA

ATLANTIC OCEAN

St Lucie Inlet
St Lucie Inlet State Park
Hobe Sound National Wildlife Refuge
Jupiter Island
Jonathan Dickinson State Park
Tequesta
Jupiter Inlet
Jupiter
Juno Beach
North Palm Beach
John D MacArthur State Park
Palm Beach Shores
Riviera Beach
West Palm Beach
Palm Beach
Lake Worth
Palm Beach Institute of Contemporary Art
Lantana
Boynton Beach
Delray Beach
Morikami Gardens
Boca Raton
Deerfield Beach
Pompano Beach
Lauderdale-by-the-Sea
Fort Lauderdale
Dania Beach
Hollywood
Hallandale
North Miami Beach

To Kennedy Space Center
Fort Pierce
Hutchinson Island
Stuart
Hobe Sound
Loxahatchee River
West Palm Beach Canal
Loxahatchee National Wildlife Refuge
Hillsboro Canal
Davie
To Miami
To Miami

Intracoastal Waterway
St Lucie Canal
Florida Turnpike (toll)
Sawgrass Expwy (toll)

0   8   16 km
0   5   10 miles

SOUTHEAST

and troops from the Tennessee Volunteers to establish a fort and stockade here in 1838.

White settlement remained stagnant until the 1870s, but by the 1890s Fort Lauderdale was large enough to support a post office, and ferry and stagecoach services. Frank Stranahan established the city's first lodge.

The real boom came with the introduction of the Florida East Coast Railroad, connecting Miami, Fort Lauderdale and St Augustine with the rest of the eastern seaboard. Immigrant groups, including large numbers of Danes, Swedes and Japanese, moved in. In 1925, Port Everglades was established – just in time for the mid-1920s bust and the 1926 hurricane, which killed dozens of people and wiped out thousands of acres.

As with Miami, WWII provided just the boost Fort Lauderdale needed. The public display of the captured German ship *Arauca* in Port Everglades served as a rallying point, and area German submarine maneuvers led to the establishment of military bases, which brought new settlers and money after the war. Prosperity grew during the 1970s construction boom, which also attracted hundreds of thousands of college students for spring break. The ritual of getting plastered as cheaply as possible was outlawed locally in the mid-1980s. Friendly police presence keeps things in order.

The days of spring break in Fort Lauderdale are gone baby, gone.

Orientation

Fort Lauderdale is set in a grid wherever physically possible (it's hard with all the water), and it's divided into three distinct sections: the beach, east of the Intracoastal Waterway; downtown, on the mainland; and Port Everglades, the cruise port south of the city.

US Hwy 1 (also called Federal Hwy) cuts through downtown, swooping under E Las Olas Blvd. Highway A1A runs along the ocean, where it's also called Atlantic Blvd (south of Sunrise Blvd) or Ocean Blvd (north of Sunrise Blvd). At its southern end, Atlantic Blvd merges into Seabreeze Blvd, and Seabreeze continues south until the curve where it becomes 17th St. The whole stretch is also known as, simply, Hwy A1A.

Streets and addresses are prefixed N, S, E or W according to their relation to Broward Blvd and Andrews Ave; Broward Blvd is the line dividing north from south, and Andrews Ave, just west of Federal Hwy, divides east from west.

The main arteries between downtown and the beach are Sunrise Blvd to the north, E Las Olas Blvd in the center and 17th St/Seabreeze Blvd to the south (Seabreeze connects the beach to Port Everglades).

Between the beach and the mainland are almost two dozen small finger islands. This is yacht country, perhaps the yacht capital of North America, and you'll notice a mooring at every house. Along with yachts, of course, come the millionaires who putter around on them. If you're waterborne, cruise by Millionaire's Row on the New River, just west of the Intracoastal Waterway – that's south of E Las Olas Blvd, west of Las Olas Isles and east of downtown.

You can easily walk 'downtown' Lauderdale-by-the-Sea. E Commercial Blvd is the town's main east-west artery, and Ocean Dr (Hwy A1A) is the main north-south route. The pier is at the end of Commercial Blvd at El Mar Dr, one block east of Ocean Dr.

Information

The excellent Greater Fort Lauderdale Convention & Visitor's Bureau (☎ 954-765-4466,

800-227-8669, W www.sunny.org), 1850 Eller Dr, is in Port Everglades. It's open 8:30am to 5pm weekdays. The CVB deliberately blurs Lauderdale neighborhood boundaries, marketing the region as a package to entice more visitors. For this reason, many pamphlets list hotels, attractions and events in the entire region within a Fort Lauderdale context.

The Lauderdale-by-the-Sea Chamber of Commerce (☎ 954-776-1000, 800-699-6764), 4201 Ocean Dr, is located in the middle of the triangle formed by the intersection of Ocean and Bougainvillea Drs. It's open 8:30am to 5pm weekdays, 9am to 3pm weekends.

The Gay & Lesbian Community Center (☎ 954-463-9005, W www.glccftl.org), 1717 N Andrews Ave, north of downtown, is quite helpful and friendly.

The main post office, 1900 W Oakland Park Blvd, is west of I-95.

Clark's Out of Town News (☎ 954-467-1543), 303 S Andrews Ave, in downtown, and the City News Stand (☎ 954-776-0940), 4400 Bougainvillea Dr, in Lauderdale-by-the-Sea, carry out-of-town and foreign newspapers. Clark's even has some travel books. Bluewater Books & Charts (☎ 954-763-6533), 1481 SE 17th St, in downtown, has an excellent selection of nautical books and charts.

The *Sun Sentinel* and the *Miami Herald* are the major area-dailies. *City Link* (W www .clo-sfl.com) is a good local weekly covering music, clubs, restaurants, art and other entertainment. *Hot Spots* covers the gay and lesbian club scene; pick it up at gay bars, clubs and guest houses.

The Broward County main public library (☎ 954-357-7444, W www.broward.org/ library) is at 100 S Andrews Ave in downtown; it has free Internet access. The library is open 9am to 9pm Monday to Thursday, 9am to 5pm Friday and Saturday, and noon to 5:30pm Sunday.

The largest public hospital in the area is Broward General Medical Center (☎ 954-355-4400), 1600 S Andrews Ave, in Port Everglades.

Downtown Fort Lauderdale

Museum of Art This museum (☎ 954-525-5500, W *www.museumofart.org, 1 E Las*

FORT LAUDERDALE AREA

1 Village Pump
2 Baja Beach Club
3 Main Post Office
4 Gay & Lesbian
   Community Center
5 Beach Hostel
6 Deauville Inn

SOUTHEAST

Olas Blvd; admission $10/8/5 adult/senior/student & child over 12 yrs; open 10am-5pm Tues-Sat, noon-5pm Sun) is simply one of Florida's best. The impressive permanent collection includes works by Pablo Picasso, Henri Matisse, Henry Moore, Salvador Dali, Frank Stella and Andy Warhol. Since the enormity of the collection far outpaces the available space, you never really know what will be showing. Don't overlook the growing and impressive collections of Cuban, ethnographic, African and South American art.

Museum of Discovery & Science Fronted by the 52-foot Great Gravity Clock, Florida's largest kinetic-energy sculpture, this environmentally oriented museum *(☎ 954-467-6637, ⓦ www.mods.org, 401 SW 2nd St; admission $14/13/12 adult/senior & student/child; open 10am-5pm Mon-Sat, noon-6pm Sun)* is one of Florida's best (of its genre). The admission price also includes one **IMAX** 3D show in the impressive five-story theater, which boasts wraparound sound. Before leaving, check out the **parabolic display** across the street: Two dishes face each other

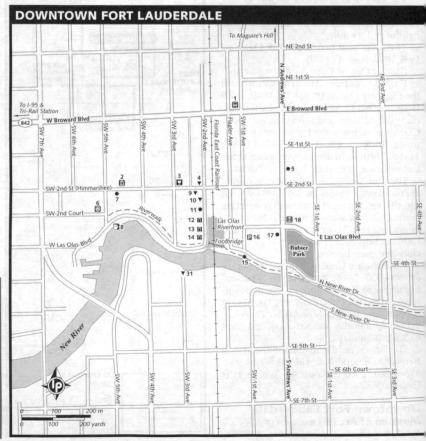

DOWNTOWN FORT LAUDERDALE

about 60 feet apart. Turn toward one dish and have a friend turn toward the other. Whisper into the dish, and you'll hear each other perfectly.

Fort Lauderdale Historical Society This organization *(219 SW 2nd Ave, W www.oldfortlauderdale.org)* maintains the 1905 **New River Inn** *(☎ 954-463-4431, 231 SW 2nd Ave; admission $5/2 adult/child 6-16 yrs; open noon-5pm Tues-Fri)*, the **Philemon Bryan House** (1905; not open to the public) and the nearby **King-Cromartie**

House (1907), which is only open for tours, at 1pm, 2pm and 3pm on Saturday. The museum mounts exhibits on Fort Lauderdale and Broward County history and Seminole folk art.

Riverwalk This meandering pathway *(☎ 954-468-1541, W www.goriverwalk.com)*, along the New River, runs from the Stranahan House to the Broward Center for the Performing Arts. It's very pleasant and lovely, and connects a number of sights.

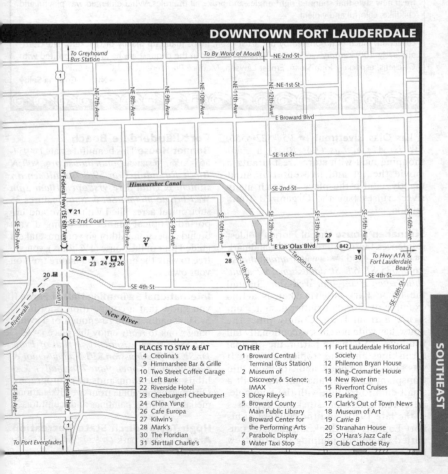

DOWNTOWN FORT LAUDERDALE

PLACES TO STAY & EAT	OTHER	11 Fort Lauderdale Historical
4 Creolina's	1 Broward Central	Society
9 Himmarshee Bar & Grille	Terminal (Bus Station)	12 Philemon Bryan House
10 Two Street Coffee Garage	2 Museum of	13 King-Cromartie House
21 Left Bank	Discovery & Science;	14 New River Inn
22 Riverside Hotel	IMAX	15 Riverfront Cruises
23 Cheeburger! Cheeburger!	3 Dicey Riley's	16 Parking
24 China Yung	5 Broward County	17 Clark's Out of Town News
26 Cafe Europa	Main Public Library	18 Museum of Art
27 Kilwin's	6 Broward Center for	19 Carrie B
28 Mark's	the Performing Arts	20 Stranahan House
30 The Floridian	7 Parabolic Display	25 O'Hara's Jazz Cafe
31 Shirttail Charlie's	8 Water Taxi Stop	29 Club Cathode Ray

SOUTHEAST

Highlights of the Museum of Art

Be sure to seek out the following artworks:

African Art The theme of the African art collection is harmony, and many of the pieces are religious, ceremonial or spiritual. The mask collection is fascinating. The detailed explanations of the pieces are very good as well.

CoBrA The museum's CoBrA collection (CoBrA is an acronym for Copenhagen, Brussels and Amsterdam, the cities where the movement originated) is the largest in the US. It was donated by Meyer and Golda Marks, who fell in love with the work in the 1960s and began procuring all they could. The movement emerged just after WWII and was led by Karel Appel, Asger Jorn and Cornelis Van Beverloo (Cornielle). These artists, disenchanted with what they felt to be the restrictive art schools of the day – mainly cubism, De Stijl and other geometric abstractionism – developed a fresh new style that shunned right angles and broke all the rules. What emerged was playful and childlike, colorful and violent.

Glackens The works of William Glackens (1870–1938) are the jewels in the museum's crown. The collection, much of it donated by the artist's son, Ira, is made up mainly of Glackens' late-19th- and early-20th-century works. Other works included in the bequest are by artists associated with Glackens, especially John Sloan, Ernest Lawson, Maurice Prendergast and George Luks.

– Nick & Corinna Selby

Las Olas Riverfront (☎ 954-522-6556, SW 1st Ave at Las Olas Blvd), a giant shopping mall with stores, restaurants, a movie theater and live entertainment nightly, is also the place to catch many river cruises (see the Organized Tours section, later).

Stranahan House One of Florida's oldest residences, this registered historic landmark (☎ 954-524-4736, W www.stranahanhouse .com, 335 SE 6th St; admission $5/2 adult/ child; open 10am-4pm Wed-Sun), behind the Hyde Park supermarket, is a fine example of Florida frontier design. Constructed from Dade County pine, the house has wide porches, exceptionally tall windows, a Victorian parlor, the original furnishings and fine tropical gardens. It was built as the home and store for Ohio transplant Frank Stranahan, who built a small empire trading with the Seminole. After real-estate and stock-market losses in the late 1920s, and the collapse of his Fort Lauderdale Bank, Stranahan committed suicide by jumping into the New River.

Fort Lauderdale Beach

Bonnet House This beautiful estate (☎ 954-563-5393, W www.bonnethouse.org, 900 N Birch Rd; admission $9/8/7 adult/senior/ student & child 6-18 yrs; open 10am-3pm Wed-Fri, noon-4pm Sat & Sun) features 35 subtropical acres filled with native and imported tropical plants, including a vast orchid collection. Although you must take a guided tour of the house (1¼ hours), you are free to walk the grounds and nature trails on your own.

International Swimming Hall of Fame If you know that a competition pool holds 573,000 gallons, you're enough of a swimming wonk to *really* enjoy this place (☎ 954-462-6536, W www.ishof.org, 1 Hall of Fame Dr/SE 5th St; admission $3/1/5 adult/senior & student/family; open 9am-7pm daily). Exhibits include thousands of photographs, Olympic memorabilia from over 100 nations, medals, uniforms, paintings and sculptures.

Hugh Taylor Birch State Recreation Area This state park (☎ 954-564-4521, 3109 E Sunrise Blvd; admission $4 per vehicle of

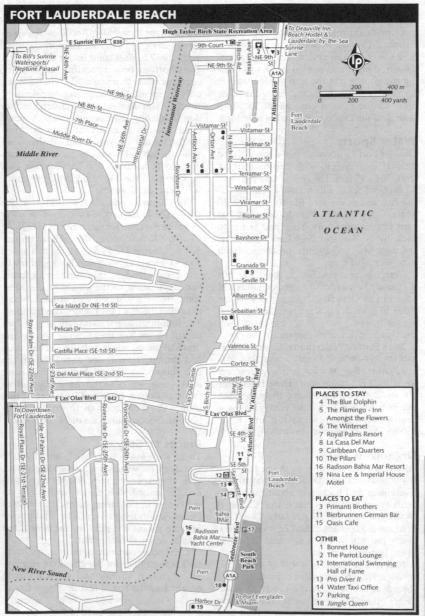

FORT LAUDERDALE BEACH

ATLANTIC OCEAN

Middle River

New River Sound

PLACES TO STAY
4   The Blue Dolphin
5   The Flamingo - Inn
    Amongst the Flowers
6   The Winterset
7   Royal Palms Resort
8   La Casa Del Mar
9   Caribbean Quarters
10 The Pillars
16 Radisson Bahia Mar Resort
19 Nina Lee & Imperial House
    Motel

PLACES TO EAT
3   Primanti Brothers
11 Bierbrunnen German Bar
15 Oasis Cafe

OTHER
1   Bonnet House
2   The Parrot Lounge
12 International Swimming
    Hall of Fame
13 Pro Diver II
14 Water Taxi Office
17 Parking
18 Jungle Queen

SOUTHEAST

2-8 people, $1 per pedestrian or bicyclist; open 8am-sunset daily) contains one of the last significant maritime hammocks left in Broward County, as well as mangroves, a freshwater lagoon system and several endangered plant and animal species (including the gopher tortoise and golden leather fern). You can fish, picnic, hike, canoe or bike. Canoe rentals cost about $5.50 an hour, and the canoe trail is half a mile long.

Water Sports
Greater Fort Lauderdale has a three-tiered natural reef system with depths ranging from 20 to 55 feet. The region also has over 75 artificial reefs, which have been attracting fish and other reef life for the last 20 years. Consequently, Fort Lauderdale has tons of dive operators. Your best bet is to pick up the 'Greater Fort Lauderdale Attractions Map and Events' brochure, which lists over 20 of them.

Waterskiing is possible on the ocean, but it's usually very expensive; check on the piers around Las Olas Blvd bridge and look for flyers in town. Jet skis are popular here, but we really wish you wouldn't use them – see the Outdoor Activities chapter for the rant.

Bill's Sunrise Watersports/Neptune Parasail *(☎ 954-462-8962 main rental, 954-761-1672 parasailing, **W** www.sunrisewatersports .com, 2025 E Sunrise Blvd)* These folks offer 10- to 12-minute parasailing flights for $65 per person, and they also rent six-person motorboats (by reservation only) for $50/85/150 per hour/two hours/four hours.

Organized Tours
For sightseeing excursions down the New River and the Intracoastal Waterway to Port Everglades and back, hop aboard the 19th-century riverboat replica, the **Carrie B** *(☎ 954-768-9920, SE 5th Ave just off Las Olas Blvd; tours $11/6 adult/child 12 yrs & under)*. Tours last about 1½ hours and depart at 11am, 1pm and 3pm daily.

Riverfront Cruises *(☎ 954-463-3372, **W** www.riverfrontcruises.com, Las Olas Riverfront at SW 1st Ave; tours $14/8 adult/ child)* offers 1½-hour yacht cruises along inland canals, past Millionaire's Row and

down to Port Everglades. Tours leave every two hours from 10:30am to 8:30pm.

Pro Diver II *(☎ 954-467-6030, **W** www.pro diveusa.com, 515 Hwy A1A/Seabreeze Blvd; tours $20/12 adult/child under 12 yrs)* is a glass-bottom boat revealing underwater ocean wonders that you could otherwise see only by snorkeling or diving. Speaking of which, if you do want to get closer, you can don snorkeling gear for an extra $9/6 adult/ child. Some people in your party can view the fish the dry way; others can splash around with the fishes. Excursions leave at 9:30am Tuesday to Saturday and 2pm Sunday. Call at 8:30am on the day of departure to check weather conditions.

You'll have to decide for yourself about the **Jungle Queen** *(☎ 954-462-5596, **W** www .junglequeen.com, Radisson Bahia Mar Yacht Center, 801 Seabreeze Blvd; dinner cruises $27, sightseeing $12.50/8.25 adult/child under 10 yrs)*. This is either a wondrous journey to a tropical island, a great meal and a funny vaudeville show, or the kitschiest, cheesiest romp into Borscht-belt glitz around. Whatever else, this is a Fort Lauderdale tradition. The four-hour dinner tour (departing at 7pm nightly) goes like this: On the way to the 'tropical' island, where you dine on barbecue and shrimp, the narrator dishes dirt on the rich folks who live on Millionaire's Row, leads group waves to the drawbridge attendants and offers trivia and local lore. If that sounds like a bit much, there are also three-hour afternoon tours, sans meal and show.

Places to Stay
There are a few youth hostels, and if you're searching for work on a foreign-flag vessel, several inexpensive crew houses, too. You'll find the most hotels, motels and B&Bs on the beach, in the '-mars' area. Lauderdale-by-the-Sea lodging tends to be a bit pricier because rooms are right on the beach, but they're definitely the nicest.

Crew houses are not for the average backpacker, but rather for those seeking employment aboard yachts and ships moored nearby (see the boxed text 'Joining a Crew,' in the Getting Around section). Generally these are the best places to pick up information on boat jobs; all have listings of the agencies in town. In most cases, backpackers just looking for lodging will not be admitted, so call first and make sure before showing up. The exception to the no-backpackers rule is Floyd's Youth Hostel & Crew House (see Port Everglades, in this section).

Wherever you go in town, be careful about advertised rates – many are for singles, with huge jumps for additional people. If you have complaints about a hotel, contact the Fort Lauderdale Division of Hotels and Restaurants (☎ 954-958-5520).

Downtown Fort Lauderdale Riverside Hotel (☎ 954-467-0671, 800-325-3280, W www.riversidehotel.com, 620 E Las Olas Blvd) Rooms $95-149/189 summer/ winter (inquire about discounts). The best option downtown, Lauderdale's oldest hotel has 105 large rooms with fluffy carpets and Jacobean oak furnishings. At press time an additional 116 rooms were under construction next door.

Fort Lauderdale Beach Beach Hostel (☎ 954-567-7275, W www.fortlauderdale hostel.com, 2115 N Ocean Blvd; see the Fort Lauderdale Area map). Dorm beds $16. Affiliated with Floyd's, this hot pink, 61-bed hostel is just one block from the beach and about a mile north of the main beach area. The mostly four-bedded dorms are both single-sex and mixed. Canned goods are set out for the taking, and breakfast foods, including eggs, are set out for the making. Free local calls, one Internet station and free snorkeling gear are also included. The hostel will pick you up anywhere in Fort Lauderdale during the day. Otherwise, bus No 11 runs by the hostel from the airport, Greyhound bus station, downtown and the beaches. Most beds are filled with international visitors, since a passport is required to stay here.

The Winterset (☎ 954-564-5614, 800-888-2639, W www.thewinterset.com, 2801 Terramar St) Rooms & efficiencies $50-65/315-410 daily/weekly summer, $60-105/380-690 winter. This old-fashioned motel has 29 units, two pools surrounded by 40 varieties of palms, and friendly management. The furnishings date back to the 1970s (and not in a hip way, either).

Gay Accommodations in Fort Lauderdale

Several charming men-only guest houses can be found in the '-mar' area, but the first entry is the only one accommodating lesbians.

Deauville Inn (☎ 954-568-5000, W www.ftlaud-deauville.com, 2916 N Ocean Blvd) Rooms/ efficiencies $60/90 summer, $70/100 winter. Two blocks from the beach, this simple 10-room place welcomes anyone gay, straight, male or female.

The Blue Dolphin (☎ 954-565-8437, 800-893-2583, W www.bluedolphinhotel.com, 725 N Birch Rd) Rooms $99-119 summer, $119-169 winter. This clean, renovated and comfortable place is just for men, who are quite comfortable around the clothing-optional pool. There are 16 rooms.

The Flamingo – Inn Amongst the Flowers (☎ 954-561-4658, 800-283-4786, W www.the flamingoresort.com, 2727 Terramar St) Rooms $100-195 summer, $140-240 winter. With a tranquil garden, 13 tidy rooms, a completely renovated interior and a friendly staff, the Flamingo keeps its guests quite satisfied.

Royal Palms Resort (☎ 954-564-6444, 800-237-7256, W www.royalpalms.com, 2901 Terramar St) Rooms $149-229 summer, $199-289 winter. The premier gay guest house is a clothing-optional place that features 12 large, airy rooms (complete with CD/TV/VCR and library), a lush tropical garden, a pool with a waterfall and lots of perks, like free parking and breakfast. It's also isolated and serene.

– Kim Grant

La Casa Del Mar (☎ 954-467-2037, W www.lacasadelmar.com, 3003 Granada St) Rooms $80-100 summer, $110-145 winter. This family-owned, homey B&B has 11 rooms, studios and one-bedroom units. They're not ultra spiffy, but they're comfortable and surrounded by a tropical garden and a little pool. A full breakfast is included.

Nina Lee & Imperial House Motel (☎ 954-524-1568, 800-646-2533, 3048 Harbor Dr) Rooms/efficiencies/two-bedrooms $49/69/89 summer, $79/99/119 winter. Just a block from the beach, in a quiet neighborhood, this very friendly and clean motel has 26 units surrounding a pool, lawn and patio. This is a good choice for families, since some rooms connect and have sleeper sofas. Guests have use of the nearby Sheraton's facilities (including the pools, gym, business center and lounge).

Caribbean Quarters (☎ 954-523-3226, 888-414-3226, W www.caribbeanquarters .com, 3012 Granada St) Rooms $135-200 summer, $150-250 winter. This three-story B&B features a lush, private patio and 12 units with wicker and rattan furnishings and gauzy netting draped over the beds. Perfect for longer stays, some suites have a balcony, living room and even a dishwasher.

Radisson Bahia Mar Resort (☎ 954-764-2233, 800-327-8154, W www.bahiamar.net, 801 Seabreeze Blvd) Rooms $119-134 summer, $199-239 winter. A standard top-end place with 300 comfortable rooms, this resort also has the requisite amenities: pool, tennis courts and health club.

The Pillars (☎ 954-467-9639, 800-800-7666, W www.pillarshotel.com, 111 N Birch Rd) Rooms $119-159 June-Oct, $149-199 Nov, Dec & May, $189-259 winter; suites $189-349 summer, $279-389 winter. Hands down the swankiest and loveliest lodging in town, this deluxe retreat is *the* place to splurge for a special occasion. It boasts 23 suave plantation-style rooms surrounding a courtyard pool, waterfront tables lining its private dock (where you can have 'room' service) on the Intracoastal Waterway and a host of amenities and pampering services.

Port Everglades

Floyd's Youth Hostel & Crew House (☎ 954-462-0631, W www.floydshostel.com, 445 SE 16th St) Dorm beds $15-16. Close to most crew placement agencies (see Boat, under Getting There & Away, later) and a short bus ride to the beach, Floyd's is friendly and protective of their property and guests. Before you can stay, you'll be vetted on the telephone. You must hold a valid passport; there's zero tolerance for illegal drug use. (Drinking is not monitored, but perhaps should be...) Floyd's provides many extras – free local calls, use of computers with DSL, incoming faxes, washer and dryer, basic food and cooking items and barbecues every couple of weeks. They'll also pick you up from the airport, bus and train stations.

Joanne's Crew House (☎ 954-527-1636, 916 SE 12th St) Rooms $135 weekly. Fort Lauderdale's most established, best organized and cleanest crew house is located in a residential area in a sprawling, ranch-style house. Fifteen people can await employment in five bedrooms (four bathrooms) in style: There's a big screened-in backyard, pool and a barbecue area on the 1-acre property. Joanne calls boat owners to tell them who's staying at their house.

Hyatt Regency Pier 66 (☎ 954-525-6666, 800-327-3796, W www.hyatt.com, 2301 SE 17 St Causeway) Rooms $179-259 summer, $269-309 winter. The Hyatt has 380 very nice rooms, good service and great views from a rotating rooftop cocktail lounge.

Lauderdale-by-the-Sea All three of these properties are right on the beach, not even a sandal's shuffle away.

A Little Inn by the Sea (☎ 954-772-2450, 800-492-0311, W www.alittleinn.com, 4546 El Mar Dr) Rooms & suites $79-149 summer, $119-199 winter. All but one of these rooms and efficiencies face the ocean. Arranged around an interior and an exterior courtyard, many rooms have balconies, and most have older bathrooms. Amenities include free bikes, free tennis, a pool and a breakfast buffet; children under age 12 stay free in their parents' room.

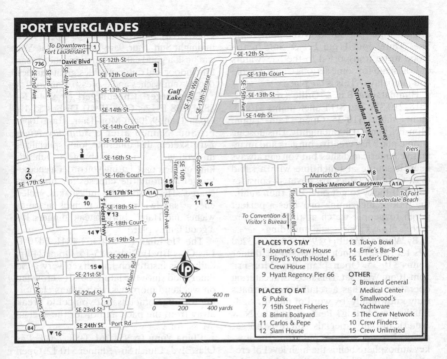

PORT EVERGLADES

Map labels:
To Downtown Fort Lauderdale
736
Davie Blvd
SE 12th St
SE 2nd Ave
SE 3rd Ave
SE 4th Ave
SE 12th St
SE 12th Court
SE 13th St
Gulf Lake
SE 14th St
SE 14th Court
SE 15th St
SE 16th St
SE 16th Court
SE 17th St
SE 18th St
SE 18th Court
SE 19th St
SE 20th St
SE 21st St
SE 22nd St
SE 23rd St
SE 24th St
S Andrews Ave
S Federal Hwy
S Miami Rd
Port Rd
84
SE 12th Way
SE 13th Terrace
Cordova Rd
SE 10th Terrace
SE 10th Ave
A1A
SE 13th Court
SE 15th Ave
SE 13th St
SE 14th St
Intracoastal Waterway
Stranahan River
Marriott Dr
St Brooks Memorial Causeway
Eisenhower Blvd
A1A
To Fort Lauderdale Beach
To Convention & Visitor's Bureau
Piers

0 200 400 m
0 200 400 yards

PLACES TO STAY
1 Joanne's Crew House
3 Floyd's Youth Hostel & Crew House
9 Hyatt Regency Pier 66

PLACES TO EAT
6 Publix
7 15th Street Fisheries
8 Bimini Boatyard
11 Carlos & Pepe
12 Siam House

13 Tokyo Bowl
14 Ernie's Bar-B-Q
16 Lester's Diner

OTHER
2 Broward General Medical Center
4 Smallwood's Yachtware
5 The Crew Network
10 Crew Finders
15 Crew Unlimited

Tropic Seas (☎ 954-772-2555, 800-952-9581, W www.tropicseasresort.com, 4616 El Mar Dr) Rooms $85-160 summer, $145-215 winter. This well-kept contemporary motel has 16 rooms. Only a few grains of sand stand between it, the pool and the ocean. Choose between simple rooms, ones that sleep three (with a kitchen), and one-bedroom suites. Children under 12 stay free in their parents' room.

Courtyard Villa (☎ 954-776-1164, 800-291-3560, W www.courtyardvilla.com, 4312 El Mar Dr) Rooms $105-135 summer, $159-175 winter. With only four courtyard suites and four oceanfront efficiencies, these distinctive and classy European-style rooms go fast – with good reason. There are many added benefits: free bikes, barbecue grills, free access to over 450 movies, free tennis, a rooftop patio and free breakfast and drinks down the street at Mulligans restaurant. You may also wish to consider two-

bedroom units ($150/250 summer/winter) and off-season weekly rates ($588).

Places to Eat
Downtown Fort Lauderdale Two Street Coffee Garage (☎ 954-523-7191, 209 SW 2nd Ave at 2nd St) Open 7am-10pm Mon-Thur, 7am-midnight Fri, 8am-midnight Sat, 8am-10pm Sun. This independent coffeehouse pumps out excellent espresso and a comfortable vibe.

Shirttail Charlie's (☎ 954-463-3474, 400 SW 3rd Ave) Dishes $9-11. Open 11:30am-10pm daily. Cantilevered over the banks of the New River, this casual outdoor eatery dishes up good fried seafood served in baskets. Service is friendly, and the prices are right. They provide ferry service from the Riverwalk that scoots you across the river to their place.

Creolina's (☎ 954-524-2003, 209 SW 2nd St) Lunch mains $7-10, dinner mains $10-18.

SOUTHEAST

Open for lunch 11:30am-2:30pm Mon-Fri, dinner 5pm-9pm Sun & Mon, 5pm-10pm Tues-Thur, 5pm-11pm Fri & Sat. In the mood to be transported to the backwaters of Louisiana for some serious Cajun, Creole and jambalaya? This is *the* place.

Himmarshee Bar & Grille (☎ 954-524-1818, 210 SW 2nd St) Lunch mains $10-13, dinner mains $16-25. Open 11am-2:30pm Mon-Fri, 6pm-10:30pm nightly. This upscale yuppie place has creative burgers and imaginative American dishes, but you can always keep it simple at lunchtime with a salad ($5). Outdoor tables are coveted; consider yourself lucky to get one. But then again, the indoor mezzanine provides a perfect perch to people-watch at the bar, where there's always a hip scene unfolding.

By Word of Mouth (☎ 954-564-3663, 3200 NE 12th Ave) Lunch mains $10-16, dinner mains $19-35. Open 11am-3pm Mon-Fri, 5pm-10pm Wed-Sat. This successful catering operation also has a retail location that's truly known only 'by word of mouth.' Self-fulfilling marketing? Perhaps, but the New American daily specials (there is no set menu) live up to the reputation. The low-key atmosphere belies the high level of creative cooking. Check out the dishes in the glass case before ordering.

Left Bank (☎ 954-462-5376, 214 SE 6th Ave) Mains $19-32, prix fixe menu $35. Open 5:30pm-9pm Sun-Thur, 5:30pm-10pm Fri & Sat. This chef-owned, elegant and romantic restaurant has certainly evolved since it opened in the early 1980s, tending away from heavier classical French to lighter Provençal-style cooking. Gravitate toward the very good seafood dishes, either à la carte or with the value-laden fixed menu that includes an appetizer, main and dessert.

Along East Las Olas Boulevard The following restaurants are all downtown along E Las Olas Blvd, which is dense with eateries.

Kilwin's (☎ 954-523-8338, 809 E Las Olas Blvd) Open 11am-10pm Sun-Thur, 11am-midnight Fri & Sat. Since 1949, these folks have made tantalizing fudge, truffles, caramel, chocolate and ice cream.

Cafe Europa (☎ 954-763-6600, 726 E Las Olas Blvd) Sandwiches $4-6. Open 9am-midnight Sun-Thur, 9am-1am Fri & Sat. You can't ask a good café for anything more than this: indoor and outdoor tables, great pastries, decent sandwiches and espresso. Can you?

Cheeburger! Cheeburger! (☎ 954-524-8824, 708 E Las Olas Blvd) Dishes $5-10. Open 11am-9:30pm Mon-Thur, 11am-10pm Fri-Sun. Named after a *Saturday Night Live* sketch, this dinerlike joint specializes in…you guessed it: cheeseburgers. Duh. It's kind on their part, letting you order a cheeseburger without the cheese 'for no extra charge.' They also make milkshakes, grilled cheese sandwiches, grilled-chicken sandwiches and Ham's 'burgersteak' dinners. It's a good family place.

The Floridian (☎ 954-463-4041, 1410 E Las Olas Blvd) Dishes $5-15. Open 24 hrs daily. This institution has served very good diner food since the late 1930s. It's crowded on weekend mornings, with diners clamoring for huge omelets, but you could break away from the pack and order the special 'Mess' for $7.

China Yung (☎ 954-761-3388, 720 E Las Olas Blvd) Lunch $6-7, dinner $10-12. Open 11:30am-10pm Mon-Sat, 4pm-10pm Sun. A classic American Chinese restaurant, this joint has cheap lunch specials that include soup, egg roll and fried rice.

Mark's (☎ 954-463-1000, 1032 E Las Olas Blvd) Lunch mains $7-18, dinner mains $16-38. Open for lunch 11:30am-2:30pm Mon-Fri, dinner 6pm-10pm Sun-Thur, 6pm-11pm Fri & Sat. Mark's has been one of the most exceptional South Florida restaurants since it opened in 1994. It's an upscale place with excellent service, a bustling open kitchen, cozy booths and rich mahogany tables. The chef uses classical cooking techniques on fresh local ingredients for his signature dishes. Look for cracked conch with black-bean mango salsa and vanilla-rum butter sauce; crab crusted grouper with wild mushroom ragout; and honey balsamic–glazed wood oven–roasted salmon.

Fort Lauderdale Beach Primanti Brothers (☎ 954-565-0605, 901 N Atlantic Blvd)

Slices $2, pies $11-15. Open 24 hrs daily. The bros have great New York–style pizza in both Neapolitan and Sicilian versions.

Bierbrunnen German Bar (☎ 954-462-1008, 425 Fort Lauderdale Beach Rd) Dishes $7-15. Open 11am-2am Sun-Fri, 11am-3am Sat. Down a little alley, this bar-cum-restaurant serves authentic schnitzel (pork loin breaded and pan fried), sauerbraten (sour roast beef with mashed potatoes and red cabbage), fresh bratwurst, and of course, excellent draft beer. You can always get something light like a mahimahi sandwich. This restaurant is a fun, partially open-air sort of place. Free appetizers lure patrons on weekdays, as do well-drink specials ($1.75).

Oasis Cafe (☎ 954-463-3130, 600 Sea-breeze Blvd) Dishes $8-17. Open 11am-10pm Sun-Thur, 11am-11pm Fri & Sat, weather permitting. Almost within a traffic island across from the beach, this palm-studded café has only outdoor seating, with shaded gliding tables. Fare consists of sandwiches, wraps, good noshing appetizers, ribs and seafood.

Port Everglades Crew-house dwellers will head to the Publix supermarket on 17th St.

Lester's Diner (☎ 954-525-5641, 250 Hwy 84) Dishes $6-8. Open 24 hrs daily. Universally hailed (in a most affectionate way) as a greasy spoon, campy Lester's has been keeping folks happy since the late 1960s. Everyone makes their way here at some point: from business types on cell phones to late-night clubbers to blue-haired ladies with second husbands.

Carlos & Pepe (☎ 954-467-7192, 1302 SE 17th St) Dishes $7-15. Open 11:30am-11pm Mon-Thur, 11:30am-11pm Fri & Sat, noon-10:30pm Sun. Ignore the strip-mall location and overlook the casual interior. This authentic Mexican place has excellent salsa, fajitas and burritos, and strong margaritas. It's the best you'll find east of New Mexico.

Tokyo Bowl (☎ 954-524-8200, 1720 S Federal Hwy) Dishes $8-9; all-you-can-eat sushi $13.50. Open 11am-11pm Mon-Thur, 11am-midnight Fri & Sat, noon-11pm Sun. This Japanese fast-food place has good cheap eats, like beef and chicken teriyaki.

Ernie's Bar-B-Q (☎ 954-523-8636, 1843 S Federal Hwy) Dishes $7-13. Open 11am-1am Sun-Thur, 11am-2am Fri & Sat. This 'blues, booze and bbq' joint has been known for its good-time squalor and good, cheap food since 1957. Ernie's has everything from burgers to ribs to enormous portions of conch chowder, which itself can make a meal. Dishes are available for takeout, too, but the atmosphere is key. You could always just come for a drink.

Siam House (☎ 954-763-1701, 1392 SE 17th St) Lunch mains $6-7, dinner mains $10-14. Open 11:30am-3pm & 5pm-10pm daily. Siam House serves Asian cuisine, great Thai specialties and seafood dishes.

Bimini Boatyard (☎ 954-525-7400, 1555 SE 17th St) Lunch mains $10-12, dinner mains $14-22. Open 11:30am-10pm Sun-Thur, 11:30am-11pm Fri & Sat. If you suffer from boat envy, avoid this Intracoastal Waterway restaurant with great views of huge yachts. It also draws loud beautiful people to a lively bar or the dining room for a predictable California/American menu. All in all, it's a lively place if you're in the mood for it.

15th Street Fisheries (☎ 954-763-2777, 1900 SE 15th St) Lunch $3-16, dinner mains $16-40. Open 11:30am-10pm daily. A casual restaurant popular with families and tourists, this Intracoastal Waterway restaurant is big into seafood and lobster. A casual lunch menu (ie, a less expensive one) is served throughout the day and evening in the lounge.

Lauderdale-by-the-Sea

Nature Boy Health Food (☎ 954-776-4696, 220 E Commercial Blvd) Sandwiches $4-6. Open 10am-5pm Mon-Sat. Your body will appreciate the healthful salads, sandwiches and fruit-and veggie-juice drinks on offer here.

Aruba Beach Cafe (☎ 954-776-0001, 1 E Commercial Blvd) Dishes $12-22. Open 11am-11pm daily. An open-air party place overlooking the ocean, with sort of a Caribbean-beach atmosphere, this place is pretty big and pretty loud. Weekday happy hour is popular, as are the Sunday breakfast buffet (9am to noon) and live music

(Wednesday to Sunday). Stick to the simpler food items like sandwiches, pasta, burgers and salads. They're fine for a quick bite.

Blue Moon Fish Co (☎ 954-267-9888, 4405 Tradewinds Ave W) Lunch mains $10-15, dinner mains $26-38. Open for lunch 11:30am-3pm daily, dinner 6pm-10pm Sun-Thur, 6pm-11pm Fri & Sat. Combine an excellent and eclectic seafood menu with good service and a spectacular waterside setting (indoor and outdoor), and you'll have this winning recipe. Come for Sunday brunch (11:30am to 3pm; $25 per person), when jazz often accompanies the spectacularly bountiful meal. Here's what you get: all-you-can-peel-and-eat shrimp and a seafood buffet, mains like seafood gumbo or salmon strudel (or both), dessert and either a bloody Mary, mimosa or champagne. Sounds too good to be true, but it's not. The raw bar and sushi (not included in the buffet) are also very good.

Entertainment

Bars There's no cover for live music at these places.

Dicey Riley's (☎ 954-522-2202, 217 SW 2nd St) Open 11am-4am daily. If you can't make it to Dublin this season, head here. This downtown restaurant and lounge is as close to an Irish pub as you'll get, with traditional cuisine ($5 to $9) and draft Guinness, Bass and others. Dicey's is particularly packed on weekends, but traditional and contemporary live Irish tunes headline Tuesday to Saturday.

Maguire's Hill (☎ 954-764-4453, 535 N Andrews Ave) Open 11:30am-2:30am Sun-Thur, 11:30am-3am Fri & Sat (kitchen closed at 10pm Sun-Thur, midnight Fri & Sat). Another classic Irish pub, this one has Irish bands Thursday to Sunday. Dishes run $6 to $14.

O'Hara's Jazz Cafe (☎ 954-524-1764, 722 E Las Olas Blvd) Open 11:30am-2am Sun-Thur, 11:30am-3am Fri & Sat. For nightly jazz in a warm, comfortable atmosphere, head over here after 9pm. The menu ($4 to $9) features crab nachos, quesadillas, chicken wings, pizzas, salads and sandwiches.

The Parrot Lounge (☎ 954-563-1493, 911 Sunrise Lane) Open 11am-2am Sun-Thur, 11am-3am Fri & Sat. A mainstay since the 1970s, this popular dive bar draws a beer-and-peanuts kind of crowd.

Village Pump (☎ 954-776-5840, 4404 El Mar Dr) Open 8am-2am daily. This is a fun local dive bar, serving full meals throughout the day.

Nightclubs 'Fort Liquordale' is still a party town, and there are tons of clubs to suit a variety of tastes, persuasions, libidos and degrees of nuttiness. One thing is for sure, though: You can expect lots less attitude here than at South Beach clubs. Cover charges vary constantly, but coupons abound. For the latest in clubland, pick up the Fort Lauderdale version of the *New Times* (W www.newtimesbpb.com), a free weekly published on Thursday, or *City Link* (W www.clo-sfl.com). The following are simply the most enduring of the available options.

Baja Beach Club (☎ 954-563-7889, 3339 N Federal Hwy) Open 9pm-2am Sun-Fri, 9pm-3am Sat. At the northwest corner of Oakland Park Blvd and US Hwy 1, Baja Beach Club looks like an orgy at King Neptune's place. The enormous multilevel club features dance music, spring-break parties (or what's left of them) and ladies' nights. Party hardy, dude.

Gay & Lesbian Venues Right up there with Provincetown, San Francisco and South Beach, Fort Lauderdale boasts dozens of gay bars and clubs scattered around town. It's best to check *Hot Spots* for the latest offerings. Again, these are simply the ones with staying power.

The Saint (☎ 954-525-7883, W www.thesaintnightclub.net, 1000 State Rd 84) Cover $4-5 Tues, Fri & Sun. Open 2pm-2am daily. This large, industrial music complex is a buzzy dance club – expect 500 people, minimum. Their cool Fetish Fridays take place on the fourth Friday of the month. Look for less buzzy and more down-home country & western bands on Tuesday and Sunday; 'ladies night' draws a crowd on Friday.

Club Cathode Ray (☎ 954-462-8611, 1307 E Las Olas Blvd) Open 2pm-2am Sun-Thur, 2pm-3am Fri & Sat. Pop over to this friendly, guppie kind of hangout for two-for-one happy 'hour' (2pm to 8pm daily). A six-hour happy hour, you gotta love it.

Performing Arts One of the state's largest and most important performing arts complexes is the **Broward Center for the Performing Arts** (☎ 954-462-0222, W www .browardcenter.org, 201 SW 5th Ave) Tickets $25-65/10-25 adult/child. Two venues, the 2688-seat Au-Rene Theater and the 588-seat Amaturro, host a wide variety of first-rate concerts, theatrical productions and kid-oriented theater. Call to see what's on.

Spectator Sports
The Fusion play major league soccer at **Lockhart Stadium** (☎ 954-717-2200, 5300 NW 12th Ave), while the Baltimore Orioles play spring-training baseball games at **Fort Lauderdale Stadium** (☎ 954-828-4980, 5301 NW 12th Ave) across from the Lockhart Stadium, a half mile west of I-95.

Shopping
Swap Shop (☎ 954-791-7927, W www.florida swapshop.com, 3291 W Sunrise Blvd) Open 6am-5pm Mon-Fri, 5am-6pm Sat & Sun. This enormous circuslike flea market, the largest indoor/outdoor flea market in the country, boasts a real circus every day. They also have a drive-in movie, a little amusement park and lots of stuff to buy.

Sawgrass Mills (☎ 954-846-2350, 800-356-4557, W www.sawgrassmillsmall.com, 12801 W Sawgrass Blvd) Open 10am-9:30pm Mon-Sat, 11am-8pm Sun. With more than 2 miles of shops (that's 400 retail shops, 30 restaurants and an entertainment area), this place overwhelms even the most intrepid shopaholics. Grab a shopping cart and make a battle plan before waging war on your credit card; otherwise, you will be very quickly defeated by the enormity of it all. Bargain hunters may wish to purchase, at the mall information desks, a $10 booklet with over $1500 worth of store coupons. (Some hotel concierges have them as giveaways.)

Getting There & Away
Air Fort Lauderdale–Hollywood International (FLL; ☎ 954-359-1200, W www.fll.net), about 30 miles north of Miami just off I-95, is smaller (though undergoing rapid expansion) and friendlier than MIA. Fort Lauderdale serves as a lower-cost alternative to MIA, especially now that the very popular Southwest Airlines services this northern neighbor. Other budget carriers include JetBlue, Air Tran and Spirit.

Bus & Shuttle The Greyhound station (☎ 954-764-6551, W www.greyhound.com), 515 NE 3rd St at North Federal, is about four blocks from Broward Central Terminal (see the Getting Around section, later), the central transfer point for Fort Lauderdale area buses. Buses to Miami leave throughout the day ($5 one-way, 30 to 60 minutes), but depending on when you arrive, you might have to wait as much as 2½ hours for the next one. It's rarely worth it.

From Miami, **SuperShuttle** (☎ 800-874-8885, W www.supershuttle.com) can take you to, but not from, Fort Lauderdale. From Miami's South Beach hotels, the cost is $22 per person.

Train Tri-Rail (☎ 800-874-7245, W www .tri-rail.com) runs between downtown Miami and the Fort Lauderdale airport ($6.75 roundtrip, 1¼ hours). A feeder system of buses at the Fort Lauderdale airport stop has connections to the airport (about 12 minutes further) for no extra charge. Free parking is provided at most stations. Since trains sometimes only run about every hour, it's best to call Tri-Rail for scheduling information.

Amtrak (☎ 800-872-7245, W www.amtrak .com) deposits passengers at 200 SW 21st Terrace in Fort Lauderdale, just south of Broward Blvd and just west of I-95.

Car & Motorcycle I-95 and Florida's Turnpike, the state's main toll road, run north-south. I-595, the major east-west artery, intersects I-95, Florida's Turnpike and the Sawgrass Expressway. It also feeds into I-75, which runs to Florida's west coast.

To reach Miami, take I-95 south (there's an airport onramp) to I-195 east for Northern Miami Beach, I-395 for South Beach, and go straight through to downtown Miami. It will take 30 to 45 minutes.

Boat Port Everglades Authority (☎ 954-523-3404) runs the enormous Port Everglades cruise port (Port Everglades is the third busiest cruise port after Miami and Port Canaveral). From the port, walk to SE 17th St and take bus No 40 to the beach or to Broward Central Terminal. If you're coming here in your own boat (not unlikely here), head for the **Radisson Bahia Mar Yacht Center** (☎ 954-764-2233).

For information on sailing to exotic points from Fort Lauderdale, see the boxed text 'Joining a Crew.'

Getting Around

To/From the Airport Fort Lauderdale-Hollywood International Airport (FLL), south of town off Federal Hwy or I-95, is about a 20-minute drive from E Las Olas Blvd. Broward County Transit's bus No 1 goes from the airport to Broward Central Terminal. Tri-Rail shuttles connect the airport terminal with the Fort Lauderdale Airport train station (you can also take BCt bus No 3 or 6); trains head from there to the Fort Lauderdale station ($3) about once an hour at rush hours (there is no train service from about noon to 3pm). The trains run from about 5:30am to 9:15pm on weekdays, with less frequent weekend service.

The official airport taxi is **Yellow Cab Co** (☎ 954-565-5400); it costs about $14 to go from the airport to a beach hotel. A ride in their metered cabs from Fort Lauderdale Airport to South Beach would run about $60. **Tri-County Transportation Airport Express** (☎ 954-561-8886) runs shuttles to hotels; a shared shuttle to most beach locations is $8 to $12. Pick up the shuttles as they circle the terminals. You must call 24 hours in advance to go *from* Fort Lauderdale *to* the airport.

Bus TMA (☎ 954-761-3543), a free shuttle with service every 15 minutes or so, runs between downtown sights (7:30am to 6pm

weekdays), between the beach and E Las Olas Blvd and the Riverfront (6pm to 1am Friday to Saturday), and between Tri-Rail and E Las Olas Blvd and the beaches (7:30am to 11pm Saturday, 7:30am to 9:30pm Sunday).

Broward County Transit (BCt; ☎ 954-357-8400), 200 W Broward Blvd, runs between downtown, the beach and Port Everglades. The fare is $1 for adults, 50¢ for seniors and children. You'll probably be better off, though, with an all-day pass ($2.50 adults, $1.25 seniors and children). From Broward Central Terminal (its main terminal), take bus No 11 to upper Fort Lauderdale Beach and Lauderdale-by-the-Sea; bus No 1 to Port Everglades; and bus No 40 to 17th St and Federal Hwy.

Car & Motorcycle Having motorized wheels is the easiest way to go, though parking is tight in high season. Pay parking lots are located north and south of E Las Olas Blvd ($1 per hour), and all-day parking at the beach costs $8 at the municipal parking lot on Hwy A1A just south of SE 5th St. All major car rental companies have offices at Fort Lauderdale–Hollywood International Airport.

Water Taxi The narrated **Water Taxi** (☎ 954-467-6677, **w** www.watertaxi.com), 651 Seabreeze Blvd, plies the canals and waterways between 17th St to the south, Atlantic Blvd/Pompano Beach to the north, the New River to the west and the Atlantic Ocean to the east. A $5 daily pass entitles you to unlimited rides. This scheduled service is a great deal because it's cheap and because it's good to get out on the water in Fort Lauderdale. Call from any commercial location downtown on the New River (it stops at many popular restaurants, attractions, hotels and shops) or along the Intracoastal Waterway (any place with a dock), and they'll swing by and pick you up. Look for maps all along the route.

AROUND FORT LAUDERDALE

We've listed the towns and cities separately because they are indeed separate entities,

Joining a Crew

There are very few ways to hop aboard a steamer these days, especially one heading to Miami. The best way to get to Miami by boat is to first get to Fort Lauderdale, America's largest transatlantic yacht harbor.

Every year, hundreds of captains look for professional or unpaid crew to help them get their boats from South Florida to wherever they're going. In late spring they're going to Europe; in summer they're heading to New England, the Mediterranean and, less frequently but gaining in popularity, the West Coast, including Alaska. At other times they could be heading just about anywhere. Boats leave for South American, Asian and Australasian destinations year-round. Best of all, it's legal for foreigners to work on a boat that's leaving the USA. Boats also leave from other marinas and ports, of course; check locally for more information.

Getting a slot on a boat is a very interesting way to arrange transportation and perhaps even earn some spending money for wherever you'll end up. Many people have been getting around the world like this for years and don't see any reason to stop. Don't get it wrong – it's hard and serious work that requires concentration, dedication, common sense and the ability to work and live with others in close quarters. But those who love it wouldn't do anything else.

Crew Information To get an idea of trends and conditions, start by perusing sailing magazines. Try *Cruising World* and *Sail*, which run ads and classifieds. Blue Seas International has a great Web site (**w** www.jobxchange.com/crewxchange) with postings for crews heading everywhere on every type of vessel. Crew placement agencies are located throughout Fort Lauderdale, and they will, for a fee, match up crew and boat owners.

The best sources for information are crew houses in Fort Lauderdale, essentially hostels or guest houses for people looking for work. Boat owners call crew houses when they have something coming up. Floyd's Youth Hostel & Crew House (☎ 954-462-0631) is an excellent source of information – see the Places to Stay section, earlier, for more information.

Agencies Fort Lauderdale's premier unofficial crew agency is the three-ring binder at Smallwood's Yachtware (☎ 954-523-2282), 1001 SE 17th St. Owners come here, list their requirements in the book and wait for crew to get in touch.

'Official' agencies include Crew Unlimited (☎ 954-462-4624), 2065 S Federal Hwy; Crew Finders (☎ 954-522-2739), 408 SE 17th St; and the Crew Network (☎ 954-467-9777), 1053 SE 17th St.

When to Go An experienced hand can pick up work within a week or two at any time of the year; in winter, the jobs go to the more experienced workers, but there's plenty of work for everyone. Inexperienced hands looking for volunteer work will also hook up in a couple of weeks. Floyd thinks that about 95% of those coming for work get it if they're serious.

What to Bring Bring as little as possible: Everything you'll need will be provided, except a toothbrush, toothpaste and a hairbrush. You will, of course, need travel documents and, if necessary, visas for your destination country.

Women Crew Members The crew world is a tight one, and both Floyd's and Smallwood's say that they haven't heard in many years of a woman being the subject of unwanted advances from boat owners. But, as with all jobs, it's a possibility. Use your intuition at the first interview to see what services will be required, and if that includes the 'personal' kind. Interview carefully and ask around about the owner before taking on an assignment. Once onboard, your options for recourse are limited.

– Kim Grant

but note that each one is within a 20-minute drive of the others. All are accessible by bus, and Tri-Rail serves Deerfield Beach, Pompano Beach and Hollywood. Many of the towns can also be accessed via the Intracoastal Waterway.

Dania Beach

Dania (pronounced **dane**-ya) Beach, 5 miles south of Fort Lauderdale, is 98% inland, 2% beach, but the beach is nice. It also has a fledgling antiques district, a fun fishing pier and the Graves Museum of Archaeology & Natural History (formerly South Florida Museum of Natural History) – the state's finest archaeological museum and collection.

The antiques district goes two blocks north and south of Dania Beach Blvd along S Federal Hwy (US Hwy 1). Dania Beach Blvd runs between the beach/fishing pier and S Federal Hwy.

The **Dania Beach Library** (☎ 954-926-2420; 255 E Dania Beach Blvd; open Mon & Thur 10am-8pm, Tues-Wed 10am-6pm & Sat 9am-5pm) may be useful.

Graves Museum of Archaeology & Natural History
This wonderful nonprofit museum (☎ 954-925-7770; W www.sfmuseumnh.org; 481 S Federal Hwy; adult/senior/student/child $10/8/7/6; open 10am-4pm Tues-Fri, 10am-6pm Sat, noon-6pm Sun), easily identified by the huge lizard skeleton on its façade, has an extensive geology and paleontology collection, a very extensive pre-Columbian pottery collection, unique pre-Columbian miniatures and museum-quality reproductions of objects discovered in Tutankhamen's tomb. It is truly worth a visit (count on about 1½ hours), and kids will love it as well.

Bus No 1 to and from Fort Lauderdale's Broward Central Terminal stops very close by.

Dania Pier The beach action is centered around this fishing pier, which stretches almost 900 feet out into the Atlantic. It's a must for fishers – perhaps you'll reel in a barracuda! The pier and tackle shop are open 24/7. Fishing-rod rental and bait is available.

Aerated saltwater tanks along the pier keep your catch swimming while you hunt down their friends.

Places to Eat Consider day trips to Dania Beach, since it's easy to reach from Fort Lauderdale, where cheaper accommodations are available.

Jaxson's Restaurant (☎ 954-923-4445; 128 S Federal Hwy; open 11:30am-11pm daily), a kid-friendly ice cream emporium, has great ice cream and lots of stuff to keep the kids entertained, like license plates on the walls.

King's Head Pub (☎ 954-922-5722; 500 E Dania Beach Blvd; dishes $8-24; open Sun-Thur 11:30am-midnight & Fri-Sat 11:30am-2am) falls short of being a real British pub (they don't overboil the vegetables or undercook the bacon), but they make a good shepherd's pie. This fun place has friendly service and several regular expats, who keep their personal beer mugs hanging around.

Getting There & Away BCt bus No 1 runs from Broward Central Terminal to Dania Beach Blvd. An eastbound bus No 7 goes from there to the beach every 20 minutes on weekdays and every 30 to 40 minutes on weekends. If you're driving, turn east down Dania Beach Blvd and follow it to the end. Metered parking is available at the beach.

Hollywood

Hollywood is directly south of Dania Beach, but the only reasons to travel this far south are the beach, the 3-mile 'broadwalk' that lines it – swarming with in-line skaters and cute hunks – and the nearby Anne Kolb Nature Center. It's worth a day trip if you're in the area.

Hollywood Blvd runs between the beach and the center of town, about 2 miles apart. Get tourist information at the **Hollywood Chamber of Commerce** (☎ 954-923-4000; W www.hollywoodchamber.org; 330 S Federal Hwy; open 9am-5pm Mon-Fri).

Anne Kolb Nature Center This nature center (☎ 954-926-2481; nature center free, recreation area $1 per person on weekends, exhibit area $1 per person all the time; exhibits open 9am-5pm daily, park open 9am-sunset daily) in West Lake Park contains 1500 acres of coastal mangrove wetland. It features an observation tower, lagoon, hiking trails, boardwalks, boat rentals and a bicycle trail, as well as a 3500-gallon aquarium. Canoe and kayak rentals are available ($7/13 hour/four hours), so you can paddle on three short (1-mile) trails through the mangrove islands. But you could always take a boat tour on West Lake; get details at the center.

Take Federal Hwy (US Hwy 1) to Sheridan St and go east for about 1½ miles.

The Beach Packed with bikes and skaters and lined with snack bars, souvenir shops and junky tourist trinket touts, the 'broadwalk' at Hollywood Beach is a scene. The sand itself is OK, and the beach has enough character to make a day here interesting.

Places to Eat Now Art Gallery Café (☎ 954-922-0506; 1820 Hollywood Blvd; open 11am-3pm Mon-Fri & Wed-Sun 7:30pm-1am) is a New Age kind of coffee place that also offers live music (folk as well as acoustic and jazz guitar) and an open-mike night (Wednesday). Visual artists aren't slighted either; their works grace the walls.

Entertainment O'Hara's Jazz Cafe (☎ 954-925-2555; w www.oharasjazzcafe.com; 1903 Hollywood Blvd; open 9pm-1am Sun & Tues-Thur, 5pm-4am Fri & Sat) has smooth live jazz, a fun atmosphere and occasional R&B acts.

Club M (☎ 954-925-8396; 2037 Hollywood Blvd; open until 3am nightly) presents a wide array of bands, from blues to acoustic to rock 'n' roll.

Getting There & Away Hollywood has two main bus-transfer points: at Young Circle at US Hwy 1, and on Hollywood Blvd, further west at the center of the city. From Broward Central Terminal (☎ 954-357-8400) take BCt bus No 1 or 9 to Young Circle, then transfer to No 6, 7 or 28 to Hollywood or to Hollywood Beach. The Greyhound bus station (☎ 800-231-2222, 1707 Tyler St) is just off US Hwy 1 and Young Circle; about six buses a day run to and from Miami ($5; 45 minutes). By car, take US Hwy 1, Hwy A1A or I-95.

Davie

If you've ever been to Dubbo, Australia, this place will look familiar. A sprawling, sparsely populated town that's slowly making the conversion from farmland to bedroom community, Davie's not a whole bunch of laughs – yeah, you'll see people on horseback, but that only takes you so far. The classic piece of tourist information is that the **McDonald's** (4101 SW 64th Ave) has a corral and hitching post. Wheee. But the town rodeo arena hosts national shows, and the Buehler Planetarium is interesting. Sleep elsewhere.

Southwest of Fort Lauderdale, the downtown – don't blink – is a short strip of Davie Rd between Griffin Rd and about SW 39th St. There's a **chamber of commerce** (☎ 954-581-0790) on Davie Rd between Griffin Rd and State Road 84 that's open 8:30am to 5pm Monday through Friday, but the folks at **Army Navy Outdoors** (☎ 954-584-7227; 4130 Davie Rd) are helpful if you need to know anything about rodeos coming to town.

Buehler Planetarium & Observatory On Broward Community College's central campus, about 1 mile south of I-595, this planetarium (☎ 954-475-6680; 2501 Davie Rd) is a cool place to spend an hour. Using a very small Zeiss star machine, the college's astronomers project fascinating night-sky displays while you lounge in comfy chairs. Shows and times change frequently, so call for information; tickets usually run $2 to $5.

Davie Rodeo Arena This arena (☎ 954-384-7075; w www.fivestarrodeo.com; 4271 Davie Rd) hosts monthly, national five-star pro rodeo events. From I-95, take Griffin Rd west to Davie Rd and turn right for the fairgrounds.

Places to Eat McDonald's (☎ 954-791-6657; 4101 SW 64th Ave) is in the 'heart' of 'downtown Davie.' Stick around long enough, and you may see someone riding through the drive-thru on horseback.

SOUTHEAST

Entertainment If you're yearning for that country & western thing, **Davie Junction** (☎ 954-581-1132; 6311 SW 45th St (Orange Dr); open 7pm-4am Thur-Sun) doesn't exactly have a mechanical bull, but it does have two-stepping rowdies and some pool tables.

Getting There & Away By car, take I-95 south to I-595 west, to exit 7. Turn south and you'll run into downtown.

BOCA RATON
pop 75,000

Boca Raton, despite its reputation as an exclusive playground of the overprivileged and surgically enhanced, has become rather democratic in recent years. Millionaires are migrating north, toward Jupiter Island and Stuart, and an influx of young professionals and working families is beginning to enjoy Boca's considerable charms.

Unlike so many built-up beaches on Florida's southeastern coast, Boca Raton's waterfront property remains relatively wild, thanks to ecologically minded benefactors. Add to these natural attractions a few fascinating museums, several inexpensive eateries and lots of kid-related activities (this town is run by grandmothers volunteering their time), and you've got one grand day or two along this lovely stretch of the Atlantic Coast.

Orientation

The name Boca Raton ('mouth of the big rat') presumably refers to the shape of that portion of the Intracoastal Waterway dividing the city. The town is a sprawler; neighborhoods stretch far west of I-95 and Florida's Turnpike.

The city's main east-west drag is Palmetto Park Rd, bisected by north-south Dixie Hwy (not to be confused with Hwy 1, here called Federal Hwy); these two roads divide city addresses into north, south, east and west. Avenues, courts and places run north and south, and streets run east and west. Highway A1A, here called Ocean Blvd, is most conveniently accessible by the bridge at Palmetto Park Rd, as well as by bridges

along Spanish River Blvd to the north and Camino Real Blvd to the south.

Boca's a beast to navigate compared to neighboring beach cities, so if you plan to explore, pick up a copy of the custom-made Dolph map available only at the chamber of commerce ($1.50).

Information

The helpful **chamber of commerce** (☎ 561-395-4433; w www.bocaratonchamber.com; 1800 N Dixie Hwy; open 9am-5pm Mon-Fri) has racks of pamphlets and the best map in town.

Bank One (☎ 561-750-1940; 225 NE Mizner Blvd), in Mizner Park, has lots of free parking.

Barnes and Noble (☎ 561-750-2134, 1400 Glades Rd), just east of I-95, has a good selection of maps and books on Florida.

The **library** (☎ 561-393-7852; 200 NW Boca Raton Blvd; open 9am-9pm Mon-Thurs, 9am-6pm Fri & Sat, noon-8pm Sun) has free Internet access.

Boca News is published daily and the breezy *Boca Raton Times* every Wednesday. Most commercial radio stations originate in West Palm Beach.

Get your laundry clean at **Boca Coin Laundry** (☎ 561-386-7322; 101 W Palmetto Rd) and mail your letters at the downtown **post office** (170 NE 2nd St).

Boca Raton Community Hospital (☎ 561-395-7100, 800 Meadows Rd, w www.brch .com) is the largest nearby.

Boca Raton Museum of Art

This fine museum (☎ 561-392-2500; w www .bocamuseum.org; 501 Plaza Real; adult/ child $8/4; open 10am-6pm Tues, Thurs & Sat, 10am-9pm Weds & Fri, noon-5pm Sun, free 5pm-9pm Wed), in Mizner Park, has an impressive permanent collection featuring contemporary works by such household names as Pablo Picasso, Henri Matisse and Andy Warhol. Also on display are collections of Asian, African and pre-Columbian art. The museum also hosts traveling exhibitions and the annual All-Florida Juried Competition, the state's oldest invitation-only art show.

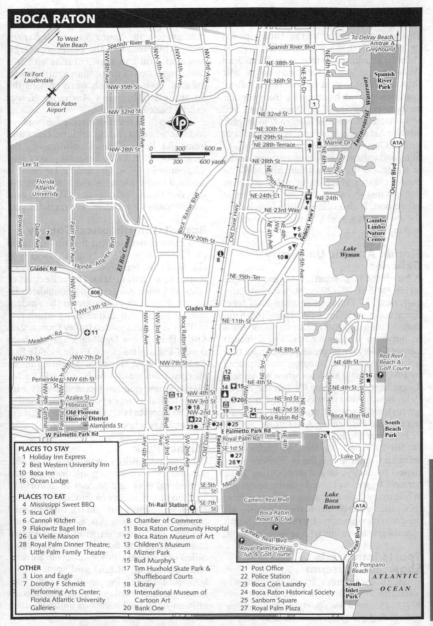

BOCA RATON

PLACES TO STAY
1 Holiday Inn Express
2 Best Western University Inn
10 Boca Inn
16 Ocean Lodge

PLACES TO EAT
4 Mississippi Sweet BBQ
5 Inca Grill
6 Cannoli Kitchen
9 Flakowitz Bagel Inn
26 La Vieille Maison
28 Royal Palm Dinner Theatre;
    Little Palm Family Theatre

OTHER
3 Lion and Eagle
7 Dorothy F Schmidt
    Performing Arts Center;
    Florida Atlantic University
    Galleries

8 Chamber of Commerce
11 Boca Raton Community Hospital
12 Boca Raton Museum of Art
13 Children's Museum
14 Mizner Park
15 Bud Murphy's
17 Tim Huxhold Skate Park &
    Shuffleboard Courts
18 Library
19 International Museum of
    Cartoon Art
20 Bank One

21 Post Office
22 Police Station
23 Boca Coin Laundry
24 Boca Raton Historical Society
25 Sanborn Square
27 Royal Palm Plaza

SOUTHEAST

International Museum of Cartoon Art

This unique tribute to the funny pages (☎ 561-391-2200; W www.cartoonart.org; 201 Plaza Real; admission free; open 10am-5pm Weds-Sun), in Mizner Park, may be the best (humanmade) reason to visit Boca Raton. Featuring artwork by everyone from popular cartoonists like Stan Lee *(Spider-Man)* and Mike Judge *(Beevis and Butthead)* to graphic novelist Art Spiegelman *(Maus)* and political satirist Gary Trudeau *(Doonesbury)*, bright films and exhibits show how cartoons make us giggle and think. The brainchild of *Beetle Bailey* creator Mort Walker, this museum doesn't just show off pen-and-ink's finest expression. It also offers a little insight into the cartoonist's world, as well as advice on making it big.

Florida Atlantic University Galleries

A bit off the beaten path, FAU has two galleries (☎ 561-297-2966; W www.fau.edu/galleries; 777 Glades Rd; admission free; open noon-4pm Tues-Fri, 1pm-5pm Sun, closed June-Aug) that attract top exhibitions in between student shows. The **Schmidt Center Gallery** is a large, adaptable space that featured enormous hanging metal pieces by FAU graduate students when we visited. To get here, use parking lot 1 at the end of Palm Beach Ave (visitors must use metered spaces), walk toward the theater and turn left into the Performing Arts Center.

Just over the hill, the **Ritter Art Gallery** (☎ 561-297-2660), on the 2nd floor of the Schmidt Center above the breezeway, is designed to exhibit larger pieces, from huge ceramic figures to carved granite sculpture. While many shows focus on student art (and this place clearly has a free-thinking art program), exhibitions by renowned South Florida artists are always a season highlight.

Sports Immortals Showcase Museum

Founded by premier sports-memorabilia collector Joel Platt, this museum (☎ 561-997-2575; W www.sportsimmortals.com; 6830 N Federal Hwy; adult/child $5/3; open 10am-6pm Mon-Fri, 11am-5pm Sat) is merely a preview of his much more ambitious project, the *Sports Immortals Experience*. While that's in the planning stages, however, you can view rotating exhibits featuring a few of more than a million mementos, many of which were part of the Smithsonian Museum's *American Heroes* exhibit back in 1981.

The top floor features interactive displays, footage of outstanding athletic feats and items like Pele's Cosmos uniform and the 'death ball' that killed baseball player Ray Chapman in 1920. The entire 1st floor is devoted to the Memorabilia Mart, where if they don't have the autographed ball or card you've always wanted, they'll get it for you.

Boca Raton Historical Society

The main reason to visit this tiny museum (☎ 561-395-6766; 71 N Federal Hwy) is to check out the building, formerly the Boca Raton town hall (1927). The collection of odds and ends is interesting enough, to be sure, but just can't compare to the golden-domed edifice and its disarming interior.

They also run a guided **trolley tour** (tickets $10; 9:15am Thurs Dec-Mar). The 1½ hour docent-led trip takes you to the **Florida East Coast Railway Depot**, a Mediterranean Revival train station built in the 1930s for Flagler's new railroad (accessible only with the historical society's permission), as well as the **Old Floresta Historic District**, a 1920s-era residential neighborhood.

Mizner Park

This upscale, outdoor shopping mall (☎ 561-362-0606, W www.miznerpark.org), bounded by Federal Hwy and Mizner Blvd north of NE 2nd street, and bookended by the Boca Raton Museum of Art and the International Museum of Cartoon Art, is hard to avoid. It's got free valet parking, the sorts of chain restaurants that would resent being called that (despite other outlets in Beverly Hills, Paris and Milan) and some lovely boutiques. There's live music here on Wednesday and Saturday nights, and Boca's affluent old guard seems to enjoy strolling the attractively lit, cobblestone sidewalks. If you want to see two of the finest museums in Florida, you'll be joining them.

Children's Museum

Boca Raton goes out of its way to cater to tiny tykes, and this small museum (☎ 561-368-6875; 498 Crawford Blvd; admission $3; open noon-4pm Tues-Sat) does a fine job. Housed in 'Singing Pines,' one of the oldest wooden structures in town, this is the toy closet you always wanted: Playthings of every description – from space shuttles to antique dolls – are available to packs of giggling children, who can try on pint-sized ethnic costumes from all over the world. The four mice on staff were very popular. The landscaped gardens outside feature native Florida plants and plenty of room for a game of tag.

Tim Huxhold Skate Park & Shuffleboard Courts

Next door to the Children's Museum, this place (☎ 561-393-7818; 400 Crawford Blvd; skateboarding/shuffleboard $6/2; open 1pm-9:30pm Mon-Fri, 10am-9:30pm Sat & Sun) seems like a unabashed bid by the city to bridge the (considerable) age gap in town. Yes, you can take the little kids to the museum, drop the older ones off at the, like, totally radical skate park, set grandma up next door with a wild game of shuffleboard and head to Mizner Park for some shopping. What more could you want?

Children's Science Explorium

It's not the most educational place (☎ 561-347-3913; 300 S Military Trail; admission free; open 9am-6pm Mon-Fri, 10am-5pm Sat & Sun), but there are exhibits on Florida ecosystems and local history, as well as brightly colored hands-on exhibits designed more to entertain than educate. Outside, however, is the very cool **Science Trail**, a series of physics experiments – many of them involving jets of water you can aim at annoying little sisters – cleverly disguised as a nifty playground. On Friday night, a maximum of 20 people can join local stargazers for telescope viewing; make arrangements in advance.

The museum is part of Sugar Sands Park, 132 acres of shady Florida scrub that's almost as nice as Boca's collection of oceanfront greenways. To get here, take Palmetto Park Rd west of I-95, then turn south on Military Trail; the park is on your left. PalmTran bus 92 will drop you off at the corner of Palmetto Park Rd and Military Trail.

Gumbo Limbo Nature Center

The best reasons to visit Boca Raton, even if (perhaps *especially* if) you're here to mingle with high society folks, are the undeveloped parks that line Ocean Blvd, leaving miles of prime beachfront remarkably condominium-free.

The crown jewel of this park system is **Gumbo Limbo Nature Center** (☎ 561-338-1473; W www.fau.edu/gumbo/; 1801 N Ocean Blvd; admission free; open 9am-4pm Mon-Sat, noon-4pm Mon), in a wild preserve of tropical hammock and dunes ecosystems. It's dedicated to educating the public about sea turtles and other local fauna.

It's a natural-history museum and educational facility of the highest caliber. Displays educate and entertain, providing simple advice for visiting snowbirds: For

---

Club Etiquette Camp

Think your kids are getting a little surly? Get even by sending them to Audrey Kardon and Rachelle Klein's **Boca Raton Resort & Club Etiquette Camp** (☎ 561-881-7733; W www.etiquetteconnection.com) for children seven to 16. The camp will indoctrinate...uh...instruct your little darlings in all they'll ever need to know about social courtesies, personal grooming, ballroom dancing (now more important than ever), French and, of course, magic and juggling. At camp's end, semiformal graduation dinners are held for the happy and now far more polite campers and their parents. The camps run twice a year, and the price is a very considerate $1000.

– Nick & Corinna Selby

SOUTHEAST

instance, don't leave your condo's lights on unnecessarily; it confuses those adorable baby sea turtles trying to make their way to the ocean. Four saltwater tanks display critters being contemplated by scientific researchers.

The preserve also has a number of interesting hikes (more like walks) through tropical foliage and along an artificial mangrove wetland, reclaimed using filtered wastewater from the city. A native flower garden attracts gemstone-colored butterflies by the bushel.

This is also one of ten places in the United States where you can (legally) observe sea turtles nesting, 9pm to 11pm every Monday and Thursday between May 20 and July 11; tickets cost $3.

Spanish River Park

This park (☎ 561-393-7815, 3001 N Ocean Blvd; carload $8 Mon-Fri, $10 Sat & Sun; open 8am-sunset daily) is a truly fine place for a picnic or relaxing on the beach. The bulk of the park – including several nature trails and a lagoon – sprawls along the west side of Hwy A1A, providing shady respite from even the hottest summer day. Campsites are off-limits unless you can convince a Girl Scout troop to accompany you. Through three tunnels under Ocean Blvd, you can walk to the wild beach, with nothing but sand dunes and surfers to distract you. Swimming, fishing and snorkeling are limited to 9am to 5pm daily.

Red Reef Beach & South Beach Park

Red Reef Beach (☎ 561-393-7815; 1 N Ocean Blvd; carload $8 Mon-Fri, $10 Sat & Sun; open 8am-sunset daily) is a top draw for snorkelers, thanks to a unique outcropping of rock and reef just offshore. Don't miss it. Above sea level, Red Reef Beach and neighboring South Beach Park together encompass some 60 acres of wild beach. Note that there are at least a dozen paths where pedestrians are welcome to enter free of charge. Look for breaks in the meandering wooden fence along Hwy A1A just north of Palmetto Park Rd.

Places to Stay

Like the rates along most of Florida's Southeastern coast, room rates in Boca Raton double between December and mid-April.

Boca Inn (☎ 561-395-7500; 1801 N Federal Hwy; rooms $35/70 summer/winter) is bright pink and the best deal in town, with clean rooms and an on-site Indian restaurant.

Ocean Lodge (☎ 561-395-7772; 531 N Ocean Blvd; rooms $55/120 summer/winter) has enormous, comfortable and somewhat threadbare rooms. Like several similar motels along Ocean Blvd, it is across the street from South Beach Park.

Best Western University Inn (☎ 561-395-5225; 2700 N Federal Hwy; rooms $69/99 summer/winter) has clean, cookie-cutter hotel rooms, a nice pool and free shuttle to their private beach.

Holiday Inn Express (☎ 561-395-7172; 2899 N Federal Hwy) is a tad more expensive but much newer, and offers a free full breakfast every morning.

Boca Raton Resort & Club (☎ 888-498-2622; W www.bocaresort.com; 501 El Camino Real; rooms from $185/260 summer/winter) is almost as nice as the Breakers (see Palm Beach, Places to Stay, later) and much more exclusive. Heck, I had to flirt like a wannabe trophy wife just to get past the gates to the uptight concierge: 'No, we do *not* offer public tours; no, you can *not* eat at any of our five-star restaurants unless you're a guest; miss, you shouldn't even *be* here.' The security guards were much more jovial. Anyway, if a fabulous (and it is fabulous) Mizner-designed Mediterranean resort with all the trimmings – spas, private beaches, golf courses – appeals to you, this is the swankiest address in town, dahlings.

Places to Eat

Folks here must not cook much, since the town boasts some of the best restaurants around for every budget. Check out the **Royal Palm Dinner Theatre** (see Entertainment, next) if you prefer a show with your meal.

Flakowitz Bagel Inn (☎ 561-368-0666; 1999 N Federal Hwy; dishes $2-6; open 7am-3pm daily) is a Boca institution. Enjoy a huge breakfast in the cramped dining room or grab any of 22 flavors of bagel at the takeout window. They also serve lunch.

Cannoli Kitchen (☎ 561-338-2929; 2001 N Federal Hwy; open 10am-10pm daily) has the best cheap eats in town, with gourmet pizza by the slice ($2 to $5) or pie ($12 to $20) and creamy-crunchy cannoli ($2) that'll make you smile.

Mississippi Sweet BBQ (☎ 561-394-6779; 2399 N Federal Hwy; mains $9-15; open 11am-9pm Mon-Fri, 4pm-10pm Sat & Sun) serves huge portions of juicy barbecued ribs and chicken, served with two classic Southern sides like deep-fried sweet potatoes or homemade applesauce. This place gets packed.

Phucket Thai (☎ 561-447-8863; 22191 Powerline Rd; lunch mains $5-8, dinner mains $10-15; open 11:30am-2:30pm Mon-Fri, 5pm-10pm daily) lives up to the enthusiastic hype: The tasty garlic chicken and fresh spring rolls made for one of my finest meals in Florida. It's hidden away in the Palm Plaza strip mall, one block south of Palmetto Park Rd.

The **Inca Grill** (☎ 561-395-3553; 515 NE 20th St; mains $10-15; open noon-10pm or so Tues-Sun) specializes in Peruvian seafood served with serious attention to presentation. You'd expect to pay twice as much for the *picante de mariscos* (seafood stew) or *cebiche de pulpo* (octopus ceviche). Reservations are highly recommended.

Culinaros (☎ 561-338-3646; 6897 SW 18th St; mains $17-28; open 5pm-10:30pm or so daily) lets you dine overlooking the golf courses with locals-in-the-know on snapper Greco (with artichokes and capers) or moussaka soufflé. Make reservations on weekends, when belly dancers prance on tables, break plates and otherwise make merry.

La Vieille Maison (☎ 561-391-6701; 770 E Palmetto Park Rd; mains $25-40, prix fixe $68) is consistently voted one of the best restaurants in Florida. The dining rooms are frilly country French and the menu mouthwatering, featuring items like crispy honey-roasted duck with sweetbreads and sesame seeds.

Entertainment

Theater A few miles north of town, **Caldwell Theatre Company** (☎ 561-930-6400;

w www.caldwelltheatre.com; 7873 N Federal Hwy; tickets $40-55) has a reputation for plays that are often alternative or even irreverent (by Boca standards), produced by local playwrights and players.

The **Royal Palm Dinner Theatre** (☎ 561-392-3755; 303 SE Mizner Blvd; tickets $55-70) is known for its critically acclaimed (if somewhat tamer than the Caldwell's) selection of musicals and plays served alongside your gourmet meal.

The **Little Palm Family Theatre** (☎ 561-394-0206), in the same plush venue, presents kid-oriented entertainment, often fairy tales, as weekend matinees.

Willow Theatre (☎ 561-347-3900, 300 S Military Trail), in Sugar Sands Park (see Children's Science Explorium, earlier) performs plays and musicals for $18 in the evening, $7/5 adult/child on weekend matinees.

Live Music The city sponsors a wide variety of free music performances at **Royal Palm Plaza**, close to Mizner Park, at 7pm on Friday, and at **Sanborn Square**, near the corner of Federal Hwy and Palmetto Park Rd, 7pm to 9pm Saturday. Call ☎ 561-393-7806 to see what's on.

The **Boca Pops Orchestra** (☎ 561-391-6777; 100 NE 1st Ave; tickets $10-50) performs at venues throughout Boca Raton and South Florida, though you can occasionally catch them for free at Royal Palm Plaza.

The **Dorothy F Schmidt Performing Arts Center** (☎ 561-297-3820, 777 Glades Rd), at FAU, hosts student ensembles and professional musicians from all over the world September to May. Tickets run $8 to $10 for student performances, more for established artists. See Florida Atlantic University Galleries, earlier, for directions.

Bars & Clubs Though Boca Raton isn't short on activities for the young and old, the bar scene still leaves something to be desired. But you'll still find a few places for a tipple.

The **Lion and Eagle** (☎ 561-394-3190; 2401 N Federal Hwy) is probably the more authentic of two British pubs in town, with Guinness, Fullers ESB and other British

Terrorists vs Tabloids: An American Tale

Shortly after the attacks of September 11, 2001, a new threat to US security emerged: anthrax, the weapon of choice for terrorists with correct postage. Ground Zero was the Boca Raton office of American Media Inc (AMI), home to popular tabloids the *National Enquirer* and *Sun*, known for their silly, scathing and sometimes accurate stories about the rich and famous.

As part of their September 11 coverage, the *Enquirer* even ran a piece revealing that Osama bin Laden's...um...private parts had been left tiny and misshapen by a childhood illness. Shortly afterward, the *Sun* received a letter containing live anthrax spores. Photo editor Bob Stevens unknowingly contracted the disease, succumbing October 5; the horrifying autopsy results suggested that he was the nation's first bioterror victim.

The Centers for Disease Control moved in, sealing off AMI headquarters and testing employees. Two had been exposed, one fell ill. And the plot thickened.

Investigators soon learned that Marwan Al-Shehhi, who flew one of the jets into the World Trade Center, had rented an apartment from the wife of the *Sun*'s editor-in-chief while enrolled at an area aviation school. She described him as a good-natured kid. He and his roommate/fellow hijacker, Hamza Alghamdi, didn't get their damage deposit back, however. They'd trashed the place.

Even as these connections were uncovered, AMI production was moved into temporary offices: The *Enquirer* never missed an issue. Editors covered subsequent anthrax attacks – which by then had reached NBC, CBS and the US Congress – with a special zeal.

Even so, they never lost sight of what the American people needed then more than ever. Yes, blurry pictures of Britney Spears adjusting her bikini and inside reports that William Shatner had passed gas on national television retained their rightful place on those colorful pages, giving proof through the night that America's spirit was still there.

– Paige Penland

brews on tap, plus bangers and mash and kidney pie on the menu.

The Duck (☎ 561-998-8288; 5903 Federal Hwy), just a few blocks north, is a tad more upscale, with a better selection of beer and live music on the weekends.

Bud Murphy's (☎ 561-447-6617; 36 SE 3rd St) is an uninspired but perfectly suitable place to throw a few back, plus it's right by Mizner Park.

Ambience (561-988-8820, 5500 N Federal Hwy) is a high-energy dance club just north of Boca Raton proper.

Aqua Lounge (☎ 561-482-9770; 21065 Powerline Blvd Rd) is another place to shake that bootie and attracts an extremely well-dressed clientele.

Getting There & Away

Boca Raton is more-or-less equidistant to Fort Lauderdale–Hollywood International Airport and Palm Beach International Airport; see corresponding Getting There & Away sections.

Amtrak (☎ 800-872-7245) is fairly close by, in Delray Beach; call for ticket information.

The Boca Raton **Tri-Rail station** (☎ 800 874-7245; 601 NW 53rd St) is close to the Embassy Suites hotel at the Yamato Rd exit of I-95. It provides shuttle service to both airports; it'll cost $4 to get to PBI, and it's free to FLL. PalmTran bus No 53 connects downtown Boca with the Tri-Rail Station; see Getting Around for more information.

Greyhound (561-272-6447) doesn't serve Boca; the closest station is in Delray Beach.

Boca Raton is about 50 miles north of Miami and sprawls several miles east and west of I-95. You can also get there from points north and south on Hwy A1A or US 1.

Getting Around

PalmTran (561-841-4287, W www.palm tran.org) serves Southeast Florida from

North Palm Beach to Boca Raton. It costs $1.25 to ride (60¢ if you're over 65 or have a student ID), and transfers are free; be sure to have exact change. From the Tri-Rail station, bus No 2 takes you to PBI and bus No 94 to FAU, where you can transfer to bus No 91 to Mizner Park. From Mizner Park, take bus No 92 to South Beach Park.

You can rent a car from **Avis** (☎ 561-241-0705) or **Enterprise** (☎ 561-852-0031), and they'll drop it off for you. Parking is usually free and plentiful, though Mizner Park can be a headache on weekend evenings. Thank goodness for that free valet service (don't forget to tip).

DELRAY BEACH
pop 52,000

Friendly Delray was founded by the Seminole Indians, who first carved the trail that's now Atlantic Ave. Settlers from Michigan walked that same beach path in the late 19th century, followed by newly freed African Americans hoping for farms of their own. Civic leaders later invited Japanese colonists to town, in the hopes of making this an agricultural stronghold. The whole citrus thing never really worked out, however.

Then the railroads came through, and this melting pot retooled itself for the tourist trade with a vengeance. Hotels and clubs along that same, now paved, road turned a blind eye to prohibition laws and accommodated everyone. Delray never looked back. Today, Atlantic Ave unites a thriving but mellow beach town with great art galleries, relaxed restaurants and, best of all, a real and welcoming sense of community.

Orientation & Information

Downtown's main drag is Atlantic Ave, which runs from Hwy A1A (Ocean Blvd), across the Intracoastal Waterway and west past I-95 to the Morikami Museum. US Hwy 1 splits into northbound Federal Hwy and southbound Old Dixie Hwy through the city center.

Delray's excellent **chamber of commerce** (☎ 561-278-0424; **w** www.delraybeach.com; 64-A SE 5th Ave; open 9am-5pm Mon-Sat) hands out free downtown maps that are as useful (if not as accurate) as the Dolph and Rand McNally versions.

The **Bank of America** (☎ 561-279-0060; 1001 E Atlantic Ave) and **SunTrust Bank** (☎ 561-243-6766; 302 Atlantic Ave) are both convenient to downtown.

The **library** (☎ 561-266-0194; 29 SE 4th Ave; open 9am-8pm Mon-Wed, 9am-5pm Thurs-Sat, 1pm-5pm Sun) has free Internet access.

Delray News & Tobacco Center (☎ 561-278-3399; 429 E Atlantic) sells foreign publications and fancy cigars. Most radio stations originate from West Palm Beach.

Delray Medical Center (☎ 561-598-4440; **w** www.delraymedicalctr.com; 5352 Linton Blvd) is just west of Military Trail.

The Morikami Museum & Japanese Gardens

This cultural landmark (☎ 561-499-2557; www.morikami.org; 4000 Morikami Park Rd; adult/child $8/4; open 10am-5pm Tues-Sun) has a fascinating history: It's the site of the Yamato settlement, brainchild of local merchants, politicians and ambitious business-school graduate Jo Sakei. The group hoped to attract Japanese families to Florida, where they would (theoretically) introduce new and profitable agricultural techniques to the region.

Yamato opened in 1905, with one big problem: Only single Japanese men volunteered; the stable families that founders had hoped for were just not interested. Sakei sold his share off during the land boom two decades later. Another settler, Sukjei 'George' Morikami, stuck around awhile longer and planted some very nice gardens. Today these skirt the outstanding Morakami Museum.

The permanent collection includes priceless Japanese antiquities and typical household items used by the Japanese colonists. The museum also hosts four traveling exhibitions each year. Tea ceremonies are held in the **Seishin-An teahouse** on the second Saturday of the month ($3).

The gardens, with more than a mile of trails, are a study in traditional Japanese landscaping techniques. More familiar

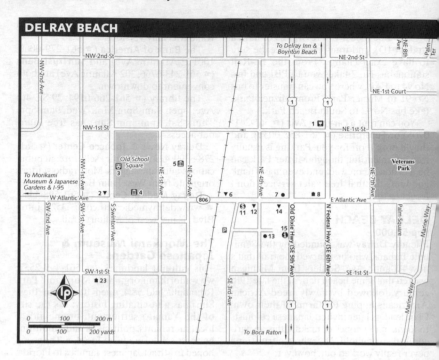

DELRAY BEACH

arts like bonsai are displayed alongside equally authentic rock gardens, waterfalls and ponds teeming with koi, all studded with monuments favored by Japanese gardeners of various eras. Free tours are available at 3pm Wednesday and Thursday.

Be sure to stop by the **Cornell Cafe** (mains $4-8), which specializes in Japanese home cooking like soba noodle soup and seaweed salad.

Morikami Gardens is about 4 miles west of I-95 on Atlantic Ave: Make a left on Jog Rd and a right on Morikami Park Rd.

International Orchid Center
Just south of Morikami Museum on Jog Rd is the headquarters of the **American Orchid Society** (☎ 561-404-2000; w www.orchidweb .org; 16700 AOS Lane; admission $6; open 10am-4pm Mon-Sat), featuring 3½ acres of landscaped gardens, including a collection of cultivated orchids from all over the world.

Old School Square
The heart of downtown and cultural center of Delray Beach, Old School Square is home to the Crest Theatre and two very different museums. It also plays host to most of the city's civic events, including live music on Friday and Saturday night.

Cornell Museum
Florida fine artists exhibit their work here (☎ 561-243-7922; 51 N Swinton Ave; adult/ child $5/1; open 1pm-4:30pm) at this small museum of art and history. The restored 1913 elementary school building is a museum piece itself; for a deeper delve into the past, ask about the **Delray Historical Archives**, available upstairs.

Palm Beach Photographic Centre
The center (☎ 561-276-9797; w www.work shop.org; 55 NE 2nd Ave; admission $3; open 10am-5pm Mon-Sat) offers classes in how

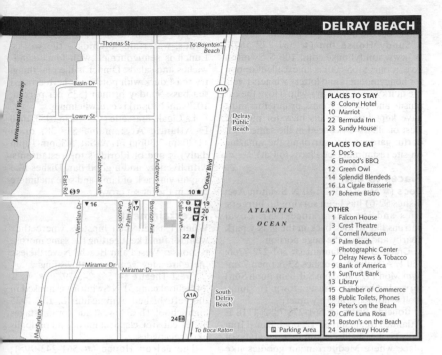

DELRAY BEACH

PLACES TO STAY
8 Colony Hotel
10 Marriot
22 Bermuda Inn
23 Sundy House

PLACES TO EAT
2 Doc's
6 Elwood's BBQ
12 Green Owl
14 Splendid Blendeds
16 La Cigale Brasserie
17 Boheme Bistro

OTHER
1 Falcon House
3 Crest Theatre
4 Cornell Museum
5 Palm Beach Photographic Center
7 Delray News & Tobacco
9 Bank of America
11 SunTrust Bank
13 Library
15 Chamber of Commerce
18 Public Toilets, Phones
19 Peter's on the Beach
20 Caffe Luna Rosa
21 Boston's on the Beach
24 Sandoway House

to use their gazillion-dollar collection of top-of-the-line equipment, and tours of facilities that will make photographers drool. The center also houses two galleries in which experimental and traditional (mostly experimental) photography is displayed and interactive tours of works by famed photographers across the globe are offered.

Sandoway House

This smallish nature center (☎ 561-274-7263; 142 S Ocean Blvd; $2 donation; open 10am-4:30pm daily) is housed in a 1936 Victorian mansion right on the beach. Exhibits are geared toward younger kids, with information on Florida's coastal ecosystems arranged for maximum color and interest. The shark show is a hit.

Places to Stay

Delray Inn (☎ 866-908-3000; W www.delrayinn.net; 297 NE 6th Ave; rooms $65/85

summer/winter) has a barbecue grill outside and full kitchenettes inside. Note that this is an alcohol-free hotel.

Budget Inn (☎ 561-276-8961; 2500 N Federal Hwy; rooms $55/85 summer/winter) is a decent place.

The **Bermuda Inn** (☎ 407-276-5288; 64 S Ocean Blvd; rooms $85/115 summer/winter), just a stone's throw (well, across Hwy A1A) from the beach, is friendly and well maintained.

The **Marriott** (☎ 561-274-3200; 101 N Ocean Blvd; rooms with/without view $149/129 summer, $259/229 winter) is a new luxury hotel that pays sincere homage to the Spanish-Mediterranean architecture of the Flagler era.

The **Colony Hotel** (☎ 561-276-4123, 800-552-2363; 525 Atlantic Ave; rooms $79/149 summer/winter) was built in 1926 and is still decorated – with wicker chairs and Gold Coast tropical grandeur – in much the same

SOUTHEAST

way. Rooms are a little small, but you just can't beat the downtown location.

Sundy House Inn (☎ 561-272-5678; W www.sundyhouse.com; 106 S Swinton Ave; rooms $165-600) is an excellent option for honeymooners and lottery winners (well, the quirky ones, anyway), who'll love the exquisite and eclectic rooms; proprietors must have kept local artisans busy for months. Best of all, it's ensconced in the same wonderful gardens that surround the amazing on-site restaurant (see Places to Eat).

Places to Eat

Doc's (☎ 561-278-3627; 10 N Swinton Ave; dishes $2-6) has been serving up burgers, fries and ice cream since 1951. Loyal patrons like to kick back in the grassy park nearby and enjoy the huge portions.

Green Owl Restaurant (☎ 561-272-7766; 330 E Atlantic Ave; dishes $3-6; open 7am-3pm Mon-Fri, 7am-2pm Sat, 8am-noon Sun) serves the best breakfast in town. The tuna-melt sandwich is also a winner.

Boheme Bistro (☎ 561-278-7882; 1118 E Atlantic Ave; mains $7-12; open 8am-11pm daily) is a casually elegant first-date type of place where Mediterranean goodies like gyros, pizza and shrimp thermador are made to order.

Elwood's BBQ (☎ 561-967-4573; 301 E Atlantic Blvd; mains $8-15; open 11am-midnight daily), in a retooled gas station, is a little touristy, but fun. The food is fine, and an Elvis impersonator shakes his pelvis on the outdoor patio Thursday night.

Splendid Blendeds (☎ 561-265-1035; 432 E Atlantic Blvd; lunch mains $7-12, dinner mains $14-25; open 11:30am-2:30pm & 5:30pm-10pm Mon-Sat) offers gourmet grub on a budget at lunch, with spicy Pahoa chicken and grilled veggie ravioli garnering raves. Prices double at dinner, as does selection. The filet mignon stuffed with roasted garlic is a favorite.

Sundy House Inn (☎ 561-272-5678; 106 S Swinton Ave; lunch mains $7-13, dinner mains $18-36; open 11:30am-2:30pm Mon-Sat, 6pm-10pm daily) is memorable. You can dine inside the refined 1902 Victorian mansion, or (better) eat at tables scattered throughout the tropical botanical gardens. They've got parrots in the trees, koi in the ponds, waterfalls, orchids – the works. Lunch is semigourmet, with fancy sandwiches and salads. Dinner is the real thing; try roast duck with polenta or herb-crusted sea bass. Sunday brunch ($35 per person; 10:30am-2:30pm) is overwhelming.

La Cigale Brasserie (☎ 561-276-6453; 1010 E Atlantic Ave; mains $17-38; open 11:30am-2:30pm Fri & Sat, 5:30pm-10pm daily) is one of Florida's top restaurants, with live jazz and a good bar. Dishes like coq au vin, rack of lamb and sole meuniere pack in the jet-set crowd.

Entertainment

When I asked area hipsters where they went for fun, I kept getting the same morose response: 'West Palm Beach.' Nevertheless, there are a few venues worth visiting.

Crest Theatre (☎ 561-243-7922; W www.oldschool.com; 51 N Swinton) is housed in the refurbished gymnasium of the 1925 high school. The 320-seat auditorium stages ballet, cabaret, classical music and oddballs like Icecapades.

The **Falcon House** (☎ 561-243-9951; W www.thefalconhouse.com; 116 NE 6th Ave; open 5pm-2am Tues-Sat, 3pm-midnight Sun) comes highly recommended for its urban atmosphere, quality cocktails, tapas menu and incredible sound system (reportedly donated by New Age musician and regular patron Yanni).

Peter's on the Beach (☎ 561-278-7878; 6 S Ocean Blvd; open 11am-10pm Mon-Fri, 11am-2pm Sat & Sun) is chromed out, serves sushi and has a great chandelier. It doesn't have the best reputation among local boozehounds, however, who say it's 'creepy.' I didn't feel it.

Caffe Luna Rosa (☎ 561-274-9404; 34 S Ocean Blvd) is a Manhattan-style Italian joint with more than 100 wines available by the bottle plus plenty of stronger stuff.

Boston's on the Beach (☎ 561-278-3364; W www.bostonsonthebeach.com; 40 S Ocean Blvd; open 7:30am-2am daily) is a grungy and very popular spot with lots of good beer and vegetarian-friendly bar food. There's free live music nightly, except on Monday (Reggae Night), when there's a $3 cover.

Getting There & Around
The **Greyhound bus station** (☎ 561-272-6447; 402 N Federal Hwy) is served by PalmTran. Bus No 2 takes you to PBI or Boca Raton; bus No 81 serves the Tri-Rail station, Amtrak and downtown Delray.

Amtrak (☎ 800-872-2745; 345 S Congress Ave), half a mile south of Atlantic Ave, shares a station with Tri-Rail (☎ 800-874-7245; www.tri-rail.com).

Delray Beach is about 20 miles south of West Palm Beach and 45 miles north of Miami on I-95, US Hwy 1 or Hwy A1A.

LAKE WORTH
pop 32,000
Lake Worth took early advantage of the sun, surf and Roaring '20s, incorporating in 1913 and bringing in the high rollers with its infamous Lake Worth Casino, built in 1925. Only three years later, however, the town was hit with a double whammy: A brutal hurricane in 1928 tore the town apart, and the Great Depression managed to squelch redevelopment for decades.

In recent years, however, downtown has attracted museums, bars and clubs, making it something of a cultural hub and a definite weekend destination for upscale area 20-somethings. The city still takes pride in its relaxed unpretentiousness, however, not to mention the fact that its forward-thinking founders managed to slip off with a sliver of the nicest beach around, a geopolitical quirk that effectively divides posh Palm Beach in two.

Orientation
Lake Worth is about 5 miles south of West Palm Beach. The small downtown lies on the mainland, straddling two one-way streets: westbound Lucerne Ave and eastbound Lake Ave. Lake Ave leads to the bridge and Lake Worth's beautiful beach and pier, and divides addresses into north and south. US Hwy 1 is called Dixie Hwy, and other north-south streets are lettered from west to east (Dixie Hwy was formerly known as I St).

Information
The **chamber of commerce** (☎ 561-582-4401; Ⓦ www.lwchamber.com; 807 Lucerne Ave; open 9am-4pm Mon-Fri) is easy to miss – it's in a tiny storefront in between J St and Old Dixie Hwy.

Bank of America (14 N Federal Hwy) is right downtown. The most convenient **post office** is on the north side of Lucerne St, between J and K Sts.

The **public library** (☎ 561-533-7354; 15 N M St; open 9:30am-8pm Mon-Wed, 9:30am-5pm Thurs-Sat) has free Internet access. **D&D Internet Kafe** (☎ 561-585-1003; 704 Lucerne Ave; open 9am-9pm Mon-Fri, 11am-6pm Sat) gets you online faster for $7 an hour.

Colonial Coin Laundry (☎ 561-585-5027, 117 N Federal) is about a block off the main drag.

The big daily is *South Florida Sun Sentinal* (Ⓦ www.sun-sentinal.com), and on Tuesday *The Forum* publishes local news. Commercial radio comes from West Palm Beach.

Palm Beach Institute of Contemporary Art
Technophiles and modern art fans will love this slick museum (☎ 561-582-0006; Ⓦ www.palmbeachica.org; 601 Lake Ave; adult/student $3/2; open noon-6pm Tues-Sun). The permanent collection can be difficult to understand, but it's easy to appreciate. Rotating exhibitions, like Fred Tomasseli's colorful studies of various hallucinogens, will have your head spinning without any added chemicals. The New Media Lounge, designed to display cutting-edge digital art, has potential to develop as the medium does.

Hibel Gallery
Recently relocated from Palm Beach, this wacky little gallery (☎ 561-533-6872; Ⓦ www.hibel.org; 701 Lake Ave; admission free; open 10am-5pm Mon-Sat) is basically a shrine to artist Edna Hibel. Her primarily figurative work has a dreamy quality overlaid with subtle social commentary and isn't everyone's cup of tea. But it's free to peruse the place and is definitely a worthwhile way to invest an hour.

Museum of the City of Lake Worth

On the 2nd floor of the utilities building, this tidy historical museum (☎ 561-586-1700; 414 Lake Ave; admission free; open 9:30am-3:30pm Mon-Fri) is packed with obscurities and ephemera, including homage to the Eastern Europeans who continue to gravitate here. Check out the life-sized photo of local farmer Erwin Smith, whose beard reached 7½ feet in 1832. They also offer a free walking tour of the city by appointment only.

In the same building, the **Lake Worth Art League Gallery** (☎ 561-586-1700; admission free; open noon-4pm Mon-Fri) has shows featuring work by local artists.

Lake Worth Beach has great surfing waves, for Florida.

Lake Worth Beach

This stretch of sand is universally agreed to be the finest beach between Fort Lauderdale and Daytona. The waves are great for surfing or swimming, the sand fine and white. If you want to risk skin cancer for a couple of days (hey, you're in Florida!) this is a great place to do it.

Island Water Sports (☎ 561-588-1728; W www.iwslakeworth.com; 728 Lake Ave) rents body boards for $10 daily and surfboards for $20 to $30 daily, depending on the board length.

Municipal Pier

This photogenic and relatively undeveloped pier (☎ 561-582-9001; adult/child $2/1 for fishing, 50¢ to look; open 7am-midnight daily) is the perfect place to watch the sun rise. You can even rent a rod and reel for $15, including bait. On weekends, you can hang out here until 2am, if you make it in by closing time.

Places to Stay

Lake Worth is a relatively inexpensive option compared to neighboring beach cities and has some interesting options. The cheapest hotels are north of town on Old Dixie Hwy, and you get what you pay for.

Southgate Motel (☎ 561-582-1544; 709 S Dixie Hwy; rooms $33/45 summer/winter) has cleanish rooms with brownish carpeting.

Budget Lodge (☎ 561-582-1379; 521 S Dixie Hwy; rooms $45/55 summer/winter) has newer rooms with similar carpeting.

New Sun Gate Motel (☎ 561-588-8110; W www.new-sungate.com; 901 S Federal Hwy; rooms $49/59 summer/winter) is a much nicer option. It caters to Finnish tourists and has an attached Mexican restaurant (seriously). Some suites have moviestar themes, which cost a tad more than the very clean regular rooms.

The **Hummingbird Hotel** (☎ 561-582-3224; 631 Lucerne Ave; rooms $66), right downtown, is a nifty little place with a B&B feel and youth hostel setup: Most of the flowery rooms share a bath, cutting your cost for a great stay.

The **Parador** (☎ 561-876-6000; 1000 S Federal Hwy; rooms from $75/125 summer/winter) isn't your typical antique-packed Victorian B&B. It's in an old hotel, but every room has been creatively redecorated. It's pet- and kid-friendly.

The **Marriott Fairfield Inn & Suites** (☎ 561-582-2585; 2870 S Ocean Blvd; rooms from $89/129 summer/winter) likes to stress that it has a *Palm Beach* address, despite its flawless location opposite Lake Worth pier. Sterile elegance, from the Continental breakfast to the large pool and business center, makes this a fair deal.

The **Gulf Stream Hotel** (☎ 888-540-0669; W www.thegulfstreamhotel.com; 1 Lake Ave; rooms from $99/179 summer/winter) is a wonderful place, housed in the former Lake Worth Casino. Despite its cultural significance, the austere outside just doesn't do the opulent-yet-cozy interior justice.

Places to Eat

The **Taco Lady** (☎ 561-502-0444; 7 N L St; dishes $2-6; open 11am-9pm Mon-Sat) serves cheap and tasty breakfast burritos and huge taco combination platters.

La Bonne Bouche (☎ 561-533-0840; 516 Lucerne Ave; open 7am-5pm Mon-Sat, 1pm-5pm Sun) is packed with French expats who line up for decadent pastries ($3 to $5) and the quiche and spinach salad combo ($6), available at lunchtime.

Benny's (☎ 561-582-9001; 10 Ocean Ave; mains $2-12; open 7am-6pm Sun-Thurs, 7am-9pm Fri & Sat), on the pier, may not have John G's rabid following, but it does have waves crashing beneath your table. Big breakfasts and fast food are available inside or at the takeout window.

John G's Restaurant (☎ 561-588-7733; 10 S Ocean Ave; dishes $4-8; open 7:30am-3pm daily), right across from the Lake Worth Pier, is the best place for breakfast in Lake Worth (and according to loyal patrons: on Earth). If the lines out the door don't convince you, try one of their 'ethnic' omelets.

European Deli & Restaurant (☎ 561-588-8052; 402 N Dixie Hwy; mains $5-12) dishes up meaty German treats like kielbasa with potato salad and kraut, and roast pork with spaetzel and cabbage. Streudel is a specialty.

Rustico Italiano (☎ 561-547-2782; 701 Lucerne Ave; mains $17-26; open 11am-10pm Mon-Sat, 5-10pm Sun) was once Lake Worth's best inexpensive Italian eatery, but it is now a white-tablecloth gourmet restaurant (and a highly recommended one at that).

Entertainment

Performing Arts On the first and third Friday of the month, Lake Worth throws **Evening on the Avenues**, a downtown street party with live music, classic cars, free food and cheap beer. The city also sponsors free big-band concerts every Thursday night at the **Bryant Park Bandshell**, on the corner of Lake Ave and Golfview.

Lake Worth Playhouse (☎ 561-586-6410; w www.lakeworthplayhouse.org; 709 Lake Ave; tickets $15-22), housed in a restored 1924 vaudeville venue, is an intimate venue that stages classic community theater. The **Stonzek Studio Theatre** (tickets $12), a 65-

seat black-box space at the same address, is a tad edgier.

Bars & Clubs Lake Worth loves to party and has more than a dozen bars and clubs within easy hopping distance of one another.

Round N' Third (☎ 561-585-8444; 509 Lake Ave) is a tiny dive bar with a patio decked out in sand and sea turtles (it's about a mile from the beach). Beer is served in plastic cups, and there's often live music, usually local rock bands, or karaoke.

Dug Rocks (☎ 561-493-1924; 6 S J St) is a local pub that packs in a primarily gay crowd for its margarita specials and Friday barbecues.

CG Café (☎ 561-585-5911; 517 Lake Ave; open 11am-11pm daily) has tables on the patio and local art in the dining room, where you can listen to acoustic musicians get their groove on.

The **Bamboo Room** (☎ 561-585-2583; w www.bambooroom.com; 25 S J St; open 4pm-2am Mon-Sat, 4pm-midnight Sun) features regional and internationally known blues acts. It's usually free, but big names justify the occasional $5 to $25 cover.

Getting There & Around

The **Tri-Rail Station** is located at 1703 Lake Worth Rd, at the intersection of A St. Palm-Tran bus Nos 60, 62 and 42 connect the station to downtown. The closest **Amtrak** and **Greyhound bus stations** are in West Palm Beach (see Getting There & Away in the West Palm Beach section); both are served by PalmTran bus No 2.

Lolly the Trolley (adult/child $1/50¢; 9am-5pm Mon-Sat) has three 'trolley' lines (they're actually buses decked out in their San Francisco–style Sunday best) that originate near city hall, at the corner of Lake Ave and H St. You can flag them down anywhere on their route. Pick up a system map at the chamber of commerce.

Downtown is designed for pedestrians, and there's free parking everywhere. Things can get tricky on Friday and Saturday night, however.

WEST PALM BEACH
pop 82,100
When Henry Flagler first decided to develop the area that would become West Palm Beach, he knew exactly what it would become: a real city that could support his glittering resort town under construction across the causeway. And so the fraternal twins were born, Palm Beach always considered the fairer of the two, West Palm working hard, playing harder, and having one heck of a lot more fun.

Some things haven't changed, and while Banyan St is no longer the den of sin that locals so loved back in the 1900s, Clematis St is enthusiastically keeping the tradition alive. And there's something of a Cinderella act afoot – the city has committed itself to an unbelievably ambitious urban renewal program. Its mission? To build a community from extremes, inclusive of insomniac hipsters and retired snowbirds, a cultural center for everyone from residents of primarily African American Riviera Beach to affluent Palm Beach and beyond.

The results – aside from way too much road construction – are impressive. The decade-old Kravis Center for the Performing Arts is now among the premier cultural attractions in Florida, and CityPlace, which could have been just another sterile shopping mall, has helped turn an already revitalized downtown into a magnet for festive folks from all over the county.

Orientation
West Palm Beach sprawls along the west bank of Lake Worth (the Intracoastal Waterway), which separates it from Palm Beach. It's a planned community and tends toward a fairly straightforward grid. The main north-south routes are I-95 and US Hwy 1, which splits into S Dixie Hwy (southbound) and Olive Ave (northbound) through much of downtown. The city plans to make Dixie Hwy the major, two-way thoroughfare, but there's a lot of construction between now and then. Major east-west roads are Okeechobee Blvd (which crosses the causeway to Palm Beach), Belvedere Rd and Southern Blvd.

Downtown is centered around Clematis St and CityPlace, and there's fantastic public transportation throughout the immediate area. Most major sites are located far from the West Palm's heart, however.

Information
The **chamber of commerce** (☎ 561-833-3711; **W** www.palmbeaches.org; 401 N Flagler Dr; open 9am-5pm Mon-Fri) is geared toward businesspeople, though they do provide some tourist information. There's a small visitor's center at the Cuillo Center for the Arts (see Entertainment, later).

The **main library** (☎ 561-659-8010, 100 Clematis St) offers free Internet access. **Clematis St Newsstand** (☎ 561-832-2302; **W** www.clematisstreetnews.com; 206 Clematis St) provides online access for $7 per hour, as well as international newspapers and magazines, tons of Lonely Planet guides, coffee and snacks.

CityPlace has two good bookstores: **Reading Etc** (☎ 561-835-0162, 700 S Rosemary Ave) may not have the same huge selection as neighboring **Barnes & Noble** (☎ 561-514-0811, 700 S Rosemary Ave), but it's got excellent overdone Egyptian decor.

The *Palm Beach Post* (**W** www.palmbeachpost.com) is the local paper of record, but the *Palm Beach Daily News* (**W** www.palmbeachdailynews.com) has more human-interest stories. Weeklies, *New Times* (**W** www.newtimesbpb.com) and *City Link* (**W** www.citylinkmagazine.com) are saucy and free, and *Closer* (**W** www.closemagazine.com) is hipper. The local chamber of commerce publishes both the annual *Guide to the Palm Beaches* and the *Palm Beach County Guide*.

Radio stations are possessed of ear-bleeding mediocrity, sandwiching three-song play lists between endless ads for breast implants, herbal Viagra and sordid legal services. A few FM stations, including 88.5 (local alternative bands), 88.9 (Latin jazz) and 90.7 (public radio) are excellent – when you can pick them up. Otherwise it's lousy rock (92.3, 98.7 and 103.1), lousy dance (101.9 and 102.3), lousy country (107.9),

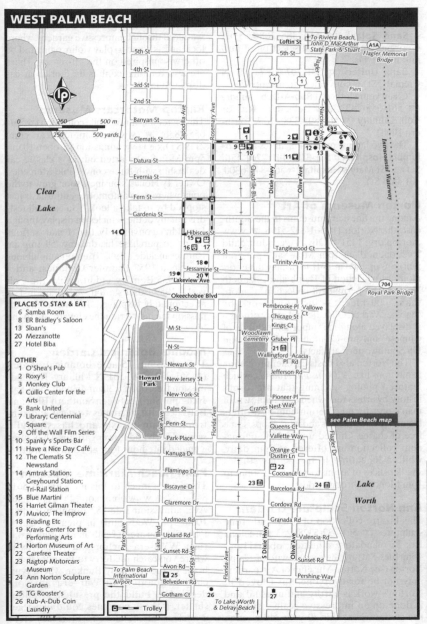

WEST PALM BEACH

PLACES TO STAY & EAT
6 Samba Room
8 ER Bradley's Saloon
13 Sloan's
20 Mezzanotte
27 Hotel Biba

OTHER
1 O'Shea's Pub
2 Roxy's
3 Monkey Club
4 Cuillo Center for the
   Arts
5 Bank United
7 Library; Centennial
   Square
9 Off the Wall Film Series
10 Spanky's Sports Bar
11 Have a Nice Day Café
12 The Clematis St
   Newsstand
14 Amtrak Station;
   Greyhound Station;
   Tri-Rail Station
15 Blue Martini
16 Harriet Gilman Theater
17 Muvico; The Improv
18 Reading Etc
19 Kravis Center for the
   Performing Arts
21 Norton Museum of Art
22 Carefree Theater
23 Ragtop Motorcars
   Museum
24 Ann Norton Sculpture
   Garden
25 TG Rooster's
26 Rub-A-Dub Coin
   Laundry

SOUTHEAST

lousy Christian (97.9) and lousy easy listening (104.3 and 105.1).

Sand Splash (☎ 561-585-7680, 5101 Georgia Ave) has a great selection of new and used CDs.

Bank United (☎ 561-707-0727, 101 N Clematis St) is convenient to downtown.

Clean your clothes at **Rub-A-Dub Laundry** (☎ 561-655-7833; 526 Belvedere Rd) or **Coin Laundry** (☎ 561-802-3388; 827 Southern Blvd).

The two largest medical facilities are **Columbia Hospital** (☎ 561-842-6141; 2201 45th St) and **St Mary's Hospital** (☎ 561-844-6300; 901 45th St).

Norton Museum of Art

Among the finest art museums in the Southeast, the Norton (☎ 561-832-5196; w www.norton.org; 1451 S Olive Ave; adult/child $6/2; open 10am-5pm Mon-Sat, 1pm-5pm Sun) was opened in 1941 to display the enormous art collection of Ralph and Elizabeth Norton. The permanent collection of more than 5000 pieces – including work by Matisse, Warhol, O'Keefe and many others – is displayed alongside important exhibits of Chinese and pre-Columbian Mexican and US Southwestern artifacts.

The Norton also hosts excellent traveling exhibitions like *A Thousand Hounds,* which featured photos spanning that art form's history, by artists renowned and unknown, of man's best friend. The museum also offers lectures, performances and workshops, some free of charge. Guided tours of the permanent collection are offered at 2pm daily, while a lunchtime lecture series studies smaller slices of art history from 12:30pm to 1pm Monday through Friday.

Ann Norton Sculpture Garden

This bizarre collection of brick and stone sculptures (☎ 561-832-5328; 253 Barcelona Rd; $5 mandatory donation; open 11am-4pm Tues-Sat) by the second wife of Ralph Norton (see Norton Museum of Art, earlier) may not be for everyone, but I loved it. Norton's work is earthy and unusual and is done on an impressive scale – stop by the studio where this 70-year-old woman climbed 15 feet or more to chisel saints and sinners from raw granite. Sculptures are scattered through impressive gardens, where local artists come to play violin, paint and be otherwise inspired on the off-season. There are also rotating exhibits by Florida artists displayed inside.

Ragtop Motorcars Museum

This incredible automobile collection (☎ 561-655-2836; w www.ragtopmotorcars.com; 2119 S Dixie Hwy; admission $5; open 10am-5pm Mon-Sat) started out as a classic car dealership with three convertible Mercedes. Owner Ty Houck's business soon grew to the point where area automotive enthusiasts just stopped by to take a look. You can still test-drive many of the vehicles on display, though I couldn't convince Ty that I had 'serious intent' to purchase his dreamy '59 Impala. Rarities include a 1967 Triumph amphibious vehicle, a 1952 Daimler Conquest and a regal 1935 Bentley. Oddities like the – oh yes! – 1959 Edsel station wagon are just as affectionately displayed. It's worth the admission fee just to ride the elevator up to the 'drive-in.'

Mounts Botanical Garden

This pleasant, 15-acre botanical garden (☎ 561-233-1749; 531 N Military Trail; admission free; open 8:30am-4:30pm Mon-Sat, 1pm-5pm Sun), between Southern Blvd and Belvedere Rd, recreates tropical and subtropical rain forests and has soulfully scented herb and flower gardens. They offer a guided one-hour tour at 11am Saturday.

Palm Beach Maritime Museum

There's not much to this museum (☎ 561-842-8202; w www.pbmm.org; 4512 N Flagler Ave; admission free ($2 donation); open 10am-2pm Weds-Sun) in pleasant Curry Park, but you aren't really here to check out rusty WWI-era anchors, anyway. This is where you catch the ferry to Peanut Island, home of the Kennedy Bunker, where typically brilliant Cold War–era advisors decided to build the president's fallout shelter. ('Those commies could *never* get a nuclear missile close to Florida.') Here you'll see JFK's decontamination shower, then you can go hiking, snorkeling or even camping (see Places to Stay) on the island. The ferry comes at 10am, noon and 2pm Wednesday through Sunday.

CityPlace

This 'entertainment destination' (☎ 561-366-1000; W www.cityplaceweb.com) is the crown jewel of West Palm Beach's recent urban renewal initiative. Part shopping center, part bar-hopping center, part cultural center, it attracts residents by the trolleyload to its pedestrian-only mall, centered on the corner of Hibiscus St and Rosemary Ave.

CityPlace's cultural centerpiece is the **Harriet Gilman Theater**, but most people show up for the free concerts held in the central plaza (see Entertainment). Shops, restaurants and bars tend to be on the upscale side, but if you're in the mood for a dive there's free public transportation to Clematis St.

Though it still feels a little sterile, City-Place really is a great idea, and successfully brings together mellow retirees, young sophisticates and, of course, hordes of hormone-addled teens looking for something to do.

Lion Country Safari

Recently voted the 'Best Tourist Trap in Southeastern Florida' by *City Link,* this oddball attraction (☎ 561-793-1084; W www .lioncountrysafari.com; 2003 Lion Country Safari Rd; adult/child $17/13; open 10am-5:30pm) is roaring your name. Here's the deal: An impressive collection of exotic and dangerous animals occupies areas designed to resemble the African habitats to which they are native. And these bison, zebras, baboons, African elephants, rhinos, giraffes, chimps and, of course, lions aren't exactly in cages.

You tour the safari section in your own car, unless it's a convertible, as a wily pride of lions could theoretically claw their way through your ragtop and eat you, your little niece and your leftover Arby's sandwiches in five seconds flat. Which poses something of an insurance risk for safari proprietors.

So if all you've got is a ragtop, they'll rent you a van for $8.50. Pets are not allowed (there's a free kennel). See the movie *Jurassic Park* for further tips.

The last car enters the safari area at 4:30pm, and admission to the small on-site amusement park is included with your admission. The park is located 18 miles west of I-95 on Southern Blvd; follow the signs.

South Florida Science Museum

If you like science museums, don't miss this one (☎ 561-832-1988; W www.sfsm.org; 4801 Dreher Trail N; adult/child $6/4; open 10am-5pm Mon-Thurs, 10am-10pm Fri, 10am-6pm Sat, noon-6pm Sun), next to the Palm Beach Zoo. Permanent exhibits are unique: You can even make your own plastic dinosaur using industrial machinery. Outside, there's a **Science Trail** with whisper dishes, a human sundial and various Florida ecosystems. Be warned, however: You'll want to spend the extra $4 when you see the **Galaxy Golf** course. It's miniature golf with a twist – each hole describes astronomical phenomena, Newtonian physics and other scientific principles to competitive siblings angling for a win. Next door, **Buzz Aldrin Planetarium** does a variety of stellar shows at 1pm and 2pm daily ($2). An on-site **observatory** is open from sunset to 10pm Friday. For directions, see the Palm Beach Zoo (following).

Palm Beach Zoo at Dreher Park

This interesting little zoo (☎ 561-547-9453; W www.palmbeachzoo.com; 1301 Summit Blvd; adult/child $6/4; open 9am-5pm daily) is worth your time and money for two big reasons: First, they have a few of the last remaining Florida panthers, North America's rarest mammal. Second, they have gator-feeding shows. There are just some things no Florida vacation is complete without. The zoo also has some other unusual residents, including Komodo dragons and Goeldi's monkeys, as well as a nice pond plied by paddleboats and a petting zoo with some very fat goats. To get here, exit Southern Blvd east from I-95, head south on Parker Ave, and follow the signs to the

Science Museum and Zoo. Dreher Park is served by PalmTran bus No 46.

Riviera Beach

If you're hoping to enjoy the sand and surf, pickings are slim in West Palm proper. But Riviera Beach, about 3 miles north of downtown, has one of the nicest beaches in the area, with wild dunes that have remained undeveloped thanks to the area's blue-collar reputation. Lifeguards are on duty from 9am to 5pm daily. To get here, take Hwy 1 north from downtown West Palm Beach until you hit Blue Heron Way (Hwy A1A); cross the causeway and continue straight ahead until you see waves. Riviera Beach is served by PalmTran bus No 30.

Boat Tours

The **Palm Beach Water Taxi** (☎ 561-683-8294; 98 Lake Dr; adult/child $17/9) isn't a taxi service at all, but instead offers guided tours along the Intracoastal Waterway: Ignore the privacy of the rich and famous on the Palm Beach Then & Now tour, or enjoy a dolphin's-eye view of John D MacArthur State Park on the Nature Lover's tour. Tours leave from both Singer Island and Clematis St in downtown West Palm Beach. They also offer a 'Wine and Cheese Sunset' cruise on Tuesday (times change with the sunset). It's $25/12 adult/child and leaves from Singer Island only.

Places to Stay

There are plenty of rather expensive and uninspiring chain hotels off I-95, but better bets (not only for price, but also for general cleanliness) are a cluster of small, family-owned places on Dixie Hwy, south of Southern Blvd and just off our map of West Palm Beach.

Camping Peanut Island (☎ 561-845-4445; tent sites $17) has great developed campgrounds by reservation only. Primitive sites on the west side of the island are free and available on a first-come, first-served basis. There are lots of restrictions, so call ahead.

KOA (☎ 561-793-9797; sites without/with hookups $14/26, kamping kabins $50) has a campground close to Lion Country Safari, 18 miles west of I-95 on Southern Blvd. It's not exactly convenient to downtown, but you do get to wake up to lions roaring.

Sunsport Gardens (☎ 561-793-0423; W www.sunsportgarden.com; 14125 North Rd; campsites without/with hookups $15/22) is perfect if you haven't done laundry in a while. Since 1965, this has been Southeast Florida's premier naturist retreat, where folks can enjoy tennis courts, saunas and camping naked. You can also come by for the day (singles/couples $25/30). From downtown, head west on Okeechobee Blvd about 11 miles, make a right on E Rd, and follow the signs.

Hotels & Motels Vali Motel (☎ 561-493-1902; 5515 S Dixie Hwy; rooms $42) is a surprisingly nice option.

Apollo Inn (☎ 561-833-1222; 4201 S Dixie Hwy; rooms $45/55 summer/winter) has basic rooms in their cheerfully painted and even more cheerfully managed hotel.

Parkview Motor Lodge (☎ 561-833-4644; 4710 S Dixie Hwy; rooms $46-74 summer, $70-88 winter) is very clean, very safe and worth the extra cash. You get a free, semi-accurate map of West Palm Beach with your room.

Hotel Biba (☎ 561-832-0094; W www.hotel biba.com; 320 Belvedere Rd; rooms $99/129 summer/winter) is definitely where Austin Powers would stay. It's super groovy: All rooms have big silver beanbags, lots of chrome and CD players. Breakfast is served in the similarly decorated on-site dance club. Make reservations well in advance.

Hibiscus House (☎ 561-863-5633, 800-203-4927; W www.hibiscushouse.com; 501 30th St; rooms $75-135 summer, $95-180 winter) is where you'd put your mom up on Mother's Day. All the rooms have terraces and bathrooms, and there's a Jacuzzi in the Red Room and a working fireplace in the suite. Have your two-course breakfast inside the antique-filled Victorian or out by the pool on the shady, flower-trimmed patio. The same people are opening another B&B close to CityPlace in 2003. Call for details.

Places to Eat

Sloan's (☎ 561-833-3335; 112 Clematis St; open 11am-9pm Sun-Thurs, 11am-11pm Fri & Sat) is a colorful place with sweets, treats and rich homemade ice cream by the pint or cone.

Howley's Restaurant (☎ 561-833-5691; 4700 Dixie Hwy; dishes $4-8; open 6:30am-9pm daily) is a popular local joint serving quality diner food.

Oriental Food Market & Takeout (☎ 561-588-4626; 4919 S Dixie Hwy; dishes $5-7; open 11am-8:30pm Mon-Sat), in tiny Raintree Plaza, may have the best takeout Thai food this side of Bangkok. Palm Beach millionaires and Thai expats alike make the pilgrimage to enjoy huge servings of pad Thai and red curry Panang, all perfectly prepared to your specified degree of spiciness.

Pit Bar-B-Q (☎ 561-835-4849; 1516 N Tamarind; dishes $6-15; open 4:30-9:45pm Tues & Weds, 11am-9:45pm Thurs, 11am-11pm Fri & Sat Ave), in a tiny brick building north of downtown, serves up huge plates of ribs, chicken and pork alongside Southern classics like collard greens. Finish off with a slice of sweet-potato pie.

ER Bradley's Saloon (☎ 561-833-3520; 104 Clematis St; mains $7-14; open 8am-3am Sun-Thurs, 8am-4am Fri & Sat) has been bringing folks from both sides of the causeway to downtown West Palm for two decades. Attractions include its expansive outdoor patio, friendly staff, happy-hour buffet and great food – the specialty is crab – at great prices. Enjoy the Bradley's benedict, crab-cake sandwich, or a just cold brew while contemplating the waterway.

391st Bomb Group Headquarters (☎ 561-683-3919; 3989 Southern Blvd; mains $12-20; open 11:30am-10pm Mon-Thurs, 11:30am-11pm Fri & Sat, 10am-2:30pm Sun), adjacent to the airport, is supposed to resemble a WWI-era, bombed-out French farm, complete with fighter planes, Willys Jeeps, sandbags and surly wenches…er…an enthusiastic waitstaff that recommends the beer cheese soup.

The **Samba Room** (☎ 561-659-3442; 1 N Clematis St; mains $17-24; kitchen open 11am-10pm Mon-Fri, 4pm-midnight Sat, 5pm-10pm Sun, bar open till 2am daily) is a Latino-fusion restaurant that aims for pre-Castro Havana elegance, complete with great mojitos and tableside cigar rollers. Try the corn cakes or grilled mussels before indulging in entrées like Argentine skirt steak and plantain-encrusted mahimahi.

Sailfish Marina (☎ 561-844-1724; 98 Lake Dr; mains $18-28; open 7am-11pm or so daily) is on Singer Island, southeast of Riviera Beach. It's a great place for a cocktail while you watch the gazillion-dollar yachts cruise by, but try the sea bass or wahoo oreganato if you're feeling hungry. Take Hwy 1 north of downtown West Palm Beach until you hit the A1A (Blue Heron Blvd). Cross the causeway and make a right on Lake Dr.

Mezzanotte (700 S Rosemary Ave; mains $24-32; open 5:30pm-11pm or so daily) attracts a gorgeous clientele with the loveliest dining room in town. The focus is Italian fusion cuisine: Chef Mauro's tuna carpaccio gets raves, as do the osso buco (veal shank) and linguini Alex-style (with crab, shrimp and asparagus) – ask for it with puttanesca sauce instead of the standard olio.

Entertainment

The Palm Beach County Cultural Council operates a 24-hour **ArtsLine** (☎ 800-882-2787; W www.palmbeaches.org) that lists cultural events for the whole county.

Performing Arts West Palm Beach sponsors free outdoor concerts year-round. **CityPlace** (☎ 561-366-1000; W www.cityplaceweb.com) hosts several, including live jazz 12:30pm-2:30pm Sunday and **City Jams**, featuring blues, acoustic rock and other musicians 7pm-11pm Friday. **Centennial Square** (☎ 561-659-8007), on Clematis St, offers **Clematis by Night**, staging all sorts of local bands from 5:30pm to 9pm Thursday, and **Friday Night Live!**, with local pop and rock bands, from 6pm to 11pm Friday.

Kravis Center for the Performing Arts (☎ 561-832-7469, 800-572-8471; 701 Okeechobee Blvd) is a three-venue complex boasting Florida's largest stage. Local organizations, including Ballet Florida, the Palm Beach Opera and Florida Philharmonic, are based here. International outfits like the Hungarian National Philharmonic and Orqestra de São Paolo also play this acoustically superior venue. Ticket prices vary widely, but most performances run $45 to $60.

The **Cuillo Center for the Arts** (☎ 561-835-9226; 201 Clematis St) stages community theater and touring off-Broadway plays, as well as regional and national bands and orchestras.

Harriet Gilman Theater (☎ 561-835-1408; W www.cityplaceweb.com; 700 S Rosemary Ave), in CityPlace, is West Palm's upscale performance space. Housed in a historic (1926) Methodist church, the Harriet is still getting its act together, but has hosted such artists as Bruce Hornsby and the Drifters.

Cinema The **Off the Wall Film Series** (☎ 561-547-6686; admission free) is the very best way to spend a Tuesday night in West Palm. Foreign, alternative and cult films are screened in an empty lot on the 500 block of Clematis St, next to Sewells, at 8:30pm. Bring a chair.

Carefree Theatre (☎ 561-833-7305; 2000 Dixie Hwy) lets you enjoy those subtitles indoors. They also stage plays and concerts. Movies are $7/5 adult/child, and tickets for other events climb as high as $55 a seat.

Muvico (☎ 561-833-2301; 550 S Rosemary St; adult/child $8/5), in CityPlace, offers a more traditional movie experience, with a bonus: For an extra $8, staff will watch your toilet-trained tot (ages 3 to 8) while you watch the movie in peace.

Bars & Clubs This town loves a night out. Upscale venues pack CityPlace, divey watering holes line Clematis St, and friendly neighborhood bars are just about everywhere you turn.

The **Monkey Club** (☎ 561-833-6500; 219 Clematis St; open 9pm-3am Sun-Thurs, 9pm-4am Fri & Sat; $5-10 cover after 11pm) has DJs spinning pulsing beats, hot body contests, college nights, drink specials, spandex dresses – you get the idea.

Have a Nice Day Café (☎ 561-835-1859; 301 Datura St), around the corner, has similar DJs, drink specials, hours and cover,

but this place has a dress code: no tank tops. If you win the wet T-shirt contest, you'll do it with sleeves, by golly.

Roxy's (☎ 561-833-2402; 209 Clematis St; open 11am-3am Sun-Thurs, 11am-4am Fri & Sat) is West Palm's oldest bar, founded in 1934 and located just across the street from its original digs. They serve edible food that the genial crowd uses to soak up the booze.

O'Shea's Pub (☎ 561-833-3865; 531½ Clematis St; open 11am-3am Sun-Thurs, 11am-4am Fri & Sat) is a quality Irish pub with good beer on tap, shepherd's pie on the menu and lots of homesick Irish people at the bar.

Spanky's Sports Bar (☎ 561-832-7964; 500 Clematis St; open 11:30am till 'whenever') gets my vote for the best bar in town. It's not really a jock crowd, despite the pool tables and ESPN – I saw more tattoos and dreadlocks than anything else. It's got an indoor stage and outdoor amphitheater where bands like Blind Side, Box Elder and 311 rock hard. The cover for big evening shows runs $6 to $20.

The **Blue Martini** (☎ 561-835-8601; 550 S Rosemary Ave; open 4pm-3am Sun-Thurs, 4pm-4am Fri & Sat) is a full-on celebrity magnet – like, ohmigod, I sat like ten feet from Sade! The swank CityPlace venue has live music (no cover) Wednesday through Sunday (usually blues, jazz or rock), plus three full bars and 18 different martini drinks for $11 a pop. Saturdays are packed. Dress to impress – it's required.

Gay & Lesbian Venues **TG Rooster's** (☎ 561-832-9119; 823 Belvedere Rd) is a popular place with bingo on Monday, free barbecue on Friday and a male dance review Sunday. They'll even hook you up with an outdated but useful map to local gay-owned and gay-friendly area businesses.

Kashmir (☎ 561-649-5557; 1651 S Congress Ave) is a trek, but it's also the best (and at press time, the only) dance spot in town catering to the gay and lesbian crowd.

Spectator Sports
The **Palm Beach County Sports Commission** (☎ 561-355-2001; W www.palmbeach

sports.org) provides listings for area sports teams, including the **Jupiter Hammerheads** (baseball; ☎ 561-775-1818), **Florida Marlins** (baseball; ☎ 305-930-4487) and **Florida Panthers** (hockey; ☎ 954-835-8326).

The **Palm Beach Polo & Country Club** (☎ 561-793-1440; Ⓦ www.palmbeachpolo .com; 13240 S Shore Blvd) is supposed to be one of the best venues in the US for the sport.

Getting There & Away

Palm Beach International Airport (PBI; ☎ 561-471-7420, Ⓦ www.pbia.org) is a convenient airport served by most major airlines and car rental companies. It's about a mile west of I-95 on Belvedere Rd. PalmTran bus No 53 (see Getting Around) runs between the airport, train station and downtown.

In a brilliant display of superior civil engineering, **Greyhound** (☎ 561-833-9636; 215 S Tamarind Ave), **Tri-Rail** (☎ 800-875-7245; 203 S Tamarind Ave) and **Amtrak** (☎ 561-832-6169; 201 S Tamarind Ave) share the same building, the historic Seaboard Train Station. Good job! This beautiful Spanish-Mediterranean complex started seeing action in 1925, when Henry Flagler's Orange Blossom Express made its first run southward. PalmTran serves the station with bus Nos 31, 43 and 53.

Getting Around

Downtown is a cakewalk: Four huge parking garages are free if you leave between 6pm and midnight; it's $6 otherwise, and there's metered parking everywhere.

A **trolley** (free; operates 11am-9pm Sun-Thurs, 11am-11pm Fri & Sat) runs between Clematis St and CityPlace.

Pedicabs (free; evenings Thurs-Sun), operated by Turtle Town Transfer Company, ply the same area; a tip of $10 or more is considered gracious.

PalmTran (☎ 561-841-4287; Ⓦ www.palm tran.org) buses are convenient and serve the entire county; the chamber of commerce and Tri-Rail station have great system maps available. Fares are $1.25; there are no transfers.

PALM BEACH

Few playgrounds of the rich and famous attract as much attention as 'The Island.' Palm Beach (population 10,000 summer, 25,000 winter) is known primarily for its stunning mansions, society events ('which disease is it tonight, dear?') and exclusivity. The entrance to this elite enclave doesn't slam down on visitors like a fortress gate, however.

The jeans-and-T-shirt set is generally made welcome, albeit with strained smiles masking the fervent hope that you won't touch anything valuable (you can't really frown right after a Botox treatment, anyway). And witness the lament of one skin-care specialist who moved her practice from Worth Ave to an almost-as-opulent West Palm Beach location: 'I've lost clients – they refuse to cross the bridge. They're afraid of crime. Or something.' It's a different world.

Regardless, the candy-colored mansions lining Ocean Blvd and glittering shops of Worth Ave are something everyone should see at least once. But other than gawking at life's lottery winners and their really great shoes, there's not really a whole lot to do here. Unless, of course, you've managed an invitation or two to the mad social swirl surrounding 'The Season.' Otherwise, it's probably best to make this a day trip; the money you save staying on the mainland might finance a week in Thailand – or Paris.

Orientation

The long, narrow island of Palm Beach sits between the Intracoastal Waterway, here called Lake Worth, and the Atlantic Ocean. It's just east of West Palm Beach and those other plebian communities stretching southward. The main north-south artery is S County Rd (Hwy A1A), and two major bridges link downtown with the mainland, Flagler Memorial Bridge (Royal Poinciana Way) and Royal Park Bridge (Royal Palm Way). Farther south, Southern Blvd and Atlantic Ave both provide entrance to the Island.

Downtown stretches from Royal Poinciana Way to Worth Ave, with most major sites scattered between. Prices tend to rise as you head southward. Ocean Blvd runs from the southern edge of the Breakers (see Places to Stay) to the tip of the Island; most of the mansions worth ogling are below Worth Ave. It's a smallish city and possible to navigate with buses and stout shoes, though you might want to rent a European luxury car for your visit. Just because.

Information

The helpful **chamber of commerce** (☎ 561-655-3282, 45 Cocoanut Row, www.palmbeachchamber.com), opposite the Royal Poinciana Chapel, has excellent maps. They also have racks of pamphlets and several gratis glossy magazines, including *Worth Avenue*, *Palm Beach Illustrated*, *Palm Beach Society* and *Vive*, all of which offer convincing arguments for indulgence at every level.

The **public library** (☎ 561-655-7226; 2 Four Arts Plaza), at the Society of the Four Arts (see Entertainment), does not offer free Internet service. Shocking.

There's a **Bank of America** (☎ 561-820-1649; 140 N County Rd) close to Royal Poinciana Way's shops; if you're strapped for cash on Worth Ave, try **Washington Mutual** (☎ 561-659-2871; 380 S County Rd). The **post office** (411 S County Rd) is also convenient to Worth Ave.

Note that many shops and restaurants are only open during high season (simply called 'The Season'), which runs roughly from November through March.

Flagler Museum

The only true museum (☎ 561-655-2833; W www.flagler.org; 1 Whitehall Way; adult/child $8/3; open 10am-5pm Tues-Sat, noon-5pm Sun) in Palm Beach is housed in the spectacular 1902 mansion built by the eponymous railroad mogul as a gift for his bride, Mary Lily Keenan. This painstakingly restored manor does not feature displays about Henry Flagler's accomplishments renovating Florida, however. Instead, it's a good, long look at the couple's understandably immodest taste in furnishings.

Persian rugs cover parquet floors packed with antiquities from every conti-

nent, all topped off with gilded woodwork of obsessive design. The 1st floor features ballrooms and banquet halls populated with marble statues and fine art; the 2nd floor has rooms bedecked in pastels of every hue. Flagler's personal railroad car, outside, is sure to impress any traveler. But, unless you're the sort of person who enjoys shows like *Lifestyles of the Rich and Famous* or MTV's *Cribs,* it might not be worth the admission fee.

As long as you're stopping by, however, why not make reservations at the Whitehall Café? For $15, you're treated to a full 'Gilded Age–Style' tea, with finger sandwiches, scones and brews custom-blended for the museum alone. It's served noon-3pm during The Season; by appointment only during the rest of the year.

Worth Ave

This quarter-mile strip of fantastically expensive boutiques and shops, including Cartier, Armani, Gucci, Chanel and many more, is worth perusing even if your credit cards are maxed. Parking is free (but difficult to find during The Season), storefronts are framed in classic Mizner-designed Spanish-Mediterranean chic, and the window displays themselves are glittering advertisements for the American dream. More than half the shops close for summer.

Worth Ave art galleries, many filled with museum-quality pieces free for the looking, often have openings with champagne, fine cheeses and attendees sporting surnames like DuPont and Lauder. Dress the part or risk having your jeans-clad ass hauled (graciously) out into the street.

Ocean Blvd

The most famous mansion overlooking this stretch of surf and sand is Donald Trump's predictably tasteful **Mar-a-Lago**, guarded by vividly painted statuettes holding golden gas lamps aloft above the wrought-iron gate. You can't help but wonder which lyrically painted fortress holds Rush Limbaugh, Rod Stewart, Vera Wang or Jimmy Buffet – and you'll never know, since the only people you'll see are servants and gardeners keeping the

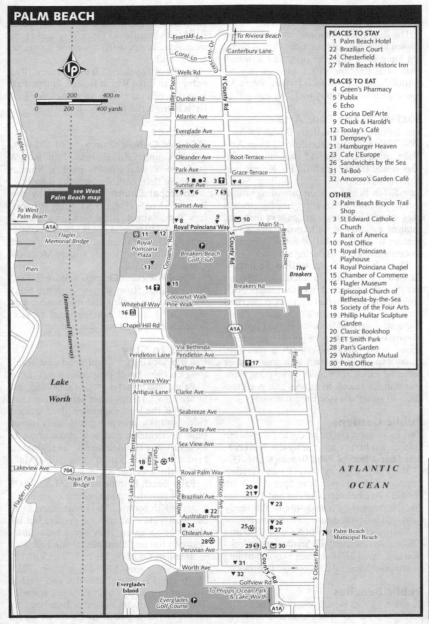

PALM BEACH

PLACES TO STAY
1 Palm Beach Hotel
22 Brazilian Court
24 Chesterfield
27 Palm Beach Historic Inn

PLACES TO EAT
4 Green's Pharmacy
5 Publix
6 Echo
8 Cucina Dell'Arte
9 Chuck & Harold's
12 TooJay's Café
13 Dempsey's
21 Hamburger Heaven
23 Cafe L'Europe
26 Sandwiches by the Sea
31 Ta-Boó
32 Amoroso's Garden Café

OTHER
2 Palm Beach Bicycle Trail Shop
3 St Edward Catholic Church
7 Bank of America
10 Post Office
11 Royal Poinciana Playhouse
14 Royal Poinciana Chapel
15 Chamber of Commerce
16 Flagler Museum
17 Episcopal Church of Bethesda-by-the-Sea
18 Society of the Four Arts
19 Phillip Hulitar Sculpture Garden
20 Classic Bookshop
25 ET Smith Park
28 Pan's Garden
29 Washington Mutual
30 Post Office

SOUTHEAST

various estates tidy (well, unless the chamber of commerce staff is feeling chatty).

The Kennedy Compound, by the way, best known for a 1991 indiscretion – see, it could not have been rape, he only had a *partial* erection at the time – by a subsequently acquitted Kennedy cousin, is farther north. All you can see is a big gray wall, anyway.

Society of the Four Arts

The cultural heart of Palm Beach (☎ 561-655-7226; W www.fourarts.com; 2 Four Arts Plaza; admission free ($5 donation); open year-round 10am-5pm Mon-Fri, November-April 10am-5pm Sat, 2pm-5pm Sun), founded in 1936, has been providing volunteer opportunities for antsy trophy spouses ever since. The on-site art gallery features rotating exhibits of well-known artists November to April, as well as artwork by area students and artisans during summer.

The adjacent **Philip Hulitar Sculpture Garden** (open 10am-5pm daily; admission free) is on land rescued from the clutches of a proletarian supermarket chain by concerned community activists (no, they didn't chain themselves to bulldozers, but instead stormed a board meeting with pens poised menacingly above open checkbooks). It's a pleasant, grassy expanse populated with some rather powerful sculptures, perfect for relaxing while you wait for tickets to movies and performances to go on sale (see Entertainment).

Public Gardens

Two more great public places to escape into landscaped luxury are run by the **Preservation Foundation of Palm Beach** (☎ 561-832-0731; 386 S County Rd). **Pan's Garden** (admission free; open 9am-5pm daily), on Hibiscus Ave between Chilean and Peruvian Aves, is fronted by a sculpture of the randy deity and is devoted entirely to native plants.

Nearby, at the corner of S County Rd and Chilean Ave, is shady **ET Smith Park** (admission free; open 24/7), starring a cool, burbling fountain and several comfortable benches.

Public Beaches

Surprise – Palm Beach boasts two beautiful public beaches, kept uncluttered with mansions by their ever-shifting white sands. **Palm Beach Municipal Beach**, along Ocean Blvd between Royal Palm Way and Hammon Ave, is open from sunrise to sunset year round.

South of Southern Blvd on Ocean Blvd, before the Lake Worth Bridge, **Phipps Park** is another place to sun your buns for free. Bicycle trails run along both beaches.

Churches

St Edward Catholic Church (☎ 561-832-0400; 142 N County Rd; services 7am, 9am & 10:30am Sunday) holds packed Sunday masses in their cathedral-quality interior.

Episcopal Church of Bethesda-by-the-Sea (☎ 561-655-4554; 141 S County Rd; services 7am, 9am & 10am Sun) is a historic landmark (1926) and holds Sunday services in their Gothic interior. Be sure to check out the small but lovely Cluett Memorial Gardens out back.

Royal Poinciana Chapel (☎ 561-655-4212; 60 Cocoanut Row; service 10:30am Sun), which is older (1895) and much more intimate, holds interdenominational services beneath its vaulted wooden ceiling.

Places to Stay

If you're looking for a deal, head west, young traveler. Palm Beach properties aren't cheap.

Palm Beach Hotel (☎ 561-659-7665; 235 Sunrise Ave; rooms from $80/125 summer/winter) is the least expensive place around. Fairly swanky suits are individually owned (and decorated), and you make arrangements to stay through an on-site real estate broker (available 9am to 5pm daily). Make reservations well in advance.

Palm Beach Historic Inn (☎ 561-832-4009; W www.palmbeachhistoricinn.com; 365 S County Rd; rooms $85-175 summer, $150-325 winter) is a tad more expensive but has character to spare. They serve breakfast – between full and Continental – in bed.

Brazilian Court (☎ 561-655-7740; 301 Australian Ave; rooms $110-175 summer, $215-350 winter) is bright, cheerful and packed with amenities. It's also *very* pet friendly: The on-site restaurant has a four-item pet menu featuring foodstuffs like bowser burgers ($6) and chancellor chow (filet mignon; $14), served with a Milk-Bone or tabby treat.

The **Chesterfield** (☎ 561-659-5800; W www .redcarnationhotels.com; 363 Cocoanut Row; rooms from $139/225 summer/winter) does its best to achieve that chummy, old-boy, 'Tally-HO! chaps, back to Blighty, what?' look, with a wood-paneled game room, green-leather chairs in the cigar lounge and elegant, overstuffed rooms. There's even a traditional English tea served 3pm to 5pm ($15).

The **Breakers** (☎ 561-659-8440, 888-273-2537; W www.thebreakers.com; 1 S County Rd; rooms $270-1950 summer, $420-3300 winter) is the uncontested grand dame of Palm Beach. It opened in 1861 as a beachfront addition to Henry Flagler's Royal Poinciana Hotel, where guests would request rooms 'over by the breakers.' The rest, as they say, is history.

An attraction in its own right, this ultra-deluxe property, modeled after the Villa Medici in Rome, has a 200-foot-long lobby with arched ceilings evocative of a Renaissance cathedral. Amenities include a full spa, fitness rooms, golf courses, tennis courts and more; during The Season, they employ two staff members per room. The finest restaurant of the seven here, **L'Escalier** (open 6pm-10pm Tues-Sun, mains $28-40) serves venison, wild-mushroom risotto and a variety of caviars.

If all this elegance is just slightly out of your price range, you can still come by for the free one-hour guided tour, offered at 3pm Wednesday. Afterward, you'll want to purchase a lottery ticket or six.

Places to Eat

As you'd expect, there are plenty of places in Palm Beach where you can pay through the perfectly sculpted nose for gourmet fare served by a starched and fawning waitstaff. But there are also several good budget options. Hey, just because your album went triple platinum doesn't mean you don't need a cheeseburger every now and then.

Publix (☎ 561-655-4120; 265 Sunset Ave) has all your picnicking needs.

Green's Pharmacy (☎ 561-832-0304; 151 N County Rd; dishes $4-7; open 7am-3:30pm Mon-Sat, 6am-2pm Sun) is a local favorite, where big breakfasts, bowls of chili, and tuna melt sandwiches are delivered to your Formica table, fast. Get there early for lunch, as Danny's daily specials always sell out.

TooJay's Café (☎ 561-659-7232; 313 Royal Poinciana Plaza; dishes $4-8; open 8am-9pm daily) caters to homesick New Yorkers in their cavernous dining room or at the deli counter, with hot pastrami sandwiches, whitefish salad, fresh-baked challah and more.

Sandwiches by the Sea (☎ 561-655-7911; 363 S County Rd; dishes $5; open 10:30am-4pm daily) is a favorite of Palm Beach's imported service-industry professionals for the huge, delicious subs and salads. The house vinaigrette dressing – get it on your sandwich – is wonderful.

Amoroso's Garden Cafe (☎ 561-805-9812; 240 Worth Ave; mains $4-9; open 8am-7pm Mon-Fri, 9am-7pm Sat, noon-5pm Sun) is tucked into a flower-filled alcove just off Worth Ave. Healthy sandwiches, soups and smoothies make for the perfect opportunity to take a load off those not-exactly-sensible heels.

Hamburger Heaven (☎ 561-655-5277; 314 S County Rd; mains $5-9; open 7:30am-8pm daily during high season, 7:30am-3pm daily low season) has been serving the rich and famous (as well as the not so rich and famous) since 1945. It's best place in town to spot celebrities in fitted designer casual wear chowing hearty breakfasts and huge burgers.

Dempsey's (☎ 561-835-0400; 50 Cocoanut Row; lunch $8-10, dinner $12-18; open 11:30am-10pm daily) serves good beer and quality pub food. Sunday brunch ($12; make reservations) is quite a spread, so bring your appetite 10am to 2pm. In the words of one server, 'The food here is very good – not spectacular – but we're, well, a very *normal* place.' Which, in this town, is exceptional.

Cucina Dell'Arte (☎ 561-655-0770; 257 Royal Poinciana Way; mains $8-15; open 7am-10pm Mon-Fri, 11:30am-10pm daily) is a relatively down-to-earth (you can wear jeans and bring your kids) Italian joint that serves pizzas and pastas ($10 to $15) with all the Palm Beach flair you'd want.

Chuck & Harold's (☎ 561-659-1440; 207 Royal Poinciana Way; mains $12-28; open 7:30am-11pm Sun-Thurs, 7:30am-midnight Fri & Sat) is an Island landmark. Try the filet mignon and eggs for breakfast, or the salmon puttanesca or macadamia-encrusted mahimahi at dinner. If you tipped well the last time, you might even score a coveted seat on the outdoor patio.

Ta-boó (☎ 561-835-3500; 221 Worth Ave; lunch $14-25, dinner $28-42) has the most coveted window seats on Worth Ave. Competition is stiff, but if you've got the Benjamins, this is *the* place to gossip over Atkins-approved appetizers while you watch the millionaires swish by.

Echo (☎ 561-802-4222; 230 Sunrise Ave; mains $24-38; open 5:30pm-9:30pm Tues-Sun) serves fine Asian-fusion cuisine in suitably upscale, feng-shuied surrounding. Recommended splurges include the Peking duck for two, crispy red snapper and their signature wok-fried green beans.

Cafe L'Europe (☎ 561-655-4020; 331 S County Rd; mains $25-45; open 11am-2:30pm Tues-Sat, 5pm-10pm Tues-Sun) may be the best restaurant in town, and that's saying something. Reservations are essential if you hope to sample their seven caviars, foie gras sautéed with huckleberries or chef Jens Dahlmann's signature Wiener schnitzel. The dining room is transcendent and the owners surprisingly friendly.

Entertainment
The **Royal Poinciana Playhouse** (☎ 561-659-3310; 70 Royal Poinciana Plaza) stages local productions, public speakers and Broadway hits. Tickets usually run $45 to $55 for the big shows, but you can catch certain matinees for as little as $8.

Society of the Four Arts (☎ 561-655-7226; W www.fourarts.com; 2 Four Arts Plaza) screens foreign and alternative flicks September to May on Friday ($3) and Saturday (free). During the summer, movies are shown Friday only. They also offer a lecture series and world-class classical music and dance performances, but these are primarily

for members only. Nonmembers can pick up tickets to lectures ($25) half an hour before the event if there are seats left, while tickets to performances ($35 to $45) are made available to the unwashed masses...er...general public one week before the show.

Getting There & Away
To get to the Palm Beach International Airport in West Palm Beach, take PalmTran (☎ 561-841-4287, www.palmtran.com) bus No 41 from Publix (see Places to Eat, earlier this section) to the Kravis Center and transfer to bus No 42; for the other three destinations, transfer to bus No 40.

By car, the two major bridges linking Palm Beach to the mainland are Flagler Memorial Bridge (Royal Poinciana Way) and Royal Park Bridge (Royal Palm Way). Farther south, Southern Blvd and Atlantic Ave in Lake Worth both provide entrance to the Island.

Getting Around
PalmTran bus No 42 covers the bulk of the island, from Lake Worth Pier to Sunrise Ave; transfer to bus No 63 at the pier to head south, bus No 41 at Publix (see Places to Eat) to go north. Though it's a fairly compact city, the two major downtown neighborhoods, centered on Royal Poinciana Way and Worth Ave, are a fair hike from one another.

Note that folks drive slowly (really, really slowly, which isn't always the same as driving well) on the Island, and there's a great bike path along the Intracoastal Waterway. Why not rent some wheels at **Palm Beach Bicycle Trail Shop** (☎ 561-659-4583; 223 Sunrise Ave)? Basic road bikes run $8 hourly, $26 daily; better bikes cost a little more.

John D MacArthur State Park to Fort Pierce

By the time many northbound travelers get to this neck of the woods, they've probably threaded nothing but urban sprawl along

I-95, enjoying asphalt and construction punctuated by billboards for luxury condominium living. After they pass North Palm Beach, however, things begin to change.

Industrialist billionaire and philanthropist John D MacArthur once owned almost everything from Palm Beach Garden to Stuart, and he kept it almost pristine during his lifetime. As he grew older, he became increasingly concerned that Florida's real estate bonanza would compromise – or destroy – what he considered paradise. In his will, he specifically stated that thousands of acres would be kept wild, and the rest would be deeded out incrementally, in order to save the oceanfront property from Miami's fate. It worked.

There are several urban attractions on this stretch, but these can't compare with a moonlight kayak trip through St Lucie Inlet State Park or the many other natural wonders along this stretch of sand and sea. Even if you're just driving through, stopping for a few hours will make for a memorable rest.

The **Jupiter Outdoor Center** (☎ 561-747-9666, 18095 Coastal Hwy A1A), in Jupiter, just north of West Palm, organizes hikes, guided tours, kayak trips and other adventures through the wild areas between Palm Beach and St Lucie Inlet, and west to Lake Okeechobee. They also rent most of the outdoor equipment you'll need to set off on your own adventure.

Getting There & Away
Though I-95 is the quickest way through this area, do yourself a favor and get off the freeway. US Hwy 1 runs consistently up the coastline, and Hwy A1A jumps back and forth between the mainland (where it's the same road as US 1) and various barrier islands.

Lack of development comes with a price: Greyhound stops only in Stuart, and there's no other convenient public transportation in the area. Bummer.

JOHN D MACARTHUR STATE PARK
While this state park (☎ 561-624-6950; 10900 SR 703; pedestrian/car $3.25; open 8am-

sunset daily) is one of the smallest in the region, it runs excellent ranger-led interpretive walks and has one of the best turtle-watching programs around. Loggerhead, green and leatherback turtles nest along the beach here from May to August. Cross Lake Worth Cove on the photogenic 1600-foot boardwalk to get to the beach, where there are dune crossovers leading out to the shore. You can't camp or canoe on your own here (there are no boat launches), but the nature center offers two-hour guided kayak trips for $15/25 single/double.

Interpretive Programs
The **William T Kirby Nature Center** (☎ 561-624-6952; open 8am-sunset Wed-Mon), just south of the main parking lot, has several aquariums and exhibits on baby sea turtles, snakes and other animals you may run into within the park. The center also screens a 15-minute video on the park's wildlife.

There are popular ranger-led trips to observe nesting turtles run Monday and Thursday evenings during June and July – but make reservations at least a month in advance. Also in summer, rangers lead snorkeling trips on the second and fourth Saturday of the month for advanced snorkelers with their own equipment. You'll see a 15-minute slide show of the area's sea life, then head off to explore the reef alongside the beach. Free guided nature walks are offered at 10am Saturday and Sunday.

Getting There & Away
The park is at the northern end of Singer Island. From the north, take PGA Blvd straight east to Hwy A1A; from the south, take Blue Heron Blvd to Hwy A1A. The entrance is just past the Blue Heron Bridge.

JONATHAN DICKINSON STATE PARK
With almost 11,500 acres to explore, this excellent state park (☎ 561-546-2771, 16450 SE Federal Hwy; pedestrian/car $1/3.25; open 8am-sunset daily), between US Hwy 1 and the Loxahatchee River (just north of Tequesta), is a great stop – either for a day, overnight or longer. There's no ocean

access within the park, which was a US army radar-instruction facility during WWII. The park's attraction lies in its several habitats: pine flatwood, cypress stands, swamp and increasingly endangered coastal sand pine scrub. Ranger-led nature walks leave 9am Sunday from the Cypress Creek Pavilion, and campfire programs are offered Saturday at dusk next to the Pine Grove Campground.

Observation Tower
You can climb to the Hobe Mountain Observation Tower (more of a hill) for an overview of the park. The tower is about 40 feet high, but 86 feet above sea level – impressive by Florida standards.

Canoeing & Kayaking
You can rent canoes and kayaks from the **concession stand** (☎ 561-746-1466; open 9am-5pm daily) at the boat launch on the Loxahatchee River. Canoes cost $10 for two hours, $4 for each additional hour; kayaks run $15/20 singles/doubles for two hours, $4 for each additional hour. You can also rent motorboats at $30 for two hours, but be careful of the manatees, OK?

Hiking & Biking
The park holds several short-loop hiking and bicycle trails, the most popular of which is the Kitching Creek Nature Trail, just north of the boat landing; it can be walked in about 1½ hours.

Advanced backpackers will appreciate an excellent network of hiking trails that lead to two primitive campsites. From the ranger station, pick up the East Loop of the white-blazed Florida Trail, which leads to the Scrub Jay campsite, 5.6 miles from the ranger station. From about there, you can pick up the Kitching Creek Hiking Trail, which continues west-southwest toward the Kitching Creek campsite, 9.3 miles from the ranger station. Get maps and instructions from the ranger station; see Camping, below, for more information.

Camp Murphy off-road bicycle trail has 2-mile and 3.5-mile loops popular with mountain bike owners; log onto Ⓦ www.club

scrub.com for more information on these and other area trails.

Organized Tours
The *Loxahatchee Queen II* offers four two-hour cruises daily to the Trapper Nelson Interpretive Site. Nelson, the son of Polish immigrants, came here around 1936 and became a local legend as the 'Wild Man' of Loxahatchee. He built a popular wildlife zoo here that still stands, though the animals are long gone. Cruises cost $12 for adults, $7 for children.

Places to Stay
The park has two developed **campgrounds** (sites $14/17 summer/winter) with hot showers, two primitive campsites and, for the tentaphobic, cabins. Sites have grills, and you can make campfires (no gathering in the park, though you can buy wood from the concession for $6 a bundle). Cabins cost $85 nightly, with a two-night-minimum stay on weekends, and sleep four people. Bring your own linens.

Two primitive riverside **sites** ($3 year-round) are also available; one is 5 miles from the ranger station, the other 10 miles. Both are accessible by boat. The trails are blazed, but pick up a map at the park entrance anyway.

HOBE SOUND NATIONAL WILDLIFE REFUGE
This refuge (☎ 561-546-6141) is a 968-acre federally protected nature sanctuary with two sections: a small slice on the mainland between Hobe Sound and US Hwy 1, opposite the Jonathan Dickinson State Park, and the main refuge grounds at the north end of Jupiter Island.

The Jupiter Island section has 3½ miles of beach (it's a favorite sea-turtle nesting ground), mangroves and sand dunes, and the mainland section is a pine scrub forest. In June and July, turtle-watching walks take place on Tuesday and Thursday evenings (reservations are necessary), and birding trips can also be arranged through the Hawley Education Center. The refuge can get crowded in winter.

Jupiter Island

The beach (carload $5, pedestrians free), with undulating and windswept dunes, is excellent for walking and swimming. There's no camping (unless you're with a Scout troop). Though most of the preserve is best accessed by boat, it's a fine stretch of public sand on an otherwise very exclusive island. Residents include sea turtles, bobcats and ospreys; if you're curious about neighboring multimillionaires, see Boat Tours, later in this section.

Blowing Rocks Preserve

This preserve (☎ 561-747-3113; admission $3; open 9am-5pm daily) encompasses a mile-long limestone outcropping riddled with holes, cracks and fissures; when the tide is high and there's a strong easterly wind (call ahead for conditions), water spews upward as if from a geyser. Even when seas are calm, you can hike through four coastal biomes: shifting dune, coastal strand, interior mangrove wetlands and tropical coastal hammock.

Across the street, **Hawley Education Center** has rotating art exhibits with nature themes, as well as two short nature trails and a butterfly garden.

Boat Tours

Jupiter Island is more famous for its *Forbes* magazine–confirmed status as the wealthiest community in the USA than its natural wonders, but voyeurs will be saddened to learn that most mansions can't be seen from the road. Never fear: **Manatee Queen Tours** (☎ 561-744-2191; 1065 N Ocean Blvd; $17/10 adult/child) offers 2½-hour tours with great views of Burt Reynold's home, among many others – and you might even see a manatee! Boats leave twice daily from the Crab House (not Charley's Crab Shack, across the street).

Getting There & Away

Finding the refuge is a little tricky, as there's no signage: From US Hwy 1, take Bridge St (708 east) to Hobe Sound, then make a left on narrow, residential Beach St (707), which terminates at the refuge parking lot. Blowing Rocks Preserve is about 4 miles south of the Hwy 707 bridge on Beach St.

ST LUCIE INLET STATE PARK

Accessible only by boat, the main part of this park (☎ 561-744-7603) protects 6 sq mi of submerged limestone rock reef in the Atlantic Ocean just off Jupiter Island. Twelve species of hard and soft coral inhabit the reef, so you're urged to anchor only on sandy bottom. Snorkeling and scuba diving are permitted. There are also excellent beaches, toilets and running water, piers, canoe trails and hiking trails. From the mainland at the eastern end of Cove Rd, a boardwalk runs from the dock opposite County Park to the beach.

STUART
pop 14,500

The self-proclaimed Sailfish Capital of the World, Stuart has long been a destination for sporty millionaires and their gleaming yachts. It wasn't until the late 1980s, however, that Stuart got its first exit off I-95, which is when the Bentley and Beemer owners started rolling through in earnest.

It's now one of the fastest-growing cities in Florida, attracting primarily affluent old money from former strongholds like Boca Raton, which is growing a tad too blue collar these days. Stuart is posh, but there are inexpensive places to stay close to the historic downtown, and no matter what you're wearing, you'll get a warm welcome from folks who make more money than the entire population of Guatemala.

Orientation

Downtown was not designed for drivers: The unavoidable intersection of the city's major throughways, Colorado Ave, Flagler Ave, Dixie Hwy (A1A) and E and W Ocean Blvd is called Confusion Corner by the locals and 'driving around the block ten times' by visitors.

Dixie Hwy slashes through the city from southeast to northwest. The town's two main drags, Flagler Ave and Osceola St, run parallel. Colorado Ave runs south of downtown, and becomes Kanner Hwy when it crosses Hwy 1. East Ocean Blvd runs along the south side of downtown, connecting the mainland with Stuart Beach on Hutchison Island. Sewell's Point is a spit of land between Stuart and Hutchison Island, separating the St Lucie River from the Intracoastal Waterway.

Information

The friendly **chamber of commerce** (☎ 772-287-1088; W www.goodnature.org; 1650 S Kanner Hwy; 8:30am-5pm Mon-Fri) is not quite a mile south of downtown. Take Colorado Ave south past Hwy 1 and look for the green building on your right. They have a few flyers and plenty of personal tips.

There's a **Bank of America** (☎ 772-288-9654; 900 S Federal Hwy) close to downtown. Get your clothes clean at **Whattawash** (☎ 772-220-7837; 2347 SE Federal Hwy).

Courthouse Cultural Center

This egregiously underpublicized art gallery (☎ 561-288-2542; 80 E Ocean Blvd; admission free ($2 donation); open 10am-4pm Mon-Fri) is inside the 1937 WPA-built Martin County Courthouse. It presents rotating exhibitions of works by local and regional artists.

Hutchison Island

Stuart's **beaches** are excellent for walking, swimming and even some snorkeling. There are plenty of other attractions, however.

Elliot Museum If you need a break from the sun, stop here (☎ 772-225-1961; 825 NE Ocean Blvd, Hutchinson Island; adult/child $6/2; open 10am-4pm daily). It's dedicated to inventor Harmon Elliott and contains an eclectic collection of exhibits. You'll see a fabulous miniature circus and recreations of old-time shops, such as an apothecary, barber shop and ice cream parlor. As you move through you'll also pass a Victorian parlor, a 1925 dining room and a typical 18th-century girl's bedroom, and another display shows off most of Elliott's 118 patent certificates. There seems to be no rhyme or reason for the selection of the displays, but they're fun all the same.

Coastal Science Center Directly across the street, the Florida Oceanographic Society's center (☎ 772-225-0505; W www.fosusa.org; 890 NE Ocean Blvd; adult/child $4/2; open 10am-5pm Mon-Sat) is absolutely great for kids, who can spend more time in this tiny place than you'd think possible. Inside are four 300-gallon aquariums filled with tropical fish, a worm reef, and touch tanks with crabs, sea cucumbers and starfish. The incredibly enthusiastic staff run guided nature walks on Wednesday and Saturday at 10am, and there's a boardwalk for self-guided tours.

Gilbert's Bar House of Refuge South along the beach, this museum (☎ 772-225-1875; 301 SE MacArthur Blvd; adult/child $4/2; open 10am-4pm daily) occupies the oldest house in Martin County (built in 1875). In more adventurous days, it was one of 10 houses that the US Life-Saving Service established as safe havens for shipwrecked sailors, who would find food and shelter here if they washed ashore. Inside are exhibits of model ships and two aquariums, and the boathouse out back holds maritime exhibits and samples of century-old lifesaving gear.

Energy Encounter About 9 miles south of the Seaway Dr bridge, Energy Encounter (☎ 561-468-4111; 877-375-4386; W www.fpl.com/encounter; Ocean Blvd; admission free; 10am-4pm Mon-Fri & Sun), inside the St Lucie Nuclear Plant (enter through gate B), is a shimmering testament to the family values of nuclear power. The 30-plus interactive displays on the history of energy give you a snuggly feeling about the American nuclear industry. To be fair, the exhibits are really first-rate, and the games are very clever, showing kids how we've come from campfires through wood and coal, electricity and finally, the pinnacle of man's creativity, nuclear power.

Places to Stay

Strangely enough, in this town that is the very definition of quaint and upscale, all the B&Bs have closed! Opportunity is knocking for some Florida-loving entrepreneur, that's for sure. In the meantime, budget travelers have more options than luxury lovers.

Royal Palm Motel (☎ 772-283-7608; 627 S Federal Hwy; rooms $52-79 summer, $65-99 winter) is good bet, with clean rooms and friendly service.

Howard Johnson (☎ 561-220-3594; 950 S Federal Hwy; rooms $55/70 summer/winter) has a rather upscale outpost with pleasantly predictable rooms.

South Wind Motel (☎ 772-287-0773; 603 S Federal Hwy; rooms from $35/89 summer/winter) is the cheapest place to stay in town, not including phone deposit (plus they cut off your 50¢ local phone calls after 10 minutes!), key deposit and other surprise charges. They inspect your room before letting you check out, too.

Holiday Inn Oceanside (☎ 772-225-3000; 3793 NE Ocean Blvd; without/with views $89/119 summer, $169/199 winter), on Hutchison Island, has windswept beaches and ocean views, plus tennis, golf, boat rentals and lot of other extras.

Places to Eat

Alice's Restaurant (☎ 772-286-9528; 2781 E Ocean Blvd; breakfast $3-7, lunch $5-8; open 7am-8pm Mon-Sat, 7am-2pm Sun) is where cops and retirees gather for big breakfasts and top-of-the-line diner food.

Nature's Way Café (☎ 772-220-7306; 25 SW Osceola St; dishes $5-8; open 10am-4pm Mon-Fri, 10am-3pm Sat) has lots of vegetarian options.

Luna (☎ 772-288-0550; 49 Flagler Ave; slices $2-4, mains $6-20; open 9am-9pm Sun-Thurs, 9am-10pm Fri & Sat) has great pizza by the slice or pie. Try the Luna veggie, with everything from cauliflower to string beans, grilled and topped with marinara sauce and fresh spinach. They also serve salads and sandwiches.

Thai Basil Garden (☎ 772-221-2522; 201 S Federal Hwy; mains $8-14; open 11:30am-2:30pm Mon-Sat, 4:30am-9:30pm daily) does excellent Thai food using fresh ingredients. Try the Panang curry or sweet basil stir-fry with your choice of meat or seafood.

Flagler Grille (☎ 772-221-9517; 47 SW Flagler Ave; mains $16-24; open 6pm-9pm Tues-Sun) is famed for its wine list and pricey nouveau-Florida cuisine. Start with lump crab cakes in Key lime aioli and move on to the grilled salmon with tropical fruit salsa.

Gusto (☎ 772-287-3334; 301 Colorado Ave; lunch $6-10, dinner $16-25; open 11:30am-2:30pm Mon-Fri, 5pm-10pm Mon-Sat) got kudos from several residents as the best restaurant in town. The friendly staff volunteered the linguini with white clam sauce and seafood pasta as their favorite dinner items. Lunch is more affordable: Try the vegetable sandwich or gnocchi alla Bolognese.

Entertainment

Every third Friday of the month from October to June, there's free jazz and folk music at **Riverwalk** (☎ 772-521-8443; W www .martinarts.com), close to downtown. There are also free concerts at **Stuart Beach** (☎ 772-221-1430) from 2pm to 4pm every third Sunday of the month, January through April.

The **Lyric Theatre** (☎ 772-286-7827; W www.lyrictheatre.com; 59 SW Flagler Ave) was built in 1926 to show silent movies. It now stages community theater, concerts and performance art. Tickets run anywhere from $25 to $40 for big events, but matinees are a bit cheaper.

Barn Theater (☎ 772-287-4884; 2400 SE Ocean Blvd; tickets $20-25), off the road a bit on a driveway just east of the Chevron station, has community theater and lots of musicals. Shows start at 7:30pm, and there are weekend matinees at 1:30pm.

Jolly Sailor Pub (☎ 772-221-1111; 1 SW Oceola St) has a raucous clientele, lots of British brews on tap and live music on weekends.

The **Osceola Cafe** (☎ 772-283-6116; 26 Osceola St) also has live music Monday and Thursday to Saturday, usually starting at around 6pm.

FORT PIERCE
pop 34,800

Fort Pierce may not have as many millionaires as its neighbors, but it does have plenty to recommend it. There are some great museums, easy access to Hutchison Island

and a recently revitalized downtown cashing in on growing numbers of snowbirds who are making this their winter home.

From Stuart, take I-95 or Hwy 1 about 25 miles north. There's no public transportation.

Orientation & Information

To get downtown from I-95, take the Orange Ave exit east, crossing US Hwy 1 (here called N 4th St). Fort Pierce's main drag (such as it is) is 2nd St, which runs a block west of Indian River Dr. Here you'll find cafés, restaurants, the landmark Sunrise Theatre (1923) and old city hall. To get to Hutchison Island, head north on 2nd St and the east on Seaway Dr, which deposits you right onto the northern terminus of Ocean Dr (Hwy A1A).

Visit the **St Lucie Chamber of Commerce** (☎ 561-595-9999; W www.stluciechamber .org; 2200 Virginia Ave; open 9am-5pm Mon-Fri) and grab their excellent $2 map of the area. There's another visitor's center in the historic **Seven Gables House** (☎ 561-468-9152), next to the Manatee Observation Center.

Manatee Observation Center

The best reason to come to Fort Pierce is this outpost (☎ 561-466-1600; 480 N Indian River Dr; admission free ($1 donation); open 10am-5pm Tues-Sat, 1pm-4pm Sun), dedicated to educating the public on the plight of the manatee. Videos, exhibits and even the gift shop teach boaters how best to avoid hurting the creatures, and the rest of us about how our lifestyle has led to environmental degradation that's wiped out most of the manatee population. Manatee sightings aren't rare in winter months, however, when waters alongside the museum's observation deck are home to between eight and 20 of the enormous creatures – they may even want you to scratch their chins.

AE Backus Gallery

Next door to the Manatee Observation Center, this interesting gallery (☎ 561-465-0630; W www.backusgallery.com; 500 N Indian River Dr; admission free; open 10am-4pm Tues-Sat, noon-4pm Sun) focuses on the life and work of artist and art educator 'Bean' Backus. Backus was a landscape artist who started teaching the trade to young African Americans in the late 1950s and early '60s, a group that came to call itself the Highwaymen. They'd sell their unusually vibrant pieces depicting Florida's natural treasures along the freeways, often for around $15 to $35. Today those same paintings are now worth thousands, and you can see some of them right here, in addition to work by the instructor himself.

Harbor Branch Oceanographic Institution

One of the most respected ocean-research institutes on Earth, this institute (☎ 561-465-2400; W hboi.edu; 5600 US Hwy 1; admission free) north of the city, runs 90-minute tours of the 500-acre facilities at 10am, noon and 2pm Monday Sunday. This is a state-of-the-art research lab that operates projects ranging from biomedical experiments to undersea exploration.

At the **Indian River Lagoon Museum** (open 9am-5pm daily), you'll see life-sized models of some of the institute's submarine research vessels, as well as aquaculture facilities with more than 450,000 specimens of marine animals and plants from around the world.

Heathcote Botanical Gardens

This small but lovingly cared for botanical garden (☎ 561-464-4672; 210 Savannah Rd; admission $3/1; open 9am-5pm Tues-Sat year-round, 1pm-5pm Sun Nov-Apr) began as a Japanese-style garden tended by Jim and Mollie Crimmins in 1955. It now features a rain forest, a great collection of palm trees from all over the world, lots of shady trails through medicinal herbs, and a 'historic agriculture garden' with heirloom species and landscaped native plants.

UDT-SEAL Museum

Get in touch with your inner Cold Warrior at the UDT-SEAL Museum (☎ 561-595-1570; 3300 Ocean Blvd; adult/child $4/2; open 10am-4pm Tues-Sat, and Mon Jan-Apr, noon-4pm Sun) on Hutchison Island, where once top-secret tools and weapons used by America's most elite combat forces are on display. Located on the site where WWII Navy Frogmen (predecessors of the SEALs) trained, this place has videos and relics from US wars since 1945, including Granada, Panama, Vietnam and Desert Storm. These exhibits may convince even die-hard pacifists to have respect for these guys (and so far, the great film *GI Jane* notwithstanding, it's been an all-male enterprise), whose photos should be featured next to your dictionary's definition for 'bad-ass.'

Urca de Lima

Just north of the UDT-SEAL Museum and east of the shoreline fronting Pepper Park is a snorkeling historian's dream, the remains of the *Urca de Lima* (☎ 850-245-6444; w dhr .dos.state.fl.us/bar/uap; admission free). Part of a doomed Spanish flotilla caught in a 1715 hurricane, the *Urca* was the only vessel to go down (relatively) intact in the fierce weather. Today, it's mapped and left somewhat exposed within easy snorkeling distance from the beach. No, if you find any doubloons (something that evidently happens fairly often), you're not supposed to keep them.

To get here, exit Ocean Blvd (Hwy A1A) at Pepper Park and walk north along the beach about 1000 yards from the park boundary. The wreck is about 20 yards from shore on the first offshore reef, under 10 to 15 feet of water.

Places to Stay & Eat

Fort Pierce is probably best seen as a day trip, but you never know when you'll fall in love with a place.

The Savannas (☎ 561-789-5776; 800-789-5776; 1400 E Midway Rd; sites without/with hookups $14/20) has camping right next to the causeway.

Days Inn (☎ 561-461-8737; 1920 Seaway Dr; rooms from $45/55 summer/winter) has clean, basic rooms.

Mana Tiki (☎ 561-460-9014; 200 N Indian River Dr; open 11am-10pm daily; mains $7-23) is a great place to enjoy a beer on the thatched-roof porch overlooking manatee-packed (well, in winter anyway) waters. Better yet, sample their crab cakes, which were lauded in no less a magazine than *Gourmet*, or a bowl of conch chowder, the tiki largo fish sandwich or anything from the raw bar.

Entertainment

During the winter, the city sponsors several public events downtown, including **ArtWalk** every fourth Wednesday of the month, when galleries break out the wine and cheese, and local artists ply their trade on the sidewalks.

Central Florida

Though Central Florida is (in)famous for Orlando's glitzy amusements (it has the densest concentration of theme parks in the world), there's much, much more to tempt you away from the water slides, movie studios, roller coasters, fairy-tale palaces and costumed characters that bring most tourists here.

Ocala National Forest is the crown jewel of Central Florida's natural treasures: Crystal clear rivers wend their way through almost untouched wilderness, and diving is exceptional in the natural springs that bubble up from the limestone here – don't miss Devil's Den, a spectacular underground spring southwest of Gainesville. Furthermore, you haven't really lived until you have seen the manatees gathering at Blue Spring State Park, an oasis less than half an hour from downtown Orlando.

Climbing down into some huge sinkholes, bicycling the fantastic network of rail trails – abandoned railroad tracks refurbished for two-wheelers – and sleeping in a famous bordello are just a few of Central Florida's charms.

You'll need a car or a good bicycle to get anywhere off the beaten path in this part of the state, as public transportation only works in the major cities and shuttle services are expensive.

Orlando

pop 190,000
If you're looking for Walt Disney World and you've opened to this section, think again: It's in its own section, where it belongs, as it's in the entirely separate city of Lake Buena Vista. Orlando is, believe it or not, a city in its own right whose locals would feel just fine, thank you very much, if all those ear-wearing yahoos would just get back in their cars and keep moving (except, of course, when they spend their money here).

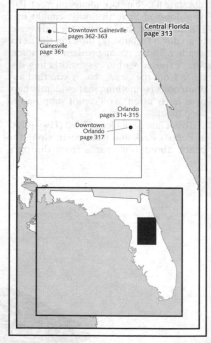

Downtown Gainesville pages 362-363

Gainesville page 361

Central Florida page 313

Orlando pages 314-315

Downtown Orlando page 317

HISTORY

At the end of the Second Seminole War, settlers and traders made their way here, eager

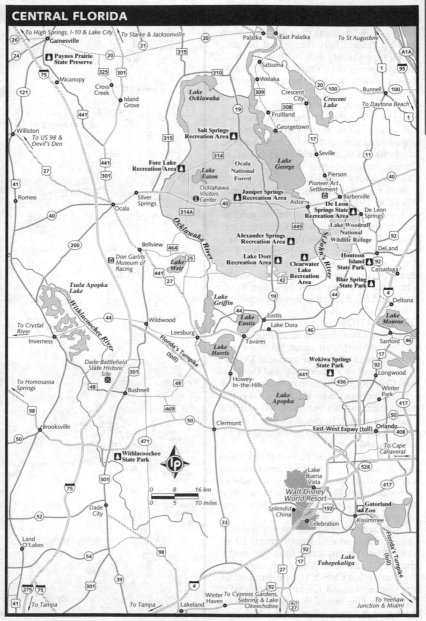

to build homes and farms in the fertile region. Originally named Jernigan (after settler Aaron Jernigan), the settlement here grew up around Fort Gatlin and became the Orange County seat in 1856. In 1857, the city was renamed Orlando for Orlando Reeves, a soldier killed by Seminole Indians on the shores of Lake Eola.

The city boomed several times; a railroad boom (which fueled a population boom), a real-estate boom and a citrus boom all helped bring prosperity to the area. And the late 1950s brought a technology boom, as Orlando manufactured the hardware for Cape Canaveral's launches.

With the establishment of Walt Disney World in 1971, the area became theme park central. Almost overnight, the median income rose by 50% and development exploded. Orlando is now the third-ranking destination of overseas visitors, after Los Angeles and New York City. To get a better idea of the drawing power of the Mouse and others, consider that Honolulu, San Francisco and Miami are all in this city's dust.

ORIENTATION

Downtown Orlando is about 23 miles north of Disney World, 10 miles north of the tourist quarter along International Dr and 4 miles south of Winter Park and the Cultural Corridor, a collection of museums and performance spaces on Mills Ave. I-4 is the main north-south connector, though it's labeled east-west: To go north, take I-4 east (toward Daytona); to go south, hop on I-4 west (toward Tampa).

The main east-west thoroughfares are Hwy 50 and Hwy 528 (Bee Line Expressway; toll road), which connect Orlando to the Space Coast. The Orlando International Airport is accessible from the Bee Line Expressway.

Downtown is centered on north-south Orange Ave and east-west Central Blvd, which divide the city's addresses into north, south, east and west. The main drags are Orange Ave and Church St. Lynx Bus Center (see Getting Around, later in this section) is between W Pine St and W Central Blvd one block west of Orange Ave.

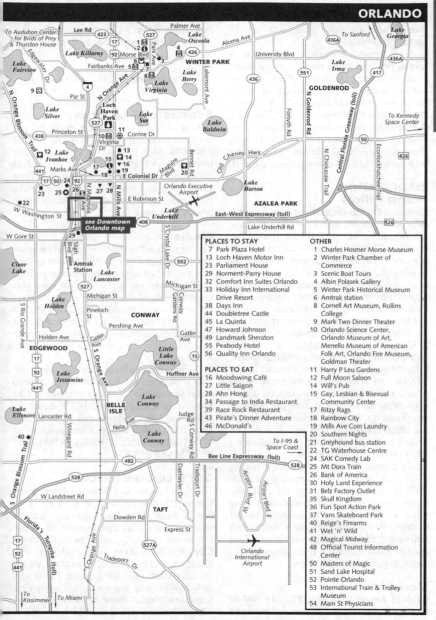

ORLANDO

PLACES TO STAY
7 Park Plaza Hotel
13 Loch Haven Motor Inn
23 Parliament House
29 Norment-Parry House
32 Comfort Inn Suites Orlando
33 Holiday Inn International
   Drive Resort
38 Days Inn
44 Doubletree Castle
45 La Quinta
47 Howard Johnson
49 Landmark Sheraton
55 Peabody Hotel
56 Quality Inn Orlando

PLACES TO EAT
16 Moodswing Café
27 Little Saigon
28 Ahn Hong
34 Passage to India Restaurant
39 Race Rock Restaurant
43 Pirate's Dinner Adventure
46 McDonald's

OTHER
1 Charles Hosmer Morse Museum
2 Winter Park Chamber of
   Commerce
3 Scenic Boat Tours
4 Albin Polasek Gallery
5 Winter Park Historical Museum
6 Amtrak station
8 Cornell Art Museum, Rollins
   College
9 Mark Two Dinner Theater
10 Orlando Science Center,
   Orlando Museum of Art,
   Menello Museum of American
   Folk Art, Orlando Fire Museum,
   Goldman Theater
11 Harry P Leu Gardens
12 Full Moon Saloon
14 Will's Pub
15 Gay, Lesbian & Bisexual
   Community Center
17 Ritzy Rags
18 Rainbow City
19 Mills Ave Coin Laundry
20 Southern Nights
21 Greyhound bus station
22 TG Waterhouse Centre
24 SAK Comedy Lab
25 Mt Dora Train
26 Bank of America
30 Holy Land Experience
31 Belz Factory Outlet
35 Skull Kingdom
36 Fun Spot Action Park
37 Vans Skateboard Park
40 Reige's Firearms
41 Wet 'n' Wild
42 Magical Midway
48 Official Tourist Information
   Center
50 Masters of Magic
51 Sand Lake Hospital
52 Pointe Orlando
53 International Train & Trolley
   Museum
54 Main St Physicians

International Dr, better known as I-Drive, is bookended by Universal Studios and Sea-World; there are three exits to this park-packed strip from I-4.

A good map is essential, as the area is so spread out, and you'll have to spend some money if you want to explore. The CVB provides several free maps that are useful for the area surrounding I-Drive and Kissimmee, but worthless for Orlando proper. The most detailed sheet map of the area is published by Map Supply, but it's unwieldy. Dolph, Universal and Rand McNally all produce useful maps ($3 to $5 at any area gas station).

INFORMATION
Tourist Offices
Orlando's **Official Tourist Information Center** (☎ 407-363-5871; 800-551-0181; ⓦ www .go2orlando.com; 8123 International Dr; open 8am-7pm daily), at the corner of Austrian Row, sells legitimate discount attraction tickets and has racks and stacks of free coupon books and handouts, including the *Official Visitors Guide, Official Accommodations Guide* and *Official Attractions Guide*.

Orlando International Airport also has an **Official Information Center** (☎ 407-825-2352; open 7am-11pm daily).

Important: There are lots unofficial 'tourist information centers,' concentrated along I-Drive and Hwy 192 in Kissimmee. Most offer a hard sell on free or discounted tickets in exchange for looking at some pricey property; however, tours are tedious and tickets are often restricted or falsified. If you're promised free parking or the right to go to the front of long lines, it's almost certainly a scam. Should you fall for it, please don't complain to harried amusement park staff; it's not their fault you thought you were slick. Call the police instead. Other venues offer deals on partially used multiple-day passes for Disney World and Universal Studios. These are *usually* real and can result in considerable savings, but it's illegal to purchase or use them.

Money
Bank of America (☎ 407-244-7041; 390 N Orange Ave) is right downtown. **American Express** (☎ 407-843-0004; Sun Bank Center, 2 W Church St) has a full-service office in **Sun Trust Bank**. Most theme parks have ATMs and foreign exchange desks.

Post
The **main post office** (46 E Robinson St) is downtown.

Bookstores & Libraries
All the chains have shops in malls around the area, including **Barnes & Noble** (☎ 407-894-6024; 8418 E Colonial Dr). The main **library** (☎ 407-835-7323; 100 E Central Blvd; open 9am-9pm Mon-Thur, 9am-6pm Fri & Sat, 1pm-6pm Sun), downtown, offers free Internet access; call to ask about other library locations.

Media
The big daily is the *Orlando Sentinel* (ⓦ www .orlandosentinel.com). Lots of free weeklies and monthlies cover local events, politics and the music scene: *Groove* (ⓦ www.you gotgroove.com) hits the dance scene; *Axis* (ⓦ www.axismag.com) is about alternative rock; *Orlando Weekly* (ⓦ www.orlando weekly.com) and *Connections* are the major free weeklies; and *Impact Press* publishes left-wing rants.

Commercial radio in Orlando is actually OK (the playlists have more than four songs in rotation): There's alternative FM rock at 101.3, 104.1 and 105.9; dance at 101.9 and 106.7; classic rock at 96.5, 98.9 and 101.5; oldies at 100.3; and country at 97.5. National Public Radio (NPR) is at 90.7 FM and 89.9 FM.

Gay & Lesbian Travelers
The **Gay, Lesbian and Bisexual Community Center** (☎ 407-228-8272; ⓦ www.glbc.org; 946 N Mills Ave) has a library and resource center, plus tips on local hot spots too numerous to mention here. **Rainbow City** (☎ 407-898-9069; 930 N Mills Ave) has a huge selection of g/l/b literature and a friendly staff; one salesperson, Matt, was only half kidding when he noted wryly that these few blocks along N Mills Ave were 'Orlando's best stab at West Hollywood.'

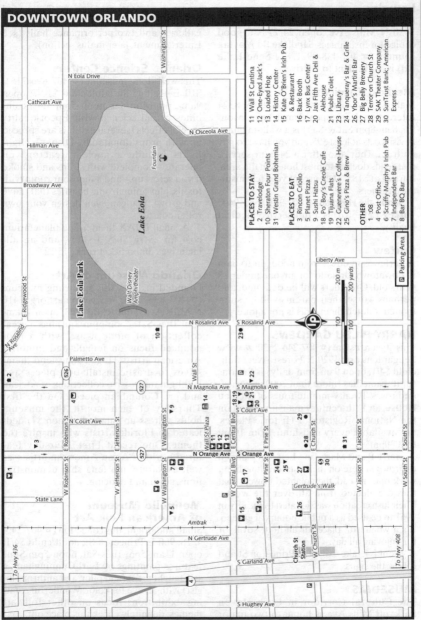

DOWNTOWN ORLANDO

PLACES TO STAY
2 Travelodge
10 Sheraton Four Points
31 Westin Grand Bohemian

PLACES TO EAT
3 Rincon Criollo
5 Planet Pizza
9 Sushi Hatsu
18 Po' Boy's Creole Cafe
19 Tijuana Flats
22 Guenevere's Coffee House
25 Gino's Pizza & Brew

11 Wall St Cantina
12 One-Eyed Jack's
13 Loaded Hog
14 History Center
15 Kate O'Brien's Irish Pub & Restaurant
16 Back Booth
17 Lynx Bus Center
20 Jax Fifth Ave Deli & Alehouse
21 Public Toilet
23 Library
24 Tanqueray's Bar & Grille
26 Ybor's Martini Bar
27 Big Belly Brewery
28 Terror on Church St
29 SAK Theater Company
30 SunTrust Bank; American Express

OTHER
1 :08
4 Post Office
6 Scruffy Murphy's Irish Pub
7 Independent Bar
8 Bar BQ Bar

Laundry

Mills Ave Coin Laundry (☎ 407-898-9059; 1030 N Mills Ave; open 24/7) is a good choice for insomniacs. **Sandlake Rd Maytag Laundry** (☎ 407-438-8911; 811 Sand Lake Rd) is convenient to I-Drive.

Medical Services

Main St Physicians (☎ 407-396-1195; 8324 International Dr; open 8am-3:30pm Mon-Fri, 8am-8pm Sat & Sun) is a walk-in clinic. A visit costs at least $95, and you have to pay up front. They also offer a 24-hour service that sends doctors to most hotels in the area, starting at $185. They accept very few insurance carriers.

Sand Lake Hospital (☎ 407-351-8550; 9400 Turkey Lake Rd) is a full-service medical facility.

Curfew

A curfew is in effect from midnight to 6am in downtown Orlando for anyone under 18 years old. Offenders will be detained, and perhaps worse, their parents will be summoned to fetch them. This is not a joke.

HARRY P LEU GARDENS

This 50-acre estate (☎ 407-246-2620; w www.leugardens.org; 1920 N Forest Ave; adult/child $4/1; open 9am-5pm daily) is famous for its camellias (more than 2000 varieties) and roses. Twenty-minute tours of the **Leu House**, an 18th-century mansion listed on the National Register of Historic Places, are available every half-hour from 10am to 3:30pm.

Harry P and Mary Jane Leu had planned to grow tea here on their estate, but it didn't work out. Instead, they planted flowers that they'd collected from all over the world. Their lush creation was donated to the city in 1961 to be used as a public botanical garden. It's a wonderful place for an hour stroll, or for enjoying all day.

From I-4, take exit 43 to Princeton St and follow the signs.

MUSEUMS

The Cultural Corridor in Loch Haven Park, off Mills Ave, is home to two major museums, the Orlando Science Center and Orlando Museum of Art, several smaller galleries and two performance halls (see Entertainment, later in this section).

Orlando Science Center

This well-done museum (☎ 407-896-7151; 810 E Rollins St; adult/child $10/7; open 9am-5pm Mon-Sat, noon-5pm Sun) combines actual science with Epcot-quality special effects (several exhibits are spruced up with props donated by Disney). Highlights include a nuclear reactor you operate – complete with sirens and smoke if you screw up – and a dinosaur room with fossils, plus animatronic beasties that move and growl. You can even design your own roller coaster.

A small IMAX theater and planetarium cost an extra $6/5 a show, and an all-inclusive combo ticket runs $15/12.

Orlando Museum of Art

Founded in 1924, this sprawling museum (☎ 407-896-4231; w www.omart.org; 2416 N Mills Ave; adult/child $6/3; open 10am-5pm Tues-Sat, noon-5pm Sun) has a great collection of modern art, with a pronounced focus on female and minority American artists. Huge rooms lend themselves to drastic installation pieces and highlight impressive collections of African and pre-Columbian pieces. On the first Thursday of each month, the museum holds a dress-up gala (admission $7) dedicated to Florida artists who inspire the theme. One recent First Thursday featured a trio of Asian American artists, as well as karate and feng shui demonstrations, sushi and dancing.

Mennello Museum of American Folk Art

Small and bright, this collection (☎ 407-246-4278; 900 E Princeton St; adult/child $4/1; open 11am-5pm Tues-Sat, noon-5pm Sun) features paintings by Earl Cunningham, a self-taught artist (and pilot, and anthropologist) with an eye for color. Wonderful rotating exhibitions focus on other folk art themes; definitely check this place out.

Orlando Fire Museum

Housed in the oldest standing firehouse in Orange County, this museum (☎ 407-898-3138; 814 E Rollins; open 10am-5pm Tues-Sat, noon-5pm Sun) was preparing to open, but still hadn't settled on the admission fee (probably adult/child $4/2). They did have some of their exhibits set up, however: The 1911 steam-engine truck and 1915 American LaFrance fire engine were two stars of the show.

History Center

Orange County's historical museum (☎ 407-836-8500; 65 E Central Blvd; adult/child $7/4; open 10am-5pm Mon-Sat, noon-5pm Sun) has permanent exhibits on prehistoric

Florida, Orange County buildings and citrus production. The excellent History of Florida Tourism exhibit pays special homage to Walt Disney (referring to swampy, backwater Orlando as 'BD' and the bustling town it is today as 'AD'). My favorite section's name says it all: 'Celebrating Giant Attractions and One-of-a-Kind Tourist Traps.' Oh yeah.

International Train & Trolley Museum

Home to the most extravagant model train set you could imagine, this museum (☎ 407-363-9002; 8990 International Dr; adult/child $9/7; open 10am-6pm daily) is probably worth the price if you're into that sort of thing.

Cracker Cuisine

The term 'cracker' is hardly politically correct – in most parts of the country, if you refer to a poor rural white person as such, you'll either get an eye rollin' or an ass kickin', depending on testosterone levels. In Florida, however, the label is worn with pride, and refers to colonial architecture, backcountry know-how and, of course, fine cooking. Most cracker cuisine runs to fried gator tail and grits, but Orlando's History Center had some authentic old-time recipes you might want to try out on the folks back home.

Baked Possum

1 possum, skinned and cleaned, with scent glands removed

6 cups water

Salt and pepper to taste

5 or 6 sweet potatoes, sliced

4 onions, chopped

½ lb collard greens

Place possum in a large skillet. Cover with water, salt and pepper. Parboil the meat until tender, then drain the water and excess oils. Put the possum into a greased pan with the potatoes and onions, cover the pan, and bake on a medium heat for 45 minutes. Add collard greens during the last 15 minutes.

Squirrel Soup

¼ lb bacon

4 to 6 squirrels, skinned and cleaned

2 onions, chopped

Salt and pepper to taste

7 cups water

1 cup sliced carrots

4 potatoes, cubed

1 large jar canned tomatoes

Fry bacon in a large pot. Remove bacon and brown squirrels on all sides. Add onions, salt and pepper and water. Cover and simmer for 1 to 2 hours, or until meat falls from the bone. Add remaining ingredients and bring to a boil. Cook over a low heat until potatoes and carrots are tender (30 to 45 minutes).

And that's a dinner party your friends will never forget.

UNIVERSAL STUDIOS FLORIDA

This combination working movie studio and theme park (☎ 407-363-8000; ⓦ www .universalorlando.com; 1000 Universal Studios Plaza; adult/child $53/44; open 9am daily, closing times vary) has a 'Ride the Movies' concept that inspires excellent 3D shows, motion simulators and rides. For real thrills, however, head to Universal's sister park, Islands of Adventure (see that section, later).

Orientation & Information

Universal Studios Florida is near the intersection of I-4 and Florida's Turnpike; the main entrance is on Kirkman Rd (Hwy 435) about half a mile north of I-4 exit 3B. A second entrance is on Turkey Lake Rd. Pick up a map at the entrance.

Guest Services is to the right of the entrance. It has foreign-language guides to the park, a lost and found and lost-kids area, a First Union bank where you can exchange most currencies and the friendliest staff around. You can rent manual/electric wheelchairs ($8/35) and single/double strollers ($8/14) here, too. Most rides are wheelchair accessible.

Lockers are available for $5 daily, and free (inconvenient) lockers are outside rides that forbid bags and purses.

Universal Studios participates in the 14-day, five-park **Flexticket** program (adult/child $203/165), which includes Islands of Adventure, SeaWorld, Wet 'n' Wild and Busch Gardens in Tampa. VIP tours ($120) take you to the front of long lines and backstage at the shows. Discount tickets and package deals are available. You can often get a second day free (stop at the information desk on your way out) during low season. Parking is $7/8 car/RV.

Things to See & Do

There's so much to see and do here that the following top ten list barely scratches the surface. Call for an *Official Studio Guide* information packet or log onto ⓦ www .universalorlando.com for more thorough coverage. Be sure to take your time strolling the different 'cities,' Hollywood, San Fran-cisco and New York. The architecture is downright remarkable and packed with neat storefronts (souvenir shops), bars and restaurants.

Terminator 2:3D CyberDyne headquarters showcases the creepy future of technology here, including fully operational examples of their brand-new, heavily armed cybernetic soldiers. Watch their PowerPoint presentation – oh wait – the signal's been interrupted! Linda Hamilton and Arnold Schwarzenegger, in glorious 3D, want you out of the building now! The evil global defense system is coming online any second, and... 'Sorry about those nutty hackers, everyone. Now, back to the presentation.'

Men in Black Can you qualify for the most elite law-enforcement agency in the galaxy? Well, you'll have to prove it. Aim your lasers at aliens of every size and description while your car swings and spins through a danger-laden downtown, and just try to beat my score of 181,000.

Nickelodeon Studios Sadly, Nickelodeon is reducing the amount of programming actually filmed here, though kids will still go wild over the **Studio Tour** of, among other sets, *Slime Time Live*. The **Green Slime Geyser** out front erupts every few minutes (on a random schedule), spewing forth GAK onto anyone standing within the clearly marked SPLAT ZONE.

Twister Despite the single most annoying preshow video in Orlando, this attraction rules! They create an 'actual' tornado – screaming wind, pouring rain, flying cows – right in front of you.

Back to the Future Hop in your DeLorean-shaped flight simulator and take off toward a seven-story, 60-foot-high (18m) screening area filled with liquid-nitrogen fog...er, to the 1950s and prehistoric times. Second for second, this is said to be one of the most expensive films (almost $4 million per minute) ever made.

ET Adventure This charming ride lets you rescue ET in flying bicycle-like contraptions: Skim the roof of a police car, then rise up over the city, past alien babies and other weird spacey stuff, to ET's home planet.

Earthquake After Charlton Heston demonstrates the now dated and creaky but then spectacular special effects from the movie *Earthquake,* you'll enter a really bitchin' replica of a San Francisco BART subway station. Suddenly, the Big One (8.3 on the Richter scale) hits: tracks buckle, the place crumbles and general mayhem ensues.

Gory Gruesome & Grotesque Horror Makeup Show This delivers, though if you're really into horror makeup it may be a little too short. If you like this, check out the enthusiastically recommended (by a crowd of hyperactive preteens) **Beetlejuice Rock 'n' Roll Graveyard Review** show, too.

Animal Planet Live! Watch as Babe the pig, Beethoven the dog, Mr Ed, Benji, an alligator named Chompers, a sea lion, Holly the stunt chimp and even a skunk reprise their acclaimed cinematic performances with video backup.

Fievel's Playland Inspired by the cartoon *An American Tail,* about a family of Russian mice who immigrate to America, this wild playground lets kids climb and slide all over giant 'garbage' that really does give you a mouse's-eye view. Plus, it'll keep them distracted from the irritating **A Day in the Park with Barney**, where they'll drag you the minute they see the plush purple dinosaur and his disturbing pal Baby Bop dancing and singing with other kids. If the Playland isn't enough, however, point them toward **Woody Woodpecker's Nuthouse Coaster**, nearby, the biggest ride in the park for wee ones.

Places to Stay & Eat

The **Hard Rock Hotel** (☎ 407-503-7625; W www.universalorlando.com; 5800 Universal Blvd; rooms $200-300 summer, $260-360 winter) is one of Universal's three partner hotels within walking (or water-taxiing)

distance from the parks and CityWalk. It's much classier than you'd think, and the pool has an underwater (!) sound system. Package deals, which include lots of extras (like no waiting in line at the parks) – make this a much better deal.

The park also holds numerous fast-food and full-service restaurants where you'll pay for just a bit more than what you get.

The **Beverly Hills Boulangerie** (dishes $7-8), in Hollywood, has healthy sandwiches and filling vegetarian options.

Lombards (dishes $5-17), at Fisherman's Wharf, reportedly has the best food in the park, with fried shrimp, fish & chips and lobster bisque served alongside cloth napkins and stemware. Make dinner reservations early in the day.

Finnegan's (dishes $8-13), in New York, is an Irish bar and grill with Cornish pasties and shepherd's pie, but sadly, no Guinness.

ISLANDS OF ADVENTURE

OK, I'll just say it: This is the best theme park in Orlando (at press time – this *is* a competitive business). Islands of Adventure (☎ 407-363-8000; W www.universalorlando.com; 1000 Universal Studios Plaza; adult/child $53/44; open 9am daily, closing times vary) has better characters than the Magic Kingdom, better rides than Universal Studios, better food than Holy Land and better architecture than Gaudi's cathedral in Spain. OK, maybe I'm going a little overboard here, but just wait until you get on that Spider-Man ride.

Orientation & Information

Islands of Adventure is the sister park of Universal Studios, and most information is identical (see Orientation & Information in the Universal Studios Florida section, earlier), although **Guest Services**, disguised as the Open Arms Motel, does not exchange foreign currency.

Things to See & Do

No one could do this place justice on paper, but the top ten list below should give you a taste of what's waiting. One thing's for sure: The fine folks at Disney World are pulling some all-nighters trying to figure out how to top this collection of rides.

Amazing Adventures of Spider-Man After the space shuttle, this may be the coolest thing in Florida. Hop onto the combination roller coaster/motion simulator quickly – Spidey needs you! Supervillains rendered in state-of-the-art 3D are on the loose (and jumping on your car, and chasing you around with giant electrical plugs), and it's up to you and your favorite webslinger to stop them.

Seuss Landing Audrey Geisel, widow of Dr Seuss (aka Ted Geisel), was heavily involved with the design and construction of this lyrical park, where the Lorax guards his trufula trees amidst incredible architecture that makes Circus McGurkis real. I've got a dollar that says the **Caro-Seuss-el** will eventually end up in the Smithsonian – or Louvre. And yes, you can get real green eggs (and ham) from concessions.

The Hulk Hands down the best roller coaster in Orlando – and watch that first hill, Dr Baxter!

Dueling Dragons Get two roller coasters in one with these synchronized thrillers – sometimes you're so close to the other cars that you'll want to pull your dangling tootsies out of the way.

Pteranodon Flyer Parents finally get their payback for having to skip all the other big rides here: If you don't have a kid with you, you can't fly. And you really do fly, carried over the jungly Jurassic Park section and all its robotic dinosaurs in a quiet hang-glider assembly.

Dudley Do-Right's Ripsaw Falls The confused Canadian Mountie has his hands full keeping logs packed with tourists from hurtling over the edge of – oh no – a huge waterfall!

Bilge Rat Barges Not wet enough for you? Head across the way, where Popeye, Bluto

and Olive Oyl operate a somewhat tamer (little kids can go), though no less drenching, raft ride.

Jurassic Park River Adventure If there's still a square inch of you that's dry, perhaps you'd like to take the boat tour of the not-at-all-dangerous velociraptor facilities here at the Jurassic Park Institute.

Poseidon's Fury More a show than a ride, this has a cheese factor of about 8.5 out of 10. You'll forgive them, though, when you see the most ingenious gimmick of entertainment technology in the park.

The Cat in the Hat Grab a couch and watch as Thing One and Thing Two instigate all sorts of mayhem. Oh, that cat!

Places to Stay & Eat
The **Hard Rock Hotel** is close by (see Places to Stay & Eat in the Universal Studios section).

All the usual fast-food suspects are sold at premium prices throughout the park, but with a commitment to theme you don't see elsewhere.

Blondie's Diner, in Toon Lagoon, sells American classics like meat-loaf sandwich and 'the Dagwood,' with ham, salami, turkey, bologna, Swiss and American cheeses, and a tomato ($7). An analogous veggie sandwich ($6) is almost as big.

Green Eggs & Ham, in Seuss Landing, does a vibrant green egg and hamwich ($6).

Mythos Restaurant (☎ 407-224-4533; dishes $15-24), in the Lost Continent, is the only restaurant where you'll need to make reservations. The dining room is an ornate underwater grotto where you'll dine on acceptable pad Thai or vegetable gnocchi while imagining yourself among the merfolk.

SEAWORLD ORLANDO
A combination amusement park, aquarium and beer garden, SeaWorld (☎ 407-351-3600; ⓦ www.seaworld.com; 7007 SeaWorld Orlando Dr; adult/child $53/44; open 9am daily, closing times vary) is fine family entertainment. It's a little pricey – more than a

Disney park – but some of that money does go to very good causes: The SeaWorld Orlando Animal Rescue Team is one of the best in the country. And if you're the sort of person who likes leaping dolphins, sliding sea lions and crashing whales, you're going to have an incredible time.

Orientation & Information

SeaWorld Orlando is near the intersection of I-4 and the Bee Line Expressway.

Guest Services, to your left as you enter the park, has an ATM and exchanges foreign currency 10am to 4pm daily. They also have a lost and found, foreign-language guides, kennel services ($7; bring your own food) and lockers ($4).

SeaWorld participates in the 14-day, five-park **Flexticket** program (adult/child $203/165), which includes the two Universal Studios parks, Wet 'n' Wild, and Busch Gardens in Tampa. Discount tickets and package deals are available. Parking is $7/8 car/RV.

All attractions are wheelchair accessible. Single/double strollers can be rented for $8/14, manual/electric wheelchairs for $8/25. There are air-conditioned child-care centers throughout the park with diapers, formula and other necessities for sale, and changing tables in all restrooms.

The park also offers special opportunities to get a little closer to the wildlife. There are several overnight camps for kids and adults; ask at guest services for a guide to more than 200 options. There are three tempting add-ons for people 13 years old and up: **Animal Care Experience** ($389) teaches basic marine animal care and feeding; **Sea-World Trainer for a Day** ($389) trains you for one of the best jobs ever; and the **False Killer Whale Interaction Program** ($200) lets you swim with Shamu. All these programs are limited to four people per day, so make reservations early.

Things to See & Do

If you'd like a more comprehensive guide to rides and attractions than this entirely subjective top list ten offers, call for a visitor's kit or log onto W www.seaworld.com.

Shamu False killer whales (several of them, all named Shamu) are the stars at SeaWorld, and this is where you watch them do their thing. The first 15 rows of Shamu Stadium are the 'splash zone,' and both whales and trainers really enjoy soaking the crowd with icy seawater. It's truly amazing, and there's a rock 'n' roll show after dark.

Kraken It's one of the best – highest, fastest, longest – roller coasters in town. A must.

Journey to Atlantis This roller coaster cum flume ride has special effects aplenty, but the reason why everyone's screaming is the 60-foot (18m) vertical drop.

Manatees: the Last Generation? The heroic SeaWorld Orlando Animal Rescue Team rescues injured and sick manatees, and this is where you'll see the recuperating cuties. It begins with a heart-wrenching film and finishes with a fine view of manatees bearing the scars of human encroachment.

Wild Arctic You're traveling to Base Station Wild Arctic in an incredibly high-powered helicopter as a bad storm front moves in. The nature-loving pilot brings you very close to some polar bears before setting down on thin ice. Of course, after hearing an awful rumbling sound, you fall through the ice and it's touch and go there for a while, but...

Dolphin Nursery Is there anything cuter than a bunch of baby dolphins leaping and playing? Well, maybe – **Stingray Lagoon**, nearby, has tiny infant stingrays.

Sea Lion & Otter Stadium This is home to *Clyde and Seamore Take Pirate Island*, a show starring sea lion, otter and walrus 'comedians.' It's excellent for kids, who find it screamingly funny. Take the tots to **Shamu's Happy Harbor** afterward, to work off some of that excitement.

Terrors of the Deep Menacing sharks, rays, barracudas, lionfish and skates swim all around the Plexiglas tube you're carried through on a conveyor belt. Aren't you glad Orlando doesn't have a beach?

Penguin Encounter People movers take you past penguin tanks with manufactured snow, the sounds of penguin calls barely audible over the hilarious and appropriate *oom-pah-pah* music. Dig the wild rockhopper penguins, which look very much like mid-1980s Rod Stewart.

Anheuser-Busch Beer School A favorite of harried single parents trying to cope with the hyperactive kids they haven't seen in six months, this 'educational' attraction teaches you how to brew beer. Afterward, you'll sample several to make sure they're OK.

DISCOVERY COVE

Adjacent to its parent park, SeaWorld, this innovative and elite attraction (☎ 407-370-1280; ⓦ www.discoverycove.com; admission $219) is limited to only 1000 guests daily; make reservations well ahead. Private beaches, a complimentary lunch and an exotic bird aviary are just a few of the diversions. As part of your day, you'll get some hands-on basic training and then swim with dolphins! There are also snorkeling opportunities in a lagoon packed with rays and tropical fish.

Reviews of Discovery Cove are mixed. One recent participant was disappointed that, after an hour of training, she only got to spend a few minutes with the dolphins. Other people I spoke with felt it was the best vacation they'd ever had.

HOLY LAND EXPERIENCE

Did you ever wonder where Rod and Todd Flanders vacation while the Simpson family, through a series of hilarious mishaps, ends up performing at Gay Day in the Magic Kingdom? They come to Holy Land Experience (☎ 407-872-3393; ⓦ www.theholy landexperience.com; 4655 Vineland Rd; adult/child $22/17; open 9am-6pm Mon-Sat, noon-6pm Sun), Orlando's only Christian theme park.

It's designed to look like Jerusalem circa 33 AD, and staff (most of whom are Israeli imports) wear flowing Bedouin robes and hawk Middle Eastern treats like mint tea, tabouli and the best falafel I have ever eaten. There aren't any rides, despite obvious Old Testament candidates like the Parting of the Red Sea, but they do serve free food 3pm to 5pm daily. And the shows are great.

Gospel choirs come from all over the Southeast to perform here, and there's a daily musical about the **Resurrection of Christ** performed at an outdoor theater built to look like Jesus' tomb. **AD 66** is a tour through an impressive scale model of ancient Jerusalem, blending history, archaeology and New Testament tales in a kid-friendly and downright educational way.

My favorite was the **Wilderness Tabernacle**, which takes you back 3400 years to see the nine different ways Aaron (Moses' older brother) sacrificed sheep to God, complete with a light-and-sound spectacular reminiscent of *Raiders of the Lost Ark*.

Rules, as you might imagine, are strict: Dress conservatively and don't smoke. Anyone yelling about evolution, gay rights or abortion will be politely escorted to the parking lot. You can rent strollers for $5 and arrange tours for the deaf and blind in advance. Parking is $3.

WET 'N' WILD

Wet 'n' Wild (☎ 407-351-1800, 800-992-9453; ⓦ www.wetnwild.com; 6200 International Dr; adult/child $33/27; hours vary seasonally) is one of Florida's first water parks, and it's still a refreshing way to spend part of your vacation.

Wet 'n' Wild participates in the 14-day, five-park **Flexticket** program (adult/child $203/165), which includes the two Universal Studios parks, SeaWorld and Busch Gardens in Tampa. Parking is $7/8 car/RV. It's perfectly located right at the heart of International Dr and is clean, safe and family oriented – not to mention packed with great rides.

Some of the attractions include **The Storm**, which dumps you into a huge whirlpool; **Mach 5**, a super-slick mat ride; **Black Hole**, enclosed for maximum disorientation; and **Hydra Fighter**, which involves bungee cords and fire hoses in a two-person car. At the center of the park is a wave pool; **Lazy River** meanders around the perimeter.

CLASSIC AMUSEMENT PARKS

Feeling nostalgic? I-Drive has a few attractions reminiscent of touring small-town carnivals, right down to the creaking machinery and carnies.

Fun Spot Action Park (☎ 407-363-3867; W www.fun-spot.com; 5551 Del Verde Way; all-inclusive armbands $30/15 adult/child) has a Ferris wheel, go-carts and the awesome Zipper, as well as the opportunity to win giant stuffed animals. You can also purchase rides separately ($3 to $6).

Magical Midway (☎ 407-370-5353; 7001 International Dr; all-inclusive armbands $20/15 adult/child) has a better location but less ambitious attractions. A game of laser tag costs $5.25 additional.

SKULL KINGDOM

You can't miss the giant skull motif on this souped-up haunted house (☎ 407-354-1564; W www.skullkingdom.com; 5933 American Way; admission $12), at the corner of I-Drive. It's not high-tech or anything, but some love went into this palace of horrors. And despite my best efforts, I did yelp a few times – the masked, knife-wielding killer had it out for me, I swear.

You can also pick up flyers for the **Orlando Ghost Tour** (☎ 407-992-1200; W www.orlandohauntings.com) here.

REIGE'S FIREARMS

Foreigners will be aghast at the ease with which this shooting range (☎ 407-859-5064; 5512 S Orange Blossom Trail; open 10am-10:30pm daily) rents handguns and semiautomatic weapons out to anyone – *anyone* – over age 21. Children over 10 can play, too, as long as they're accompanied by an adult.

Here's how it works: Rent the range for an hour ($6) and a gun ($6) – choose anything from a Glock to a Smith & Wesson .44 magnum. Semiautomatics cost a bit more. It's $2 for the necessary safety equipment and extra for ammo. They'll give you a quick

basic training course on safety and shooting, then it's all up to you. Blammity-blam-blam!

VANS SKATEBOARD PARK

Adrenaline junkies will love this enormous skateboard and BMX park (☎ 407-351-3881; 5220 International Dr; 2-hour session $11-14), at the intersection of Touchstone Dr. You can rent a skateboard ($5) and all the necessary safety equipment, right after you (or your *legal* guardian if you're under 18) sign a comprehensive waiver.

WEKIWA SPRINGS STATE PARK

If Orlando is your only stop in the region, do yourself a favor and see this sliver of the real Central Florida (☎ 407-884-2006; 1800 Wekiwa Circle; pedestrian/car $1/4). It's got miles of hiking, bicycle and canoe trails through palmetto wilderness, not to mention a natural spring welling up at 72°F year-round. You can rent bikes ($9 for two hours, $18 all day) and canoes ($14 for two hours, $25 all day) to better take it all in. Best of all, the only mice you'll see will be trying to raid your picnic basket. There's camping (see Places to Stay) here, too.

Head north from downtown Orlando on I-4 East about 6 miles, and exit 49 west on Sanlando Rd. Make a right at Wekiwa Springs Rd and follow the signs three more miles to the park.

PLACES TO STAY

Hotels in downtown Orlando are geared to business travelers. It's usually a much better deal to stay on International Dr, close to the theme parks, or (even cheaper) in Kissimmee, along Hwy 192 (see Places to Stay in the Kissimmee section). Most places on I-Drive are small, basic, independently run motels or absolutely standard chain places with perks like free shuttles to the amusement parks. The rack rates quoted here vary widely according to demand, and can usually be lowered by bargaining, or as part of a package deal.

Camping

Raccoon Lake (☎ 407-239-4148, 800-776-9644; 9200 Turkey Lake Rd; sites without/

with hookups $15/25, cottages $45-50) is in Orlando.

Wekiwa Springs (☎ 407-884-2006; 1800 Wekiwa Circle; sites without/with hookups $17/19) is completely inconvenient without a car, but a much more beautiful place to pitch a tent. (See Wekiwa Springs State Park, earlier.) There are also free walk-in sites 4 miles from the parking lot.

KOA (☎ 407-277-5075, 800-562-3969; 12343 Narcoossee Rd; sites without/with hookups $25/30) has a campground 5 miles south of the Bee Line Expressway at exit 13.

Downtown

Loch Haven Motor Inn (☎ 407-896-3611; 1820 N Mills Ave; rooms $40) is clean enough, friendly and convenient to Winter Park and the Cultural Corridor.

Travelodge (☎ 407-423-1671; 409 N Magnolia Ave; rooms $55-65) is pleasant and has a pool.

Parliament House (☎ 407-425-7571; 410 N Orange Blossom Trail; rooms $59-99 summer, $99-139 Gay Days) is a gay resort and an Orlando institution.

The **Norment-Parry House** (☎ 407-648-5188, 800-444-5289; W www.orlando historicinn.com; 211 N Lucerne Circle E; rooms $89-120) is a friendly, four-house B&B with colorful and comfortable rooms.

Sheraton Four Points (☎ 407-841-3220; 151 E Washington; rooms $99-129) is well located right on Lake Eola, but the rooms are somewhat aged; it's a little too expensive for what you get.

Westin Grand Bohemian (☎ 407-313-9000; W www.grandbohemianhotel.com; 325 S Orange Ave; singles/doubles $109/139 weekends, $159/189 weekdays) is downtown's most luxurious option, with spas, restaurants and very nice rooms. Oh, and they've got one of two gold-plated Bösendorfer pianos in the world, played nightly along with a jazz quartet.

International Drive

Hotels lining I-Drive usually include a 'free' (you'll actually pay about $10 more per room for this service) shuttle to area amusement parks.

Comfort Suites Orlando (☎ 407-351-5050; No 5825; rooms $49/89 summer/winter) is very comfortable.

Days Inn (☎ 407-351-1200; No 7200; rooms $39/99 summer/winter) has basic rooms but no free shuttle.

Doubletree Castle (☎ 407-345-1511; No 8629; rooms $79/199 summer/winter) wins for presentation, a huge castle with lots of kid-oriented amenities.

Holiday Inn International Drive Resort (☎ 407-351-3500; No 6515; rooms $49/69 summer/winter) is nicer than average, with shuffleboard courts!

Howard Johnson (☎ 407-351-2000; W www .howardjohnsonhotelorlando.com; 7050 S Kirkman Rd; rooms $45/79 summer/ winter) has a free shuttle and miniature golf course ($1).

Landmark Sheraton (☎ 407-351-2100, 800-327-1366; W www.sheratonstudiocity.com; No 5905; rooms $99/119 summer/winter) is flashy.

La Quinta (☎ 407-345-1365; 8504 Universal Blvd; rooms $69/109 summer/winter) has rooms with microwaves and fridges.

Quality Inn Orlando (☎ 407-996-8585; No 9000; rooms $89) has standard rooms, a free shuttle and a big pool.

The **Peabody Hotel** (☎ 407-352-4000; W www.peabodyorlando.com; 9801 International Blvd; rooms $345-1400) is the big exception. It's got all the amenities you'd expect at these prices, plus one famous extra: At 11am a line of ducks marches into the lobby fountain, then they head single file back to their ceiling nests at 5pm. And yes, you can just drop by to see the parade.

PLACES TO EAT

Orlando has few outstanding restaurants worth dressing up for (see Places to Stay & Eat in the Winter Park section for more of these), and there's a never-ending supply of fast-food and chain restaurants.

Downtown

Guenevere's Coffee House (☎ 407-992-1200; 37/39 S Magnolia; open 8pm-midnight daily) has caffeine in all its guises, sugary treats and live acoustic music.

Planet Pizza (☎ 407-839-5998; 14 W Washington St; slices $2-4, pies $15-25; open 6pm-3am daily) is perfect for late-night club munchies.

Gino's Pizza & Brew (☎ 407-999-7827; 120 S Orange Ave; slices $3-4, pies $16-20; open 9:30am-4:30am daily) has late hours and good pizza for hard drinkers and downtown businesspeople.

Rincon Criollo (☎ 407-872-1128; 331 N Orange Ave; sandwiches $5-7; open 8am-3pm daily) does vegetarian Cuban cuisine like meatless meatball sandwiches and pressed veggie Cubans.

Po' Boy's Creole Cafe (☎ 407-839-5852; 50 E Central Blvd; sandwiches $4-8; open 11am-3pm Mon, 11am-10pm Tues-Thur, 11am-midnight Fri, noon-10pm Sat) has good pressed sandwiches with a Creole zing.

Tijuana Flats (☎ 407-839-0007; 50 E Central Blvd; dishes $4-9; open 11am-6pm Sun & Mon, 11am-9pm Tues-Thur; 11am-midnight Fri & Sat), right next door, is a better bet for lunch. Huge burritos and gooey quesadillas come with your choice of 12 different hot sauces, from 'Georgia Peach & Vidalia Onion' to 'Smack My Ass and Call Me Sally.'

Sushi Hatsu (☎ 407-422-1551; 24 W Washington St; mains $8-13; open 11am-2:30pm Mon-Fri, 5pm-10pm Mon-Sat) gets several thumbs up. It's a Korean-Japanese place that serves excellent kimchee and sushi.

International Drive

It's buffet central – Chinese, seafood, Southern cuisine, etc – on I-Drive, and even the locals recommend chain restaurants. But everyone's got to eat, right?

McDonalds (☎ 407-351-2185; 6875 Sand Lake Blvd) – I know, I know, it's the evil empire. Whatever. But get this – it's the biggest McDonalds in the world!

Race Rock Restaurant (☎ 407-248-9876; 8186 International Dr; mains $7-15; open 11:30am-11:30pm daily) is a NASCAR theme restaurant with cars hanging from the ceiling, a museum-quality collection of racing memorabilia, burgers, fried chicken and steaks.

Passage to India Restaurant (☎ 407-351-3456; 5532 International Dr; lunch $8-13, dinner $13-22; open 11:30am-10pm daily) is heaven sent for vegetarians needing a break from the salad bars. It's a little pricey but worth it – try the bhaigan bharta (baked eggplant) or tandoori chicken.

Pirate's Dinner Adventure (☎ 407-248-0590; 6400 Carrier Dr; adult/child $44/27) has a full-sized Spanish galleon where actors swing from ropes, have sword fights and rescue damsels in distress while you eat mediocre food. It's actually pretty enthralling, especially for kids, who get to participate in all the action. Check the tourist rags for coupons offering 50% discounts.

Elsewhere

Little Saigon (☎ 407-423-8539; 1106 E Colonial Dr; dishes $5-9), just off N Mills, is an Orlando institution (the menu is on display at the Historical Center). It's got excellent service and quality charbroiled beef and pho.

Ahn Hong Restaurant (☎ 407-999-2656; mains $5-9; open 9am-9:30pm daily), nearby, serves more traditional Vietnamese food – have a durian smoothie with your meal. The spring rolls are excellent.

Moodswing Café (☎ 407-895-9777; 815 N Mills; mains $7-13; open 11:30am-9pm Mon-Thur, 11am-10:30pm Fri & Sat) has great burgers, sandwiches and Lonnie's famous meat loaf. On the first and third Monday of the month, it becomes a 'drag diner,' with extra-dazzling servers, entertainers and even customers ($5 cover).

ENTERTAINMENT

Orlando has a taste for fun, not to mention a healthy local music scene – Creed came up through these bars. From the manufactured merrymaking at Universal Studios' City-Walk and Disney's Pleasure Island (see Walt Disney World Resort, later) to downtown's excellent and organic collection of clubs, there's just no reason to stay home at night. Local theater and dance troupes entertain at some spectacular venues, too.

The collection of bars, shops and night-clubs on Church St near Garland Ave is housed in beautifully renovated, century-old buildings called Church St Station, done up in an Old South/Grand Ole Opry theme.

It was closed for much-needed renovations when I went by, however, but promises to reopen before this book expires (late 2003 was the goal).

Most of the bars and clubs listed in this section are downtown.

Bars & Pubs

Tanqueray's Bar & Grille (☎ 407-649-8540; 100 S Orange Ave; open 11am-2am Mon-Fri, 6pm-2am Sat & Sun), a few steps down from street level, is friendly, packed with regulars and has live music, usually reggae or blues, on weekends ($2 cover).

Scruffy Murphy's Irish Pub (☎ 407-648-5460; 9 W Washington St) is the best Irish place, and has a great selection of Irish beers and a fun crowd.

Bar BQ Bar (☎ 407-648-5441; 64 N Orange Ave; open 6pm-2am daily) has cheap beer and a menu worth reviewing (but don't order anything, OK?) and local bands getting busy Tuesday and some other nights. There's never a cover.

Back Booth (☎ 407-999-2570; W www.back booth.com; 37 W Pine St; open 9pm-2am Sat-Wed; 5pm-2am Thur & Fri) was, at the time of research, *the* place to see local and national bands. There's usually a cover.

Big Belly Brewery (☎ 407-649-4270; 33 W Church St; open 4pm-2am daily) has scantily clad servers and a mostly male clientele who only come here for the happy-hour buffet, really.

Will's Pub (☎ 407-898-5070; W www.wills pub.com; 1850 N Mills) is off the beaten path but worth it for the great live music and atmosphere refined to the tastes of Orlando's tattooed masses.

Ybor's Martini Bar (☎ 407-316-8006; 41 W Church St; open 5pm-2am Mon-Fri, 7pm-2am Sat) is upscale, with cigars in the humidor and premium drinks like Louis 13th cognac, Macallan 18-year-old scotch and 45 types of martini.

Jax Fifth Ave Deli & Ale House (☎ 407-841-5322; 11 S Court Ave) is a comfy, divey place with 200 different beers.

Kate O'Brien's Irish Pub & Restaurant (☎ 407-649-7646; 42 W Central Blvd; open 11:30am-2am Mon-Sat, 7pm-2am Sun) has

live music Thursday to Saturday (no cover), lots of good beer on tap and standards like fish & chips on the menu.

Clubs

:08 (☎ 407-839-4800; 100 W Livingston St) is an insanely popular country bar – you have to stay on the mechanical bull for eight seconds, get it?

Independent Bar (☎ 407-839-0457; 68 N Orange Ave; cover $10; open 9pm-3am Wed-Sat) is hip, crowded and loud, with DJs spinning underground dance and alternative rock until the wee hours; ladies drink free until midnight on Wednesday.

The **Loaded Hog** (☎ 407-420-1515; 11 N Orange Ave; open 6pm-2am Tues-Sat), **One-Eyed Jack's** (☎ 407-648-2050; 15 N Orange Ave; open 11am-2am Mon-Fri, 6pm-2am Sat) and the **Wall St Cantina** (☎ 407-420-1515; 19 N Orange Ave) are owned by the same people and share one of Orlando's most impressive music calendars between them. Cover varies, but hovers around $5 for bands like Skeeter Biscuit, the Joint Chiefs and Heart Lung Machine.

Gay & Lesbian Venues

Orlando's gay and lesbian scene is growing, and explodes during the weeks around Gay Day (see the boxed text 'Gay Day at Disney'). Before you transgendered cuties head out on the town, stop by **Ritzy Rags** (☎ 407-897-2117; W www.ritzyrags.com; 928 N Mills), where owner and performer Leigh Shannon offers makeup and wardrobe tips for making the most of what you were born with. Wigs, dresses and size-14 pumps are also available.

John & Jason's Coffee Shoppe (☎ 407-447-1578; 932 N Mills; open 7am-10pm Mon-Thur, 7am-2am Fri & Sat, 10am-11pm Sun) serves coffee and sandwiches alongside acoustic entertainment most weekend nights.

Southern Nights (☎ 407-898-0424; 375 Bennet Rd), just north of the Orlando Executive Airport, attracts more of a mixed crowd.

Faces (☎ 407-291-7571; 4910 Edgewater Dr), north of downtown on the west side of I-4, is a well-established lesbian bar.

Parliament House (☎ 407-425-7571; 410 N Orange Blossom Trail) is a gay resort (see Places to Stay) with cruisey country, piano and poolside bars, along with drag shows and other live entertainment.

Full Moon Saloon (☎ 407-648-8725; 500 N Orange Blossom Trail) is a leather/Levi's place next door.

Universal CityWalk

Right by Universal Studios, this pedestrian mall is a little plastic but certainly fun. It's a collection of (mostly theme) restaurants and bars with great live music, and it's packed with tourists, buskers and Orlando teens looking for something to do. After 6pm parking is free, and you can get a pass to all the clubs for $10, a good deal considering cover is $5 to $10 each after 9pm.

Margaritaville (☎ 407-224-6916; W www .margaritaville.com; open 11am-2am daily; mains $8-15) serves tamed Caribbean cuisine and has live music nightly, usually classic rock but sometimes steel drum players.

City Jazz (☎ 407-224-2189; cover $5; open 8pm-1am Sun-Thur, 7pm-2am Fri & Sat) has good live jazz every night.

Motown Restaurant (☎ 407-224-2500; mains $12-20; open 11:30am-11pm Sun-Thur, 11:30am-2am Fri & Sat) specializes in barbecue and has a great collection of Motown memorabilia. DJs and dancing start at around 8pm.

Hard Rock Live (☎ 407-351-5483; tickets $20-30; box office open 10am-9pm daily) is a 2800-seat auditorium that draws some fairly big names: Ruben Blades, Jethro Tull and They Might Be Giants were on the schedule when I was there.

Performing Arts

The **Orlando Fringe Festival** (☎ 407-648-0077; W www.orlandofringe.com) features performance art, community theater and

---

Gay Day at Disney

Gay Day was conceived in 1991, when Orlando gay activist Doug Swallow and a handful of friends posted an invitation online saying, 'Hey, if you're into Disney, show up and wear red.' Some 2500 gays and lesbians made it. Ever since, the first Saturday in June has seen the Magic Kingdom transformed into the gayest place on Earth.

Disney (whose recent record of fair treatment to gay and lesbian employees has been exemplary, going so far as to extend health-care benefits to same-sex partners) stresses very publicly that this is *not* an official Disney event. Still, they tolerate – even help organize – Gay Day, and in 2002 an estimated 125,000 gay and lesbian visitors descended on Cinderella's Castle for what is now an entrenched Florida tradition.

At 1pm, bears (um, hirsute gentlemen) head to the Country Bear Jamboree to sing along with their animatronic friends. And at 3pm everyone gathers for the Main St parade, where characters put on an especially enthusiastic show as they navigate a truly awesome sea of red.

The festivities have now grown to encompass almost every attraction in Orlando. On the Thursday before the event, party people pack Pleasure Island, and Friday at SeaWorld is de rigueur. Friday night is the Beach Ball at Disney's Typhoon Lagoon, with DJs and dancing. So much for getting to Magic Kingdom early and beating the lines!

Saturday night sees a bash at Arabian Nights Dinner Theater, and Universal Studios is actively trying to get in on the action, offering discounts on Sunday at Islands of Adventure. And all weekend long, downtown Orlando clubs and bars cater to the crowds.

Log on to W www.gayday.com for more information, and to register for regular email updates. Good Time Gay Productions (W www.goodtimegaytravel.com) books Gay Day packages – make reservations early, as this is the most popular event in Disney World history.

other (stranger) offerings at venues throughout the city in May.

The **TD Waterhouse Centre** (☎ 407-849-2001 events listings, 407-849-2020 box office; 1 Magic Place (600 W Amelia Ave)) hosts sporting events and concerts. It also holds two more major performing arts venues, the **Bob Carr Performing Arts Centre** and the **Civic Theater of Central Florida**, both of which stage performances of opera, classical music and theater.

Goldman Theater (☎ 407-447-1700; 812 E Rollins St), in the Cultural Corridor, is a 120-seat venue that stages locally produced plays and musicals as well as hosting touring troupes. Also here is **Studio B**, a black box theater specializing in performance art.

Lowndes Shakespeare Center (☎ 407-836-5540; 812 E Rollins St), in the same complex, is home to the UCF Shakespeare Festival (W www.shakespearefest.org), which performs here and at the **Walt Disney Amphitheater**, on Lake Eola in downtown Orlando.

The **University of Central Florida Theatre Guild** (☎ 407-823-1500; 4000 Central Florida Blvd; adult/student $10/6) stages performances at the University of Central Florida and other area venues.

Southern Ballet Theatre (☎ 407-426-1739; W www.southernballet.org; 1111 N Orange Ave) offers dance performances year-round at various locations in the area.

SAK Comedy Lab (☎ 407-648-0001; 398 W Amelia St) is a comedy/improv troupe that packs 'em in on weekends; make reservations.

The **Mark Two Dinner Theater** (☎ 407-843-6275; W www.themarktwo.com; 3376 Edgewater Dr; tickets $35-50) does daily performances like *Titanic* and *Annie Get Your Gun* while you eat.

Masters of Magic (☎ 407-352-3456; 8815 International Dr; adult/child $20/15) stages a 90-minute magic show starring Typhoon Low, who served in the Navy for 22 years and also attended clown school. He disappears in midair on a Harley!

SPECTATOR SPORTS
The **Orlando Magic** (☎ 407-896-2442; W www.nba.com/magic) is Orlando's powerhouse professional men's basketball team and plays home games at the TD Waterhouse Centre (see Performing Arts).

The **Orlando Miracle** (☎ 407-916-9622; W www.wnba.com/miracle), a Women's National Basketball Association team, plays here as well.

The TD Waterhouse Centre is also home to the Arena Football League's **Orlando Predators** and the IHL **Solar Bears**.

SHOPPING
All the museums have gift shops, as do all the theme parks – probably more shops than rides by a factor of ten – packed with tempting, overpriced merchandise. Be careful out there.

International Dr is lined with grungy storefronts hawking everything from discount Disney gear and cheap electronics to specialty stores for science fiction, movie and beanie baby buffs. It's bookended by two malls.

Pointe Orlando (☎ 407-248-2838; W www.pointeorlandofl.com; 9101 International Dr), to the south, is a popular mall that was clearly designed by someone who'd done way too much acid at Disney World.

Belz Factory Outlet (☎ 407-354-0126) is an enormous place with discount designer duds; I scored a pair of DKNY leather pants for $55, marked down from $230. Sweet.

Park Ave in Winter Park (see Around Orlando) has upscale chain stores interspersed with the sorts of boutiques where you can purchase gowns suitable for accepting an Oscar.

GETTING THERE & AWAY
Air
It is almost always cheaper to fly here as part of a package than to purchase airfare and everything else separately: More packages are available to Orlando than to any other Florida city, and cross-marketing plans with the theme parks, hotels and airlines lower the final tally.

Orlando International Airport (MCO; ☎ 407-825-2001; W www.orlandoairports.net/goaa/main.htm), in the far southeastern corner of the city, is the largest airport in central Florida. The easiest way here from I-Drive is via the Bee Line Expressway (Hwy 528), a toll road. Lynx bus Nos 11 and 42 (see Getting Around, below) serve the airport.

Bus
The **Greyhound bus station** (☎ 407-292-3424; 555 N John Young Parkway (Hwy 423)) is in the middle of nowhere, with direct service to every major city in Florida. It's served by Lynx bus No 25 (see Getting Around); a cab to downtown costs about $10, to I-Drive $20.

Train
Amtrak (☎ 407-843-7611; 1400 Sligh Blvd) is about a mile south of downtown and three blocks west of Orange Ave. It has direct service to Miami, Gainesville and points north. It's served by Lynx bus No 4, and there's a **Hertz Rental Car** (☎ 407-872-0112) outlet on-site.

Car & Motorcycle
I-4 runs north-south through Orlando, though it's labeled east-west; head north to Daytona on I-4 East and south to Tampa via I-4 West.

From Miami, the fastest and most direct route to Orlando is via Florida's Turnpike (toll), about a 4½-hour drive. To get to the Space Coast, take I-95 to Hwy 528, the Bee Line Expressway (toll); to avoid the tolls, at the cost of about an hour, take I-95 to Hwy 50 (Colonial Dr), which goes directly to Titusville.

GETTING AROUND
Bus
Lynx (☎ 800-344-5969 general information, 407-841-8240 route information; W www.golynx.com; rides $1, transfers 10¢; buses run 4am-3am Mon-Fri, 4am-1am Sat, 4am-10pm Sun) is convenient and covers all of Orlando. Bus stops are marked with a sign bearing a Lynx paw print of sorts along with the number of the route(s) that stop there. **Lymmo** is their free bus service, which circles downtown Orlando.

The **Lynx Bus Center** is in the alley between W Pine St and W Central Blvd,

one block west of Orange Ave. You can buy tickets and get system maps and specific route information from the **information booth** (open 6:30am-8pm Mon-Fri, 7:30am-6pm Sat, 8am-6pm Sun).

Lynx serves Orlando International Airport (Nos 11 and 42), Winter Park (Nos 1 and 9, hourly), Kissimmee (Nos 4 and 18), Walt Disney World (Nos 50 and 56), International Dr (No 38) and Colonial Dr (No 30), among many other places.

Trolley
I-Ride Trolley (☎ 407-248-9590; W www.iride trolley.com; rides 75¢; operates 24/7) operates trolleys (really just buses in drag) that run along International Dr and Universal Blvd. It serves Universal Studios, Wet 'n' Wild, SeaWorld, and the gazillion hotels, restaurants and tourist traps in between.

Shuttle & Limo Services
The biggest shuttle service in the area is **Mears Transportation** (☎ 407-423-5566), which runs vans between most major hotels, the youth hostel, campsites and the major theme parks. Expect to pay between $10 and $15 roundtrip for shuttle service, unless your hotel has a special deal – many do.

Car & Motorcycle
The major car-rental companies all have offices at the airport and many hotels (see the Getting Around chapter). If you're in the midst of a midlife crisis, **Orlando Harley Davidson** (☎ 407-944-3938; W www.orlando harley.com) will drop off and pick up rental bikes at your hotel.

Note that many major throughways are toll roads, including Hwy 528, which connects I-Drive with the airport and Space Coast. Bring quarters: If you have correct change (50¢ to $1.50), you can breeze through the booths a lot faster.

Downtown Orlando has an infuriating one-way street system that would seem to have been taken right out of either Kafka or Boston. Bring a map and expect to do a loop or two while looking for the freeway on-ramps. Metered parking downtown is fairly easy to find and costs 25¢ for 30 minutes. Several public parking facilities are available for $6 to $10 daily.

Taxi

Fares are $3 for the first mile plus $1.50 for each additional mile. You need to call for a cab (as opposed to hailing one on the street). Major companies include **City Cab** (☎ 407-422-5151) and **Checker & Yellow Cab Co** (☎ 407-699-9999).

AROUND ORLANDO
Winter Park

The self-proclaimed 'Venice of America,' so named for its numerous canals, is one of Central Florida's best-kept secrets, a favorite weekend destination for the state's more Epicurean leisure seekers.

Shaded cobblestone streets are lined with posh shops and restaurants, historic buildings and a handful of remarkable museums. Exclusive Rollins College – worth a stroll for its impressive architecture – adds an intellectual flavor. It's Flagler-era Florida still thriving, right down to the picturesque Amtrak station in the pedestrian-friendly city center. It makes for the perfect vacation from the frantic glitter of the theme parks.

Winter Park is about 4 miles north of downtown Orlando. The city's main drag is Park Ave, bisected by Morse Blvd downtown. Rollins College is at the intersection of Park Ave and Osceola Ave (Hwy 426).

The **Winter Park Chamber of Commerce** (☎ 407-644-8281; W www.winterparkcc.org; 150 N New York Ave; open 9am-5pm Mon-Fri) has free maps and a pamphlet outlining self-guided tours to the town's historic landmarks. Next door is the **post office** (300 New York Ave). There's a **Bank of America** (☎ 407-646-3524; 250 Park Ave) downtown.

The **library** (☎ 407-326-6600; 460 E New England) does not offer free Internet access. **Brandywine Books** (☎ 407-644-1711; 114 E Park Ave; open 10am-5:30pm Mon-Sat) has a huge collection of new and used tomes.

Cornell Fine Arts Museum The collection at this small museum (☎ 407-646-1595; 1000 Holt Ave; admission free; open 10am-5pm Tues-Fri, 1pm-5pm Sat & Sun), on the Rollins College campus, easily outclasses many larger, more famous galleries: Oldenburg, De Kooning and Rauschenberg works are just part of the permanent file. Rotating exhibitions are spectacular.

Charles Hosmer Morse Museum of American Art I was astounded by this beautiful museum (☎ 407-645-5311; 445 Park Ave N; adult/student $3/1; open 9:30am-4pm Tues-Sat, 1pm-4pm Sun) and its unparalleled collection of Tiffany glass. Lamps are the least of the treasures you'll see: The *Four Seasons* may be the pinnacle of the art form, but the elaborate (some say garish, but they have no taste) Tiffany Chapel is certainly the most impressive. Oh yeah, there's lots of other art here, too, mostly from the 1920s.

Albin Polasek Galleries Scattered through the grounds of this stately home and serene garden (☎ 407-674-6294; W www.polasek.org; 633 Osceola Ave; adult/child $4/2; open 10am-4pm Mon-Sat, 1pm-4pm Sun) are the works of Czech sculptor Albin Polasek, an artist obsessed with our ability to carve our own destiny. The sculptures are heavy, thoughtful and, in some cases, quite moving. Impromptu tours through the statues and small chapel are available from informative docents at the door, as long as they're not too busy.

Audubon Center for Birds of Prey Fierce feathered friends are taken care of when wounded and available for observation at this center (☎ 407-644-0190; 1101 Audubon Way; adult/child $5/4; open 10am-4pm Tues-Sun), in Eatonville, just down the road from Winter Park. They also offer classes on the basics of bird watching ($10).

Maitland Art Center Since 1937, this art center (☎ 407-539-2181; W www.maitartctr.org; 231 W Packwood Ave; admission free; open 9am-4:30pm Mon-Fri, noon-4:30pm Sat & Sun) has provided classes and studio space to area artists, as well as galleries where they can display their work for the public. The facilities also have some lovely gardens where live music, usually classical, is performed on an irregular basis.

Scenic Boat Tours This company (☎ 407-644-4056; W www.scenicboattours.com; 1 E Morse Ave; adult/child $8/4; open 10am-4pm daily) takes you down through 12 miles of tropical canals, lined with mansions and the stunning campus of Rollins College. Be warned, however: Sandra, who now works

Fiction & Folklore: Zora Neale Hurston

Zora Neale Hurston (1901–60) was born in Eatonville, the first black incorporated town in the US, about 5 miles from Orlando. Her family broke apart when she was young, and she supported herself from the age of 14, working odd jobs and finding her way in 1919 to all-black Howard University in Washington, DC. In 1925 she moved to Harlem, the cultural capital of black America, and distinguished herself quickly as a bright young literary voice. Along with poet Langston Hughes and others, she rose to the forefront of what came to be known as the Harlem Renaissance, a flowering of black creative and intellectual achievement and a celebration of the African American experience.

Hurston came from a background of storytelling. As a child she'd listened to the men gathered on the porch of Joe Clark's store tell their 'big ol lies' to entertain one another. In later years, she became a good storyteller herself, which made her the life of every party in Harlem. Her interest in storytelling also led her to Barnard College, where she met Franz Boas – the father of modern American anthropology – and discovered the study of folklore. Under Boas' guidance, Zora won a research fellowship from Columbia University and headed back to the South to record the songs, tales, superstitions, games and traditions she'd grown up with.

In pursuit of folklore, she traveled from Florida to New Orleans and eventually into the rich culture of the Caribbean; she posed as a runaway bootlegger's moll, lived in the shantytowns of migrant turpentine workers and was poisoned nearly to death by a voodoo witch doctor in Haiti. But despite her travels and wild, far-flung adventures, Eatonville and the porch of Joe Clark's store would remain at the center of her work, appearing again and again in both her folklore and her fiction.

Mules and Men was published in 1935 and is considered by many the greatest work on black American folklore ever written. In Southern vernacular, it recounts tales of conjure men and hoodoo cures; Ol Massa and his favorite slave, John; Brer Rabbit and Brer Gator (like Disney has never seen them); and more. Before Hurston, white folklorists had portrayed black culture as the product of childish, silly and unsophisticated minds. Hurston instead revealed its wit, humor, imagination and complexity.

Her most famous novel, *Their Eyes Were Watching God*, was published in 1937. It is one of the earliest black feminist novels, telling the story of Janie Crawford, an independent black woman who loved who and how she wanted. The book was savaged by contemporaries like Richard Wright, author of *Black Boy* and *Native Son*, because it did not address race relations and black oppression but rather black community and black folk.

Hurston died in a welfare home in 1960 and was buried in an unmarked grave in the Garden of Heavenly Rest, in Fort Pierce. In the 1970s, a few dedicated black writers and scholars began the 'Hurston Renaissance' – her seven books were reissued, and Alice Walker made a pilgrimage to Fort Pierce to place a memorial stone on her grave. It reads:

Zora Neale Hurston
'A Genius of the South'
Novelist/Folklorist/Anthropologist
1901–1960

– Laini Taylor

at the Park Plaza Hotel, had to uproot her family and move here after taking this trip. They also rent canoes, $5 for the first hour, $1 for each additional hour.

Places to Stay & Eat Winter Park's hotels don't exactly cater to the budget traveler.

Best Western (☎ 407-647-1166; 110 S Orlando Ave; rooms $97) takes full advantage of its location by charging premium prices for clean, standard rooms.

Park Plaza Hotel (☎ 407-647-1072, 800-228-7220; 307 Park Ave S; rooms without/with a view $100/194) is easily the most elegant property in the Orlando area. Its 1920s ambience is palpable, and some lushly appointed rooms have balconies overlooking the cobblestoned downtown.

The **Thurston House** (☎ 407-539-1911; W www.thurstonhouse.com; 851 Lake Ave; rooms $140-150), in nearby Eatonville, is a rambling Victorian B&B on the shores of Lake Eulalia.

Power House Cafe (☎ 407-645-3616; 111 E Lyman Ave; dishes $4-6; open 9am-7pm Mon-Fri, 10am-5pm Sat) serves truly outstanding sandwiches with a vegetarian focus and Middle Eastern flavor. The fruit smoothies are excellent.

Briarpatch Restaurant (☎ 407-628-8651; 252 Park Ave N; dishes $7-12; open 7am-9pm Mon-Sat, 8am-5pm Sun) does great specialty omelettes and homemade breads, plus lots of vegetarian dishes for lunch and dinner.

Restaurant du Parc (☎ 407-647-4469; 348 Park Ave N; prix fixe $45; open 11:30am-2pm & 6pm-9pm Mon-Sat) is a fine French restaurant tucked into a hidden garden off Park Ave. The same proprietors offer more affordable crepe-based cuisine at **Maison des Crepes** (mains $15-20) next door.

Getting There & Away Service by **Lynx Buses** (see Getting Around in the Orlando section) runs between downtown Orlando and Winter Park; bus Nos 1 and 9 make the trip hourly.

Amtrak (☎ 407-645-5055; 150 Morse Blvd) stops right downtown and offers regular service to Orlando, Miami and all points on the Eastern Seaboard.

By **car**, head north on I-4 to exit 46, go east on Lee Rd and take a right on Orlando Ave (Hwy 92). Make a left onto Morse St, which takes you right downtown.

Mount Dora

Strolling that fine line between township and a theme park, Mount Dora attracts tourists eager to escape, via Civil War–era steam train, urban Orlando for what amounts to Central Florida World. It's a sugary concoction of gingerbread Victorian B&Bs, shady parks, a beautiful lake plied by photogenic pontoon boats and a cutthroat knickknack market that has elegant matrons providing free coffee and fresh-baked cookies to lure you inside their adorable shops and galleries.

It really is, however, a taste of what awaits visitors that have the time to explore Central Florida's hinterlands, complete with that sense of luxurious indolence endemic to this beautiful region. But it's all right here, an hour from Orlando, perfect for visitors budgeting their time – and you don't need a rental car to experience it.

Orientation & Information Mount Dora's main drag is Donnelly St, which runs from US Hwy 441 south to the shores of Lake Dora. East-west avenues are numbered, beginning at the lake's shore; shops and restaurants are concentrated in between 3rd and 6th Aves. The train station is a block south of Donnelly on 3rd St.

The **chamber of commerce** (☎ 352-383-2165; W www.mountdora.com; 341 Alexander St), in the 1915 Atlantic Coastline train depot, has racks of pamphlets and colorful free maps of town. The free *Railway Gazette*, published fortnightly, has events listings and train schedules.

Bank of America (163 W 5th St) is at the corner of Alexander St.

Dickens-Reed (☎ 352-735-5950; 140 5th Ave; open 9am-6pm Mon-Sat, 11am-5pm Sun) is an excellent bookstore with an attached coffee shop that serves outstanding apple pie. They show free foreign flicks at 8pm Saturday.

Organized Tours The Mount Dora Road Trolley (☎ 352-357-9123; 100 N Alexander St; adult/child $8/6) offers a one-hour tour that takes you to the 'lighthouse,' along a small nature trail and past lots of historic buildings. It leaves several times daily from the Lakeside Inn; you can also get package deals that include a meal or room at the hotel.

Rusty Anchor Water Tours (☎ 352-383-3922; 400 W 4th Ave; tours $8, $15 with lunch) navigates Lake Dora's canal system in a pontoon boat. You'll see alligators, bald eagles and mansions.

Places to Stay For a complete list of lodging options (with a heavy emphasis on B&Bs) contact the chamber of commerce. If you're taking the train, let them know that you'll be staying overnight when you purchase your tickets.

Mount Dora Inn (☎ 352-735-1212; W www .mountdorahistoricinn.com; 221 E 4th St; rooms $75-135) is a typically lovely 1880s Victorian mansion walking distance from downtown.

The **Lakeside Inn** (☎ 352-383-4101; W www .lakeside-inn.com; 100 N Alexander St; rooms $92-210) is a rustic hotel that packs in the tourists (there's a popular package deal included with your train ticket); it's a little rough around the edges but has ambience to spare.

Coconut Cottage Inn (☎ 352-383-2627; W www.coconutcottageinn.com; 1027 McDonald St; rooms $129-149), in a 1920s arts & crafts home, is a bit different: Rooms are decorated with African, Asian and Middle Eastern motifs.

Places to Eat If you're looking for local gems undiscovered by tourists, you've come to the wrong place.

Sunshine Mountain Bakery (☎ 352-735-5227; 115 W 3rd Ave; dishes $3-8; open 7am-4pm daily) has pastries, sandwiches and salads.

The **Frosty Mug** (☎ 352-383-1969; 411 N Donnelly St; dishes $6-20; open noon-midnight Tues-Thur & Sun, noon-1am Fri & Sat), in the Renaissance Mall, is a cozy Icelandic pub serving gravlax (cured salmon),

pickled herring and more. There's live jazz and blues on Wednesday and Thursday night.

O'Neil's Irish Pub (☎ 352-735-7755; 421 Baker St; lunch $6-10, dinner $10-20; open 11am-midnight Sun-Wed, 11am-2am Thur-Sat) has all the Irish standards (cottage pie, bangers and mash), plus burgers, steaks and tasty Buffalo wings. There's live acoustic music Thursday through Saturday.

Entertainment The Mount Dora Theatre Company (☎ 352-383-4616; W www.mount doratheatrecompany.com; 1100 N Unser St; adult/child $15/7) stages local and professional plays and musicals.

Courtyard Rendezvous sponsors free live music nightly at the Arbors & Eyebrows retail complex, at the corner of 4th Ave and Alexander St.

Getting There & Away The Cannonball (☎ 352-735-4667; W www.mtdoratrain.com; adult/child $12/8; runs Tues-Sun) is a historic 'steam' train (it's now electric) that runs between Mt Dora and the Centroplex Railway Station at the corner of Hughley and Robinson Sts in downtown Orlando. It's photogenic enough to have appeared in *Oh Brother, Where Art Thou?* and makes the hour-long trip through the orange groves four times daily.

By car (but that's sort of missing the whole point, isn't it?) from Orlando, take Hwy 441 north from downtown and make a left on CR 44B (Donnelly St) shortly after the turnoff to Eustis. There's lots of free parking downtown.

Kissimmee

The area around Kissimmee (pronounced kih-**sih**-mee) was once a peaceful landscape of swamps and green, but the extraordinary growth of theme parks has had a profound effect on the surroundings. Kissimmee's main strip, Hwy 192 (called Irlo Bronson Memorial Hwy and Vine Ave), is a sprawling ribbon of endless concrete, motels, shopping malls, wanna-be attractions and discount ticket stands of dubious reliability. It is also the area's cheapest place to bed down for the night.

For tourist information, contact the **Kissimmee/St Cloud Convention & Visitors Bureau** (☎ 407-847-5000, 800-327-9159; W www.floridakiss.com; 1925 W Hwy 192). There's a **post office** (601 Market St) in Celebration: Head south on Celebration Ave from Hwy 192, it's about 2 miles down on your left.

Kissimmee is about 25 miles southwest of downtown Orlando; take bus Nos 4 and 18 from the Lynx Bus Center (see Getting Around in the Orlando section, earlier). It's about a half-hour drive on I-4.

Splendid China This Chinese-owned-and-operated theme park (☎ 407-396-7111, 800-244-6226; W www.floridasplendidchina.com; 3000 Splendid China Blvd; adult/child $27/17; open 9:30am-7pm daily), just off Hwy 192 west of I-4, is definitely a different sort of dazzling. Exhibits, arranged throughout the manicured grounds, are miniature replicas of famous Chinese sights done in meticulously detailed, hand-painted ceramic. It attracts lots of Chinese-American families hoping to force-feed the kids some history, and they've come to the right place: The Stone Forest, Great Wall, Temple of Confucius, and Forbidden City are just a few of the dramatic displays populated by five-inch-tall inhabitants.

A recorded history of each site is provided in English and Spanish, and a free tram circles the park, hitting most sites. There are also performances of folk music, martial arts and traditional theater, including a 90-minute Broadway-style show called *Mysterious Kingdom of the Orient*. Admission includes a meal at one on-site restaurant.

Gatorland You're in Florida, so you've got to see gators. And this is a fine place (☎ 407-855-5496, 800-393-5297; W www.gatorland .com; 14501 S Orange Blossom Trail; adult/child $18/9; open 9am-6pm daily) to do it. A warning though: This place probably isn't PETA-approved, and the **Wrestlin' Gator Show** may have more empathic folks squirming. If you can handle it, however, try to catch Babs Steorts, Gatorland's first female wrestler, take on one of the toothy critters.

Ethical issues aside, Gatorland is fun. The **Jumparoo Show** has 10-foot-long (3m) alligators leaping almost entirely out of the water to grab chunks of rotting meat from the trainer's hand – like Shamu, only creepy. The **breeding marsh**, with 100 females and 25 lucky guys, is, well, one whole heck of a lot of alligators. The **Gatorland Express Train** will give you a tour of the place for an extra $1. And there are lots of crocodiles and other reptiles imported from all over the world.

Hungry? Gatorland breeds alligators for food, and you can get the freshest gator nuggets and smoked gator ribs around at **Pearl's Smokehouse**.

Flying Tigers Warbird Air Museum A must for WWII buffs, this museum (☎ 407-933-1942; 231 N Hoagland Blvd; adult/senior or child $9/8; open 9am-5:30pm Mon-Sat, 9am-5pm Sun), in Hangar No 5 at Kissimmee Regional Airport, displays WWII fighter planes in various stages of restoration. Workers can take up to several years per plane, and some of the finished products can be seen before they fly away to join air shows and air-tour-company fleets.

From I-4, go east on W Hwy 192 to the second light after the Medieval Times dinner theater and turn right; the entrance to the airport is about three-quarters of a mile down.

Places to Stay At Tropical Palms (☎ 407-396-4595; 2650 Holiday Trail; sites without/with hookups $24/39, cabins $59-149) they cater to the RV crowd but welcome tenters with a pool, volleyball court, nature trail and grocery store. Shuttles to area amusement parks cost extra.

HI/AYH Orlando/Kissimmee Resort (☎ 407-396-8282, 800-909-4776; 4840 W Hwy 192; dorm beds HI/AYH members/non-members $16/19, rooms $28/31) looks more like a motel than a hostel, but it has a large common area and kitchen, a swimming pool and a lake out back. It's clean, safe and fun, but it's inconvenient to get here without a car. From downtown, take Lynx bus No 50 to Disney and transfer to No 56, which stops right by the hostel.

For those seeking motel and hotel lodging, accommodations are cheap and tend to be a tad tattered. The farther you get from I-4, the less you'll pay. Of more than 100 hotels and motels along the W Hwy 192 strip, the following are as good as any:

Casa Rosa Motel (☎ 407-396-2020; w www .hotel4you; No 4600; rooms $50) has friendly service but no free shuttles.

Gator Motel (☎ 407-396-0127; No 4576; rooms $25/60 summer/winter) has room fridges and a giant alligator next door, but no free shuttles.

Howard Johnson (☎ 407-396-4762; No 4836; rooms $44/79 summer/winter) has a picnic area by the lake and a free shuttle to Disney.

Knights Inn (☎ 407-396-8186; 2880 Poinciana Blvd; rooms $35/60 summer/winter) has spacious rooms and a free shuttle to Epcot.

Magic Castle Inn & Suites (☎ 407-396-1212; No 4559; rooms $34/39 summer/winter) looks like a castle and has a free shuttle to Disney.

Masters Inn (☎ 407-396-4020; No 5367; rooms $35/50 summer/winter) has a free shuttle to Disney and lots of French tourists.

Ramada Inn (☎ 407-396-1111; w www .ramadainneastgate.com; No 9200; rooms $49/99 summer/winter) has miniature golf, tennis courts and a free shuttle.

Sevilla Inn (☎ 800-367-1363; w www .sevillainn.com; No 4640; rooms $30/60 summer/winter) is attractive, but offers no free shuttles.

Sun Motel (☎ 407-396-6666, No 5020; rooms $37/55 summer/winter) is cleaner than average.

Places to Eat Highway 192 has lots fast food chains and gut-busting buffets that will unite body and soul.

Cracker Barrel (☎ 407-396-6521; 5400 W Hwy 192; dishes $4-8; open 6am-10pm Sun-Thur, 6am-11pm Fri & Sat) is my favorite chain, and Kissimmee's lousy restaurant selection gives me an excuse to include it. Breakfasts are legendary – don't skip the hash brown casserole or biscuits and gravy. Try the catfish, chicken 'n' dumplings and

perfect fried okra, too. If you don't stop by here, well, they're everywhere.

Old San Juan Restaurant & Bakery (☎ 407-343-9213; 407 W Hwy 192; mains $8-10; open 7am-10pm daily) has authentic Borriqua dishes like carne frita and bistec encebollado, but save room for their great pastries, pies and flans.

Havana's Cafe (☎ 407-846-6771; 3628 W Hwy 192; lunch $6-8, dinner $7-13) includes pepper steak and chicken filet skillet on the menu.

Giordano's Pizza (☎ 407-397-0044; 7866 W Hwy 192; dishes $10-13; open 11am-midnight Mon-Sat, noon-midnight Sun), close to Splendid China, has great stuffed and thin-crust pizzas plus hearty pasta dishes.

For some reason, Kissimmee is dinner theater central. *Always* check the tourist rags for coupons, which will save you a bundle.

Medieval Times (☎ 407-396-1518; w www .medievaltimes.com; 4510 W Hwy 192; adult/child $44/28) takes you back to the Middle Ages, when everyone ate with their hands (kids dig this) while watching jousting tournaments. There's also a **museum** (open 4:30pm-8:30pm daily; adult/child $8/6) with torture devices used during the Spanish Inquisition.

Arabian Nights (☎ 407-239-9223, 800-553-6116; 6225 W Hwy 192; adult/child $46/27) has acrobats, gypsies, unicorns and, according to a horse trainer I spoke to, some impressive equestrian stunts. Dinner is your choice of prime rib or vegetable lasagna.

Capone's Dinner & Show (☎ 407-397-2378; 4740 W Hwy 192; adult/child $40/24), a mile east of Hwy 535, is a gangland revue set in a 'cabaret and speakeasy' in Prohibition-era Chicago. There's an unlimited Italian buffet.

Dade Battlefield Historic Park

Just west of Orlando, this small state park (☎ 352-793-4781; 603 S Battlefield Dr; adult/child $2/1; open 8am-sunset daily) has a few small nature trails, a great little **museum** (open 9am-5pm daily) and one of the most interesting historical reenactments in Florida.

In 1835, the US government tried to move the Seminole nation to concentration camps…er, reservations in Oklahoma. Seminole chief Osceola was not about to go quietly, and organized 180 warriors and escaped slaves to fight back. On December 28, they ambushed a column of soldiers led by Major Francis L Dade, killing all but two of them; Osceola lost three men. Every year, on the anniversary of the battle, reenactors (including several enthusiastic Seminole Indians) gather here to re-create the carnage.

There's great camping nearby at **Withlacoochie Trail State Park** (☎ 352-726-2251; 3100 Old Floral City Rd; sites without/with hookups $10/13) on the shores of Silver Lake next to an awesome rail trail.

To get here, take US Hwy 50 (Colonial Dr) east of downtown about 40 miles; Withlacoochie Trail State Park is at the intersection with I-75, Dade Battlefield Historic Park about 10 miles north on the interstate.

Cypress Gardens

Billed as Florida's first theme park, Cypress Gardens (☎ 800-282-2123; W www.cypress gardens.com; adult/child $37/21; hours vary) is a mellow attraction that aims to recreate antebellum Florida amidst an absolutely stunning array of formal gardens. Paddleboats, aviaries, butterfly gardens and lots of shows make up for the underwhelming assortment of rides, which include a small water park. It's still a quirky and enjoyable place, though admission is steep for what you get. But, the park features daily reenactments of the endangered (this is probably for the best) Southern custom of 'belles.'

What's a belle? Pubescent girls, ages 15 to 17, are chosen by civic leaders (the girls are traditionally selected from 'good' families), briefed on the intricacies of ballroom dance, etiquette and hairspray application, and dressed up in puffy ball gowns. They're then introduced to the community (ie, displayed to potential spouses) in a formal ceremony that's followed by a cotillion dance. And you can enroll your own little beauty queen in Cypress Gardens' **Junior Belle** program, which may or may not scar her for life.

Cypress Gardens is about 25 miles south of Kissimmee in the town of Winter Haven;

take I-4 west and exit Hwy 27; head south and follow the signs.

Yeehaw Junction
pop approximately 100

There's not much going on at Yeehaw Junction, about 60 miles south of Orlando on Florida's Turnpike, but the town has two die-hard tourist attractions that pack 'em in. First is the **Yeehaw Travel Center** (☎ 407-436-1616, 800-493-3492; 3100 SR 60; open 7am-8pm Sun-Thur, 7am-9pm Fri & Sat), which sells discount tickets to Orlando attractions and specializes in getting good deals on rooms. They also have free coffee.

The second attraction has charm, character and the dignity of having been placed on the National Register of Historic Places. The **Desert Inn** (☎ 407-436-1054; W www.desert innandrestaurant.com; 5570 S Kenansville Rd; rooms $39) was once Central Florida's favorite bordello. Room service isn't what it used to be, but you can still stay the night, or just stop at the **restaurant** (dishes $3-5; open 9am-10pm Mon-Thur, 8am-11pm Sat, 9am-11pm Sun) for a burger or a beer.

Ask owner Beverly Zichek to show you the **museum** (admission $1). In several of the rooms, it shows the bedrooms as they looked during the place's heyday from 1889 to 1953, complete with red satin bedspreads, swings and saddles.

Walt Disney World Resort

When Disneyland opened in Southern California, it took off in a huge way, fundamentally transforming the concept of theme parks. Walt Disney, however, was unsatisfied, and irritated at the hotels and concessions that were springing up around his property in a manner that he felt was entirely parasitic. So in the mid-1960s, under the nom de guerre Reedy Creek Development Company, Walt bought up thousands of acres of land in central Florida.

His goal was no less than the creation of a family vacation 'city,' every aspect of which – hotels, resorts, restaurants, parking and transportation – he controlled. He even convinced the state of Florida to grant Disney the right to self-govern the municipality. The park opened in 1971 and in its first year saw more than 10 million visitors. Today, the park's almost 40,000 employees welcome an average of 70,000 people daily.

It is indeed its own city, complete with an elaborate transportation system (featuring buses, trams, ferries, shuttles and a monorail), a fire department, several medical centers, an efficient and incorruptible police force, an energy plant – even a florist. All this is designed to make the theme park as isolated, self-sufficient and perfectly happy as it can be.

What follows is just a highlights description of the park, and in no way covers the seemingly infinite options for entertainment, dining, shopping and more. You could easily vacation here for two weeks without seeing the same thing twice. And you'd never even know that Orlando was there.

PLANNING
When to Go
As far as accommodations go, the cheapest time of year is from the beginning of August to mid-December. July and August are hot, but cooling (and line-shortening) downpours occur frequently. Visiting between late June and early August, or around the Christmas and New Year's holidays, guarantees spending an extra three hours per day in line. During the summer, weekends are the least crowded days; the rest of the year the opposite is true.

No matter what season you arrive, get to the parks early. They open about an hour before the schedule says they do, and staff gets the most popular rides running early. Note that certain night events like fireworks and laser shows are seasonal, so if you have your heart set on seeing something, check with Disney early to make sure it will be on when you visit.

Prices for everything are raised regularly, so pay for accommodations and tickets as soon as possible to beat the hikes.

What to Bring
Even when it's raining, temperatures are (usually) warm, so bring a lightweight rain poncho, comfortable clothing that you don't mind getting wet, a bathing suit, sunscreen and sunglasses. Carry it all in a backpack compact enough to keep on your lap during rides. Also bring a solidly resealing bottle of drinking water (refills are free). Food from outside is technically not permitted in the parks.

Maps
The free *Walt Disney World Resort Map*, available throughout the park and at any Orlando visitor's center, has an overview of the whole resort, breakdown maps of the main parks, and a useful transportation network chart. Get free handout maps of each particular park at the entrance.

ORIENTATION
Walt Disney World Resort is north of Hwy 192, roughly west of I-4 and skirted on its east and some of the north by Hwy 535. It's about 23 miles southwest of Orlando and 4 miles northwest of Kissimmee.

There are four main parks (Magic Kingdom, Epcot, Disney-MGM Studios and Disney's Animal Kingdom), three water parks (Blizzard Beach, Typhoon Lagoon and River Country), a shopping and entertainment district (Downtown Disney), several specialized attractions (including the Disney Institute, DisneyQuest and Disney's Wide World of Sports) and numerous other destinations. There are 22 Disney-owned resorts on the property.

The main Ticket & Transportation Center (TTC) is off of Seven Seas Dr, as are the main bus station and parking lots for Magic Kingdom. Many Orlando and Kissimmee hotels provide shuttle buses to this complex, which is simple to find by car from either I-4 or Hwy 192.

INFORMATION
Disney World (☎ 407-934-7639; TDD 407-939-7670; **w** www.disneyworld.com) does *not* have a toll-free information or reservations telephone number. The information/

reservations line is also usually backed up at least fifteen minutes, especially for English-speaking operators. The Web site, however, is easy to use and often has better prices on accommodations. By mail, send requests for brochures or other information to **Walt Disney Guest Communications** (PO Box 10000, Lake Buena Vista, FL 32830-1000).

Money

Guest Relations in all four parks exchanges foreign currency up to $50, at slightly worse rates than you'd get at the bank. They can point you toward numerous ATM machines.

Disney Dollars can be purchased at a 1:1 exchange with US dollars at parks and Disney stores all over the world, then used to buy souvenirs. In fact, Disney hopes you'll keep several of them as souvenirs themselves.

Admission Prices

Disney raises its prices every year, so these will be low by the time you read them. Purchasing your park tickets in advance – at any Disney store, by mail, phone, or through the Web site – may save you considerable cash.

There are several types of tickets: The One-Day One-Park ($51/40 adult/child) can only be purchased at the gate of the one park you're going to visit. A better idea (this really isn't a one-day destination) are Park Hopper tickets, which get you into the four main parks, or Park Hopper Plus tickets, which add other attractions you choose, including Pleasure Island, Wide World of Sports and the water parks. Children's prices cover kids under 10 years old; kids under three are free. Unused days can be redeemed as long as Disney World exists.

Four-Day Park Hopper Pass
  (adult/child $204/161)

Five-Day Park Hopper Pass ($230/182)

Five-Day Park Hopper Plus
  (two add-ons; $262/209)

Six-Day Park Hopper Plus
  (three add-ons; $294/235)

Seven-Day Park Hopper Plus
  (four add-ons; $325/262)

Wide World of Sports ($10/8)

Walt Disney World Speedway ($90 to $1200)

Pleasure Island (admission $21)

DisneyQuest ($31/24)

Blizzard Beach ($34/28)

Typhoon Lagoon ($34/28)

River Country ($19/12)

Parking costs an extra $6/7 car/RV. You can buy slightly discounted tickets at the Orlando CVB. Florida residents are occasionally given hefty discounts, as are students and members of the US military.

Oh, and if you really, *really* like Disney, you can purchase a 40-year membership to the Disney Vacation Club for only $11,250 down and $50 a month, which gets you all sorts of discounts on tickets and everything else. Go ahead and laugh – there were 60,000 members at press time.

Books

Before you start planning, order a free copy of the *Walt Disney World Vacations Brochure* online or by calling ☎ 800-327-2996. You can also request a free vacation planning video.

The most complete book to the resort is Birnbaum's propaganda-packed *Walt Disney World,* Disney's Official Guide. The slightly more critical *Unofficial Guide to Disney World* is much better. For the alternative view, check out Carl Hiaasen's *Team Rodent: How Disney Devours the World.*

Organized Tours

There are at least a dozen guided tours (☎ 407-939-8687) available throughout the park, ranging from the tempting *Keys to the Kingdom,* which takes you through the Magic Kingdom's network of underground tunnels, to *Epcot Dive Quest,* which lets certified divers frolic with dolphins. Attendance is limited and prices vary widely; call for more information.

Medical Services

There are excellent, nurse-staffed clinics in all the parks.

Disabled Travelers

The excellent *Guidebook for Guests with Disabilities,* available at Guest Services, has maps and ride-by-ride guides with information on closed captioning and accommodating wheelchairs and seeing-eye dogs. On many rides, wheelchair-bound folks (plus all 10 of their friends) will be waved to the front of the line. You can borrow Braille guides and audiotape guides with a $25 deposit, and wheelchairs are available for $8/40 manual/electric all over the resort. All public transportation is wheelchair accessible.

Baby Centers & Sitters

Excellent Baby Centers are located in every park. They're air-conditioned, packed with toys and run Disney cartoons constantly (for the older kids). They also sell diapers, formula, baby powder, over-the-counter medicine – the works. Nursing rooms are also available: Note that nursing children in public may attract uncomfortable stares in this part of the USA.

For private baby-sitting for kids under 12, call **KinderCare** (☎ 407-827-5437); if you're staying at a Disney resort, they can watch children under 12 in your hotel room (☎ 407-827-5444). Disney also offers supervised activities for potty-trained tots ages four to 12, which run $5 to $8 hourly between 5pm and midnight. Call ☎ 407-939-3463 for more information.

You can rent strollers ($8/15 single/double). This is a good idea – you'll be walking a lot more than you think, and even active kids over five will get tired.

Lockers

Each park has a set of lockers for visitors' use. The cost is $7 daily, with a $2 deposit.

Kennels

There are kennels at the four major parks available to pets with proof of vaccinations for $6 daily, $9 overnight. Food is extra, and dog owners are expected to return twice daily to walk their pets. Pets can also stay with you at Fort Wilderness campsites.

Lines

Crowds can get amazing, especially in high seasons. Approximate wait times (usually slightly overestimated) are posted at the beginning of each line. Fastpass lets you swipe your ticket at the entrance to popular attractions, then return at a predetermined time (usually an hour or two later), when you'll be waved to the front of the line. Disney also has a child swap program, which allows parents with small children to hand the kid off to one another while the other rides. Single riders often have separate, and much shorter, lines.

The best strategy is get to the park early and get in line for the most popular rides first. Downpours and parades also tend to shorten lines considerably.

Autograph Books & Passports

These things are very popular with kids; you can buy them here or bring your own. They are used to collect character autographs and stamps from the different 'lands' in Epcot. Do the characters a favor and bring a large, thick pen – it's hard to grab a skinny little ballpoint in a 50lb rubber suit.

MAGIC KINGDOM

When most people think of Disney World, they're thinking of Magic Kingdom: This is Mickey and Minnie's home base, and where you'll find such classic attractions as It's a Small World, Pirates of the Caribbean and Space Mountain. The centerpiece is Cinderella's Castle, instantly recognizable to most of the world's population. Magic Kingdom is also the single most anticipated destination on the Disney property for the under-12 set. Save it for last or risk eye-rolling aplenty when you drag the kids to Epcot.

Orientation & Information

The Magic Kingdom is divided into seven 'lands' arranged around the central hub of Cinderella's Castle. You enter onto **Main St**, with lots of restaurants and souvenir shops. **Tomorrowland** and **Frontierland** have most of the big rides (and most of the long lines). **Fantasyland** and **Mickey's Toontown Fair** (where characters congregate) have rides for smaller children. **Liberty Square** and **Adventureland** seem somewhat neglected, but still have their charms. Walt Disney World

Why Don't We Do It in the Moat?

Disney cast members, as chipper as they may be, are a little like New York City cops: they've seen it all. But admirable company loyalty makes them uncomfortable when asked about anything that may be construed as being 'against' Disney.

So when we asked around about the most outrageous thing that's happened at Disney, there were lots of tight-lipped smiles and not too much else.

But then: pay dirt. A former cast member (and we won't tell you their nationality or sex) laughingly mentioned one incident in which a young couple smoked marijuana and then stripped naked and tried to have sex under a bridge on the banks of the moat surrounding Cinderella's Castle in Magic Kingdom. A couple of months later, we met a member of that very party and got more of the story.

It was a group of Floridians on holiday with their teenagers, and yes, the parents admit that their then-14-year-old son (let's call him 'James') met a teenage woman in the park, shared his marijuana with her, and, after a little discussion, the two agreed to have sex under the bridge.

They say that the teens were nabbed by undercover officers, posing as tourists, who popped up out of nowhere before any serious action had taken place, forced the naked teens to dress and then hauled them into custody. And as in Beverly Hills, the officers were forceful yet exceedingly polite. Disney won't really comment on its security forces, though it is generally believed that they have the power of arrest and that they operate as undercover agents who mingle with crowds, watching for pickpockets and other miscreants – including, apparently, copulating couples.

As for James, he says he was told by the Disney security that not only was he being ejected from the park – which is pretty much par for the course – he was also being declared persona non grata at all Disney property worldwide – forever. If this is true, Disney may have succeeded where several noteworthy American politicians have failed: deportation of troublemakers.

Don't mess with the Mouse.

– Nick & Corinna Selby

Railroad, a steam-driven locomotive, circumnavigates the entire park in a long, boring loop, stopping at Main St, Frontierland and Mickey's Toontown Fair.

Guest Services is in City Hall, immediately after you enter the park. There are **ATMs** and **storage lockers** at the Main St Railroad Station. **First Aid** and the park's **Baby Care Center** are located, as you enter the park, on the left side of Main St by the Crystal Palace restaurant. Magic Kingdom is on the Monorail line.

Things to See & Do

The Magic Kingdom has been the pet project of some of the world's finest artists and engineers for more than 30 years, and this top ten list doesn't even include the infectious It's a Small World. Which should give you some idea of what I've had to omit.

Splash Mountain Talk about Disney magic: This ride, based on the movie *Song of the South,* depicts the misadventures of Brer Rabbit, Brer Bear and Brer Fox, complete with chatty frogs, singing ducks and other colorful critters. Awww. Then it drops you a screaming 50 feet (15m) at nearly 40mph into the river, making for one of the biggest thrills in the park.

ExtraTERRORestrial Alien Encounter

This can scare the daylights out of younger kids, who will then ask to do it again. Watch as money-hungry scientists ('profit is just a by-product we've learned to live with') test new, painful transporter technology on an unspeakably adorable little alien. Then head into the main demonstration room, where even more ambitious experiments are – oh no…NO!

Big Thunder Mountain Railroad Someone who truly loves the desert designed the sets for this ride – and someone else, who lives to make people scream, engineered the hairpin turns and steep drops through this abandoned Old West mine.

Tomorrowland Indy Speedway Race gas-powered Grand Prix–style cars around a figure eight track – without your parents! Get here early – this one had a two-hour wait when I was here.

Buzz Lightyear You're inside the film – well, the spin-off video game for the film – letting loose with your laser cannon at almost anything that moves. Steer your own ship (in a 360° circle) as it races through space, with the Evil Emperor Zirg close behind. Tip: If you hold the trigger down, rather than firing in rapid bursts, you'll score much higher.

Space Mountain It's *the* classic coaster – it even has its own fan club – and hurtles you through the darkness of outer space. Yes, it's tame by today's standards, but I challenge you to get through this ride without screaming.

Pirates of the Caribbean Flashback to St Augustine: You're on a boat, negotiating some very tame rapids, watching as grinning pirates pillage, plunder and burn a small seaside town, all while singing happy pirate songs. Yo ho ho!

Peter Pan's Flight This is for the wee ones, but I thought it was beautiful. Board a pirate ship and fly over London, enchanted in stars and fog, to Never Neverland.

Haunted Mansion This attraction is less a chilling haunted house (even little kids will be fine) than a showpiece for what Disney's special-effects geniuses can come up with when their hearts are in it.

Hall of Presidents This attraction only supplanted It's a Small World because you really ought to go in prepared. After a heartwarming and (disturbingly) patriotic film that

depicts (read: distorts) US history, you'll see every US president posed on stage, all of them shifting and nodding in unison, while select presidents say a few words. It's weird. President George W Bush, like President Clinton before him, actually made time to record a message for his animatronic double to lip-sync along with. And that, friends, is the power of Disney.

Places to Eat
As in all the parks, expect lots of perfectly edible fast food, cafeteria cuisine and snacks at premium prices. Don't miss the delicious turkey legs ($5). All the coffee at Disney World is just horrible.

This list only includes sit-down restaurants where reservations (☎ 407-969-3463) are recommended.

Tony's Town Square Restaurant (Main St; mains $10-24) serves Italian cuisine, including good vegetarian options.

Liberty Tree Tavern (Liberty Square; dishes $8-15; adult/child $16/9 for character dinners) serves American cuisine (clam chowder, prime rib) and at dinner, a buffet with Minnie Mouse, Goofy, Chip and Dale!

Crystal Palace (adult/child $16/9) has a good-looking buffet with the coolest characters in town, Winnie the Pooh and Tigger, too!

Cinderella's Royal Table (mains $16-30) is the most popular restaurant in Disney World – make reservations 90 days ahead of time. A host of characters keep the kids entertained while you eat gourmet(ish) American cuisine.

DISNEY-MGM STUDIOS
Compared to the other parks, MGM Studios seems a little in need of some fresh Disney sparkle. Smaller kids – who can't take advantage of the absolutely awesome rides on offer here – will probably find it dull. Adults, unless they're movie buffs, may agree by the end of the day. But there are definitely some diamonds worth digging for.

Orientation & Information
You enter this smallish park on **Hollywood Blvd**, basically a cluster of movie-themed gift

shops. Make a right onto **Sunset Blvd** to hit the big thrill rides, left toward **New York** for the movie-based attractions. **Mickey Ave**, straight ahead, is designed for kids.

Guest Relations, to your right as you enter, also houses the park's **First Aid**, **Baby Care** and **banking** facilities. This park is accessible by bus or car only.

Things to See & Do
Rock 'n' Roller Coaster This is the best coaster at Disney World, hitting you with 5Gs around the loop – more than the space shuttle.

Fantasmic! Get here *at least* an hour early to get good (or any, on crowded days) seats for what's generally agreed to be the best show at Disney World. It's epic: Mickey Mouse faces Disney's assembled dark side, including a 50-foot (15m), fire-breathing dragon, with a soaring score and light show to match.

Twilight Zone Tower of Terror Follow the screams to creepy Hollywood Tower Hotel, where Rod Serling takes you to a strange, new, special-effects-laden dimension – one where you drop 13 stories in two seconds!

Jim Henson's Muppet Vision 3D Miss Piggy plays a gorgeous diva; Beaker plays with dangerous chemicals; Kermit plays the straight man; and the rat keeps trying to play the audience by putting on fake ears and masquerading as Mickey Mouse. Aging 3D technology is helped along with animatronic hecklers and live-action trolls, but this movie's so hilarious that it doesn't even need 'em.

Indiana Jones Epic Stunt Spectacular Professional stuntpeople show you the tricks of the trade…well, sort of, anyway. At any rate, they blow things up and crash motorcycles while kids scream and gasp. Tip: If you want to be part of the action, sit up front and start jumping around and yelling immediately when they ask for volunteers.

Who Wants to Be a Millionaire Admit it – you've always wanted to face down

Regis on this, the cheesiest of all game shows. Now you can: Everyone gets a 'fastest finger' ticker at their seat, and top scorers compete for pins, hats and even tickets for two to New York City.

Star Tours How can you not have a blast on a flight simulator that takes you on a fast and frantic ride through the *Star Wars* saga? The gift shop is a budget buster.

Disney-MGM Studios Backlot Tour Earthquakes, artillery fire, tidal waves, flaming oil rigs, the original house from the *Golden Girls* – all this and more awaits you on this entertaining tour. Check out the old spaceship props left to rust in the Florida rain.

Honey, I Shrunk the Kids Movie Set Adventure This fantastic playground area is scaled to bring you down to sub-ant size, with mountainous weeds, gigantic insects, huge Lego pieces and an oversized, water-sprinkling garden hose (oh boy, do kids like this one – there are triggers in the floor).

Voyage of the Little Mermaid This 15-minute musical about Ariel and her finned friends gets rave reviews for the singing, set and underwater effects: It's a definite 'can't miss' attraction. I missed it, though, opting instead to see the not-quite-as-acclaimed *Hunchback of Notre Dame* – hey, I'm a sucker for stories starring saucy gypsy dancers. And it was so good – elaborate costumes, inspired acting, catchy songs – definitely the best 15 minutes of my day. If the *Mermaid* show is better, you should probably check it out.

Places to Eat
There are lots of places to eat, and these restaurants recommend making reservations (☎ 407-969-3463).

Mama Melrose's Ristorante Italiano (mains $8-15), behind New York St, bakes its pizzas in a brick oven and serves all kinds of other Italian food, including spaghetti just like Lady and the Tramp shared on their big date.

Sci-Fi Dine-In Theater (mains $9-15), across from Star Tours, is a 'drive-in' where you eat in abbreviated Cadillacs and watch classic sci-fi flicks.

Hollywood Brown Derby (Sunset Blvd; mains $13-25) serves gourmet cuisine and a great-looking Cobb salad in semi-upscale surroundings modeled after the LA original.

EPCOT

Epcot, which stands for the 'Experimental Prototype Community of Tomorrow,' attempts to infuse high-concept entertainment with educational merit. Results, in my mind, are mixed.

Half the park is devoted to **Future World**, where rides and attractions have scientific themes and often corporate underwriters. Exxon Mobil, for example, sponsors the Universe of Energy (see later), which describes fossil fuels in, shall we say, more glowing terms than some experts would use. The rides are awesome and certainly inspire, but consider taking the kids to the excellent Orlando Science Center (see Orlando, earlier) afterward for second opinions on some of this stuff.

The **World Showcase**, on the other hand, is flawless. Disney has done an extraordinary job in re-creating the very best of 11 countries. Staff members from the nations represented come here on one-year contracts, and operate authentic-feeling villages that serve some of the best food in Disney World.

Orientation & Information

You enter the park in **Future World**, centered on the landmark geodesic dome of Spaceship Earth. The **World Showcase** is farther back, arranged country by country around the lagoon where fireworks are held.

Guest Services is to your left as you enter the park, **lockers** and an **ATM** to your right. **First Aid** and the **Baby Center** are located in the Odyssey Center, on the left before you cross the bridge from Future World to the World Showcase. This park is served by monorail.

Things to See & Do

Several of Epcot's best attractions aren't really 'doable' – they're edible! So see Places to Eat for more information.

IllumiNations: Reflections of Earth This is the best evening fireworks show in Disney World – the heat coming off flaming barges in the lagoon is palpable and the roar of explosives is deafening. Add to this 'Tapestry of Dreams,' an artsy parade featuring gauzy two-story-tall puppets, and that's a great ending to your day.

Test Track Test General Motors' latest model cars here, in the most extreme conditions those wacky engineers can come up with. You'll appreciate the antilock breaks.

Universe of Energy I've already registered my complaints about the science, so let me continue by saying that this was one of my favorite rides in Orlando. Join Bill Nye (the Science Guy) and Ellen DeGeneres as they explain various energy sources, from solar to nuclear to fossil fuels – which, of course, necessitates a trip into the Cretaceous period (yes!), because oil and coal and stuff are all made out of really cool dinosaurs.

Honey, I Shrunk the Audience It's not just a 3D film starring the cast of *Honey, I Shrunk the Kids,* it's a full-on sensory experience. Your children will finally forgive you for making them spend all day at Epcot.

Maelstrom Tucked away in the Norway pavilion, this fun little ride has Vikings, trolls and a couple of good waterfalls.

Living Seas Featuring one of the largest aquariums in the world, this excellent attraction gives you a good dose of SeaWorld without paying separate admission.

Living with the Land This (splash-free) water ride educates you about – farming! It's much more interesting than it sounds, though, and lots of the herbs and veggies you see growing onshore will soon be served at the Garden Grille restaurant upstairs.

Wonders of Life Despite needing an update, there are two amusing attractions here. **Body Wars** is a dated but fun motion simulator ride based on the movie *Inner Space,* and **Cranium Command** is a totally hilarious look at the command and control systems of a 12-year-old boy's brain and body.

Innoventions If your corporation can't come up with the cash to sponsor a whole ride, you can always purchase a booth here. Free Sega games are a highlight, the one-sided display celebrating genetically modified organisms (sponsored by agribusiness giant Monsanto) a lowlight. This is a great place to have the 'advertising versus information' talk with your kids.

Mission Space Still under construction when I was there, this huge attraction will soon compete with the Kennedy Space Center (see the Space Coast chapter). Even behind a chain-link fence, it was more entertaining than the tedious Spaceship Earth.

Places to Eat
The World Showcase has different pavilions – some with rides, some with shows, all with shops hawking crafts from the exhibiting country, plus at least two great restaurants – representing (clockwise as you cross the bridge) Mexico, Norway, China, Germany, Italy, USA, Japan, Morocco, France, UK and Canada. If you've got a Park Hopper pass, spend your day anywhere, but come here for dinner.

Make reservations (☎ 407-939-3462) to eat in any of their lavish dining rooms (Mexico's is outstanding) as soon as you get to the park. Though sit-down meals generally run $14 to $30, all the pavilions have a counter-service option outside that costs about half that. The most popular (read: make reservations *well* in advance) restaurants are as follows:

Le Cellier, in the Canada pavilion, is hands down the most requested eatery. Servers, who bemoan the lack of poutine on the menu, recommend the steak burger ($10) and barbecued beef tips ($16), as well as the *Oh Canada* film next door. Veg-

etarians shouldn't even bother – head to Morocco's **Tangierine Café** instead.

Mitsukoshi, one of four restaurants at this lavish pavilion, has been serving fine cuisine in Japan (the country, not the theme park attraction) since 1673, cooked right at your table ($12 to $30). Other on-site eateries serve sushi ($7 to $10 per roll) and tempura plates ($13 to $28). Try to get there for the drumming demonstrations.

Chefs de France is the obvious choice, with an appropriately snooty staff that likes the salade niçoise ($11), foie gras ($19) and marmite du pêcheur (Mediterranean seafood casserole; $27). All options come with wine recommendations, *bien sur.*

Garden Grille (adult/child $21/10), in The Land section of Future World, serves catfish, barbecue and fresh veggies – with Mickey, Pluto, Chip and Dale! The food didn't look nearly as good as what's on offer in the World Showcase, but your kids won't care. Make reservations 60 days out, and save room for dessert at Norway's **Kringla Bakeri**.

DISNEY'S ANIMAL KINGDOM
It's a matter of taste, but this was my favorite park at Disney World. There are rides and shows, of course, but this place is all about the animals: The safari tours sometimes have to stop in their tracks to let elephants and zebras get by. The Asia and Africa sections display an obsession with detail endemic to Disney, right down to the staff – as in the World Showcase (see Epcot, earlier), many people working here are on one-year contracts from Cambodia, Côte d'Ivoire and other regionally appropriate countries.

Though you'd think your children might get bored here, most of the kids I talked to (especially *Lion King* fans, who thought their heroic parents had somehow provided them with tickets to paradise) were having a great time.

Orientation & Information
You enter the park at the **Oasis**, which features lovely gardens and giant anteaters. To your left is **Camp Minnie-Mickey**, with characters and rides for little kids, and to your right **DinoLand USA**, which caters to the

preteen crowd. The park is centered on **Discovery Island** and its landmark Tree of Life, which is definitely worth a closer look. You'll have to cross the island to get to **Asia** and **Africa**, where the very popular safari begins. **Rafiki's Planet Watch** is accessible only by a train that leaves from Africa.

Guest Services is to your left as you enter the park, as is an **ATM** and **lockers**. Both **First Aid** and the **Baby Center** are on Discovery Island, on your left as you make your way to Africa.

Things to See & Do

Despite a multimillion-dollar public relations blitz that claims the contrary, the majority of Animal Kingdom is basically a zoo. Sure, it's the most amazing zoo you could ever imagine, souped up with all sorts of bells and whistles, but you'll enjoy yourself more if you don't expect a thrill-packed amusement park. Instead, take it as a grand tour of the world's biodiversity, refracted through that rose-colored Disney lens.

Kilimanjaro Safaris This ride is so worth the wait – it could compete with almost any zoo in the country for the animals and their 'natural' habitats. And it's got that Disney touch: You're barreling down rutted roads in your rickety bus, past zebras, lions and more, when suddenly there's word that poachers are on the loose! Local law enforcement can't do it alone, so you've got to help.

It's Tough to Be a Bug It's the best 3D show in Disney World, with lots of creepy crawly critters leaping right at you. It will terrify at least a few preschoolers into hysterical screaming fits.

Festival of the Lion King This classic Disney spectacular has everything: real animals, animatronic animals, a big stage production, audience participation, and best of all, the *Hakuna Matata* song. Which is exactly what you need after waiting for an hour to get seats.

Dinosaur The most thrilling ride in the park takes you back in time, where you've

got to rescue a (huge, scary) dinosaur specimen before the meteor hits…

Rafiki's Conservation Station Take a pleasant train ride past concrete animal care facilities to this bizarre attraction, which highlights Disney-funded ecosystem conservation projects all over the world. You can watch veterinary procedures (I saw a lion tamarin have an exploratory laparoscopy), visit the petting zoo and learn lots about saving the planet from the environmental degradation caused by humankind's addiction to unnecessary goods and services. Ahem.

Pagani Forest Exploration Trail On the first of two walking trails that put a Disney spin (outrageous architecture, nifty exhibits) on the typical zoo experience, this lush and landscaped path passes gorillas, hippos, a great aviary and – my favorite – a hive of naked mole rats, the only mammals who organize themselves like insects.

Maharaja Jungle Trek See Bengal tigers, huge fruit bats, Komodo dragons and other Asian critters lounging around in habitats designed to look like Angkor Wat. Neat.

Kali River Rapids Feeling overheated? This ride will get you soaking wet (souvenir shops nearby sell extra socks) while you scream. Bonus: It has some of the best in-line entertainment around.

Primeval Whirl Yeah, so it's a kid's coaster. It's still a whirly twirly good time.

The Boneyard This may be the most inspired sandbox on Earth: Just try to drag the kids away from their frantic digging for mastodon skeletons, or their seat atop massive rib cages and other fossils.

Places to Eat

The only restaurant here that takes reservations is **Restaurantosaurus** (☎ 407-939-3463), which does a character breakfast featuring Donald, Mickey, Goofy and Pluto. Yes, your kids would rather eat with Timon and Simba, but at press time this wasn't an option.

OTHER ATTRACTIONS

It would only take, oh, two weeks to experience (almost) everything in the four major parks, but Disney would like you to stick around a little longer. So they've provided several other entertainment options, many of which are listed here. There are also five golf courses, parasailing and surfing lessons, waterskiing options and more – call ☎ 407-939-7529 for more information.

Blizzard Beach

This is the home of **Summit Plummet**, Disney's tallest (120 feet) and fastest freefall slide. Themed to look like a ski resort, it features things like a ski lift and snow-capped mountains, but mainly it's a slide and raft park that is a great way to spend at least half a day. Don't miss **Run-Off Rapids**, with three crazily curving slides, or **Teamboat Springs**, which increases speed with every person you pile onto your mat.

Typhoon Lagoon

The slides themselves are a tad less radical than those at Blizzard Beach, but this tropical-rain-forest-themed water park has a couple of big bonuses: The **Surf Pool** features 6-foot-tall (2m) breakers, and the **Shark Reef** offers instruction and equipment for snorkeling among tropical fish.

River Country

Though aged, River Country is still a popular water park. Near Fort Wilderness, it offers small water slides, ropes and tube rides, all built around an enormous swimming pool. Though a nice place for a picnic, it doesn't hold a candle to the other two. It's a bit cheaper, though.

Walt Disney's Wide World of Sports

This huge complex (☎ 407-828-3267; **w** www .disneyworldsports.com) is home to the **NFL Experience**, where you can take on the same obstacle courses and other challenges as your favorite American football players. The complex also hosts a mind-boggling array of professional and amateur sports events, including the Atlanta Braves, Orlando Rays and the Harlem Globetrotters. Events tickets are not included in the price of admission.

This is also where you'll find the **Walt Disney World Speedway**, where you can race Winston Cup–style cars (see NASCAR in the Daytona chapter), operated by the Richard Petty Experience (☎ 800-237-3889), around a real track.

DisneyQuest

This attraction, located in Downtown Disney, features five floors of exhibits designed to indulge Ritalin-addled video-game addicts. Virtual reality rides, arcades, alien invasions, flight simulators and other technological delights will satisfy even folks with the most limited attention spans. Note that some rides here cost a little extra on top of the admission fee, and you must be 51 inches tall (130cm) to hop onto the really good ones.

On slow nights, management may offer discounted tickets ($15) at the gate for the last two hours of operation.

Disney Institute

Created as an educational approach to vacationing, the Disney Institute offers guests scores of classes and programs covering everything from culinary arts and interior decorating to canoeing and storytelling. Some are taught by experts in the field; other classes are run by B-list celebrities with an interest in, say, bread making. This is hugely popular among adult Disney regulars, who recommend these classes highly.

Downtown Disney

Basically a shopping mall with upscale chain restaurants and venues staging great live music, Downtown Disney eliminates any temptation to leave the resort property should you, say, need to buy a bathing suit, Dominican cigars or museum-quality original art. There are several entertainment options:

Cirque du Soleil: La Nouba (☎ 407-939-7600; **w** www.cirquedusoleil.com; adult/

child $72/42) is the big draw here, an artistic circus with no animals. Many people say this is the best thing at Disney World.

House of Blues (☎ 407-934-2583; **w** www .hob.com) is one of a chain of Southern soul-food-style restaurants that features great live shows: Tenacious D, George Thorogood and No Doubt were on the schedule at press time.

Bongos Cuban Café (☎ 407-828-0999) has live Latin music and dancing Thursday to Saturday.

Pleasure Island

It's New Year's Eve every night at this complex of eight bars and clubs, open to folks 18 and older. It's adjacent to Downtown Disney and free for all Disney employees, which means you'll get all the real dirt about the parks over a beer or three. Oh, and you can carry your drinks from bar to bar. Two Magic Kingdom characters taking a break from signing autographs told me that **Mannequins Dance Palace**, with a rotating dance floor and live DJs nightly, was the single best attraction in all of Disney World. I think they really needed a drink.

PLACES TO STAY

The best source for full descriptions of all 22 (at press time) Disney-run accommodation options is Birnbaum's *Walt Disney World,* which lists each resort's features and services. You can also get resort-by-resort descriptions and the latest rates online. Make reservations online or by calling ☎ 407-934-7639.

The rack rates quoted are a tad misleading, as you can get good deals on multiple-day packages that include admission to the theme parks and other attractions. One veteran Disney-goer said she paid the same price for five nights at a deluxe resort as was originally quoted for four nights at a value resort – just by asking. Still, it's always cheaper to stay in Orlando or Kissimmee.

The main advantage to staying at the resorts is convenience: Public transportation throughout Disney World and free parking are part of the deal. Some days Disney offers early entry to the parks. All properties have on-site eateries, lounges and bars, pools and playgrounds. Hotels are broken down into four main categories.

Value Resort Hotels

The least-expensive properties available, these have thousands of very small rooms that may be difficult to maneuver should you ask for a refrigerator or crib. All are lavishly (garishly?) decorated according to the theme. Rates run $77 to $124, depending on the season.

The **All-Star Sports Resort** has enormous footballs everywhere.

The **All-Star Music Resort** has giant guitars.

The **All-Star Movies Resort** is perfect for the cinemaphile in the family.

The **Pop Century Resort** is the largest, with more than 5000 rooms.

Moderate Resort Hotels

These hotels have slightly larger rooms, less-ostentatious themes and access to beaches and the marina. Rooms run $133 to $219 for four people.

Caribbean Beach Resort was my favorite for the brightly hued decor.

Coronado Springs Resort has a Mexican/Southwestern theme and is convenient to Animal Kingdom.

Port Orleans Resort includes a Disneyfied version of New Orleans' French Quarter.

Deluxe Resort Hotels

These upscale resorts have everything: large rooms designed to sleep at least five, kids' programs, room service and health clubs, not to mention characters in all their plush glory roaming the lobby and food courts every morning.

Wilderness Lodge (rooms $194-500) has a beach, marina, 'hiking' trails and easy access to Magic Kingdom.

Animal Kingdom Lodge (rooms $204-599) abuts the African Safari section of Animal Kingdom, so you can see zebras, giraffes and other exotic critters from your hotel window.

Contemporary Resort (rooms $234-525) has futuristic architecture, character dining and monorail access.

Polynesian Resort (rooms $289-650) has tropical landscaping and an evening luau feast (adult/child $47/24) Tuesday to Saturday.

The **Yacht Club Resort** (rooms $289-650) has a nautical theme.

Beach Club Resort (rooms $289-650) offers the best opportunities to participate in water sports.

The **Boardwalk Inn** (rooms $289-650) has child-care facilities and is convenient to Epcot.

The **Grand Floridian Resort & Spa** (rooms $329-815), which looks for all the world like the hotel from *Some Like it Hot*, has full kitchens in the rooms, monorail access and almost any other amenity you could dream up.

Home-Away-From-Home Resorts

These properties vary widely in price and amenities, but generally sleep at least eight people.

Fort Wilderness Resort & Campground (campsites $34-80, cabins $224-314, rooms $289-990) is in a shady natural preserve where programs include hayrides and sing-alongs. All campsites have full hookups.

Villas at the Disney Institute (rooms $214-550) has the most comprehensive spa treatments at Disney World.

Boardwalk Villas (rooms $289-990) is the most convenient of these choices to the parks.

Non-Disney Properties

There are several non-Disney properties in the area, and some of them are excellent. Rates change dramatically on an almost daily basis, depending on demand.

Club Hotel by Doubletree (☎ 407-239-4646, 800-521-3297; 12490 Apopka-Vineland Rd; rooms $79-139) is an attempt at a budget place.

Courtyard by Marriott Downtown Disney Hotel (☎ 407-828-8888, 800-223-9930; 1805 Hotel Plaza Blvd; rooms $89-139) is a very good deal with standard hotel rooms.

Doubletree Guest Suites Downtown Disney Resort (☎ 407-934-1000, 800-222-

8733; 2305 Hotel Plaza Blvd; suites $138-279) is right nearby.

Wyndham Palace Resort & Spa (☎ 407-827-2727; 1900 Buena Vista Dr; suites $189-199) is walking distance to Downtown Disney and a favorite for Gay Day participants.

GETTING THERE & AWAY

If you're flying into Orlando International Airport and staying at a Disney Resort, and have no urge to visit Orlando or the surrounding area, you don't need to rent a car. Mears Airport Shuttle (☎ 407-423-5566; w www.mearstransportation.com; $16 one way, $28 roundtrip) provides transportation between the airport and Disney World, where you can use free public transportation throughout the park.

Most hotels in Kissimmee and Orlando offer shuttles to Disney World. If yours doesn't, call around to see if you can catch a ride (usually $10 to $12) on a nearby hotel's shuttle.

From Orlando's Lynx Bus Center, in the alley between W Pine St and W Central Blvd, one block west of Orange Ave, you can catch buses to the Disney parks (No 50, every two hours), but it's a long ride.

The entire complex is designed for clueless out-of-town drivers: Signage and civil engineering are spectacular. From Orlando, take I-4 south and follow the signs, which are marked for easy access to each of the four major theme parks. From Kissimmee, take Hwy 192 west and follow the signs.

North from Orlando

Following Hwy 17 north from the Orlando area brings you into a charming rural region with several parks, recreation areas and notable small towns. Here watch endangered manatees at Blue Spring State Park or get a spiritual reading at Cassadaga.

BLUE SPRING STATE PARK

Blue Spring State Park (☎ 386-775-3663; 2100 French Ave; pedestrian/car $2/4) is the best place in the state to see manatees in their natural habitat. Visit between November and March, when the St John's River gets cold enough to make the peaceful mammals seek the relative warmth of Blue Spring's 72°F spring. During the peak season, an average of 25 to 50 manatees are here daily. Swimming is prohibited when manatees are present.

Even if you're not here during manatee season, there are plenty of reasons to come by: This is one of the most singularly beautiful swimming holes in Florida. For certified divers, there's a real treat: You can make your way through the narrow fissure at the source of the spring, past railroad tracks, abandoned car parts and fossils, to 'cork rock,' a boulder suspended in the upwelling water. You can rent snorkeling equipment

Blue Spring State Park is manatee central.

and canoes ($10 for the first hour, $5 for subsequent hours) at concessions. If you'd rather not paddle, **St Johns River Cruises** (☎ 386-917-0724; w www.sjrivercruises.com; adult/child $16/10) offers two-hour nature cruises through the park.

There's also **camping** (without/with hookups $15/17; four-person cabins $50) in the developed campground. Primitive campsites (adult/child $3/2) are at the end of a scenic 4-mile hike into the wilderness. You can make reservations up to a year in advance, the earlier the better.

The park is off French Ave at the northern end of Orange City. The 5 feet by 10 feet sign is impossible to miss if you're looking.

CASSADAGA

About 20 minutes north of Winter Park, this registered historic district is home to the Cassadaga (pronounced kassuh-**day**-guh) Spiritualist Camp, established in 1884 to further research into our elusive sixth sense. The camp houses a group of about 25 spiritualist-mediums who live and work here. The church, the **Southern Cassadaga Spiritualist Camp Meeting Association** (SCSCMA; ☎ 904-228-3171), believes in infinite intelligence, everlasting life on many planes of existence and the precepts of prophecy and healing.

For what it's worth, these folks genuinely believe in what they are doing and don't practice witchcraft or black magic; they don't condone hypnotism or promise to tell you your future; and they don't call themselves psychics but rather mediums.

There's no public transportation to Cassadaga. By car, take I-4 to exit 54, head to the light, go east on County Rd 4101 for a quarter mile, then turn right onto County Rd 4139.

Orientation & Information

The camp is mainly south of County Rd 4139, bordered roughly by Horseshoe Park to the west, by Lake St to the south, and by Marion St to the east. There's not much here – not even an ATM or gas station – and the main attraction is having your fortune told. Note that SCSCMA-certified mediums do not use tarot or other tools to do their readings; while they aren't morally opposed to such things, they believe that cards and crystal balls tend to block or channel energy rather than allowing it to flow naturally.

There are dozens of tarot card readers in town, however, who will be more than happy to tell your future if you'll cross their palms with silver (usually about $50 for half an hour). You can arrange a reading in advance through the Cassadaga Hotel (see Places to Stay & Eat, below), but there are plenty of walk-in places along CR 4139.

Get more information in the **Cassadaga Camp Bookstore** (☎ 386-228-2880; Ⓦ www .cassadaga.org; cnr Steven St & Cassadaga Rd; open 10am-5:30pm Mon-Sat, noon-5:30pm Sun), which sells New Age books, crystals and incense and serves as the de facto visitor's center for the town, with a community bulletin board and informative staff.

Places to Stay & Eat
Cassadaga Hotel (☎ 386-228-2323; 355 Cassadaga Rd; rooms $50/60 Sun-Thur/Fri & Sat) is on the site of a convalescence home that burned down in 1925, killing most of the patients. So, as you'd expect, there are plenty of ghosts: Sarah and Caitlin are two young girls who enjoy playing with visiting children; Henry, who has a flair for the dramatic, tends to wander around in long dark robes looking mysterious; and Mary, who died of a heart attack, likes to sit in the green chair outside the gift shop and greet early risers. Disclaimer: I also write horoscopes for Lonely Planet's excellent City-Sync guides (Ⓦ www.citysync.com), and I like to think I'm pretty sensitive to this stuff. If ghosts really do exist, this place is packed with them, and I swear I felt Mary sitting right across from me. Anyway, the hotel offers **Spirit Tours** (adult/child $10/5; 7:30pm Fri, 3pm & 7:30pm Sat), so you can judge for yourself.

The hotel also hosts about ten **psychics and tarot card readers**, and you can make an appointment through the hotel reservations number. The cost is $50 for half an hour, and it's considered gracious to tip. There's also an

on-site restaurant, **Lost in Time Cafe** (dishes $5-8; open 11am-3pm Mon-Fri, 11am-5pm Sat & Sun) that serves light lunches.

Old Cassadaga Grocery (☎ 386-228-3797; 1083 Stevens St; dishes $3-6; open 11:05am-5pm Sun-Thur, 11:05am-7pm Fri & Sat), across the street, is the other place to eat in town. It's refreshingly Enya-free and serves decent sandwiches and vegetarian chili.

DELAND
pop 60,000
Most people stop into DeLand for its easy access to the amazing wilderness areas that surround it, and for skydiving, the town's claim to fame. But the beautiful historic district, incorporated in 1882, represents the best of small-town Central Florida: A university town and county seat, it boasts impressive architecture, a handful of interesting museums and, this being Central Florida, lots of antique shops. It may not exactly live up to its nickname, 'Athens of America,' but it's a fine place to spend an afternoon.

New York Ave is the main street, with the historic district, museums and Stetson University located just west of the intersection with Hwy 17; the latter has most of the fast food chains. The small downtown is eminently strollable.

The **Welcome Center** (☎ 386-734-4331; Ⓦ www.delandchamber.org; 336 N Woodland Blvd; open 8:30am-5pm Mon-Fri) has pamphlets for area attractions including a self-guided walking tour of the historic district. Don't miss the beautiful Athens Theatre, the copper-domed County Courthouse or the attractive **post office** (cnr New York & Amelia Aves).

There's no public transportation to DeLand. To get here by car, take US Hwy 17 north from Orlando or south from Jacksonville; from Daytona, head west on Hwy 92.

Stetson University
DeLand was just beginning to profit from area citrus plantations when, in 1885, a bad freeze destroyed the entire crop. Times were tight and it looked like brand-new

DeLand University would have to shut its doors. That's when John B Stetson, the man who created the famed Stetson hat, stepped in, taking over the facility's endowment and renaming it Stetson University (☎ 386-822-7100; W www.stetson.edu; 421 N University Blvd).

Today, Florida's first private university has had its entire 165-acre (66-hectare) campus listed on the National Register of Historic Places, and features several significant buildings. The **Gillespie Museum of Minerals** (☎ 386-822-7330; W www.gillespiemuseum .stetson.edu; 234 E Michigan St; open 9am-4pm Mon-Fri) has a comprehensive collection of rocks, fossils, crystals and gemstones – check out the fluorescent collection, displayed under a black light – and makes a good destination as you wander the shady campus.

DeLand House Museum

Housed in a lovely 1886 mansion, this museum (☎ 386-740-6813; 137 W Michigan Ave; adult/child $4/2; open noon-4pm Tues-Sat) has the same stuff you'll find in historic homes all over the state: lovely antiques, lovely exhibits, lovely period clothes. Yay. Though, to be fair, it does have some outstanding stained glass. Behind the museum is a monument to the man who saved DeLand's, and arguably Central Florida's, agricultural sector.

Lue Gim Gong, the 'Citrus Wizard,' moved to DeLand in 1885, the same year that cold weather devastated local crops and threw most of the city into bankruptcy. The Chinese immigrant had a talent for botany, and, in 1911, he successfully crossed two different types of fruits to create the Lue Gim Gong orange, which ripened in early fall and was resistant to frost. The new crop was planted successfully throughout the state, Lue was awarded a medal by the US Department of Agriculture, and then…his accomplishments were swept under the rug. I wonder why. Finally, in 1999, area residents corrected this lapse into amnesia and built this shady place perfect for enjoying a tall glass of Florida orange juice.

African American Museum of the Arts

This tiny, jam-packed museum (☎ 386-736-4004; W www.africanmuseumdeland.org; 325 South Carolina; admission free (donations appreciated); open 10am-4pm Wed-Sat) features art and artifacts from Africa and the Caribbean, as well as a collection of 150 original pieces by African American artists. There's also a revolving gallery where new and established artists hang their work. They're currently in the process of moving to more spacious digs, so call ahead.

DeLand Memorial Hospital Museum

This strange collection (☎ 386-740-5800; 230 N Stone St; admission free; open 10am-3pm Wed-Sun) includes more than 1000 ceramic, wicker, glass and stone elephants; an entire room dedicated to the history of the ice-making industry (which in steamy Florida was serious business); a black heritage room; Nazi china and stemware; and uniforms from almost every major US war. If that's not eclectic enough for you, step into the Operating Room, where department store mannequins use 1920s-era medical technology to operate on one another. It's definitely worth stopping by.

Skydiving

Skydive DeLand (☎ 386-738-3539; W www .skydivedeland.com; 1600 Flightline Blvd; jumps $169) invented the tandem jump: A seasoned professional is strapped to your back, so if you freak out on the way down, there's going to be someone right there to pull the ripcord for you. What this means is that, with only half an hour of training and a pair of comfortable running shoes, you'll be able to experience the least boring two minutes of your entire life. Experienced skydivers are, of course, welcome to make the jump solo.

From downtown, take Hwy 17 (Woodland Blvd) north to Hwy 92; head east and exit Lexington Ave to DeLand Municipal Airport. Continue to Flightline Blvd and make a right; Skydive Deland is at the end of the street.

Places to Stay & Eat

Most of the cheap hotels are along Hwy 17 (Woodland Blvd), north of New York Ave. There's camping in Ocala National Forest, nearby.

DeLand Motel (☎ 386-734-5177; 1340 N Woodland Blvd; rooms $60) has cleanish rooms and discounts for skydivers.

Best Inn University (☎ 386-734-5711; 644 N Woodland Blvd; rooms $70, $180 for special events) is much nicer, with a pool and coffee makers in the very pleasant rooms.

Boston Gourmet Coffee House (☎ 386-738-2326; 109 E New York Ave; dishes $3-7; open 7am-6pm Mon-Thur, 7am-10pm Fri & Sat) has a fine assortment of bagels, pastries and healthy sandwiches with a few vegetarian options.

Hunter's Restaurant (☎ 386-736-7954; 202 N Woodland Blvd; mains $3-8; open 6am-midnight Mon-Thur, 6am-2am Fri & Sat) does home-style Southern cooking, with big breakfasts and dinners like chicken 'n' dumplings with veggies on the side.

The **Main St Grill** (☎ 386-740-9535; 100 E New York Ave; dishes $5-12; open 11am-10pm Mon-Sat, 10am-9pm Sun) has fat burgers and satisfying salads. It's a magnet for area businesspeople.

LAKE WOODRUFF NATIONAL WILDLIFE REFUGE

This 19,000-acre protected refuge (admission free; open 9am-sunset daily), just north of DeLand, is open to canoeists, anglers and, September through October, bow hunters (bright orange is *very* fashionable during those months). The majority of the park is made up of freshwater marshes, lakes and streams, and it's home to lots of alligators, bald eagles and manatees. Note that any clear, beautiful springs you might find bubbling up along clearly marked hiking trails are technically off-limits to swimmers, especially naked ones, as the presence of alligators make such transgressions an insurance risk. So if you're breaking federal law (for shame!) and see a ranger, be sure to let him or her know that you lost a contact lens and were wearing dry-clean-only clothes.

To get here, take Hwy 17 to Retta St, go one block to Grand Ave and turn left. The office is about a quarter mile down on your right. To reach the park, continue past the office to Mud Lake Rd, turn right and drive about 1 mile; the entrance is across the railroad tracks.

DE LEON SPRINGS STATE RECREATION AREA

The natural springs here (☎ 386-985-4212; pedestrian/car $1/4; open 9am-sunset daily) are a year-round 72°F, and developed into a huge and aesthetically challenged cement-lined swimming pool that's an absolutely fantastic place to take the kids. Except on weekends, it's usually pretty free of people. You can (and really should, if you have the chance) rent a canoe or kayak ($10 hourly, $28 daily) from concessions.

Overlooking the manicured grounds, the **Old Spanish Grill & Griddle House** (☎ 386-985-5644; dishes $4-6; open 9am-3pm daily) is the finest breakfast joint in Florida. In a beautiful old sugar mill, they've installed electric griddles into the center of sturdy wooden tables where you make yourself all-you-can-eat pancakes served with honey, molasses or maple syrup. You can also cook your own eggs, bacon and sausage at the table. Cool.

Picnicking is OK, but camping is not. The entrance is just off Hwy 17 and is very well signed.

PALATKA
pop 3500

A pleasant little town about 30 miles from St Augustine, Palatka (pronounced puhl-**at**-kuh) has an Amtrak station (which, more than likely, is why you're here), a lovely state garden and some of the best onion rings in Florida.

The main drag is Hwy 17, here called Reid St. Get tourist information at the **chamber of commerce** (☎ 386-328-1503; ⓦ www.putnamcountychamber.com; 1100 Reid St), just next to the **Amtrak station** (11th St), which is just north of Reid St. They hand out pamphlets with walking and driving tours to the town's historical sites.

David Browning Railroad Museum

This museum (☎ 386-325-7425; admission free; open 1pm-4pm 1st & 3rd Sunday each month) in the Amtrak station is run by the **Palatka Railroad Preservation Society**. Inside, you'll see railroad paraphernalia like schedules and maps of the railroads that came through Florida. But the star of the show is definitely the RailRodeo model train set. Built by a reporter from Pennsylvania, this was the largest HO-scale transportable model railroad in the state. Highlights are its animated objects: lights, crossings, bridges, a little girl in a tire swing, kites, cranes and front-end loaders, and handmade circus wagons. Donations are accepted.

Ravine State Gardens

This state park (☎ 904-329-3721; pedestrian/car $1/4, open 8am-sundown daily), at the southeastern end of town, was officially created as a WPA project in 1933. But the ravine itself was created over millions of years by water flowing from the St John's River. The 182-acre park has a 2-mile loop road and walking trails along the creek. In March and April, this is the home of the Palatka Azalea Festival.

The loop drive is open to cars from 9am to 4pm, which means your best bet is to get here at 4pm and walk this beautiful stretch in peace. To get here, drive west on Reid St to 9th St, turn left, follow the bend and continue after it becomes Crill Ave; turn left at Moseley Ave and left again at Twigg St. The park entrance is on the right-hand side of the road.

Other Attractions

In the Northside Historic District, the 1884 **Bronson-Mulholland House** (☎ 904-329-0140; open 2pm-5pm Tues, Thur & Sun), the former home of Judge Isaac Bronson, is open as a historic museum. **St Mark's Episcopal Church** (☎ 386-328-1474; 200 Main St), built in 1854, was the missionary center of the Episcopal Church in St John's Valley and a Union troop barracks during the Civil War. It's open for services Sunday at 8am and 10:30am.

Places to Stay & Eat

Azalea House (☎ 386-325-4547; 220 Madison St; rooms $75-105 Sun-Thur, $90-135 Fri & Sat) is a very nice B&B in a restored old home. On weekends you get a full gourmet breakfast; during the week it's expanded continental.

Angel's Dining Car (☎ 386-325-3927; 209 Reid St; dishes $2-6; open 5am-midnight Mon-Thur, 5am Fri-midnight Sun) is an aluminum diner and claims to be the oldest in Florida. Maybe yes, maybe no, but it does serve delicious and enormous sweet-onion onion rings handmade from St Augustine onions, huge burgers and Pusalow (pronounced **puss**-uh-loh), which is chocolate milk with a little vanilla syrup and some crushed ice.

Ocala & Ocala National Forest

If you're in search of the *real* Central Florida, with gingerbread Victorian townships populated with down-to-earth folks just a generation removed from subsistence farming, surrounded by palmetto wilderness where manatees and gators swim wild and free through clear, natural springs, you've found it. Saddle up your horse, car or bicycle and get ready for a little adventure, Central Florida style.

OCALA

Ocala, in a region famed for its beautiful scenery and plethora of natural springs, has been continuously occupied for at least 4000 years, first by Timucuan Indians, who greeted explorer Hernando de Soto in the village of Ocali, probably located just east of the current city center. Fort King was erected here in 1827 as the base of military operations in the Seminole War, and in 1846 the town incorporated as the seat of Marion County.

Today, this interesting and often overlooked city has plenty to recommend it: a couple of fine museums and a unique theme park, a thriving and compact downtown, decent public transportation and the best backyard in Florida, Ocala National Forest. It's also an equestrian center, surrounded by more than 1000 ranches that raise some of the finest thoroughbred horses in the USA.

Orientation & Information

Ocala's main drag, which connects it with the neighboring resort town of Silver Springs and Ocala National Forest, due east, is Silver Springs Blvd (Hwy 40). It's bisected by Pine Ave (Hwy 441), which runs between Gainesville to the north and Orlando to the south. The two roads divide addresses into north, south, east and west, and the downtown square is centered at their crossroads.

The **chamber of commerce** (☎ 352-629-8051; W www.ocalacc.com; 110 E Silver Springs Blvd; open 9am-5pm Mon-Fri) has useful free maps and lots of pamphlets, including a self-guided tour to the nearby Tuscawilla Historic District.

There's a **Bank of America** (☎ 352-620-1220; 35 SE 1st Ave) right downtown. Clean up at **Hillside Center Laundry** (☎ 352-351-0466; 2673 E Silver Springs Blvd).

The major daily is the *Star-Banner* (W www.starbanner.com); *Ocala* magazine (W www.ocalamagazine.com) is a glossy monthly.

Silver Springs

Built around seven natural springs and the resultant stunningly clear Silver River, this unusual attraction (☎ 352-236-2121, 800-234-7458; 5656 E Silver Springs Blvd; adult/child $32/23; open 9am-5:30pm daily) is allegedly where glass-bottomed boats were invented in 1878. If that's not enough of a claim, try this one: Tarzan movies and portions of *The Abyss* were shot here as well.

There aren't really any thrill rides here, as this park was built to show off the Florida wilderness. The **glass-bottom boat ride** is spectacular: As you slowly cruise over the eel grass, you'll pass over six small spring formations before the grand finale: a pass over Mammoth Spring, the world's largest artesian limestone spring.

There are other tours as well, including the **Lost River Voyage**, a boat ride through

dense jungle; **Jeep Safari**, a trailer ride through 35 acres (14 hectares) of African and Asian animals; Florida panther exhibits; and **Gator Lagoon**, with some very large alligators. There are also wildlife shows featuring birds, snakes, bears and creepy-crawlies like hissing cockroaches.

Twin Oaks Mansion is a concert venue that features both kinds of music: country *and* western. Jim Nabors was playing when I was there. Concerts are included with the price of admission. Parking is an extra $5.

Wild Waters Water Park

Next door to Silver Springs, this good-sized water park (☎ 352-236-2121; W www.wildwaterspark.com; 5656 E Silver Springs Blvd; adult/child $25/22; open 9am-5:30pm daily) has plenty to keep you cool: five huge water slides, a couple of smaller ones for little kids, a wave pool and a few small thrill rides. You can get a combo ticket to both Silver Springs and Wild Waters for $35/26 adult/child.

Appleton Museum of Art

Featuring a surprisingly impressive collection of fine art, the Appleton (☎ 352-236-7100; W www.appletonmuseum.org; 4333 NE Silver Springs Blvd; adult/child $12/5; open 10am-6pm daily) is worth a stop. In an imposing edifice between Ocala and Silver Springs, curators rotate permanent collections of American and European art (think Van Gogh, Matisse, Cezanne) with even better exhibits featuring Middle Eastern, North African and pre-Columbian American art and artifacts. The museum also offers free (with cost of admission) lectures and films throughout the year.

Don Garlits Museum of Drag Racing

This excellent automotive attraction (☎ 352-245-8661; W www.garlits.com; 13700 SW 16th Ave; adult/child $12/3; open 9am-5pm daily) features an absolutely outstanding collection of race cars, including the seminal dragster Swamp Rat I, 'Big Daddy' Don Garlits' own prize-winning speedster. The cluttered and comprehensive array of trophies and mementos from the sport's 50-year history is unparalleled. Also on-site is the **Drag Racing Hall of Fame**, a shrine to the fastest men and women around.

Garlits, a legend who designed and raced some of the sport's most impressive pieces of machinery, and his wife, Pat, a trophy-winning racer herself, run this museum. Stock cars, long-nosed top fuel rides, and antique classics and customs, mostly pre-WWII Fords, are displayed alongside involved explanations of how they were bored and blown for maximum horsepower. Bonus: You may even get to meet Don's mom, who just hates the fact that her son has started hitting the raceways again in recent years.

The museum is located about 10 minutes south of downtown Ocala on I-75; take exit 67 (CR 484) and follow the signs.

Organized Tours

Ocala Carriage & Tours (☎ 352-867-8717, 877-996-2252; w www.ocalacarriage.com) offers one-hour tours in carriages pulled by Clydesdales through the countryside, visiting different area horse farms, for $95 per carriage (four to six people). They also offer tours of Ocala's historic districts on weekends, by reservation only, for $50.

Many Marion County horse farms open their gates for private tours, some offering trail rides, others just letting you look at more than 40 breeds of horses raised here. Try **Double Diamond** (☎ 352-237-3834), **Paso Fino** (☎ 352-867-5305; w www.pasobeat .com/farms/youngs) or **Ocala Foxtrotter Ranch** (☎ 352-347-5551; w www.ocalafox trotter.com).

Places to Stay

There's a cluster of cheap lodgings just south of downtown Ocala on Hwy 441 (S Pine Ave) and more hotels within walking distance of Silver Springs. Camping opportunities in Ocala National Forest (see that section, later) are endless.

Comfort Motel (☎ 352-622-3060; 1850 S Pine Ave; rooms $25-35) is a very basic place with clean enough rooms and friendly owners.

Cloister Court Motel (☎ 352-236-1723; 5460 E Silver Springs Blvd; rooms $35-40) is

the best deal near Silver Springs, with small, decent rooms arranged around a nice pool, all accented with stone arches.

Sun Plaza (☎ 352-236-2343; 5461 E Silver Springs Blvd; rooms $55-70) boasts that this is where country artists performing at nearby Silver Springs stay. It's got basic rooms with refrigerators and microwaves.

The **Ritz Historic Inn** (☎ 352-671-9300, 888-382-9390; w www.ritzhistoricinn.com; 1205 E Silver Springs Rd; rooms $70-125), in a striking Spanish colonial building, has theme rooms (African safari, floral gardens) arranged around gardens and a courtyard. There's an on-site restaurant and bar (see Entertainment).

Seven Sisters Inn B&B (☎ 352-867-1170; w www.7sistersinn.com; 820 SE Fort King St; rooms $119-269), in a very large, very pink Victorian mansion, has beautiful rooms, expansive flower gardens and gourmet candlelight breakfasts.

Places to Eat

The restaurant scene in Ocala runs primarily to steakhouses, greasy buffets and fast food, but there are some exceptions.

The **Brass Rooster** (☎ 352-402-0097; 30 S Magnolia St; dishes $3-6; open 8am-4pm Mon-Thur, 8am-9pm Fri, 11am-3pm Sat) is a classic soda fountain and café with salads, sandwiches and ice cream floats, right on the square downtown.

Yen Lin Chinese Buffet (☎ 352-236-2226; 5436 E Silver Springs Blvd; buffet $7, dishes $5-13; open 11am-9pm Tues-Sat, noon-8pm Sun) was a surprise: I didn't think I'd include it in Ocala coverage, I just needed some vegetables, fast. But the buffet was still fresh at 1:30pm and featured some great stir-fries and excellent dumplings. A winner.

El Ranchito Mexican Restaurant (☎ 352-622-4808; 1655 S Pine Ave; dishes $6-15; open 11am-10pm Mon-Fri, noon-10pm Sat & Sun) serves huge portions of great Mexican grub, and there's a mariachi band on Wednesday night.

Tea with Lee (☎ 352-867-5530; 944 E Silver Springs Blvd; prices & hours by arrangement) is different. Lee serves high teas with

CENTRAL

spectacular trimmings, including the single most beautiful pastry I have ever seen (she called it a Napoleon, but that's like calling Don Garlits a commuter), in a frilly dining room decked out with about fifty shimmering portraits of Jesus.

Felix's Restaurant (☎ 352-629-0339; 917 E Silver Springs Blvd; lunch $7-13, dinner $12-24; open 11am-2:30pm Tues-Fri, 4:30pm-10pm Tues-Sat) has a beautiful, dark-wood dining room perfect for impressing your prom date. It's gourmet Southern cuisine, and at dinner, you can order two 'petite entrées,' exactly half of a regular entrée, if you can't decide on just one.

Entertainment

The square in downtown Ocala has half a dozen different bars and clubs within easy hopping distance of one another.

O'Malley's Alley (☎ 352-690-2262; 24 S Magnolia Ave) is your basic Irish pub with Guinness on tap and live music on weekends.

Harry's Seafood Bar & Grill (☎ 352-840-0900; W www.hookedonharrys.com; 24 SE 1st Ave) has a great happy hour.

The **Ritz Historic Inn** (☎ 352-671-9300, 888-382-9390; W www.ritzhistoricinn.com; 1205 E Silver Springs Blvd) has live jazz on Friday and Saturday nights, and karaoke on Wednesdays.

Ocala Civic Theatre (☎ 352-236-2274; W www.ocalacivictheatre.com; 4337 E Silver Springs Blvd) hosts dance and classical music performances, and community and professional theater.

Getting There & Around

Both **Greyhound** (☎ 352-732-2677; 512 N Magnolia Ave) and **Amtrak** are in the Central Transfer Station, at the corner of NW 5th St in Ocala just a few blocks from the downtown square. The SunTran transfer station is here as well.

By car from Gainesville, take either I-75 or Hwy 441 south to Silver Springs Blvd (Hwy 40), where Ocala is centered; go east to get to Silver Springs. From Orlando, take Florida's Turnpike to I-75, and that to Silver Springs Blvd.

SunTran (☎ 352-401-6999; adult/child $1/75¢) is a good public transportation option, although buses only run between 6am and 7pm. The Central Transfer Station is a few blocks from downtown at the corner of 5th St and Magnolia. The Orange Route serves the cheap hotels on S Pine Ave, and the Green Route connects downtown Ocala with Silver Springs.

OCALA NATIONAL FOREST

One of Florida's most important natural treasures is 400,000-acre (160,000-hectare) Ocala National Forest, a confederation of national, state and locally administered wilderness areas that work with private landowners to preserve and manage one of the most incredible ecosystems in the USA. There are 18 developed campgrounds, 219 miles of trails, 600 lakes (30 open for boating), and countless opportunities for biking, horseback riding, canoeing, bird watching or just meditating on how great it is that the government got here before the theme parks did.

Visitors unfamiliar with the concept of a national forest, as opposed to a national park, should be aware that this is a very different setup from, say, the Everglades. There's no single admission fee and no one number to call and reserve campsites. Some areas of the forest are extremely well developed, with paved roads and easy-to-follow trails, while others may only be accessible by dirt roads or blazed trails. And you'll find lots of things here you won't see in a national park: logging trucks, western bars, school buses and signs that say 'Private Property.' You'll also find dozens of natural springs, several very different biomes – from sand pine scrub to palmetto wilderness to subtropical forest – and more species of endangered flora and fauna than you could take in over a two-week stay. Don't miss this.

Orientation & Information

Two highways cross the park: Hwy 19 runs north-south and Hwy 40 runs east-west. You can pick up free maps at any of the visitor's centers, or order them through **Ocklawaha Visitor Center** ($7.42; 3199 NE Hwy 315, Silver Springs, FL 34488). Topographical maps, hiking guides, wildlife guides and other books are also available at any of the visitor's centers.

Of the many trails crisscrossing the park, the most popular are the 66-mile Florida National Scenic Trail (orange blazes), the 22-mile Paisley Woods Bicycle Trail (yellow blazes; off-road bikes highly recommended), and the 7-mile St Francis Trail (blue blazes), which leads to the abandoned 1880s town of St Francis. During hunting season (November to January), hikers should wear a bright orange vest or hat. Seriously. And if you're planning to do much trekking into the forest's vast interior, invest in a topographical map; there's a naval bombing range here, too, and it just takes one little missile to ruin your whole vacation.

The following three visitor's centers are open from 8am to 5pm daily:

Ocklawaha Visitor Center (☎ 352-236-0288; 3199 NE Hwy 315), your first stop if you're coming from Ocala and Silver Springs

Pittman Visitor Center (☎ 352-669-7495; 45621 State Rd 19), on the major throughway from Orlando and Mt Dora

Salt Springs Visitor Center (☎ 352-685-3070; 14100 N Hwy 19), in Salt Springs, accessible from Jacksonville and Palatka

Rangers serve most of the forest, and all campgrounds have volunteers (usually chatty retirees) who live on-site year-round and are great sources of information. Sites at developed campgrounds cost between $4 and $25 per night, and day-use areas are generally open from 8am to 8pm daily. Note that the areas listed are just a few of the many here; pick up a free park guide at the visitor's center for many other camping, hiking, swimming and wildlife-watching opportunities.

Juniper Springs Recreation Area

This is the forest's most popular and easily accessible area (☎ 352-625-3147; admission $3; open 8am-8pm daily; campsites $13-15) and was first developed in the mid-1930s. Concessions sell groceries and firewood and rent kayaks and canoes ($20 daily) for making the 7-mile run down Juniper Creek; there's a pick-up and a return shuttle at the bottom. This area also has the most comprehensive wheelchair access in the forest.

The main attractions are two of the most beautiful springs around, Juniper Spring (where swimming is permitted) and Fern Hammock Spring, which is followed by an unbelievably lovely little nature trail. You can also pick up the Florida National Scenic Trail here.

Salt Springs Recreation Area

Rumored to have curative powers and home to an interesting array of wildlife, Salt Springs (☎ 352-685-2048; admission $3; open 8am-8pm daily; campsites without/with hookups $13/17) is home to lots of black bears and alligators, and is a favorite with the RV set. There's a 2-mile nature trail, but the real attraction here is that, in addition to canoes ($28 daily), you can rent pontoon boats ($110 daily) and powerboats ($45 daily), perfect for making mischief on enormous Lake Kerr.

Alexander Springs Recreation Area

This beautiful region (☎ 352-669-3522; admission $3; open 8am-8pm daily; campsites $15) has one of the last untouched subtropical forests left in Florida, home to several endangered species, and has suffered more than the rest of the park during the drought of the past several years. Still, the stunning freshwater spring attracts wildlife, swimmers, scuba divers (extra $5 fee) and sunbathers, and there's a 1.1-mile nature trail that accesses the Florida National Scenic Trail and Paisley Woods Bicycle Trail. Renting a canoe ($10 for two hours, $26 daily) is an excellent idea.

Lake Eaton & Lake Eaton Sinkhole

Accessible by a well-maintained dirt road, this isolated area (no phone; admission $2; open 6am-10pm daily; campsites $6-8) has the excellent Lake Eaton sinkhole, which is 80 feet deep and about 450 feet in diameter. A 2.2-mile interpretive walking trail leads past it, a boardwalk runs around it, and a staircase leads down into it. I was there on a

Saturday afternoon and had the whole sinkhole to myself. Lake Eaton, nearby, doesn't rent boats but does have a launch.

Clearwater Lake Recreation Area

Another relatively isolated area (☎ 352-669-0078; admission $3; open 8am-8pm daily; campsites $15), this lovely little lake marks the southern terminus of the Florida National Scenic, Paisley Woods Bicycle and St Francis Trails. There's a 1-mile trail around the lake, which you can also enjoy in a rental canoe ($20 daily).

Getting There & Away

SunTran (☎ 352-401-6999; adult/child $1/75¢) runs between Ocala's Greyhound and Amtrak stations (see Getting There & Around in the Ocala section, earlier) and the western edge of the national forest; buses will transport your bicycle free of charge. But keep in mind that this is an enormous wilderness area – more than twice as big as Orlando – and once here, there's no public transportation.

The only way for nonathletes to get around is by car. All public roads are well maintained; even dirt roads are fine for 2WD cars. However, if you get lost, you may find yourself on private dirt roads (I did this), which are not as firmly packed: If the sand looks soft, don't stop, OK?

There are several different entries to the park, all convenient to different urban areas: From Orlando, take Hwy 441 north to the Eustis turnoff and continue north on Hwy 19 (about 40 miles); from Daytona, take Hwy 92 west to DeLand, then head north on Hwy 17 to Barberville and west on SR 40 (about 30 miles); from Ocala, take Silver Springs Blvd due west about 5 miles to the forest's main entry.

Gainesville

pop 105,000
Gainesville is a college town, and most of the action focuses around the sprawling University of Florida (UF) campus. It's got everything a college town should: Lots of great inexpensive eateries, excellent museums, a *wide* selection of bars and clubs, 77 miles of bike trails and an anarchist bookstore.

Hemming all the festivities in are some of Florida's finest wilderness areas, including Paynes Prairie, Devil's Millhopper State Geological Site and, just an hour away, Ocala National Forest. So stop in, have a Gatorade (invented right here) and stay a while.

ORIENTATION

The city is laid out on a grid system. Avenues run east-west and streets run north-south. University Ave is the main drag as well as the north-south divider; its intersection with Main St, the east-west divider, is considered the center of town. Downtown Gainesville is roughly bordered by 13th St to the west, 2nd St to the east, 2nd Ave to the north and 4th Ave to the south. The university is southwest of the center.

Addresses and streets are given a N, S, E, W or NE, SE, NW, SW prefix dependent on their relation to the intersection of Main and University. It's confusing, even to locals, whose trick is the mnemonic device APRIL (actually APRL) which means: Avenues,

---

Boiled Peanuts

As you crisscross the county roads of Central Florida, you're bound to come across steaming kettles of the region's favorite treat, boiled peanuts. They're cheap, packed with protein and often a vegetarian's best option in the outback, but…boiled peanuts?

The key to enjoying your first taste of this unusual item is to think of them not as nuts, but as something more akin to boiled potatoes: They're soft and flavorful (green peanuts are a tad firmer), and even tastier with Cajun seasoning.

You'll be presented with a Crock-Pot (or giant metal barrel, or anything else that can be kept warm over an open flame) of the nuts: Grab the requisite Styrofoam cup, stacked to the side, and ladle them in. Then enjoy!

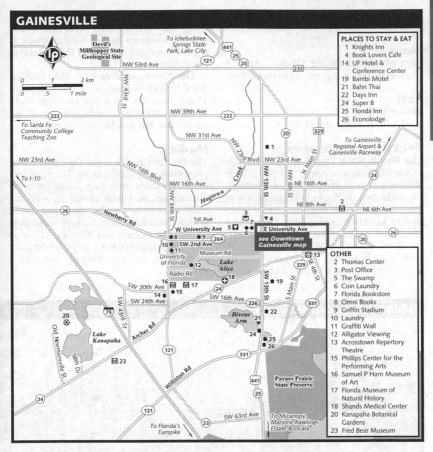

GAINESVILLE

0   1   2 km
0   .5   1 mile

To Ichetucknee Springs State Park, Lake City

Devil's Millhopper State Geological Site

To Santa Fe Community College Teaching Zoo

To I-10

To Gainesville Regional Airport & Gainesville Raceway

see Downtown Gainesville map

Bivens Arm

Lake Kanapaha

Old Newmansville St.

Paynes Prairie State Preserve

To Micanopy, Marjorie Rawlings Estate & Ocala

To Florida's Turnpike

PLACES TO STAY & EAT	
1	Knights Inn
4	Book Lovers Cafe
14	UF Hotel & Conference Center
19	Bambi Motel
21	Bahn Thai
22	Days Inn
24	Super 8
25	Florida Inn
26	Econolodge

OTHER	
2	Thomas Center
3	Post Office
5	The Swamp
6	Coin Laundry
7	Florida Bookstore
8	Omni Books
9	Griffin Stadium
10	Laundry
11	Graffiti Wall
12	Alligator Viewing
13	Acrosstown Repertory Theatre
15	Phillips Center for the Performing Arts
16	Samuel P Harn Museum of Art
17	Florida Museum of Natural History
18	Shands Medical Center
20	Kanapaha Botanical Gardens
23	Fred Bear Museum

Places, Roads and Lanes run east-west while everything else runs north-south. Addresses denote cross streets – a No 7150 would be between 71st and 72nd.

Alachua County Tourist Development (see Tourist Offices) sells copies of Rand McNally's *Gainesville City Map* and gives out some tourist maps, including a map to the Gainesville bikeway system (see Getting There & Around, later in this section). The Florida Book Store has an absolutely fantastic selection of maps, including topographical sheets for Ocala National Forest and other natural preserves.

INFORMATION
Tourist Offices

Alachua County Visitors & Convention Bureau (VCB; ☎ 352-374-5231; W www .visitgainesville.net; 30 E University Ave; open 8:30am-5pm Mon-Fri), just east of Main St, stocks the usual tourist flyers and literature. The amazing **Civic Media Center** (CMC; ☎ 352-373-0010; W www.civicmedia center.org; 1021 W University Ave; open noon-7:30pm Mon-Sat) has heaps of information on politics, culture, history, gay and lesbian resources, music and nightlife. It also hosts open-mike poetry readings and guitar concerts throughout the week. Admission is $3 to $5, depending on your income.

Money

Bank of America (☎ 352-335-0411; 1116 W University Ave) is convenient to downtown.

Post

The **post office** (☎ 352-371-6748; cnr 1st Ave & 17th St) is across from UF.

Bookstores & Libraries

The **Florida Book Store** (☎ 352-336-7466; ⓦ www.flbookstore.com; 1614 W University Ave), close to campus, has an outstanding collection of books and guides about Florida, hundreds of maps and a nice selection of Lonely Planet guides. Downtown you'll find several good used-book stores; try **Omni Books** (☎ 352-375-3755; 99 SW 34th St at University Ave), located a bit inconveniently at the Westgate Publix Shop-

ping Center. **Wild Iris Books** (☎ 352-375-7477; 802 W University Ave) sells feminist and women's studies books, as well as a good selection of gay and lesbian travel books and fiction.

The downtown **library** (☎ 352-334-3977; 401 E University Ave; open 10am-9pm Mon-Thurs, 10am-5pm Fri & Sat, 1pm-5pm Sun), at the corner of SE 3rd St, just east of the courthouse, has free Internet access.

Media

The big daily paper is the *Gainesville Sun* (ⓦ www.gainesvillesun.com). There are lots of fun freebies, including *Moon* (ⓦ www.moonmag.com), with events listings and political scandals, and *Insite,* with music reviews, entertainment listings and more. The daily *Independent Florida Alligator* (ⓦ www.alligator.org) is published by students at, but not officially associated with, UF.

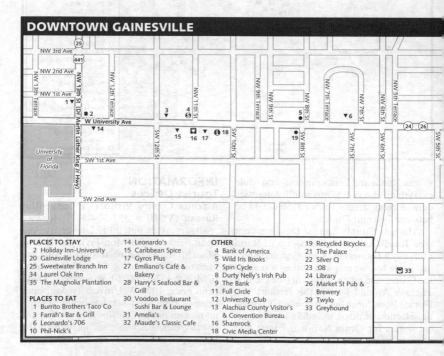

DOWNTOWN GAINESVILLE

PLACES TO STAY
2 Holiday Inn-University
20 Gainesville Lodge
25 Sweetwater Branch Inn
34 Laurel Oak Inn
35 The Magnolia Plantation

PLACES TO EAT
1 Burrito Brothers Taco Co
3 Farrah's Bar & Grill
6 Leonardo's 706
10 Phil-Nick's

14 Leonardo's
15 Caribbean Spice
17 Gyros Plus
27 Emiliano's Café & Bakery
28 Harry's Seafood Bar & Grill
30 Voodoo Restaurant Sushi Bar & Lounge
31 Amelia's
32 Maude's Classic Cafe

OTHER
4 Bank of America
5 Wild Iris Books
7 Spin Cycle
8 Durty Nelly's Irish Pub
9 The Bank
11 Full Circle
12 University Club
13 Alachua County Visitor's & Convention Bureau
16 Shamrock
18 Civic Media Center

19 Recycled Bicycles
21 The Palace
22 Silver Q
23 :08
24 Library
26 Market St Pub & Brewery
29 Twylo
33 Greyhound

Feeling political? Try the *Mahogany Review* or *Gainesville Iguana,* two leftist rags with events listings, or *Onward,* publishing the anarchist take on Gainesville events, all available at the CMC.

Gainesville commercial radio is great: 105.3 FM has a huge dance playlist and 103.7 FM has new and old hard rock. National Public Radio (NPR) can be heard on 89.1 FM; don't miss the morning show, when UF students (attempt to) read the day's events.

Gay & Lesbian Travelers
For gay and lesbian information and resources, call the **Gay Switchboard** (☎ 352-332-0700) or the **LGB Union at UF** (☎ 352-392-1665 x310).

Laundry
Spin Cycle (420 W University Ave) is just across from the Gainesville Lodge. **Coin Laundry** (1636 W University Ave) is close to UF.

Medical Services
Shands Medical Center (☎ 352-265-8000, 800-749-7424; ⓦ www.shands.org; 1600 SW Archer Rd) is just south of the UF campus.

UNIVERSITY OF FLORIDA
The state's oldest university (UF; ☎ 352-392-3261) was established in 1853 as the East Florida Seminary in Ocala and moved to Gainesville after the Civil War. It's one of the 10 largest universities in the country, with more than 30,000 students and a 2000-acre campus packed with historic landmarks.

The Holland Law Center building stands near the site of Native American burial mounds, and archaeologists have discovered artifacts from pre-Columbian settlements along Lake Alice, just east of the campus center. Lake Alice also has lots of friendly

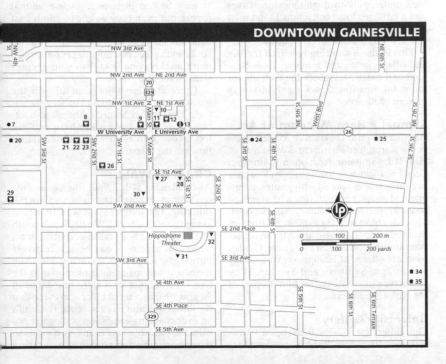

DOWNTOWN GAINESVILLE

alligators swimming wild and free; you can view them from shore near the intersection of Museum and Radio Rds. Keep rambunctious children close.

The main reasons to visit the campus during your visit are the museums – unless, of course, you're here to see a football game. Griffin Stadium (also called Florida Field) is home to the Fightin' Gators, major players in the highly competitive Southeastern Conference. If you still haven't figured out how important college football is in the South, just try getting a hotel room on game day.

Florida Museum of Natural History

This museum (☎ 352-846-2000; w www.flmnh .ufl.edu; cnr SW 34th St & Hull Rd; admission free; open 10am-5pm Mon-Sat, 1pm-5pm Sun & holidays) is a blast. Colorful galleries highlight Florida ecosystems with exhibits like a grub-and-worm-infested log that kids can look under, walk-through limestone caves and a fabulous fossil collection. Don't miss the children's gallery, which features art inspired by the museum's collections.

This is also a working research facility and offers classes and seminars from September through May; check the Web site for more information. Special exhibits may require admission.

Samuel P Harn Museum of Art

Another UF prize, the Harn (☎ 352-392-9826; w www.arts.ufl.edu/harn; cnr SW 34th St & Hull Rd; admission free; open 11am-5pm Tues-Fri, 10am-5pm Sat, 1pm-5pm Sun) has sweeping spaces packed with photos, paintings and sculptures displaying a pronounced concentration in 20th-century American art. They also have rotating exhibitions from all over the world. The Asian and African collections are among the finest in the state. Guided tours are offered at 12:30pm on Wednesday and at 2pm Saturday and Sunday. They also screen international art films as part of the Risk Cinema series.

University Gallery

This gallery (☎ 352-392-0201; open 10am-8pm Tues, 10am-5pm Wed-Fri, 1pm-5pm Sat)

hangs six shows annually by both students and nationally known artists. In the spring, it presents works of faculty and MFA candidates. The gallery is in the Fine Arts Building complex on campus, in Building B. Public exhibitions of local art also rotate through city hall, the Gainesville airport, the county administration building and the downtown library.

FRED BEAR MUSEUM

This truly unique attraction (☎ 352-376-2411; 4600 SW 41st Blvd; adult/child $5/3; open 10am-6pm daily) bills itself as a natural history museum, which it is – sort of. Fred Bear, an expert bow hunter and innovator, founded Bear Archery, the largest manufacturer of hunting bows in the USA. And here, next to the factory, you'll see many, many examples of creative taxidermy (check out the lion wrestling a water buffalo) concocted from animals Bear and others took down. It may be too intense for some animal lovers, but even they've got to admit that a 60-year-old man taking on a full-grown male Kodiak bear, armed basically with two sticks and a piece of string, makes for a much more level playing field than your average slaughterhouse.

There are also bows from all over the world, some bejeweled and others prehistoric. Every other Saturday, there's a shooting competition out back, where you can lob arrows into rubber animals scattered through the forest.

GRAFFITI WALL

Also called the 34th St Wall, this is one of the city's finest examples of right, and liberal, thinking. The long cement wall that runs along the east side of SW 34th St just south of SW 2nd Ave is a graffiti-permitted zone, whose management has been effectively turned over to students and artists. The main focus is a well-maintained memorial to the five UF students who were murdered in August 1990 by a serial killer – an event that continues to haunt city residents. The wall's an ever-changing exhibition of slogans, political manifestos, and thank-you notes to parents paying for students' education

('Thanks, Mom and Dad!'). While it's legal to tag here, the central memorial panel is strictly off-limits.

THOMAS CENTER

This historical museum (☎ 352-334-2197; 302 NE 6th Ave; admission free; open 8am-5pm Mon-Fri), in a restored 1920s Mediterranean-revival hotel (it also houses city offices), has period rooms, a small history display and art galleries with rotating exhibitions.

DEVIL'S MILLHOPPER STATE GEOLOGICAL SITE

Welcome to one of Florida's most famous holes in the ground (☎ 352-955-2008, 352-462-7905; 4732 Millhopper Rd; pedestrian/car $1/2, open 9am-5pm daily). The geology works like this: Limestone is susceptible to weak acids that are formed when rainwater mixes with decomposing plant matter, and over time comes to resemble Swiss cheese. When the holes – caverns – get extensive enough, the whole limestone structure collapses on itself and presto! It's a sinkhole.

That's just one theory, of course: Some say that when the Devil stole a beautiful Indian maiden, a handful of braves decided to track him down. So the wily old Devil conjured up a millhopper-shaped hole and trapped those braves at the bottom. Fossilized bones discovered here by early European settlers seem to corroborate this hypothesis, but UF geologists still lean toward explanation A.

No matter how it formed, this hole is impressive, more than 120 feet deep and 500 feet across. Walk down the 232-step wooden staircase into the hole, feeling the temperature decreasing and watching the ecosystem changing with every step. It all amounts to a cutaway section of Florida's geological formation. Ranger-led tours are held every Saturday morning at 10am.

To get to the park, take University Ave west to NW 39th Rd, which becomes NW 43rd St; follow that to its intersection with Hwy 232, which is Millhopper Rd.

KANAPAHA BOTANICAL GARDENS

The most wonderful thing about these 62-acre gardens (☎ 352-372-4981; 4700 SW 58th Dr; adult/child $4/2; open 9am-5pm Mon, Tues & Fri, 9am-dusk Wed, Sat & Sun), aside from the volunteers, is the water garden: Four waterfalls and a long babbling brook meandering through the landscape come courtesy of reclaimed wastewater from the regional utilities board. Apparently, when they tried to just, well, shove the water back into the ground, it wreaked havoc with the local pH balance. The gardens and the utility came up with this ingenious, environmentally friendly and lovely method of reintroducing the stuff into the ground slowly and gently. This is a very serene place to take a stroll any time of year. It also features a vinery, an herb garden and butterfly and hummingbird gardens.

From downtown, take University Ave west to 13th St and turn left; continue to Archer Rd and turn right, following Archer 1 mile past I-75; the entrance is up the little dirt road on the right-hand side (look for the sign).

PLACES TO STAY

Prices soar during special events such as football games, car races and graduation. Check in newspapers or with the VCB to see if any such special events are planned during your stay, and, if so, call *well* in advance for reservations!

Paynes Prairie State Preserve (☎ 352-466-3397) has rustic camping, 10 miles south (see Around Gainesville later in this chapter).

Hotels & Motels

Most of the cheapie motels are just east of UF, along SW 13th St or on approach roads.

Bambi Motel (☎ 352-376-2622, 800-342-2624; 2119 SW 13th St; rooms $30, during special events $70) has nicer rooms than the exterior would lead you to believe; they're large and have TVs with HBO included.

Florida Inn (☎ 352-376-3742; 2603 SW 13th St; rooms $33, special events $70) has a classic motel sign and shoddy but acceptable rooms; local calls are 25¢.

EconoLodge (☎ 352-373-7816; 2649 SW 13th St, rooms $36, special events $80), right next door to the Florida Inn (they share a nice pool), has smaller, newer rooms.

Gainesville Lodge (☎ 352-376-1224; 413 W University Ave; rooms $40, special events $70) has a great location on the main drag of W University Ave, within easy stumbling distance of the downtown club scene.

Super 8 (☎ 352-372-3654; 2000 SW 13th St; rooms $50, special events $80) has clean, cookie-cutter rooms with one great amenity: The hotel is adjacent to the excellent Bahn Thai Restaurant (see Places to Eat later in this section).

Days Inn University Motel (☎ 352-376-2222; 1901 SW 13th St; rooms $50, special events $100) is surprisingly nice by the chain's standards, with a large pool, big backyard and attractive rooms, some with refrigerators.

Holiday Inn–University (☎ 352-376-1661; 1250 W University Ave; rooms from $85, special events $140) is a little tattered for the price, but you can walk to the big game.

University of Florida Hotel & Conference Center (☎ 352-371-3600; Ⓦ www.ufhotel .com; 1714 SW 34th St; rooms $90-120 Mon-Fri, $75-100 Sat & Sun) is as close as you'll come to a luxury hotel in town. It's packed with amenities geared toward the businessperson, including conference centers, DSL hookups and discounts at area golf courses.

B&Bs

Of the several B&Bs in town, most are east of Main St. The VCB has a complete list.

Sweetwater Branch Inn (☎ 352-373-6760; 625 E University Ave; rooms $80-110 Mon-Fri, $90-155 Sat & Sun) is a rather professional operation, with six rooms, a cottage and a carriage house, two with hot tubs and three with fireplaces. Crepes are the specialty at breakfast.

Laurel Oak Inn (☎ 352-373-4535; 221 SE 7th St; rooms $90-145) is a brand-new place (though you wouldn't know it from their antique collection) built by friendly do-it-yourselfers who can cook a mean breakfast.

The Magnolia Plantation (☎ 352-375-6653; 309 SE 7th St; rooms $95-110, cottages $125-175) has a fantastic breakfast, and there's a free fridge filled with snacks and soft drinks if you're ever hungry again. Wine and hors d'oeuvres are served in the evening. There are also several cuddly cats, a dog and a duck who thinks it's a dog patrolling the pond out back, next to the two cottages with Jacuzzis and fireplaces.

PLACES TO EAT

Vegetarians who have subsisted on boiled peanuts (see the boxed text 'Boiled Peanuts,' earlier) while traversing the outback of central Florida will be thrilled. Note that service isn't always what it could be; many servers have exams to cram for and 'Hey, dude, we're puttin' the *band* back together!' attitudes, and are therefore far too busy to bring your barbecued tofu sandwich.

Budget

Maude's Classic Cafe (☎ 352-335-1204; 101 SE 2nd Place) serves tea and coffee (including one of the best lattes I've ever had) to students and overworked resident doctors just steps from the Hipp.

Burrito Brothers Taco Co (☎ 352-378-5948; 16 NW 13th St; dishes $2-6; open 11am-10pm daily) has burritos so good that crowds form. None of the beans or tortillas contain animal fat, and you can get your meal dairy-free on request.

Caribbean Spice (☎ 352-377-2172; 1121 W University Ave; lunch special $5; open 11am-7pm daily) has a tiny but tasty selection of savory pastries packed with meat or vegetable fillings. The popular lunch special includes a pastry, soft drink and slice of banana bread.

Gyros Plus (☎ 352-336-5323; 1011 W University Ave; dishes $4-6; open 11am-10pm Mon-Sat, noon-8pm Sun) makes their own pita bread, which they then fill with tasty meaty or vegetarian fillings.

Book Lover's Cafe (☎ 352-384-0090; 505 NW 13th St; dishes $3-7; open 10am-10pm daily) serves light vegetarian fare in a dining room surrounded by stacks of used books, including lots of Lonely Planet guides.

Phil-Nick's (☎ 352-376-8269; 37 N Main St; dishes $4-7; open 6:30am-3:30pm Mon-Sat) serves hearty pastas and casseroles cafeteria style, and makes fresh pressed sandwiches while you wait.

Leonardo's (☎ 352-375-2007; 1245 W University Ave; open 11am-11pm Mon-Thur, 11am-midnight Fri & Sat) serves inspired pizzas by the (enormous) slice ($2 to $5) or pie ($9 to $18).

Farrah's Bar & Grill (☎ 352-378-5179; 1120 W University Ave; dishes $6-9; open 11am-10pm Mon & Tues, 11am-midnight Wed-Sat) serves five-star (my rating, not Michelin's) Mediterranean food, from gyros to huge maza platters featuring falafel, kibbie, kifta and more, in a high-ceilinged atrium. There's live jazz on Friday and Saturday night.

Mid-Range & Top End

Bahn Thai Restaurant (☎ 352-335-1204; 1902 SW 13th St; lunch buffet $7, dishes $11-14; open 11am-2:30pm Mon-Fri, 5pm-10pm Mon-Sat) has the best Thai food in town, especially anything made with Banyang or Panang curry. The lavish lunch buffet is a great deal.

Emiliano's Café & Bakery (☎ 352-375-7381; 7 SE 1st Ave; lunch $7-10, dinner $10-22; open 5:30pm-9:30pm Tues-Thur, 11:30am-9:30pm Fri & Sat, 8am-3pm Sun) is a great tapas bar that serves big portions of Latin-Caribbean fusion finger foods worth writing home about. Highly recommended.

Voodoo Restaurant Sushi Bar & Lounge (☎ 352-381-1999; 112 S Main; mains $10-19; open 5pm-2am) is a slick, dark place with lots of chrome and a sense of sterile romance. There's a full sushi bar and entrées that feature lots of steak and seafood. It turns into an upscale bar by 10pm.

Leonardo's 706 (☎ 352-378-2001; 706 W University Ave; mains $13-24; open 5pm-11pm Mon-Thur, 5pm-midnight Fri & Sat, 11am-3pm Sun) is supposed to have the finest food in town, though my friend Barbara (who knows gourmet cuisine) considers it overrated.

Amelia's (☎ 352-373-1919; 235 S Main St; mains $12-24; open 11:30am-2:30pm Thur & Fri, 5pm-10pm or so Tues-Sun), behind the

Hipp, is a romantic spot with good Italian food and stellar bills. Don't skip the antipasti.

ENTERTAINMENT
Performing Arts

The **Hippodrome** (☎ 352-375-4477; W http://hipp.gator.net; 25 SE 2nd Place), in an imposing historic edifice (1904–11) that was formerly a federal building, is now one of Gainesville's most loved stages. Over the past 20 years, the Hipp has been the city's main cultural center, hosting theatrical productions, experimental cinema, teen theater programs, kids' productions and more. Admissions vary.

The **Phillips Center for the Performing Arts** (☎ 352-392-2787 for tickets, 352-392-1900 for information; W www.performing arts.ufl.com) is actually a complex of four performance spaces located on the UF campus, ranging from 80 seats to 1800. You'll see anything from student performance art to the Moscow Grigorovich Ballet (not to mention David Copperfield, a Philip Glass film festival and the Men's Glee Club Choral). Contact the Phillips Center for information on performances at these and UF's other stages.

Acrosstown Repertory Theatre (☎ 352-378-9166; 619 S Main St; shows at 8pm Tues-Sat) is an intimate, 80-seat black-box theater that stages unusual plays and performance art.

Bars & Pubs

This is a truly fine town for barhopping, with dozens of festive options packed to the rafters with college students, drag queens, cowboys and tattooed hipsters all dressed to impress. It's so worth the hangover.

The Swamp (☎ 352-377-9267; 1642 W University Ave; open 11am-2am daily) will be remembered by countless UF alumni as the first place they ever threw up from alcohol poisoning. Domestic beer in plastic cups, edible food and underage coeds giggling behind marginal fake IDs make this a fine place to contemplate the real meaning of higher education.

Durty Nelly's Irish Pub (☎ 352-374-9567; 208 W University Ave; open 11:30am-2am Mon-Fri, 4pm-2am Sat, 5pm-11pm Sun) is a relaxing place to enjoy all those Irish and English brews on tap, perfect with some live entertainment, usually Irish folk music, on stage Wednesday through Saturday.

Market St Pub & Brewery (☎ 352-377-2929; 120 SW 1st Ave) has a tasty selection of microbrews made on the premises and an understated meat-market atmosphere. There's live music Wednesday and Friday nights.

Silver Q (☎ 352-371-4644; 225 W University Ave) is a mellow sports bar with 12 pool tables, 20 TVs tuned into sports events, and happy hour Monday through Saturday.

Shamrock (☎ 352-374-6777; W www .gainesvilleshamrock.com; 1017 W University Ave) is a decent Irish pub – good beer, live music – with one big bonus: All the Irish specials on the menu – shepherd's pie, colcannon, corned beef and cabbage – are either vegetarian or vegan. Two, if you consider Grateful Dead night (Monday; it involves drum circles) a bonus.

Brew-Ha's (☎ 352-367-9191; open 6pm-2am Mon-Sat, 4pm-11pm Sun) lets you party in the comfort of your hotel room by delivering beer (by the six-pack or keg), cigarettes and something called cheesy bread right to your door. Gainesville rules.

Clubs & Live Music

:08 (☎ 352-384-0888; 201 W University Ave; open 9pm-2am daily) is an enormous cowboy/cowgirl (cowperson?) club with long, long lines outside and lots of line dancing inside. Can't dance? No worries – they offer lessons every Saturday night.

Twylo (☎ 352-379-9003; 210 SW 2nd Ave) has DJs most nights and a Latin dance extravaganza on Friday.

The Palace (☎ 352-336-8360; W www.gama productions.com; 233 W University Ave) is one of the best places in town to see live music, from local bands to internationally known acts. Ticket prices vary widely.

Full Circle (☎ 352-377-8080; 6 E University Ave; open 10pm-2am nightly) is an artsy, gay-friendly, all-welcome kind of place that plays old-wave, disco and house and progressive. Regulars go through a lot of eyeliner.

University Club (☎ 352-378-6814; W www .ucclub.com; 18 E University Ave) is pre-dominantly gay, but it's open to everyone provided they have the 'proper attitude.' Lady Pearl and her Pussy Cabaret host a very popular drag show that attracts loud and lovely entertainers from all over the state. The entrance is around the back at NE 1st Ave.

The Bank (☎ 352-271-0333; 22 W University Ave) is where displaced Miamians head when they're homesick for exclusive, chromed-out clubs. It's a nice place, cool and comfortable, but jeans and sneakers are strictly *verboten*.

SPECTATOR SPORTS

Griffin Stadium (Florida Field; ☎ 352-375-4683; W www.ufl.edu) is the home of the UF Gators football team, which plays in the 85,000-seat venue between September and December. Tickets cost about $30, but this is an entirely academic point: You will *not* get tickets unless you pay scalpers (get there early) three times that much – more, if you want to see bitter SEC rivals the Tennessee Vols trounce the Fightin' Gators in person. (Go Big Orange!) The Gators have men's baseball and men's and women's basketball teams as well; call the above number for ticket information to all Gators athletic events.

The **Gainesville Raceway** (☎ 352-377-0046; W www.gainesvilleraceway.com; 1211 N County Rd 225) is one of the fastest tracks on the National Hot Rod Association circuit – the first 300mph Top Fuel runs happened here. In March it hosts the Mac Tools Gatornationals, which in 2002 attracted a crowd of 132,000 to see dragsters, funny cars, pro stock cars and pro stock bikes tear up the track. It also sponsors a slew of other racing events and car shows throughout the year.

GETTING THERE & AROUND

Gainesville Regional Airport (☎ 352-373-0249) is a midsize airport about 10 miles northeast of downtown, served by a handful of domestic carriers. Bus No 24 connects the airport with downtown Gainesville.

There is a **Greyhound bus station** (☎ 352-376-5252; 516 SW 4th Ave) with daily service to Miami, Orlando, Tallahassee, Atlanta and points north. **Gainesville Regional Transit System** (RTS; ☎ 352-334-2600; W www.go-rts.com; adult/student $1/50¢) runs an excellent network of buses throughout the city. Bus No 1 operates between downtown and the cluster of motels on SW 13th St. Bus Nos 5, 43 and 10 ply University Ave. Although service to greater Gainesville winds down at around 9pm nightly, the **Later Gator** lines, which serve downtown and the UF area, run until 3am Thursday to Saturday. All buses have bicycle racks.

The nearest **Amtrak station** (☎ 352-468-1403) serving the Gainesville area is in Waldo, 13 miles northeast. A taxi from the station to the center of Gainesville costs about $35.

If you're driving, downtown Gainesville is about 3 miles east of I-75, a little more than halfway between Tallahassee and Orlando.

The two big taxi companies in town are **Gator Cab** (☎ 352-375-0313) and **City Cab** (☎ 352-375-8294).

Gainesville has 77 miles of bike lanes painted onto roads; 19 miles of bike lanes separated from the roads by a curb; and many bike trails completely independent of city streets. In the city, bike lanes are marked with signs or with diamonds painted on the street. In rural areas, bike trails or rail trails are signed. The largest of these is the 17-mile Gainesville-Hawthorne Rail Trail (mountain bikes only), which cuts across the northern end of Paynes Prairie State Preserve (see the Around Gainesville section below).

Recycled Bicycles (☎ 352-372-4890; 805 W University Ave; open 9:30am-6pm Mon-Fri, 10am-5pm Sat) rents bikes for $14 daily. **Spin Cycle** (☎ 352-373-3355; W www.spinracing.com; 424 W University Ave) rents bikes for $18 plus a deposit based on the worth of the bike.

Around Gainesville

HIGH SPRINGS
This small town with quaintness to spare is a magnet for antique junkies, nature lovers and motorcycle enthusiasts, who all find plenty to do in this historic burg. Mainly,

however, it's a great jumping-off point for several state parks and wild and developed springs.

The main drag is Main St, lined with shops, art galleries and restaurants; it's the major north-south divider. Hwy 441, here called 1st Ave, is the major east-west throughway, intersecting Main St downtown. Addresses are labeled NW, NE, SW and SE as they relate to these two roads. Numbered streets tend to run north and south, similarly numbered avenues east and west. There are no visitor's center, but pamphlets and free maps of downtown are available at area shops and restaurants. For more information you can go to W www.highsprings.com.

Public transportation? Not a chance. By car, High Springs is about 20 miles northwest of Gainesville on Hwy 441 (NW 13th St), a straight shot from UF.

San Felasco Hammock State Preserve
About halfway between Gainesville and High Springs, this wilderness area (☎ 352-955-2008; pedestrian/car $1/3.25; open 9am-dusk daily) has dozens of sinkholes, some dry and some filled with water. The area is populated by bobcats, foxes, deer and, of course, lots of gators. It has 10 miles of hiking trails, and while there's no camping per se, overnight ranger-led tours are offered every Saturday from April to October.

Poe Springs Park
Opened in 1991 along the banks of the winding Santa Fe River, the centerpiece of this pleasant, manicured park (☎ 352-454-1992; 28800 NW 182nd Ave; admission $4; open 9am-sundown daily) is Poe Springs, where you're welcome to swim in the developed pools or canoe down the Santa Fe River. There are also several miles of hiking trails.

Poe Springs is located off CR 340, a few minutes west of High Springs.

Ginnie Springs
If you like your clear, natural springs served up with something of a party atmosphere

(but *no* beer kegs without prior written permission, OK?), head to Ginnie Springs (☎ 386-454-7188; W www.ginniesprings outdoors.com; 7300 NE Ginnie Springs Rd; adult/child $8/3; hours vary, but generally open 8am-sunset Sun-Thur, 8am-10pm Sat & Sun). In addition to seven springs and a swath of the Santa Fe River, this outdoor entertainment complex has sundecks, heated pools, volleyball courts, a convenience store, a deli and a restaurant.

Concessions rents just about every sort of scuba diving equipment you might want (a package without/with dive light runs $50/60), plus canoes and kayaks ($8 for two hours) and tubes ($5 all day). Divers pay an extra $19 to $25 daily. There's also on-site **camping**, $14 per adult and $6 per child. Electrical hookups are an extra $4 daily.

Ginnie Springs is about 5 miles west of High Springs on CR 340.

Activities

There are two things for the visitor to do when they visit High Springs. First is shop, and there's no end to the number of adorable little knickknacks you'll find at the gazillion antique shops and art galleries in town. Second is commune with nature, and with 34 natural springs within an easy drive of downtown, that generally means canoeing, kayaking and diving.

Adventure Outpost Ecotours (☎ 386-454-0611; 815 Santa Fe Blvd) rents and sells canoes, kayaks and other gear. They also organize more than 30 guided river runs of varying degrees of difficulty around High Springs.

Santa Fe Bicycle Outfitters (☎ 386-454-2453; 10 N Main St; open 10:30am-6pm Mon-Sat) rents 21-speed bikes for $20 daily and arranges three-hour guided group bike tours to Ichetucknee or nearby O'Leno State Park for $30 per group plus rentals. Longtime owner and area expert Jim Gabriel also can help arrange overnight biking/camping trips throughout the region from this full-service bike store.

Bird's Underwater Dive Center (☎ 386-563-2763; W www.birdsunderwater.com; 320 NW Hwy 19) is another dive shop that pro-

vides instruction and rentals, and also organizes manatee snorkeling adventures.

Places to Stay

High Springs Campground (☎ 386-454-1688; 24004 NW Old Bellamy Rd) offers cheap camping.

Blue Springs Park (☎ 386-454-1369; 7450 NE 50th St; adult/child $10/4, electrical hookups $4) has its own spring. They also rent canoes for $6 an hour, $10 for two hours. Head south on CR 340 from Main St (it's a right if you're coming from Gainesville) and go straight for 4 miles.

The **Cadillac Motel** (☎ 386-454-1701; 405 NW Santa Fe Blvd; rooms $40) has clean, basic rooms in the middle of paradise.

The **Rustic Inn** (☎ 386-454-1223; W www .rusticinn.net; 3105 S Main St; rooms $79-89 Mon-Fri, $99-109 Sat & Sun) sits on a 5-acre (2-hectare) ranch and is more convenient to Ichetucknee Springs than downtown High Springs. All the rooms come with kitchenettes.

Grady House Bed & Breakfast (☎ 386-454-2206; W www.gradyhouse.com; 420 NW 1st Ave; rooms $85-185), right downtown, has beautiful gardens, rooms in the big Victorian house, and a two-story cottage out back.

Places to Eat

Silver Moon Cycles (☎ 386-454-3766; Hwy 441; open 11am-6pm 'usually'), just east of High Springs on Hwy 441, is a combination Harley-Davidson repair shop, clothing store and Internet café; online access is free with the purchase of a latte or muffin. Dr Love asked me to mention that women's apparel comes with free installation.

The **Station Bakery & Cafe** (☎ 386-454-4943; 20 NW Railroad Ave; dishes $4-7; closed Sun), housed in the old train station, has pastries, ice cream and deli sandwiches.

Great Outdoors Trading Company (☎ 386-454-2900; W www.greatoutdoorscafe.com; 65 N Main St; dishes $6-15; open 10am-8:30pm Sun-Thur, 10am-9:30pm Fri & Sat) is a rustic place right at the city center and a gathering place for area spring divers. Sandwiches and salads are your best bet, although more expensive options include

Szechuan eggplant and lasagna. They also have live music, plays and storytellers on Friday and Saturday night – check the Web site to see what's on.

ICHETUCKNEE SPRINGS STATE PARK

A trip to these waters (☎ 386-497-4690, recording ☎ 386-497-2511; open 8am daily) is mandatory for summer visitors, unless it's a crowded weekend. The Ichetucknee (meaning 'beaver pond') River is fed by the Ichetucknee Spring group, nine springs that together produce 233 million gallons of clear water daily, flowing downstream at about 1¼mph and maintaining a constant temperature of 73°F. The park runs regular trams bringing tubers to the river and also a shuttle service between the north and south park entrances.

The park also offers swimming, snorkeling and diving. For $5 per certified diver, the Blue Hole Spring scuba diving season runs October 1 to March 31. There are also hiking and interpretive programs. Camping is prohibited, but private campgrounds line park access roads. Bringing in alcohol, tobacco, pets, bottles, cans or disposable *any*thing is forbidden. Inner tubes can't be over 5 feet in diameter. Rangers check bags as tubers board trams, and they patrol; carriers of contraband can be ejected from the park.

Tubing

The park limits the number of tubers coming in the north entrance to 750 daily, though on weekends you may see some 3000 people along the river. Rent tubes from concessionaires along Hwys 238 and 47 for about $5 (or one/two-person rafts for $10/15).

The longest ride, three to 3½ hours, begins at the north entrance and ends at the south (the north entrance is south off Hwy 238). Drive in (admission for tubers for this run is $4.25 per person) and drop your party at the upper tube launch. Leave the park and drive 7 miles to the south entrance. Turn left on Hwy 238 and follow signs to the south entrance, about half a mile past the Ichetucknee River bridge. At the south entrance, leave the car and shuttle back to the north entrance to rejoin your party. The north entrance is open for tubing from Memorial Day weekend to Labor Day.

Two shorter floats are available. Instead of the north entrance, start at the **Midpoint Tube Launch** (about a two-hour float from the south entrance) or **Dampier's Landing** (about an hour). For these runs, park at the south entrance (which has free lockers and $1 locks to rent) and walk over to Dampier's or take a tram to Midpoint (trams run Memorial Day weekend to Labor Day), otherwise it's a 12-minute walk. South entrance admission for tubers is $3.25. The south entrance is open for tubing all year.

Canoeing

Canoes, available from nearby concessions for $25 to $45 daily, transportation included, can be launched at the north entrance year-round. Rangers lead sunrise and sunset trips from October to March. Lasting about two hours, the trips cost $10 per person (minimum two per canoe). Canoer admission is $4.25 per person.

PAYNES PRAIRIE STATE PRESERVE

Made up of wet prairie, swamp, hammock and pine flatwoods, this wonderful and eerie preserve (☎ 352-466-3397; pedestrian/car $1/3.25; open 8am-sunset year-round) offers world-class birding (bald eagles, raptors, sandhill cranes) and herds of wild horses and bison. There are also extensive opportunities for hiking and mountain biking (more than 34 trails). And it's all just minutes from Gainesville.

From November to April, guided tours leave from the main visitor's center at 8am Saturday and Sunday. The park also offers ranger-led overnight outings for $10 per person, including marshmallows. The 17-mile **Gainesville-Hawthorne Rail Trail** is, as its name suggests, a rail trail: Popular throughout central Florida, these are built atop abandoned railbeds.

The park's **camping** (without/with hookups $11/14) options include drive-in family sites and walk-in tent sites (which are close to the parking lots). You can reserve up to 60 days in advance, which is a good idea if there are any football games or drag races on during your stay.

The preserve is between Gainesville and Micanopy on Hwy 441 (SW 13th St).

RAWLINGS ESTATE

Marjorie Kinnan Rawlings (1896–1953) was author of the Pulitzer prize–winning novel *The Yearling*, a coming-of-age story set in what is now the Ocala National Forest, and *Cross Creek*, a book about her life at this estate (☎ 352-466-3672; pedestrian/car $1/3.25; open 9am-5pm daily) just north of Orange Lake, off Hwy 325 between Island Grove and Micanopy.

Rawlings came to the area with her first husband in 1928, and she remained in the area after they divorced in 1933. She remarried in 1941 and continued to write at Cross Creek until her death.

The cracker-style house is open for guided tours only (adult/child $3/2, 10am-4pm Thur-Sun) on the hour, limited to 10 people. The rest of the estate, including the orange groves and farmhouse guarded by an amorous rooster, can be perused on your own.

MICANOPY

The oldest landlocked town in Florida, Micanopy (pronounced mick-a-**nope**-ee) has been continuously inhabited for at least 10,000 years. When naturalist William Bertram visited in 1774, Seminole Indians called the village Cuscowilla; they were eventually displaced by European settlers who renamed it Micanope, in honor of the then-chief of the Seminole tribe.

The entire downtown was listed on the Register of Historic Places in 1983, and residents have decided to make that a theme, siphoning antiques and art from the rest of Florida to create a museum-quality collection of stuff that's displayed in the windows of buildings well over a century old. This is no exaggeration: **Delectable Collectibles** (☎ 352-466-3327) on Cholokka Blvd has the second-largest collection of cameos in the world. Down the street, **O Brisky Books** (☎ 352-466-3910) has thousands of rare old books, a few of which are priced at thousands of dollars.

Cholokka Blvd (Hwy 234) is Micanopy's main street; exit Hwy 441 (a right turn if you're coming from Gainesville) and follow the signs. Note that most Micanopy businesses don't use street addresses.

Micanopy Historical Society Museum

One of the few places with rarities that aren't on sale, this museum (☎ 352-466-3200; cnr Cholokka Blvd & Bay St; admission free; open 1pm-4pm daily) is housed in a 1890s barn built by John Early Thrasher. The focus here is on the travels of locally famous botanist William Bertram, who explored the wilds of inland Florida throughout the late 1700s. Artifacts from the original Seminole settlement and relics from the Seminole wars are also on display.

The historical society publishes a free map and walking tour of Micanopy, which you can pick up here. It gives backgrounds to all the interesting old homes and storefronts you've been ignoring while you shop; some of them date back to the early 1800s.

Places to Stay & Eat

There's **camping** at Paynes Prairie State Preserve (earlier this section).

Herlong Mansion Bed & Breakfast (☎ 352-466-3322; 402 NE Cholokka Blvd; rooms $89-179 Sun-Thur, $99-189 Fri & Sat) is in a huge columned edifice built by a lumberman in the early 1900s; the extravagant woodwork includes exotics like mahogany and cypress from all over the world.

Shady Oaks Ice Cream Parlor (☎ 352-466-0725; Cholokka Blvd; dishes $4-8; open 10:30am-6pm daily) serves light sandwiches and salads, so you'll save room for their phenomenal ice cream.

DEVIL'S DEN

Devil's Den (☎ 352-528-3322; open 9am-6pm Mon-Thur, 8am-6pm Fri-Sun) is an underground spring about 18 miles southeast of Gainesville.

Divers simply do not want to miss this fantastic cave-dive opportunity, in one of the most spectacularly odd and beautiful places in the state. Swimming ($9 daily) is also permitted unless too many divers are in the water. It's a fine spot for an overnighter – you can camp at the site.

The spring bubbles up at a constant 72°F, so you can swim comfortably year-round. Divers used to lower themselves down to the springs on rope ladders, but now a staircase has been dug into the ground – it's a wonderful sensation to enter a hole in the ground, walk down through solid rock and emerge into something right out of the movie *The Abyss*. The eerie blue water is illuminated by the sunlight that shines through an opening in the ground, about 20 feet above the surface of the water. The park also has activities like volleyball and horseback riding, all designed to keep the families of obsessed divers entertained while their loved one stays under.

Diving

Certified divers can dive here for $27 daily, and a full line of rental equipment is available (you can even get certified here in four days; prices vary at the discretion of the instructor, but generally run $250 to $300 per person). A basic rental package (not including flashlight, booties or hood) is $67 daily, including admission to the park. The spring has a maximum depth of 56 feet (though droughts compromised this somewhat) and numerous tunnels to explore. You'll see six species of fish in the spring, as well as prehistoric fossils embedded in the cave walls and floor.

Sunset dives on Saturday cost an additional $10 if you've been there all day, or $15 if you show up after 3pm. Night dives can be arranged for groups of six or more.

Places to Stay & Eat

Tent **camping** costs $7 for each adult. Campfires are permitted, but they must be in a fire circle. Cabins with kitchens are $85 to $95 a night and sleep up to four people.

Williston Motor Inn (☎ 352-528-4801; 606 W Noble Ave; rooms $33) caters to the diving crowd with clean rooms and weekly rates. The attached **Hilltop Family Market** (open 7am-9pm daily) serves breakfast all day.

The **Winn-Dixie supermarket** (727 W Noble Ave), on the corner at Hwy 27 in downtown Williston, has groceries and some camping supplies.

Getting There & Away

No public transportation is available. To get here by car from Gainesville take I-75 then Hwy 121 south for 15 miles to the junction of US Hwy 27, which will bring you into downtown Williston. Turn west on Hwy 27A (toward the town of Bronson), turn at the sign and drive past Stonehedge Ranch; the Den is on the right-hand side of the road (look for the dive flag). From Orlando, take Florida's Turnpike north to I-75 north, to exit 70, and then take Hwy 27 north to Williston.

Space Coast

The major attraction on the Space Coast is the Kennedy Space Center – one of two places on Earth from which humans have been launched into space. But the area is also famed for its natural treasures: Bird watchers have a field day at Merritt Island National Wildlife Refuge, and whales have been spotted off Canaveral National Seashore. Some of Florida's finest sea turtle observation programs are also run here. And the strip between Sebastian Inlet and Cocoa Beach has the state's best surfing.

Regardless, the Space Coast is obsessed with its celestial objectives, a theme you won't be able to escape: Rock stations broadcast launch updates; shuttles adorn gas stations, banks and bakeries; even the area code is ☎ 321 (liftoff!).

Consider this typical day in Titusville: The space shuttle launch I'd hoped to see was delayed *again* for three days, and NASA wouldn't announce the specific time until four hours prior to liftoff. I was bemoaning my busy schedule at the gas station when an attendant spoke up: 'Well, STS 110 is headed for the space station, and that's a tight launch window.' His thick Southern drawl paused for some quick calculations. 'Since it moves back about, oh, seven to ten minutes a day, I'd say it'll go up at around 4:30, maybe a quarter to five.'

Sure enough, at 4:44pm Thursday, that beauty blasted into the air. And just about everyone on the Space Coast – surfers, salespeople and scientists alike – felt a certain pride in what had been wrought right here.

KENNEDY SPACE CENTER

KSC (☎ 321-449-4444; W www.kennedy spacecenter.com; adult/child $26/16; open 9am-sundown) is among the most popular attractions in Florida, drawing more than two million people a year. The KSC is also a working spaceport, with missions operating at all times. The robot- and rocket-packed complex is Disney World for scientists and

Highlights

- Watch the space shuttle blast off for orbit

- Visit the Kennedy Space Center and have your awe inspired by the massive Saturn V rocket

- Attend Space Camp to learn rocket science – or offload the kids for a week while you soak in the sun on the nearby beaches

- See birds and wildlife at the Merritt Island National Wildlife Refuge, home to more endangered and protected species than any other refuge in the country

- Surf the best breaks in Florida, between Cocoa Beach and Sebastian Inlet, dude

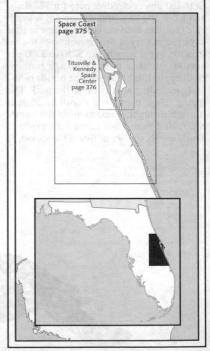

Space Coast
page 375

Titusville &
Kennedy
Space
Center
page 376

space junkies, albeit with only one ride (see the boxed text 'So You Wanna Be an Astronaut…', later in this chapter, for more information), and is a worthwhile diversion for anyone interested in the ultimate form of travel. Plan to spend a day seeing the massive launch apparatus, IMAX theater and absolutely stellar exhibits, including an enormous Saturn V rocket.

History

Early Rocket Science In 1865, French science fiction author Jules Verne published *From Earth to the Moon,* in which three men in a five-stage rocket are shot from Florida's 27°7' north parallel to the lunar surface. In 1969, Neil Armstrong, Michael Collins and Buzz Aldrin would take the five-stage Saturn V rocket from Kennedy Space Center (27°27' north) to the Moon.

It wasn't prophecy, simply logical scientific conjecture (Verne felt the USA had the edge in technology, and the closer you are to the equator, the easier it is to get to the Moon). And in the 1890s, Verne fan and Russian scientist Konstantin Tsiolkovsky built on some of the book's other theories and designed a completely new rocket. It abandoned the use of solid fuel – that'd be gunpowder – in favor of multiple engines powered by liquid hydrogen and oxygen. Modern rocketry was born.

American scientist Robert Goddard launched the first successful guided rocket in 1926. Then, during WWII, Nazi Germany decided to explore the technology's potential. German scientists led by Wernher von Braun perfected the V2 rocket in 1942, which had a range of about 200 miles and could drop bombs from an altitude of 50 miles. After Germany surrendered, US war spoils included von Braun (who would become NASA's deputy chief) and about 100 V2s. The USSR acquired a somewhat less prestigious selection of scientists and equipment.

The Soviets, however, surprised everyone, launching the unmanned satellite *Sputnik* on October 4, 1957. *Vanguard* was launched from Cape Canaveral on March 17, 1958; Soviet premier Khrushchev reportedly called it 'Rearguard.' The race was on.

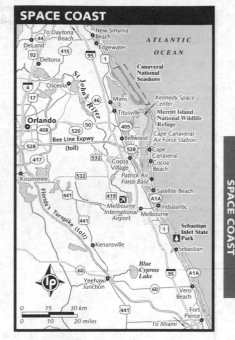

SPACE COAST

The Space Race The National Aeronautics & Space Administration (NASA) was established on October 1, 1958, at Cape Canaveral Air Force Base. They announced Project Mercury the following week. The mission: manned space flight. NASA put 110 American test pilots through an unprecedented battery of physical and psychological tests. Seven were chosen: Virgil 'Gus' Grissom, Deke Slayton, John Glenn, Wally Schirra, Alan Shepard, Scott Carpenter and Gordon Cooper. None would be the first person in space. Soviet cosmonaut Yury Gagarin took that honor on April 12, 1961. A month later, Shepard completed a 15-minute suborbital flight, followed by Glenn's successful orbit, but NASA – and the USA – was wiping egg off its face.

On May 25, 1961, President John F Kennedy announced that the US intended to land a man on the Moon by the end of the decade. As part of the ambitious initiative, a new facility on Merritt Island, just north of

TITUSVILLE & KENNEDY SPACE CENTER

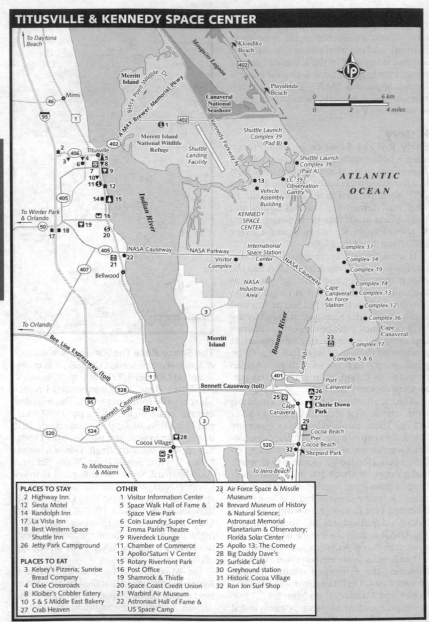

PLACES TO STAY
2 Highway Inn
12 Siesta Motel
14 Randolph Inn
17 La Vista Inn
18 Best Western Space
   Shuttle Inn
26 Jetty Park Campground

PLACES TO EAT
3 Kelsey's Pizzeria; Sunrise
   Bread Company
4 Dixie Crossroads
8 Kloiber's Cobbler Eatery
10 S & S Middle East Bakery
27 Crab Heaven

OTHER
1 Visitor Information Center
5 Space Walk Hall of Fame &
   Space View Park
6 Coin Laundry Super Center
7 Emma Parish Theatre
9 Riverdeck Lounge
11 Chamber of Commerce
13 Apollo/Saturn V Center
15 Rotary Riverfront Park
16 Post Office
19 Shamrock & Thistle
20 Space Coast Credit Union
21 Warbird Air Museum
22 Astronaut Hall of Fame &
   US Space Camp

23 Air Force Space & Missile
   Museum
24 Brevard Museum of History
   & Natural Science;
   Astronaut Memorial
   Planetarium & Observatory;
   Florida Solar Center
25 Apollo 13: The Comedy
28 Big Daddy Dave's
29 Surfside Café
30 Greyhound station
31 Historic Cocoa Village
32 Ron Jon Surf Shop

Cape Canaveral Air Force Station, opened in 1962: NASA's Launch Operations Center. After the forward-thinking president's assassination in 1963, the facility was renamed the John F Kennedy Space Center (KSC).

Soon after, NASA initiated Project Gemini, which would develop the skills and technology necessary for a Moon landing. Gemini used huge Titan II intercontinental ballistic missiles to achieve those goals: space walks, two-week endurance flights, serious piloting, and the rendezvous of Gemini VI-A and Gemini VII. Gemini was declared successful in January 1967, and Project Apollo was announced. NASA was shooting for the Moon. It began tragically. During a test run for the Apollo I, astronauts Gus Grissom, Edward White and Roger Chaffee were killed when their capsule caught fire. Yet the horrible accident inspired upgrades that would culminate with the Apollo 11 flight: On July 20, 1969, the *Eagle* module landed on the Moon's surface. As the world watched, Neil Armstrong delivered one of the best lines ever: 'That's one small step for man, one giant leap for mankind.'

Moving Ahead A total of six Apollo expeditions had landed on the Moon by 1972. (Apollo 13 had suffered a debilitating explosion in one of its oxygen tanks and was unable to land; just making it home was an Odyssean ordeal dramatized in the excellent eponymous movie.) Despite these successes, the taxpaying public was losing interest in yet another (yawn) Moon landing, so NASA turned its attention to creating a space station. Skylab was completed in 1973 and, despite numerous technical difficulties, hosted three crews and 79 successful experiments before falling back to Earth in 1979.

The 1970s marked several historic moments for the space program: The Soviet *Soyuz 19* and *Apollo 18* rendezvous on July 17, 1975, witnessed the first international handshake in space. The Viking and Voyager probes, which have since collected data from Mars, Jupiter and Saturn, were launched. And NASA built its first reusable spacecraft, a delta-winged space plane called an orbiter better known as the space shuttle.

In 1981, space shuttle *Columbia* lifted off from the KSC for its maiden voyage. Designed as transport vehicles, shuttles carried everything from military and commercial satellites to scientific experiments into space. Shuttles also took the first female American, Sally Ride, and the first African American, Guion S Bluford Jr, into zero gravity. Orbiters could also carry civilians. In 1985, charismatic Christa McAuliffe was chosen from a field of 11,000 applicants to be the first 'Teacher in Space.' The world fell in love with McAuliffe, and with the idea that regular people could fly. It was the public relations coup that NASA, reeling from budget cuts, desperately needed.

On January 28, 1986, about 73 seconds after liftoff, the space shuttle *Challenger* suffered an explosion in the external fuel tank; all aboard, including McAuliffe, were killed. The event, televised worldwide, was the worst accident in NASA's history.

Space on a Shoestring The loss of the *Challenger* set the shuttle program back three years, as investigations and redesigns devoured the agency's waning resources. Lucrative contracts with private companies and the Department of Defense were pulled. Civilian passengers would not be considered again until 2002, when NASA chief Sean O'Keefe announced the revival of the Teacher in Space program.

Well, except for one 77-year-old gentleman, that is. But he had a little pull with the agency. In 1998, Ohio Senator John Glenn, who had been the first American in orbit, became the oldest man in space. Though his stated mission was to collect data on how space affects the aging process, it was also hoped that his successful flight would rekindle interest in the space program among taxpayers and, more importantly, among Glenn's congressional colleagues.

Despite contributions like hurricane tracking, global communications and, of course, Tang, many public officials seem to consider NASA little more than an expensive Cold War relic. US politicians often run for office on a platform of cutting taxes, and

SPACE COAST

NASA – run by scientists, not lobbyists – has been an easy target.

When you tour the KSC, note how many offices are in temporary trailers. The landmark Vehicle Assembly Building needs millions of dollars worth of maintenance and repair. The Lunar Base, the Manned Mission to Mars – these programs have essentially been shelved. NASA has been forced to reassess its priorities (see the boxed text 'At What Cost the Stars?' in this chapter).

Results of necessary cost-cutting initiatives have been mixed. While the 'Cheaper, Faster, Better' program was lauded by politicians for streamlining the agency, two of its high-profile Mars probes were lost in 1999. And the flagship shuttle program

runs on technology outclassed by your home computer.

Today, most of the shuttles leaving the KSC are headed for the International Space Station (ISS), a joint venture between the USA, Russia, Brazil, Canada, Japan and the 14 members of the European Space Agency. The ISS has been plagued with difficulties since the beginning. Russia, by far NASA's most important partner, couldn't reach the proposed orbit from its Baikonur Cosmodrome in Kazakhstan; the compromise orbit has been an expensive headache affecting all KSC launches. Worse, the collapse of the Russian economy in the early 1990s stuck NASA with an extra $600 million bill. Other partners complain loudly (and endlessly)

At What Cost the Stars?

And NASA thought putting men on the Moon was challenging. Heck, that was just rocket science. Those old-timers should try begging the US congress for enough cash to achieve what's considered possible: sending humans, and lots of us, to the stars.

At the height of the Cold War, the US space program got 4% of the US federal budget; today it receives only 0.7%, about $15 billion annually. Massive layoffs and aging equipment now compromise NASA's once cutting-edge capabilities. Gravity is no longer our biggest obstacle to becoming a space-faring species. Today's hurdles are financial.

In 1995, hoping to stretch their resources, NASA announced the 'Faster, Cheaper, Better' program, launching two probes – the Mars Observer and Mars Climate Orbiter – on Delta II launch vehicles instead of the recommended Titans. The savings? Three hundred million dollars a shot. But the discount launches necessitated using an experimental Aero-braking system upon entering Mars atmosphere; neither probe made it. There are other explanations for the failures that can't be blamed on budget cuts, such as a fuel leak and engineering flaws (some scientists were using imperial measurements, others metric – d'oh!). Still, the adage 'you get what you pay for' had humans, hopeful for a permanent Mars colony in our lifetimes, sighing over opportunities lost.

More embarrassing, the space shuttle, NASA's de facto symbol, runs almost entirely on obsolete technology. Scientists must now scour eBay for ancient Intel 8086 chips (circa 1981) to keep America aloft. The folks that brought us the Saturn V have mastered the art of garbage picking.

NASA is finally learning to play politics, however. By awarding International Space Station (ISS) contracts to companies in 20 different states, they've managed to keep key members of congress somewhat interested. This strategy, unsurprisingly, has produced a ridiculously expensive station with huge technical problems. But at least it's there. Critics also note that new spacecraft designs aren't chosen for their engineering excellence but for their appeal to private contractors – whose lobbyists keep NASA in business. Sad, but shrewd.

The next challenge? Getting funding for a Pluto mission in time for the January 2006 launch window (the next one is in 2018). But congress has more generous donors to feed. 'The conquest of space is worth the risk of life,' said astronaut Gus Grissom, who perished in Apollo I's flames. But is it worth risking reelection? That's a tougher call.

about delays but have their own budgets to stick to.

Regardless, NASA has learned to make due, moving the space program forward in spite of cutbacks and layoffs. Mars, which probably has everything necessary for permanent human habitation, is now the agency's most important extraorbital focus. NASA has long had the skills and technology to get us there. But whether humans walk on the Red Planet in our lifetimes depends on the rest of us.

Orientation

The Kennedy Space Center (KSC) takes up about 46,000 acres on Merritt Island. Much of it is used for NASA facilities, but the northern third of the island is wilderness area, comprising Merritt Island National Wildlife Refuge and Canaveral National Seashore.

The Visitor Complex is located on the east side of the Intracoastal Waterway (here called Indian River), accessible from Titusville via Columbia Blvd (Hwy 405; NASA Pkwy) and from Cocoa Beach and Orlando on Hwy 528 (Bee Line Expressway). The Banana River separates the KSC from Cape Canaveral Air Force Station.

All commercial maps of the facility are distorted to protect sensitive areas, but colorful handouts at the information desk are helpful for finding your way around. Facilities outside the Visitor Complex are accessible by tour bus only.

Information

There's an **information desk** (☎ 321-449-4444; 9am-sundown) at the Visitor Complex. In addition to pamphlets and a friendly, multilingual staff, they provide lockers and audio guides in several languages. Guests with disabilities can call ☎ 321-449-4364 (voice) or ☎ 321-454-4198 (TDD) to arrange special tours in advance.

There are **ATMs** at the Visitor Complex, Apollo/Saturn V Center and, of course, the Space Shop. The Space Shop also has an enormous selection of hard-to-find books on NASA and space travel. NASA broadcasts countdowns and other space news on 920 AM, available throughout the Space

Coast. Television channel 15, also available throughout the Space Coast, has a constant video feed of NASA operations.

Note that security has increased dramatically since September 11, 2001. Do yourself a favor and leave your backpack at the hotel.

Visitor Complex

The entryway to America's Spaceport is no longer free – you pay your admission, which covers all IMAX shows and a bus tour, at the Skylab-inspired ticket plaza before entering the facilities. The Visitor Complex features excellent – nay, mind-blowing – exhibits accompanied by explanations geared for the average spaceaholic with a high school education; for more technical discussions of events and hardware, visit the Space Shop bookstore and prepare to be overwhelmed.

Overpriced eateries abound, including the Moon Rock Café at the Apollo/Saturn V Center, which enhances your dining experience with a chunk of Earth's oldest satellite. Tour buses to the LC-39 Observation Gantry, Apollo/Saturn V Center and International Space Station Center leave the Visitors Complex every 15 minutes from 10am to 2:45pm daily.

NASA for Kids Several exhibits at the Visitor Complex are designed to lure youngsters into the world of math and science, using the promise of potential space travel as bait. You can help by picking up an Interplanetary Passport at the gift shops, which kids can have stamped throughout the KSC. The **Kid's Play Dome** is for smaller children, who like the climbable versions of the space shuttle and ISS, and **Exploration in the New Millennium** will entertain older kids with interactive displays and the opportunity to touch a rock from Mars. Don't miss **Robot Scouts**, which introduces young people to talkative 'trailblazers for human exploration.'

Rockets & Spacecraft The **Rocket Garden**, visible from anywhere in the complex, is an inspiring collection of Redstone, Atlas and Titan rockets, originally developed by the military to blow people up but adapted by NASA to send them into outer space. The massive Apollo Saturn 1B rocket is the exception, designed specifically to carry astronauts up, up and away.

Inside the Visitor Complex are dozens more spacecraft and scale models, including the *Gemini 9* and a mockup of the Apollo-Soyuz rendezvous (the Apollo capsule is real, the Soyuz is a full-scale model). Some vessels are covered with transparent plastic, allowing you to peer inside and wonder just how astronauts could stand being cooped up in those things for so long.

The **Shuttle Plaza** features a full-size model of a space shuttle, dubbed *Explorer*. Walk through the cockpit and check out the cargo bay, which was recently refitted with a mock-up of the new Canadian-engineered payload arm. Don't miss the steering rockets or the custom-fitted heat tiles outside, which must be replaced after each reentry using an exacting process that would send Henry Ford into conniption fits.

Next to the Shuttle Plaza is the **Astronaut Memorial**, its black granite expanse inscribed with the names of those who have given their lives so that, one day, our own planet might not feel quite so lonely.

IMAX Theater The five-story-high screens of the Complex's two IMAX theaters show films throughout the day. *The Dream Is Alive* includes footage taped during various missions, and *L5: First City in Space* features a truly awesome sequence depicting a space shuttle launch in 3D.

In the same building, the **NASA Art Gallery** has works commissioned by the agency to render data they've collected from other celestial bodies into images – landscapes, really – that nonscientists can comprehend. Many of the Hubble Space Telescope's best shots are also on display.

Astronaut Encounter Yes, the 'I Want to Be an Astronaut' song hurts, but it's just the introduction to a guaranteed highlight of your visit: A question-and-answer period with a real, live astronaut. Story Musgrave, who helped repair the Hubble Telescope in orbit, was speaking when I was there – what a treat! Inevitable questions about bathroom

breaks aside, it's interesting to hear tales of weightlessness and radiation from the people who've experienced them. Please, *please* don't ask if we really got to the Moon (see the boxed text 'Was the Moon Landing a Hoax?'). You'll sound like a moron, and even if it was a hoax, it's not like they're going to tell you.

LC-39 Observation Gantry
The first stop on the bus tour into the real meat of the KSC facility is this 60-foot (18m) observation tower, with great views of Launch Pads 39A and 39B, from which the space shuttle is hurled into space. A couple of films show simplified explanations of how shuttles are loaded and prepped for flight once they've made it to the launch pad. More interesting is the 14-foot-long, 7000lb main engine from one of the shuttles.

Launch Facilities
The bus continues its tour through the launch facilities themselves. As you might imagine, there are plenty of superlatives involved. My favorite factoid predates the Shuttle: When Apollo 5 left the facility in 1967, it produced the loudest sound humans have ever made. Yes, including the nuclear bomb.

The **Vehicle Assembly Building** (VAB), where Saturn rockets and later space shuttles have been assembled and stored, is among the largest in the world. The **Crawler Transporters**, which carry the Shuttle at a blistering 1mph from the VAB to the launch pad, weigh 6 million pounds (2.7 metric tons) apiece and are two of the world's heaviest vehicles. Even the runway where the space shuttle lands, at 15,000 feet (4572m) long, is in the record books.

Apollo/Saturn V Center
The **Saturn V** rocket is still one of the most complex pieces of machinery we simians have ever come up with: It's big, it's bad, and it put us on the Moon. And you can see one of the few remaining examples right here, in all of its lovingly restored glory. And that's just the beginning. The center contains some of the most important relics of the space race, including the **Lunar**

Was the Moon Landing a Hoax?

Some conspiracy theorists claim that the Moon landings were actually filmed right here on Earth. Well, this is the same government that – ahem – didn't have troops in Cambodia at the time, so let's take quick look at the debate.

Conspiracy Theorists: The flag rippled, but there's no wind on the Moon.

NASA: *The Moon's gravity is a fraction of Earth's; thus, the flag continued to vibrate for longer than you'd expect after being planted.*

CTs: There are no stars in any of the pictures.

NASA: *Those photos were taken in full sunlight, requiring a narrow aperture that couldn't register faint daytime stars*

CTs: There were no flames during takeoff.

NASA *The lander used a mixture of hydrazine and dinitrogen tetroxide for fuel, which doesn't produce flames.*

CTs: Some photos show objects in front of the lens crosshairs.

NASA: *This effect is common in overexposed film.*

Why would NASA paint giant crosshairs on the back of the set, anyway? Sheesh. The agency also points to its 1000lb (450kg) Moon rock collection as proof they were there, as well as the fact that the USSR and other less-than-friendly nations monitored, and verified, all communications. I'm convinced.

Module and **Command Service Module** from the Apollo program.

Even better is the **Firing Room Theater**, preceded by a movie that will impress upon people too young to remember the Cold War the drive those tensions inspired. The main feature is a remarkable multimedia recreation of the frenetic Apollo 8 launch. It uses the original equipment from mission command as props, plus video footage on three huge screens and a sound-and-light show that approximates what technicians experienced at the moment of liftoff. Wow.

The **Lunar Theater** attempts to dramatize Neil Armstrong's riveting Moon landing with equal flair but ends up feeling a little too sticky sweet. Don't miss the preview footage, however, with Walter Cronkite's classic coverage of the event.

International Space Station Center

This center is so cutting-edge that it was off-limits because of new and hopefully temporary antiterrorism protocols. Drat. If it's open, you'll see the actual facility where NASA is processing ISS components, as well as replicas of living quarters and work modules on the station.

Organized Tours & Programs

In addition to the bus tour included with your admission, the KSC offers several other special tours and programs, most costing a bit extra. You can order tickets by calling ☎ 321-249-2444 or logging on to ⓦ www.ksctickets .com. There's a free tour of the **Rocket Garden** at 11am and 3pm daily.

NASA Up Close (adult/child $46/36) includes regular admission plus a two-hour tour of 'restricted areas,' where the space shuttle is refitted after landing and is prepped for launch. This is supposed to be an excellent option, but note that just prior to a launch, this tour is cut short (no refunds).

Cape Canaveral Then and Now (adult/child $46/36) tops off your visit with a two-hour tour of the sites where Alan Shepard and John Glenn blasted off on their historic Mercury missions. 'Hanger S,' where early astronauts lived and trained, and the Cape Canaveral Lighthouse are also included on this tour.

The best place to watch a **space shuttle launch** is from the KSC. Car passes to the viewing site have been suspended indefinitely, but you can still purchase bus tickets (order early) from NASA (☎ 321-867-4636). The KSC also offers a package that combines launch tickets with another (ful)filling experience: **Dine with an Astronaut** (adult/child $72/51) before or after liftoff.

Note that all launch tickets must be tracked for security reasons, and shipping within the USA costs at least $10, overseas $30. If a launch is delayed, your tickets may be used for subsequent attempts (same mission only) or exchanged for one movie at the IMAX theater. If you didn't get your tickets in time, there are still plenty of places outside the KSC with fine views (See the boxed text 'Let's Do Launch,' in this chapter).

Getting There & Away

From I-95, Hwy A1A or US Hwy 1, Kennedy Space Center is almost impossible to miss. From Orlando, take Hwy 528 (the Bee Line Expressway) straight east to the entrance.

Getting here without a car is difficult. Greyhound only has service as close as Cocoa and Titusville; from Orlando it's $18, though that doesn't include the taxi (about $15) from Cocoa to the KSC.

AROUND KENNEDY SPACE CENTER

The area around the KSC is federally protected wilderness area and usually open to the public. Many of these areas are closed the day before a launch – days, if there are delays or terrorism alerts. Call ahead. You can camp on Apollo Beach, if you've got a canoe or kayak, on several islands within the Canaveral National Seashore.

Great information about the area is available on the web at **W** www.space-coast.com.

Merritt Island National Wildlife Refuge

NASA uses only about 5% of its total land-holdings for making things that go boom. In 1963, NASA turned management of its unused land over to the US Fish & Wildlife Service (USFWS), who then established this refuge (☎ 321-861-0667; admission free; open 8am-4:30pm Mon-Fri, 9am-5pm Sat & Sun, closed Sun Apr-Oct). At press time, ramped-up security closed the park three days prior to launch and one day before a landing.

The **visitor's center**, located 4 miles east of Titusville on SR 402 (exit 80 off I-95) has lots of informative pamphlets, including a self-guided tour around the refuge's most popular and easily accessible attraction, the **Black Point Wildlife Drive**, a 6-mile loop. **Boardwalk Trail** is a quarter-mile nature trail next to the center.

Three other hiking trails begin about a mile east of the main visitor's center: the half-mile **Oak Hammock Trail**; the 2-mile **Palm Hammock Trail**, which winds through hardwood forest and has boardwalks above the open marsh; and the 5-mile **Cruickshank Trail**, which begins at stop 8 along the Black Point Wildlife Drive.

The refuge is notable because its mangrove swamps, marshes and hardwood hammocks are home to more endangered and threatened species than any other refuge in the continental USA. Along with Canaveral National Seashore, the area is also one of the best birding spots in the country. Located on the Atlantic Flyway, this is migration central, as birds head back and forth between North and South America. You can pick up a free bird-spotting guide at the visitor's center.

The best time to visit is from October to May, as that's the height of migratory bird season and also when the climate is most comfortable. From March to September, thousands of wading birds can be seen in spectacular breeding plumage throughout the park.

Canaveral National Seashore

The 25 miles of windswept beaches along this seashore (☎ 321-267-1110; **W** www.nps.gov/

cana; open 6am-6pm daily winter, 6am-8pm summer; pedestrian/car $1/5) are a favorite haunt of surfers, campers and nature lovers.

All of the park's visitor programs and information services are handled by the **North District Visitors Center** (☎ 321-267-1110), located 7 miles south of New Smyrna Beach on Hwy A1A. It shows an excellent 12-minute video of the park's facilities, campsites and trails, and has pamphlets and monthly activity schedules available. **Sea Turtle Watching** programs take small groups (a strict maximum of 20 people) along the beach between June and July starting at about 10:30pm. Call for reservations up to eleven months in advance.

The park also maintains a **South District Office** (☎ 321-867-4077), located 12 miles east of Titusville on SR 402. Note that the South District is closed for four days around shuttle launches.

The real reason you're here, however, is the seashore. **Apollo Beach**, to the north, is favored by families because of the calm surf (watch out for riptides, though). **Klondike Beach**, the 12-mile stretch between Apollo and Playalinda Beaches, is as pristine as it gets, with nary a nature trail to mar it. **Playalinda Beach**, at the southern end, is surfer headquarters, with decent (for Florida) breaks and lots of guys named Dude.

You can canoe or kayak through Mosquito Lagoon, though winds can get strong. **Village Outfitters** (see Activities in the Cocoa Village & Cocoa Beach section, later) operates kayak tours through the area.

You can **camp** (☎ 386-428-3384; $10 daily for up to 6 people) at Apollo Beach from November to mid-April. If you've got a boat, there are 11 primitive campsites, open year-round and scattered throughout the islands. Make reservations early, and note that there is no camping during shuttle launches.

Air Force Space & Missile Museum

Located on the grounds of Space Launch Complex 5/6, where Alan Shepard took off to become the first American in space, this museum (☎ 321-853-3245; Complex 26 at Cape Canaveral Air Station; open 10am-2pm

Mon-Fri, 10am-4pm, closed on launch days; admission free) sounds amazing. It's got restored hardware from the early days of space travel, mementos from the Mercury missions, and Jupiter and Redstone rockets on display. Military launches still blast off nearby, so it's been closed since September 11, 2001, for security reasons. Darn it. Give them a call to see if it's reopened.

TITUSVILLE

Titusville is the main gateway to both the Kennedy Space Center and the wildlife refuge, and it has excellent vantage points for watching a launch. NASA cutbacks (see the boxed text 'At What Cost the Stars,' in this chapter) have been hard on the city, which now boasts some of the most affordable real estate on Florida's Atlantic Coast.

Information
The **Chamber of Commerce** (☎ 321-267-3036; Ⓦ www.space-coast.com; 2000 S Washington Ave; open 9am-5pm Mon-Fri) is geared primarily toward businesspeople and residents but has some helpful information.

Banks are plentiful, but check out the **Space Coast Credit Union** (☎ 321-724-5730; 5445 S Washington Ave), with a logo remarkably similar to Lonely Planet's. There's a **post office** (686 Cheney Hwy) in the Winn-Dixie shopping plaza.

Florida Today (Ⓦ www.floridatoday.com) is the major daily and publishes a map to shuttle-viewing sites the day of a launch. The *Star-Advocate* is their more in-depth weekly publication. *Brevard Live* has events listings for the entire county.

The **Coin Laundry Super Center** (☎ 321-383-1358; 600 S Park Dr) actually is pretty super, especially if you like video games.

Astronaut Hall of Fame
This entertaining museum (☎ 321-269-6100; Ⓦ www.astronauthalloffame.com; 6225 Vectorspace Blvd; adult/child $14/10; open 9am-5pm daily, until liftoff on launch days) is open for launch (unlike the Kennedy Space Center) and has one of the prime viewing spots in Titusville. If NASA scrubs the flight, they'll even let you in with your old ticket

for the next attempt(s). Launch days are packed, but you may get to see 'Mod' Maury Hersom's Space Shuttle Columbia – a rare 1942 Chevrolet with a NASA paint job and (oh yes!) propane-fueled booster engines – parked outside.

Much of the museum is kid-oriented, but it's definitely of interest to any space junkie. Pass the mural painted by astronaut Alan Bean to enter the theater, where sitting through the smarmy film is worth what's waiting on the other side.

A room filled with spinning rides and motion simulators (obsolete for astronauts but still packing a 4G wallop) is the highlight of the show. Colorful and technologically impressive displays transform physics problems into video games. Exhibits include a life-sized model of the space shuttle, a tribute to the astronauts lost in the Apollo I disaster and the actual Apollo 14 module. All are accompanied by explanations that make no bones about where this museum stands in the 'small probes versus human explorers' debate.

'Some came to believe the old fallacy that robots can explore space as well as people, but more cheaply,' they note, discussing early problems with the shuttle program. Newly appointed NASA chief Sean O'Keefe, a proponent of robot exploration, will (hopefully) have his hands full with folks who've experienced this fine attraction.

The **Hall of Fame** is well done but oddly only includes American astronauts – Yury Gagarin, the first person in space, is not mentioned.

US Space Camp

One of the most innovative ideas in summer camp is this program (☎ 321-269-6100, 800-897-5798; W www.spacecamp.com; 6225 Vectorspace Blvd), on the grounds of the Astronaut Hall of Fame. Rocket pioneer Wernher von Braun came up with the idea as a way of encouraging kids to study math and science. The original space camp opened in Huntsville, Alabama, in 1982, and this one opened in 1988. Since then, more than 30,000 kids have attended programs here.

Courses teach space science and rocket propulsion, and require simulated shuttle missions and astronaut training from different eras of the space program. Participants also perform experiments in physics, chemistry and space science. You can see many of the facilities free with your admission to the Astronaut Hall of Fame; if you want a closer look, you'll need to enroll.

Five-day programs run $700 to $800, including room and board, but they're only for nine to 14 year olds. Jealous? Find a willing kid to accompany you for the three-day parent/child program ($350). Still no luck? There's a space camp for adults ($900) in Huntsville.

Warbird Air Museum

In the TICO (pronounced Ti-tus-ville Co-coa) Space Center Airport, this museum (☎ 321-

---

So You Wanna Be an Astronaut...

Think you've got the right stuff? NASA picks new astronauts about every two years, and US citizens have first priority. You'll need at the very least a degree in biology, physics or mathematics and three years of related professional experience. Pilot astronaut applicants must have logged at least 1000 hours of pilot-in-command time on jet aircraft and must be able to pass a NASA Class 1 space physical. Mission specialists must pass a Class 2 space physical.

Wanna try? Download the appropriate forms at W www.nasajobs.nasa.gov/jobs/astronauts/aso/application.htm, fill them out and send them in to the Astronaut Selection Office, Mail Code AHX, Johnson Space Center, 2101 NASA Rd One, Houston, TX 77058.

May the force be with you.

– Nick & Corinna Selby

268-1941; 6600 Tico Rd; adult/child $9/5; open 10am-6pm daily) offers exhibits of historic war aircraft. The star here is a functioning C-47, built in October 1942, that's a veteran of the Normandy invasion. Other highlights include an F-14 Tomcat, a supersonic Crusader that flies using the computer that originally operated Apollo I, and the last UH-1 to make it out of Vietnam after the fall of Saigon. You can also see planes in various stages of restoration; when I was there, they were working on a wildcat that had spent 50 years underwater. Each year, the museum holds an air show as a fundraiser for itself and its aviation scholarship program; the show is held the second week of March, and more than 100 warbirds take part.

To get here from I-95, take exit 79 to Hwy 405 east and follow the signs; the airport's on the right.

Space Walk Hall of Fame

Located on the Indian River at Broad St, just south of SR 406 at Space View Park, this monument and museum (☎ 321-264-0434; w www.spacewalkoffame.com; free admission; open 10am-5pm Mon-Sat, noon-5pm Sun) celebrates the achievements of the Mercury and Gemini programs with stately monoliths. At the base of the monuments, topped with the astrological symbols for Mercury and Gemini, are the bronzed handprints of the astronauts of those programs. The small museum features the handprints of various Apollo astronauts (a monument is in the works), models on loan from the KSC and other space relics that different astronauts have donated from their private collections. The park, open 24/7, is a great place to view a shuttle launch.

Places to Stay

Accommodations here aren't cheap for what you get, and prices rise astronomically during the week of a shuttle launch. There's a cluster of chain places around exit 79 (Cheney Hwy) off I-95, and a string of older hotels along Washington Ave (Hwy 1), some with great views of takeoff.

Manatee Hammock Park (☎ 321-264-5083; sites without/with hookups $20/22),

just south of Titusville at 7275 S US Hwy 1 in Bellwood, is a family-oriented campground with laundry facilities, a pool and a nature trail running straight through the place.

KOA Cape Kennedy Campground (☎ 321-269-7361, 800-848-4562; 4513 W Main St;

Tourists in Space

So you forgot to join the military and got your degree in art history. Now you'll never get to go up into space. Right? Don't be so sure. San Diego equity-fund manager Dennis Tito made history in 2001, spending a reported $20 million for eight days on the International Space Station (ISS) as a guest of the Russian space program. NASA fought against it, but eventually accepted that the Russians are just die-hard capitalists – they even let Pizza Hut advertise on a Proton rocket in 2000. And so the era of space tourism begins.

The Russians have since hosted the coincidentally named Mark Shuttleworth, a South African Internet millionaire (well, he *was* a millionaire) on Soyuz, making him the first person born in Africa in space. At press time, they were training Lance Bass, member of boy band N'Sync, to fly. Right alongside him (and the envy of preteen girls everywhere) is former NASA official Lori Garver; even she couldn't land a spot on the space shuttle.

Why isn't cash-strapped NASA interested in space tourism? For one, the US government forbids it. Second, it costs around $450 million to launch a shuttle, while Soyuz catches air for about $25 million. It's just not worth it to NASA to have art historians on board, getting in the astronauts' way. So it's either Soyuz or stay home.

If you don't have $20 million to blow on a weeklong vacation, there are other options: Space Adventures (book through w www.realbuzz.co.uk), Incredible Adventures (w www.incredible-adventures.com) and Novac Space Travel (w www.novacspacetravel.com) are all offering seats on as-yet-unproven spacecraft for $50,000 to $650,000 a pop. Make reservations well in advance.

sites without/with hookups $20/23, Kamping Kabins $30-40) is up in the town of Mims, just north of Titusville.

Highway Inn (☎ 321-269-9310; 3480 Garden St; rooms $40/55 nonlaunch/launch) has the best deal in town on clean, no-frills rooms. It's right off I-95, exit 80.

La Vista Inn (☎ 321-269-7110, 800-715-7110; w www.lavistainn.com; 3655 Cheney Hwy; $55/70 nonlaunch/launch) has clean, spacious rooms and a groovy faux-natural pool with a waterfall.

Siesta Motel (☎ 321-267-1455; 2006 S Washington Ave; rooms $39/95 nonlaunch/launch) has basic rooms with good launch views, and they *love* Canadians. So swing by, eh?

The Randolph Inn (☎ 321-269-5945; 3810 S Washington Ave; rooms $64/99 nonlaunch/launch) is nicer than the average Washington Ave hotel, with a pool and great Continental breakfast.

Best Western Space Shuttle Inn (☎ 321-269-1000, 800-523-7654; w www.space shuttleinn.com; rooms $75/112 nonlaunch/launch) has typically pleasant rooms – and a few strange ones. For a little extra cash, you can stay in their Evergreen Rooms, with filtered drinking systems and custom air cleaners, or the Space Shuttle Fantasy Room, where you get to sleep in your very own orbiter.

Places to Eat
Sunrise Bread Company (☎ 321-268-1009; 2825 Garden St; open 6am-6pm Mon-Sat) has great coffee to wash down cinnamon buns, scones and other breakfast treats, as well as loaves of excellent bread.

S&S Middle East Bakery (☎ 321-269-0702; 1309 S Washington; sandwiches $2-4; open 8am-7pm Mon-Sat) is great for vegetarians: Falafel, homemade hummus and excellent tabouli are just some of the good stuff in the deli case; try a spinach pie.

Kloiber's Cobbler Eatery (☎ 321-383-0689; 337 S Washington Ave; dishes $3-7; open 8am-4pm Mon, 8am-8pm Tues-Sat) has more substantial breakfasts and an excellent chicken-salad sandwich. Delicious fresh-fruit cobbler is made from scratch daily.

Kelsey's Pizzaria (☎ 321-268-5555; 2845 Garden St; dishes $5-9; open 11am-10pm daily) has great pizza and a hearty Greek salad.

Dixie Crossroads (☎ 321-268-5000; 1475 Garden St; mains $9-18; open 11am-10pm daily), 2 miles east of exit 80 off I-95, is always packed with tourists and locals. The specialty is rock shrimp ($9 dozen, $12 two dozen), but all sorts of seafood and steak dishes are on the menu.

Entertainment
Titusville is more an abandoned blue-collar burg than a thriving beach town, and most evening options involve cheap beer at dive bars. There are a few exceptions, however.

Emma Parish Theatre (☎ 321-268-1125; 301 Julia St; adult/child $15/13), in the historic district, does community theater in addition to hosting dance troupes and orchestras. *Delicious Demise Survival Style* is the latest incarnation of their signature murder-mystery series, which features audience participation, snacks and prizes.

Riverdeck Lounge (☎ 321-383-1288; 1829 Riverside Dr; open noon-2am Mon-Sat, 1pm-midnight Sun) has pool tables, a pleasant outdoor patio and karaoke Monday and Tuesday, as well as other special events.

Shamrock & Thistle (☎ 321-385-9611; 2035 Cheney Hwy; open 11am-2am Mon-Sat, 1pm-midnight Sun) is your basic traditional Irish pub with 19 brews on tap, darts and pub grub like fish & chips ($6) to soak up all that Guinness. They have live music on 'special nights.'

Getting There & Around
Greyhound (☎ 321-267-8760; 100 S Hopkins Ave) serves Titusville; you can catch a Space Coast Area Transit (SCAT) bus nearby to almost anywhere in the county (not the Kennedy Space Center, however).

SCAT (☎ 321-633-1878, 952-4672; w www .ridescat.com; ticket $1) is an inconvenient public bus system that serves the entire Space Coast. Titusville is served Monday to Friday only. Bus No 2 infrequently operates along Cheney Hwy, Washington Ave (US Hwy 1) throughout downtown and Garden St.

COCOA VILLAGE & COCOA BEACH

Snuggled between Cape Canaveral and Patrick Air Force Base is the optimistically named city of Cocoa Beach. As *I Dream of Jeannie* fans may already suspect, this is basically a service town for NASA and the air force bases, albeit with a hard-packed sand beach filled with partiers and surfers.

Historic Cocoa Village, due west across the causeway, has upscale restaurants, shops and lots of historic buildings; pick up a brochure with a self-guided tour at the chamber of commerce.

Information

Cocoa Beach's **Chamber of Commerce** (☎ 231-459-2200; 400 Fortenberry Rd; open 9am-5pm Mon-Fri) is located on Merritt Island.

Cocoa Beach Public Library (☎ 321-868-1104; 550 N Brevard Ave; open 10am-5pm Tues-Sat) has free Internet access.

There's a **Washington Mutual** (☎ 888-497-3287; 505 Brevard Ave) nearby.

Cocoa Village is a bimonthly paper covering local stories.

The **post office** (cnr 4th St & N Brevard Ave) is one block west of Hwy A1A.

Cocoa Beach Coin Laundry (☎ 321-783-0336; 66 S Atlantic; open 24/7) is in downtown Cocoa Beach.

Astronaut Memorial Planetarium & Observatory

This excellent planetarium and observatory (☎ 321-634-3732; W www.brevard.cc.fl.us/planet; 1519 Clearlake Rd; adult/student $6/5 single show, $10/8 two shows; open 7pm-10:30pm Fri & Sat) houses Florida's largest public-access telescope. Budget cuts, however, have limited hours to Friday and Saturday night only. The observatory is open from sunset until 10:30pm.

Planetarium shows start at 7pm and show off what's billed as the world's only tandem team of Digistar planetarium projectors and America's only Minolta Infinium star projector. Afterward, at 8pm, films are shown in the three-story-high IWERKS (it's like IMAX, but smaller) theater. Laser light shows ($6) start at 9pm. The planetarium is on the Broward Community College (BCC) campus, off Clearlake Rd between Michigan Ave and Rosetine St; from US Hwy 1 take Dixon Blvd west to Clearlake and turn north; the campus is on the left.

Brevard Museum of History & Natural Science

BCC's other claim to fame, this museum (☎ 321-632-1830; 2201 Michigan Ave; adult/child $3/2.50; open 10am-4pm Tues-Sat, 1pm-4pm Sun) has a permanent collection including local historical artifacts, archaeological items including 7000-year-old Indian artifacts and exhibits on area wildlife. It also holds special exhibits on subjects as diverse as arachnids, powder horns and early-20th-century weaponry. A pleasant, shady trail around the lake (closed at sunset) links the museum and observatory.

Florida Solar Energy Center

This working research facility (☎ 321-638-1015; 1679 Clearlake Rd; open 9am-5pm Mon-Sat; free admission), also on the BCC campus, has a warehouse-sized room full of exhibits relating to solar energy and one of the world's largest research libraries devoted to the technology. Call ahead to arrange tours.

Ron Jon Surf Shop

You've seen the billboards, now visit the store (☎ 321-799-8888; W www.ronjons.com; 4151 N Atlantic Ave; open 24/7). It's more than just a shop: Live music (think Beach Boys cover bands), classic cars and a warehouse packed to the rafters with swimsuits, surfboards and more make this an experience. Next door, Ron Jon Watersports rents all manner of equipment; see Activities, below.

Cocoa Beach Pier

This festive pier (adult/child $4/3 to fish, spectator 50¢) is 800 feet long and often features live music on weekends. Parking is $5. You can rent a rod and reel for $10, which includes pier access, and buy bait for $3. Restaurants and bars pack the first (free) half of the pier, and the **Tiki Bar** at the very tip may be the finest spot in Cocoa Beach to watch a launch.

Beaches

Cocoa has three public beaches. **Shepard Park**, at the end of Hwy 580, is more family oriented, while **Cocoa Beach**, by the pier, is by far the busiest and caters to space tourists and the surf crowd. **Downtown Cocoa Beach**, at the intersection of Minuteman Causeway and Hwy A1A, is geared toward adults, with a collection of cool bars and upscale restaurants abutting the sand.

Let's Do Launch

It's the modern equivalent of watching those first ambitious fish haul themselves up onto dry land, topped off with the explosive power of the world's most expensive firework. If you ever need a little inspiration, a space shuttle launch will make you appreciate how remarkable human beings really are.

Begin by contacting the Kennedy Space Center (☎ 321-867-4636; Ⓦ www.kennedyspace center.com/html/see_launch.html) to find out if there's a launch during your visit (you can also order tickets to view the launch; see Organized Tours & Programs in the Kennedy Space Center section of this chapter). If you can't get tickets to KSC facilities, don't worry. There are plenty of great places to see shuttles soar: Try the Astronaut Hall of Fame, Jetty Park Campground, Cherie Down Park, Rotary Riverfront Park, Space View Park, Cocoa Beach Pier, Bennet Causeway (Hwy 528) and the Brewer Pkwy bridge in Titusville.

Make hotel reservations early, and plan to stay for a while. The launch I viewed, STS-110, was delayed three times due to mechanical problems and windy weather, a week which culminated with a nail-biting countdown that had technicians reloading software onto space shuttle *Atlantis* in the final minutes.

It's worth checking launch status throughout the day (☎ 231-867-4636) if you're, say, in Orlando, but Space Coast news stations cover NASA operations obsessively: Weather broadcasts begin with 'There's a 40% chance of a successful launch,' rather than boring us with hurricane warnings. Most area radio stations also have regular updates.

Get to your viewing site early, and bring binoculars and extra beer – it's an international tailgate party no matter where you end up. Vendors sell ice cream, soda and even mission-specific T-shirts ($10; they make great souvenirs). Tune into 920 AM for up-to-the-minute reports and, five minutes before the big event, the countdown.

At the launch I viewed, the anticipation was thicker than solid fuel in a pressurized tank for STS-110. I was parked at the Brewer Pkwy bridge, blocked in by dozens of cars – no one cared, no one was going anywhere. Folks from all over the world were taking turns with my friend Linda's telescope, examining *Atlantis* from across the bay, imagining it straining against the launch apparatus, eager to fly. 'The wind may be too strong today,' announced one man, his ear to the radio. We had 28 minutes until the launch window opened. Prayers to various deities ensued. 'The shuttle's computers went down,' another woman yelled. The window would close in nine minutes.

But NASA came through with seconds to spare, and the whole Space Coast started chanting: 'Three, two, one – LIFTOFF!' And there were flames, then clouds of steam, and then a silent ascent into the stratosphere. 'Here comes the noise,' a father whispered to his son. Windshields rattled in response to the roar; not one of us covered our ears. And *Atlantis* was gone.

Activities

Village Outfitters (☎ 231-633-7245; **W** www
.villageoutfitters.com; 113 Brevard Ave; open
10am-6pm Mon-Fri, 10am-4pm Sat), in
Cocoa Village, runs half-day kayak tours
(single/double kayak $30/45) to Merritt
Island Refuge, Pine Island and elsewhere, including tours of wild beaches with awesome
views of the shuttle launch. They also do
more challenging trips throughout the area.

Ron Jon's Watersports (☎ 321-799-8840;
4151 N Atlantic Ave; open 8am-8pm daily),
next to the larger Ron Jon Surf shop in
Cocoa Beach, rents just about anything
water-related you'd want: fat-tired beach
bikes ($15 daily), kayaks (singles/doubles
$30/35), wetsuits ($10), oxygen tanks ($6)
and other diving equipment, surfboards
($30 daily) and much, much more.

Don't know how to surf? Contact
Surfguy's Surfing School (☎ 321-956-3268;
W www.surfguyssurf.com)], and they'll
teach you. Private classes run $35 per hour,
three or more people $25 each per hour.
They also offer four-day 'camps' for $130.
The **Cocoa Beach Surfing School** (☎ 321-
868-1980; www.cocoabeachsurfingschool
.com) is a little more expensive, but boasts
members of the US National Surfing Team
as instructors.

Places to Stay

Cocoa Beach attracts surfers at spring break
and space junkies during launches, so expect
higher prices during those times.

Jetty Park Campground (☎ 321-783-7111;
400 E Jetty Rd; without/with hookups
$19/26), in the nearby city of Cape Cana-
veral, has some of the best shuttle-launch
views in the area.

Budget Inn (☎ 321-632-5721; 4150 W
King St; $49/89 nonlaunch/launch) provides
clean, basic rooms right off the freeway for
(relatively) cheap.

Silver Sands Motel (☎ 321-783-2415; 225
N Atlantic Ave; rooms $65/90 nonlaunch/
launch) has clean rooms, friendly service and
a beachfront location.

Fawlty Towers (☎ 321-784-3870; 100 E
Cocoa Beach Causeway; $60/140 non-
launch/launch) is garishly overdressed in

Pepto-Bismol pink but has really nice rooms
and a tropical-themed pool fronted by their
Tiki Bar.

The **Inn at Cocoa Beach** (☎ 321-799-3460;
4300 Ocean Beach Blvd; rooms $135/295
nonlaunch/launch) isn't the quaintest B&B
in the world, but it does have onsite spa
treatments and a great beachside location.

Places to Eat

Mama D's Deli (☎ 321-638-1338; 109 Brevard
Ave; mains $3-6; open 8am-5pm Mon-Sat)
does salads, sandwiches and big breakfasts
with Italian flair. Have yours with a Torani
fizz and top it off with their homemade
tiramisu.

Crab Heaven (☎ 321-783-5001; 6910 N
Atlantic Ave (Hwy A1A); open 11am-10pm
Mon-Sat, 11am-9pm Sun) is technically in
Cape Canaveral and worth the trip for crab
lovers. Huge, wonderful fish sandwiches
($6) and crab soup ($4) are perfect for lighter
appetites, but the all-you-can-eat crab specials ($25 blue crab, $28 snow crab) are the
real draw.

Heidelberg Restaurant (☎ 321-783-6806; 7
N Orlando Ave; mains $15-20; kitchen open
10am-10pm Tues-Sat, 5pm-10pm Sun) serves
authentic German cuisine, including Jaeger-
bratten and Wienerschnitzel, along with
German wines and great jazz nightly.

The **Black Tulip** (☎ 231-631-1133; 207
Brevard Ave; mains $13-24; open 11:30am-
2:30pm daily & 5pm-9:30pm Mon-Sat), across
the street, serves New American cuisine:
Veal Oscar and roast duck are recommended, as is the Sunday jazz brunch ($13).

Café Margaux (☎ 321-639-8343; 222
Brevard Ave; lunch $9-12, dinner $18-26;
open 11am-3pm & 5pm-9pm or so daily) is
a French gourmet restaurant. Lunch – try
the curried scallops – is affordable. At
dinner, prices and selection double; servers
recommend the artichoke Asiago pasta.

Entertainment

Cocoa Village has a great community playhouse, and Cocoa Beach is where the Space
Coast comes to party. Some bars are a
typical beach scene, but others showcase
great local music.

SPACE COAST

Cocoa Village Playhouse (☎ 321-636-5050; 300 Brevard Ave; tickets $12-15) stages locally produced plays on the site of the old and ornate Aladdin Theatre (1924).

Apollo 13: The Comedy (☎ 800-888-8388; 8701 Astronaut Blvd (Hwy 528)), at the Radisson at the Port, in Cape Canaveral, is a long-running dinner theater that involves guitar-playing astronauts and audience participation. Oh dear.

Murdock's Bistro & Char Bar (☎ 321-633-0600; 600 Brevard Ave; open 11am-10pm Mon-Thur, 11am-midnight Sat & Sun) has an outdoor patio where you can drink, dine on catfish tacos and listen to some great music. On Wednesday, the Phat Cats play the blues, and there's live oldies on Thursday and big bands on Friday and Saturday.

Big Daddy Dave's (☎ 321-633-7653; 401 Delannoy Ave; open 5pm-2am Tues-Sat), next to Riverfront Park, is the premier jazz venue on the Space Coast. Get dressed up in your snazzy best and listen to tunes while you get started on that two-drink minimum.

Surfside Café (☎ 321-799-3566; 211 E Cocoa Beach Blvd; 11am-2pm daily) is the quintessential beach bar, with Budweiser on tap, live music nightly and the occasional bikini contest or DJ competition.

Getting There & Around

The **Greyhound bus station** (☎ 321-636-6531; 302 Main St) is not served by local public transportation.

SCAT (☎ 321-633-1878, 321-952-4672; W www.ridescat.com; ticket $1) is an inconvenient public bus system that serves the entire Space Coast. Well, not Cocoa Village, but most of the coast, including Cocoa Beach, where buses operate Monday to Friday only. Bus No 9 runs along Hwy A1A, connecting Cocoa Beach to Cape Canaveral.

MELBOURNE & INDIALANTIC

Melbourne and Indialantic make a good base for turtle watchers and more affluent surfers sick of battling the crowds at Cocoa Beach. For the latter, it's well located between the breaks at Patrick Air Force Base and Sebastian Inlet. Most of the Melbourne area's life is centered along the

beach – on the east side of the Intracoastal Waterway – and in the towns of Melbourne Beach, Indialantic and Melbourne.

Information

The **Melbourne Chamber of Commerce** (☎ 321-724-5400, W www.melpb-chamber .org; 1005 E Hwy 192; open 9am-5pm Mon-Fri) has the usual pamphlets.

Eau Gallie Public Library (☎ 321-255-4304; 1521 Pineapple Ave; open 9am-9pm Mon-Thur, 9am-5pm Fri & Sat) has free Internet access and one of the nicest views of the Indian River imaginable.

Coin Laundry (826 Hwy A1A) lets you clean your clothes while you catch some rays.

Historic Downtown

The Historic Downtown area, along E New Haven Ave right behind the chamber of commerce, is a pleasant enough antique shop–lined street. Nearby is the **Crane Creek Manatee Sanctuary**, just two blocks west of the chamber of commerce, where you'll definitely see lots of river turtles and catfish and, if you're lucky, manatees.

Brevard Museum of Art & Science

This small museum (☎ 321-242-0798; W www .artandscience.org; 1463 Highland Ave; 10am-5pm Tues-Sat, 1pm-5pm Sun; adult/student $5/2, free 1pm-5pm Thur) has a few interesting art exhibits and some very nice volunteers; call in advance to arrange a tour. Across the street is the **Clemente Science Center** (☎ 321-254-7782; 1520 Highland Dr), which is included in the admission fee. It has hands-on exhibits and experiments for smaller children.

The Brevard Zoo

This excellent if small zoo (☎ 321-254-9453; W www.brevardzoo.org; 8225 N Wickham Rd; adult/senior/child $7/6/5), remodeled largely by volunteer labor, focuses on Latin American jungles and has good exhibits on sloths, spider monkeys and jaguars. They also have a few Florida panthers, North America's rarest mammal. Kids will love the aviary, where they can feed exotic birds by hand.

Andretti Thrill Park

This race car–themed attraction (☎ 321-956-6706; W www.andrettithrillpark.com; 3960 S Babcock St; admission \$5, for all rides \$22) is sure to keep kids who are bored with all that space stuff happy. It'll hold them over until you get to Orlando, anyway. Three go-cart tracks, bumper boats, laser tag and an 18-hole miniature golf course are just a few of the attractions.

Beach & Boardwalk

The area's main public beach and boardwalk, at the end of Hwy 192 in Indialantic, isn't the world's largest, but it's got great surfing (see Activities) and white sand speckled with sunbathers. There are a few restaurants and bars that cater to the locals – not too many tourists make it down this far.

Activities

The **Longboard House** (☎ 321-951-0730; W www.longboardhouse.com; 101 5th Ave; open 9am-9pm Mon-Sat, 9am-6pm Sun), in Indialantic, sells a huge selection of new and used surfboards and rents longboards for \$25 per day, bodyboards for \$10 per day. They also run a surfing information hotline (☎ 321-953-0392).

The best breaks in the area (arguably, in Florida) are 18 miles south of Indialantic at Sebastian Inlet, which has strong currents and, on good days (as in, when storms brew in the Atlantic), 10-foot breaks. In Indialantic, surf is good behind the Comfort Suites Hotel; on Patrick Air Force Base (to the north), good waves can generally be found behind the Officer's Club.

Beach Bicycle Works (☎ 231-725-2500; 113 5th Ave) rents mountain/road bikes for \$10/15 per half day, \$30 for three days and \$50 weekly.

Places to Stay

Oceanside Motel (☎ 321-727-2723; 745 Hwy A1A; rooms \$55) is a good deal, with clean rooms, a pool and giant sea turtles nesting outside June to September.

Melbourne Harbor Suites (☎ 800-242-4251; 1207 E 1st St; rooms \$48/58 summer/winter), in the 'heart of Historic Downtown

Melbourne,' is a great option, close to some excellent restaurants and the Crane Creek Manatee Sanctuary.

Windmere Inn By the Sea (☎ 321-728-9334; 800-224-6853; W www.windmereinn.com; 815 Hwy A1A; rooms \$95-195) is a highly recommended oceanfront B&B with all the trimmings: country English antiques, Jacuzzis in some rooms, afternoon sherry and a full breakfast.

Melbourne Quality Suites Hotel (☎ 321-723-4222, 800-876-4222; 1665 N Hwy A1A; suites \$99/129 summer/winter) has very nice two-room oceanfront (yes, all of them) suites with balconies.

Places to Eat

Community Harvest Café (☎ 321-242-2398; 1405 Highland Ave; dishes \$3-5; open 9am-7:30pm Mon-Fri, 9am-4pm Sat), next to the library and art museum, serves unusual vegetarian and vegan fare – try the pita pizzas or tempuna (tempeh with kelp salad) sandwich.

Oceanview Diner (☎ 321-723-2270; 1 5th Ave; dishes \$3-7; open 24/7) serves basic diner food on a great outdoor patio overlooking the beach anytime – unless you're a Indialantic city official, in which case you've been permanently banned from the premises.

Pop's Casbah (☎ 321-723-9811; 2005 S Waverly Place; dishes \$4-7; open 6am-2:30pm Sat-Wed; 6am-8:30pm Thur & Fri), in the historic downtown, serves food just like grandma's (assuming your grandmother is an outstanding Southern cook) in a cool, low-ceiling dining room decorated with Highwaymen art. Breakfasts are huge, and the meat-and-three plates (\$7) come with truly divine cornbread.

Cantina Dos Amigos (☎ 321-724-2183; 990 N Hwy A1A; mains \$8-15; open 4pm-10pm Sun-Thur, 4pm-11pm Fri & Sat) has a breezy patio, more than 50 different kinds of tequila, and magnificent, authentic Mexican food. Try the pollo borracho or vegetables Acapulco for a real treat.

Djon's (☎ 321-722-2737; 522 Ocean Ave; mains \$16-40; open 5pm-10pm or so daily) is a wonderful place to be treated to a three-star, dress-up, gourmet dinner. Start with yummy seafood crêpes (\$9) and continue with delectable sea bass with mussels in lobster broth ($22), both *highly* recommended. Don't miss the dramatic bananas Foster flambé ($9) for dessert.

Entertainment

Friday Fest (☎ 231-724-1741; open 6pm-9pm Fri; cnr E New Haven Ave & Waverly St), on the second Friday of the month, closes historic downtown Melbourne off to traffic and brings in live bands, carnival games, drinking in the streets and all manner of merrymaking. If you're around, check it out.

King Performance Center (☎ 321-242-2219; 3865 N Wickham Rd) is home to performances by the Brevard Symphony Orchestra. It's also a good resource for children's performances in spring and fall. Take I-95 south to exit 73, and Wickham Rd east for 7 miles to Post Rd, then continue east to the center.

Meg O'Malley's (☎ 321-952-5510; w www .megomalleys.com; 810 E New Haven Ave) has 20 brews on tap, including their own Irish cider, and live music – usually Irish bands or local jazz and blues groups – every night at around 8pm. This place gets packed.

Getting There & Around

Melbourne International Airport (☎ 321-723-6227; w www.mlbair.com) is a growing airport served by Delta, Spirit, Comair and Atlantic Southeast Airlines, as well as a handful of rental car companies. The airport is also the future site of the sorely needed Space Coast Amtrak station. It's served by SCAT bus No 21 daily.

There is a **Greyhound bus station** (☎ 321-723-4329; 460 S Harbor), but it's not served by local transportation.

SCAT (☎ 321-633-1878, 952-4672; w www .ridescat.com; ticket $1) is an inconvenient public bus system that serves the entire Space Coast. Melbourne buses run seven days a week. Bus No 21 serves the airport, while bus No 26 runs from the transfer point at Babcock and Hibiscus to serve Indialantic and the beaches.

AROUND MELBOURNE & INDIALANTIC

About 20 miles south of Indialantic on Hwy A1A is Sebastian Inlet. There are a couple of small museums, but the main attractions are the fishing, surfing and camping opportunities at Sebastian Inlet State Park.

Sebastian Inlet State Park

This laid-back park (☎ 321-984-4852; 9700 S A1A; open 8am-sunset daily; pedestrian/car $3.25/1), on a narrow stretch of the barrier island chain, attracts folks who love the ocean. There's great surfing, and you can snorkel or scuba dive the remains of Spanish galleons (and perhaps find a doubloon of your very own). Regular visitors also say that this is a great place for fishing or clam-digging your own dinner.

The Indian River and Atlantic Ocean also provide ample opportunities for boating. Visit the **Inlet Marina** (☎ 321-724-5424; 9502 S A1A; open 8am-6pm daily) to rent canoes (half day/day $21/30), kayaks ($25/35 single, $29/39 double), catamaran sailboats ($75/119) or even a 10-passenger pontoon boat ($139/179). The concession stand also runs ranger-led, two-hour boat tours at 2pm daily (adult/child $16/10) and serves cheap meals ($3-6).

There's a **campground** (☎ 561-984-4852; 9700 S Hwy A1A; without/with hookups $19/24) right on the water.

Mclarty Treasure Museum

This small museum (☎ 561-589-2147; open 9am-5pm daily; 9700 S A1A; adult/child $1/free), within Sebastian Inlet State Park, displays Spanish treasures from 11 galleons that were destroyed in a hurricane just off the coast back in 1715. The exhibits are fascinating and silver-sparkly, but the best reason to come takes place during 'salvage season,' from May through September. From the galleon-shaped pier behind the museum, you can watch divers and treasure-hunters moored right offshore do their thing.

Northeast Florida

For centuries, Northeastern Florida was contested territory, the site of bloody battles between European powers France, Spain and Britain, and later the staging ground for some of the fiercest fighting in the American Civil War. Because of its strategic position along these contested and ever-shifting borders, it was long home to pirates, smugglers and soldiers of fortune, who built their own private empires of bars and brothels along the beautiful coastline.

For the past century or so, however, things have been (relatively) quiet. But the region's remarkable history has left a legacy reflected in the architecture and attitudes of some of Florida's finest destinations.

Jacksonville is the commercial heart of Northeastern Florida: It's a business center, not a tourist town, and visitors have to work to uncover the treasures this sprawling metropolis contains. To the north is Amelia Island, one of the state's finest destinations for its natural and historic treasures, an often overlooked gem worth discovering for yourself.

Most visitors make their way here to see St Augustine. Its charming cobblestone streets and old Spanish- and English-built buildings (old not just by US standards but even by those of chilly, damp countries in which people drive on the left: many structures here date to the late 1700s) make it an irresistible stop.

Northeast Florida is also home to the Birthplace of Speed: Daytona Beach. Spring breakers, stock-car-racing fans and motorcycle enthusiasts all stake out their time in the sun making this one of Florida's most festive destinations. Join them and drive the hard-packed sands of the most celebrated beach track in the history of American auto racing.

JACKSONVILLE
pop 740,000
Unlike many Florida cities possessed of so much prime real estate along the Atlantic, Jacksonville is not what you'd call a tourist

Highlights

- Get to the heart of Florida's history in lovely St Augustine, the USA's first European settlement
- View the impressive collection at the Cummer Museum of Art in Jacksonville
- Check out the 31-degree bank at the Daytona Speedway, then drive on the hard-packed sands of the original track, Daytona Beach itself
- See a Civil War reenactment at Fort Clinch or Olustee Battlefield
- Wander the islands, trails and waterways of the Timucuan Preserve along the mighty St John's River

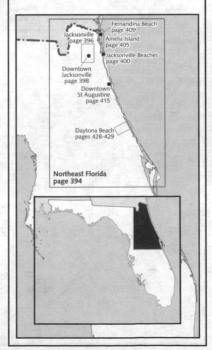

NORTHEAST

NORTHEAST FLORIDA

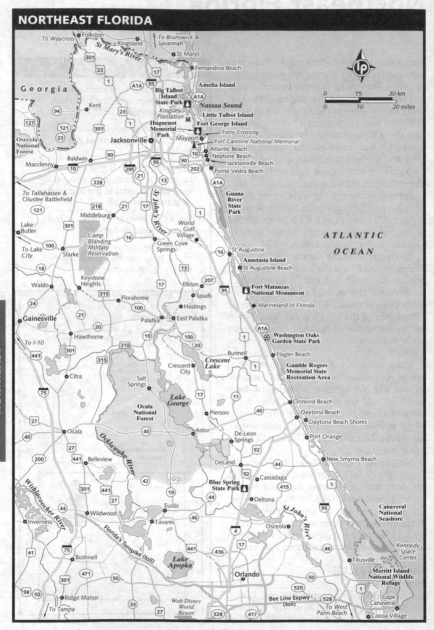

town. It's a working city, with lots of asphalt and traffic, skyscrapers and strip malls, and more business opportunities than B&Bs.

Even if your company didn't send you here, there are plenty of good reasons to visit. It sprawls along three meandering rivers, the Trout, Broward and mighty St John's, with sweeping bridges and city lights that silhouette the nighttime sky. The beaches are lined with bungalows and bars, not mansions and condominiums, and packed with party people unconcerned with anything except the next wave.

It also boasts one of the Southeast's best art museums and easy access to the Timucuan Preserve, a collection of parks and historical sites unlike any in the USA. Jacksonville is all but unavoidable if you're visiting northeast Florida, but why fight it? Get off the freeway and enjoy some Southern hospitality and a tall glass of sweet tea.

History

Jacksonville Beach was first occupied between 12,000 and 4000 years ago by Paleo-Indians, who left behind shell mounds and spear points for future archaeologists to puzzle over. They lived along the river, close to present-day King St downtown, and were among the first in North America to use pottery, starting about 4000 years ago. When Europeans first got here, locals called the town Wacca Pilatka (a place where cows could ford the river); in 1816 the name was Anglicized to Cowford.

The French made the first attempt at a permanent European settlement in 1562. They founded Fort Caroline, just north of present-day Jacksonville, a military base and colony that knowingly trespassed on Spain's new territory. Most of the settlers were Huguenots, an unpopular religious sect back home.

When local Indian chief Saturiba first approached the newcomers with food and aid, he suggested forming a military alliance. The French refused. In 1565, Spanish admiral Menendez de Avilés attacked the poorly guarded colony and killed some 140 settlers (he lost one soldier), later capturing those who had escaped at Matanzas (see the St Augustine section of this chapter to find out what happened to them).

France, Spain, Great Britain and the USA all claimed the region at various times throughout the next 300 years, even as a steady trickle of British and then US settlers crept across the contested border to occupy the region. Spain ceded Florida to the USA in 1821, and Jacksonville, named for provisional governor Andrew Jackson, was incorporated in 1822.

Jacksonville was one of the first Florida towns on Henry Flagler's railroad system, and was attracting some 65,000 tourists annually by 1886. Then came a triple whammy: A yellow fever epidemic decimated the local population in 1888; the railroad system started serving the much nicer beaches to the south in the decade that followed; and a fire leveled most of downtown – 2300 buildings, $15 million in damages – in 1901. The town was just beginning to recover when the Great Depression hit.

Today locals speak in terms of pre-Jaguars and post-Jaguars culture: Prior to 1993, when the NFL awarded this city the Jacksonville Jaguars, their very own professional football franchise, a local church had all but banned alcohol sales downtown. When Sundays started being devoted to more secular pursuits, however, the football fans fought for, and won, the right to enjoy a cold brew at the games. And downtown became a place to party once again.

Today, despite suffering from serious urban sprawl (Jacksonville is the one of the largest cities in the USA in terms of square mileage), it's becoming much more cosmopolitan, with great neighborhoods and entertainment venues that take full advantage of the city's bustling economy and beautiful location.

Orientation

The city of Jacksonville is trisected by a very rough T formed by the St John's River – which runs north-south, with a little east and then north jig, through the city and then banks almost due east – and the Trout River, which joins the St John's from the west. Downtown Jacksonville is

NORTHEAST

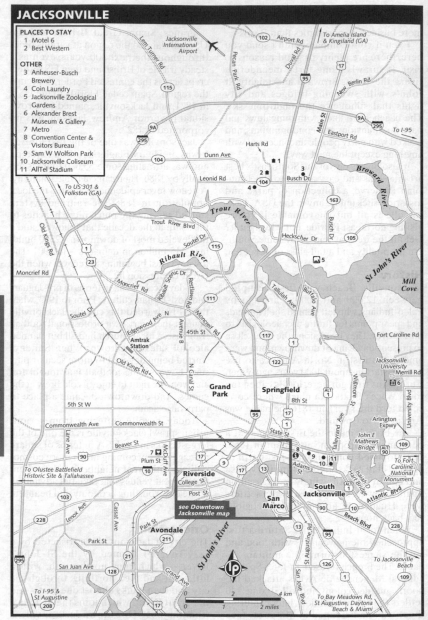

JACKSONVILLE

PLACES TO STAY
1 Motel 6
2 Best Western

OTHER
3 Anheuser-Busch Brewery
4 Coin Laundry
5 Jacksonville Zoological Gardens
6 Alexander Brest Museum & Gallery
7 Metro
8 Convention Center & Visitors Bureau
9 Sam W Wolfson Park
10 Jacksonville Coliseum
11 AllTel Stadium

on the west side of the St John's River on the little jig.

I-95 comes in straight from the north to a junction just south of downtown with I-10. Follow I-10 east into downtown, with a well-signed but still confusing maze of state highways offering access to surrounding areas; Hwy 17 takes you to Five Points. Three major bridges cross the river here, Fuller Warren (I-10), Acosta (Hwy 13) and Main St. All will take you to San Marco. I-295 breaks off from I-95 and forms a half circle around the western edges of the city.

Though the city is enormous, most sites of interest to the visitor are concentrated along the St John's River's narrowest point: downtown, just north of the jig; Five Points, just south of downtown along the river; and the San Marco Historical District along the southern shore.

The Jacksonville beaches – from Ponte Vedra Beach at the south to Atlantic Beach at the north – are about a 40-minute drive east of the city center. I-10, which becomes Hwy 10 shortly after crossing the St John's River, takes you to Atlantic Beach, and Hwy 90 (Beach Blvd) goes directly to Jacksonville Beach. Highway A1A (3rd St) is the main north-south road along the beaches, jogging inland a bit along Hwy 10, then becoming Mayport Rd as it heads north to Hanna Park and the St John's River Ferry.

Information

The **Jacksonville & the Beaches Convention & Visitors Bureau** (☎ 904-798-9111, 800-733-2668; W www.jaxcvb.com; 201 E Adams St) has useful tourist pamphlets, discount coupon books and bus maps. There's a more convenient visitors information center upstairs at **Jacksonville Landing** (☎ 904-353-1188; open 10am-8pm Mon-Thur, 10am-9pm Fri & Sat, noon-5:30pm Sun).

First Union (☎ 904-361-2455; 225 Water St) has its most luxurious branch downtown. **Gordon Bank** (☎ 904-873-7220; 363-16 Atlantic Blvd) is by the beach. There is a **post office** (cnr Julia & Duval Sts) downtown.

Five Points News Center (☎ 904-354-4470; 1060 Park St) carries out-of-town and international publications. The **Jacksonville**

Public Library (☎ 904-241-1141; 602 3rd St; open 10am-9pm Mon-Fri, 10am-6pm Sat, 1pm-6pm Sun) has free Internet service.

The conservative *Florida Times-Union* (W www.times-union.com) is the big daily paper and produces *Weekend*, featuring family-oriented events listings, every Friday. *Folio Weekly* and *Entertainer* are free weeklies with club, restaurant and events listings. *Out in the City* covers Jacksonville's gay and lesbian scene. *Jacksonville* magazine (W www .jacksonvillemag.com) has lots of human-interest stories, and *San Marco* magazine really wishes it was covering Palm Beach.

Commercial radio conforms to corporate standards, with rock at 96.9, 100.7 and 104.5; 'smooth jazz' at 97.9; country at 99.1 and 107.3; alternative rock at 93.3, 95.1 and 102.9; dance at 95.1; excellent old school funk at 101.5; adult contemporary at 96.1 and 105.3; and Christian rock (an oxymoron? you decide…) at 106.5. National Public Radio (NPR) is at 89.9 FM.

Coin Laundry (926-1 Baymeadows Rd) is close to the chain hotels off I-95 (see Places to Stay, later). **Park and Wash** (no telephone; 1333 N 3rd St) is convenient to the Jacksonville beaches. **Maytag Laundry** (☎ 904-634-4768; 1012 Margaret St) is in Five Points.

Cummer Museum of Art & Gardens

Northeast Florida's best collection of Western art is housed in this beautifully appointed museum (☎ 904-356-6857; W www .cummer.org; 829 Riverside Ave; adult/student $6/3, free 4pm-9pm Tues; open 10am-9pm Tues & Thur, 10am-5pm Wed, Fri & Sat, noon-5pm Sun), in the Five Points area, just southwest of downtown. The Southern Tudor building was originally constructed for Ninah May Holden Cummer, who bequeathed her home, a collection of more than 60 paintings and administrative funds to run the museum after her death in 1958.

The interior is beautiful and the art outstanding, including woodcuts by Albrecht Du\"rer, Rubens' *The Entombment of Christ*, Winslow Homer's *Waiting for a Bite* and George PA Healy's famous and untitled portrait of President Andrew Jackson close

DOWNTOWN JACKSONVILLE

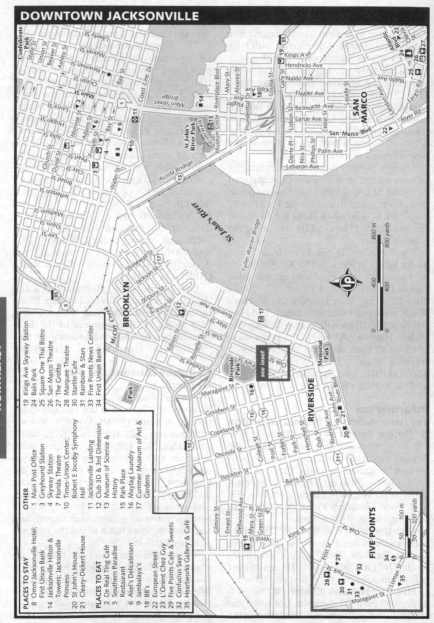

PLACES TO STAY
8 Omni Jacksonville Hotel;
   First Union Bank
14 Jacksonville Hilton &
   Towers; Jacksonville
   Princess
20 St John's House
21 Cleary-Dickert House

PLACES TO EAT
2 De Real Ting Café
5 Southern Paradise
   Restaurant
6 Akel's Delicatessen
9 Jambalaya's
18 BB's
22 European Street
23 L'Orient Chez Guy
29 Five Points Cafe & Sweets
32 Confucius Says
35 Heartworks Gallery & Café

OTHER
1 Main Post Office
3 Greyhound Station
4 Skyway Station
7 Florida Theatre
10 Times-Union Center;
   Robert E Jocoby Symphony
   Hall
11 Jacksonville Landing
12 Club 3D & 3rd Dimension
13 Museum of Science &
   History
15 Park Place
16 Maytag Laundry
17 Cummer Museum of Art &
   Gardens
19 Kings Ave Skyway Station
24 Balis Park
25 Square One Thai Bistro
26 San Marco Theatre
27 The Grotto
28 Marquee Theatre
30 Starlite Cafe
31 Rainbow & Stars
33 Five Points News Center
34 First Union Bank

FIVE POINTS

to death. There are also various collections of antiquities, from European furniture to Japanese *inro* and *tonkatsu,* small metal or lacquer purses for men.

The gardens, a popular spot for wedding photographers, are draped with wisteria and shaded by massive, mossy oaks, a great place to unwind after trying to absorb all the handmade beauty inside.

Museum of Science & History

MOSH (☎ 904-396-6674; W www.themosh .org; 1025 Museum Circle; adult/senior/child $7/5.50/5; open 10am-5pm Mon-Fri, 10am-6pm Sat, 1pm-6pm Sun) is an outstanding museum. It features comprehensive exhibits about Jacksonville's pre-Columbian history and Spanish, French and US settlements, as well as the natural history of the St John's River system, one of two rivers in the world that flows north (the other is the Nile).

Extras include a flight simulator ($4) that takes you through the mineshafts of Mercury. The planetarium explains astronomical events during the day, and has rockin' laser light shows ($6) on Friday and Saturday, including (proof that Western Civilization is crumbling) an 'N Sync and Backstreet Boys show at 4pm.

Jacksonville Zoological Gardens

Northeast Florida's only major zoo (☎ 904-757-4462; W www.jaxzoo.com; 8605 Zoo Rd; adult/child $8/5; open 9am-5pm daily), off exit 124A from I-95, just completed a $17 million expansion. It was worth every penny. The zoo opened in 1914 with one deer, and today has 73 acres of animals, most in three areas: Wild Florida, with really fat alligators and rare Florida panthers; Australian Adventure, packed with kangaroos and charming, despite the rampant overuse of 'G'day'; and the Plains of East Africa. There's also an excellent great apes exhibit (which completes the collection with a mirror) and a reptile house with poisonous slitherers. A train ride through the grounds costs an extra $5 for adults, $3 for children.

Anheuser-Busch Brewery

Very close to the zoo, the brewery (☎ 904-696-8373; W www.budweisertours.com; 111 Busch Dr; open 9am-4pm Mon-Sat) offers free tours and, if you're over 21, free beer. The exhibits are fine, showing how hops are grown, Dale Earnhardt Jr's No 8 Budweiser stock car (see the boxed text 'NASCAR,' in the Daytona Beach section) and that sort of thing. What really inspires, however, is the sight of 950 bottles of Bud per minute meandering through machinery that would look at home in a nuclear power plant, all on its way to you and me. Tours depart on the hour. Exit I-95 at Busch Dr and follow the billboards.

Alexander Brest Museum & Gallery

The Brest Museum (☎ 904-744-3950 x3371; 2800 University Blvd N; admission free; open 9am-4:30pm Mon-Fri, noon-5pm Sat), in the Philips Fine Arts building on the manicured campus of Jacksonville University, probably isn't worth the trip – unless you'll appreciate the astounding collection of carved ivory from all over the world (Japan, China, India, the Netherlands and so on), some dating back to the 1600s. From downtown, take the Matthews Bridge east to Hwy 109 north, which becomes University Blvd.

Fort Caroline National Memorial

This memorial (☎ 904-641-7155; 12713 Fort Caroline Rd; admission free; open 9am-5pm daily) is the administrative headquarters of the Timucuan Ecological and Historical Preserve, a confederation of federal, state and local parks working with private landowners to maintain the St John's River ecosystem. If Ranger Rhonda – corporate America lost a fine CEO when she joined the NPS, that's for sure – gets her way, all 46,000 acres will soon be Timucuan National Park.

The memorial itself is an approximately two-thirds-scale model of the original fort built here by French Huguenots in 1562. The re-creation, made from earth and wood, stands on the site where it is believed the original fort was erected. The park also features several hundred acres of pristine wilderness along the St John's River. Keep your eyes open for artifacts, too – a couple of years ago, two teenagers found a Spanish musket.

NORTHEAST

About half a mile east of the main visitor's center is a monument, on the bluff 75 feet above the St John's River, that reproduces the original column left here by Jean Ribault, who first landed at the inlet. In the visitor's center, videos discussing the Fort Caroline story and the preserve run continually throughout the day.

To reach the main visitor's center from downtown, take Matthews Bridge to the Atlantic Blvd Expressway (Hwy 10 east) and then turn left onto Monument Rd; follow that to Fort Caroline Rd and turn right. The entrance is about half a mile ahead. From the north, take I-95 to Hwy 9A (essentially an eastern extension of I-295) and follow that to Merrill Rd (there are big signs all the way). Turn left on Merrill, which becomes Fort Caroline Rd.

Jacksonville Landing

This popular shopping mall (☎ 904-353-1188; W www.jacksonvillelanding.com; open 10am-8pm Mon-Thur, 10am-9pm Fri & Sat, noon-5:30pm Sun), in the heart of downtown, has tables overlooking the St John's River where you can enjoy your food-court meal. They often stage free entertainment here on weekends and holidays, usually local jazz, country and rock bands. It's on the north side of the river, at the northwestern foot of the Main St Bridge.

Riverwalk

This 1.2-mile boardwalk on the south side of the St John's River opposite downtown and Jacksonville Landing is a somewhat pleasant city park, but definitely underutilized.

Beaches

The beaches, approximately 15 miles east of downtown, are about 25 miles of white sand stretching from Ponte Vedra Beach to the south to Atlantic Beach to the north. Moving from south to north, **Ponte Vedra Beach** is posh, with golf courses and resorts, and not much else. **Jacksonville Beach** is loud, urban and fun: Huge bars blast dance music into the night, and weekends bring out the flashy custom cars. **Neptune Beach** makes a stab at upscale, but is just too relaxed to quite get

there. And if you want some sand all to yourself, **Atlantic Beach**, with several entrances off Seminole Beach Rd, is perfect.

Organized Tours

Jacksonville Haunted History Tours (☎ 904-276-9098; adult/child $10/5; 7:30pm Fri & Sat) is a 1½-hour tour of the city's spookiest sites, operated by North Florida Paranormal Research, Inc.

River Cruises Inc (☎ 904-396-2333; W www.rivercruise.com; 1511 Montana Ave) runs lunch and dinner buffet cruises. You can take

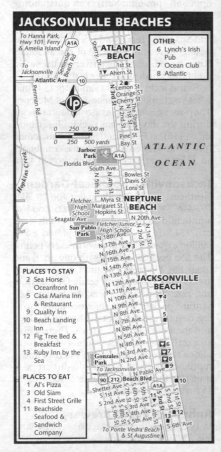

JACKSONVILLE BEACHES

OTHER
6 Lynch's Irish Pub
7 Ocean Club
8 Atlantic

PLACES TO STAY
2 Sea Horse Oceanfront Inn
5 Casa Marina Inn & Restaurant
9 Quality Inn
10 Beach Landing Inn
12 Fig Tree Bed & Breakfast
13 Ruby Inn by the Sea

PLACES TO EAT
1 Al's Pizza
3 Old Siam
4 First Street Grille
11 Beachside Seafood & Sandwich Company

15-mile to 20-mile chugs up the St John's River aboard the *Lady St Johns* or the *Annabelle Lee.*

La Cruise Casino (☎ 904-241-7200; W www .lacruise.com; admission free) disembarks on daily five-hour gambling cruises from Mayport, next to the St John's River Ferry. Not only is it free, you might even come back a winner!

The **Jacksonville Hilton and Towers** (☎ 904-398-8800; 1201 Riverplace Blvd; adult/child $35/20 for dinner cruises, other prices vary) runs the *Jacksonville Princess,* a 149-passenger yacht that offers Sunday brunch, a sunset cocktail party and romantic dinner cruises throughout the year.

Places to Stay

Hanna Park (☎ 904-249-4700; 500 Wonderwood Dr; campsites without/with hookups $14/18, 4-person cozy cabins $34), in Atlantic Beach, has a shady campground 200 yards from the ocean. Huguenot Memorial Park and Little Talbot and Fort George Islands also have camping (see the Talbot & Fort George Islands section, later).

Jacksonville's accommodation scene is pretty institutional: Except for a couple of B&Bs, it's all chains, average in everything. You can often bargain for city rooms on weekends, and beach rooms on weekdays.

The cheapest rooms are along I-95 and I-10, where chains congregate. Among them are **Studio Six** (☎ 904-731-7317; 8765 Baymeadows Rd; rooms $49); **Best Western** (☎ 904-751-5600, 800-528-1234; 10888 Harts Rd; rooms $65); and **Quality Inn** (☎ 904-281-0900, 800-842-1348; 4660 Salisbury Rd; rooms $90). Baymeadows Rd (Hwy 152) is about 30 miles south of downtown off I-95; Harts Rd is north, off Hwy 104 on the opposite side of I-95 from the Anheuser-Busch Brewery.

Sea Horse Oceanfront Inn (☎ 904-246-2175; W www.seahorseresort.com; 120 Atlantic Blvd; rooms $89-129) has nice rooms and a pool overlooking the ocean in downtown Neptune Beach.

Beach Landing Inn (☎ 904-249-9778; 97 S 1st St; rooms $99), in Jacksonville Beach, has basic rooms and a flawless location (if

you want to party, dude), with the Atlantic on one side and the bars and cars of the 1st St cruise on the other.

Jacksonville Hilton & Towers (☎ 904-398-8800, 800-445-8667; W www.hilton.com; 1201 Riverplace Blvd; rooms from $99 Fri-Sun, $129 Mon-Thur) has a great pool overlooking the river and downtown, and all the amenities you'd expect from a luxury property geared toward businesspeople.

Omni Jacksonville Hotel (☎ 904-355-6664, 800-843-6664; 245 Water St; rooms $155), in the heart of downtown, has amenity-laden rooms, acres of marble, a fitness room and free video games, just perfect for decompressing after the big meeting.

Casa Marina Inn (☎ 904-270-0025; W www .casamarina.cc; 691 N 1st St; rooms $155), by the beach, isn't as nice as the rates imply, but the historic 1925 hotel has all the Spanish-Mediterranean elegance you'd want.

Ponte Vedra Inn and Club (☎ 904-273-9500; W www.pvresorts.com; 607 Ponte Vedra Blvd; rooms from $190/250 summer/winter) is in swish Ponte Vedra Beach, the southernmost stretch of sand claimed by Jacksonville. They offer package deals (most involving their acclaimed golf courses) that are a much better value.

If you're looking for a B&B, consider the following options.

St John's House (☎ 904-384-3724; 1718 Osceola St; rooms $70-100; closed June-Aug), near downtown and Five Points, has three rooms.

The **Fig Tree B&B** (☎ 904-246-8855; 185 4th Ave; rooms $75-150), in Jacksonville Beach, is a pleasant 1915 cottage with five rooms. In addition to breakfast, they do an afternoon tea on the shady porch.

Ruby Inn by the Sea (☎ 904-241-5551; W www.rubyinnbythesea.com; 802 2nd St S; rooms $95-145), also in Jacksonville Beach, is a lovely old Nantucket-style place right near the ocean, and offers garden rooms with courtyards.

Cleary-Dickert House (☎ 904-387-4762; 1804 Copeland St; singles/doubles $99/129, suite $139) is a 1914 prairie-style B&B just off the river. From downtown, take Riverside Ave and turn left onto Copeland; it's at the corner of St John's Rd. Free wine and snacks in the afternoon and a full hot breakfast each morning are included. The friendly owners bake their own breads and biscuits.

Places to Eat

Downtown At **Jacksonville Landing** (☎ 904-353-1188) there are several choices, mostly chains like the **Ruby Tuesday** and **Hooters**. A better bet is **Jambalaya's Southern Kitchen** (mains $4-8), with gumbo, jambalaya and excellent po' boys. It's just to the left as you enter the mall via Water St.

Akel's Delicatessen (☎ 904-356-5628; 130 N Hogan St; dishes $1-5; open 7am-4pm daily) is a very popular downtown lunch spot with huge sandwiches, decent pasta salads and outstanding cheesecake. Try the Akel's special, marinated chicken in a pita.

Southern Paradise Restaurant (☎ 904-358-1082; 229 W Forsyth St; dishes $5; open 7am-3pm Mon-Fri) serves heaping helpings of Southern classics like chicken 'n' dumplings alongside your choice of some 21 vegetable sides – only four of which are deep fried. Don't let the cafeteria atmosphere dissuade you.

De Real Ting Café (☎ 904-633-9738; 45 W Monroe St; mains $5-10; open 11am-3pm Tues-Thur, 11am-2am Fri, 6pm-late Sat & Sun) serves awesome and, during the week, toned-down Caribbean cuisine like jerk chicken and curried shrimp. The chef does more authentic specials on the weekend, when the place packs up for reggae shows (see Entertainment).

Five Points The counterculture loves Five Points' collection of cheap, healthy and eclectic restaurants.

Heartworks Gallery & Café (☎ 904-355-6210; 820 Lomax St; dishes $4-8; open 11am-3pm Mon-Fri, noon-4pm Sat, 10am-2pm Sun) is a very cool gallery/café with exhibits of works by local artists and some of the best vegetarian cuisine in town. Specials like carrot dogs and veggie pizza are winners.

Five Points Cafe & Sweets (☎ 904-356-8380; 1005 Park St; dishes $5-7) has small

salads and excellent baked goods; try the muffins.

Confucius Says (☎ 904-355-9333; 1023 Park St; mains $9-25; open 11am-2:30pm Mon-Fri, 5pm-9:30pm daily) is popular for its groovy tropical decor and Mongolian barbecue.

San Marco Historical District A combination chocolatier, deli, bar and upscale market, **European Street** (☎ 904-398-9500; 1704 San Marco Blvd; dishes $5-10; open 10am-10pm daily) is known for its desserts and prized for its busy but mellow atmosphere. Whether their beer list or pastry selection is the more astounding could be debated for hours.

BB's (☎ 904-306-0100; 1019 Hendricks Ave; mains $14-24; open 11am-10:30pm Mon-Thur, 11am-midnight Fri & Sat, 10am-2pm Sunday brunch) has a huge wine list, elaborate grilled pizzas and entrées like Indian spiced duck breast and tempura scallops – make reservations.

L'Orient Chez Guy (☎ 904-348-2440; 1540 Atlantic Blvd; mains $18-30; open 6pm-10pm Tues-Sat) has an haute-austere dining room where you can start with sesame encrusted fried oysters with tobiko caviar in a wasabi vinaigrette before settling on an even more adventurous Asian-fusion entrée.

Jacksonville Beaches The **Beachside Seafood & Sandwich Company** (☎ 904-241-4880; 120 3rd St S; dishes $4-8; open 11am-6:30pm Mon-Sat, 11am-5pm Sun) is a seafood market and world-class hole-in-the-wall, serving excellent perch sandwiches and other fresh seafood with cold beer.

Al's Pizza (☎ 904-249-0002; 303 Atlantic Blvd; dishes $4-10; open 11am-11pm Mon-Thur, 11am-midnight Fri & Sat, noon-10pm Sun) serves New York–style thin-crust pizza and more to hordes of happy beachgoers.

First Street Grille (☎ 904-246-6555; 807 N 1st St; dishes $6-12; open 11:30am-4pm & 5pm-10pm daily) is a great outdoor place that shoots for Cajun cuisine; you can fill up on small main courses. You can order more expensive seafood dishes at night, when a Caribbean steel-drum band plinks away.

Old Siam (☎ 904-247-7763; 1716 N 3rd St; mains $8-12; open 5pm-10pm Tues-Sun) is an excellent, family-run Thai place.

Entertainment

Music & Theater The **Jacksonville Symphony Orchestra** (☎ 904-354-5547; W www .jaxsymphony.org; 300 Water St) plays at the Robert E. Jacoby Symphony Hall.

The **Times-Union Center** (☎ 904-633-6110; 300 Water St; box office open 10am-4pm daily) hosts major performers like…um… 'N Sync and Barry Manilow.

Florida Theatre (☎ 904-355-2787; 1128 E Forsyth St) does rock shows, community and alternative theater, musicals and other events; ticket prices vary widely.

Alhambra Dinner Theater (☎ 904-641-1212, 800-688-7469; 12000 Beach Blvd; tickets $36-45), about halfway between downtown and the beach, is something of a Jacksonville institution: a buffet dinner and show.

Jacksonville Landing (☎ 904-353-1188; W www.jacksonvillelanding.com), downtown, often has free entertainment, usually jazz, country or rock bands on holidays and weekends, at the outside amphitheater between the food court and river. Many of the restaurants and bars here also offer evening entertainment.

San Marco Theatre (☎ 904-398-1186; 2032 San Marco Blvd; adult/child $7/5), a landmark 1938 art deco creation, has got to be the best place to catch a flick in Jacksonville. Order beer, wine, pizza and sandwiches to munch while you watch.

Bars & Clubs Downtown, **De Real Ting Café** (☎ 904-633-9738; 45 W Monroe St; open 11am-3pm Tues-Thur, 11am-2am Fri, 6pm-late Sat & Sun) has live reggae and acid jazz shows on weekends, often featuring house band Pili Pili. There's a happy hour buffet from 7pm to 11pm Friday. They also do a poetry slam session Sunday, from 6pm 'until there are no more rhymes.'

The **Starlite Cafe** (☎ 904-356-444; 1044 Park St) has good beer, edible food (sandwiches $6 to $8) and live music, usually very good jazz, in the evenings.

The **Marquee Theatre** (☎ 904-356-5555; W www.marqueetheatre.com; 1028 Park St), within a former theater, hosts local and national acts like Nashville Pussy, Cheap Trick, Guar and the Wailers – how's that for variety? Covers vary widely, and when no bands are in town they have DJs, dancing and the occasional Goth night.

Square One Thai Bistro (☎ 904-306-9004; W www.squareonejax.com; 1974 San Marco Blvd; open noon-2am Mon-Fri, 5pm-2am Sat) has a Latin dance night Wednesday and live jazz and rock bands the rest of the week. They also serve fairly good pad Thai ($15).

The Grotto (☎ 904-398-0726; W www.jax wines.com; 2012 San Marco Blvd; open 11am-5pm Mon, 11am-midnight Tues-Sat) has more than 100 wines available by the bottle and several by the glass, which you can enjoy with a cheese plate (3/6 cheeses $13/23) or other fine snacks.

In Jacksonville Beach, the **Ocean Club** (☎ 904-242-8884; W www.oceanclubjax.com; 401 N 1st St) has all that in spades plus a Tuesday ladies' night, with $1 draft beers and free manicures!

The **Atlantic** (☎ 904-249-3338; W www .the-atlantic.com; 333 N 1st St) is slightly more sophisticated and does live dance music. Check their Web site to see what's on.

Lynch's Irish Pub (☎ 904-249-5181; 514 N 1st St) is a somewhat more sedate beach watering hole, with 25 brews on tap and Irish standards like bangers and mash ($9) on the menu.

Gay & Lesbian Venues A good resource for gay and lesbian listings of clubs, bars and community services is available online at **Club Jax** (W www.clubjax.com/info/gay.htm). You could also drop by **Rainbows and Stars** (☎ 904-356-7702; 1046 Park St), in Five Points, and check out their community bulletin board, not to mention their selection of flags, books and toys.

Club 3D & Third Dimension (☎ 904-353-6316; 711 Edison Ave; open 3pm-2am Tues-Fri, 8pm-2am Sat, 6pm-2pm Sun) has entertainment at 11:30pm nightly: Tuesday is talent night, Wednesday is the amateur strip show, Sunday is a male review, and drag shows keep the place hopping Thursday to Saturday.

Park Place (☎ 904-389-6616; 931 King St; open noon-2am daily) has more of a neighborhood bar feel to it, right down to the pool tables.

Metro (☎ 904-388-8719, 800-380-8719; 2929 Plum St), with four enormous bars, calls itself a gay-entertainment complex, complete with disco, cruise bar, piano bar and leathery boiler room. For special events, there are drag shows and cabaret.

Spectator Sports
The **Jacksonville Jaguars** (☎ 904-633-6000; W www.jaguarsnfl.com) became the NFL's 30th team in 1993 and qualified for the playoffs twice in its first three seasons. Their star has dimmed somewhat since the blistering 1997 upset that saw them slam the Denver Broncos during playoffs, but fans still pack the 73,000-seat **AllTel Stadium** during the pro-football season, from August to January – get your tickets early.

The **Jacksonville Lizard Kings** (☎ 904-358-7825; W www.lizardkings.com) are an East Coast Hockey League team and hope to join the NHL; they play at the **Jacksonville Coliseum** (1000 W Bay St).

The **Jacksonville Suns** (☎ 904-358-2846; W www.jaxsuns.com; tickets $5-8) are a minor-league baseball team that plays from April to September in **Sam W Wolfson Park** (1201 E Duval St).

Getting There & Away
The **Jacksonville International Airport** (JAX; ☎ 904-741-4902; W www.jaxairports.com) has a sparkling terminal that's sensibly laid out and served by several major and some regional airlines. Most domestic airlines and all major car-rental companies serve JAX (see Rental under Car & Motorcycle in the Getting Around chapter for information), about 18 miles north of downtown Jacksonville off the Airport Rd exit from I-95. There's no public transportation to the airport, but you can take the Northside No 8 bus from downtown to the DePaul stop and call a cab ($7) to take you out to JAX.

The **Greyhound bus station** (☎ 904-356-9976; 10 Pearl St) is at the western end of downtown. Jacksonville is a major Greyhound hub, and you can get direct buses to most cities on the eastern seaboard and throughout Florida.

The **Amtrak station** (☎ 904-766-5110; 3570 Clifford Lane) is in the middle of nowhere, about 5 miles northwest of downtown. JTA (see Getting Around) bus No NS4 runs between here and downtown, but if they're crowded they might hassle you about a full-sized backpack. You can take a taxi downtown ($10) or to the beaches ($30) – they meet every train.

Jacksonville is at the intersection of I-10, which connects Jacksonville to Tallahassee and the Pacific Ocean, and I-95, a straight shot down the East Coast to Miami. Hwy A1A is the scenic route and runs north-south along the beaches using various aliases: Mayport Rd, Atlantic Blvd and 3rd St among them. It connects directly to St Augustine, to the south. If you're heading north, however, you'll need to catch the **St John's River Ferry** (☎ 904-251-3331; pedestrian/car 50¢/$2.75; operates 6:30am-10pm daily), also called the Mayport Ferry. It runs every half-hour.

Getting Around
Jacksonville Transportation Authority (JTA; ☎ 904-630-3100; W www.jtaonthemove.com) runs the local bus service in town (bus fare 75¢) and to the beaches ($1.35). The main downtown transfer center is at 201 State St opposite the FCCJ main building, which is also the terminus of the Skyway monorail line.

Downtown is served by two limited but entertaining public transportation options. The **Skyway** (☎ 904-743-3582; W www.ridejta.net; monorail fare 35¢; operates 6am-11pm Mon-Fri, 10am-11pm Sat) connects downtown, which sprawls across the St John's River, via a very scenic monorail. Downtown San Marco is strolling distance from the Kings Ave station; you can connect to JTA at the FCCJ station. The free **trolley** (☎ 904-743-3582; W www.ridejta.net; operates 6:30am-7pm Mon-Fri) has 12 stops throughout downtown's northern shore.

Despite Jacksonville's admirable attempts at an adequate public transportation system, your own personal internal combustion engine is the best way to navigate this city. The morning rush hour (7am to 10am weekdays) backs up traffic headed into the city; evenings (4pm to 6pm) are much worse trying to leave. Roads linking downtown with the beaches are always congested.

Parking, on the other hand, is generally easy to find, and unmetered everywhere except downtown. There, several lots charge $6 to $8 daily.

OLUSTEE BATTLEFIELD

About a half-hour's drive west of Jacksonville on I-10, the **Olustee Battlefield Historic Site** (☎ 386-758-0400; pedestrian/car $1/3.25; open 9am-sunset daily) marks the site of the largest Civil War battle to take place in Florida.

Union strategists knew that it would be a bloodbath: This was wild country, and homegrown Confederate militias controlled the area. But they needed to cut off supply lines to enemy forces in Georgia. On February 20, 1864, some 10,000 troops (about 30% of Union forces were African American) faced off in an unbelievably brutal five-hour battle that had some of the highest casualty rates in the war: 1860 Union dead, 946 Confederate dead. Union troops retreated to Jacksonville, where they would remain until the end of the war.

Each February, thousands of Civil War buffs gather here for a play-by-play reenactment of the battle, which is well worth seeing if you're in the area. The **visitor's center museum** (open 9am-5pm Thur-Mon) has some neat exhibits on period uniforms, money and the like, but probably isn't of much interest to anyone but military historians.

AMELIA ISLAND
pop 20,000

This richly historic area is one of northern Florida's finest destinations. It's home to Fernandina Beach, an attractive shrimping village with a hugely intricate history, and to American Beach, the first resort for blacks

AMELIA ISLAND

PLACES TO STAY & EAT
1 Ocean View Inn
4 Elizabeth Pointe Lodge
7 Hampton Inn
8 Best Western
9 KP's Deli
10 Beachside Motel Inn
13 Ritz-Carlton
16 Amelia Island Plantation

OTHER
2 Atlantic Ave Recreation Center
3 Driftwood Surf Shop
5 Maytag Laundry
6 Baptist Medical Center-Nassau
11 Fernandina Beach Golf Club
12 Island Aerial Tours
13 Island Watersports
15 Black Heritage Museum
17 Kelly Seahorse Ranch

in Florida (a must-see on the Black Heritage Trail, a guide to which is available at Florida bookstores or through Florida tourist information centers). Civil War–era forts, tony resorts and miles of shark-tooth-covered coastline fringe the island, and just south is the tropical wilderness of Little Talbot Island and Fort George Island, two excellent state parks. And it's all just a ferry ride away from Jacksonville.

History

The French first established a settlement in the St John's River delta in 1564, two years after founding their first colonial outpost in present-day South Carolina. They built Fort Caroline here, in territory claimed by the Spanish crown, drawing a line in the sand that quickly became the Spanish-French DMZ.

Upon arriving in St Augustine to defend the Spanish claim, Don Pedro Menendez de Avilés launched two attacks against the French. The second led to the slaughter of some 600 French settlers (see the St Augustine History section, later in this chapter) and neutralized the French threat.

Amelia Island's strategic location remained key through centuries of colonial struggle. Between 1807 and 1809, when President Jefferson's Embargo Act forbade legal

Amelia Island was a popular roost for
pirates in the early 19th century.

trade between the US and European nations, Amelia Island became a bastion of black-market shipping: pirates, cutthroats and smugglers traded slaves and rum, and prostitutes took tips in half a dozen different currencies.

Then, in 1812, US-backed guerillas seized the island and turned over control to the US the next day. But after the Spaniards hit the roof, the US quickly returned it. In 1817, Sir Gregor MacGregor, a Scottish mercenary with revolutionary experience in Venezuela, rounded up some soldiers of fortune who again took the island from the Spanish. When the money ran out, so did MacGregor, who left two lieutenants in command. But wait…there's more!

The two left holding the bag, Lieutenants Ruggles Hubbard and Jared Irwin, formed a joint venture with a Mexican-backed French pirate named Louis Aury, and these three managed to turn the place into an even *more* scandalous town. It's said that there were more bars and brothels than street corners.

Perhaps using moral outrage as an excuse to nab some nifty real estate, US troops moved in and took over in December 1819. In a face-saving compromise, Spain officially turned Florida over to the US in 1821 in exchange for US promises to pay claims to Spanish subjects (none of which, by the way, were ever paid). A homegrown Confederate militia held the town for one year during the Civil War, setting up camp in the partially completed Fort Clinch, after which the Union regained control. Amelia Island has been in US hands ever since.

In the years following the Civil War, hotels popped up like mad to accommodate tourists brought here on the trans-Florida railroad. Henry Flagler's north-south railroad killed the boom in the 1890s, sucking more and more northern tourists directly to the resorts at St Augustine, Palm Beach and Miami. And it all happened so fast. In a Pompeii-like flash, the boomtown was frozen in time, and much of what you'll see here today remains practically unchanged.

Orientation & Information

Amelia Island is Florida's northernmost barrier island, located just south of the

Ten Flags

Local lore holds that since the Europeans showed up, Amelia Island has been ruled under eight flags. There are several problems with that, though, because of interrupted Spanish rule and the US Civil War. If you're going to count Spain twice in the beginning, as several tourist pamphlets do, then we say you should count the US twice in the end, as the US rule was indeed interrupted for a full year by the Confederates, who decidedly had a flag of their own.

And then there's argument about flags themselves: 'There's no documentation,' says James Perry, formerly the curator of the Amelia Island Museum of History, 'that the French ever even flew a flag.' And what is a flag, anyway – the Patriots flew one, while representing not a sovereign nation but a group of mercenaries and hotheads.

To settle the argument, we say that there were eight different flags flown at 10 different times:

French – 1562–1565

Spanish – 1565–1763

British – 1763–1783

Spanish – 1783–1821

Patriots – US spy-backed rebels, who captured the island on March 17, 1812, and gave it to the US the next day, who promptly gave it back to Spain

Green Cross of Florida – MacGregor's gang, 1817

Mexican Rebel Flag – Also in 1817, Aury and the boys, until the US moved in and took over the island, holding it in trust for Spain, which finally ceded Florida to the US in 1821

US – In 1821, happily running things until the Civil War

Confederate – In 1861, holding the island for a year; but on March 3, 1862, the US took over again

US – Under continuous US rule since 1862

– Nick & Corinna Selby

Georgia border and 30 miles northeast of Jacksonville. It's about 13½ miles long. The Downtown Fernandina Beach Historic District, at the northern end of the island, is where most of the action takes place. It's laid out in a grid, with east-west streets given names and north-south streets numbers. Centre St is the main drag and the north-south divider; it becomes Atlantic Ave east of 8th St.

The best free map for downtown is on the rate sheet for the Florida House Inn (see Places to Stay later in this section).

The **visitor's center** (☎ 904-261-3248, 800-226-3542; **w** www.ameliaisland.com; open 10am-3pm Mon-Sat) is in the old railroad depot at the west end of Centre St. The volunteer staff will help you sort through the zillions of flyers outlining what this small town has to offer.

Bank of America (☎ 904-321-1000; 520 Centre St) is right downtown. The main **post office** (cnr 4th & Centre Sts) is nearby. A great

bookstore, for both conversation and selection, is the **Book Loft** (☎ 904-261-8991; 214 Centre St). The main **library** (☎ 904-277-7365; 25 N 4th St; open 10am-6pm Mon-Sat, until 8pm Mon & Thur) has free Internet access.

The *Florida Times-Union* (**w** www .jacksonville.com) is the big daily; *Fernandina News Leader* is 'Florida's oldest weekly newspaper.' Commercial radio stations originate from Jacksonville.

Try **Maytag Laundry** (☎ 904-277-3730; 913 S 14th St) on Hwy A1A for washing.

Baptist Medical Center – Nassau (☎ 904-261-3627; 1250 S 18th St at Lime St) is the largest area medical facility. **Nassau City Health Center** (☎ 904-277-7280; 30 S 4th St; open 8am-5pm Mon-Fri) is a small clinic convenient to downtown.

Fort Clinch State Park

The US Government began construction of Fort Clinch (☎ 904-277-7274; pedestrian/car

$1/3.25; open 8am-sundown daily, fort open 9am-5pm daily) in 1847. It was state-of-the-art engineering at the time, but rapid advancements in military technology had already rendered its masonry walls – which new cannons could easily shatter – obsolete by the Civil War. A Confederate militia occupied the almost-complete fort early on in the conflict, but General Robert E Lee ordered an evacuation in 1862 following reports that well-armed, professional Union troops were just offshore. Federal troops again occupied the fort in 1898, following the detonation of the USS *Maine* in Havana, and during WWII, when the fort served as a surveillance and communications station for the US Coast Guard.

You may be lucky enough to wander in during a reenactment of the Confederate evacuation: Authentically outfitted troops (bare feet and 'gray' uniforms that had almost faded to the yellow of that era's popular and temporary vegetable dyes) had been stationed there all weekend when I visited.

These reenactors keep it as real as possible: They were cooking breakfast in the old kitchen's massive iron cauldron and sleeping on straw mats in the soldiers' barracks (though there was some discussion about how to file taxes online). When they raised the Bonnie Blue over the thick double walls of the massive fort, while the rest of the troops performed military drills in the grassy courtyard, it was something else. It's worth planning your visit around one of these events; call the park for a schedule. On regular days, rangers wear Union blue, cook meals on-site and pull sentry duty. If you make reservations in advance, they'll even take you on a candlelit tour.

Fort Clinch Rd is just west of the beach off Atlantic Ave.

Fernandina Beach

Fernandina Beach residents, who refer to the rest of the world as being 'off-island,' eat well in very good restaurants, live well in lovely Victorian houses, and guests can stay well in any of the many spectacular B&Bs. The only drawback is the paper mill just upwind of the city, which sends whiffs of production aroma townward.

Amelia Island Museum of History The state's only oral-history museum (☎ 904-261-7378; 233 S 3rd St; adult/student $4/2; open 10am-5pm Mon-Fri, 10am-4pm Sat), in the former city jail (1879–1975), offers docent-led tours at 11am and 2pm Monday through Saturday, which at press time was the only way to access the 1st floor. They hope to open those rooms to everyone as soon as they've adequately protected certain artifacts from the additional traffic. Even if it's open, keep in mind that the excellent exhibits are secondary to the oral history from the volunteers.

The museum also conducts two-hour walking tours of the Downtown Historic District, by appointment only (adult/student $10/5). At 3pm Thursday and Friday, they also hold a Centre St Stroll ($8/3) that leaves from the visitor's center.

St Peter's Parish This neo-Gothic Episcopal church (☎ 904-261-4293; cnr 8th St & Atlantic Ave), built 1881–84, features impressive stained-glass windows and a magnificent Harrison organ. Services are held Sunday at 7:30am, 9am and 11:15am.

American Beach

In 1901, AL Lewis (1865–1947) opened Florida's first insurance company, and it catered to black people. Business was so successful that in 1935 Lewis, an African American, bought up land on Amelia Island and founded American Beach, the first African American beach along Florida's segregated shores.

At its heyday, American Beach catered to throngs of Northern blacks, who came by the busload to enjoy the beaches and black-owned motels, restaurants and nightclubs, where shows with Ray Charles, Count Basie, Duke Ellington and other stars made for some of the biggest bills in Florida.

After desegregation, however, beaches closer to home opened up and the crowds stopped coming south. One by one, the clubs and restaurants lining the windswept coast shut their doors. In recent years, what's left of American Beach has become tightly sandwiched between golf courses and gated communities, raising the double-edged sword of skyrocketing property values: This historic landmark loses ground with each passing year. Famed **American Beach Villas** is 'closed for repairs' and could not say when they might reopen.

Local resident, great-granddaughter of Lewis and 'unofficial mayor' MaVynee Betsch (pronounced may-**veen** bech) has been leading the fight to protect the beach from further development, most recently saving a portion of Nana, the town's 55-foot sand dune. Ms Betsch is always happy to

guide tours personally, and she operates the **Black Heritage Museum** out of her small mobile home, parked at the corner of Gregg and Lewis Sts. For tour or any other information, contact MaVynee at the trailer when you get here, or write her at MaVynee Betsch, Black Heritage Museum, Gregg St, American Beach, Florida 32034.

Activities

There are free municipal tennis courts at the corner of Atlantic Ave and 13th St in Fernandina Beach. Get the key ($5 deposit) at

FERNANDINA BEACH

PLACES TO STAY
14 Hoyt House
17 Hampton Inn & Suites
18 Florida House Inn

PLACES TO EAT
1 Marina Restaurant
3 Amelia Island Gourmet Coffee
4 Café Karibo
16 Joe's 2nd St Bistro
20 T-Ray's Burger Station
23 Beech St Grill

OTHER
2 Palace Saloon
5 Main Library
6 Main Post Office
7 St Peter's Parish
8 Voyager Ventures
9 Visitor's Center
10 Public Toilets
11 Book Loft
12 O'Kane's Irish Pub & Eatery
13 Bank of America
15 Tennis Courts
19 Nssau City Health Center
21 Police
22 Fernandina Beach Bike & Fitness
24 Amelia Community Theatre
25 Amelia Island Museum of History

the **Atlantic Ave Recreation Center** (☎ 904-277-7350; 2500 Atlantic Ave; open 8am-8pm Mon-Fri, noon-8pm Sat, 2pm-4:30pm Sun). Amelia Island, known for its expansive private golf courses, also has an outstanding public option, **Fernandina Beach Golf Club** (☎ 904-277-7370; 2800 Bill Melton Rd; games $36-40 each; open 7am-6pm daily). They rent clubs for $25 per game.

Take surfing lessons through **Driftwood Surf Shop** (☎ 904-321-2188; 31 S Fletcher Ave), or just rent a longboard ($25) or body board ($10) and try the waves on your own.

Kelly Seahorse Ranch (☎ 904-451-5166), down the path that's the last left turn at the southern tip of the island, before you reach the bridge over Nassau Sound, does beach-side **horseback riding** tours atop some very mellow horses. One-hour rides ($35) leave four times daily; call in advance for 1½ hour ($50) and two-hour ($65) trips. Children must be at least 4 feet 6 inches tall, and there's a 230lb weight limit. Reservations are recommended on weekends and holidays.

Kayak Amelia (☎ 904-321-0697, 888-305-2925; ⓦ www.kayakamelia.com) offers half-day and full-day **kayaking** trips – they even provide cookies. **Down Under Guide & Booking** (☎ 904-261-9099; ⓦ www.fishinmusician.com; 4883 Otis Trail; open 4pm-8pm Wed-Sat), next to Down Under Restaurant (see Places to Eat), also offers kayak trips.

Voyager Ventures (☎ 904-321-1244; adult/child $35/16) runs sunset cruises year-round and afternoon sails April through September on the *Voyager,* a replica of a 19th-century ship. It leaves from the Fernandina Harbor Marina opposite the visitor's center.

Island Aerial Tours (☎ 904-321-0904) at Fernandina Beach Municipal Airport (take Hwy A1A to Parkway to Airport Rd and then follow the signs to the yellow hangar) can take up to three people in their Cessna 172 for a 40-minute tour ($100), or in the Warbird for a full hour ($200).

Places to Stay

Most places to stay are in Fernandina Beach. Room rates vary widely, rising about 50% during high season (March to September) and for special events.

Camping At Fort Clinch State Park (☎ 800-326-3521; without/with hookups $19/21) you'll find tent sites beneath sweeping oak trees draped with Spanish moss, but make reservations 11 months in advance. Fires are in grills only, and you'll need to bring your own firewood, as gathering it in the park is forbidden; some supermarkets sell bundles.

Motels & Hotels The Best Western (☎ 904-277-2300; 2707 Sadler Rd; singles/doubles $40/60 winter, $70/90 summer) has clean rooms, free admission to a local health club when you stay, and the friendliest staff around.

Ocean View Inn (☎ 904-261-0193; 2801 Atlantic Ave; rooms $85 winter, 'much higher' summer) has basic rooms, three free phone calls and a pool.

Beachside Motel Inn (☎ 904-261-4236; 3172 S Fletcher Ave; rooms $99-159 winter, $129-169 summer) doesn't take people under 25, but has crisp rooms and a great pool for everyone else.

Hampton Inn & Suites (☎ 904-491-4911; ⓦ www.hamptoninnandsuites.net; 19 S 2nd St; singles/doubles $134/154) is brand new and right downtown. It's also much more luxurious than the chain's sister property in town.

Amelia Island Plantation (☎ 904-261-6161, 800-874-6878; singles/doubles $158/194 winter, $224/292 summer), at the southern end of the island, is a 550-room resort primarily based around their golf courses, designed by Pete Dye and Tom Fazio. It's off Amelia Island Parkway south of American Beach – follow the signs.

The **Ritz-Carlton** (☎ 904-277-1100, 800-241-3333; ⓦ www.ritzcarlton.com; 4750 Amelia Island Pkwy; rooms from $148/188 winter/summer) is the finest resort on the island. Children's programs ('Ritz kids'), croquet, Jet-Skis, cooking classes, an 18-hole golf course, spa services and special events are just a few of the things that make this place worth the price. Heck, there's even a bonfire, with s'mores, on Saturday night.

B&Bs Amelia Island might well win the coveted 'Most B&Bs per Square Inch in Florida' award, if it existed. For *many* more options, log onto the Amelia Island Bed & Breakfast Association Web site (W www .ameliaislandinns.com).

Florida House Inn (☎ 904-261-3300, 800-258-3301; W www.floridahouse.com; 20 & 22 S 3rd St; rooms $80-180) is allegedly Florida's oldest hotel (1857), and in its heyday hosted luminaries including President Ulysses S Grant and poet José Martí. Rooms are beautifully decorated with antiques and artwork, and many have fireplaces. Loaner bikes are available. There's a friendly pub downstairs, and their restaurant serves up remarkably good Southern cooking (see Places to Eat, below).

Hoyt House (☎ 904-277-4300, 800-432-2085; W www.hoythouse.com; 804 Atlantic Ave; rooms $99-149), in a fabulously renovated Victorian home (1905), has nine rooms and serves homemade cookies and wine in the afternoons.

Elizabeth Pointe Lodge (☎ 904-277-4851; W www.elizabethpointelodge.com; 98 S Fletcher Ave; rooms $145-185, cottages for eight people $270) is even nicer than it looks from the outside. Rooms with ocean views are furnished with fresh flowers and the breakfast buffet is unreal. Rent a bike ($5) for the day, but be back in time for the wine-and-snacks social hour, 6pm to 7pm daily.

Places to Eat

T-Ray's Burger Station (☎ 904-261-6310; 202 S 8th St; dishes $3-6; open 7am-3pm Mon-Fri, 8am-1pm Sat), inside the Exxon station, is the real reason all those people are lined up outside. There's no sign, but that doesn't keep people away from the Big Breakfast (two eggs, grits, biscuit and bacon or sausage), famed burgers or daily specials. Word to the wise: T-Ray's chicken 'n' dumplings sell out every Thursday.

Amelia Island Gourmet Coffee Co (☎ 904-321-2111; 207 Centre St; open 7:30am-7pm Mon-Fri, 7:30am-9pm Sat & Sun) does caffeinated beverages right, as well as pastries, desserts and sandwiches like jerk chicken panini ($5 to $6).

Café Karibo (☎ 904-277-5269; 27 N 3rd St; mains $5-9; open 11am-9pm or so Mon-Sat, 11am-2pm Sun) is an oasis for vegetarians, where the freshest ingredients go into their chili with corn bread, fancy sandwiches and the excellent 'loaded' lentil salad. Carnivores have plenty of options, too. Don't skip dessert.

Fernandina Seafood Market (☎ 904-491-0476; 315 N Front St; dishes $6-8; open 11am-3:30pm Mon-Wed, 11am-5pm Fri-Sun), just a takeout window on the pier overlooking a flotilla of fishing boats, is worth the 10-minute walk on Front St from downtown. Enjoy the freshest fried seafood imaginable – oysters, fish and shrimp, among other choices. There are outdoor tables where you can watch the day's catch being unloaded.

KP's Deli (☎ 904-261-6251; 2124 Sadler Rd; dishes $5-10; open 10:30am-9pm Mon-Sat), at the scroungy Sadler Square shopping center, is a local favorite. Seeing all those huge portions of great food made ordering difficult, so I traded some of my delicious calypso chicken salad to the guy sitting next to me for a bite of his tender French dip sandwich. Both were flawless. Our server also recommended the spectacular assortment of desserts, all baked by KP's mother-in-law.

The **Florida House Inn** (☎ 904-261-3300; 20 & 22 S 3rd St; dishes $7-12; open lunch 11:30am-2:30pm Mon-Sat, dinner 5:30pm-8:30pm Tues-Sat, brunch 10am-2pm Sun) does amazing boardinghouse-style meals: Platters of stewed okra, fried chicken, catfish, collard greens, mashed potatoes and on and on just keep coming. Sit down at big tables with locals and other travelers for great conversation, and don't forget to take your dishes back to the kitchen when you're done.

Marina Restaurant (☎ 904-261-5310; 101 Centre St; mains $15-18; open 7am-10am & 11:30am-9pm daily) was packed with cops (the barometer with which I judge fine fried cuisine) enjoying the enormous seafood entrées.

Down Under Restaurant (☎ 904-261-1001; 4883 Otis Trail, Hwy A1A; mains $14-24; open 5pm-9:30pm Sun-Thur, 5pm-10pm Fri & Sat) gets raves for their simple but spectacular seafood entrées. Try the grouper Monterey (with onions, tomatoes and Jack cheese) or shrimp scampi. Getting here is a little tricky: Take Hwy A1A north from town and cross the bridge (you'll see the sign on your right), then make an immediate left into what looks like the parking lot of another restaurant. Follow the signs back under the bridge.

Joe's 2nd St Bistro (☎ 904-321-2558; 14 S 2nd St; mains $16-28; open 6pm-9:30pm daily), serves gourmetified Southern cuisine like pan-fried mahimahi with jalapeño grits.

Beech St Grill (☎ 904-277-3662; 801 Beech St; mains $21-30; open 6pm-10pm daily) has exquisite seafood. While they are not cheap, you get what you pay for: crab stuffed local shrimp, seared veal and daily fresh seafood specials for about the same price (some a bit cheaper), plus fine service.

Entertainment

Many of the restaurants on Fernandina Beach's downtown 'strip' double as pubs, and all are within easy crawling distance of one another.

O'Kane's Irish Pub & Eatery (☎ 904-261-1000; 318 Centre St; dishes $7-16) has serviceable Irish food, better Irish beer, and often live music (8pm to midnight), usually 'Jimmy Buffet–type stuff,' as well as a saxophone player Friday night.

Palace Saloon (☎ 904-261-6320; 113-117 Centre St) is a scene, where regulars include shrimpers from the nearby docks and area service-industry folks – it's got the latest hours in town, open 'reliably' until 2am – come by for brew and bands. Live shows usually have a $3 cover.

Amelia Community Theatre (☎ 904-261-6749; 209 Cedar St; tickets $3-12) is a quirky local theater now in its 18th season. On average, they perform eight plays a year, sometimes as part of dinner theater productions.

Getting There & Away

There's no public transportation between the mainland and the island, so you'll need a car, bicycle or a very expensive taxi.

By car, take exit 129 from I-95 to Hwy A1A east; follow this straight out to the island, about 15 miles. If coming from the west, take I-10 to the Baldwin exit, stay on Hwy 301 through Baldwin to Callahan and take Hwy A1A for about 40 miles.

From Jacksonville, head north along Hwy A1A from Jacksonville Beach to the town of Mayport, where you can catch the **St John's River Ferry** (☎ 904-251-3331; pedestrian/car 50¢/$2.75; operates 6:30am-10pm daily), also called the Mayport Ferry, which runs to Fort George Island. To Amelia Island, continue up Hwy A1A – there's no public transportation. **Island Trails** (☎ 904-491-8934, 904-459-1671) (see Getting Around) can drop off a bicycle at the ferry and pick it up anywhere on the island; make arrangements in advance.

Getting Around

For Fernandina Beach, walking is the best bet, but a car or bike is necessary to get around the island. Parking is easy and free. **Benjamin's Cab Service** (☎ 904-261-7278) provides transportation throughout the island and to Jacksonville Airport.

It's a great biking town and island – very flat and no major distances. **Fernandina Beach Bike & Fitness** (☎ 904-277-3227; 115 8th St; open Mon & Wed-Sat), just behind the BP station, rents bikes for $5 hourly, $14 daily or $65 weekly. Reserve early.

Another good place to rent bikes is **Island Trails** (☎ 904-491-8934, 904-459-1671). A three-day minimum rental ($35) is required, but by the week ($65) is a better deal. Brian can drop off and pick up the bike almost anywhere on the island.

TALBOT & FORT GEORGE ISLANDS

Just to the south of Amelia Island, these two islands contain a couple of very interesting state parks and a historic site. **Ft George Island Surf Shop** (☎ 904-251-3483; 10030 Heckscher Dr (Hwy A1A)) rents kayaks ($40 per day) and is also the island's post office.

Big Talbot Island State Park

There's not much to do here at this beautiful park (☎ 904-251-2320; pedestrian/car $1/2; open 8am-sundown daily) except see one of Florida's truly amazing natural wonders. Pull into the lone parking lot and follow a short, shady trail to the wild beach, where by some trick of the tides, enormous, tree-sized driftwood – polished and regal in sharp contrast to the white sands – litters the shoreline.

Little Talbot Island State Park

This treasure of an island (☎ 904-251-2320; pedestrian/car $1/4; open 8am-sundown daily) has plenty to recommend it: Five miles of beaches, canoeing ($5 hourly, $15 daily), hiking trails and elevated bike trails. Canoeing permission is granted depending on the tides.

There are campsites ($10/14 Oct-Feb/ Mar-Sept) right on the beach. You won't find a nicer place to pitch your tent on Florida's east coast. The park entrance is on the east side of Hwy A1A.

Kingsley Plantation

Zephaniah Kingsley and his wife, Anna Jai (whom he originally purchased as a slave and later married in a tribal African ceremony), established this plantation (☎ 904-251-3537; admission free; open 9am-4:45pm daily) here on Fort George Island in 1814. Today, you can tour the remains of 23 slave cabins and the main house, which features exhibits on natural history, slavery, and the couple's life, a show that recently toured Jai's native Senegal.

Kingsley was an unusual slave trader, less because he married and subsequently freed Jai and their three children (a fourth was born free) than for his vocal criticism of state law. He certainly wasn't against slavery as an institution, but argued in the Florida legislature that slaves and free blacks deserved *some* rights – like, say, they shouldn't be beaten to death without due legal process. Much eye-rolling (not to mention a couple of death threats) ensued. In 1835, he finally gave up on slavery altogether, freed everyone and moved the family to Haiti. After his death in 1860, Jai returned to Florida just in time to see the Emancipation Proclamation delivered.

The plantation is now your basic tropical paradise and a great place for a picnic. There are ranger-led tours at 1pm daily and 3pm Saturday and Sunday.

Huguenot Memorial Park

This excellent little regional park (☎ 904-251-3335; admission 50¢), just past the north-

ern St John's Ferry launch on Hwy A1A, has the best deal around on campsites ($6/8 interior/riverfront). The mellow atmosphere, cheap rates and wide beaches attract Jacksonville teens on weekends, so bring your earplugs. There are a few hiking trails, lots of sand dunes and a great shoreline with one unique feature: You can drive on the beach for free! It's even more fun than it sounds, but be sure to get some speed before negotiating the soft dunes at the entrance – don't worry, my teeny 2WD Toyota did just fine.

ST AUGUSTINE
pop 14,000

The oldest European settlement in the USA, St Augustine was founded by the Spanish in 1565. It's Europe by Disney without the admission fees: an American city with, at least in the downtown area, more cobblestone than asphalt, more coquina than cement, and more time and patience for the pleasures of living than one generally runs across. Spanish-colonial architecture combined with the period costumes required for many workers render the downtown one huge, permanent Renaissance fair.

Through the 144-block National Historic Landmark District clop horse-drawn carriages, and throngs of pedestrians gawk at the architecture and fill sidewalks lined with crafts shops, cafés, restaurants and pubs. It all adds up to a living time capsule (and tourist trap, but of the very highest quality) that's a real pleasure to visit.

History

St Augustine was settled by Spanish explorer Don Pedro Menendez de Avilés, who named the new settlement for the day he first sighted land, August 28, the saint's feast day. He had come to battle the French military (and Huguenot settlers) who had established Fort Caroline near present-day Jacksonville. The French fleet did him the favor of getting caught in a hurricane; the surviving troops were butchered by Menendez's men, inspiring the name of a nearby inlet: *Matanzas* (slaughter).

By the time Spain ceded Florida to the US in 1821, the city had been sacked, looted,

NORTHEAST

burned and occupied by Spanish, British, Georgian and South Carolinian forces. Many of these events are reenacted in a series of city-sponsored events throughout the year.

The British first occupied and torched the town in 1586 under the command of Sir Francis Drake, and again in 1668. Spain responded to the second assault by breaking ground for the Castillo de San Marcos in 1672. Now the oldest masonry fort in North America, it has never fallen to attack, though it has been at various times under command of Spanish, British, US and Confederate troops.

In 1702, the British again burned the city, but the fort held unscathed. In 1740, British, Georgian and South Carolinian troops attacked again, this time from the south at Matanzas inlet. Though the siege eventually failed, the Spanish realized that the unfortified inlet was as inviting to invaders as a large welcome mat, so they constructed tiny Fort Matanzas in 1742.

Beaten finally by fighting elsewhere in the French & Indian War, the Spanish ceded Florida to Great Britain in 1763 as a swap for Cuba. The British would stay for 20 years, leaving their mark in many ways. Under their rule, residents of the failed New Smyrna Beach colony (south of present-day Daytona Beach), established in 1768 by London physician Andrew Turnbull, brought about 1500 Greek, Italian and Minorcan laborers to Florida. Most fell prey to malaria, but descendants of the survivors remain to this day. As part of the Treaty of Paris, however, the fort was returned to Spain in 1783.

The Spanish, battered and bankrupt from centuries of war, ceded Florida to the USA in 1821. Henry Flagler brought his railroad to town in the late 1880s, and started a building boom of luxury hotels, gambling halls and restaurants. But as the railroad headed south, so did the tourists, leaving behind lots of very expensive and very empty buildings.

Today, the city retains much of its European flair. The coquina and tabby buildings, made of a locally popular concrete that uses crushed seashells as mortar, lend a faded, pastel but somewhat magical quality to the narrow streets, and the city's long and colorful history is palpable.

Orientation

St Augustine is about 35 miles southeast of Jacksonville, served by both US Hwy 1, which runs through the city, and I-95, about 10 miles west. The compact Downtown Historic District is the area roughly bordered by Orange St and the Old City Gate to the north, Bridge St to the south, Av Menendez and Matanzas Bay to the east, and Cordova St to the west. St George St is a pedestrian-only zone from Cathedral Place at the south to Orange St at the north.

North of downtown, Av Menendez becomes San Marco Ave, which intersects Ponce de Leon Blvd (US Hwy 1). King St connects US Hwy 1 and Beach Blvd (Hwy A1A) via the Bridge of Lions, becoming Anastasia Blvd on Anastasia Island, on the east side of Matanzas River. Both Anastasia State Park and St Augustine Beach are on Anastasia Island.

Information

The main **visitor information center** (☎ 904-825-1000; W www.visitoldcity.com; 10 Castillo Dr; open 8:30am-5:30pm daily) displays an overwhelming number of pamphlets and sells tickets for sightseeing trains, trolleys and horse-drawn carriages (see Organized Tours later in this section). There are smaller tourist information booths all over town.

There's a **Bank of America** (☎ 904-819-1300; 60 Cathedral Place) at the corner of Cordova St. The main **post office** (99 King St) is a short walk from downtown.

St Augustine has about a dozen used-bookstores. **Wolf's Head Books** (☎ 904-824-9357; 48-50 San Marco Ave) is one of the best.

The **public library** (☎ 904-823-2651; 1960 N Ponce de Leon Blvd; open 9:30am-9pm Mon-Wed, 9:30am-6pm Thur & Fri, 9:30am-5pm Sat, 1pm-5pm Sun) has free Internet access. Delve into the area's rich history at the **St Augustine Historical Society Research Library** (☎ 904-825-2333; 6 Artillery Lane; open 9am-4:30pm Tues-Fri).

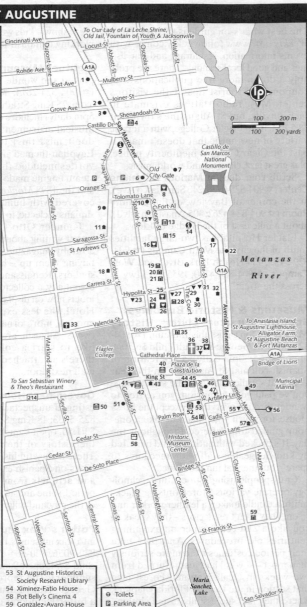

DOWNTOWN ST AUGUSTINE

PLACES TO STAY
- 11 Southern Wind
- 17 Monterey Inn
- 18 Old Powder House Inn
- 30 Secret Garden Inn
- 32 Casablanca Inn
- 34 Pirate Haus
- 43 Casa Monica
- 57 Marion Motor Lodge

PLACES TO EAT
- 12 Spanish Bakery
- 23 Schmagel's Bagels
- 27 Bunnery Café
- 29 Pizza Garden
- 31 Tea Room
- 37 Athena Restaurant
- 41 Café Alcazar
- 47 DeNoël French Pastry
- 55 OC White's
- 56 Santa Maria Restaurant

OTHER
- 1 3D World
- 2 Solano Scooter Rental
- 3 Wolf's Head Books
- 4 Ripley's Believe It or Not!
- 5 Visitor Information Center
- 6 Huguenot Cemetery
- 7 Rosario Defense Wall
- 8 Mill Top Tavern
- 9 Tomolato Cemetery
- 10 Oldest Wooden Schoolhouse
- 13 Spanish Quarter Living History Museum
- 14 Tourist Information
- 15 Casa Avero; St Photios National Greek Orthodox Shrine
- 16 The Monk's Vineyard
- 19 Casa de Nicholas de Ortega
- 20 Villalonga House
- 21 Acosta House
- 22 Horse-drawn carriages
- 24 Backstreet Coffee House & Lounge
- 25 Rendezvous
- 26 St George Tavern
- 28 Rodriguez-Avero-Sánchez House
- 33 Flagler Memorial Presbyterian Church
- 35 Peña-Peck House
- 36 Cathedral Basilica of St Augustine
- 38 TradeWinds Lounge
- 39 Hotel Ponce de León
- 40 Government House Museum
- 42 Lightner Museum
- 44 Trinity Parish Church
- 45 Potter's Wax Museum
- 46 Spanish Military Hospital
- 48 A1A Ale House
- 49 Victory III Scenic Cruises; Schooner Freedom; Sail Boat Adventures
- 50 Museum of Weapons
- 51 Flagler College Auditorium
- 52 Oldest Store Museum
- 53 St Augustine Historical Society Research Library
- 54 Ximinez-Fatio House
- 58 Pot Belly's Cinema 4
- 59 Gonzalez-Avaro House

To Our Lady of La Leche Shrine, Old Jail, Fountain of Youth & Jacksonville

Cincinnati Ave
Locust St
Dupont Lane
Abbott St
Osceola St
Water St
A1A
Rohde Ave
East Ave
Mulberry St
Joiner St
San Marco Ave
Grove Ave
Shenandoah St
Castillo Dr
Castillo de San Marcos National Monument
Old City Gate
Orange St
Tolomato Lane
Fort Al
St George St
Spanish St
Fletcher Lane
Saragossa St
St Andrews Ct
Cuna St
Sevilla St
Charlotte St
Matanzas River
Hypolita St
Cordova St
Carrera St
Court
Avenida Menendez
Valencia St
Markland Place
Flagler College
Treasury St
To Anastasia Island, St Augustine Lighthouse, Alligator Farm, St Augustine Beach & Fort Matanzas
Cathedral Place
Bridge of Lions
Plaza de la Constitution
King St
To San Sebastian Winery & Theo's Restaurant
Granada St
Artillery Ln
Avenida Menendez
Municipal Marina
214
Sevilla St
Palm Row
Cadiz St
Bravo Lane
Cedar St
Historic Museum Center
Cedar St
De Soto Place
Ribiera St
Weeden St
Sanford St
Central Ave
Dumas St
Oneida St
Washington St
St George St
Cordova St
Bridge St
St Francis St
Marine St
Charlotte St
Maria Sanchez Lake
San Salvador St

NORTHEAST

Toilets
Parking Area

The paper of record is the *St Augustine Record* (W www.staugustinerecord.com). The best what's-on guide is the free *Folio Weekly* (W www.folioweekly.com), with events information, restaurant and bar listings and good local scandals. There are probably a dozen more free publications with coupons and tourist tips at the visitor's center. Most radio stations originate in Jacksonville, but St Augustine's own is at 88.5 FM, from Flagler College, with a terrific variety of new music that doesn't make it past the Clear Channel mediocrity police, plus great jazz, classical and world music.

Scrub your duds at **Mariotti's Cleaning Center** (☎ 904-825-0738; 240 San Marco Ave), at the corner of Bayview, or the **Laundry Room** (☎ 904-824-4262; 405 Anastasia Blvd), about a mile east of the Bridge of Lions.

Flagler Hospital has two large facilities south of the city: the **Main Campus** (☎ 904-829-5155; 400 Health Park Blvd) and **West Campus** (☎ 904-826-4700; 1955 US Hwy 1) across the street.

Museums & Historic Buildings
Spanish Quarter Living History Museum Don't miss this museum (☎ 904-825-6830; St George St; adult/child $6.50/4; open 9am-5:30pm daily), a re-creation of Spanish-colonial St Augustine in the year 1740 that's walled off from the street. Once you've paid your admission, you're free to wander through everything except the Mesa House, for which you'll need to take a one-hour guided tour, offered throughout the day. It's packed with antiques and narrated by knowledgeable staff with anecdotes to spare – but the real fun is outside.

Craftspeople using 18th-century technology operate various 'storefronts': a blacksmith, a candle maker, a leather worker and so on. They aren't reenactors – they speak to you like a 21st-century person explaining centuries-old procedures. And they take their period costumes a tad more seriously than most – several had just returned from two weeks in Ocala National Forest (see that section in the Central Florida chapter), where they had successfully tested clothing and tools they'd made here. So this is all

potentially very useful information, in the event of an apocalypse. And they put on a great show – kids went crazy over the metalworking demonstrations.

Lightner Museum This majestically displayed and wonderfully bizarre collection (☎ 904-824-2874; W www.lightnermuseum.com; 75 King St; adult/child $6/2; open 9am-5pm daily) includes everything from antique musical instruments (played 11am daily – don't miss this) to matchbox labels to Egyptian-themed art deco sculpture. My favorites included the *Excelsior*, a working steam engine made entirely of blown glass, and the 1898 *Monkey Vase* by Inoue Ryosai, covered with hundreds of small ceramic simians. Eclectic, to say the least.

Founder Otto C Lightner started his career writing about different collections for a hobby magazine, and eventually started buying them up – buttons, salt and pepper shakers, Renaissance art, etc – becoming, essentially, a collector of collections. All this loot is now on display at the restored Alcazar Hotel, the less expensive (though oddly enough, more ornate) of Henry Flagler's two St Augustine resorts. Inspired? If you'd like to start a collection of your own, there's an attached antique (and junque) mall next door.

Government House Museum This interesting, if unspectacular, collection (☎ 904-825-5033; 48 King St; adult/student or child $3/1.50; open 9am-4:30pm daily) spotlights the history of the settlement of the city. There's a useful historical timeline and exhibits on Spanish explorers (including coins and artifacts from galleons), the British period, some archaeological finds, early plans of the city, and military architecture.

Potter's Wax Museum If you're really into wax museums, this is a good one (☎ 904-829-9056, 800-584-4781; 17 King St; adult/child $7/4; open 9am-5pm winter, 9am-9pm summer). The reproduction of President George 'Dubya' Bush, sculpted by either a bitter Democrat or *Mad* magazine fan, sold me. If you're gonna go, you've gotta see

Creative touches on Orlando signage

Curious manatee

Fountain and dome at Walt Disney World

Kennedy Space Center's Rocket Garden

Cape Canaveral honors US astronauts.

Space shuttles, US Astronaut Hall of Fame

Dude! Driving on the beach, St Augustine

Sun, sand and surf at Daytona Beach

Casa Monica, St Augustine

Light and water displays at Jacksonville's Friendship Park

the 'tyrant room': Nixon, Hitler, Mussolini, Harry Truman (?) and others.

Oldest Wooden School House This museum (☎ 904-824-0192, 800-653-7245; 14 St George St; adult/child $3/2; open 9am-5pm daily) is housed in a 200-year-old structure purchased by Juan Genoply, who conducted classes here. It has a very nice garden and animatronic teachers and students who'll teach you a lot about 18th-century life and education.

Spanish Military Hospital A different sort of attraction (☎ 904-825-6808; 3 Aviles St; adult/child $3/2; open 10am-4pm daily), this hospital doesn't appear to be much, but the volunteers are wonderful: If you get a good one, plan on spending an hour hearing history, tales of Spanish explorers and perhaps the origin of the term 'sleep tight.' The building is a reconstruction of a military hospital that stood on the site during the second Spanish-colonial period (1784–1821). The herb garden out back grows potent medicines common back then and coming back into style today; one hopes the fierce-looking amputation equipment will never again be in vogue.

Oldest Store Museum This wacky museum (☎ 904-829-9729; 4 Artillery Lane; adult/child $5/2; open 10am-4pm Mon-Sat, noon-4pm Sun) has a fascinating collection of clutter including everything from a colonial-era dentistry tool (ouch!) to a dog-powered butter churn. Among the standouts are a disturbingly graphic 19th-century chart discussing health risks associated with alcoholism and an excellent collection of old vehicles, including a real Conestoga covered wagon that negotiated the brutal Oregon Trail.

Museum of Weapons Owners Donna Lee and Delilah Walton are well known among area military archaeologists and relic hunters, who bring their treasures here (☎ 904-829-3727; 81-C King St; adult/child $4/1; open 9:30am-5pm daily) first. This means that you get to enjoy an unparalleled collection of guns, knives, ammunition, sniper glasses and the like, all crammed into one very small room.

Exhibits include *Feared One,* a Remington rolling caliber rifle hand-beaded by the Sioux brave who bore it, and the 1⅝₁₆-inch-long, 2mm Pinfire pistol from Austria, designed for ladies to use at very close range. The focus here, however, is the Civil War. CSA (Confederate States of America) uniforms and military equipment are displayed alongside slave-traders' documents and the signature of General Robert E Lee. This museum isn't for everyone, but military and gun buffs will be astounded.

Old Jail The former town prison and residence of the town's first sheriff, Charles Joseph 'the Terror' Perry (who stood 6 feet, 6 inches tall and weighed more than 300lb), is now a museum (☎ 904-829-3800, 800-397-4071; 167 San Marco Ave; adult/child $5/4; open 8:30am-5pm daily). Built in 1892, the simple structure housed up to 64 bad seeds in very cramped cells. Upstairs, there's a firearms collection. Narration makes it more interesting than it sounds, such as the explanation of the area out back beneath the 'bird cage,' where locals used to picnic while harassing the unhappy occupant of the man-sized cage suspended above the lawn. Nice.

St Augustine Lighthouse You can see light produced by the first-order lens from this lighthouse (☎ 904-829-8172; 81 Lighthouse Ave (Old Beach Rd); adult/child $7/4, $4/2 for the house & grounds only; open 9am-7pm daily) all the way from downtown. The black-and-white-striped St Augustine Lighthouse (219 steps to the top) is a great place to bring kids older than seven and more than 4 feet tall (none younger or shorter are allowed). The adjacent museum contains things nautical.

Hotel Ponce de León Henry Flagler was a visionary, but if he ever envisioned 175 college students chowing down on sloppy joes and fish sticks in his flagship luxury hotel's dining room – the one with all the Tiffany glass and the ornate 35-foot vaulted ceiling – he certainly never said so in his memoirs.

The hotel, which was completed in May 1887, quickly became the most exclusive winter resort in the USA. Flagler College, the pricey private university that has taken over the property and extensively renovated it, offers tours (☎ 904-823-3378; adult/child $4/1) from May to August and over the Christmas holidays. Do try to see the Flagler Room, which makes the dining room look positively common.

Historic Remains
Old City Gate This gate, at the northern end of St George St, was built in 1739 to defend the northern St Augustine line from attacks by the British. The coquina pillars were built in 1808.

Rosario Defense Wall Opposite the Huguenot Cemetery is a re-creation of a section of the Rosario Defense Wall, an earth barrier constructed by the Spaniards in the early 1700s to fend off British attack. The wall, which successfully stopped the Brits, was originally topped with spiky yucca plants and prickly-pear cacti.

Plaza de la Constitution Opposite the Bridge of Lions in the heart of downtown, this grassy expanse has a gazebo, a couple of cannons and a Civil War memorial, as well as the remains of the town well and a centuries-old marketplace. It was the central market for food, and (though this goes unmentioned on the historical marker) for slaves.

An interesting historical note: When St Augustine was ruled by the Spanish, many escaped slaves from Georgia and points north would make their way here. While the Spanish did have slavery, they tweaked the Brits with a law guaranteeing that any slave escaping from a British colony would be granted freedom on arrival.

Castillo de San Marcos National Monument In 1672, after the British had burned the city down around them one time too many, the Spanish began work on this coquina fort (☎ 904-829-6506; adult/child

$5/2; open 8:45am-4:45pm daily). It was completed 23 years later, and is now the oldest masonry fort in the continental US. It's an impressive feat of military engineering, and rangers wearing Spanish-colonial-era uniforms (some accessorized with sneakers and cell phones) just add to the medieval ambience of the place. Reenactments, complete with pirate ships, firefights and villagers running amok, take place here occasionally, and the cannons are fired every Sunday. You can hear the ancient iron beasts all over town.

Historic Homes
Antique lovers and history buffs alike will go gaga over the many impressive old homes restored by organizations and individuals. Some you can tour in their entirety, but you'll have to content yourself with the outside view of others.

Gonzalez-Alvarez House (☎ 904-824-2872; 14 St Francis St; adult/student $5/3; open 9am-5pm daily) claims continuous occupancy from the early 1600s to today, making it the oldest house in the USA. True or not, it has some lovely gardens and exhibits on early residents and the British sacking of the city.

Peña-Peck House, (☎ 904-829-5064; 143 St George St; adult/student $5/3; open 12:30pm-4:30pm Tues-Sun), run by the Women's Exchange, was built in the 1740s as the home of the Spanish royal treasurer, Juan Estaban de Peña. It was later renovated by Dr Seth Peck, whose family lived here until the 1930s.

Ximinez-Fatio House (☎ 904-829-3575; w www.ximinezfatiomuseum.org; 20 Aviles St; open 11am-4pm Thur-Mon) is a coquina block house built in the late 1700s that served as the general store and home of merchant Andres Ximinez. It later became an inn owned by Louisa Fatio.

St George St has several old buildings that deserve a longer look. Though there are shops and museums in them now, plaques offer abbreviated historical narratives. From north to south, these include the Casa de Nicholas de Ortega (1740), Villalonga House (1803–20), Acosta House (1803–12) and Rodriguez-Avero-Sánchez House (circa 1762).

The **Historic Museum Center** comprises eight houses on a city block bounded by Palm Row at the north, St George on the east, Cordova on the west and Bridge St at the south. The free *St Augustine Historic Museum Center* pamphlet, found at the visitor's center and in bins by the historic center, has maps and a self-guided tour to the homes, including interesting historical accounts of each edifice.

Churches & Shrines
Cathedral Basilica of St Augustine
This magnificent 1797 Spanish mission–style Catholic cathedral (☎ 904-824-2807; w www .thefirstparish.com; Cathedral Place; admission free), near the Plaza de la Constitution on the northeast corner of St George and King Sts, stands on the site of what was likely the first Catholic house of worship in the New World. The coquina church became a cathedral in 1870, but a fire destroyed much of it in 1887, which was a good excuse to build much of the soaring structure you see today. Mass is held at 8am Monday through Saturday, 11am and 6pm Sunday; there's an evening vigil at 5pm Saturday. Special events like the Blessing of the Animals bring in the crowds.

Trinity Parish Church
The first Protestant church in Florida (☎ 904-824-2876; 215 St George St; admission free; open 9am-4pm daily), directly south across Plaza de la Constitution, was built in 1821. The revelatory stained glass was designed and constructed either by Tiffany personally or by his company; note the window in St Peter's Chapel, in the main building, signed by Tiffany himself. Services are held at 7:45am, 9am and 11:15am Sunday, and at 10am Wednesday. Free tours are usually available in the afternoons Monday through Saturday.

Flagler Memorial Presbyterian Church
If Henry Flagler wanted to outdo the cathedral builders at their own game, this extravagant church (☎ 904-829-6431; 36 Sevilla St; admission free; open 9am-4:30pm Mon-Sat, 12:30pm-4:30pm Sun), at the corner of Valencia St, arguably succeeded. Built as a memorial to his daughter, Jennie, who died at birth, the spectacular Venetian-Renaissance edifice (1889–90) illuminates its trademark dome at night. The floor is Sienna marble, the wood is Santo Domingo mahogany and the pipe organ, which is played 11am Sunday and 12:15pm Wednesday, is enormous. Services are at 8:30am and 10:55am Sunday.

St Photios National Greek Orthodox Shrine
In memory of the Greek immigrants who labored at New Smyrna Beach (see History earlier in this section), this shrine and museum (☎ 904-829-8205; 41 St George St; admission free; open 9am-4:30pm daily) has amazing and ornate Byzantine murals covering the vaulted ceiling and walls. You can light candles and make an offering in the shrine, which has piped-in chanting. There are also exhibits elucidating area history, with old maps, mementos and diaries of settlers. Back in the lobby, watch an 18-minute video about the history of the colony. And remember that this is indeed a shrine: While shorts and T-shirts are fine, food and drink are not; ask permission before taking photographs. Donations are appreciated.

Our Lady of La Leche Shrine
Pro-choicers shouldn't be put off by the oh-so-tasteful memorial to aborted fetuses/children near the entrance of Mission Nombre de Dios (☎ 904-824-2809; 27 Ocean Ave; admission free). Wander past it instead, along a shady trail that passes several interesting sculptures and monuments, including the 208-foot-tall stainless-steel cross that's visible from many parts of downtown, to the serene Shrine to Our Lady of La Leche. The small chapel houses a very maternal-looking image of the Virgin Mary, which according to local tradition washed ashore in the early 1600s and has been helping women with every aspect of childbirth since. If you're pregnant (or want to be), ladies of any faith or none are welcome to pick up a candle at the gift shop and illuminate her altar accordingly.

Other Attractions
Anastasia State Recreation Area
This recreation area (☎ 904-461-2033; 1340 Hwy A1A; pedestrian/car $1/3.25), on Anastasia Island (the entrance is on Anastasia Blvd) is

NORTHEAST

a very nice state park with beach access at its eastern end, nature and hiking trails and a campground (see Places to Stay). Concessions rents umbrellas, bikes and canoes and can arrange sailboard lessons along the 4 miles of perfect beach.

Ripley's Believe It or Not!

Yes, it's a chain. Yes, it's cheesy. But inside the old (1887) Castle Warden is the first and flagship Ripley's Believe It or Not! (☎ 904-824-1606; 19 San Marco Ave; adult/child $10/6; open 9am-10pm daily), a monument of sorts to the culture of modern tourism. It has pretty much the same fun stuff you'll see in any of Ripley's fine outposts, so if you've never given in to your curiosity (c'mon, admit it, you want to check out that two-headed calf for yourself), St Augustine is the place to do it.

Robert Ripley, seeker of the amazing and bizarre

Fountain of Youth

This shady, pleasant park (☎ 904-829-3168, 800-356-8222; 11 Magnolia Ave; adult/senior/student or child $5.75/4.75/2.75; open 9am-6pm daily) has flocks of peacocks, guides dressed in full Spanish military regalia, a planetarium show and a working archaeological dig of Seloy, the Timucuan village that predates European St Augustine. It also has the *actual* fountain of youth sought by Spanish explorer Juan Ponce de León! Before you start stocking up at the gift shop, however, note that some of the people working here have…um…wrinkles. Claims may be a little overstated. Regardless, kids love the enthusiastic narrative,

over-the-top props and bright exhibits, not to mention all the farm animals running around, and adults with a taste for the absurd will have a ball.

San Sebastian Winery

The winery (☎ 904-826-1594; 157 King St; open 10am-6pm Mon-Sat, 11am-6pm Sun) has free, one-hour tours topped off with wine tastings, and shows a short video about Florida wine making since the 1600s.

3D World

This 3D-themed place (☎ 904-829-9849; 28 San Marco Ave; admission $10; open 9am-8pm daily) is bemoaned by almost everyone as 'cheesy' or 'lame' – everyone, that is, except for dozens of eight- to 12-year-olds I interviewed outside, who enthusiastically agree that this is the coolest thing since GameCube. Hyperactive children and adults diagnosed with ADD may want to check it out.

Alligator Farm

This farm (☎ 904-824-3377; Anastasia Blvd; adult/child $15/9; open 9am-5pm daily), about a mile east of the bridge, is a blast. You'll cross ponds packed with American alligators and see caged examples of rarer reptiles like the Nepalese gharial and Siamese crocodile, extinct in the wild. Don't miss Gomek, the biggest (stuffed) gator in Florida. Other wildlife includes several rare bird species that are quite a sight when mating and nesting. There are talks and shows at the Reptile Theater throughout the day, starring a couple of baby beasties and Regi the Burmese python. And hey, no pets, OK?

St Augustine Beach

The 7-mile stretch of St Augustine Beach is a great place to get tan, and the strip of Hwy A1A fronting it has budget hotels, family restaurants and boisterous bars to spare. If you need an excuse to relax in the Florida sunshine, head to the **St John's Pier** (☎ 904-461-0119; 350 Beach Blvd (Hwy A1A); open 6am-10pm daily), where you can rent a rod and reel ($3 for two hours, $1 for each additional hour).

Take Anastasia Blvd to Hwy A1A right out to the beach; there's a visitors information booth right at the foot of the pier.

Organized Tours

There are dozens of guided tours through this historic town, all with slick, bright pamphlets scattered like confetti through hotel lobbies, museums and visitor's centers. These are just a few.

Roland Loveless (☎ 904-797-9733), who is very friendly and knowledgeable, runs several different walking tours through downtown, bedecked in full early-1700s Spanish costume. Get information and make reservations directly.

There's a serious obsession with the supernatural in this city, and several tours cater to the spiritually sensitive. **Ghostly Experience Walking Tours** (☎ 904-461-1009, 888-461-1009; tours $8) covers downtown, and also offers a tour of the 'haunted' St Augustine Lighthouse on Friday. **Ghost Walk** (☎ 904-829-2396; tours $8) also covers downtown.

You could take a **horse-drawn carriage tour** through town, but keep in mind that animal activists take issue with the steeds' long working hours. **St Augustine Transfer** (☎ 904-829-2818, 904-829-2391; adult/child $15/7, private carriage $55) leaves from Av Menendez just south of the fort for a 2½ hour ride with opinionated anecdotes aplenty.

Motorized Tours There are two fiercely competitive tourist choo-choos plying city streets, **Old Town Trolley Tours** (☎ 904-829-3800; w www.trolleytours.com/staugustine; 167 San Marco Ave; adult/child $15/5) and **St Augustine Sightseeing Trains** (☎ 904-829-6545; w www.redtrains.com; 170 San Marco Ave; adult/child $12/5). Both offer free parking at their headquarters, free shuttles from most area hotels, more expensive packages with discount admission tickets to area attractions and lively narratives of city history. There are ticket booths at the visitor's center (see Information) and at dozens of stands in town. You can get on and off your company's vehicle as often as you'd like at any of 20 stops, but remember to wear your admission sticker at all times. Tourists foolish enough to try boarding the wrong company's vehicle risk being chastised severely by loyal employees.

If you'd prefer to see the city from an air-conditioned van, **Fiesta Tours** (☎ 904-825-0519, 888-275-8902; w www.fiestatours .com; 41 Cathedral Place; tickets $10-70) offers similar services (with less freedom to roam) plus trips farther afield, including the Kennedy Space Center (see the Space Coast chapter) and Daytona USA (see the Daytona Beach section, later in this chapter).

Boat Tours Victory III Scenic Cruises (☎ 904-824-1806, 800-542-8316; adult/senior/child $11/9/7) offers narrated 1¼-hour cruises in huge 120-person boats along the waterfront. Cruises leave four to six times daily from the Municipal Marina, just south of the Bridge of Lions.

For a more romantic ride, try **Schooner Freedom** (☎ 904-810-1010; tours $28), also at the Municipal Marina, where 50 people enjoy two-hour tours aboard a replica 19th-century tall ship; folks wearing pirate costumes get 10% off Thursday night.

Sail Boat Adventures (☎ 904-347-7183; w www.villavoyager.com; 308 Segovia Rd; tours $35) has a six-person limit on their four-hour, wind-driven trips.

Places to Stay

St Augustine is a popular weekend escape for Florida residents, so expect room rates to rise about 25% on Friday and Saturday. It's fairly pricey, but you'll definitely find decent doubles for $50 during the wintertime low season (roughly October to March) and $80 summertime high season (May to August).

Camping The **Anastasia State Recreation Area** (☎ 904-461-2033; 1340 Hwy A1A; sites without/with electricity $18/20), on Anastasia Island, has beautiful campgrounds, but make reservations months in advance, particularly for weekends. For more information see Other Attractions earlier in this section.

KOA (☎ 904-471-3113, 800-562-4022; 525 W Pope Rd; tent sites $26, full hookups $35-41), just across the Mickler O'Connell Bridge on Anastasia Island, isn't as scenic but is much more likely to have sites available. There's a $4 shuttle to downtown.

NORTHEAST

Hostels The **Pirate Haus** (☎ 904-808-1999; W www.piratehaus.com; 32 Treasury St; dorm beds $15, rooms $36-56) is a truly fine place, with clean, bright rooms that are nicer than many hotels', a full kitchen and rooftop barbecue, festive common room and rotating door code with no lockout. Laundry service ($3), bike rentals ($5) and Internet access are all part of the package. About 30 area businesses also grant guests special discounts, too. And what a location: two blocks north of King St downtown (though parking is limited, which can be a hassle). What more could you want? Well, how about an all-you-can-eat breakfast featuring 'pirate pancakes'? Sorry, I can't go into details. Bob and Ellie, the owners, are great sources of local information and appreciate hostelling and pirates with equal enthusiasm. Highly recommended.

Motels There are plenty of choices in motels, running the gamut from as sleazy as you'd imagine to as nice as you'd want. The better ones are in the center, the cheaper ones along San Marco Ave and Anastasia Blvd. Motels and chain hotels line San Marco Ave, near the area near where it meets US Hwy 1.

Scottish Inns (☎ 904-824-2871, 800-251-1962; 110 San Marco Ave; rooms winter/summer $45/55 Mon-Fri, $65/75 Sat & Sun) has basic, comfortable rooms and staff that goes way beyond the call of duty: They even taped an 'urgent' message from Mom to my door.

The **Monterey Inn** (☎ 904-824-4482; W www.themontereyinn.com; 16 Av Menendez; singles/doubles $46/69 Mon-Fri, $79/99 Sat & Sun) has perfectly acceptable rooms and a great location.

Marion Motor Lodge (☎ 904-829-2261, 800-258-2261; 120 Av Menendez; rooms $58-78 Sun-Thur, $98 & up Fri & Sat) is a pleasant enough place and right on the water.

Ramada Inn (☎ 904-824-4352; 116 San Marco Ave; rooms from $60/100 winter/summer) has big rooms and a great hot tub.

La Fiesta Oceanside Inn (☎ 904-471-2220; W www.lafiestainn.com; 810 Beach Blvd (Hwy A1A); rooms from $99 winter, $199 summer), just steps from St Augustine Beach, has ocean views, a pier and free shuttles to downtown.

Edgewater Inn (☎ 904-825-2697; 2 St Augustine Blvd; rooms $95 Sun-Thur, $105 Fri & Sat), at the eastern terminus of the Bridge of Lions, has the nicest view in town; some of the spotless rooms have large bay windows to take it all in. You can also dock at their private marina.

EconoLodge (☎ 904-471-2330; 311 Beach Blvd (Hwy A1A)); rooms $49/109 winter/summer) is the best deal on the beach, with very basic accommodations across Hwy A1A from the sand.

Casa Monica (☎ 904-827-1888, 800-648-1888; rooms from $199-239 winter, $219-259 summer), in the former Cordova Hotel (circa 1880), is a grand restoration project done right. It's got amenity-packed rooms, a spectacular lobby and a truly grand swimming pool, as well as gourmet restaurants, art galleries, clothing shops, jewelry stores…need I go on?

B&Bs There are *at least* 25 registered B&Bs in town, all with outstanding reputations. For more options you can contact **Historic Inns of St Augustine** (W www.visitoldcity.com).

Southern Wind (☎ 904-825-3626, 800-781-3338; W www.southernwind.com; 18 Cordova St; rooms $115-215) is mellow and spacious, with wide verandas made for sipping iced tea while you listen to the horse-drawn carriages clop by. Their buffet breakfast is seasoned with herbs from the organic gardens out back.

Casablanca Inn (☎ 904-826-1892, 800-826-2626; W www.casablancainn.com; 24 Av Menendez; rooms $90-200 Sun-Thur, $130-225 Fri & Sat) lets you enjoy a big breakfast on the expansive veranda overlooking the water. Even the less expensive rooms are lovely.

Old Powder House Inn (☎ 904-824-4149; W www.oldpowderhouse.com; 38 Cordova St; rooms $90-120 Sun-Thur, $150-160 Fri & Sat) is as frilly as a litter of perfumed pink poodles and serves a truly outstanding breakfast. The no-kids policy and complimentary bicycles are just two of the reasons why guests keep coming back.

Secret Garden Inn (☎ 904-829-3678; 56½ Charlotte St; rooms from $105 Sun-Thur, $150 Fri & Sat), tucked way back in the alley, is shady and romantic. With only three suites, you won't have to worry about finding quiet time in the gardens.

Places to Eat

There's plenty to keep you full, and cheaply. And cheap doesn't mean bad: case in point, the Spanish Bakery's filling lunches and pastries. Note that laid-back St Augustine restaurants often close a bit earlier or later than the hours listed.

Snacks, Pizza & Fast Food The **Spanish Bakery** (☎ 904-471-3046; 47½ St George St; dishes $1-3; open 9:30am-3pm daily) is quicker, cheaper and much, much better than any chain. Check out cases of tasty fresh-baked empanadas, cookies and smoked-sausage rolls ($3). The filling lunch special includes soup, mini bread and a soft drink ($5).

Schmagel's Bagels (☎ 904-824-4444; 69 Hypolita St; dishes $2-5; open 7am-3pm, closes 2pm in summer) serves your choice of 10 different bagels and 14 types of toppings, as well as sandwiches prepared with your bagel of choice. There are lovely courtyard tables.

Pizza Garden (☎ 904-825-4877; 21 Hypolita St; slices $3-5, pies $7-18; open 11am-9pm Sun-Thur, 11am-10pm Fri & Sat) has a relaxing outdoor patio and good 'n' greasy pizza by the slice or pie.

DeNoël French Pastry (☎ 904-829-3974; 212 Charlotte St; dishes $5-7; open 9am-7pm daily) has been serving decadent homemade baked goods since 1966. They also have sandwiches on fresh croissants, but why spoil your appetite for dessert?

Bunnery Café (☎ 904-829-6166; 121 St George St; dishes $7-9; open 8am-6pm daily) serves healthy salads and sandwiches, then immediately sabotages whatever health gains were made with their surreally delectable sticky pecan buns and cinnamon rolls.

Restaurants & Cafés A classic Greek diner, **Athena Restaurant** (☎ 904-823-9076; 14 Cathedral Place; dishes $2-8; open 7am-9pm Sun-Thur, 7am-10pm Fri & Sat) does excellent breakfasts, good burgers and the best tzatziki around. Don't mind the line – it's worth the wait.

Theo's Restaurant (☎ 904-824-5022; 169 King St; dishes $3-6; open 6:30am-3pm Mon-Fri, 6:30am-2pm Sat, 7:30am-2pm Sun) is a local favorite for breakfast. It's a family-run Greek place that bakes all its own bread and cinnamon buns daily and serves up excellent Greek and American food for cheap at lunch; try the pastitsio.

Café Alcazar (☎ 904-824-7813; 25 Granada St; dishes $4-7; open 11:30am-3pm Tues-Sat), adjacent to the Lightner Museum, serves sandwiches, salads and other café standards in one really awesome 'room': It was once the world's largest indoor pool, done up in that patented Flagler opulence.

Manatee Café (☎ 904-826-0210; 179A San Marco Ave; dishes $4-8; open 8am-3pm Tues-Thur), at the corner of May St, does excellent vegetarian and vegan cuisine. The veggie pita, with the extra hummus recommended by my server, was the best meal I had in St Augustine – and I ate *well* in St Augustine.

Treasure Ship Restaurant (☎ 904-471-0889; 7001 Hwy A1A S; mains $5-10; open 8am-7pm daily), on the way to Fort Matanzas, has edible food and the amazing Norman, who may perform one of his impromptu comedy/magic acts if you're friendly. Shrimp and other dishes are available; note that despite how tasty some of the items on his road-kill menu might sound, the restaurant doesn't actually serve pickled possum tails.

Tea Room (☎ 904-808-8395; 15 Hypolita St; dishes $6-10; open 11am-4pm Wed-Sun) is a delightful, *trés* European place (the owner speaks French, Dutch and German) serving afternoon tea, 'dainty' sandwiches and scones, as well as lighter options, in their lacy dining room.

Jack's Pit Bar-B-Que (☎ 904-460-8100; 691 Beach Blvd (Hwy A1A); mains $5-12; open 10am-10pm Mon-Fri, 8am to at least 10pm Sat & Sun), out by the beach, serves outstanding barbecue sandwiches and full entrées with cold beer on their sandy porch. Both the turkey and pork are tops.

NORTHEAST

OC White's (☎ 904-824-0808; 118 Av Menendez; lunch mains $5-8, dinner mains $12-20) is a party place with a pleasant outdoor patio and live music every night, usually classic rock cover bands, and reggae on Saturday night. Serviceable fish and pasta dishes are another excuse for lounging around here for a while, and the staff says the specials are always tops.

Fusion Point (☎ 904-823-1444; 237 San Marco Ave; open 5pm-10pm daily) is a satisfying splurge on beautifully prepared sushi. Very fresh sashimi runs $1 to $2 per piece, $3 to $6 for a roll, and fully cooked entrées, mostly curries and stir-fries, set you back $9 to $20.

Santa Maria Restaurant (☎ 904-829-6578; 135 Av Menendez; mains $12-20; open noon-9pm Thur-Tues, 5pm-9pm Wed), just south of the Marina at the end of a wooden pier, serves filling (read: fried) family-style fish dishes. But that's not why you're here: After you order, open up the trapdoor in your table and drop bread crumbs (they bring a bowl to your table) to the hordes of hungry catfish below. Catfish basking by the floodlight to the right of the pier, outside the restaurant, enjoy such snacks as well.

Gypsy Cab Co (☎ 904-824-8244; 828 Anastasia Blvd; mains $12-20; open 4:30pm-11pm daily, lunch 11am-3pm Sat, brunch 10:30am-3pm Sun) is absolutely worth crossing the bridge for, not the least for the superb house dressing. Entrées like blackened grouper and baked ziti get raves, and Saturday lunches are a deal, with an abbreviated menu of their gourmet fare for almost half off.

The Raintree (☎ 904-824-7211; 102 San Marco Ave; mains $12-30; open 5pm-10pm daily) is a fine choice for decked-out dining. Evening entrées include beef Wellington and raspberry-glazed roast duck. The dining room glows, giving the large Victorian house something of an enchanted feel.

Entertainment
Theater & Cinema
The **Flagler College Auditorium** (☎ 904-824-2874, 866-352-4537; W www.flaglerauditorium.com; tickets $5-15), on the Flagler College campus just west of the Lightner Museum, stages student pro-

ductions as well as classical music and jazz performances from September to May.

St Augustine Amphitheater (☎ 904-471-1965; 1340 Hwy A1A S), about half a mile east of the entrance to the Anastasia State Recreation Area on Anastasia Blvd, does professional and community theater and often has free live music (parking is $5).

Limelight Theatre (☎ 904-825-1164; W www.limelight-theatre.com; 11 Old Mission Ave; adult/student $22/20 musicals, $16/14 dramas or comedies) also stages professional performances.

Pot Belly's Cinema 4 Plus (☎ 904-829-3101; 31 Granada St) shows first-run movies for $3.75, which you'll watch from the comfort and luxury of a reclining easy-chair while the waitstaff brings you sodas, beer or wine, plus pizzas, sandwiches and other deli delights.

Bars & Clubs
Locals and tourists mingle downtown at a variety of pleasant watering holes.

TradeWinds Lounge (☎ 904-829-9336; W www.tradewindslounge.com; 124 Charlotte St) is the classic St Augustine local bar, under the same management for about 50 years. It's got live music every night by Southern-rock outfit Matanza, the house band, or other local musicians.

St George Tavern (☎ 904-824-4204; 116 St George St; open 11am-1am) is a rowdy local bar and gets packed with college students and downtown's period-costumed workforce during their great happy hour, from 4pm to 7pm Monday through Thursday.

Mill Top Tavern (☎ 904-829-2329; 19½ St George St) may be touristy, but it has a great location in a restored grist mill with a covered deck overlooking the fort and St George St scene. Grab a brew or two and listen to live music almost daily, with acoustic stuff during the day and more rockin' bands at night.

The Monk's Vineyard (☎ 904-824-5888; 56 St George St; open 11am-6pm Thur-Tues) serves their own line of alcoholic beverages: Try the Blushing Monk wine or the very yummy Buzzing Monk mead. Their narrow patio hosts some of the last remaining

Sax in St Augustine

Though most street performers have been banned from downtown St Augustine (some shows were deemed too risqué for public consumption, and palm weavers were stripping the trees bare to make hats and flowers for the tourists), others have found places where they're welcome. One melody you'll still hear as you wend your way down St George St is that of Jim Brock.

Brock's handmade flutes, saxophones and other wind instruments have enchanted an impressive following, including musicians like Yanni, Bela Fleck, Grover Washington Jr and Richard Elliot. But it's the St George St scene that keeps Brock captivated. When he starts to play, plying his wares, onlookers gather, eager to hear more of the eerie intonations his custom creations breathe.

Brock began as a collector, and taught himself to play the exotic instruments he'd found. One day, he had an epiphany: 'I was contemplating making my own musical instruments and found myself in a bamboo patch, watching the ants,' he remembers with a small smile. 'They had eaten a hole through one piece. I cut it and tried it, and it made a note.'

That was in 1980; Brock estimates that he's made 140,000 instruments since. He first found success on the crafts show circuit, then began following Renaissance fairs all over the country. He loved his trade, but missed Florida terribly. And then it hit him – why not settle in St Augustine? He already had all the period costumes. It's one of those rare places that soothes restless souls and considers gypsies and pirates respectable, perfect for a piper called to his task. And like his spiritual brother in Hamlin, he had, along the way, learned to draw crowds rather than follow them.

Today, you can often catch Brock at the Monk's Vineyard (see Bars & Clubs), where a private porch protects him from the city's antibusking laws. Interested in learning to play a saxophone as different as St Augustine? Contact Jim Brock (e bamboo@staugustine.com).

---

buskers (see the boxed text 'Sax in St Augustine') on St George St.

Rendezvous (☎ 904-824-1090; 106 St George St, suite H; open 11am-6pm Mon-Thur, 11am-12:30am Fri-Sun) is another place catering to brew connoisseurs, and has at least 160 varieties of beer in stock at all times.

Backstreet Coffee House and Lounge (☎ 904-827-0990; 61 Spanish St; open 10:30am-midnight daily), hidden on a service throughway one block west of St George St, is one of the hippest venues around for rock and alternative bands. Comfy, mismatched couches are abandoned for all-ages shows (though there's a great selection of beer) and packed for spoken word performances (first and third Monday of the month).

A1A Ale House (☎ 904-829-2977; 1 King St) has seven microbrews from $3 a pint, cheaper during happy hour (4pm to 7pm daily). They also brew fresh root beer for the kids. They do ragtime and other live music, and have an expensive restaurant upstairs.

Oasis (☎ 904-471-3424; w www.world famousoasis.com; 4000 Beach Blvd; open 11am-1am daily) has a raucous family restaurant downstairs topped by a breezy, busy bar. When the kitchen closes, DJs and local bands like Rezolution turn it up for drunk college students on the prowl and downtown wait-staff taking out the day's aggressions on the dance floor.

Sunset Grille (☎ 904-471-5555; w www .sunsetgrilleala.com; 421 Beach Blvd; open 11am-midnightish) lets you display your Harley right next to the outdoor bar, so you might impress potential love interests.

Getting There & Away

The Pirate Haus youth hostel (see Places to Stay, earlier) posts Greyhound and Amtrak schedules on their Web site (w www.pirate haus.com).

The cheapest transportation option is challenging: Sunshine Buses ($1; see Getting Around) will take you to the Ruby Tuesday restaurant in Avenues Mall, on Hwy 1. From there, JTA buses ($1.35; see Getting Around in the Jacksonville section) can take you downtown, where you'll transfer to the Northside No 8 bus. Get off at the DePaul stop and call a cab ($7). Good luck!

Much, much easier are **Airport Express** (☎ 904-471-0106) or **Al's Airport Shuttle** (☎ 904-794-2024), both of which get you there for about $30.

The **Greyhound bus station** (☎ 904-829-6401; 100 Malaga St) is one block north of King St, just east of the bridge over the San Sebastian River. It's a quick walk to downtown. There are at least five buses daily to Miami, Jacksonville and Orlando.

Amtrak, infuriatingly, does not serve St Augustine but rather the thoroughly inconvenient town of Palatka, 25 miles west (see the Central Florida chapter).

By car, take the Hwy 16 exit off I-95 and head east past US Hwy 1 to San Marcos Ave; turn right and you'll end up at the Old City Gate, just past the fort. Alternately, you can take Hwy A1A along the beach, which intersects with San Marco Ave, or US Hwy 1 south from Jacksonville.

Getting Around

The brand-new **Sunshine Bus Company** (☎ 904-823-4816; $1) is a great first step toward providing public transportation throughout the city. There weren't any regular stops when I was there (it's a goal), but you could flag down the bright yellow buses at the Bridge of Lions. Buses run approximately 6:30am to 6pm daily and serve downtown, the beaches and the outlet malls, as well as many points in between. Most hotels offer free or reasonably priced shuttles to downtown and the beaches.

Cars are a lousy idea downtown, where one-way and pedestrian-only streets collude with highly competitive metered parking (25¢ per hour; enforced 8am to 6pm Monday through Saturday) to give unsuspecting visitors very serious migraines. But outside the city center, cars are all but necessary. Both **Enterprise** (☎ 904-829-1662; 1050 S Ponce de Leon Blvd) and **Hertz** (☎ 904-826-1374; 4900 US 1) will drop off and pick up your car anywhere in St Augustine.

Other motorized options are available at **Solano Scooter Rental** (☎ 904-825-6766; W www.solanocycle.com; 32 San Marco Ave; open 10am-6pm daily), where you can rent one-seat mopeds ($14/50 for two hours/day), two-seat scooters ($28/75) or regular bicycles ($8/18). You'll need a credit card or $300 deposit, plus a driver's license from any country. The rental company can't offer insurance, so you'll be fully liable for any damage done to the equipment.

Ancient City Cabs (☎ 904-824-8161) charges $3 per person downtown, $6 to St Augustine Beach, and $55 per carload to JAX.

AROUND ST AUGUSTINE

There are some lovely areas and little towns to the west of St Augustine, including Palatka and, farther south, Blue Spring State Park and Cassadaga; see the Central Florida chapter for information on those.

World Golf Village

A vision in synthetic stucco, this is the ultimate monument to a good walk spoiled. It's a full-service resort (☎ 904-221-0027, 800-948-4653; W www.wgv.com; 21 World Golf Place) and home to the World Golf Foundation (WGF) and PGA Productions, the media entity responsible for televising golf events when you'd rather be watching infomercials.

There are several attractions here: shops selling unfathomable golfing accessories, an IMAX theater and, of course, lots of prestigious and pricey golf courses. The reason you'll want to jump off the freeway, however, is the **World Golf Hall of Fame** (adult/senior/child $7/6/5; open 10am-6pm daily), a must-see museum if you're at all interested in the sport. I'm emphatically *not* and still had a fantastic time.

There are 18 exhibits (like 18 holes, get it?), nine covering the history of the sport and the rest examining modern professional golf. Separating them is the actual Hall of Fame, a shiny space-age tribute to scores of men and women; if you're curious about any one of them, simply call them up on the computer to initiate a multimedia exhibit detailing their life and career. Other highlights include astronaut Alan Shepard's club from his 1971 tee off on the lunar surface, and the most elegant miniature-golf gimmick ever – take a swing with century-old wooden clubs and try to drop an 1880s-style rubber ball in the hole.

Though staying here would be sort of like vacationing at a suburban gated community, **Renaissance Resort** (☎ 904-940-8000; 500 S Legacy Trail; rooms $129-289 Jan-May & Oct & Nov, $109-259 Jun-Sept & Dec) does the job nicely, with spa treatments, package deals and TVs in the bathrooms. Skip the hotel restaurant, however, and have a burger at **Caddy Shack** (☎ 904-940-3673; 455 S Legacy Trail; mains $7-14). The theme restaurant and bar is named for the movie in which half-owner Bill Murray plays a hapless yet heroic golf-course groundskeeper obsessed with catching a dancing animatronic gopher.

World Golf Village is just off I-95.

Berry Picking

About 13 miles west of I-95 on Hwy 207, the town of Elkton offers peace and quiet and the chance to pick your own strawberries for $1.50 a quart at Tommy Howle's Vegetable Bin & Garden, on the right-hand side of the road on the eastern end of town. You can also get fresh tomatoes, boiled peanuts, used romance novels and sweet St Augustine onions, not to be confused with the famed Vidalia onions grown in Georgia. As

one farmer said: 'I work too hard for them to be called that!'

Fort Matanzas National Monument

Though it doesn't have the Castillo's monumental scale, this small fort (☎ 904-471-0116; 8635 Hwy A1A; open 9:30am-6pm daily) has character. It stands near the site where Menendez de Avilés executed several hundred shipwrecked French soldiers and colonists who had surrendered to him; historians suggest that this brutal act was necessary, as food stores at St Augustine were running low. The fort itself wasn't constructed until 1742, after wily Brits used the inlet as a base in one almost successful attack; the Spanish learned their lesson and erected the two-story edifice to better survey the swamps and sandbars.

Today, the fort is only accessible by a free ferry ride (donations are appreciated) that leaves every half-hour. Once there, the ranger gives a great talk and lets you wander at your leisure for a while. They also offer torch-lit evening tours, by reservation only ($5), where rangers get dudded up in their Spanish military uniforms and fire cannons as part of the show. How cool is that?

DAYTONA BEACH
pop 65,000

Daytona's early history is typical of Florida: Timucuan Indians had the run of the place until the late 1700s, when Europeans settlers moved in. Henry Flagler built a railroad, Matthias Day (hence Daytona) built a hotel, and the city got a few tourists, though not as many as St Augustine. Then, in 1902, Daytona had a high-speed date with destiny.

Playboy racecar drivers Ransom Olds and Alexander Winston realized that the unusually hard-packed sands of Daytona Beach were good for more than just sunbathing. They waged a high-profile race along the water to prove it, reaching an unheard-of 57mph. Suddenly, it all became clear: God and Mother Nature had created this beach for racing, an epiphany that Daytona's public-relations machinery trumpeted in every national forum they could find.

Dat'l Do It

Be sure and try the fiery and flavorful locally grown datil (rhymes with that'll) peppers, available in mustard, vinegar (for splashing on collard greens) and sauces like Dat'l Do It and Dixie Datil (motto: 'Ain't killed no one yet'). All are available at Publix and some other local markets.

– Nick & Corinna Selby

The Florida East Coast Automobile Association was founded in 1903, the Winter Speed Carnival (predecessor to today's Daytona 500) began in 1904, and for the next 30 years, Daytona Beach was where speed records were made and smashed.

Stock-car racing came into vogue during the late 1930s, and Race Weeks packed the beaches with fans. On December 14, 1947, at the Streamline Hotel, Bill France Sr founded NASCAR (see the boxed text 'NASCAR') with the then-unbelievable statement, 'I believe stock-car racing can become a nationally recognized sport.' Civic leaders felt that this was a fine dream, and in 1959 they opened the Daytona Speedway.

Today, Daytona Beach thrives on racing- and party-based tourism: It has one of the last Atlantic Coast Spring Breaks (arrests, hookers, drunk kids, fire engines) and, during Bike Week, the town goes absolutely insane, as hordes of Harleys – and their remarkably well-behaved owners – roar into town. But the heart and soul of Daytona remain committed to the pursuit of one thing: speed.

DAYTONA BEACH

PLACES TO STAY
1 The Villa
6 Thunderbird Beach Motel
9 Adam's Mark Resort
20 Hilton Garden
26 Streamline Hotel;
   Streamline Lounge
33 Bermuda Villas
37 Travelodge Ocean
   Jewels Resort
39 Coquina Inn B&B
40 Live Oak Inn; Rosario's
   Restaurant

PLACES TO EAT
5 Anna's Italian Trattoria
7 Starlight Diner
27 Pasha
31 Dancing Avocado Kitchen

OTHER
2 First Union Bank
3 Razzles
4 Diplomatic Laundromat
8 Municipal Band Shell
10 Ocean Center Landing
11 Peabody Auditorium

12 Bank & Blues
13 Dirty Harry's Pub
14 Boardwalk
15 Froggy's Saloon
16 Cinematique of Daytona
17 Halifax Medical Center
18 Barnes & Noble
19 Daytona USA
21 Seaside Music Theater
22 Southeast Museum of
   Photography
23 Martinis on Bay
24 Groove Dance Lounge

25 Love Bar
28 Mandala Bookstore
29 SunTrust Bank
30 Greyhound
32 Library
34 Halifax Historical Museum
35 Jackie Robinson Ballpark
36 Daytona Beach
   Convention Center &
   Visitors Bureau
38 Museum of Arts &
   Sciences
41 A Tiny Cruise Line

Orientation

Daytona lies at the intersection of I-95 and I-4, sprawling across the Intracoastal Waterway to the Atlantic Ocean. The main east-west drag, International Speedway Blvd (US Hwy 92) connects the beaches with the Daytona Speedway, Daytona International Airport and I-95.

The main north-south road on the barrier island is Atlantic Ave (Hwy A1A), while US Hwy 1, on the mainland, is called Ridgewood Ave. Beach St runs parallel and is the main north-south road through downtown. Main St is the north-south divider. Mason Ave, Main St, International Blvd and Orange Ave, as well as Dunlawton Ave to the south, all have bridges connecting the mainland with the beaches.

Information

The **Daytona Beach Convention & Visitor's Bureau** (CVB; ☎ 386-255-0415, 800-544-0415; ⓦ www.daytonabeach.com; 126 E Orange Ave; open 9am-5pm Mon-Fri) is excellent. There's another visitor's center at the Daytona International Speedway.

DAYTONA BEACH

NORTHEAST

If your wallet's feeling light, head to **Sun-Trust Bank** (☎ 386-258-2306; 120 S Ridgewood Ave) or **First Union** (☎ 386-323-1475; 441 Seabreeze Blvd). The **post office** (220 N Beach St) is convenient to downtown.

Mandala Bookstore (☎ 386-255-6728; 127 W International Speedway Blvd) has 150,000 used books. The main **library** (☎ 386-257-6036; 105 E Magnolia Ave; open 9:30am-5:30pm Mon & Wed, 9:30am-8pm Tues & Fri, 9am-5pm Sat) on City Island, in the Intracoastal Waterway just south of Hwy 92, offers free Internet access.

The *Daytona News-Journal* (**W** www.news-journalonline.com) is the daily paper of record, while several free publications serve niche markets: *Full Throttle* (**W** www.fullthrottleonline.com) and *Dixie Biker* (**W** www.dixiebiker.com) are for motorcycle enthusiasts; *Backstage Pass* (**W** www.backpassmag.com) covers the local music scene; *Seniors Today* is for active oldsters; and the *Daytona Beach Business Guide* (**W** www.gaydaytona.com) serves the gay and lesbian community. National Public Radio (NPR) is at both 90.7 FM and 89.9 FM.

Wash up at **Diplomatic Laundromat** (☎ 386-254-2974; 4101 Seabreeze Blvd).

The **Halifax Medical Center** (☎ 386-254-4000; 303 N Clyde Morris Blvd) is next to Daytona Community College.

When planning your trip to Daytona, keep in mind that several large, annual events can quadruple your costs, even if you don't participate. Of course, they can also double your fun:

Speed Weeks (first two weeks in February): Between the Rolex 24 Hour Race and Daytona 500, there's a lot of partying to be done.

Bike Week (early March): It's 10 days of motorcycle racing, leather wearing and breast baring fun.

Spring Break (March): College kids on a mission to drink more than they have ever drunk before: Some will succeed, others will fail. All will wake up confused and dehydrated.

Black College Reunion (second week in April): See Spring Break, above.

Easter & Memorial Day: Even more of the same for a broader age group.

Pepsi 400 Meet (Fourth of July weekend): NASCAR fans fly the checkered flag.

Biketoberfest (mid-October): Raise a glass because it's finally cool enough (by Florida standards) to wear leather again!

Turkey Run (late November): The custom car crowd enjoys its weekend in the sun.

World Karting Racing (last week in December): What else is there to do until New Year's Eve?

Daytona International Speedway & Daytona USA

The most famous raceway in the USA, **Daytona International Speedway** (☎ 386-947-6782, box office ☎ 386-253-7223; **W** www.daytonaintlspeedway.com) is a pilgrimage-worthy destination for auto aficionados and worth seeing even if you're not. Events tickets (see Information, earlier, for a partial list of events) range from $30 to $220, though scalpers get three times that for the big races. If nothing's on, the complex is designed to make you think that you need to enter excellent but pricey Daytona USA (☎ 386-947-6800; **W** www.daytonausa.com; adult/child $20/14; open 9am-7pm daily) just to see the track. This is an illusion: Go through the gift shop, located just to the right of the ticket counter, and wander into the grandstands for free.

If you're a car person, however, you'll happily fork over the cash to see Daytona USA, a very flashy shrine to a very flashy sport. Stock cars driven by NASCAR's biggest names are the stars of the show, but there's much, much more. See how sneaky teams try to circumvent Winston Cup weight regulations with lead goggles and helmets (every ounce counts in NASCAR). Try to change a tire in 16 seconds at the **Pit-Stop Challenge** or drive your own virtual vehicle in **Acceleration Alley**. It's well worth the extra $7 to tour the Speedway and see the 31° bank negotiated three cars wide by the best drivers in the nation.

If you're so inspired, you could even try the **Richard Petty Experience** (☎ 800-237-3889; **W** www.1800bepetty.com), where you'll drive a 600-horsepower Winston Cup–style car ($350 to $2500, depending on the program) or ride shotgun for only $106, including admission to Daytona USA.

NASCAR

To understand the American South, one must first understand stock-car racing (well, that and college football, fried okra and rocking chairs, but you've got to start somewhere). The National Association for Stock Car Auto Racing (NASCAR) was founded in Daytona Beach back in 1947, but that's not where this story begins.

During Prohibition, moonshine (a potent corn liquor) production was an important segment of the rural Southern economy, and young people with cars fast enough to outrun local cops handled distribution. On their off-time, they tried to outrun each other. When alcohol was relegalized, the races continued, and the most glamorous venue was the Beach St track in Daytona. There, an entrepreneurial driver named Bill France began promoting 'Race Weeks,' which brought fans to Daytona by the thousands.

The sport grew like kudzu, though it was often dismissed by other automotive enthusiasts as upstart rednecks racing cars that any mechanic could build in their own garage. France knew better, however, and organized NASCAR with the aim of transforming his obsession into a world-class sport. He succeeded beyond his wildest dreams.

Today, despite the acronym, these cars aren't even close to stock: Beneath the myriad product endorsements covering each colorful contender, the bodies are still recognizably Mustangs and Monte Carlos, but the similarity ends there. Each auto (teams typically have several) is stripped to the frame, with only the required safety and speed equipment remaining. Each conforms to strict regulations that guarantee the driver and pit crew, *not* the car, are being tested. Sanctioned races take place at tracks large and small throughout the country, and the granddaddy of them all is the Winston Series.

Just finishing a Winston Cup race (heck, just qualifying for one) is an impressive feat, and the winner isn't really determined by who gets there first. Points, which accumulate throughout the season, are doled out for a variety of reasons, such as how many laps the driver led. It's not unusual for a third-place team to 'win.'

The real appeal for many fans, however, is less the competition than the fact that this is a quintessentially Southern family affair. Shawna Robinson's two kids come down to the track and cheer her on, while racing dynasties like the Pettys, Jarretts and Earnhardts (see the boxed text 'The Intimidator's Last Run') are legendary. More than that, it's a down-to-earth sport – none of your polo snobs around here – with open arms for anyone who wants to join the NASCAR family – even Yankees.

Klassix Auto Museum

This wonderful museum (☎ 386-252-0940; w www.klassixauto.com; 2909 W International Speedway Blvd; adult/child $9/4; open 9am-6pm daily) has a rotating collection of classic cars with an emphasis on mouthwatering muscle, including every Corvette from 1953 to 1994 (and an explanation of why there was no '83 'Vette). The tastiest treat, however, is the selection of masterworks by (arguably) the greatest automotive artisan of all time, George Barris: the Batmobile, Drag-u-la, Greased Lightning and the Flintstones car, as well as a few of his seamlessly chopped and dropped Mercs and a hybrid that splits into two motorcycles. If you're not an automobile enthusiast, understand that this is comparable to walking into a small-town museum and finding a handful of Louvre-quality da Vincis.

Other delectables include vintage Winston Cup pace cars, the Blues Brother's Crown Victoria and a Harley Davidson powered by a Chevy 350 small block engine. If you're only going to see one car museum while you're here, I recommend this one over Daytona USA (though you should still check out the Speedway itself).

Museum of Arts & Sciences

You might not think of Daytona as a cultural center, but this place (☎ 386-255-0285;

1040 Museum Blvd; adult/student or child $7/2; open 9am-4pm Tues-Fri, noon-5pm Sat & Sun), off Nova Rd, is an incredible surprise. The **Cuban Museum** alone, with an amazing variety of paintings by artists from the island, is worth the entry fee. The museum is heavy on arts, with stunning artifacts from Africa and China in their own galleries, as well as the **Dow Gallery of American Art**, with noteworthy paintings and examples of antique furniture and silver. **Root Hall**, sponsored by the family that bottled Coca-Cola from the beginning, has a surreal assortment of relics from the soda's history, from ancient vending machines to 1920s delivery vans. Oh, and this is Daytona, where no museum would be complete without autos; experimental speedsters have been restored to perfection.

The **Science Center** has a giant sloth skeleton unearthed only a few miles from here, as well as other exhibits on Florida's natural history. Its 96-seat **planetarium** (admission $3; shows 2pm Tues-Fri) does astronomy presentations and also offers free films every Saturday.

The Beach

Beautiful Daytona Beach (☎ 386-239-7873) is great for sunbathing, swimming, springbreaking and a host of other outdoor activities, but that's not what made this 18-mile stretch of sand world famous. The beach itself was once the raceway where, in 1935, Sir Malcolm Campbell reached a blistering 276mph. Today, *you* can drive these hallowed sands for $5, $3 after 3pm, although the (strictly enforced) top speed

---

The Intimidator's Last Run

The heat was on: Would Dale Earnhardt, winner of seven Winston Cups, take the 2001 Daytona 500? This was the one race that had beaten the NASCAR legend and his famous No 3 car – 20 times – until a 1998 upset. And competition was stiff. Arch-rival Jeff Gordon, No 24, was finally in sync with his pit crew and hungry for victory. Also revving their engines were heavy hitters like Dale Jarrett, Michael Waltrip and Bobby LaBonte, as well as Dale Earnhardt Jr, the Intimidator's son.

The elder Earnhardt earned his nickname with an aggressive driving style that bordered on homicidal: If it was the last lap, competitors would complain, he'd wreck his own mom. That's why the crowd loved him. And there was just a little more pressure. This was NASCAR's first major event on network television, hailed as a coming-of-age for a sport started by backwoods bootleggers. The Intimidator was ready.

The race was an exciting one, with Gordon, then Waltrip, then Earnhardt taking the lead. But on the last lap, the No 3 car got too close to the wall; Earnhardt flipped onto the infield. It wasn't the worst wreck Daytona had ever seen – not by a long shot – but fans knew that Dale would be pissed as all hell.

Michael Waltrip took the checkered flag and made his way, one big ruddy smile, to Victory Lane. Then a friend grabbed him; he went gray. An announcement was made. Dale Earnhardt would not be climbing out of his twisted Monte Carlo as he had so many times, growling about the other lousy drivers. The Intimidator was gone. The speedway fell silent with disbelief – how could this happen? It just didn't look that bad. But a security harness had snapped, leaving the fragile human being inside unprotected. Real men, a racing nation was reminded, do cry.

Some say that an athlete is not a true hero, not like a firefighter or astronaut. Perhaps. But Dale Earnhardt, like so many who have left their skidmarks on that speedway, devoted his life to reminding the rest of us what humans can endure: heat and torque, fear and focus, all that crushes the driver of a machine pushed to its limits. And by that measure, one hero left us that day, hitting heaven at an easy 200mph. We can only hope that the angels were ready for the cussing and spitting that followed.

is only 10mph. Oh well. There are six well-marked entries between Granada Blvd and Beach St; the area between Seabreeze Blvd and International Speedway Blvd is traffic-free.

Don't have a car? You can rent ATVs (some painted like your favorite NASCAR) from half a dozen vendors on the beach for around $35 to $45 an hour. You can also rent boogie boards (usually $5 hourly, $10 daily), fat-wheeled pedal trikes ($10 hourly, $25 daily) and umbrellas and chairs ($8 to $10 daily) from various stands. If you're feeling extra adventurous, contact **Daytona Beach Parasail** (☎ 386-547-6067; W www.daytona parasailing.com; $55).

Most beachside vendors are open from 8am to 5pm, later during special events, when all these prices rise according to demand.

The Boardwalk
Daytona does it up right, with thrill rides, go-carts and beachside patios where you sip beer from plastic cups. It's good family fun with just a hint of sleaze to keep things interesting.

Southeast Museum of Photography
This museum (☎ 386-254-4475; 1200 International Speedway Dr, Daytona Beach Community College, Bldg 37; admission free; open 10am-6pm Mon & Wed-Fri, 1pm-8pm Tues, 1pm-5pm Sat & Sun) features fascinating rotating exhibitions of photography in two galleries. When I was there, they had a traveling exhibit featuring photographs of New York City on September 11, 2001, as well as a graduate student's photos of Afghanistan, Pakistan and India. My compliments to the curators.

Jackie Robinson Ballpark
Off Beach St on City Island, opposite the CVB, Jackie Robinson Ballpark is where Robinson broke the color barrier in professional sports, playing his first MLB spring training game in 1946. The Class A **Daytona Cubs** (☎ 386-257-3172), a farm team of the Chicago Cubs, play here April through September.

Halifax Historical Museum
Come here (☎ 386-255-6976; W www.halifax historical.org; 252 S Beach St; adult/child $4/1) just to see the great model of Daytona Beach Pier, circa 1938. There's lots of other stuff, including a comprehensive exhibit of local black history, housed in an old bank building. Check out the old-school vault.

Ponce de León Inlet Lighthouse Museum
This lighthouse museum (☎ 386-761-1821; 4931 S Peninsula Dr; adult/child $7/1; open 10am-7pm daily), about 5 miles south of Daytona, is an interesting place to spend an afternoon, and climbing the 203 steps to the top makes for a splendid view. Also on display are rickety Cuban rafts that were found on Ormond Beach, nautical navigation tools and photos of lighthouses from all over the USA. You'll also learn to appreciate the difference between Fresnel lens orders!

Little Chapel by the Sea
Check out this photo op: the chapel (☎ 386-767-8716; 3140 S Atlantic Ave; admission free) is a drive-in Christian church. Really. Attach a speaker to your car (tourists love this) or be like the locals and tune in to 680 AM or 88.5 FM to hear Reverend Larry G Deitch do his thing. He and the choir hold service on a balcony overlooking the autos at 8:30am and 10am Sunday. There's free coffee and donuts between services.

This used to be the Neptune Drive-In Theater, but when that closed down, area church leaders felt that the venue would appeal to car-crazy Christians here to see the races. They opened in 1954 and have been preaching to a packed parking lot ever since.

Organized Tours
A Tiny Cruise Line (☎ 386-226-2343; 425 S Beach St; tickets $10-15 adult, $6-8 child) runs one-hour cruises up the Halifax River at varying times and at sunset daily.

Next to Aunt Catfish's (see Places to Eat), **Sunny Daze & Starry Nights Cruises** (☎ 386-253-1796; W www.sunnydazeriver-cruises.com; tours $10-30) offers a variety of

NORTHEAST

guided ecological and historical tours on the Halifax River.

Places to Stay

Daytona has more hotels than you can shake a crankshaft at, and you'll find that they're fairly predictable: For $35, you'll get a basic, cleanish room with laundry and a swimming pool; for $55, you'll find a newer room and perhaps some wacky amenity, like miniature golf or a water slide; and for $80, a relatively luxurious chain hotel. Prices quadruple for events like Race Week, and rooms fill up weeks in advance.

These are just a few of Daytona's more than 400 hotels; for more choices contact the convention center about their *Superior Small Lodging* booklet, or log onto w www .daytonalodging.com. And pay attention to the architecture and neon along the Atlantic Ave strip: Daytona is a living museum of 1950s pop culture.

Motels & Hotels The Travelodge Ocean Jewels Resort (☎ 386-252-2581; 935 S Atlantic Ave; rooms $49/99 year-round/special events) has two pools and nice rooms with coffeemakers.

Dream Inn (☎ 386-767-2821; 3217 S Atlantic Ave; rooms $49/99 year-round/special events) is a bit off the main strip but worth the drive for its flowery courtyard and big pool.

Bermuda Villas (☎ 386-255-2438; 505 S Atlantic Ave; rooms $55/125 year-round/special events) has airy rooms and a much better location.

The **Monterey Inn** (☎ 386-255-1991; 2403 S Atlantic Ave; rooms $30/140 year-round/special events) has tattered but clean and spacious rooms.

Streamline Hotel (☎ 386-258-6937; 140 S Atlantic Ave; rooms $21/150 year-round/special events) is no longer a hostel, but it's still the cheapest place in town. Rooms are marginally cleaner than you'd guess from the lobby. New management, however, has grand plans afoot for restoring the historic art deco edifice where NASCAR was born: They want to develop the building into a race-themed luxury hotel that caters to the gay and lesbian crowd. Well, the gay pride and NASCAR flags *are* remarkably similar...

Thunderbird Beach Motel (☎ 386-253-2562; 500 N Atlantic Ave; rooms $55 year-round, whatever they can get high season) has large rooms and free cookies at reception.

Sun Viking Lodge (☎ 386-252-5463; w www.sunviking.com; 2441 S Atlantic Ave; quads $70/300 year-round/special events) has a 60-foot (18m; that's long, not high) water slide.

Hilton Garden (☎ 386-944-4000; 187 Midway Ave; rooms $94 year-round, $300-450 special events), convenient to the airport and International Speedway, has all the amenities you'd expect, including an airport shuttle.

Adam's Mark Resort (☎ 386-254-8200, 800-444-2326; w www.adamsmark.com; 100 N Atlantic Ave; rooms from $135 year-round, $385 special events) is a fabulously luxurious resort, with heaps of amenities and a traffic-free beach that's all but private, what with their patrols and activities.

B&Bs The **Coquina Inn B&B** (☎ 386-254-4969; w www.coquinainndaytonabeach.com; 544 S Palmetto Ave; rooms $90-140) features fireplaces in some rooms, a lush garden patio and a Jacuzzi. Bicycles are available.

The Villa (☎ 386-248-2020; w www.the villabb.com; 801 N Peninsula Drive; rooms $100-150) is one of the nicest B&Bs I've ever seen. It's in a Spanish-colonial-style mansion with stained glass, shady gardens, lots of antiques, two cats and Andy the dog. It's gay-owned and a grand place for anyone.

Live Oak Inn (☎ 386-252-4667; 444-448 S Beach St; rooms without/with Jacuzzi $90/120 year-round, $110/150 special events), in a sprawling 1881 Victorian close to the marina, has relaxing rooms and lots of regulars.

Places to Eat

Pasha (☎ 386-257-7753; 919 W International Speedway Blvd; dishes $4-6; open 10am-7:30pm Mon-Sat, noon-6pm Sun) has unusually authentic Middle Eastern food: Fatoush, foulemudammas and labriah join standards like hummus and tabouli on a combination plate of your design. It's also a deli.

Starlight Diner (☎ 386-255-9555; 401 N Atlantic Ave; dishes $4-8; open 7am-9pm daily) looks like an Airstream trailer and has a great jukebox, huge burgers and real malts.

Dancing Avocado Kitchen (☎ 386-947-2022; 110 S Beach St; mains $5-8; open 8am-4pm Mon-Sat) has absolutely stellar vegetarian dishes, including five different meatless burgers and the recommended dancing avocado melt sandwich.

Lighthouse Landing (☎ 386-761-9271; 4940 S Peninsula Dr; mains $5-15; open 11:30am-10pm daily), near the Ponce de León Inlet Lighthouse, has a pleasant outdoor patio overlooking the water and kitsch to spare. Good fish sandwiches and seafood entrées come with fries, but spend the extra 50¢ for onion rings.

Aunt Catfish's on the River (☎ 386-767-4768; 4009 Halifax Dr; mains $8-16; open 11:30am-9pm or so daily) serves fried, grilled and Cajun-style catfish (Cajun-style is the best); all meals include a great salad bar. A huge Sunday brunch ($11) is served from 9am to 2pm.

Anna's Italian Trattoria (☎ 386-239-9624; 304 Seabreeze Blvd; mains $13-20; open 5pm-10pm Tues-Sun) is a great place to splurge on veal marsala or fettuccini Alfredo, unless they have the shrimp cognac on special – it's the chef's favorite.

Rosario's Restaurant (☎ 386-258-6066; 444 S Beach St; mains $16-28; open 5pm-10pm Tues-Sat) has a 175-item wine list and dishes like filet mignon in whiskey sauce and veal shank, though the chef recommends the specials.

Entertainment

Performing Arts An enormous multipurpose facility, **Ocean Center Landing** (☎ 386-254-4500; W www.oceancenter.com; 101 N Atlantic Ave) stages country and rock concerts, ice-hockey matches, wrestling, art shows and more.

Seaside Music Theater (☎ 386-252-6200; W www.seasidemusictheater.org, 1200 W International Speedway Blvd; tickets $35-55) stages professional musicals at the Daytona Beach Community College.

Peabody Auditorium (☎ 386-255-1314; 600 Auditorium Blvd) holds mainly classical, but also pop, concerts. Daytona Beach Civic Ballet performances are staged here, as are touring Broadway productions and a biannual performance by the London Symphony Orchestra.

Municipal Bandshell (☎ 386-673-2080; W www.bandshell.org; 420 S Beach St) has been throwing free concerts since 1937. Shows – which range from swing to rock to classical – usually happen from 7pm to 10pm on Saturday and Sunday.

Cinematique of Daytona (☎ 386-323-9807; 331 Bill France Blvd; adult/child $6/4), tucked away in the Speedway Business Center, screens art films in the MFC Cinema Six on select evenings. You can also catch mainstream movies here for $2.50.

Bars & Clubs There are almost as many bars as hotels in this town, and that's saying something.

Dirty Harry's Pub (☎ 386-252-9877; 705 Main St) provides the perfect excuse to wear leather, with live music Wednesday and Saturday night and an impressive collection of automatic weapons on the wall.

Froggy's Saloon (☎ 386-254-8808; 800 Main St), down the street, also caters to the biker crowd. Shirts are required after 7pm.

Razzles (☎ 386-257-6236; 611 Seabreeze Blvd; cover $5-10; open 8pm-3am daily) is a high-energy dance club. Ladies drink free Wednesday and Friday till midnight.

Love Bar (☎ 386-252-7600; 116 N Beach St; open 10pm-3am Fri & Sat), next door, is a Gothic-kitsch, couch-laden meat market with a groovy dance lounge.

Groove Dance Lounge (☎ 386-252-7600; 124 N Beach St) is in the same complex, and has a shag (the material, not the British verb) bar.

Martinis on Bay (☎ 386-258-1212; 101 Bay St; open 11am-1am Mon-Thur, 5pm-3am Fri & Sat) attracts an upscale crowd with classic movies on Tuesday, DJs on weekends, and ladies night on Thursday, complete with complimentary chair massages from 8pm to 1am.

Streamline Lounge (☎ 386-258-6937; 140 S Atlantic Ave; open 11am-3am daily) is a threadbare gay bar that attracts an older male crowd. Patrons here also recommend **TomBoys Bar & Grill** (☎ 386-257-6464; 322 Seabreeze Blvd) and **Rumors Nite Club & Bar** (☎ 386-252-3776; 1376 N Nova Rd).

Bank and Blues (☎ 386-257-9272; 701 Main St) has lots of good blues events throughout the year and an open jam on Wednesday night.

Getting There & Away

Daytona Beach International Airport (☎ 386-248-8030), just east of the Speedway, is served by Continental, Northwest and Delta airlines and all major car-rental companies.

The **Greyhound bus station** (☎ 386-255-7076, 800-231-2222; 138 S Ridgewood Ave) has four buses daily to DeLand, seven to Miami and others to just about anywhere you'd like to go on the seaboard.

Daytona is close to the intersection of two of Florida's major interstates, I-95 and I-4. I-95 is the quickest way to Jacksonville (about 70 miles) and Miami (200 miles), though Hwy A1A and US Hwy 1 are more scenic. Beville Rd, an east-west thoroughfare south of Daytona proper, becomes I-4 after crossing I-95; it's the fastest route to Orlando and Tampa.

Getting Around

Votran (☎ 386-761-7700; w http://velusia.org/votran; adult/child $1/50¢) runs buses and trolleys throughout the city. Exact change is required. Ask for a free transfer when you get on the bus. Buses run 6am to 7:30pm daily, trolleys noon to midnight Monday through Saturday from January through Labor Day. The CVB and most hotels have schedules and system maps.

Bus No 10 connects the airport with downtown and the beaches, while bus No 11 will get you to the International Speedway. Take bus No 17AB to the lighthouse. The trolley runs along Atlantic Ave (Hwy A1A) from Granada Blvd in Ormond to Dunlawton Ave in Daytona Beach Shores.

Parking is free and easy in most places, but in downtown, watch out for meter agents – use store-provided lots when you can. During major events, the speed limits in

this speed capital are steady-as-she-goes or she-goes-to-jail.

AROUND DAYTONA BEACH
Flagler Beach

Thirty miles north of Daytona Beach is the charming and isolated town of Flagler Beach, a 6-mile-long protected island on the Intracoastal Waterway. The draws here are the beaches themselves and a very nice state recreation area (see Gamble Rogers Memorial State Recreation Area).

At the southern end of town is the **Flagler Beach Pier** (☎ 386-439-2200; 215 S A1A; fishers/spectators $3/1; open 6:30am-dark daily), where you can rent a pole for $14 daily, including bait and pier admission.

There are several cheap motels along the A1A, but a standout is the **Topaz Motel** (☎ 386-439-3301; 1224 A1A; rooms $55/145 winter/summer), with antiques enough for any B&B and a great view.

King's Oceanshore Restaurant (☎ 386-439-0380; 208 S A1A; mains $4-12; open 8am-8pm Mon-Sat, 8am-2pm Sun), across from the pier, has great breakfasts: Try the King's Benedict or blueberry pancakes, served on a breezy patio. The haddock sandwich and crab cakes come highly recommended.

The only way to get to the Flagler Beach area is by car; take exit 91 off I-95 and then go east for 6 miles, or take Hwy A1A directly north from Daytona or south from St Augustine.

Gamble Rogers Memorial State Recreation Area

Three miles south of Flagler Beach on Hwy A1A, this great place (☎ 386-517-2086; 3100 A1A; pedestrian/car $1/3.25) has hiking, swimming and alligator and manatee watching. You can also camp right on the beach (without/with electricity $19/21), but make reservations at least 11 months in advance.

If you're hungry for food or local beach culture, stop into **High Tide Snack Jacks** (☎ 386-439-3344; 2805 A1A; dishes $5-15; open 11am-11pm daily), where rest rooms are labeled 'dudes' and 'dudettes.' Fish sand-

NORTHEAST

wiches and fried seafood combos are the order of the day.

Washington Oaks Gardens State Park

If you're traveling up Hwy A1A, definitely make a pit stop here (☎ 386-446-6780; 6400 N Oceanshore Blvd; admission per carload $3.25 to park, $2 beach). It's got coarse and boulder-strewn wild beaches, very different from the manicured expanses of sand you've seen elsewhere. Follow your nose to the huge formal gardens, with spectacular collections of roses, fruit trees, bromeliads and other showy plants arranged around koi ponds, bridges and fountains. The native Florida section is really well done. Paths are a little rough, so if you're worried that your wheelchair won't handle it, rangers can hook you up with an all-terrain model at the station. The park has 5 miles of hiking trails, picnic areas and ranger-led walks on Saturday and Sunday. Take Hwy A1A north about 5 miles from Flagler Beach.

Marineland of Florida

Just north of Washington Oaks Gardens State Park is one of Florida's first family attractions (☎ 877-326-7539; W www.marineland.net; 9600 Ocean Shore Blvd (Hwy A1A); adult/child $12/8; open 9:30am-4:30pm Wed-Mon). This forerunner to Sea-World was opened in 1938, and certainly shows its age. But it has the world's first oceanarium; dolphin, penguin and sea lion shows; and tours of the **Whitney Lab** (☎ 904-461-4000), a University of Florida research facility, by reservation only. Certified divers can swim with dolphins ($100).

Southwest Florida

With the warm, calm waters of the Gulf of Mexico lapping its white-sand beaches, southwest Florida is perhaps the state's most beautiful region, and contains arguably America's finest collections of beaches – yes, including Hawaii. It also offers some of the best opportunities in the state for getting out into nature.

The area was developed at the end of the 19th century, when Henry B Plant, Florida's west-coast version of Henry Flagler, built a railroad line connecting the area with the northeast and ran a steamship line between Tampa and Havana, which brought in the tobacco that made Tampa America's cigar-making capital.

Henry Ford, Thomas Edison, John Ringling (who was as serious about art as he was about circuses – don't miss his museum in Sarasota) and a fascinating religious commune all set down roots here, and the region is rich with cultural attractions. You can tour Edison's rubber laboratories and winter home and gawk at fantastic museum collections in both Tampa and St Petersburg. In fact, the Tampa–St Petersburg area is becoming one of the hottest tourist draws in Florida. St Petersburg has three excellent museums (including Salvador Dalí's) that together rival any others the state has to offer. And you can still watch cigars being hand rolled in Tampa's hip *and* historic Ybor City district, before drinking and dancing the night away.

For exploring nature, splendid Gulf barrier islands from Naples to Clearwater Beach offer unparalleled canoeing, kayaking, hiking and biking opportunities. The Pinellas Trail, around Clearwater Beach, for instance, is the longest urban trail in the country. Inland, don't overlook the exceptional Myakka River State Park around Sarasota and the Audubon Society's jewel, the Corkscrew Swamp Sanctuary, around Naples. And even in a place as developed as Fort Myers Beach, you're never more than a half-hour away from total immersion in

Highlights

- Hunt for shark's teeth in Venice
- Gather an extraordinary variety of seashells on Sanibel and Captiva Islands
- Shop for cigars in Ybor City, one-time US cigar capital
- Kayak among the pristine barrier islands of Matlacha Pass Aquatic Preserve
- Experience African wildlife and terrifying roller coasters at Busch Gardens

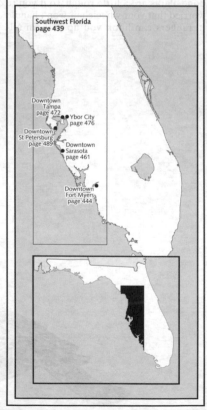

Southwest Florida
page 439

Downtown Tampa page 472
Ybor City page 476
Downtown St Petersburg page 489
Downtown Sarasota page 461
Downtown Fort Myers page 444

SOUTHWEST

wilderness. Fantastic souvenirs are found right along the coast, from the mounds of shark's teeth that wash up on Venice's beaches to the unparalleled shelling at Sanibel, Captiva and Pine Islands. As for beaches, Fort Desoto, Sand Key and Caladesi Island win awards and entice swimmers with phenomenal white-sand beaches.

The area's two theme parks are also definitely worth a visit: Busch Gardens has the best roller coasters in the southeastern USA, and Weeki Wachee Springs is famous for its weirdly campy underwater mermaid shows.

Visit Homosassa Springs State Park for a close-up look at some of Florida's wildlife. The tourist trap of Tarpon Springs is less than an hour away, but you may consider it a waste of time: the once-quaint town is now made up of tourist shops, junk stands, expensive parking lots.

Hotels and motels in the region are priced a little higher than in other areas of the state, but there's inexpensive camping in several of the state parks and historic sites (best on some of the barrier islands west of Fort Myers) and a fantastic youth hostel in Clearwater Beach.

But the best part is that there's less development here than on the east coast. Much of the coastline is protected, and the residents on the barrier islands and in beach communities are quite content to leave the screaming hordes of spring breakers and the gaggles of fashion plates where they are in the Panhandle.

NAPLES
population 21,000
Affluent Naples is worth a look for its great beaches and restaurants, a superb nature center and an even better Audubon sanctuary.

Orientation & Information
Downtown Naples is laid out in a grid: streets run north and south, avenues run east and west. Old Naples (bounded by 10th Ave S at the north, 14th Ave S at the south, the Gulf of Mexico at the west and the Gordon River at the east) is the epicenter, and 5th Ave S is the central artery. Gulf Shore Blvd runs

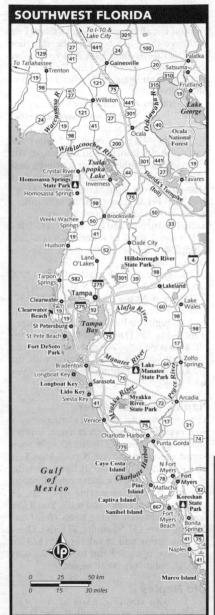

north-south along the beach, from the southern tip at Gordon Pass, where it becomes Gordon Dr, all the way north to Clam Pass (although there is a break in the shoreline north of Lowdermilk Park and you'll have to jog east on Mooring Line Dr to US 41 and back west again via Harbor Dr to Gulf Shore Blvd).

The **Naples Area Chamber Visitors Center** (☎ 239-263-1858; ⓦ www.napleschamber .org; 895 5th Ave S; open 9am-5pm Mon-Sat), at Hwy 41, is not open on Sunday and has less useful information than most. You might instead try the **outdoor concierge desk** (☎ 239-434-6533; 3rd St S; open 10am-6pm Mon-Sat & noon-5pm Sun in winter, 11am-4pm Wed-Fri & 11am-6pm Sat in summer), between Broad Ave and 12th Ave S. It's staffed by friendly and knowledgeable folks.

Per usual, **Bank of America** (☎ 800-299-2265; 796 5th Ave S) has many branches around town.

There are branch **post offices** (1200 Goodlette Rd N; 4th Ave S at 9th St).

Barnes & Noble (☎ 239-598-5200; 5377 Tamiami Trail N) carries the whole gamut.

Although the local area code changed from 941 to 239 (and call forwarding of the old area code stops after March 2003), you may still see brochures printed with the old area code. Substitute 239 whenever you see 941.

Naples Nature Center

The environmental nonprofit Conservancy of Southwest Florida runs great nature centers, including this one (☎ 239-262-0304; ⓦ www .conservancy.org; 14th Ave N; open Mon-Sat), off Goodlette-Frank Rd. It has a museum of natural history, a wildlife rehabilitation center, a 3000-gallon marine aquarium, an aviary with bald eagles and trails. You'll also find naturalist-led hiking tours (free) and boating tours ($7.50 adults, $2 kids). There are also canoe and kayak rentals ($13 for two hours; open 9:30am to 1pm Tuesday through Saturday). By all means, visit.

Old Naples

For in-town strolling, parts of ritzy Old Naples are right up there with Rodeo Drive.

Along 5th Ave S, between 3rd and 9th Sts S, you'll find a collection of shops, restaurants and cafés. Over on 3rd St S, at Broad Ave, another cluster lies in wait.

Beaches

Naples' beaches are wonderful. Because construction was forbidden close to the water, that all-too-familiar Florida condo cluster along the seashore doesn't exist here. Yahoo. We can breath easier now. As such, the downtown beach is arguably the finest city beach in Florida – spotless, white sand and very popular. Access it at the Gulf end of each avenue, and bring quarters for parking meters. At the western end of 12th Ave S, locals congregate at **The Pier**, a center of fishing activity, especially on weekends. It's a great place to watch pelicans.

Lowdermilk Park (Millionaire's Row at Gulf Shore Blvd), north of Old Naples, has restrooms, vending machines, picnicking places and volleyball courts showcasing some of the best players around. If you're a world-class player visiting from, say, Hawaii, you might be able to join them. Otherwise, just watch the buff bods. And again, bring quarters.

Clam Pass County Park (☎ 239-353-0404; at the end of Seagate Dr from US 41; open 8am-sunset daily), north of Old Naples, has a three-quarter-mile boardwalk through a mangrove forest that leads out to a white powdery sand beach. There's a free electric tram from the parking lot, but you'll have to pay $3 to park. The Registry Resort runs a concession stand (☎ 239-597-3232) near the beach where you can rent canoes ($25 hourly) and kayaks (single/double $20/30 hourly).

Delnor-Wiggins Pass State Recreation Area (☎ 239-597-6196; 111th Ave N; admission per carload $3.25, per pedestrian or cyclist $1; open 8am-sunset daily), also north of Old Naples, boasts gorgeous, pristine white sands, food concessions, showers and every rental item you might need for a day in the sun (chairs, umbrellas, snorkeling, kayaks, et al). There's great snorkeling at a reef just offshore.

Other Things to See & Do

Immediately east of the pier, the late-19th-century **Palm Cottage** (☎ 239-261-8164; 137 12th Ave S; 'donation' $6; open 1pm-4pm Tues-Fri & Sun), home to the Collier County Historical Society, offers tours. It's one of the last remaining 'tabby mortar' homes in southwest Florida. Tabby was a kind of paste made from burning shells.

You can't miss **Tin City**, a waterfront shopping mall that surrounds the city docks at the eastern end of 12th Ave S on the Gordon River. Over 40 shops sell everything from fine crafts to kitsch. You can also catch a good boat tour from here (see below).

Formerly a 52-acre botanical oasis, **Caribbean Gardens** (☎ 239-262-5409; 1590 Goodlette-Frank Rd; adult/child $14/9) is now the jungle-like home to some exotic animals including Bengal tigers, zebras, panthers and huge snakes. You can also take a narrated cruise to observe monkeys and apes living freely in an island habitat. All activities are included in the admission price. And even though it's not the focus of the place, kids love the petting zoo and a myriad of daily animal presentations.

Just so you know, the **Teddy Bear Museum** (☎ 239-598-2711; 2511 Pine Ridge Rd; adult/child $6/2; open 10pm-5pm Tues-Sun), which displays a whopping 4000 bears, draws tens of thousands of visitors annually – visitors who prefer their animals soft and cuddly to wild and unpredictable. Are you a closet softie? The museum is about 2½ miles west of I-75 off exit 16.

Hotel Escalante Spa (☎ 239-659-3466; 290 5th Ave S), a low-key place, is open to the public for massages, scrubs and enriching wraps. Fees range from $55 to $90 depending on the service and length. You'd never guess how much stress guidebook writers are under when traveling around reviewing places. This place soothed it out of the system and was worth every penny.

Organized Tours

Naples Trolley Tours (☎ 239-262-7300), with anecdotal and historical narration, make a 1¾-hour circuit through the city, stopping at many hotels and the Chamber. It's pricey

($16 for adults, $7 for kids) but because you can ride all day and get on and off as often as you'd like, it's worth it. Trips run from 10am to at least 3pm daily.

Sweet Liberty (☎ 239-793-3525; W www .sweetliberty.com), a quarter-mile east of Tin City on the Gordon River, offers relaxing three-hour catamaran trips past luxe Naples Bay homes and on to Key Island, where you'll have about an hour to swim and collect shells. You'll probably see some dolphins along the way. Afterwards, stop in for a quick bite at **The Waterfront Cafe** (☎ 239-775-8115), a casual and breezy open-air seafood eatery.

Places to Stay

Wellesley Inn & Suites (☎ 239-793-4646, 800-888-4444; W www.wellesleyinnandsuites.com; 1555 5th Ave S; rooms $49-79/89-129 summer/winter) has 105 well-kept rooms (some of which are a bit small) and a pool.

Red Roof Inn & Suites (☎ 239-774-3117, 877-508-6391; W www.redroof.com; 1925 Davis Blvd; rooms $45-70/90-120 summer/winter), just east of US 41, has 157 modern units, about 30 of which have kitchens. It's a very good value, considering what town we're in.

Holiday Inn (☎ 239-262-7146, 800-325-1135; W www.hinaples.com; 1110 9th St N; rooms $56-66/130-140 summer/winter) has a nicely landscaped pool and 137 typically clean and quiet rooms, although the place does have a popular happy-hour bar.

Inn by the Sea (☎ 239-649-4124, 800-584-1268; W www.innbythesea-bb.com; 287 11th Ave S; rooms $94-104/149-169 summer/winter), on the National Register of Historic Places, boasts 1937 architecture, five bright and airy rooms, warm hosts and beautiful woodwork. It's a very good choice.

Lemon Tree Inn (☎ 239-262-1414, 888-800-5366; W www.lemontreeinn.com; 250 9th St S; rooms $59-79/149-199 summer/winter), conveniently situated, has friendly staff, free lemonade and 35 spotless, well-appointed rooms around a breakfast gazebo and gardens.

Comfort Inn & Marina (☎ 239-649-5800, 800-382-7941; W www.comfortinnnaples.com;

1221 5th Ave S; rooms $66-100/140-250 summer/winter), downtown on the bay, has 150 good units and a heated pool that's close to Tin City.

Hotel Escalante (☎ 239-659-3466; W www .hotelescalante.com; 290 5th Ave S; rooms $165-210/250-320 summer/winter, suites more), a boutique villa-style hotel designed to look like it's been there for a hundred years, boasts absolutely stunning tropical horticultural gardens. If you're not staying here, you should at least walk around to appreciate the rare plantings. As for the 70 rooms, they're outfitted with luxurious Frette linens and decadent showerheads. Go all out and get one with a patio. An expanded Continental breakfast is thoroughly enjoyed around the pool and lush courtyard, complete with stucco walls and wrought iron work. For relaxing, there's no better place. Period. They greet you with champagne on arrival, and it's only one block from the beach, and they'll send chairs and beach towels down for you.

If money is no object, the **Registry Resort** (☎ 239-597-3232, 800-247-9810; W www .registryhotel.com; 475 Seagate Dr; rooms $250-390, suites more) has 474 large rooms, enormous suites, a friendly staff and very good and very expensive restaurants (Lafite, with French cuisine, and Brass Pelican, serving seafood with Asian overtones). On Clam Pass Beach, the resort manages the county park's concessions, including canoe and kayak rentals.

Places to Eat

Cheeburger Cheeburger! (☎ 239-435-9796; 505 5th Ave S; burgers $4-6; open 11am-9pm daily) has fantastic onion rings. Oh yeah, the burgers are good, too.

Lindburgers (☎ 239-262-1127; 330 Tamiami Trail S; dishes $5-9; open 11am-9pm Mon-Sat), just a couple blocks east of 5th Ave, boasts over 50 kinds of burgers, including vegetarian ones, as well as sandwiches, salads and soups. Their patties are topped with just about anything you can think of.

5th Ave Deli Cafe (☎ 239-262-4106; 467 5th Ave S; dishes $6-7; open 10am-6pm Mon-Sat), perfect when you're preparing a

beach picnic, has enormous sandwiches big enough to share, salads and excellent pastries and pizzas. (Hint: don't take the pizza to the beach.)

Old Naples Grill (☎ 239-649-8200; 255 13th Ave S; dishes $6-14; open 11am-10pm Mon-Sat, noon-9pm Sun), a small American-style neighborhood pub, has a nice courtyard tucked behind the upscale shops. For the area, its nachos, salads, grouper and chips, ribs, tuna Caesar salads and catch-of-the-day are a great value. There is live entertainment most nights in season, and on weekends in the summer.

Dock at Crayton Cove (☎ 239-263-9940; 825 12th Ave S; dishes $8-25; open 11am-midnight daily), specializing in fried seafood on the open-air city docks, is a rustic place. They also have hefty sandwiches, good daily specials and some Caribbean-style dishes. The bar is quite popular with the locals. Watch the boats cruise by and munch on some apps and a refreshing drink.

Wynn's on Fifth (☎ 239-261-0901; 745 5th Ave S; dishes $10-19; open 8am-6pm Mon-Thur, 8am-9pm Fri, 8:30am-4pm Sat), a longtime fixture in town, excels at gourmet take-out food, European pastries and other baked goods. If you're staying in an efficiency with a microwave, you'll come here at least once.

Bistro 821 (☎ 239-261-5821; 821 5th Ave S; mains $14-30; open 5pm-10pm nightly), the old New American kid on the block, has staying power. Come for Mediterranean-influenced cuisine, bouillabaisse, steaks, lobster tails, creative pastas, risotto and an open kitchen, or, if you're lucky, sidewalk dining.

Yabba Island Grill (☎ 239-262-5787; 711 5th Ave S; mains average $16-18; open 5:30pm-10pm daily), a lively and bustling in-town eatery, almost feels like a beachside bar. Perhaps that's because of the fun bar and prevalence of rum drinks. As for the wide-ranging and well-executed Caribbean dishes, portions are large and flavored with island fruits and spices like mango and curry. You can always get one of their few inexpensive sandwiches for less than $10.

Zoe's (☎ 239-261-1221; 720 5th Ave S; mains $17-29; open 6pm-10pm nightly) attracts an energetic yuppie crowd with an eclectic bistro menu that changes weekly, and also serves comfort foods like meat loaf and gussied-up down-home mac-and-cheese. Singles congregate at the big bar and you'll feel comfortable dining alone here, as long as you're dressed to be seen. High-energy dancing takes over on weekend nights.

Chop's City Grill (☎ 239-262-4677; 837 5th Ave S; mains $17-29; open 5:30pm-10pm nightly), a cosmopolitan eatery with innovative preparations, serves very good grilled fish and high-quality beef, aged on the premises. Look for Asian-influenced combinations and seasonings. Their extensive wine list can also be enjoyed at the popular bar.

Ridgeway Bar & Grill (☎ 239-262-5500; 13th Ave S; lunch $8-14, dinner mains $18-27; open 11:30am-9:30pm daily), serving large portions of very good American food, has a prime outdoor patio. Lunchtime salads and sandwiches are nicely prepared; dinner choices are wide-ranging and creative – from lamb osso buco and swordfish piccata to simple seafood, grilled or sautéed. Regardless, save room for fabulous desserts and enjoy the well-chosen wine list. The piano bar is popular late at night.

Getting There & Away
A Greyhound bus station (☎ 239-774-5660; 2669 Davis Blvd; open 8:30am-6pm Mon-Sat) serves the region. The trip from Naples to Miami takes 3½ hours ($24.50/41.50 one-way/roundtrip); to Orlando takes 5¾ hours ($38.50/77); to Tampa takes 5½ to 6 hours ($34.50/69).

Naples is about 40 miles southwest of Fort Myers via I-75, at the southwestern end of the Tamiami Trail (Hwy 41), just northwest of Marco Island and the Everglades.

AROUND NAPLES
Corkscrew Swamp Sanctuary
This National Audubon Society property (☎ 239-348-9151; adult/student/child $8/5.50/3.50; open 7am-5:30pm daily Oct–mid-Apr, 7am-7:30pm daily mid-Apr–Sept) is the crown jewel of their national holdings. It provides a rare opportunity to go back 500 years to experience a pristine swamp and jungle forest. Be sure not to miss it, even if you've been to the Everglades. The enormous 11,000-acre property teems with wildlife, including alligators, otters, Florida black bears, red-bellied turtles, white-tailed deer and more than 200 species of birds. You can explore the world's largest subtropical-growth bald cypress forest via a 2¼-mile-long boardwalk trail that cuts right through the center of the action. (Bald cypresses, by the way, are relatives of the mighty redwoods and have a girth of 25 feet and tower to 130 feet.) It provides a cool respite from Florida's heat and is virtually free of mosquitoes, thanks to the tiny fish that eat the larvae. The preserve is northeast of Naples and southeast of Fort Myers; take I-75 to exit 17 and head east on Hwy 846; follow the signs. It's remote, so bring a lunch.

FORT MYERS
Dubbed the City of Palms for the 2000 royal palm trees that line McGregor Blvd, Fort Myers was a sleepy resort town in 1885 when Thomas Alva Edison decided to build a winter home and laboratory here. It was Edison who began planting the palms: he made a deal to plant them if the city agreed to maintain them after his death. He planted 543 as seedlings, and he imported another 270 from the Everglades, which lined the first mile of the avenue. Today McGregor is lined with palms for 14 miles!

Edison moved here in 1886 and expanded his estate over the years. In 1914, Henry Ford visited him and liked the place so much that he bought the house next door. Today, both houses are open as museums, yet Fort Myers is known more for its beach life and excellent parks than for Edison's grand experiments.

But a grand experiment is in the works today with a high-speed ferry linking Fort Myers and Key West – see the Getting There & Around section later for more information.

Orientation
The sprawling greater Fort Myers area consumes the southwest corner of Florida,

SOUTHWEST

DOWNTOWN FORT MYERS

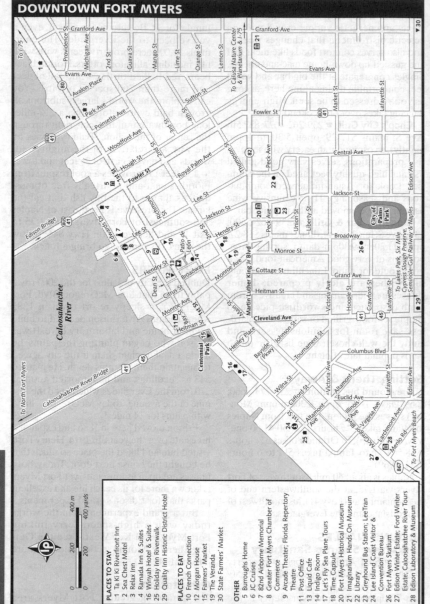

PLACES TO STAY
1 Ta Ki Ki Riverfront Inn
2 Sea Chest Motel
3 Relax Inn
4 Ramada Inn & Suites
16 Winyah Hotel & Suites
25 Holiday Inn Riverwalk
29 Quality Inn Historic District Hotel

PLACES TO EAT
10 French Connection
12 Morgan House
15 Farmers' Market
19 The Veranda
30 State Farmers' Market

OTHER
5 Burroughs Home
6 JC Cruises
7 82nd Airborne Memorial
8 Greater Fort Myers Chamber of
   Commerce
9 Arcade Theater; Florida Repertory
   Theatre
11 Post Office
13 Liquid Cafe
14 Indigo Room
17 Let's Fly Sea Plane Tours
18 Time Capsule
20 Fort Myers Historical Museum
21 Imaginarium Hands On Museum
22 Library
23 Greyhound Bus Station; LeeTran
24 Lee Island Coast Visitor &
   Convention Bureau
26 Fort Myers Skatium
27 Edison Winter Estate; Ford Winter
   Estate; Caloosahatchee River Tours
28 Edison Laboratory & Museum

northwest of Naples and the Everglades. Fort Myers sits on the southern banks of the Caloosahatchee River, North Fort Myers on the north bank; Cape Coral sits to the west. To the southwest lie San Carlos and the Estero Islands (which includes the city of Fort Myers Beach).

Distances in the Fort Myers area are incredible: the Lee County Parks Department told us that the Lee County Manatee Park, 8 miles northeast of downtown, was 'pretty much downtown Fort Myers.' Anywhere you'll want to go beyond the immediate vicinity ends up being at least 40 minutes away by car. Traffic doesn't help. Stay at Fort Myers Beach if you're after sun and surf, but if you're primarily planning to canoe around the Matlacha Pass Aquatic Preserve (see Pine Island & Matlacha later in this chapter) or to hit the Edison and Ford Winter Estates, you're in for a long drive.

Downtown is broken up by two intersecting grids. Streets in the historic district run kitty-corner to the standard east-west grid system that makes up the rest of the city. It's bounded on the south by ML King Jr Blvd, on the east by Evans Ave and on the west by Cleveland Ave (US Hwy 41, the Tamiami Trail), which runs into the Caloosahatchee Bridge and on to North Fort Myers.

Downtown doesn't really have a main drag, but what action there is (ie, not much) is concentrated along 1st St, which is one block in from the waterfront. A little pedestrian mall called Patio de León is bounded by Main, 1st and Hendry Sts and Broadway.

Information

Although they're not really geared toward walk-ins, the **Lee Island Coast Visitor & Convention Bureau** (☎ 239-338-3500, 800-237-6444; W www.leeislandcoast.com; 2180 W 1st St, Suite 100) has some good planners and information kits, including a Lee Island Coast nature guide.

The helpful **Greater Fort Myers Chamber of Commerce** (☎ 239-332-3624; W www.fort myers.org; cnr Lee St & Edwards Dr; open 9am-4:30pm Mon-Fri) has the usual array of glossy tourist magazines and brochures, including one highlighting downtown public art.

You can reach **AAA** (☎ 239-939-6500; 2516 Colonial Blvd), which has an enormous local office, by taking Cleveland Ave (US Hwy 41) south to Colonial, which is a major connector.

Bank of America (☎ 239-335-1225; 2400 1st St) has many branches in the city. The main downtown **post office** is at the corner of Bay St and Monroe Ave.

As usual, **Barnes and Noble** (☎ 239-437-0654; US 41 at Daniels Rd) will have most anything you need.

Although the local area code changed from 941 to 239 (and call forwarding of the old area code stops after March 2003), you may still see brochures printed with the old area code. Substitute 239 whenever you see 941.

Head to the main **library** (☎ 239-338-3155; 2050 Central Ave; open 9am-9pm Mon-Thur, 9am-6pm Fri & Sat) for free web surfing on 10 computers. The daily newspaper is the *News-Press* (W www.news-press.com). National Public Radio (NPR) dials in at 90.1 FM.

The area's largest public hospital is **Lee Memorial Hospital** (☎ 239-332-1111; 2776 Cleveland Ave).

Edison & Ford Winter Estates

The town's primary tourist attraction, the 14-acre **Edison Winter Estate** (☎ 239-334-7419; W www.edison-ford-estate.com; adult/child/family $12/6/30; open 9am-4pm Mon-Sat, noon-4pm Sun) was the winter home of Thomas Edison from 1885 until his death in 1931. As you probably know, Edison was one of America's most prolific inventors, but you may not know that he was also an avid botanist. The grounds are lovely, brimming with more than 1000 varieties of plants. Check out the Dynamite Tree, which spreads its seeds through pods that explode, and the enormous banyan tree, which has a reach of more than 400 feet. It's the largest in Florida.

Edison's laboratory here was devoted mainly to crossbreeding an American rubber tree at the behest of car and tire makers Ford and Firestone, who wanted to establish a reliable domestic supply. After experimenting with thousands of plants, Edison successfully created a hybrid goldenrod plant that grew to a height of almost 12 feet in a season and contained 12% rubber – an unprecedented quantity. Unfortunately, the production process was too expensive and nothing commercial came of it. The remarkable laboratory has been kept pretty much as Edison left it – the array of gizmos is amazing.

Adjacent to the laboratory (and included in the admission price), the **Edison Laboratory & Museum** contains a fascinating collection of hundreds of Edison's inventions and possessions. Look for his 1908 four-cylinder Cadillac coupe, tons of office equipment, movie projectors and kinescopes, Edison lightbulbs, phonographs and the first three-wire generator system. Guided tours through the estate also include a visit to the adjacent **Ford Winter Estate**, where the famed automaker and sometime philanderer resided. Ford and Edison were longtime friends, but didn't become neighbors until Ford built this genteel bungalow in 1916.

Fort Myers Historical Museum

This museum (☎ 239-332-5955; 2300 Peck Ave; adult/senior/child $6/5.50/3; open 9am-4pm Tues-Sat) is a hit with kids if only to tour the Esperanza, a private Pullman railroad car. Permanent exhibits document the city's history and include Calusa and Seminole artifacts, models of the local military bases and a display on Colonel Myers – the man for whom the city is named (though he never actually visited his namesake fort). Other exhibits include a Spanish cannon, a complete saber-toothed cat *(Smilodon)* skeleton, a pioneer 'cracker' house, and an exhibit on Fort Myers' two WWII training bases, which trained British, American, Canadian, Russian and Yugoslavian pilots and gunners.

Imaginarium Hands On Museum

The excellent Imaginarium (☎ 239-337-3332; 2000 Cranford Ave; adult/senior/child under 13 yrs $7/6.50/4; open 10am-5pm Mon-Sat, noon-5pm Sun), off ML King Jr Blvd, is just past the *News-Press* and *USA Today* plant – look for the big water tower. With over 60 exhibits, this hands-on science museum is favored by the wide-eyed kid in everyone. Check out the hot-air balloon exhibition and take a spin across an electronic obstacle course in a chemical-abuse simulator jeep to test your reflexes after a couple of virtual snoots. Or, through weather-forecasting tech-

---

Thomas Alva Edison

Thomas Edison (1847–1931), a tireless and entirely commercially minded inventor, held 1093 patents in his name (17 of which were co-patents with another inventor).

In Robert Conot's *A Streak of Luck*, Edison is quoted as having said, 'Anything that won't sell I don't want to invent. Its sale is proof of utility, and utility is success.'

And utilitarian Edison most certainly was: his patents include 389 under the category of 'Electric Light and Power,' 195 for phonographs, 150 for the telegraph, 141 for batteries, 62 for ore separators, 40 for cement, 34 for railroads, nine for motion pictures, eight for automobiles, five for 'electric pen' and mimeograph, three for typewriters, one for vacuum preservation, three for chemicals, one for an autogiro (a cross between a helicopter and an airplane), three for military projectiles, two for radio and one for rubber.

To get an idea of his energy, consider that he patented at least one gizmo a year for 65 consecutive years: he was issued 34 patents in 1872, 75 in 1882, 23 in 1907, and in 1931, the year of his death, he was issued two. But even death was not enough to completely sap his relentless pursuit: four patents were issued to him posthumously.

(Source: Historical Division, Edison and Ford Winter Estates)

nology, kids can then see themselves in the center of a hurricane video. There are also excellent exhibits on ozone depletion and weather – touching a cloud is neat – and a tornado machine. A 3D theater runs shows at 1pm and 3pm. Outside, a 'dig pit' lets kids look for fossils and shark teeth, while the lagoon teems with tons of freshwater fish and other Florida aquaculture. Check out the coral reef tank, aquariums and reptile retreat.

Burroughs Home

Call 'em hokey, but the 'living history' tours at this historic landmark Georgian Revival home (☎ 239-332-6125; 2505 1st St; adult/child $4/2; open 11am-3pm Tues-Fri) are still popular. You'll be led through the gracious turn-of-the-20th-century house by the costumed characters of Jettie and Mona Burroughs, daughters of Nelson Burroughs. A businessman, Burroughs bought the house from a Texas cattleman named Murphy in 1918, and the house remained in the family until it was donated to Naples in 1983. The house is on 2½ acres of shady lawn that runs down to the river; it's a nice place to have lunch. Guided tours (for an extra $2/1 adult/child) run as needed.

Other Downtown Attractions

The **82nd Airborne Memorial** (cnr Lee & Edwards Dr) stands as a monument to the Gulf Coast chapter of the Army's 82nd Airborne Division.

In 1976, the town elders gathered to make a **time capsule** (cnr 2nd St & Broadway) of items readily available during that year, to be opened on July 4, 2076.

On the banks of the Caloosahatchee River, **Centennial Park** has riverfront paths, good picnicking potential and a playground.

Calusa Nature Center & Planetarium

This complex (☎ 239-275-3435; ⓦ www.calusa nature.com; 3450 Ortiz Ave; adult/child museum & trails $5/2.50, planetarium $3/2; open 9am-5pm Mon-Sat, 11am-5pm Sun) features a series of winding boardwalks through a cypress swamp, an Audubon aviary, a (decrepit) faux Seminole village and his-

torical exhibitions documenting the formation of southwestern Florida. But kids really want to see the venomous snakes and alligator demonstrations (call for times). Nature trails abound on the 105-acre grounds. The **planetarium** stars southwest Florida's night sky; astronomy shows take place on Friday, Saturday and Sunday afternoons.

The complex is north of the intersection of Ortiz Ave, Colonial Blvd and Six Mile Cypress Pkwy.

Lakes Park

This innovative and scenic county park (7330 Gladiolus Dr, South Fort Myers) encompasses two original creations: the **Fragrance Garden** (☎ 239-432-2000; parking $3 daily; open 8am-6pm daily) and a **miniature train village** (train rides over age 6/under $2.50/50¢; open 10am-2pm Mon-Fri, 10am-4pm Sat, noon-4pm Sun). The garden was created in 1991 as a place where visually impaired and wheelchair-bound visitors could smell, feel and even eat herbs and flowers. While it's fully wheelchair accessible, and signs are in print and braille, the park is open to all. It's a nice place for a picnic. The gardens, by the way, were built by volunteers from the Master Gardeners Club, Boy and Girl Scouts and at-risk students from a nearby high school.

The miniature train (7½-inch gauge) makes little tootles around the 1¼-mile track every 15 minutes. In case you're looking for something else to do, you can rent boats here, too. **Lakeside Marina** (☎ 239-432-2017) rents canoes ($8 hourly) daily. There are alligators in the lake and on the small islands – ask at the marina where the best areas to see them are. See the 'Alligator Attacks' boxed text in the Facts about Florida chapter for safety tips.

From downtown, take US Hwy 41 south to Gladiolus Dr.

Six Mile Cypress Slough Preserve

This 2000-acre woodland and wetland (☎ 239-432-2004; admission free, parking $3 daily; open 8am-6pm daily) acts as a filter collecting run-off water during heavy rains.

Before making its way out to the Estero Bay Aquatic Preserve, the water is filtered by the slough, where sediment and pollutants settle or are absorbed by the plants. It's an interesting place to visit during the wet season (June through October), when water up to 3 feet deep flows through the area. The preserve also has an otter pond, a mile-long boardwalk lined with benches, free guided walks, a picnic area and an amphitheater used for interpretive flora and fauna talks.

From downtown Fort Myers, take Cleveland Ave south to Colonial Blvd (Hwy 884) east, to Ortiz Ave and turn south; this road will become Six Mile Cypress Pkwy.

Seminole-Gulf Railway

Founded in 1888, this railway (☎ 239-275-8487, 800-736-4853; W www.semgulf.com) operated between Arcadia and Naples with a second line running between Bradenton, Sarasota and Venice. Today, it offers five-course, murder mystery dinner tours on the line's restored trains. The 3½-hour twilight dinner rides ($52 to $64 for adults, depending on the night), which depart Wednesday through Sunday, require reservations.

The station is near the intersection of Colonial Blvd and Metro Pkwy; from downtown, take Cleveland Ave south to Colonial Blvd east until you think you'll run out of gas; the terminal is on the left.

Activities

Fort Myers Skatium (☎ 239-461-3145; W www .fortmyersskatium.com; 2250 Broadway), with ice and in-line skating, offers a change of pace. Since the management presumes you're not traveling with a pair of skates in your backpack, fees include rentals (adult/senior & child $5/4). There are daily public skates from 1pm to 3:30pm and on some evenings (Tuesday 7:30pm to 9:30pm and Friday and Saturday 7:30pm to10:30pm). Laser tag and a video arcade round out the offerings.

Organized Tours

The Edison Winter Estate offers **Caloosahatchee River tours** (☎ 239-334-7419; $4 per person; 9am-3pm Mon-Fri) aboard a replica of Edison's very own *Reliance,* an electric

launch. Meet at the estate, where trips depart every 30 minutes.

JC Cruises (☎ 239-334-7474; 2313 Edwards Dr), at the Fort Myers Yacht Basin, offers two-hour and full-day lunch and dinner cruises, as well as manatee excursions (but only November through April), up and down the Caloosahatchee River and Intracoastal Waterway.

Page Field, off Cleveland Ave, just south of downtown Fort Myers, is flight-tour central. Among the outfits, **Classic Air Ventures** (☎ 888-852-9226; open 10am-5pm Thur-Sat Nov-Apr) operates a restored 1940 open-cockpit biplane (that's right, goggles, leather helmet and all!). They offer six different flights from six to 45 minutes in length. Prices range from $50 to $200 for two people.

True to their word, **Let's Fly Sea Plane Tours** (☎ 239-332-4746; W www.fortmyerssea planes.com; 2044 W 1st St) offers 'Alaskan-style bush flying in a tropical setting' from $35 per person (there are three different tours available). It's fun.

Special Events

The annual **Edison Festival of Light** (☎ 239-334-2999; W www.edisonfestival.org) takes place during the two weeks preceding Edison's birthday on February 11. There are dozens of mostly free events, block parties with live music and tons of food, high school band concerts, hymn sings, fashion shows and the Thomas A Edison Regional Science and Inventors Fair, which features more than 400 student finalists from the southwest Florida school systems. It could be a blast – especially considering how Thomas himself blew up his railroad car/laboratory as a child. The fair culminates in the enormous Parade of Light, the last major nighttime parade in the USA, drawing up to 400,000 spectators.

Places to Stay

Most people stay at Fort Myers Beach (see Around Fort Myers later in this chapter), but businesspeople gravitate downtown to chain hotels. Of these, try the **Holiday Inn Riverwalk** (☎ 239-334-3434, 800-465-4329; 2220 W 1st St; rooms $89/129 summer/winter), with a fitness center, pool and 147 rooms near

Hanging out at Bonita Beach Pier, near Fort Myers Beach

Beach stroll on Sanibel Island

Dolphin sculpture at Sarasota's Island Park

Wakulla Springs State Park, near Tallahassee

Kayaking along Tampa's Hillsborough River

Lovely evening south of Tallahassee

Tampa skyline

the Edison and Ford Estates; and the **Ramada Inn & Suites** (☎ 239-337-0300, 800-833-1620; 2500 Edwards Dr; rooms $89/170 summer/winter), with 417 rooms near the Burroughs Home.

Relax Inn (☎ 239-334-3743; 2568 1st St; rooms $40/45 summer/winter), a few blocks from the Burroughs Home, has 23 rooms and a small pool. It'll do in a pinch.

Quality Inn Historic District Hotel (☎ 239-332-3232, 800-424-6423; 2431 Cleveland Ave (Tamiami Trail); rooms $55-70/59-110 summer/winter), with art deco overtones and 124 largish rooms, has all the standard amenities.

Sea Chest Motel (☎ 239-332-1545; 2571 1st St; rooms $40-50/70-80 summer/winter), on the river and sporting a fishing pier, has 32 cheap rooms and a heated pool.

Ta Ki Ki Riverfront Inn (☎ 239-334-2135, 866-453-0016; 2631 1st St; rooms $46/79 summer/winter), the king of downtown motels, has a good pool and 23 doubles; in-room fridges cost extra.

Winyah Hotel & Suites (☎ 239-332-2048; w www.winyah.com; 2038 W 1st St; rooms $65-115/89-159 summer/winter), with 27 rooms and one- and two-bedroom suites, is nicely situated on the marina and river.

Built in 1912, the nicely renovated and restored **Li-Inn Sleeps B&B** (☎ 239-332-2651; 2135 McGregor Blvd; rooms $70-95/105-115 summer/winter) has five smoke-free rooms with private bath, full breakfast and a very welcoming owner.

Generally, Cleveland Ave (US Hwy 41) has somewhat seedier motels. There are two exceptions: **Days Inn Fort Myers South** (☎ 239-936-1311, 800-329-7466; 11435 S Cleveland Ave; rooms $51-121), with 121 rooms; and **La Quinta Inn Fort Myers** (☎ 239-275-3300, 800-531-5900; 4850 S Cleveland Ave; rooms $55-95), with 129 largish rooms next to Mel's Diner.

Places to Eat

Mel's Diner (☎ 239-275-7850; 4820 Cleveland Ave; dishes $2-12; open 6:30am-9:30pm Sun-Thur, 6:30am-10:30pm Fri & Sat), about 4 miles south of downtown, is an old-fashioned diner. Look for open-faced hot platters and

tons of burgers by day, and specials like chicken and biscuits and prime rib by night.

The **French Connection** (☎ 239-332-4443; 2282 1st St; dishes $4-8; open 11am-2am Mon-Sat) features good service, big sandwiches and quiches, crepes, a killer French onion soup, daily soups and salads. Outdoor tables and a friendly bar (with an eight-hour happy hour from 11am to 7pm) rounds out the appeal.

Morgan House (☎ 239-337-3377; 2207 1st St; lunch $6-8, dinner mains $13-18; open 11:30am-9pm Tues-Fri, 5pm-9pm Sat), a casual but fine dining establishment, draws loyal patrons for sandwiches, salads and burgers. At night the menu ranges from chicken and steaks to seafood and pastas, so you're bound to find something that'll be okay.

The Veranda (☎ 239-332-2065; 2122 2nd St; lunch $7-13, dinner mains average $25; open 11am-2:30pm Mon-Fri, 5:30pm-11pm Mon-Sat), which wins for ambience, is located in two beautiful houses dating to 1902 and brimming with history (see the back of the menu). Considering the quality, lunch is a real bargain. Dinner is more serious and formal, with Southern regional cuisine like grilled grouper over crab hash.

On Thursdays from 7am to 3pm, visit the colorful **farmers market** underneath the entrance to the Caloosahatchee River Bridge. This is not to be confused with the **State Farmers' Market** (☎ 239-332-6910; 2744 Edison Ave; open 8:30am-5:30pm Mon-Sat, 10am-2pm Sun), which is a hotel buyers' hangout with two retail produce stands and a simple restaurant specializing in Southern dishes like grits, fried chicken and barbecue.

Entertainment

Theater The **Barbara B Mann Performing Arts Hall** (☎ 239-481-4849, 800-440-7469; w www.bbmannpah.com; season Dec-May) is the area's biggest player, on the Edison Community College campus, just northwest of the intersection of Summerlin Rd and Cypress Lake Dr. It hosts touring Broadway productions, classical and pops series and easy-listening singers. Ticket prices vary considerably.

The beautifully renovated 1908 **Arcade Theater** hosts popular comedies, dramas, musicals and ever-increasing local productions, including those by the year-round **Florida Repertory Theatre** (☎ 239-332-4488; W www.floridarep.org; 2267 1st St; tickets $15-28).

Foulds Theater (Royal Palm Square Blvd), south of Colonial Blvd between Summerlin Rd and McGregor Blvd, houses the year-round **Theatre Conspiracy** (☎ 239-936-3239; W www.theatreconspiracy.org; adult/student $16/7), a troupe that stages productions from the classic to the cutting edge.

Broadway Palm Dinner Theatre (☎ 239-278-4422; W www.broadwaypalm.com; 1380 Colonial Blvd), about a block from Royal Palm Square, stages long-running and nationally touring shows like *Nunsense* and *Forever Plaid*. Matinee and evening performances ($21) run Wednesday through Sunday. If you want some buffet-style sustenance with your acting, it'll cost you $33 (matinee) or $37 to $40 (evening).

Bars & Clubs In **Patio de León** there's an ever-changing lineup of nightclubs and cafés – **Gotham Hall**, with live bands; **Club Varian's**, with indoor-outdoor dining and late-night DJs spinning international grooves; **Cigar Bar**, a martini, humidor and wing chair sort of place; and **Cool Beans**, a coffee bar. It's best to wander down the short alley and see for yourself what's had staying power.

By day, the cool **Liquid Cafe** (☎ 239-461-0444; W www.liquidcafe.com; 2236 1st St; open 1pm-2am Mon-Sat, 6pm-2am Sun) has very good pies, specialty sandwiches, salads and coffee, as well as local art on the walls and funky chess chairs. By night, sample over 60 different bottled beers, and check out the open mike on Tuesday, the 'Skinny Dippers' (the fun house band) on Friday, and other bands on Wednesday and Saturday nights. Do stop in, and hang a while on the outdoor patio.

Indigo Room (☎ 239-332-0014; 2219 Main St; open until 2am nightly), in Patio de León, is a popular pub-bar-club with DJs and bands on some nights. In the contest for beer boasting rights, Indigo claims over 100 different brands.

Bottom Line Lounge (☎ 239-337-7292; 3090 Evans Ave; open 2pm-2am nightly), just north of Winkler Rd, is predominantly gay with a healthy mix of lesbians, but all are welcome. Bartop dancers gyrate all the time and drag queens come out nightly except Thursday and Saturday. Meanwhile, the gloves (and everything else for that matter) come off on Sunday night with guest strippers. Thursday is 'Sink or Swim,' when unlimited draft beer ($5) and well drinks ($10) rule from 9pm to closing.

Spectator Sports

City of Palms Park (2201 Edison Ave), the spring-training field for baseball's hallowed **Boston Red Sox** (☎ 239-334-4700; W www.redsox.com), is hopping in March. The **Minnesota Twins** (☎ 239-768-4270; W www.mntwins.com) play at Lee County Sports Complex, just southwest of the intersection of Daniels Pkwy and Six Mile Cypress Pkwy. During the regular season, the Fort Myers Miracles (the Minnesota Twins minor-league-baseball farm team) play here.

Getting There & Around

Southwest Florida International Airport (RSW; ☎ 239-768-1000; W www.swfia.com; Daniels Pkwy), east of I-75, is served by upwards of 15 airlines.

The **Greyhound bus station** (☎ 239-334-1011; 2250 Peck Ave) serves most places you'd want to go. The trip from Fort Myers to Miami takes 4 hours ($26/47 one-way/roundtrip); to Orlando takes 2½ to 6½ hours ($32/64); to Tampa takes 2½ to 4½ hours ($24/43).

There is a decent public transport system that can get you around, albeit slowly. **LeeTran** (☎ 239-275-8726; 2250 Peck Ave) buses run throughout Lee County, but not to Sanibel or Captiva Islands, and they take a while (like an hour and a half from downtown Fort Myers to Fort Myers Beach). Fares are $1, transfers 15¢. From downtown, bus No 20 runs (every 30 minutes) between the downtown station and the Edison and Ford Winter Estates.

Amtrak (☎ 800-872-7245) shuttles stop throughout the city and bring passengers to the Tampa terminal.

Because of the sadistic distances between everything you'll want to see, a car is key. Downtown Fort Myers is about 40 minutes from Fort Myers Beach; the main connecting artery is Summerlin Rd (Hwy 869), which dead-ends into Colonial Blvd. Another main connector between downtown and the beach is McGregor Blvd (Hwy 867), which forks away from Summerlin as it heads into downtown Fort Myers and becomes ML King Jr Blvd after it passes beneath US Hwy 41. Both Summerlin Rd and McGregor Blvd intersect with San Carlos Blvd, which continues to Fort Myers Beach and southward.

Fort Myers, between I-75 and US Hwy 41 (the Tamiami Trail), is about 140 miles from Miami and 123 miles from Tampa. Most major car rental companies have offices at the airport; see the Getting Around chapter for more information.

The ferry **Express to Key West** (☎ 239-765-0808, 800-273-4496; **W** www.keywest ferry.com; Fisherman's Wharf) will save you 300 miles of driving and 7 hours in the car. The daily high-speed ferry leaves Fort Myers Beach at 7:45am and arrives in Key West at noon; it then returns at 5:30pm to arrive in Fort Myers Beach at 10pm. Roundtrip tickets (adult/senior/child $129/119/89) cost the same even if you're not returning same-day. The price includes Continental breakfast, free parking in Fort Myers Beach and discount coupons to Key West attractions. Head south on San Carlos Blvd (Hwy 865) toward the Sky Bridge to Fort Myers Beach; just before the bridge, turn right on Main St and left on Fisherman's Wharf.

AROUND FORT MYERS
On Estero Island, Fort Myers Beach manages to be both a party town (at its Times Square section) and a quiet beach resort (farther south near the Outrigger Beach Resort). Many people make this their base for exploring the area.

Although the local area code changed from 941 to 239 (and call forwarding of the old area code stops after March 2003), you may still see brochures printed with the old area code. Substitute 239 whenever you see 941.

Lee County Manatee Park
This park (☎ 239-432-2038; admission free, parking $3 daily; park open 8am-5pm daily year-round; visitor's center open during winter park hours and 9am-4pm Sat & Sun in summer) on the Orange River draws visitors with a manatee-viewing platform, picnic shelters, guided viewing programs, summer kayak rentals ($10 hourly), native plant habitats and an 'Eco-Torium' with manatee displays and information. Keep in mind that this is a non-captive habitat and West Indian manatees only hang around when the water temperatures dip below 70° (ie, from about December through March). Call the manatee viewing line at ☎ (239) 694-3537 for updates. The park is off of Hwy 80, about 8 miles east of downtown Fort Myers and about 1½ miles east of I-75 exit 25.

Organized Tours
Within the largest contiguous cattle ranch east of the mighty Mississippi River, **Babcock Wilderness Adventures** (☎ 800-500-5583; **W** www.babcockwilderness.com) offers swamp-buggy rides billed as ecotours (see the 'Air Boats & Swamp Buggies' boxed text in the Everglades chapter for information on swamp buggies and their effect on the environment). The popular nature tours, through the enormous 90,000-acre Crescent B Ranch on the Telegraph Cypress Swamp, are naturalist-led 90-minute tours. They promise sightings of bison, quarter horses, Texas cougars, alligators, panther, deer, wild turkey and boar. And they traverse five different ecosystems. Tours depart from 9am to 3pm November through May, but in the summer, they only depart in the morning. Reservations are required; the cost is $18 for adults, $10 for children.

They also have three-hour bike tours ($35 for adults, $30 for children) at 9am and 1pm daily; reservations are required for these trips, too. The ranch is about 10 miles northeast of Fort Myers; take I-75 to exit 26 and take Hwy 78 east, then take Hwy 31 north for 6 miles.

Fort Myers Beach
Except for the beach (which is very nice), tons of hotels and condos, a fishing pier, and

bars, there isn't much here. That said, anyone who thinks that the sunsets at Key West are the bee's knees should get a gander at these. If you want action and turmoil, head to the **Times Square** party area surrounding the Estero Island side of the Sky Bridge. Although it's wishful thinking to employ the Times Square comparison, there are a number of lively bars and eateries here. Otherwise, prepare for sunning, drinking, parasailing and scootering around.

Estero Island, a 7-mile-long sliver of an island, is about a 40-minute drive southwest from downtown Fort Myers. The main drag – actually the *only* drag – is Estero Blvd, which eventually leads across a bridge to Lover's Key State Recreation Area (see Lover's Key later in this section), Bonita Beach and US Hwy 41.

The **Greater Fort Myers Beach Chamber of Commerce** (☎ 239-454-7500, 800-782-9283; W www.fmbchamber.com; 17200 San Carlos Blvd; open 8am-5pm Mon-Fri, 10am-5pm Sat, 11am-5pm Sun), about 3 miles north of the Sky Bridge, has all the requisite pamphlets, menus and a voluminous list of beachside condo rentals.

The **library** (☎ 239-463-9691; Bay Rd; open 9am-8pm Mon & Wed, 9am-5pm Tues, Thur & Fri, 9am-1pm Sat), across from Seagrape Plaza, has free Internet access.

If you need to wash your clothes and rental car (not together please), head to **Mid-Island Laundry and Car Wash** (☎ 239-463-7452) near the Outrigger Beach Resort (see Places to Stay below).

Places to Stay The **San Carlos RV Park** (☎ 239-466-3133; 18701 San Carlos Blvd; sites $28/33-38, mobile homes weekly $355/580 summer/winter), right before the bridge between the mainland and San Carlos Island, has friendly folks who rent 140 tent and RV/van sites with hookups and 19 trailers. Although it's built on dead-end causeways, lined with palms and pines, sites are really close together.

The 250-site **Red Coconut RV Resort & Campground** (☎ 239-463-7200; 3001 Estero Blvd; parkside sites $32/48 summer/winter, beach sites $45-59/51-65 summer/winter),

between Lovers Lane and Donora Blvd, is the area's only beachside campground, but they have far more sites on the 'park' side so don't get your hopes up. It's also very commercial.

Palm Terrace Apartments (☎ 239-765-5783, 800-320-5783; W www.palm-terrace.com; 3333 Estero Blvd; units $49-81/85-130 summer/winter), another fine choice near the beach, has nine efficiencies and apartments, most with a deck or screened porch. They also have a pool and barbecue facilities.

Island House Motel (☎ 239-463-9282, 800-951-9975; W www.edgewaterfmb.com; 701 Estero Blvd; units $59-99/99-115 summer/winter), just north of Matanzas Pass Bridge and within walking distance of the action, has complimentary bikes and beach chairs, a pool, and a mere five units with kitchens. It's a very good choice.

Outrigger Beach Resort (☎ 239-463-3131, 800-749-3131; W www.outriggerfmb.com; 6200 Estero Blvd; units $85-150/100-185 summer/winter), with 144 rooms and efficiencies and a fun beachfront tiki bar with great sunset views, is worth the extra expense.

Chain hotels include **Holiday Inn Fort Myers Beach** (☎ 239-463-5711, 800-650-9350; 6890 Estero Blvd; rooms from $95/185 summer/winter), with a pool and 103 rooms that either face an ugly parking lot or a nice courtyard, and **Best Western Pink Shell Resort** (☎ 239-463-6181, 800-237-5786; 275 Estero Blvd; rooms from $135/239 summer/winter), with 208 family-friendly rooms on the quiet northern tip of the island.

Places to Eat Fresh seafood is a smart choice here, since 'daily catch' equates to truth-in-advertising: there's a sizable fishing port at Matanzas Pass.

Split Rail (☎ 239-466-3400; 17943 San Carlos Blvd; breakfast $1-5, lunch & dinner mains $7-13; open 6am-9pm daily), a dependable breakfast source, has a weird mix of Greek, Mexican (which predominates) and American food (sandwiches and seafood). It's off the beach, about a mile and a half back toward Fort Myers.

Düsseldorf's on the Beach (☎ 239-463-5251; 1113 Estero Blvd; dishes $10-12; open

11am-1am daily), just by the Sky Bridge, is known more for its 100 varieties of beer and oom-pah-pah atmosphere than for its cheap but decent food. Nonetheless, look for a German sausage sampler or the kassler rippchen (smoked pork chop either fried or boiled in sauerkraut), both served with German potato salad, kraut and German bread.

Loggerheads (☎ 239-463-4644; Santini Marina Plaza; lunch $5-6, dinner mains from $13; open 11am-10pm daily), at the southern end of the beach, is a great choice for casual seafood specialties. But they also have a bit of everything, from Cobb salads and burgers to pasta and very good ribs. Here's a fun twist: kids' meals are served on a Frisbee.

Snug Harbor Seafood Restaurant (☎ 239-463-4343; 645 Old San Carlos Blvd; lunch $7-12, dinner mains $10-39; open 11:30am-3pm & 4:30pm-closing daily), also at the foot of the Sky Bridge and popular among locals (who especially like to hang out at the dockside bar), features Caesar salads, salmon cakes, sautéed grouper and blackened chicken breast. As mentioned earlier, though, fresh-caught seafood specials are usually a good bet.

Matanzas Inn (☎ 239-463-3838; 416 Crescent St; lunch $7-10, dinner mains $13-19; open 11am-10pm daily), with dockside and deck dining, is a very good casual option for fresh seafood (particularly stuffed grouper, mahimahi and beer battered shrimp). You can see fish being unloaded from the adjacent docks.

Papa Mondo (☎ 239-765-9660; 1821 Estero Blvd; mains $11-17; open 3:30pm-10pm daily), a northern Italian eatery with pasta made on the premises, serves authentic dishes like pesto and pomodoro gnocchi or ravioli stuffed with ricotta and spinach in a sage and butter sauce. Early specials ($8 to $11) from 3:30pm to 6pm make this an even better value.

Getting There & Around From downtown Fort Myers, take McGregor Blvd to San Carlos Blvd and cross the Sky Bridge. From the south on US Hwy 41, turn west on

Bonita Beach Rd at the southern end of Bonita Springs and head north.

By bus from downtown Fort Myers, take the No 140 south to Bell Tower ($1, every 20 minutes), where you change for the No 50 (15¢ transfer, hourly at 20 minutes past the hour) and then to a beach trolley (25¢, hourly) for Fort Myers Beach.

A red **LeeTran trolley** (☎ 239-275-8726; 25¢, every half-hour from about 7am to 9pm) runs daily between the pier (opposite the Sky Bridge) and Bowditch Point Regional Park at the northwestern end of the island, all the way southeast to Villa Santini Plaza at the 7000 block of Estero Blvd. At Villa Santini Plaza, you can catch another tram that runs south between Fort Myers Beach and Bonita Beach, past Lover's Key.

Lover's Key State Recreation Area

Between Fort Myers Beach and Bonita Beach, this four-island park (☎ 239-597-6196; admission per carload $4, per pedestrian or bicyclist $1; open 8am-sunset) is quieter than Fort Myers Beach and offers very good shelling, 2½ miles of good beaches and bird watching. Wooden walkways from the parking area lead across Inner Key out to the Gulf beach at Lover's Key. Canoe and kayak rentals are available.

Koreshan State Park

This pioneer settlement (☎ 239-992-0311, 800-326-3521; Koreshan State Park, cnr US Hwy 41 & Corkscrew Rd, Estero; admission per carload $3.25, per pedestrian or bicyclist $1; open 8am-sunset), a state historic site, offers access to the Estero River Canoe Trail.

Led by Cyrus R Teed, the Koreshans were a religio-scientific movement that settled in the area in 1893 to build a New Jerusalem (see 'The Koreshans' boxed text). In 1961, the last four Koreshans donated the group's 305 acres to Florida in exchange for a promise to maintain the settlement in perpetuity. The last Koreshan died in 1982. And sure enough, to this day, the park contains the members' cottage, machine shops and the art hall from the early 1900s.

The site is west of US Hwy 41; from I-75, take exit 19, which becomes Corkscrew Rd, and head west 2 miles. From Fort Myers Beach, take Estero Blvd south past Bonita Beach and over to US Hwy 41; go north to Corkscrew Rd, then west.

Mound Key If you're canoeing the Estero River, Mound Key makes an interesting destination. It's a mile into Estero Bay from the junction of the river (about 4¼ miles from the Koreshan site). Surrounded by mangrove forests, the island was, in essence, formed from mounds of discarded oyster shells left by Calusa Indians about 2000 years ago. These folks ate a *lot* of oysters: many mounds that make up the key (which supported at least a thousand homes) are more than 30 feet high! The area is now a state archaeological site. One of the largest mounds was actually a town, Calos, which researchers theorize was the capital of the Calusa Indians' region. In 1567, Jesuit missionaries founded the San Antonio de Carlos mission on one of the mounds. As you can imagine, the Calusa were not amused and the mission failed.

Although the tides are generally calm from Mound Key to the site, check with rangers before making the trip. And remember that since this is a working archaeological site, it's illegal to remove shells.

Canoeing The Estero River Canoe Trail passes through the northern end of the park, and you can rent canoes here for $3 per hour or $16 for five or more hours. The canoe trail is about 1½ miles upriver and 1¾ miles downriver to its junction with Estero Bay.

Places to Stay Scrub Oak Camping Area (sites without/with electric $11/13 May-Nov, $18/20 Dec-Apr), at the Koreshan site, has 60 tent and RV sites with picnic tables, fire rings, water, hot showers and laundry facilities. Campers are allowed unlimited access to the park, while day-use guests must depart at sunset. If you plan to arrive after sunset to camp, call the ranger station (see Koreshan State Park above) between 8am and 5pm for the gate key combination.

If Koreshan is full, **Woodsmoke Camping Resort** (☎ 239-267-3456; 19551 S US Hwy 41; sites with hookups $29/34-40 summer/winter) is the nearest commercial camping. But they only serve RVs and pop-ups set 'among permanent park models.' It's just south of San Carlos Park, about 2 miles north of Estero and 9 miles south of Fort Myers.

SANIBEL & CAPTIVA ISLANDS

The southernmost Gulf barrier islands, Sanibel and Captiva make excellent day trips from Fort Myers. Staying out here is a tad expensive (read: understatement), if you're

---

The Koreshans

Inspired by a vision, Cyrus R Teed changed his name to Koresh (which is Hebrew for Cyrus, 'the anointed of God,' and has no connection to the ill-fated movement led by David Koresh near Waco, Texas). The Koreshans believed that although the earth was round, it was concave, not convex. They also believed that humankind lived inside the earth and viewed the solar system within it. Under this theory (they never argued with the belief that the earth was 25,000 miles in circumference), the sun would have been placed at the center of the earth, about 4000 miles from the inner crust on which people lived.

While a lot of pseudoscientific mumbo jumbo involving the use of a 'Pullman-built rectilineator' was used to explain this theory, the Koreshan Unity Foundation, Inc (☎ 239-992-2184) maintains that the universe was God's greatest creation; talk in scientific circles of a 'limitless universe' disturbed the group.

Their religion was based (like the Shakers') around a God of male and female essences. Adherents practiced a restricted form of celibacy and one of a community of goods and effort. If simply joining the cooperative effort, members could maintain a family. To join the advanced ecclesia, and be allowed to live within the confines of the settlement, members had to let go of their personal property and live a celibate life.

– Nick & Corinna Selby

even lucky enough to get a room. Everyone comes for the glorious beaches, which also cough up some of the Western Hemisphere's best shells. In fact, the shelling is so good and so diverse that there's a shell museum. Sanibel's also got an eccentric, isolated and very clique-prone populace that can sometimes be haughty toward tourists. But if you can manage to get acquainted with some locals, you'll have a great time. Good kayaking and canoeing abound within the JN 'Ding' Darling National Wildlife Refuge and within the islands.

Unless you're coming by boat, private plane or helicopter, there's only one way to get here: the Sanibel Causeway (Hwy 867), which has a $3 toll for cars, $1 for motorcycles. Fare collectors get you coming but not going. At the end of the causeway, follow Periwinkle Way to its end at Tarpon Bay Rd (look for the post office), turn right, and then left onto Sanibel-Captiva Rd. The shell museum is on the left, the 'Ding' Darling Refuge on the right. It'll seem to take forever and you'll probably think you've missed it, but you won't have.

The **Sanibel Island Chamber of Commerce** (☎ 239-472-1080; **W** www.sanibel-captiva.org; 1159 Causeway Blvd; open 9am-7pm Mon-Sat, 10am-5pm Sun) has mountains of tourist information.

Bailey Matthews Shell Museum

This museum (☎ 239-395-2233; **W** www.shell museum.org; 3075 Sanibel-Captiva Rd; adult/child $5/3; open 10am-4pm Tues-Sun) is dedicated to all things shell-related. With over 30 exhibits, the wide-reaching galleries will educate you about edible scallops of the world; shells in tribal art; medicinal (and poisonous) properties of mollusks; and about shells from the Pacific Northwest, Japan, Saudi Arabia and South Africa. A giant globe indicates where in the world the shells originated from. Check out the cool sculpture – made from shells, of course – called *Horse Racing at a State Fair*. The library boasts everything from an environmental coloring book and *Synopsis Omnium Methodica Molluscorum Generum* to a computerized research center with an enormous conchological data bank and a 35mm slide collection.

JN 'Ding' Darling National Wildlife Refuge

Named for cartoonist Jay Norwood 'Ding' Darling, an environmentalist who helped establish more than 300 sanctuaries across the USA, this fascinating 6300-acre refuge (☎ 239-472-1100, 888-679-6450; **W** www.ding darling.fws.gov; Sanibel-Captiva Rd at MM 2; admission per carload $5, per pedestrian or

She Finds Seashells Down by the Seashore

You can find about 160 varieties of shells on Sanibel Island beaches, and although it's so corny it's embarrassing, people really do refer to the act of bending over to pick them up as the 'Sanibel Stoop.'

Head out to Blind Pass at the northwesternmost section of Sanibel at low tide, preferably low tide in winter, or better yet, low tide in winter after a storm. You won't be alone, and locals, while sometimes standoffish in restaurants and bars, will cheerfully offer advice and counsel on shell-gathering strategies. So start hanging your head and stooping over. You'll come up with boatloads of conch shells, cat's paws, slippers.

Anything that's dead is yours for the taking, but make certain that nothing's living inside your shell – taking live shell inhabitants or sand dollars, sea stars or sea urchins is grounds for a big fine and jail time. That same penalty applies to any shells taken from the 'Ding' Darling Refuge, where shelling is prohibited. These people are incredibly serious about enforcement, so use your head.

If you're really interested in shelling, the Bailey Matthews Shell Museum has plenty of literature describing all the varieties of shells as well as techniques for collecting, cleaning, preserving and displaying them.

bicyclist $1; see open hours below), at the northern end of Sanibel, is home to a huge variety of fish and wildlife. You'll see alligators, green-backed and night herons, red-shouldered hawks, spotted sandpipers, roseate spoonbills, pelicans and anhinga. The refuge also has canoe trails, an outstanding educational center and exhibition space, a 5-mile Wildlife Drive, alligator observation platforms and walking trails. Note that shelling is strictly prohibited here. The best time to visit is low tide, when birds are feeding. The Bailey Trail, off Tarpon Bay Rd, is accessible on Fridays when the rest of the park isn't.

Wildlife Drive tram tours (☎ 239-472-8900) depart from the visitor's center parking lot at 10:30am and 2pm Saturday through Thursday; there's an additional trip at 6pm Tuesday through Thursday. The refuge is open Sunday to Thursday for cars (7:30am to 7:30pm) and for bicycles and pedestrians (sunrise to sunset). Regardless of transport, the **visitor's center** is open 9am to 4pm daily.

Canoeing & Kayaking

The friendly folks at **Tarpon Bay Recreation** (☎ 239-472-8900; 900 Tarpon Bay Rd), within the refuge on Sanibel, rent canoes and kayaks for $20 for two hours. There is plenty of time to paddle your way around the marked mangrove waterways. Pick up rentals from 8am to 2pm daily, or join a guided group ecotour (adult/child $25/12.50) and then paddle around on your own (no additional charge).

'Tween Waters Marina (☎ 239-472-5161), on Captiva north of the refuge at the 'Tween Waters Inn, rents canoes ($20 for two hours). Although it's close enough to the refuge to paddle from the marina, ask about the tides. Even if you're just paddling around the resort, you can zip across to Buck Key, which has two canoe trails. 'Tween also offer three-hour guided kayak tours at Buck Key for $40.

Biking

With over 23 miles of dedicated paths, biking is an excellent way to get around; the Chamber of Commerce has a detailed bike

map. Head to **Billy's Rentals** (☎ 239-472-5248; 1470 Periwinkle Way, Sanibel) or **Jim's Rentals** (☎ 239-472-1296; Andy Rosse Lane, Captiva), at southern and northern ends of their respective islands. Rates are competitive and depend on what kind of bike you want. Figure about $5 hourly, $12 daily and $35 weekly.

Beaches & Shelling

The main beaches (parking costs 75¢ hourly) are Bowman's Beach, Sanibel Lighthouse, Turner Beach (limited parking) and Gulfside Park. You can't enter the wooden **Sanibel Island Lighthouse**, but there's a fishing pier there and parking lots. East, Middle and West Gulf Drives provide Gulf beach access.

Places to Stay

For a complete listing of charming motels alternatives, contact the **Sanibel-Captiva Small Inns and Cottages Association** (W www.sanibelsmallinns.com).

Seahorse Cottages (☎ 239-472-4262; W www.seahorsecottages.com; 1223 Buttonwood Lane, Sanibel; units $64-95/90-185 summer/winter), near the lighthouse and beach, is a great option, with a small pool, five pleasant and tiled cottages, a studio and laundry facilities.

Buttonwood Cottages (☎ 239-395-9061, 877-395-2688; W www.buttonwoodcottages .com; 1234 Buttonwood Lane, Sanibel; units $75-160/125-220 summer/winter) is basically a cheery motel with eight comfortable 'cottagey' units, complete with kitchens and screened porches. It's a short walk to either Gulf or bay beaches.

The charming **Tarpon Tale Inn** (☎ 239-472-0939, 888-345-0939; W www.tarpontales.com; 367 Periwinkle Way, Sanibel; rooms $99-189/149-229 summer/winter), with lush gardens in an old neighborhood, has five fresh and contemporary units with lots of amenities: beach chairs, barbecue grills, bicycles and a hot tub.

Waterside Inn on the Beach (☎ 239-472-1345, 800-741-6166; W www.watersideinn thebeach.com; 3033 W Gulf Dr, Sanibel; units $138-171/160-230 summer/winter), which has 37 modestly furnished units (most with kitchenettes), is perched on the edge of the beach. Expect lush landscaping, two pools and a coin laundry.

Casa Ybel Resort (☎ 239-472-3145, 800-276-4753; w www.casaybelresort.com; 2255 W Gulf Dr, Sanibel; units from $210/400 summer/winter), a condo community with one- and two-bedroom units with kitchens, is a real splurge. A few of the numerous amenities include a pool, beach, tennis and manicured grounds.

Captiva Island Inn (☎ 239-395-0882, 800-454-9898; w www.captivaislandinn.com; 11509 Andy Rosse Lane, Captiva; cottages $130-160/220-250 summer/winter) has 10 cottages (one-bedroom units with a sleeper sofa) in a wonderful setting.

Places to Eat

Service is generally bad, but the food is OK if you keep it simple. Grilled fish is always better than the bourbon-glazed whatever over pan-fried yadda yadda.

Bailey's General Store (☎ 239-472-1516; Periwinkle Way at Tarpon Rd, Sanibel; open 7am-9pm daily), when you need picnic fixings, has the gourmet goods.

The Bean (☎ 239-395-1919; 2240 Periwinkle Way, Sanibel; dishes $5-7; open 7:30am-9pm daily, until 10pm in winter), stepping up to the plate where Starbucks doesn't venture, serves light breakfast bagels, lunchtime salads and panini and the namesake coffee bean drinks in an outdoor setting.

The Lazy Flamingo (☎ 239-472-6939; 1036 Periwinkle Way, Sanibel; ☎ 239-472-5353; 6520 Pine Ave, Captiva; dishes $6-13; both open 11:30am-1am daily) is a casual option with a sports bar atmosphere. Look for great raw oysters, good smoked fish, mesquite-grilled grouper sandwiches and grilled chicken breasts. Their specialty is 'The Pot,' two dozen oysters or clams steamed in beer and seasonings ($16). For a good value and a casual atmosphere, they're hard to beat.

McT's Shrimp House & Tavern (☎ 239-472-3161; 1523 Periwinkle Way, Sanibel; mains $17-23; open 5pm-10pm nightly), something of an island institution, specializes in shrimp, shrimp and shrimp. The tavern is open until

midnight. Shrimp anyone? Okay, you can get grouper, pasta and steaks, but you shouldn't. Get the shrimp.

The Jacaranda (☎ 239-472-1771; 1223 Periwinkle Way, Sanibel; mains average $22; open 5pm-10pm daily), which works hard at being chic, specializes in fresh seafood, black Angus steaks and pastas.

The Bubble Room (☎ 239-472-5558; 15001 Captiva Dr, Captiva; lunch $8-15, dinner mains $15-25; open 11:30am-2:30pm & 5:30pm-9:30pm daily) is either amusing or bizarre, depending on your perspective. It's packed with memorabilia from the 1930s and '40s, flashing lights, movie photos, bric-a-brac and hoo-has. It's a totally insane place (with service to match), worth a stop simply for some apps (large Gulf shrimp in garlic butter or she-crab soup made with cream) and a drink or two.

Chadwick's Restaurant (☎ 239-472-7575; Captiva Dr, Captiva; buffet $19-25; open 11am-2pm Sun & 5:30pm-9:30pm nightly), at the northern tip of the island at the entrance of South Seas Resort, draws patrons with big appetites to its extensive all-you-can-eat buffet. Expect to be zapped with an 18% service charge, which could still make it a value if you can *really* pack away food. The champagne Sunday brunch is an all-you-can-eat-and-drink affair.

Otter's Island Eats (☎ 239-395-1142; Andy Rosse Lane, Captiva; breakfast & lunch $6-12, dinner mains $10-20; open 7:30am-10:30pm daily), ensconced in an old wooden cottage, is a cheap and casual eatery with indoor and outdoor dining. The extensive menu ranges from good sandwiches and burgers, to excellent and creative breakfasts, to soft-shell crabs and old-fashioned country-fried steaks.

AROUND SANIBEL & CAPTIVA

Some of Florida's best natural attractions are here. From excellent county parks to the undeveloped splendor of Cayo Costa Island and the Matlacha Pass Aquatic Preserve, you can spend days soaking up the nature, kayaking or canoeing, watching alligators, dolphins and manatees and really getting away from it all.

Pine Island & Matlacha

Just north of Captiva Island, the gorgeous barrier islands surrounding the pristine Matlacha (pronounced mat-la-**shay**) Pass Aquatic Preserve are perfect for kayak and canoe exploration. The preserve, along with the Pine Island Sound Aquatic Preserve, covers 90 sq mi and more than 70 miles of coastline, and it's made up of islands, mangrove swamps, shallow lagoons and bays.

Pine Island, at 17 miles long, is the area's largest, and while it's officially broken up into several communities, everyone calls the whole thing Pine Island. Fortunately, it's been spared development because of its location and by Florida height and density zoning limits.

Communities include the tiny fishing village of Matlacha; Bokeelia (pronounced bow-**keel**-ya), at the northern tip of Pine Island, which is the commercial fishing center and home of the *Tropic Star* (see Getting There & Away under Cayo Costa Island, later in this section); and Pine Island Center, the commercial district at the center of the island.

The island was inhabited by Calusa Indians from AD 300 to 1513, when Ponce de León landed here. After that, the Indians who weren't killed by soldiers were killed by disease.

Orientation & Information Pine Island is due west of North Fort Myers and not accessible by public transportation. By car, take either US Hwy 41 north to Pine Island Rd (Hwy 78) or I-75 north to exit 26 (Bayshore Rd, which becomes Pine Island Rd). Follow Pine Island Rd west until you get there; you'll pass Matlacha and Little Pine Island.

Volunteers at **Greater Pine Island Chamber of Commerce** (☎ 239-283-0888; ⓦ www.pineislandchamber.org; Pine Island Rd; open 10am-4pm Mon-Fri, 10am-1pm Sat), just east of Matlacha, dispense reliable information like 'there's a coin laundry next to the pizza place as you come into town on the right.'

Kayaking At **Gulf Coast Kayak** (☎ 239-283-1125; ⓦ www.gulfcoastkayak.com; 4882 NW Pine Island Rd), on Little Palm Island, Matlacha, they offer several year-round wildlife and nature tours as well as kayak and canoe rentals (single $25 daily, double $35). Bruce, the friendly owner, spouts fountains of valuable information. Consider renting for several days since you could take camping trips to Cayo Costa State Park (see Cayo Costa Island later in this section). Reservations are recommended.

Places to Stay A full-service commercial campground, **Fort Myers/Pine Island KOA** (☎ 239-283-2415, 800-992-7202; sites without/with hookups $20/28-30 summer, $35/41-45 winter, 1-/2-room Kamping Kabins $40/50 summer, $48/55 winter) has 365 sites that are difficult to obtain in winter unless you call months in advance. They offer a free beach and attraction shuttle in winter. From I-75, take exit 26 and head west on Hwy 78 to the first four-way stop. Turn left and head 5 miles down Stringfellow Rd.

Bridge Water Inn (☎ 239-283-2423, 800-378-7666; ⓦ www.bridgewaterinn.com; 4331 Pine Island Rd; rooms $49-119/49-129 summer/winter), a great family-run place built on a pier, has three motel rooms and five large efficiencies. The two corner efficiencies have huge sliding-glass doors that look out onto the aquatic preserve and the waterfront. With dolphins and manatees swimming by regularly, it's as close to a perfect Florida experience as you'll get.

Beach House Motel (☎ 239-283-4303, 800-348-6306; 7202 Bocilla Lane; units $70-100 summer, room $80 winter), with its own private pier, has three nice apartments and one simple room, but the apartments are only rented weekly in winter ($750).

Knolls Court (☎ 239-283-0616; ⓦ www.knollscourtmotel.com; 4755 Pine Island Rd; roadside/waterside efficiencies $55/65-75 summer, $75/85-95 winter) has seven units and offers daily and weekly rentals.

Places to Eat A bunch of mom-and-pop restaurants (with a low tourist tolerance and consistently reliable seafood and burgers) are within walking distance of the motels along Pine Island Rd NW.

Mulletville (☎ 239-283-5151; 9745 Pine Island Rd; dishes $3-6; open 5:30am-12:30pm in summer, for all 3 meals in winter), the biggest local hangout for entertainment, is also good for shooting pool. While they have great breakfasts, head elsewhere for better afternoon and evening eats.

Matlacha Oyster House (☎ 239-283-2544; 3930 Pine Island Rd NW; lunch $6-9, dinner mains $9-21; open 11am-3pm & 4:30pm-9pm daily) offers daily seafood specials like grouper fingers, seafood-stuffed flounder, poached salmon and seafood strudel.

Sandy Hook Restaurant (☎ 239-283-0113; 4875 Pine Island Rd; dishes $12-16; open 4pm-9pm Tues-Sat, noon-8pm Sun), with excellent water views, offers good baby back ribs and combo platters with grouper and ribs.

Cayo Costa Island

One of Florida's largest undeveloped barrier islands, Cayo Costa lies west of Pine Island and north of Captiva Island. The 2500-acre **state park** (☎ 941-964-0375, 800-326-3521; tent sites $14, 4-person cabins $23 plus $5 per extra person) offers great shelling, swimming, kayaking and canoeing. As if that wasn't enough, Atlantic bottle-nosed dolphins live around here and frolic just offshore. With white sand, sabal palms, gumbo-limbo hammocks, clear water and cheap accommodations, the 30-site park offers arguably one of the best deals for enjoying Florida's sun and fun. There are three catches: you have to bring your own food (though cooking and picnic facilities are available); you have to get there by boat (see below); and there's no hot water or electricity in the cabins. Bring your own linen, utensils and, definitely, insect repellent. Reservations are required.

Getting There & Away The island is accessible only by boat. Park rangers run a tram between the island dock and the camping area, or you can walk the mile.

Gulf Coast Kayak (☎ 239-283-1125), which rents kayaks (see Gulf Coast Kayak earlier in this section) and camping equipment, also runs guided tours that include everything you'll need except a toothbrush and sleeping bag. Prices vary depending on the length of stay.

The *Tropic Star* (☎ 239-283-0015), departing from Knight's Landing in Bokeelia at the northern tip of Pine Island, cruises year-round to Cayo Costa. You can get off and camp here, or just bring a lunch and beach gear and take the boat back at 3pm. The roundtrip costs $21 for adults, $16 for children. From November through April, the same boat is called a nature cruise and continues up to the Cabbage Key Inn (see below), where you can buy lunch before enjoying two hours on Cayo Costa. From May through October the Cabbage Key trip runs when there are enough people. Reservations are required.

The other option is a private water taxi. **Island Charters** (☎ 239-283-2008; ⓦ www.islandcharters.com) runs water taxis from Pineland Marina to the Cabbage Key Inn (see below; about 15 minutes) for $25 per person.

Cabbage Key

Supposedly, Jimmy Buffet's song 'Cheeseburger in Paradise' was inspired by this 100-acre key. The most notable sight here, though, is the hotel and restaurant.

Cabbage Key Inn (☎ 239-283-2278; ⓦ www.cabbage-key.com; rooms $89, cottages $145-189; open for all 3 meals daily) boasts a long list of celebrities who have stayed here – from Julia Roberts to JFK Jr to Johnny Carson sidekick Ed McMahon to Ernest Hemingway. The home was constructed atop a Calusa shell mound by writer Mary Roberts Rinehart in 1938. The wackiest thing about the place is the wallpaper: twenty to thirty thousand $1 bills festoon the walls. The story goes like this: in the 1940s, commercial fishermen used to eat here, and when they were feeling fat, they autographed a dollar and stuck it to the wall. When they felt broke, they could always yank one down from the wall and buy themselves a bowl of chowder. Today, many guests do the same (yeah, right).

The inn's lunch menu – homey soups, burgers, large salads and the popular homemade smoked-salmon appetizer – is priced reasonably (dishes are mostly $7 to $8). If nothing else, you could always hop aboard the *Tropic Star* (see Cayo Costa Island earlier in this section), which stops here for lunch on its daily cruise.

For a wonderfully romantic dinner of grouper with crabmeat, Gulf shrimp on angel-hair pasta or Szechuan salmon, you'll fork over about $20 per entree. If you're not staying here, don't forget to factor in the cost of a water taxi (see Cayo Costa Island). If you do want to stay here, reserve early. There are only six rooms and six cottages; the latter have kitchens.

SARASOTA
population 52,700
The largest city between Fort Myers and Tampa–St Petersburg, Sarasota is an affluent but welcoming place with many first-rate attractions, excellent beaches, the nearby Myakka River State Park, lots of live music and one of the best bookstores in the South. If that's not enough, it's also circus central: John Ringling made this the winter home of his famous circus, and the Flying Wallendas, the Sarasota Sailor Circus and the National Circus School of the Performing Arts are based here today.

Many travelers skip Sarasota because it looks too expensive, but appearances can be deceptive. While you can pay as much as you want, you also can sleep fairly cheaply without too much inconvenience. Sarasota also has heaps of restaurants churning out great and often inexpensive food. Additionally, the Selby Botanical Gardens and Mote Aquarium are must-see attractions, as is Ringling's home and museum. His circus may have made him famous, but he also gathered one fine art collection.

Orientation
The Tamiami Trail (US Hwy 41) zooms north straight as a die from Venice to the southern end of Sarasota, then it follows the southwest curve of downtown and skirts the east coast of Sarasota Bay before slashing northwest toward Tampa. Within town, it's called N Tamiami Trail north of Gulf Stream Ave and S Tamiami Trail south of Bay Front Dr.

Downtown Sarasota streets and roads run east-west; avenues and boulevards run north-south. The main drag downtown is Main St, which runs northeast from Bay Front Park, then due east from Central Ave. Head south on Pineapple Ave to the tiny but hippish historic district of Burns Court, with its burgeoning number of galleries and shops.

From downtown, head east across the John Ringling Causeway to St Armand's Circle on Lido Key. From there head south to Lido Beach or north to Mote Marine Laboratory and Pelican Man's Bird Sanctuary. Continue northward to pricey Longboat Key and Anna Maria Island.

To reach residential Siesta Key from downtown, head south on US 41 (Tamiami Trail) and east on Siesta Dr, which will take you right onto the barrier island. Midnight Pass Rd (SR 789) is the main thoroughfare, but Ocean Blvd skirts the northeastern portion of the key. The funkier Siesta Village, laid out along curvy canals, is wedged in between Ocean Blvd and Midnight Pass Rd. Stickney Point Rd (SR 72), about halfway down the key, will also take you back out to US 41.

The Ringling Estate and airport are north of downtown; Myakka River State Park is southeast of downtown (see Around Sarasota later in this chapter).

Information
The **Sarasota Convention & Visitors Bureau** (☎ 941-957-1877; W www.sarasotafl.org; 655 N Tamiami Trail; open 9am-5pm Mon-Sat, 11am-3pm Sun) and the **Sarasota Chamber of Commerce** (☎ 941-955-8187, 800-522-9799; W www.sarasotachamber.org; 1945 Fruitville Rd; open 8:30am-5pm Mon-Fri) both hand out reams of information, including a detailed beach guide and the *Gulf Coast Heritage Trail* brochure with a good overview of area attractions all perfectly mapped. For recorded information on music, jazz and film festivals, call the **Sarasota ArtsLine** (☎ 941-953-4636 x6000).

The **Longboat Key Chamber of Commerce** (☎ 941-383-2466; W www.longboatkey chamber.com; 6854 Gulf of Mexico Dr; open 9am-5pm Mon-Fri) has more key-specific

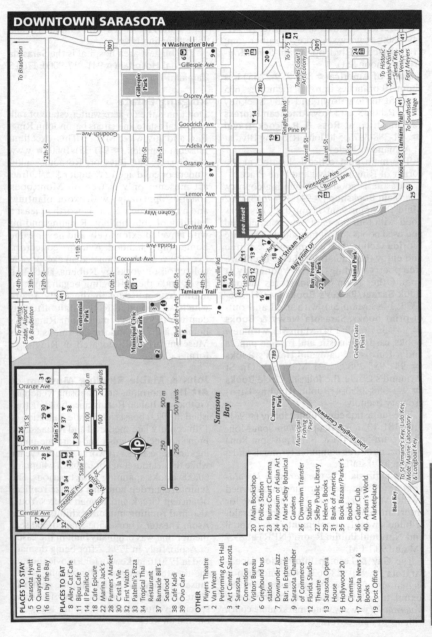

DOWNTOWN SARASOTA

PLACES TO STAY
5 Sarasota Hyatt
10 Quayside Inn
16 Inn by the Bay

PLACES TO EAT
8 Alley Cat Cafe
11 Bijou Cafe
14 Il Panificio
18 Cafe Epicure
22 Marina Jack's
28 Farmers' Market
30 C'est la Vie
32 First Watch
33 Patellini's Pizza
34 Tropical Thai
    Restaurant
37 Barnacle Bill's
    Seafood
38 Café Kaldi
39 Ovo Cafe

OTHER
1 Players Theatre
2 Van Wezel
   Performing Arts Hall
3 Art Center Sarasota
4 Sarasota
   Convention &
   Visitors Bureau
   Greyhound bus
   station
6 Downtowner Jazz
   Bar; In Extremis
9 Sarasota Chamber
   of Commerce
12 Florida Studio
   Theatre
13 Sarasota Opera
   House
15 Hollywood 20
   Cinemas
17 Sarasota News &
   Books
19 Post Office
20 Main Bookshop
21 Police Station
23 Burns Court Cinema
24 Museum of Asian Art
25 Marie Selby Botanical
   Gardens
   Downtown Transfer
   Station
27 Selby Public Library
29 Helen's Books
31 Bank of America
35 Book Bazaar/Parker's
   Books
36 Gator Club
40 Artisan's World
   Marketplace

Sarasota Bay

SOUTHWEST

lodging and restaurant information, as does the **Siesta Key Chamber of Commerce** (☎ 941-349-3800; W www.seistakeychamber.com; 5100 B Ocean Blvd; open 9am-5pm Mon-Fri, 9am-noon Sat).

Bank of America(☎ 800-299-2265) has about 10 branches in town, including 1605 Main St in downtown and 1237 Stickney Point Rd on Siesta Key. **American Express** has an office at **Ross & Babcock Travel** (☎ 941-388-3975; 540 John Ringling Blvd at St Armand's Circle).

The main **post office** is located at the corner of Ringling Blvd and Pine Place.

Sarasota is good book-hunting country. The **Main Bookshop** (☎ 941-366-7653; 1962 Main St; open 9am-11pm daily) is very good, with four floors of new, remaindered and used books, lots of maps and a first-rate Florida section. Have a cup of free coffee and enjoy the fine atmosphere. There are free poetry readings every Wednesday at 8pm. Other Main St bookstores include **Book Bazaar/Parker's Books** (☎ 941-366-1373; 1488 Main St), with used and out-of-print books; **Sarasota News & Books** (☎ 941-365-6332; 1341 Main St), with new books, cards, domestic and foreign papers and a Euro-style café; and **Helen's Books** (☎ 941-955-2989; 1531 Main St). On St Armand's Circle, the folks at **Circle Books** (☎ 941-388-2850; 478 John Ringling Blvd) are very friendly.

The fantastic **Selby Public Library** (☎ 941-316-1181; 1331 1st St; open 9am-9pm Mon-Thur, 9am-5pm Fri & Sat, 1pm-5pm Sun) has dozens of free computer terminals and a very helpful staff.

The main daily is the *Sarasota Herald-Tribune* (W www.heraldtribune.com), owned by the *New York Times*. Pick up *Elipse* for entertainment information or the Herald-Tribune's weekly supplement *Ticket*. You'll find National Public Radio (NPR) at 89.7 FM and 90.1 FM.

The **Gay & Lesbian Information Line – Sarasota** (☎ 941-923-4636) has information on matters of interest to gay, lesbian and bisexual travelers. Look for the biweekly *Watermark* (W www.watermarkonline.com), with up-to-date coverage.

Try **Violet Ray Laundry** (☎ 941-954-1348; 2287 Lime Ave), between Fruitville Rd and John Ringling Blvd.

The biggest area hospital is the **Sarasota Memorial Hospital** (☎ 941-917-9000; 1700 S Tamiami Trail).

Ringling Estate

Don't miss the 66-acre winter estate of railroad, real estate and circus baron John Ringling and his wife, Mable. This excellent museum complex (☎ 941-351-1660; W www.ringling.org; 5401 Bayshore Rd; adult/senior/student or child age 12 & under $15/12/free, art museum only is free on Mon; open 10am-5:30pm daily), with exotic plantings and a rose garden, is easily worth at least a half-day of your holiday. Ringling and his wife traveled extensively and never came home empty-handed. Avid art collectors, over the years they amassed an exceptional collection of works by Rubens, Hals, Van Dyck and others. Ringling began work on a fine-arts museum in the early 1920s, which was donated to the state after his death in 1936. You can also tour Ringling's home, Cà d'Zan, and the enormous Circus Museum originally located in Ringling's former garage.

John & Mable Ringling Museum of Art This enormous and imposing Venetian-Gothic and Italian Renaissance building (finished in 1929) boasts a first-rate collection of 17th-century, late-medieval and Renaissance French, Dutch, Spanish and Baroque paintings and tapestries. Art works span 500 years, while the art museum library has a whopping 60,000 books spanning all art periods. The sculpture garden contains bronze replicas of ancient Greek and Roman figures. You'll also find rotating modern exhibits and the **Asolo Theater**, a horseshoe-shaped, 300-seat theater that was originally built in the castle of Asolo, Italy, in 1798. After being dismantled in 1930 to make way for a movie theater, the theater was eventually bought by the museum from a Venetian antique dealer in 1950. Today, it's open for lectures, films and special events. Guided museum tours are offered on weekdays.

Cà d'Zan After undergoing a substantial renovation, this palatial home reopened with deserved fanfare in spring 2002. Said to be 'House of John' in Venetian dialect, Cà d'Zan (1924–26) was the grand winter home of the Ringlings. Fronting Sarasota Bay, it's a spectacular combination of Italian and French Renaissance, Baroque, Venetian-Gothic and modern architecture. There's a catwalk around the 30-foot-high court, or living room, with very fine tapestries throughout. In fact, the whole stupendous place is filled with eclectic and opulent decorative arts and furnishings. It exemplifies the lifestyles of the rich and famous, à la the Roaring Twenties. The lavish house has a ballroom, dining room, and taproom (with vaulted ceilings and stained-glass panels); the ballroom and playroom had their ceilings painted by Willy Pogany, a set designer for the Ziegfeld Follies. John's bedroom features an enormous ceiling painting, *Dawn Driving Away the Darkness* by Jacob de Wit. The bathroom contains such necessities as a bathtub hewn from a solid block of Siena marble, which also covers the walls.

Circus Museum This fascinating place contains the wild Barlow Animated Miniature Circus, original and elaborately carved circus wagons, the cannon used to blast the Flying Zacchinis into low orbit, sequined costumes, calliopes and dozens of rare circus posters. Circus fans will be pleased to know that the spirit of the circus is still alive and kicking in Sarasota, though it's no longer the winter home of Ringling Bros Circus (see Entertainment later in this section).

Marie Selby Botanical Gardens

This 9-acre, indoor-outdoor botanical oasis (☎ 941-366-5730; ⓦ www.selby.org; 811 S Palm Ave; adult/child $10/5; open 10am-5pm daily) specializes in orchids (more than 6000 of them) but they also have an incredible selection of other botanical attractions. There's a hibiscus garden, cacti and succulent garden, a tropical display house, bromeliad display, bamboo pavilion, koi pond, butterfly garden, waterfall garden and tropical food gardens, where everything's edible. There's also a

mangrove walkway. All in all, it's a great place to sit quietly and soak in the peaceful aura.

Mote Marine Laboratory

One of the USA's premiere organizations for shark study, this laboratory (☎ 941-388-4441, 800-691-6683; ⓦ www.mote.org; 1600 Ken Thompson Pkwy; age 13 & up/child 4-12 yrs $12/8; open 10am-5pm daily), just east of the drawbridge between Lido and Longboat Keys, operates the excellent *and* educational Mote Aquarium. Volunteers expertly guide you through the museum, where you'll see sea turtles, Florida lobsters, skates, nurse sharks (see 'Research at the Mote' boxed text) and a 135,000-gallon shark tank containing bull sharks, barracuda and groupers. Ever look a shark in the eye and live to talk about it? You can also learn all about the intricate Florida reef systems and check out sea horses, squid, octopuses and fireworms. Or check out the 25-foot preserved giant squid. There's also an enormous contact-cove touch-tank filled with horseshoe crabs and stingrays. Check out the minimizing glass: when you look at the tank from above, everything gets bigger.

Admission to the Mote includes the adjacent **Marine Mammal Center**, dedicated to research and rehabilitation of marine mammals. In the visitor's center, across the street from the museum just past the boatyard, you can watch staff (on video screens) work with injured dolphins.

Sarasota Baywalk

These shell paths and boardwalks circle a series of ponds surrounded by red, black and white mangroves. Though interesting, the lagoons were man-made and excavated by the Sarasota Bay Natural Estuary Program to different depths to attract different animals. The Baywalk is adjacent to the Mote, next to the bridge between Lido and Longboat Keys.

Pelican Man's Bird Sanctuary

Dale Shields is the Pelican Man, and his sanctuary (☎ 941-388-4444; ⓦ www.pelicanman .org; admission by donation; open 10am-5pm

Research at the Mote

The Mote's biomedical program concentrates primarily on researching the shark's immune system. As researchers try to understand the role that the immune system plays in conferring sharks and skates with a natural resistance to diseases, they hope to advance immunology research in humans. Since a shark's skeletal structure is made of cartilage, not bone, it has no bone marrow, which is the source of immune cells in mammals.

Since the program began in 1990, Mote scientists have established the existence of thymus glands in sharks, skates and rays as well as the existence of T-cells (thymus-derived lymphocytes). These discoveries have encouraged researchers looking for clues to human immune systems. Other research includes work on coastal resources, fisheries and aquaculture, environmental assessment and enhancement, and marine mammals and sea turtles.

The Mote Aquarium is the outreach program run by the laboratory to get the public more involved in its work.

– Nick & Corinna Selby

daily) rehabilitates injured wildlife; it's just east of the Mote, on the south side of Ken Thompson Pkwy. Although all injured animals are helped, pelicans are their primary customers (90% of all injured pelicans are hurt by fishing line). Since its humble beginnings in 1985 when Shields' first pelican rehabbed in a bathtub, the sanctuary now rehabilitates upwards of 6000 animals annually. Still, some animals cannot be released; about 250 birds including hawks, gulls, egrets, owls, storks and pelicans and other indigenous area wildlife now live here permanently.

Museum of Asian Art

This focused collection (☎ 941-954-7117; 640 S Washington Blvd; adult/child & student $5/free; open 11am-5pm Wed-Fri) highlights art from China, Thailand, Cambodia, Nepal and Myanmar (Burma). It boasts the famous Yangtze River Collection of Chinese jades.

St Armand's Circle

John Ringling bought land on St Armand's Key from Charles St Amand with the intention of developing it into exactly what it is today: an upscale shopping center surrounded by posh residences. Then Ringling employed circus elephants to haul timber for the construction of the causeway between the mainland and the key, and the area was opened to the public in 1926. Today, St Armand's Circle (☎ 941-388-1554) – yes, they misspelled St Amand's name for posterity – is a fancy-schmancy shopping center surrounded by a glorified traffic circle, packed with posh shops and cafés. It's a handy transfer point between buses to the beach (bus No 4) and the Mote Aquarium and the Pelican Man's Bird Sanctuary (bus No 18).

Beaches

The area's excellent powdery, white-sand beaches are located on barrier islands west of town; see Orientation earlier. Parking is generally a snap; there are public lots, and there's public transport from the mainland (see Getting Around, later in this section). Lido Key, just west of St Armand's Circle, is divided into **North and South Lido Beaches**, the latter of which is huge and also shaded for picnicking. **Siesta Key Beach**, an absolutely deservedly famous strip of sand, accommodates 800 cars in its parking lot...and all the soon-to-be-tanned-or-burned bodies that pile into those cars. Head south on Midnight Pass Rd to the end of Siesta Key for the quieter **Turtle Beach**. **Crescent Beach**, perfectly fine, is wedged in between those two. **Longboat Key**, north of St Armand's Circle, also has lovely beaches with lots of access points, many of which are backed by upscale condo developments.

Art Centers

The **Towles Court Art Colony** (☎ 941-330-9817; w www.towlescourt.com), on Morrill and Adams Sts between Osprey Ave and SR 301, is a community of dozens of artists. Their working studios and galleries range from jewelry and mixed media installations to watercolors and water gardens. You'll also find a few restaurants and even a yoga studio. On the third Friday of each month, galleries open their doors for an evening stroll (6pm to 10pm).

Founded in 1926 as the Sarasota Visual Art Center, **Art Center Sarasota** (☎ 941-365-2032; W www.artsarasota.org; 707 N Tamiami Trail; open 10am-4pm Tues-Sat) is a community art gallery center. It's something of a one-stop-shopping-experience for those interested in local art who also happen to be short on time.

Artisan's World Marketplace (☎ 941-365-5994; 104 S Pineapple Ave; open 10am-5pm Mon-Fri, 9am-2pm Sat), a one-room retail outlet in the basement of the First United Methodist Church, is a fair-trade store for worldwide artisans. For every $1200 worth of goods sold here, an artist in a developing country can work for one year and support a family of four. Wow.

Classic Car Museum

This sexy place (☎ 941-355-6228; W www .sarasotacarmuseum.org; 5500 N Tamiami Trail; adult/senior/child $8.50/8/6; open 9am-6pm daily), with over 75 exotic and curvaceous cars, appeals to nostalgic travelers. Among the Rolls-Royces, you'll find a 1905 Rapid Depot Wagon, an '81 DeLorean, a 1932 Auburn speedster, a tiny 1958 Metropolitan, and that most sought-after transporter, a 1976 Plymouth Voyager Van. A small music room contains romantic radios, turntables and other ancient noise-makers. You can't miss it as you drive north on US Hwy 41 – look for the Flintstones' car outside.

Historic Spanish Point

This museum and archaeological site (☎ 941-966-5214; adult/child $7/3; open 10am-4pm Mon-Sat, noon-4pm Sun), about 2 miles south of Sarasota in Osprey, crams about 4000 years of history into a two-hour, mile-long tour offered at various times (call ahead, since times vary with the day and month). Walking tours are free but tram tours cost an extra buck. The 31-acre site

contains walking trails, a Native American burial mound and two 1867 pioneer homesteads (with a reconstructed citrus packing plant). Five formal gardens were created in 1913 when the land was part of the winter estate of a Mrs Parker. Purchase tickets at the **visitor's center** (337 S Tamiami Trail) and then head to the gatehouse.

Organized Tours

Sarasota Bay Explorers (☎ 941-388-4200) operates Sea Life Encounter Cruises that leave from the Mote Aquarium daily at 11am, 1:30pm and 4pm. The 1¾-hour hands-on eco-tours cost $24/20 for adults/children. While trawling under the supervision of marine biologists, you'll pick up and touch sponges, sea horses, puffers and cowfish. You'll also inspect rookeries and stop on an uninhabited island for a short nature walk. Maybe you'll even see manatees and dolphins; you never know what ocean mysteries will rear their heads. Guided three-hour kayak tours from the Mote cost $50/40.

Places to Stay

It's always cheaper to stay in or near downtown as opposed to on the beaches, but these beach options give good value for the money.

Downtown The **Quayside Inn** (☎ 941-366-0414; W www.quaysideinn.com; 270 N Tamiami Trail; rooms $60-80/65-86 summer/winter), at Fruitville Rd and within walking distance of the bay, has tidy, value-laden rooms. The 'Old South' style motel has a mere 27 rooms and a sundeck. Give 'em a jingle.

Inn by the Bay (☎ 941-365-1900; W www .stayinsarasota.com; 1 N Tamiami Trail; rooms $39-69/89-104 summer/winter), with an outdoor pool, has 100 reasonably clean rooms within walking distance of downtown eateries.

Sleep Inn (☎ 941-359-8558, 800-281-5917; 900 University Pkwy; rooms $69-89/99-110 summer/winter), a fine choice with 80 units and a pool, is directly across from the airport.

Wellesley Inn (☎ 941-366-5128, 800-444-8888; W www.wellesleyonline.com; 1803 N

Tamiami Trail; $69/109 summer/winter), with 106 nice and spotless rooms, also offers free local calls and HBO. Some rooms have marina views.

Sarasota Hyatt (☎ 941-953-1234, 800-233-1234; W www.hyatt.com; 1000 Blvd of the Arts; rooms from $165/240 summer/winter), overlooking the bay and marina, has 297 upscale Hyatt-esque rooms, many with balconies.

You'll find a spate of similar chain motels halfway between the airport and downtown on N Tamiami Trail. Look for **Best Western Golden Host Resort** (☎ 941-355-5141, 800-722-4895; 4675 N Tamiami Trail), a two-story building with 80 rooms and weekly rates (it's the nicest of the lot); **Super 8 Motel** (☎ 941-355-9326, 800-800-8000; 4309 N Tamiami Trail), with 52 rooms; and **Days Inn Airport** (☎ 941-355-9721, 800-329-7466; 4900 N Tamiami Trail), with 121 rooms. Expect rooms to cost about $50/80 summer/winter.

Siesta Key South of downtown and *on the way* to Siesta Key as opposed to right *on* Siesta Key, **Calais Motel Apartments** (☎ 941-921-5797; 1735 Stickney Point Rd; rooms $49-55/85-99 summer/winter) has 26 efficiencies and a pool.

Sunsets on the Key (☎ 941-312-9797; 5203 Avenida Navarre; rooms $79-119/129-199 summer/winter), with a mere eight units, has some of the cheapest beds on the Key. They're wedged between Ocean Blvd and the beach.

Longboat Key Beachside **Harrington House** (☎ 941-778-5444, 888-828-5566; W www.harringtonhouse.com; 5626 Gulf Dr; rooms $129-199 midweek off-season, $189-249 other times), north of Longboat Key (call for directions – it's about 30 minutes north of St Armand's Circle) on Anna Maria Island, is unmatched in the area. The first-rate B&B features large rooms (some with fireplaces and Jacuzzi-type tubs), full breakfasts, private baths, good beaches and lots of extras – including kayaks, canoes, bicycles and heated pool. Many rooms have balconies overlooking the water. The inn has 21 rooms, but also operates another nearby inn with 27 rooms.

Resort at Longboat Key Club (☎ 941-383-8821, 800-237-8821; W www.longboatkeyclub.com; 301 Gulf of Mexico Dr; rooms $195-225/315-410 summer/winter), at the southern end of Longboat Key, has 232 stunningly deluxe hotel rooms, all with balconies and oodles of services. Ask about packages at this harborside golf and tennis resort.

Places to Eat

Downtown For the most part, you needn't look farther than Main St for a good place to eat, although if you do look farther, you'll find some really excellent places.

A **Farmers' Market** (Lemon Ave between Main & 1st Sts), with seasonal fruit and vegetables and some arts and crafts, is held from 7am to noon Saturday.

Morton's Gourmet Market (☎ 941-955-9856; 1924 S Osprey Ave; open 8am-8pm Mon-Sat, 10am-5pm Sun), purveyors of upscale picnic fixings (although you can eat at one of their outdoor tables), has excellent sandwiches, pastries, salads and hot items. About 15 blocks south of downtown in the Southside Village area, Morton's is one of a few upscale places here frequented by neighborhood gourmands. Osprey Ave runs parallel to the Tamiami Trail, so this place is really on the way to Siesta Key from downtown.

The cozy **Café Kaldi** (☎ 941-366-2326; 1568 Main St; open 7am-7pm Mon-Thur, 7am-midnight Fri & Sat) offers coffee and pastry to accompany web surfing ($6 hourly).

Patellini's Pizza (☎ 941-957-6433; 1410 Main St; slices $2, pies $10-14; open 11am-9pm Mon-Sat, 1pm-9pm Sun), still going strong with New York–style pizza slices and overstuffed calzones, has some of the best pizza in the southwest.

Il Panificio (☎ 941-366-5570; 1703 Main St; dishes $3-6; open 9:30am-9pm Mon-Sat, 9:30am-7pm Sun) bakes *really* good bread and pastries. But for real meals, order a large focaccia or deli sandwich.

C'est la Vie (☎ 941-906-9575; 1553 Main St; dishes $4-7; open 7:30am-4:30pm Mon-Sat), an honest-to-goodness French bakery (with flaky croissants) and café with popular outdoor seating, also has friendly service. Try some crepes or less adventurous but quite tasty salads and sandwiches.

The casual **First Watch** (☎ 941-954-1395; 1395 Main St; dishes $4-7; open 7am-2:30pm daily), with good omelettes and friendly service, is also quite popular. Perhaps that's because breakfast and lunch dishes are available no matter what the time.

Cafe Epicure (☎ 941-366-5648; 1298 N Palm Ave; lunch $6-12, dinner mains $9-18; open 11am-10:30pm daily), a bakery and specialty market, also serves creative continental bistro and pasta dishes in bright and airy surroundings.

Tropical Thai Restaurant (☎ 941-364-5775; 1420 Main St; lunch $6-7, dinner mains average $10; open 11:30am-3pm & 4:15pm-10pm daily) has a sushi bar and the best area Thai served in pleasant surroundings.

Barnacle Bill's Seafood (☎ 941-365-6800; 1526 Main St; lunch $7-8, dinner mains $12-30; open 11:30am-9pm Mon-Sat, 4pm-9pm Sun) features very good seafood dishes (choose the creative daily specials), pastas and stir-fry dishes. Baskets of fried seafood dominate the lunch menu. Even without a waterfront view, crowds still gather.

Michael's on East (☎ 941-366-0007; 1212 East Ave S; lunch $8-10, dinner mains average $21; open 11:30am-2pm Mon-Fri, 6pm-10pm Mon-Sat), within the Midtown Plaza off US 41, serves exceptionally creative cuisine in elegant digs. The menu changes seasonally but the patrons are loyal throughout the year. To experience Michael's deservedly award-winning cuisine while still hanging onto your wallet, come for a fancy lunchtime sandwich or partake of the lighter bar menu.

Marina Jack's (☎ 941-365-4232; at the Marina at Central Ave; lunch $8-15, dinner mains $16-35; open 11:30am-11pm daily), which can't be matched for waterfront views of Sarasota Bay, has a popular outdoor raw bar, where you can also get good burgers. If you decide to eat indoors (although there are better places to eat indoors) after a few too many drinks, choose simple seafood preparations.

Alley Cat Cafe (☎ 941-954-1228; 1558 4th St; lunch $9-13, dinner mains $19-29; open 11:30am-2:30pm and, 6pm-9pm Tues-Thur, 6pm-10pm Fri & Sat) has charming garden seating and serves creative new American dishes like pan-seared halibut.

Ovo Cafe (☎ 941-954-6029; 35 S Lemon Ave; lunch averages $10, dinner mains $21-27; open 11am-9pm Mon-Thur, 5pm-11pm Fri & Sat, 5pm-10pm Sun), an urbane eatery, serves excellent martinis. As for the food, try the signature drunken lobster pillows, Thai chicken salad and shrimp bisque.

Bijou Cafe (☎ 941-366-8111; 1287 1st St; lunch $9-16, dinner mains $18-30; open 11:30am-2pm Mon-Fri, 5pm-9pm Mon-Thur, 5pm-10:30pm Fri & Sat), a stylish chef-owned eatery with nice service and an excellent wine list, offers substantial lunchtime salads, steak frites, famously delectable pommes gratin and mains like spicy shrimp piri piri. It's the hands-down favorite in the immediate area.

Siesta Key Siesta Key is lined with dozens of eateries of the same ilk – none really bad, none really outstanding. You certainly won't go without.

The Broken Egg (☎ 941-346-2750; 210 Avenida Madera; dishes $5-8; open 7:30am-2:30pm daily), a charming family-style breakfast place, serves the best hash browns in the world and a huge variety of Paul Bunyan–sized pancakes. Also, as you might expect but don't always receive, they serve fresh orange juice. The indoor-outdoor seating is nice, and the lunchtime meat loaf tasty.

The resort casual **Lobster Pot** (☎ 941-349-2323; 5157 Ocean Blvd; lunch $6-12, dinner mains $11-30; open 11am-9pm Mon-Thur, 11am-9:30pm Sat), boasting *enormous* lobster rolls made with sweet Maine crustaceans, is informal, lunchy and worth stopping for a sandwich.

Longboat Key A longtime bayfront eatery at the northern end of the key, **Morton's Stone Crab** (☎ 941-383-1748; 800 Broadway; dishes $7-23; open 11:30am-9:30pm daily, closed Mon-Fri for lunch in summer) serves stone crabs in season (October to March) and informal seafood and sandwiches the rest of the time.

St Armand's Circle With a couple of tiny balconies overlooking the action, **Hemingways** (☎ 941-388-3948; 325 John Ringling Blvd; lunch $6-10, dinner mains $16-22; open 11:30am-10pm daily) also has lots of indoor seating. Good for families as well as couples, these well-served and well-prepared dishes range from salads and grilled chicken breast sandwiches to surf-and-turf specials. Nothing's going to knock your sandals off, but it's a pretty good place. How's that!

Entertainment
Performing Arts On the Ringling Estate, the regional **FSU Center for the Performing Arts** (☎ 941-351-8000; **w** www.asolo.org; 5555 N Tamiami Trail; tickets $10-45; season Nov-May) hosts the **Asolo Theater Company**, visiting companies and the annual Asolo Theatre Festival at its 19th-century Italian playhouse. More daring productions are staged in a smaller theater; check to see what's playing at the Mertz Theatre, a 1900 Scottish theater dismantled and moved here in 1987. Day-of-performance student tickets are usually available for $8; call ahead. Tours of the center are available (when performances are scheduled) Wednesday to Saturday at 10am and 11am.

Florida West Coast Symphony (☎ 941-953-3434; **w** www.fwcs.org; tickets $11-55; season Oct-May), which also sponsors the Sarasota Music Festival in June, performs classical concerts at venues throughout the area, as well as masterworks and ensemble performances with the Florida String Quartet.

Players Theatre (☎ 941-365-2494; **w** www.theplayers.org; 838 N Tamiami Trail; tickets about $20), a highly regarded nonprofit, stages six well-known musicals, a couple of plays and summertime specials. Perhaps you'll discover the next Pee Wee Herman (who was, in turn, discovered here).

Sarasota Opera House (☎ 941-953-7030, 800-826-9303; **w** www.sarasotaopera.org; 61 N Pineapple Ave; tickets $17-82; season Feb-Mar), a 1000-seat 1926 Mediterranean Revival theater, has served the opera well

since the early 1960s. Don't understand Italian? No worries; English translations are projected above the stage.

The city-run **Van Wezel Performing Arts Hall** (☎ 941-953-3368; **w** www.vanwezel.org; 777 N Tamiami Trail; season Nov-May) hosts some 200 events, from big band to easy listening, classical to pop, touring Broadway musicals to modern dance. You can't avoid the big pink and purple building.

Florida Studio Theatre (☎ 941-366-9000; **w** www.fst2000.org; 1241 N Palm Ave; tickets $26-30; season mid-Oct–Aug) stages contemporary musicals and plays. They also have an early-20th-century European-style cabaret supper club (tickets $18 to $22, plus the cost of à la carte dining).

Cinemas The **Burns Court Cinema** (☎ 941-364-8662; 506 Burns Lane), in a sweet alleyway between Palm and Pineapple Aves, is a happenin' cinema that shows foreign and art films. In November, don't miss the **Sarasota Film Society's** (**w** www.filmsociety.org) annual 10-day CINE-World Film Festival, which screens over 40 of the year's best international films.

Hollywood 20 Cinemas (☎ 941-365-2000; 1993 Main St) has 20 screens. If you can't find something worth seeing, the movie industry is in big, big trouble.

Circuses The **Sarasota Sailor Circus** (☎ 941-361-6350; **w** www.sailorcircus.org; 2075 Bahia Vista St), under a big blue-and-white dome top, east off S Tamiami Trail, is nothing short of wonderful. Comprised of Sarasota County students, this extracurricular school activity teaches kids high-flying, tumbling and clowning. The circus performs in late December and from late March to early April, but there are free rehearsals on weekdays at about 4:30pm from September through November, and in January and February.

Bars & Live Music Head down to Siesta Key, along Ocean Blvd and Beach Rd, and follow your ears. Most restaurants have an outdoor bar with live music nightly.

Downunder Jazz Bar (☎ 941-951-2467; Sarasota Quay), at Michael's Mediterranean Grille, is the place for contemporary jazz.

In Extremis (☎ 941-954-2008; Sarasota Quay), which draws 'em in with a wicked cool sound-and-light show, spins Top 40 high-energy dance tunes. To really get your money's worth, head over on Friday or Saturday night, which offers all-you-can-drink-all-night-long buzzes for $12.

Gator Club (☎ 941-366-5969; 1490 Main St; open until 2am nightly) has live music nightly, from Motown to salsa to reggae to alternative dance tunes. Call to see what's up when you're ready to go.

Café Kaldi (☎ 941-366-2326; 1568 Main St) occasionally brings in acoustic guitar players (see Places to Eat above).

Getting There & Away
The **Sarasota-Bradenton International Airport** (SRQ; ☎ 941-359-2770; W www.srq-airport.com; 6000 Airport Circle) is served by many major airlines. Take N Tamiami Trail north to University Ave (near the Ringling Estate), and turn right.

A **Greyhound bus station** (☎ 941-955-5735; 575 N Washington Blvd) serves the area. The trip from Sarasota to Miami takes 7 hours ($29/55 one-way/roundtrip); to Fort Myers takes 2½ hours ($9/18); and to Tampa takes 2 hours ($11/20).

Amtrak (☎ 800-872-7245) provides shuttle buses between the Tampa station and Sarasota (1995 Main St).

Sarasota is 60 miles south of Tampa and about 75 miles north of Fort Myers. The main roads into town are the Tamiami Trail (US Hwy 41) and I-75. The most direct route from I-75 is exit 39 to Hwy 780 west for about 8 miles; Hwy 780 turns into Fruitville Rd.

The usual suspects rent cars at the airport terminal.

Getting Around
Driving from the airport, take University Pkwy west to US Hwy 41, then head south straight into downtown. Major car rental companies are located at the airport.

Bus No 10 runs between the airport and downtown via the Ringling Estate; buses depart once an hour 7am to 6pm Monday to

Saturday, but there is no service Sunday. From the **downtown transfer station**, buses leave on the same schedule from about 6:15am to 6:15pm.

Sarasota County Area Transit (SCAT; ☎ 941-316-1234) operates area buses; the fare is 50¢. There are no transfers or Sunday services. From the downtown transfer station at 1st St and Lemon Ave, bus Nos 4 and 18 go to St Armand's Key; bus No 4 then goes to south Lido Key and the beach, and bus No 18 goes north on City Island Rd, near the Mote Marine Lab and Pelican Man's Bird Sanctuary, and up to Longboat Key. Both buses run hourly. Note that the last bus back from the beach leaves south Lido Key at 6:30pm. Bus No 2 also runs hourly, between downtown and the Ringling Estate.

The Sarasota Trolley (☎ 941-316-1234), with two lines, operates a red route ($1) to the Ringling Estate, Marie Selby Botanical Gardens, Mote Marine Laboratory, St Armand's Circle and Lido Beach. The blue route (25¢) heads down Main St. Here's a no-brainer: purchase an unlimited daylong pass for a mere $2 that gets you on both. Trolleys run from 10am to 6pm Monday through Saturday.

Parking's a snap, driving's a breeze and the streets are pretty safe. To reach the beaches, take the John Ringling Causeway (Hwy 789) in front of Golden Gate Point and Bay Front Park west, around St Armand's Circle and then follow Ben Franklin Dr. For the Mote Marine Laboratory and Pelican Sanctuary, turn right off the circle and right again just before the drawbridge to Longboat Key.

AROUND SARASOTA
Myakka River State Park
This excellent 47-sq-mi wildlife preserve (☎ 941-361-6511; admission $4 per carload) is comprised of dense woodlands, hammocks and prairies. Florida's largest state park offers great bird and alligator watching, 40 miles of boardwalks and trails and a few touring options. The airboat ride (on an enclosed, pontoon-type boat that remains in the upper lake area and doesn't damage wildlife but sure is loud) draws 'em in, but there is also a

nature tram tour. Airboats depart at 10am, 11:30am, 1pm and 2:30pm (no 2:30pm tour in summer) and cost $8 for everyone over age 6. Trams depart at 1pm and 2:30pm in wintertime only and cost the same.

Seriously consider **canoeing** the Myakka River. Park canoes (☎ 941-923-1120) rent for $15 for two hours, $25 for four and $40 for eight. Or take a guided 2½ to 5½ hour tour with **Discover Kayaking** (☎ 941-922-9671) for $45 to $75 per person, depending on the trip. Trips into the primitive wilderness area of the lower lake depart early in the morning (all gear is included); meet at the park after making reservations (a minimum of four people is required).

Camping (sites $15/20 summer/winter, cabins $61) is primo here. There are five cabins with kitchens and linens and 76 RV and tent sites. None have showers.

Venice Campground (☎ 941-488-0850; 4085 E Venice Ave; sites $26-30, cabins $45) is a fine alternative and boasts 104 RV sites, 28 shaded tent sites and 3 cabins on the banks of the river.

From downtown Sarasota, take US Hwy 41 south to Hwy 72 (Clark Rd) and head east for about 14 miles; the park is about 9 miles east of I-75.

VENICE

With a quiet, lovely stretch of Gulf Coast white sand, Venice happens to be the shark's tooth capital of Florida. Shark's teeth have washed up on the shores for centuries due to coastal contours, and you can still find them if you're willing to walk with your head down and back hunched over. Head to the southern two-thirds of **Caspersen Beach**, south of town on Harbor Dr, to find the largest stash of teeth. If you have a bad back or would rather gaze out onto the horizon, you can always buy bags of teeth at roadside stands and in some tourist shops.

Most people come to the beach for day trips, but if you stay, you'll find some decent motel deals, sunset dining and old-fashioned root beer.

Contact the **Venice Chamber of Commerce** (☎ 941-488-2236; w www.venice chamber.com; 597 S Tamiami Trail; open 8am-5pm Mon-Fri) for more information.

To reach Venice, take US Hwy 41 south from Sarasota for about 25 miles and turn west to the beach (bear right) and Business 41. Parking at the beach lots is free.

Air Tours

Florida Flight Training Center (☎ 941-484-3771; w www.fftc.info; 150 E Airport Ave) offers hour-long air tours that'll give you a bird's-eye view of the area for about $109 for one to three people. If you've got a strong stomach, their aerobatics instructor will flip you silly and safely for $150 – but only in the winter. And if you really fall for it, the pilot (a licensed instructor) will let you take controls of the plane. Note: this is not the place where they taught terrorist Mohammed Atta to fly planes but not to land them. That's Huffman Aviation School, which is also located at the Venice Airport.

Places to Stay & Eat

Motel 6 (☎ 941-485-8255; 281 S Tamiami Trail; rooms $46-56/61-71 summer/winter), just north of Venice Ave on Business 41 rather than Hwy 41, has 103 of the cheapest rooms in town.

Gondolier Inn (☎ 941-488-4417; 340 S Tamiami Trail; $45/80 summer/winter), also on Business 41, offers 21 spotless and comfortably welcoming rooms, a pool and a hefty Continental breakfast. It happens to be the oldest motel on the island, but it's also one of the best and quietest.

The Banyan House (☎ 941-484-1385; w www.banyanhouse.com; 519 S Harbor Drive; rooms and apartments $99-139, closed July-Sept), a lovely B&B in a sprawling 1926 house, has Venice's first swimming pool and a great climbing tree in its lushly shaded courtyard. Breakfast is 'continental plus' – there's always one main hot dish plus fruit and pastries, all served on china. All five units have private baths and TVs; most have balconies.

The Frosted Mug (☎ 941-497-1611; 1856 S Tamiami Trail; open 11am-4pm Sun-Thur, 11am-8pm Fri & Sat), a roadside root beer stand south of Venice, has been here since

1957 and serves real frosted-mug root beer ($1.29) and root beer floats ($2.10). For the uninitiated, a float is a mug of root beer with a scoop of vanilla ice cream floating on top, and root beer is a traditional American soda that some love and some say tastes like carbonated toothpaste – there's no accounting for taste. It's worth a stop, if just for the ambience.

The Soda Fountain (☎ 941-412-9860; 349 Venice Ave W; open 11am-9pm Mon-Sat, noon-9pm Sun) offers a big taste of the past: a long wooden bar, spinning counter stools, black-and-white photos and retro light fixtures and appliances. Old-fashioned specialties include 25 different ice cream sodas and sundaes, expertly blended milk shakes, mom-style chicken salad, and a myriad of hot dog variations (including a PBJ one). You can't beat it for good, quick food.

Sharky's on the Pier (☎ 941-488-1456; 1600 Harbor Dr S; lunch $4-12, dinner mains $10-27; open 11:30am-10pm Sun & Tues-Thur, 11:30am-midnight Fri & Sat), at the Venice Fishing Pier, has a primo waterfront location and a fun-loving sunset crowd at the tiki bar. Their seafood isn't going to rock your world, but it's fresh.

TAMPA
population 303,400

Tampa is a city that's no longer on the rise – it's newly risen and it likes its newfound status, thank you very much. At the center of its revitalization is Ybor City, the national historic landmark district built within the heart of the old cigar industry, which once dominated this town. But Busch Gardens is undeniably a strong draw, as it combines an excellent zoo with some of the best roller coasters you'll ever encounter. Tampa also offers a great hands-on science museum, a wonderful aquarium, several high-quality art museums, a large performing-arts center and the elegant but haunted Tampa Theatre. And it all sits on a nice bay and is sliced in half by a tranquil, lazy Hillsborough River.

History

An Indian fishing village when Hernando de Soto arrived in 1539, Tampa wasn't really settled by Europeans (who drove off and killed – by war or disease – most of the natives) until the late 18th century, and it didn't become a city of consequence until 1855, when Fort Brooke was established here.

Towards the end of the 19th century, Cuban cigar makers moved into the area en masse, and over the next 50 years, the city would be known as the Cigar Capital of America. Vicénte Martínez Ybor and Ignacio Haya put Tampa on the cigar-making map. In 1885, they moved their considerable cigar factories – Principe de Gales (Prince of Wales) and La Flor de la Sanchez y Haya, respectively – to present-day Ybor City. Haya's factory actually opened first, in February 1886, and Ybor's soon after. (Ybor's opening had been delayed due to a strike by factory workers.) The move from Key West – which had until then been the cigar-making capital of the USA due to its proximity to Cuba – was precipitated by the strong organization of workers there: the cigar barons decided that moving was the only way to break the union's grip on their factories.

Workers were imported to the new (and un-unionized) factories from Key West and directly from Havana. And as if to send a message to Key West that its cigar-making days were over, a fire broke out there on April 1, 1886, that destroyed several cigar factories, including Ybor's Principe de Gales Key West branch. Ybor City became the largest functioning production facility, and the cigar business never looked back.

As the factories drew thousands and thousands of workers – such as cutters and support staff like packers and shipping personnel – Ybor City grew to have the largest concentration of Cubans outside Cuba. These Cubans began organizing into leagues and clubs – notably El Liceo Cubano and La Liga Patriotica Cubana (the Cuban Lyceum and the Cuban Patriotic League). These organizations, and later others like the Ignacio Agramonte Cuban Revolutionary Club, formed the backbone of revolutionary organization through fund-raising and propaganda.

José Martí (see 'José Martí' boxed text) became a member of the Patriotic League

DOWNTOWN TAMPA

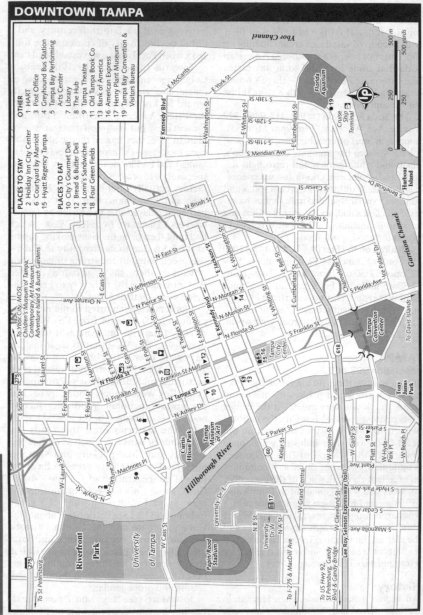

OTHER
1   HART
3   Post Office
4   Greyhound Bus Station
5   Tampa Bay Performing
    Arts Center
7   Library
8   The Hub
9   Tampa Theatre
11 Old Tampa Book Co
13 Bank of America
16 American Express
17 Henry Plant Museum
19 Tampa Bay Convention &
    Visitors Bureau

PLACES TO STAY
2   Holiday Inn City Center
6   Courtyard by Marriott
15 Hyatt Regency Tampa

PLACES TO EAT
10 City's Gourmet Deli
12 Bread & Butter Deli
14 Lonni's Sandwiches
18 Four Green Fields

(there is a statue of him across the street from the Ybor Cigar Factory building today) and stayed in Tampa when not traveling around Florida. In mid-November 1892, agents of the Spanish government attempted to assassinate Martí by poisoning him.

The prosperity of the area made it attractive to other immigrant groups, Italians chief among them. Blacklisted from working in the Cuban factories, the Italians founded their own 'buckeye' factories, in which they manufactured cheap cigars known as cheroots (see any Clint Eastwood film made prior to 1976 for more information).

These Italians, along with Cubans and Spaniards, created mutual aid societies here to provide health care for the workers. In the earliest example of cooperative social health care in the USA, several societies – among them El Porvenir, El Círculo Cubano and L'unione Italiana – provided medicine and hospitalization to their members.

Spanish, Germans and Jews from various countries also migrated to the area.

During the Cuban Revolution and the Spanish-American War, Tampa was an important staging area for revolutionaries and troops to Havana, since it had the most developed communication with the island (well-established steamship routes supplied the area with Cuban tobacco).

Ybor City remained America's cigar-making capital until the 1959 Castro Revolution and the resulting US embargo of Cuban products. Over the next three decades, Ybor City and the entire city of Tampa hit the skids; crime increased and the abandoned factories and housing became dangerous and dilapidated.

Tampa's resurgence of late is due in large part to the renovation, rehabilitation and gentrification of historic Ybor City, which was named a National Historic Landmark District in 1990 and is the center of Tampa nightlife. Tampa's excellent museums and Busch Gardens, and the popularity of nearby beaches along the Gulf, have turned southwest Florida's oldest city into a prime tourist destination once again. Its economy also thrives on a revitalized seaport and a well-developed banking industry; and although it's

José Martí

Havana-born José Martí (1853–95) was exiled to Spain in 1870 for 'opposition to Colonial rule.' He eventually made his way to North and South America, where his antiracist writings relentlessly extolled his vision of a free Cuba. He stirred up anti-Spanish sentiment wherever he could, including Florida. Although he was allowed to return to Cuba in 1878, he was quickly booted out by angry Spanish authorities. In 1895, Martí returned to Cuba again, this time to participate in the war for Cuban independence. Considered one of Cuba's leading writers and a hero of its independence, Martí was also one of the first to die in the conflict.

Some hail it as his greatest accomplishment, others damn him eternally for it, but the fact remains that a Martí poem provided the lyrics for *Guantanamera*.

– Nick & Corinna Selby

not the economic engine it once was, over a half billion cigars are produced here annually.

Orientation

Tampa is crisscrossed by major highways and interstates. US Hwy 41 (the Tamiami Trail) cuts straight north through the center of the city. The Hillsborough River runs roughly north-south through the western side of downtown before turning eastward.

I-75 runs north-south and skirts the eastern edge of Tampa. I-275 also runs north-south and cuts through downtown before it heads west, across the Howard Frankland Bridge over Tampa Bay, south through St Petersburg and on to Sarasota.

Northeast of downtown, I-275 breaks off from I-75 as it goes south into downtown, until it meets up with I-4 – this intersection is lovingly referred to by local motorists as Malfunction Junction. I-4 runs east and then northeast to Orlando and on to meet I-95 on Florida's east coast.

Downtown Tampa is bordered by I-275 at the north, the Hillsborough River at the west, Garrison Channel at the south and Meridian Ave at the east. Franklin St, in the center of downtown, is a pedestrian zone. Between 6am and 7pm, Marion St is closed to all vehicular traffic except buses. Ybor City is just northeast of downtown; Channelside and the Port of Tampa are due east, just beyond the railroad tracks.

Davis Island and Harbour Island are situated in Hillsborough Bay, on the southern edge of downtown.

South Tampa is really old Tampa, the peninsula southwest of downtown (south of Kennedy Blvd) and reached via the northeast-southwest Bayshore Blvd and the north-south S Dale Mabry Hwy. MacDill Air Force Base, where the Joint Chiefs of Staff's Central Command is located ('CenCom' covers the Middle East, so ostensibly the US war on terrorism is headquartered here), occupies the southern tip of this peninsula; Bay-to-Bay Blvd and Gandy Blvd (which heads over the bridge to St Petersburg) run east-west across it. North Tampa feels like the set of *The Truman Show.*

Information

The **Tampa Bay Convention & Visitors Bureau** maintains a very good visitor's center (☎ 813-223-1111, 800-448-2672; w www .visittampabay.com; 615 Channelside Dr; open 9:30am-5:30pm Mon-Sat, 11am-5pm Sun) near the Florida Aquarium. Their free map shows how all the neighborhoods and interstates fit together. The **Ybor City Chamber of Commerce** (☎ 813-248-3712;

w www.ybor.org; 1600 E 8th Ave; open 10am-6pm Mon-Sat, noon-6pm Sun) has tons of information on this National Landmark Historic District and very good historical displays on the cigar connection. Pick up their excellent historic walking tour brochure, which illuminates Ybor City's former cultural and working heritage.

Call **Bank of America** (☎ 800-299-2265; 101 E Kennedy Blvd) for other Tampa branches. Change money at **American Express** (☎ 813-273-0310; One Tampa City Center).

The **post office** (925 N Florida Ave; 1900 E 12th Ave, Ybor City) has a number of branches.

Downtown, the **Old Tampa Book Co** (☎ 813-209-2151; 507 N Tampa St) has a huge selection of used books and some remainders. **Books for Thought** (☎ 813-988-6363; 10910 N 56th St), two blocks south of Fowler Ave, specializes in books by or about African Americans. The gay and lesbian **Tomes and Treasures** (☎ 813-251-9368; 406 S Howard Ave; open 11am-midnight Mon-Fri, 10am-midnight Sat & Sun) also has a coffeehouse.

Downtown Tampa hosts the main **library** (☎ 813-273-3652; 900 N Ashley Dr), while Ybor City gets a branch **library** (☎ 813-272-5747; 1505 Nebraska Ave); both have free web surfing.

The major daily is the *Tampa Tribune* (w www.tampatrib.com), though the *St Petersburg Times* (w www.sptimes.com) and the *Miami Herald* are available everywhere. In the hotel, tune into Bay News 9, the nation's first all-Spanish cable station. In the car, tune into National Public Radio (NPR) at 89.7 FM.

Try **Laundromat Express** (☎ 813-837-9100; Phar Mor Plaza, 4306 S Dale Mabry Hwy) with pool tables, snacks and beer.

Tampa General Hospital (☎ 813-251-7000), south of downtown on Davis Island, is the biggest area hospital.

The gay and lesbian scene is big but hard to pin down: things are always in a state of flux. Look around the city for the biweekly *Watermark* (w www.watermarkonline.com), with up-to-date listings of gay, lesbian and bisexual community groups and resource centers.

The **Center of Tampa Bay** (☎ 813-875-8116; w www.tampacenter.org; 3708 W Swann Ave) has information on the Tampa Film Festival.

Museum of Science & Industry

MOSI (☎ 813-987-6000; w www.mosi.org; 4801 E Fowler Ave; adult/senior/child $14/12/10, includes one IMAX film; open 9am-5pm Mon-Fri, 9am-7pm Sat & Sun) is deservedly one of the biggest draws around, and it's definitely in contention for Florida's best hands-on science museum. With upwards of 450 'minds-on' activities, hyperactive kids will think they're in heaven. Look for varied traveling exhibits and a (permanent) cool hot-air balloon exhibit, as well as ones on the human body, Florida, and the amount of garbage the average American generates annually. Enter a flight avionics simulator or a Gulf Coast hurricane before taking to a 1-mile trail within the on-site wetland preserve.

Tampa Museum of Art

This mod museum (☎ 813-274-8130; w www.tampamuseum.com; 600 N Ashley Dr; adult/senior/child & student $5/4/3, admission by donation 5pm-8pm Thur & 10am-noon Sat; open 10am-5pm Tues, Wed, Fri & Sat, 10am-8pm Thur, 1pm-5pm Sun) belies an impressive abundance of classical Greek and Roman antiquities. It also features a wide range of rotating exhibitions – from avant-garde to old masters, from sculpture and photography to works by emerging Florida artists. Overlooking the Hillsborough River, the glassed-in Terrace Gallery provides a great backdrop for sculptures. The grounds make a nice place for a picnic.

Channelside

This huge entertainment megaplex (☎ 813-223-4250; w www.channelside.com; Channelside Dr), directly on Ybor Channel, boasts a fun sports bar (Newk's Cafe), an IMAX theater, an upscale billiards hall (Pop City), a movie theater, lots of eateries, some clubs and open-air shops. You'll also find cruise ships pulling into the Port of Tampa here, as well as the Florida Aquarium (see below).

Channelside Dr is southeast of downtown and southwest of Ybor City. From I-4, get off at exit 1 and follow the signs.

Florida Aquarium

This great fish bowl (☎ 813-273-4000; w www.flaquarium.net; 701 Channelside Dr; adult/senior/child $15/13/10; open 9:30am-5pm daily), with exhibits on three floors, traces how water travels from its freshwater source to the open sea. Take the elevator to the top to start at the beginning, Florida Wetlands, where you'll find itty-bitty fish, a limestone cavern, a mangrove forest and alligator hatchlings. In Bays & Beaches, the indoor beach is complete with dunes, waves, sea oats and live seabirds. The Coral Reef Gallery is the best, though. Its 500,000-gallon tank teems with colorful coral and thousands of fish. Divers jump into the coral reef and shark tank and speak to crowds via intercom several times daily (11am to 3pm), providing a window onto the undersea world. It's interactive: the audience asks questions of the diver, who swims around pointing out the answers.

The aquarium also has a 64-foot catamaran, the *Dolphin Quest Eco Tour*, that heads out into Tampa Bay looking for the 400 or so bottle-nosed dolphins who live here. Along the way you'll also see manatees and a bird island, too. Tickets cost $18/17/13 adult/senior/child, but there are combo tickets with the aquarium, too, which will save you about $3 per person. Adjacent parking is $4. An average visit takes 2½ hours.

Ybor City

Once a dangerous and scary place because of muggers and car thieves, the renaissance of Ybor City (pronounced **ee**-bore) almost matches that of Miami Beach. For power-drinkers and 20-somethings, the area is a must-see for its energy and drink-till-you-barf potential; there are 60-plus bars and clubs within a small area, plus a few tattoo parlors. Indeed, you might want to visit twice: it's G-rated during the day with conventioneers and business lunches, PG-rated with middle-aged folks during the dinner hour and often X-rated late at night when

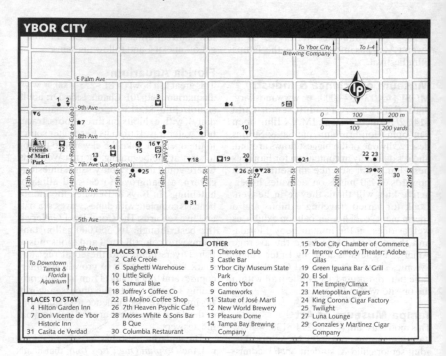

YBOR CITY

To Ybor City
Brewing Company

To I-4

E Palm Ave

0   100   200 m
0   100   200 yards

PLACES TO EAT
2 Café Creole
6 Spaghetti Warehouse
10 Little Sicily
16 Samurai Blue
18 Joffrey's Coffee Co
22 El Molino Coffee Shop
26 7th Heaven Psychic Cafe
28 Moses White & Sons Bar
   B Que
30 Columbia Restaurant

PLACES TO STAY
4 Hilton Garden Inn
7 Don Vicente de Ybor
   Historic Inn
31 Casita de Verdad

OTHER
1 Cherokee Club
3 Castle Bar
5 Ybor City Museum State
   Park
8 Centro Ybor
9 Gameworks
11 Statue of José Martí
12 New World Brewery
13 Pleasure Dome
14 Tampa Bay Brewing
   Company

15 Ybor City Chamber of Commerce
17 Improv Comedy Theater; Adobe
   Gilas
19 Green Iguana Bar & Grill
20 El Sol
21 The Empire/Climax
23 Metropolitan Cigars
24 King Corona Cigar Factory
25 Twilight
27 Luna Lounge
29 Gonzales y Martinez Cigar
   Company

To Downtown
Tampa &
Florida
Aquarium

E 7th Ave is closed to vehicular traffic. For everyone else, it's a must-see for its history (see History earlier in this section) and sheer success at recreating itself. You'll find palm-lined and brick-paved streets, wrought iron balconies à la New Orleans' Bourbon Street and handsome former cigar factories and social clubs.

Ybor City is in the northeast section of Tampa. The main drag, 7th Ave (La Septima), is closed to vehicles on Friday and Saturday from about 9pm to 4am. The area is roughly bordered by 23rd St at the east, 13th St at the west, Palm Ave (between 10th and 11th Aves) at the north and the railroad tracks along 6th Ave at the south. 14th St is also called Avenida República de Cuba.

An Ybor City **market** (☎ 813-241-2442) takes place every Saturday from 9am to 3pm at Centennial Park, at the corner of 8th Ave and 18th St, offering arts and crafts, fruits and veggies.

Ybor City Museum State Park Covering about half a city block, this park (☎ 813-247-6323; 1818 9th Ave; admission $2; open 9am-5pm daily) includes La Casita (a typical but reconstructed 'shotgun'-style abode that housed immigrant cigar workers), the Ferlita Bakery (with its original brick ovens and exhibits on the bakery and cigar industry), cigar-rolling demonstrations and fascinating photographs of the cigar factories and of late-19th-century Ybor City. Informative walking tours ($4) are offered on Saturdays at 10:30am.

Centro Ybor Converted in 1999, this dominating upscale shopping, dining and entertainment emporium runs along 8th Ave between 15th and 17th Sts, but it also cuts through what would have been 16th St down to 7th Ave.

Friends of Martí Park The Parque Amigos de José Martí (cnr 13th St & 8th Ave) contains a not-very-good but life-size monument to Martí that was dedicated by Martí's son, actor Cesar Romero. The park is sited at Paulina Pedroso's house, where Martí stayed after the Spanish government attempted to assassinate him in 1892.

Cigar Shops To listen in on a thoroughly fascinating discussion of the merits of particular cigars and the paraphernalia that's necessary for their enjoyment, tune into **The Cigar General**, a radio talk show on Saturdays from noon to 2pm on 970 AM. But if someone lights up and you can't see, taste or smell it, does that make a radio sound? Somehow this metaphysical question is answered through passionate commentary and your ability to close your eyes and imagine. Perhaps afterwards you'll be able to answer this compelling variation of the ancient Zen riddle: what is the sound of one man smoking?

One of the country's only shops to be set up as a humidor, **Metropolitan Cigars** (☎ 813-248-3304; 2014 E 7th Ave) is the best cigar shop in this former cigar capital of America. They sell Arturo Fuente and Cuesta Rey cigars.

The largest is **King Corona Cigar Factory** (☎ 813-241-9109, 1523 E 7th Ave), complete with an old-fashioned cigar bar and live entertainment. They carry Honduran and Dominican-made cigars.

El Sol (☎ 813-248-5905; 1728 E 7th Ave), established in 1929, is the oldest cigar store in Ybor City. They sell mainly Dominican cigars.

The **Gonzales y Martinez Cigar Company** (☎ 813-247-2469, 2025 E 7th Ave) has cigar-rolling demonstrations Monday through Saturday.

The most well-known of the Tampa brands is Havatampa, whose mass-marketed Tampa Sweets are available in supermarkets and tobacco shops throughout the state and the country.

Ybor City Brewing Company Within the former cigar factory of Seidenberg & Co (1894), this microbrewery (☎ 813-242-9222; 2205 N 20th St) produces 8000 barrels of beer annually, including their Hurricane Reef products, Key West Sunset Ale and Lager, Ybor Gold, Ybor Calusa Wheat, Ybor Brown Ale and Gaspar's Ale. Brews are available throughout Ybor City and Florida. Thirty-minute brewery tours are given daily at 11am, noon and 1pm (call for the off-season schedule from May through August). Tours ($3) include a look at the brewing and bottling process, a history of the building and a beer tasting (it's not enough to get you drunk).

Tampa Theatre
This atmospheric movie palace (☎ 813-274-8286; ⓦ www.tampatheatre.org; 711 N Franklin St; adult/senior, student or child $7/5), on the National Register of Historic Places, was built in 1926 by John Eberson. These days it screens independent and classic films and hosts concerts and other special events. The interior is special. Come early to hear the mighty Wurlitzer organ played before every movie; it features sirens, boat horns, cymbals, sleigh bells and other wacky sounds. Stars (though no star formations), some of which twinkle, are painted onto the ceiling. All the furniture (like old Broadway seats) in the 1446-seat theater is original, and, oh yes, the place is haunted by one Hank Fink, a projectionist here for 25 years who died in the late 1960s. Stories abound: some claim to have seen apparitions; a projectionist apparently quit because he heard strange noises in the booth; other staff members have heard keys rattling.

SOUTHWEST

Lowry Park Zoo

The lush zoo's best feature (☎ 813-932-0245; W www.lowryparkzoo.com; 7530 North Blvd; adult/senior/child $9.50/8.50/6; open 9:30am-5pm daily) is the manatee encounter and aquatic center, but there are also good exhibits on panthers, alligators, Komodo dragons, pandas, primates and bison. The Asian domain highlights a rare Indian rhinoceros, while families love the Wallaroo Station, an Australian theme area with kangaroos and wallabies that kids can pet. They can also pet and feed stingrays elsewhere in the park. Before leaving, don't miss the 18,000-sq-ft, free-flight aviary. To reach the zoo from downtown, take I-4 west to I-275 north to exit 31; go west on Fly Ave to North Blvd.

Henry Plant Museum

Railroad magnate Henry Plant's Tampa Bay Hotel, which opened in 1891, was one of the most luxurious places imaginable in the early days of the city, when Tampa was about as remote as Miami at the southern tip of the state. All 500 guest rooms had private baths and electricity, and the extravagant hotel contained all the furniture, sculptures and mirrors Plant's wife had collected during their European and Oriental travels.

After the hotel failed in the early 20th century, the city of Tampa took over and today the National Historic Landmark is a museum (☎ 813-254-1891; W www.plantmuseum.com; 401 W Kennedy Blvd; adult/child $5/1; open 10am-4pm Tues-Sat, noon-4pm Sun), across the river from downtown on the University of Tampa campus. You can gawk at the luxury and tour the hotel's grand salon, guest room, solarium and lobby, among others. Even if you don't go in, look for the dramatic Moorish revival architecture and silver minarets. The annual Victoria Christmas Stroll takes place from December 1 to 21, and it includes dramatizations of fairy tales by actors in period costume in different rooms of the hotel. Tickets are $6 adults, $3 children.

Children's Museum of Tampa

Also known as Kid City (☎ 813-935-8441; 7550 North Blvd; admission over age 2 yrs $4; open 9am-5:30pm Mon-Fri, 10am-5:30pm Sat, noon-5:30pm Sun), this place has rotating, hands-on interactive displays and a permanent, 45,000-sq-ft outdoor exhibition that kids love: child-size replicas of 13 municipal buildings, each with activities. Care to try your hand as a judge in the courthouse or a reporter at a TV station? Follow directions to the Lowry Park Zoo, above.

South Tampa

The world's longest contiguous **boardwalk**, measuring a whopping 6 miles, is a great place to bike, walk or run along the water. While you're in the area, drive or walk around the **Old Hyde Park** neighborhood, a residential area with brick streets, gas lanterns and renovated Victorian-style architecture. Head up Rome, Dakota or Oregon Aves from Bayshore Blvd. You'll also find an upscale, outdoor retail and dining complex where these three roads intersect with Swann Ave. Look for the old-time fruit stands in South Tampa, too.

Davis Island

The only reason to pop over here for a few minutes is to get a glimpse of real Tampa. And the little village straddling the roadside will provide just such a window. Take Davis Island Blvd off Bayshore Blvd and then at the split, take E Davis Blvd. Grab a coffee and hang around a bit; or settle in with some chips and salsa at **Estela's Mexican Restaurant** (☎ 813-251-0558; 209 E Davis Blvd; open daily for lunch & dinner; dishes max out at $12), with sidewalk seating. Portions are big, but stick with the basics.

Contemporary Art Museum

The University of South Florida's museum (CAM; ☎ 813-974-2849; W www.usfcam.usf.edu; USF campus, 4202 E Fowler Ave; admission free; open 10am-5pm Mon-Fri, 1pm-4pm Sat) mounts six to eight exhibitions by university students and alumni. Weekday parking costs $2.

Busch Gardens

Sprawling over 300 acres, the area's biggest theme park (☎ 813-987-5082, 866-353-8622;

W www.buschgardens.com; 10000 McKinley Dr; adult/child $50/41; although hours vary throughout the year, it's roughly open 9:30am-7pm daily) draws crowds with the state's best roller coasters and one of the state's best zoos. Despite the woolly mammoth–sized admission price, a trip to Busch Gardens is worth it, although you should probably cough up $11 more per person, which will entitle you to a return visit the following day. Also consider getting a combination ticket to Busch Gardens/Adventure Island (see later in this section). And add another $7 for parking. Several rides have height restrictions, which vary from 42 to 56 inches. In general, lines at Busch Gardens are far shorter than their Orlando counterparts; on a high-season day, you'll probably only have to wait about 10 minutes for a ride. Themed shows, performances and craft demonstrations occur several times daily and change often; check at the ticket window for the day's shows and activities. The same goes for animal acts starring alligators, elephants and tortoises, orangutans and warthogs and tigers; they occur at various villages around the park.

Additionally, Busch Gardens, in an attempt to stay ahead of the curve, is always inventing new rides and theme areas. Check at the gate. Also check for details on two tours once you're inside: the Animal Adventure Tour and the Serengeti Safari Tour.

It's about 7 miles north of downtown and accessible from both I-75 and I-275, both of which have Busch Blvd exits. From I-75 head west at the exit; from I-275 head east. The entrance to the park is on McKinley Dr, which juts north from Busch Blvd.

Crown Colony You can catch the monorail and Skyride here, to use as an orientation tour or for transportation. The Crown Colony House Restaurant overlooking the Serengeti Plain has a welcoming Hospitality Center, where you can get a 10oz cup of Anheuser-Busch beer (limit two per person per day, 21 and older). The Clydesdale Hamlet features trademark Budweiser Clydesdale horses.

Egypt The star of Egypt, Montu, claims to be the southeast USA's largest inverted steel roller coaster. The three-minute killer ride features an inverse loop – a 104-foot vertical loop that is the world's largest on an inverted coaster. As if that wasn't enough, there are two more vertical loops at a 45¼-degree angle. These coasters don't coast; speeds reach 60mph, and the G-force hits a maximum of 3.85 (minimum height 54 inches).

Other attractions include a replica of King Tutankhamen's tomb, a gigantic wall inscribed with hieroglyphics, and a Sand Dig area, where children can discover Egyptian antiquities in the sand. There are, of course, shopping bazaars and Egyptian-costumed characters roaming around.

Serengeti Plain The most authentic area, this 80-acre habitat is populated by about 500 animals that are best seen from the monorail (a bumpy 15- to 20-minute ride) and pretty well seen from the Skyride (more peaceful) and steam locomotive. Although giving animals free range makes it harder to see them, the zebras, giraffes, kudus, hippos, lions, camels and buffalo are in a more natural setting. Hip-hip, hooray. Take the Skyride so you can hear the wind and animal sounds; it's much more relaxing.

Edge of Africa You can get close up with big animals here, sometimes getting nose-to-nose with lions, hyenas, ostriches, zebras, hippos and giraffes. The viewing is similar to that of Myombe Reserve, with glass between the visitor and the animal habitat. Inquire about wildlife tours led by park zoologists.

Myombe Reserve The 3-acre reserve resembles the western lowlands of Africa, complete with gorillas and chimpanzees. It all feels very tropical and rainforesty, complete with waterfalls and piped-in tropical fog. From here you can participate in a Rhino Rally, cruising around the 'plains' in 4WD vehicles like you see on safaris and then racing other Rovers.

Nairobi Nairobi is home to the Animal Nursery, a petting zoo and the kid-favorite

Nocturnal Mountain,' where nocturnal creatures are exposed (so to speak). Other exhibits include the Show Jumping Hall of Fame and feature reptiles, tortoises and elephants.

Timbuktu This area draws 'em in with **Scorpion** – a 50mph ride with a 360-degree loop and 62-foot drop (minimum height 42 inches) – and Phoenix, a boat-swing ride (minimum height 48 inches). There are also kiddie rides and a video-game arcade. The Dolphin Theater stages live entertainment.

Congo Everyone is trying to get to the northwest corner of Busch Gardens for one reason: **Kumba**, one of the best roller coasters anywhere. It's a crazy ride, featuring a diving loop that plunges from a height of 110 feet, a camelback loop (spiraling 360 degrees and creating three seconds of weightlessness) and a 108-foot vertical loop. In addition, there are ducks, dips and swirls around pedestrian walkways and a generally terrifying vibe (minimum height 54 inches).

The other roller coaster ride here is the relatively tame (ha!) **Python**, a double spiral corkscrew that hits speeds of 50mph (minimum height 48 inches). Rafts take you down the **Congo River Rapids** (height restriction 39 inches, or at least two years old), but note you *will* get wet – if not from the current splashing against the raft, from the water cannons that line the route. People actually *pay* to shoot water at innocent rafters as they float by.

Claw Island is home to heartbreakingly beautiful Bengal tigers. Feeding times are posted near the fence, and it's gruesomely fascinating to watch these fluffy, elegant creatures ripping into lunch. There are more kiddie rides here, including the Ubanga-Banga Bumper Cars.

Stanleyville Prepare to get wet, since this African village features the **Tanganyika Tidal Wave** – a boat ride that plunges over a 55-foot waterfall (minimum height 48 inches). Stanley Falls is a log-flume ride with a 40-foot drop (height restriction 46 inches or with guardian). Catch a kid-friendly show at the Zambezi Pavilion or Stanleyville Theater. Or

walk through the Orchid Canyon, where there are orangutans and warthogs.

Bird Gardens & Land of the Dragons

Busch Gardens originated at the ever-so-humble Bird Gardens, which was merely a minor detour from the main action at the Anheuser-Busch Brewery tour: you'd guzzle some free beer and walk outside to see the birds. These days the old brewery and Bird Gardens site features Gwazi, a double, wooden roller coaster (the largest in the southeast USA). Standing at a mere 90 feet tall, this just may be the coaster to ride if you're normally queasy about these topsy-turvy machines. You'll also want to check out the interactive Land of the Dragons, an enchanted forest filled with colorful dragons. Or climb around a three-story-tall tree house, hop on the Ferris wheel, climb aboard a flume ride or a waterfall and dragon carousel (kids' rides have a 56-inch height restriction). Other draws include exotic birds and birds of prey, which are seen in the lush, walk-through aviary. Flamingos and pelicans abound. A koala habitat features all manner of Australian animals, including Queensland koalas.

Adventure Island

This 25-acre water park (☎ 813-987-5600; Ⓦ www.adventureisland.com; 10001 McKinley Dr; adult/child age 3-9 yrs $28/26, combination Busch Gardens & Adventure Island for 2/3 days $59/70; open 10am-5pm Mon-Fri, 9:30am-6pm Sat & Sun), also run by Anheuser-Busch, has 16 different areas, including Key West Rapids, on which rafters go down a six-story twist, ending in a 60-foot-long pool. Other slide rides include the Aruba Tuba (portions are in total darkness, others in daylight) and Rambling Bayou, where you go through weather 'effect' areas (parts are foggy, others have heavy rain). There's also a 9000-sq-ft swimming pool with waterfalls, diving platforms and translucent tube slides. And don't forget the 76-foot, free-fall body slide, Tampa Typhoon.

Parking is $5. With the combo Busch Gardens/Adventure Island ticket get one day at each park.

Activities

Ice-Skating There are afternoon and evening sessions at **Town and Country Skateworld** (☎ 813-884-7688; 7510 Paula Dr; open year-round), one block north of Hillsborough Ave (call for specific times). Fees are $4.50 for afternoon sessions, $7 to $8 for evening sessions. Rental is included, unless you want in-line or speed skates ($3 and $2.50, respectively). From downtown, take I-275 south to the Veteran's Expressway (Tampa International Airport exit off the interstate) to Hillsborough Ave. Then head about 2 miles west to Hanley Rd and turn right on Hanley Rd.

Cruises From the Port of Tampa's cruise ship terminal, **Carnival Cruise Lines** (☎ 800-438-6744; w www.carnival.com) operates *Sensation*; the seven-night trip heads to New Orleans, Grand Cayman and Cozumel, Mexico, and departs every Sunday. It also sails on similar four- and five-day cruises, perhaps adding a stop in Key West.

Holland America Cruise Line (☎ 206-281-3535, 800-426-0327; w www.hollandamerica .com) operates the *Noordam* (February through April), a 14-day sailing with stops in San Juan, St Thomas, Dominica, St Lucia, Bonaire and Georgetown.

Organized Tours

Ybor City Ghostwalk (☎ 813-242-4660) runs scheduled tours hosted by an actor in period costume telling tales of Ybor City past. They depart at 4pm Thursday and Saturday. Reservations are highly recommended (the tours can be canceled for lack of interest and besides, you have to know where to meet). Tickets are $10 for adults, $8 per child (it's not recommended for children under age 7).

Narrated **Duck Tours** (☎ 813-310-3825; w www.ducktoursoftampabay.com; 514 Channelside Dr at Newk's Cafe), which take place within authentic WWII army amphibious vehicles, waddle around Ybor City, downtown sites and then plunge into the Hillsborough River for a view of Tampa from the water. The 80-minute tours depart frequently throughout the day in winter (call for off-season schedule) and cost

$18.50 for adults, $16.50 for seniors and $10 for children.

Places to Stay

There's good camping at Hillsborough River State Park (see Around Tampa later in this chapter). Otherwise, you'll be stuck at mega sites. Like the others in the area, **Sunburst Super Park Tampa East** and **Encore RV Park Tampa East** (☎ 813-659-0002, 877-917-2757; 12720 Hwy 92; sites $25-33/33-41 summer/winter) cater to tourists traveling along I-4 and winter snowbirds. This superstore RV park has hundreds of sites, amenities galore and a pool that's open 24/7. From I-75, take the I-4 exit east 3 miles to exit 9 (McIntosh Rd), turn right (south) and drive an eighth of a mile, or continue south to Hwy 92, turn right and drive for about a quarter-mile.

Downtown In the immediate downtown area, you'll find **Holiday Inn City Center** (☎ 813-223-1351; 111 W Fortune St; rooms $89-129/109-153 summer/winter), a three-story place with 312 units behind the Tampa Bay Performing Arts Center; **Courtyard by Marriott** (☎ 813-229-1100, 800-321-2211; w www.marriott.com; 102 E Cass St; rooms from $99/159 summer/winter), with 141 typically good rooms; and the 521-room **Hyatt Regency Tampa** (☎ 813-225-1234, 800-233-1234; w www.hyatt.com; 211 N Tampa St; rooms $125-294), which is geared toward business travelers.

Economy Inn Express (☎ 813-253-0851; 830 W Kennedy Blvd; rooms $45-50/50-55 summer/winter), near the University of Tampa, has 50 decent rooms; HBO is free.

Ybor City At press time a new Hampton Inn (normally a moderately priced chain) was scheduled to open; ask at the Chamber of Commerce.

Don Vicente de Ybor Historic Inn (☎ 813-241-4545; w www.donvicenteinn.com; 1915 República de Cuba; rooms $99-129/129-159 summer/winter), with 16 boutique-style rooms, was built in 1895 by the founder of Ybor City. It's a good choice.

Hilton Garden Inn (☎ 813-769-9267, 877-367-4458; w www.hiltonybor.com; 1700 E

9th Ave; rooms & suites from $89/149 summer/winter), with 95 rooms and suites in a four-story building, has more of a homey feel than you might expect.

Casita de Verdad (☎ 813-654-6087; [W] www .yborguesthouse.com; 1609 E 6th Ave; whole house $180/250 weekday/weekend), a lovingly restored 1908 cigar maker's house, has just two period rooms, with either an antique sleigh bed or four-poster bed and a claw-foot bathtub. Features include a courtyard deck, multi-night discounts, a plethora of packages (perhaps including a flamenco show at Columbia Restaurant) and full breakfast.

Busch Gardens Chains here include **Economy Inn** (☎ 813-933-7831; 11414 N Central Ave; rooms $31), with 48 rooms; a nicely renovated **Motel 6** (☎ 813-932-4948, 800-466-8356; 333 E Fowler Ave; rooms $44), with 150 rooms; **Red Roof Inn** (☎ 813-932-0073, 800-733-7663; 2307 E Busch Blvd; rooms $39-55/49-70 summer/winter), with 108 rooms, a pool and free local phone calls; **Holiday Inn** (☎ 813-971-4710, 800-465-4329; 2701 E Fowler Ave; rooms $75-80), with 408 rooms; and **Howard Johnson Maingate** (☎ 813-988-9191, 800-446-4656; 4139 E Busch Blvd; rooms $69-79/89-99 summer/winter), with 100 rooms and a pool.

Less than a mile from Busch Gardens, the excellent 150-room **Best Western All Suites** (☎ 813-971-8930, 800-786-7446; [W] www.that parrotplace.com; 3001 University Center Dr; rooms $109/119 summer/winter) has a nice heated pool and spa, friendly staff and enough perks to satisfy most everyone. Look for two TVs, a refrigerator, a microwave, VCR, a boom box, and a bedroom and living room. Breakfast is an all-you-can-eat hot buffet. They also have a 99¢ happy hour from 4:30pm to 6:30pm daily.

South Tampa Neither here nor there, South Tampa may split the difference nicely for you. The prices are decent at **EconoLodge Midtown** (☎ 813-254-3005, 800-553-2666; 1020 S Dale Mabry Hwy; rooms $50-70/60-80 summer/winter), with 74 rooms and a pool.

Tahitian Inn (☎ 813-877-6721, 800-876-1397; [W] www.tahitianinn.com; 601 S Dale Mabry Hwy; rooms $69-99/89-119 summer/winter), with 62 rooms and suites, also has a nice heated pool and workout room.

Places to Eat
Downtown If you're downtown, you'll find standard lunch places.

Bread & Butter Deli (☎ 813-301-0505; 507 N Franklin St; dishes $4-7; open 6am-4pm Mon-Fri), a Greek-run deli with a lot more than the name implies, has good homemade soups, upwards of 20 salads, sandwiches from 'A to Z' and Greek and Lebanese specials.

City's Gourmet Deli (☎ 813-229-7400; 514 Tampa St; sandwiches $5-6; open 10:30am-3pm Mon-Sat), with homemade everything, is an excellent choice. From salads and soups to wraps and sandwiches heaped with good stuff, this is not your average deli. For instance, they roast their own meats and use French chocolate in their brownies.

Lonni's Sandwiches (☎ 813-223-2333; 513 E Jackson St; dishes $5-8; open 9am-4pm Mon-Fri) swarms with county workers who flock here for enormous, cheap and sometimes creative sandwiches, with Cuban, American and sometimes Asian blends.

Four Green Fields (☎ 813-254-4444; 205 W Platt St; dishes $10-12; open 11am-3am Mon-Sat, noon-3am Sun) looks like a traditional Irish cottage (with, yes, a thatched roof). Sure enough, it features traditional Irish cooking, thick brogues, Irish music, 30-weight Guinness, pints that pack a punch and friendly folk.

Ybor City Head to Ybor City if you want an interesting meal.

El Molino Coffee Shop (☎ 813-248-2521; 2012 E 7th Ave; open 8am-4pm Mon-Fri) boasts serious Cuban coffee, not that wimpy American stuff.

7th Heaven Psychic Cafe (☎ 813-242-0400; 1725 E 7th Ave; open 6pm-midnight Tues & Wed, noon-'whatever' Thur-Sat, 3pm-8pm Sun) couldn't psychically determine why we wanted their prices, but that doesn't mean their readings ($25 for 15 minutes) aren't up and up. You can get coffee and snacks here.

Little Sicily (☎ 813-248-2940; 1724 E 8th Ave; dishes $3-6; open 8am-5pm Mon-Sat), a good Italian-style deli with a few small outside tables, has huge sandwiches, good calzones, pasta dishes and very friendly service.

Joffrey's Coffee Co (☎ 813-248-5282; 1616 E 7th Ave; sandwiches $5; open 7:30am-6pm Mon & Tues, 7:30am-midnight Wed & Thur, 7:30am-3am Fri & Sat) has croissant and bagel sandwiches, pastries and lots of coffee and tea. Or better yet, how about some pure oxygen for $8 for 10 minutes.

The friendly **Cephas** (☎ 813-247-9022; 1701 E 4th Ave; dishes $5-11; open 11:30am-9pm Tues-Thur, 11:30am-3:30am Fri & Sat), a little piece of Jamaica in Ybor City, is run by Cephas Gilbert, who showed up in America in 1982 with $37 in his pocket. If you're a fan of huge plates of jerk chicken wings, curry goat or chicken and brown stew, start jumping up and down.

Moses White & Sons Bar B Que (☎ 813-247-7544; 1815 E 7th Ave; platters $7-10; open 11am-6pm Mon-Thur, 11am-3am Fri & Sat), with a real oak-fired pit and some of Florida's best barbecue sauce, has platters (half a chicken or ribs) with two side dishes and a half slab o' ribs.

Spaghetti Warehouse (☎ 813-248-1720; 1911 N 13th St; dishes under $10; open noon-10pm daily) doles out serviceable Italian in a renovated warehouse behind Ybor Square. The atmosphere is cool enough, regardless of whether you've got an indoor or outdoor table.

The chic **Café Creole** (☎ 813-247-6283; 1330 E 9th Ave; lunch $6-14, dinner mains $9-18; open 11:30am-10pm Mon-Fri, 4pm-11pm Sat), within some of the most sumptuous digs in Ybor City, features excellent and authentic Creole and Cajun dishes (jambalaya, Louisiana crab cakes, crawfish), good service, Southern-style praline cheesecake and excellent beans and rice as side dishes. You'll also get live jazz and gospel Tuesday through Saturday nights. There is also outside seating.

Samurai Blue (☎ 813-242-6688; 1600 E 8th Ave; lunch $10-13, dinner mains $15-22; open 11am-2pm Mon-Sat, 5pm-11pm Sun-Thur, 5pm-2am Fri & Sat), with cool architecture, boasts a remarkable 30-foot sushi bar, an unusual sake bar and a creative Asian fusion menu for the less adventurous.

Columbia Restaurant (☎ 813-248-4961; 2117 E 7th Ave; set lunch $9-22, dinner mains $15-22; open 11am-10pm Mon-Sat, noon-9pm Sun), family-owned since it opened in 1920, is the oldest restaurant in Florida and a legitimate historical place. It's a gaudy, glitzy place that many people write off as a tourist trap. You shouldn't; you should go. Just make sure you're in a fun mood. The interior is gorgeous, with 11 dining rooms decorated lavishly with tiled scenes from *Don Quixote* and a center fountain. Salads and the black bean appetizers are excellent (especially the '1905' salad), paella a la Valenciana is a specialty and dinner is better than lunch. Consider catching the hot flamenco show (twice nightly except Sunday) for an extra $6. Or pop into the Cigar Bar for some tapas, smokes and jazz (Thursday through Saturday).

Busch Gardens The mainstay of the classic **Mel's Hot Dogs** (☎ 813-985-8000; 4136 E Busch Blvd; open 11am-8pm Sun-Thur, 11am-9pm Fri & Sat), made by the Chicago Vienna Beef Company, is the Mighty Mel Hot Dog ($3), a flabbergastingly large dog with relish, mustard and pickles on a poppyseed bun. For wiener-haters who travel with wiener-devotees, there are veggie burgers.

Taj (☎ 813-971-8483; 2734-B E Fowler Ave; lunch buffet $8, dinner mains $8-16; open 11:30am-2:30pm & 5pm-10pm Tues-Sun), which can get very crowded, serves good Indian food and has an all-you-can-eat lunch buffet. Try the chicken tandoori and chicken curry.

South Tampa Referred to by locals as SoHo (ie, South Howard Ave), this burgeoning dining area offers a number of varied choices.

Bean There Traveler's Coffee House (☎ 813-837-7022; 3203 Bay-to-Bay Blvd; dishes $3-6; open 7am-3pm Mon-Fri, 8am-3pm Sat, 8am-2pm Sun) serves breakfast (all day), sandwiches and coffee alongside their maps, globes and the big 'Where You Bean' bulletin board where guests put up photos, postcards and other travel mementos. Take Bayshore Blvd from downtown to Bay-to-Bay Blvd and turn right; it's on the right side of the road, past MacDill Ave.

The Yellow Door (☎ 813-258-3074; 311 S Howard Ave; dishes $7-13; open 6pm-11pm Mon-Sat) serves Southeast Asian–style tapas dishes bursting with flavor (shrimp rolls, Mongolian sea bass) in low-key, minimalist surroundings. This is a very good choice.

Mise en Place (☎ 813-254-5373; 442 W Kennedy Blvd; mains $16-27; open 5:30pm-10pm Tues-Thur, 5:30pm-11pm Fri & Sat), a longtime chef-owned bistro across from the University, is arguably Tampa's brightest culinary shooting star. The creative and seasonal menu, with Floribbean twists, is decidedly eclectic and always a treat. Always. Put on some trendy black and saunter over; you won't be disappointed. Or head next door (in that same black garb) for some appetizers and jazz at their adjacent **442** club. Or settle for takeout at their **Mise en Place Market** (2616 S MacDill Ave).

Side Bern's (☎ 813-258-2233; 1002 S Howard Ave; mains $24-26; open 6pm-10pm Tues-Sun), the Bern's Steak House spin-off, is nothing like its parent. What, you never thought that could happen? You'll find contemporary fusion cuisine here, which utilizes spices from around the world to enliven the mostly seafood dishes. Ostrich or lamb devotees need not worry, though; you'll find those on the menu.

Bern's Steak House (☎ 813-251-2421; 1208 S Howard Ave; steaks from $27, desserts from $4; open 5pm-10:30pm daily), Tampa's landmark restaurant, serves some of the best steaks east of the west. Perhaps you're in the mood to share a 60oz slab with five of your closest friends? No problem, if you have $225. Downstairs the slick atmosphere is heavy on red velvet, gold leaf and statuary; upstairs, where all patrons head for sweets in the cigar-friendly dessert room, the tables are made from redwood wine casks. Reservations are a must. Not widely known, you can always just order a steak sandwich at the bar. Or you can always just come for one of a hundred desserts (a scoop of vanilla ice cream, flaming cherries jubilee or bananas

Foster served in paneled booths) to get a sneak peek at the place, but they don't take reservations for just dessert, and you may find yourself waiting for the privilege. Bern's wine list boasts more than 7000 labels and 1800 dessert wines, but the cellars stash upwards of a million bottles. Take Bayshore Blvd from downtown to Howard Ave, and then turn right on Howard.

Entertainment

For up-to-the-minute Tampa Bay cultural events, call the **arts line** (☎ 813-229-2787) operated by the Arts Council of Hillsborough County. There's no shortage of printed information, either: get local news and entertainment listings in the free Wednesday *Weekly Planet* (W www.weeklyplanet.com); the pull-out Thursday *Weekend* section of the *St Petersburg Times*; and the pullout Friday *Extra* section of the *Tampa Tribune*.

Gameworks (☎ 813-241-9675; 1600 E 8th Ave; open 11am-midnight Sun-Wed, 11am-2am Thur-Sat), a high-tech play place with virtual reality free-falling simulators and the like, has plenty of eateries and bars to keep you spending money.

Seminole Indian Casino (☎ 813-621-1302, 800-282-7016; W www.casino-tampa.com; 5223 N Orient Rd; open 24/7) is about 15 minutes from downtown Tampa off I-4 (head east to Orient Rd and then head left). This casino sucks in those who love the thrill of winning big time, instantly. But don't bet on it. Like a spider spinning a web with high-stakes bingo and stud poker, this place has it all and has designed on keeping it.

Performing Arts Beautifully sited on a river park, the **Tampa Bay Performing Arts Center** (☎ 813-229-7827, 800-955-1045; 1010 N MacInnes Place; tickets $10-50) is the largest performing-arts center south of the Kennedy Center in Washington, DC. It's home to major concerts, touring Broadway productions, plays, the Tampa Ballet and special events. There are four theaters in the complex: Festival Hall (a 2500-seat venue where touring Broadway shows and headliners perform), Ferguson Hall (with 1000 seats), the Jaeb (a three-floor cabaret) and the 100-seat Shimberg Playhouse, a 'black box' venue that's home to cutting-edge performances by local and national artists and groups. Free backstage guided tours (☎ 813-222-1000) are offered Wednesday and Saturday at 10am, by reservation.

UT Falk Theater (☎ 813-253-3333; 428 W Kennedy Blvd), a 900-seat theater, is operated by the University of Tampa.

Florida Orchestra (☎ 813-286-2403, 800-662-7286; tickets $20-42), a 90-piece orchestra, plays at the Performing Arts Center as well as venues in St Petersburg and Clearwater and at free park concerts.

USF School of Music (☎ 813-974-2311; USF campus, Fowler Ave; tickets $2-4; season Sept-Mar), where the USF Theater also performs, is accessible from Fowler Ave exits on I-275 and I-75. They stage a variety of concerts and recitals open to the entire community.

Sun Dome (☎ 813-974-3111; W www.sun dome.org; 4202 E Fowler Ave), also on the USF campus, hosts rock, jazz, pop and other concerts – from Jimmy Buffet to 'N Sync, from Luciano Pavarotti to the World Wrestling Federation (now there's some 'performing arts' for you!).

Raymond James Stadium (☎ 813-350-6500; W www.tampasportsauthority.com; 4201 N Dale Mabry Hwy) often presents concerts, too.

Ticketmaster (☎ 813-287-8844) sells tickets to most events and tacks on a surcharge for its trouble.

Bars & Clubs If the words 'party central,' 'meat market' and 'bouncers' show up regularly in your conversations, Ybor City is your kind of place. Intense weekend crowds and partyers revel into the wee hours. Locals suggest showing up early, getting your hand stamped and coming back later to push through the crowds like you're a celebrity. Check flyers on walls and lampposts – they're the most reliable source of up-to-date party, concert and nightclub information. Nightly drink specials and cover charges change more quickly than a leopard changes spots, so it's pointless to include them here (for the most part). Cruise E 7th Ave

between 15th and 20th Sts on Friday and Saturday night between 9pm and 3am and you might not be able to control yourself.

Adobe Gilas (☎ 813-241-8588; 1600 E 8th Ave; open 11am-3am Mon-Sat, 1pm-3am Sun) mixes margaritas. The 2nd-floor balconies are also a very good vantage point from which to take in the street scene below.

The name, **Pleasure Dome** (☎ 813-247-2711; W www.pleasuredomeonline.com; 1430 E 7th Ave; open Tues, Fri & Sat), says it all — from Taboo Tuesday (with female impersonators at 12:30am) to Friday night's 'Shake your Naked Ass' (with DJs spinning hip-hop and booty) to Saturday 'X-Factory' (with a DJ spinning break, beat and house music). What's in a name? Everything here.

Improv Comedy Theater (☎ 813-864-4000; W www.tampaimprov.com; 1600 E 8th Ave; tickets $10-22) puts on good doses of nightly comedic schtick. Some national acts come to town.

Tampa Bay Brewing Company (☎ 813-247-1422; 1812 N 15th St; open 11:30am-midnight Mon & Tues, 11:30am-2am Wed-Sat) is a fun place with microbrews, $4 liters on Wednesday and weekday happy hours (4pm to 7pm).

New World Brewery (☎ 813-248-4969; 1313 E 8th Ave; open 3pm-3am Sat-Wed, 11:30am-3am Thur & Fri), a bar and disco with a great jukebox, draws a hugely lubricated crowd with its great dance music. DJs and live music grace the place a few nights weekly.

Green Iguana Bar & Grill (☎ 813-248-9555; W www.greeniguana.net; 1708 E 7th Ave; open 11am-2am nightly) is a cool but laidback bar and restaurant by day (with Floribbean food and sandwiches and burgers). By night, it's really two clubs in one – deal with either high-energy cover bands or high-energy, DJ-driven dance music and $1 drinks on Wednesday.

Castle Bar (☎ 813-247-7547; 2004 16th St; open 9:30pm-3am Fri-Mon), popular for years, draws a decidedly artsy and interesting mix of people.

Twilight (☎ 813-247-4225; 1507 E 7th Ave; open 9pm-3am Wed-Sat) reels 'em in with college nights, live music, hot DJs and hotter dancing on two floors. Soul and funk, anyone?

The Empire/Climax (☎ 813-247-2582; 1902 E 7th Ave; open from 9pm Fri & Sat) attracts a diverse crowd with techno, hip-hop and booty. Downstairs is ruled by a DJ and color laser lights; head upstairs to Climax with R&B and reggae.

Cherokee Club (☎ 813-247-9966; 1320 E 9th Ave; open 8pm-3am Fri & Sat), with dancing and infrequent live music, is a predominantly lesbian (but gay as well) club. Exuding a satisfying irony, this former 'gentlemen only' club was frequented by such luminaries as José Martí, Winston Churchill and Teddy Roosevelt. Bully, ladies!

So you've decided to forgo Ybor City to see what the rest of Tampa has to offer? Here are two dependable choices.

The Hub (☎ 813-229-1553; 701 N Florida Ave), a fun local hangout with a jukebox and cheap drinks, looks like a hole in the wall. But the bar gets packed on weekends with a Jack Daniels and Coke drinking crowd. Be prepared to call a cab after ordering a few too many.

The all-around scene at **Hyde Park Cafe** (☎ 813-254-2233; W www.thehydeparkcafe .com; 1806 W Platt St; open from 8pm Tues-Sat), a late-night pizza place ($10 to $15), indoor-outdoor cafe and VIP club, gets really packed on Tuesday nights with eclectic music. Other nights see a good DJ spinning tunes behind the rack; happy hour (and no cover) dominates from 8pm to 10pm. Silicone implants and South Beach–slick attire dominate the club. See also Four Green Fields, under Downtown Places to Eat, above.

Spectator Sports

Football The NFL's **Tampa Bay Buccaneers** (☎ 813-870-2700; W www.buccaneers.com) play at Raymond James Stadium (4201 N Dale Mabry Hwy). Games are played from August (pre-season) to December, but unfortunately you'll probably have to catch them on television since season ticket holders grab all the stadium seats.

The Outback Bowl (☎ 813-874-2695; W www.outbackbowl.com), an NCAA (National College Athletic Association) football game on New Year's Day, is played at Raymond James Stadium. If you've never seen an American college football game, this shouldn't be missed (but at $50 per ticket, it may have to be!).

The USF Bulls (☎ 813-974-2125, 800-462-8557; W www.gousfbulls.com), a Division I-AA football team, play at Tampa Stadium; tickets run about $20.

Baseball The **New York Yankees** (☎ 813-875-7753; W www.legendsfieldtampa.com) play spring-training games at Legends Field (3802 ML King Jr Blvd at Dale Mabry Hwy) in March. Tickets cost $10 to $14. The 10,000-seat stadium is modeled after the House that Ruth Built, or Yankee Stadium, which is in the Bronx, New York. The Yankees' minor-league team, the Tampa Yankees, plays at Legends Field from April to September. Tickets cost $3 to $5; parking is free.

Hockey The **Tampa Bay Lightning** (☎ 813-301-6600; W www.tampabaylightning.com) play at the Ice Palace in the Channel District from October through March. Tickets cost $15 to $60. The entertainment complex also hosts NHL hockey games, basketball games, concerts and ice shows.

Shopping

Oversized flea markets are a Florida fixture, but this one north of downtown is special. **Big Top Flea Market** (☎ 813-986-4004; W www.bigtopfleamarket.com; 9250 E Fowler Ave; open 9am-4:30pm Sat & Sun) redefines 'bargain' with a capital 'B.' Forget retail when these 1000 enclosed and covered stalls can provide every essential and nonessential item ever produced. You gotta love it…or hate it.

Getting There & Away

Air The **Tampa International Airport** (TPA; ☎ 813-870-8700; W www.tampaairport.com) is about 13 miles west of downtown, off of Hwy 589. Since it's the major regional airport, most flights to the Tampa area land here – as opposed to at St Petersburg–Clearwater International Airport.

Bus Tampa's **Greyhound bus station** (☎ 813-229-2112, 800-231-2222; 610 Polk St) serves the region. The trip from Tampa to Miami takes 7 to 9 hours ($36/65 one-way/roundtrip); to Orlando takes 2 to 3 hours ($16/28); to Sarasota takes 2 hours ($11/21); and to Gainesville takes 3 to 3½ hours ($18/36).

Train Several times daily **Amtrak** (☎ 813-221-7600; 601 Nebraska Ave) has shuttle buses running between Tampa and Orlando. The ticket office is open from 5:45am to 9:50pm daily except from 10:30am to 11:30am and 7:30pm to 8:30pm. Now that you know, don't get caught empty handed.

Car & Motorcycle Tampa is 245 miles northwest of Miami, 135 miles southwest of the Space Coast and 85 miles south of Orlando. Between Tampa and Orlando, take I-4. Between Tampa and Miami, the fastest way is to take I-75 south to Fort Lauderdale and then I-95 south, though the more scenic route is US Hwy 41 (Tamiami Trail) south to Everglades City and due east to Calle Ocho in Miami. Major car rental agencies are located at the airport.

Getting Around
To/From the Airport
The No 30 HART bus picks up and drops off at the Red Arrival Desk on the lower level; exact change is required. From the airport, buses run to the downtown terminal (see Bus below) about every half-hour from 6am to 8:30pm. The trip takes about 40 minutes. From downtown to the airport, buses run about every half-hour from 5:45am to 7pm.

Super Shuttle (☎ 800-282-6817; W www .supershuttle.com) plies the road outside the arrival areas; it generally costs from $15 to $19 to downtown Tampa.

All major car agencies have desks at the airport. By car, take I-275 to N Ashley Dr, turn right and you're in downtown.

Bus The **Uptown-Downtown Connector** (☎ 813-254-4278) is free and runs up and down Florida Ave, Tampa St and Franklin St

every 10 minutes from 6am to 6pm Monday through Friday.

Hillsborough Area Regional Transit (HART; ☎ 813-254-4278; W www.hart line.org) buses converge on the Morgan St terminal. Buses cost $1.25 one-way, $3 for an all-day pass. To take your bike on the bus, you'll need to go to the terminal and buy a photo ID permit ($2); from then on, there's no extra charge. Check out these popular destinations by bus (all leave from the main terminal):

destination	bus no	departs
Ybor City	8, 46	half-hourly
Busch Gardens & USF	5	half-hourly
Lowry Park Zoo	7	half-hourly
Henry Plant Museum	10	half-hourly
MOSI	6 to University Transit Center*	hourly

*Note there are two routes on bus No 6, so check the destination.

Express rush-hour buses ply the route between Tampa and the coast: bus No 100x goes to St Petersburg and bus No 200x to Clearwater.

Trolley Beginning in late 2002, electric streetcars (☎ 813-242-5491; W www.hart line.org) will tootle around Ybor City from Channelside on a 2.3-mile route.

AROUND TAMPA
Hillsborough River State Park
This appealing 3400-acre state park (☎ 813-987-6771; 15402 N Hwy 301; admission $3.25 per carload; open 8am-sunset daily) offers inexpensive camping and canoeing, a noble way to spend an afternoon or an overnight. You'll find picnic facilities, 8 miles of nature and hiking trails and a half-acre swimming pool (adult/child $2/1; open 10am-5pm Fri-Sun summer, daily winter).

Within the park, the reconstructed **Fort Foster** was originally built in 1836–37 as a bridge defense during the Second Seminole War, as the area was on a supply trail running from Fort Brooke in Tampa to Fort

SOUTHWEST

King in present-day Ocala. There were skirmishes here, but no major battles, and over the years the original fort deteriorated and was vandalized. The fort, the east side of Hwy 301, is only open for **guided tours** (2pm Sat & 11am Sun).

Camping at the 106 sites costs $13/15 without/with hookups; each site has a fire ring, picnic table and water source. There are also hot showers.

From downtown Tampa, take Fowler Ave east to Hwy 301, and go north for 9 miles.

Canoeing The river's current isn't challenging here, and you can rent canoes for an easy paddle ($8 hourly, $20 for four hours). Lots of wildlife lives along the river and the best time for sightings is early morning or around dusk. Keep your eyes peeled for bobcats, white-tailed deer, opossums, raccoons, gray foxes, red-tailed hawks, ospreys, armadillos, water birds and alligators.

Canoe Escapes! (☎ 813-986-2067; **w** www .canoeescape.com; 9335 E Fowler Ave), near the Hillsborough River in Thonotosassa, a half-mile east of I-75, is the area's largest outfit. Canoes come in two sizes, which can hold a family of four for two- and four-hour jaunts. These easy, self-guided adventures downstream include stops along the way for picnicking (bring a cooler). You'll get river maps and, if necessary, paddling instructions. The cost is $32 per canoe for the two-hour trip, and $38 for four hours, including transport to and from the river. The first boat out on weekdays is at 9am, last out is 2pm, last pickup from the river is 5pm; on Saturday and Sunday, they start an hour earlier, but last out and pickup are the same.

ST PETERSBURG
population 248,000
Rejuvenated St Petersburg, a lovely city set on a peninsula, boasts a collection of museums that, together, form what may be the state's cultural powerhouse. The Dalí Museum is the largest collection of that artist's works outside Spain; the St Petersburg Fine Arts Museum has one of the finest collections in the state; and the Florida International Museum's blockbuster rotating exhibitions have brought national attention with groundbreaking international shows. And, to boot, they're all connected by a convenient trolley and intermingled with fine bistros and cafés. Throw in about 7 miles of accessible waterfront and you've got yourself one serious destination.

Orientation
St Petersburg is a typically sprawling southwest Florida town. For instance, it's a good 25 minutes to the beach in the best of traffic. Downtown is about 10 miles northeast of St Pete Beach and about 20 miles southwest of Tampa across Old Tampa Bay.

The city is oriented on the ever-familiar grid: avenues run east-west and streets and boulevards run north-south. The north-south dividing line is Central Ave, and 34th St (Hwy 19) is the east-west divider, though people usually ignore the east-west designation. The directional indicator is placed after the street. Avenues count upward away from Central Ave, so 1st Ave N is one block north of Central, and 1st Ave S is one block south.

Downtown is the area roughly bordered by the bay at the east, ML King Jr Blvd (9th St) at the west, 10th Ave N at the north and 17th Ave S at the south.

Information
For advance information, contact the **St Petersburg/Clearwater Area Convention & Visitors Bureau** (☎ 727-464-7200, 800-345-6710; **w** www.floridasbeach.com; 14450 46th St N); their location across from the airport is inconvenient for drop-ins.

Once in town, head to the **St Petersburg Area Chamber of Commerce** (☎ 727-821-4715; **w** www.stpete.org; 100 2nd Ave N; open 9am-5pm Mon-Fri, 10am-4pm Sat, noon-4pm Sun) for brochures, pamphlets and maps. They produce a good downtown arts guide as well as a general map with pullouts of different neighborhoods. The Chamber also has an information booth at The Pier (see later in this section) and at 2001 Ulmerton Rd (exit 18 off I-275 south, just beyond the Howard Frankland Bridge).

Bank of America has many branches downtown.

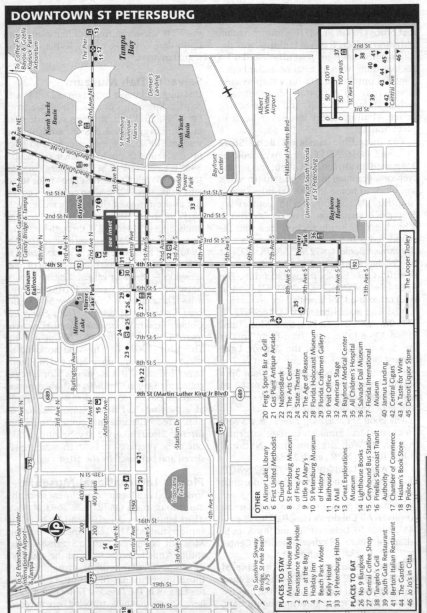

DOWNTOWN ST PETERSBURG

PLACES TO STAY
1 Mansion House B&B
2 Renaissance Vinoy Hotel
3 Inn at the Bay
7 Holiday Inn
10 Beach Park Motel
31 Kelly Hotel
33 St Petersburg Hilton

PLACES TO EAT
26 No 9 Bangkok
27 Central Coffee Shop
38 Tangelo's Grill
39 South Gate Restaurant
41 Bertoni Italian Restaurant
44 The Garden
46 Jo Jo's in Citta

OTHER
5 Mirror Lake Library
6 First United Methodist
   Church
8 St Petersburg Museum
   of Fine Arts
9 Little St Mary's
10 St Petersburg Museum
   of History
11 Bathhouse
12 Mall
13 Great Explorations
   Museum
14 Lighthouse Books
15 Greyhound Bus Station
16 Pinellas Suncoast Transit
   Authority
17 Chamber of Commerce
18 Haslam's Book Store
19 Police

20 Ferg's Sports Bar & Grill
21 Gas Plant Antique Arcade
22 NationsBank
23 The Arts Center
24 State Theatre
25 The Age of Reason
28 Florida Holocaust Museum
29 Florida Craftsmen Gallery
30 Post Office
32 American Stage
34 Bayfront Medical Center
35 All Children's Hospital
36 Salvador Dalí Museum
37 Florida International
   Museum
40 Jannus Landing
42 Central Cigars
43 A Taste for Wine
45 Detroit Liquor Store

SOUTHWEST

The main post office (3135 1st Ave N) is less convenient than the open-air downtown **post office** (76 4th St N). This branch, within a Mediterranean Revival building, was the nation's first open-air post office, and it's a glorious thing, with a keystone-arched open front. It contains an itty-bitty display case in the rear with postal paraphernalia such as stamps, inkwells and a numbering device. Mailing letters has never been so educational!

The incredible **Haslam's Book Store** (☎ 727-822-8616; 2025 Central Ave) could be designated an attraction without raising any eyebrows. Founded in 1933, the shop needs a half block to house its 300,000 titles (who's counting?), all arranged with a surprising degree of organization. To no one's surprise, it has a good Florida section, new and remaindered books and a core of used books. **Lighthouse Books** (☎ 727-822-3278; 1735 1st Ave N) has Florida and Caribbean sections as well as rare books, maps and prints. **The Age of Reason** (☎ 727-821-0892; 621 Central Ave) offers used books with friendly service.

Visit the main **library** (☎ 727-893-7724; 3745 9th Ave N; open 9am-9pm Mon-Thur, 9am-5:30pm Fri & Sat, 10am-6pm Sun) or the downtown branch, the **Mirror Lake Library** (☎ 727-893-7268; cnr 5th St & 2nd Ave N; open 9am-6pm Mon-Fri, 9am-5pm Sat) for web surfing. Call ahead to make an appointment, or take your chances with a couple of walk-in computers.

The good *St Petersburg Times* (W www.sptimes.com) has great up-to-date information on its Web site. Tune into National Public Radio (NPR) at 89.7 FM.

Try **Angel Laundromat** (☎ 727-822-9021; 1117 4th St N), about nine blocks north of downtown.

For medical emergencies, the area's largest hospital is **All Children's Hospital** (☎ 727-898-7451; 6th St S), between 8th and 9th Aves S; otherwise, there's **Bayfront Medical Center** (☎ 727-823-1234; 701 6th St S).

Those in need should call **The Line of Tampa Bay** (☎ 727-586-4297), a crisis hotline that is answered from 7pm to 11pm nightly. There's plenty more information on bars, restaurants and community events if you're willing to keep pressing keys on your Touch-Tone phone. Look for the biweekly *Watermark* (W www.watermarkonline.com), with up-to-date coverage of gay, lesbian and bisexual matters.

Salvador Dalí Museum

Boasting the largest collection of Dalí's work outside Spain, this must-see treasure trove (☎ 727-823-3767; W www.salvadordalimuseum.org; 1000 3rd St S; adult/senior/student $10/7/5, half price after 5pm on Thur; open 9:30am-5:30pm Mon-Sat, noon-5:30pm Sun) is easily one of St Petersburg's star attractions. While Dalí is best known for surrealist work, this $125 million collection covers the entire range of the artist's work: from early impressionism, cubism, still lifes and landscapes (1914 to 1927), through his transitional period (1928), onto surrealism (1929 to 1940) and back to classical works (1943 to 1989)…not to mention the collection of masterworks – 18 major oil paintings produced between 1948 and 1970. Of these, don't miss *The Discovery of America by Christopher Columbus* (1958–59); *The Ecumenical Council* (1960); *Galacidalacidesoxiribunucleicacid* (1962–63); and *The Hallucinogenic Toreador* (1969–70). How the heck did all these paintings end up in little old St Petersburg? Industrialist A Reynolds Morse began collecting Dalí in the 1940s and when he was searching for a location that would be suitable, the town had the common sense to woo him. Free, illuminating guided tours are offered throughout the day; be sure to take one or be prepared to be even more bewildered and bemused by the artist's work.

Florida International Museum

Ensconced in a former department store, this enormous space (☎ 727-822-3693; W www.floridamuseum.org; 100 2nd St N; adult/senior/student $12/11/6; open 10am-5pm Mon-Sat, noon-5pm Sun), a Smithsonian Institute Affiliate, hosts some of the country's most spectacular temporary exhibits. All those international blockbusters that you read about in the *London Times* make a stop here. Shows that have traveled here in recent years include: Norman Rockwell's Saturday

Evening Post Covers, Treasures of the Tzars, Splendors of Ancient Egypt, Alexander the Great and Treasures of the Titanic. The only two permanent exhibits – on the Cuban Missile Crisis and the Kennedy Collection (with a scale replica of the Oval Office, Rose Garden and Dallas motorcade) – are excellent and alone worth the price of admission.

St Petersburg Museum of Fine Arts

This is one of the state's best fine-arts museums (☎ 727-896-2667; w www.fine-arts.org; 255 Beach Dr NE; adult/senior/student $6/5/2, suggested donation on Sunday $3; open 10am-5pm Tues-Sat, 1pm-5pm Sun), with an enormous permanent collection that constitutes a very diverse and well-rounded history of art. Look for Asian, Indian and African art, pre-Columbian sculpture, photographic works, Cycladic sculpture from the 3rd century BC and American and European paintings and sculpture. Perhaps you non-Americans will get lucky and see some O'Keefe, Stella, Lichtenstein and Rauschenberg. Americans would be fortunate to admire fine European impressionists. Free regular tours and special events like concerts, plays and films are often scheduled; check with the front desk on arrival. The waterfront location is appealing, as are the courtyards.

St Petersburg Museum of History

This museum (☎ 727-894-1052; w www.museumofhistoryonline.org; 335 2nd Ave NE; adult/senior & student/child $5/4/2; open 10am-5pm Mon-Sat, 1pm-5pm Sun) features upwards of 60 permanent and rotating exhibits celebrating the town's long history. Check out a dog-powered butter churn, million-year-old fossils, a 400-year-old carved cypress canoe and a pioneer-era general store, not to mention taking a trip back in time to St Petersburg's Victorian influences. It also has a great display on the early days of aviation – St Petersburg was the takeoff site for America's first scheduled airline flight on January 1, 1914. The plane used for that flight, the Benoist Airboat

(restored in 1984), now hangs in the First Flight Gallery, which also has some interesting early aviation artifacts.

Florida Holocaust Museum

This memorial (☎ 727-820-0100; w www.flholocaustmuseum.org; 55 5th St S; adult/senior & student/child $6/5/2; open 10am-5pm Mon-Fri, noon-5pm Sat & Sun), the fourth largest in the USA, is worth a visit not just for its Holocaust exhibits but for those of Jewish life around the world. It also exhibits one of three boxcars in the USA used to transport prisoners to death camps in Poland. Visit the quiet meditation court before leaving and vow to make the museum's mission your own: promote tolerance today.

Coffee Pot Bayou

This old northeast neighborhood, the heart of which is between 19th and 30th Aves NE (but it's also very sweet around 9th Ave NE), east of 4th St, was developed in the 1920s and is lined with brick streets and authentic architecture. A 30-minute drive will reward you with an insider's view of St Petersburg beyond the museums and marinas. While you're in the area, drive over the Venetian-style Snell Island Bridge (at Coffee Pot Blvd and 21st Ave NE) to appreciate some Mediterranean-style architecture. To reach Coffee Pot, follow the waterfront north of downtown; take Bayshore Dr to North Shore Dr to Coffee Pot Blvd.

BayWalk

The downtown revitalization continues with this upscale shopping mall, bounded by 2nd and 3rd Aves N and 1st and 2nd Sts. The open-air emporium has lots of shops, eateries and the 20-screen **Muvico Theater** (☎ 727-502-9573), complete with stadium seating.

The Pier

Formerly a railroad pier (☎ 727-821-6164; 800 2nd Ave NE; open 10am-9pm Mon-Sat, 11am-9pm Sun), this dominating inverted pyramid is something of a tourist trap. It's, well, a long pier with a fishing platform at the end. And it's been converted to hold a five-story shopping mall with three restaurants, a free 2nd-floor **aquarium** (open 11am-7:30pm Mon-Sat, noon-6pm Sun) and a kids' museum (see below). Pier parking (including valet) costs $3, and there's a shuttle that runs between the parking lots and the action.

You can feed resident pelicans (who are standing around waiting for you) with fish food from the **baithouse** (☎ 727-821-3750); ten fish cost $5. Or you can rent a fishing rod for $10 a day; the price includes bait.

The story of **Little St Mary's** begins with Henry Taylor, who was never paid for his design work at St Mary's Church, located at 515 4th St S. Out of spite he built this Romanesque-revival miniature church and dubbed it Little St Mary's. The only rub: it's a toilet. This is perhaps the only toilet in Florida that is also a historic landmark.

South of the pier, **Demen's Landing** waterfront park (Bayshore Dr SE at 1st Ave S), with picnic facilities, hosts **American Stage in the Park** (☎ 727-822-8814), a Shakespeare festival that takes place from mid-April to mid-May. The park, by the way, was named for a Russian-born railroad developer who brought passengers to the area in the late 1880s.

Great Explorations Museum 'Hands-on' reaches new heights at this fun science museum (☎ 727-821-8992; W www.greatexplorations.org; 800 2nd Ave NE; age 3 to 54 yrs/senior $4/2; open 10am-8pm Mon-Sat, 11am-5pm Sun). It really lets kids get down and dirty with a Touch Tunnel, an 8-foot-long, pitch-black maze and a dino dig (where kids dig for fossils in the sand and try to reconstruct the creature). Fire up the imagination with interactive computer games, a reptile room (snakes, scorpions and spiders, anyone?) and a floor maze.

First United Methodist Church

This 1925 Gothic Revival church (☎ 727-894-4661; 212 3rd St N), listed on the National Register of Historic Places, has some pretty nice Tiffany-style stained-glass windows. Sunday services are held at 8am and 11am.

Gizella Kopsick Palm Arboretum

This 2-acre arboretum (☎ 727-893-7335; cnr N Shore Dr & 10th Ave NE; admission free;

open dawn to dusk daily) contains upwards of 300 different exotic and rare palms and cycads representing about 75 worldwide species. Follow the brick walkways to inspect the wildly diverse jelly palm, windmill palm and triangle palm, but don't overlook the garden-variety gru gru palm.

Sunken Gardens

Opened in 1935, this garden (☎ 727-551-3100; 1825 4th St N; adult/senior/child $7/5/3; open 9:30am-5pm daily), with lots of water features, consists of four tropical acres and a walk-through butterfly aviary. The city of St Petersburg took over the site recently and plans to revamp it.

Biking

The **Friendship Trail Bridge** (☎ 727-549-6099), aka the old Gandy Bridge and US 92, is basically a 2.6-mile-long dedicated biking, walking and in-line skating path that runs alongside the Gandy Bridge, which connects St Petersburg and Tampa. Look for the trailhead on 34th St S near 8th Ave.

See also Pinellas Trail under Around Clearwater Beach, later in this chapter.

Organized Tours

Biplane Rides (☎ 727-895-6266), at Albert Whitted Airport near Bayfront Center, offer downtown tours in a 1933 WACO biplane originally owned by William Randolph Hearst. Tours start at $90 for up to three people, for 15 to 20 minutes; they're best taken in the morning.

Narrated **Duck Tours** (☎ 727-432-3825; W www.ducktoursoftampabay.com; 200 2nd Ave NE at The Pier), which take place within authentic WWII army amphibious vehicles, waddle by downtown attractions and then plunge into the bay near Demen's Landing for a view of St Petersburg from the water. Tours depart daily in winter (call for off-season schedule) and cost $18.50 for adults, $16.50 seniors and $10 for children.

Places to Stay

For camping options, see Fort Desoto Park under Around St Petersburg and Places to

Stay under St Pete Beach, both later in this chapter.

Hotels & Motels The **Kelly Hotel** (☎ 727-822-4141; 326 1st Ave N; dorm beds $15/20, singles/doubles $39/49 daily, $145/165 weekly), on the National Register of Historic Places, has a nice staff, 65 spartan rooms and hostel-style dorms. Rooms on higher floors are cheerier, but all are basically clean, and many have a view of adjacent brick walls. One hostel-style floor has eight rooms, some of which have four bunks and some of which are semiprivate rooms. Dorm rooms, while clean enough and air-conditioned, are not the cheeriest in the world.

Beach Park Motel (☎ 727-898-6325, 800-657-7687; 300 Beach Dr NE; rooms $74) has 26 older but good rooms with fridges and a great location.

St Petersburg Hilton (☎ 727-894-5000, 800-774-1500; **W** www.stpetehilton.com; 333 1st St S; rooms from $89/139 summer/winter) has 333 Hilton-ish rooms with a fine downtown location, restaurants, bars and a pool and fitness center.

Holiday Inn (☎ 727-822-4814, 800-283-7829; **W** www.holiday-inn.com; 234 3rd Ave N; rooms $109/139 summer/winter), a great choice with 70 rooms, is *almost* more like a B&B than a motel, since it's partially housed in a 1926 Victorian, complete with a wraparound porch and some antiques.

There are a bunch of cheap motels of varying quality on 4th St N (which runs right into downtown) and 34th St N (which is just west of I-275). Here are the best of the bunch: **Tops Motel & Apartments** (☎ 727-526-9071; 7141 4th St N; units $35-40/40-50 summer/winter), with 16 rooms and apartments; **Days Inn Central** (☎ 727-321-2958, 800-325-2525; 650 34th St N; rooms $60-66), with 28 rooms, a third of which have kitchens; and **Comfort Inn** (☎ 727-323-3100, 800-228-5150; 1400 34th St N; rooms $59-79/69-89 summer/winter), with 75 rooms, half of which are efficiencies.

Resorts A large, pink and flashy grande dame on the bay, **Renaissance Vinoy Resort** (☎ 727-894-1000, 800-468-3571, **W** www .renaissancehotels.com; 501 5th Ave NE; rooms from $179/199 summer/winter) is reminiscent of a bygone era. Built in 1925 the national historic landmark boasts 360 richly furnished guest rooms (many with bay views), a day spa, huge fitness center, excellent golf and tennis and opulent dining and entertainment areas.

B&Bs One of St Petersburg's least-expensive B&Bs, **Bay Shore Manor** (☎ 727-822-3438; **W** www.bayshoremanor.com; 635 12th Ave NE; rooms $69-84) includes a German-style breakfast with coffee, milk, juice, breads, cold cuts, cheese, eggs and cereal. Each of the seven rooms has a TV, coffeemaker, microwave and mini-refrigerator.

Inn at the Bay (☎ 727-822-1700, 888-873-2122; **W** www.innatthebay.com; 126 4th Ave NE; rooms & suites $109-250), with 12 guest rooms in an old northeast neighborhood house that dates to 1910, offers a full breakfast, feather beds, data ports and robes. Most bathrooms have two-person whirlpool tubs.

Bayboro House B&B (☎ 727-823-4955, 877-823-4955; **W** www.bayborohousebandb .com; 1719 Beach Dr SE; rooms $129/149-229 summer/winter), a waterfront B&B built in 1907 in a quiet neighborhood on Tampa Bay, has lots of Victorian charm (read: lace and antiques) and a wraparound verandah. Each of the eight rooms and suites has a private bath and a VCR/TV. You'll also appreciate beach chairs, beach towels and a pool and spa.

Mansion House B&B (☎ 727-821-9391, 800-274-7520; **W** www.mansionbandb.com; 105 5th Ave N; rooms $99-165/149-220 summer/winter), with a tranquil pool and courtyard garden, has 12 rooms and a suite in two wonderful old houses. Other pluses include gracious hosts, complimentary afternoon wine, full breakfast and a great location.

Places to Eat
Biff-Burger/Buffy's BBQ (☎ 727-527-5297; 3939 49th St N; dishes $1-6; open 6am-10:30pm Sun-Thur, 6am-midnight Fri & Sat), kitschy with a 1957 Chevy on the roof, is worth going out of your way for. The classic drive-in has live bands and entertainment

SOUTHWEST

along with the burger and BBQ Grub. Friday night is car night, when everyone brings their souped-up wheels and vies for prizes and kids compete in hula hoop contests; Saturday night is the same deal – for bikers.

Central Coffee Shop (☎ 727-821-1125; 530 Central Ave; dishes $2-6; open 6:30am-1pm Mon-Fri) is the place for no-frills meals.

South Gate Restaurant (☎ 727-823-7071; 29 3rd St N; dishes $3-7; open 7am-5:30pm daily) serves cheap breakfasts all day, cheap sandwiches at lunch, and good Greek salads and chicken gyros.

Tangelo's Grill (☎ 727-894-1695; 226 1st Ave N; dishes $4-10; open 11am-6pm Mon, 11am-8pm Tues-Thur, 11am-9pm Fri & Sat) serves Cuban-style sandwiches like roast pork on grilled Cuban bread, Spanish grouper and some Caribbean dishes.

The Garden (☎ 727-896-3800; 217 Central Ave; lunch $5-8, dinner mains $9-15; open 11:30am-2am daily), the oldest restaurant in town, makes a good lunchtime pesto pasta and Lebanese sampler plate. Mediterranean-influenced dinner dishes might include grilled lamb chops or wild mushroom pasta. Otherwise, just choose a few dishes from the tapas menu. The Garden also hosts live jazz (see Entertainment below).

Number 9 Bangkok (☎ 727-894-5990; 571 Central Ave; dishes $7-11; open 11am-3pm & 5pm-10pm Mon-Sat) has decent Thai food like pad Thai and yellow curry with beef or shrimp.

Just north of downtown, **Fourth Street Shrimp Store** (☎ 727-822-0325; 1006 4th St N; dishes $7-16; open 11am-9pm daily) is a fun place with murals as far as the eye can see. It's perfect for quick dinners like fresh grouper (and duh, shrimp). In addition to baskets of fried fish, their big seller (and a great bargain) is a 22-piece shrimp platter with fries and slaw for a mere $7. But you could go all out with a platter of grouper, clams and shrimp for $16.

Jo Jo's in Citta (☎ 727-894-0075; 200 Central Ave; lunch specials $6, dinner mains $9-15; open 11am-10pm Sun-Thur, 11am-11pm Fri & Sat) has decent Italian dishes like baked pasta and veal piccata. Midday subs and pizza are cheaper.

Bertoni Italian Restaurant (☎ 727-822-5503; 16 2nd St N; mains $12-20; open 5pm-10pm Mon-Sat) offers fancier Italian dishes along with fine service, a nice bar and comfortable surroundings.

Entertainment

The local entertainment scene is less dynamic than its Russian counterpart's, and that says a lot! For recorded information on upcoming events, call the **Hotline** (☎ 727-892-5700).

Theater The area's oldest professional theater ensemble, **American Stage** (☎ 727-822-8814; W www.americanstage.org; 211 3rd St S) stages American classics and Broadway shows.

The **Bayfront Center** (☎ 727-892-5767; 400 1st St S) houses the 8400-seat Times Bayfront Arena and the 2000-seat Mahaffey Theater as well as hosting Broadway shows, concerts and some sporting events.

Live Music Also called the Palace of Pleasure, the **Coliseum Ballroom** (☎ 727-892-5202; 535 4th Ave N) opened in 1924 and, over the years, big bands, classical orchestras and rock bands have all played here. It also hosts indoor tennis matches, and in 1985, it made its film debut in *Cocoon* in that incredible ballroom scene. The red oak dance floor is classic. If you're here on a Wednesday, definitely hit the big band Tea Dance sessions, which run from 1pm to 3:30pm. Most events are BYOB.

State Theatre (☎ 727-895-3045; W www.statemedia.com; 687 Central Ave), a restored art deco theater (1927), has live music regularly – from the acoustic stylings of unplugged women to 'old wave' to new bands. Buy your tickets at the bar ($5 to $10) and head upstairs.

Ticketmaster (☎ 813-287-8844) sells tickets with a surcharge to most events.

Bars & Clubs At **Jannus Landing** (☎ 727-896-1244; W www.jannuslanding.net; 200 1st Ave N), an outdoor courtyard behind the Bertoni Italian Restaurant (see Places to Eat earlier), there are several weekly concerts by local and national bands. It's very casual – shorts, T-shirts and jeans. There is a full cash bar, and all ages are admitted – but you'll be carded if you look under 30 and try to buy alcohol. They also serve burgers, hot dogs and such catered by Harvey's 4th St Grill. Tickets are generally about $15. You can get tickets from the nearby **Detroit Liquor Store** (☎ 727-821-7466; 201 Central Ave).

The 2nd-floor **A Taste for Wine** (☎ 727-895-1623; 241 Central Ave; open 1pm-9pm Tues-Thur, 2pm-midnight Fri & Sat, 2pm-6pm Sun), with a New Orleans–style balcony, is a fun place with wine tastings, wines by the glass, appetizers (unless you *want* to drink on an empty stomach) and a very nice atmosphere.

The Garden (see Places to Eat earlier), with indoor and outdoor seating and a martini bar, also has live jazz outdoors with the Buster Cooper Jazz Trio every Friday and Saturday from 9pm to 1:30am. On some Thursdays, they have a DJ or live music, too.

Ferg's Sports Bar & Grill (☎ 727-822-4562; 1320 Central Ave; open 11am-2am Mon-Sat, noon-10pm Sun), a friendly neighborhood place with an outdoor bar, really gets hopping before and after gametime.

Central Cigars (☎ 727-898-2442; 273 Central Ave; open 10am-10pm Sun-Thur, 10pm-midnight Fri & Sat) carries an enormous selection of cigars (Arturo Fuente, Ous X, Padrón, Partagas) as well as a full line of humidors and accessories. Stop into their cigar bar, where you can sink into an overstuffed leather chair, sample smokes, sip port and catch up on all your cigar-related reading.

Spectator Sports

From April through September, **Tropicana Field** (☎ 727-825-3333; w www.devilrays.com; 1 Stadium Dr; tickets $2-19) is home to the Tampa Bay Devil Rays, one of major-league baseball's newest expansion teams and also, sadly, one of its worst. But the games are fun anyway. You'll find parking (about $5) all over the place around 10th St and 4th Ave S. The Devil Rays play spring-training games at **Florida Power Park** (☎ 727-822-3384; 230 1st St S) in March.

You can take a behind-the-scenes tour of Tropicana Field ($5 adults, $3 seniors and children) and check out the dugouts, press box, batting tunnels, weight room and field. On non-game days, the 45- to 90-minute tours are given from 10am to 4pm Monday through Friday; on game days, they run from 10am to noon Monday through Friday.

Shopping

Antique stores litter downtown, especially on the north side of Central Ave between 6th and 11th Sts (it's a street waiting to happen, really), and along 4th St. If you're really interested, pick up a good brochure at the Chamber of Commerce. Specifically check out the **Gas Plant Antique Arcade** (☎ 727-895-0368; 1246 Central Ave), with 150 dealers on four floors.

Florida Craftsmen Gallery (☎ 727-821-7391; 501 Central Ave) features over 150 statewide artists and craftspeople in this retail and exhibition space.

The Arts Center (☎ 727-822-7872; 719 Central Ave), with five galleries, shows paintings, ceramics, printmaking, drawing and mixed media art.

Tyrone Square (☎ 727-345-0126; 66th St & 22nd Ave N), the area's big shopping mall, has 150 retail stores, including a Burdines, Dillard's, Sears, Gap, Borders, Disney Store and Sunglass Hut.

Getting There & Around

Although **St Petersburg–Clearwater International Airport** (☎ 727-453-7800; w www.fly2pie.com; Roosevelt Blvd & Hwy 686 in Clearwater) is served by several major carriers, if you're flying into the region, you'll probably land in Tampa; see the Tampa Getting There & Away section earlier in the chapter. If you're in the mood for a quick jaunt to Key West, check flights out of here.

The **Greyhound bus station** (☎ 727-898-1496; 180 9th St N) dispatches regular service to and from all over Florida. The trip from St Petersburg to Miami takes 6 to 10 hours ($35.50/64.50 one-way/roundtrip); to Orlando takes 3 to 4 hours ($15.25/27.25); to Tampa takes a half-hour to 1½ hours ($7.25/11.25).

Amtrak (☎ 800-872-7245) provides a continuing rail shuttle-bus link between Tampa and St Petersburg; it'll drop you at the inconvenient Parkside Mall at the intersection of Hwy 19 and Park Blvd. From there take PSTA (see below) bus No 75 (hourly departures) to Madeira Beach, where you catch the Suncoast Beach Trolley north to Sand Key and change to PSTA bus No 80 for Clearwater Beach, or you take the Suncoast Beach Trolley south to St Pete Beach.

Several **car rental** companies have offices at the airport. St Petersburg is 289 miles from Miami, 84 miles from Orlando. From Tampa, the best route is I-275 south, which runs right through downtown St Petersburg and continues across the Sunshine Skyway Bridge; it connects with I-75 and US Hwy 41 (Tamiami Trail) on the south side of Tampa Bay. From Sarasota, take I-75 north to I-275 across the Sunshine Skyway. From Orlando, take I-4 south to I-75 to I-275.

PSTA bus No 79 connects the airport to downtown. By car to downtown, take Roosevelt Blvd (Hwy 686) south, across the jig on Ulmerton Rd, to I-275 south.

To Clearwater, take Roosevelt Blvd north to the Bayside (49th St) Bridge and go west on Causeway Blvd.

Pinellas Suncoast Transit Authority (PSTA; ☎ 727-530-9911; W www.psta.net; 340 2nd Ave N; open 7am-5:45pm Mon-Sat, 8am-11:30am & 12:30pm-4pm Sun) has a downtown bus station at Williams Park, between 3rd and 4th Sts. They sell daily/weekly/monthly unlimited-ride Go Cards ($3/12/40) and give transit information.

PSTA serves Clearwater and Tarpon Springs from St Petersburg; consult the very good system map available from most Chambers of Commerce. Hourly departures from St Petersburg to St Pete Beach take about an hour on trolley No 35 (fare $1, bills accepted).

The excellent **Looper** (☎ 727-821-5166), which you can use as a 30-minute orientation tour since there is narration, is a bargain since it stops at a dozen popular museums, hotels and shops (including The Pier) around downtown. Tickets cost $1 per ride (50¢ for seniors). The service operates 10am

to 5pm Monday through Friday and 11am to 5pm Saturday and Sunday.

Getting around and parking here is a cinch. Just be sure to have a lot of quarters since you'll be feeding the hungry meters. Consider parking at The Pier and taking the Looper trolley.

To get to St Pete Beach, take I-275 to Hwy 682, which connects to the Pinellas County Pkwy and west to the beach, or take Central Ave due west to either the Treasure Island Causeway or turn south on 66th St to the Corey Causeway.

AROUND ST PETERSBURG

The following are all south of downtown, near the southern tip of the peninsula.

Boyd Hill Nature Park

This great 245-acre park (☎ 727-893-7326; 1101 Country Club Way S; adult/child $2/1; open 9am-5pm daily Nov-Mar, 9am-5pm Fri-Mon & Wed, 9am-8pm Tues & Thur Apr-Oct) is an oasis hidden in the midst of an urban area. Partly on the shores of Lake Maggiore, this natural butterfly habitat has about 3½ miles of nature trails and boardwalks that traverse scrubland, pine flatwoods, swamp woodlands and coastal willows. On Willow Marsh Trail you'll likely hear young alligators squeaking and see bald eagles, snowy egrets, box turtles and opossums among the live oaks, cypress trees and ferns. The friendly rangers here offer lots of good walks (check at the entrance when you arrive); daily tram tours depart at 10:30am April through October, 3pm daily November through March. There's a picnic area, a playground and paths for bicycles, but not in-line skates or skateboards.

From downtown take I-275 south to exit 4, turn east onto 54th Ave S to ML King Jr Blvd S, then north to the first traffic signal (Country Club Way S) and turn left (west).

Fort DeSoto Park & Beach

With a beach that consistently ranks among the top 20 in the US, this 1100-plus-acre county park (☎ 727-582-2267; W www.fortdesoto.com; admission free; open dawn to dusk daily) is located on Mullet Key south of downtown, kind of between St Pete Beach and St Petersburg. It has 4 miles of self-guided nature and recreational trails for biking, blading, walking and hiking, and about 7 miles of swimmable and shallow shoreline. North Beach is on the Gulf side, and has lifeguards; East Beach fronts Tampa Bay; both have fast-food concessions. There are also two fishing piers with bait shops and rod rentals, if you're so inclined. The fort, by the way, was built during the Spanish-American War. To get here from St Petersburg, take I-275 south to exit 4 and follow the signs; it's at 3500 Pinellas Bayway S. There is an 85¢ toll on the approach road.

Fort DeSoto Park Campground (☎ 727-582-2267; 3500 Pinellas Bayway S; sites $23/33 summer/winter) has 235 shaded tent and RV sites, many of which are waterside. Make reservations for two- to 14-day stays, within 30 days of your stay, *in person only* at the camp office above (open 8am-9pm daily), the Clearwater office (631 Chestnut St; open 8am-5pm Mon-Fri) or the St Petersburg office (courthouse, 501 1st Ave N, Room A116). Reserve well in advance; yeah, right.

Sunshine Skyway Bridge

Okay, it's not exactly an attraction, but it's impressive nonetheless: the 4-mile-long Sunshine Skyway Bridge ($1 toll) spans Tampa Bay south of St Petersburg. It's dramatic on approach and once you're on it. It's actually the continuation of I-275, which meets up with I-75 on the south side of the bay. Built to replace the old span, which was destroyed in 1980 when the *Summit Venture* rammed into its base, the Sunshine Skyway is a shimmering modern bridge. Each of its supports are surrounded by 'dolphins': gigantic shock absorbers capable of withstanding the force of an 87,000-ton vessel traveling at 10 knots (talk about shutting the barn door after the…ah, never mind). The *Summit Venture* weighed 34,500 tons and was traveling at 8 knots when it struck the old bridge.

Much of the old bridge still stands, and has been converted into supposedly the world's largest fishing pier, spanning almost 2 miles.

ST PETE BEACH
population 9000

With a great white-sand beach and clear, blue water, St Pete Beach (they officially changed the name in the early 1990s) makes a great day or overnight trip from St Petersburg. Pass-a-Grille, a more quiet and residential neighborhood with sandy streets and little houses, is at the southernmost tip of St Pete Beach.

See the St Petersburg Getting There & Around section for information on how to get here by bus and car. Excellent PSTA Suncoast Beach Trolleys frequently ply Gulf Blvd, from Pass-a-Grille (just south of St Pete Beach) north to Sand Key, where you can connect with the Clearwater Beach Jolley Trolley.

Orientation & Information

Part of a 30-mile-long string of barrier beaches west of St Petersburg, St Pete Beach is on Long Key, about 10 miles west of downtown St Petersburg across the Corey Causeway or the Pinellas County Bayway. The island is long and narrow, and the main (and only) artery is Gulf Blvd (Hwy 699).

The **St Pete Beach Chamber of Commerce** (☎ 727-360-6957; **w** www.tampabaybeaches .com; 6990 Gulf Blvd; open 9am-5pm Mon-Fri) has tons of pamphlets and coupons and an excellent (free) area beach map.

Change money at **Bank of America** (4105 Gulf Blvd & 7500 Gulf Blvd).

Wash at the **Washboard Laundry** (☎ 727-360-0674; 6350 Gulf Blvd).

Bikers should head to **Beach Cyclist** (☎ 727-367-5001; 7517 Blind Pass Blvd), where rentals cost $5 hourly, $20 daily and $50 weekly.

Don CeSar Beach Resort & Spa

This 275-room landmark resort (☎ 727-360-1883, 800-282-1116; **w** www.doncesar.com; 3400 Gulf Blvd; rooms from $209/244 summer/winter) occupies a strategic stretch of prime beachfront. It'll probably be the first thing you'll notice when you pull into St Pete Beach: built in 1928, this monster of a hotel was a hot spot for F Scott Fitzgerald, Clarence Darrow, Lou Gehrig and Al

SOUTHWEST

Capone. In 1942 the enormous pink palace was bought by the US Army and turned into a hospital and convalescent center for army personnel. Stripped of all its splendor, the building was abandoned in 1967 by the Veterans Administration, which had taken it over after the war. It was then reopened in 1973, and from 1985 to 1989 it was completely restored. Today, the resort hotel is complete with a European-style spa, fine dining and a extensive kids' program. They don't make 'em like this anymore. If you want an excuse to loiter, have a drink at the poolside Beachcomber Bar. Or rent $10 chairs in front of the hotel on the beach.

Gulf Beaches Historical Museum

This museum (☎ 727-552-1610; 115 10th Ave at Pass-a-Grille Beach; admission free; open 10am-4pm Thur & Sat, 1pm-4pm Sun), about 2 miles south of the Don CeSar hotel, is located in the former Pass-a-Grille Church (1917) – the first to be built on a west coast barrier island. In addition to a large collection of beach photographs and artifacts dating from the early 1800s, the museum has a good selection of old postcards and church memorabilia. Take Gulf Blvd south past the Don CeSar; the road becomes Pass-a-Grille Blvd, which runs into 10th Ave.

Organized Tours

Dolphin Landings Charter Boat Center (☎ 727-367-4488; w www.dolphinlandings .com; 4737 Gulf Blvd) offers several tours, including two-hour daily dolphin-watching excursions ($25 for adults, $15 for kids), four-hour shelling excursions ($35/25) and sunset sails ($25 per person). Prices include free soft drinks (and a cooler, so you can BYO beer); reservations are required.

Places to Stay

KOA St Petersburg/Madeira Beach (☎ 727-392-2233, 800-562-7714; 5400 95th St N; sites without/with hookups $30/39 summer, $40/49 winter, Kamping Kabins $58-68), set on the Pinellas bike trail north of St Pete Beach, is about 2 miles from Madeira Beach and has a whopping 350 shaded and grassy sites, 60 'kamping kabins,' canoe rentals and a pool.

From downtown St Petersburg, take I-275 north to 38th Ave N and go west for 5½ miles; take a left onto 66th St, then a right onto Tyrone Blvd, and go 1½ miles to 95th St. Turn right and it's about a half-mile ahead.

Lamara Motel Apartments (☎ 727-360-7521, 800-211-5108; w www.lamara.com; 520 73rd Ave; units $44-49/65-75 summer/winter), with a pool and 16 units featuring kitchens, is just west of Gulf Blvd.

Palm Crest Motel (☎ 727-360-9327, 888-558-1247; w www.palmcrest.com; 3848 Gulf Blvd; rooms $57-76/85-103 summer/winter) has 18 units with kitchens and a pool.

Travel Lodge of St Pete Beach (☎ 727-367-2711, 800-237-8918; 6300 Gulf Blvd; rooms from $80/104 summer/winter) has 200 very nice rooms and an Olympic-sized heated pool. Sound familiar?

Pasa Tiempo B&B (☎ 727-367-9907; w www.pasa-tiempo.com; 7141 Bay St; rooms & suites $110-150) has eight units (one with a kitchen, one with a private terrace) facing east toward the Intracoastal Waterway. Afternoon wine and cheese are included and the lush, brick-paved courtyard makes a nice respite.

The best and less expensive motel beachside chain is **Howard Johnson** (☎ 727-360-7041, 800-231-1419; 6100 Gulf Blvd; rooms $90/115 summer/winter), with 130 contemporary rooms and a large pool on a quiet stretch of beach.

Alden Beach Resort (☎ 727-360-7081, 800-237-2530; w www.aldenbeachresort .com; 5900 Gulf Blvd; units $97-179/125-254 summer/winter), a step up from their neighbors, has two pools, tennis courts, a Jacuzzi, bar, barbecue area and good service. The six-story family-owned resort has 143 waterfront rooms and one-bedroom suites.

Places to Eat

Aunt Heidi's Italian Restaurant (☎ 727-367-3448; 6340 Gulf Blvd; lunch $4-7, dinner mains $9-11; open 11am-10pm Mon-Sat, 2pm-10pm Sun) is fine for a quick bite. Hoagies, pizza or baked ziti, anyone?

Bruno's (☎ 727-367-4420; 432 75th Ave; mains $10-17; open 4pm-10pm Mon-Sat), a decent Northern Italian place, dishes up fettuccine primavera, veal rollatini and chicken cacciatore.

Hurricane's Seafood Restaurant (☎ 727-360-9558; 807 Gulf Way; lunch $8-10, dinner mains $14-20; open 8am-1am daily), in the Pass-a-Grille neighborhood, has been a popular seafood eatery and hangout for locals and visitors since forever. Even though the food's sometimes inconsistent, you can't beat the sunset views. They offer live entertainment Wednesday through Sunday and a happenin' rooftop deck-cum-bar. Gulf Way, by the way, is on the opposite side of the peninsula from Gulf Blvd and runs parallel to it.

Ted Peter's Famous Smoked Fish (☎ 727-381-7931; 1350 Pasadena Ave; dishes $10-15; open 11:30am-7:30pm Wed-Mon), on the way to St Pete Beach from St Petersburg, has been smoking fish since the 1950s. It's an institution. Their smoked salmon, mackerel and mullet, straight from the little smoke-house, are succulently fresh. Get takeout for the beach, or head next door where they serve more smoked seafood specialties and patrons drink lots of beer by the fireplace.

Crabby Bill's (☎ 727-360-8858; 5100 Gulf Blvd; dishes $10-29; open 11:30am-10pm daily), a casual place with picnic tables (or inside dining) and water views, serves all kinds of fried seafood but obviously specializes in crab.

Maritana Grille (☎ 727-360-1882; 3400 Gulf Blvd; mains $27-32; open 5:30pm-10pm daily), serving creative American cuisine with slight Caribbean overtones, is one of the area's better restaurants. Try the pan-seared sea scallops with a lemongrass and ginger risotto.

CLEARWATER BEACH

Despite being overdeveloped and lined with beachfront cookie-cutter hotels, Clearwater Beach draws visitors because of incredible white-sand beaches, a large fishing fleet (read: fresh fish dinners), and its proximity to Tampa and St Petersburg. It also has a great HI/AYH-member hostel and is a prime area for kayaking, shelling, bicycling and broiling yourself on the beach – which just about sums up the local 'tourist attractions.'

Backpackers will appreciate the scale of the island; unlike many Florida towns, it's only 3½ miles long, and it's easy to get around by foot or bicycle.

Orientation & Information

This northernmost barrier island is about 22 miles north of St Pete Beach and 2 miles west of downtown Clearwater (a separate city on the mainland) over the Memorial Causeway (Hwy 60), which to the east becomes Causeway Blvd. From here the road south is S Gulfview Blvd and north is Mandalay Ave, Clearwater Beach's main drag. Pier 60 is right at the roundabout where these three roads meet. From St Petersburg, it's about a half-hour drive or a 1½-hour bus ride.

The **Clearwater Beach Welcome Center** (☎ 727-461-0011; W www.beachchamber .com; open 9am to one hour prior to sunset daily) is located at Pier 60. This and the youth hostel (see Places to Stay) are the best sources of local information.

The **Clearwater Beach Public Library** (☎ 727-462-6890; 483 Mandalay Ave; open 9am-5pm Mon-Fri) has free Internet access, but it's limited to 30 minutes daily.

Wash clothes 24/7 at **Beach Coin** (575 Mandalay Ave), north of the rotary.

Clearwater Marine Aquarium

This nonprofit aquarium (☎ 727-447-0980, 888-239-9414; W www.cmaquarium.org; 249 Windward Passage; adult/child $8.75/6.25; open 9am-5pm Mon-Fri, 9am-4pm Sat, 11am-4pm Sun) is a very nice place, dedicated to educating the public and to rescuing and rehabilitating marine animals like dolphins, fish, sea otters and threatened loggerhead and endangered Kemp's ridley turtles. Informative presentations run throughout the day. Inquire about their two-hour Sea Life Safari with an onboard biologist; their dolphin trainer-for-a-day program; and their trips to monitor loggerhead nests (May through October). Between Clearwater and Clearwater Beach, off Memorial Causeway (Hwy 60), it's conveniently located since the Jolley Trolley stops here.

Pier 60

Sunset celebrations at Pier 60 are equivalent to those at Key West's Mallory Square. Jugglers and magicians perform, musicians play and craftspeople and artists hawk their wares. Head down to the pier nightly, two hours before and after sunset. The pier is also a favorite spot for fishing and the public beach is popular with college students and watersports concessionaires.

Activities

The bay side of the beach, filled with mangrove islands, is prime for **canoeing**. The calm Gulf waters also promote easy paddling up to the beautiful retreat of Caladesi Island (see Around Clearwater Beach later in this chapter). The hostel has free canoes for its guests.

Just south of the rotary on Coronado Dr and across from the pier, activity booths hawk their services, including **Parasail City** (☎ 727-449-0566), which will get you up for $40 to $60, depending on how high you want to go.

You can **bike** along the beach or the Pinellas Trail, a 47-mile bicycle path (see Around Clearwater Beach later in this chapter); the hostel rents bicycles ($5 daily). Otherwise, head to **Transportation Station** (☎ 727-443-3188; 652 Gulfview Blvd), which rents them for $5 to $8 hourly, $20 to $26 daily; the higher prices are for mountain bikes and bikes with more gears.

Organized Tours

See Resorts, later, for the historical tour of the Belleview Biltmore hotel.

Dolphin Encounter (☎ 727-442-7433; w www.dolphinencounter.org), opposite Pier 60, runs very good, frequent, daily, 80-minute dolphin-watching cruises into the Gulf of Mexico ($13 for adults, $7.50 for kids). They also have daily sunset cruises for the same price.

Captain Memo's Pirate Cruise (☎ 727-446-2587; w www.captainmemo.com), opposite Pier 60, operates daily two-hour cruises aboard a replica pirate ship ($28 for adults, $18 for kids). Mom and Dad get blurry eyed with free beer and wine, while

the kids go treasure hunting and take home swashbuckler fantasies.

Places to Stay

Hostels A resort-style hostel, **Clearwater Beach International Youth Hostel** (☎ 727-443-1211; w www.clearwaterbeachhostel.com; 606 Bay Esplanade; dorms HI/AYH members/nonmembers $12/13 nightly, $75/84 weekly) has 38 beds, a swimming pool surrounded by lush gardens, a picnic area and tiki huts. Private rooms are also available ($39-43/47-51 summer/winter). Best of all, it's only a three-minute walk to the beautiful beach. In addition to having kitchen and laundry facilities, the air-conditioned hostel rents linens and offers free canoes (as long as you fork over a $50 deposit). For diversion, there is table tennis, shuffleboard and a barbecue; a nearby recreation center has tennis, basketball and volleyball.

Motels & Hotels The **Patio Motel** (☎ 727-442-1862; w www.patiomotel.com; 15 Somerset St; rooms $45/55 summer/winter, apartments $46-74/55-88 summer/winter), about a mile north of Pier 60 (at the quiet end of town), has 14 clean units, many of which look right out to the Gulf. Even though there isn't a pool, the motel is on the water and has a private beach.

Koli-Bree Motel (☎ 727-461-6223; 440 E Shore Dr; units $56/82 summer/winter), with only 10 apartments, is a clean and tidy choice northeast of the rotary. It doesn't have a pool, but it's only three blocks from the beach.

Palm Pavilion Inn (☎ 727-446-6777; w www.palmpavilioninn.com; 18 Bay Esplanade; rooms $59-89/87-125 summer/winter) has a pool and 29 units, only a few of which have a kitchen. It's across from the beach, but its adjacent Grill and Bar is on the beach and has live music most nights. Light sleepers need not apply.

There's a denser concentration of louder, more action-oriented hotels south of the rotary. Chains all along the beach include the ultra-pricey **Hilton Clearwater Beach Resort** (☎ 727-461-3222, 800-753-3854; 400 Mandalay Ave; rooms $159-299), with 425 rooms;

the medium-pricey **Holiday Inn Sunspree Resort** (☎ 727-447-9566, 800-465-4329; 715 S Gulfview Blvd; rooms $139-199), with 216 rooms; and the cheaper **Days Inn** (☎ 727-447-8444, 800-329-7466; 100 Coronado Dr; rooms $69/110 summer/winter), with 80 rooms.

Resorts The 21-acre **Belleview Biltmore Resort & Spa** (☎ 727-373-3000, 800-237-8947; **w** www.belleviewbiltmore.com; 25 Belleview Blvd; rooms from $99), off Hwy 60 and Fort Harrison Ave, in Belleair on the mainland, was built in the 1890s by railroad magnate Henry Plant as a retreat for wealthy northeasterners. In the 1950s, the Duke of Windsor, his dogs and possibly Mrs Simpson stayed here. The Duke even wrote part of his memoirs here while dancing with the bandleader's wife and the staff; he was apparently a hit at costume balls. As was, we assume, Lady Thatcher, who stayed here. It's not exactly a backpacker's hangout: while the pool and opulent spa are certainly charming, the atmosphere is akin to a swanky golf retreat. The best rates are actually bed and breakfast packages.

If these 300 or so rooms and suites are too rich for your blood, take a tour; there's one daily at 11am for $5. For a mere $10 more, it'll include a buffet lunch at their restaurant. You'll get to see the tunnels underneath the hotel, a museum and a section devoted to the Army Air Corps, which was stationed here during WWII. Still not striking the right chord? You could always just soak away your troubles at the spa.

Places to Eat
There are plenty of places, but Frenchy's really has a lock on the market; in fact, there are even more Frenchy's outlets than mentioned here.

Computer Port Cafe (☎ 727-441-2667; 432 Poinsettia Ave; open 9am-6pm Sun-Thur, 9am-10pm Fri & Sat) has smoothies, sweets, fast Internet connections, coffee and an open mike night on Saturday (7pm to 10pm). It's a block north of the roundabout.

Frenchy's Original Cafe (☎ 727-446-3607; 41 Baymont; dishes $5-10; open 11:30am-11pm Sun-Thur, 11:30am-midnight Fri &

Sat), 'the original hole in the wall' dating *way* back to 1981, is a tiny local hangout with picnic benches. Specials include seafood gumbo, smoked fish spread, grouper sandwiches and crabby shrimp sandwiches. It's off Mandalay Ave north of the rotary.

Frenchy's Rockaway Grill on the Beach (☎ 727-446-4844; 7 Rockaway St; dishes $8-14; open 11am-midnight daily), off Mandalay Ave north of the center of town, serves salads, excellent she-crab soup, burgers, seafood and a few Mexican and Jamaican dishes. Alternately, check out the live music on most nights, pool tables and a happy hour (4pm to 7pm).

Entertainment
The beachfront tiki bar at **Shephards** (☎ 727-441-6875; 601 S Gulfview Blvd) has reggae on Saturday and Sunday afternoons. Let's get together and feel alright.

Storman's (☎ 727-571-2202; 2675 Ulmerton Rd), in Largo just south of Clearwater, hosts a Friday night party (5pm to 8pm) with two-for-one well drinks, cheap draft beers and a free buffet.

Singles mingle at **Old New York New York** (☎ 727-539-7441; 18573 US Hwy 19) on Friday and Saturday nights.

Getting There & Around
A Greyhound bus station (☎ 727-796-7315; 2811 Gulf-to-Bay Blvd, Clearwater) services six buses daily that make the half-hour trip from Tampa to Clearwater ($7/14 one-way/roundtrip). But then you'll have to get to Clearwater Beach.

From Clearwater, take **PSTA** (☎ 727-530-9911) bus No 60 from the stop across Causeway Blvd westbound to the Park St Bus Depot, and change there to bus No 80 to Clearwater Beach. Buses run every 30 to 60 minutes. For the hostel, get off at the tennis courts at the corner of Mandalay Ave and Bay Esplanade; it'll be a two-minute walk to the hostel.

From Tampa, take Hwy 60 (Courtney Campbell Causeway) through Clearwater and west out to the beach. From St Petersburg, take Hwy 19 (34th St N) north to Hwy

60 and go west. From St Pete Beach, take Gulf Blvd north.

The red **Jolley Trolley** (☎ 727-445-1200; adult/child & senior $1/50¢) runs around Clearwater Beach and onward to Sand Key. The beach route runs 10am to 10pm daily; pick up maps at the trolley office (483 Mandalay Ave). A second Jolley Trolley runs between the beach and Clearwater's Park St Station during the same time frame.

AROUND CLEARWATER BEACH

Ready for some excellent beaches and great biking?

Heritage Village

Just south of Clearwater in Largo, this 21-acre historical park and open-air museum (☎ 727-582-2123; 11909 125th St; admission free; open 10am-4pm Tues-Sat, 1pm-4pm Sun) has period craft demonstrations and 22 structures. You can visit the county's oldest house, two Victorian houses, a one-room schoolhouse, mercantile store, doctor's office, a mill, barn and a church. By car or bike (it's about 10 miles), take Alt Hwy 19 south to Ulmerton Rd, turn right, and left on 125th St. From Clearwater Beach, take bus No 80 to Park St Station and then change for bus No 52 or 61 to the stop at Walsingham and 125th St; the entrance is very close by.

Pinellas Trail

This 47-mile paved bicycle trail, built on the abandoned CSX railway bed, runs from St Petersburg to Tarpon Springs. To date, it's the longest urban trail in the country. It's also very smooth – smooth enough for in-line skates or roller skates as well as bicycles. There are lots of stops along the way, with cafés, pubs, bike shops, skate shops, and fast-food places. As it's on the route of the old railway, the corridor cuts through widely varied terrain: sometimes you're in the middle of downtown (as in Dunedin), sometimes along waterways, sometimes among orange groves (near Pinellas Park) and sometimes you're riding practically through people's backyards in bedroom communities.

From the Clearwater Beach International Youth Hostel, which rents bikes (see the Clearwater Beach section, earlier in this chapter), head over the causeway, and ride north on Fort Harrison Ave and east on Jones St for about three blocks. You'll pick up the southern end of the Clearwater to Tarpon Springs section of the path. It's 13.2 miles from Jones St to Tarpon Ave.

Contact the **Pinellas County Planning Department** (☎ 727-464-4751; W www.co.pinellas .fl.us/mpo) for their free guidebook to the Pinellas Trail, which lists rest stops and local attractions and has a mileage chart.

Sand Key Park & Beach

This 65-acre beach park (☎ 727-464-3347), at the southern end of Clearwater Beach just south of the Clearwater Pass Bridge (or, depending on your perspective – it's always about perspective, isn't it – at the northern end of a long barrier island on the Gulf of Mexico) is often voted one of the top 20 beaches in the country. The half-mile-long beach is the widest in the area. It's also a great spot for dolphin watching, especially on the channel side, and a pretty good spot for shelling (best at low tide, especially during new and full moons and after storms). The Jolley Trolley (see Getting Around later in this section) passes by; otherwise, it's an easy bicycle ride. Be prepared to feed quarters to the parking meters.

Founded in 1971, the **Suncoast Seabird Sanctuary** (☎ 727-391-6211; W www.seabird sanctuary.org; 18328 Gulf Blvd; admission free; open 9am-sunset daily), south of Indian Shores, is the largest wild-bird hospital in North America (1½ acres). About 40 species of crippled birds have found a home here, and at any given time there are usually between 400 to 600 sea and land birds being treated and recuperating. Whenever possible, the birds are released back into the wild. When it's not, their offspring are re-leased. Procreation doesn't stop with recuperation. Tours take place Wednesday and Sunday at 2pm.

Honeymoon & Caladesi Islands

Honeymoon Island State Recreation Area (☎ 727-469-5942; 1 Dunedin Causeway; admission $4 per carload; open 8am-sunset daily) began life as a grand prize in a 1940s contest. Paramount newsreels and *Life* magazine were giving away all-expense-paid honeymoons here to newlyweds, who would stay in the 50 or so thatched huts lining the beach. During the war, Honeymoon Island served as a prime R&R site for exhausted war factory workers, and after that, the place was never a honeymoon spot again. After a road connecting the island to the mainland was built in 1964, the state bought the land in the early 1970s.

Today, the park offers diverse birding, good swimming and great shelling. Coastal plants include mangrove swamps, rare virgin slash pine, strand and salt marshes. There are also nature trails and bird observation areas, as well as a ferry to Caladesi Island. Take Alt Hwy 19 north to the city of Dunedin (pronounced dun-**eden**) and go west on Curlew Rd (Hwy 586), the Dunedin Causeway, which leads to the island.

Just south of Honeymoon Island, **Caladesi Island State Park** (☎ 727-469-5918; admission free; open 8am-sunset daily) always ranks at the top of national surveys for best natural beaches. It can actually be reached on foot from Clearwater Beach, although it's a 3-mile beach walk – a 1921 hurricane and a 1985 storm filled in the gap between north Clearwater Beach and the island. Perhaps better yet, you canoe there or take a ferry from Honeymoon Island. In addition to nature trails and an unspoiled, palm-lined 3-mile beach (with rental umbrellas and chairs available), it's nice for picnicking beneath shaded pavilions, swimming and shelling. You'll probably see armadillos, threatened gopher tortoises, raccoons, snakes, turtles, pelicans, ibis, ospreys, cormorants and others. Keep your eyes open and stay light on your feet.

Caladesi Connection (☎ 727-734-5263), at the western end of Curlew Rd (Hwy 586) in Honeymoon Island State Recreation Area, operates hourly weekday ferries to Caladesi. On weekends the 30-minute ferries run on the half-hour, starting at 10am; the last departure from Caladesi is around 4:30pm. The roundtrip fare is $7 for adults, $3.50 for children. One note: to manage passengers coming and going, you'll get a card stamped

with your return-trip departure time (no more than four hours later). If you want to stay longer, you can, but other folks with that time will be taken first. It's rather like an airline standby.

It's Our Nature (☎ 727-441-2599, 888-535-7448; Ⓦ www.itsournature.com) runs guided eco-heritage and bird watching trips in Caladesi Island State Park and Honeymoon Island. Fees are $15 to $25, plus the cost of the park fee or boat ride.

TARPON SPRINGS
About 15 miles north of Clearwater, the tidy little tourist trap (Ⓦ www.tarponsprings .com) is touted as an authentic Greek sponging village. But it's more akin to a collection of tourist attractions and touristy restaurants. If you've never been to Crete or don't have a passport, though, you might find it ever-so-slightly appealing. Regardless, after seeing the rest of southwest Florida, Tarpon Springs *is* a fish out of water.

Once upon a time, the city was indeed a sponging center, and attracted the Greek immigrants who made up so much of the town's culture from the early 1900s until the sponge died off in the 1940s. After new sponge beds were discovered in the 1980s, the sponge docks are again bustling, though you may find items overpriced and shopkeepers cynical. If you've never tried Greek appetizers, it may be interesting to sample some at the dozens of Greek restaurants and bakeries around the docks. If you've had baklava on Rhodes, though, you probably won't hang around long.

The seven-block Tarpon Springs Downtown Historic District, however, is a charming 19th-century area, with brick streets, lots of antique stores and the fabulous **St Nicholas Church**. The Greek Orthodox church, built with 60 tons of Greek marble and featuring Czech stained glass, is the focal point of the annual Epiphany Day celebration on January 6. Before leaving, take a little drive along the riverfront Spring Bayou (off Tarpon Ave west of downtown), where manatees linger and big Victorian estates line the road.

The **Chamber of Commerce** (☎ 727-937-6109; Ⓦ www.tarponsprings.com; on the sponge docks; open 8am-5pm Mon-Fri) has more details than you'll ever need. Speaking of which, if you can't get enough, pop in to the free **Spongeorama** museum on the main drag, Dodecanese Blvd.

From Clearwater, Alt Hwy 19 heads straight north to Tarpon Springs.

WEEKI WACHEE SPRINGS

'The City of Mermaids,' Weeki Wachee Springs (☎ 352-596-2062, 877-469-3354; W www.weekiwachee.com; adult/child $17/13; open 10am-5:30pm daily) is about 30 miles north of Tarpon Springs and 80 miles northwest of Orlando. Most people come to this 200-acre theme park as a day trip from the Clearwater/Tampa area, but there's a **Best Western** (☎ 352-596-2007, 800-490-8268; rooms $65-89) across from the park entrance, with 122 rooms.

Hold it...Mermaids? Yup. Since 1947, families and celebrities, such as Esther Williams, Danny Thomas and Elvis Presley, have been coming here to see the star attraction: an underwater show starring long-haired women in mermaid costumes who swim in the natural spring (there are also mermen).

The spring has a constant temperature of 72°F, measures about 100 feet across and produces about 170 million gallons of water a day; it's the headwater of the Weeki Wachee River. The mermaids perform in the spring, alongside fish, turtles, otters, snakes and eels.

The shows here are the height of kitsch, a trip straight back to the 1950s. You watch the mermaids, about 20 of them, perform their mainstay show, *The Little Mermaid,* in an underwater theater – the audience watches through glass panels, making this the world's only underwater artesian spring theater. The theater was built in 1946 by Newton Perry, an ex-Navy frogman. Remarkably, the mermaids flail and swim about with what appears to be the greatest of ease.

Don't be fooled. Performing underwater requires incredible stamina, and the breathing apparatus is tricky. There are submerged air hoses on the sides of the theater: the mermaids swim over, grab some air, hold their breath while swimming around performing and then zip back for more air – for *half an hour* at a time! They train first on land and then in the water without the tail, practicing the moves of the 30-minute shows. It takes about six to eight months to get the whole thing to look as effortless as it does. If it looks easy, *you* try lip-synching to music underwater next time you're snorkeling!

The park also has a Wilderness River Cruise, a Buccaneer Bay water park, a petting zoo, and two bird shows (Birds of Prey and Exotic Birds). To see all the shows, budget five hours. You can also rent **canoes** (☎ 352-597-0360) on the river from the rear of the parking lot. Take the crystal clear 7-mile canoe trail, which would take 2½ hours without stopping (but you *will* stop to picnic, right?), and you'll probably see manatees. Flowing at 4mph, the twisting and turning river is one of the fastest in central Florida. Reservations are highly recommended. Double canoes rent for $33, single kayaks $24 (no doubles are available); rentals include a pick-up service.

Drive north on rural Hwy 19 to the intersection of Hwy 50, about a half-hour north of Tarpon Springs; from I-75, take exit 61 and go west about 20 miles. If you're coming directly from Tampa, it takes about 45 minutes.

HOMOSASSA SPRINGS

The headwater of the Homosassa River, these springs (☎ 352-628-2311; W www.hsswp .com; adult/child $8/5; open 9am-5:30pm daily) are home to the Homosassa Springs State Wildlife Park, in essence, the state's largest all-natural theme park. The 168-acre park (actually it's 180, but some of it's submerged) is made up of wetlands, hydric hammock and spring-run streams that bubble out of the 45-feet-deep Homosassa Spring.

The park showcases and gives educational demonstrations about its diverse and often rehabbing wildlife – manatees, black bears, bobcats, white-tailed deer, alligators, American crocodiles and river otters. Interpretive programs include alligator and crocodile demonstrations, animal encounter programs on snakes or birds of prey, and one on manatees. But best of all, you can also watch manatees and 10,000 fish within a floating underwater observatory. A pontoon boat will take you on an orientation tour, after which you're free to wander on the nature trails. Plan on spending about three to four hours here.

If you find yourself up here late in the day, **Homosassa Riverside Resort** (☎ 352-628- 2474, 800-442-2040; w www.riversideresorts .com; 5295 Cherokee Way; rooms $55-85) has 75 rooms (half of which are truly riverside) about 3 miles from the park. It's a perfectly fine place to lay your head.

The park is about 20 miles north of Weeki Wachee, 65 miles north of Clearwater and 75 miles north of Tampa; take Hwy 19 north right to the entrance of the park.

Northwest Florida & the Panhandle

From the historical and military traditions of Pensacola to the canopy roads and posturing politicians of Tallahassee, the Panhandle offers something for every traveler. In the almost 200 miles between these two cities lie glorious white-sand beaches, alligator-ridden bayous, fishing villages, great restaurants, sophisticated nightlife and many charming Floridians eager to share their homeland.

The Panhandle is known for the best beaches in the US; the Appalachian quartz sand is dazzling white, so fine it 'barks' as you walk. The warm, turquoise and emerald waters of the Gulf of Mexico are always clear. Also, the Panhandle is known as spring break central, with Panama City Beach sometimes called the Redneck Riviera, for its popularity with visitors from nearby counties and states. And the Panhandle is known for hurricanes, which blow through with frightening regularity.

But it also boasts pristine nature, from Gulf Islands National Seashore dunes to the waters of Blackwater River State Park to the caves at Florida Caverns State Park.

Many areas can be explored as day trips, going out from Pensacola, Panama City Beach, Tallahassee or Apalachicola.

The founding of Pensacola predates even St Augustine (the cities argue over which is the nation's oldest settlement). Pensacola has three historic districts and incredible beaches. You can also see the Blue Angels precision-flying team at the Pensacola Naval Air Station.

Tallahassee is the state capital, though don't expect to see lawmakers running around cutting deals – the legislature meets for less than three months a year. Some 60 miles east of the capital, the Stephen Foster State Folk Cultural Center on the Suwannee River is a worthy destination.

Don't miss exploring the Forgotten Coast and the Nature Coast. Along this stretch you'll pass through oyster-rich Apalachicola and experience Steinhatchee, which offers serious fishing and a chance to chow down

Highlights

- Enjoy the stunning beaches at Pensacola, Destin, Fort Walton Beach and Grayton Beach – known for their sugar-white sand, clear water and spectacular sunsets and moonrises

- Swim, hike and camp at St Andrews or Grayton Beach State Recreation Areas – both voted best beach in the USA by *Condé Nast Traveler*

- Stroll or drive along Tallahassee's lovely canopy roads

- Traipse through Florida Caverns State Park, among eerie stalactite and stalagmite formations

- Canoe on the Blackwater River, which, despite its name, is one of the clearest sand-bottom rivers in the world

- Relax in the peace and tranquillity of secluded St George Island

- Marvel at the Cedar Key State Museum's eclectic collections

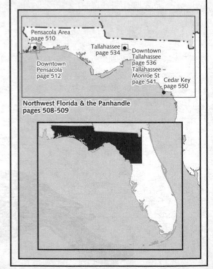

Pensacola Area
page 510

Tallahassee
page 534

Downtown
Tallahassee
page 536

Downtown
Pensacola
page 512

Tallahassee –
Monroe St
page 541

Cedar Key
page 550

Northwest Florida & the Panhandle
pages 508-509

on the freshest possible catch. Nearby, historic Cedar Key beckons.

Gulf Coast

PENSACOLA
population 412,000; time zone CST

Pensacola is an ancient city, for the USA. The Spanish tried to colonize here in 1559, but the hurricane-plagued settlement was abandoned after two years, leaving St Augustine to claim the title of first European settlement, in 1565.

Pensacola became a permanent settlement in 1698. The city came under various governments until, in 1821, it was where Florida was officially turned over to the US by Spain. Today Pensacola celebrates its multinational past by displaying its five former flags: Spain, France, Britain, the Confederacy and the US. Much of today's downtown area dates to the 1800s, though there are remnants of British and Spanish buildings from the 1700s.

Reasons to travel to Pensacola are many. The beaches are a treasure, gently sloped, sugar-white sand lapped by calm waters. In the city proper, there are three renovated historic districts. And the Naval Air Station, home to thousands of people and also the Blue Angels, offers the National Museum of Naval Aviation, Fort Barrancas and the Pensacola Lighthouse.

History

Written records of the native population that made the area home for some 10,000 years are unfortunately scant. Most accounts begin with the area's exploration in the 1540s by Hernando de Soto and the unsuccessful settlement attempt in 1559 by Spanish explorer Don Tristan de Luna.

In the 17th century, hostilities escalated between Spain and France. The French had settlements at nearby Mobile, Alabama, and in 1719, Pensacola was taken by the French and surrendered back to Spain four times.

During the period of British rule (1763–81), much of the city planning took place; remnants of British-built structures – including the government house and officers' compound – can still be seen in the British-designed Seville Historic District. When the Spanish took over again, they changed all the street names, thus the presence today of Alcaniz, Palafox and Intendencia Sts.

General Andrew Jackson swept in unsanctioned after the War of 1812 and took Pensacola for the US. During the war, Spain had allowed British ships to dock – and the Brits had trained the Creek Indians Jackson was fighting. The US initially gave the area back, but it was returned when the Spanish ceded Florida to the US in 1821. Andrew Jackson returned to Florida as its first governor.

The city's harbor and geographical position were key in its development as a military city; construction of the first navy base was begun after the US took control, and forts were built to defend Pensacola Bay.

Those forts would become a major focus during the Civil War, when fighting over them led to a stalemated battle in the harbor. After the war and a yellow fever epidemic that reduced the population, Pensacola went through a number of booms, probably the biggest being lumber.

The navy had abandoned the Pensacola base in the early 1900s, but reopened it as an air base in 1914 to train pilots for long-range flight and antisubmarine warfare. The area gained prominence in WWII, when the navy flight instruction school began working overtime, training thousands of American and foreign pilots. Pensacola Beach, connected to the mainland by a 3-mile-long bridge, became a tourist spot.

Restoration of the historic districts began in the 1960s; North Hill was listed on the National Register of Historic Places in 1972. Redevelopment of the waterfront area is underway, including a new festival park and replacement of the decaying Bayfront Auditorium. City movers and shakers continue to haggle over the waterfront, with developers squaring off against various community advocates. Despite growing pains, Pensacola remains a city with a strong military economy. It's home to interesting museums,

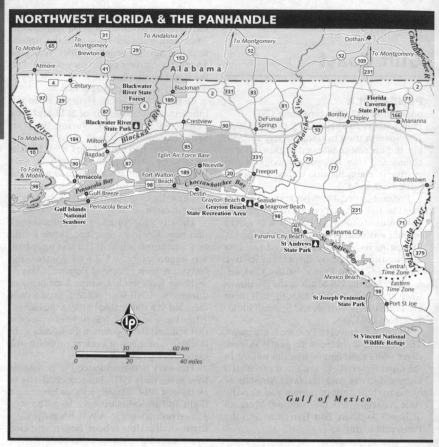

NORTHWEST FLORIDA & THE PANHANDLE

a strong gay community, a vibrant arts scene, good restaurants, an opera center and major theatrical offerings.

Orientation

Downtown Pensacola, from the historic districts to the waterfront, is walkable. But it's difficult to get around outside of downtown without a car. Interstate Highway I-110, a thoroughfare to chain motels away from the downtown, starts near the city center and shoots north to I-10.

Palafox St, sometimes called Palafox Place south of Garden St, is the east-west divider,

Garden St the north-south. The North Hill Preservation District, just northwest of downtown, is bordered by Palafox St to the east, Reus St to the west, Blount St to the north and Wright St to the south.

In the southeast downtown quadrant is the Palafox Historic District, a collection of smaller districts making up one large preservation area bounded by Cervantes St to the north, the waterfront to the south, Florida Blanca St to the east and Spring St to the west. Within the Palafox district is Historic Pensacola Village, with Government St to the north, Main St to

NORTHWEST FLORIDA & THE PANHANDLE

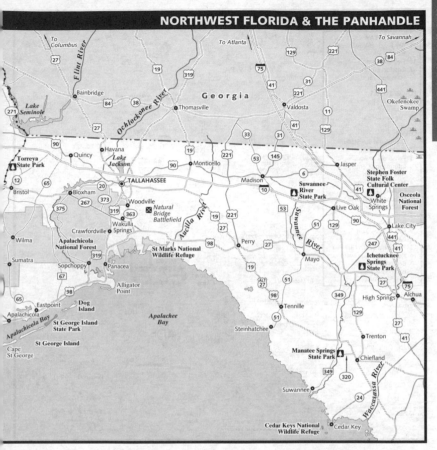

the south, Palafox St to the west and Alcaniz St to the east.

The Naval Air Station (NAS) is southwest of the city.

Pensacola Beach is on Santa Rosa Island, southeast of Pensacola and Gulf Breeze. Gulf Breeze is connected to Pensacola by the Pensacola Bay Bridge (the Three Mile Bridge) and to Pensacola Beach by the Bob Sikes Bridge ($1 toll). A string of older bridges alongside the Three Mile Bridge on the eastern side is open for fishing – it's reachable only from the south.

The Pensacola Visitors Information Center sells city maps for $3, and gives out placemat-size maps showing the historic districts and an area map.

Information

The **Pensacola Visitors Information Center** (☎ 850-434-1234, 800-874-1234; ⓦ www.visit pensacola.com; 1401 E Gregory St; open 8am-5pm daily), at the foot of the Pensacola Bay Bridge, has a bounty of tourist information and knowledgeable staff. Another information source is the **Pensacola Beach Visitors Center/Chamber of Commerce**

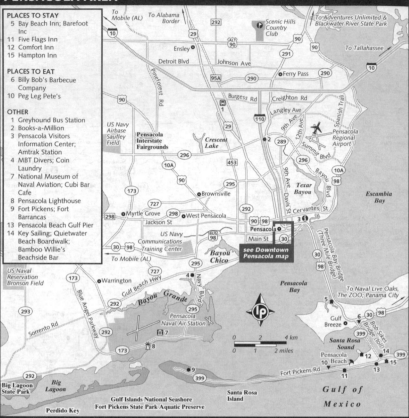

PENSACOLA AREA

PLACES TO STAY
5 Bay Beach Inn; Barefoot Inc
11 Five Flags Inn
12 Comfort Inn
15 Hampton Inn

PLACES TO EAT
6 Billy Bob's Barbecue Company
10 Peg Leg Pete's

OTHER
1 Greyhound Bus Station
2 Books-a-Million
3 Pensacola Visitors Information Center; Amtrak Station
4 MBT Divers; Coin Laundry
7 National Museum of Naval Aviation; Cubi Bar Cafe
8 Pensacola Lighthouse
9 Fort Pickens; Fort Barrancas
13 Pensacola Beach Gulf Pier
14 Key Sailing; Quietwater Beach Boardwalk; Bamboo Willie's Beachside Bar

(☎ 850-932-1500, 800-635-4803; 735 Pensacola Beach Blvd; open 9am-5pm daily). Skip the Pensacola Chamber of Commerce on W Garden St; it's geared toward business and development.

The **Pensacola Historical Society Resource Center & Library** (☎ 850-434-5455; 117 E Government St), opposite Seville Quarter, is what it sounds like. The **Arts Council of Northwest Florida** (☎ 850-432-9906) is useful – see Entertainment later in this section for more information.

Change money at **Whitney Bank** (☎ 850-435-2481; 101 W Garden St) downtown and at its outlying branch (☎ 850-435-6740; 6200 N Davis Hwy). The main **post office** (101 S Palafox St) is downtown.

Arcade News (☎ 850-438-1796; 194 Palafox St) has magazines, books, area newspapers and the *New York Times*.

Tony's Pipe Rack (☎ 850-432-2055; 13 E Garden St) sells tobacco, books, the *New York Times*, *Wall Street Journal* and other out-of-town papers.

At **Books-a-Million** (☎ 850-478-4849; 6235 N Davis Hwy), a warehouse store in the Village Oaks center, you'll find regional history, guidebooks and local-interest authors. It also stocks newspapers and magazines; the espresso bar is nice, too.

The **public library** (☎ 850-435-1760; 200 W Gregory St; open 9am-8pm Tues-Thur, 9am-5pm Fri & Sat) may be useful, and you can check your email or get on the Web for free.

The *Pensacola News Journal* is the daily; look for the Friday 'Weekender' section. There's also the *New American Press,* offering regional African American news. National Public Radio (NPR) is at 88.1 FM.

It's not easy finding a coin laundry downtown. There's one out toward the naval air station at 43A S Navy Blvd, next to MBT Divers, and another on Santa Rosa Island (☎ 850-932-3005) at 37 Via de Luna.

Three area hospitals are **Baptist Hospital** (☎ 850-434-4011; 1000 W Moreno St), closest to downtown; **Sacred Heart Hospital** (☎ 850-416-7000; 5151 N 9th Ave); and **West Florida Regional Medical Center** (☎ 850-494-4000; 8383 N Davis Hwy).

Historic Pensacola Village

This village (☎ 850-595-5985; w www.historic pensacola.org; adult/senior or military/child $6/5/2.50; open 10am-4pm Tues-Sat) is a collection of homes and museums. Two-hour walking tours run Monday to Friday in winter and Monday to Saturday in summer, leaving at 11am and 1:30pm from the main ticket office at the Tivoli House, 205 E Zaragoza St. The tour goes to many district buildings, such as the **Lavalle House** (205 E Church St) and the **Julee Cottage** (210 E Zaragoza St), the former home of freed slave Julee Paton. Included are the TT Wentworth Museum, the Museum of Commerce and the Museum of Industry.

Get tour tickets at the TT Wentworth Museum. You don't have to take the tour to see many buildings; one admission is for all village buildings except the Lear-Rocheblave House (1890), the Dorr House (1871), the Lavalle House (1805) and Old Christ Church (1832).

TT Wentworth Museum The Wentworth (330 S Jefferson St) is an elaborate 1907 yellow-brick Renaissance Revival building, originally Pensacola City Hall.

Across from the Plaza Ferdinand (where Florida was accepted into the US), it dominates the block with its wide eaves, red tile roof and deep second-story arcade. The museum contains some quirky displays, including a Coca-Cola room. It also features a thought-provoking exhibit on black life, and one on the five flags period in Pensacola, which ran from the Spanish exploration through the Civil War.

Museum of Industry Across the street from the Museum of Commerce, Industry (200 E Zaragoza St) displays photographs and equipment from the city's 19th-century industries, including brickmaking, timber, fishing and the railroad.

Pensacola Museum of Art

This museum (☎ 850-432-6247; 407 S Jefferson St; adult/student or military $2/1, free Tues; open 10am-5pm Tues-Fri, 10am-4pm Sat, 1pm-4pm Sun), founded in 1954 and housed in the old jail (1906–08), mounts about 18 exhibitions a year; call for what's on.

Civil War Soldiers Museum

Displays in this museum (☎ 850-469-1900; 108 Palafox Place; adult/military/child $5/4.50/2.50; open 10am-4:30pm Mon-Sat) are arranged in chronological order. Note the battlefield hospital display, complete with life-sized bloody soldiers, and the photographs of field hospitals and amputations. There's also a re-creation of a soldier's campsite, weapons, uniforms, tobacco, drugs and currency, and the Confederate flag captured by New York Zouaves during the 1861 Battle of Santa Rosa Island. Displays are easy to comprehend; a small bookstore is packed with offerings on local history and the Civil War.

Veterans Memorial Park

A moving monument to veterans of all American wars, this 5½-acre park (cnr Bayfront Pkwy & 9th Ave) overlooks Pensacola Bay (take Main St east from downtown to the 'Huey' helicopter). At the end is Wall South, a replica of the Vietnam

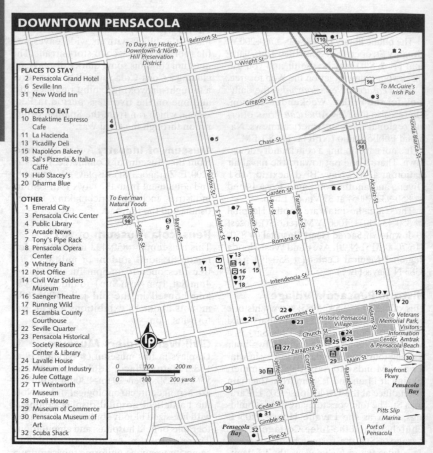

DOWNTOWN PENSACOLA

PLACES TO STAY
2 Pensacola Grand Hotel
6 Seville Inn
31 New World Inn

PLACES TO EAT
10 Breaktime Espresso
   Cafe
11 La Hacienda
13 Picadilly Deli
15 Napoléon Bakery
18 Sal's Pizzeria & Italian
   Caffé
19 Hub Stacey's
20 Dharma Blue

OTHER
1 Emerald City
3 Pensacola Civic Center
4 Public Library
5 Arcade News
7 Tony's Pipe Rack
8 Pensacola Opera
   Center
9 Whitney Bank
12 Post Office
14 Civil War Soldiers
   Museum
16 Saenger Theatre
17 Running Wild
21 Escambia County
   Courthouse
22 Seville Quarter
23 Pensacola Historical
   Society Resource
   Center & Library
24 Lavalle House
25 Museum of Industry
26 Julee Cottage
27 TT Wentworth
   Museum
28 Tivoli House
29 Museum of Commerce
30 Pensacola Museum of
   Art
32 Scuba Shack

Memorial in Washington, DC, erected in 1991 and displaying the names of the more than 58,000 US soldiers who died in the war; among them are eight women nurses, 'Angels on the Wall.'

Pensacola Naval Air Station

Every US WWII pilot was trained at the Pensacola Naval Air Station (☎ 850-452-0111). On any given day, there are some 6000 aviators-in-training at Pensacola NAS.

Take Hwy 295 to the NAS entrance, south of the bridge at the end of Navy Blvd, across Bayou Grande. You'll be stopped at the gate

for a security check of your car. Once you are deemed free of seditious materials, enter the base on Navy Blvd, which becomes Duncan Rd. Turn right at the second light onto Taylor Rd, which runs toward the Advanced Redoubt ruins and Fort Barrancas, the National Museum of Naval Aviation and the Pensacola Lighthouse.

National Museum of Naval Aviation This museum (☎ 850-453-3604, 800-327-5002; ⓦ www.naval-air.org; 1750 Radford Blvd; admission free; open 9am-5pm daily) is the largest of the navy's museums, and Florida's most attended museum of *any* kind. In the foyer, hanging above you are four A-4 Skyhawk jets that the Blue Angels retired when they upgraded to F/A-18s in 1986. At the entrance, hop a shuttle for a free 20-minute tour of the flightline. Buses to the tarmac leave twice hourly; check at the desk for exact times and to get a ticket. Every day one tour includes the restoration hangar, where dedicated volunteers refurbish historic aircraft for later exhibits.

There's an IMAX cinema (adults/senior, military, child $6.25/5.75, shows every hour 10am-3pm), featuring 'The Magic of Flight' to launch the viewer on a 360-degree audiovisual journey into the skies. Other exhibits include flight simulators, cockpit trainers, and a replicated carrier flight deck. A walk through the somber POW exhibit will keep you from getting entirely enchanted with the military marvels that fill this 107,000-sq-ft museum.

When you need a break (publicists claim the average visit lasts five hours), have lunch at the Cubi Bar, decorated with hundreds of hand-carved Vietnam War–era squadron plaques brought here from the officers' club in Cubi, the Philippines (see Places to Eat, later in this section).

Blue Angels This group (☎ 850-452-4784; w www.blueangels.navy.mil), which performs for about 15 million people yearly, is a flying team based at NAS Pensacola. The Angels, organized in 1946, today visit about 35 show sites a year, where four jets fly in tight formation and perform rolls, loops and other precision maneuvers. Two other F/A-18s are used for solo flights, and the shows culminate with all six planes flying in trademark Delta formation. The Angels practice frequently (as would you if you were doing 300mph stunts with $180 million worth of aircraft); check the Web site for the schedule, or write to the Blue Angels Public Affairs Office, 390 San Carlos Rd, Suite A, Pensacola, FL 32508. Practices are at 8:30am, and some are followed by pilot autograph sessions. Park at the aviation museum; the viewing area is behind it.

Pensacola Lighthouse Florida's second oldest lighthouse (built in 1858 on the site of the first) is run by the US Coast Guard. At the time of research the landmark was closed for repairs and scheduled to reopen in July 2002.

Gulf Islands National Seashore

Covering many of the barrier islands for 150 miles between West Ship Island (Mississippi) and Santa Rosa Island, the seashore (☎ 850-934-2600, w www.nps.gov/guis; vehicle/pedestrian or cyclist $8/3) has many natural and historical attractions. In Florida, it covers Perdido Key, two sections of Santa Rosa Island (extending to the NAS across the Fort Pickens State Park Aquatic Preserve) and a small beach in the Okaloosa Island area (see Fort Walton Beach, later in this chapter).

The Gulf Islands are vulnerable to hurricanes – Opal in October 1995 buried the western half of Santa Rosa Island, including Fort Pickens, in sand.

Fort Barrancas Accessed through the NAS, this fort (☎ 850-455-5167; admission free; open 9:30am-5pm daily winter, 8:30am-4pm summer) has been built, destroyed, remodeled and occupied by Spanish, French, British, Confederate and American forces – there's been some incarnation of Fort Barrancas here since 1698. The British built another fort, the Advanced Redoubt, nearby. Pick up the brochure at the visitor's center and walk up to the fort, where you can slither through a dark tunnel under a dry ditch and peer through slit windows in the walls. Guided tours happen daily in winter at 2pm; in summer a 10:30am tour is added. Advanced Redoubt is open Saturday and Sunday noon to 2pm, with extended hours and Saturday tours at 11am during the summer.

From the main NAS gate, take Duncan Rd to Taylor Rd and turn right; the visitor's center is up the road.

Fort Pickens This pentagonal brick fort (☎ 850-934-2621), built in 1829–34, was the site of Geronimo's incarceration in 1886–87. Inside, take a self-guided tour. There's camping near the fort (see Places to Stay, later in this section). There are guided tours daily at 2pm; on Saturday and Sunday there's a parade ground rifle-firing. Fort Pickens offers swimming, and nature and bike trails. Admission is good for seven days, and also grants entry to other fee areas of the seashore.

You can dive the wreck of the USS *Massachusetts* at the Underwater Archaeological Preserve in Fort Pickens State Park Aquatic Preserve. The ship, launched in 1893 and sunk in 1921, is in 26 feet of water, 1½ miles south-southwest of the Pensacola Pass at latitude 30°17'45"N and longitude 87°18'45"W.

Naval Live Oaks The visitor's center (☎ 850-934-2600; 1801 Gulf Breeze Pkwy; admission free; open 8:30am-sunset daily), about 6 miles east of Gulf Breeze, is the Florida headquarters for the Gulf Islands National Seashore. Here you'll get information on all of the Florida seashore sites. At Naval Live Oaks, an area where settlers found strong ironwood for building warships, Native American shell mounds and burial sites have been found. The park has nature trails, and visitor's center rangers can tell you about the park, the region and local Native American artifacts. Public camping is prohibited.

The ZOO

At The ZOO (☎ 850-932-2229; w www.the-zoo.com; 5701 Gulf Breeze Pkwy; adult/senior/child $10/9/7; open 9am-5pm daily), Hwy 98, about 10 miles east of Gulf Breeze, visit the Farm, a petting area where you can feed giraffes. There are more than 700 animals, such as cougars, zebras, white tigers and snow leopards, at The ZOO, and a 15-minute Safari Line Train ($3) through the nature preserve. Animals – including llamas, brown deer, addaxes, scimitar-horned oryx, fallow deer and sable antelope – walk up to the cars. A boardwalk out over the preserve provides sightings of many animals you'd see from the train, but free.

Pensacola Beach

Don't leave the area without seeing a sunset or a moonrise from Pensacola Beach. It's a shimmering, white-sand crescent, with stunningly clear Gulf water.

Many streets in Pensacola Beach have Spanish names. The east-west drag running from Fort Pickens to the Bob Sikes Bridge is Fort Pickens Rd, which becomes Via de Luna heading east. Via de Luna is crossed by north-south-running avenidas, numbered up to 23.

The 1950s-era flashing neon sign welcoming all to the 'World's Whitest Beaches' was created for the corner of Gregory and Palafox Sts in Pensacola and moved to the Bob Sikes Bridge entry in the 1960s. It's a bit worse for wear, but is a beloved landmark; the **water tower** (cnr Via de Luna & Avenida 23) is another one.

The **Pensacola Beach Gulf Pier** (☎ 850-934-7200; 41 Fort Pickens Rd; observer/adult fishing/senior fishing/youth fishing $1/6.50/5.50/3.50; open 24/7), replaced the old Pensacola Beach Pier in 2001. At 1471 feet, it's called 'the longest and friendliest pier on the Gulf of Mexico,' and it's probably worth a buck to get way out on the water without having to boat or surf.

Activities

With gin-clear waters and generally balmy temperatures, Pensacola is a natural for watersports and all kinds of other outdoor exertions.

Watersports At MBT Divers (☎ 850-455-7702; w www.mbtdivers.com; 43B S Navy Blvd; open 9am-5pm Mon-Thur, 8am-6pm Sat, 8am-2pm Sun) they offer trips for novices, experts and everyone in between, including spearfishers and ecodivers. Prices range from $65 to $90. MBT also offers certification courses and equipment rental. Its Web site lists more than 1000 dive sites and has information on historic diving.

The **Scuba Shack** (☎ 850-433-4319; 711 S Palafox St; charters $55-70; open at 9am daily), on the Pensacola waterfront, has a 50-foot diving and fishing boat and a full range of rental equipment. On the same site since 1981, the Scuba Shack folks, specializing in moonlight excursions, are the experts.

Barefoot Inc (☎ 850-932-7887; 49 Gulf Breeze Pkwy; open 9am-6pm daily, shorter winter hours), in Gulf Breeze, rents kayaks for $10 an hour and pontoon boats for $95 for four hours; they also rent bicycles.

Go to **Key Sailing** (☎ 850-932-5520; 500 Quietwater Beach Rd), in Pensacola Beach by the Quietwater Beach Boardwalk at the end of the Bob Sikes Bridge, for kayaks ($15 per hour), Hobie Cats ($40 per hour, $60 for two), pontoon boats ($90 to $198) and fishing/ski boats ($150 for four hours). Key Sailing also offers parasailing, a dizzy 20-minute trip above the waves that's almost worth the $50.

Running The store **Running Wild** (☎ 850-435-9222; 126 Palafox Place; open 10am-6pm Mon-Fri, 10am-5pm Sat), next to the Saenger Theatre, is your link to Pensacola's running community. Store owners Paul and Russell can send you to the best trails and the best upcoming runs. They'll also sell you shoes and duds and give you expert advice on both.

Places to Stay

The cheapest camping in the area is at Big Lagoon State Park and at Adventures Unlimited; see Around Pensacola, later in this chapter.

Fort Pickens (☎ 850-934-2621; sites without/with hookups $15/20), on the tip of Santa Rosa Island, has picnic tables, grills, showers and water and electric hookups.

Perdido Key (☎ 850-492-7278; free) offers limited primitive camping, but a permit is required (see Around Pensacola, later in this chapter).

Gulf Breeze & Pensacola Beach Waterfront room rates tend to be high, but the payoff is proximity to the beaches.

Five Flags Inn (☎ 850-932-3586; 299 Fort Pickens Rd; rooms $55/95 winter/summer), in Pensacola Beach, is a reasonable place with a heated pool and 49 Gulfside units. Turn right at the traffic light after the bridge and go west; the hotel's on the left.

Bay Beach Inn (☎ 850-932-2214, 866-932-2214; 51 Gulf Breeze Pkwy; rooms $59-99), off the Three Mile Bridge, is family friendly. There's a restaurant, pool, wading pool and almost a mile of private Pensacola Bay beach outside the door.

Comfort Inn – Soundside (☎ 850-934-5370, 800-934-5400; 40 Fort Pickens Rd; rooms $99-109/119-129 winter/summer), on the water, has a pool and 100 units, some with kitchenettes.

Hampton Inn (☎ 850-932-6800, 800-320-8108; 2 Via de Luna; rooms $80-120/120-170 winter/summer) is a comfortable hotel, and the sunset views will knock you out. There's a pool. It's after the first traffic light on the way to the beach from Sikes Bridge.

Clarion Suites Resort & Convention Center (☎ 850-932-4300, 800-874-5303; 20 Via de Luna; rooms $82-110/125-175 winter/summer), which has a pool, is on the beach.

Downtown The **Seville Inn** (☎ 850-433-8331, 800-277-7275; 223 E Garden St; rooms/suites $55/80 winter, $75/119 summer) is a good downtown option, just four blocks off Palafox St. It has clean rooms, two pools, and two free online computers in the lobby.

Days Inn Historic Downtown (☎ 850-438-4922; 710 N Palafox St; rooms $58/68 winter/summer), with 102 units, is the your best value downtown. Rates include a full breakfast. The staff exudes good cheer, and there's a pool and a lounge.

New World Inn (☎ 850-432-4111; 600 S Palafox St; rooms/suites $75/125), well located between downtown and waterfront, has clean rooms and a helpful staff.

Pensacola Grand Hotel (☎ 850-433-3336, 800-348-3336; w www.pensacolagrandhotel.com; 200 E Gregory St; doubles/triples/quads $135/145/155, suites higher) offers luxury. The Grand certainly is, with many sections surviving from the 1912-era L&N Railroad Depot. You get a lounge, restaurant, pool, and a library with leather chairs and a set of Detective Book Club mysteries.

Greater Pensacola One of many chains out along the I-110 corridor, **Motel 6** (☎ 850-474-1060; 7226 Plantation Rd; rooms $38/44 winter/summer) has 80 standard motel units with queen beds and there's a pool.

Red Roof Inn (☎ 850-476-7960; 7340 Plantation Rd; rooms $45/51 winter/summer) is also not bad, although there's no pool. Two pluses: rooms have data ports and children stay free.

Ramada Inn (☎ 850-477-0711; 6550 Pensacola Blvd; rooms $69-79) has 106 comfortable units, a pool, and a restaurant and lounge.

Places to Eat
Here on the Gulf of Mexico, fresh seafood abounds. Cuisine in Pensacola benefits from myriad influences, manifesting Cajun, Deep South, Hispanic, European and contemporary US trends that often blend in intriguing ways. On a typical day, you might eat grits and biscuits for breakfast, spinach-and-mushroom wraps for lunch and blackened grouper for dinner.

Pensacola Beach The happening place in Pensacola Beach is **Peg Leg Pete's** (☎ 850-932-4139; 1010 Fort Pickens Rd; Cajun specialties $8-14, fried seafood mains $14-16; open 11am to late evening daily). The old pirate dishes up burgers and sandwiches, and features oysters shucked to order (try the spicy Lafitte, $11 a dozen). In summer there's live music in the Underwhere Bar.

Billy Bob's Barbecue Company (☎ 850-934-2999; 911 Gulf Breeze Pkwy; open 11am-9pm daily) specializes in hand-pulled Carolina-style barbecue 'without the fat.' Daily specials include a rib lunch ($8).

Downtown **Breaktime Espresso Cafe** (☎ 850-438-7788; 34 S Palafox St; coffee drinks $1-3.50, wraps $4-5; open 7:30am-5:30pm Mon-Fri, 9am-5pm Sat) has a large, varied menu – and the same goes for the clientele. Smoothies keep the health nuts happy, but gooey desserts like brownies à la mode ($3) are available, too.

Napoléon Bakery (☎ 850-434-9701; 101 S Jefferson St; breakfast $4-6, lunch $5-7; open 7am-5pm Mon-Fri, 7am-2pm Sat) is like a Parisian boulangerie; French accents float across the counter and the buttery smell of fresh pastry turns a notion into a craving. Have a croissant with preserves for breakfast, with coffee, juice or tea ($5), or get one at lunchtime stuffed with

ham, cheese and béchamel sauce ($5). *C'est bon!*

Ever'man Natural Foods (☎ 850-438-0402; 315 W Garden St; sandwiches, salads & stir-fries $6; store open 7am-7pm Mon-Sat; deli open 8am-6:30pm Mon-Sat) sells natural foods and is your source for vegetarian lunches and premade sandwiches and wraps. Six tables tucked in by the deli counter invite you to stick around. If all this bliss sounds like California, remind yourself it's the South by picking up a Bible Bar (it's made with the seven foods from Deuteronomy 8:8: wheat, barley, vines, figs, pomegranates, olive oil and honey).

Picadilly Deli (☎ 850-438-3354; 102 Palafox Place; sandwiches $4-6; open 11am-3pm Mon-Sat) does a hopping lunch business. Specialties are sandwiches and salads; vegetarians will like the eight nonmeat options.

Sal's Pizzeria & Italian Caffé (☎ 850-433-5385; 128 S Palafox St; slices $2-4, whole pies $4-20; open 11am-6pm Mon-Thur, 11am-9pm Fri) makes a great early dinner stop if you're headed out. The Boscaiola (slice $2.50) melts in your mouth.

Hub Stacey's (☎ 850-469-1001; 312 E Government St; salads $3-7, sandwiches $6-10; deli open 11am-9pm Mon-Sat) dishes up hefty lunch salads, sandwiches and veggie options. The Spring Street ($7), pita bread with seasoned shrimp and veggies topped with Creole mayo, is tasty; wash it down with a microbrew.

Dharma Blue (☎ 850-433-1275; 300 S Alcaniz St; lunch $6-9, dinner $7-23; open 11am-4pm Mon-Fri, 11am-3pm Sat & 5pm-10pm Mon-Thur, 5pm-11pm Fri & Sat) is across from Hub Stacey's. Enjoy the aqua-washed living room of this old house, hung with tropical paintings by local artists. The food's good, too – a roasted portobello wrap served with salad and walnut-feta pasta ($7) makes a filling lunch.

La Hacienda (☎ 850-429-0126; 21 W Romana St; lunches & dinners $6-10; open 11am-2:30pm Mon-Sat, 2:30pm-9:30pm Mon-Thur, 2:30pm-10.30pm Fri & Sat) is an aromatic, mural-bedecked space where young servers in ethnic dress whirl out of the kitchen laden with sizzling fajitas ($9) or combination plates ($6 to $8) or other traditional Mexican favorites. The five vegetarian options are also good.

Greater Pensacola The **Cubi Bar Cafe** (1750 Radford Blvd; sandwich with salad $6), in the National Museum of Naval Aviation, serves good, reasonable lunches (children may go for the T-4 Trainer dog, $3). Commemorative plaques from the original Cubi Bar in the Philippines cover the walls.

Entertainment
Performing Arts The **Saenger Theatre** (☎ 850-444-7686; Ⓦ www.pensacolasaenger .com; 118 S Palafox St; box office open 10am-5pm winter, 10am-4pm summer), pronounced **sayn**-ger, a Spanish-Baroque beauty, was reconstructed in 1925 using bricks from the Pensacola Opera House, which was destroyed in a 1916 hurricane. It's home to Broadway productions and performances by the Northwest Florida Ballet, the Pensacola Symphony Orchestra and Pensacola Opera.

Pensacola Opera Company (☎ 850-433-6737; Ⓦ www.pensacolaopera.com; 75 S Tarragona St; box office open 9am-5pm Mon-Fri), founded more than 20 years ago and housed in the Pensacola Opera Center, stages three yearly opera productions, featuring singers from around the country. Call or drop by the opera center, or contact the Saenger for ticket information.

Pensacola Symphony Orchestra (☎ 850-435-2533; Ⓦ www.pensacolasymphony-orchestra.com), with more than 70 musicians, has been performing since 1926. The season runs September through April, with five masterworks concerts, a 'pops' series, special Sunday matinees and a Christmas show, all held at the Saenger.

Jazz Society of Pensacola (☎ 850-433-8382, 850-432-6821; Ⓦ www.jazzpensacola.com) is a wide-ranging appreciation society. It sponsors the Pensacola JazzFest in April and a jazz picnic in June at the Pensacola Yacht Club. It also hosts 'Jazz Gumbo' nights every third Monday at the Seville Quarter (see Bars & Clubs later in this section) during winter.

Gallery Walks The Arts Council of Northwest Florida (☎ 850-432-9906; Ⓦ www.art snwfl.org; Seville Tower, 226 S Palafox St, Suite 204) runs **Gallery Nights**, held in March, July and November. These walks among openings at art galleries have been held since 1991. The galleries, all downtown, include the following:

Historic Pensacola Photographs
  ☎ 850-434-1122, 122 S Palafox St
Jeweler's Trade Shop
  ☎ 850-432-4433, 26 S Palafox St
A Means of Expression
  ☎ 850-434-6300, 215 E Zaragoza St
Blue Dolphin Gallery
  ☎ 850-435-7646, 23 S Palafox St
Casa de Cosas
  ☎ 850-433-5921, 732 W Garden St

Bars & Clubs Pensacola has a lively night scene, from the beaches to the waterfront to downtown.

McGuire's Irish Pub (☎ 850-433-6789; 600 E Gregory St; open from 11am daily) is a tradition. Happy hour is 4pm to 6pm; live entertainment starts at 9pm.

Seville Quarter (☎ 850-434-6211; 130 E Government St; open from 11am daily) is an entertainment/restaurant complex. Its several establishments have varying closing hours. There's billiards at **Fast Eddie's**, music at **Rosie O'Grady's** and karaoke in **Lili Marlene's**. Pick up a brochure at the Quarter.

Bamboo Willie's Beachside Bar (☎ 850-916-9888; 400 Quietwater Beach Rd; open from 11 am daily) is the place to watch the boardwalk scene. It offers food and drink specials and live entertainment Wednesday to Sunday in winter. Think bands, bikini contests and crawfish boils.

Gay & Lesbian Venues Drawing a mixed crowd (heavy on the gay men Saturday), **Emerald City** (☎ 850-433-9491; 406 E Wright St; open 5pm-3am Wed-Sun, 9pm-3am Mon) features drag shows at 11pm and 1am Sunday, Monday and Wednesday, with entertainment the other nights, too (dances, wet underwear contests and amateur-talent nights). Cover charges vary.

Red Carpet (☎ 850-453-9918; 937 N New Warrington Rd; open 5pm-2:30am daily), to the west of downtown off Hwy 295, has action every night. Saturday live music rules ($3 cover), while Wednesday there's karaoke.

Round Up (☎ 850-433-8482; 706 E Gregory; open 2pm-3am daily) mostly attracts a gay male crowd. Videos and music run most nights, and the patio opens Friday and Saturday.

The gay community rocks Pensacola with a Memorial Day weekend bash; check W www.gaypensacola.com.

Spectator Sports The **Pensacola Barracudas** (☎ 850-432-7825; W www.pensacola barracudas.com) play arena football (tickets $9 to $25) April to November at the **Pensacola Civic Center** (☎ 850-432-0800; W www.pensacolaciviccenter.com; 201 E Gregory St).

The **Pensacola Ice Pilots** (☎ 850-432-7825; W www.pensacolaicepilots.com) play hockey at the Civic Center October to April.

Getting There & Away

Pensacola Regional Airport (☎ 850-436-5005, 850-436-5000; W www.flypensacola .com), served by many major airlines, is 4 miles northeast of downtown, near the bay; the terminal is off 9th Ave on Airport Blvd.

By bus, consider the following routes, travel times and one-way/roundtrip prices for buses departing from the **Greyhound station** (☎ 850-476-4800; 505 W Burgess Rd at Pensacola Blvd). Pensacola to Jacksonville takes 8¼ to 9½ hours and costs $57/110; to Miami takes 16¼ to 20 hours ($83/168); to Mobile takes 1 hour ($13/26); to New Orleans takes 4 to 5¾ hours ($28/52); to Panama City Beach takes 2½ hours ($21/42); and to Tallahassee takes 5 to 7 hours ($21/42).

Pensacola is an Amtrak *Sunset Limited* stop, connecting Los Angeles (for instance) and Orlando, with a stop here. The **Amtrak station** (☎ 850-433-4966; 980 E Heinberg St at 15th Ave) is just north of the visitors information center.

If you're driving, for New Orleans, Louisiana, or Mobile, Alabama, take I-10

west. To the rest of Florida and to the Panhandle, take either I-10 east or the coastal route (Hwy 98, through Gulf Breeze, Fort Walton Beach and Panama City Beach). From Pensacola, it's about 200 miles to New Orleans, 650 miles to Miami, 103 miles to Panama City Beach, 192 miles to Tallahassee and 364 miles to Jacksonville.

Getting Around

From the airport, take ECAT bus No 2 to the downtown transfer station (it departs on the hour), and then bus No 16 (it runs every half-hour, starting at 6:26am) to downtown Pensacola (see Escambia County Transit, below). A taxi costs $12 to $14 to downtown, $22 to $24 to the beach. Driving, take Airport Blvd to 9th Ave or I-110 south, which go downtown and join Hwy 98, which continues over the Three Mile Bridge to Gulf Breeze and Pensacola Beach.

Escambia County Transit (ECAT; ☎ 850-436-9383 ext 611, ADA ext 12) has limited bus service around Pensacola, none to the beach. No 16 runs between Palafox St and the transfer station (at the corner of Fairfield Drive/Hwy 295 and L St, northwest of downtown), from where you can catch bus No 2 to/from the airport or bus No 14 to the NAS. The fare is $1, transfers 10¢.

The Tiki Trolley is a free weekend shuttle up and down Pensacola Beach running 10am to 3am Friday and Saturday and to 10pm Sunday. Catch it at trolley signs along Via de Luna.

There are a few one-way streets downtown, but driving is fairly easy. Downtown is 20 minutes from Pensacola Beach; find car-rental companies at the airport.

Taxi rates in Pensacola are $1.50 at flagfall, $1.60 each mile. Cab companies include **Airport Express** (☎ 850-572-5555) and **Yellow Cab** (☎ 850-433-3333).

You can rent bikes at **Key Sailing** (see Activities, earlier in this section), in Pensacola Beach, for $10 for four hours. For $50 you can eschew fossil fuels and bike around for a week. Try the Seashore Bicycle Trail, which runs along the south side of Hwy 98 to Navarre Beach, 15 miles east of Fort Walton Beach.

AROUND PENSACOLA
Big Lagoon State Park & Perdido Key

On 700 acres along the Gulf Intracoastal Waterway, Big Lagoon (☎ 850-492-1595, 800-326-3521; 12301 Gulf Beach Hwy; vehicle/pedestrian or cyclist $3.25/1; tent sites without/with electric $13/15 summer, $11/13 winter) has nature trails, observation towers, a boat launch, camping and incredible spans of beaches.

Perdido Key (admission $2 or receipt from Big Lagoon), the easternmost Florida piece of the Gulf Island National Seashore, has an ends-of-the-earth feel, with only windswept dunes between you and crystalline Gulf waters. Look for an endangered Perdido Key beach mouse scurrying through the grass. Boardwalks leading to the beach provide handicapped access.

Camping fees includes admission to both Big Lagoon and Perdido Key. They're about 12 miles southwest of Pensacola, off Hwy 292.

Blackwater River State Park

There's canoeing, camping and swimming here (☎ 850-983-5363, 800-326-3521), one of the world's clearest sand-bottom rivers. The shallows are clear; the 'blackwater' parts are dusky with tannin (the substance that colors tea). Canoers can camp anywhere along the riverbank – but must gather only dead wood for fires, bury human waste 6 inches deep and take out everything brought in.

Nature trails run throughout the park, and the rangers present summer interpretive programs. The park is in the Blackwater River State Forest, the state's largest, running south from the Alabama state line to just north of I-10. The river itself begins in the Conecuh National Forest in Alabama; its tributaries, the Sweetwater, Juniper and East Coldwater Creeks, run through the park as well.

Things to See & Do At **Blackwater Canoe Rental and Outpost** (☎ 850-623-0235, 800-967-6789) you can rent canoes for Blackwater River day trips for $16 per person and $22 overnight. You pay (get a receipt), staff drives you upriver from 4 miles to 36 miles, and you paddle back downriver. For day trips, canoes are due 30 minutes before sunset. The Outpost offers a three-night canoe rental for $33 per person. If you want a mini-adventure, rent a tube and float for 4 miles ($11).

Adventures Unlimited (☎ 850-623-6197, 800-239-6864; Route 6), a camping resort 12 miles north of Milton, offers canoeing and tubing, with hourly to three-day trips on the Coldwater and Blackwater Rivers and Juniper Creek. Short trips and day trips are $16; special 18-mile, five-hour trips are $18. Overnighters, including canoe, tent, sleeping bags, stove, cooking kit (but not food) and lantern, are $48 per person per night, $64 per person for two nights.

From Pensacola, take I-10 east to Avalon Blvd (exit 7) north to Hwy 90 east into Milton, turn left at Burger King and go 12 miles north – Adventures Unlimited is well signed.

Places to Stay Thirty sites (with water) are available within the state park; tent and RV sites are $8 plus tax, $10 with electricity.

The **campground** at Adventures Unlimited is on the Coldwater River. Primitive sites are $15 nightly; it also has air-conditioned camping 'tree houses' (on stilts). Bunk cabins cost $39 winter and $49 summer; cabins with kitchens and bathrooms cost $109 winter, $119 summer.

Getting There & Away To get to the park and to Blackwater Canoe Rental from Pensacola, take I-10 east to exit 10 (Hwy 87), turn left and go north for 1 mile to Hwy 90; turn right (east) and go 5½ miles to the canoe/state park sign. Turn left (north) and drive 1½ miles; Blackwater Canoe Rental and Outpost is on the right.

US Air Force Armament Museum

This museum (☎ 850-882-4062; admission free; open 9:30am-4:30pm daily), outside the west gate of Eglin Air Force Base, is surrounded by aircraft on the lawn, including an A-10A Warthog, an F-16A, a cool B-17

Rattlesnakes? In Florida?

Picture a rattlesnake 6 feet long and weighing 10lb. You may not see one on your Panhandle visit, but they do exist. The largest rattlesnake in the world, the eastern diamondback (*Crotalus adamanteus*) has ranged throughout Florida for at least 2 million years. Although rattlers are thought of as living in dry sandhills and scrub, they also dip into swamps and marshes, especially when water levels are low. Scientists have even seen rattlers miles out at sea, apparently attempting to swim between islands (doing the snake paddle?).

Sadly, the eastern diamondback is declining rapidly, some say to the verge of being endangered. Loss of habitat is partly to blame; the snakes frequently make use of gopher tortoise burrows as shelter, the homes of a species currently on the run from humans. Unmolested rattlers may live to be 20 years old, but attaining such advanced years is becoming increasingly difficult for the reptiles. Even as development fragments and destroys their habitat, the snakes themselves are also subject to destruction, both by automobiles and by hunters who harvest snakeskin to turn into saleable skins and curios.

The Gopher Tortoise Council (PO Box 117800, University of Florida, Gainesville, FL 32611) has taken up the rattlesnakes' cause as part of its fight to 'work for the wise management and perpetuation of the gopher tortoise, the animals that live with it, and their natural habitats.' If you send a donation, the council will thank you, and so will the snakes.

Flying Fortress and the SR-71A Blackbird reconnaissance plane, which owns the transcontinental speed record of 68 minutes, 17 seconds. Inside, there are tons of weapons, a Warthog simulator and a terrifying F-105 Thunderchief missile. There's information on the history of Eglin (which one volunteer characterizes as the largest military base in the free world) along with planes, cannons, missiles and a huge hand-weapon display vault. Don't miss the airborne battlefield command center, with worn leather seats that look as if the occupants just stepped away for a minute to wipe their brows.

From Pensacola, take I-10 east to exit 12 (Crestview) and go south on Hwy 85 for about 2 miles to Hwy 123. Go 5 miles until you pick up Hwy 85 again, and follow the signs.

FORT WALTON BEACH & DESTIN
time zone CST

The resort region of Fort Walton Beach (population 22,000) and Destin (population 11,000) stretches mid-Panhandle, between Pensacola and the Walton County line, from where a strip dubbed The Beaches of South

Walton runs east to Panama City Beach. The beaches along two sections (called the Emerald Coast by the PR types) are undeniably stunning, with the whitest Appalachian quartz sand on the Panhandle. But development in the region has been nonstop, and, while officials trumpet 'ecofriendly tourism,' the reality is multiplying condominiums, land-eating golf courses and ever-larger tourist attractions.

But not all is lost: a few human-sized attractions, such as the Indian Temple Mound Museum, are worth visiting. The beachfront between Fort Walton Beach and Destin, owned by the US Air Force, is pristine. The Beaches of South Walton are stunning, and Grayton Beach State Park is an oasis. Fort Walton Beach and Destin work fine as bases for exploring this entire region.

Orientation & Information

Fort Walton Beach, the hometown of Eglin Air Base, is 60 miles east of Panama City Beach and about 35 miles west of Pensacola, along Hwy 98/Alt 98. The beach is on Okaloosa Island, a barrier island at the southern end of Choctawhatchee Bay, separated from the downtown area to the north by the Santa Rosa Sound. Destin, about 5 miles east along Miracle Strip Pkwy (Hwy 98), is on the barrier island.

Emerald Coast Visitors Welcome Center (☎ 850-651-7131 x227, 800-322-3319; 1540 Miracle Strip Pkwy; open 8am-5pm Mon-Fri, 10am-4pm Sat & Sun) has useful literature.

South Walton Tourist Development Center (☎ 850-267-3511, 800-822-6877; 25771 Hwy 331 at Hwy 98; open 8am-4:30pm daily) is on Santa Rosa Beach. The **Destin Area Chamber of Commerce** (☎ 850-837-6241; Ⓦ www.destinchamber.com; 4484 Legendary Dr at Hwy 98; open 9am-5pm Mon-Fri) offers accommodations brochures.

Change money at **Whitney Bank** in Fort Walton Beach (☎ 850-769-1400; 412 Mary Esther Cutoff NW), on the mainland, or in Destin (☎ 850-269-3400; 14060 Emerald Coast Pkwy, Suites 100-200).

Check email at the **Internet Cafe** (☎ 850-269-9864; 1988 Scenic Gulf Coast Dr, Miramar Beach; 15 min/1 hr $3/8).

The daily newspaper is the *Destin Log,* which publishes a Saturday 'Time Out' entertainment section. Look for the free weekly *Beachcomber* for happenings. For beach reading, visit the **Book Rack** (☎ 850-243-8020; 29 Miracle Strip Pkwy), a mine of used paperbacks so cheap you can leave them behind for the next traveler.

At **The Shores** (cnr Hwy 98 & Main St) center is **Bruno's** supermarket, a coin laundry, a bank ATM and a used bookstore.

Fort Walton Beach Medical Center (☎ 850-862-1111; 1000 NW Mar-Walt Dr) is on the mainland.

Things to See & Do

Indian Temple Mound Museum (☎ 850-833-9595; 139 Miracle Strip Pkwy; adult/child $2/1; open 11am-4pm Mon-Fri, 9am-4pm Sat winter, 9am-4:30pm Mon-Sat, 12:30pm-4:30pm Sun summer) is a look into the prehistoric past. Exhibits include Native American flutes, pottery and a display of Indian dwellings by region. Children will like the 'touchable' clothing and tool displays, and who wouldn't want to see a dog skeleton dating from AD 500? Outside the museum are the temple mound and a small nature

trail. In the gift shop, pick up a free brochure for a self-guided walking tour of historic Fort Walton that will take about 45 minutes.

The **Gulfarium** (☎ 850-244-5169, 800-247-8575; Ⓦ www.gulfarium.com; 1010 Miracle Strip Pkwy; adult/senior/child $17/15/10; open 9am-4pm winter & 9am-6pm summer) is a typical dolphins-jumping-through-the-hoops sea-life attraction.

A better option is the **Emerald Coast Science Center** (☎ 850-664-1261; 139 Brooks St; adult & child/senior $3.50/3; open 10am-4pm Mon-Fri, 11am-4pm Sat & Sun), where the wonders of physics come alive through interactive exhibits. Explore the computer room, or master air, elasticity and the science of 'bubbleology' by blowing a 4-foot-bubble. The center is next to **Fort Walton Landing Park**, on the water. Brooks St is one block south of and parallel to Miracle Strip Pkwy.

The 208-acre **Henderson Beach State Park** (☎ 850-837-7550; 17000 Emerald Coast Pkwy/Hwy 98, Destin; vehicle/pedestrian or cyclist $3.25/1) is a gem among the condos – 1¼ miles of shoreline along the Gulf of Mexico. There are outside showers and camping (see Places to Stay, later in this section).

Twenty miles north of Fort Walton Beach, at Niceville, the **Fred Gannon Rocky Bayou State Park** (☎ 850-833-9144; 4281 SR 20) invites you to tramp 1½ miles through sand-pine forest on the banks of Rocky Bayou, an arm of Choctawhatchee Bay that is part freshwater and part salt. You'll find Native American artifacts, and a freshwater lake for boaters. There is camping here (see Places to Stay, later in this section) and a playground.

Activities

Harborwalk Marina (Hwy 98 just east of East Pass Bridge) can be your marine headquarters. Hop aboard the glass-bottomed *Southern Star* (☎ 850-87-7741) for dolphin excursions or sunset cruises; fares run adult/senior/child $17/14/7.

Or stroll to the nearby **Reef Runner** kiosk (☎ 850-654-4655) to take a snorkeling cruise (adult or child $22) or sunset cruise (adult/child $12/5). Fishing charter boats, starting at $70 per person for four hours, also tie up here, and parasailing is available. All this happens next to the Lucky Snapper Grill & Bar (see Places to Eat, later in this section).

Paradise II (☎ 850-837-0123; next to June's Dunes restaurant at 1780 Hwy 98) is a kiosk with a large stock of kayaks (four hours $20), small sailboats (one hour/two hours $35/60) and bright blue beach chairs and umbrellas. You'll know you're there from the bodies bouncing off the waterside trampoline. Paradise also offers parasailing, for $60 to $70.

Diving is phenomenal in the Gulf of Mexico, with small sponge beds, natural and artificial reefs and wrecks, and a limestone ledge. There's 25 to 40 feet summer visibility – up to 80 feet in winter.

ScubaTech (☎ 850-837-2822, 850-837-1933; 301 Hwy 98) has staff who know the entire area and arrange dive trips. Driving from the west, you'll see a mural on the building's east wall. A four-hour, two-tank, 58- to 90-foot dive is $55 per person. A buoyancy compensator rents for $10, regulator for $15 and weight belt for $4. A complete package, including all that plus fins, mask and snorkel, is $45. ScubaTech also offers two-hour snorkel trips aboard the *Mongoose* for $22 a person including gear and wetsuit.

Places to Stay

Henderson Beach State Park (☎ 850-837-7550, 800-326-3521; 17000 Emerald Coast Pkwy/Hwy 98) has 60 campsites without/ with hookups for $8/10, while **Fred Gannon Rocky Bayou State Park** (☎ 850-833-9144, 800-326-3521; 4281 SR 20) has 42 (same rates).

Camping on the Gulf (☎ 877-226-7485; **w** www.campgulf.com; 10005 Emerald Coast Pkwy/Hwy 98; sites winter/spring/summer $45/52/65) is a mammoth campground with ample tent and RV sites. Skip it if you're looking for solitude, but don't underrate the park's helpful staff or many amenities (private beach, heated pool, store, activities center, proximity to shopping).

Howard Johnson (☎ 850-244-8663; 203 Miracle Strip Hwy; rooms $49/99 winter/ summer) has a 100 motel rooms, a pool and guest laundry facilities. It works fine as a home base.

EconoLodge (☎ 850-243-7123; 1284 Marler Dr; rooms $45-70/60-80 winter/summer), on Okaloosa Island, has no pool, but is on the water, next to the Marler Park picnicking area.

Leeside Inn (☎ 850-243-7359; 1350 Miracle Strip Hwy/Hwy 98E; rooms $55-90/75-120 winter/summer), which has a pool, is also on Okaloosa Island, by the National Seashore, and has a marina.

Sea Isle Motel (☎ 850-243-5563; 1214 Hwy 98E; rooms $74/94 winter/summer) is large, pink and friendly, and up the road from the Leeside.

Destin Holiday Beach Resort (☎ 850-837-6112, 800-874-0402; **w** www.condosinc.com; 1006 Hwy 98E; rooms $70-170/115-220 winter/summer) rents decent condominiums. It's on the beach; rates vary depending on apartment size and whether it faces the water.

Places to Eat

Shoney's Restaurant (☎ 850-244-3101; 201 Miracle Strip Pkwy; open 6am-11pm daily) is good for the budget-minded. The best choices are the imaginative breakfast bar, costing $6 and running till 2pm, and the dinner bar, for only $7. Guests at HoJo's next door get 10% off.

Donut Hole (☎ 850-267-8824; 635 Hwy 98E; breakfast $5-9, sandwiches $5-9; open 24/7), a cheerful Destin eatery, serves awesome donuts and good coffee. Get breakfast around the clock.

Another Broken Egg Cafe (☎ 850-644-0499; 104 Hwy 98E; breakfast $6-9, sandwiches $7-8; open 7am-2pm Tues-Sun) is an upscale eatery specializing in egg dishes. Savor the Floridian, with fresh crabmeat ($9), or the blackberry grits ($2).

The **Lucky Snapper Grill & Bar** (☎ 850-654-0900; 76 Hwy 98E; mains $6-22; open 11am-10pm daily), a dockside joint on Destin harbor, features a monster menu and a good-time atmosphere. Fare runs to generous portions of fried fish. The Caribbean jerk seasoned mahimahi, over rice and topped with mango-pineapple corn relish, will reward your adventurous spirit. Live banjos rock Wednesday to Saturday.

For the **Back Porch** (☎ 850-837-2022; 1740 Hwy 98E; mains $15-24; open 11am-11pm daily), shake the sand from your flip-flops and dress a little upmarket. This seafood and oyster bar has a smashing view of the Gulf and a seafood menu ranging from amberjack to shrimp. Or, you can order a cheeseburger with fries and slaw ($7).

SEASIDE & GRAYTON BEACH
time zone CST

The area between Destin and Panama City is less commercial than the Fort Walton Beach area and is home to the small, planned city of Seaside.

Orientation & Information

Grayton Beach, Seaside and Seagrove Beach are 35 miles west of Panama City Beach along County Hwy 30A (called Scenic 30A or Scenic Gulf Coast Dr), which splits south off Hwy 98 just before State Hwy 393 in the west and right after Panama City Beach in the east. Look for a bulletin board with tourist brochures on the eastern end of the Seaside Town Square. The ranger booth at Grayton Beach State Park is also a local information resource.

Explore the area by pedaling the 9-mile-long bike trail running parallel to Hwy 30A from just west of Grayton Beach clear to the road's end at Hwy 98.

Seaside

This collection of more than 300 dwellings (**W** www.seasidefl.com) is a planned community begun in 1981 as a pedestrian-friendly enclave evoking the traditional architectural styles of northwest Florida. The master plan called for an 80-acre city, with houses clustered around the Town Square, a model that has been lauded by architectural observers. The overall effect is pleasant. The uniformity of the houses isn't jarring, and individuality peeps through the building codes. People are welcoming, shops are cheery, service peppy. There is aggressive growth underway here, however, evidenced by ubiquitous construction and hard-sell real estate brochures everywhere. One caveat: Seaside is not your budget beachside paradise. If you plan to do more than explore the streets or lie on the beach, bring money.

Seaside Bike Rentals (☎ 850-231-2314; north side, Town Square) can equip you for a pedal-powered tour. Geared bikes are $10 an hour, $20 for 24 hours and $65 per week. Here are also wagons, tricycles and adult trikes.

Grayton Beach State Recreation Area

One of the finest beaches on the planet is at Grayton (☎ 850-231-4210; 357 Main Park Rd, Santa Rosa Beach; vehicle/pedestrian or cyclist $3.25/1), a 1133-acre stretch of dunes rolling down to the emerald water's edge. The Grayton Beach Nature Trail (get a self-guiding tour at the gate) runs from the east side of the parking lot through the dunes and pine flatwoods and onto a boardwalk to a return trail along the beach. Summer brings interactive campfire programs. Rent a canoe ($10 a half-day or $15 daily), or just relax on the beach.

Places to Stay

Grayton Beach State Recreation Area (☎ 850-231-4210, 800-326-3521; sites winter/summer $8/14, electricity $2 extra) is the best camping option. The park also rents 30 housekeeping **cabins** (night/week $85/536 winter, $110/693 summer, minimum 2 nights). The cabins have no maid service, no TV and one central phone – sounds nice, huh? A full kitchen, linens, dishes and heating are included.

Seagrove Villas and Motel (☎ 850-837-4853; 3040 Scenic Hwy 30A; units $78-146/109-268 winter/summer, weekly rates available), east of Grayton and Seaside, is the place to avoid the condo trap in a spacious motel room. There's a pool and free bicycles.

The **Old Pier Motel & Apartments** (☎ 850-837-6442; 65 Pomano St, Crystal Beach; rooms $85-200), run by the affable Kathi McGowan and her husband, offers one- and two-bedroom units with kitchens. Beach access, rare along this condo-lined stretch, is close.

Emerald Sun Properties, Inc (☎ 850-231-3554, 888-750-3554; **W** www.emeraldsun

.com; Seagrove Beach) handles vacation rentals for the South Walton area.

Places to Eat

Heavenly Shortcakes & Ice Cream (☎ 850-231-2029; on the Town Square; treats $3-7) is a good stop for gelato, cookies and cappuccino.

Roly Poly Wraps (☎ 850-231-3799; sandwich wraps $5-8; open 10am-7pm Sun-Thur, 10am-8pm Fri & Sat), in Market West (Seaside's upscale shopping cluster), has rolled sandwiches, including veggie options. The French Twist (warm and gooey grilled brie and Swiss) isn't low-fat, but it's tasty.

Cafe Spiazzia (☎ 850-231-1297; breakfast $7-13, lunch $9-13, dinner $8-25; open 8am-9pm daily), also in Market West, does lunch salads from $8 to $13 and pizzas squares for $6. As you eat, peruse the area map this place gives out.

Criolla's (☎ 850-267-1267; 170 Scenic Hwy 30A; open dinner only) is a quarter-mile east of Hwy 283 and 2 miles west of Seaside. Here are inventive dishes, fusing Creole and Caribbean flavors. Try the wood-grilled Yucatan grouper ($24) or the pan-seared salmon with skewered soft-shell crawfish ($25).

PANAMA CITY BEACH
population 7600; time zone CST

Dazzling white-sand beaches, plentiful watersports, abundant and inexpensive motel rooms and miles of tacky attractions all combine to make Panama City Beach one of the best spring break destinations in the USA. Throw in a tolerant attitude toward alcohol, and you have paradise for the party-hearty crowd.

If you're over 25, dude, and happen to hit town during March or early April, you may wonder why anyone comes here, *ever*. But this town has other faces: it's home to a number of religious retreats, and you'll find clean-living, upstanding citizens here, along with bookstores and shops selling religious items. And, while nightlife is definitely in the 'party with thousands' category and fast-food places line the strip, there's some unspoiled nature here.

St Andrews State Park, at the eastern tip of the barrier island containing Panama City Beach, is a haven of sand and sea. The Surfrider Foundation, a nonprofit dedicated to protection of the world's oceans, waves and beaches, in 2000 ranked Panama City Beach third on a list of 10 US coastal areas setting a good example in urban beach management.

Orientation

The barrier island containing Panama City Beach is just west of the separate Panama City, a military town tied to Tyndall Air Force Base. Hwy 98, the main southern coastal road, splits at Panama City Beach and becomes Hwy 98 in the north and Hwy 98A along the beach. The upper road is Panama City Beach Pkwy, the lower is Front Beach Rd.

The island is 27 miles long, from St Andrews State Park in the east to the Philips Inlet Bridge in the west. Hwy 98 connects Panama City Beach to Panama City via the Hathaway Bridge, across St Andrew Bay. The split of Hwys 98 and 98A occurs at the northeastern end of the beach, just south of the bridge, and cuts almost due west at Thomas Dr. Hwy 392 runs coastside between Front Beach Rd and St Andrews. Front Beach Rd is lined with fast-food joints, motels, miniature golf and cheesy amusement parks.

Information

The **Panama City Beach Convention & Visitors Bureau** (☎ 850-233-5070, 800-722-3224; 🄦 www.800pcbeach.com; 17001 Panama City Beach Pkwy; open 8am-5pm daily) has a good visitors information center and a useful map. Skip the PCB Chamber of Commerce and just come here, at the corner of Hwys 79 and 98, next to city hall.

For money exchange, **Bay Bank & Trust Co** (☎ 850-235-3333; 7915 Panama City Beach Pkwy; ☎ 850-235-4078; 17255 Panama City Beach Pkwy) has two branches on the beach. American Express has a representative office in Panama City at **Nervig Travel Service** (☎ 850-763-2876; 569 Harrison Ave).

Panama City Beach has more than one **post office** (268 S Arnold Rd ☎ 850-234-

9101; 420 Churchwell Dr). The **Panama City Beach Public Library** (☎ 850-233-5055; 110 Arnold Rd; open10am-8pm Mon, 10am-5pm Tues-Fri, 10am-4pm Sat) provides free Internet access.

The *Panama City News-Herald* is the daily. *Bay Arts & Entertainment* is a local events calendar published quarterly by the Bay Arts Alliance.

Do laundry at **Beachside Laundry and Dry Cleaning** (☎ 850-234-1601; 21902 Front Beach Rd) or at the **Express Coin Laundry** (275 S Arnold Rd).

The largest medical facility is **Bay Medical Center** (☎ 850-769-1511; 615 N Bonita Ave), in Panama City.

Museum of Man in the Sea

This museum (☎ 850-235-4101; 17314 Panama City Beach Pkwy; adult/child $5/2; open 9am-5pm daily) is a serious look at diving. Ever wonder how those hand-pumped diving systems work? You can crank up a Siebe pump, used for dives down to 30ft. Or climb into a Beaver Mark IV submersible, and see models of Sealab III, an underwater laboratory. The place is a refreshing throwback in an age of high-tech science museums. One staffer, named Greg, obviously cares about the museum, standing by to answer questions as you amble around the circle of exhibits. There's a cave-diving section, and video and interactive computer displays, and a collection of old diving suits. When you get to the aquarium, you can crawl under a table and come up with your head in a diver's helmet – and find yourself staring a big mullet in the face!

Zoo World Zoological & Botanical Park

This park (☎ 850-230-1243; 9008 Front Beach Rd; adult/senior/child $11/8/7; open 9am-dusk daily) is home to more than 300 animals, including 20 endangered species. The zoo participates in the Species Survival Plan (SSP), governed by the American Zoological Association, which brings together zoos and parks to protect and breed endangered animals. The Sumatran tiger is heart-breakingly beautiful, as are the lions; the cages for these big cats seem too small.

Zoo World also has a Swan Lake, with black and white versions of the graceful bird. You'll see reptiles, chimpanzees and other primates, an aviary and a petting zoo.

Gulf World

This marine park (☎ 850-234-5271; W www .gulfworldmarinepark.com; 15412 Front Beach Rd; adult/child $20/14; open 9am-4pm daily) has predictable marine-attraction shows, including a sea lion–kissing session. The river otters and the black-footed penguins are smile makers.

St Andrews State Recreation Area

St Andrews (☎ 850-233-5140, 800-326-3521; 4607 State Park Lane; vehicle/single-occupancy vehicle/pedestrian or cyclist $4/2/1) is1260 acres graced with nature trails, swimming beaches and camping (see Places to Stay, later in this section). During WWII it was part of the St Andrews Sound Military Reservation (see the circular cannon platforms on the beach near the jetties). If you move quietly, there's lots of wildlife, including foxes, coyotes, snakes, alligators and seabirds.

Try a snorkeling getaway trip to nearby Shell Island. The *Shell Island Shuttle* leaves from near the jetties daily at least every hour (9am to 5pm in summer, 10am to 4pm weekdays only in winter). A snorkel package including gear and the roundtrip costs $18. If you just want sunbathing, the roundtrip is adult/child $9.50/5.50. Get takeout snacks and bottled water from the store at the shuttle pier; it also sells hot dogs and ice cream.

The park is at the eastern end of the island. From Panama City cross the bridge, turn left on Thomas Dr and cross the Grand Lagoon; the entrance is on the left. From the beach, take Front Beach Rd to Thomas Dr to the end.

Activities

Panama City Dive Center (☎ 850-235-3390; 4823 Thomas Dr) offers daily boat rentals and dive charters – for snorkeling, you pay

$27 with rental gear, $19 with your own. Boats leave at 10am and 2pm.

Dixie Divers (☎ 850-914-9988; 109 B W 23rd St) runs three-day dive trips ($75 to $85), and open-water certification plus five dives (to get a PADI gold card) for $350, including equipment rental. Offshore there are shipwrecks, including a WWII liberty ship and a 220-foot tugboat, and 50 artificial reefs.

Lighthouse Marina (☎ 850-236-0056; N Lagoon Dr next to Captain Anderson's Restaurant) is a one-stop-shopping watersports center. Here are charter boats for bay and deep-sea fishing, dive charters (four hours, $60 per person), pontoon boat rentals (half-day, $149) and parasailing ($35 to $115).

Treasure Island Marina (☎ 850-230-9222; 3605 Thomas Dr at Grand Lagoon) can set you up for a day or three on the water. See **Island Time** (☎ 850-234-7377) to charter sailing catamarans, take snorkel and dolphin trips ($20 with coupon available at dock – includes lunch and gear), or cruise to a sunset (adult/child $12/8). This marina offers **The Glass Bottom Boat** (☎ 850-234-8944), running Shell Island and dolphin-encounter trips (adult/senior/child $15/14/8, discount coupons available), deep-sea fishing boats, as well as food concessions.

Organized Tours
Bay Seaplanes (☎ 850-234-1532; W www.bay seaplanes.com; 14856 Bayview Circle) gives the best air tours on the Panhandle, via Captain Dick Gregg's Cessna 180, which takes off from West Bay, north of PCB on Hwy 79. He'll fly you on a 10-mile, 20-mile or 50-mile trip, starting at adult/child $30/15 (two-adult minimum).

Places to Stay
St Andrews State Recreation Area (☎ 850-233-5140; nonwaterfront sites without/with hookups $10/12 winter; $17/19 summer; waterfront sites $12/14 winter, $19/21 summer) has campsites for tents and RVs. **Raccoon River Campground** (☎ 850-234-0181; 12209 Hutchinson Blvd; primitive/with electricity $16/18 winter, $24/18 summer) isn't a wilderness experience (two pools, cable hookups, a

playground, store, laundry room, game room and rec hall), but has some vegetation and a pond. Thirty primitive sites are available; 13 tent sites have electricity. RV sites with 50-amp electric are $2 extra.

Marriott (☎ 800-228-9290), **Holiday Inn** (☎ 800-465-4329) and **Howard Johnson** (☎ 800-654-2000) are among the dozen or so chains in Panama City Beach.

PCB motels are plentiful, and prices change often, so search for discounts and weekly rates.

Fiesta Motel (☎ 850-235-1000, 800-833-1415; 13623 Front Beach Rd; rooms & suites $30-120) divides its rates into eight mini-seasons, and charges a lower price for non-seaview units. The staff are personable; enjoy the pool and the clean rooms.

Sea Witch Motel (☎ 850-234-5722, 800-322-4571; 21905 Front Beach Rd; singles/doubles $35-40/50-60 winter, $50-60/75-80 summer), at the western end of PCB, has one/two-bedroom apartments ($59/125) and comfy motel rooms. It has a pool and is on the beach.

Island Breeze (☎ 850-234-8841, 800-874-6617; 17281 Front Beach Rd; rooms & suites $45-155) has a complicated rate structure and a list of house rules almost as Byzantine. The list of amenities is also long (heated pool, kids' pool, hot tub, full kitchens, private beachfront balconies, guest laundry), and the place is immaculate – you could do worse.

Sugar Sands Beach Resort (☎ 850-234-8802, 800-367-9221; 20723 Front Beach Rd; beachfront suites $50-135, economy kitchenettes $40-70) is also on the beach. Perks include a heated pool, barbecue area, playground and guest laundry. Ask about discount specials.

Places to Eat
As in the rest of the Panhandle, culinary emphasis here is on seafood. It tends to be good – especially oysters, which are cheap and plentiful. Check with the visitors information center for information on new restaurants; it also stocks a selection of restaurant menus.

The **Sunnyside Grill** (☎ 850-233-0729; 21828 Front Beach Rd; breakfast $2-4.50, lunch & dinner $2-11; open 6am-9pm Wed-Mon, 6am-2pm Tues), across from the Sea Witch Motel, dishes up what one server calls 'just good down-home cooking.' For breakfast, eggs come with home fries or grits, and a specialty is the Western Hash, topped with ham, cheese, onions, green peppers and tomatoes and served with biscuits ($5). Come back later for the fish platter, available fried or grilled ($9).

Mike's Diner (☎ 850-234-1942; 17554 Front Beach Rd; breakfast $4-6, lunch & dinner $4-13; open 6am-9pm daily) is the place for local fish, shrimp and oysters. Burgers and sandwiches, starting at $4, are on hand for the unconverted.

The **All-American Diner** (☎ 850-233-6007; 15404 Front Beach Rd; breakfast $3-8, lunch $3-7, dinner $7-11; open 24/7) is the place for typical US fare. Behind the All-American's chrome-quilted facade, the omelettes are named Marilyn, Elvis, Dean and Bogart. Lunch consists mainly of sandwiches and burgers, while for dinner, steaks, chops and chicken dishes rule.

Panama City Brewery (☎ 850-230-2739; 11040 Hutchinson Blvd; lunch specials $10-14, dinner mains $15-18) has good food and house-made beers in a chic setting. Try the beer sampler ($7) – small glasses of its five beers, all which have clever names (eg, 'Mullet Head Red').

Captain Anderson's Restaurant (☎ 850-234-2225; 5551 North Lagoon Dr; dinner mains $15-35; open at 4:30pm Mon-Fri, 4pm Sat) is a sprawling family restaurant on the water. Heavily but tastefully decorated with many things nautical, it specializes in seafood, which is also for sale in the waterfront market. What steaks there are come certified angus, and are cooked to order.

Entertainment
Along the beach, every bar does a happy hour and drink specials, especially during spring break. The two big nightclubs, **Spinnaker** (☎ 850-234-7822; 8795 Thomas Dr) and **Club La Vela** (☎ 850-234-3866; 8813 Thomas Dr), adjacent to one another, are famous around the Panhandle for their jam-packed, meat-market atmosphere and for rocking the beach with ear-splitting music.

Harpoon Harry's (☎ 850-234-6060; W www.harpoonharrys.com; 12627 Front Beach Rd; open 11am-late daily) has a café, but no one comes here just to eat. You'll find a Gulfside bar, a dance floor often fueled by live music, and disc jockeys or karaoke going loud and long into the night. There's also a sports bar and video games.

Getting There & Away
The nearest airport is **Panama City Bay County Airport** (☎ 850-763-6751; 3173 Airport Rd) in Panama City, served only by a small number of carriers. There's no public transport from the airport; a taxi or rental car is your only choice.

Amtrak's *Sunset Limited* stops at Chipley (57 miles away) on Sunday, Tuesday and Thursday at 9:51pm coming from Orlando, and on Wednesday, Saturday and Monday at 9:10am from Los Angeles.

Greyhound has a flag stop in Panama City Beach at the Hwy 98/Hwy 79 stoplight; there's a **station** (☎ 850-785-6111; 917 Harrison Ave) in Panama City. For planning purposes, consider the following routes, travel times and one-way/roundtrip prices for buses departing from Panama City: to Gainesville takes 5½ to 9 hours and costs $54/108; to Miami takes 13½ to 14½ hours ($83/168); to Jacksonville takes 5½ to 6½ hours ($58/116); to New Orleans takes 7 to 8½ hours ($28/52); to Pensacola takes 2½ to 4 hours ($23/45); and to Tallahassee takes 3½ to 4½ hours ($13/26).

By car, Panama City is 98 miles from Tallahassee; 287 miles from Atlanta, Georgia; 305 miles from New Orleans, Louisiana; 339 miles from Tampa; 340 miles from Orlando; and 562 miles from Miami. From the south, take Hwy 98 into town; from the east or west take I-10 to either Hwys 231 or 79, which run south to the beach.

Getting Around
The **Bay Town Trolley** (☎ 850-769-0557) makes a 2½-hour roundtrip up and down Front Beach Rd five times daily (50¢).

From the airport, a taxi costs about $16; call **Yellow Cab** (☎ 850-763-4691). By car, take Hwy 390 south to Hwy 98 west, straight to the beach.

Affordable Limousine (☎ 850-233-0029) will pick up and drop off up to six people in a luxury van or a stretch limo anywhere along the beach – between the Hathaway Bridge and Hwy 79 – for $10. It's open and on call 24/7.

California Cycle (☎ 850-233-1391; 10624 Front Beach Rd), putting spring breakers on wheels for 19 years, has three shops along the main drag and is the source of those yellow scooters buzzing the streets like so many bees. Rentals start at $7 per hour (three hours minimum). Full-sized cycles are available, starting at $30 per hour. You can also rent a bicycle, starting at $15 daily.

Classic Scooter Rental (☎ 850-234-0170; 8307 Thomas Dr) is the real deal, biker style. Scooters start at $10 per hour, but why stop there? A full-sized Harley Davidson can be yours for only $50 hourly or $150 daily, plus $100 deposit and $900 insurance (motorcycle license required).

ST JOSEPH PENINSULA STATE PARK

This park (☎ 850-227-1327, 800-326-3521; 8899 Cape San Blas Rd; vehicle with boat/vehicle/pedestrian or cyclist $5/3.25/1; camping without/with electric $8/10 winter, $15/17 summer; open 8am-sunset daily) is spectacular. It's a 2500-acre finger of land jutting into the Gulf of Mexico, with 10 miles of wilderness trails, long expanses of dune-rimmed beaches, plus canoeing and camping. In 2002, it was ranked first in the 12th annual America's Best Beaches list, a popular rating based on 50 criteria including sand quality, water temperature and amount of litter (see W www.topbeaches.com).

Accommodations include eight furnished cabins ($55 per night winter, $70 per night summer; two-night minimum on weekends or holidays). Get canoes from the rangers for $3 an hour or $15 a day.

The park is east of Mexico Beach and west of Apalachicola, off Hwy 98 on County Hwy 30, which veers south just east of the city of Port St Joe. Follow that road for about 10 miles to a fork, then bear left (there's a sign saying St Joseph Peninsula State Park). Drive about 8 miles to the end, and you're in the park.

APALACHICOLA
population 3500; time zone EST

The oyster capital of Florida, Apalachicola is a gem of a town for seafood aficionados and for nature lovers. It's a quaint Southern town on a stately river, with a rich history and a fascinating natural environment. Apalachicola Bay, fed daily by 16 billion gallons of freshwater from the Chattahoochee, Flint and Apalachicola Rivers, teems with sea life.

Within the town are a number of attractions, and its peaceful streets and proximity to the river and the beaches make it a better base for excursions than, say, Panama City Beach. Apalachicola is also the former home of refrigeration pioneer Dr John Gorrie, who invented air conditioning here (he was granted his patent in 1851). Gorrie was at various times the mayor, postmaster, treasurer, councilor, bank director and the founder of Trinity Episcopal Church. Today, Gorrie's home is a museum.

Orientation

Apalachicola is at the end of the southward bulge in the Panhandle, about halfway between Tallahassee and Panama City, south of the Apalachicola National Forest. Hwy 98 runs from the west through the center of town and east toward St George Island (see later in this chapter). Downtown Apalachicola and the Apalachicola Historic District are on the eastern end of the spit leading toward the Gorrie Bridge (Hwy 98), and the streets lie in a grid that's on a 45-degree angle to compass points.

Market St is the primary southeast-northwest street; other streets west of Market St are numbered, beginning with 4th St. Streets are bisected by avenues, which are lettered beginning at Ave B, one block northwest of Bay Ave at the waterline. Ave E is the main drag and the continuation of Hwy 98, running from Market St in the northeast all the way out of town and beyond.

Information

Get tourist information and city maps at the **Apalachicola Bay Chamber of Commerce** (☎ 850-653-9419; 99 Market St; open 9am-5pm Mon-Fri).

The municipal **library** (☎ 850-653-8436; 76 6th St; open 10am-5pm Mon, 10am-noon & 2pm-5pm Tues, Thur & Fri, 10am-noon Wed) has two computers with free Internet access.

Hooked on Books (☎ 850-653-2420; 54 Market St) specializes in area history, nature guides and children's literature.

Things to See & Do

Walking Tour The chamber of commerce hands out a 35-site walking tour, which could take days if you were to hit every spot. So be selective and use the brochure as a rough guide; many sites are close together. The following are some highlights.

Looking like a Southern plantation, the columned **Raney House** (☎ 850-653-9749; 46 Ave F), built in 1838, was the home of Harriet and David Raney, the latter a two-time mayor of the city. It was under renovation at the time of research; call to see if tours are available.

Watch the shrimp boats coming in and out at the piers by the waterfront. In the block between Aves D and F, from Water St to Market St, are two interesting sites, the **Sponge Exchange** (1840) and the **Cotton Warehouse** (1838). Strolling around downtown makes for a pleasant hour or two.

Dr John Gorrie (1803–55) was one of the pioneers of refrigeration, which he developed to keep yellow fever patients cool. His house is now the **Gorrie House Museum** (☎ 850-653-9347; 46 6th St; admission $1; open 9am-5pm Thur-Sun), one block south of Ave E. Inside, you can see and use a model of his condensing pumps. There are other displays on cotton and long-gone cotton warehouses that used to trade along the Apalachicola River, and tiny exhibits of tools, pine resin samples and sea sponges. The museum is closed Thanksgiving, Christmas and New Year's Day.

Trinity Episcopal Church (79 6th St) feels very New England, with its columns and large windows. It was built in New York state and cut into sections that were shipped down the Atlantic coast, around the Keys and up to this spot, where it was assembled in 1836.

St Patrick Catholic Church (cnr Ave C & 6th St), close to the Gorrie House Museum, is another interesting church (from 1929), this one Romanesque.

The **St Vincent National Wildlife Refuge headquarters and visitor's center** (☎ 850-653-8808; north end of Market St; admission free; open 8am-4:30pm Mon-Fri) has interactive exhibits and information, and occupies an island a quarter-mile offshore at the west end of Apalachicola Bay, west of Cape St George. Staff can tell you where to catch a boat to the island, and what to look for (dune ridges that reveal 5000-year-old geological records, red wolves, sea turtles, peregrine falcons and other endangered species).

The **Apalachicola National Estuarine Research Reserve** (☎ 850-653-8063; 261 7th St; admission free; open 8am-5pm Mon-Fri) is across the way from the refuge headquarters. Allot substantial time for appreciating the Gulf of Mexico, Apalachicola Bay and River and Ocean Reef habitat-simulating aquariums. In them you'll see all the critters of the river and the bay close up, and then you can take the half-mile nature trail boardwalk out to the wonderful river (look for turtles along the way), where you'll find free binoculars on a turret.

Organized Tours At **Broke-A-Toe's Outdoor Guide Service** (☎ 850-229-9283, 850-227-9534) they offer sightseeing charters ($240, limit six people) and bay and deep-sea fishing trips ($250 to $650, bait, ice, tackle and licenses included).

EcoVentures, Inc (☎ 850-653-2593; 301 Market St; ⓦ www.apalachicolatours.com) runs two-hour cruises on the 40-foot *Osprey* through the shallow rivers, marshes and swamps of the estuary reserve (adult/child $20/10).

Places to Stay

Apalachicola Bay Campground (☎ 850-670-8307; Hwy 98; tent/RV sites $15/17) in Eastpoint, across the Gorrie Bridge from Apalachicola, has sites with electricity and water; RV/van sites have sewer hookups. (See St George Island later in this section for more camping.)

The **Rancho Inn** (☎ 850-653-9435; 240 Hwy 98W; rooms $60/70 Sun-Thur/Fri & Sat) attracts boaters driving big pickups and has a down-home feel. Every room has a fridge, a microwave and a coffeemaker.

Best Western Apalach Inn (☎ 850-653-9131, 800-528-1234; 249 Hwy 98W; rooms $75) is a spiffy chain motel with ordinary rooms and a pool.

Apalachicola River Inn (☎ 850-653-8139; 123 Water St; rooms $85-110) provides clean riverside rooms. More than a motel, here you'll find a full restaurant (see Places to Eat, below), an oyster bar and a lounge, not to mention a seafood store, a package store and a marina with charter boats.

Gibson Inn (☎ 850-653-2191; Ⓦ www.gibsoninn.com; 51 Ave C; rooms $90-105), an enormous 1907-vintage downtown centerpiece, is a B&B with Victorian-style rooms, a wraparound porch and a cat named Sylvester who snoozes on the reception counter. The Gibson, which is on the National Historic Register, is convenient to everything.

Places to Eat

Dolores' Sweet Shoppe (☎ 850-653-9081; 29 Ave E; open 7am–mid-afternoon Mon-Fri) is an old-fashioned ice cream parlor and café in a crumbling brick building – look for the large 'EAT' sign. It has homemade pastries (try the key lime pie), subs and sandwiches ($3 to $5).

The **Red Top Cafe** (☎ 850-653-8612; 238 Hwy 98W; open 6am–mid-afternoon Tues-Sat), by the Rancho Inn, serves hearty breakfasts in the $4 to $6 range (pecan pancakes are good).

Risa's Pizza (☎ 850-653-8578; 83 Market St; open 11am-9:30pm Mon-Tues, 11am-3pm Wed, 11am-9:30pm Thur-Sat) offers salads from $4.25 to $6, sandwiches from $4 and 16-inch cheese pizzas for $9.

The **Apalachicola Seafood Grill** (☎ 850-653-9510; 100 Market St; open 11:30am-8pm Mon-Sat) is the heart of downtown. Serving up baskets of fried seafood ($8 to $14) and

meal-sized salads ($6 to $8), it's always bustling. It has a full bar and a gift shop with those hard-to-find tacky souvenirs.

Caroline's (☎ 850-653-8239; 123 Water St, at the Apalachicola River Inn) is an elegant motel dining room serving three meals daily. At breakfast, country ham and red-eye gravy with two eggs, grits and biscuits goes for $8; come back for dinner and enjoy seared salmon and black mussels with a cilantro lime sauce, jasmine rice and sautéed Asian vegetables ($24).

Getting There & Around

There's no Greyhound service within 50 miles of here. Driving, you'll come into town from either direction from Hwy 98. Once you're here, walking will get you around downtown, but you'll need to get back in the old gasburner to go anywhere else.

ST GEORGE ISLAND
population 700

Discovered by Europeans in the 1500s, St George Island is a 28-mile-long barrier island, secluded across a long bridge, flat as a pancake and fringed with white sand. Unless you're camping, St George Island isn't a budget destination – the cheapest room in the only motel is $50 in low season. But the camping, in the state park or on Cape St George (the island to the west of St George), is excellent.

The island is south of the city of Eastpoint, across a 3-mile-long causeway. When you get to the beach, go straight until you can't anymore – this is known as Gulf Beach Dr and also as Front Beach Dr. If you turn left, the road will eventually take you to St George Island State Park; a right turn will take you to Government Cut, which separates Little St George Island from the big island.

St George Island State Park

This 1962-acre park (☎ 850-927-2111, 800-326-3521; vehicle/pedestrian or cyclist $4/1; tent sites without/with electricity $8/10 winter, $12/14 summer) is at the northeast end of St George Island. Throughout the pine woods, you'll find hiking trails and boardwalks, marshes and live oak hammocks, and there's excellent swimming.

Cape St George
If you're looking for peace and quiet, search no more: there's free camping on the eastern and western ends of the Cape St George Reserve on Little St George Island, just across Sikes Cut. The area is idyllic, and the only sounds during the day (other than the occasional motorboat) are made by wildlife, including the snowy plover, least tern, black skimmer willet and osprey, and the standard Florida-issue raccoons.

Though camping is free, there are no facilities – bring everything you'll need, including a gallon of water per person a day and food in a plastic (not Styrofoam) cooler. Take your trash out, and set campfires (use downed wood) only on the beach. You don't need to reserve ahead, but park rangers request you let them know if you're going there (call the Apalachicola National Estuarine Research Reserve at ☎ 850-653-8063).

Jeanni's Journeys (☎ 850-927-3259; 240 E 3rd St), on St George Island, rents kayaks ($30 to $55 daily), sailboats ($95 daily) and canoes ($35 daily); all are good ways to reach Cape St George.

Places to Stay & Eat
Buccaneer Inn (☎ 850-927-2585, 800-847-2091; 160 W Gorrie Dr; rooms $50-105/80-140 winter/summer) is the only motel on the island; room rates depend on the view and season. Rooms with kitchenettes cost $15 to $20 more nightly than those without. Rooms are clean and adequate; there's a pool.

St George Inn (☎ 850-927-2903, 800-322-5196; w www.stgeorgeinn.com; 135 Franklin Blvd at Pine St; singles/doubles $70/90) is a well-appointed, three-story B&B complete with heated pool.

Many people stay in condominiums, cottages and houses, which rent for an average of $700 weekly in the winter, $850 weekly in fall, $1100 weekly in spring and $1400 weekly in summer. Contact **Collins Vacation Rentals** (☎ 850-927-2900, 800-423-7418).

Blue Parrot Oyster Bar & Grill (☎ 850-927-2987; 216 W Gorrie Dr; open 10am-9pm winter, 11am-10pm summer) is an oceanfront café and local hangout. A dozen raw oysters are $6, steamed $7. Sandwiches run $5 to $10, platters such as chicken tenders are $11, and the seafood combo is $17.

Paradise Cafe (☎ 850-927-4898; 65 W Gorrie Dr; dinners $11-17) is good for breakfast, featuring omelettes from the simple ($3) to the sublime (the $9 seafood omelette). It also has sandwiches and burgers ($5 to $8).

Island Oasis (☎ 850-927-2639; 101 E Gulf Beach Dr; open at 7:30am daily, dinner served after 2pm) serves a full menu, emphasizing fried or grilled seafood. Breakfasts are inexpensive ($3 for a Belgian waffle, $5 for a seafood omelette) and tasty.

Getting Around
Beach Bike Rentals (☎ 850-927-3993; 139 E Gorrie Dr at Franklin Blvd) rents bikes for just $25 to $30 weekly, and will pick up and deliver. It's a great way to see St George Island – use the bike path that runs for miles along E Gulf Beach Dr.

I-10 Corridor

DEFUNIAK SPRINGS
population 6500; time zone CST
DeFuniak Springs, the Walton County seat, is becoming popular as a stopover destination for northerners on their way to the Emerald Coast beaches. It's home to historic buildings, a winery and a lovely downtown hotel.

The historic district consists of 39 buildings that ring **Lake DeFuniak**, a perfectly round, spring-fed lake with a mile-long circumference. The **Walton County Chamber of Commerce** (☎ 850-892-3191; 95 Circle Dr; open variable hours) is in the Chautauqua Building, a colonnaded 1909 landmark (off Hwy 90, follow the chamber of commerce signs). If it's closed, you can get a brochure from an outside rack for a self-guided tour around the lake.

Begin at the **Chautauqua Building**, the summer home of the New York Chautauqua, a cultural and educational organization, from 1885 to 1922. Moving counterclockwise around the lake, you'll see the 1896 **St Agatha's Episcopal Church** (144 Circle Dr), which has handsome stained-glass windows, followed by other architectural beauties, from Victorian and Queen Anne to traditional Florida vernacular.

The **Chautauqua Vineyards & Winery** (☎ 850-892-5887; 364 Hugh Adams Rd), near I-10, is worth a visit. It grows its own grapes and other fruits for some interesting wines – including a blueberry wine. Tours and tastings happen daily, 9am to 5pm.

The **Book Store** (☎ 850-892-3119; 640 Baldwin St), downtown, carries used and new books.

Super 8 (☎ 800-800-8000), **Best Western** (☎ 800-528-1234) and **Days Inn** (☎ 800-325-2525) line the Hwy 90 exit to DeFuniak Springs off I-10.

Hotel DeFuniak (☎ 850-892-4383, 877-333-8642; 400 Nelson Ave; rooms/suites $80/100) is the best place to stay. It's in a 1920 Victorian building, with eight rooms and four suites. The **Restaurant** (open 7am-9am & 11am-2pm daily, 5pm-closing Mon-Sat) serves Sunday brunch (11am to 2pm) and is excellent. Lunch offerings include salads and sandwiches ($4 to $7); dinners range from fresh vegetable pasta ($9) to potato-crusted salmon ($13) and pork medallions with fruit chutney ($13). There's an ice cream parlor, too.

FLORIDA CAVERNS STATE PARK
time zone CST
Three miles north of Marianna, on County Hwy 166, is **Florida Caverns State Park** (☎ 850-482-1228, 850-482-9598, camping reservations 800-326-3521; 3345 Caverns Rd; vehicle/pedestrian or cyclist $3.25/1, cave tours adult/child $5/2.50; campsites without/with electricity $8/10 winter, $12/14 summer), a 1300-acre park on the Chipole River that has some fascinating caves. Eerie stalactites, stalagmites and flowstone formations that look like rock waterfalls fill the lighted caves, along with calcified shapes formed over the centuries as calcite has bubbled through the rocks. Only 10 of the many cavern rooms are open. The Florida Parks Service zealously protects the caves, as well as the endangered gray bats that live there. The other caves are open only to scientists and archaeologists. In the visitor's center are archives and artifacts taken from archaeological digs in the park.

Dipping underground for a couple of hundred feet within the park, the Chipole River is a nice surprise. There's a boat ramp and facilities for camping, canoeing, swimming and riding (if you brought your horse!). The visitor's center rents canoes at $15 for eight hours, $10 for four. There's also camping. Motels and restaurants can be found in nearby Marianna.

Guided tours of the caves lasting 45 minutes leave the visitor's center at least once an hour (more often if staff is available) from 9am to 4:30pm daily. The tours are limited to 25 people each; go to the ticket office at the cave right when you arrive.

TORREYA STATE PARK
Fifty miles west of Tallahassee, this little park (☎ 850-643-2674, 800-326-3521; vehicle/pedestrian or cyclist $3/1; open 8am-sunset daily; tent camping adult/student or child $3/2, RV sites $8) is set on high bluffs along the Apalachicola River. It's home to a pre–Civil War plantation mansion, where tours start daily at 10am, and Saturday and Sunday at 2pm and 4pm also. The park is south off I-10, just off Hwy 12, near Bristol.

SUWANNEE RIVER STATE PARK
At the junction of the Suwannee and Withlacoochee Rivers, this 1800-acre state park (☎ 386-362-2746; vehicle/pedestrian or cyclist $2/1; open 8am-sunset daily; campsites without/with electricity $8/10 winter, $10/12 summer) features the confluence of rivers and a bubbling spring you can swim in. You'll see the Confederate fortifications built to protect the railroad bridge over the Suwannee, which was used to shuttle supplies to the front.

The park has canoes ($15 daily) and camping. Interpretive signs mark the Suwannee River Nature Trail through hardwood hammock, and the Sandhills Trail, which leads to the Old Stage Road, a historic Pensacola-Jacksonville transport route. The park is 13 miles northwest of Live Oak, on Hwy 90.

STEPHEN FOSTER STATE FOLK CULTURAL CENTER
time zone EST

About an hour and a half east of Tallahassee, off I-10, the Stephen Foster State Folk Cultural Center (☎ 386-397-2733, 800-326-3521; vehicle/pedestrian or cyclist $3.25/1) is a 247-acre center honoring the composer of Florida's state song, 'Old Folks at Home' (see the boxed text 'Stephen C Foster'), a man who never came near here.

The park has a 5-mile biking/hiking trail, a museum of Florida history that you'd swear is a 19th-century plantation, and a huge carillon. Ten dioramas illustrating Foster songs and peopled by tiny mechanical characters line the walls of the museum and the carillon tower. Each took some 1500 hours of work to complete. Tours run frequently, sometimes led by guides in antebellum dresses and ser-enaded by bagpipers. Special events happen throughout the year, culminating in the Florida Folk Festival Memorial Day weekend. Other festivals are Rural Folklife Days in November and Stephen Foster Day in January.

The Stephen Foster Memorial Carillon, installed in 1958, is behind the museum. Its 97 bells, which make it the largest tubular carillon in the world, ring periodically throughout the day and during programs of Foster's more than 200 compositions.

To enjoy the river, rent canoes from **American Canoe Adventures** (☎ 386-397-1309). Tent camping costs $8 per site ($2 extra for electricity). The campground is closed Memorial Day weekend.

From I-10, take Hwy 41 north past the town of White Springs and follow the signs.

Stephen C Foster

While Stephen Collins Foster (1826–64) could be considered a true American legend (he was even born on the Fourth of July), his work in minstrel shows and his popularity at the height of slavery have meant that his legacy has been tainted with political incorrectness.

Yet his performances and variations on slave songs of the era are undeniably offset by his contribution to American culture. Foster brought us 'Oh, Susanna!' – as familiar to listeners now as it was when released in 1846. And he brought the world's attention to the Suwannee River – a river Foster never set eyes on.

The song is 'Old Folks at Home,' with lyrics in simulated dialect: 'Way down upon the Swannee Ribber, far, far away/Dere's wha my heart is turning ebber/Dere's where the old folks stay.' Foster chose the Suwannee on a whim: it's said he was considering the Pedee and the Yazoo Rivers as well ('Way down upon the Yazoo River'?!?), but a misspelled map drew him to the 'Swannee,' which runs through north-central Florida and empties into the Gulf of Mexico.

Despite what contemporary sensibility recognizes as racist tone and lyrics (one line is 'Oh! darkeys how my heart grows weary/Far from de old folks at home'), it was so popular worldwide in its day that it was adopted by Florida as the state song.

Today, visitors to the Stephen Foster State Folk Cultural Center are treated to wildly disparate imagery: on one hand, the center is dedicated to the life and work of a man who spent most of his career writing 'plantation melodies.' On the other, the center is host to many fine programs that increase visitors' understanding of black and Native American heritage.

In any event, it's interesting to note that here, in the southernmost Southern state, this center is dedicated to the memory of a man who wrote a song of the South from his home in Allegheny, Pennsylvania. It could be worse – 'Oh Susanna!' was written in Cincinnati, Ohio.

– Nick Selby

Tallahassee & Around

TALLAHASSEE
population 149,000; time zone EST

Tallahassee usually is a medium-sized Southern town, a sleepy place of elegant buildings and shade-dimpled thoroughfares that invite the visitor to stroll and linger. The streets are so tree lined – many are completely canopied – that when viewed from the air the town looks like a small settlement in the middle of a forest. But this is a planned city, and a quick glance at a map reveals that 'all roads lead to Tallahassee.' The capitol is the hub of a loose network of roads snaking outward in all directions.

Tallahassee became the capital of the Florida territories in 1824, when Pensacola and St Augustine, the two biggest cities, could not agree on a capital. Tallahassee, midway between the two, benefited from the dispute, and the hilly little settlement became the state business center.

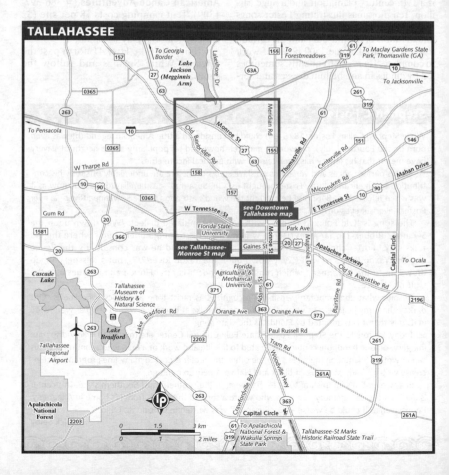

TALLAHASSEE

'Tallahassee' is an Apalachee word meaning 'old town.' The Apalachees, original settlers in the area, were killed off by disease and Spaniards, who followed Hernando de Soto's arrival in 1539.

By the 19th century, the area was rich agriculturally, and relying heavily on slaves to work the farms. During the Civil War, Tallahassee was the only Confederate city east of the Mississippi River not to fall to Union troops – though there was a battle at nearby Natural Bridge (see History in the Facts about Florida chapter).

Today, twice a year the streets, hotels and restaurants of Tallahassee fill up and the limpid air becomes electric: when the state legislature meets (March to May) and when college football season rolls around (in the fall). When Florida State University hosts football, thousands of avid football fans materialize, conspicuously supporting their beloved team.

As a stop for a day or week, Tallahassee is definitely rewarding, politicians and football fans notwithstanding. Attractions are many and the citizens gracious. And, despite being the capital of one of the fastest-growing states in the nation, it moves forward at a languorous pace, and doesn't neglect to treasure its past.

Orientation

The main north-south drag is Monroe St; it's the east-west dividing line for addresses. Tennessee St is the north-south divider. The downtown is the center of the city, bounded by Tennessee St on the north, Van Buren St on the south, the FSU campus to the west and Magnolia Drive on the east.

Thomasville Rd forks to the right off Monroe St, just north of Brevard St, and runs northeast, toward Maclay Gardens State Park.

The Civic Center is west of the Florida State Capitol and the Old Capitol. Florida State University is about three-quarters of a mile west of Monroe St; massive Doak Campbell Stadium is at the southwest corner of campus.

Florida Agricultural & Mechanical University is south of downtown, bordered by Orange Ave on the south, Canal St on the north, Adams St on the east and Perry St on the west.

Information

Tourist Offices The **Tallahassee Area Convention & Visitors Bureau** (☎ 850-413-9200, 800-628-2866; 106 E Jefferson St; open 8am-5pm Mon-Fri, 9am-1pm Sat) runs the excellent Visitor Information Center. The center has two helpful brochures, *Touring Tallahassee,* a walking guide to the downtown district, and *Canopy Roads and Country Lanes,* a county driving tour. (See Getting Around, later in this section, for a canopy roads list.) The visitors bureau also staffs an **information desk** in the Tallahassee Mall (2415 N Monroe St; open 10am-6pm Mon-Sat, 12:30pm-5:30pm Sun), but it's no substitute for the excellent downtown office.

The **Florida Welcome Center** (☎ 850-488-6167; ⓦ www.flausa.com; open 8am-5pm Mon-Fri, 11am-3pm Sat), in the New Capitol, is a must-visit resource. Manager Don Hardy, here since 1989, is a mine of information, which he'll share with a friendly drawl as he dispenses coupons and flyers on statewide attractions. The center also arranges free 35-minute guided tours of the capitol Monday to Friday – you'll see the chambers and get the building's history.

A hotel reservation hotline (☎ 850-488-2337) has updated accommodation availability information during the busier times.

The **Chamber of Commerce** (☎ 850-224-8116; ⓦ www.talchamber.com; 100 N Duval St; open 9am-5pm Mon-Fri) is only useful if you're thinking of relocating. It's in The Columns (circa 1830), Tallahassee's oldest surviving home.

Leon County has an excellent Tallahassee Web site (ⓦ www.co.leon.fl.us/visitors).

Money The **Bank of America** has a downtown branch (315 S Calhoun St), and other branches (2262 N Monroe St, 1321 W Jefferson St) where you can exchange money. ATMs are sprinkled throughout town.

Post The main **post office** (2800 S Adams St) is on the edge of downtown; there's another closer to the center (216 W College Ave) and one on the north side, closer to the Monroe St motels (1845 Martin Luther King Jr Blvd). Information on all branches is available at ☎ 800-275-8777.

Bookstores & Libraries You'll find new and used books at **Bill's Books**, with one location at the northeast end of the FSU campus (☎ 850-224-3178; 102 S Copeland St) as well as two others (☎ 850-561-1495; 1411 E Tennessee St ☎ 850-222-6653; 649 W Gaines St).

Barnes & Noble (☎ 850-877-3878; 1480 Apalachee Pkwy ☎ 850-383-0600; 2415 N Monroe in the mall) has a café in both stores.

The **Paperback Rack** (☎ 850-244-3455; 105 N Monroe St) has new and used literature, fiction and some travel books, while the **House of Books** (☎ 850-681-0774; 1215 N Monroe St) is a good stop for new and used light reading, as well as used audio books, for your Panhandle auto trip.

The main **library** (☎ 850-487-2665; 200 W Park Ave; open 10am-9pm Mon-Thur, 10am-6pm Fri, 10am-5pm Sat, 1pm-6pm Sun) is

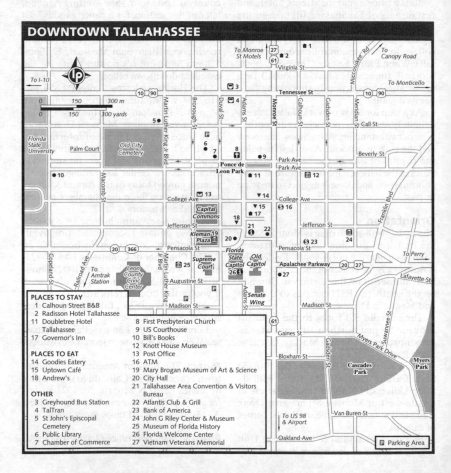

DOWNTOWN TALLAHASSEE

PLACES TO STAY
1 Calhoun Street B&B
2 Radisson Hotel Tallahassee
11 Doubletree Hotel Tallahassee
17 Governor's Inn

PLACES TO EAT
14 Goodies Eatery
15 Uptown Café
18 Andrew's

OTHER
3 Greyhound Bus Station
4 TalTran
5 St John's Episcopal Cemetery
6 Public Library
7 Chamber of Commerce

8 First Presbyterian Church
9 US Courthouse
10 Bill's Books
12 Knott House Museum
13 Post Office
16 ATM
19 Mary Brogan Museum of Art & Science
20 City Hall
21 Tallahassee Area Convention & Visitors Bureau
22 Atlantis Club & Grill
23 Bank of America
24 John G Riley Center & Museum
25 Museum of Florida History
26 Florida Welcome Center
27 Vietnam Veterans Memorial

good for checking email, offering 20 free online computers. It's on Park St; the parking lot entrance is on Call St.

Media The *Tallahassee Democrat* (W www .tallahassee.com) is the daily newspaper. National Public Radio (NPR) is at 88.9 FM.

Universities Tallahassee is a college town, with two universities. **Florida State University** (FSU; ☎ 850-644-2882; W www.fsu.edu) is a liberal arts school of over 35,000 students, concentrating on sciences, computing and performing arts (and football), with undergraduate and graduate studies. From September to April, there are free guided tours of the campus leaving from **Visitor Services** (☎ 850-644-3246; 100 S Woodward Ave) Monday to Friday at 10am, 11am, 1pm and 3pm.

The city's other university, **Florida Agricultural & Mechanical University** (☎ 850-599-3000) – also Florida A&M or FAMU (pronounced 'fam-you') – was founded in 1887 as State Normal College for Colored Students, with 15 students and two instructors. Today, about 10,000 students of all races go here, home of the Black Archives Research Center & Museum (see later in this chapter).

Laundry The **Northwood Coin Laundry** (☎ 850-385-9121; 1940 N Monroe St), in the Northwood Centre, has many washers and dryers. Also try **Plaza Laundromat** (☎ 850-422-0262; 1911 N Monroe St).

Medical Services The largest hospital is **Tallahassee Memorial Hospital** (☎ 850-431-1155; 1300 Miccosukee Rd), northeast of downtown.

Florida State Capitol
Welcome to the most unusual state capitol in the US (New Capitol; ☎ 850-488-6167; cnr Pensacola & Duval Sts). This home of the Florida legislature is a 22-story monolithic slab. If you're here during session, you can enjoy the scene, as movers and shakers bustle in and out of offices and restaurants, hands waving and cell phones ringing. If the big shots aren't around, at least take the free

tour. Without the tour, you can still visit the observation deck, which affords a cool panoramic view, revealing just how much forest surrounds the city. You'll find landmarks like the Vietnam Veterans Memorial and the First Presbyterian Church; the arresting chisel-shaped building to the south is the Florida Education Center.

Old Capitol
The Old Capitol (☎ 850-487-1902; 400 S Monroe St; admission free; open 9am-4:30pm Mon-Fri, 10am-4:30pm Sat, noon-4:30pm Sun & holidays) is a grand structure, and home to the **Florida Center for Political History and Governance**, with rotating exhibits. Senior museum specialist Robin Turner is a trove of information on the building and on Florida legislative history. The building, with its luminous 1902 art-glass dome and candy-striped awnings, adjoins the New Capitol.

Vietnam Veterans Memorial
Opposite the Old Capitol, on S Monroe St, a huge, billowing US flag marks the Vietnam War memorial honoring Floridians who died or went missing in the conflict. The flag hangs between twin granite towers inscribed with the names of 1869 Floridians listed as killed and 83 missing in action.

Black Archives Research Center & Museum
This museum (☎ 850-599-3020; cnr Martin Luther King Jr Blvd & Gamble St; admission free; open 9am-4pm Mon-Fri), in the Carnegie Library on the FAMU campus, has one of the country's largest collections of African American and African artifacts, and is a center on black influence on US history and culture. There's a hands-on Underground Railroad display, a 500-piece Ethiopian cross collection and a huge collection of papers, photographs, paintings and documents pertaining to American black life.

John G Riley Center & Museum
The **John G Riley Center & Museum of African American History & Culture** (☎ 850-681-7881; 419 E Jefferson St; adult/child $2/1;

open 10am-4pm Mon-Fri), in the 1890-vintage former residence of a black Tallahassee high school principal, is an archival black history center. The center's museum features artifacts and documents.

First Presbyterian Church

Tallahassee's oldest church (1835–38), the Greek Revival First Presbyterian (☎ 850-222-4504; 102 N Adams St), is open to the public. During the 19th century, it accepted slaves as members, with or without their masters' consent, though seating was segregated.

Museum of Florida History

This worthwhile museum (☎ 850-245-6450; 500 S Bronough St; admission free; open 9am-4:30pm Mon-Fri, 10am-4:30pm Sat, noon-4:30pm Sun & holidays) is in the RA Gray Building. The star attraction is an American mastodon skeleton more than 4 feet across, but it also houses Native American artifacts, objects from the Spanish period and the Civil War (including a reconstructed Confederate campsite from 1861 and a climb-aboard steamboat), historic farm equipment, quilts, cigar box labels and clothing. This is also the home of the State Archives and State Library.

Mary Brogan Museum of Art & Science

This museum (☎ 850-513-0700; ⓦ www.thebrogan.org; 350 S Duval St; adult/child, senior & military $6/3.50; open 10am-5pm Mon-Sat, 1pm-5pm Sun), called both MOAS and The Brogan, is in Kleman Plaza. It houses a science center on the 1st and 2nd floors and the Tallahassee art museum on the 3rd. The science center features hands-on exhibits and Saturday classes for children. Displays include a weather station and hydrogeology lab. Rotating exhibits, such as a recent physics-of-football demo, are worth checking out. The art museum mounts exhibitions throughout the year. Parking is available under Kleman Plaza.

Cemeteries

The **Old City Cemetery** (open sunrise-sunset), bounded by Park Ave, Macomb and

Call Sts and Martin Luther King Jr Blvd, is a shady place to stroll beneath moss-draped live oaks. Grab a walking tour brochure at the gate to find out who's buried where, including both Union and Confederate Civil War casualties.

Though it's posted No Trespassing, you can look over the fence into the 1840 **St John's Episcopal Cemetery** (cnr Call St & Martin Luther King Jr Blvd).

Knott House Museum

With a colonnaded portico, this museum (☎ 850-922-2459; 301 E Park Ave; admission free) is a restored Victorian house occupied during the Civil War by Confederate and then Union troops. On May 20, 1865, Union General Edward McCook read the Emancipation Proclamation from here; the date is still celebrated locally as Emancipation Day. In 1928, politico William V Knott bought the house. It's called 'the house that rhymes' because his wife, poet and temperance advocate Luella Knott, wrote poetry on the evils of drink, which she attached to many of her furnishings. You can see the poems and decor on guided hour-long tours 1pm to 3pm Wednesday to Friday and 10am to 3pm Saturday.

Alfred B Maclay Gardens State Park

A 30-minute drive north of downtown is the 1930s estate of financier Alfred B Maclay (☎ 850-487-4556; 3540 Thomasville Rd; open 8am-sunset; vehicle/pedestrian or cyclist $3.25/1). During peak blooming season, from January to April, there are more than 200 varieties of flowers. Don't miss the little walled garden and the reflecting pool, as well as nature trails and a lakeside pavilion. The gardens are open year-round, the house only in blooming season. It's a charming, airy place holding Maclay's artifacts, which reveal him as a man of many interests. From I-10, take exit 30 to Thomasville Rd north; follow the signs – the entrance is on your left.

Tallahassee Museum of History & Natural Science

This history museum (☎ 850-576-1636, 850-575-8684; ⓦ www.tallahasseemuseum.org;

3945 Museum Dr; adult/senior/child; $6.50/ 6/4.50; open 9am-5pm Mon-Sat, 12:30pm-5pm Sun), about 4 miles southwest of downtown near Lake Bradford, has hands-on nature displays and a working 1880s farmhouse with animals. From the natural habitat zoo, with its red wolf, Florida panthers and black bears, to its re-created Bellevue plantation and outbuildings, it's a captivating place. Walking out of the small, dark, heart-constricting slave huts and into the richly appointed plantation house is an effective US history lesson for both children and adults. Wildlife demonstrations and creative programs run throughout the year – such as sing-alongs and shows like Spring Farm Days (which features historic farming technique demonstrations).

Take Gaines St to Lake Bradford Rd (Hwy 371), go south, and then bear right at the fork and follow Orange Ave to Rankin Rd, turn left and follow the signs.

Tallahassee Antique Car Museum

This museum (☎ 850-942-0137; w www.tacm .com; 3550-A Mahan Dr; adult/child $7.50/5; open 10am-5pm Mon-Sat, 1pm-5pm Sun), at Car Nations Plaza northeast of downtown, showcases classic American cars, including a 1931 Deusenberg and, of course, a DeLorean. The 1948 Tucker Torpedo, one of only 51 made, is a treat.

Courthouse & Ponce de Leon Park

This 1936 building (110 W Park Ave) once housed the US Courthouse and post office.

Lake Ella

Walk around Lake Ella and you may cross the line that divides the here and now from the then and there. Just off the very urban Monroe St, the lake is a sylvan, spring-fed pool two-thirds of a mile around that has been an integral part of Tallahassee life for more than a century. Look past the blanket of seagulls on the green, across the water, and you can almost see the baptismal candidates on the far shore, dressed in their Sunday best and standing in water up to their knees as they prepare to wade in and meet God.

Originally known as Bull's Pond, in the 19th century Lake Ella was renamed by planter Jabez Bull for his daughter. It has long been a swimming hole, baptismal site and picnic spot. It was here, in 1867, that more than 2000 newly freed slaves celebrated Emancipation Day.

Lake Ella roared during the 1920s. In 1924 Gilbert Sewell Chandler built the Lakeside Motel (the cottages still line the east shore today, housing boutiques and shops), and in 1929 the American Legion Hall Claude Sauls Post No 13 went up on the north side. The hall was a social center during WWII, and still hosts community events today. In 1982, the Department of Natural Resources paid for picnic facilities, parking and landscaping. Park supporters EC Allen and his wife donated a high-spurting floating fountain, and decorative streetlights were put up around the perimeter.

Lake Ella is where you'll find the town's Vietnam Memorial, alongside a monument sent to the city by the French government in appreciation for help during WWII. The most moving monuments, however, are the dozens of memorial plaques and plantings that rim the lake, evoking the ghosts of those who once enjoyed Lake Ella and now are gone. 'For Ellah Chodorov, who adds beauty to the world,' reads one plaque. 'Natalia Casas…99 years in our lives, forever in our hearts,' reads another. And then there's 'In fond memory of our favorite singing cat, Kacukiukas (Chooke) Sparkis.'

The past is everywhere as you walk around the lake. But so is the present – Lake Ella is constantly in use. Sometimes rainstorms combine with the high water table here, causing flooding that covers the trail. No one is deterred, however, and you'll still see the lovers of Lake Ella as they walk around their pond, umbrellas bobbing in the rain.

Note the neoclassical columns, the cupola and the WPA murals. Across the street is Ponce de Leon Park (circa 1880), a pleasant sward of green with a fountain.

From March to November here, come to the **Downtown Marketplace** (☎ 850-297-3945; **w** www.downtownmarketplace.com), where art, live music and gourmet food await you.

Tallahassee–St Marks Historic Railroad State Trail

This 16-mile path (☎ 850-922-6007; admission free; open 8am-dark year-round), for runners, bicyclists, skaters and horseback riders, is flat the entire length. At the time of research, bids were out from the park service for a bike-rental concession. If you want to ride, call to see if rental bikes are available. From downtown Tallahassee, take Monroe St south, which becomes Woodville Hwy (Hwy 363). After you cross Capital Circle; the trailhead is 100 yards ahead on the right.

Activities

Forestmeadows Park & Athletic Center (☎ 850-891-3920; 4750 N Meridian Road; open 8am-10pm Mon-Fri, 8am-7pm Sat & Sun) is a city recreation center where non-residents can drop in for tennis ($3 per 1½ hours), racquetball/squash/wallyball ($4.50 per hour), weight room ($3) or sauna ($2.25). In summer, you can use the **swimming pool** (☎ 850-891-3927; open 12:30pm-6pm; $3). Forestmeadows is north of I-10 about 3½ miles, on the west side of Meridian Road.

Elinor Klapp-Phipps Park, containing more than 10 miles of multiuse trails (for hikers, bicycles and horses) and 7 miles of dedicated hiking trails, is just east of Forestmeadows. In March the Red Hills Horse Trials (☎ 850-893-2497; **w** www.rhht.org), an international equestrian competition in dressage, cross country and stadium jumping, take place here.

The **Lake Overstreet Trails** trailhead (see Alfred B Maclay Gardens State Park, earlier in this section) is directly across Meridian Road from Forestmeadows. These trails loop around within the 877-acre area, circling Lake Overstreet and winding through deer, gray fox and bobcat habitat.

Lake Ella, just east off N Monroe St to the south of W Tharpe St, is a well-used urban park, great for a brisk half-mile walk (see the boxed text 'Lake Ella').

Organized Tours

Downtown walking tours leave from Capitol West Plaza in summer Monday to Saturday. The Florida Welcome Center in the New Capitol (☎ 850-488-6167) has more information.

Tours With A Southern Accent (☎ 850-513-1000) runs van tours and guided walks of downtown for $20 (multilingual tours are available). The two-hour tours run 10am to 2pm Monday to Friday. This company also offers half- or full-day special tours by arrangement – call for details.

Places to Stay

Most of the hotels and motels in the area are clumped at exits along I-10 or lined along Monroe St, between I-10 and downtown. Scour the Florida Welcome Center for discount coupons. Most places offer free local calls and provide at least coffee and a breakfast snack.

Budget The **Tallahassee RV Park** (☎ 850-878-7641; 6504 Mahan Drive/Hwy 90; sites with hookups $25) is 10 minutes east of Tallahassee. From I-10, take exit 31A and go west a mile on Hwy 90.

Florida State University Seminole Reservation (☎ 850-644-6083, 850-644-6892; 3226 Flastacowo Rd; cabins FSU student/non-student $35/45) is 73 acres on Lake Bradford, near the airport. 'The Rez' offers rustic cabins (kitchens, but no TV or telephone). You can try and get the student rate with an ISIC. It also has two dormitory cabins, each with 12 bunk beds; the cost is $60 per night or $8 per person, whichever is greater.

Motel 6 (☎ 850-386-7878, 800-466-8356; 2738 N Monroe St; rooms $40) amenities include a pool, coffee and guest laundry.

Executive Suites Motor Inn (☎ 850-386-2121, 800-342-0090; 522 Silver Slipper Lane; rooms $49-69) is spotless, if bland. All rooms have bathroom Jacuzzis. There's a pool.

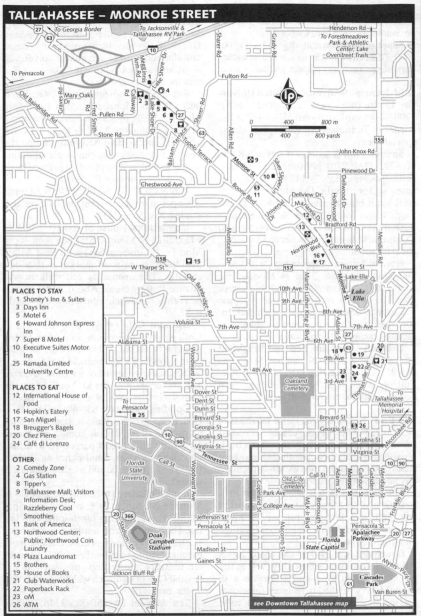

TALLAHASSEE – MONROE STREET

PLACES TO STAY
1 Shoney's Inn & Suites
3 Days Inn
5 Motel 6
6 Howard Johnson Express Inn
7 Super 8 Motel
10 Executive Suites Motor Inn
25 Ramada Limited University Centre

PLACES TO EAT
12 International House of Food
16 Hopkin's Eatery
17 San Miguel
18 Breugger's Bagels
20 Chez Pierre
24 Café di Lorenzo

OTHER
2 Comedy Zone
4 Gas Station
8 Tipper's
9 Tallahassee Mall; Visitors Information Desk; Razzleberry Cool Smoothies
11 Bank of America
13 Northwood Center; Publix; Northwood Coin Laundry
14 Plaza Laundromat
15 Brothers
19 House of Books
21 Club Waterworks
22 Paperback Rack
23 oM
26 ATM

Days Inn (☎ 850-386-9376, 800-329-7466; 2800 N Monroe St; rooms $54) often features discount specials. There's a pool.

Super 8 Motel (☎ 850-386-8818; 800-800-8000; 2702 N Monroe St; rooms $50) is a standard Super 8 in every respect, including price.

Mid-Range The **Ramada Limited University Centre** (☎ 850-224-7116, 800-272-6232; 1308 W Brevard St; rooms $50-90) is at the corner of Tennessee St. Rates rise during special events.

Shoney's Inn & Suites (☎ 850-386-8286, 800-222-2222; 2801 N Monroe St; rooms/suites/poolside $59/79/113) is a pleasant surprise, for a chain. The Mediterranean-style inn is built around tree-shaded courtyards, where fountains bubble and Spanish moss trails down. The rooms are bright, and Continental breakfast is served in a big, cheerful room.

Howard Johnson Express Inn (☎ 850-386-5000, 800-446-4656; 2726 N Monroe St; rooms $59) is a cozy place under impressive oaks. The staff are congenial; a free gym pass to Legends, down the street, is included. In-room refrigerators, a pool and guest laundry facilities complete the package.

Calhoun Street Inn Bed and Breakfast (☎ 850-425-5095; 525 N Calhoun St; rooms $65-95) is on a tree-lined street downtown. Full breakfast is included; fireplaces and flowers enliven the common areas.

Top End The **Doubletree Hotel Tallahassee** (☎ 850-224-5000; 101 S Adams St; rooms $79-150, higher during busy times) is a businessperson's high-rise, with 243 modern rooms. A restaurant serves three meals a day and a Sunday brunch.

The **Radisson Hotel Tallahassee** (☎ 850-224-6000; 415 N Monroe St; rooms $109/119 weekend/weekday) is a full-service hotel near downtown, with a dining room, lounge and fitness center.

Governor's Inn (☎ 850-681-6855; 209 S Adams St; rooms & suites $129-229) is the poshest place in town and a favorite with capital heavyweights. It features turndown service, free drinks, newspapers and valet service.

Places to Eat

Breugger's Bagels (☎ 850-224-1409; 1216 N Monroe St) has good bagels for $6 a dozen. Get them to go, or have one sliced, toasted and slapped with cream cheese so you can sit at an outdoor table with a large coffee and the Sunday *Democrat*.

Razzleberry Cool Smoothies (☎ 850-297-0626; 2415 N Monroe St; open 10am-6pm Mon-Sat, 12:30pm-5:30pm Sun), in the center of the Tallahassee Mall, is good to know about if you've dropped in to escape the heat. A mango-orange-pineapple smoothie with a shot of protein powder ($4) sure beats the junk-food-heaven food court.

Publix (☎ 850-385-5121; 1940 N Monroe St), a popular supermarket, has take-out deli sandwiches ($4 to $6).

International House of Food (☎ 850-386-3433; 2013 N Monroe St; open 8am-10pm Mon-Fri, 10am-6pm Sat) is an East Asian/Middle Eastern food market with a deli counter. The aroma as you walk in will ensure that you eat. About $2.50 buys a heavenly sandwich; platters are $4, dahl is $3.50.

Uptown Cafe (☎ 850-219-9800; 111 E College Ave; open 7am-3pm Mon-Fri) is great for breakfast, and its soups are the toast of the town ($3.50 small, $4 large). Sandwiches, some vegetarian, are good ($4.50 to $6), and cookies go for $1. You'll know the Uptown by the colorful mural on the front.

Goodies Eatery (☎ 850-681-3888; 116 E College Ave; open 7:30am-4:30pm Mon-Sat), across the street, isn't as homey, but makes up for it with a yogurt bar, espresso drinks and cheery servers. Sandwiches and salads ($4 to $6) are hearty, and a light breakfast is served all day.

Hopkin's Eatery (☎ 850-386-4252; 1840 N Monroe St; lunch $4-6; open 11am-5pm Mon-Fri) is a bustling lunch joint with latticework booths and a mixed clientele of students and office workers. Choose from excellent garden sandwiches, salads, vegetarian platters and grilled subs, such as the toasted Cuban sandwich with pork, ham and all the extras ($6).

San Miguel (☎ 850-385-3346; 200 W Tharpe St; lunch specials $4-6, dinners

$7-9.50; open 11am-2pm & 5pm-10pm Mon-Fri, noon-11pm Sat, noon-9pm Sun) is where locals go for authentic Mexican food. Servers whisk traditional (or four different vegetarian) *platos Mexicanos* to your table. Try the generous veggie quesadillas, two for $7.

Andrew's (☎ 850-222-3444; 228 S Adams St; open 11:30am-10pm Mon-Thur, 11:30am-11pm Fri & Sat, 11:30am-2pm Sun) sits in the shadow of the New Capitol and feeds most of its denizens on a regular basis while the legislature is in session. Movers and shakers spill over to sidewalk tables for lunch (mostly sandwiches, running $7 to $9, and some fish and pasta dishes). At dinner, choices include 13 kinds of burger (two veggie) for about $7, and 'Executive Branch' main dishes from salmon ($16) to the 'Secretary of Steaks' delmonico ($24).

Café di Lorenzo (☎ 850-681-3622; 1001 N Monroe St; open 11am-9pm Mon-Thur, 11am-11pm Fri & Sat, 11am-8pm Sun) serves pasta, pizza and other Italian dishes ($12 to $18) in an artsy black-and-white dining room under a sky-blue awning. The exuberant Lorenzo Amato presides over the restaurant, art gallery and piano bar that make up this eclectic establishment.

Chez Pierre (☎ 850-222-0936; 1215 Thomasville Rd; open 11am-2:30pm daily, 5:30pm-10pm Mon-Sat, 5:30pm-9pm Sun) is an elegant yet unpretentious French place in a fine old house with original art on the walls and an outdoor terrace. Lunches ($7 to $12) range from a quiche du jour to a sturdier duck cassoulet, while the dinner selection ($15 to $23) is wide, with vegetarian pasta on the conservative end and *filet de boeuf* for the hungrier. Desserts ($4 to $8) are divine, and there's an extensive wine list.

Entertainment

Check the Friday 'Limelight' in the *Tallahassee Democrat* for theater and entertainment listings. For an ongoing calendar of cultural events, check the Web site Ⓦ www.netcrc.org/calendar.html.

Theater The **Leon County Civic Center** (☎ 850-222-0400, 800-322-3602; 505 W Pensacola St) is the main venue for touring theater productions and big-time music concerts.

FSU Theatre Department (☎ 850-644-6500; box office open 11am-5:30pm Mon-Fri) has three venues. The **Richard G Fallon Mainstage Theater** in the Fine Arts Building, north of Call St on the campus, does large productions of plays and musicals. The **Studio**, in the Williams Building on campus, stages various free student productions and MFA-candidate works. Off campus, at the corner of Lafayette and Copeland Sts, **The Lab** does a range of works from Shakespeare to musicals in its 150-seat thrust-stage setting.

Tallahassee Little Theater (☎ 850-224-8474; Ⓦ www.tallytown.com/TLT; 1861 Thomasville Rd; box office open 10am-2pm Mon-Sat) is a lively community theater offering several productions a year. It also puts on 'Readers Theatre,' expressive readings from children's literature such as *Winnie the Pooh.*

Capital Commons Amphitheatre (Kleman Plaza, S Duval St) hosts the annual **Spring Shakespeare Fest** (☎ 850-671-0742) and the annual **Caribbean Fest** (☎ 850-878-2198) in August.

Live Music The **Tallahassee Symphony Orchestra** and **Tallahassee Symphony Youth Orchestra** (☎ 850-224-0461) both perform at the **FSU Ruby Diamond Auditorium** (cnr College Ave & Copeland St).

Bars & Clubs At **Club Waterworks** (☎ 850-224-1887; 1133 Thomasville Rd; cover $3) happy hour is 4pm to 7pm Monday to Friday. There's live music Monday and Saturday; Friday is cha-cha night. It's dimly lit, there are couches, and it has a good beer selection.

Atlantis Club and Grill (☎ 850-224-9711; 220 S Monroe St; open 8pm-late nightly) features dance lessons 9pm to 10pm. Live music, discs and karaoke happen regularly; Saturday is Latin night, and the fun goes until 5am.

Comedy Zone (☎ 850-386-1027; 2900 N Monroe St), at the Ramada Inn, presents two comedy shows Friday and Saturday night ($10 cover); it's a bar at other times.

Brothers (☎ 850-386-2399; 926 W Tharpe St) is a gay and lesbian venue featuring a DJ nightly, from 4pm to 2am. Note the terrace bar.

oM (☎ 850-577-0017; 1026 N Monroe St; open at 11am Mon-Sat) features poetry readings, live acoustic and electronic music, jazz and soul. There's also open mike Tuesday night, and new art exhibits every six weeks.

Tippers (☎ 850-531-9787; 2698 N Monroe St; open 9:30pm-late nightly) is a raucous, smoky bar, where you can dance to live bands every night. Expect a young, energetic crowd.

Spectator Sports

Football is king, queen, prince and deity in Tallahassee. From September to November, the FSU Seminoles play to 80,000-plus at Doak Campbell Stadium on the FSU campus. Tickets (which sell out months in advance) are $27, all seats.

And, oh yes, FSU baseball happens in the spring at Dick Howser Stadium, where game tickets run $2 to $5. For more FSU sports information, call the athletic department (☎ 850-644-1830, 888-378-6653).

On the FAMU campus, the FAMU Rattlers play football from August to November at Bragg Memorial Stadium (☎ 850-599-3141).

Getting There & Away

Air The Tallahassee Regional Airport (☎ 850-891-7800, 800-610-1995) is served by Delta, US Airways, American Eagle, Airtran and several smaller airlines. It's about 5 miles southwest of downtown, off Hwy 263.

Bus The Greyhound station (☎ 850-222-4249, 800-231-2222; 112 W Tennessee St; open 24/7) is at the corner of Duval, opposite the downtown TalTran transfer center. Buses to/ from Tallahassee include the following: The trip to Gainesville takes 3 to 3½ hours and costs $25/49 one-way/roundtrip; to Jacksonville takes 3 to 4 hours ($29/55); to Miami takes 12 to 15 hours ($60/115); to Panama City takes 1 to 2 hours ($13/26); and to Pensacola takes 2¼ to 4 hours ($21/42).

Train There is an Amtrak station (☎ 850-244-2779, 800-872-7245; 918½ Railroad Ave). The Sunset Limited passes through three times weekly on its way from Orlando to Los Angeles.

Car & Motorcycle It's 98 miles to Panama City Beach, 163 miles to Jacksonville, 192 miles to Pensacola and 470 miles to Miami. The main access road is I-10 from the east and the west. To get to the Gulf Coast towns along the Panhandle, take Hwy 319 south to Hwy 98. From Gainesville, it's about 120 miles; take I-75 north to I-10 west.

Getting Around

To/From the Airport There's no public transportation to and from the airport. A regular cab will cost $14 to $16; call Yellow Cab (☎ 850-580-8080).

By car, take Capital Circle Rd (Hwy 263) to Lake Bradford Rd, north to downtown.

Bus TalTran (☎ 850-891-5200) has a main transfer point downtown on Tennessee St at Adams St. The fare is adult/child & senior $1/50¢, and transfers are free. Other convenient routes include:

Bus No 15 – Tallahassee Museum of History & Natural Science

Bus No 1 – Monroe St to I-10

Bus Nos 3, 23 – Doak Campbell Stadium

FSU shuttle, bus Nos 5, 11, 14 – FAMU campus

Bus No 16 – north on Thomasville Rd to a half-mile south of Maclay Gardens State Park

Trolley The Old Town Trolley (☎ 850-891-5200) is a free shuttle running around downtown every 20 minutes 7am to 6:30pm Monday to Friday. Look for the trolley signs. It runs north to Brevard St, then south to Madison St on Adams St and around the Civic Center and back. Pick up route maps on the trolley or at the Visitor Information Center on E Jefferson St.

Car & Motorcycle There are several canopy roads (those almost completely covered by foliage) in the area, and the best way to see them is by driving. They include Old St Augustine Rd, Centerville Rd, Meridian Rd, Miccosukee Rd and Old Bainbridge Rd.

Parking is not hard downtown, once you know where to look. There are a couple of four-hour metered parking garages between Duval and Bronough Sts, behind the New Capitol; parking here is free Saturday and Sunday. The one-way streets (see the Downtown Tallahassee map) can be a challenge, so observe the signs. During the legislative session, parking is harder. The pols don't work Friday, which makes it the best weekday to visit downtown attractions.

If you stop in the morning at the library on Park Ave to check email, consider leaving your car in the lot here and making the short walk downtown – the cost is minimal, and you won't need to return every four hours.

AROUND TALLAHASSEE
Natural Bridge Battlefield
Fifteen miles southeast of Tallahassee, this historic site (☎ 850-922-6007; admission free; open 8am-sunset daily) is where a ragtag group of Confederate soldiers prevented Union troops from reaching Tallahassee in 1865 (see the Facts about Florida chapter). The park is peaceful, with long-silent earthworks, a Daughters of the Confederacy memorial and picnic tables. In March costumed villagers and soldiers stage a battle re-enactment, complete with booming cannon. From Tallahassee, take Hwy 363 south to Natural Bridge Rd in Woodville.

Wakulla Springs State Park
This 2860-acre state park (☎ 850-922-3633; 550 Wakulla Park Dr; vehicle/pedestrian or cyclist $3.25/1) features a natural spring covering about 3 acres and producing at peak times 1.2 billion gallons of water daily. Scenes from old Johnny Weismuller Tarzan movies were filmed here, as were parts of *The Creature from the Black Lagoon*. There's a glass-bottom boat ride (when the water's clear) as well as a riverboat cruise.

The riverboat cruise is a must-do. You glide by an array of birds: ospreys, tricolor herons, white ibises, double-crested cormorants, for instance. You get up close to alligators, brown water snakes and tribes of turtles comically lined up nose-to-tail, basking on a sunny log. Both tours run daily 11am to 3pm and last 30 minutes; the cost is $4.50 for adults, $2.25 for children. There's also swimming and a 6-mile hiking trail.

In 1850, scientist Sarah Smith discovered the bones of an ancient mastodon at the bottom of the spring here; since then the remains of at least nine other Ice Age mammals have been found. There are more than 55 recorded archaeological sites on the property, with artifacts dating back almost 15,000 years. Almost 15 miles of underwater cave systems have been mapped by research divers.

Wakulla Springs Lodge (☎ 850-224-5950; singles/doubles $79/99) is the only place to stay in the park. It's an immense 1937-vintage Spanish building with a walk-in fireplace in the lobby. The comfortable rooms have marble floors and bathrooms and no TV. The huge **Ball Room Restaurant** (☎ 850-224-5950; open 7:30am-10am, 11:30am-2pm, 6pm-8pm daily) is good, with lunches running $8 to $15 and dinners $8 to $18. The Cajun shrimp fettuccine ($15) is especially tasty.

The park is about 17 miles south of Tallahassee. Take Hwy 319 south to Hwy 61 south and follow the signs; the entrance is on Hwy 267.

APALACHICOLA NATIONAL FOREST
The largest of Florida's three national forests, Apalachicola (day-use areas $3; open 8am-sunset) occupies almost 938 sq mi of the Panhandle, from just west of Tallahassee to the Apalachicola River. The forest is lowlands and pine in the higher parts; other areas are made up of cypress hammocks and oaks. Dozens of species call the area home, including mink, gray and red foxes, coyotes, eastern moles, six bat species, beavers, Florida black bears and possibly Florida panthers.

Orientation & Information
The park is bisected by the Ochlockonee River, which flows south through the center of the park; the eastern half is controlled by the Wakulla Ranger District, the western half

The People's Archaeologist

Calvin Jones (1938–98) had a long career as state archaeologist for Florida. His name comes up virtually every time a Florida archaeological site is mentioned, and those sites are many. Among his more than 1000 documented discoveries were coins, jars, beads and chain mail from the 1539 winter campground of Hernando de Soto near Myers Park, and a rare Paleo-Indian knife blade (called a Simpson preform) found at Wakulla Springs. Identifying the blade enabled scientists to confirmed the existence of a flourishing human community at Wakulla Springs dating back 10,000 to 12,000 years.

Who was Calvin Jones? He was a lifelong collector of artifacts, pursuing a passion that led him as a child to spend his summer days 'collecting' treasures and carting them home at the end of the day in his Radio Flyer wagon. Jones was part Cherokee and part Creek; biographers have speculated that his career was in a way a search for his own roots. The past spoke to him – his colleagues marveled at his ability to spot and unearth lost civilizations.

'The archaeologist must be like a shaman,' Jones wrote. 'He must have a communion with people who lived thousands of years ago.' Jones seems to have been such a shaman. He is honored by a plaque at Wakulla Springs State Park as 'The People's Archaeologist.'

by the Apalachicola Ranger District. The **Apalachicola Ranger Station** (☎ 850-643-2282) is just south of the city of Bristol, northwest of the park near the intersection of Hwys 12 and 20; the **Wakulla Ranger Station** (☎ 850-926-3561) is just north of Crawfordville on Hwy 319.

The forest's boundaries are Hwy 20 on the north, Hwy 319 on the east, the Franklin County line on the south and the Apalachicola River on the west. Several highways traverse the park. You'll need maps of the forest, available at the Visitor Information Center at the New Capitol in Tallahassee or either of the ranger stations, which also supply pamphlets and sell topographical maps. 'Canoeing the National Forests in Florida' provides maps and descriptions of all the creeks in the forest – and it's waterproof.

Things to See & Do

The huge forest invites hiking, horseback riding, walking and canoeing, although powerboats are also permitted. For information on canoe rentals, contact either ranger station.

In the western section, **Fort Gadsden Historic Site** is an old fort on the Apalachicola River, which was blown to pieces by a horrendous munitions magazine explosion in 1816 that killed more than 200 people. It's

now a green, serene picnic area with some interesting artifacts. Check with the ranger station before you come here – at the time of research, Fort Gadsden was slated for possible closure, although there was stiff local opposition. Also on the western side of the forest, south of Tallahassee, is the **Munson Hills Loop**, a tough 7½-mile bicycle trail through the hilliest section of the forest in an area made up of hammock, dunes, hills and brush. If you run out of steam halfway through, take the Tall Pine Shortcut out of the trail, for a total distance of 4½ miles.

The forest is filled with water and sinkholes, and the best place to see both is the **Leon Sinks Geological Area** ($3 per vehicle; open 8am-6pm winter, 8am-8pm summer), where more than 6 miles of trails wind through the forest, past sinks and swamps, all which are named (how about the Big Dismal?) and bear interpretive signs. The sinks are at the eastern end of the park, just east of Hwy 319, about 10 miles south of Tallahassee.

Swim at Camel Lake, Wright Lake, Silver Lake and Lost Lake.

Places to Stay

All facilities are primitive, some without toilets. There are primitive hunting camps;

check at the ranger stations. For $5 per campsite, family camping is available on the western (Apalachicola) side of the forest at Camel Lake (from Bristol, near the ranger station, take Hwy 12 south for 11 miles and turn east on Forest Rd 105 for 2 miles). Also, you can camp, for $8 per vehicle, at Hickory Landing (from Sumatra, take Hwy 65 south; turn right on Forest Rd 101 and left on 101B). Wright Lake, at $8 per campsite, is just northeast of Hickory Landing.

A warning: at the time of research, the district ranger was proposing to close both Wright Lake and Camel Lake to camping. Check first (☎ 850-643-2282) if you're planning to camp in these areas.

In the eastern (Wakulla) section of the forest, family camping is $8 per vehicle at Wood Lake (from Sopchoppy, take Hwy 375 to Hwy 22 west, to Hwy 340 south to Hwy 338).

Eastern Panhandle

STEINHATCHEE
population 1400; time zone EST

In Steinhatchee (pronounced **steen**-hatchie), you won't find high-rise condominiums, white-sand beaches, amusement parks, Olympic-size swimming pools, a Home Depot, Wal-Mart or even a Winn Dixie. What you *will* find is a lovely, lazy river, wetlands teeming with birds and wildlife, lots of boats, a half-dozen marinas, some motels, a handful of restaurants serving hearty meals of fried fish, a citizenry of down-home folks and a light-up-the sky sunset almost nightly. And, oh yes: cobia, sea trout, amberjack, mackerel, grouper, sheepshead and scallops, all in the water, waiting to be caught. Scallop season, the busiest time for the town, runs July 1 to Sept 20. Everyone shows for opening day. As one old marina hand puts it, 'It's like an Easter egg hunt,' with every generation wading into the fun.

If you want a real getaway, this little river town about 90 miles southeast of Tallahas-

see is the place to come. For ideas, check W www.steinhatchee.com.

Boating

Sea Hag Marina (☎ 352-498-3008; 322 Riverside Dr) rents 20-foot-long motorboats for $125 daily or six-person pontoon boats for $155.

Ideal Marina & Motel (☎ 352-498-3877; 114 Riverside Dr SE) has similar rental rates, or fishing charters for four ($250 daily). Half-day charters are available, but as they say at Ideal, 'Fish being fish, they tend to move around and if it takes a while to find a "sweet" spot, you want to have time to enjoy the fishing.'

Gulfstream Motel & Marina (☎ 352-498-8088; Hwy 358 just over the bridge) is another good marina, with competitive rentals, charters and motel rooms, and a waterside bar for relaxing after your river trip.

Places to Stay & Eat

Fisherman's Rest (☎ 352-498-3877), across from and operated by the Ideal Marina and Motel (see Boating, above), offers tent camping ($8 per person), RV camping ($20 per couple, $7.50 each additional person) and motel rooms ($59 to $79). There's a grill area and free boat dockage.

Steinhatchee River Inn (☎ 352-498-4049; 600 Riverside Dr; rooms $55-65/65-75 winter/summer) is run by Steinhatchee Landing Resort and presided over by Rick and Nancy Zimmer. Rooms have TV, coffeemaker and fridge and are phoneless, but there's a central pay phone. Upstairs rooms have full kitchens.

Steinhatchee Landing Resort (☎ 352-498-3513; Hwy 51, 8 miles north of Steinhatchee; 1–3-bedroom units $120-615) has cottages with screened-in porches, full kitchens, washer/dryers, dishwashers, TVs, VCRs, stereo systems and fireplaces. Weekly rates are available; during holidays there's a three-night minimum. For your money there's also a pool, tennis courts, bicycles and a jogging trail.

Lynn-Rich Restaurant (☎ 352-488-0605; Hwy 51; breakfasts $3-5; open 6am-2pm Sun-Tues, 6am-9pm Wed-Sat) is the place for breakfasts like skillet-sized pancakes or eggs, biscuits and gravy.

The **Bridge End Cafe** (☎ 352-498-2002; 310 Tenth St; open 6am-9pm daily), tucked under the trees at the north end of Steinhatchee's only bridge, is the best restaurant in town. It's off the main drag, yet always bustling. Breakfasts range from a fruit bowl and a large biscuit ($4) to country-fried steak and eggs ($7). A veggie omelette is $4. For Friday or Saturday lunch, try the all-you-can-eat buffet ($7), including fish, meats, soup, salads, vegetables and breads (try a corn muffin). For dinner, all-you-can-eat catfish is $10, or you can enjoy the surf 'n' turf ($21).

Roy's (☎ 352-498-5000; cnr Hwys 51 & 351) has a salad bar, and seafood running $10 to $14, while **Fiddler's** (☎ 352-498-7427; 1306 SE Riverside Dr; open 11am-10pm Tues-Sun) has a large dinner menu ($11 to $17) that includes $14 fish entrees, all served with salad, potatoes or grits. The Peanut Butter Moose pie ($2) is decadent.

Getting There & Away
You have to drive. From Tallahassee, take Hwy 19 (also called Hwy 19/27 and, later, Hwy 19/98) to the crossroads with a blinking light and a sign saying 'Tennille,' and drive west on Hwy 51 to the end, about 12 miles.

MANATEE SPRINGS STATE PARK
Every day, 117 million gallons of cold water gush from the springhead here (☎ 352-493-6072, 800-326-3521; 11650 NW 115th St; vehicle/pedestrian or cyclist $3.25/1; open 8am-sundown daily). The spring, where diving and swimming are permitted, flows through cypress, maple and ash groves before emptying into the Suwannee River and, 25 miles farther, into the Gulf of Mexico. There's an 8½-mile-long hiking/biking trail, but the best thing is the viewing platform and boardwalk. From here, look down and see manatees, alligators, snapping turtles and big old snub-nosed mullets. There's canoeing along the spring run; canoes are available here for $5 for the first hour, $4 each additional hour (park campers get discounts). **Camping** costs $10, with electricity $12.

The park is at the end of Hwy 320, off Hwy 98, 6 miles west of Chiefland.

CEDAR KEY
population 1000; time zone EST
Once an important fishing port and the wood source for Eagle and Eberhard-Faber pencils, Cedar Key was one of the largest towns in Florida in its heyday in the late 19th century, when it became the western terminal of Florida's first transstate railroad. (See Amelia Island, in the Northeast Florida chapter, for more information.) But the town and port were decimated by an 1896 hurricane; the factory closed and the port couldn't meet the growing need for deep harbors. Today, Cedar Key is blessed with great beaches nearby, good seafood and an impressive museum of local history.

Orientation & Information
There are some 100 islands in the Cedar Keys, 12 of them in the Cedar Keys National Wildlife Refuge. Cedar Key is at the southwestern end of Hwy 24, some 23 miles southwest of Hwy 19/98. Hwy 24 turns into C St in town; the main commercial drag is 2nd St, which is a short walk or bike ride from the docks. There are three noteworthy annual festivals: the Sidewalk Art Festival (April), the Fourth of July celebration and the Seafood Festival, held the third weekend in October.

The **Cedar Keys Chamber of Commerce** (☎ 352-543-5600; ⓦ www.cedarkey.org; 2nd St next to City Hall; open 10am-1pm Mon, Wed & Fri) offers local information. The Cedar Key State Museum rangers are also knowledgeable about the area (see below).

The **post office** (518 2nd St) is nearby, and the **library** (☎ 352-543-5777; open noon-4pm & 6pm-8pm Tues, 10am-2pm Wed & Sat, 10am-4pm Thur), with three free Internet-ready computers, is behind the chamber of commerce.

Cedar Key State Museum
This museum (☎ 352-543-5350; 12231 SW 166th St; admission $1; open 9am-5pm

Thur-Mon) features excellent historical exhibits and the collections of St Clair Whitman, a main player in both the pencil factory and the local fiber mill, who at 14 arrived in the area in 1882 and started collecting everything he saw. Displays include insects, butterflies, glass, sea glass, bottles, and what's labeled the largest seashell collection in Florida.

For gardeners interested in native vegetation, the museum grounds show a riot of sand pine, slash pine, red cedar, live oak, sabal palm and saw palmetto.

Cedar Key Historical Museum

This very local museum (☎ 352-543-5549; cnr D & 2nd Sts; adult/child $1/50¢; open 1pm-4pm Sun-Fri, 11am-5pm Sat) rewards a careful look, especially at the extensive photographic record of Cedar Key. See also the exhibit on a once-thriving Cedar Key industry, brushmaking.

Cedar Keys National Wildlife Refuge

This refuge (☎ 352-493-0238; 16450 NW 31st Place, Chiefland) is on 12 islands in the Gulf of Mexico, 5 miles from Cedar Key. Established as a bird breeding ground, today the refuge – home to 50,000 birds and 12 species of reptiles – is closed to the public. Except for Seahorse Key, however, refuge beaches are open to the public during daylight hours. Seahorse Key, including a 300-foot zone around the island, is closed from March 1 to June 30.

The keys can be accessed only by boat, and shallow water and mudflats make that tough. To explore the area, contact the rangers' office or Wild Florida Adventures or Island Hopper (see below).

Organized Tours

Wild Florida Adventures (☎ 352-373-6047, 877-945-3928; **w** www.wild-florida.com)

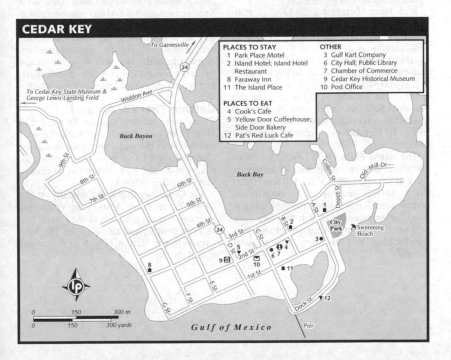

CEDAR KEY

PLACES TO STAY
1 Park Place Motel
2 Island Hotel; Island Hotel Restaurant
8 Faraway Inn
11 The Island Place

PLACES TO EAT
4 Cook's Cafe
5 Yellow Door Coffeehouse; Side Door Bakery
12 Pat's Red Luck Cafe

OTHER
3 Gulf Kart Company
6 City Hall; Public Library
7 Chamber of Commerce
9 Cedar Key Historical Museum
10 Post Office

To Gainesville

To Cedar Key State Museum & George Lewis Landing Field

Widdon Ave

Back Bayou

Back Bay

9th St
8th St
7th St
6th St
5th St
4th St
3rd St
2nd St
1st St

Collins St
Old Mill Dr
Depot St
A St
B St
C St
D St
E St
F St

City Park
Swimming Beach

Dock St
12

0 150 300 m
0 150 300 yards

Gulf of Mexico Pier

offers organized kayak tours, focusing on the Lower Suwannee and Cedar Keys National Wildlife Refuges. Tours ($50) include boat, paddles, life vests, drinking water and snacks. Tours vary in time and in distance; contact the company for details.

Island Hopper (☎ 352-543-5904; City Marina) runs pontoon boat trips and also rents skiffs and pontoon boats.

Places to Stay

Sunset Isle Park (☎ 352-543-5375; sites $14), on the north side of Hwy 24 a mile west of the first bridge from the mainland, has tent and RV campsites, water and electric hook-ups included.

The **Faraway Inn** (☎ 352-543-5330; cnr 3rd & G Sts; rooms $45-75) has individually decorated rooms, some with kitchens. Rates include use of bicycles, canoes and paddleboats; the water's across the street. Gregarious owners Oliver and Doreen Bauer have made the Faraway a garden spot.

Park Place Motel (☎ 352-543-5737, 800-868-7963; 211 2nd St; rooms $60-90) has generic motel rooms with kitchenettes; all units face the water.

Island Hotel (☎ 352-543-5111, 800-432-4640; w www.islandhotel-cedarkey.com; 224 2nd St at B St; rooms $80-125) is a step back in time. This two-story 1859 beauty (on the National Register of Historic Places) has immaculate rooms, a fine restaurant (see Places to Eat, below) and a wraparound balcony.

The **Island Place** (☎ 352-543-5306, 800-780-6522; w www.islandplace-ck.com; cnr 1st & B Sts; units $80-135/95-150 Sun-Thur/ Fri & Sat), a beachfront condominium complex that's less obstructive than most, is good for an extended stay. It features one- and two-bedroom condos with balconies overlooking the Gulf; there's a pool and Jacuzzi.

Places to Eat

The **Yellow Door Coffeehouse** (☎ 352-543-8008; 597 2nd St; open 7am-5pm daily, later Fri & Sat) is run by some nice and helpful folks (Molly can tell you what's happening). They also make great coffee. The café shares space with the **Side Door Bakery**.

Cook's Cafe (434 2nd St; breakfasts $4-8; open 6:30am-2pm daily, 5pm-8pm Tues-Sat) is good at breakfast, when you can get everything from biscuits and gravy to a groaning plate of pork chops, eggs, grits and toast.

Pat's Red Luck Cafe (☎ 352-543-6840; 590 Dock St; open 7am-9pm Mon-Sat, 7am-3pm Sun), hanging over the water, starts your day with a hearty breakfast ($4 to $6) and provides burgers or fish sandwiches for lunch ($4 to $8) – the grilled grouper sandwich, with potatoes and slaw ($7), is divine. End your day with seafood ($13 to $18).

The **Island Hotel Restaurant** (☎ 352-543-5111; 224 2nd St at B St; breakfast $9-13, dinner mains $14-26; open 8am-10am Sat & Sun, 6pm-9pm Wed-Mon) combines contemporary cooking with historical recipes passed down through the hotel. The results are imaginative; try the vegetarian *atsena otie* of sautéed artichokes, mushrooms and other fresh vegetables combined with sherry in a cream cheese and parsley sauce ($16).

Getting There & Around

There is no public transport. Driving, take Hwy 19/98 or I-75 to Hwy 24 and follow it southwest to the end. Private pilots can use George Lewis Landing Field, a strip on the island of Cedar Key with no aviation services (parking is free).

Let **Cedar Key Gulf Kart Company** (☎ 352-543-5300; cnr 1st & A Sts) keep you out of your car. It rents golf carts seating three, four or eight people, and also bicycles. The rates vary with the season, length of rental and size of the cart.

LONELY PLANET

You already know that Lonely Planet produces more than this one guidebook, but you might not be aware of the other products we have on this region. Here is a selection of titles which you may want to check out as well:

Miami & the Keys
ISBN 1 74059 183 6
US$16.99 • UK£9.99

Diving & Snorkeling Florida Keys
ISBN 0 86442 774 3
US$16.99 • UK£10.99

Miami City Map
ISBN 1 86450 177 4
US$5.99 • UK£3.99

Bahamas, Turks & Caicos
ISBN 1 86450 199 5
US$19.99 • UK£12.99

Cuba
ISBN 0 86442 750 6
US$19.99 • UK£11.99

Georgia & the Carolinas
ISBN 1 86450 383 1
US$19.99 • UK£12.99

Louisiana & the Deep South
ISBN 1 86450 216 9
US$21.99 • UK£12.99

USA
ISBN 1 86450 308 4
US$24.99 • UK£14.99

Puerto Rico
ISBN 1 74059 274 3
US$15.99 • UK£9.99

Available wherever books are sold.

You already know that Lonely Planet produces. More than this one guidebook, but you might not be aware of the other product, we have on this region. Here is a selection of titles which you may want to check out as well.

Index

Bold indicates maps.

Bold indicates maps.

Bold indicates maps.

Boxed Text

MAP LEGEND

ROUTES

City Regional

...............Freeway
...............Toll Freeway
...............Primary Road
...............Secondary Road
...............Tertiary Road
...............Dirt Road

...............Pedestrian Mall
...............Steps
...............Tunnel
...............Trail
...............Walking Tour
...............Path

TRANSPORTATION

...............Train
...............Metro

...............Bus Route
...............Ferry

HYDROGRAPHY

...............River; Creek
...............Canal
...............Lake

...............Spring; Rapids
...............Waterfalls
...............Dry; Salt Lake

ROUTE SHIELDS

80 Interstate Freeway
101 US Highway
95 State Highway
G4 County Road

BOUNDARIES

...............International
...............State

...............County
...............Disputed

AREAS

...............Beach
...............Building
...............Campus
...............Cemetery
...............Forest
...............Garden; Zoo
...............Golf Course
...............Park
...............Plaza
...............Reservation
...............Sports Field
...............Swamp; Mangrove

POPULATION SYMBOLS

○ NATIONAL CAPITAL ... National Capital
◉ State Capital .... State Capital
● Large City .... Large City
● Medium City .... Medium City
● Small City .... Small City
● Town; Village .... Town; Village

MAP SYMBOLS

■ ....Place to Stay
▼ ....Place to Eat
● ....Point of Interest

...............Airfield
...............Airport
...............Archeological Site; Ruin
...............Bank
...............Baseball Diamond
...............Battlefield
...............Bike Trail
...............Border Crossing
...............Buddhist Temple
...............Bus Station; Terminal
...............Cable Car; Chairlift
...............Campground
...............Castle
...............Cathedral
...............Cave

...............Church
...............Cinema
...............Dive Site
...............Embassy; Consulate
...............Footbridge
...............Gas Station
...............Hospital
...............Information
...............Internet Access
...............Lighthouse
...............Lookout
...............Mine
...............Mission
...............Monument
...............Mountain

...............Museum
...............Observatory
...............Park
...............Parking Area
...............Pass
...............Picnic Area
...............Police Station
...............Pool
...............Post Office
...............Pub; Bar
...............RV Park
...............Shelter
...............Shipwreck
...............Shopping Mall
...............Skiing - Cross Country

...............Skiing - Downhill
...............Stately Home
...............Surfing
...............Synagogue
...............Tao Temple
...............Taxi
...............Telephone
...............Theater
...............Toilet - Public
...............Tomb
...............Trailhead
...............Tram Stop
...............Transportation
...............Volcano
...............Winery

Note: Not all symbols displayed above appear in this book.

LONELY PLANET OFFICES

Australia
Locked Bag 1, Footscray, Victoria 3011
☎ 03 8379 8000 fax 03 8379 8111
email talk2us@lonelyplanet.com.au

USA
150 Linden Street, Oakland, California 94607
☎ 510 893 8555, TOLL FREE 800 275 8555
fax 510 893 8572
email info@lonelyplanet.com

UK
10a Spring Place, London NW5 3BH
☎ 020 7428 4800 fax 020 7428 4828
email go@lonelyplanet.co.uk

France
1 rue du Dahomey, 75011 Paris
☎ 01 55 25 33 00 fax 01 55 25 33 01
email bip@lonelyplanet.fr
www.lonelyplanet.fr

World Wide Web: www.lonelyplanet.com *or* AOL keyword: lp
Lonely Planet Images: lpi@lonelyplanet.com.au